W9-AQI-343

Index of American Periodical Verse: 1987

Rafael Catalá

and

James D. Anderson

assisted by

Sarah Park Anderson

and

Martha Park Sollberger

The Scarecrow Press, Inc.
Metuchen, N.J., & London
1989

Library of Congress Catalog Card No. 73-3060
ISBN 0-8108-2243-1

Contents

Preface

This, the seventeenth annual volume of the *Index of American Periodical Verse*, was produced with the cooperation of 258 participating English and Spanish language periodicals from Canada, the United States, and Puerto Rico. More than 6,100 entries for individual poets and translators are included, with more than 17,400 entries for individual poems and the same number of title or first line entries.

The importance of the *Index* grows as its necessity becomes more apparent in circles of contemporary poetry research. The increasing demand for inclusion corroborates this fact. The *Index* constitutes an objective measure of poetry in North America, recording not only the publication of our own poets in Canada, the U.S. and Puerto Rico, but also those from other lands and cultures and from other times. Of course, the *Index*'s primary purpose is to show what poems have been published by particular poets, what poems have been translated by particular translators, and who wrote poems with particular titles or first lines. But taken together, the *Index* reveals trends and influences: the ebb and flow of particular poets, as well as the influence of cultures of other lands and times as represented by their poets published in North American journals.

James D. Anderson has made a major contribution to the *Index* by designing and refining computer programs that have greatly facilitated the indexing process, control of necessary cross references, and typesetting. Also, I want to express my sincere appreciation to Sarah Park Anderson and Martha Park Sollberger for their valuable assistance.

Rafael Catalá
Co-Editor

Introduction

Compilation

The 1987 *Index* was compiled on an Osborne 4 Vixen CP/M microcomputer using the Wordstar wordprocessing program. Once all indexing was complete, entries, including cross-references, were transferred to an IBM personal computer for sorting by "IOTA Big Sort," written by Fred A. Rowley. Title entries were then extracted, and formatted author and title entries were transferred to a Macintosh computer with lazer printer for typesetting and page formatting.

The principal advantage of computer-based compilation is the elimination of repetitive data entry. Within a single issue of a journal, for example, the journal citation will be the same for every poem, yet with the old card-based method, the citation had to be rewritten on every card. With the computer, it is simply copied, without re-keying, to each entry. Similarly, translations no longer call for a completely new entry for the translator. Instead, the original entry is simply copied and modified, moving the name of the translator to the lead position, and the author to the note.

Persons interested in the precise details of compilation, including the computer programs used, should write to the editors at P.O. Box 38, New Brunswick, NJ 08903-0038. The 1982, 1983, 1984, 1985, 1986, and 1987 *Indexes* are available from the editors on 5-1/4" floppy disks.

Names and Cross References

With the addition of many more poets with compound surnames and surnames containing various prefixes, we have recognized the need for systematic cross references from alternative forms of surname to the form chosen for entry in the *Index*. We have included these references whenever the form used for entry did not fall under the last element. In addition, many poets publish under different forms of the same name, for example, with or without a middle initial. Often these forms will file next to each other in the *index*. When two or more different names refer to the same poet, one name will be chosen, with "see" references to the chosen name from other names. When it is not possible to determine with assurance whether a single poet is using variant forms of name or different poets have similar names, both names may be used. In such cases, "see also" references are added to headings to remind users to check the variant name forms which might possibly refer to the same poet. When poets are known to use different forms of the same name, alternative forms may be indicated using the format authorized by the *Anglo-American Cataloguing Rules*, Second Edition. For example:

WHEATLEY, Pat (Patience)

This heading indicates that this poet has poems published under two forms of name: Pat Wheatley and Patience Wheatley.

Format and Arrangement of Entries

The basic format and style of the *Index* remain unchanged. Poets are arranged alphabetically by surname and forenames. In creating this alphabetical sequence, we have adopted principles of the filing rules issued in 1980 by the American Library Association and the Library of Congress. Names are arranged on the basis of their spelling, rather than their pronunciation, so that, for example, names beginning with 'Mac' and 'Mc' are no longer interfiled. Similarly, the space consistently counts as a filing element, so that similar compound and prefixed surnames are often separated by some distance, as illustrated in the following examples. Note that "De BOLT" precedes "DeBEVOISE" by a considerable number of entries.

De ANGELIS	Van BRUNT
De BOLT	Van DUYN
De GRAVELLES	Van HALTEREN
De LOACH	Van TOORN
De PALCHI	Van TROYER
De RONSARD	Van WERT
De VAUL	Van WINCKEL
DEAL	VANCE
DeBEVOISE	Vander DOES
DeFOE	VANDERBEEK
DEGUY	VanDEVENTER
Del VECCHIO	
DeLISLE	
DeMOTT	
DENNISON	
Der HOVANESSIAN	
DESY	
DeYOUNG	

Abbreviations are also arranged on the basis of spelling, rather than pronunciation, so that "ST. JOHN" is *not* filed as "SAINT JOHN", but as "S+T+space+JOHN". Punctuation, signs and symbols other than alphabetic letters and numerals are not considered; a hyphen is filed as if it were a space and apostrophes and accents are ignored for purposes of filing. In title entries, initial articles are also ignored. Finally, numerals are arranged in numerical order preceding alphabetical letters rather than as if they were spelled out.

Under each poet's name, poems are arranged alphabetically by title or, if there is no title, by first line. Poem titles and first lines are placed within quotation marks. All significant words of titles are capitalized, but in first lines, only the first word and proper nouns are capitalized. Incomplete excerpts from larger works are followed by the note "Excerpt" or, if they consist of complete sections, by "Selection". The title, first line or number of the excerpt follows if given in the publication. For example:

WALCOTT, Derek
"Midsummer" (Selections: XXXIV-XXXVI). [Agni] (18) 83, p. 5-7.

WEBB, Phyllis
"The Vision Tree" (Selection: "I Daniel"). [PoetryCR] (5:2) Wint
83-84, p. 11.

WAINWRIGHT, Jeffrey
"Heart's Desire" (Excerpt: "Some Propositions and Part of a
Narrative"). [Agni] (18) 83, p. 37.

WATTEN, Barret
"One Half" (Excerpts). [ParisR] (24:86) Wint 82, p. 112-113.

If an excerpt is treated as a complete "sub-work", it receives an
independent entry, with reference to the larger work in a note. For example:

ANDERSON, Jack
"Magnets" (from The Clouds of That Country). [PoNow] (7:2,
#38) 83, p. 23.

Notes about dedications, joint authors, translators, and sources follow the
title, enclosed in parentheses. A poem with more than one author is entered
under each author. Likewise, a translated poem is entered under each
translator, as well as its author(s). Each entry includes the names of all authors
and all translators. Multiple authors or translators are indicated by the
abbreviation "w.", standing for "with". Translators are indicated by the
abbreviation "tr. by", standing for "translated by", and original authors are
indicated by the abbreviation "tr. of", standing for "translation of". For
example:

AGGESTAM, Rolf
"Old Basho" (tr. by Erland Anderson and Lars Nordström).
[NewRena] (16) Spr 83, p. 25.

ANDERSON, Erland
"Old Basho" (tr. of Rolf Aggestam, w. Lars Nordström).
[NewRena] (16) Spr 83, p. 25.

NORDSTRÖM, Lars
"Old Basho" (tr. of Rolf Aggestam, w. Erland Anderson).
[NewRena] (16) Spr 83, p. 25.

The journal citation includes an abbreviation standing for the journal
title, followed by volume and issue numbers, date, and pages. The journal
abbreviation is enclosed in square brackets. An alphabetical list of these
journal abbreviations is included at the front of the volume, followed by the
full journal title, name of editor(s), address, the numbers of the issues indexed
for this volume of the *Index*, and subscription information. A separate list of

ix

indexed periodicals is arranged by full journal title, with a reference to the abbreviated title. Volume and issue numbers are included within parentheses, e.g., (16:5) stands for volume 16, number 5; (21) refers to issue 21 for a journal which does not use volume numbers. Dates are given using abbreviations for months and seasons. Year of publication is indicated by the last two digits of the year, e.g., 87. Please see the separate list of abbreviations at the front of the volume.

Compiling this year's *Index* has been an adventure into the wealth and variety of poetry published in U. S., Puerto Rican and Canadian periodicals as well as the intricacies of bringing this wealth together and organizing it into a consistent index. The world of poetry publication is a dynamic one, with new journals appearing, older journals declining, dying, reviving and thriving. This year saw the loss of 13 journals and the addition of 22 new ones, with a net gain of 9 journals. Both deleted and newly added journals are listed at the front of the volume. Keeping up with these changes is a big job, and we solicit our readers' suggestions as to journals which should be included in future volumes of the *Index*, and also, journals which could be dropped. Editors who would like their journals considered for inclusion in future volumes should send sample issues to:

Rafael Catalá, Editor
Index of American Periodical Verse
P.O. Box 38
New Brunswick, NJ 08903-0038

Although indexing is indispensable for the organization of any literature so that particular works can be found when needed and scholarship and research facilitated, it is a tedious business. I know that we have made mistakes. We solicit your corrections and suggestions, which you may send to me at the above address.

James D. Anderson
Co-Editor

Abbreviations

dir., dirs.	director, directors
ed., eds.	editor, editors
(for.)	price for foreign countries
(ind.)	price for individuals
(inst.)	price for institutions
(lib.)	price for libraries
NS	new series
p.	page, pages
po. ed.	poetry editor
pub.	publisher
(stud.)	price for students
tr. by	translated by
tr. of	translation of
U.	University
w.	with

Months

Ja	January	Jl	July
F	February	Ag	August
Mr	March	S	September
Ap	April	O	October
My	May	N	November
Je	June	D	December

Seasons

Aut	Autumn	Spr	Spring
Wint	Winter	Sum	Summer

Years

84	1984	86	1986
85	1985	87	1987

Periodicals Added

Periodical acronyms are followed by the titles.

AlphaBS : ALPHA BEAT SOUP
BambooR : BAMBOO RIDGE
Bomb : BOMB MAGAZINE
Chat : CHATTAHOOCHEE REVIEW
Colum : COLUMBIA
CuadP : CUADERNOS DE POÉTICA
FiveFR : FIVE FINGERS REVIEW
Footwork : FOOTWORK
FourQ : FOUR QUARTERS
Gambit : GAMBIT MAGAZINE
GreensboroR : THE GREENSBORO REVIEW
HampSPR : THE HAMPDEN-SYDNEY POETRY REVIEW
Lactuca : LACTUCA
LightY : LIGHT YEAR
Lyra : LYRA
Margin : MARGIN
Phoenix : PHOENIX
Sequoia : SEQUOIA
WeberS : WEBER STUDIES
WilliamMR : THE WILLIAM AND MARY REVIEW
Witness : WITNESS
Writer : THE WRITER

Periodicals Deleted

EvergR: EVERGREEN REVIEW, Barney Rosset & Fred Jordan, eds., c/o Grove Press, 196 W. Houston St., New York, NY 10014; "Discontinued."

Imagine: IMAGINE: International Chicano Poetry Journal, Tino Villanueva, ed., 89 Mass. Ave., Suite 270, Boston, MA 02115. None published since vol. 2, no. 1, Summer 1985.

LittleBR: THE LITTLE BALKANS REVIEW, Gene DeGruson, po. ed., The Little Balkans Press, Inc., 601 Grandview Heights Terr., Pittsburg, KS 66762. No 1986 or 1987 issues received.

Oink: OINK! Superseded by New American Writing, first issue, 1987. See NewAW.

Open24: OPEN 24 HOURS, Kate Pipkin and Chris Toll, eds, 702 Homestead St., Baltimore, MD 21218. No 1986 or 1987 issues received.

Origin: ORIGIN. National Poetry Foundation. Cid Corman, ed., Michael Heller, USA ed., P.O. Box 981, Stuyvesant Sta., New York, NY 10009. Ceased publication.

PoetryCR: POETRY CANADA REVIEW, Robert Billings, ed., 307 Coxwell Ave., Toronto, Ontario M4L 3B5 Canada. No 1986 or 1987 issues received.

PortLES: THE PORTABLE LOWER EAST SIDE, Kurt Hollander, ed., 463 West St., #344, New York, NY 10014. No 1986 or 1987 issues received.

Sam: SAMISDAT, Merritt Clifton, ed., Box 129, Richford, VT 05476. Deleted by editorial decision.

SanFPJ: SAN FERNANDO POETRY JOURNAL, Richard Cloke, ed., 18301 Halsted St., Northridge, CA 91325. Deleted by editorial decision.

SecC: SECOND COMING, A. D. Winans, ed./pub., Box 31249, San Francisco, CA 94131. No longer publishing in standard periodical format.

Tendril: TENDRIL, George E. Murphy, Jr., managing ed., Box 512, Green Harbor, MA 02041. No 1986 or 1987 issues received; P.O. Box closed.

WritersL: WRITER'S LIFELINE, Stephen Gill, managing ed., Vesta Publications Limited, Box 1641, Cornwall, Ontario K6H 5V6 Canada. Deleted by editorial decision.

Periodicals Indexed

Arranged by acronym, with names of editors, addresses, issues indexed, and subscription information. New titles added to the *Index* in 1987 are marked with an asterisk (*).

Abraxas: ABRAXAS, Ingrid Swanberg, ed., 2518 Gregory St., Madison, WI 53711. Issues indexed: (35/36). Subscriptions: $12/4 issues; Single issues: $3; Double issues: $6.

Acts: ACTS: A Journal of New Writing, David Levi Strauss, ed. & pub., 514 Guerrero St., San Franisco, CA 94110. Issues indexed: (6-7). Subscriptions: $12/yr. (2 issues, ind.), $16/yr. (2 issues, inst. & for.); $20/2 yrs. (4 issues, ind.), $28/2 yrs. (4 issues, inst. & for.); Single issues: $8.

Agni: THE AGNI REVIEW, Askold Melnyczuk, ed., Creative Writing Dept., Boston U., 236 Bay State Rd., Boston, MA 02115. Issues indexed: (24/25). Subscriptions: $29/3 yrs., $19/2 yrs., $10/yr., plus $1/yr. (for.); Single issues: $5; Double issues: $10.

*AlphaBS: ALPHA BEAT SOUP, Dave Christy, ed., 5110 Adams St., Montreal, Quebec H1V 1W8 Canada. Issues indexed: (1-2). Subscriptions: $5/yr. (2 issues); Single issues: $3.

Amelia: AMELIA, Frederick A. Raborg, Jr., ed., 329 "E" St., Bakersfield, CA 93304. Issues indexed: (4:1/2-3, issues 9-10). Subscriptions: US, Canada, Mexico, $56/3 yrs., $38/2 yrs., $20/yr.; $92/3 yrs., $62/2 yrs., $32/yr. (for. air mail); Single issues: $5.95, $9 (for. air mail).

Americas: THE AMERICAS REVIEW, A Review of Hispanic Literature and Art of the USA (formerly Revista Chicano-Requeña), Julián Olivares, ed., U. of Houston, University Park, Houston, TX 77004. Issues indexed: (14:3/4, 15:1-3/4). Subscriptions: $15/yr. (ind.), $20/yr. (inst.); Single issues: $5.

AmerPoR: THE AMERICAN POETRY REVIEW, David Bonanno, Stephen Berg, Arthur Vogelsang, eds., World Poetry, Inc., Temple U Center City, 1616 Walnut St., Room 405, Philadelphia, PA 19103. Issues indexed: (16:1-6). Subscriptions: $26/3 yrs., $31/3 yrs. (for.), $19/2 yrs., $23/2 yrs. (for.), $11/yr., $13/yr. (for.); classroom rate $6/yr. per student; Single issues: $2.25.

AmerS: THE AMERICAN SCHOLAR, Joseph Epstein, ed., United Chapters of Phi Beta Kappa, 1811 Q St. NW, Washington, DC 20009. Issues indexed: (56:1-4). Subscriptions: $42/3 yrs., $32/2 yrs., $18/yr. plus $3/yr. (for.); Single issues: $5.

AmerV: THE AMERICAN VOICE, Frederick Smock, ed., The Kentucky Foundation for Women, Inc., Heyburn Bldg., Suite 1215, Broadway at 4th Ave., Louisville, KY 40202. Issues indexed: (6-9). Subscriptions: $12/yr. Single issues: $4.

AnotherCM: ANOTHER CHICAGO MAGAZINE, Lee Webster & Barry Silesky, eds., Box 11223, Chicago, IL 60611. Issues indexed: (17). Subscriptions: $9/yr., $40/5 yrs., $150/lifetime; Single issues: $5.

Antaeus: ANTAEUS, Daniel Halpern, ed., The Ecco Press, 26 W. 17th St., New York, NY 10011. Issues indexed: (58-59). Subscriptions: $20/4 issues, $37/8 issues, $53/12 issues; plus $3 per issue (for., surface mail), $6 per issue (for. air mail); Single issues: $10.

AntigR: THE ANTIGONISH REVIEW, George Sanderson, ed., St. Francis Xavier U., Antigonish, Nova Scotia B2G 1C0 Canada. Issues indexed: (68, 69/70, 71/72). Subscriptions: $16/4 issues; Single issues: $4.50.

Periodicals Indexed

AntR: THE ANTIOCH REVIEW, Robert S. Fogarty, ed., David St. John, po. ed., P.O. Box 148, Yellow Springs, OH 45387. Issues indexed: (45:1-4). Subscriptions: $18/yr., $34/2 yrs., $48/3 yrs. (ind.); $25/yr., $48/2 yrs., $69/3 yrs. (inst.); plus $5/yr. (for.); Single issues: $4.75.

Aréito: ARÉITO, Andrés Gómez, Director, P.O. Box 44-1403, Miami, FL 33144. Issues indexed: Segunda Epoca (1:1). Subscriptions: $20/yr. (inst.), $30/yr. (for. inst.), $12/yr. (ind.), $18/yr. (ind. for.).

ArizQ: ARIZONA QUARTERLY, Albert Frank Gegenheimer, ed., U. of Arizona, Tucson, AZ 85721. Issues indexed: (43:1-4). Subscriptions: $10/3 yrs., $5/yr.; Single issues: $1.50.

Ascent: ASCENT, Daniel Curley, et al ., eds., English Dept., U. of Illinois, 608 South Wright St., Urbana, IL 61801. Issues indexed: (12:2-3, 13:1). Subscriptions: $3/yr. (3 issues), $4.50/yr. (for.); Single issues: $1 (bookstore), $1.50 (mail).

Atlantic: THE ATLANTIC, William Whitworth, ed., Peter Davison, po. ed., 8 Arlington St., Boston, MA 02116. Issues indexed: (259:1-6, 260:1-6). Subscriptions: $29.95/3 yrs., $15.95/2 yrs., $9.95/yr., plus $3/yr. (Canada), $5/yr. (for.); Single issues: $2; $2.50 (Canada).

BallSUF: BALL STATE UNIVERSITY FORUM, Bruce W. Hozeski, ed., Darlene Mathis-Eddy, po. ed., Ball State U., Muncie, IN 47306. Issues indexed: (28:1-4). Subscriptions: $20/yr. (4 issues), Single issues: $6.

*BambooR: BAMBOO RIDGE: The Hawaii Writers' Quarterly, Eric Chock, Darrell H. Y Lum, eds., P.O. Box 61781, Honolulu, HI 96822-8781. Issues indexed: (31-36). Subscriptions: $12/yr.; Single issues, $3-$9.

BellArk: BELLOWING ARK, Robert R. Ward, ed., P.O. Box 45637, Seattle, WA 98145. Issues indexed: (3:1-6). Subscriptions: $12/yr.; Single issues: $2.

BellR: THE BELLINGHAM REVIEW, Randy Jay Landon, ed., 932 Monitor Ave., Wenatchee, WA 98801. Issues indexed: (10:1-2). Subscriptions: $4/yr. (2 issues), $7.50/2 yrs., $10.50/3 yrs.; Single issues: $2.

BelPoJ: THE BELOIT POETRY JOURNAL, Marion K. Stocking, ed., RFD 2, Box 154, Ellsworth, ME 04605. Issues indexed: (37:3-4, 38:1-2). Subscriptions: $22/3 yrs., $8/yr., 4 issues (ind); $33/3 yrs., $12/yr. (inst.); Single issues: $2.

BilingR: THE BILINGUAL REVIEW/LA REVISTA BILINGUE, Gary D. Keller, ed., Hispanic Research Center, Arizona State U., Tempe, AZ 85287. Issues indexed: (12:3) 1985, c1988. Subscriptions: $15/yr., $28/2 yrs., $39/3 yrs. (ind.); $24/yr. (inst.).

BlackALF: BLACK AMERICAN LITERATURE FORUM, Joe Weixlmann, ed., Thadious David, Sterling Plumpp, po. eds., Parsons Hall 237, Indiana State U., Terre Haute, IN 47809. Issues indexed: (21:1/2-4). Subscriptions: $15/yr. (ind.), $21/yr. (inst.), $18/yr. (for.), $24 (for. inst.). Single issues: $6.

BlackWR: BLACK WARRIOR REVIEW, Amber Vogel, ed., Jeff Mock, po. ed., U. of Alabama, P.O. Box 2936, Tuscaloosa, AL 35487-2936. Issues indexed: (13:2, 14:1). Subscriptions: $6.50/yr. (ind.), $9/yr. (inst.); Single issues: $3.50.

BlueBldgs: BLUE BUILDINGS: An International Magazine of Poetry and Translations, Tom Urban, Ruth Doty, Michaela Haberkern, David Smith, Cathy Colver, eds., Dept. of English, Drake U., Des Moines, IA 50311. Issues indexed: (10). Subscriptions: $4/2 issues; Single issues: $2; Back issues: $1.50.

Blueline: BLUELINE, Alice Gilborn, ed., Blue Mountain Lake, NY 12812. Issues indexed: (7:2/3 [i.e. 8:2/3?]). Subscriptions: $5/yr., $9/2 yrs. (U.S. & Canada), $6/yr., $11/2 yrs. (for.); Back issues: $3.

Bogg: BOGG, John Elsberg, ed., 422 N. Cleveland St., Arlington, VA 22201; George Cairncross, ed., 31 Belle Vue St., Filey, N. Yorkshire YO14 9HU, UK. Issues indexed: (57-58). Subscriptions: $8/3 issues; Single issues: $3.

*Bomb: BOMB MAGAZINE, Betsy Sussler, ed., New Art Publications, 177 Franklin St., New York, NY 10013. Issues indexed: (18-21). Subscriptions: $22/yr., $20/2 yrs.; $26/yr. (for.); Single issues: $6.

BostonR: BOSTON REVIEW, Margaret Ann Roth, ed. & pub., Matthew Gilbert, po ed., 33 Harrison Ave., Boston, MA 02111. Issues indexed: (12:1-6). Subscriptions: $12/yr., $20/2 yrs. (ind.); $15/yr., $25/2 yrs. (inst.); plus $6/yr. (for.); Single issues: $3.

Boulevard: BOULEVARD, David Brezovec, executive ed., Richard Burgin, ed., Opojaz, Inc., 4 Washington Square Village #9-R, New York, NY 10012. Issues indexed: (2:1/2-3). Subscriptions: $10/yr., $17.50/2 yrs., $21/3 yrs.; Single issues: $4-$4.50.

Bound: BOUNDARY 2, William V. Spanos, ed., Dept. of English, State U. of New York, Binghamton, NY 13901. Issues indexed: (14:1/2-3, 15:1/2). Subscriptions: $25/yr. (inst.), $15/yr. (ind.), $13/yr (stud.), plus $2 (for.); Single issues: $8, Double issues: $10.

Caliban: CALIBAN, Lawrence R. Smith, ed., P.O. Box 4321, Ann Arbor, MI 48106. Issues indexed: (2-3). Subscriptions: $8/yr., 2 issues (ind.), $15/yr. (inst.); $11/yr. (ind.), $15/yr. (inst.), Canadian currency; $12/yr. (for. ind.), $21/yr. (for. inst.). Single issues: $5.

Callaloo: CALLALOO: A Journal of Afro-American and African Arts and Letters, Charles H. Rowell, ed., Dept. of English, Wilson Hall, U. of Virginia, Charlottesville, VA 22903. Issues indexed: (9:4, 10:1-3; #29-32). Subscriptions: $15/yr. (ind.), $30/yr. (inst.); plus $5.50 (Canada, Mexico); plus $11 (outside North America); The Johns Hopkins University Press, Journals Publishing Division, 701 W. 40th St., Suite 275, Baltimore, MD 21211.

CalQ: CALIFORNIA QUARTERLY, Elliot L. Gilbert, ed., Carlos Rodriguez, po. ed., 100 Sproul Hall, U. of California, Davis, CA 95616. Issues indexed: (30). Subscriptions: $10/yr. (4 issues); Single issues: $2.50.

Calyx: CALYX: A Journal of Art and Literature by Women, Margarita Donnelly, Lisa Domitrovich, Managing eds., P.O. Box B, Corvallis, OR 97339-0539. Issues indexed: (10:2/3, 11:1). Subscriptions: $18/yr., $32/2 yrs., $42/3 yrs., plus $4/yr. (for.), $9/yr. (for. airmail); $22.50/yr. (inst.); $15/yr. (low income individual); Single issue: $6.50-$12.

CanLit: CANADIAN LITERATURE, W. H. New, ed., U. of British Columbia, 2029 West Mall, Vancouver, B.C. V6T 1W5 Canada. Issues indexed: (112, 113/114, 115). Subscriptions: $20/yr. (ind.), $25/yr. (inst.) plus $5/yr. outside Canada; Single issues: $7.50.

CapeR: THE CAPE ROCK, Harvey Hecht, ed., Southeast Missouri State U., Cape Girardeau, MO 63701. Issues indexed: (22:1-2). Subscriptions: $3/yr. (2 issues); Single issues: $2.

CapilR: THE CAPILANO REVIEW, Dorothy Jantzen, ed., Sharon Thesen, po. ed., Capilano College, 2055 Purcell Way, North Vancouver, B.C. V7J 3H5 Canada. Issues indexed: (42-45). Subscriptions: $22/8 issues (ind.), $12/4 issues (ind.), $14/4 issues (lib.); plus $1/4 issues (for.); Single issues: $5.

CarolQ: CAROLINA QUARTERLY, Robert Rubin, ed., Greenlaw Hall 066-A, U. of North Carolina, Chapel Hill, NC 27514. Issues indexed: (39:2-3, 40:1); Spine of 39:3 has "Volume 4 Number 3" in error. Subscriptions: $12/yr. (3 issues) (inst.), $10/yr. (ind.), $11/yr. (for.); Single issues: $4, plus $1 postage.

CentR: THE CENTENNIAL REVIEW, Linda Wagner-Martin, ed., 110 Morril Hall, Michigan State U., East Lansing, MI 48824-1036. Issues indexed: (31:1-4). Subscriptions: $10/2 yrs., $6/yr., plus $3/yr. (for.); Single issues: $2.

CentralP: CENTRAL PARK, Stephen-Paul Martin, Richard Royal, Eve Ensler, eds., Box 1446, New York, NY 10023. Issues indexed: (11-12). Subscriptions: $9/yr., 2 issues (ind.), $10/yr. (inst.); Single issues: $5 (ind), $5.50 (inst).

CharR: THE CHARITON REVIEW, Jim Barnes, ed., Division of Language and Literature, Northeast Missouri State U., Kirksville, MO 63501. Issues indexed: (13:1-2). Subscriptions: $7/4 issues; Single issues: $2.

*ChatR: THE CHATTAHOOCHEE REVIEW, Lamar York, ed., DeKalb College, 2101 Womack Road, Dunwoody, GA 30338-4497. Issues indexed: (8:1). Subscriptions: $15/yr. (4 issues), $25/2 yrs.; Single issues: $4.

Chelsea: CHELSEA, Sonia Raiziss, ed., P.O. Box 5880, Grand Central Station, New York, NY 10163. Issues indexed: (46). Subscriptions: $9.50/2 issues or double issue, $10.50 (for.); Single issues: $6, $6.50 (for.).

ChiR: CHICAGO REVIEW, Robert Sitko, ed., Paul Baker, Jane Hoogestraat, Elizabeth Arnold, po. eds., U. of Chicago, Faculty Exchange, Box C, Chicago, IL 60637. Issues indexed: (35:4). Subscriptions: $54/3 yrs., $36/2 yrs., $18/yr., $14/yr. (ind.), plus $4/yr. (for.); Single issues: $4.50.

ChrC: THE CHRISTIAN CENTURY, James M. Wall, ed., 407 S. Dearborn St., Chicago, IL 60605. Issues indexed: (104:1-39). Subscriptions: $28/yr.; Single issues: $1.25.

CimR: CIMARRON REVIEW, Neil J. Hackett, ed., Janemarie Luecke, Nuala Archer, po. eds., 208 Life Sciences East, Oklahoma State U., Stillwater, OK 74078-0273. Issues indexed: (78-81). Subscriptions: $10/yr.; Single issues: $2.50.

ClockR: CLOCKWATCH REVIEW: A Journal of the Arts, James Plath, ed., 737 Penbrook Way, Hartland, WI 53029. Issues indexed: (4:1). Subscriptions: $6/yr.; Single issues: $3.

ColEng: COLLEGE ENGLISH, National Council of Teachers of English, James C. Raymond, ed., James Tate, po. ed., P.O. Drawer AL, Tuscaloosa, AL 35487. Issues indexed: (49:1-8). Subscriptions: $40/yr. (inst.), $35/yr. (ind.), plus $4/yr. (for.); Single issues: $4.50; NCTE, 1111 Kenyon Rd., Urbana, IL 61801.

ColR: COLORADO REVIEW, Bill Tremblay, ed., English Dept., Colorado State U., 360 Eddy Bldg., Fort Collins, CO 80523. Issues indexed: (NS 14:1-2). Subscriptions: $9/yr. (2 issues), $17.50/2 yrs.; Single issues: $5.

*Colum: COLUMBIA: A Magazine of Poetry & Prose, Michael S. Kirkpatrick, Elizabeth Lerner, eds., Karen Blomain, Campbell McGrath, po. eds., 404 Dodge Hall, Columbia Univ., New York, NY 10027. Issues indexed: (12). Subscriptions: $4.50/yr.

Comm: COMMONWEAL, Peter Steinfels, ed., Rosemary Deen, po. ed., 15 Dutch St., New York, NY 10038. Issues indexed: (114:1-22). Subscriptions: $49/2 yrs., $53/2 yrs. (Canada), $59/2 yrs. (for.), $28/yr., $30/yr. (Canada), $33/yr. (for.); Single issues: $1.50.

ConcPo: CONCERNING POETRY, Ellwood Johnson, L. L. Lee, eds., Robert Huff, po. ed., Dept. of English, Western Washington U., Bellingham, WA 98225. Issues indexed: (20). Subscriptions: "Terminates publication with this issue."

Cond: CONDITIONS: A Feminist Magazine of Writing by Women with an Emphasis on Writing by Lesbians, Cheryl Clarke, Dorothy Randall Gray, Pam A. Parker, Annette Peláez, Sabrina, eds., P.O. Box 150056, Van Brunt Station, Brooklyn, NY 11215-0001. Issues indexed: (14). Subscriptions: $34/3 issues (inst.), $24/3 issues (ind), $32 (for.); Single issues: $8.95 (ind.), $10.95 (inst.).

Confr: CONFRONTATION, Martin Tucker, ed., English Dept., C. W. Post Campus of Long Island U., Greenvale, NY 11548. Issues indexed: (35/36). Subscriptions: $30/3 yrs., $20/2 yrs., $10/yr.; Single issues: $6-7.

Conjunc: CONJUNCTIONS: Bi-Annual Volumes of New Writing, Bradford Morrow, ed., 33 West 9th St., New York, NY 10011. Issues indexed: (10-11). Subscriptions: $16/yr. (2 issues), $30/2 yrs.; $20/yr., $40/2 yrs. (inst., for.); $45/yr., $85/ 2 yrs. (cloth binding); Single issues: $8.95.

ConnPR: THE CONNECTICUT POETRY REVIEW, J. Clair White, James Wm. Chichetto, eds., P.O. Box 3783, Amity Station, New Haven, CT 06525. Issues indexed: (6:1). Single issues: $3 (including postage).

Contact: CONTACT II: A Poetry Review, Maurice Kenny, J. G. Gosciak, eds., P.O. Box 451, Bowling Green, New York, NY 10004. Issues indexed: (9:44/45/46). Subscriptions: $8/yr. (ind.); $14/yr. (inst.); Single issues: $6.

CrabCR: CRAB CREEK REVIEW, Linda Clifton, ed., 4462 N. 42nd, Seattle WA 98103. Issues indexed: (4:2-3). Subscriptions: $15/2 yrs., $8/yr.; Single issues: $3.

Crazy: CRAZYHORSE, Zabelle Derounian, managing ed., Ralph Burns, po. ed., Dept. of English, U. of Arkansas, Little Rock, AR 72204. Issues indexed: (32-33). Subscriptions: $8/yr., $15/2 yrs., $22/3 yrs. Single issues: $4.

CreamCR: CREAM CITY REVIEW, Peter Blewett, ed., Renee Deljon, po. ed., English Dept., P.O. Box 413, U. of Wisconsin, Milwaukee, WI 53201. Issues indexed: (11:2/3). Single issues: $4.50; Double issues: $7.50.

CrescentR: THE CRESCENT REVIEW, Bob Shar, ed., P.O. Box 15065, Winston-Salem, NC 27113. Issues indexed: (5:1-2). Subscriptions: $7.50/yr. (2 issues); Single issues: $4.

CrossC: CROSS-CANADA WRITERS' QUARTERLY, Ted Plantos, ed., George Swede, po. ed., Box 277, Station F, Toronto, Ontario M4Y 2L7 Canada. Issues indexed: (9:1-3/4). Subscriptions: $14/yr. (ind.), $16/yr. (inst.), $18/yr (for.); Single issues: $3.95.

CrossCur: CROSSCURRENTS, Linda Brown Michelson, ed., Elizabeth Bartlett, po. ed., 2200 Glastonbury Road, Westlake Village, CA 91361. Issues indexed: (6:4-5, 7:1-3). Subscriptions: $15/yr., $22.50/2 yrs.; Single issues: $6.

*CuadP: CUADERNOS DE POÉTICA, Diógenes Céspedes, Director, Apartado Postal 1736, Santo Domingo, República Domincana; US Editors: Kate Nickel, 111 Oldfather Hall, U. of Nebraska, Lincoln, NE 68588-0315, Rafael Catalá, 10610 Cielo Vista del Sur N.W., Corrales, NM 87048. Issues indexed: (4:12, 5:13). Subscriptions: $25/yr. (ind.), $30/yr. (inst.).

CumbPR: CUMBERLAND POETRY REVIEW, Bob Darrell, Sherry Bevins Darrell, Donald Davie, Malcolm Glass, Jeanne Gore, Michael Kreyling, Laurence Lerner, Alison Reed, Eva Touster, eds., Poetics, Inc., P.O. Box 120128, Acklen Station, Nashville, TN 37212. Issues indexed: (6:2, 7:1). Subscriptions: $12/yr, $22/2 yrs. (ind.); $15/yr., $27/2 yrs. (inst.); $21/yr., $33/2 yrs. (for.); Single issue: $6.

CutB: CUTBANK, Joseph Martin, Bronwyn G. Pughe, eds., Bronwyn G. Pughe, Jennifer Hiebert, po. eds., Dept. of English, U. of Montana, Missoula, MT 59812. Issues indexed: (27/28). Subscriptions: $9/yr.; Single issues: $3.75.

Dandel: DANDELION, Christopher Wiseman, John McDermid, managing eds., Claire Harris, John McDermid, po eds., Alexandra Centre, 922 - 9th Ave., S.E., Calgary, Alberta T2G 0S4 Canada. Issues indexed: (14:1-2). Subscriptions: $18/2 yrs., $10/yr., $15/yr. (inst.); Single issues: $6.

DekalbLAJ: THE DEKALB LITERARY ARTS JOURNAL, Frances S. Ellis, ed., DeKalb College, 555 N. Indian Creek Dr., Clarkston, GA 30021. Issues indexed: (20:1/4). Subscriptions: $15/volume, $17/volume (for.)

DenQ: DENVER QUARTERLY, David Milofsky, ed., Bin Ramke, po. ed., U. of Denver, Denver, CO 80208. Issues indexed: (21:2/4, 22:1-2). Subscriptions: $28/2 yrs., $15/yr., $18/yr. (inst.), plus $1/yr. (for.); Single issues: $5.

Descant: DESCANT, Karen Mulhallen, ed., P.O. Box 314, Station P, Toronto M5S 2S8, Ontario, Canada. Issues indexed: (18:1/2-4, issues 56/57-59). Subscriptions: $18/yr., $32/2 yrs. (ind.); $26/yr., $52/2 yrs. (inst.); plus $4/yr. (for.); Single issues: $8.50-$12.

Electrum: ELECTRUM MAGAZINE, Roger Suva, ed., 2222 Silk Tree Drive, Tustin, CA 92680-7129. Issues indexed: (39). Subscriptions: $10/4 issues, $17/8 issues, plus $5 (for.); Single issues: $3.

Periodicals Indexed

EngJ: ENGLISH JOURNAL, National Council of Teachers of English, Ben F. Nelms, ed., 215-216 Townsend Hall, U. of Missouri, Columbia, MO 65211; Paul Janeczko, po. ed., P.O. Box 1079, Gray, ME 04039. Issues indexed: (76:1-8). Subscriptions: $40/yr. (inst.), $35/yr. (ind.), plus $4/yr. (for.); Single issues: $4.50; NCTE, 1111 Kenyon Rd., Urbana, IL 61801.

Epoch: EPOCH, C. S. Giscombe, ed., 251 Goldwin Smith Hall, Cornell U., Ithaca, NY 14853-3201. Issues indexed: (36:1-3). Subscriptions: $9.50/yr.; Single issues: $3.50.

Event: EVENT: The Douglas College Review, Dale Zieroth, ed., Douglas College, P.O. Box 2503, New Westminster, B.C., V3L 5B2 Canada. Issues indexed: (16:1-3). Subscriptions: $9/yr., $17/2 yrs.; $17/2 yrs. (lib.); Single issue: $4.

Farm: FARMER'S MARKET, Jean C. Lee, John E. Hughes, Gail Nichols, eds., Midwest Farmer's Market, Inc., P.O. Box 1272, Galesburg, IL 61402. Issues indexed: (4:1-2). Subscriptions: $7/yr. (2 issues).

Field: FIELD: Contemporary Poetry and Poetics, Stuart Friebert, David Young, eds., Rice Hall, Oberlin College, Oberlin, OH 44074. Issues indexed: (36-37). Subscriptions: $16/2 yrs., $10/yr.; Single issues: $5.; Back issues: $10.

*FiveFR: FIVE FINGERS REVIEW, Kim Addonizio, Lori Callies, Carol Dorf, John High, Jonathan Merritt, eds., 553 25th Ave., San Francisco, CA 94121. Issues indexed: (5). Subscriptions: $20/4 issues, $11/2 issues, plus $5 (for.); Single issues: $6.

FloridaR: THE FLORIDA REVIEW, Pat Rushin, ed., Tom George, po. ed., Dept. of English, U. of Central Florida, Orlando, FL 32816. Issues indexed: (15:1-2). Subscriptions: $7/yr., $11/2 yrs.; Single issues: $4.50.

*Footwork: FOOTWORK, A Literary Collection of Contemporary Poetry, Short Fiction, and Art, Maria Gillan, ed., Passaic County Community College, College Boulevard, Paterson, NJ 07509. Issues indexed: (1987). Subscriptions: $5/issue + $1 for postage and handling.

*FourQ: FOUR QUARTERS, John J. Keenan, ed., La Salle U., Philadelphia, PA 19141. Issues indexed: Second Series (1:1-2). Subscriptions: $8/yr. (2 issues), $13/2 yrs.; Single issues: $4.

*Gambit: GAMBIT MAGAZINE: A Journal of the Ohio Valley, a joint publication of the Ohio Valley Literary Group and Parkersburg Community College, Jane Somerville, ed., P.O. Box 1122, Marietta, OH 45750. Issues Indexed: (20-21). Single issues: $3.

Gargoyle: GARGOYLE MAGAZINE, Richard Peabody, Jr., ed./pub., Gretchen Johnsen, po. ed., Paycock Press, P.O. Box 30906, Bethesda, MD 20814. Issues indexed: (32/33); According to the publisher, No. 30/31 was "fiction only." It was not indexed. Subscriptions: $10/2 issues (ind.), $12/2 issues (inst.). Single issues: $5.95-7.95.

GeoR: GEORGIA REVIEW, Stanley W. Lindberg, ed., U. of Georgia, Athens, GA 30602. Issues indexed: (41:1-4). Subscriptions: $20/2 yrs., $12/yr., plus $3/yr. (for.); Single issues: $5, $6 (for.).

Germ: GERMINATION, Allan Cooper, ed. & pub., Leigh Faulkner, Assoc. ed., 428 Yale Ave., Riverview, New Brunswick E1B 2B5, Canada. Issues indexed: (10:2, 11:1). Subscriptions: $6/2 issues (ind.), $8/2 issues (inst.); Single issues: $3.50.

GrahamHR: GRAHAM HOUSE REVIEW, Peter Balakian & Bruce Smith, eds., Colgate U. Press, Box 5000, Colgate U., Hamilton, NY 13346; Issues indexed: (10). Subscriptions: $17/2 yrs; Single issues: $4.50.

Grain: GRAIN, Saskatchewan Writers Guild, Brenda Riches, ed., Garry Radison, po. ed., Box 3986, Regina, Saskatchewan S4P 3R9 Canada. Issues indexed: (15:1-4). Subscriptions: $20/2 yrs., $12/yr.; Single issues: $4.

GrandS: GRAND STREET, Ben Sonnenberg, ed., 50 Riverside Dr., New York, NY 10024. Issues indexed: (6:2-4, 7:1). Subscriptions: $20/yr. (ind.), $24/yr. (for.); $24/yr. (inst.), $28/yr. (for. inst.); Single issues: $5; Back issues, $6..

GreenfR: GREENFIELD REVIEW, Joseph Bruchac III, ed., 2 Middle Grove Road, Greenfield Center, NY 12833. Issues indexed: (14:1/2-3/4). Volume 14, numbers 3 & 4 is the final issue.

*GreensboroR: THE GREENSBORO REVIEW, Jim Clark, ed., Elizabeth Gayle, po. ed., Dept. of English, U. of North Carolina, Greensboro, NC 27412. Issues indexed: (39-43). Subscriptions: $5/yr. (2 issues), $12/3 yrs.; Single issues: $2.50.

GWR: THE G. W. REVIEW, The Editor, Box 20, Marvin Center, The George Washington U., 800 21st St., N.W., Washington, DC 20052 (Editor changes annually). Issues indexed: No 1987 issues received. Subscriptions: $6/yr.; Single copies: $1.50.

*HampSPR: THE HAMPDEN-SYDNEY POETRY REVIEW, Tom O'Grady, ed., P.O. Box 126, Hampden-Sydney, VA 23943. Issues indexed: 1986, 1987. Subscriptions: $5/yr. (single issue).

HangL: HANGING LOOSE, Robert Hershon, Dick Lourie, Mark Pawlak, Ron Schreiber, eds., 231 Wyckoff St., Brooklyn, NY 11217. Issues indexed: (50/51) Special issue: Hang Together, The Hanging Loose Press 20th Anniversary Anthology. Subscriptions: $25/9 issues, $17.50/6 issues, $9/3 issues; Single issues: $3.50 plus $1 postage and handling.

Harp: HARPER'S MAGAZINE, Lewis H. Lapham, ed., 666 Broadway, New York, NY 10012. Issues indexed: (274:1640-1645, 275:1646-1651). Subscriptions: $18/yr., plus $2/yr. (USA possessions, Canada), plus $3/yr. (for.); Single issues: $2; P.O. Box 1937, Marion, OH 43305.

HarvardA: THE HARVARD ADVOCATE, Dan Buchanan, Managing ed., K. Michèle Walters, po. ed., 21 South St., Cambridge, MA 02138. Issues indexed: (120:2 Mr 87; 121:3 My 87; 122:1 N '87; 122:2 D 87) volume numbering appears to be erratic! Subscriptions: $15/yr. (ind.), $17/yr. (inst.), $20/yr. (for.).

HawaiiR: HAWAII REVIEW, Faye Kicknosway, John Rieder, Robert Shapard, Faculty Readers, U. of Hawaii at Manoa, Dept. of English, 1733 Donaghho Rd., Honolulu, HI 06822. Issues indexed: (19-22). Subscriptions: $6/yr. (2 issues); Single issue: $4.

HayF: HAYDEN'S FERRY REVIEW, Marcia Hamilton, Managing ed., John Graves Morris, Paul Morris, po. eds., Student Publications, Matthews Center, Arizona State U., Tempe, AZ 85287. Issues indexed: (2). Subscriptions: $4/yr. (1 issue) plus $1 postage & handling.

HeliconN: HELICON NINE: The Journal of Women's Arts & Letters, Gloria Vando Hickok, ed., P.O. Box 22412, Kansas City, MO 64113. Issues indexed: (17/18). Subscriptions: $18/yr. (3 issues), $33/2 yrs., $22/yr. (inst.), plus $1/issue (for.); Single issues: $8-12.

HighP: HIGH PLAINS LITERARY REVIEW, Robert O. Greer, Jr., ed., Joy Harjo, po. ed., 180 Adams St., Suite 250, Denver, CO 80206. Issues indexed: (2:1-3). Subscriptions: $20/yr. (3 issues), $38/2 yrs., plus $5/yr. (for.); Single issues: $7.

HiramPoR: HIRAM POETRY REVIEW, English Dept., Hiram College, Hale Chatfield & Carol Donley, eds., P.O. Box 162, Hiram, OH 44234. Issues indexed: (43). Subscriptions: $4/yr. (2 issues); Single issues: $2.

HolCrit: THE HOLLINS CRITIC, John Rees Moore, ed., Hollins College, VA 24020. Issues indexed: (24:1-5). Subscriptions: $6/yr., $10/2 yrs., $14/3 yrs.; $7.50/yr., $11.50/2 yrs., $15.50/3 yrs. (for.).

Hudson: THE HUDSON REVIEW, Paula Deitz, Frederick Morgan, eds., 684 Park Ave., New York, NY 10021. Issues indexed: (39:4, 40:1-3). Subscriptions: $18/yr., $34/2 yrs., $50/3 yrs., plus $3/yr. (for.); Single issues: $5.

IndR: INDIANA REVIEW, Elizabeth Dodd, ed., Krista Adams, Lynda 2Hull, Kathy May, po. eds., 316 N. Jordan Ave., Bloomington, IN 47405. Issues indexed: (10:1/1-3, 11:1). Subscriptions: $10/3 issues, $12/3 issues (inst.); $18/6 issues (ind.), $20/6 issues (inst.); plus $5/3 issues (for.). Single issues: $4.

Periodicals Indexed

Interim: INTERIM, A. Wilber Stevens, ed., Dept. of English, U. of Nevada, Las Vegas, NV 89154. Issues indexed: (6:1-2). Subscriptions: $5/yr. (ind.), $8/yr. (inst.), $10/yr. (for.); Single issues: $3.

InterPR: INTERNATIONAL POETRY REVIEW, Evalyn P. Gill, Raymond Tyner, eds., Box 2047, Greensboro, NC 27402. Issues indexed: (13:1-2). Subscriptions: $7/yr. (2 issues); Single issues: $3.50.

Inti: INTI, Revista de Literatura Hispanica, Roger B. Carmosino, ed., Dept. of Modern Languages, Providence College, Providence, RI 02918. Issues indexed: (22/23-24/25). Subscriptions: $20/yr. (ind.), $25/yr. (for.); $30/yr. (inst.)); Single issues: $15, $25 (double issues).

Iowa: IOWA REVIEW, David Hamilton, ed., 308 EPB, U. of Iowa, Iowa City, IA 52242. Issues indexed: (17:1-3). Subscriptions: $20/yr. (inst.), $15/yr. (ind.), plus $3/yr. (for.); Single issues: $6.95.

Jacaranda: THE JACARANDA REVIEW, Laurence Roth, ed., Dept. of English, U. of California, Los Angeles, 90024. Issues indexed: (2:2). Subscriptions: $5/yr. (2 issues), $8/yr. (inst.).

JamesWR: THE JAMES WHITE REVIEW, A Gay Men's Literary Journal, Greg Baysans, David Lindahl, eds., P.O. Box 3356, Traffic Station, Minneapolis, MN 55403. Issues indexed: (4:2-4, 5:1). Subscriptions: $10/yr., $17/2 yrs.; $12/yr. (Canada); $15/yr. (other for.); Single issues: $2.50; Back issues, $3.

JlNJPo: THE JOURNAL OF NEW JERSEY POETS, Marjorie Keyishian, Managing ed., English Dept., Fairleigh Dickinson U., 285 Madison Ave., Madison, NJ 07940. Issues indexed: No 1987 issue published. Subscriptions: $3/2 issues; Single issues: $1.50.

Kaleid: KALEIDOSCOPE, International Magazine of Literature, Fine Arts, and Disability; Darshan Perusek, ed., Chris Hewitt (228 W. 71 St., Apt. F, New York, NY 10023), po. ed., United Cerebral Palsy and Services for the Handicapped, 326 Locust St., Akron, OH 44302. Issues indexed: (14-15). Subscriptions: $8/yr. (2 issues); $12/yr. (for.); Single issues: $4; $6 (for.); Back issues: $3; $5 (for.).

KanQ: KANSAS QUARTERLY, Harold Schneider, Ben Nyberg, W. R. Moses, John Rees, eds., Dept. of English, Denison Hall, Kansas State U., Manhattan, KS 66506. Issues indexed: (19:1/2-4). Subscriptions: $15/yr., $27/2 yrs. (USA, Canada, Latin America); $16/yr., $29/2 yrs. (other countries); Single issues: $5.

KenR: KENYON REVIEW, Philip D. Church, Galbraith M. Crump, eds., Kenyon College, Gambier, OH 43022. Issues indexed: (NS 9:1-4). Subscriptions: Kenyon Review, P.O. Box 1308 L, Fort Lee, NJ 07024; $15/yr., $28/2 yrs., $39/3 yrs. (ind.); $18/yr. (inst.); plus $5 (for.); Single issues: $6.50; Back issues: $5.

*Lactuca: LACTUCA, Mike Selender, ed., P.O. Box 621, Suffern, NY 10901. Issues indexed: (5-8). Subscriptions: $10/yr.; Single issues: $3.

LakeSR: THE LAKE STREET REVIEW, Kevin FitzPatrick, ed., Box 7188, Powderhorn Station, Minneapolis, MN 55407. Issues indexed: (21). Subscriptions: $4/2 yrs. (2 issues); Single issues: $2.

LaurelR: LAUREL REVIEW, Craig Goad, ed., Green Tower Press, Dept. of English, Northwest Missouri State U., Maryville, MO 64468. Issues indexed: (20:1/2-21:1/2). Subscriptions: $8/yr. (2 issues), $14/2 yrs.; Single issues: $3.50.

LetFem: LETRAS FEMENINAS, Asociación de Literatura Femenina Hispánica, Adelaida López de Martínez, Directora., Dept. of Modern Languages, Texas A & M U., College Station, TX 77843-4238. Issues indexed: (13:1/2). Membership/Subscription: $20/yr; $25/yr. (lib.).

*LightY: LIGHT YEAR: The Biennial of Light Verse & Witty Poems, Robert Wallace, ed., Bits Press, Dept. of English, Case Western Reserve U., Cleveland, OH 44106. Issues indexed: ('87). Subscriptions: '87, $13.95; '88/9, $15.95.

LindLM: LINDEN LANE MAGAZINE, Belkis Cuza Malé, ed., P.O. Box 2384, Princeton, NJ 08540-0384. Issues indexed: (6:1, 2/3, 4). Subscriptions: $12/yr. (ind.), $18/yr. (inst.), $22/yr. (for.); Single issues: $2.

Lips: LIPS, Laura Boss, ed., P.O. Box 1345, Montclair, NJ 07042. Issues indexed: (13). Subscriptions: $9/yr. (3 issues), $12/yr. (inst).; Single issues: $3, $4 (inst.).

LitR: THE LITERARY REVIEW, Walter Cummins, ed., Fairleigh Dickinson U., 285 Madison Ave., Madison, NJ 07940. Issues indexed: (30:2-4, 31:1). Subscriptions: $12/yr., $15/yr. (for.); $22/2 yrs., $28/2 yrs. (for.); Single issues: $4.50, $5.50 (for.).

LittleM: THE LITTLE MAGAZINE, Kathryn Cramer, et al ., eds, Dragon Press, P.O. Box 78, Pleasantville, NY 10570. Issues Indexed: No issues published in 1987. Next issue (15:3/4) published in 1988.

*Lyra: LYRA, Lourdes Gil, Iraida Iturralde, eds., P.O. Box 3188, Guttenberg, NJ 07093. Issues indexed: (1:1-2). Subscriptions: $10/yr. (4 issues, ind.), $15/yr. (inst.), plus $5/yr. (for.); Single issues: $3, $5 (for.).

Mairena: MAIRENA: Revista de Crítica y Poesía, Manuel de la Puebla, director, Himalaya 257, Urbanización Monterrey, Río Piedras, PR 00926. Issues indexed: (9:23-24). Subscriptions: $6/yr., $10/yr. (inst.), $10/yr. (for.), $15/yr. (for. inst.).

MalR: THE MALAHAT REVIEW, Constance Rooke, ed., P.O. Box 1700, Victoria, B. C., Canada V8W 2Y2. Issues indexed: (78-81). Subscriptions: $40/3 yrs., $15/yr. (USA, Canada), $50/3 yrs., $20/yr. (other countries), $10/yr. (stud.); Single issues: $7 (USA, Canada), $8 (other countries).

ManhatPR: MANHATTAN POETRY REVIEW, Elaine Reiman-Fenton, ed., F.D.R. P.O. Box 8207, New York, NY 10150. Issues indexed: (9). Subscriptions: $10/yr. (2 issues), $20/yr. (for.), $18/2 yrs., $38/2 yrs. (for.); Single issues: $5.80; Back issues: $25.

ManhatR: THE MANHATTAN REVIEW, Philip Fried, ed., 304 Third Ave., Suite 4A, New York, NY 10010. Issues indexed: No 1987 issues published. Next issue 4:2, 1988. Subscriptions: $8/2 issues (ind.), $12/2 issues (inst.), plus $2.50/2 issues (outside USA & Canada); Back issues: $4 (ind.), $6 (inst).

*Margin: MARGIN: A Quarterly Magazine of Literature, Arts and Ideas, Robin Magowan, ed., 46 Shepard St., #42, Cambridge, MA 02138. Issues indexed: (1-5). Subscriptions: $20/4 issues; $24/4 issues (Canada); Single issues: $7.

MassR: THE MASSACHUSETTS REVIEW, Mary Heath, Fred Robinson, eds., Anne Halley, Paul Jenkins, po. eds., Memorial Hall, U. of Massachusetts, Amherst, MA 01003. Issues indexed: (28:1-4). Subscriptions: $12/yr. (ind.), $15/yr. (lib.), $17/yr. (for.); Single issues: $4.

MemphisSR: MEMPHIS STATE REVIEW, William Page, ed., Dept. of English, Memphis State U., Memphis, TN 38152. Issues indexed: (7:2, 8:1). Subscriptions: $5/yr. (ind., 2 issues), $6/yr. (inst).; Single issues: $3.

Mester: MESTER, Maria-Luiza Carrano, ed., Dept. of Spanish and Portuguese, U. of California, Los Angeles, CA 90024. Issues indexed: (16:1-2). Subscriptions: $17/yr. (inst.), $10/yr. (ind.), $6/yr. (stud.), plus $2/yr. outside U.S., Canada, Mexico; Single issues: $7 (inst.), $4 (ind.)

MichQR: MICHIGAN QUARTERLY REVIEW, Laurence Goldstein, ed., 3032 Rackham Bldg., U. of Michigan, Ann Arbor, MI 48109. Issues indexed: (26:1-4). Subscriptions: $24/2 yr., $13/yr. (ind.), $15/yr. (inst.); Single issues: $3.50; Back issues: $2.

MidAR: MID-AMERICAN REVIEW, Robert Early, ed., Sally Kraine, po. ed., 106 Hanna Hall, Dept. of English, Bowling Green State U., Bowling Green, OH 43403. Issues indexed: (7:2). Subscriptions: $6/yr. (2 issues), $10/2 yrs., $14/3 yrs.

MidwQ: THE MIDWEST QUARTERLY, James B. M. Schick, ed., Stephen E. Meats, po. ed., Pittsburg State U., Pittsburg, KS 66762-5889. Issues indexed: (28:2-4, 29:1). Subscriptions: $8/yr. plus $2 (for.); Single issues: $2.50.

Periodicals Indexed

MinnR: THE MINNESOTA REVIEW, Helen Cooper, Marlon Ross, Michael Sprinker, Susan Squier, eds, Helen Cooper, po. ed., Dept. of English, State U. of New York, Stony Brook, NY 11794-5350. Issues Indexed: (NS 28-29). Subscriptions: $24/2 yrs. (inst. & for.), $12/2 yrs. (ind.); $14/yr. (inst. & for.), $7/yr. (ind.); Single issues: $4.

MissouriR: THE MISSOURI REVIEW, Speer Morgan, ed., Sherod Santos, Garrett Kaoru Hongo, po. eds., Dept. of English, 231 Arts and Science, U. of Missouri, Columbia, MO 65211. Issues indexed: (10:1-3). Subscriptions: $21/2 yrs. (6 issues), $12/yr. (3 issues). Single issues: $5.

MissR: MISSISSIPPI REVIEW, Frederick Barthelme, ed., The Center for Writers, U. of Southern Mississippi, Southern Station, Box 5144, Hattiesburg, MS 39406-5144. Issues indexed: (15:3, issue 45). Subscriptions: $26/3 yrs., $18/2 yrs., $10/yr., plus $2/yr. (for.); Single issues: usually $5.

MoodySI: MOODY STREET IRREGULARS, Joy Walsh, ed., P.O. Box 157, Clarence Center, NY 14032. Issues indexed: (18/19). Subscriptions: $10/4 single, 2 double issues (ind.), $15/4 single, 2 double issues (lib.); Single issues: $3, double issues: $5.

MSS: MSS, L. M. Rosenberg, ed., Box 530, State U. of NY at Binghamton, Binghamton, NY 13901. Issues indexed: (5:2-3, 6:1). Subscriptions: $18/2 yrs. (ind.), $35/2 yrs. (lib.); $10/yr. (ind.), $20/yr. (lib.); Single issues: $4., Double issues: $6.

Nat: THE NATION, Victor Navasky, ed., Grace Schulman, po. ed., 72 Fifth Ave., New York, NY 10011. Issues indexed: (244:1-25, 245:1-22). Subscriptions: $67/2 yrs., $36/yr., plus $9/yr. (for.); Single issues: $1.25; Back issues: $3, $4 (for.). Send subscription correspondence to: P.O. Box 1953, Marion, OH 43305.

NegC: NEGATIVE CAPABILITY, Sue Walker, ed., 62 Ridgelawn Dr. East, Mobile, AL 36608. Issues indexed: (7:1/2-3/4). Subscriptions: $12/yr. (ind.), $16/yr. (inst., for.); Single issues: $4.

NewAW: NEW AMERICAN WRITING, Maxine Chernoff, Paul Hoover, eds., OINK! Press, 1446 West Jarvis, Chicago, IL 60626. Issues indexed: (1-2). Subscriptions: $6/issue.

NewEngR: NEW ENGLAND REVIEW AND BREAD LOAF QUARTERLY, Sydney Lea, Maura High, eds., Middlebury College, Middlebury, VT 05753. Issues indexed: (9:3-4, 10:1-2). Subscriptions: $12/yr. (4 issues), $22/2 yrs., $33/3 yrs. (ind.); $18/yr., $26/2 yrs., $33/3 yrs. (inst.); plus $3/yr. (for.); Single issues: $4.

NewL: NEW LETTERS, James McKinley, ed., U. of Missouri-Kansas City, 5216 Rockhill Rd., Kansas City, MO 64110. Issues indexed: (53:2-4, 54:1-2). Subscriptions: $50/5 yrs., $25/2 yrs., $15/yr. (ind.); $60/5 yrs., $30/2 yrs., $18/yr. (lib.); Single issues: $4.

NewOR: NEW ORLEANS REVIEW, John Biguenet, John Mosier, eds., Box 195, Loyola U., New Orleans, LA 70118. Issues indexed: (14:1-4). Subscriptions: $25/yr. (ind.), $30/yr. (inst.), $35/yr. (for.); Single issues: $9.

NewRena: THE NEW RENAISSANCE, Louise T. Reynolds, ed., Stanwood Bolton, po. ed., 9 Heath Road, Arlington, MA 02174. Issues indexed: (7:1, #21). Subscriptions: $20/6 issues, $10.50/3 issues; $24/6 issues, $12.50/3 issues (Canada, Mexico, Europe); $26/6 issues, $13.50/3 issues (elsewhere); Single issues: $5.

NewRep: THE NEW REPUBLIC, Martin Peretz, ed., 1220 19th St. N.W., Washington, DC 20036. Issues indexed: (196:1-26, 197:1-26). Subscriptions: $56/yr., $70 (Canada), $81 (elsewhere). Back issues: $2.50. Single issues: $2.25. Subscription Service Dept., The New Republic, P.O. Box 56515, Boulder, CO 80322.

NewYorker: THE NEW YORKER, 25 W. 43rd St., New York, NY 10036. Issues indexed: (62:46-52, 63:1-45). Subscriptions: $52/2 yrs., $32/yr.; $50/yr. (Canada); $56/yr. (other for.); Single issues: $1.75; Subscription correspondence to: Box 56447, Boulder, CO 80322.

NewYRB: THE NEW YORK REVIEW OF BOOKS, Robert B. Silvers, Barbara Epstein, eds., 250 W. 57th St., New York, NY 10107. Issues indexed: (33:21/22, 34:1-20). Subscriptions: $34/yr., $64/2 yrs, $95/3 yrs; plus $6/yr. (N. & S. America); plus $8 (other for.); Single issues: $2; Subscription Service Dept., P.O. Box 940, Farmingdale, NY 11737.

Nimrod: NIMROD, Francine Ringold, ed., Joan Flint, Manly Johnson, po. eds., Arts and Humanities Council of Tulsa, 2210 S. Main St., Tulsa, OK 74114. Issues indexed: (30:2, 31:1). Subscriptions: $11/yr. (2 issues), $18/2 yrs., $26/3 yrs., plus $3/yr. (for.); Single issues: $5.50, $7 (for.).

NoAmR: THE NORTH AMERICAN REVIEW, Robley Wilson, Jr., ed., Peter Cooley, po. ed., U. of Northern Iowa, Cedar Falls, IA 50614. Issues indexed: (272:1-4). Subscriptions: $11/yr., $12/yr. (Canada, Latin America), $14/yr. (elsewhere); Single issues: $3.

NoDaQ: NORTH DAKOTA QUARTERLY, Robert W. Lewis, ed., Jay Meek, po. ed., Box 8237, U. of North Dakota, Grand Forks, ND 58202. Issues indexed: (55:1-4). Subscriptions: $10/yr.; Single issues: $4.

Northeast: NORTHEAST, John & JOANNE Judson, ed., Juniper Press, 1310 Shorewood Dr., La Crosse, WI 54601. Issues indexed: (Ser. 4:5-6). Subscriptions: $30 (ind.), $35 (inst.), includes Juniper Books, a haiku-short poem booklet, W.N.J. Series Books, and a gift book in additiona to NORTHEAST; Single issues: $3.

Notus: NOTUS, New Writing, Pat Smith, ed., 2420 Walter Dr., Ann Arbor, MI 48103. Issues indexed: (2:1-2); volume 1 consisted of number 1 only. Subscriptions: $10/yr., 2 issues, U.S. & Canada (ind.), $14/yr. (elsewhere), $20/yr. (inst.).

NowestR: NORTHWEST REVIEW, John Witte, ed. & po. ed., 369 PLC, U. of Oregon, Eugene, OR 97403. Issues indexed: (25:1-3). Subscriptions: $30/3 yrs., $21/2 yrs., $11/yr., 3 issues; $20/2 yrs., $10/yr. (stud.); plus $2/yr. (for.); Single issues: $4-10.

Obs: OBSIDIAN II: Black Literature in Review, Gerald Barrax, ed., Dept. of English, Box 8105, North Carolina State University, Raleigh, NC 27695-8105. Issues indexed: No 1987 issues received. Subscriptions: $10/yr., $18/2 yrs.; $11/yr. (Canada), $13/yr. (other for.); Single issues: $4; Double issues: $8.

OhioR: THE OHIO REIVEW, Wayne Dodd, ed., Ellis Hall, Ohio U., Athens, OH 45701-2979. Issues indexed: (38-39). Subscriptions: $30/3 yrs. (9 issues), $12/yr. (3 issues); Single issues: $4.25.

Oink: OINK! Superseded by New American Writing, first issue, 1987. See NewAW.

OntR: ONTARIO REVIEW, Raymond J. Smith, ed., 9 Honey Brook Dr., Princeton, NJ 08540. Issues indexed: (26-27). Subscriptions: $8/yr. (2 issues), $15/2 yrs., $21/3 yrs., plus $1/yr. (for.); Single issues: $3.95.

OP: OPEN PLACES, Eleanor M. Bender, ed., Box 2085, Stephens College, Columbia, MO 65215. Issues indexed: Sum 87, final issue.

OroM: ORO MADRE, Loss and Jan Glazier, eds., 4429 Gibraltar Dr., Fremont, CA 94536. Issues indexed: No 1986 or 1987 issues received. Subscriptions: $12/4 issues; Single issues: $3.95.

Os: OSIRIS, Andrea Moorhead, ed., Box 297, Deerfield, MA 01342. Issues indexed: (24-25). Subscriptions: $7/2 issues, $10/2 issues (inst.). Single issues: $3.50.

Outbr: OUTERBRIDGE, Charlotte Alexander, ed., Linda Principe, po. ed., English Dept. (A323), College of Staten Island, 715 Ocean Terrace, Staten Island, NY 10301. Issues indexed: (18/19). Subscriptions: $5/yr. (1 issue); double issues: $2.

Paint: PAINTBRUSH: A Journal of Poetry, Translations, and Letters, Ben Bennani, ed., Division of Language and Literature, Northeast Missouri State U., Kirksville, MO 63501. Issues indexed: (14:27/28). Subscriptions: $6/yr. (ind.), $8/yr. (inst.); Single issues: $5; Back issues: $5.

PaintedB: PAINTED BRIDE QUARTERLY, Louis Camp, Joanna DiPaolo, Louis McKee, eds., Painted Bride Art Center, 230 Vine St., Philadelphia, PA 19106. Issues indexed: (30-31). Subscriptions: $12/yr. (4 issues), $20/2 yrs., $16/yr. (lib, inst.); Single issues: $5. Distributed free to inmates.

ParisR: THE PARIS REVIEW, George A. Plimpton, Peter Matthiessen, Donald Hall, Robert B. Silvers, Blair Fuller, Maxine Groffsky, eds., Jonathan Galassi, po. ed., 541 East 72nd St., New York, NY 10021. Issues indexed: 102-105. Subscriptions: $1000/life, $60/12 issues, $40/8 issues, $20/4 issues, plus $4/4 issues (for.); Single issues: $5; Subscription address: 45-39 171 Place, Flushing, NY 11358.

PartR: PARTISAN REVIEW, William Phillips, ed., Boston U., 141 Bay State Rd., Boston, MA 02215. Issues indexed: (54:1-4). Subscriptions: $47/3 yrs., $33/2 yrs., $18/yr. (4 issues); $36/2 yrs., $21/yr. (for.); $28/yr. (inst.); Single issues: $5.

PassN: PASSAGES NORTH, Elinor Benedict, ed., Bay Arts Writers' Guild of the William Bonifas Fine Arts Center, Inc., Escanaba, MI 49829. Issues indexed: (8:1-2). Subscriptions: $2/yr., $5/3 yrs; Single issues: $1.50.

Pax: PAX: A Journal for Peace through Culture, Bryce Milligan, ed., Center for Peace through Culture, 217 Pershing Ave., San Antonio, TX 78209. Issues indexed: No 1987 issues received. Subscriptions: $15/3 issues (U.S., Canada, Mexico); $20/3 issues (inst.); $25/3 issues (other for.).

Pembroke: PEMBROKE MAGAZINE, Shelby Stephenson, ed., Box 60, Pembroke State U., Pembroke, NC 28372. Issues indexed: (19). Subscriptions: $3/issue (USA, Canada, Mexico), $3.50/issue (for.).

PennR: THE PENNSYLVANIA REVIEW, Ed Ochester, executive ed., James Gyure, po. ed., 526 Cathedral of Learning, U. of Pittsburgh, Pittsburgh, PA 15260. Issues indexed: (3:1-2); Vol. 2, no. 2 never published. Subscriptions: $9/yr., $15/2 yrs.; Single issues: $5.

Pequod: PEQUOD, Mark Rudman, ed., Dept. of English, Room 200, New York U., 19 University Place, New York, NY 10003. Issues indexed: (23/24). Subscriptions: $17/2 yrs. (4 issues), $9/yr. (2 issues) (ind.); $30/2 yrs., $15/yr. (inst).; plus $3/yr. (for.); Single issues: $5.

*Phoenix: PHOENIX, Joan S. Isom, ed., Division of Arts & Letters, Northeastern State U., Tahlequah, OK 74464. Issues indexed: (7:1-2). Subscriptions: $9.50/yr. (2 issues), $11/yr. (for.); Single issues: $5, $6.50 (for.).

Pig: PIG IRON, Rose Sayre & Jim Villani, eds., Pig Iron Press, P.O. Box 237, Youngstown, OH 44501. Issues indexed: (14). Single issues: $6.95.

PikeF: THE PIKESTAFF FORUM, Robert D. Sutherland, James R. Scrimgeour, eds./pubs., P.O. Box 127, Normal, IL 61761. Issues indexed: (8). Subscriptions: $10/6 issues; Single issues: $2; Back issues: $2.

Ploughs: PLOUGHSHARES, DeWitt Henry, Peter O'Malley, Directors, Div. of Writing, Publishing and Literature, Emerson College, 100 Beacon St., Boston, MA 02116; send manuscripts to Box 529, Cambridge, MA 02139-0529. Issues indexed: (13:1, 2/3, 4). Subscriptions: $15/yr. (ind.), $18/yr. (for. ind.); $18/yr. (inst.), $21/yr. (for. inst.). Single issues: $5.95.

Poem: POEM, Huntsville Literary Association, Nancy Frey Dillard, eds., c/o English Dept., U. of Alabama, Huntsville, AL 35899. Issues indexed: (57-58). Subscriptions: $7.50/yr., $10/yr. (for.); Sample issue: $2.50; Back issues: $5; Huntsville Literary Association, P.O. Box 919, Huntsville, AL 35804.

PoetC: POET AND CRITIC, Neal Bowers, ed., Mary Swander, Anita Helle, po eds., 203 Ross Hall, Iowa State U., Ames, IA 50011. Issues indexed: (18:2-3, 19:1). Subscriptions: Iowa State U. Press, South State St., Ames, IA 50010, 12/yr., plus $3/yr. (for.); Single issues: $4; .

PoeticJ: POETIC JUSTICE: Contemporary American Poetry, Alan Engebretsen, ed., 8220 Rayford Dr., Los Angeles, CA 90045. Issues indexed: (17). Subscriptions: $10/4 issues (irregular); Single issues: $3.

PoetL: POET LORE, Philip K. Jason, Barbara Lefcowitz, Roland Flint, Executive eds., The Writer's Center, 7815 Old Georgetown Rd., Bethesda, MD 20814. Issues Indexed: (81:3-4, 82:1-4). Subscriptions: $12/yr., $20/yr. (inst.), plus $5/yr. (for.); Single issues: $4.

Poetry: POETRY, Joseph Parisi, ed., 60 W. Walton St., Chicago, IL 60610. Issues indexed: (149:4-6, 150:1-6, 151:1/2-3). Subscriptions: $22/yr., $27/yr. (for.); Single issues: $2.50 plus $.75 postage; Back issues: $3 plus $.75 postage.

PoetryE: POETRY EAST, Richard Jones, Kate Daniels, eds., Dept. of English, 802 W. Belden Ave., DePaul Univ., Chicago, IL 60614. Issues indexed: (22-23/24). Subscriptions: $10/yr.; Single issues: $4-$7.

PoetryNW: POETRY NORTHWEST, David Wagoner, ed., U. of Washington, 4045 Brooklyn Ave., NE, Seattle, WA 98105. Issues indexed: (28:1-4). Subscriptions: $10/yr., $12/yr. (for.); Single issues: $3, $3.50 (for.).

PottPort: THE POTTERSFIELD PORTFOLIO, Peggy Amirault, Barbara Cottrell, Robin Metcalfe, Donalee Moulton-Barrett, eds., Crazy Quilt Press, c/o 19 Oakhill Drive, Halifax, Nova Scotia B3M 2V3 Canada. Issues indexed: No 1987 issues published. Subscriptions: $12/3 yrs. (ind.), $15/3 yrs. (inst.); $15/3 yrs. (USA, for. ind.), $18/3 yrs. (USA, for. inst., USA); Single issues: $4.50.

PraF: PRAIRIE FIRE, Andris Taskans, ed., Kristjana Gunnars, po. ed., 208-100 Arthur Street, Winnipeg, Manitoba R3B 1H3 Canada. Issues indexed: (8:1-4). Subscriptions: $18/yr. (ind.), $24/yr. (inst.), plus $6 (for.); Single issues: $5.95.

PraS: PRAIRIE SCHOONER, Hilda Raz, ed., Sally Herrin, Marcia Southwick, po. readers, 201 Andrews Hall, U. of Nebraska, Lincoln, NE 68588-0334. Issues indexed: (61:1-4). Subscriptions: $39/3 yrs., $28/2 yrs., $15/yr. (ind.); $19/yr. (lib.); Single issues: $4.

Prima: PRIMAVERA, Ann Grearen, Lisa Grayson, Jeanne Krinsley, Karen Frankfather Peterson, Julie Weissman, Ruth Young, eds., 1212 East 59th, Chicago, IL 60637. Issues indexed: No 1987 issues published. Next issue: (11/12) 1988. Single issues: $5.

Puerto: PUERTO DEL SOL, Joe Somoza, po. ed., English Dept., Box 3E, New Mexico State U., Las Cruces, NM 88003. Issues indexed: (22:2). Subscriptions: $7.75/yr. (2 issues), $15/2 yrs., $22/3 yrs.; Single issues: $4.

Quarry: QUARRY, Bob Hilderley, ed., Box 1061, Kingston, Ontario K7L 4Y5 Canada. Issues indexed: (36:1-4). Subscriptions: $18/yr. (4 issues), $30/2 yrs. (8 issues); Single issues: $4.50.

QRL: QUARTERLY REVIEW OF LITERATURE, T. & R. Weiss, 26 Haslet Ave., Princeton, NJ 08540. Issues indexed: Poetry series 8, vol. 27. Subscriptions: $15/2 volumes (paper), $20/volume (cloth, inst.).

QW: QUARTERLY WEST, Kevin Cantwell, Jonathan Maney, eds.; Beth Tornes, Ralph Wilson, po. eds., 317 Olpin Union, U. of Utah, Salt Lake City, UT 84112. Issues indexed: (24-25). Subscriptions: $17/2 yrs. (4 issues), $8.50/yr. (2 issues); Single issues: $4.50.

Raccoon: RACCOON, David Spicer, ed., 3387 Poplar Ave., Suite 205, Memphis, TN 38111. Issues indexed: (24/25). Subscriptions: $12.50/yr.; Single issues: $2-5.

RagMag: RAG MAG, Beverly Voldseth, ed., Box 12, Goodhue, MN 55027. Issues indexed: No 1987 issues published. Subscriptions: $7/yr.; Single issues: $3 plus $1 postage.

Rampike: RAMPIKE, Karl Jirgens, ed., 95 Rivercrest Road, Toronto, Ontario M6S 4H7 Canada. Issues indexed: (5:3). Subscriptions: $12/yr. (2 issues); Single issues: $6.

Periodicals Indexed

Raritan: RARITAN, Richard Poirier, ed., Rutgers U., 165 College Ave., New Brunswick, NJ 08903. Issues indexed: (6:3-4, 7:1-2). Subscriptions: $16/yr., $26/2 yrs. (ind.); $20/yr., $30/2 yrs. (inst.); plus $4/yr (for.); Single issues: $5; Back issues: $6.

RedBass: RED BASS, Jay Murphy, ed., 2425 Burgundy St., New Orleans, LA 70117. Issues indexed: (12). Subscriptions: $10/4 (ind.), $15 (inst., for.); Single issues: $4.

RevChic: REVISTA CHICANO-RIQUENA. See Americas: THE AMERICAS REVIEW.

RevICP: REVISTA DEL INSTITUTO DE CULTURA PUERTORRIQUENA, Marta Aponte Alsina, Directora, Apartado 4184, San Juan, PR. Issues indexed: No 1987 issues received. Subscriptions: $6/yr.; Single issues: $2.

RiverS: RIVER STYX, Carol J. Pierman, ed., 14 South Euclid, St. Louis, MO 63108. Issues indexed: (22-24). Subscriptions: $14/yr. (3 issues, ind.); $24/yr. (3 issues, inst.); Single issues: $5.

Salm: SALMAGUNDI, Robert Boyers, ed., Skidmore College, Saratoga Springs, NY 12866. Issues indexed: (72-74/75, 76/77). Subscriptions: $12/yr., $18/2 yrs. (ind.); $16/yr., $25/2 yrs. (inst.); Plus $2/yr. (for.); Single issues: $4-10.

SenR: SENECA REVIEW, Deborah Tall, ed., Hobart & William Smith Colleges, Geneva, NY 14456. Issues indexed: (17:1-2). Subscriptions: $6/yr. (2 issues), $10/2 yrs.; Single issues: $3.50.

*Sequoia: SEQUOIA, Marianne Burke, ed., Storke Publications Building, Stanford, CA 94305. Issues indexed: (30:3, 31:1). Subscriptions: $10/yr. (2 issues), $11/yr. (for.), $15/yr. (inst.); Single issues: $4.

SewanR: THE SEWANEE REVIEW, George Core, ed., U. of the South, Sewanee, TN 37375. Issues indexed: (95:1-4). Subscriptions: $48/3 yrs., $33/2 yrs., $18/yr. (inst.); $28/3 yrs., $20/2 yrs., $12/yr. (ind.); plus $3/yr. (for.); Single issues: $4; Back issues: $5-10, plus $1/copy postage & handling.

Shen: SHENANDOAH, James Boatwright, ed., Richard Howard, po. ed., Washington and Lee U., Box 722, Lexington, VA 24450. Issues indexed: (37:1-4). Subscriptions: $25/3 yrs., $18/2 yrs., $11/yr.; $33/3 yrs., $24/2 yrs., $14/yr. (for.); Single issues: $3.50; Back issues: $6.

SilverFR: SILVERFISH REVIEW, Rodger Moody, ed., P.O. Box 3541, Eugene, OR 97403. Issues indexed: (14). Subscriptions: $9/3 issues (ind.), $12/3 issues (inst.), Single issues: $4.

SingHM: SING HEAVENLY MUSE!: Women's Poetry and Prose, Sue Ann Martinson, Carol Masters, eds., P.O. Box 13299, Minneapolis, MN 55414. Issues indexed: No 1987 issues published. Subscriptions: $17/3 issues (ind.), $21/3 issues (inst.); Single issues: $7 + $2 postage & handling.

Sink: SINK, Spencer Selby, ed., P.O. Box 590095, San Francisco, CA 94159. Issues indexed: No 1987 issues published. Subscriptions: $12/3 issues; Single issues: $4.

SinW: SINISTER WISDOM, Melanie Kaye/Kantrowitz, ed. & pub., P.O. Box 1308, Montpelier, VT 05602. Issues indexed: (31). Subscriptions: $15/yr. (4 issues), $27/2 yrs. (ind.); $28/yr. (inst.); $17/yr. (for.); $6/yr. (hardship); Free on request to women in prisons and mental institutions; Single issues: $4.75-9.95.

SlipS: SLIPSTREAM, Robert Borgatti, Dan Sicoli, eds., Box 2071, New Market Station, Niagara Falls, NY 14301. Issues indexed: (7). Subscriptions: $5.50/2 issues; Single issues: $3.

SmPd: THE SMALL POND MAGAZINE OF LITERATURE, Napoleon St. Cyr, ed./pub., P.O. Box 664, Stratford, CT 06497. Issues indexed: (24:1-3, issues 66-68). Subscriptions: $6.25/yr. (3 issues), $11.50/2 yrs., $16.75/3 yrs.; Single issues: $2.50.

SnapD: SNAPDRAGON, Gail Eckwright, D'Wayne Hodgin, Ron McFarland, Tina Foriyes, eds., Dept. of English, U. of Idaho, Moscow, ID 83843. Issues indexed: (10:1/2). Subscriptions: Karen Buxton, c/o Library, U. of Idaho, Moscow, ID 83843, $3.50 (ind.), $4.50 (inst.).

Sonora: SONORA REVIEW, Heather Aronson, Michael Magoolaghan, eds, Amy Pence, po. ed., Dept. of English, U. of Arizona, Tucson, AZ 85721. Issues indexed: (12-13). Subscriptions: $6/yr. (2 issues); Single issues: $4.

SoCaR: SOUTH CAROLINA REVIEW, Richard J. Calhoun, ed., Dept. of English, Clemson U., Clemson, SC 29634-1503. Issues indexed: (19:2, 20:1, + special Sum 87 issue). Subscriptions: $9/2 yrs., $5/yr. (USA, Canada, Mexico); $10/2 yrs., $5.50/yr. (elsewhere); Back issues: $5.

SoDakR: SOUTH DAKOTA REVIEW, John R. Milton, ed., Dept. of English, U. of South Dakota, Box 111, U. Exchange, Vermillion, SD 57069. Issues indexed: (25:1-4). Subscriptions: $17/2 yrs., $10/yr. (USA, Canada); $20/2 yrs., $12/yr. (elsewhere); Single issues: $3.

SouthernHR: SOUTHERN HUMANITIES REVIEW, Dan R. Latimer, Thomas L. Wright, eds., 9088 Haley Center, Auburn U., AL 36849. Issues indexed: (21:1-4). Subscriptions: $12/yr.; Single issues: $4.

SouthernPR: SOUTHERN POETRY REVIEW, Robert Grey, ed., English Dept., U. of North Carolina, Charlotte, NC 28223. Issues indexed: (27:1-2). Subscriptions: $5/yr.; Single issues: $3.

SouthernR: SOUTHERN REVIEW, Fred Hobson, James Olney, eds., Louisiana State U., 43 Allen Hall, Baton Rouge, LA 70803. Issues indexed: (23:1-4). Subscriptions: $30/3 yrs., $21/2 yrs., $12/yr.; Single issues: $5.

SouthwR: SOUTHWEST REVIEW, Willard Spiegelman, ed., Southern Methodist U., 6410 Arline Rd., Dallas, TX 75275. Issues indexed: (72:1-4). Subscriptions: $40/3 yrs., $32/2 yrs., $16/yr.; $20/yr. (inst.). Single issues: $5.

Sparrow: SPARROW PRESS POVERTY PAMPHLETS, Felix Stefanile, ed./Pub., Sparrow Press, 103 Waldron St., West Lafayette, IN 47906. Issues indexed: (52). Subscriptions: $7.50/3 issues; Single issues: $2.50.

Spirit: THE SPIRIT THAT MOVES US, Morty Sklar, ed., P.O. Box 1585, Iowa City, IA 52244. Issues indexed: (8:2 -- Editor's Choice II: Fiction, Poetry & Art from the U.S. Small Press, ed. by Morty Sklar and Mary Biggs). Subscriptions: Vol. 8 -- $14.80 (paper), $26 (cloth); Vol. 9 -- $10.80 (paper), $20.40 (cloth).

SpiritSH: SPIRIT, David Rogers, ed., Seton Hall U., South Orange, NJ 07079. Issues indexed: (53:1). Subscriptions: $4/yr.; Single issues: $2.

SpoonRQ: THE SPOON RIVER QUARTERLY, Lucia Getsi, ed., Dept. of English, Illinois State U., Normal, IL 61761. Issues indexed: (12:1-3). Subscriptions: $10/yr.; $12/yr. (inst.); Single issues: $3.

Stand: STAND, Jon Silkin, Lorna Tracy, eds., 179 Wingrove Road, Newcastle upon Tyne NE4 9DA, U.K.; Jack Kingsbury, USA ed., English Dept., U. of North Alabama, Florence, AL 35632-0001; Howard Fink, Canadian ed., 4054 Melrose Ave., Montreal, Quebec H4A 2S4 Canada; Issues indexed: (28:1-4). Subscriptions: $14/yr.; $12/yr. (students, unwaged); Single issues: $3.50; Stand Magazine USA, Anton J. Mikovsky, 57 West 84th St., #1-C, New York, NY 10024.

StoneC: STONE COUNTRY, Judith Neeld, ed., The Nathan Mayhew Seminars of Martha's Vineyard, P.O. Box 132, Menemsha, MA 02552. Issues indexed: (14:1/2, 15:1/2). Subscriptions: $16/4 issues, $8.50/2 issues; Single issues: $4.75; Back issues: $3.50.

Sulfur: SULFUR, Clayton Eshleman, ed., English Dept., Eastern Michigan U., Ypsilanti, MI 48197. Issues indexed: (6:3, 7:1-2, issues 18-20). Subscriptions: $22/yr., 3 issues (inst.), $15/yr., 3 issues (ind.), plus $3/yr. (for.) or $12 for airmail postage; Single issues: $6.

TarRP: TAR RIVER POETRY, Peter Makuck, ed., Dept. of English, East Carolina U., Greenville, NC 27858-4353. Issues indexed: (26:2, 27:1). Subscriptions: $6/yr., $10/2 yrs.; Single issues: $3.

Temblor: TEMBLOR, Contemporary Poets, Leland Hickman, ed., 4624 Cahuenga Blvd., #307, North Hollywood, CA 91602. Issues indexed: (5-6). Subscriptions: $16/2 issues, $30/4 issues (ind.); $20/2 issues, $40/4 issues (inst.); plus $2.50/issue (for.); Single issues: $7.50.

TexasR: TEXAS REVIEW, Paul Ruffin, ed., Division of English and Foreign Language, Sam Houston State U., Huntsville, TX 77341. Issues indexed: (7:3/4 = "special release: Contemporary New England Poetry: A Sampler"; 8:1/2-3/4). Subscriptions: $4/yr., $7/2 yrs., $10/3 yrs.; $4.25/yr. (Canada), $4.50/yr. (for.); Single issues: $2.

ThRiPo: THREE RIVERS POETRY JOURNAL, Gerald Costanzo, ed., Three Rivers Press, P.O. Box 21, Carnegie-Mellon U., Pittsburgh, PA 15213. Issues indexed: (29/30). Subscriptions: $10/4 issues; Single issues: $2.50; Double issues: $5.

Thrpny: THE THREEPENNY REVIEW, Wendy Lesser, ed., pub., P.O. Box 9131, Berkeley, CA 94709. Issues indexed: (28-31). Subscriptions: $16/2 yrs., $10/yr., $18/yr. (surface for.), $24/yr. (airmail for.); Single issues: $3.

Trans: TRANSLATION, The Journal of Literary Translation, Frank MacShane, Franklin D. Reeve, William Jay Smith, eds., The Translation Center, 307A Mathematics Bldg., Columbia U., New York, NY 10027. Issues indexed: (18-19). Subscriptions: $17/yr. (2 issues), $30/2 yrs., $42/3 yrs., plus $1.50/yr. (for. except Canada, Mexico); Single issues: $8.

TriQ: TRIQUARTERLY, Reginald Gibbons, ed., Northwestern U., 2020 Ridge, Evanston, IL 60208. Issues indexed: (68-70). Subscriptions: $150/life (ind.), $300/life (inst.), $28/2 yrs. (ind.), $44/2 yrs. (inst.), $16/yr. (ind.), $26/yr. (inst.), plus $4/yr. (for.); Single issues: usually $6.95-8.95; Sample copies: $4.

US1: US 1 WORKSHEETS, Cynthia Gooding, ed., Lynn Powell, Mark Scott, po eds., US 1 Poets' Cooperative, 21 Lake Dr., Roosevelt, NJ 08555. Issues indexed: (20/21). Subscriptions: $5/4 issues; Single issues: $2; Back issues: Prices on request.

Verse: VERSE, Henry Hart, U. S. ed., Dept. of English, College of William and Mary, Williamsburg, VA 23185. Issues indexed: (4:1-3). Subscriptions: $9/yr. (3 issues); Single issues: $3.

VirQR: THE VIRGINIA QUARTERLY REVIEW, Staige D. Blackford, ed., Gregory Orr, po. consultant., One West Range, Charlottesville, VA 22903. Issues indexed: (63:1-4). Subscriptions: $24/3 yrs., $18/2 yrs., $10/yr., plus $.50/yr. (Canada), $1/yr. (elsewhere); Single issues: $3.

Vis: VISIONS, Bradley R. Strahan, po. ed./pub., Black Buzzard Press, 4705 South 8th Rd., Arlington, VA 22204. Issues indexed: (23-25). Subscriptions: $10/yr., $19/2 yrs.; $30/3 yrs. (lib).; Single issues: $3.50.

Waves: WAVES, Bernice Lever, ed., Gay Allison, po. ed., 79 Denham Drive, Richmond Hill, Ontario L4C 6H9 Canada. Issues indexed: 14:4, 15:1/2, 3-4). Ceased publication following v. 15, no. 4.

*WeberS: WEBER STUDIES: An Interdisciplinary Humanities Journal, Neila Seshachari, ed., Weber State College, Ogden, UT 84408. Issues indexed: (4:1-2). Subscriptions: $5/yr. (2 issues), $10/yr. (inst.); Back issues: $5; Single issues: $2.75.

WebR: WEBSTER REVIEW, Nancy Schapiro, ed., Pamela White Hadas & Jerred Metz, po. eds., Webster U., 470 E. Lockwood, Webster Groves, MO 63119. Issues indexed: (12:1-2). Subscriptions: $5/yr. (2 issues); Single issues: $2.50.

WestB: WEST BRANCH, Karl Patten & Robert Taylor, eds., Dept. of English, Bucknell U., Lewisburg, PA 17837. Issues indexed: (20). Subscriptions: $5/yr. (2 issues), $8/2 yrs.; Single issues: $3.

WestCR: WEST COAST REVIEW, a Literary Quarterly, Harvey De Roo, ed., Charles Watts, po. ed., Dept. of English, Simon Fraser U., Burnaby, B.C. V5A 1S6 Canada. Issues indexed: (21:3-4, 22:1-2). Subscriptions: $14/yr. (ind., 4 issues), $18/yr. (inst.); Single issues: $4.

WestHR: WESTERN HUMANITIES REVIEW, Barry Weller, ed., Larry Levis, po. ed., U. of Utah, Salt Lake City, UT 84112. Issues indexed: (41:1-4). Subscriptions: $20/yr. (4 issues, inst.), $15/yr. (ind.); Single issues: $4.

*WilliamMR: THE WILLIAM AND MARY REVIEW, Bruce Hainley, ed., College of William and Mary, Williamsburg, VA 23185. Issues indexed: (25). Subscriptions: $4/issue.

WillowS: WILLOW SPRINGS, John Keeble, ed., Edward Parris, po. ed., PUB P.O. Box 1063, Eastern Washington U., Cheney, WA 99004. Issues Indexed: (19-20). Subscriptions: $8/yr. (2 issues), $15/2 yrs., $22/3 yrs.; Single issues: $4.

Wind: WIND, Quentin R. Howard, ed., RFD Route 1, Box 809K, Pikeville, KY 41501. Issues indexed: (17:59-61). Subscriptions: $7/3 issues (inst.), $6/3 issues (ind.), $10.50/3 issues (for.); Single issues: $2; $3 (for.).

WindO: THE WINDLESS ORCHARD, Robert Novak, ed., English Dept., Indiana U.-Purdue U., Fort Wayne, IN 46805. Issues indexed: (48-49). Subscriptions: $7/yr. (4 issues), $20/3 yrs., $4/yr. (stud.); Single issues: $2.

*Witness: WITNESS, Peter Stine, ed., 31000 Northwestern Highway, P.O. Box 9079, Farmington Hills, MI 48333-9079. Issues indexed: (1:1-4). Subscriptions: $16/yr. (4 issues), $28/2 yrs.; $22/yr., $40/2 yrs. (inst.); plus $4/yr. (for.); Single copies: $5.

WoosterR: WOOSTER REVIEW, Stuart Safford, Carrie Allison, Jonathan Barclay, eds., The College of Wooster, Wooster, OH 44691. Issues indexed: (7) Final issue.

WorldO: WORLD ORDER, Firuz Kazemzadeh, Betty J. Fisher, Howard Garey, James D. Stokes, eds., National Spiritual Assembly of the Baha'is of the United States, 415 Linden Ave., Wilmette, IL 60091. Issues indexed: (20:2). Subscriptions: $18/2 yrs., $10/yr. (USA, Canada, Mexico); $28/2 yrs., $15/yr. (elsewhere); Single issues: $3.

WormR: THE WORMWOOD REVIEW, Marvin Malone, ed., P.O. Box 8840, Stockton, CA 95208-0840. Issues indexed: (27:1, 2/3, 4 - issues 105, 106/107, 108). Subscriptions: $24/4 issues (patrons), $7/4 issues (ind.), $9/4 issues (inst.); Single issues: $3.

Writ: WRIT, Roger Greenwald, ed., Innis College, U. of Toronto, 2 Sussex Ave., Toronto, Canada M5S 1J5. Issues indexed: (19). Subscriptions: $12/2 issues (US funds outside Canada); Back issues: $5-10.

*Writer: THE WRITER, 120 Boylston St., Boston, MA 02116. Issues indexed: (99:1-12, 100:1-12). Subscriptions: $20/yr., $39/2 yrs., $57/3 yrs. (USA); $26/yr., $51/2 yrs. (for.); $8/6 issues for new subscribers; Single issues: $1.75.

WritersF: WRITERS' FORUM, Alexander Blackburn, Victoria McCabe, Craig Lesley, Bret Lott, eds., P.O. Box 7150, U. of Colorado, Colorado Springs, CO 80933-7150. Issues indexed: (13). Subscriptions: $8.95/yr; Back issue sample: $5.95.

YaleR: THE YALE REVIEW, Kai Erikson, ed., J. D. McClatchy, po. ed., Yale U., 1902 A Yale Station, New Haven, CT 06520. Issues indexed: (76:2-4, 77:1). Subscriptions: $25/yr. (inst.), $16/yr. (ind.), plus $3/yr. (for.); Single issues: $6; Back issues: Prices on request; Subscription office: Yale University Press, 92A Yale Station, New Haven, CT 06520.

YellowS: YELLOW SILK, Journal of Erotic Arts, Lily Pond, ed., P.O. Box 6374, Albany, CA 94706. Issues indexed: (22-25). Subscriptions: $15/yr. (ind.), $20/yr. (lib., inst.), plus $5/yr. (for. surface), plus $10/yr. (for. air). Single issues: $4..

YetASM: YET ANOTHER SMALL MAGAZINE, Candace Catlin Hall, ed., Andrew Mountain Press, Box 14353, Hartford, CT 06114. Issues indexed: No 1987 issues received. Single issues: $1.98.

Periodicals Indexed

Zyzzyva: ZYZZYVA: The Last Word, West Coast Writers & Artists, Howard Junker, ed, 41 Sutter St., Suite 1400, San Francisco, CA 94104. Issues indexed: (3:1-4). Subscriptions: $20/yr. (4 issues), $32/2 yrs; $28/yr. (inst.).; $30/yr. (for.); Single copies: $8 post paid.

Alphabetical List of Journals Indexed, with Acronyms

Abraxas : Abraxas
Acts: A Journal of New Writing : Acts
The Agni Review : Agni
Alpha Beat Soup : AlphaBS
Amelia : Amelia
The American Poetry Review : AmerPoR
The American Scholar : AmerS
The American Voice : AmerV
The Americas Review : Americas
Another Chicago Magazine : AnotherCM
Antaeus : Antaeus
The Antigonish Review : AntigR
The Antioch Review : AntR
Areito : Areito
Arizona Quarterly : ArizQ
Ascent : Ascent
The Atlantic : Atlantic

Ball State University Forum : BallSUF
Bamboo Ridge : BambooR
The Bellingham Review : BellR
Bellowing Ark : BellArk
The Beloit Poetry Journal : BelPoJ
The Bilingual Review/la Revista Bilingue : BilingR
Black American Literature Forum : BlackALF
Black Warrior Review : BlackWR
Blue Buildings: An International Magazine of Poetry and Translations : BlueBldgs
Blueline : Blueline
Bogg : Bogg
Bomb Magazine : Bomb
Boston Review : BostonR
Boulevard : Boulevard
Boundary 2 : Bound

Caliban : Caliban
California Quarterly : CalQ
Callaloo: A Tri-annual Journal of Afro-american and African Arts and Letters : Callaloo
Calyx: A Journal of Art and Literature by Women : Calyx
Canadian Literature : CanLit
The Cape Rock : CapeR
The Capilano Review : CapilR
Carolina Quarterly : CarolQ
The Centennial Review : CentR
Central Park : CentralP
The Chariton Review : CharR
The Chattahoochee Review : ChatR
Chelsea : Chelsea
Chicago Review : ChiR
The Christian Century : ChrC
Cimarron Review : CimR
Clockwatch Review : ClockR
College English : ColEng
Colorado Review : ColR
Columbia : Colum
Commonweal : Comm
Concerning Poetry : ConcPo

Alphabetical List

Conditions : Cond
Confrontation : Confr
Conjunctions : Conjunc
The Connecticut Poetry Review : ConnPR
Contact II : Contact
Crab Creek Review : CrabCR
Crazyhorse : Crazy
Cream City Review : CreamCR
The Crescent Review : CrescentR
Cross-Canada Writers' Quarterly : CrossC
Crosscurrents : CrossCur
Cuadernos de Poética : CuadP
Cumberland Poetry Review : CumbPR
Cutbank : CutB

Dandelion : Dandel
The Dekalb Literary Arts Journal : DekalbLAJ
Denver Quarterly : DenQ
Descant : Descant

Electrum Magazine : Electrum
English Journal : EngJ
Epoch : Epoch
Event: Journal of the Contemporary Arts : Event

Farmer's Market : Farm
Field: Contemporary Poetry and Poetics : Field
Five Fingers Riview : FiveFR
The Florida Review : FloridaR
Footwork : Footwork
Four Quarters : FourQ

The G. W. Review : GWR
Gambit Magazine : Gambit
Gargoyle Magazine : Gargoyle
Georgia Review : GeoR
Germination : Germ
Graham House Review : GrahamHR
Grain : Grain
Grand Street : GrandS
Greenfield Review : GreenfR
The Greensboro Review : GreensboroR

The Hampden-Sydney Poetry Reivew : HampSPR
Hanging Loose : HangL
Harper's Magazine : Harp
The Harvard Advocate : HarvardA
Hawaii Review : HawaiiR
Hayden's Ferry Review : HayF
Helicon Nine: The Journal of Women's Arts & Letters : HeliconN
High Plains Literary Review : HighP
Hiram Poetry Review : HiramPoR
The Hollins Critic : HolCrit
The Hudson Review : Hudson

Indiana Review : IndR
Interim : Interim
International Poetry Review : InterPR
Inti : Inti
Iowa Review : Iowa

The Jacaranda Review : Jacaranda
The James White Review : JamesWR
The Journal Of New Jersey Poets : JlNJPo

Kaleidoscope : Kaleid
Kansas Quarterly : KanQ
Kenyon Review : KenR

Lactuca : Lactuca
The Lake Street Review : LakeSR
Laurel Review : LaurelR
Letras Femeninas : LetFem
Light Year : LightY
Linden Lane Magazine : LindLM
Lips : Lips
The Literary Review : LitR
The Little Magazine : LittleM
Lyra : Lyra

Mairena : Revista de Crítica y Poesía : Mairena
The Malahat Review : MalR
Manhattan Poetry Review : ManhatPR
The Manhattan Review : ManhatR
Margin : MarginMARGIN
The Massachusetts Review : MassR
Memphis State Review : MemphisSR
Mester : Mester
Michigan Quarterly Review : MichQR
Mid-American Review : MidAR
The Midwest Quarterly : MidwQ
The Minnesota Review : MinnR
Mississippi Review : MissR
The Missouri Review : MissouriR
Moody Street Irregulars : MoodySI
Mss : MSS

The Nation : Nat
Negative Capability : NegC
New American Writing : NewAW
New England Review And Bread Loaf Quarterly : NewEngR
New Letters : NewL
New Orleans Review : NewOR
The New Renaissance : NewRena
The New Republic : NewRep
The New York Review Of Books : NewYRB
The New Yorker : NewYorker
Nimrod : Nimrod
The North American Review : NoAmR
North Dakota Quarterly : NoDaQ
Northeast : Northeast
Northwest Review : NowestR
Notus : Notus

Obsidian Ii: Black Literature in Review : Obs
The Ohio Reivew : OhioR
Oink: OINK! : *See* New American Writing
Ontario Review : OntR
Open Places : OP
Oro Madre : OroM
Osiris : Os
Outerbridge : Outbr

Paintbrush: A Journal of Poetry : Paint
Painted Bride Quarterly : PaintedB
The Paris Review : ParisR
Partisan Review : PartR
Passages North : PassN
Pax: A Journal for Peace through Culture : Pax
Pembroke Magazine : Pembroke
The Pennsylvania Review : PennR

Alphabetical List

Pequod : Pequod
Phoenix : Phoenix
Pig Iron : Pig
The Pikestaff Forum : PikeF
Ploughshares : Ploughs
Poem : Poem
Poet And Critic : PoetC
Poet Lore : PoetL
Poetic Justice: Contemporary American Poetry : PoeticJ
Poetry : Poetry
Poetry Canada Review : PoetryCR
Poetry East : PoetryE
Poetry Northwest : PoetryNW
The Pottersfield Portfolio : PottPort
Prairie Fire : PraF
Prairie Schooner : PraS
Primavera : Prima
Puerto Del Sol : Puerto

Quarry : Quarry
Quarterly Review Of Literature : QRL
Quarterly West : QW

Raccoon : Raccoon
Rag Mag : RagMag
Rampike : Rampike
Raritan : Raritan
Red Bass : RedBass
Revista Chicano-Riqueña : *See* The Americas Review
Revista Del Instituto De Cultura Puertorriquena : RevICP
River Styx : RiverS

Salmagundi : Salm
Seneca Review : SenR
Sequoia : Sequoia
The Sewanee Review : SewanR
Shenandoah : Shen
Silverfish Review : SilverFR
Sing Heavenly Muse!: Women's Poetry and Prose : SingHM
Sink : Sink
Sinister Wisdom : SinW
Slipstream : SlipS
The Small Pond Magazine Of Literature : SmPd
Snapdragon : SnapD
Sonora Review : Sonora
South Carolina Review : SoCaR
South Dakota Review : SoDakR
Southern Humanities Review : SouthernHR
Southern Poetry Review : SouthernPR
Southern Review : SouthernR
Southwest Review : SouthwR
Sparrow Press Poverty Pamphlets : Sparrow
Spirit : SpiritSH
The Spirit That Moves Us : Spirit
The Spoon River Quarterly : SpoonRQ
Stand : Stand
Stone Country : StoneC
Sulfur : Sulfur

Tar River Poetry : TarRP
Temblor : Temblor
Texas Review : TexasR
Three Rivers Poetry Journal : ThRiPo
The Threepenny Review : Thrpny
Translation : Translation
Triquarterly : TriQ

Us 1 Worksheets : US1

Verse : Verse
The Virginia Quarterly Review : VirQR
Visions : Vis

Waves : Waves
Weber Studies : WeberS
Webster Review : WebR
West Branch : WestB
West Coast Review : WestCR
Western Humanities Review : WestHR
The William and Mary Review : WilliamMR
Willow Springs : WillowS
Wind : Wind
The Windless Orchard : WindO
Witness : Witness
Wooster Review : WoosterR
World Order : WorldO
The Wormwood Review : WormR
Writ : Writ
The Writer : Writer
Writers' Forum : WritersF

The Yale Review : YaleR
Yellow Silk : YellowS
Yet Another Small Magazine : YetASM

Zyzzyva: The Last Word : Zyzzyva

The Author Index

A, Pak Yul
   See PAK, Yul A
1. AAL, Katharyn Machan
   "Angry." [Footwork] 87, p. 20.
   "The Beets Poem." [LightY] '87, c86, p. 44-45.
   "Cayuga" (for Paula Gunn Allen). [Blueline] (7:2/3 [i.e. 8:2/3?]) 87, p. 98.
   "Hazel Tells Laverne." [PikeF] (8) Fall 87, p. 35.
   "In 1929." [Amelia] (4:3, issue 10) 87, p. 93.
   "Nearing Divorce." [Amelia] (4:3, issue 10) 87, p. 93.
   "Nothing Like" (for Arthur Tobias). [CrabCR] (4:2) Spr 87, p. 11.
   "Office Hours." [LightY] '87, c86, p. 175.
   "Plath's Last Home" (for Rosemary Campbell). [Bogg] (58) 87, p. 24.
   "Quail." [LightY] '87, c86, p. 174-175.
   "Red Haven." [Phoenix] (7:1) 87, p. 41.
   "The Things of This World" (1986 Finalist, Eve of Saint Agnes Poetry Competition).
      [NegC] (7:1/2) 87, p. 180.
   "Upstate." [Footwork] 87, p. 20.
   "When Our Mothers Die" (1986 Honorable Mention, Eve of Saint Agnes Poetry
      Competition). [NegC] (7:1/2) 87, p. 133.
2. AARNES, William
   "In Summer Dark, Waiting for Change." [SouthernR] (23:3) Jl 87, p. 628.
3. ABBE, Kate
   "The Flood." [WoosterR] (7) Spr 87, p. 10.
4. ABBEY, Lloyd
   "At Lions Gate Hospital." [Event] (16:2) Sum 87, p. 56-57.
5. ABBOT, Louise Hardeman
   "Homage" (to William Carlos Williams). [GeoR] (41:1) Spr 87, p. 34.
6. ABBOTT, Anthony
   "Dust Beneath My Shoe." [TarPR] (27:1) Fall 87, p. 24.
7. ABBOTT, Steve
   "Conversations with Aliens" (a sonnet sequence for Jack Spicer). [Acts] (6) 87, p.
      56-57.
8. ABERNETHY, Nugh
   "Modernists." [CharR] (13:2) Fall 87, p. 82-83.
ABID IBN AL-ABRAS
   See Al-ABRAS, Abid Ibn
ABRAS, Abid Ibn al-
   See Al-ABRAS, Abid Ibn
9. ABSE, Dannie
   "Of Itzig and His Dog." [Spirit] (8:2) 87, p. 219.
   "Of Two Languages" (For Hanoch Bartov). [Poetry] (151:1/2) O-N 87, p. 1-2.
   "Sky in Narrow Streets." [QRL] (Series 8, vol. 27) 87, 61 p.
10. ABSHER, Tom
   "August Poem." [Nat] (245:5) 29 Ag 87, p. 168.
   "Day Poem." [BlackWR] (14:1) Fall 87, p. 17.
   "The End of It All." [BlackWR] (14:1) Fall 87, p. 48.
   "Learning to Sail." [BlackWR] (14:1) Fall 87, p. 89.
   "Migration." [Agni] (24/25) 87, p. 136.
   "Newsreel." [Witness] (1:1) Spr 87, p. 9.
11. ACCAME, Vincenzo
   "Nuova Scrittura" (New Writing). [Caliban] (2) 87, p. 69.
12. ACKER, W. H.
   "A Christmas Eve in Bastogne, 1944." [MidAR] (7:2) 87, p. 92.
13. ACKERMAN, Diane
   "Gramercy Park." [Poetry] (150:1) Ap 87, p. 30.
   "Lady Canute." [PraS] (61:1) Spr 87, p. 12-13.
   "Lament of the Banyan Tree." [Poetry] (150:1) Ap 87, p. 31-32.
   "The Manure Gatherers." [PraS] (61:1) Spr 87, p. 11.

"Opening the Locket." [PraS] (61:1) Spr 87, p. 13-14.
"St. Louis Botanical Gardens" (The orchid exhibit). [Poetry] (150:1) Ap 87, p. 29-30.
14. ACKERMAN, Stephen
"Unknown." [AntR] (45:4) Fall 87, p. 443-444.
15. ACORN, Milton
"Captain Neal MacDougal in Nineteen-Fourteen." [Grain] (15:1) Spr 87, p. 9.
16. ACOSTA, Cipriano
"Y sin embargo, llueve." [Mairena] (9:24) 87, p. 118-119.
ACOSTA, Ramon Zapata
See ZAPATA ACOSTA, Ramon
17. ACZEL, Tamas
"Idyll" (tr. of Igor Khomin, w. Joseph Langland and Laszlo Tikos). [NowestR] (25:3)
87, p. 132-133.
18. ADAM, Dawne
"In Lucia's House." [BelPoJ] (38:2) Wint 87-88, p. 26-29.
"Photograph of the End of the War." [Witness] (1:2) Sum 87, p. 141-142.
19. ADAM, Helen
"In and Out of the Horn-Beam Maze." [RiverS] (24) 87, p. 24-25.
20. ADAMSON, Arthur
"The River" (Franklin's route to the Arctic, by canoe, 1970). [PraF] (8:3) Aut 87, p.
78.
"The Weight of the Potatoes." [PraF] (8:3) Aut 87, p. 76.
21. ADAMSSON, Slade
"The Last Kiss." [Bogg] (57) 87, p. 28.
22. ADCOCK, Betty
"The Case fo Gravity." [HeliconN] (17/18) Spr 87, p. 25.
"Corner of Pawnee and Broadway." [CarolQ] (39:3) Spr 87, p. 37-38.
"Cycladic." [TarPR] (27:1) Fall 87, p. 13-16.
"The Kinds of Sleep." [HeliconN] (17/18) Spr 87, p. 26-27.
"Woman in a Series of Photographs." [GeoR] (41:4) Wint 87, p. 761-762.
23. ADELL, Tim
"The Musicians Play Hoops" (1986 Honorable Mention, Eve of Saint Agnes Poetry
Competition). [NegC] (7:1/2) 87, p. 125.
24. ADELSPERGER, Jocelyn
"Wild and Free." [Gambit] (20) 86, p. 46.
25. ADIGA, M. Gopal Krishna
"Song of the Earth." [Bomb] (18) Wint 87, p. 60-61.
26. ADILMAN, Mona Elaine
"Brain-Death" (for Sheila Martindale). [CrossC] (9:1) 87, p. 25.
27. ADKINS, Vincent
"The Road to Damascus." [ChrC] (104:11) 8 Ap 87, p. 331.
28. ADLER, Carol
"Image-Making." [BallSUF] (28:4) Aut 87, p. 72-73.
"Priorities." [BallSUF] (28:4) Aut 87, p. 70.
29. ADLER, Cori
"Mussulman." [HighP] (2:2) Fall 87, p. 184-187.
30. ADNAN, Etel
"Poem IX" (From the Arab Apocalypse). [RedBass] (12) 87, p. 27.
"Poem XXXII" (From the Arab Apocalypse). [RedBass] (12) 87, p. 14.
"Poem XXXIV" (From the Arab Apocalypse). [RedBass] (12) 87, p. 46.
"Poem XXXVII" (From the Arab Apocalypse). [RedBass] (12) 87, p. 43.
"Poem XLVI" (From the Arab Apocalypse). [RedBass] (12) 87, p. 49.
ADORNO, Pedro López
See LOPEZ-ADORNO, Pedro
31. ADRIAN, Loretta
"Abortion." [CrescentR] (5:1) 87, p. 13.
"Bon Voyage." [CrescentR] (5:1) 87, p. 12.
"The Chairs Remember." [ManhatPR] (9) Sum 87, p. 61.
"Love Like Alice." [LaurelR] (21:1/2) Wint-Sum 87, p. 16.
32. ADRIAN, Vonna
"Clerihews" (3 poems). [LightY] '87, c86, p. 66.
"A Plaguey Thing." [LightY] '87, c86, p. 192-193.
"The Rake's Progress." [LightY] '87, c86, p. 150.
33. AGGESTAM, Rolf
"Towards the Pole" (tr. by Erland Anderson and Lars Nordstrom). [GreenfR] (14:1/2)
Wint-Spr, p. 103.

AGHA SHAHID ALI
See ALI, Agha Shahid
34. AGOOS, Julie
"Affliction." [WilliamMR] (25) Spr 87, p. 22.
"Age" (for my father). [WilliamMR] (25) Spr 87, p. 19-20.
"Franklin." [WestHR] (41:1) Spr 87, p. 30-33.
"Lunar Eclipse at a New England Funeral." [PartR] (54:1) Wint 87, p. 123-125.
35. AGOSIN, Marjorie
"Mi Estomago (My Belly)" (tr. by Cola Franzen). [Calyx] (10:2/3) Spr 87, p. 115-116.
36. AGRICOLA, Sandra
"Anna." [OhioR] (39) 87, p. 61-62.
"Body and Soul." [MidAR] (7:2) 87, p. 24-25.
"Chronologaic." [OhioR] (39) 87, p. 58-60.
"Ode on Carbon 14." [GeoR] (41:3) Fall 87, p. 494-495.
"White Geraniums." [GreensboroR] (39) Wint 85-86, p. 58-59.
37. AGTE, Bruce
"Salamander." [Raccoon] (24/25) My 87, p. 100.
38. AGUERO, Kathleen
"Firemen's Picnic." [HangL] (50/51) 87, p. 13.
"Metal Detector." [HangL] (50/51) 87, p. 10.
"Old Stories." [HangL] (50/51) 87, p. 11.
"Sister Dominic." [HangL] (50/51) 87, p. 12.
"The Wind and the Sun." [HangL] (50/51) 87, p. 9.
39. AI
"Boys & Girls, Lenny Bruce, or Back From the Dead" (For Willem Dafoe, Ron Vawter
& The Wooster Group). [Ploughs] (13:4) 87, p. 13-17.
"Family Portrait." [Ploughs] (13:4) 87, p. 11-12.
"Interview with a Policeman." [Poetry] (151:1/2) O-N 87, p. 2-4.
40. AIELLO, Kate
"Waiting in Puerto." [Bogg] (57) 87, p. 45.
41. AIGLA, Jorge H.-
"The Maelstrom." [Americas] (15:2) Sum 87, p. 74.
"Mi Mamá Cecilia." [Americas] (15:2) Sum 87, p. 76.
"The Power of the Word." [Americas] (15:2) Sum 87, p. 75.
42. AIKEN, William
"Cataracts and Memories." [HampSPR] Wint 86, p. 56.
"Fishing." [Bogg] (57) 87, p. 30.
"Our Hands Our Coffee Cups." [HampSPR] Wint 86, p. 56.
"Rest, Art, Politics." [HampSPR] Wint 86, p. 57.
43. AINSWORTH, J. Alan
"Carnival." [Shen] (37:1) 87, p. 77.
44. AIRD, Paul
"My Legacy." [Waves] (15:4) Spr 87, p. 95.
45. AISENBERG, Katy
"Excavations." [Ploughs] (13:1) 87, p. 12-15.
"No Aubade." [Agni] (24/25) 87, p. 55.
46. AISENBERG, Nadya
"Now, Somebody Hold the World Together." [PraS] (61:1) Spr 87, p. 15-17.
"Roses of Sharon." [PraS] (61:1) Spr 87, p. 14-15.
"Southwest Harbor." [TexasR] (7:3/4) 87, p. 2.
"Tellurian." [Agni] (24/25) 87, p. 201-202.
47. AKAMINE, Sheri Mae
"We saw three different store-ladies." The Best of [BambooR] [(31-32)] 86, p. 13.
48. AKERS, Deborah
"Pele's Sleep" (Mauna, Hawaii). [YellowS] (22) Spr 87, p. 21.
49. AKHMADULINA, Bella
"I've forgotten nothing" (tr. by Katya Olmsted and John High). [FiveFR] (5) 87, p.
102.
"Night Fantasies" (tr. by Katya Olmsted and John High). [FiveFR] (5) 87, p. 103.
50. AKHMATOVA, Anna
"I have a certain smile" (No. 70, in Russian and English, tr. by Judith Hemschemeyer).
[Gargoyle] (32/33) 87, p. 54-55.
"It is simple, it is clear" (No. 218, in Russian and English, tr. by Judith
Hemschemeyer). [Gargoyle] (32/33) 87, p. 56-57.
"The Legatee" (tr. by Eugene Dubnov and John Heath-Stubbs). [ChiR] (35:4) 87, p.
103.

"Marina Tsvetayeva (1892-1941)" (tr. by Eugene Dubnov and John Heath-Stubbs). [ChiR] (35:4) 87, p. 104.
"Parting (2)" (Zh. 328, tr. by Judith Hemschemeyer). [NowestR] (25:3) 87, p. 423.
"Sergei Esenin" (tr. by Eugene Dubnov and John Heath-Stubbs). [ChiR] (35:4) 87, p. 106.
"Sergei Esenin (1895-1925)" (tr. by Eugene Dubnov and John Heath-Stubbs). [ChiR] (35:4) 87, p. 105.
"Song of the Last Meeting" (Sept. 29, 1911, tr. by Marianne Andrea). [Waves] (14:4) Spr 86, p. 78.
"Three Poems" (1944-1960, tr. by Marianne Andrea). [Waves] (14:4) Spr 86, p. 78.
"To a Future Reader" (tr. by Eugene Dubnov and John Heath-Stubbs). [ChiR] (35:4) 87, p. 107.
AKIKO, Yosano
    See YOSANO, Akiko
51. AKIN, Gülten
    "The Cliff Dwellers" (in Turkish & English, tr. by Dionis Coffin Riggs). [InterPR] (13:2) Fall 87, p. 42-43.
    "Rain" (tr. by Talat Sait Halman). [Trans] (19) Fall 87, p. 102.
52. AKSAL, Sabahattin Kudret
    "All Red" (tr. by Murat Nemet-Nejat). [Trans] (19) Fall 87, p. 150.
    "Blond" (tr. by Murat Nemet-Nejat). [Trans] (19) Fall 87, p. 150.
    "Crows" (tr. by Talat Sait Halman). [Trans] (19) Fall 87, p. 151-153.
    "Masts" (tr. by Murat Nemet-Nejat). [Trans] (19) Fall 87, p. 150.
    "Rifle" (tr. by Murat Nemet-Nejat). [Trans] (19) Fall 87, p. 149.
    "Table" (tr. by Murat Nemet-Nejat). [Trans] (19) Fall 87, p. 149.
53. Al-ABRAS, Abid Ibn
    "An Arab Chieftain to His Young Wife" (tr. by Omar S. Pound). [AntigR] (69/70) 87, p. 72.
54. Al-HUTAY'A
    "It Is New, Therefore a Pleasure" (tr. by Omar S. Pound). [AntigR] (69/70) 87, p. 73.
55. Al-RUMI, Ibn
    "Slow Giving" (tr. by Omar S. Pound). [AntigR] (69/70) 87, p. 73.
56. Al-YUSUFI, Amir Manjak Ibn Muhammad
    "Hair" (tr. by Arthur Wormhoudt). [Paint] (14:27) Spr 87, p. 39.
57. ALABAU, Magaly
    "Un Cuarto Oscuro Blanco." [LindLM] (6:4) O-D 87, p. 5.
    "Dos gotas de calma." [Mairena] (9:24) 87, p. 112.
58. ALARCON, Francisco X.
    "Mi Pelo." [Zyzzyva] (3:3) Fall 87, p. 27.
    "My Hair" (tr. by Francisco Aragon). [Zyzzyva] (3:3) Fall 87, p. 26.
59. ALBERT, Zsuzsa
    "Vault" (tr. by Zsuzsanna Ozsvath and Martha Satz). [WebR] (12:1) Spr 87, p. 87.
60. ALBERTI, Rafael
    "White" (tr. by Carolyn Tipton). [Trans] (18) Spr 87, p. 294-297.
    "Zurbarán" (tr. by Carolyn Tipton). [Trans] (18) Spr 87, p. 298-299.
61. ALBIACH, Anne-Marie
    "Distance: 'Analogy'" (tr. by Joseph Simas). [LitR] (30:3) Spr 87, p. 338-347.
    "'H-II' Linear" (tr. by Anthony Barnett and Joseph Simas). [Temblor] (5) 87, p. 66-77.
    "Supreme Love" (on Danielle Collobert, from *Anawratha*, tr. by Merle Ruberg). [Act] (7) 87, p. 19.
62. ALBRECHT, Michael von
    "De Lacu Aliciae" (ad Richardum Eberhart). [NegC] (7:1/2) 87, p. 255.
    "Lake Alice" (To Richard Eberhart). [NegC] (7:1/2) 87, p. 254.
63. ALBRIGHT-CASSEL, Ben
    "Actors' Night." [EngJ] (76:3) Mr 87, p. 34.
64. ALBUCASIS
    "An Arab on Cauteries (ca. 980 A.D.)" (Adapted from a prose treatise on medicine, tr. by Omar S. Pound). [AntigR] (69/70) 87, p. 74.
65. ALCALAY, Ammiel
    "After Ecclesiastes" (In Memoriam: Dan Pagis). [Sulfur] (18) Wint 87, p. 84-87.
66. ALCOSSER, Sandra
    "The Anatomy of Air." [Nimrod] (30:2) Spr-Sum 87, p. 2.
    "Approaching August." [Nimrod] (30:2) Spr-Sum 87, p. 1.
    "But This Is Not the Yucatan." [Poetry] (151:3) D 87, p. 275.
    "Rags." [Nimrod] (30:2) Spr-Sum 87, p. 3.

67. ALDRICH, Jonathan
    "A Shaker Girl" (New England, c. 1850). [TexasR] (7:3/4) 87, p. 3-5.
68. ALDRIDGE, Richard
    "Quantities and Qualities" (To M.G.). [Outbr] (18/19) Fall 86-Spr 88, p. 152.
    "A Sharing of Silences." [TexasR] (7:3/4) 87, p. 6-7.
69. ALEIXANDRE, Vicente
    "Between Two Darknesses, One Lightning Flash" (tr. by Nathaniel Smith). [InterPR]
        (13:1) Spr 87, p. 7, 9.
    "Como Moíses Es el Viejo." [CrossCur] (6:4) 87, p. 24.
    "Entre Dos Oscuridades, un Relámpago." [InterPR] (13:1) Spr 87, p. 6, 8.
    "The Old Man Is Like Moses" (tr. by David Garrison). [CrossCur] (6:4) 87, p. 25.
70. ALEJANDRO, Ann
    "Migrations." [Puerto] (22:2) Spr 87, p. 68-69.
71. ALESHIRE, Joan
    "Marcus Aurelius." [AmerS] (56:3) Sum 87, p. 330.
    "This Far." [QRL] (Series 8, vol. 27) 87, 76 p.
    "To Charlotte Brontë." [AmerS] (56:4) Aut 87, p. 576.
72. ALEXANDER, Cheryl Ann
    "Most People Have Some Brown." [Electrum] (39) Fall-Wint 87, p. 37.
73. ALEXANDER, Elizabeth
    "Ala." [SouthernR] (23:4) O 87, p. 825.
    "Ladders." [SouthernR] (23:4) O 87, p. 824.
    "Omni-Albert Murray." [SouthernR] (23:3) Jl 87, p. 605-609.
74. ALEXANDER, Floyce
    "Diptych." [WritersF] (13) Fall 87, p. 191-193.
    "Serenade." [ColR] (NS 14:2) Fall-Wint 87, p. 90-91.
75. ALEXANDER, Meena
    "Her Garden." [Chelsea] (46) 87, p. 182-183.
    "Invitation." [Chelsea] (46) 87, p. 185.
    "Sidi Syed's Architecture." [Chelsea] (46) 87, p. 181-182.
    "To Balasore." [Chelsea] (46) 87, p. 184.
76. ALEXANDER, Pamela
    "Acuity." [Atlantic] (260:2) Ag 87, p. 42.
77. ALEXANDROU, Aris
    "The Book" (tr. by Robert Crist). [Raccoon] (24/25) My 87, p. 169.
    "From 'I Converse, Therefore I Exist'" (tr. by Robert L. Crist). [GreenfR] (14:1/2)
        Wint-Spr, p. 187.
    "In Full Knowledge" (tr. by Robert L. Crist). [GreenfR] (14:1/2) Wint-Spr, p.
        188-189.
    "In the Rocks" (tr. by Robert L. Crist). [GreenfR] (14:1/2) Wint-Spr, p. 187.
    "No Man's Land" (tr. by Robert L. Crist). [GreenfR] (14:1/2) Wint-Spr, p. 188.
    "Unsent Letters" (tr. by Robert Crist). [Raccoon] (24/25) My 87, p. 162-168.
78. ALGARDI, Alessandro
    "Manoscritto" (Manuscript). [Caliban] (2) 87, p. 66.
79. ALI, Agha Shahid
    "Death Row." [Sonora] (12) Spr 87, p. 9.
    "Desert Landscape." [Chelsea] (46) 87, p. 188.
    "Palm Reading" (Said Sultanpour, Iranian poet, was executed on 21 June 1981).
        [Chelsea] (46) 87, p. 189.
    "Stationery." [Chelsea] (46) 87, p. 187.
    "The Tiger at 4 a.m." [Chelsea] (46) 87, p. 186.
    "A Wrong Turn." [Chelsea] (46) 87, p. 187.
    "The Youngest of the Graeae." [Sonora] (12) Spr 87, p. 7-8.
80. ALI, Ahmed
    "In Exile I Remember My People and Feel Sad." [Chelsea] (46) 87, p. 251-252.
    "The Year of the Rat." [Chelsea] (46) 87, p. 252.
    "Youth and Age." [Chelsea] (46) 87, p. 251.
81. ALI, Kareem
    "Looking at Summer from a Train." [StoneC] (14:3/4) Spr-Sum 87, p. 24.
82. ALICECHILD
    "Old Man." [CentR] (31:1) Wint 87, p. 59-60.
83. ALIESAN, Jody
    "Omens." [CrabCR] (4:3) Sum 87, p. 4.
84. ALLAIS, Alphonse
    "Scientia Liberatrix, or, The Exploding Mother-in-Law" (tr. by Rachel Stella). [Notus]
        (2:2) Fall 87, p. 18-19.

85. ALLARDT, Linda
   "Wish Me Dust" (1986 Honorable Mention, Eve of Saint Agnes Poetry Competition).
      [NegC] (7:1/2) 87, p. 138.
86. ALLBERY, Debra
   "Background, 1969." [WestHR] (41:1) Spr 87, p. 34-35.
   "Children's Story." [Poetry] (150:5) Ag 87, p. 275.
   "Lapse." [Poetry] (150:5) Ag 87, p. 277.
   "Offering." [Poetry] (150:5) Ag 87, p. 276-277.
87. ALLEGRE, Marla Rowe
   "Artichoke." [NegC] (7:3/4) 87, p. 153.
88. ALLEN, Boyd C.
   "A Piece of the Moon." [CrabCR] (4:3) Sum 87, p. 28.
89. ALLEN, Deborah
   "Apples." [ManhatPR] (9) Sum 87, p. 8.
   "Winter Landscape." [ManhatPR] (9) Sum 87, p. 9.
90. ALLEN, Dick
   "Another Knowledge." [Poetry] (151:1/2) O-N 87, p. 4-5.
   "Barge Lights on the Hudson" (For Dana and Mary Gioia). [Poetry] (150:1) Ap 87, p.
      8.
   "The Clergyman's Wife Composes a Spring Letter." [TexasR] (7:3/4) 87, p. 8-9.
   "The Commuter." [Poetry] (150:1) Ap 87, p. 9.
   "Flight & Pursuit" (2 selections). [OntR] (27) Fall-Wint 87, p. 72-74.
   "If You Visit Our Country." [TexasR] (7:3/4) 87, p. 10-11.
   "Lost Love." [NewYorker] (63:19) 29 Je 87, p. 34.
   "Notes After Ether." [Poetry] (150:1) Ap 87, p. 6-7.
91. ALLEN, George C., Jr.
   "Petri Dish Self-Portrait." [Witness] (1:3) Fall 87, p. 144.
92. ALLEN, Gilbert
   "In Old Salem" (Winston-Salem, North Carolina). [Interim] (6:2) Fall 87, p. 45.
93. ALLEN, John S.
   "Work." [MoodySI] (18/19) Fall 87, p. 19.
94. ALLEN, Paul
   "Hypothesis Contrary to Fact" (John Ciardi, 1916-1986). [NowestR] (25:1) 87, p.
      13-14.
   "Hypothesis Contrary to Fact" (John Ciardi, 1916-1986). [NowestR] (25:3) 87, p.
      446-447.
   "Note for in the Morning." [NowestR] (25:1) 87, p. 15.
   "One up by Clinton." [NewEngR] (10:2) Wint 87, p. 149.
   "Youngblood Tells Beekman and Jimmy Jr. About Crow" (1986 John Williams
      Andrews Poetry Prize Winner). [PoetL] (82:1) Spr 87, p. 5-8.
95. ALLEN, Paula Gunn
   "Weed." [Calyx] (10:2/3) Spr 87, p. 77.
96. ALLEN, Richard
   "Epitaph for the Western Intelligentsia." [Chelsea] (46) 87, p. 37.
   "India Song." [Chelsea] (46) 87, p. 36-37.
   "White." [Chelsea] (46) 87, p. 38-43.
97. ALLEN, Robert
   "E Mente Turpe Corpus Sanum." [SmPd] (24:1) Wint 87, p. 16.
98. ALLEN, William
   "Cochiti Lake." [PraS] (61:3) Fall 87, p. 89-90.
   "Dead Communists in their Coffins, 1871." [DenQ] (22:1) Sum 87, p. 33-34.
   "On Hearing Geese Fly Over Manhattan." [PraS] (61:3) Fall 87, p. 88-89.
   "Stalking Dragonflies on Mt. Wachusett." [PraS] (61:3) Fall 87, p. 87.
99. ALLEY, Rick
   "South Grove." [PoetL] (82:3) Fall 87, p. 162.
100. ALLGREN, Joe
   "Salvadore Dali with a Tube Up His Nose." [Pig] (14) 87, p. 82.
101. ALLISON, Carrie
   "Cattle." [WoosterR] (7) Spr 87, p. 79.
102. ALLISON, Dorothy
   "When I Drink I Become the Joy of Faggots." [Spirit] (8:2) 87, p. 138-139.
103. ALLISON, Gay
   "Holding the World." [Waves] (15:1/2) Fall 86, p. 63.
   "Memory Is an Animal That Hides in Your Heart." [Waves] (15:1/2) Fall 86, p. 65.
   "Night Life." [Dandel] (14:2) Fall-Wint 87, p. 28.
   "The Truth of My Body." [Waves] (15:1/2) Fall 86, p. 64.

"Winter Night in Peterborough" (for H.K. in memory of Margaret Laurence).
[Dandel] (14:2) Fall-Wint 87, p. 26-27.
104. ALLMAN, John
"Necessities of Two." [NoDaQ] (55:1) Wint 87, p. 1.
"The Nuclear Reactors at Indian Point." [NoDaQ] (55:1) Wint 87, p. 2.
"On the Harmony of Number and Utterance." [NoDaQ] (55:1) Wint 87, p. 1-2.
105. ALLOULA, Malek
"I Might Perhaps Restate Tonight" (tr. by Eric Sellin). [LitR] (30:3) Spr 87, p. 396.
ALMEDA, Antonio Pérez
See PEREZ ALMEDA, Antonio
106. ALMON, Bert
"Cultural Revolutions." [CrossC] (9:2) 87, p. 13.
"A Little Girl in Kingston Town." [CumbPR] (7:1) Fall 87, p. 21.
107. ALTHAUS, Keith
"The View." [VirQR] (63:2) Spr 87, p. 273-274.
108. ALTIOK, Metin
"Avalanche" (tr. by Nermin Menemencioglu). [Trans] (19) Fall 87, p. 127.
109. ALVAREZ, A.
"Craft" (tr. of Primo Levi, w. Gaia Servadio). [NewYorker] (63:34) 12 O 87, p. 46.
110. ALVAREZ, Ernesto
"Cesar Vallejo." [Mairena] (9:24) 87, p. 46-47.
111. ALVAREZ, Julia
"Against Cinderella." [Calyx] (10:2/3) Spr 87, p. 174.
ALVARES BECKER, Leda
See BECKER, Leda Alvares
112. AMABILE, George
"Don't Get Stuck in the Snow and If You Do, Why Not?" [PraF] (8:3) Aut 87, p. 57.
"Inventing *Nogales*." [Margin] (1) Wint 86, p. 70-71.
"Northern Sonnet." [Margin] (1) Wint 86, p. 72.
"Sticks and Stones." [Margin] (1) Wint 86, p. 69.
"Synergy Triad" (to Alison, for Lloyd). [Margin] (1) Wint 86, p. 68.
"This Business of Getting Through the Night." [PraF] (8:3) Aut 87, p. 31.
113. AMALI, Odumu Onche
"Lizards by Live Bulbs." [Chelsea] (46) 87, p. 119.
114. AMBRUSO, Diane
"Pool's Edge" (1986 Finalist, Eve of Saint Agnes Poetry Competition). [NegC]
(7:1/2) 87, p. 215.
115. AMICHAI, Yehuda
"Half-Sized Violin" (tr. by Chana Bloch). [CrossCur] (7:3) 87, p. 16.
"A House" (tr. by Chana Bloch). [CrossCur] (7:3) 87, p. 15.
"Once More" (tr. by the author). [AmerPoR] (16:6) N-D 87, p. 14.
"The Opening of the School Year" (tr. by Chana Bloch). [CrossCur] (7:3) 87, p.
18-19.
"Statistics" (tr. by Chana Bloch). [CrossCur] (7:3) 87, p. 17.
"Try Again" (tr. by the author). [AmerPoR] (16:6) N-D 87, p. 14.
"The Water's Surface" (tr. by the author). [AmerPoR] (16:6) N-D 87, p. 14.
AMICO, Maureen di
See DiAMICO, Maureen
116. AMIDON, Richard
"Trying to Reason with Her on a Tuesday Morning in July, After the Fourth." [SlipS]
(7) 87, p. 98-99.
"You've Bought a Telescope." [SlipS] (7) 87, p. 100-101.
117. AMJAD, Amjad Islam
"The Night Gasps for Breath" (tr. by Salim-ur Rehman). [Vis] (23) 87, p. 12.
118. AMMONS, A. R.
"Ah." [Hudson] (40:2) Sum 87, p. 293.
"The Eternal City." [SouthwR] (72:2) Spr 87, p. 162-163.
"Fall's End." [Harp] (274:1651) D 87, p. 32.
"Fall's End." [Hudson] (40:2) Sum 87, p. 294.
"Forerunners." [Hudson] (40:2) Sum 87, p. 290-291.
"Inclinations." [Hudson] (40:1) Spr 87, p. 59-70.
"Loving People." [Hudson] (40:2) Sum 87, p. 292-293.
"Motion Which Disestablishes Organizes Everything." [Hudson] (40:2) Sum 87, p.
288-290.
"Slights of Sight." [Hudson] (40:2) Sum 87, p. 293-294.
"The Time Rate of Change." [Hudson] (40:2) Sum 87, p. 291-292.

"Tow Possibilities." [SouthwR] (72:2) Spr 87, p. 161.
"Why Is It Always the Way It Always Is." [Hudson] (40:2) Sum 87, p. 286-288.
119. AMONG, Michael Darnay
"Taking a chance at night." [HawaiiR] (19) Spr 86, c87, p. 57.
120. AMOS, Patricia
"Anne Tanner." [LaurelR] (20:1/2) Sum 87, p. 67-68.
121. AMROUCHE, Jean
"Words from the Star" (Excerpt, tr. by Eric Sellin). [LitR] (30:3) Spr 87, p. 396.
122. ANDAY, Melih Cevdet
"Startling Encounter" (tr. by Talat Sait Halman). [Trans] (19) Fall 87, p. 128.
"Vertigo" (tr. by Talat Sait Halman). [Trans] (19) Fall 87, p. 129.
123. ANDERMANN, Guri
"Syllogisms." [Calyx] (10:2/3) Spr 87, p. 11.
124. ANDERS, Jaroslaw
"Mass for the Imprisoned" (tr. of Zbigniew Herbert, w. Michael March). [NewYRB] (33:21-22) 15 Ja 87, p. 15.
125. ANDERS, Shirley
"A Silence." [SouthernPR] (27:2) Fall 87, p. 57.
126. ANDERSON, Barbara
"A Life of Lives." [IndR] (10:3) Spr 87, p. 73-74.
127. ANDERSON, Barbara Rine
"Taking Tea" (To my grandmother, Lila Mae Chittick Rine, 1890-1982, who lived women's rights). [BellArk] (3:6) N-D 87, p. 6.
128. ANDERSON, Bobby
"Type of Darkness." [Thrpny] (31) Fall 87, p. 18.
129. ANDERSON, Bruce
"Cézanne: The Ruined Chateau" (from The Motives). [Agni] (24/25) 87, p. 34-35.
130. ANDERSON, Catherine Corley
"On Tasting a Perfect Orange." [Writer] (100:1) Ja 87, p. 22.
"Time." [Writer] (99:11) N 86, p. 17.
131. ANDERSON, Chris
"Three Stages of the Body" (The Greensboro Review Literary Award, Honorable Mention). [GreensboroR] (41) Wint 86-87, p. 33-34.
132. ANDERSON, Claes
"Why All These Answers" (tr. by Lennart Bruce). [CrossCur] (7:3) 87, p. 69.
133. ANDERSON, Debbie
"Maybe the Cows." [Gambit] (21) 87, p. 19.
134. ANDERSON, Doug
"A Late October's Lowell" (for Jack Kerouac). [MoodySI] (18/19) Fall 87, p. 38.
135. ANDERSON, Erland
"Blind Indians" (tr. of Joaquin Pasos). [NewRena] (7:1, #21) Fall 87, p. 55.
"Lagoon" (tr. of Ernesto Gutierrez). [NewRena] (7:1, #21) Fall 87, p. 53.
"My Two Hands" (tr. of Alvaro Menen Desleal). [NewRena] (7:1, #21) Fall 87, p. 59.
"North-South" (for Betty La Duke). [GreenfR] (14:1/2) Wint-Spr, p. 104-105.
"Old Papers." [HawaiiR] (19) Spr 86, c87, p. 21-23.
"Questions about Hogs and Their Abusive Names" (tr. of Jose Emilio Pacheco). [NewRena] (7:1, #21) Fall 87, p. 56.
"Towards the Pole" (tr. of Rolf Aggestam, w. Lars Nordstrom). [GreenfR] (14:1/2) Wint-Spr, p. 103.
136. ANDERSON, Jack
"American Romantic." [HangL] (50/51) 87, p. 21.
"The Caves." [BelPoJ] (38:1) Fall 87, p. 36.
"The Drama." [HangL] (50/51) 87, p. 22-23.
"Here You Are Walking Forty Years Ago." [HangL] (50/51) 87, p. 14-16.
"The Invention of New Jersey." [Spirit] (8:2) 87, p. 55-56.
"A Journey by Railroad." [HangL] (50/51) 87, p. 19-20.
"Poem for a Birthday." [BelPoJ] (38:1) Fall 87, p. 35-36.
"Social Studies Problems." [HangL] (50/51) 87, p. 17-18.
137. ANDERSON, Jon
"Drowning." [NowestR] (25:3) 87, p. 174.
138. ANDERSON, Lori
"On the Last Page of Her Diary She Said She Was Two Severed Selves." [DenQ] (22:2) Fall 87, p. 68-71.
"Water." [DenQ] (22:1) Sum 87, p. 37-38.

139. ANDERSON, Maggie
"Walker Evans: Mining Camp Residents, West Virginia, July, 1935." [NowestR]
(25:3) 87, p. 399.
140. ANDERSON, Mark
"Carpentry." [CapeR] (22:1) Spr 87, p. 43.
"Summer Evening on the Porch." [CapeR] (22:1) Spr 87, p. 42.
141. ANDERSON, Mia
"The Apotheosis." [MalR] (80) S 87, p. 66-75.
142. ANDERSON, Murray
"Mink Farming." [BellR] (10:2) Fall 87, p. 59-60.
143. ANDERSON, Robert
"Chain of Days." [JamesWR] (5:1) Fall 87, p. 9.
144. ANDERSON, Rod
"Breakfast." [AntigR] (71/72) Aut 87-Wint 88, p. 173.
"Circles." [Germ] (11:1) Fall 87, p. 36.
"Guilty as Charged." [AntigR] (71/72) Aut 87-Wint 88, p. 175.
"Michael." [AntigR] (71/72) Aut 87-Wint 88, p. 174.
"Plane Trip." [AntigR] (71/72) Aut 87-Wint 88, p. 172-173.
"Suitor." [Germ] (10:2) Spr 87, p. 34.
"Sunday." [Germ] (10:2) Spr 87, p. 35.
145. ANDERSON, Skip
"Sister Trees." [Pembroke] (19) 87, p. 145.
146. ANDERSON, T. J., III
"The Message of Fire" (1987 Ratner-Ferber-Poet Lore Honorable Mention). [PoetL]
(82:2) Sum 87, p. 85-86.
147. ANDRADE, Eugenio de
"IV. You lean your face on sorrow, don't even" (tr. by Alexis Levitin). [StoneC]
(14:3/4) Spr-Sum 87, p. 23.
"XLVI. É inverno, as mãos mal podem." [StoneC] (14:3/4) Spr-Sum 87, p. 22.
"XLVI. It is winter, hands can hardly hold" (tr. by Alexis Levitin). [StoneC] (14:3/4)
Spr-Sum 87, p. 22.
"Against the Shadow" (tr. by Alexis Levitin). [BostonR] (12:3) Je 87, p. 4.
"The Color of Those Days" (tr. by Alexis Levitin). [GrahamHR] (10) Wint-Spr 87, p.
55.
"Encostas a face à melancolia e nem sequer." [StoneC] (14:3/4) Spr-Sum 87, p. 23.
"Just a Glance" (tr. by Alexis Levitin). [SenR] (17:1) 87, p. 45.
"March Has Returned" (tr. by Alexis Levitin). [GrahamHR] (10) Wint-Spr 87, p. 54.
"No, I Cannot Find the Photograph" (tr. by Alexis Levitin). [GrahamHR] (10)
Wint-Spr 87, p. 53.
"September Sea" (tr. by Alexis Levitin). [CrossCur] (7:3) 87, p. 95.
"They Touched the Earth" (tr. by Alexis Levitin). [SenR] (17:1) 87, p. 44.
"White on White" (tr. by Alexis Levitin). [QRL] (Series 8, vol. 27) 87, 60 p.
"With the Birds" (tr. by Alexis Levitin). [SenR] (17:1) 87, p. 46.
148. ANDRASICK, Kathleen
"Dishwasher Fears." [HawaiiR] (22) Fall 87, p. 17.
"Listening." [BambooR] (33) Spr 87, p. 16-17.
149. ANDRE, Michael
"The Unfeathered Bird." [Abraxas] (35/36) 87, p. 33.
150. ANDREA, Marianne
"After Reading Linda Pastan." [StoneC] (15:1/2) Fall-Wint 87-88, p. 68.
"November Mums." [CrossCur] (7:2) 87, p. 91.
"Song of the Last Meeting" (Sept. 29, 1911, tr. of Anna Akhmatova). [Waves] (14:4)
Spr 86, p. 78.
"Three Poems" (1944-1960, tr. of Anna Akhmatova). [Waves] (14:4) Spr 86, p. 78.
151. ANDRESEN, Sophia de Mello Breyner
"The Smooth Beach with Eurydice Dead" (tr. by Alexis Levitin). [Vis] (24) 87, p. 4.
"Women by the Seashore" (tr. by Lisa Sapinkopf). [HampSPR] Wint 86, p. 28.
152. ANDREW, Victor
"In the Back of the Little Grocery Store." [WindO] (49) Fall 87, p. 58.
"Memory, Slender & Silver." [BallSUF] (28:4) Aut 87, p. 45-46.
"Paris No. 4 — Felix Potin." [WindO] (49) Fall 87, p. 59.
"Paris, No. 13 — Conversation with the Duchess D'Harcourt, October, 1985."
[WindO] (49) Fall 87, p. 60.
153. ANDREWS, Bruce
"Be Careful Now You Know Sugar Melts in Water." [Temblor] (6) 87, p. 122-125.
"Bomb Then, Bomb Now." [NewAW] (1) 87, p. 93-94.

"Could Darwin Instruct Those Turtles?" [ParisR] (29:105) Wint 87, p. 150-152.
"The Distancing Device Is the Staff of Life" (Hugo Ball). [Temblor] (6) 87, p. 125.
"How to Attract Love." [NewAW] (1) 87, p. 91-92.
"I Want Educated Oxen" (from "I Don't Have Any Paper So Shut Up . . ."). [Bound]
    (14:1/2) Fall 85-Wint 86 [c87], p. 109-110.
"In This Charming Little Room." [Temblor] (6) 87, p. 126-127.
"Strictly Confidential" (Excerpt). [CentralP] (11) Spr 87, p. 26.
154. ANDREWS, Jenné
    "The Horse Flower." [Abraxas] (35/36) 87, p. 27.
155. ANDREWS, Linda
    "Images of the Absent Father." [CumbPR] (7:1) Fall 87, p. 24-25.
    "My Daughter in the Surf." [CumbPR] (7:1) Fall 87, p. 22-23.
156. ANDREWS, Michael
    "Children, Plaza de Armas, Cusco." [DekalbLAJ] (20:1/4) 87, p. 31.
    "Generations" (A Cliff Dwelling, the San Juan River). [DekalbLAJ] (20:1/4) 87, p.
      32.
    "In the Auto Parts Store." [WormR] (27:4, issue 108) 87, p. 111.
    "In Tucson We Said Adios." [Abraxas] (35/36) 87, p. 76-77.
    "Peppers: On a Newspaper Review of a Robert Altman Film: 'Three Women,' . . ."
      [WormR] (27:4, issue 108) 87, p. 109-110.
    "Xmas in Love." [Abraxas] (35/36) 87, p. 77.
157. ANDREWS, Nancy
    "There, Where the Ground Swells." [HampSPR] Wint 86, p. 11.
158. ANDREWS, Tom
    "Song of a Country Priest." [WilliamMR] (25) Spr 87, p. 37-39.
    "Spring Dialogue." [LaurelR] (20:1/2) Sum 87, p. 93.
159. ANDROLA, Ron
    "How the Days Look." [Bogg] (58) 87, p. 33.
    "Over the Fields." [SlipS] (7) 87, p. 44.
160. ANDRUS, Pat
    "For Clara on Her First Christmas." [BellArk] (3:6) N-D 87, p. 6.
    "Geranium." [BellArk] (3:5) S-O 87, p. 1.
161. ANDRYCHUK, Kristin
    "Dirty Tricks." [Quarry] (36:1) Wint 87, p. 12-13.
    "Gone to Ground." [Quarry] (36:1) Wint 87, p. 13-14.
162. ANGEL, Ralph
    "And the Grass Did Grow." [Poetry] (149:4) Ja 87, p. 196.
    "Don't." [AmerPoR] (16:6) N-D 87, p. 55.
    "How Long Can We Go on Winning." [IndR] (10:3) Spr 87, p. 76.
    "The Loneliest Man in the World." [Poetry] (149:4) Ja 87, p. 195.
    "Shadow Play." [Poetry] (149:4) Ja 87, p. 197-198.
163. ANGELAKI-ROOKE, Katerina
    "Jealousy" (tr. by Rae Dalven). [LitR] (31:1) Fall 87, p. 47.
    "Penelope Says" (tr. by Helen Kolias). [Paint] (14:27) Spr 87, p. 30-31.
    "Penelope Says" (tr. by Rae Dalven). [PartR] (54:2) Spr 87, p. 267-269.
ANGELI, Milo de
    See De ANGELIS, Milo
ANGELIS, Milo de
    See De ANGELIS, Milo
164. ANGELL, Roger
    "Greetings, Friends!" [NewYorker] (63:45) 28 D 87, p. 39.
165. ANGKUW, Rietje Marie
    "Peelings." [HiramPoR] (42) Spr-Sum 87, p. 10.
ANGLADA, Luis Lopez
    See LOPEZ ANGLADA, Luis
166. ANGLE, Lily D.
    "Seedam." [LightY] '87, c86, p. 244.
167. ANGLESEY, Zoë
    "Acreage and Distance." [NoDaQ] (55:3) Sum 87, p. 73.
    "And in This Coming and Going" (tr. of Diana Avila). [Cond] (14) 87, p. 195.
    "Ars Poetica" (tr. of Mirna Martinez). [StoneC] (15:1/2) Fall-Wint 87-88, p. 51.
    "Being Guerrillera" (tr. of Ana María Rodas). [Cond] (14) 87, p. 191.
    "The Cat" (tr. of Carmen Naranjo). [Cond] (14) 87, p. 173, 175.
    "Criteria for Post-Interrogation Status." [StoneC] (15:1/2) Fall-Wint 87-88, p. 48.
    "The Days Are the Cities" (tr. of Ana María Rodas). [Cond] (14) 87, p. 187.
    "Death Is a Retreat" (tr. of Ana Istarú). [Cond] (14) 87, p. 205, 207.

"Everyone Has the Right" (tr. of Ana María Rodas). [Cond] (14) 87, p. 185.
"Look at Me" (tr. of Ana María Rodas). [Cond] (14) 87, p. 189.
"Lullaby for a Salvadoran Child" (tr. of Carmen Naranjo). [Cond] (14) 87, p. 179,
   181.
"Perhaps the Flower, the Bee" (tr. of Carmen Naranjo). [Cond] (14) 87, p. 177.
"Rhythm & Blues." [StoneC] (15:1/2) Fall-Wint 87-88, p. 49.
"We Need Time" (tr. of Etelvina Astrada). [CrossCur] (7:3) 87, p. 31.
"While U.S. Helicopters Land as 'Gifts' in Costa Rica." [Electrum] (39) Fall-Wint
   87, p. 26.
"Word" (tr. of Mirna Martínez). [Cond] (14) 87, p. 197.
168. ANGST, Bim
"Knowing." [Farm] (4:2) Spr-Sum 87, p. 48.
"Liturgy of the Midwest Home." [Farm] (4:2) Spr-Sum 87, p. 49.
169. ANNHARTE
"Banana Moon." [PraF] (8:3) Aut 87, p. 14.
"Jumper Moon." [PraF] (8:3) Aut 87, p. 15.
170. ANONYMOUS
"An Anglo-Saxon Riddle: 66" (from "The Exeter Book," in Anglo-Saxon & English,
   tr. by Nan Fry). [StoneC] (14:3/4) Spr-Sum 87, p. 74.
"Did You See the Modest Girl?" (tr. from the Gaelic by Iain Crichton Smith). [Stand]
   (28:2) Spr 87, p. 50.
"Images" (tr. from the Japanese by Graeme Wilson). [LitR] (31:1) Fall 87, p. 87.
"Marquesas Islands Songs" (tr. by Margaret Orbell). [Trans] (19) Fall 87, p.
   174-176.
"The Mourning Songs of Greece" (Selections, tr. by Konstantinos Lardas).
   [AmerPoR] (16:5) S-O 87, p. 28-29.
"The Mourning Songs of Greek Women" (tr. by Konstantinos Lardas). [ColEng]
   (49:1) Ja 87, p. 37-41.
"Pity That I Was Not Born Blind" (tr. from the Gaelic by Iain Crichton Smith).
   [Stand] (28:2) Spr 87, p. 49.
"Seathan Son of the King of Ireland" (tr. from the Gaelic by Iain Crichton Smith).
   [Stand] (28:2) Spr 87, p. 50-53.
"Song from Kanteletar" (collected by Lonrot in the 19th century, tr. from the Finnish
   by Jascha Kessler and Kirsti Simonsuuri). [Nimrod] (31:1) Fall-Wint 87, p.
   130.
171. ANONYMOUS, 5th grader
"In my body there are caves." The Best of [BambooR] [(31-32)] 86, p. 14.
172. ANSEN, Alan
"Jaws." [Shen] (37:1) 87, p. 32.
173. ANTHONY, Frank
"The Moment." [NegC] (7:3/4) 87, p. 80.
174. ANTIN, Amy
"The Poor in the Bus Depot" (tr. of Lêdo Ivo). [NewYorker] (63:43) 14 D 87, p. 44.
175. ANTLER
"The Darkness Within." [GreenfR] (14:1/2) Wint-Spr, p. 186.
"Happenstance." [AlphaBS] (2) D 87, p. 14.
"Raising My Hand." [GreenfR] (14:1/2) Wint-Spr, p. 184.
"What the God Says Through Me." [GreenfR] (14:1/2) Wint-Spr, p. 185.
176. ANTON, K. H.
"The Black Ship" (tr. of Pablo Antonio Cuadra). [CutB] (27/28) 87, p. 103.
"The Pyramid of Quetzacoat" (tr. of Pablo Antonio Cuadra). [CutB] (27/28) 87, p.
   100-102.
177. ANTONIO, Norberto
"Lirio y Delirio (1) y (2)." [Mairena] (9:24) 87, p. 68.
178. APATOVSKY, Pat
"For the Bayman." [PaintedB] (30) 87, p. 20.
179. APOLLINAIRE, Guillaume
"Snow White" (tr. by Bernhard Frank). [WebR] (12:2) Fall 87, p. 42.
180. APPEL, Cathy
"The Debt." [PassN] (8:2) Sum 87, p. 26.
181. APPLEFIELD, David
"A Bit of Flesh" (tr. of Alain Bosquet). [LitR] (30:3) Spr 87, p. 437.
"Das Ewig Weibliche" (for E.M. Cioran, tr. of Edouard Roditi). [LitR] (30:3) Spr 87,
   p. 434.
"Fabeltier" (tr. of Edouard Roditi). [LitR] (30:3) Spr 87, p. 434.
"A Funeral" (tr. of Alain Bosquet). [LitR] (30:3) Spr 87, p. 436.

"A Mother's Death" (tr. of Alain Bosquet). [LitR] (30:3) Spr 87, p. 436.
"Windesbraut" (for Kenneth Rexroth, tr. of Edouard Roditi). [LitR] (30:3) Spr 87, p. 435.

182. APPLEMAN, Philip
"Gathering by the River." [Poetry] (151:1/2) O-N 87, p. 6.
"Gertrude C. Appleman (1901-1976)." [PartR] (54:3) Sum 87, p. "426-427.
"Parables." [BelPoJ] (38:2) Wint 87-88, p. 14-15.

183. APPLEWHITE, James
"Deciphering the Known Map." [TarPR] (27:1) Fall 87, p. 25-26.
"The Forest." [Confr] (35/36) Spr-Fall 87, p. 61.
"Good As Dad." [Confr] (35/36) Spr-Fall 87, p. 62.
"Jonquils." [NowestR] (25:2) 87, p. 150.
"Lessons in Soaring." [TarPR] (27:1) Fall 87, p. 27.
"Observing the Sun." [CarolQ] (39:3) Spr 87, p. 97.

184. AQUILAR-CARIÑO, Maria Luisa
"After Movies." [BlackWR] (13:2) Spr 87, p. 47.
"From an Album." [BlackWR] (13:2) Spr 87, p. 42-43.
"Improvisation." [BlackWR] (13:2) Spr 87, p. 48.
"Monsoon." [BlackWR] (13:2) Spr 87, p. 44.
"Omaira." [BlackWR] (13:2) Spr 87, p. 45-46.
"A Sense of Balance." [BlackWR] (13:2) Spr 87, p. 40-41.

185. ARAGON, Francisco
"My Hair" (tr. of Francisco X. Alarcón). [Zyzzyva] (3:3) Fall 87, p. 26.

186. ARBOLEAS, Héctor
"Tzompantli de Conciencias." [Mester] (16:1) Spr 87, p. 61.

187. ARCHER, Nuala
"Adrift in a Coracle of Ash" (for Marjorie). [ColEng] (49:2) F 87, p. 171.
"Bizarre, the Boojum." [ColEng] (49:2) F 87, p. 172-173.
"A Breaking, a Bread-Colored Light" (Award Poem — 3rd Place). [Phoenix] (7:1) 87, p. 3.
"Cello Strings & Chick Peas." [CreamCR] (11:2/3) 87?, p. 91-92.
"Coal-Colored Giraffe." [ColEng] (49:2) F 87, p. 174.
"From a Mobile Home: Black Mesa Rendezvous." [MidAR] (7:2) 87, p. 50-51.
"Glossolalia." [Calyx] (11:1) Wint 87-88, p. 42-43.
"Riant Quiet." [Nimrod] (30:2) Spr-Sum 87, p. 4-5.
"She Had Licked Her Name." [Calyx] (11:1) Wint 87-88, p. 40-41.

188. ARCHIBEQUE, Leanne
"Machaca" (Dedicated to Irma, my children's Foster Mother from 3/86 to 5/87). [Witness] (1:3) Fall 87, p. 27.

189. ARDERIU, Clementina
"Distant Deaths" (tr. by Lynette McGrath and Nathaniel B. Smith). [WebR] (12:2) Fall 87, p. 22.
"Song of Perfect Trust" (tr. by Lynette McGrath and Nathaniel B. Smith). [WebR] (12:2) Fall 87, p. 21.

190. ARENA, Adri Anna
"Isle of Eriska, Scotland." [StoneC] (14:3/4) Spr-Sum 87, p. 21.

191. ARFAA, Anne Leonard
"Toward Evening." [Phoenix] (7:1) 87, p. 29-30.

192. ARGÜELLES, Ivan
"After the Coma." [CapeR] (22:2) Fall 87, p. 9.
"The Age of Englightenment." [Margin] (5) Wint 87-88, p. 49-50.
"Argonautica." [Margin] (1) Wint 86, p. 67.
"Because There Are Reasons" (for CZ). [YellowS] (23) Sum 87, p. 9.
"The Big Chair." [Margin] (5) Wint 87-88, p. 50-51.
"Bird in Flight." [FiveFR] (5) 87, p. 10.
"Borracho Perdido." [Sonora] (12) Spr 87, p. 23.
"Bride of My Unreason." [YellowS] (25) Wint 87, p. 30.
"A Career in Music." [Abraxas] (35/36) 87, p. 21.
"Childhood." [Abraxas] (35/36) 87, p. 22.
"The Death of Sokrates." [Abraxas] (35/36) 87, p. 23.
"Free Form." [Wind] (17:59) 87, p. 1.
"From the Hymn to Persephone" (for Christina). [YellowS] (23) Sum 87, p. 11.
"The History of the Alphabet." [Margin] (1) Wint 86, p. 63-64.
"I Love Coffee I Love Espresso I Love Death" (for George Hitchcock). [Caliban] (2) 87, p. 150-151.
"Kama Sutra." [YellowS] (25) Wint 87, p. 31.

"Koré." [Margin] (5) Wint 87-88, p. 51-52.
"Lady Murasaki." [Margin] (1) Wint 86, p. 61.
"A Love Poem." [Margin] (1) Wint 86, p. 62.
"Love with the Perfect Stranger" (for CZ). [YellowS] (23) Sum 87, p. 7.
"Lunacy" (for Christina). [YellowS] (23) Sum 87, p. 10.
"Tellurian Enigmas." [Margin] (1) Wint 86, p. 65-66.
"We Love the Wounds We Give Each Other" (for Christina Zawadiwsky). [YellowS] (23) Sum 87, p. 8.
"Yellow Silk." [YellowS] (23) Sum 87, p. 6.
193. ARGÜELLO, Jorge Eduardo
    "The Brain of Ruben Dario" (tr. by John Oliver Simon). [PikeF] (8) Fall 87, p. 30.
    "El Cerebro de R.D." [PikeF] (8) Fall 87, p. 30.
194. ARGYROS, Alex
    "Cait Loses." [Grain] (15:3) Fall 87, p. 64-65.
    "Digging Up Spring Bulbs." [Grain] (15:4) Wint 87, p. 70-71.
    "In the Valley of the Rondout." [CumbPR] (7:1) Fall 87, p. 14-15.
    "The Last Gift." [Grain] (15:3) Fall 87, p. 63.
    "Ogygia." [Grain] (15:3) Fall 87, p. 66.
    "Remembering a Childhood Friend." [StoneC] (15:1/2) Fall-Wint 87-88, p. 31-32.
    "Stevens' Tree." [Grain] (15:4) Wint 87, p. 68-69.
    "Walking Past a Friend's Grave." [Grain] (15:4) Wint 87, p. 66.
    "Without." [Grain] (15:4) Wint 87, p. 67.
195. ARIDJIS, Homero
    "The Dead of the Revolution" (tr. by Joel Zeltzer). [Abraxas] (35/36) 87, p. 47.
    "Los Muertos de la Revolución." [Abraxas] (35/36) 87, p. 46.
196. ARISUKE, Miharu No
    "The Power of Suggestion" (tr. by Graeme Wilson). [LitR] (31:1) Fall 87, p. 86.
197. ARIZAGA, Carlos Manuel
    "Volver sobre tu cuerpo." [Mairena] (9:24) 87, p. 113.
198. ARK, Laurine
    "Resurrection." [NegC] (7:3/4) 87, p. 157.
199. ARKELL, Chris
    "I Hide My Face Against the Tramcar Window" (tr. of Eugene Dubnov, w. John Heath-Stubbs). [SenR] (17:1) 87, p. 19.
200. ARMAND, Octavio
    "Doorknob" (tr. by Carol Maier). [NewOR] (14:1) Spr 87, p. 55.
201. ARMANTROUT, Rae
    "Begin." [Bound] (14:1/2) Fall 85-Wint 86 [c87], p. 47.
    "The Panoply of." [Bound] (14:1/2) Fall 85-Wint 86 [c87], p. 48.
    "Wake Up." [CentralP] (12) Fall 87, p. 81.
202. ARMER, Sondra
    "Nude Ascending a Pillowcase." [TexasR] (8:3/4) Fall-Wint 87, p. 102.
203. ARMITAGE, Barri
    "Fittings." [GeoR] (41:2) Sum 87, p. 348.
    "Self-Portrait." [Poetry] (149:5) F 87, p. 264.
    "Trading on Gravity." [Poetry] (149:5) F 87, p. 264-265.
204. ARMOUR, Richard
    "The Conscience." [LightY] '87, c86, p. 82.
    "Hiding Place." [LightY] '87, c86, p. 248.
    "Money." [LightY] '87, c86, p. 20.
    "Sequence." [LightY] '87, c86, p. 138.
    "To Have and Too Old." [LightY] '87, c86, p. 130.
205. ARMSTRONG, Gene
    "The Heavenly Hell of It." [HampSPR] Wint 86, p. 42.
    "Over and On." [HampSPR] Wint 86, p. 42.
    "Scherzo for a Summer Afternoon." [HampSPR] Wint 86, p. 42.
206. ARNDT, Dorla D.
    "Eight Ways of Looking at Loneliness." [InterPR] (13:2) Fall 87, p. 66-67.
    "No Letter." [InterPR] (13:2) Fall 87, p. 65.
207. ARNDT, Walter
    "The Island" (tr. of Rainer Maria Rilke). [NewEngR] (10:2) Wint 87, p. 215-216.
208. ARNETT, Harold
    "Sassafras." [Gambit] (20) 86, p. 111-112.
    "Tobacco Stripping." [Gambit] (20) 86, p. 70.

209. ARNOLD, Madelyn
"On Reading the Entire Oxford Anthology of English Verse in a Single Sitting, While Crabby." [BellArk] (3:4) Jl-Ag 87, p. 5.
ARPINO, Tony d'
See D'ARPINO, Tony
210. ARROWSMITH, William
"Arsenio" (tr. of Eugenio Montale). [Pequod] (23/24) 87, p. 295-296.
"Eclogue" (tr. of Eugenio Montale). [SouthernHR] (21:2) Spr 87, p. 156-157.
"End of Childhood" (tr. of Eugenio Montale). [Pequod] (23/24) 87, p. 292-294.
"Falsetto" (tr. of Eugenio Montale). [SouthernHR] (21:2) Spr 87, p. 132-133.
"Now and Then" (tr. of Eugenio Montale). [SouthernHR] (21:2) Spr 87, p. 134.
"Ossi di Seppia" (Selections: 4 poems in Italian and English, tr. of Eugenio Montale). [CrossCur] (7:2) 87, p. 26-33.
"Satura" (Selections: 4 poems, tr. of Eugenio Montale). [Interim] (6:2) Fall 87, p. 3-6.
"Seacoasts" (tr. of Eugenio Montale). [Pequod] (23/24) 87, p. 290-291.
"A Wild Squall" (tr. of Eugenio Montale). [SouthernHR] (21:3) Sum 87, p. 230.
211. ARROYO, Rane
"Kierkegaard, on Faith." [WindO] (48) Spr 87, p. 29.
"Spirits in Flight." [Vis] (23) 87, p. 18.
212. ARTAUD, Antonin
"To Have Done with the Judgment of God" (Excerpt, tr. by Guy Wernham). [NowestR] (25:3) 87, p. 65-67.
213. ARVIO, Sarah
"Library at Los Milagros." [YaleR] (76:4) Sum 87, p. 554-555.
214. ASEKOFF, L. S.
"After the Deluge." [Shen] (37:1) 87, p. 40-42.
"Babel." [NewYorker] (62:48) 19 Ja 87, p. 34.
"Winter Oranges." [NewYorker] (62:48) 19 Ja 87, p. 34.
215. ASH, Karin
"Cornucopias." [VirQR] (63:2) Spr 87, p. 272.
216. ASHBERY, John
"Adam Snow." [Poetry] (150:5) Ag 87, p. 250-251.
"Amid Mounting Evidence." [Poetry] (150:5) Ag 87, p. 253-255.
"April Galleons." [NewYorker] (63:9) 20 Ap 87, p. 34.
"Art Songs." [NewRep] (197:17) 26 O 87, p. 32.
"Bilking the Statues." [Boulevard] (2:3) Fall 87, p. 19-21.
"Drab Shutters" (from *For Nelson Mandela, a Festscrift*). [Harp] (274:1649) O 87, p. 26.
"Dreams of Adulthood." [Sulfur] (19) Spr 87, p. 70-71.
"Finnish Rhapsody." [Conjunc] (10) 87, p. 91-92.
"Forgotten Sex." [Sulfur] (19) Spr 87, p. 72-73.
"Frost." [NewYorker] (63:11) 4 My 87, p. 36.
"The Ice Storm." [Temblor] (5) 87, p. 3-4.
"A Mood of Quiet Beauty." [NewYRB] (34:4) 12 Mr 87, p. 8.
"Morning Jitters." [Poetry] (150:5) Ag 87, p. 252.
"Never to Get It Really Right." [NewYRB] (34:2) 12 F 87, p. 4.
"One Coat of Paint." [Shen] (37:3) 87, p. 51.
"Ostensibly." [Poetry] (150:5) Ag 87, p. 249-250.
"The Revised Weather Report." [Shen] (37:3) 87, p. 50.
"Riddle Me." [Poetry] (150:5) Ag 87, p. 255-256.
"Sighs and Inhibitions." [NewYorker] (63:19) 29 Je 87, p. 30.
"Someone You Have Seen Before." [Sulfur] (19) Spr 87, p. 73-75.
"Unreleased Movie." [Poetry] (151:1/2) O-N 87, p. 7-10.
217. ASHEAR, Linda
"Congratulations: Chords & Other Poems" (for Ruth Lisa Schechter). [Footwork] 87, p. 51.
218. ASHTON, Jennifer
"After Light." [PoetryNW] (28:3) Aut 87, p. 29-30.
"Curator." [PoetryNW] (28:3) Aut 87, p. 30-31.
219. ASHWORTH, Peggy
"Collage with Paint" (For H.B.). [BlueBldgs] (10) 87?, p. 26.
220. ASPENBERG, Gary
"The Desert." [Caliban] (3) 87, p. 42.
"Memories of Hiroshima" (for Stomu Yamash'ta). [Caliban] (3) 87, p. 43.
"Visage" (for Luciano Berio). [Caliban] (3) 87, p. 40-41.

221. ASPENSTRÖM, Werner
"The Child Asks About the Sun" (tr. by D. L. Emblen). [CrossCur] (7:3) 87, p. 133.
"The Lakes in Scandinavia" (tr. by D. L. Emblen). [PoetL] (81:3) Fall 86, p. 180.
222. ASPER, Douglas
"You Tell Me We're Having a Baby." [KanQ] (19:1/2) Wint-Spr 87, p. 39.
223. ASPINWALL, Dorothy
"To Live" (tr. of Pierre Béarn). [WebR] (12:2) Fall 87, p. 17.
"The Violinist" (tr. of Jean-Pierre Lemaire). [CumbPR] (6:2) Spr 87, p. 9.
224. ASTOR, Susan
"Bending to Her Bath." [PoetL] (82:1) Spr 87, p. 25.
"Erection." [PoetL] (81:3) Fall 86, p. 171.
"Johnny Appleseed Gets a Sign." [PoetL] (82:1) Spr 87, p. 22-23.
"Women in Love." [PoetL] (82:1) Spr 87, p. 24.
225. ASTRADA, Etelvina
"We Need Time" (tr. by Zoe Anglesey). [CrossCur] (7:3) 87, p. 31.
226. ATENCIA, María Victoria
"Among Those Who Have Gone Away" ("Entre Los Que Se Fueron," tr. by Joanna
Courteau). [PoetC] (18:2) Wint 87, p. 33.
"The Day of Anger" ("Dia de la Ira," tr. by Joanna Courteau). [PoetC] (18:2) Wint 87,
p. 32.
"The Hard Bread" ("El Duro Pan," tr. by Joanna Courteau). [PoetC] (18:2) Wint 87,
p. 31.
"Leave Me Alone" ("Dejame," tr. by Joanna Courteau). [PoetC] (18:2) Wint 87, p.
30.
227. ATKINS, Kathleen
"Enisled." [HayF] (2) Spr 87, p. 32.
228. ATKINSON, Alan
"At the Movie." [Margin] (4) Aut 87, p. 111.
"Twilight Zone." [Margin] (4) Aut 87, p. 110.
229. ATKINSON, Charles
"Chopping a Mother's Piano." [SouthernPR] (27:2) Fall 87, p. 55-56.
"Concert, After a Friend's Death." [DenQ] (22:1) Sum 87, p. 29-30.
"Family Album" (for two brothers, 1987 Ratner-Ferber-Poet Lore Honorable
Mention). [PoetL] (82:2) Sum 87, p. 81-82.
"For the Dreamer Who Makes Nothing of Dreams." [PoetryNW] (28:1) Spr 87, p.
31.
"Nicaraguan Ceremonial" (For the Sandanistas). [NegC] (7:3/4) 87, p. 105-107.
"Solstice at the Tidepools." [KanQ] (19:1/2) Wint-Spr 87, p. 270.
"The Sprit Willing." [CapeR] (22:2) Fall 87, p. 45.
"Translations from the Olfactory." [CapeR] (22:2) Fall 87, p. 46-47.
"Writing Tutorial" (for Lisa). [CapeR] (22:2) Fall 87, p. 44.
230. ATKINSON, Donald
"Food for the Gods." [Stand] (28:2) Spr 87, p. 60-62.
231. ATKINSON, Jennifer
"Afterward." [Poetry] (150:6) S 87, p. 329.
"The Dogwood Tree." [Poetry] (150:6) S 87, p. 328.
"Resolution." [Sonora] (12) Spr 87, p. 5-6.
"Winter Apples." [Sonora] (12) Spr 87, p. 3-4.
232. ATLIN, Gary
"Notes on the Long-Expected Death, in 1984, of the Marxist Mayor of Huancayo."
[NewL] (54:1) Fall 87, p. 114.
233. ATTILA, József
"The Man Spoke" (tr. by Susan Tomory and Reynold Stone). [AntigR] (71/72) Aut
87-Wint 88, p. 158.
"You Should Not Be Sorry" (tr. by Susan Tomory and Reynold Stone). [AntigR]
(71/72) Aut 87-Wint 88, p. 158.
234. ATWOOD, Margaret
"Ageing Female Poet Sits on the Balcony." [OP] (final issue) Sum 87, p. 89-90.
"An Angel." [Verse] (4:1) Mr 87, p. 19.
"Werewolf Movies." [OP] (final issue) Sum 87, p. 90-91.
"You Begin." [MidwQ] (28:4) Sum 87, p. 525-526.
235. AUBERT, Jimmy
"Artist, Muttering." [MidwQ] (28:2) Wint 87, p. 205.
236. AUDEN, W. H. (Wystan Hugh)
"Musée des Beaux Arts." [MassR] (28:2) Sum 87, p. 197-198.

"The Platonic Blow" (Generally attributed to W. H. Auden). [Margin] (1) Wint 86, p. 46-50.
"Thanksgiving." [WindO] (48) Spr 87, p. 34.
237. AUER, Benedict
"An Annunciation: On Giving Birth to God." [Interim] (6:2) Fall 87, p. 46.
"Changes." [DekalbLAJ] (20:1/4) 87, p. 33.
"The Confessor." [Paint] (14:28) Aut 87, p. 7.
"An Elegy." [BallSUF] (28:4) Aut 87, p. 53.
"February Fog." [ManhatPR] (9) Sum 87, p. 28.
"Firenze from the 'Dickens View'." [Wind] (17:61) 87, p. 1-2.
"Ionesco Visits a Monastery." [Paint] (14:28) Aut 87, p. 6.
"A Memoried Odor." [KanQ] (19:3) Sum 87, p. 264.
"My Pagan Baby." [SpoonRQ] (12:2) Spr 87, p. 43.
"A Predawn Ride into Morning." [KanQ] (19:3) Sum 87, p. 265.
"The Real Presence." [Phoenix] (7:1) 87, p. 16.
"Star Catching." [BlueBldgs] (10) 87?, p. 25.
238. AUGUST, Edmund
"On the New Road to Hazard." [Wind] (17:61) 87, p. 3.
239. AUSTIN, David Craig
"Animals." [BlackWR] (13:2) Spr 87, p. 26.
"Autobiography." [BlackWR] (13:2) Spr 87, p. 25.
"Elizabeth in 1945." [PoetryE] (23/24) Fall 87, p. 122.
"Good Friday." [YaleR] (76:4) Sum 87, p. 553.
"In the Country of the Eye." [ManhatPR] (9) Sum 87, p. 59.
"Solace." [BlackWR] (13:2) Spr 87, p. 27.
"Two Prayers." [ColR] (NS 14:1) Spr-Sum 87, p. 74-75.
240. AUSTIN, Jerry
"Bass Lake" (Circa 1974). [BellArk] (3:4) Jl-Ag 87, p. 4.
"Centerpiece." [BellArk] (3:2) Mr-Ap 87, p. 18.
"Image Homage." [BellArk] (3:1) Ja-F 87, p. 10.
"Snow Geese." [BellArk] (3:6) N-D 87, p. 5.
241. AUSTIN, Kathy M.
"Friday: Finding My Way to School — Alone." [Kaleid] (14) Wint-Spr 87, p. 72.
242. AUSTIN, Penelope
"Going Back." [NewRep] (197:11/12) 14-21 S 87, p. 52.
"Modernism." [NewRep] (196:26) 29 Je 87, p. 38.
AVE JEANNE
See JEANNE, Ave
243. AVELINE, Claude
"Punctuations" (tr. by Lawrence W. Lynch). [AntR] (45:3) Sum 87, p. 297.
244. AVERILL, Diane
"A Woman and Two Birds." [ColR] (NS 14:2) Fall-Wint 87, p. 85.
245. AVERILL, Kelly
"Remembered Feast." [MidwQ] (28:3) Spr 87, p. 355-356.
246. AVERY, Brian C.
"Eve at the Beach." [PoetL] (82:3) Fall 87, p. 166-167.
247. AVIGNONE, June
"The (Dis)Advantages of Stars." [Footwork] 87, p. 52-54.
248. AVILA, Diana
"And in This Coming and Going" (tr. by Zoë Anglesey). [Cond] (14) 87, p. 195.
"Y en Este Ir y Venir." [Cond] (14) 87, p. 194.
249. AVINS, Carol
"I'll live through this, survive, and they'll ask me" (tr. of Irina Ratushinskaya, w. Frances Padorr Brent). [NewYRB] (34:8) 7 My 87, p. 19.
"Two Poems from Prison" (tr. of Irina Ratushinskaya, w. Frances Padorr Brent). [NewYRB] (34:8) 7 My 87, p. 19.
"Well, we'll live as the soul directs" (tr. of Irina Ratushinskaya, w. Frances Padorr Brent). [NewYRB] (34:8) 7 My 87, p. 19.
250. AVIS, Nick
"Tuaimetuaime . . ." [CrossC] (9:3/4) 87, p. 8.
251. AWAD, Joseph
"Windows." [Wind] (17:61) 87, p. 2.
252. AXELROD, David
"First Days at Bear Creek Ranch." [CutB] (27/28) 87, p. 50-51.
253. AYALA, Elena
"Aire en la Calle." [Mairena] (9:24) 87, p. 69-70.

254. AYHAN, Ece
    "A Blind Cat Black" (tr. by Murat Nemet-Nejat). [Trans] (19) Fall 87, p. 130.
    "Epitafio" (tr. by Murat Nemet-Nejat). [Trans] (19) Fall 87, p. 131.
255. AZPADU, Dodici
    "Urban Development." [Lactuca] (5) Ja 87, p. 16.
256. AZZOPARDI, Mario
    "April Song" (tr. by Oliver Friggieri). [Vis] (25) 87, p. 17.
BAASTAD, Erling Friis
    See FRIIS-BAASTAD, Erling
257. BAATZ, Ronald
    "Like a Young Shelley Winters." [YellowS] (24) Aut 87, p. 10.
    "A Strange Habit." [YellowS] (24) Aut 87, p. 11.
258. BABAD, Katharine Heath
    "Aubade." [Interim] (6:1) Spr 87, p. 24.
    "Beyond the Wind." [CapeR] (22:2) Fall 87, p. 4.
    "Foreign Territory." [CapeR] (22:2) Fall 87, p. 5.
    "Past All Seeking." [CapeR] (22:1) Spr 87, p. 50.
259. BABB, Sanora
    "The Last Year" (to James Wong Howe). [HawaiiR] (21) Spr 87, p. 20.
260. BABER, Bob Henry
    "The Lobotomized Man Tries to Recall His Name" (For Major). [LaurelR] (20:1/2)
        Sum 87, p. 12-14.
    "Richwood." [Gambit] (20) 86, p. 69.
261. BACA, Jimmy Santiago
    "Green Chile." [Puerto] (22:2) Spr 87, p. 138-139.
    "Gregorio Cortez." [QW] (24) Wint 87, p. 96-97.
262. BACHHUBER, Daniel
    "In Memoriam: Professor Merle Brown." [Iowa] (17:2) Spr-Sum 87, p. 126.
263. BÄCHLER, Wolfgang
    "Another Low Pressure System?" (tr. by Rainer Schulte). [NewOR] (14:3) Fall 87, p.
        32.
    "Anticipation" (for Michael Krüger, tr. by Rainer Schulte). [NewOR] (14:3) Fall 87,
        p. 22.
    "Branching Out" (tr. by Rainer Schulte). [NewOR] (14:3) Fall 87, p. 36.
    "The Days Are Growing Shorter" (tr. by Rainer Schulte). [NewOR] (14:3) Fall 87, p.
        26.
    "Erwartung" (für Michael Kruüger). [NewOR] (14:3) Fall 87, p. 23.
    "Fruitless Retreat" (tr. by Rainer Schulte). [NewOR] (14:3) Fall 87, p. 34.
    "I Carry Earth in Me" (tr. by Rainer Schulte). [NewOR] (14:3) Fall 87, p. 30.
    "Ich Trage Erde in Mir." [NewOR] (14:3) Fall 87, p. 31.
    "Ein Neues Tief?" [NewOR] (14:3) Fall 87, p. 33.
    "Roads" (tr. by Rainer Schulte). [NewOR] (14:3) Fall 87, p. 20.
    "Ein Schrei." [NewOR] (14:3) Fall 87, p. 25.
    "A Scream" (tr. by Rainer Schulte). [NewOR] (14:3) Fall 87, p. 24.
    "Die Tage Fallen." [NewOR] (14:3) Fall 87, p. 27.
    "Veitshöchheim." [NewOR] (14:3) Fall 87, p. 29.
    "Veitshöchheim" (tr. by Rainer Schulte). [NewOR] (14:3) Fall 87, p. 28.
    "Vergeblicher Rückzug." [NewOR] (14:3) Fall 87, p. 35.
    "Verzweigungen." [NewOR] (14:3) Fall 87, p. 37.
    "Wege." [NewOR] (14:3) Fall 87, p. 21.
264. BACHLUND, Linda
    "Annie Listens to Her Plants." [Electrum] (39) Fall-Wint 87, p. 27.
265. BACHMANN, Ingeborg
    "Rome at Night" (tr. by Peter Filkins). [Trans] (18) Spr 87, p. 281.
    "A Type of Loss" (tr. by Peter Filkins). [PartR] (54:3) Sum 87, p. 425-426.
    "Wood and Shavings" (tr. by Peter Filkins). [Trans] (18) Spr 87, p. 282.
266. BACKBURN, Paul
    "Lo Dous Cossire Que'm Don' Amors Soven" (tr. of Guilhem de Cabestanh).
        [NewAW] (2) Fall 87, p. 55-57.
267. BACKEN, B.
    "Mr. Winner likes to take connie out to dinner." [Bogg] (57) 87, p. 10.
268. BADIKIAN, Beatriz
    "Mapmaker." [Americas] (15:2) Sum 87, p. 73.
    "Rituals at Bennington: The Elusive Joy of Writing." [Americas] (15:2) Sum 87, p.
        71.
    "Words." [Americas] (15:2) Sum 87, p. 72.

269. BAEHR, Anne-Ruth Ediger
      "Amish Adolescent" (Bird in Hand, Pennsylvania). [KanQ] (19:3) Sum 87, p. 171.
      "Guests." [KanQ] (19:3) Sum 87, p. 170.
      "Monster." [KanQ] (19:3) Sum 87, p. 169.
270. BAER, William
      "Futurist Exhibit." [BellR] (10:2) Fall 87, p. 33.
271. BAGG, Robert
      "White Shoulders." [Agni] (24/25) 87, p. 132-133.
272. BAGGETT, Rebecca
      "Strawberries." [HeliconN] (17/18) Spr 87, p. 162.
      "Walking the Sick Baby." [HeliconN] (17/18) Spr 87, p. 163.
273. BAGLOW, John
      "Babel." [CapilR] (44) 87, p. 46.
      "How to Understand What Is Happening in South Africa." [CanLit] (113/114)
          Sum-Fall 87, p. 27.
      "Mediated View." [CapilR] (44) 87, p. 48.
      "Memory." [CapilR] (44) 87, p. 47.
274. BAHAN, Lee Harlin
      "A Picture of Moses Not Being Rescued from Bulrushes." [LaurelR] (21:1/2)
          Wint-Sum 87, p. 75.
      "Why I Teach Senior English by Ann Hammond." [LaurelR] (21:1/2) Wint-Sum 87,
          p. 76.
275. BAIDEN, Larry
      "The Coppertone Guide to Philosphy." [Rampike] (5:3) 87, p. 57.
276. BAKER, Alison
      "Hunting." [Interim] (6:2) Fall 87, p. 11.
      "The Slough." [Interim] (6:2) Fall 87, p. 10.
277. BAKER, David
      "Breakdown." [Crazy] (32) Spr 87, p. 18-19.
      "Dig." [PoetryE] (23/24) Fall 87, p. 209.
      "Dixie." [SouthernR] (23:1) Ja 87, p. 119-124.
      "Starlight." [Poetry] (149:4) Ja 87, p. 203.
      "Your Wildest Imagination." [PoetryE] (23/24) Fall 87, p. 210.
278. BAKER, June Frankland
      "Related." [CentR] (31:1) Wint 87, p. 63-64.
      "Trying Silence." [CrabCR] (4:3) Sum 87, p. 13.
279. BAKER, Keith
      "Patient." [LightY] '87, c86, p. 222.
BAKER, Marie
      See ANNHARTE
280. BAKER, Peter
      "Blue Monk." [PoetC] (18:2) Wint 87, p. 8.
      "Far Cry." [PoetC] (18:2) Wint 87, p. 7.
      "Forgetting." [PoetC] (18:2) Wint 87, p. 9.
      "One Whose Exile Is Water." [Interim] (6:2) Fall 87, p. 40.
      "Pharoah's Dance." [PoetC] (18:2) Wint 87, p. 5.
      "Welcome Honor to John Coltrane." [PoetC] (18:2) Wint 87, p. 6.
281. BAKER, Will
      "On the Level." [GeoR] (41:4) Wint 87, p. 796-797.
282. BAKKEN, Dick
      "How to Eat Corn." [Spirit] (8:2) 87, p. 336.
      "Saturday Morning." [Amelia] (4:1/2, issue 9) 87, p. 124.
283. BAKTI, John
      "With a Pure Heart" (tr. of Attila Jozsef). [SpiritSH] (53:1) 87, p. 35.
284. BALABAN, Camille
      "Ahab." [EngJ] (76:5) S 87, p. 111.
      "For Nana." [PoeticJ] (17) 87, p. 14.
285. BALABAN, John
      "Eliseo's Cabin." [PaintedB] (30) 87, p. 78.
      "Eliseo's Cabin, Taos Pueblo." [PaintedB] (30) 87, p. 77.
      "Passing Through Albuquerque." [PaintedB] (30) 87, p. 76.
      "Snowbound." [PoetL] (81:3) Fall 86, p. 198.
286. BALAKIAN, Peter
      "Domestic Lament." [Poetry] (151:1/2) O-N 87, p. 10-12.
      "Father, 4-F, 1941." [Poetry] (150:4) Jl 87, p. 214.
      "Flat Sky of Summer." [Poetry] (150:4) Jl 87, p. 211-213.

"Pacysandra." [Verse] (4:3) N 87, p. 17.
287. BALASHOVA, Elena
"Nasturium as Reality" (tr. of Arkadii Dragomoshchenko, w. Lyn Hejinian). [Sulfur] (19) Spr 87, p. 94-107.
288. BALAZ, Joseph P.
"Lounge Lizard." [HawaiiR] (21) Spr 87, p. 44-46.
"When I Get to Heaven." [HawaiiR] (19) Spr 86, c87, p. 54-55.
"When I Turn Out Hawaiian Electric." [HawaiiR] (20) Fall 86, c87, p. 79-80.
289. BALAZS, Mary
"Bulimic." [CapeR] (22:2) Fall 87, p. 28.
"Feathers." [CapeR] (22:2) Fall 87, p. 29.
"Jewel: A Conceit." [Outbr] (18/19) Fall 86-Spr 88, p. 56.
"Strangler Tree." [KanQ] (19:3) Sum 87, p. 327.
"Yachts." [KanQ] (19:3) Sum 87, p. 327-328.
"Your Aging: A Conceit." [CapeR] (22:2) Fall 87, p. 30.
290. BALBO, Ned
"Late August Light" (In memory of my mother). [AntR] (45:3) Sum 87, p. 340.
291. BALDWIN, Barbara
"October Light." [Calyx] (10:2/3) Spr 87, p. 72.
292. BALDWIN, Beth Williams
"Ferry" (The Greensboro Review Literary Award Poem). [GreensboroR] (43) Wint 87-88, p. 17-18.
"Summer Rain at Three A.M." [GreensboroR] (43) Wint 87-88, p. 19.
293. BALDWIN, Joseph
"Green Sky at Late Night." [KanQ] (19:3) Sum 87, p. 157.
"In Full Stride." [KanQ] (19:1/2) Wint-Spr 87, p. 100-101.
"Returned." [KanQ] (19:3) Sum 87, p. 157.
294. BALDWIN, Neil
"Fantasia." [Contact] (9:44/45/46) Fall-Wint 87, p. 35.
295. BALDWIN, Tama
"Excavation." [Raccoon] (24/25) My 87, p. 170.
296. BALESTRIERI, Elizabeth
"In Mexico There Is No East or West." [WilliamMR] (25) Spr 87, p. 70-72.
"Torch Lake." [CreamCR] (11:2/3) 87?, p. 78.
297. BALESTRINI, Nani
"Mrs. Richmond Gets Sick of Dogs and Leaves for Greenland" (tr. by Nicolo Fabrizi). [Caliban] (3) 87, p. 96-98.
"Mrs. Richmond's Film: The Last Beach" (tr. by Nicolo Fabrizi). [Caliban] (3) 87, p. 99-101.
298. BALK, Christianne
"Elegy." [Harp] (274:1642) Mr 87, p. 37.
"John Muir Remembers Eliza Hendricks." [NewYorker] (63:42) 7 D 87, p. 46.
299. BALL, Angela
"Address." [Boulevard] (2:3) Fall 87, p. 172.
"Ancient Monument." [MalR] (80) S 87, p. 93-94.
"Embrace." [DenQ] (21:3) Wint 87, p. 9.
"House of Many Rooms." [MalR] (80) S 87, p. 91-92.
"A Man Considers Himself." [MalR] (80) S 87, p. 89-90.
300. BALL, Richard
"Cynghanedd at Eventide" (To the memory of J.M. Sherby, Poet, New York City, died 1985). [Pembroke] (19) 87, p. 242.
"Earth-Man Soliloquy." [Pembroke] (19) 87, p. 189.
"Poem for Alison Bielski and Your Stay at Tenby." [Pembroke] (19) 87, p. 241.
301. BALOIAN, Jimmy
"In the San Joaquin." [GrahamHR] (10) Wint-Spr 87, p. 10-11.
302. BALTENSPERGER, Peter
"First Snow." [Germ] (10:2) Spr 87, p. 24.
303. BANANI, Sheila
"Nairobi" (1969). [CrossCur] (7:1) 87, p. 145.
"Spring Cleaning." [CrossCur] (7:1) 87, p. 144.
304. BANKS, Stanley E.
"The Game." [NewL] (54:1) Fall 87, p. 110.
"Jazz Dancing." [NewL] (54:1) Fall 87, p. 111.
305. BANUS, Maria
"Not by Design" (tr. by Diana Der Hovanessian and the author). [CrossCur] (7:3) 87, p. 97.

306. BAPTISTA, Amadeu
   "A Terra e o Mar." [Mester] (16:1) Spr 87, p. 57-58.
307. BARAKA, Amiri
   "1929: Y You Ask?" [CreamCR] (11:2/3) 87?, p. 51-52.
308. BARANCZAK, Stanislaw
   "History" (tr. by Michael and Aleksandra Parker). [Verse] (4:1) Mr 87, p. 6.
   "In an Empty Parking Lot, Setting the Hand Brake" (tr. by Regina Grol-Prokopczyk).
      [Paint] (14:27) Spr 87, p. 35.
   "The Return to Order" (tr. by Michael and Aleksandra Parker). [Verse] (4:3) N 87, p.
      9-14.
309. BARANOW, Joan
   "Night Guard." [US1] (20/21) Wint 86-87, p. 9.
310. BARANSKY, Laszlo
   "The Applause" (tr. of Tillye Boesche-Zacharow, w. Istvan Eorsi, Anna Saghy and
      Bob Rosenthal). [Rampike] (5:3) 87, p. 70.
   "Beer: For Leising" (tr. of Karl Mickel, w. Istvan Eorsi, Anna Saghy and Bob
      Rosenthal). [Rampike] (5:3) 87, p. 66.
   "A Career" (tr. of Istvan Eorsi, w. Anna Saghy and Bob Rosenthal). [Rampike] (5:3)
      87, p. 69.
   "Change of Location" (tr. of Uwe Kolbe, w. Istvan Eorsi, Anna Saghy and Bob
      Rosenthal). [Rampike] (5:3) 87, p. 66.
   "German Woman '46" (tr. of Karl Mickel, w. Istvan Eorsi, Anna Saghy and Bob
      Rosenthal). [Rampike] (5:3) 87, p. 66.
   "Metamorphosis" (tr. of Uwe Kolbe, w. Istvan Eorsi, Anna Saghy and Bob
      Rosenthal). [Rampike] (5:3) 87, p. 67.
   "The Modern Quarter" (tr. of Karl Mickel, w. Istvan Eorsi, Anna Saghy and Bob
      Rosenthal). [Rampike] (5:3) 87, p. 67.
   "The Myth of the Cave" (tr. of Volker Braun, w. Istvan Eorsi, Anna Saghy and Bob
      Rosenthal). [Rampike] (5:3) 87, p. 69.
   "Orderly Hair" (tr. of Karl Mickel, w. Istvan Eorsi, Anna Saghy and Bob Rosenthal).
      [Rampike] (5:3) 87, p. 67.
   "Zeno Black" (tr. of Noah Zacharin, w. Istvan Eorsi, Anna Saghy and Bob
      Rosenthal). [Rampike] (5:3) 87, p. 70.
311. BARBARESE, J. T.
   "Schuyler Street." [Boulevard] (2:3) Fall 87, p. 91-94.
312. BARBER, David
   "The Dark Ages." [NoAmR] (272:3) D 87, p. 9.
313. BARBOUR, Douglas
   "Acrostic: gentle creatures such as these." [CrossC] (9:3/4) 87, p. 12.
314. BARDEN, Tom
   "While Hitchhiking on Monroe Street." [Gambit] (20) 86, p. 118.
315. BARDSLEY, Beverly
   "Persephone" (tr. of Yannis Ritsos, w. Peter Green). [GrandS] (6:4) Sum 87, p.
      143-156.
316. BARFIELD, Randall
   "Armero, Colombia." [Ploughs] (13:1) 87, p. 16-17.
317. BARGEN, Walter
   "Cain Returns Home from the Tobacco Fields." [Wind] (17:60) 87, p. 1.
   "Father's Day." [Farm] (4:1) Wint 87, p. 40.
   "Jukebox Blues." [CapeR] (22:2) Fall 87, p. 32.
   "Shaw's Gardens." [LaurelR] (21:1/2) Wint-Sum 87, p. 14.
   "Twice Told Tale." [Wind] (17:60) 87, p. 1-2.
318. BARGER, Kim R.
   "The Afternoon." [Pembroke] (19) 87, p. 186-187.
319. BARI, Karoly
   "Mumbling" (tr. by Endre Farkas). [Rampike] (5:3) 87, p. 68.
320. BARKAN, Stanley H.
   "Derech Emunoh." [Lips] (13) 87, p. 32-33.
   "Ladders." [Vis] (25) 87, p. 20.
   "Saying Nothing." [Lips] (13) 87, p. 31.
321. BARKER, Christine
   "A New Love." [AntigR] (69/70) 87, p. 126.
322. BARKER, Diane
   "Looking for the Scissors in the Dark" (The Greensboro Review Literary Award,
      Honorable Mention). [GreensboroR] (41) Wint 86-87, p. 18.

323. BARKER, Wendy
"Coming Through December." [Nimrod] (30:2) Spr-Sum 87, p. 11-14.
"Disappearing Acts." [Nimrod] (30:2) Spr-Sum 87, p. 7-8.
"Lost Dog." [Nimrod] (30:2) Spr-Sum 87, p. 6.
"Once More, Squam Lake." [PassN] (8:2) Sum 87, p. 27.
"One Lemon." [PoetL] (81:3) Fall 86, p. 161.
"You, Arthritis Fusing Your Joints." [Nimrod] (30:2) Spr-Sum 87, p. 9-10.
324. BARLOW, George
"The Girl with Tourette's." [Caliban] (2) 87, p. 159.
"In My Father's House." [Caliban] (2) 87, p. 157-158.
"A Vigil in Reno." [RiverS] (22) 87, p. 67.
325. BARNARD, Mary
"On Arriving" (A Poem for *Poetry* on Its 75th Anniversary). [Poetry] (151:1/2) O-N
87, p. 12.
326. BARNES, Dick
"A Day on the Desert." [CrossCur] (7:1) 87, p. 27-28.
"Helendale." [LightY] '87, c86, p. 80-81.
"A Meditation on the Desert Fathers: Five Poems." [OhioR] (39) 87, p. 113-117.
327. BARNES, Jane
"Captions" (for LANAC). [WormR] (27:4, issue 108) 87, p. 96.
"Even a Poet's Mind." [HangL] (50/51) 87, p. 25.
"Pretending to Write a Poem While Being Filmed for 'The Poet's Corner' for TV."
[HangL] (50/51) 87, p. 24.
328. BARNES, Jim
"Dog Days 1978." [Spirit] (8:2) 87, p. 282.
"Fourche Maline Bottoms." [HighP] (2:2) Fall 87, p. 190.
"Night Letter to the Secretary of the Interior." [BambooR] (36) Fall 87, p. 43-44.
"The Planting: For Carolyn." [MemphisSR] (7:2) Spr 87, p. 45.
"Touching the Rattlesnake." [PoetryNW] (28:3) Aut 87, p. 28-29.
329. BARNES, Kate
"The End of October." [TexasR] (7:3/4) 87, p. 12.
"The Night Tide." [TexasR] (7:3/4) 87, p. 13.
330. BARNES, Mike
"Accident." [Waves] (15:3) Wint 87, p. 77.
"Working in the O.R." [Waves] (15:3) Wint 87, p. 76.
331. BARNES, Richard (*See also* BARNES, Richard A.)
"Elegy." [SlipS] (7) 87, p. 31.
"The Fool." [SlipS] (7) 87, p. 31.
332. BARNES, Richard A. (*See also* BARNES, Richard)
"The Birthday Party." [Farm] (4:1) Wint 87, p. 33.
"Proust's Cake." [BlueBldgs] (10) 87?, p. 53.
333. BARNETT, Anthony
"'H-II' Linear" (tr. of Anne-Marie Albiach, w. Joseph Simas). [Temblor] (5) 87, p.
66-77.
"The Immensity of the Firmament" (tr. of Alain Delahaye). [Temblor] (5) 87, p.
57-59.
334. BARNETT, Cathy
"The Summer People." [Footwork] 87, p. 25.
"Traffic Jam, I-95 South." [Footwork] 87, p. 25.
335. BARNSTONE, Tony
"Darling" (tr. of Mang Ke, w. Willis Barnstone). [AmerPoR] (16:4) Jl-Ag 87, p. 40.
"Return" (tr. of Mang Ke, w. Willis Barnstone). [AmerPoR] (16:4) Jl-Ag 87, p. 40.
"To Children" (tr. of Mang Ke, w. Willis Barnstone). [AmerPoR] (16:4) Jl-Ag 87, p.
40.
"Yesterday and Today" (tr. of Mang Ke, w. Willis Barnstone). [AmerPoR] (16:4)
Jl-Ag 87, p. 41.
336. BARNSTONE, Willis
"Catullus." [SouthernR] (23:1) Ja 87, p. 128-129.
"Dark and White Song of Theodore Roethke." [Nimrod] (30:2) Spr-Sum 87, p. 18.
"Darling" (tr. of Mang Ke, w. Tony Barnstone). [AmerPoR] (16:4) Jl-Ag 87, p. 40.
"Isaiah." [SouthernR] (23:1) Ja 87, p. 127-128.
"Pablo Neruda: Pilgrimage of My Bones." [Nimrod] (30:2) Spr-Sum 87, p. 15-16.
"Renaissance Figures." [SewanR] (95:4) Fall 87, p. 553-557.
"Return" (tr. of Mang Ke, w. Tony Barnstone). [AmerPoR] (16:4) Jl-Ag 87, p. 40.
"Richard Wilbur Tossing in His Bed." [Nimrod] (30:2) Spr-Sum 87, p. 19.

"Thinking of the Underground Poet Bei Dao and of Myself, Whom No One Will Put in Prison . . ." [PraS] (61:2) Sum 87, p. 29.
"To Children" (tr. of Mang Ke, w. Tony Barnstone). [AmerPoR] (16:4) Jl-Ag 87, p. 40.
"Uncle Vania and the Train to Moscow." [NowestR] (25:3) 87, p. 318.
"Wallace Stevens Examining His First Spring in France." [Nimrod] (30:2) Spr-Sum 87, p. 20-21.
"William Carlos Williams Back in Puerto Rico." [Nimrod] (30:2) Spr-Sum 87, p. 17.
"With Bei Dao and His Painter Friend in a Place Halfway Down a Hutong in South Beijing." [PraS] (61:2) Sum 87, p. 30.
"Yesterday and Today" (tr. of Mang Ke, w. Tony Barnstone). [AmerPoR] (16:4) Jl-Ag 87, p. 41.

337. BARON, Enid L.
"Seduction at the Villa del Sol." [WoosterR] (7) Spr 87, p. 62.

338. BARON, Todd
"Return of the World." [Act] (7) 87, p. 53-57.

339. BARONE, Patricia
"August: Seeds Grow Heavy and Fall." [Germ] (11:1) Fall 87, p. 21.

340. BARQUET, Jesus J.
"A la Primavera." [LindLM] (6:1) Ja-Mr 87, p. 24.

341. BARR, Bob
"In Sabbato Sancto." [KanQ] (19:3) Sum 87, p. 328.

342. BARR, John
"Articles of War." [NewEngR] (10:2) Wint 87, p. 152-155.
"Flounder." [GrahamHR] (10) Wint-Spr 87, p. 43.
"R & R" (Selections: 1, 3, 5). [NewEngR] (10:2) Wint 87, p. 150-151.

343. BARR, Tina
"Entrenched." [HighP] (2:1) Spr 87, p. 29-30.
"Mowing." [PoetryNW] (28:3) Aut 87, p. 36-37.

344. BARRERA VALVERDE, Alfonso
"Existence" (tr. by H. J. Van Peenen). [SenR] (17:1) 87, p. 47.
"A Letter to My Brother from the Old Quarter" (tr. by H. J. Van Peenen). [SenR] (17:1) 87, p. 48-49.
"Penumbra" (tr. by H. J. Van Peenen). [SenR] (17:1) 87, p. 56.
"Regards to a White Mare" (tr. by H. J. Van Peenen). [SenR] (17:1) 87, p. 50-52.
"Sonnet: You have copied water's way of voyaging" (tr. by H. J. Van Peenen). [SenR] (17:1) 87, p. 55.
"The Sparrow's Daily Round" (tr. by H. J. Van Peenen). [SenR] (17:1) 87, p. 53.
"Stone Cross" (For My Brother Wilfrido, tr. by H. J. Van Peenen). [SenR] (17:1) 87, p. 54.

345. BARRESI, Dorothy
"Comeuppance" (For Michael, fallen through a sky-light). [Poetry] (150:6) S 87, p. 339-340.
"Late Summer News." [Poetry] (150:6) S 87, p. 337-338.
"Lifting." [Poetry] (150:6) S 87, p. 335-336.

346. BARRETO, Néstor
"Vision de Ti." [Mairena] (9:24) 87, p. 114.

347. BARRETO-RIVERA, R.
"Alphanumericuns" (from "The Invisible A(r)mada). [Rampike] (5:3) 87, p. 43.

348. BARRETT, Carol
"Penance." [Phoenix] (7:1) 87, p. 35.

349. BARRETT, Joseph
"A Final Decree." [Bogg] (58) 87, p. 17.
"Woodgathering in Long Shadows." [Bogg] (58) 87, p. 31.

350. BARROWS, Brenda
"Introduction to the Opera." [OhioR] (38) 87, p. 109.
"Weather." [OhioR] (38) 87, p. 108.

351. BARRY, S.
"Before a Solar Eclipse." [AntigR] (69/70) 87, p. 181-182.

352. BARSOTTI, Richard
"In Praise of Snakes." [StoneC] (15:1/2) Fall-Wint 87-88, p. 30.

353. BARST, Fran
"The Old House." [Wind] (17:60) 87, p. 3-4.

354. BARTLETT, Elizabeth
"1 + 1 = 2." [PoetL] (81:3) Fall 86, p. 167-168.
"Instead of a Mass." [CumbPR] (7:1) Fall 87, p. 16-17.

"Letter from Australia." [CumbPR] (7:1) Fall 87, p. 18.
"Silk Cut" (for Fleur Adcock). [CumbPR] (7:1) Fall 87, p. 19-20.
"Spell Beauty." [CrossCur] (7:3) 87, p. 59-60.
"Stone Heart." [CrossCur] (7:1) 87, p. 42.
"Voices." [CrossCur] (7:1) 87, p. 43.
355. BARTLETT, Paul
"Mountain Village." [Wind] (17:61) 87, p. 4.
356. BARTON, Bruce
"Atlanta Child Murders." [IndR] (10:3) Spr 87, p. 75.
357. BARTON, David
"Midnight in the Republic of Praise" (Thomas Lovell Beddoes, 1803-1849).
[JamesWR] (4:3) Spr 87, p. 8-9.
"Seahorses in August" (for T. D.). [PoetryNW] (28:4) Wint 87-88, p. 11-12.
358. BARTON, Marcia
"Hurricane Season." [CrabCR] (4:2) Spr 87, p. 14.
359. BARTOW, Stuart, Jr.
"Christ in Turtles." [LitR] (31:1) Fall 87, p. 40.
360. BARTRA, Agustí
"The Prodigal Son" (In Memory of León Felipe, tr. by Peter Cocozzella). [Paint]
(14:27) Spr 87, p. 18-22.
361. BARTUL, Rose-Mary
"Summer Sunday." [EngJ] (76:7) N 87, p. 99.
362. BASINSKI, Michael
"Mantra for Kerouac." [MoodySI] (18/19) Fall 87, p. 43.
"Street of Poets." [WormR] (27:1, issue 105) 87, p. 34-35.
"The Yearbook." [WormR] (27:1, issue 105) 87, p. 33-34.
363. BASMAJIAN, Shaunt
"hhhhhhh . . ." (fr jw curry). [CrossC] (9:3/4) 87, p. 4.
364. BASNEY, Lionel
"Workhouse Poems" (Selections: 2, 4, 6, 7). [Nimrod] (31:1) Fall-Wint 87, p.
115-118.
365. BASS, Ellen
"Even This." [Calyx] (10:2/3) Spr 87, p. 32-33.
"To Praise." [Calyx] (10:2/3) Spr 87, p. 148-149.
366. BASSO, Eric
"Avowals and Aversions" (tr. of E. M. Cioran). [Margin] (5) Wint 87-88, p. 90-91.
367. BASTIEN, Mark
"From Prague." [Event] (16:3) Fall 87, p. 25.
368. BATEMAN, Claire
"5:30 A.M." [CumbPR] (6:2) Spr 87, p. 30.
"Adam's Child." [CimR] (78) Ja 87, p. 46.
"Economics." [WoosterR] (7) Spr 87, p. 26.
"In the Icicle Garden." [Poem] (58) N 87, p. 25.
"Morning Tactics." [Poem] (58) N 87, p. 24.
369. BATES, Randolph
"Dolphin Island." [PraS] (61:1) Spr 87, p. 84-85.
370. BATES, Scott
"As I Was Dining at the Steak House, My Sirloin Said to Me." [LightY] '87, c86, p.
42.
"Bird Notes on a Beautiful But Noisy April Morning." [LightY] '87, c86, p. 120.
"Fable of the Curious Crow and the Devious Weevil." [LightY] '87, c86, p. 105.
"Fable of the Terrorist Mouse." [LightY] '87, c86, p. 248-249.
"Guide to Paris: Eiffel Tower, Versailles." [LightY] '87, c86, p. 168.
371. BATHANTI, Joseph
"Courting the Chatham Girls." [Pembroke] (19) 87, p. 191.
"Entering an Abandoned House." [TexasR] (8:3/4) Fall-Wint 87, p. 100-101.
"Her Name." [Vis] (23) 87, p. 26.
"In the Eye of the Admirer" (For Flannery O'Connor). [Poem] (57) Mr 87, p. 29.
"Off South Carolina 9 in Little Rock." [Poem] (57) Mr 87, p. 20.
372. BATISTA, Liony E.
"Absence." [ConnPR] (6:1) 87, p. 23.
"Brenda Speaks of Having Babies as We Ride the Subway." [Footwork] 87, p. 43.
"Heroes" (for Susan). [Footwork] 87, p. 43.
"The Photograph." [Footwork] 87, p. 42.
"The Poets Wife" (for my sister). [Footwork] 87, p. 42.

373. BATT, Herb
   "A Red Guard Meditates on His Past." [Quarry] (36:3) Sum 87, p. 33-35.
374. BATTEN, Amy
   "A Roller-Coaster Affair." [Gambit] (20) 86, p. 43.
375. BATTIN, Wendy
   "Calling & Singing." [YaleR] (76:3) Spr 87, p. 412.
376. BAUDELAIRE, Charles
   "Abyss" (tr. by David Ferry). [Raritan] (7:1) Sum 87, p. 31.
   "Le Gouffre." [Raritan] (7:1) Sum 87, p. 30.
   "The Pipe" (tr. by Stephen Meats). [PoetryE] (23/24) Fall 87, p. 219.
377. BAUER, Grace
   "La Belle Dame Sans Merci" (tr. of Rosario Castellanos). [InterPR] (13:1) Spr 87, p.
      47.
   "Commentary on the Sculptor" (tr. of Rosario Castellanos). [InterPR] (13:1) Spr 87,
      p. 43.
   "Disregard" (tr. of Rosario Castellanos). [InterPR] (13:1) Spr 87, p. 43.
   "Elegy" (tr. of Rosario Castellanos). [InterPR] (13:1) Spr 87, p. 45.
   "Evocation of Aunt Elena" (tr. of Rosario Castellanos). [InterPR] (13:1) Spr 87, p.
      41.
   "Nazareth" (tr. of Rosario Castellanos). [InterPR] (13:1) Spr 87, p. 41.
   "Nymphomania" (tr. of Rosario Castellanos). [InterPR] (13:1) Spr 87, p. 45.
   "The Return" (tr. of Rosario Castellanos). [InterPR] (13:1) Spr 87, p. 37, 39.
378. BAUER, Steven
   "Hint of Spring." [MissouriR] (10:2) 87, p. 144-145.
379. BAUERBACH, David
   "Ebony Tunnel." [Gambit] (20) 86, p. 49.
380. BAUERLE, Claire
   "The Glass Blower." [PennR] (3:1) Spr-Sum 87, p. 61.
381. BAUMEL, Judith
   "At the Tomb of the Venerable Bede in Durham Cathedral." [DenQ] (22:1) Sum 87, p.
      12-13.
   "The *Fruition* of Berneray, Hebrides." [AmerPoR] (16:4) Jl-Ag 87, p. 34.
   "Ginestra" (To Count Giacomo Leopardi). [NewYorker] (63:25) 10 Ag 87, p. 26.
   "Half-Way There." [DenQ] (22:1) Sum 87, p. 14-15.
   "Roches Moutonnees." [ParisR] (29:103) Sum 87, p. 176.
   "The Split Bulb and Philandering Sigh of Ocean." [Boulevard] (2:3) Fall 87, p.
      108-109.
   "Thirty-Six Poets" (after Sokai Hoitsu). [ParisR] (29:103) Sum 87, p. 175.
382. BAUMGAERTNER, Jill
   "1930-32." [CentR] (31:1) Wint 87, p. 60-61.
383. BAUSCH, Victor H.
   "The Death of Bed." [SlipS] (7) 87, p. 39.
384. BAUSKA, Barry
   "Visions." [CumbPR] (7:1) Fall 87, p. 54.
385. BAWER, Bruce
   "The Jogger." [Boulevard] (2:1/2) Spr 87, p. 171-712.
   "A Letter to Cambridge" (to S.E.B.). [Hudson] (40:3) Aut 87, p. 449-450.
   "River Phoenix in 'The Mosquito Coast'." [KanQ] (19:4) Fall 87, p. 50.
   "Thirteen." [PoetryE] (23/24) Fall 87, p. 134-135.
386. BAXTER, Andrea-bess
   "Dolly Jean." [GreensboroR] (40) Sum 86, p. 72-73.
   "For Annie Jump Cannon (1863-1941)." [GreensboroR] (40) Sum 86, p. 74.
387. BAXTER, Charles
   "The Fables." [ParisR] (29:102) Spr 87, p. 210.
   "Machines That Make Men Happy." [ParisR] (29:102) Spr 87, p. 207.
   "The Photographer." [ParisR] (29:102) Spr 87, p. 208-209.
   "The Slow Classroom." [ParisR] (29:102) Spr 87, p. 206.
388. BAYES, Ronald H.
   "4th Porpoise: Eighth Book." [Pembroke] (19) 87, p. 234.
   "Chapter" (from "The Casketmaker"). [Pembroke] (19) 87, p. 232.
   "Guises: A Chainsong to the Muse" (for Joshu). [Pembroke] (19) 87, p. 216-218.
   "Homage to Rod McEwen, E. A. Guest & Mrs. Browning." [Pembroke] (19) 87, p.
      234.
   "Returning in January." [Pembroke] (19) 87, p. 233.
389. BAYSA, Fred O.
   "Rapture: A Dream of Dying." [Nat] (244:16) 25 Ap 87, p. 545.

390. BAYSANS, Greg
"Fanta-Scene." [JamesWR] (4:2) Wint 87, p. 7.
391. BEACH, Norman
"Gift." [InterPR] (13:2) Fall 87, p. 68-69.
"Man and Woman at Home." [InterPR] (13:2) Fall 87, p. 70-71.
392. BEAGLE, Donald
"Fossils." [CarolQ] (39:3) Spr 87, p. 94.
393. BEAKE, Fred
"Poem: Captain Blankness had to piss." [Bogg] (57) 87, p. 46.
BEAR, Ray A. Young
See YOUNG BEAR, Ray A.
394. BEARD, Philip
"A Friend Speaks to Me in a Poem." [HampSPR] Wint 86, p. 37.
395. BEARDEN, Nancy
"Without a Name." [PassN] (8:2) Sum 87, p. 24.
396. BEARDSLEY, Doug
"Winter Journal: Winnipeg Dream." [AmerPoR] (16:1) Ja-F 87, p. 32.
397. BÉARN, Pierre
"To Live" (tr. by Dorothy Aspinwall). [WebR] (12:2) Fall 87, p. 17.
398. BEASLEY, Bruce
"In Rodin." [SouthernPR] (27:1) Spr 87, p. 50.
"Miserére." [Amelia] (4:1/2, issue 9) 87, p. 78.
"The Reliquary." [QW] (24) Wint 87, p. 83-85.
399. BEASLEY, Sherry
"New Parents." [SouthernPR] (27:2) Fall 87, p. 32.
400. BEAUMONT, Alison
"She Thinks About Drowning" (WQ Editors' First Prize Winner — Poetry). [CrossC]
(9:1) 87, p. 16.
401. BEAUSOLEIL, Claude
"Au Sujet d'une Exposition de Diego Rivera." [Os] (24) 87, p. 19.
"Hommage á Jorge-Luis Borges." [Os] (24) 87, p. 17-18.
"The Journal of Nights" (tr. by Andrea Moorhead). [Os] (24) 87, p. 7-9.
402. BECERRA, José Carlos
"Affairs in Order" (tr. by Robert L. Jones). [WestHR] (41:3) Aut 87, p. 258.
"Autumn Traverses the Islands" (tr. by Robert L. Jones). [WestHR] (41:3) Aut 87, p.
260.
"The Drowned Man" (tr. by Robert L. Jones). [WestHR] (41:3) Aut 87, p. 262.
"Outskirts of the World" (tr. by Robert L. Jones). [WestHR] (41:3) Aut 87, p. 261.
"Your Face Disappearing" (tr. by Robert L. Jones). [WestHR] (41:3) Aut 87, p. 259.
403. BECK, Art
"Cemetery Strike." [PaintedB] (31) 87, p. 22.
"First Rain." [PaintedB] (31) 87, p. 23.
"Fog City." [PaintedB] (31) 87, p. 21.
404. BECKER, Anne
"The Transmutation Notebooks: Poems in the Voices of Charles and Emma Darwin"
(4 selections). [Gargoyle] (32/33) 87, p. 126-142.
405. BECKER, Carol
"Molly Bolts." [AmerV] (8) Fall 87, p. 60-61.
406. BECKER, Leda Alvares
"Primavera." [LetFem] (13:1/2) Primavera-Ontoño 87, p. 131.
407. BECKER, Robin
"Living in the Barn" (for Marianne Weil). [AntR] (45:1) Wint 87, p. 34.
408. BECKETT, Samuel
"Sébastien Chamfort" (in French & English). [LitR] (30:3) Spr 87, p. 416-417.
409. BECKETT, Tom
"For Spicer." [Acts] (6) 87, p. 58.
"A Name, A Shape, A Stasis." [Bound] (14:1/2) Fall 85-Wint 86 [c87], p. 62-63.
"A Theory of Pictures." [Act] (7) 87, p. 59.
"A Theory of Systems." [Act] (7) 87, p. 58.
410. BECKWITH, E. P.
"My New Rooms." [Amelia] (4:3, issue 10) 87, p. 69.
411. BEDWELL, Carol
"Saüre" (Selections: 10, 36, 57, tr. of Christoph Meckel). [PoetL] (81:3) Fall 86, p.
175-177.
412. BEE, Earle
"Funeral Parlor Flowers." [Gambit] (20) 86, p. 96.

413. BEEDE, Gayle Jansen
   "Restoration" (after a snapshot of my father). [CumbPR] (6:2) Spr 87, p. 11.
414. BEETHOVAN, Paul
   "Sitting Next to Emily." [PoeticJ] (17) 87, p. 41.
415. BEH, Terry P.
   "Zebras." [LightY] '87, c86, p. 117.
416. BEHLEN, Charles
   "The Drunk's Widow." [Puerto] (22:2) Spr 87, p. 46-47.
   "Rex." [Puerto] (22:2) Spr 87, p. 44-45.
417. BEHM, Richard
   "The Anthropologist's Tale." [SouthernR] (23:1) Ja 87, p. 148-149.
   "A Message for Summer in the Suburbs." [Spirit] (8:2) 87, p. 206.
   "Perhaps." [SouthernR] (23:1) Ja 87, p. 147-148.
   "Sandusky River Mornings." [Farm] (4:2) Spr-Sum 87, p. 67.
   "That Quick." [Farm] (4:2) Spr-Sum 87, p. 66.
418. BEHN, Bettina
   "From the Program" (tr. by Stuart Friebert). [ConnPR] (6:1) 87, p. 32.
419. BEHN, Robin
   "The Angel in Sandusky." [Gambit] (21) 87, p. 9.
   "Land's End." [DenQ] (22:1) Sum 87, p. 26.
   "Leavetaking in Winter." [DenQ] (22:1) Sum 87, p. 27-28.
   "To the City of San Cristobal de las Casas." [IndR] (10:3) Spr 87, p. 82-83.
   "Two Waves." [Gambit] (21) 87, p. 11.
   "Vestigial Kisses." [Gambit] (21) 87, p. 10.
420. BEHRAMOGLU, Ataol
   "Letters to My Daughter" (Selection: "In Exile" 12-19, tr. by Talat Sait Halman).
      [Trans] (19) Fall 87, p. 83-87.
421. BEHRENDT, Stephen C.
   "Autumnal Cadence." [KanQ] (19:1/2) Wint-Spr 87, p. 64.
   "Spring Garden." [KanQ] (19:1/2) Wint-Spr 87, p. 63.
422. BEHUNIN, Judith R. (See also BEHUNIN, Judy)
   "October Mood (in July)." [Amelia] (4:3, issue 10) 87, p. 46.
423. BEHUNIN, Judy (See also BEHUNIN, Judith R.)
   "Computer Language." [PoeticJ] (17) 87, p. 38.
424. BEI, Dao
   "Answer" (tr. by Donald Finkel and Xueliang Chen). [SenR] (17:2) 87, p. 25.
   "Border" (tr. by Donald Finkel and Xueliang Chen). [SenR] (17:2) 87, p. 26.
   "Country Night" (tr. by Donald Finkel and Xueliang Chen). [SenR] (17:2) 87, p. 27.
   "Let's Go" (tr. by Donald Finkel and Xueliang Chen). [Antaeus] (58) Spr 87, p. 160.
   "The Oranges Are Ripe" (tr. by Donald Finkel and Xueliang Chen). [Antaeus] (58)
      Spr 87, p. 158.
   "Snow Line" (tr. by Donald Finkel and Xueliang Chen). [SenR] (17:2) 87, p. 24.
   "Testament" (tr. by Donald Finkel and Xueliang Chen). [Antaeus] (58) Spr 87, p.
      157.
   "A Ticket" (tr. by Donald Finkel and Xueliang Chen). [Antaeus] (58) Spr 87, p.
      159-160.
425. BEINING, Guy R.
   "Stoma 1649." [Caliban] (3) 87, p. 63.
   "Stoma 1748. (After the Fact)." [Caliban] (3) 87, p. 64.
   "Stoma 1749. (After the Facts)." [Caliban] (3) 87, p. 64.
   "Stoma 1752." [Caliban] (3) 87, p. 65.
   "Stoma 1755." [Caliban] (3) 87, p. 66.
   "Stoma 1756. The Right Century at Last." [Caliban] (3) 87, p. 67.
   "Stoma 1767." [Caliban] (3) 87, p. 68.
426. BEKER, Ruth
   "In the Wet, Wet Ground" (Kansas Quarterly / Kansas Arts Commission Awards
      Honorable Mention Poem, 1986/1987). [KanQ] (19:1/2) Wint-Spr 87, p. 24.
   "Studs." [KanQ] (19:1/2) Wint-Spr 87, p. 25.
427. BEKTAS, Cengiz
   "Sisyphus" (tr. by Talat Sait Halman). [Trans] (19) Fall 87, p. 103.
428. BELCHER, Charles, Jr.
   "Reba on All Hallows Eve." [MemphisSR] (8:1) Fall 87, p. 38.
429. BELIÉS, Erríkos
   "Recognition" (tr. by Yannis Goumas). [Verse] (4:2) Je 87, p. 61.
430. BELIN, Mel
   "Anniversary." [CapeR] (22:1) Spr 87, p. 8.

51

"The Mephisto Waltz." [Vis] (25) 87, p. 37.
431. BELITT, Ben
"Displaced Person." [YaleR] (76:4) Sum 87, p. 518-519.
432. BELL, Elouise
"Overheard in Amherst." [EngJ] (76:5) S 87, p. 111.
433. BELL, Jo
"Fairy-Tale Princesses." [TexasR] (8:1/2) Spr-Sum 87, p. 59.
"Haiku" (2 poems). [TexasR] (8:1/2) Spr-Sum 87, p. 58.
434. BELL, Marvin
"8287." [Ploughs] (13:4) 87, p. 20.
"161286." [Ploughs] (13:4) 87, p. 18-19.
"Broken Egg." [Ploughs] (13:4) 87, p. 21.
"The Moon Is Visible Tonight." [Poetry] (151:1/2) O-N 87, p. 13.
"Pages." [AntR] (45:1) Wint 87, p. 22-32.
"Replica." [GeoR] (41:2) Sum 87, p. 344-345.
"Ten Thousand Questions Answered" (Section 3. "Nothing is sadder than a book of
poetry"). [AmerPoR] (16:5) S-O 87, p. 34.
"Trinket." [DenQ] (22:2) Fall 87, p. 82-83.
435. BELL, Melissa
"Outside Cafe." [Vis] (25) 87, p. 26.
436. BELLA DONNA (See also FOSTER, Barbara)
"Jose: d. 1985." [HighP] (2:1) Spr 87, p. 31-32.
BELLAGENTE LAPALMA, Marina de
See LaPALMA, Marina de Bellagente
437. Ben JELLOUN, Tahar
"Harrouda" (Excerpt, tr. by Rafika Merini). [Paint] (14:27) Spr 87, p. 8-10.
438. BEN-LEV, Dina
"After the Playground Suicides." [MSS] (5:3) 87, p. 180.
"Brooklyn and After." [GreensboroR] (40) Sum 86, p. 92-93.
"Feeling for Seatbels." [MSS] (5:3) 87, p. 178-180.
"The Planetarium." [MalR] (79) Je 87, p. 115.
BENAVIDES, Manuel Terrin
See TERRIN BENAVIDES, Manuel
439. BENDER, Christina
"Bedtime Stories." [Wind] (17:61) 87, p. 43.
440. BENEDETTI, Mario
"Another Sky" (tr. by Richard Zenith). [PoetL] (81:3) Fall 86, p. 155.
"Love Is a Center" (tr. by Richard Zenith). [PoetL] (81:3) Fall 86, p. 154.
441. BENEDIKT, Michael
"Of Making Large Decisions Calmly (Disquisition at a Picnic)." [PartR] (54:1) Wint
87, p. 135-138.
"Of Poetry, My Friend" (1977, Revision 1987). [Lips] (13) 87, p. 1-2.
"Public Ode #1: To the People / Poets in the Countryside." [GreenfR] (14:1/2)
Wint-Spr, p. 190-192.
442. BENEDIKTSSON, Tom
"Aunt Marie at 99." [Footwork] 87, p. 48.
"Bone." [Footwork] 87, p. 48.
"Hawks Are Always from Somewhere Else." [Paint] (14:28) Aut 87, p. 11.
"Natirar." [Paint] (14:28) Aut 87, p. 10.
443. BENEVENTO, Joe
"A Human Condition." [CentR] (31:2) Spr 87, p. 189.
444. BENFEY, Chris
"Opening." [BostonR] (12:6) D 87, p. 4.
445. BENGSTON, David
"Just the Right Tree." [Northeast] (Ser. 4:5) Sum 87, p. 21.
446. BENN, Gottfried
"Songs: I" (adapted from the German by Peter Viereck). [Ploughs] (13:4) 87, p. 133.
447. BENNANI, Ben
"P.M. Rates." [CharR] (13:2) Fall 87, p. 77.
"Psalms for Palestine" (tr. of Mahmud Darwish). [Paint] (14:27) Spr 87, p. 42-44.
"Roundness & Length." [MSS] (5:3) 87, p. 138.
448. BENNETT, Allyson
"Black Earth, Wisconsin." [Farm] (4:2) Spr-Sum 87, p. 64-65.
449. BENNETT, Bruce
"Against Waking Early." [LightY] '87, c86, p. 227-228.
"A Cow's Life." [LightY] '87, c86, p. 111.

"The Dangerous Cliffs." [LightY] '87, c86, p. 131.
"Epitaph for the Lemon Lady." [LightY] '87, c86, p. 241.
"Garza." [LightY] '87, c86, p. 49.
"Getting Along." [PaintedB] (30) 87, p. 69.
"The Passionate Businessman to His Love." [LightY] '87, c86, p. 150.
"The Poet Redgrove." [LightY] '87, c86, p. 215.
"The Road and the Feet." [RiverS] (24) 87, p. 74.
"The Stones of Florence." [LightY] '87, c86, p. 166.
"Taking the Cure." [PaintedB] (30) 87, p. 68.
450. BENNETT, Elizabeth
"Small Explosion, August 6th, 1985." [PoetL] (81:3) Fall 86, p. 196.
451. BENNETT, John M.
"My Underwear" (For Ling). [Pig] (14) 87, p. 80.
"Shirking." [Bogg] (57) 87, p. 14.
"Toiletseat." [Pig] (14) 87, p. 80.
452. BENNETT, Maria
"Men in the City" (tr. of Alfonsina Storni). [StoneC] (15:1/2) Fall-Wint 87-88, p. 27.
"Nothingness" (tr. of Julia de Burgos). [StoneC] (14:3/4) Spr-Sum 87, p. 37.
453. BENNETT, Paul
"Fishing Again the Evolutionary Stream." [Gambit] (20) 86, p. 98.
"Of Voices: the Give and Take." [Gambit] (20) 86, p. 99-100.
454. BENSEN, Robert
"Tokiwa and Her Children" (A painted screen by Yokoyaman Kazan, Japan, 19th
century). [AntR] (45:1) Wint 87, p. 35.
"We've Been Domesticated, I Tell You." [Ploughs] (13:1) 87, p. 18-20.
455. BENSKO, John
"The Hotel Mayaguez." [ChiR] (35:4) 87, p. 108-109.
"The Implied Author." [Poetry] (150:2) My 87, p. 68-71.
456. BENSKO, Rosemary
"An Envious Mood with Wild Ponies." [Phoenix] (7:1) 87, p. 43.
457. BENSON, Steve
"We're constantly floating past each other into new lights." [Bound] (14:1/2) Fall
85-Wint 86 [c87], p. 64-66.
458. BENTHUL, Herman F.
"Bluebird for My Garden." [Writer] (100:1) Ja 87, p. 24.
459. BENTLEY, Beth
"Abraham's Wife." [Calyx] (10:2/3) Spr 87, p. 30.
"Marcel" (1986 Winner, Eve of Saint Agnes Poetry Competition). [NegC] (7:1/2) 87,
p. 118-121.
"Signing." [PoetryNW] (28:4) Wint 87-88, p. 36-38.
"Undelivered Mail." [PoetryNW] (28:4) Wint 87-88, p. 38-39.
460. BENTLEY, Nelson
"Tracking the Transcendental Moose" (Book Five: The Rockies, Auden, & Price).
[BellArk] (3:1) Ja-F 87, p. 11-18.
"Tracking the Transcendental Moose" (Book Six: Rackham Check and Information
Desk). [BellArk] (3:2) Mr-Ap 87, p. 11-16.
"Tracking the Transcendental Moose" (Book Seven: Early Seattle Years). [BellArk]
(3:3) My-Je 87, p. 11-17.
"Tracking the Transcendental Moose" (Book Eight: Sean, Yeates and Lear." [BellArk]
(3:4) Jl-Ag 87, p. 11-17.
"Tracking the Transcendental Moose" (Book Nine: Sean and Julian). [BellArk] (3:5)
S-O 87, p. 11-18.
"Tracking the Transcendental Moose" (Book Ten: Sea Lion Caves Becomes a Book).
[BellArk] (3:6) N-D 87, p. 11-18.
461. BENTLEY, Roy
"On Horseback D. V. Bentley Carries Home News and Something More." [MidAR]
(7:2) 87, p. 26-27.
462. BENTTINEN, Ted
"Bloomsday in Provincetown." [SewanR] (95:2) Spr 87, p. 238.
"A Child Is Coming." [KanQ] (19:1/2) Wint-Spr 87, p. 331.
"Coronach" (Weddell Sea, Antarctica). [SewanR] (95:2) Spr 87, p. 239.
"Courtesan." [KenR] (NS 9:1) Wint 87, p. 75.
"Memory." [BallSUF] (28:4) Aut 87, p. 35.
"Tiger Fugu." [KenR] (NS 9:1) Wint 87, p. 74-75.
463. BENTZMAN, Bruce Harris
"Necktie Moan." [Pig] (14) 87, p. 71.

464. BERENGUER, Amanda
"The Blow" (tr. by Deborah Bonner). [AmerPoR] (16:2) Mr-Ap 87, p. 17.
"Moebius Strip" (tr. by Deborah Bonner). [AmerPoR] (16:2) Mr-Ap 87, p. 16-17.
465. BERG, Lora
"Baiting the Jug." [BelPoJ] (38:2) Wint 87-88, p. 4-5.
"Electricity." [BelPoJ] (38:2) Wint 87-88, p. 6.
"Lions." [ColR] (NS 14:2) Fall-Wint 87, p. 33.
"Mombassa Tale." [BelPoJ] (38:2) Wint 87-88, p. 5.
"Shadow Play." [CarolQ] (40:1) Fall 87, p. 55.
466. BERG, Stephen
"Clouded Sky" (tr. of Miklós Radnóti, w. Steven Polgar and S. J. Marks. Entire
issue). [PoetryE] (22) Spr 87, 113 p.
"The Voice." [AmerPoR] (16:5) S-O 87, p. 32.
467. BERGER, Bruce
"Bitter Grapes." [LightY] '87, c86, p. 212.
"Death Florentine" (1986 Honorable Mention, Eve of Saint Agnes Poetry
Competition). [NegC] (7:1/2) 87, p. 135.
"Family Reading." [Poetry] (150:5) Ag 87, p. 282.
"Gaspard" (1986 Finalist, Eve of Saint Agnes Poetry Competition). [NegC] (7:1/2)
87, p. 170.
"MSG." [LightY] '87, c86, p. 40.
"One-Up." [LightY] '87, c86, p. 193.
"To Answer Your Question." [Poetry] (150:5) Ag 87, p. 283.
"Vespers" (1986 Finalist, Eve of Saint Agnes Poetry Competition). [NegC] (7:1/2)
87, p. 168-169.
"The Wedding Gift." [Poetry] (150:5) Ag 87, p. 284.
468. BERGER, Donald
"I Said." [MassR] (28:2) Sum 87, p. 271-272.
469. BERGHASH, Rachel
"School" (tr. of Avner Treinin). [ColR] (NS 14:1) Spr-Sum 87, p. 35.
470. BERGMAN, David
"A Family Likeness" (to Bob). [JamesWR] (5:1) Fall 87, p. 12.
"Old Voices at a New Number." [JamesWR] (4:3) Spr 87, p. 3.
471. BERGMAN, Petter
"Game of Chance" (tr. by Daniel Ogden). [Vis] (23) 87, p. 14.
472. BERGMAN, Susan
"Tell Me about Him (Bellevue)." [IndR] (10:3) Spr 87, p. 28.
473. BERK, Ilhan
"Poem: Yellow, Loveliest, enters my city" (tr. by Talat Sait Halman). [Trans] (19)
Fall 87, p. 126.
"Women" (tr. by Talat Sait Halman). [Trans] (19) Fall 87, p. 127.
474. BERKE, Judith
"Composite." [MissouriR] (10:3) 87, p. 190-191.
"Hasidic Wedding." [OhioR] (39) 87, p. 63.
"The Invention of the Printing Press." [OhioR] (39) 87, p. 64.
"Jonah." [Shen] (37:4) 87, p. 36-37.
475. BERKSON, Bill
"Dear Consumer, the Estimate Is High." [NewAW] (2) Fall 87, p. 40.
"In a Hand Not My Own." [Notus] (2:2) Fall 87, p. 68.
"Mandate: Archie to Jughead." [NewAW] (2) Fall 87, p. 39.
"Melting Milk." [NewAW] (1) 87, p. 27.
"Night Straits" (after Clark Coolidge). [Notus] (2:2) Fall 87, p. 70.
"Under a Cloud and After the Waves" (after Lyn Hejinian). [CreamCR] (11:2/3) 87?,
p. 2.
"Under a Cloud and After the Waves" (after Lyn Hejinian). [Notus] (2:2) Fall 87, p.
69.
476. BERLIND, Bruce
"The Fantasy." [SenR] (17:2) 87, p. 50.
"I Didn't Tell You Then" (tr. of Imre Orvecz, w. Maria Körösy). [Rampike] (5:3) 87,
p. 70.
"Seventh Symphony: The Assumption of Mary" (To my mother's memory, tr. of
Sandor Weöres, w. Mária Körösy). [GrahamHR] (10) Wint-Spr 87, p. 64-72.
477. BERMAN, Barbara
"After Jerusalem." [Vis] (24) 87, p. 17.
478. BERMAN, Lisa
"Falling Asleep." [Outbr] (18/19) Fall 86-Spr 88, p. 88-89.

479. BERMAN, Ruth
   "Nick Chopper the Tin Woodman." [KanQ] (19:3) Sum 87, p. 126.
   "Star Wheels." [KanQ] (19:3) Sum 87, p. 125.
480. BERNARD, April
   "Miss — — —." [Boulevard] (2:3) Fall 87, p. 73.
481. BERNARD, Pam
   "Bacteria." [StoneC] (14:3/4) Spr-Sum 87, p. 61.
482. BERNHARD, J.
   "Greyhound Bus Depot." [BellArk] (3:4) Jl-Ag 87, p. 5.
   "Marilyn." [BellArk] (3:4) Jl-Ag 87, p. 6.
   "Sasha." [BellArk] (3:5) S-O 87, p. 10.
   "Waiting for Sasha." [BellArk] (3:5) S-O 87, p. 10.
483. BERNSTEIN, Charles
   "Blow-Me-Down Etude." [Sulfur] (18) Wint 87, p. 95-109.
   "How to Disappear." [Conjunc] (11) 87?, p. 176.
   "Nina's Party at Judy's Gym." [Conjunc] (11) 87?, p. 175.
   "The Puritan Ethic and the Spirit of Capitalization." [CentralP] (12) Fall 87, p. 16-17.
   "Reading the Tree" (1 & 2). [Temblor] (5) 87, p. 136-142.
   "Riddle of the Fat Faced Man." [Conjunc] (11) 87?, p. 176.
   "Riot at 111 Station." [NewAW] (1) 87, p. 81.
   "Romance." [Bound] (14:1/2) Fall 85-Wint 86 [c87], p. 89.
   "Rowing with One Oar." [Bound] (14:1/2) Fall 85-Wint 86 [c87], p. 89.
   "Saltmines Regained." [Bound] (14:1/2) Fall 85-Wint 86 [c87], p. 88.
   "Seven for Aotearoa." [Notus] (2:2) Fall 87, p. 48-54.
   "Slowed Reason" (w. Nick Piombino). [NewAW] (1) 87, p. 82-83.
   "Verdi and Postmodernism." [Conjunc] (11) 87?, p. 175-176.
   "The Voyage of Life." [Bound] (14:1/2) Fall 85-Wint 86 [c87], p. 87.
   "Wait." [NewAW] (1) 87, p. 79-80.
   "Whose Language." [CentralP] (12) Fall 87, p. 5.
   "Whose Language." [Conjunc] (11) 87?, p. 177.
484. BERNSTEIN, Lisa
   "Diabetic, Testing Blood." [Antaeus] (58) Spr 87, p. 86.
   "The Family Rage." [FiveFR] (5) 87, p. 41.
   "The Sentence." [FiveFR] (5) 87, p. 42-43.
485. BERNSTEIN, Sylvia
   "Jealousy" (tr. of Roque Dalton, w. Harold Black). [Vis] (23) 87, p. 13.
486. BERRIGAN, Ted
   "Blue Galahad" (for Jim Carroll). [NewAW] (2) Fall 87, p. 36.
   "A Certain Slant of Sunlight." [NewAW] (2) Fall 87, p. 29.
   "Eileen (Detail)" (for George Schneeman). [NewAW] (2) Fall 87, p. 38.
   "For Robt. Creeley." [NewAW] (2) Fall 87, p. 36.
   "Give Them Back, Who Never Were." [NewAW] (2) Fall 87, p. 30.
   "In Your Fucking Utopias." [NewAW] (2) Fall 87, p. 32.
   "Montezuma's Revenge." [NewAW] (2) Fall 87, p. 37.
   "My Autobiography." [NewAW] (2) Fall 87, p. 33.
   "Ode" (w. Joanne Kyger). [NewAW] (2) Fall 87, p. 34.
   "Stars & Stripes Forever" (for Dick Jerome). [NewAW] (2) Fall 87, p. 35.
   "To Sing the Song, That Is Fantastic." [NewAW] (2) Fall 87, p. 31.
   "Turk" (for Erje Ryden). [NewAW] (2) Fall 87, p. 32.
487. BERRIS, Sandra
   "No Return." [MidwQ] (28:2) Wint 87, p. 210.
488. BERRY, D. C.
   "Covey." [Confr] (35/36) Spr-Fall 87, p. 229.
489. BERRY, Wendell
   "Except." [Spirit] (8:2) 87, p. 76.
   "The Fear of Love." [Spirit] (8:2) 87, p. 76.
   "Horses." [NowestR] (25:1) 87, p. 115-117.
   "The Three." [Sequoia] (31:1) Centennial issue 87, p. 13.
   "To My Mother." [Poetry] (151:1/2) O-N 87, p. 14.
490. BERSSENBRUGGE, Mei-Mei
   "Ala Kanak Break-Up — 3." [Caliban] (3) 87, p. 8.
   "Chinese Space." [Conjunc] (10) 87, p. 209-210.
   "The Hill Is Consumed." [RiverS] (23) 87, p. 74.
   "Honeymoon" (Drawing by Richard Tuttle). [Conjunc] (11) 87?, p. 104-112.
   "The Margin." [Conjunc] (10) 87, p. 211-212.
   "Recitatif." [Temblor] (6) 87, p. 83.

"The Swan." [Conjunc] (10) 87, p. 212-214.
"The Wind." [RiverS] (23) 87, p. 73.
491. BERTOLINO, James
"A Boy and His Dog." [Caliban] (2) 87, p. 77.
"A Crystal." [BellR] (10:1) Spr 87, p. 9.
"Double Eclipse." [BellR] (10:1) Spr 87, p. 6.
"Frog Voices" (for Philip McCracken). [Spirit] (8:2) 87, p. 70.
"The Interview" (For William Stafford). [BellR] (10:1) Spr 87, p. 10.
"The Lives of a Chicken." [BellR] (10:1) Spr 87, p. 7.
"Lullaby." [Caliban] (2) 87, p. 77.
"Maroon." [Caliban] (2) 87, p. 76.
"Smile on the Face of Awe" (For Jane Armitage). [BellR] (10:1) Spr 87, p. 8.
492. BERZINS, Rai
"Breakfast." [Waves] (15:3) Wint 87, p. 65.
493. BESS, Robert
"Domestic Birds." [LightY] '87, c86, p. 121-123.
494. BETHEL, Gar
"At Variety Mart." [KanQ] (19:1/2) Wint-Spr 87, p. 75.
"The Coffee Shop." [KanQ] (19:1/2) Wint-Spr 87, p. 76.
495. BETTENCOURT, Michael
"Blue Jay." [BallSUF] (28:4) Aut 87, p. 74.
496. BEVAN, Jack
"Here and Elsewhere" (tr. of Giuliano Dego). [BlueBldgs] (10) 87?, p. 38.
497. BEY, Rachid
"Destiny" (tr. by Eric Sellin). [LitR] (30:3) Spr 87, p. 398-399.
498. BEYER, William
"Journey After Passing." [Wind] (17:61) 87, p. 5-6.
"Mood for Grief: Autumn." [Wind] (17:61) 87, p. 5.
499. BEZNER, Kevin
"How She Danced." [HolCrit] (24:5) D 87, p. 11-12.
500. BHATT, Sujata
"Search for My Tongue." [Calyx] (10:2/3) Spr 87, p. 58-64.
501. BIALI, Harvey
"In Vitriol." [Notus] (2:2) Fall 87, p. 79-94.
502. BIEHL, Michael
"On Shakespeare's Sonnet CXXX." [Bogg] (58) 87, p. 10.
503. BIELSKI, Alison
"Raider." [Pembroke] (19) 87, p. 239.
"Rondeau Redouble for Raglan Castle." [Pembroke] (19) 87, p. 239-240.
"Rondel for Idwal" (Llyn Idwal, North Wales). [Pembroke] (19) 87, p. 240.
504. BIERDS, Linda
"Erebus." [NewYorker] (63:33) 5 O 87, p. 42.
"The Neon Artist in December." [Field] (37) Fall 87, p. 55-56.
"Quickly and Fully" (homage to Louis Pasteur). [Field] (37) Fall 87, p. 57-58.
"Strike." [NewYorker] (63:12) 11 My 87, p. 46.
"The White Ponies" (Cmdr. R. F. Scott, b. June 1868, d. South Pole Exploration
    Party, March 1912). [PoetryNW] (28:3) Aut 87, p. 4-6.
"Winter Fire: Minneapolis." [PoetryNW] (28:3) Aut 87, p. 3-4.
"Wonders." [Field] (37) Fall 87, p. 53-54.
505. BIESPIEL, David
"Bus Stop." [EngJ] (76:5) S 87, p. 110.
506. BIGGINS, Michael
"The Blue Vault" (tr. of Tomaz Salamun). [Ploughs] (13:4) 87, p. 112.
"The Boat" (tr. of Tomaz Salamun). [WillowS] (20) Spr 87, p. 80.
"The Cross" (tr. of Tomaz Salamun). [WillowS] (20) Spr 87, p. 78-79.
"Dead Men" (tr. of Tomaz Salamun). [MissR] (15:3, issue 45) Spr-Sum 87, p. 28-30.
"Help Me!" (tr. of Tomaz Salamun). [MissR] (15:3, issue 45) Spr-Sum 87, p. 27.
"Lips" (tr. of Tomaz Salamun). [ParisR] (29:105) Wint 87, p. 149.
"Pont-Neuf" (tr. of Tomaz Salamun). [ParisR] (29:105) Wint 87, p. 148.
507. BILGERE, George
"6 O'Clock." [NewEngR] (9:3) Spr 87, p. 347.
"Back to Earth." [LitR] (31:1) Fall 87, p. 62.
"Cropduster." [NewEngR] (9:3) Spr 87, p. 345-346.
"Sheep Grazing." [ChiR] (35:4) 87, p. 122-123.
508. BILLINGS, Phil
"Provincialism" (George Struble). [StoneC] (14:3/4) Spr-Sum 87, p. 12-13.

509. BILLINGS, Robert
"Dark Eyes." [Waves] (14:4) Spr 86, p. 74.
"Two Hands with the Water Card." [Waves] (14:4) Spr 86, p. 74-75.
"White City Poems" (Selections: 1, 3, 4, 6, 8, 13). [MalR] (79) Je 87, p. 143-148.
510. BILLINGS, Timothy
"To My Ledge, to My Ledge." [ManhatPR] (9) Sum 87, p. 52.
511. BINGHAM, Ginger
"My Cousins From Brazil." [DenQ] (22:1) Sum 87, p. 10-11.
512. BIRCHARD, Guy
"Coup de Hache." [WestCR] (21:4) Spr 87, p. 11.
"Destroyed After Something Delicious." [WestCR] (21:4) Spr 87, p. 11.
"Monograph: Leo Mirau, Carver, Painter." [WestCR] (21:4) Spr 87, p. 5-7.
"Palliser's Triangle." [WestCR] (21:4) Spr 87, p. 8-9.
"Scrying." [WestCR] (21:4) Spr 87, p. 10.
513. BIRNEY, Earle
"For George Johnston." [MalR] (78) Mr 87, p. 147.
"Seadancers." [Grain] (15:1) Spr 87, p. 12.
514. BISHOP, Elizabeth
"Three Sonnets for the Eyes" (Sonnets I. "Tidal Basin" & III). [Verse] (4:3) N 87, p.
    22-23.
"Visits to St. Elizabeths (1950)." [Verse] (4:3) N 87, p. 43-44.
"Wading at Wellfleet." [Verse] (4:3) N 87, p. 28.
515. BISHOP, Ellen
"Legacy." [MinnR] (NS 28) Spr 87, p. 12-13.
516. BISHOP, Rand
"Ama Ata Aidoo in Florida." [FloridaR] (15:2) Fall-Wint 87, p. 90.
517. BISHOP, Wendy
"Afternoon Decisions" (after Weldon Kees). [PraS] (61:2) Sum 87, p. 61-62.
"Bowl." [PraS] (61:2) Sum 87, p. 62-63.
"First Marriage." [PraS] (61:2) Sum 87, p. 61.
"Futility Sestina: Getting Housing in Kano, Nigeria." [KanQ] (19:3) Sum 87, p. 296.
"The Light at the End of the Year." [Poem] (58) N 87, p. 42.
"A Myth of Absence." [EngJ] (76:3) Mr 87, p. 32.
"Nothing Happened." [ColEng] (49:7) N 87, p. 776.
"Picnic." [ArizQ] (43:3) Aut 87, p. 230.
"Why Sing of a Father Unathletic." [KanQ] (19:3) Sum 87, p. 303.
518. BISSETT, Bill
"The silvr hors." [CrossC] (9:3/4) 87, p. 12.
"Splintrs th virgin mary is popular in a poplar tree in th sault." [CrossC] (9:3/4) 87,
    p. 13.
519. BISSONETTE, David
"Orbiting: The Block, the Seasons, the Unknown Planet." [CrossCur] (7:1) 87, p.
    128-129.
"Rumours of Moving." [Waves] (14:4) Spr 86, p. 52.
520. BITTNER, Richard
"Chasing Rainbows" (Macedonia Brook, Ken Falls, Conn., Finalist, Eve of St.
    Agnes Poetry Competition). [NegC] (7:1/2) 87, p. 147.
521. BJØRNVIG, Thorkild
"The Grebe" (tr. by Marilyn Nelson Waniek). [LitR] (30:4) Sum 87, p. 509-510.
"Isak Dinesen" (On the centennial of her birth, tr. by William Jay Smith and Leif
    Sjöberg). [GrahamHR] (10) Wint-Spr 87, p. 50-52.
"Morning Darkness" (tr. by Marilyn Nelson Waniek). [LitR] (30:4) Sum 87, p.
    507-508.
522. BLACK, Candace
"The River Took the Woman Down." [CapeR] (22:2) Fall 87, p. 22.
523. BLACK, Harold
"Jealousy" (tr. of Roque Dalton, w. Sylvia Bernstein). [Vis] (23) 87, p. 13.
524. BLACK, J. David
"Bareskin." [Waves] (15:3) Wint 87, p. 74.
525. BLACK, Ralph
"A Piece of Window." [PoetL] (81:3) Fall 86, p. 162.
526. BLACK, Star
"Rendezvous." [Ploughs] (13:4) 87, p. 22-23.
"Unassuming." [Boulevard] (2:1/2) Spr 87, p. 135-136.
527. BLACKBURN, Cathy
"The Lake." [TexasR] (8:1/2) Spr-Sum 87, p. 82.

BLACKBURN, Inés Dölz
    See DÖLZ-BLACKBURN, Inés
528. BLACKBURN, Michael
    "Neighbours in Soho" (from *Why Should Anyone Be Here and Singing: Capital Sonnets*). [Bogg] (57) 87, p. 25.
529. BLACKBURN, Thomas
    "Brynhyfryd." [Interim] (6:1) Spr 87, p. 19.
    "Morituri." [Interim] (6:1) Spr 87, p. 18-19.
    "Purgatorial." [Interim] (6:1) Spr 87, p. 20.
530. BLACKSHEAR, Helen
    "Heritage." [NegC] (7:3/4) 87, p. 97.
531. BLACKWELL, Barry
    "AIDS" (Excerpts). [MichQR] (26:2) Spr 87, p. 332-336.
532. BLADES, Joe
    "Found Synthetic Adventure Clues." [CrossC] (9:3/4) 87, p. 9.
533. BLAEUER, Mark
    "Leafing Through the Bible on a Winter's Morning." [Paint] (14:28) Aut 87, p. 25.
534. BLAIR, John
    "Swimming in Winter." [KanQ] (19:1/2) Wint-Spr 87, p. 40.
535. BLAIR, Peter
    "Kitchen Surgery." [Poem] (57) Mr 87, p. 34.
    "The Stars." [Poem] (57) Mr 87, p. 35.
536. BLAKE, George
    "After the Vigils." [KanQ] (19:1/2) Wint-Spr 87, p. 49.
    "Winter Song." [KanQ] (19:1/2) Wint-Spr 87, p. 50.
    "Winter Watch." [KanQ] (19:1/2) Wint-Spr 87, p. 50.
537. BLAKE, Patricia
    "Over a dark and quiet empire" (tr. of Andrei Voznesensky, w. William Jay Smith). [Trans] (18) Spr 87, p. 316.
    "To hang bare light bulbs from a ceiling" (tr. of Andrei Voznesensky, w. William Jay Smith). [Trans] (18) Spr 87, p. 316.
538. BLAKER, Margaret
    "Hernando DeSoto" (Clerihew). [LightY] '87, c86, p. 66.
539. BLANCO, Alberto
    "El Autobus Descompuesto." [Puerto] (22:2) Spr 87, p. 48-52.
    "The Broken-Down Bus" (tr. by John Oliver Simon). [Puerto] (22:2) Spr 87, p. 49-53.
540. BLANKENBURG, Gary
    "Mr. Electric." [SmPd] (24:1) Wint 87, p. 28.
541. BLASING, Randy
    "Calling." [Poetry] (151:1/2) O-N 87, p. 15-16.
    "Divining Rod." [Poetry] (150:6) S 87, p. 317.
    "Golden Valley." [Poetry] (150:6) S 87, p. 316.
    "The Luminist." [MichQR] (26:3) Sum 87, p. 505.
    "The Only Child." [MichQR] (26:3) Sum 87, p. 503-504.
    "Refuge." [Poetry] (150:6) S 87, p. 315.
542. BLEA, Irene I.
    "Damn, Sam." [BilingR] (12:3) 1985, c1988, p. 245-246.
    "Female Learning." [BilingR] (12:3) 1985, c1988, p. 241-242.
    "Fire Color." [BilingR] (12:3) 1985, c1988, p. 243-244.
    "He Never Wrote." [BilingR] (12:3) 1985, c1988, p. 244.
    "Married." [BilingR] (12:3) 1985, c1988, p. 242.
    "An Occasional Baby." [BilingR] (12:3) 1985, c1988, p. 242-243.
    "Why." [BilingR] (12:3) 1985, c1988, p. 244-245.
543. BLEHERT, Dean
    "Pinochio had a cricket for a conscience." [Bogg] (57) 87, p. 45.
544. BLESSING, Richard
    "Homecoming" (for Marlene). [MinnR] (NS 28) Spr 87, p. 108.
    "Tumor." [MinnR] (NS 28) Spr 87, p. 105-106.
545. BLESSING, Tom
    "The Lovers." [Bogg] (57) 87, p. 14.
546. BLESSINGTON, Francis
    "Fall Term." [CumbPR] (7:1) Fall 87, p. 10.
547. BLISS, Alice
    "De Haut en Bas." [Poem] (57) Mr 87, p. 31.

548. BLOCH, Chana
    "Half-Sized Violin" (tr. of Yehuda Amichai). [CrossCur] (7:3) 87, p. 16.
    "A House" (tr. of Yehuda Amichai). [CrossCur] (7:3) 87, p. 15.
    "The Opening of the School Year" (tr. of Yehuda Amichai). [CrossCur] (7:3) 87, p.
        18-19.
    "Statistics" (tr. of Yehuda Amichai). [CrossCur] (7:3) 87, p. 17.
549. BLOCH, Ingram
    "Science Is Easy When You're Eighty." [CumbPR] (6:2) Spr 87, p. 86.
550. BLOCK, Laurie
    "Peanuts, Here." [Grain] (15:3) Fall 87, p. 31.
551. BLODGETT, E. D.
    "Leavings." [Bound] (15:1/2) Fall 86-Wint 87, p. 298-300.
    "Song of Silences." [Bound] (15:1/2) Fall 86-Wint 87, p. 293-297.
    "Wintering Over." [Bound] (15:1/2) Fall 86-Wint 87, p. 301-304.
552. BLOMAIN, Karen
    "Abandoned Farm, Hop Bottom, Pa." [GreenfR] (14:1/2) Wint-Spr, p. 111.
    "Music Lesson." [GreenfR] (14:3/4) Sum-Fall 87, p. 88.
553. BLOOMFIELD, Maureen
    "Lotto." [NewRep] (196:20) 18 My 87, p. 32.
    "Rock and Tree and Water." [Shen] (37:3) 87, p. 18.
554. BLOSSOM, Lavina
    "Mr. Berg Waves to the Sky." [ParisR] (29:102) Spr 87, p. 205.
555. BLOUNT, Roy, Jr.
    "Gutes and Eulas." [LightY] '87, c86, p. 50-52.
    "On Instant Lives" (Howard Moss's Capsules of Great Figures in the Arts). [LightY]
        '87, c86, p. 216.
556. BLUE, Jane
    "The Room That Does Not Exist" (for D.B. and P.F.). [Vis] (25) 87, p. 13-14.
    "The Waltz." [Vis] (24) 87, p. 22-25.
    "Zen and the Birds of Appetite." [ThRiPo] (29/30) 87, p. 17-18.
557. BLUMBERG, Michele
    "The Heron." [CapeR] (22:1) Spr 87, p. 33.
558. BLUMENTHAL, Fritz
    "Blind Passenger." [GreenfR] (14:3/4) Sum-Fall 87, p. 51.
    "The Old Man Speaks." [GreenfR] (14:3/4) Sum-Fall 87, p. 52.
559. BLUMENTHAL, Jay A.
    "The Canonization: August 16, 1948." [Footwork] 87, p. 47.
560. BLUMENTHAL, Michael
    "At Lucy Vincent Beach, Easter Sunday 1986" (Martha's Vineyard). [TexasR] (7:3/4)
        87, p. 16.
    "The Dangers of Metaphor." [Nimrod] (30:2) Spr-Sum 87, p. 41.
    "First Snow: Cambridge, Mass." [Poetry] (151:1/2) O-N 87, p. 16-17.
    "The Heart of Quang Duc" (Saigon, 11 June 1963). [AmerV] (6) Spr 87, p. 47-48.
    "It Happens." [TexasR] (7:3/4) 87, p. 14-15.
    "Poem by Someone Else." [Nimrod] (30:2) Spr-Sum 87, p. 33-34.
    "The Walkers of Hurricanes." [Nimrod] (30:2) Spr-Sum 87, p. 40.
    "The Wasp in the Study." [MassR] (28:1) Spr 87, p. 145-146.
    "The Word 'Love'" (For Katherine). [Nat] (244:1) 10 Ja 87, p. 26.
561. BLUNK, Jonathan
    "Certain Trees." [PoetryE] (23/24) Fall 87, p. 120.
    "Song of the Rails." [PoetryE] (23/24) Fall 87, p. 121.
562. BLY, Robert
    "A Bed of Tulips." [OhioR] (38) 87, p. 90.
    "A Black Crab on a Searock." [Caliban] (3) 87, p. 47.
    "A Cattail in Athens, Ohio." [OhioR] (38) 87, p. 91.
    "Conversation with a Holy Woman Not Seen for Many Years." [Field] (36) Spr 87,
        p. 94.
    "Cornpicker Poem." [Field] (36) Spr 87, p. 92-93.
    "Dolly." [PaintedB] (30) 87, p. 40.
    "The March Buds." [AmerPoR] (16:5) S-O 87, p. 33.
    "A Piece of Dried Lichen." [Caliban] (2) 87, p. 15.
    "Poem for Sam at Assateague Island." [Raccoon] (24/25) My 87, p. 160-161.
    "Prayer for My Father." [Poetry] (151:1/2) O-N 87, p. 17-18.
    "A Private Fall." [Germ] (11:1) Fall 87, p. 20.
    "The Small Ant Heap." [PaintedB] (30) 87, p. 41.
    "Snowstorm Coming." [Witness] (1:2) Sum 87, p. 82.

"The Turtle." [AmerPoR] (16:5) S-O 87, p. 33.
"What We Provide." [AmerPoR] (16:5) S-O 87, p. 33.
"Who Is This One?" [OntR] (26) Spr-Sum 87, p. 34.
563. BLYSTONE, Sandra
"Poet Class." [BelPoJ] (38:1) Fall 87, p. 26-29.
564. BLYTHE, Randy
"Early Spring." [Poem] (57) Mr 87, p. 1.
"Inheritance." [Poem] (57) Mr 87, p. 2.
"October." [DekalbLAJ] (20:1/4) 87, p. 33.
565. BOB, Indiana
"Borrowings from Ernest Kroll." [WindO] (48) Spr 87, p. 11.
566. BOBROWSKI, Joannes
"Horses" (tr. by Rich Ives). [ColR] (NS 14:2) Fall-Wint 87, p. 6.
567. BOBYSHEV, Dmitri
"Prayer to a Guardian Angel" (tr. by Michael Van Walleghen). [Vis] (25) 87, p. 18.
568. BOCHO, Yamamura
"Light" (tr. by Graeme Wilson). [LitR] (31:1) Fall 87, p. 87.
569. BOE, Deborah
"About Lazarus." [Poetry] (150:4) Jl 87, p. 196-197.
"And Yahweh Closed the Door Behand Noah." [Poetry] (150:4) Jl 87, p. 193-194.
"Branches." [HangL] (50/51) 87, p. 29-30.
"The Carpenter's Level." [HangL] (50/51) 87, p. 32.
"The Changeling." [PoetryNW] (28:1) Spr 87, p. 8-9.
"The Genealogy of Despair." [HangL] (50/51) 87, p. 28.
"In Proof of the Existence of Angels." [HangL] (50/51) 87, p. 31.
"Mary of Bethany." [Poetry] (150:4) Jl 87, p. 194-195.
"My Sister, Afraid." [HangL] (50/51) 87, p. 33.
"The Predictions." [HangL] (50/51) 87, p. 35.
"Snow Light in the Mojave." [DenQ] (22:1) Sum 87, p. 35.
"Walking All Night." [OhioR] (38) 87, p. 118.
"Where She Will Wait." [HangL] (50/51) 87, p. 34.
570. BOE, Marilyn J.
"Everlasting Fielder." [Outbr] (18/19) Fall 86-Spr 88, p. 73.
571. BOEGEHOLD, Alan
"Steps" (tr. of C. P. Cavafy). [Margin] (5) Wint 87-88, p. 40.
572. BOEHRER, Bruce
"Exequy." [NegC] (7:1/2) 87, p. 82.
"For an Unborn Child." [KanQ] (19:1/2) Wint-Spr 87, p. 100.
"Thomas the Doubter." [NegC] (7:1/2) 87, p. 81.
"William Gardiner, Martyr for God's Cause." [KanQ] (19:1/2) Wint-Spr 87, p. 99.
573. BOESCHE-ZACHAROW, Tillye
"The Applause" (tr. by Laszlo Baransky, Istvan Eorsi, Anna Saghy and Bob Rosenthal). [Rampike] (5:3) 87, p. 70.
574. BOETTCHER, Monika
"The Funeral." [Waves] (15:3) Wint 87, p. 70.
"The Statue." [Waves] (15:3) Wint 87, p. 70.
575. BOGAN, James
"Black and Black" (tr. of Max Martins). [NewL] (53:3) Spr 87, p. 115.
"Musicstone" (tr. of Max Martins). [NewL] (53:3) Spr 87, p. 113.
"This for That" (tr. of Max Martins). [NewL] (53:3) Spr 87, p. 113.
"To Shan-Hui" (tr. of Max Martins). [NewL] (53:3) Spr 87, p. 115.
576. BOGARD, William
"Daedalethics" (A Manifesto, w. Philip Turetzky). [ColR] (NS 14:2) Fall-Wint 87, p. 68-80.
577. BOGEN, Don
"The Freedom of the Press." [MissouriR] (10:2) 87, p. 166-167.
"The Known World." [Shen] (37:4) 87, p. 82-107.
"Literacy." [MissouriR] (10:1) 87, p. 158.
578. BOGGS, Mildred Williams
"Coming Out of Appalachia." [Wind] (17:61) 87, p. 19.
579. BOGIN, Nina
"It Was Not a Star." [Iowa] (17:2) Spr-Sum 87, p. 60-61.
"Like a wound." [Iowa] (17:2) Spr-Sum 87, p. 62.
"Once Again the Moon." [Iowa] (17:2) Spr-Sum 87, p. 63.
"A Sky of Dark Furrows." [Iowa] (17:2) Spr-Sum 87, p. 64.

580. BOHM, R.
"Folk Episodes: Keeping a Record" (for Mickey Tyson, 1986 Finalist, Eve of Saint Agnes Poetry Competition). [NegC] (7:1/2) 87, p. 195-196.
581. BOISSEAU, Michelle
"Partial Eclipse." [Poetry] (150:5) Ag 87, p. 281.
"Pinwheel." [MissouriR] (10:1) 87, p. 166.
"We Return to a Plain Sense of Things." [Poetry] (150:5) Ag 87, p. 280-281.
582. BOLAND, Eavan
"Another Country." [MassR] (28:3) Aut 87, p. 363-364.
"The Black Lace Fan My Mother Gave Me." [NewYorker] (63:35) 19 O 87, p. 40.
"The Bottle Garden." [PartR] (54:4) Fall 87, p. 583-584.
"The Emigrant Irish." [MassR] (28:3) Aut 87, p. 363.
"Envoi." [NowestR] (25:1) 87, p. 69.
"Fever." [MassR] (28:3) Aut 87, p. 366-367.
"Fever." [NowestR] (25:1) 87, p. 70.
"Fever." [NowestR] (25:3) 87, p. 449.
"The Fire in Our Neighbourhood." [MassR] (28:3) Aut 87, p. 364-365.
"Fond Memory." [MassR] (28:3) Aut 87, p. 365-366.
"The Glass King." [MalR] (79) Je 87, p. 141-142.
"I Remember." [AmerPoR] (16:5) S-O 87, p. 41.
"The Journey." [NowestR] (25:1) 87, p. 62-65.
"Lace." [Agni] (24/25) 87, p. 272-273.
"Lace." [MassR] (28:3) Aut 87, p. 369-370.
"Nocturne." [Agni] (24/25) 87, p. 276.
"Nocturne." [MassR] (28:3) Aut 87, p. 367.
"Nocturne." [NowestR] (25:1) 87, p. 68.
"Re-Reading the Middle English One Summer Night in Ireland." [NowestR] (25:1) 87, p. 66-67.
"Self-Portrait on a Summer Evening." [MalR] (79) Je 87, p. 135-136.
"Suburban Woman: A Detail." [Agni] (24/25) 87, p. 274-275.
"Suburban Woman: A Detail." [MassR] (28:3) Aut 87, p. 368-369.
"Tirade for the Lyric Muse." [AmerPoR] (16:5) S-O 87, p. 40.
"The Unlived Life." [AmerPoR] (16:5) S-O 87, p. 40.
"The Unlived Life." [NowestR] (25:1) 87, p. 71-72.
"The Wild Spray." [MalR] (79) Je 87, p. 139-140.
"The Women." [MalR] (79) Je 87, p. 137-138.
583. BOLLS, Imogene
"The Bones Hold the Answer." [SouthernPR] (27:1) Spr 87, p. 34.
"Hole." [LightY] '87, c86, p. 220-221.
"Living on the Edge." [Paint] (14:28) Aut 87, p. 9.
"Mapping My Mother." [CentR] (31:1) Wint 87, p. 62-63.
584. BOLTON, Joe (Joseph Edward)
"American Variations" (Guy Owen Poetry Prize Winner). [SouthernPR] (27:2) Fall 87, p. 5-7.
"The Blue World." [HayF] (2) Spr 87, p. 82.
"Breckinridge County Suite: To a Young Kentucky Woman" (To Rebecca). [Crazy] (32) Spr 87, p. 44-60.
"Celebration" (tr. of Enrique Huaco). [InterPR] (13:2) Fall 87, p. 17.
"Historically This Man" (tr. of Enrique Huaco). [WillowS] (20) Spr 87, p. 34-35.
"Little Testament I-III" (tr. of Enrique Huaco). [InterPR] (13:2) Fall 87, p. 19-25.
"Loca Sancta #1." [YellowS] (24) Aut 87, p. 11.
"Ode to a Relative I Never Met." [HighP] (2:2) Fall 87, p. 167-168.
"Party." [Crazy] (32) Spr 87, p. 61-63.
"Sestina: Anonymous Spanish Drawing." [CumbPR] (6:2) Spr 87, p. 42-43.
"Sonnet: Bored Cop Leaning against Abstract Sculpture on Plaza below Skyscraper." [CumbPR] (6:2) Spr 87, p. 44.
"The Southern Quartet: Improvisations on Themes from Vallejo's *Trilce*." [ChatR] (8:1) Fall 87, p. 7-10.
"A Wreath of Stars: Symsonia, Kentucky, 1914." [SouthernPR] (27:2) Fall 87, p. 7-8.
585. BOLZ, Judy
"Bonsai." [SouthernPR] (27:2) Fall 87, p. 63.
BOMBARD, Joan La
See LaBOMBARD, Joan
586. BONAFFINI, Luigi
"Every Night" (tr. of Guiseppe Jovine). [PoetL] (82:3) Fall 87, p. 174.

"The Peacock" (To Miserere, tr. of Guiseppe Jovine). [PoetL] (82:3) Fall 87, p. 173.
587. BOND, Bruce
"Ives." [PoetryNW] (28:4) Wint 87-88, p. 25.
"Matisse: The Red Studio." [Sonora] (12) Spr 87, p. 25.
"Night Pools." [StoneC] (14:3/4) Spr-Sum 87, p. 38.
"Vermeer: The Maidservant." [Sonora] (12) Spr 87, p. 26-27.
588. BOND, Harold
"Advice Against Thumbers." [LightY] '87, c86, p. 141.
589. BOND, Pearl
"Jewish Mother" (for Della). [Calyx] (10:2/3) Spr 87, p. 114.
590. BONDS, Diane
"Counterparts." [SouthernHR] (21:2) Spr 87, p. 115.
"Harvest Scene" (from "Days of Heaven"). [SouthernHR] (21:4) Fall 87, p. 352.
591. BONNEFOY, Yves
"The Art of Poetry" (tr. by Lisa Sapinkopf). [HampSPR] Wint 86, p. 29.
592. BONNELL, William
"Canadian Landscape." [Waves] (14:4) Spr 86, p. 66-67.
"Foreigner." [Waves] (14:4) Spr 86, p. 65.
593. BONNER, Deborah
"The Blow" (tr. of Amanda Berenguer). [AmerPoR] (16:2) Mr-Ap 87, p. 17.
"Moebius Strip" (tr. of Amanda Berenguer). [AmerPoR] (16:2) Mr-Ap 87, p. 16-17.
594. BONO, Jeremy
"My Baseball." [Gambit] (20) 86, p. 39.
BONTE, Karen La
   See LaBONTE, Karen
595. BOOTH, Philip
"Chapter One." [Pequod] (23/24) 87, p. 184.
"Garden." [NoDaQ] (55:3) Sum 87, p. 74-75.
"Presence" (After George Oppen). [Poetry] (151:1/2) O-N 87, p. 18-19.
"Seeing" (postcards from Maine to Kansas and back). [GeoR] (41:4) Wint 87, p.
   718-719.
"Visiting Grandma: Omaha 1932." [Pequod] (23/24) 87, p. 185-187.
596. BORDAO, Rafael
"Pronostico." [LindLM] (6:4) O-D 87, p. 5.
597. BORDEN, Jonathan
"Signing Herself Fangs" (North Hanover Street, Carlisle, Christmas 1895). [Iowa]
   (17:3) Fall 87, p. 167.
598. BORGES, Jorge Luis
"Ajedrez, I-II." [InterPR] (13:2) Fall 87, p. 26.
"Chess, I-II" (tr. by Nathaniel Smith). [InterPR] (13:2) Fall 87, p. 27.
"One of Lee's Soldiers" (tr. by Hardie St. Martin). [AmerV] (9) Wint 87, p. 63.
"El Suicida." [InterPR] (13:1) Spr 87, p. 56.
"The Suicide" (tr. by Susan Schreibman). [InterPR] (13:1) Spr 87, p. 57.
"Tankas" (6 poems in Spanish). [InterPR] (13:1) Spr 87, p. 54, 56.
"Tankas" (6 poems, tr. by Susan Schreibman). [InterPR] (13:1) Spr 87, p. 54, 56.
599. BORICH, Valerie
"A Mother Pauses Before a Photograph" (after Jonathan Borofsky's South Africa
   installation). [GreenfR] (14:3/4) Sum-Fall 87, p. 155-156.
600. BORINSKY, Alicia
"En un Bar" (from "Mujeres Timidas," tr. by Cola Franzen). [Rampike] (5:3) 87, p.
   40.
"I Miss Her Already" (tr. by Cola Franzen). [StoneC] (15:1/2) Fall-Wint 87-88, p.
   67.
"Immortalities of the Marionette" (tr. by Cola Franzen). [StoneC] (15:1/2) Fall-Wint
   87-88, p. 65.
"In Buenos Aires" (tr. by Cola Franzen). [NewAW] (2) Fall 87, p. 48.
"Inmortalidades de Marioneta" (from "Mujeres Tímidas). [StoneC] (15:1/2) Fall-Wint
   87-88, p. 64.
"Proverbio" (from "Mujeres Timidas," tr. by Cola Franzen). [Rampike] (5:3) 87, p.
   41.
"Strip-Tease" (tr. by Cola Franzen). [NewAW] (2) Fall 87, p. 47.
"Ya La Extrão." [StoneC] (15:1/2) Fall-Wint 87-88, p. 66.
601. BOROWSKI, Tadeusz
"Dead Poets" (tr. by Tadeusz Pioro). [Trans] (19) Fall 87, p. 224.
"Dear Diary" (tr. by Tadeusz Pioro). [Trans] (19) Fall 87, p. 219.
"Friends" (tr. by Tadeusz Pioro). [Trans] (19) Fall 87, p. 223.

"I Think of You" (tr. by Tadeusz Pioro). [Trans] (19) Fall 87, p. 219.
"It's the Same Each Night" (tr. by Tadeusz Pioro). [Trans] (19) Fall 87, p. 220.
"My Friend, I Think of You at Night" (tr. by Tadeusz Pioro). [Trans] (19) Fall 87, p. 222.
"Night Over Birkenau" (tr. by Tadeusz Pioro). [Trans] (19) Fall 87, p. 221.
"Return to Life" (tr. by Tadeusz Pioro). [Trans] (19) Fall 87, p. 221.
602. BORSON, Roo
    "The Irony." [CutB] (27/28) 87, p. 44.
    "The Merchants' Song" (after "Foxfire" by Hiroshige). [CutB] (27/28) 87, p. 45.
603. BORST, Steve
    "My Angel." [Abraxas] (35/36) 87, p. 25.
604. BORUCH, Marianne
    "Buick." [MassR] (28:4) Wint 87, p. 735.
    "Delphinium." [Iowa] (17:2) Spr-Sum 87, p. 68.
    "The Funny Looking Biscuit." [MassR] (28:4) Wint 87, p. 736-737.
    "Monkshood." [Iowa] (17:2) Spr-Sum 87, p. 67.
    "Moon" (after a painting by Doris Lee, 1935). [NowestR] (25:3) 87, p. 400.
    "My Son and I Go See Horses." [AmerPoR] (16:3) My-Je 87, p. 6.
    "Napping in Trees." [Nat] (244:18) 9 My 87, p. 622.
    "November Garden with Moon." [Nat] (245:11) 10 O 87, p. 384.
    "Purple Iris." [Iowa] (17:2) Spr-Sum 87, p. 66.
    "White Rose." [Iowa] (17:2) Spr-Sum 87, p. 65.
    "Wine Lily." [Iowa] (17:2) Spr-Sum 87, p. 69.
605. BORUM, Poul
    "The Four Cradles" (tr. of Pia Tafdrup, w. Roger Greenwald). [Writ] (19) 87, p. 28-30.
    "In Spite of Everything" (tr. of Pia Tafdrup, w. Roger Greenwald). [Writ] (19) 87, p. 31.
    "The Inmost Membrane of My Brain" (tr. of Pia Tafdrup, w. Roger Greenwald). [Writ] (19) 87, p. 24.
    "Just My Blood" (tr. of Pia Tafdrup, w. Roger Greenwald). [Writ] (19) 87, p. 26-27.
    "No Longer Afraid" (tr. of Pia Tafdrup, w. Roger Greenwald). [Writ] (19) 87, p. 32.
    "Sharp Tugs" (tr. of Pia Tafdrup, w. Roger Greenwald). [Writ] (19) 87, p. 33.
    "Skin" (tr. of Pia Tafdrup, w. Roger Greenwald). [Writ] (19) 87, p. 35.
    "So As Not to Stand in Our Own Way" (tr. of Pia Tafdrup, w. Roger Greenwald). [Writ] (19) 87, p. 25.
    "Spring Tide" (tr. of Pia Tafdrup, w. Roger Greenwald). [Writ] (19) 87, p. 34.
    "What Comes" (tr. of Pia Tafdrup, w. Roger Greenwald). [Writ] (19) 87, p. 23.
606. BOSNICK, David
    "Rebecca and the Marriage of Swans." [FloridaR] (15:2) Fall-Wint 87, p. 54.
607. BOSQUET, Alain
    "A Bit of Flesh" (tr. by David Applefield). [LitR] (30:3) Spr 87, p. 437.
    "A Funeral" (tr. by David Applefield). [LitR] (30:3) Spr 87, p. 436.
    "A Mother's Death" (tr. by David Applefield). [LitR] (30:3) Spr 87, p. 436.
608. BOSS, Laura
    "The Children Are Listening." [Lips] (13) 87, p. 52-53.
    "My Mother's Toughness." [Footwork] 87, p. 15.
    "Tugboat Man." [GreenfR] (14:1/2) Wint-Spr, p. 193-194.
609. BOSTON, B. H.
    "Apiary." [WestHR] (41:1) Spr 87, p. 36-37.
610. BOSWELL, Terri J.
    "Big-Chested Man." [Pig] (14) 87, p. 62.
    "To Her Coy Mister." [Pig] (14) 87, p. 39.
611. BOTTOMS, David
    "Armored Hearts." [Poetry] (151:1/2) O-N 87, p. 19-20.
    "Christmas Stars." [VirQR] (63:1) Wint 87, p. 81-83.
    "Face Jugs: Homage to Lanier Meaders." [AmerPoR] (16:2) Mr-Ap 87, p. 55.
    "Fiddle Time." [VirQR] (63:1) Wint 87, p. 80-81.
    "The Ice Pasture." [VirQR] (63:1) Wint 87, p. 83-84.
    "In Heritage Farms, Settled." [Poetry] (150:3) Je 87, p. 135.
    "A Night, Near Berkeley Springs." [Poetry] (151:3) D 87, p. 271.
    "Rats at Allatoona." [Poetry] (150:3) Je 87, p. 136.
612. BOUCHER, Alan
    "Delicate Scent" (tr. of Olafur Johann Sigurdsson). [Vis] (25) 87, p. 36.
    "The Sun" (tr. of Steinn Steinarr). [Vis] (24) 87, p. 21.
    "Wood" (tr. of Steinn Steinarr). [Vis] (23) 87, p. 12.

613. BOUCHERON, Robert
    "Attis" (tr. of Catullus: *Poems* 63). [JamesWR] (4:2) Wint 87, p. 13.
614. BOUDJEDRA, Rachid
    "The Café" (tr. by Eric Sellin). [LitR] (30:3) Spr 87, p. 400.
615. BOUDREAU, Jean
    "New England News." [Interim] (6:2) Fall 87, p. 23.
    "The Owl." [Interim] (6:2) Fall 87, p. 22.
616. BOUGHN, Mike
    "Recalcitrant Music" (3 selections). [Notus] (2:2) Fall 87, p. 57-59.
617. BOULLATA, Kamal
    "The Echo Is an Arch." [Vis] (23) 87, p. 33.
618. BOURAOUI, Hédi
    "Tree of Words" (tr. by the author). [Paint] (14:27) Spr 87, p. 7.
619. BOURASSA, Alan
    "Hearing of Nakasone's Apology in the UN for Japanese Involvement in World War
       Two." [Quarry] (36:3) Sum 87, p. 37.
    "A Medieval Nobleman Travels from Paris to Orleans." [Quarry] (36:3) Sum 87, p.
       36.
    "Small Towns." [Germ] (11:1) Fall 87, p. 49.
    "Thinking of White Magic I Hear Reports of Fighting in South Yemen." [Quarry]
       (36:3) Sum 87, p. 37.
620. BOURNE, Daniel
    "The Air Between Us" (tr. of Bronislaw Maj). [StoneC] (14:3/4) Spr-Sum 87, p. 59.
    "Board" (tr. of Tomasz Jastrun). [NowestR] (25:2) 87, p. 109.
    "Boys Who Go Aloft" (16 poems). [Sparrow] (52) 87, 25 p.
    "Elevator" (tr. of Tomasz Jastrun). [PraS] (61:1) Spr 87, p. 49-50.
    "Feathers" (tr. of Tomasz Jastrun). [PraS] (61:1) Spr 87, p. 50.
    "The First Night" (tr. of Tomasz Jastrun). [NowestR] (25:2) 87, p. 102.
    "Five Year Plan" (tr. of Tomasz Jastrun). [QW] (25) Spr 87, p. 133.
    "Forty-Eight Hours" (tr. of Tomasz Jastrun). [NowestR] (25:2) 87, p. 110-111.
    "Hunters Are Magnificent Animals." [KanQ] (19:1/2) Wint-Spr 87, p. 185.
    "I Hold My Family" (1986 Finalist, Eve of Saint Agnes Poetry Competition). [NegC]
       (7:1/2) 87, p. 154-161.
    "Interrogation with Map" (tr. of Tomasz Jastrun). [NowestR] (25:2) 87, p. 106.
    "Is It Right" (tr. of Bronislaw Maj). [CrossCur] (7:3) 87, p. 58.
    "The Journey Forever" (tr. of Tomasz Jastrun). [QW] (25) Spr 87, p. 133.
    "Leaving Prison" (tr. of Tomasz Jastrun). [NowestR] (25:2) 87, p. 112.
    "Light" (tr. of Tomasz Jastrun). [NowestR] (25:2) 87, p. 107.
    "Low." [LaurelR] (21:1/2) Wint-Sum 87, p. 9.
    "Milk" (tr. of Tomasz Jastrun). [Salm] (72) Fall 86, p. 196.
    "On the Crossroads" (tr. of Tomasz Jastrun). [NowestR] (25:2) 87, p. 103.
    "Once Again." [CarolQ] (40:1) Fall 87, p. 84.
    "Our Grammar" (tr. of Tomasz Jastrun). [NowestR] (25:2) 87, p. 114.
    "The Pharoah Who Knew Not Joseph." [Poem] (57) Mr 87, p. 50.
    "Scrap" (tr. of Tomasz Jastrun). [NowestR] (25:2) 87, p. 113.
    "A Secret Meeting" (tr. of Tomasz Jastrun). [Salm] (72) Fall 86, p. 196-197.
    "Small Fires" (tr. of Tomasz Jastrun). [NowestR] (25:2) 87, p. 108.
    "Snow" (tr. of Tomasz Jastrun). [PartR] (54:2) Spr 87, p. 271-272.
    "Survivalist Pantoum." [Poem] (57) Mr 87, p. 48-49.
    "To My Son" (tr. of Tomasz Jastrun). [NowestR] (25:2) 87, p. 105.
    "Trial" (tr. of Tomasz Jastrun). [PartR] (54:2) Spr 87, p. 272-273.
    "Visitation" (tr. of Tomasz Jastrun). [PartR] (54:2) Spr 87, p. 273.
    "Windows" (tr. of Tomasz Jastrun). [NowestR] (25:2) 87, p. 104.
621. BOURNE, Lesley
    "The Voice Says in Such a Way." [Event] (16:1) Mr 87, p. 30-31.
622. BOUVARD, Marguerite
    "Ballad of the Back." [PartR] (54:2) Spr 87, p. 273-274.
    "Blanche's Dream." [CentR] (31:1) Wint 87, p. 61-62.
    "Triptych" (for Mary Todd Shaw). [MidwQ] (28:2) Wint 87, p. 206-207.
623. BOUZAHER, Hocine
    "Imperfect and Present Tense" (tr. by Eric Sellin). [LitR] (30:3) Spr 87, p. 401.
624. BOVE, Armand D.
    "The Garden." [Writer] (99:7) Jl 86, p. 20.
625. BOWER, Roger
    "On Door Jambs." [Spirit] (8:2) 87, p. 325.

626. BOWERING, George
    "Jacket Too Big." [Pig] (14) 87, p. 76.
627. BOWERS, Beth Baker
    "Last Note on Letting Go." [US1] (20/21) Wint 86-87, p. 6-7.
BOWERS, Cathy Smith
    See SMITH-BOWERS, Cathy
628. BOWERS, Edgar
    "AA." [Sequoia] (31:1) Centennial issue 87, p. 15.
    "Thirteen Views of Santa Barbara." [Thrpny] (29) Spr 87, p. 14-15.
629. BOWERS, Neal
    "Aliens." [Poetry] (150:5) Ag 87, p. 271.
    "Apple Mechanics." [Poetry] (150:5) Ag 87, p. 270.
    "Being Philosophical." [SoDakR] (25:2) Sum 87, p. 76.
    "Breaking Silence." [GeoR] (41:3) Fall 87, p. 484.
    "Dead Weight." [SouthernPR] (27:2) Fall 87, p. 60.
    "Driving in Greenwood Cemetery." [SewanR] (95:2) Spr 87, p. 240-241.
    "For the Piano Tuner." [Hudson] (40:3) Aut 87, p. 431.
    "For the South." [SouthernR] (23:2) Ap 87, p. 380.
    "How We Get Our Names." [SoDakR] (25:2) Sum 87, p. 77.
    "Jesse James in Hell." [WebR] (12:2) Fall 87, p. 64-66.
    "The Man with the Left-Handed Tools." [MidwQ] (28:2) Wint 87, p. 208-209.
    "Night Builder." [Poetry] (150:4) Jl 87, p. 223.
    "Space Burial." [Hudson] (40:3) Aut 87, p. 427-430.
    "Sympathies." [NewL] (53:2) Wint 86-87, p. 85.
    "Words for a Fireman's Funeral." [SewanR] (95:2) Spr 87, p. 241.
630. BOWIE, Robert
    "Author, Author." [ArizQ] (43:3) Aut 87, p. 217.
    "Bridges." [ArizQ] (43:1) Spr 87, p. 52.
    "Equus Caballus." [Abraxas] (35/36) 87, p. 57.
    "Gallery." [DenQ] (21:3) Wint 87, p. 77-78.
    "If I Find a Field." [DenQ] (21:3) Wint 87, p. 75-76.
    "Lambs in Spring." [Phoenix] (7:2) 87, p. 1.
    "Song of the Robin." [Abraxas] (35/36) 87, p. 56.
    "Surviving the Seduction of Nature's Beauty." [HawaiiR] (22) Fall 87, p. 44-45.
631. BOWMAN, Catherine
    "Marge Margerie." [WebR] (12:1) Spr 87, p. 20-21.
    "Sunflower Revival in Potato Town." [WebR] (12:1) Spr 87, p. 22-23.
632. BOWMAN, L. MacF.
    "Failure." [Sequoia] (31:1) Centennial issue 87, p. 103.
633. BOYCE, Robert C.
    "An Ever-Expanding Universe." [Bogg] (57) 87, p. 51.
634. BOYD, Greg
    "Evolution." [HawaiiR] (22) Fall 87, p. 46.
635. BOYER, Jeff
    "At Crums Beauty College (Five-Fifty a Cut)." [KanQ] (19:1/2) Wint-Spr 87, p. 136.
    "Scalding Hogs." [KanQ] (19:1/2) Wint-Spr 87, p. 137.
636. BOYLE, Kevin
    "Pointlessly Losing Control." [AnotherCM] (17) 87, p. 5-6.
637. BRACKENBURY, Alison
    "To Market." [Verse] (4:1) Mr 87, p. 54.
638. BRACKENRIDGE, Valery
    "Broken Glass." [Footwork] 87, p. 81.
    "Complete Consummation." [Footwork] 87, p. 82.
    "Even in Sleep." [Footwork] 87, p. 81.
    "The Flower by My Bed." [Footwork] 87, p. 81.
    "For Beth." [Footwork] 87, p. 81.
    "In the Morning." [Footwork] 87, p. 83.
    "Lady in White." [Footwork] 87, p. 81.
    "Nightwatchman." [Footwork] 87, p. 82.
    "Sometime Later." [Footwork] 87, p. 82.
    "Watching Maria Read." [Footwork] 87, p. 82.
639. BRADLEY, Ardyth
    "Hope." [NegC] (7:3/4) 87, p. 109.
640. BRADLEY, Bob
    "Message to Father in Pork Pie Hat, with Cocktail." [AntR] (45:1) Wint 87, p. 36-37.

641. BRADLEY, George
"Cyclopean Wall in the Alto-Molise." [YaleR] (76:4) Sum 87, p. 551-552.
"Life As We Know It." [Field] (36) Spr 87, p. 72.
"M31 in Andromeda." [Field] (36) Spr 87, p. 69-70.
"Noch Einmal, an Orpheus." [GrandS] (7:1) Aut 87, p. 141.
"Objects of Art." [GrandS] (7:1) Aut 87, p. 140-141.
"Second Thoughts in Twilight." [GrandS] (7:1) Aut 87, p. 142.
"Versicles." [GrandS] (7:1) Aut 87, p. 143.
"The Year of the Comet." [Shen] (37:4) 87, p. 29-32.
642. BRADLEY, John
"For the American Dead." [Germ] (11:1) Fall 87, p. 26.
"For the Angel of Memory, in Her Sickness and in Her Grief." [Germ] (11:1) Fall 87,
    p. 27.
"From Chile." [HighP] (2:3) Wint 87, p. 253-254.
"Insomnia of the News of South Africa" (For Jay Griswold). [Germ] (11:1) Fall 87,
    p. 29.
"Invisibility." [Germ] (11:1) Fall 87, p. 28.
"Moonrise: Hernandez, New Mexico, 1941." [Raccoon] (24/25) My 87, p. 146.
643. BRADLEY, Robert
"Cataract." [PoetryE] (23/24) Fall 87, p. 201.
"The Dolphins." [PoetryE] (23/24) Fall 87, p. 199.
"The Frame." [PoetryE] (23/24) Fall 87, p. 200.
644. BRADY, Stephen
"Judith." [BellArk] (3:6) N-D 87, p. 5.
"October." [BellArk] (3:6) N-D 87, p. 10.
645. BRAGANZA, Brian
"Desolation." [Waves] (15:4) Spr 87, p. 26.
646. BRAMBACH, Rainer
"Endangered Landscape" (tr. by Stuart Friebert). [Iowa] (17:3) Fall 87, p. 106.
647. BRAND, Alice
"Caught at the Curve." [CapeR] (22:1) Spr 87, p. 25.
"We Only Piece It Together from Scraps of Germany or Poland." [Event] (16:3) Fall
    87, p. 64.
648. BRANDER, John
"Auntie and Dai in Clydach." [Amelia] (4:1/2, issue 9) 87, p. 112-113.
"In a Druid Wood." [Amelia] (4:1/2, issue 9) 87, p. 113-116.
649. BRANDT, Anthony
"Walls." [Boulevard] (2:1/2) Spr 87, p. 58.
650. BRASFIELD, James
"Arcadia." [PoetryE] (23/24) Fall 87, p. 205.
"The Denial" (tr. of Arturo Fontaine, w. the author). [CutB] (27/28) 87, p. 104.
"Lagoons" (tr. of Arturo Fontaine, w. the author). [CutB] (27/28) 87, p. 105.
"Monuments." [PoetryE] (23/24) Fall 87, p. 206-207.
"Waynesboro." [QW] (24) Wint 87, p. 94-95.
"Your Dresses" (tr. of Arturo Fontaine, w. the author). [CutB] (27/28) 87, p. 105.
651. BRASHLER, Ann
"Amen." [NewL] (54:1) Fall 87, p. 104.
652. BRASS, Deborah
"Adore the God Who Gives and Takes Away" (Phillis Wheatley 1753-1784).
    [CrescentR] (5:1) 87, p. 125.
653. BRATHWAITE, Edward Kamau
"Stone" (for Mikey Smitt, Stoned to death in Stony Hill, Kingston, Jamaica, 1983 /
    1987). [Chelsea] (46) 87, p. 296-299.
"Twoom." [NewEngR] (9:3) Spr 87, p. 262-264.
654. BRAUN, Henry
"In Memory of Benjamin E. Linder" (young engineer and clown of Portland, USA
    and . . . Nicaragua). [AmerPoR] (16:6) N-D 87, p. 20.
655. BRAUN, Volker
"The Myth of the Cave" (tr. by Laszlo Baransky, Istvan Eorsi, Anna Saghy and Bob
    Rosenthal). [Rampike] (5:3) 87, p. 69.
656. BRAVERMAN, Kate
"Obscenities of Green." [Electrum] (39) Fall-Wint 87, p. 43.
657. BRAVERMAN, Melanie
"Education." [Calyx] (11:1) Wint 87-88, p. 13.
"Etymon." [Calyx] (11:1) Wint 87-88, p. 14.

658. BRAXTON, Charlie R.
"Working the Nightshift" (At B.C. Roger's chicken plantation). [MinnR] (NS 28) Spr 87, p. 28-29.
659. BRAZIER, John
"The Disappearances of Guevara." [WestCR] (21:4) Spr 87, p. 23-26.
660. BREBNER, Diana
"All for the Burning Bodies." [Grain] (15:4) Wint 87, p. 22.
"The Dark Ages." [Grain] (15:4) Wint 87, p. 23.
"Laborare Est Orare." [AmerV] (9) Wint 87, p. 87.
"A Migratory Gift." [MalR] (80) S 87, p. 35.
"Pauper Sum Ego." [MalR] (80) S 87, p. 36.
"Pink Hearts with No Teeth." [Event] (16:1) Mr 87, p. 32.
661. BREEDEN, David
"Down at This End of the Ohio" (for Kevin). [MidAR] (7:2) 87, p. 30-31.
"Poem: Thermos, he says." [PoetL] (82:4) Wint 87-88, p. 223.
"Surprised at the Fading of a Memory." [MidAR] (7:2) 87, p. 32.
662. BREIT, Luke
"Sacramento." [Spirit] (8:2) 87, p. 256-257.
663. BRENNAN, Karen
"A Beautiful Way of Looking at Something Starts." [Ploughs] (13:4) 87, p. 24.
"The Black Puppy Story." [Ploughs] (13:4) 87, p. 25.
"Chaucer's Black Knight Is Still Weeping in the 14th Century." [Colum] (12) 87, p. 66.
"Rocketing Back and Forth the Rabbits." [SenR] (17:1) 87, p. 67.
664. BRENT, Frances Padorr
"I'll live through this, survive, and they'll ask me" (tr. of Irina Ratushinskaya, w. Carol Avins). [NewYRB] (34:8) 7 My 87, p. 19.
"Two Poems from Prison" (tr. of Irina Ratushinskaya, w. Carol Avins). [NewYRB] (34:8) 7 My 87, p. 19.
"Well, we'll live as the soul directs" (tr. of Irina Ratushinskaya, w. Carol Avins). [NewYRB] (34:8) 7 My 87, p. 19.
665. BRETT, Peter
"Ice Chunks (Gold Run, California)." [FloridaR] (15:1) Spr-Sum 87, p. 120.
"Manzanilla Heat." [Lactuca] (6) Ap-My 87, p. 17.
"Needles." [Lactuca] (6) Ap-My 87, p. 18.
"Walking at Dawn" (Farmington, N.M.). [Lactuca] (6) Ap-My 87, p. 16.
666. BREWER, Gay
"Everybody's with Sam Tonight." [Bogg] (57) 87, p. 60.
667. BREWER, Kenneth W.
"Letter to My Daughter." [KanQ] (19:1/2) Wint-Spr 87, p. 66-67.
668. BREWSTER, Elizabeth
"Fiction Class: Exercise One (with Credit to John Gardner)." [Event] (16:1) Mr 87, p. 70-71.
"Letter to T.S. Eliot." [Event] (16:1) Mr 87, p. 72-74.
"Metamorphosis." [Waves] (15:1/2) Fall 86, p. 62.
"Poems for Old Women" (Selections: 2, 4). [Waves] (15:1/2) Fall 86, p. 60-61.
669. BREWTON, Butler E.
"Full Measure." [Nimrod] (30:2) Spr-Sum 87, p. 42.
"Peach Orchard." [Nimrod] (30:2) Spr-Sum 87, p. 43.
670. BREWTON, Catherine
"My Father's Mistress." [CumbPR] (7:1) Fall 87, p. 55-56.
"A View of the Bay" (For Catrina). [ManhatPR] (9) Sum 87, p. 30-31.
BREYNER ANDRESEN, Sophia de Mello
See ANDRESEN, Sophia de Mello Breyner
671. BRICCETTI, Lee Ellen
"Sacred Heart." [AmerV] (9) Wint 87, p. 24.
672. BRIDGES, Lawrence
"Mail." [Outbr] (18/19) Fall 86-Spr 88, p. 128.
673. BRIDGFORD, Kim
"The Basics." [PoeticJ] (17) 87, p. 40.
"Leaf on Leaf." [BallSUF] (28:4) Aut 87, p. 11.
"Obsessions." [Event] (16:3) Fall 87, p. 85-87.
"This Light." [NewOR] (14:2) Sum 87, p. 16.
"The Way We See Planets." [Outbr] (18/19) Fall 86-Spr 88, p. 129.
674. BRIGHAM, Besmilr
"Accusation." [HangL] (50/51) 87, p. 26-27.

675. BRINGHURST, Robert
"Conversations with a Toad." [Descant] (59) Wint 87, p. 7-14.
"Parsvanatha." [Verse] (4:1) Mr 87, p. 14.
"Sengzhao." [Verse] (4:1) Mr 87, p. 15.
676. BROACH, Charlee Carter
"Generations." [Electrum] (39) Fall-Wint 87, p. 24.
677. BROADHEAD, Marlis Manley
"Last Rites of Spring." [WoosterR] (7) Spr 87, p. 80.
678. BROBST, Richard
"All Things Dance." [Pembroke] (19) 87, p. 145.
"Dreamscape." [Pembroke] (19) 87, p. 146.
679. BROCK, Randall
"Cold Fire." [Wind] (17:59) 87, p. 9.
"I Am." [Wind] (17:59) 87, p. 16.
"Solid." [Wind] (17:59) 87, p. 37.
680. BROCK-BROIDO, Lucie
"Autobiography." [Agni] (24/25) 87, p. 183.
"Birdie Africa." [NewL] (53:2) Wint 86-87, p. 9-11.
"Constellation of the Birds." [Agni] (24/25) 87, p. 186-187.
"Domestic Mysticism." [Ploughs] (13:1) 87, p. 22-23.
"Elective Mutes" (Winner, NER/BLQ Narrative Poetry Competition). [NewEngR]
(10:1) Aut 87, p. 3-7.
"I Think Deeply of Ruin." [Agni] (24/25) 87, p. 185.
"In the Economy of Diminishing Resources" (on attending a Tuesday colloquium,
Harvard Univ.). [NewL] (53:2) Wint 86-87, p. 5-7.
"A Little Piece of Everlasting Life." [Agni] (24/25) 87, p. 179.
"Magnum Mysterium." [Ploughs] (13:1) 87, p. 21.
"Noctilucent." [Agni] (24/25) 87, p. 184.
"Ohio & Beyond." [NewL] (53:2) Wint 86-87, p. 8.
"Put Your Little Shoes Away." [Agni] (24/25) 87, p. 180-182.
681. BROCKLEBANK, Ian
"The End of the Pony Express." [Bogg] (58) 87, p. 14.
682. BROCKLEY, Michael
"Goal." [BallSUF] (28:4) Aut 87, p. 32.
"Waitress." [BallSUF] (28:4) Aut 87, p. 19.
683. BRODETSKY, Martin
"All the Poets." [Bogg] (58) 87, p. 25.
684. BRODINE, Karen
"Letter from My Grandmother to My Mother" (Detroit, March 29, 1942). [Contact]
(9:44/45/46) Fall-Wint 87, p. 32.
"Letter from Myself to My Mother" (July 26, 1984). [Contact] (9:44/45/46) Fall-Wint
87, p. 33-34.
685. BRODKEY, Harold
"Between 6:37 PM and 9:04 PM." [NewYorker] (63:17) 15 Je 87, p. 32.
686. BRODSKY, Joseph
"The Belfast Tune." [NewYorker] (63:21) 13 Jl 87, p. 28.
"The Bust of Tiberius" (tr. by Alan Myers and the author). [NewYRB] (34:11) 25 Je
87, p. 18.
"Eclogue V: Summer" (tr. by the author and George L. Kline). [NewYorker] (63:24)
3 Ag 87, p. 22-24.
"The Fifth Anniversary." [Ploughs] (13:1) 87, p. 36-40.
"The Hawk's Cry in Autumn." [ParisR] (29:103) Sum 87, p. 30-33.
"In Memoriam." [NewYorker] (63:38) 9 N 87, p. 48.
"Kelomyakki." [NewYorker] (62:49) 26 Ja 87, p. 26-27.
"Lithuanian Nocturne: To Thomas Venclova." [Ploughs] (13:1) 87, p. 24-35.
"The New Jules Verne" (To Leo and Nina Loseff, tr. by the author). [PartR] (54:4)
Fall 87, p. 576-582.
"October Tune." [NewYorker] (63:33) 5 O 87, p. 38.
"Polonaise: a Variation." [NewYorker] (63:31) 21 S 87, p. 40.
"Slave, Come to My Service" (Dialogue between a master and his slave, 10th c. BC,
tr. from the Sumerian). [NewYRB] (34:18) 19 N 87, p. 23.
"To Urania" (I.K.). [ParisR] (29:103) Sum 87, p. 187.
687. BRODSKY, Louis Daniel
"Elementary Teacher" (For John Lents and Dr. Bill Hardin). [BallSUF] (28:4) Aut 87,
p. 31.

688. BRODY, Harry
    "Fields." [Raccoon] (24/25) My 87, p. 309-315.
    "The Gallery." [MidAR] (7:2) 87, p. 87.
BROIDO, Lucie Brock
    See BROCK-BROIDO, Lucie
689. BROMIGE, David
    "Lines." [Bound] (14:1/2) Fall 85-Wint 86 [c87], p. 69-71.
    "A Sense of Humor's Soliloquy." [NewAW] (1) 87, p. 77-78.
690. BROMLEY, Anne (Anne C.)
    "Anniversary in Your Absence." [PoetC] (18:3) Spr 87, p. 30.
    "Dusting His Mahogony Destk." [PoetC] (18:3) Spr 87, p. 29.
    "Mountain Temple." [ColR] (NS 14:2) Fall-Wint 87, p. 15.
    "The Scream of Water Enters Her Body" (Tsegi Canyon, the Navajo Nation). [ColR]
        (NS 14:2) Fall-Wint 87, p. 16-17.
    "Voice in the Bowl." [HolCrit] (24:3) Je 87, p. 18-19.
691. BROOK, Donna
    "Losing (Three Poems)." [HangL] (50/51) 87, p. 40-42.
    "The School of Pain." [Spirit] (8:2) 87, p. 280.
    "What Being Responsible Means to Me" (for my sister-in-law). [HangL] (50/51) 87,
        p. 43.
692. BROOKS, Alan
    "Poets in Spring." [BelPoJ] (37:3) Spr 87, p. 2.
693. BROOKS, Connie
    "Genesis." [Bogg] (58) 87, p. 24.
    "On Communicating." [Bogg] (57) 87, p. 27.
694. BROOKS, David
    "The Maps at Midnight." [WestB] (20) 87, p. 70.
    "Storing the Bulbs." [WestB] (20) 87, p. 68-69.
695. BROOKS, Gwendolyn
    "Winnie." [Poetry] (151:1/2) O-N 87, p. 20-21.
696. BROSMAN, Catharine Savage
    "Apples." [Interim] (6:1) Spr 87, p. 37.
697. BROSNAHAN, Nick
    "Sea of China" (Age 17). [PikeF] (8) Fall 87, p. 20.
698. BROSNAN, Michael
    "Birds in the Dark." [NewL] (54:2) Wint 87-88, p. 61-62.
    "Green." [NewL] (54:2) Wint 87-88, p. 60-61.
    "Phone Call." [NewL] (54:2) Wint 87-88, p. 57-59.
699. BROSSARD, Nicole
    "Polynesia of the Eyes." [Notus] (2:1) Spr 87, p. 7-16.
    "Polynésie des Yeux." [Notus] (2:1) Spr 87, p. 7-16.
700. BROST, Carole
    "Beyond Repair." [PraF] (8:1) Spr 87, p. 33.
    "Home." [Phoenix] (7:1) 87, p. 36.
    "Spring Is Born." [PraF] (8:1) Spr 87, p. 32.
701. BROUGHTON, T. Alan
    "Aeneas Through the Looking Glass." [Poetry] (149:5) F 87, p. 283-284.
    "Amish Market." [ThRiPo] (29/30) 87, p. 21.
    "Brook Changes." [CharR] (13:1) Spr 87, p. 92-93.
    "Family History." [DenQ] (22:1) Sum 87, p. 41-42.
    "Freeze." [SenR] (17:1) 87, p. 10-11.
    "Guardian of the Dump." [TexasR] (7:3/4) 87, p. 20-21.
    "Heroics." [Poetry] (149:5) F 87, p. 282.
    "Ice Fisher." [TexasR] (7:3/4) 87, p. 17-19.
    "Losing Argument." [FourQ] (1:1) Wint 87, p. 57.
    "Vacant Lot." [CharR] (13:1) Spr 87, p. 92.
    "The Woman Under Us." [ThRiPo] (29/30) 87, p. 19-20.
    "Writer at Work." [BelPoJ] (38:1) Fall 87, p. 2-3.
702. BROUMAS, Olga
    "Amazon Twins." [Calyx] (10:2/3) Spr 87, p. 156-157.
    "Bliss." [Calyx] (10:2/3) Spr 87, p. 235-236.
    "Evensong." [AmerV] (6) Spr 87, p. 10-12.
    "Exile." [NowestR] (25:3) 87, p. 276.
    "Eye of Heart." [AmerV] (8) Fall 87, p. 73-74.
    "Lying In." [Sonora] (13) Fall 87, p. 82-83.
    "Nikonos." [Sonora] (13) Fall 87, p. 85.

"Parity." [Sonora] (13) Fall 87, p. 84.
"Slow Birds." [Caliban] (2) 87, p. 81-82.
"Something Else." [Caliban] (2) 87, p. 82.
"Song / For Sanna." [Calyx] (10:2/3) Spr 87, p. 146-147.
"With God." [Caliban] (2) 87, p. 80.
703. BROUWER, Joel, II
"Recognition for an English Teacher's Son." [EngJ] (76:1) Ja 87, p. 50.
704. BROWN, Allan
"Eyes, the Dark." [Quarry] (36:1) Wint 87, p. 114.
"Pause." [Quarry] (36:1) Wint 87, p. 113.
705. BROWN, Ashley
"The Poet Thomas Hardy Speaks" (tr. of João Cabral de Melo Neto). [Verse] (4:3) N
87, p. 57.
706. BROWN, Betsy
"It Might Be Deep Blue." [ColEng] (49:7) N 87, p. 775.
"This Pulls on Choice." [Sonora] (12) Spr 87, p. 21-22.
707. BROWN, Bill
"The Right to Drown" (for Roger). [PassN] (8:1) Wint 87, p. 14.
"Sleep's Companions." [Vis] (23) 87, p. 39.
"Telling the Bees." [CumbPR] (6:2) Spr 87, p. 88.
"Traffic Salvation." [Vis] (24) 87, p. 37.
708. BROWN, D. F.
"For the Duration." [FiveFR] (5) 87, p. 14.
"Keeping Days and Numbers Together." [FiveFR] (5) 87, p. 12.
"Lawn." [FiveFR] (5) 87, p. 11.
"Twenty Lines." [FiveFR] (5) 87, p. 13.
709. BROWN, Derek
"A Kite." [Gambit] (20) 86, p. 45.
710. BROWN, George MacKay
"Shrove Tuesday." [Verse] (4:2) Je 87, p. 5-6.
711. BROWN, Jeffrey
"The Dog in Chains." [NewAW] (2) Fall 87, p. 90.
"Novel in Progress." [NewAW] (2) Fall 87, p. 91.
712. BROWN, Julie
"Still Swimming." [CimR] (79) Ap 87, p. 21-22.
713. BROWN, K. Margaret
"Untitled: There go the fences." [Kaleid] (15) Sum-Fall 87, p. 25.
"Untitled: They said the only way to go is up." [Kaleid] (15) Sum-Fall 87, p. 25.
714. BROWN, Lee Ann
"Prunes" (for C. D. Wright). [SouthernPR] (27:2) Fall 87, p. 56.
715. BROWN, LoVerne
"Amadeus." [LightY] '87, c86, p. 242.
716. BROWN, Melissa
"Trinity Street." [Ploughs] (13:4) 87, p. 26-27.
717. BROWN, Norman O.
"Homage to Robert Duncan" (Cleveland State Univ. Poetry Center Jubilation of Poets
Panel, 10/23/86). [Sulfur] (19) Spr 87, p. 11-23.
718. BROWN, Polly
"The Old Poet Walks Home with a New Goat." [BelPoJ] (37:4) Sum 87, p. 30-31.
719. BROWN, Robert
"New Moon." [Puerto] (22:2) Spr 87, p. 108.
720. BROWN, Simon
"Homo Superior." [Bogg] (58) 87, p. 49.
721. BROWN, Stephen Ford (Steven Ford)
"The Conformist" (tr. of Angel González, w. Pedro Gutierrez Revuelta). [CrossCur]
(7:3) 87, p. 33.
"Do You Know That Paper Can?" (tr. of Angel González, w. Pedro Gutierrez
Revuelta). [CrossCur] (7:3) 87, p. 32.
"Harp Boys." [PaintedB] (31) 87, p. 24.
"Love Poem." [PaintedB] (31) 87, p. 25-26.
"Man and Woman." [PaintedB] (31) 87, p. 24.
"Promise." [PaintedB] (31) 87, p. 27.
724. BROWN, Thomas J.
"The Competitor." [InterPR] (13:1) Spr 87, p. 97.

725. BROWN-DAVIDSON, Terri Lynette
    "Minot Train Station." [CentR] (31:3) Sum 87, p. 286.
726. BROWNE, Michael Dennis
    "His Toys." [LightY] '87, c86, p. 95.
    "Peter and Thunder." [TriQ] (68) Wint 87, p. 105.
    "Potatoes, October." [VirQR] (63:3) Sum 87, p. 449-450.
    "To My Wife in Time of War." [NowestR] (25:3) 87, p. 359-362.
    "What He Says." [TriQ] (68) Wint 87, p. 106.
    "Wind, Fourth of July." [VirQR] (63:3) Sum 87, p. 450-451.
727. BROX, Jane
    "First Night, Squam." [Hudson] (39:4) Wint 87, p. 616.
    "Squam." [Hudson] (39:4) Wint 87, p. 617.
728. BRUCE, Debra
    "After Dinner, She Discusses Marriage with Her Friends." [MassR] (28:1) Spr 87, p.
        43-44.
    "The Clock in the Museum." [PassN] (8:1) Wint 87, p. 15.
729. BRUCE, Lennart
    "Chinatown." [Margin] (3) Sum 87, p. 22-23.
    "Off the Record." [Margin] (3) Sum 87, p. 23.
    "On the Commuter Train." [Margin] (3) Sum 87, p. 19.
    "Speculation." [CrossCur] (7:1) 87, p. 120.
    "The Translation." [Margin] (3) Sum 87, p. 21.
    "Why All These Answers" (tr. of Claes Anderson). [CrossCur] (7:3) 87, p. 69.
730. BRUCHAC, Joseph
    "Directions." [RiverS] (23) 87, p. 29.
    "Fixing the Barn" (for Robert Morgan). [AmerV] (6) Spr 87, p. 92-93.
    "Pages." [RiverS] (24) 87, p. 51.
    "Seeing Animals." [RiverS] (23) 87, p. 28.
    "South Greenfield Road" (October 1984). [Raccoon] (24/25) My 87, p. 223-224.
    "Walking at Night in Slade Brook Swamp." [Lips] (13) 87, p. 46-47.
    "Wind in November at Saranac Lake Inn." [CrossCur] (7:2) 87, p. 61.
731. BRUCK, Edith
    "Equality, Father" (tr. by Ruth Feldman). [Spirit] (8:2) 87, p. 164-165.
732. BRUGALETTA, John J.
    "How Do You Like Monet?" [GreenfR] (14:3/4) Sum-Fall 87, p. 136.
    "A Lust for the Quaint Old Ways" (an acrostic). [LightY] '87, c86, p. 177.
    "An Ordinary Curtain Rod." [NegC] (7:3/4) 87, p. 163.
    "Photograph: Brown Thresher" (1986 Finalist, Eve of Saint Agnes Poetry
        Competition). [NegC] (7:1/2) 87, p. 172-173.
733. BRUMMELS, J. V.
    "A Cool Evening in September." [Iowa] (17:1) Wint 87, p. 4-5.
    "The Country Turns Inside Out." [WestB] (20) 87, p. 44-45.
    "Eulogy." [Iowa] (17:1) Wint 87, p. 2-4.
    "Rape." [WestB] (20) 87, p. 46.
    "Something for the Telling" (for Bob Carpenter). [Iowa] (17:1) Wint 87, p. 5-9.
734. BRUNK, Juanita
    "Leaving Crete." [AmerPoR] (16:1) Ja-F 87, p. 6.
    "Valentine." [AmerPoR] (16:5) S-O 87, p. 48.
BRUNT, H. L. van
    See Van BRUNT, Lloyd
BRUNT, Lloyd van
    See Van BRUNT, Lloyd
735. BRUSH, Thomas
    "Why I Won't Contribute to the Renovation of the Pike Place Market" (Seattle 1985).
        [IndR] (10:3) Spr 87, p. 33-34.
736. BRYAN, Sharon
    "Cinéma Verité." [QW] (24) Wint 87, p. 46-47.
    "The End of Rose's Streak." [MemphisSR] (8:1) Fall 87, p. 19.
    "Out of Mind." [MemphisSR] (8:1) Fall 87, p. 18.
    "Pictures of Nothing." [MemphisSR] (8:1) Fall 87, p. 20-21.
737. BRYANT, Ben
    "Vision" (For Nancy Green d. 1812, age 24). [BellArk] (3:1) Ja-F 87, p. 18.
738. BUCHANAN, Paul
    "A Father Considers His Infant Son." [Poem] (57) Mr 87, p. 36.
    "The Love of Motherhood" (For Her First Mother's Day). [Poem] (57) Mr 87, p. 37.

739. BUCK, Dan
    "In the Edge of My Eye." [Kaleid] (15) Sum-Fall 87, p. 37.
740. BUCKAWAY, Catherine M.
    "All the High Breaks of Noon." [Phoenix] (7:1) 87, p. 40.
741. BUCKHOLTS, Claudia
    "As Hitler Marches into the Sudetenland" (Prague, 1938). [ConnPR] (6:1) 87, p.
       38-39.
    "The Transfer of Populations." [MinnR] (NS 28) Spr 87, p. 20-21.
742. BUCKINGHAM, Hugh
    "The Unexploded Mine." [Stand] (28:1) Wint 86-87, p. 51.
743. BUCKLEY, Christopher
    "Blue Autumn" (Santa Barbara, 1986). [Poetry] (150:6) S 87, p. 311-314.
    "Clouds in Summer." [Poetry] (150:3) Je 87, p. 125-127.
    "Extempore" (5 poems). [IndR] (10:1/2) 87, p. 109-124.
    "Four Monologues on Klaus Schnitzer & Robert Sennhauser's . . . Photographs of
       Ellis Island." [OntR] (26) Spr-Sum 87, p. 41-49.
    "The Inverse Square Law of the Propagation of Light" (With apologies to Carl
       Sagan). [Poetry] (151:1/2) O-N 87, p. 22-23.
    "October Visiting: Fresno, 1985" (for Jon Veinberg). [QW] (25) Spr 87, p. 122-125.
    "Old Spanish Days — Santa Barbara, 1955." [PennR] (3:2) Fall-Wint 87, p. 70-71.
    "On the Eiffel Tower." [Poetry] (150:3) Je 87, p. 127-129.
    "Playing for Time" (for Gary Young). [Crazy] (33) Wint 87, p. 59-61.
    "To Giordano Bruno in the Campo di Fiori." [DenQ] (21:3) Wint 87, p. 53-56.
744. BUDENZ, Julia
    "In the Copernican system." [WilliamMR] (25) Spr 87, p. 41-47.
745. BUDY, Andrea Hollander
    "Trying to Explain" (1986 Finalist, Eve of Saint Agnes Poetry Competition). [NegC]
       (7:1/2) 87, p. 220.
746. BUETTNER, Shirley
    "Behind the Motherhouse." [CreamCR] (11:2/3) 87?, p. 60.
    "The Disarray That Trees Once Made." [Farm] (4:2) Spr-Sum 87, p. 75.
747. BUGEJA, Michael J.
    "Ars Poetica: In Defense of Matthew Arnold." [PikeF] (8) Fall 87, p. 38.
    "Dolphins." [GeoR] (41:4) Wint 87, p. 767-768.
    "Heresy." [AntR] (45:4) Fall 87, p. 442.
    "I Know." [NewEngR] (9:3) Spr 87, p. 328.
    "Justice, Divine or Otherwise" (for Rita). [KanQ] (19:1/2) Wint-Spr 87, p. 68.
    "Moon, Love: Whereof I Swear Never Again to Write." [NewEngR] (9:3) Spr 87, p.
       327.
    "Moral" (for William Stafford). [Amelia] (4:1/2, issue 9) 87, p. 67.
    "The Night That Should Have Been Ours." [PoetC] (18:2) Wint 87, p. 15.
    "Silence." [ManhatPR] (9) Sum 87, p. 64.
    "These Days, Even the Pond." [KanQ] (19:1/2) Wint-Spr 87, p. 68.
748. BUISSON, Justine
    "Chapman Field" (1986 Honorable Mention, Eve of Saint Agnes Poetry Competition).
       [NegC] (7:1/2) 87, p. 136.
749. BUKOWSKI, Charles
    "A Drawer of Fish." [NowestR] (25:3) 87, p. 45-47.
    "First Day, First Job." [SlipS] (7) 87, p. 24-26.
    "Funny Man." [Spirit] (8:2) 87, p. 78-79.
    "Going On." [WormR] (27:1, issue 105) 87, p. 36-37.
    "He's Probably Ripping and Tearing in Hell Right Now." [SlipS] (7) 87, p. 20.
    "How I Got Started." [WormR] (27:1, issue 105) 87, p. 38.
    "Looking for the Hit Man." [Raccoon] (24/25) My 87, p. 65-66.
    "A Magician, Gone." [SlipS] (7) 87, p. 21-23.
    "The Melt-Down." [Raccoon] (24/25) My 87, p. 67.
    "My Cat, the Writer." [Raccoon] (24/25) My 87, p. 62-64.
    "An Ordinary Poem of Mispent Feelings." [SlipS] (7) 87, p. 23.
    "Paris." [Gargoyle] (32/33) 87, p. 53.
    "Practice." [WormR] (27:1, issue 105) 87, p. 37-38.
    "Release." [WormR] (27:4, issue 108) 87, p. 117.
    "A Sensible Fellow." [SlipS] (7) 87, p. 26.
    "Speed!!!!!!!!!!!" [WormR] (27:4, issue 108) 87, p. 116.
750. BULLA, Hans Georg
    "Against Heaven" (tr. by D. H. Wilson and the author). [PoetL] (81:4) Wint 86-87, p.
       250.

"Back in Cellars" (tr. by D. H. Wilson and the author). [PoetL] (81:4) Wint 86-87, p. 244.

"Back to Happiness" (tr. by D. H. Wilson and the author). [PoetL] (81:4) Wint 86-87, p. 249.

"Dog-Paddle" (tr. by D. H. Wilson and the author). [PoetL] (81:4) Wint 86-87, p. 251.

"Father" (tr. by D. H. Wilson and the author). [PoetL] (81:4) Wint 86-87, p. 248.

"Father from the Tree" (tr. by D. H. Wilson and the author). [PoetL] (81:4) Wint 86-87, p. 247.

"Fresh Loam" (tr. by D. H. Wilson and the author). [PoetL] (81:4) Wint 86-87, p. 248.

"From Dernekamp" (tr. by D. H. Wilson and the author). [PoetL] (81:4) Wint 86-87, p. 252.

"From the Shore" (tr. by D. H. Wilson and the author). [PoetL] (81:4) Wint 86-87, p. 249.

"Greetings to Rafael Alberti" (tr. by D. H. Wilson and the author). [PoetL] (81:4) Wint 86-87, p. 246.

"Landscape with Feather" (tr. by D. H. Wilson and the author). [PoetL] (81:4) Wint 86-87, p. 243.

"Late Ice" (tr. by D. H. Wilson and the author). [PoetL] (81:4) Wint 86-87, p. 244.

"Night Return" (tr. by D. H. Wilson and the author). [PoetL] (81:4) Wint 86-87, p. 247.

"Night Train" (tr. by D. H. Wilson and the author). [PoetL] (81:4) Wint 86-87, p. 245.

"The Old Man" (tr. by D. H. Wilson and the author). [PoetL] (81:4) Wint 86-87, p. 246.

"Snowfall" (tr. by D. H. Wilson and the author). [PoetL] (81:4) Wint 86-87, p. 252.

"Through the Village" (tr. by D. H. Wilson and the author). [PoetL] (81:4) Wint 86-87, p. 243.

"Toads on the March" (tr. by D. H. Wilson and the author). [PoetL] (81:4) Wint 86-87, p. 245.

"Village End" (tr. by D. H. Wilson and the author). [PoetL] (81:4) Wint 86-87, p. 250.

"The Wicked Village" (tr. by D. H. Wilson and the author). [PoetL] (81:4) Wint 86-87, p. 251.

751. BULLIS, Jerald
"Consolation." [SouthernHR] (21:4) Fall 87, p. 358.
"This & That." [SouthernHR] (21:2) Spr 87, p. 146.

752. BULLOCK, Michael
"The Grey Fleece." [CanLit] (115) Wint 87, p. 106.

753. BUNN, David
"Lovesong After the Music of K. E. Ntsane" (tr. of Antjie Krog, w. Jane Taylor and the author). [TriQ] (69) Spr-Sum 87, p. 334-335.
"Poem: The storm troopers are in the streets" (tr. of Hein Willemse, w. the author). [TriQ] (69) Spr-Sum 87, p. 180-181.

754. BURCH, F. F.
"In a Station of the IRT." [LightY] '87, c86, p. 31.

755. BURD, Cindy
"From the Fisherman I Learn." [US1] (20/21) Wint 86-87, p. 10.

756. BURDEN, Jean
"Against the Night" (for Father Raymond Roseliep). [GeoR] (41:2) Sum 87, p. 364.

BURESH, Anne Squire
See SQUIRE-BURESH, Anne

757. BURGESS, Puanani
"The 'Ahu." [BambooR] (36) Fall 87, p. 80.
"Pono'i Hawai'i." [BambooR] (36) Fall 87, p. 75-79.

758. BURGESS, Richard A., II
"A Day at the Beach" (Age 11). [PikeF] (8) Fall 87, p. 20.

759. BURGGRAF, Linda Parsons
"All Other Ground" (For A.C.). [InterPR] (13:1) Spr 87, p. 94-95.
"Exile." [InterPR] (13:1) Spr 87, p. 95-96.

760. BURGHARDT, John
"Dr. Ruth Reingold Descends the Stairs." [BelPoJ] (37:4) Sum 87, p. 6-8.
"Learning to See." [BelPoJ] (37:4) Sum 87, p. 6.

761. BURGOS, Julia de
"Nada." [StoneC] (14:3/4) Spr-Sum 87, p. 36.

"Nothingness" (tr. by Maria Bennett). [StoneC] (14:3/4) Spr-Sum 87, p. 37.
762. BURKARD, Michael
"Bay Window." [Pequod] (23/24) 87, p. 190.
"Behind the Rain." [DevQ] (21:2) Fall 86, p. 6-7.
"Lament upon Hearing of a Wedding." [Pequod] (23/24) 87, p. 189.
"Night Fog." [Pequod] (23/24) 87, p. 188.
"A Series of Judgments." [ParisR] (29:105) Wint 87, p. 99.
"Two Chimneys." [NewL] (53:3) Spr 87, p. 96-97.
763. BURKE, Anne
"Look Homeward, Angel" (an irreverent look at grants). [CrossC] (9:3/4) 87, p. 29.
764. BURKE, Brian
"Baked Beans." [AntigR] (71/72) Aut 87-Wint 88, p. 203.
"Mound Presence." [AntigR] (71/72) Aut 87-Wint 88, p. 202.
765. BURKE, Daniel
"The Writing Teacher." [FourQ] (1:1) Wint 87, p. 59.
766. BURKETT, Thomas D.
"Blackberries." [PoetL] (82:3) Fall 87, p. 147.
"Moving Targets." [SoDakR] (25:3) Aut 87, p. 45.
"Virginia Suburb Blues." [PoetL] (82:3) Fall 87, p. 146.
767. BURKIN, Ivan
"How the Hours Talk to Each Other" (from "God May Be Around," tr. of Aleksandr
Vvedensky). [FiveFR] (5) 87, p. 25-26.
768. BURLINGAME, Robert
"Birds That Burn." [HighP] (2:3) Wint 87, p. 282.
"Words on the Tree Named Madrone" (For Del). [HighP] (2:3) Wint 87, p. 283-284.
769. BURN, Skye
"Home Birth." [BellArk] (3:2) Mr-Ap 87, p. 10.
"Through the Crib Slats." [BellArk] (3:2) Mr-Ap 87, p. 10.
770. BURNETT, David
"Thais" (Selection: IV). [Margin] (2) Spr 87, p. 76.
"Thais" (Selections: XXX, XXXV). [Margin] (2) Spr 87, p. 97.
771. BURNETT, Maud (Maud Gwynn)
"After Closing Time." [Witness] (1:2) Sum 87, p. 18.
"Culta Inculta." [Witness] (1:2) Sum 87, p. 17-18.
"The Necropolis at St. Pierre L'Estrier." [Descant] (59) Wint 87, p. 15.
"The Necropolis at St. Pierre L'Estrier." [Witness] (1:2) Sum 87, p. 16.
"Sapphics (More or Less)." [Descant] (59) Wint 87, p. 17.
"The Seventh Wave." [Descant] (59) Wint 87, p. 16.
772. BURNEY, Jeanette
"After the Birth" (for Allison). [AntigR] (69/70) 87, p. 24-25.
773. BURNHAM, Deborah
"Calling My Daughter." [NegC] (7:1/2) 87, p. 62.
"Fire in the Onion field." [WestB] (20) 87, p. 48.
"Persons from Porlock." [NegC] (7:1/2) 87, p. 63.
"Shooting a Woodchuck." [Farm] (4:2) Spr-Sum 87, p. 11.
774. BURNS, Gerald
"A Chain for Madeleine." [Temblor] (5) 87, p. 94-96.
"Clarke on the Fo'c'sle, to Him, Burns." [Sulfur] (20) Fall 87, p. 145-147.
775. BURNS, Michael
"An Apology and a Kind of Prayer" (for R.S., 1950-1984). [KanQ] (19:3) Sum 87,
p. 226.
"The Local News." [Farm] (4:2) Spr-Sum 87, p. 73.
776. BURNS, Nancy
"April." [Wind] (17:59) 87, p. 2.
"Indian Summer" (for Cathy). [Wind] (17:59) 87, p. 2-3.
777. BURNS, Richard
"Austin Mini" (tr. of Radomiro Spotorno). [Margin] (1) Wint 86, p. 52-53.
"The Manager" (Excerpts). [AnotherCM] (17) 87, p. 7-12.
"The Manager" (Selections). [Margin] (2) Spr 87, p. 44-56.
778. BURNS, Robert
"The Many Worlds of the Wide-Eyed Future Made Clear." [WritersF] (13) Fall 87, p.
120.
"Sign of the Cross." [WritersF] (13) Fall 87, p. 119.
779. BURNS, William
"Alice, Parkinsonian." [Interim] (6:2) Fall 87, p. 25.
"Else's." [Interim] (6:2) Fall 87, p. 28.

"Haven House, Pasadena" (A Temporary Refuge for Families of Violent Alcoholics). [Interim] (6:2) Fall 87, p. 26.
"Maneuvers Ago." [Interim] (6:2) Fall 87, p. 27.
"Pulse." [Interim] (6:2) Fall 87, p. 27.
780. BUROKAS, Cecelia
"Ancient Music" (tr. of Cecilia Meireles). [ColR] (NS 14:1) Spr-Sum 87, p. 36.
781. BURRIS, Sidney
"Very True Confessions." [Poetry] (149:6) Mr 87, p. 330-331.
782. BURRITT, Mary
"Flight." [Raccoon] (24/25) My 87, p. 307.
"From the Poem of Houses." [Raccoon] (24/25) My 87, p. 297.
783. BURROUGHS, E. G.
"Misadventure." [PaintedB] (30) 87, p. 75.
784. BURROUGHS, J. Robert
"Romancing the Cove." [Pembroke] (19) 87, p. 169.
785. BURROWS, E. G.
"First Mate." [BelPoJ] (37:4) Sum 87, p. 15.
"Tacoma Downtime." [Ascent] (12:2) 87, p. 11-14.
786. BURRS, Mick
"Simple Journeys to Other Planets." [Grain] (15:2) Sum 87, p. 20.
787. BURSK, C. (See also BURSK, Christopher)
"Adjusting." [US1] (20/21) Wint 86-87, p. 5.
788. BURSK, Christopher (See also BURSK, C.)
"The Museum of Fine Arts." [Poetry] (151:1/2) O-N 87, p. 23-24.
"Third Person Singular." [MassR] (28:4) Wint 87, p. 717-722.
789. BURTON, Sue D.
"Margaret Bope Perkins." [Phoenix] (7:1) 87, p. 24-25.
"The Millet Poem." [SinW] (31) 87, p. 84-86.
790. BUSAILAH, Reja-e
"At the Battlefront." [InterPR] (13:1) Spr 87, p. 104.
"The Miracle." [InterPR] (13:1) Spr 87, p. 105.
791. BUSCH, Trent
"Clytemnestra at the Palace Wall." [Hudson] (40:3) Aut 87, p. 446-447.
"The Descent." [SoDakR] (25:2) Sum 87, p. 85.
"Europa Perceived: Young Man Without a Name." [InterPR] (13:2) Fall 87, p. 96.
"Forget Horses." [InterPR] (13:2) Fall 87, p. 94.
"Hands." [ConnPR] (6:1) 87, p. 29-30.
"The Hollow." [Abraxas] (35/36) 87, p. 74.
"The Hound at the Gate." [PraS] (61:4) Wint 87, p. 15-16.
"Lookout Point." [InterPR] (13:2) Fall 87, p. 95.
"Promises Not Promises." [SouthwR] (72:2) Spr 87, p. 246.
"Pupils of Discipline." [Interim] (6:2) Fall 87, p. 8.
"Summer Day." [Confr] (35/36) Spr-Fall 87, p. 240.
"This Day." [Interim] (6:2) Fall 87, p. 7.
"Trolls." [Interim] (6:2) Fall 87, p. 9.
792. BUSH, Duncan
"Coming Back." [SouthernR] (23:3) Jl 87, p. 615-618.
"The News of Patroclus." [SouthernR] (23:3) Jl 87, p. 614.
793. BUSHELLE, David
"All the Days Come Fast." [StoneC] (14:3/4) Spr-Sum 87, p. 71.
794. BUSHKOWSKY, Aaron
"Another Way We Remember." [PraF] (8:1) Spr 87, p. 17.
"At Bay." [AntigR] (69/70) 87, p. 49.
"Dusting." [AntigR] (69/70) 87, p. 48.
"E i e i o." [AntigR] (69/70) 87, p. 51-52.
"The Fabled Wind." [AntigR] (69/70) 87, p. 52-53.
"Part About Parting." [PraF] (8:1) Spr 87, p. 18.
"The Same Wait." [AntigR] (69/70) 87, p. 50-51.
"She Insisted She Wasn't." [PraF] (8:1) Spr 87, p. 16.
"Untitled: We are serious the trees insist." [PraF] (8:1) Spr 87, p. 19.
795. BUSTAMANTE, Cecilia
"Camino Real." [LetFem] (13:1/2) Primavera-Ontoño 87, p. 117.
"Cuánto Te Amara." [LetFem] (13:1/2) Primavera-Ontoño 87, p. 117-118.
"Premio Nobel de la Paz a Madre Teresa." [LetFem] (13:1/2) Primavera-Ontoño 87, p. 116.
"Si Será la Paz." [LetFem] (13:1/2) Primavera-Ontoño 87, p. 115.

796. BUTCHER, Grace
"Another Year, Another Festive Season." [Gambit] (20) 86, p. 87.
"Double Dutch." [Gambit] (20) 86, p. 89-90.
"How, in Darkness, the Runner Feels Invisible." [Northeast] (Ser. 4:5) Sum 87, p. 19.
"I Am More Comfortable with Fierce Things." [SouthernPR] (27:2) Fall 87, p. 39.
"My Mother and the Bums." [Gambit] (20) 86, p. 88.
"On Falling." [CumbPR] (6:2) Spr 87, p. 34-35.
"Playing Statues." [Northeast] (Ser. 4:5) Sum 87, p. 20.
"Saving All Questions Till the End." [Gambit] (20) 86, p. 86.
"Voyage Using an Ancient Map." [WestB] (20) 87, p. 24-25.
797. BUTKIE, Joseph
"Waiting Room Meditation." [Amelia] (4:1/2, issue 9) 87, p. 81.
"With AIDS." [JamesWR] (5:1) Fall 87, p. 10.
798. BUTLER, Jack
"A Way with Words." [PoetryNW] (28:3) Aut 87, p. 27-28.
799. BUTLER, Lynne
"The Daily News." [Outbr] (18/19) Fall 86-Spr 88, p. 154.
"The Dream Thief." [SouthernPR] (27:2) Fall 87, p. 53.
"Hearts and Flowers." [BelPoJ] (37:4) Sum 87, p. 8.
"The Man Who Said Be Patient." [CapeR] (22:2) Fall 87, p. 24.
"The Professor Speaks of Tragedy." [CapeR] (22:2) Fall 87, p. 25.
"Sleeper." [SouthernPR] (27:2) Fall 87, p. 52.
800. BUTOR, Michel
"Laundry for Marie-Jo" (tr. by Karlis Racevskis). [AntR] (45:3) Sum 87, p. 286-290.
801. BUTTERFIELD, Martha
"Inuit Woman." [Quarry] (36:4) Fall 87, p. 70.
"Monarch." [Quarry] (36:4) Fall 87, p. 69-70.
802. BUTTERICK, George
"More Repartee with the Mummy." [NewAW] (1) 87, p. 70-73.
"Repartee with the Mummy" (Excerpts). [Sulfur] (19) Spr 87, p. 78-80.
"Repeatedly." [Sulfur] (19) Spr 87, p. 80-81.
803. BUTTS, Bill
"Clerihew for Wystan Hugh." [HolCrit] (24:2) Ap 87, p. 12.
804. BYER, Kathryn Stripling
"Burning Wing Gap." [CarolQ] (39:3) Spr 87, p. 83.
"Queen Anne's Lace." [CrescentR] (5:1) 87, p. 84.
"Wildwood Flower" (Selections: 12 poems, Dedicated to Lee Smith). [Nimrod] (31:1) Fall-Wint 87, p. 42-53.
805. BYERLY, Alison
"Poem (Revised)." [NegC] (7:1/2) 87, p. 90.
806. BYERS, Eleanor
"Summer with Foxglove." [CrabCR] (4:3) Sum 87, p. 26.
807. BYRKIT, Rebecca
"The Effluvial Mood." [Ploughs] (13:4) 87, p. 28.
808. BYRNE, Edward
"In Your Memory, We Move." [BlackWR] (13:2) Spr 87, p. 34.
"Words Spoken, Words Unspoken." [BlackWR] (13:2) Spr 87, p. 32-33.
809. BYRNE, Edward R., Jr.
"A Dream." [ArizQ] (43:3) Aut 87, p. 276.
810. BYRNE, Elenakarina
"The Possibility of War" (For Stephen). [CalQ] (30) Wint 87, p. 31.
811. BYRNES, Fred
"Published." [MoodySI] (18/19) Fall 87, p. 43.
812. BYRON, Catherine
"Pattern Day." [MalR] (79) Je 87, p. 70-76.
813. CABESTANH, Guilhem de
"Lo Dous Cossire Que'm Don' Amors Soven" (tr. by Paul Backburn). [NewAW] (2) Fall 87, p. 55-57.
CABRAL DE MELO NETO, João
See NETO, João Cabral de Melo
814. CADDELL, Marsha
"Dragon Wings" (for Renée). [GreensboroR] (40) Sum 86, p. 118.
815. CADER, Teresa
"Open Letter to the Polish Government, 1986: On the Subject of Putting Highways through Cemeteries." [Ploughs] (13:1) 87, p. 41-42.

"Return to Poland" (1986 Finalist, Eve of Saint Agnes Poetry Competition). [NegC] (7:1/2) 87, p. 223-224.
"Unanswered Questions" (for my grandparents, Poland, 1914. Finalist, Eve of St. Agnes Competition). [NegC] (7:1/2) 87, p. 221-222.
816. CADNUM, Michael
"Abandoned Slaughterhouse." [Footwork] 87, p. 25.
"Cities on the Other side of the World." [StoneC] (15:1/2) Fall-Wint 87-88, p. 72.
"Columbus Leaves the New World for the Last Time." [Wind] (17:59) 87, p. 4-5.
"Driving Through the Desert." [WritersF] (13) Fall 87, p. 175.
"Exile." [BelPoJ] (37:3) Spr 87, p. 20-21.
"Feeding Geese." [GeoR] (41:3) Fall 87, p. 530-531.
"The Guava Garden at Lahainaluna." [PoetryNW] (28:2) Sum 87, p. 12-13.
"House-Sitting During the Festival of Angels." [PoetryNW] (28:2) Sum 87, p. 13-14.
"It's Not the Heat." [PoetryNW] (28:2) Sum 87, p. 11-12.
"The Little House Made of Food." [MidwQ] (29:1) Aut 87, p. 71-72.
"Napa: August." [SouthernHR] (21:3) Sum 87, p. 244.
"A Painting by Patinir." [IndR] (10:3) Spr 87, p. 84.
"Prairie." [WritersF] (13) Fall 87, p. 174.
"Sunbathing in Winter." [PoetC] (18:2) Wint 87, p. 20.
"Two Hundred Miles Before Breakfast." [Wind] (17:59) 87, p. 4.
"Vacation Coup." [PoetryNW] (28:2) Sum 87, p. 10-11.
"Waiting for the Detective." [LightY] '87, c86, p. 57.
CAEIRO, Alberto
  See PESSOA, Fernando
817. CAFAGNA, Marcus
"The Other World." [NegC] (7:3/4) 87, p. 94.
818. CAIN, Michael Scott
"Melanie, Harborplace, 1987." [CapeR] (22:2) Fall 87, p. 38.
819. CAINE, Shulamith Wechter
"Aubade" (The Greensboro Review Literary Award, Honorable Mention). [GreensboroR] (43) Wint 87-88, p. 38.
"Scar." [SouthernPR] (27:2) Fall 87, p. 38.
820. CAIRNS, Barbara
"The Magician Lectures." [ThRiPo] (29/30) 87, p. 22-23.
"Memory." [ThRiPo] (29/30) 87, p. 24.
"Settling a New House." [TarPR] (27:1) Fall 87, p. 29-30.
821. CAIRNS, Scott
"Acts." [NewRep] (197:26) 28 D 87, p. 42.
"Archaeology: The First Lecture." [TexasR] (8:1/2) Spr-Sum 87, p. 32.
"In Praise of Darkness." [NewRep] (197:15) 12 O 87, p. 40.
"A Lost City for Calvino." [DenQ] (21:3) Wint 87, p. 91-93.
"Memory." [QW] (25) Spr 87, p. 126.
822. CAJINA-VEGA, Mario
"The Old Poet" (a map poem of Nicaragua, tr. by Richard Elman). [Witness] (1:4) Wint 87, p. 76-77.
823. CALABRESE, John Michael
"Camouflage." [ManhatPR] (9) Sum 87, p. 32.
824. CALBERT, Cathleen
"Exercise." [Shen] (37:4) 87, p. 40-41.
"For Darwin." [PoetryNW] (28:2) Sum 87, p. 31-32.
"The Vampire Baby." [PoetryNW] (28:2) Sum 87, p. 30-31.
825. CALDERON, Enriqueta
"Antes de Irme." [LetFem] (13:1/2) Primavera-Ontoño 87, p. 119.
"Comienzo a Despedirme." [LetFem] (13:1/2) Primavera-Ontoño 87, p. 119-120.
"En la Sombra." [LetFem] (13:1/2) Primavera-Ontoño 87, p. 119.
"Sueños." [LetFem] (13:1/2) Primavera-Ontoño 87, p. 120.
826. CALIBAN
"Afterthoughts." [Caliban] (2) 87, p. 165.
827. CALMAN, Nancy Harris
"The Woman Who Sells Cross-Stitch Supplies" (1987 Ratner-Ferber-Poet Lore Honorable Mention). [PoetL] (82:2) Sum 87, p. 87-88.
828. CALVERT, Laura
"Night." [KanQ] (19:1/2) Wint-Spr 87, p. 219.
829. CAMBRONNE, Tom
"A Monologue Before Sleep." [JamesWR] (4:3) Spr 87, p. 12.
"A Sheltered Man." [NoAmR] (272:3) S 87, p. 92.

830. CAMERON, Juan
"O" (from "Apuntes," tr. by Cola Franzen). [Rampike] (5:3) 87, p. 41.
831. CAMILLE, Pamela
"For My Man with the Grey Swirlies in His Beard." [CrossCur] (6:5) 87, p. 110.
"Freedom and Light." [CrossCur] (6:5) 87, p. 39.
"One of the Seven Deadlies." [CrossCur] (6:5) 87, p. 82-83.
832. CAMP, James
"The Dinosaurs" (For those who perished under the volcano). [OP] (final issue) Sum
87, p. 72.
"From an Athlete Living Old." [LightY] '87, c86, p. 28.
"Mary's Color." [OP] (final issue) Sum 87, p. 70-71.
"A Note Toward a Definition of Culture." [LightY] '87, c86, p. 211.
"The Race." [LightY] '87, c86, p. 132-133.
"The Rose and the Worm." [LightY] '87, c86, p. 209.
"Waterbugs and Politicos." [OP] (final issue) Sum 87, p. 71.
833. CAMPBELL, Anneke
"Cutting the Body Loose." [SouthernR] (23:4) O 87, p. 832-835.
"Echoes." [SouthernR] (23:4) O 87, p. 831-832.
"Quarry." [SouthernR] (23:4) O 87, p. 830.
834. CAMPBELL, Carolyn E.
"A Proper Tea." [Bogg] (58) 87, p. 23-24.
835. CAMPBELL, Don
"San Gabriel" (with thanks to Henri Coulette and William Carlos Williams). [SmPd]
(24:2) Spr 87, p. 21.
836. CAMPBELL, Joan
"Boats Out of Water." [MSS] (5:3) 87, p. 132.
"Tryptich." [OhioR] (39) 87, p. 106-107.
837. CAMPBELL, Kevin
"Fogbound." [Margin] (5) Wint 87-88, p. 64.
838. CAMPBELL, Mark
"The Image" (Age 10). [PikeF] (8) Fall 87, p. 21.
"The Keeper of All Secrets" (Age 10). [PikeF] (8) Fall 87, p. 21.
839. CAMPBELL, Nicholas
"Astronomer." [CrossCur] (7:1) 87, p. 95.
"Littoral." [Waves] (15:3) Wint 87, p. 66.
840. CAMPBELL, Robin
"Blue Table / Stay Cool." [PaintedB] (30) 87, p. 35.
"Let." [PaintedB] (30) 87, p. 35.
841. CAMPION, Dan
"Dreams Are of the Body." [Caliban] (2) 87, p. 53.
"The Red Pencil." [Caliban] (2) 87, p. 54.
"The Veil." [PoetL] (81:3) Fall 86, p. 199.
842. CAMPO PÉREZ, Rebeca
"Among the Ashes" (tr. by Susan Schreibman). [InterPR] (13:1) Spr 87, p. 53.
"Entre las Cenizas." [InterPR] (13:1) Spr 87, p. 52.
"If There Were a Whiteness" (tr. by Susan Schreibman). [InterPR] (13:1) Spr 87, p.
51.
"Nightdreams" (tr. by Susan Schreibman). [InterPR] (13:1) Spr 87, p. 51.
"Si Hubiera una Blancura." [InterPR] (13:1) Spr 87, p. 50.
"Sueños de Noche." [InterPR] (13:1) Spr 87, p. 50.
CAMPOS, Alvaro de
See PESSOA, Fernando
843. CANALES, Jaque
"Un trono que se oculta." [Mairena] (9:24) 87, p. 116.
844. CANDELARIA, Fred
"Honest Man" (for Ronald Reagan). [AntigR] (69/70) 87, p. 127.
845. CANIZARO, Vincent, Jr.
"Autumn Wind." [BallSUF] (28:4) Aut 87, p. 48.
"Islam." [CrossCur] (6:5) 87, p. 11.
"Rain Moth." [BallSUF] (28:4) Aut 87, p. 54.
"Wings." [BallSUF] (28:4) Aut 87, p. 40.
846. CANNON, Maureen
"Sponge." [LightY] '87, c86, p. 137.
847. CANTRELL, Charles
"Zymurgy." [SoCaR] (19:2) Spr 87, p. 39.

848. CANTWELL, Kevin
"Color and Chance in the Experimental Garden." [Shen] (37:4) 87, p. 33-35.
"In a Field of Lanterns." [Puerto] (22:2) Spr 87, p. 42.
849. CANZONERI, Robert
"Syntax." [LightY] '87, c86, p. 220.
850. CARB, Alison B.
"The Daughter Makes Dinner for Her Boyfriend." [Amelia] (4:1/2, issue 9) 87, p. 125.
CARBEAU, Mitchell les
See LesCARBEAU, Mitchell
851. CARDENAL, Ernesto
"From Nicaragua, with Love: Poems 1979-1986" (Selections: 4 poems, tr. by Jonathan Cohen). [Trans] (18) Spr 87, p. 246-253.
"Psalm 5" (tr. by Nathaniel Smith). [InterPR] (13:1) Spr 87, p. 11.
"Salmo 5." [InterPR] (13:1) Spr 87, p. 10.
"Tahirassawichi in Washington" (tr. by Steven F. White). [Spirit] (8:2) 87, p. 244-246.
852. CARDILLO, Joe
"The Book of Jonysha." [Lactuca] (7) Ag 87, p. 29-34.
"Desire Was a Gift from the Dead." [Lactuca] (7) Ag 87, p. 36.
"Her Children." [Lactuca] (5) Ja 87, p. 33.
"Making Love." [Lactuca] (5) Ja 87, p. 32.
"Most of All." [Lactuca] (5) Ja 87, p. 31.
"Noa." [Lactuca] (7) Ag 87, p. 34-35.
"Old Man." [Lactuca] (5) Ja 87, p. 31-32.
"Outside the Wind." [Lactuca] (5) Ja 87, p. 34.
"Psalm for the Pagan Christian, the Barbaric Jew." [Lactuca] (5) Ja 87, p. 29-30.
"She Enters the Dark." [Lactuca] (7) Ag 87, p. 37.
"Something Inside Us Waits." [Lactuca] (7) Ag 87, p. 36.
"This morning, the wind is full." [Lactuca] (7) Ag 87, p. 36.
"Wanting So Much, So Close." [Lactuca] (7) Ag 87, p. 37.
853. CARDOZO, Manoel
"Epura" (tr. of Ronald de Carvalho). [Vis] (24) 87, p. 14.
854. CARDOZO, Nancy
"At the Open Air Market: Eurydice Lost." [RiverS] (23) 87, p. 64.
"Dead of Winter" (for Anna Daria — aged six). [Hudson] (39:4) Wint 87, p. 613.
855. CAREY, Barbara
"Afraid of the Dark." [PraF] (8:1) Spr 87, inside back cover.
"In the Garden for the Last Time." [CrossC] (9:1) 87, p. 21.
"Why Gray." [Waves] (15:1/2) Fall 86, p. 89.
856. CAREY, John
"Cook Book" (7 poems, tr. of Teresa de Jesús). [MinnR] (NS 29) Fall 87, p. 7-15.
857. CAREY, Michael A.
"Driving Home, the Essentials." [LaurelR] (21:1/2) Wint-Sum 87, p. 42.
"The Naming of Trees." [CapeR] (22:2) Fall 87, p. 12.
"Weather Report." [LaurelR] (21:1/2) Wint-Sum 87, p. 43.
"The Wild Place." [ColR] (NS 14:2) Fall-Wint 87, p. 32.
"Winter Chores: December 25, 1986." [SpoonRQ] (12:2) Spr 87, p. 44.
CARIÑO, Maria Luisa Aquilar
See AQUILAR-CARIÑO, Maria Luisa
858. CARIS, Jane Godard
"Best Burn a Dry, Old Love." [CrescentR] (5:1) 87, p. 111.
"Like Shafts of Wheat Gone Wild." [CrescentR] (5:1) 87, p. 110.
859. CARLILE, Henry
"Another Low Dishonest Decade." [AmerPoR] (16:5) S-O 87, p. 27.
"Desire." [AmerPoR] (16:5) S-O 87, p. 27.
"Hugo." [Poetry] (151:1/2) O-N 87, p. 24-25.
860. CARLSON, Barbara Siegel
"A Poem Without Loss." [Outbr] (18/19) Fall 86-Spr 88, p. 103-104.
861. CARLSON, Michael
"The Goodbye Look." [MissR] (15:3, issue 45) Spr-Sum 87, p. 85.
862. CARLSON, R. S.
"O What'll We Do When the Virgins Are Gone?" [Amelia] (4:1/2, issue 9) 87, p. 66-67.
"Tommy Akmitaluk." [TexasR] (8:1/2) Spr-Sum 87, p. 75.

863. CARLSON, Robert
"Photo ca. 1900." [InterPR] (13:1) Spr 87, p. 93.
865. CARLSON, Tom (Thomas C.)
"Adolescents on the Sea" (tr. of Nichita Stanescu, w. Vasile Poenaru). [LitR] (30:4)
Sum 87, p. 589.
"Autumn Twilight" (tr. of Nichita Stanescu, w. Vasile Poenaru). [LitR] (30:4) Sum
87, p. 588.
"Distance" (tr. of Nichita Stanescu, w. Vasile Poenaru). [LitR] (30:4) Sum 87, p.
588.
"The Market" (tr. of Vasile Poenaru). [Raccoon] (24/25) My 87, p. 294.
"Ninth Elegy: Of the Egg" (tr. of Nichita Stanescu, w. Vasile Poenaru). [Raccoon]
(24/25) My 87, p. 106-107.
"Second Elegy: The Ghetica" (for Vasile Parvan, tr. of Nichita Stanescu). [BlueBldgs]
(10) 87?, p. 37.
"Song" (tr. of Nichita Stanescu, w. Vasile Poenaru). [LitR] (30:4) Sum 87, p. 589.
"Unwords" (tr. of Nichita Stanescu, w. Vasile Poenaru). [Raccoon] (24/25) My 87,
p. 105.
867. CARPATHIOS, Neil
"By the Iowa River." [KanQ] (19:3) Sum 87, p. 292-293.
"Those Nights." [StoneC] (15:1/2) Fall-Wint 87-88, p. 38.
868. CARPENTER, Carol
"The Farthest House." [CapeR] (22:1) Spr 87, p. 22.
"A Still Shot." [CapeR] (22:1) Spr 87, p. 21.
869. CARPENTER, J. D.
"Profiles." [Waves] (15:1/2) Fall 86, p. 88.
870. CARPENTER, Lucas
"Kid Pictures." [BelPoJ] (38:2) Wint 87-88, p. 12.
871. CARPER, Thomas
"The Abductors." [Poetry] (150:3) Je 87, p. 137.
"The Attraction." [Poetry] (150:3) Je 87, p. 137-138.
"Burning Her Past." [Poetry] (150:3) Je 87, p. 139.
"A Farmstead with a Hayrick and Weirs Beside a Stream" (Rembrandt Poems).
[AmerS] (56:3) Sum 87, p. 399.
"Play on a French Beach." [Poetry] (150:3) Je 87, p. 138.
"Rembrandt Prepares for a Walk along the Amstel River" (Rembrandt Poems).
[AmerS] (56:3) Sum 87, p. 398.
872. CARR, Dan
"Light Moving Under Clouds." [ConnPR] (6:1) 87, p. 35.
873. CARRACINO, Nicholas
"Long Time." [Footwork] 87, p. 40.
874. CARREGA, Gordon
"Loss of Face." [FiveFR] (5) 87, p. 91.
"Phone Call at Three A.M." [FiveFR] (5) 87, p. 90.
875. CARREGA, Ugo
"10 Proposizioni per la Poesia Materica" (10 Propositions for a Material Poetry).
[Caliban] (2) 87, p. 64.
876. CARRELL, Don
"For Annie." [InterPR] (13:2) Fall 87, p. 103.
"Wild Beauty Annie." [InterPR] (13:2) Fall 87, p. 102.
877. CARREÑO, Alfonso
"Las Estancias." [LindLM] (6:4) O-D 87, p. 8.
"Panoramica Finisecular" (a Sieghild Bogumil, tan desasosegada por la historia).
[LindLM] (6:4) O-D 87, p. 8.
878. CARRIER, Constance
"Pro Patria." [TexasR] (7:3/4) 87, p. 22-23.
879. CARRINO, Michael
"Outside the Infirmary Window." [HayF] (2) Spr 87, p. 72.
"The Valet Parking Attendant Contemplates Escaping Vermont." [Vis] (24) 87, p. 29.
880. CARROLL, Rhoda
"Morphine." [MSS] (5:3) 87, p. 74-75.
881. CARRUTH, Hayden
"The Bearer." [Poetry] (151:1/2) O-N 87, p. 25-26.
"Homage to John Lyly and Frankie Newton." [NowestR] (25:2) 87, p. 60.
"Just Recently in California, Where Else." [Caliban] (3) 87, p. 39.
"Mix the Ingredients." [NowestR] (25:2) 87, p. 61.

882. CARRUTHERS, Ben Frederic
"Don't Know No English" (tr. of Nicolás Guillén, w. Langston Hughes). [Callaloo] (10:2) Spr 87, p. 171.
"High Brown" (tr. of Nicolás Guillén, w. Langston Hughes). [Callaloo] (10:2) Spr 87, p. 175.
"My Gal" (tr. of Nicolás Guillén, w. Langston Hughes). [Callaloo] (10:2) Spr 87, p. 179.
"Pass On By" (tr. of Nicolás Guillén, w. Langston Hughes). [Callaloo] (10:2) Spr 87, p. 177.
"Thick-Lipped Cullud Boy" (tr. of Nicolás Guillén, w. Langston Hughes). [Callaloo] (10:2) Spr 87, p. 173.
883. CARSON, Anne
"Short Talk on Chromo-luminarism." [Bomb] (20) Sum 87, p. 76.
"Short Talk on Geisha." [Bomb] (20) Sum 87, p. 76.
"Short Talk on Homo Sapiens." [Bomb] (20) Sum 87, p. 76.
"Short Talk on Major and Minor." [Bomb] (20) Sum 87, p. 76.
"Short Talk on the Rules of Perspective." [Bomb] (20) Sum 87, p. 76.
"Short Talk on Trout." [Bomb] (20) Sum 87, p. 76.
"Short Talk on Vicuñas." [Bomb] (20) Sum 87, p. 76.
884. CARSON, Jeffrey
"Diary of an Invisible April" (Selections, tr. of Odysseus Elytis). [AmerPoR] (16:2) Mr-Ap 87, p. 34.
"With Both Light and Death" (Selections, tr. of Odysseus Elytis). [AmerPoR] (16:2) Mr-Ap 87, p. 35.
885. CARSON, Jo
"Tears." [AmerV] (9) Wint 87, p. 77-78.
886. CARSON, Meredith S.
"Fish." [HawaiiR] (19) Spr 86, c87, p. 71.
"Jellyfish." [HawaiiR] (22) Fall 87, p. 22.
"The Letter." [BambooR] (36) Fall 87, p. 38.
"Windows." [HawaiiR] (22) Fall 87, p. 23.
887. CARSON, Mike
"Holy Name School, 1951." [Comm] (114:17) 9 O 87, p. 566.
888. CARTER, Jared
"Galleynipper." [Poetry] (150:6) S 87, p. 347-348.
"Improvisation." [Poetry] (151:1/2) O-N 87, p. 26.
889. CARTIER, Marie
"Between My Palms." [ColR] (NS 14:1) Spr-Sum 87, p. 57.
"Protect." [Outbr] (18/19) Fall 86-Spr 88, p. 116-124.
890. CARVALHO, Ronald de
"Epura" (tr. by Manoel Cardozo). [Vis] (24) 87, p. 14.
891. CARVER, Raymond
"Evening." [Poetry] (150:4) Jl 87, p. 231.
"The Net." [Poetry] (151:1/2) O-N 87, p. 28.
"The Phone Booth." [NowestR] (25:3) 87, p. 324-325.
"Slippers." [Raccoon] (24/25) My 87, p. 176.
"The Toes." [Poetry] (151:1/2) O-N 87, p. 27-28.
892. CARY, Kelly M.
"Dad." [Footwork] 87, p. 83.
893. CASARJIAN, Bethany
"Letter to a Friend's Mother." [KanQ] (19:1/2) Wint-Spr 87, p. 119.
"Love Distance." [KanQ] (19:1/2) Wint-Spr 87, p. 120.
894. CASAS, Walter de las
"Calidoscopio de la Vida." [LindLM] (6:4) O-D 87, p. 24.
"Nueva Emperatriz de la China." [LindLM] (6:4) O-D 87, p. 24.
895. CASAVIS, Dave
"The Other End." [Lactuca] (5) Ja 87, p. 35-36.
896. CASE, Robert
"Caterpillar climbing." [Waves] (15:1/2) Fall 86, p. 37.
"Tiger outside cage." [Waves] (15:1/2) Fall 86, p. 37.
897. CASEY, Crysta
"Breaking the Silence." [BellArk] (3:5) S-O 87, p. 19.
"Forgiveness." [BellArk] (3:2) Mr-Ap 87, p. 9.
"On My Way." [BellArk] (3:6) N-D 87, p. 5.
898. CASEY, Deb
"Round and Round." [PraS] (61:2) Sum 87, p. 58-59.

"Wet Dream." [PraS] (61:2) Sum 87, p. 60.
899. CASH, Les
"Leota, the Larruping Lady." [Amelia] (4:3, issue 10) 87, p. 82-84.
CASSEL, Ben Albright
See ALBRIGHT-CASSEL, Ben
900. CASSELLS, Cyrus
"Down from the Houses of Magic." [Callaloo] (10:3) Sum 87, p. 369-374.
"Lament for Lorca." [Callaloo] (10:3) Sum 87, p. 380-384.
"Night and Mist" (for Carolyn Forché). [Callaloo] (10:3) Sum 87, p. 375-379.
901. CASSELMAN, Barry
"I Think About a Past and an Uncertain Future." [MemphisSR] (8:1) Fall 87, p.
   10-11.
902. CASSIAN, Nina
"Ghost" (tr. by Christopher Hewitt). [NewYorker] (63:7) 6 Ap 87, p. 42.
"The Green Elephant" (tr. by Christopher Hewitt). [NewYorker] (63:7) 6 Ap 87, p.
   42.
"September." [NewYorker] (63:30) 14 S 87, p. 36.
"That Animal" (tr. by Christopher Hewitt). [NewYorker] (63:7) 6 Ap 87, p. 42.
"What Is Keeping the Clouds?" (tr. by Naomi Lazard). [CrossCur] (7:3) 87, p. 120.
"The Young Bat" (tr. by Christopher Hewitt). [NewYorker] (63:7) 6 Ap 87, p. 42.
903. CASSITY, Turner
"Between the Chains." [Sequoia] (31:1) Centennial issue 87, p. 75.
"Deco Mauresque." [Sequoia] (30:3) Wint 87, p. 40.
"A Different Perspective on a Rebours." [Sequoia] (31:1) Centennial issue 87, p. 74.
"Eljen a Magyar." [Sequoia] (30:3) Wint 87, p. 41.
"Lazy Afternoon." [ChiR] (35:4) 87, p. 111.
"Method." [ChiR] (35:4) 87, p. 110.
"Open Wounds." [Sequoia] (31:1) Centennial issue 87, p. 74.
"Prometheus in Polynesia." [Poetry] (151:1/2) O-N 87, p. 29.
904. CASTELLANOS, Rosario
"Bella Dama sin Piedad." [InterPR] (13:1) Spr 87, p. 46.
"La Belle Dame Sans Merci" (tr. by Grace Bauer). [InterPR] (13:1) Spr 87, p. 47.
"Comentario al Escultor." [InterPR] (13:1) Spr 87, p. 42.
"Commentary on the Sculptor" (tr. by Grace Bauer). [InterPR] (13:1) Spr 87, p. 43.
"Commission" (tr. by Carolyne Wright). [AmerPoR] (16:2) Mr-Ap 87, p. 41.
"Desamor." [InterPR] (13:1) Spr 87, p. 42.
"Disregard" (tr. by Grace Bauer). [InterPR] (13:1) Spr 87, p. 43.
"Elegia." [InterPR] (13:1) Spr 87, p. 44.
"Elegy" (tr. by Grace Bauer). [InterPR] (13:1) Spr 87, p. 45.
"Evocacion de la Tia Elena." [InterPR] (13:1) Spr 87, p. 40.
"Evocation of Aunt Elena" (tr. by Grace Bauer). [InterPR] (13:1) Spr 87, p. 41.
"Nazareth." [InterPR] (13:1) Spr 87, p. 40.
"Nazareth" (tr. by Grace Bauer). [InterPR] (13:1) Spr 87, p. 41.
"Ninfomania." [InterPR] (13:1) Spr 87, p. 44.
"Nymphomania" (tr. by Grace Bauer). [InterPR] (13:1) Spr 87, p. 45.
"El Retorno." [InterPR] (13:1) Spr 87, p. 36, 38.
"The Return" (tr. by Grace Bauer). [InterPR] (13:1) Spr 87, p. 37, 39.
905. CASTELLOTE, Carmen
"Admiro al pjaro que conoce su vuelo." [LetFem] (13:1/2) Primavera-Ontoño 87, p.
   121-122.
"De recuerdos y de tiempo era." [LetFem] (13:1/2) Primavera-Ontoño 87, p. 122-123.
"Hubo un tiempo en que las cosas fueron mías." [LetFem] (13:1/2) Primavera-Ontoño
   87, p. 121.
"Mi casa es una mesa servida de gente." [LetFem] (13:1/2) Primavera-Ontoño 87, p.
   123-124.
906. CASTERTON, Julia
"Daughters at the Lake." [MinnR] (NS 28) Spr 87, p. 23.
907. CASTILLO, Horacio
"This Bitter Matter" (9 poems, tr. by Jason Wilson). [Trans] (18) Spr 87, p. 90-94.
908. CASTILLO, Ofelia
"Chronicles" (for Luis Bassani, tr. by H. E. Francis). [BlackWR] (13:2) Spr 87, p.
   167.
"Cronicas" (a Luis Bassani). [BlackWR] (13:2) Spr 87, p. 166.
909. CASTILLO, Otto René
"Exilio." [Areíto] (1:1) Primavera 87, inside back cover.
"Frente al Balance Mañana." [Areíto] (1:1) Primavera 87, inside front cover.

82

CASTILLO

"Satisfaccion" (Dedicado a Carlos, en el octavo aniversario de su muerte). [Areíto] (1:1) Primavera 87, p. 23.
910. CASTLEBURY, John
"Lynchburg Travelogue, Night Two." [SouthernPR] (27:1) Spr 87, p. 23-28.
911. CASTLEMAN, Rebecca
"The Pier" (1986 Finalist, Eve of Saint Agnes Poetry Competition). [NegC] (7:1/2) 87, p. 225.
912. CASTO, Keith
"Oh, Now I See." [LightY] '87, c86, p. 97.
"She Don't Bop." [LightY] '87, c86, p. 174.
913. CASTRO, Jan Garden
"The Divide." [GreenfR] (14:1/2) Wint-Spr, p. 117-118.
914. CASTRO, Michael
"After Vallejo." [Vis] (25) 87, p. 29-30.
"If Not You, Who?" (for Trish). [Vis] (24) 87, p. 18.
"The United States of America." [RiverS] (24) 87, p. 47.
CASTRO, Victoria Scharf de
See DeCASTRO, Victoria Scharf
915. CASTRO RIOS, Andrés
"Celebracion de Vallejo." [Mairena] (9:24) 87, p. 51.
916. CATHERS, Ken
"These Are the Houses." [Event] (16:2) Sum 87, p. 102.
917. CATHERWOOD, Mike
"Dead Man in a Field." [KanQ] (19:3) Sum 87, p. 211.
"If You Turned Around Quickly" (title of a painting by Rich Hauge). [MidwQ] (28:2) Wint 87, p. 211.
918. CATLIN, Alan
"The Ancient Mariner of Western Avenue." [Lactuca] (6) Ap-My 87, p. 8.
"And Agamemnon Dead." [CrabCR] (4:3) Sum 87, p. 5.
"Black and White Punk Rockette on the Schenectady to Albany Bus 1984." [FloridaR] (15:1) Spr-Sum 87, p. 77.
"The Breather." [Lactuca] (8) N 87, p. 13-14.
"The Collector." [Lactuca] (6) Ap-My 87, p. 7.
"The Graduate of Harvard University, Oneonta, N.Y." [Lactuca] (8) N 87, p. 14.
"High Shoes." [Lactuca] (6) Ap-My 87, p. 9.
"Long Island Kid." [Lactuca] (6) Ap-My 87, p. 10.
"Modern Love: The Iliad as Retold by Menelaus." [CrabCR] (4:3) Sum 87, p. 5.
"On the Corner of Flatbush and Fifth." [Lactuca] (6) Ap-My 87, p. 10-11.
"The Shark." [Lactuca] (6) Ap-My 87, p. 5-6.
"Streetwalking." [Lactuca] (6) Ap-My 87, p. 1-2.
"Urban Renewal." [Lactuca] (8) N 87, p. 13.
"Why I Wear Two Wedding Rings." [Lactuca] (6) Ap-My 87, p. 2-3.
"Wimpy." [Lactuca] (6) Ap-My 87, p. 4-5.
"Y-Y-Yo!" [Lactuca] (6) Ap-My 87, p. 10.
919. CATTAFI, Bartolo
"Deeds" (tr. by Rina Ferrarelli). [Trans] (18) Spr 87, p. 323.
"The Flood" (tr. by Rina Ferrarelli). [Trans] (18) Spr 87, p. 321.
"In There" (tr. by Rina Ferrarelli). [Trans] (18) Spr 87, p. 322.
"The Line the Thread" (tr. by Rina Ferrarelli). [Trans] (18) Spr 87, p. 321.
"Thickets of Shade" (tr. by Rina Ferrarelli). [Trans] (18) Spr 87, p. 320.
"The Tin Box" (tr. by Rina Ferrarelli). [Trans] (18) Spr 87, p. 322.
"To My Shadow" (tr. by Rina Ferrarelli). [Trans] (18) Spr 87, p. 321.
"To Repeat the Image" (tr. by Rina Ferrarelli). [Trans] (18) Spr 87, p. 323.
"Venus" (tr. by Rina Ferrarelli). [Trans] (18) Spr 87, p. 322.
920. CATULLUS, Gaius Valerius
"Attis" (tr. of Poems 63, by Robert Boucheron). [JamesWR] (4:2) Wint 87, p. 13.
"Poems" (Selections: II, III, LXXV, LXX, LII, XCVIII, XI, tr. by Sam Hamill). [CrabCR] (4:2) Spr 87, p. 3-4.
921. CAVAFY, C. P. (Constantine)
"Beneath the House." [GrandS] (6:2) Wint 87, p. 132.
"Half an Hour." [GrandS] (6:2) Wint 87, p. 137.
"Hidden Things." [GrandS] (6:2) Wint 87, p. 130-131.
"Making Sense." [GrandS] (6:2) Wint 87, p. 136.
"Steps" (tr. by Alan Boegehold). [Margin] (5) Wint 87-88, p. 40.
"Their Beginning." [GrandS] (6:2) Wint 87, p. 136.

922. CAVIS, Ella
    "Nicholas and Christopher." [ManhatPR] (9) Sum 87, p. 29.
    "Nicholas and Christopher." [PoeticJ] (17) 87, p. 18.
923. CAWLEY, Kevin
    "Train." [LaurelR] (21:1/2) Wint-Sum 87, p. 15.
924. CECIL, Richard
    "Greed." [WestB] (20) 87, p. 82-83.
    "The Happy New Year." [AmerPoR] (16:3) My-Je 87, p. 20-21.
    "The Merry Christmas." [AmerPoR] (16:3) My-Je 87, p. 20.
    "One Year Leases." [Jacaranda] (2:2) Spr 87, p. 21-22.
    "Walking Home in the Rain." [MissouriR] (10:2) 87, p. 137.
    "Winter Physical." [Verse] (4:1) Mr 87, p. 52-53.
925. CEDERQUIST, Druzelle
    "Other Realms." [WorldO] (20:2) Wint 85-86 c88, p. 62.
    "The Prophets." [WorldO] (20:2) Wint 85-86 c88, p. 62.
926. CELAN, Paul
    "Atemwende" (Selections: 3 poems in German & English, tr. by Michael Hamburger).
        [SouthernHR] (21:3) Sum 87, p. 224-229.
    "Discus" (tr. by Katherine Washburn and Margaret Guillemin). [AntR] (45:1) Wint
        87, p. 96.
    "Grown Weary" (tr. by Katherine Washburn and Margaret Guillemin). [AntR] (45:1)
        Wint 87, p. 97.
    "Wurfscheibe." [AntR] (45:1) Wint 87, p. 96.
927. CELLI, Roberto
    "18th-Century Mirrors." [PoetL] (81:3) Fall 86, p. 194.
    "Palmistry." [PoetL] (81:3) Fall 86, p. 193.
    "Woods." [PoetL] (81:3) Fall 86, p. 192.
928. CERNUDA, Luis
    "Farewells" (tr. by Andrew Harvey). [SenR] (17:2) 87, p. 35.
    "The Lover Babbles" (tr. by Andrew Harvey). [SenR] (17:2) 87, p. 33-34.
CERTAIN, Miguel Falquez
    See FALQUEZ-CERTAIN, Miguel
929. CERVANTES, Lorna Dee
    "Astro-no-mía." [Americas] (15:3/4) Fall-Wint 87, p. 44.
    "Bird Ave." [Americas] (15:3/4) Fall-Wint 87, p. 41-43.
930. CHACE, Joel
    "Falling Waitress" (For A. R. Ammons). [Pembroke] (19) 87, p. 177-181.
    "For My Grandmother in America." [Wind] (17:59) 87, p. 6.
931. CHADWICK, Joseph
    "And My Body?" (tr. of José Lezama Lima). [HawaiiR] (20) Fall 86, c87, p. 13.
    "A King's Whiskers" (tr. of José Lezama Lima). [HawaiiR] (20) Fall 86, c87, p. 11.
932. CHAFFIN, Lillie D.
    "Following." [CrossCur] (6:4) 87, p. 41.
    "Severance." [Footwork] 87, p. 46.
    "Traveling with You." [CrossCur] (6:4) 87, p. 40.
933. CHALLEM, Jack J.
    "Old Floors." [Phoenix] (7:2) 87, p. 15-16.
934. CHALLENDER, Craig
    "All It Says." [HampSPR] Wint 87, p. 27.
    "Flood." [SouthernPR] (27:2) Fall 87, p. 45-46.
    "Pot of Gold." [HampSPR] Wint 87, p. 28.
    "Words for My Daughter." [PikeF] (8) Fall 87, p. 13.
935. CHAMBERLAIN, Karen
    "Stepping in the Same River." [Nat] (244:19) 16 My 87, p. 660.
936. CHAMBERS, George
    "August 18." [NowestR] (25:3) 87, p. 182.
937. CHAMBERS, Leland H.
    "I'll Hang a Line." [Nimrod] (31:1) Fall-Wint 87, p. 84.
938. CHANDRA, G. S. Sharat
    "The Absent." [WeberS] (4:1) Spr 87, p. 67.
    "An Alien's Day After in Kansas." [DenQ] (21:3) Wint 87, p. 39.
    "Assassination" (to Indira Gandhi). [Chelsea] (46) 87, p. 227.
    "Barbers of Nanjangud." [WeberS] (4:1) Spr 87, p. 68.
    "Coffee Break." [Chelsea] (46) 87, p. 229.
    "The Emmy Award." [DenQ] (21:3) Wint 87, p. 40-41.
    "Fable of the Home Cooked Lunch." [DenQ] (21:3) Wint 87, p. 42.

"Fate, a Hindi Movie." [Chelsea] (46) 87, p. 226.
"Indian Fillybuster." [Chelsea] (46) 87, p. 228.
"Midlife." [WeberS] (4:1) Spr 87, p. 69.
"Unable to Visit My Mother, I Drink Myself to Sleep." [HighP] (2:2) Fall 87, p. 193.
939. CHANG, Diana
"Apples, Stars." [StoneC] (14:3/4) Spr-Sum 87, p. 35.
940. CHANG, Soo Ko
"On a Snowy Night." [Pembroke] (19) 87, p. 212.
"The Surrealist's Diary." [Pembroke] (19) 87, p. 212.
"To Marc Chagall." [Pembroke] (19) 87, p. 213.
"A Visionary's Song." [Pembroke] (19) 87, p. 213.
941. CHAPERO, Rene
"Antofagasta" (tr. by John Vincent Smith). [Vis] (24) 87, p. 13.
942. CHAPMAN, R. S.
"A Circle for Morning." [BelPoJ] (38:2) Wint 87-88, p. 24.
"High School." [BelPoJ] (38:2) Wint 87-88, p. 22.
"What Went Wrong." [BelPoJ] (38:2) Wint 87-88, p. 23.
943. CHAPPELL, Fred
"At the Feast" (An Afterword to Annie Dillard's *Pilgrim at Tinker Creek*). [Confr]
(35/36) Spr-Fall 87, p. 58-59.
"Feast." [Raccoon] (24/25) My 87, p. 47-48.
"The Voices at Sunset" (Untitled etching by Mary Ann Sloane, 1902). [Confr] (35/36)
Spr-Fall 87, p. 60.
944. CHARACH, Ron
"And the Shoeshine Man Dreams." [Descant] (59) Wint 87, p. 30.
"Dagwood at Seven a.m." [Grain] (15:3) Fall 87, p. 34-35.
"In the Room of Airtight Windows" (WQ Editors' Second Prize Winner — Poetry).
[CrossC] (9:1) 87, p. 17.
"Julius Dithers in the Morning." [Grain] (15:3) Fall 87, p. 36-37.
"Listen: It Is Dagwood." [Grain] (15:3) Fall 87, p. 32-33.
"To See My Friends." [Descant] (59) Wint 87, p. 27-28.
"A Welder's Dream." [Descant] (59) Wint 87, p. 29.
945. CHARRIERE, Gérard
"To the Consciousness of a Shooting Star" (w. David Rattray). [Bomb] (18) Wint 87,
p. 44-47.
946. CHASE, Aleka
"Oh, Mother." [FiveFR] (5) 87, p. 40.
947. CHASE, Karen
"My House." [YellowS] (24) Aut 87, p. 26.
"Somewhat a Visitor." [YellowS] (24) Aut 87, p. 6.
"Stubborn Sheets." [YellowS] (24) Aut 87, p. 8.
"This Can Happen When You're Married." [YellowS] (24) Aut 87, p. 7.
948. CHATFIELD, Hale
"Deep River." [NewEngR] (10:1) Aut 87, p. 133.
"Fields III." [HiramPoR] (43) Fall-Wint 87-88, p. 17.
"A Lament." [Gambit] (20) 86, p. 68.
"A Lament." [NewEngR] (10:1) Aut 87, p. 132.
"Lifesongs" (I-IV). [NewEngR] (10:1) Aut 87, p. 124-125.
"Migrations." [NewEngR] (10:1) Aut 87, p. 131.
"A Random Lifesong." [NewEngR] (10:1) Aut 87, p. 126.
"Sestina." [Gambit] (20) 86, p. 65-66.
"Statewide Artists' Meeting." [NewEngR] (10:1) Aut 87, p. 120-122.
"Tape Recorder: May 13, Interstate 71." [Gambit] (20) 86, p. 67.
"Theodicy." [NewEngR] (10:1) Aut 87, p. 132.
949. CHAVEZ, Denise
"Artery of Land." [Americas] (15:3/4) Fall-Wint 87, p. 70.
"Birth of Me in My Room at Home." [Americas] (15:1) Spr 87, p. 56-58.
"Chekhov Green Love." [Americas] (15:3/4) Fall-Wint 87, p. 79.
"Cloud." [Americas] (15:3/4) Fall-Wint 87, p. 69.
"Cuckoo Death Chime." [Americas] (15:3/4) Fall-Wint 87, p. 76-77.
"Door." [Americas] (15:3/4) Fall-Wint 87, p. 78.
"Everything You Are Is Teeth." [Americas] (15:3/4) Fall-Wint 87, p. 75.
"The Feeling of Going On." [Americas] (15:3/4) Fall-Wint 87, p. 81.
"For My Sister in Paris." [Americas] (15:1) Spr 87, p. 59-61.
"I Am Your Mary Magdalene." [Americas] (15:3/4) Fall-Wint 87, p. 66.
"Lagaña of Lace." [Americas] (15:1) Spr 87, p. 48-49.

85

"Mercado Day." [Americas] (15:1) Spr 87, p. 52-54.
"La Pesadez." [Americas] (15:3/4) Fall-Wint 87, p. 65.
"Purgatory Is an Ocean of Flaming Hearts." [Americas] (15:1) Spr 87, p. 55.
"Saying 'Oh No'." [Americas] (15:3/4) Fall-Wint 87, p. 74.
"Silver Ingots of Desire." [Americas] (15:3/4) Fall-Wint 87, p. 71.
"Starflash." [Americas] (15:3/4) Fall-Wint 87, p. 73.
"The State of My Inquietude." [Americas] (15:3/4) Fall-Wint 87, p. 80.
"The Study." [Americas] (15:3/4) Fall-Wint 87, p. 72.
"Tears." [Americas] (15:3/4) Fall-Wint 87, p. 68.
"This River's Praying Place." [Americas] (15:3/4) Fall-Wint 87, p. 67.
"This Thin Light." [Americas] (15:3/4) Fall-Wint 87, p. 82.
"Two Butterflies." [Americas] (15:3/4) Fall-Wint 87, p. 83.
"Ya." [Americas] (15:1) Spr 87, p. 50-51.

950. CHAY, John
"At a London Museum" (to a Japanese friend, tr. of Hwang Tong-Gyu, w. Grace Gibson). [Pembroke] (19) 87, p. 21.
"The Exit" (tr. of Hwang Tong-Gyu, w. Grace Gibson). [InterPR] (13:1) Spr 87, p. 60.
"For Two to Fly Together in the Sky" (tr. of Hwang Tong-Gyu, w. Grace Gibson). [Pembroke] (19) 87, p. 24.
"From an Alien Land 4" (tr. of Hwang Tong-Gyu, w. Grace Gibson). [Pembroke] (19) 87, p. 22.
"Iowa Diary 1" (to Ma Chinggi, tr. of Hwang Tong-Gyu, w. Grace Gibson). [Pembroke] (19) 87, p. 22-23.
"A Joyful Letter" (tr. of Hwang Tong-Gyu, w. Grace Gibson). [Pembroke] (19) 87, p. 25.
"The Last Solgo" (tr. of Hwang Tong-Gyu, w. Grace Gibson). [Pembroke] (19) 87, p. 23-24.
"A Little Autumn Day" (tr. of Hwang Tong-Gyu, w. Grace Gibson). [Pembroke] (19) 87, p. 24.
"Separate, But Standing Around Together" (tr. of Hwang Tong-Gyu, w. Grace Gibson). [Pembroke] (19) 87, p. 22.
"Short Poem" (poems 4 & 5, tr. of Hwang Tong-Gyu, w. Grace Gibson). [Pembroke] (19) 87, p. 25.
"A Small Poem #5" (tr. of Hwang Tong-Gyu, w. Grace Gibson). [InterPR] (13:1) Spr 87, p. 60.
"Snowfall on the Harbor" (tr. of Hwang Tong-Gyu, w. Grace Gibson). [Pembroke] (19) 87, p. 26.
"A Snowy Night" (tr. of Kim Do Sung, w. Grace Gibson). [InterPR] (13:1) Spr 87, p. 62.
"Song" (tr. of Hwang Tong-Gyu, w. Grace Gibson). [Pembroke] (19) 87, p. 26.
"Walking the Tightrope" (tr. of Hwang Tong-Gyu, w. Grace Gibson). [Pembroke] (19) 87, p. 21.
"The Wind" (tr. of Pak Yul A, w. Grace Gibson). [InterPR] (13:1) Spr 87, p. 63.
"Wind Burial" (poems 1-11, tr. of Hwang Tong-Gyu, w. Grace Gibson). [Pembroke] (19) 87, p. 26-31.
"Winter Morning" (tr. of Lee Sung Hyung, w. Grace Gibson). [InterPR] (13:1) Spr 87, p. 64.
"The Year Is Getting Late" (tr. of Kim Do Sung, w. Grace Gibson). [InterPR] (13:1) Spr 87, p. 61.

951. CHEADLE, Brian
"Independence." [CumbPR] (7:1) Fall 87, p. 58.
"Momentum." [CumbPR] (7:1) Fall 87, p. 57.
"The Watchmaker." [CumbPR] (7:1) Fall 87, p. 59-60.

952. CHEATAM, Karyn
"When the Northers Come." [CrossCur] (6:4) 87, p. 99.

953. CHEN, Xueliang
"Answer" (tr. of Bei Dao, w. Donald Finkel). [SenR] (17:2) 87, p. 25.
"Border" (tr. of Bei Dao, w. Donald Finkel). [SenR] (17:2) 87, p. 26.
"Country Night" (tr. of Bei Dao, w. Donald Finkel). [SenR] (17:2) 87, p. 27.
"Let's Go" (tr. of Bei Dao, w. Donald Finkel). [Antaeus] (58) Spr 87, p. 160.
"The Oranges Are Ripe" (tr. of Bei Dao, w. Donald Finkel). [Antaeus] (58) Spr 87, p. 158.
"Snow Line" (tr. of Bei Dao, w. Donald Finkel). [SenR] (17:2) 87, p. 24.
"Testament" (tr. of Bei Dao, w. Donald Finkel). [Antaeus] (58) Spr 87, p. 157.
"A Ticket" (tr. of Bei Dao, w. Donald Finkel). [Antaeus] (58) Spr 87, p. 159-160.

954. CHENEY, Sally
"Calligraphy." [PoetL] (81:3) Fall 86, p. 195.
955. CHENG, Anne A.
"Aunt Jenny in Shanghai, 1940." [OntR] (27) Fall-Wint 87, p. 97-98.
"Aunt Jenny's Painting." [OntR] (27) Fall-Wint 87, p. 99.
CHENG, Gu
    See GU, Cheng
956. CHERKORSKI, Neel
"In Shul." [Contact] (9:44/45/46) Fall-Wint 87, p. 51.
957. CHESTER, Laura
"Eating Alone." [Notus] (2:2) Fall 87, p. 55.
"The Good Time Is Now." [Notus] (2:2) Fall 87, p. 56.
958. CHEYFITZ, Eric
"The Continent." [HampSPR] Wint 87, p. 29.
"Silent Movie." [HampSPR] Wint 87, p. 29-30.
CHI, Li
    See LI, Chi
959. CHICHETTO, James William
"De-Centering Myths" (Selections: 12, 14-15, 17, 19-20). [ConnPR] (6:1) 87, p.
    25-28.
960. CHIESA, Carmen
"Abandonada." [Mairena] (9:24) 87, p. 108.
961. CHILD, Abigail
"Blueprint for a Scenario (1)." [Bound] (14:1/2) Fall 85-Wint 86 [c87], p. 24-26.
962. CHILDISH, Billy
"No Reason." [Bogg] (57) 87, p. 50.
"Tushunka Witko" (Crazy Horse). [Bogg] (58) 87, p. 29.
963. CHIN, Marilyn
"And All I have Is Tu Fu." [Caliban] (2) 87, p. 37.
"Art Wong Is Alive and Ill and Struggling in Oakland California." [Zyzzyva] (3:1) Spr
    87, p. 64-65.
"Composed Near the Bay Bridge" (after a wild party). [Caliban] (2) 87, p. 38.
"How We Saved the Other" (to the beat of a Tartar drum). [Caliban] (2) 87, p. 35-36.
"The Narrow Roads of Oku" (after Basho). [Iowa] (17:3) Fall 87, p. 80-83.
"Vandals, Early Autumn" (for Donald Justice). [Iowa] (17:3) Fall 87, p. 85.
"We Are Americans Now, We Life in the Tundra." [Iowa] (17:3) Fall 87, p. 84.
CHINCHILLA, Freddy Villalobos
    See VILLALOBOS CHINCHILLA, Freddy
964. CHINELLY, Cynthia
"The Coralroot." [GrahamHR] (10) Wint-Spr 87, p. 35.
965. CHINN, Daryl
"Not Translation, Not Poetry" (for those who felt "cheated" at reading "The Laws" in
    CHINA MEN). [GreenfR] (14:3/4) Sum-Fall 87, p. 157-159.
966. CHINWEIZU
"Apprentice Dowager" (for an aging actress on the train). [RiverS] (22) 87, p. 41-43.
967. CHITWOOD, Michael
"Goats." [HampSPR] Wint 86, p. 48.
"Leaving Saltville." [SouthernPR] (27:2) Fall 87, p. 23.
"Leaving the House of the Enchantress" (For Jean). [HampSPR] Wint 86, p. 49.
"Martyrdom of the Onions." [ChatR] (8:1) Fall 87, p. 15.
"Seeing the Lights." [MalR] (80) S 87, p. 113.
"Slipping into Another Skin." [HampSPR] Wint 86, p. 49.
"Thinking of Rome in Fair Lea, West Virginia." [SouthernHR] (21:4) Fall 87, p. 353.
"Wreck and Attempted Rescue." [HampSPR] Wint 86, p. 48.
968. CHOCK, Eric
"The Mango Tree." The Best of [BambooR] [(31-32)] 86, p. 19-20.
"Poem for George Helm, Aloha Week 1980." The Best of [BambooR] [(31-32)] 86,
    p. 21-23.
"Termites." The Best of [BambooR] [(31-32)] 86, p. 17-18.
"Tutu on the Curb." The Best of [BambooR] [(31-32)] 86, p. 24.
969. CHOE, Wolhee
"Another's Light" (for poets, tr. of Chong Hyon-Jong, w. Constantine Contogenis).
    [Nimrod] (31:1) Fall-Wint 87, p. 133.
"Family" (tr. of Chong Hyon-Jong, w. Constantine Contogenis). [Nimrod] (31:1)
    Fall-Wint 87, p. 133.

970. CHONG, Hyon-Jong
    "Another's Light" (for poets, tr. by Wolhee Choe and Constantine Contogenis).
        [Nimrod] (31:1) Fall-Wint 87, p. 133.
    "Family" (tr. by Wolhee Choe and Constantine Contogenis). [Nimrod] (31:1)
        Fall-Wint 87, p. 133.
971. CHORLTON, David
    "Alien Freight." [PoetL] (82:4) Wint 87-88, p. 203.
    "Anyone's Army." [Lactuca] (7) Ag 87, p. 25-26.
    "Coming Home from Gino." [SlipS] (7) 87, p. 75.
    "Corner Hotel." [SlipS] (7) 87, p. 76.
    "Field Work." [Lactuca] (7) Ag 87, p. 24.
    "Franz Probst Sketches the Ghetto." [PoetL] (81:4) Wint 86-87, p. 239.
    "Hotel Revolution." [Lactuca] (7) Ag 87, p. 24-25.
    "In the Next Country." [PoetL] (82:3) Fall 87, p. 138.
    "Kien-Wu Drinking." [DekalbLAJ] (20:1/4) 87, p. 34.
    "Kien-Wu in a Nocturnal Storm." [Poem] (58) N 87, p. 66.
    "Kien-Wu's Retreat." [DekalbLAJ] (20:1/4) 87, p. 35.
    "Kien-Wu's Ways." [WebR] (12:2) Fall 87, p. 51.
    "Marina Tsvetayeva" (for Joan Silva). [Pembroke] (19) 87, p. 102-105.
    "Ownership." [Poem] (58) N 87, p. 65.
    "The Sage and the Courtesan." [Poem] (58) N 87, p. 64.
    "The Sage, Kien-Wu." [PikeF] (8) Fall 87, p. 3.
    "The Uncarved Block." [WebR] (12:2) Fall 87, p. 52.
    "The Vine." [Lactuca] (7) Ag 87, p. 23-24.
972. CHOYCE, Lesley
    "Control." [Germ] (11:1) Fall 87, p. 35.
    "A Degree in Nothingness." [Germ] (11:1) Fall 87, p. 31.
    "President Marcos and the 3000 Pairs of Shoes." [Germ] (11:1) Fall 87, p. 30.
    "This Poem." [Germ] (11:1) Fall 87, p. 32-34.
973. CHRISTENSEN, Erleen J.
    "Night Song." [Wind] (17:59) 87, p. 7.
    "Notes for Travelers." [Wind] (17:59) 87, p. 7.
974. CHRISTENSEN, Peter A.
    "Hard Dollars." [Footwork] 87, p. 50.
    "Mathematics." [Footwork] 87, p. 51.
    "Saturday's Children." [Footwork] 87, p. 50.
    "Smokey." [Footwork] 87, p. 50.
975. CHRISTENSON, Michael
    "Walt Whitman in the Parking Lots of America." [Pig] (14) 87, p. 38.
976. CHRISTHILF, Mark
    "Lines." [KanQ] (19:3) Sum 87, p. 208.
    "Wave." [KanQ] (19:1/2) Wint-Spr 87, p. 62.
977. CHRISTIAN, Eddena
    "Gone." [PoeticJ] (17) 87, p. 12.
    "Stone." [PoeticJ] (17) 87, p. 12.
978. CHRISTIANSON, Norah
    "Night." [KanQ] (19:3) Sum 87, p. 295.
979. CHRISTIE, Linda
    "A Series of Filth." [AntigR] (69/70) 87, p. 203.
980. CHRISTINA, Martha
    "Supporting Evidence." [BelPoJ] (38:1) Fall 87, p. 3.
981. CHRISTOPHER, Nicholas
    "Atlantic Avenue." [Lips] (13) 87, p. 3.
    "Blizzard." [Nat] (244:1) 10 Ja 87, p. 22.
    "Circe Revisited." [NewRep] (197:24) 14 D 87, p. 48.
    "Collecting Stamps in Port-au-Prince." [YaleR] (76:4) Sum 87, p. 555-556.
    "Desperate Character." [NewYorker] (63:28) 31 Ag 87, p. 30.
    "Elegy for My Grandmother." [MissouriR] (10:3) 87, p. 110-111.
    "Krazy Kat's Confession." [Nat] (245:8) 19 S 87, p. 280.
    "Miranda in Reno." [NewRep] (196:4) 26 Ja 87, p. 40.
    "Notes at Summer's End." [Field] (36) Spr 87, p. 62-63.
982. CHRISTOPHER, Renny
    "Vanishing Traces" (title corrected in 7:2, p. 175). [CrossCur] (7:1) 87, p. 117.
983. CHRISTY, Jim
    "Island Boys." [AlphaBS] (1) Je 87, p. 21.
    "A Mexican Tale." [AlphaBS] (1) Je 87, p. 18-19.

"Nuestra Senora de Guadelupe." [AlphaBS] (1) Je 87, p. 17.
"They're Smooching in Wildwood." [AlphaBS] (1) Je 87, p. 20.
"Tonight in the World." [AlphaBS] (2) D 87, p. 25.
984. CHRYSTOS
"The Wings of a Wild Goose." [Cond] (14) 87, p. 167-168.
985. CHUN, Herbert
"Pa-ke." The Best of [BambooR] [(31-32)] 86, p. 25-26.
986. CHUNN, Ian
"Immanuel Kant Lectures at Hubei University." [Rampike] (5:3) 87, p. 53.
987. CHUTE, R. M. (See also CHUTE, Robert M.)
"The Homestead." [GreenfR] (14:1/2) Wint-Spr, p. 114.
988. CHUTE, Robert M. (See also CHUTE, R. M.)
"Ansel Adams: Classic Images (1986)" (Plate #41 — Mrs. Gunn on Porch, Plate #40
— Mount Williamson). [AntigR] (69/70) 87, p. 26.
"Blackberries." [Northeast] (Ser. 4:5) Sum 87, p. 22.
"Carpenter's Apprentice." [WormR] (27:4, issue 108) 87, p. 95.
"Dark Iron Spring." [AntigR] (69/70) 87, p. 27.
"George Celebrates the Solstice." [Northeast] (Ser. 4:5) Sum 87, p. 23.
"Inquest." [LitR] (30:4) Sum 87, p. 576.
"Lucky Shots." [SmPd] (24:3) Fall 87, p. 24.
"March, 1724." [TexasR] (7:3/4) 87, p. 24.
"Summers Past." [HiramPoR] (42) Spr-Sum 87, p. 12.
"Veterans' Day." [KanQ] (19:3) Sum 87, p. 226.
"Voyager." [HiramPoR] (42) Spr-Sum 87, p. 11.
"What Vaudeville Killed." [WormR] (27:4, issue 108) 87, p. 95.
989. CIESLINSKI, L. John
"Zamboanga." [NegC] (7:3/4) 87, p. 135.
990. CIMON, Anne
"Beachcomber." [Waves] (15:3) Wint 87, p. 67.
991. CIORAN, E. M.
"Avowals and Aversions" (tr. by Eric Basso). [Margin] (5) Wint 87-88, p. 90-91.
992. CIRINO, Leonard
"The Bound Man." [Amelia] (4:1/2, issue 9) 87, p. 95.
"Unified Fields" (for Duncan). [Amelia] (4:1/2, issue 9) 87, p. 95-96.
"Winter Letter to Loretta in L.A." [Electrum] (39) Fall-Wint 87, p. 20.
993. CIRIPOMPA, Patricia
"To the Songwriter." [Writer] (99:9) S 86, p. 26.
994. CITINO, David
"At the Harding Memorial" (for James Wright). [CentR] (31:4) Fall 87, p. 381-382.
"The Family in the Suburbs: A Situation Comedy." [LightY] '87, c86, p. 154-155.
"For Working Fifty Years on the B&O, Grandfather Receives a Watch." [Gambit]
(20) 86, p. 14.
"Giovanni De'Dondi, Master John of the Clock." [Salm] (73) Wint 87, p. 148-149.
"Going Downtown to Draw Up Our Will." [SenR] (17:2) 87, p. 51-52.
"High Water." [KanQ] (19:3) Sum 87, p. 18.
"Homage to the Frostbelt." [KanQ] (19:3) Sum 87, p. 17.
"The Hot Fish." [WestB] (20) 87, p. 102-103.
"Howard Carter Unwraps King Tut: Or, Curse of the Mummy's Tomb."
[MemphisSR] (7:2) Spr 87, p. 47.
"In Drumcliff Churchyard." [TarPR] (27:1) Fall 87, p. 18-19.
"Letter From the Shaman: The History of Shooting Stars." [TexasR] (8:1/2) Spr-Sum
87, p. 17.
"The Life and Death of Fields." [CentR] (31:4) Fall 87, p. 380-381.
"Loving the Stars." [Nimrod] (30:2) Spr-Sum 87, p. 45.
"Luigi Galvani Discovers Animal Electricity, 1791." [DenQ] (21:3) Wint 87, p.
25-26.
"The Man Who Couldn't Believe." [PraS] (61:4) Wint 87, p. 37-38.
"Meditation on U.S. 75." [MemphisSR] (7:2) Spr 87, p. 46.
"The Muscle of God." [SouthernR] (23:1) Ja 87, p. 159-160.
"The News." [SouthernR] (23:1) Ja 87, p. 160-161.
"The Nocturnal Migration of Songbirds." [Nimrod] (30:2) Spr-Sum 87, p. 44.
"The Poet in Residence Moves into the Dorm." [HolCrit] (24:4) O 87, p. 11.
"Rita Hayworth over Hiroshima." [BelPoJ] (38:2) Wint 87-88, p. 24-25.
"Sister Mary Appassionata on the History of Madness." [MemphisSR] (8:1) Fall 87,
p. 26-27.

"Sister Mary Appassionata on the Invention of Soap." [MemphisSR] (7:2) Spr 87, p.
48.
"Sister Mary Appassionata Writes to Wilhelm Reich Rgarding the Nature of the
Orgone." [OhioR] (39) 87, p. 40-41.
"Starting the Garden, I Remember That the Citizens of Purgatory Knew Dante Was
Alive . . ." [PoetryNW] (28:3) Aut 87, p. 26.
"While Crooning 'Love Me Tender,' Ghost of Elvis Makes Love to Me: Now I Carry
His Baby." [SouthernPR] (27:1) Spr 87, p. 31-32.
995. CLAIRE, William
"Misty Meadows." [Confr] (35/36) Spr-Fall 87, p. 290.
996. CLAMPITT, Amy
"Dorothy and William at Coleorton." [GrandS] (6:2) Wint 87, p. 22-25.
"The Field Pansy." [WilliamMR] (25) Spr 87, p. 8-9.
"Man Feeding Pigeons." [NewYorker] (62:49) 26 Ja 87, p. 30.
"Meadowlark Country." [NewYorker] (63:21) 13 Jl 87, p. 32.
"Notes on the State of Virginia." [GrandS] (6:3) Spr 87, p. 48-51.
"Perseus Airborne." [NoDaQ] (55:1) Wint 87, p. 41.
"Westward." [Poetry] (151:1/2) O-N 87, p. 30-34.
997. CLARE, Josephine
"The Rain" (In memory of Ben Atkinson). [SenR] (17:2) 87, p. 54-55.
998. CLARENCE, Judy
"Conversion" (for Dan O'Hanlon). [WebR] (12:1) Spr 87, p. 48-49.
999. CLARK, J. P.
"The Death of Samora Machel." [Chelsea] (46) 87, p. 113-114.
"Dele Giwa." [Chelsea] (46) 87, p. 113.
"The News from Ethiopia and the Sudan." [Chelsea] (46) 87, p. 114.
1000. CLARK, J. Wesley
"Autobiography." [Notus] (2:1) Spr 87, p. 89.
"Lady." [Notus] (2:1) Spr 87, p. 87.
"Outlaws." [Notus] (2:1) Spr 87, p. 86.
"A Pretty Black Woman with Yellow Shoes." [Notus] (2:1) Spr 87, p. 88.
1001. CLARK, Naomi
"The Muse of Circuses" (title corrected in 7:2, p. 175). [CrossCur] (7:1) 87, p. 41.
1002. CLARK, Patricia
"After Stone Lions Are Gone." [TarPR] (27:1) Fall 87, p. 31.
1003. CLARKE, Cheryl
"Stuck." [Cond] (14) 87, p. 182-183.
1004. CLARKE, George Elliott
"How Exile Melts to a Hundred Roses: Postscript." [Germ] (11:1) Fall 87, p. 15.
"Look Homeward, Anti-Hero, and Be Enraged." [Germ] (11:1) Fall 87, p. 10.
"Love Poem / Song Regarding Weymouth Falls: Postscript." [Germ] (11:1) Fall 87,
p. 14.
"Monologue for Selah Bringing Spring to Weymouth Falls." [Germ] (11:1) Fall 87,
p. 12.
"Night Train to Weymouth Falls." [Germ] (11:1) Fall 87, p. 11.
"Proverbs of Weymouth Falls." [Germ] (11:1) Fall 87, p. 13.
1005. CLARKE, Gerald
"No Way." [NegC] (7:3/4) 87, p. 102.
1006. CLARKE, John
"Fourteen Sonnets." [Temblor] (5) 87, p. 15-21.
1007. CLARKE, Kevin Jeffery
"The Gift." [JamesWR] (5:1) Fall 87, p. 14.
"Walking Papers." [ParisR] (29:105) Wint 87, p. 94.
CLARKE, William Comer
See COMER-CLARKE, William
1008. CLARY, Bruce W.
"Cloudburst: Stanton County, Kansas." [Wind] (17:59) 87, p. 8-9.
"January Night." [Wind] (17:59) 87, p. 8.
1009. CLARY, Killarney
"Clouds of birds rise above the upper bay." [MissouriR] (10:3) 87, p. 69-70.
"Mr. Dooms would meet us across the Oakland Bay Bridge." [MissouriR] (10:3) 87,
p. 68-69.
1010. CLAUDEL, Paul
"A Hundred Sentences Written on Fans" (Excerpts, tr. by Robin Magowan).
[Margin] (1) Wint 86, p. 14-21.

1011. CLAUSEN, Jan
"Diptych: Northwest Corner." [HangL] (50/51) 87, p. 44-46.
"Sestina, Winchell's Donut House." [Calyx] (10:2/3) Spr 87, p. 73-74.
1012. CLAVIJO PEREZ, Elena
"Nos Llevo la Muerte Tu Silencio." [LindLM] (6:1) Ja-Mr 87, p. 5.
1013. CLEMENTE, Vince
"In Ciardi's Attic Study." [Interim] (6:1) Spr 87, p. 13.
1014. CLEMENTS, Arthur (See also CLEMENTS, Arthur L.)
"He Said." [Lips] (13) 87, p. 16-18.
1015. CLEMENTS, Arthur L. (See also CLEMENTS, Arthur)
"Eddie Ferguson Watches TV" (for Barry Targan). [Footwork] 87, p. 10-11.
"Why I Don't Speak Italian." [Footwork] 87, p. 12.
1016. CLEMENTS, Susan (See also CLEMENTS, Susan Hauptfleisch)
"Aruba." [Lips] (13) 87, p. 12-13.
"Grace." [Footwork] 87, p. 23.
"Nottingham Lace." [Lips] (13) 87, p. 11.
"On the Hill." [Lips] (13) 87, p. 14-15.
"Snow Country." [Footwork] 87, p. 23.
"The Year You Died." [Blueline] (7:2/3 [i.e. 8:2/3?]) 87, p. 97.
1017. CLEMENTS, Susan Hauptfleisch (See also CLEMENTS, Susan)
"Vietnam Veterans Memorial, Spring." [Contact] (9:44/45/46) Fall-Wint 87, p. 57.
1018. CLEVELAND, Odessa
"Life." [BlackALF] (21:4) Wint 87, p. 450.
1019. CLEVER, Bertold
"Exile." [JamesWR] (5:1) Fall 87, p. 1.
1020. CLIFFORD, Deborah Ann
"Mother's Earrings." [CentR] (31:2) Spr 87, p. 188-189.
1021. CLIFFORD, Wayne
"On Abducting the Cello" (Excerpt, for Rilke's musty funnybone). [Quarry] (36:1)
Wint 87, p. 109-111.
1022. CLIFTON, Leigh
"Boulangerie." [CrabCR] (4:2) Spr 87, p. 16.
1023. CLIFTON, Linda J.
"90° in the Shade." [SouthernHR] (21:3) Sum 87, p. 236.
1024. CLIFTON, Lucille
"Crazy Horse Names His Daughter." [AmerPoR] (16:5) S-O 87, p. 4.
"Cruelty. Don't talk to me about cruelty." [AmerPoR] (16:5) S-O 87, p. 4.
"The Death of Thelma Sayles" (2/13/59, age 44). [AmerPoR] (16:5) S-O 87, p. 5.
"Here is another bone to pick with you." [AmerPoR] (16:5) S-O 87, p. 4.
"If Our Grandchild Be a Girl." [AmerPoR] (16:5) S-O 87, p. 5.
"L. at Gettysburg." [AmerPoR] (16:5) S-O 87, p. 4.
"L. at Jonestown." [AmerPoR] (16:5) S-O 87, p. 4.
"L. at Nagasaki." [AmerPoR] (16:5) S-O 87, p. 4.
"The Lost Women." [AmerPoR] (16:5) S-O 87, p. 4.
"The Message of Crazy Horse." [AmerPoR] (16:5) S-O 87, p. 4.
"My Dream About the Poet." [AmerPoR] (16:5) S-O 87, p. 5.
"Shapeshifter Poems." [AmerPoR] (16:5) S-O 87, p. 3.
"Sorrow Song." [AmerPoR] (16:5) S-O 87, p. 5.
"This belief." [AmerPoR] (16:5) S-O 87, p. 5.
"What spells raccoon to me." [AmerPoR] (16:5) S-O 87, p. 5.
1025. CLIMENHAGA, Joel
"Beautiful Armenian Women." [Pig] (14) 87, p. 94.
"Ninety-Nine Messages from Separate Places" (Selections: 4 poems). [KanQ] (19:3)
Sum 87, p. 74-75.
"Ripening Silences Greet My Ears." [Pig] (14) 87, p. 94.
"Starting from Eighty-Six Thousand Five Hundred and Fifty-Three" (Selections: 3
poems). [KanQ] (19:3) Sum 87, p. 75-76.
1026. CLINTON, Michèlle T.
"Migration of the Rats" (1985 Alice Jackson Poetry Prize: Third Prize). [Electrum]
(39) Fall-Wint 87, p. 90-10.
1027. CLOUD, Darrah
"Inmates." [Witness] (1:3) Fall 87, p. 122.
1028. CLOUTIER, Cécile
"Il fait BLANC partout." [Os] (25) 87, p. 7.
1029. CLOUTIER, David
"Nightscripts." [Pembroke] (19) 87, p. 214.

CLUE, Charlotte de
    See DeCLUE, Charlotte
1030. COADY, Michael
    "Letting Go." [Pembroke] (19) 87, p. 81.
    "The Mouth of Time" (at Muckross Abbey, Killarney). [Pembroke] (19) 87, p.
        63-64.
1031. COAKER, Evan
    "Fame." [LitR] (30:4) Sum 87, p. 620.
1032. COATES, Carrol
    "Something Is Circulating" (tr. of Marthe Jalbert). [Paint] (14:27) Spr 87, p. 13-14.
1033. COBARRUBIAS, Norberto Abel
    "Olor." [Mairena] (9:24) 87, p. 77.
1034. COCCIMIGLIO, Vic
    "Orders." [MSS] (5:3) 87, p. 150-151.
1035. COCHRAN, Leonard
    "Acts." [ChrC] (104:29) 14 O 87, p. 877.
1036. COCOZZELLA, Peter
    "The Prodigal Son" (In Memory of León Felipe, tr. of Agustí Bartra). [Paint] (14:27)
        Spr 87, p. 18-22.
1037. COE, Dina
    "Islands of New York." [US1] (20/21) Wint 86-87, p. 4.
    "The Maggot." [KanQ] (19:3) Sum 87, p. 209.
1038. COFER, Judith Ortiz
    "Betrayal Is." [ChatR] (8:1) Fall 87, p. 16.
    "Dear Odysseus." [SouthernR] (23:4) O 87, p. 809-810.
    "Old Women." [SouthernPR] (27:2) Fall 87, p. 59.
    "Penelope." [SouthernR] (23:4) O 87, p. 808.
    "Unspoken" (to my daughter). [PraS] (61:2) Sum 87, p. 64.
1039. COGGESHALL, Rosanne
    "Advent, 1985." [SoCaR] (20:1) Fall 87, p. 22.
    "Walking: Pawleys Island, January, 1985." [SouthernR] (23:2) Ap 87, p. 364-369.
1040. COGSWELL, Fred
    "Wordsworth County." [AntigR] (69/70) 87, p. 164.
1041. COHEN, Andrea
    "Story of the Tattoo." [Ploughs] (13:4) 87, p. 29-30.
1042. COHEN, Carole
    "I Swear It!" [Ascent] (12:3) 87, p. 28-29.
    "Slack-Jawed Moon." [CapeR] (22:1) Spr 87, p. 17.
    "We Who Wait." [Ascent] (12:3) 87, p. 29-30.
1043. COHEN, Helen Degen
    "The Children of War Smile and Are Happy." [Outbr] (18/19) Fall 86-Spr 88, p.
        45-46.
    "Class." [Pig] (14) 87, p. 71.
    "The Doll, Waiting for Revison." [Outbr] (18/19) Fall 86-Spr 88, p. 44.
    "Light." [PartR] (54:4) Fall 87, p. 584-585.
    "The Little Poet." [Outbr] (18/19) Fall 86-Spr 88, p. 43.
    "The Red House." [Outbr] (18/19) Fall 86-Spr 88, p. 47.
1044. COHEN, Jeff
    "The Golden Boys." [ChatR] (8:1) Fall 87, p. 17.
1045. COHEN, Jonathan
    "From Nicaragua, with Love: Poems 1979-1986" (Selections: 4 poems, tr. of
        Ernesto Cardenal). [Trans] (18) Spr 87, p. 246-253.
    "Walt Whitman in Ohio." [Agni] (24/25) 87, p. 241.
1046. COHEN, Marc
    "Breakawayer." [AnotherCM] (17) 87, p. 15-16.
    "A Journey Back to Where It Started." [AnotherCM] (17) 87, p. 13-14.
    "Mecox Road" (for Darragh Park). [Verse] (4:2) Je 87, p. 53-57.
COHEN, Maree Zukor
    See ZUKOR-COHEN, Maree
1047. COHEN, Rhea L.
    "Resonance" (A Poem Sequence, For Stephen J. Gould). [Lyra] (1:1) 87, p. 19-21.
1048. COKINOS, Christopher
    "Water Night." [MidwQ] (29:1) Aut 87, p. 73.
1049. COLAKIS, Marianthe
    "Helen" (tr. of Yannis Ritsos). [WebR] (12:1) Spr 87, p. 59-77.

1050. COLANDER, Valerie Nieman
"Feeding Cattle at Night, Jan. 16." [BellR] (10:2) Fall 87, p. 31.
"Hanging Up Clothes." [GreenfR] (14:3/4) Sum-Fall 87, p. 41.
"Hearing That My Piano Teacher Died." [LaurelR] (20:1/2) Sum 87, p. 14-15.
"Never Wear a Hat." [LaurelR] (20:1/2) Sum 87, p. 15.
"November." [GreenfR] (14:3/4) Sum-Fall 87, p. 42.
"A Raccoon Saved." [BellR] (10:2) Fall 87, p. 30.
"A September Evening, Farmington, W. Va." [BellR] (10:2) Fall 87, p. 32.
"Three Lectures on Bird Songs." [SouthernPR] (27:1) Spr 87, p. 13-14.

1051. COLE, E. R.
"Anosmiac." [InterPR] (13:2) Fall 87, p. 53-54.
"Summer Company." [InterPR] (13:2) Fall 87, p. 51-52.
"These Solemn Turnings." [InterPR] (13:2) Fall 87, p. 55-56.

1052. COLE, Henri
"Saint Stephen's Day with the Griffins." [YaleR] (76:2) Wint 87, p. 256-257.
"Three Look at One Another." [WilliamMR] (25) Spr 87, p. 89.

1053. COLE, James
"Grandma, On Rose Street." [MSS] (5:3) 87, p. 117.
"Late March." [SouthwR] (72:2) Spr 87, p. 236.

1054. COLE, Norma
"Il Donc" (Selection: II, tr. of Danielle Collobert). [Act] (7) 87, p. 20-28.
"Paper House" (part two, p-x). [Sulfur] (19) Spr 87, p. 82-85.
"The Provinces" (for Jack Purdom "Nick" Latham). [Act] (7) 87, p. 34-40.

1055. COLE, William
"Literary River Rhyme." [LightY] '87, c86, p. 212.
"Marriage Couplet." [LightY] '87, c86, p. 131.
"Ribald River Rhyme." [LightY] '87, c86, p. 175.
"What a Friend We Have in Cheeses! or Sing a Song of Liederkranz." [LightY] '87,
c86, p. 36-38.

1056. COLEMAN, John
"Body Craters." [Poem] (57) Mr 87, p. 13.
"Jarts." [WindO] (49) Fall 87, p. 6.
"Players." [StoneC] (15:1/2) Fall-Wint 87-88, p. 54.
"Porch Light." [WindO] (49) Fall 87, p. 6.

1057. COLEMAN, Mary Ann
"At the Hospital." [NegC] (7:3/4) 87, p. 169.
"Autumn Camping." [OhioR] (39) 87, p. 42-43.
"Lakescape: After the Funeral." [Pembroke] (19) 87, p. 211.
"Waking in Athens, Georgia." [Amelia] (4:1/2, issue 9) 87, p. 124.

1058. COLEMAN, Wanda
"All About a Humbug." [HighP] (2:1) Spr 87, p. 53-56.
"Bottom Out Blues." [Electrum] (39) Fall-Wint 87, p. 38.
"In the Kitchen My Potatoes Are Polemical." [MassR] (28:4) Wint 87, p. 705.

1059. COLES, Katharine
"Demeter." [Shen] (37:4) 87, p. 46-47.

1060. COLETTI, Edward
"Nuthatch." [LightY] '87, c86, p. 121.

1061. COLLIER, Michael
"Burial." [Boulevard] (2:3) Fall 87, p. 74-75.
"The Diver." [Poetry] (149:4) Ja 87, p. 212.
"Feedback." [NewYorker] (62:50) 2 F 87, p. 34.
"North Corridor." [Antaeus] (58) Spr 87, p. 95-96.
"A Private Place." [Poetry] (149:4) Ja 87, p. 213.
"The Problem." [Boulevard] (2:3) Fall 87, p. 75-76.

1062. COLLIER, Phyllis K.
"The Cost of Living." [InterPR] (13:1) Spr 87, p. 98.
"Digging into the Darkness." [InterPR] (13:1) Spr 87, p. 99.

1063. COLLIGAN, Elsa
"Full Moon Man" (For Eric). [Phoenix] (7:2) 87, p. 40.

1064. COLLINS, Billy
"The Brooklyn Museum of Art." [NewYorker] (63:13) 18 My 87, p. 109.
"Cancer" (1985 Alice Jackson Poetry Prize: 2nd Honorable Mention). [Electrum]
(39) Fall-Wint 87, p. 12.
"Come Running." [BlackWR] (14:1) Fall 87, p. 91.
"The Life of Riley: A Definitive Biography" (special section: 13 poems). [WormR]
(27:4, issue 108) 87, p. 97-104.

"Night Sand." [BlackWR] (14:1) Fall 87, p. 65.
"Pensée." [BlackWR] (14:1) Fall 87, p. 37.
1065. COLLINS, Caroline
"Nina's Place." [Poem] (58) N 87, p. 4.
1066. COLLINS, Floyd
"Border Town." [MemphisSR] (7:2) Spr 87, p. 35.
"Riding Accident." (for Michael Gills). [MemphisSR] (7:2) Spr 87, p. 34.
1067. COLLINS, Loretta
"The Mother's Song" (for Douglas). [AntR] (45:4) Fall 87, p. 448-450.
"Storm" (for "Johnboy" Lopez). [AntR] (45:4) Fall 87, p. 445-447.
1068. COLLINS, Martha
"Aesthetics I." [PoetryE] (23/24) Fall 87, p. 198.
"Before Spring." [Agni] (24/25) 87, p. 100.
"Dotted Line." [PoetryE] (23/24) Fall 87, p. 195-196.
"Leaf." [Agni] (24/25) 87, p. 99.
"Pentecost." [DenQ] (21:3) Wint 87, p. 43-44.
"Plot." [WestB] (20) 87, p. 81.
"Slug." [Ploughs] (13:4) 87, p. 31.
"Testimony." [PoetryE] (23/24) Fall 87, p. 197.
"Wings." [Agni] (24/25) 87, p. 98.
1069. COLLOBERT, Danielle
"Il Donc" (Selection: II, tr. by Norma Cole). [Act] (7) 87, p. 20-28.
1070. COLLOM, Jack
"Factory Crumb." [HangL] (50/51) 87, p. 54.
"Father Demo Square" (for Fred Worden). [HangL] (50/51) 87, p. 50-52.
"Sick & Sexy." [HangL] (50/51) 87, p. 53.
1071. COLON RUIZ, José O.
"Imagenes Incongruentes." [Mairena] (9:24) 87, p. 115.
1072. COLT, Scott
"Untimely Confrontation: Argument After a Clockwork Orange." [ChatR] (8:1) Fall 87, p. 18.
1073. COLTHARP, Duane
"Almost." [KanQ] (19:1/2) Wint-Spr 87, p. 188.
1074. COLTMAN, Paul
"First Gentleman." [CumbPR] (6:2) Spr 87, p. 50-51.
"The Road." [CumbPR] (6:2) Spr 87, p. 52-53.
"Tog's Trip." [CumbPR] (6:2) Spr 87, p. 54-55.
1075. COLUMBUS, Claudette
"Coronary" (In Memoriam, tr. of Rosa Elena Maldonado, w. David Weiss). [SenR] (17:1) 87, p. 40.
"Desire" (tr. of Rosa Elena Maldonado, w. David Weiss). [SenR] (17:1) 87, p. 42.
"Dreams on a Nonexistent Shore" (tr. of Rosa Elena Maldonado, w. David Weiss). [SenR] (17:1) 87, p. 43.
"Inheritance" (tr. of Rosa Elena Maldonado, w. David Weiss). [SenR] (17:1) 87, p. 39.
"Not the City" (tr. of Rosa Elena Maldonado, w. David Weiss). [SenR] (17:1) 87, p. 41.
1076. COMER-CLARKE, William
"Sensation." [Bogg] (57) 87, p. 17.
1077. COMFORT, Alex
"Curriculum Vitae." [Interim] (6:1) Spr 87, p. 14-15.
"O do not take my towel, Sir." [Interim] (6:2) Fall 87, p. 29-30.
1078. COMPTON, Gayle
"Old Woman Walking." [Wind] (17:61) 87, p. 8.
"Storm." [Wind] (17:61) 87, p. 7.
1079. CONDINI, Ned
"And the Wolf" (tr. of Mario Luzi). [PartR] (54:3) Sum 87, p. 427-428.
"Don't ask us the word that will give shape" (tr. of Eugenio Montale). [PraS] (61:3) Fall 87, p. 70-71.
"I often met evil in life" (tr. of Eugenio Montale). [PraS] (61:3) Fall 87, p. 72.
"I would have liked to feel scoured, bared" (tr. of Eugenio Montale). [PraS] (61:3) Fall 87, p. 72.
"North Wind" (tr. of Eugenio Montale). [PraS] (61:3) Fall 87, p. 71.
1080. CONE, Jon
"Abstract." [Rampike] (5:3) 87, p. 74.

1081. CONN, Jan
"Correll." [PraF] (8:2) Sum 87, p. 41-42.
"Farm-aid, Champaign-Urbana, September, 1985" (for Cookie & Carl & the two
Ls). [PraF] (8:2) Sum 87, p. 40.
1082. CONN, Stewart
"In Monte Mario." [Verse] (4:2) Je 87, p. 9.
1083. CONNELLAN, Leo
"Maine." [Raccoon] (24/25) My 87, p. 94.
"Pulling Oar." [GreenfR] (14:3/4) Sum-Fall 87, p. 148-149.
"Verplanck." [GreenfR] (14:3/4) Sum-Fall 87, p. 150.
"Wawenock." [TexasR] (7:3/4) 87, p. 25.
1084. CONNER, Ann
"Storm." [MidwQ] (28:2) Wint 87, p. 212-213.
1085. CONNER, Debra
"Persephone." [LaurelR] (20:1/2) Sum 87, p. 132.
1086. CONNOLLY, Geraldine (See also CONNOLLY, Gerry)
"Rouen." [Vis] (24) 87, p. 14.
"Silhouette." [CrossCur] (7:2) 87, p. 116-117.
"To Welcome the Soul." [SouthernR] (23:4) O 87, p. 826.
1087. CONNOLLY, Gerry (See also CONNOLLY, Geraldine)
"Irwin, Pennsylvania, 1955." [HighP] (2:2) Fall 87, p. 188-189.
1088. CONNORS, Bruton
"Englym" (reprinted from Bogg 28-29). [Bogg] (58) 87, p. 42.
1089. CONNORS, Marie
"Centennial Park." [Raccoon] (24/25) My 87, p. 234.
1090. CONOLEY, Gillian
"Ahkmatova and Tsvetaeva." [WillowS] (20) Spr 87, p. 69.
"Country Music." [SouthernPR] (27:1) Spr 87, p. 6-7.
"Harvest." [WillowS] (20) Spr 87, p. 70.
"July 5, 1985." [Confr] (35/36) Spr-Fall 87, p. 251.
"Leah Callahan: 1882-1972." [WillowS] (20) Spr 87, p. 71-72.
"The Native." [SouthernPR] (27:1) Spr 87, p. 5-6.
"Snow." [SouthernPR] (27:2) Fall 87, p. 35-36.
1091. CONOVER, Carl
"The Discovery of Morbidezza." [MidAR] (7:2) 87, p. 85.
"Obituary." [CarolQ] (39:2) Wint 87, p. 79.
"Paradise." [BelPoJ] (38:1) Fall 87, p. 4.
1092. CONSTANTINE, David
"Adam Confesses an Infidelity to Eve." [Waves] (14:4) Spr 86, p. 90.
"Butterfly." [Waves] (14:4) Spr 86, p. 89.
"Pillbox." [Waves] (14:4) Spr 86, p. 89.
"The Trees." [Waves] (14:4) Spr 86, p. 91.
1093. CONTI, Edmund
"Bears Repeating." [SmPd] (24:2) Spr 87, p. 26.
"Cross Words." [LightY] '87, c86, p. 233.
"Emphasis Mine." [LightY] '87, c86, p. 221.
"Haiku: How do I love thee?" [Bogg] (57) 87, p. 5.
"Haiku: Seventeen sylla-." [LightY] '87, c86, p. 193.
"Mala—Plop!" [Bogg] (58) 87, p. 39.
"My Son, the Tuba Player." [LightY] '87, c86, p. 98.
"On First Looking into Chapman's Refrigerator." [LightY] '87, c86, p. 56.
1094. CONTOGENIS, Constantine
"Another's Light" (for poets, tr. of Chong Hyon-Jong, w. Wolhee Choe). [Nimrod]
(31:1) Fall-Wint 87, p. 133.
"Family" (tr. of Chong Hyon-Jong, w. Wolhee Choe). [Nimrod] (31:1) Fall-Wint
87, p. 133.
1095. CONTOSKI, Victor
"Autumn House." [HangL] (50/51) 87, p. 56.
"White Shadows." [HangL] (50/51) 87, p. 55.
1096. CONWAY, Jack
"Every Possibility." [NewRena] (7:1, #21) Fall 87, p. 119.
"Skeletons in a Tree." [NewRena] (7:1, #21) Fall 87, p. 118.
1097. COOK, Dennis C.
"The wheel was a marvelous fad." [Amelia] (4:1/2, issue 9) 87, p. 42.
1098. COOK, Jane W.
"My Dancing Shadow." [Footwork] 87, p. 35.

1099. COOK, Paul
"Before She Left." [CharR] (13:2) Fall 87, p. 85.
"The Moon in the Phonebooth." [CharR] (13:2) Fall 87, p. 84.
1100. COOK, R. L.
"George Watson's College Revisited." [BallSUF] (28:4) Aut 87, p. 15-16.
1101. COOK, William W.
"The Children's Hair." [InterPR] (13:2) Fall 87, p. 80-82.
"Homecoming: North Carolina." [InterPR] (13:2) Fall 87, p. 84.
"Shy Lover" (For Ossie Davis). [InterPR] (13:2) Fall 87, p. 85.
"Zinnias." [InterPR] (13:2) Fall 87, p. 83-84.
1102. COOK-DARBY, Candice
"Late Mourning." [BelPoJ] (38:1) Fall 87, p. 1.
1103. COOLEY, Dennis
"Driving Home." [CrossC] (9:1) 87, p. 27.
"The Muse of Absence." [PraF] (8:4) Wint 87-88, p. 34.
"Parchment." [PraF] (8:4) Wint 87-88, p. 35.
"Planting" (Selection: vi). [PraF] (8:4) Wint 87-88, p. 33.
1104. COOLEY, Peter
"The Boy Child." [Poetry] (150:4) Jl 87, p. 207.
"Elegy." [Crazy] (32) Spr 87, p. 43.
"The Enclosed Field." [Raccoon] (24/25) My 87, p. 141.
"An Epiphany." [HayF] (2) Spr 87, p. 85.
"Fathers and Sons." [Poetry] (150:4) Jl 87, p. 205.
"Harvest Landscape: Blue Cart" (on Van Gogh). [SewanR] (95:2) Spr 87, p. 243.
"Iron Bridge at Trinquetaille" (on Van Gogh). [SewanR] (95:2) Spr 87, p. 242.
"The Pathetic Fallacy." [Crazy] (32) Spr 87, p. 42.
"Seascape with Attendant Premonitions." [Poetry] (150:4) Jl 87, p. 206.
"Self-Portrait in Front of an Easel." [TarRP] (26:2) Spr 87, p. 30.
"To a Willow Waist-high in the Mississippi." [HayF] (2) Spr 87, p. 86.
"Van Gogh, 'Garden of the Hospital at Arles'." [PraS] (61:1) Spr 87, p. 45.
"Van Gogh 'L'Arlesienne: Madame Ginoux'." [HayF] (2) Spr 87, p. 84.
"Van Gogh, 'Le Mousmé'." [Raccoon] (24/25) My 87, p. 142-143.
"Van Gogh, 'Meadow with Butterflies'." [CharR] (13:1) Spr 87, p. 89.
"Van Gogh, 'Olive Trees in a Mountain Landscape'." [PraS] (61:1) Spr 87, p. 43-44.
"Van Gogh, 'Orchard Bordered by Cypresses'." [PraS] (61:1) Spr 87, p. 44.
"Van Gogh, 'Portrait of Dr. Gachet'." [Raccoon] (24/25) My 87, p. 144-145.
"Van Gogh, 'The Drawbridge'." [SouthernPR] (27:1) Spr 87, p. 49.
"Van Gogh, 'The Woman at Cafe Tambourin'." [CharR] (13:1) Spr 87, p. 90-91.
"A Wheat Field." [TarRP] (26:2) Spr 87, p. 30.
1105. COOLIDGE, Clark
"Art & Life & Times." [FiveFR] (5) 87, p. 61.
"Ashbery Explains." [Conjunc] (10) 87, p. 78-80.
"At Egypt." [NewAW] (2) Fall 87, p. 1-18.
"Barely, Twombly." [Conjunc] (10) 87, p. 80-81.
"Cats Mounted on Cots." [Conjunc] (10) 87, p. 81-84.
"For Ed Ruscha." [FiveFR] (5) 87, p. 62.
"Literal Landscapes" (Selections: 20 poems). [Temblor] (6) 87, p. 41-50.
"Powers That Be Too." [Bound] (14:1/2) Fall 85-Wint 86 [c87], p. 54-55.
1106. COONEY, Ellen
"A Short Satyre Upon This Noysesome Age (1711)." [Bogg] (58) 87, p. 22.
1107. COOPER, Allan
"The Holy Place of the Spawn." [Germ] (11:1) Fall 87, p. 54.
"The Orchard." [Germ] (10:2) Spr 87, p. 52-53.
"A Presence in the Earth." [Germ] (10:2) Spr 87, p. 50.
"The Residue of Love." [Germ] (11:1) Fall 87, p. 54-55.
"Ten Yellow Daffodils." [Germ] (10:2) Spr 87, p. 51.
1108. COOPER, Bernard
"Aphorism." [WestHR] (41:4) Wint 87, p. 351.
"Ark." [MalR] (81) D 87, p. 96.
"Don't Think About Breathing." [WestHR] (41:4) Wint 87, p. 352.
"Gravitational Attraction." [MalR] (81) D 87, p. 94.
"Live Wire." [WestHR] (41:4) Wint 87, p. 353.
"Rain Rambling Through Japan." [WestHR] (41:4) Wint 87, p. 354-355.
"Temple of the Holy Ghost." [MalR] (81) D 87, p. 95.
"The Theory of Relativity." [MalR] (81) D 87, p. 97.

1109. COOPER, Darius
"Under the Gravity of Some Thirty Odd Years." [Chelsea] (46) 87, p. 236-239.
1110. COOPER, Irene
"Red Truck Farm." [Wind] (17:59) 87, p. 40.
1111. COOPER, Jane Todd
"The Nazi's Widow." [WebR] (12:2) Fall 87, p. 81-82.
"Sonogram." [WebR] (12:2) Fall 87, p. 83.
1112. COOPER, M. Truman (Marsha Truman)
"And Then I Knew I'd Always Be Alone." [Outbr] (18/19) Fall 86-Spr 88, p. 100.
"The Baby." [Outbr] (18/19) Fall 86-Spr 88, p. 98.
"Bao Chi." [Puerto] (22:2) Spr 87, p. 81.
"Black Bananas." [KanQ] (19:3) Sum 87, p. 275.
"The Broken Book." [CentR] (31:3) Sum 87, p. 287-289.
"The Cellar." [KanQ] (19:3) Sum 87, p. 275.
"The Courage of Children." [Outbr] (18/19) Fall 86-Spr 88, p. 99.
"The Day Pain Stops." [Outbr] (18/19) Fall 86-Spr 88, p. 101.
"The Dowser." [Blueline] (7:2/3 [i.e. 8:2/3?]) 87, p. 13.
"Eating Alone." [Farm] (4:2) Spr-Sum 87, p. 16.
"An Equal and Opposite Reaction." [SoDakR] (25:2) Sum 87, p. 74.
"The Fifth Bullet." [NewL] (54:2) Wint 87-88, p. 11-13.
"Firewood." [Puerto] (22:2) Spr 87, p. 80.
"Letting Go." [CrossCur] (7:1) 87, p. 29.
"The Mirage." [SoDakR] (25:2) Sum 87, p. 73.
"A Mondo." [MemphisSR] (8:1) Fall 87, p. 59.
"The New Bicycle." [Outbr] (18/19) Fall 86-Spr 88, p. 97.
"One More Small Wonder." [CentR] (31:3) Sum 87, p. 286-287.
"Opening Day at the California-Indochina Market." [NewL] (54:2) Wint 87-88, p. 5-7.
"Pain." [Raccoon] (24/25) My 87, p. 196.
"Phantom Limb Syndrome." [NewL] (54:2) Wint 87-88, p. 15.
"Picking Up a Black Marble." [Outbr] (18/19) Fall 86-Spr 88, p. 102.
"The Private." [NewL] (54:2) Wint 87-88, p. 10-11.
"The Reed Mat." [Phoenix] (7:2) 87, p. 50-51.
"The Specter." [PennR] (3:1) Spr-Sum 87, p. 63.
"Theater Means a Place to See." [NewL] (54:2) Wint 87-88, p. 14.
"This Will Break Your Heart." [NewL] (54:2) Wint 87-88, p. 8-9.
"Waking Up by an Oven." [MemphisSR] (8:1) Fall 87, p. 60.
1113. COOPER, Patricia
"There Is Rain." [PoetL] (82:3) Fall 87, p. 172.
1114. COOPER, Wyn
"The Country of Here Below." [HolCrit] (24:4) O 87, p. 14.
"Desert, with Train." [AntR] (45:4) Fall 87, p. 434.
1115. COOPER-FRATRIK, Julie
"A Celebrated Fiction Writer Reads from His Poetry" (Raymond Carver, 1984). [StoneC] (15:1/2) Fall-Wint 87-88, p. 22-23.
"Metamorphosis." [CapeR] (22:1) Spr 87, p. 15.
1116. COOPERMAN, Robert
"An American Uncle to His French Nephew." [Wind] (17:59) 87, p. 10.
"Aphrodite's Aunt." [GreensboroR] (43) Wint 87-88, p. 125.
"At the Nursing Home." [SouthernPR] (27:1) Spr 87, p. 33-34.
"The Cost." [HampSPR] Wint 87, p. 56.
"Dorothy Wordsworth." [GreensboroR] (40) Sum 86, p. 48.
"The Empress of the Laundromat." [Comm] (114:11) 5 Je 87, p. 357.
"Faces on the Post Office Wall." [PoetC] (19:1) Fall 87, p. 18.
"The Firing Squad." [PoetC] (19:1) Fall 87, p. 17.
"From 'The Ballad of Geordie'." [PikeF] (8) Fall 87, p. 3.
"Good-By and Keep Cold." [CharR] (13:2) Fall 87, p. 70.
"The Gothic Cathedral At Bourges." [InterPR] (13:2) Fall 87, p. 92.
"Hitchhiker's Nightmare." [PikeF] (8) Fall 87, p. 12.
"Lady Leicester Miscarries, 1776." [Poem] (57) Mr 87, p. 66-67.
"The Man Who Captured Eichmann." [CapeR] (22:1) Spr 87, p. 11.
"Medusa." [InterPR] (13:2) Fall 87, p. 91.
"The Mouse Sonata." [SnapD] (10:1/2) Wint 87, p. 18-19.
"The Music Man." [TarPR] (27:1) Fall 87, p. 43.
"O. Henry's Funeral." [CumbPR] (7:1) Fall 87, p. 4-5.
"Odysseus Remembers the Sacrifice of Iphigenia." [ChatR] (8:1) Fall 87, p. 19.

"Peter Tondee on His Death Bed, Savannah, Georgia, 1775." [HampSPR] Wint 87, p. 57-58.
"The Pony Express." [ColEng] (49:6) O 87, p. 652-653.
"The Promise." [PaintedB] (31) 87, p. 10.
"Quarters." [PaintedB] (31) 87, p. 8.
"Roland Thibidoux Travels by Stage Coach from Denver to Salida." [SnapD] (10:1/2) Wint 87, p. 16-17.
"The Root." [HampSPR] Wint 87, p. 56-57.
"The Secrets of the Virgin of Medjugorje, Yugoslavia." [Poem] (57) Mr 87, p. 64-65.
"Snow." [SmPd] (24:1) Wint 87, p. 10.
"A Talk with My Uncle." [PoetL] (82:3) Fall 87, p. 148.
"The Thrill of the Hunt." [StoneC] (15:1/2) Fall-Wint 87-88, p. 60.
"The Vietnam War Memorial." [PaintedB] (31) 87, p. 9.
"Views of the General." [Outbr] (18/19) Fall 86-Spr 88, p. 48-49.
"Your Cousin Donnie." [CapeR] (22:1) Spr 87, p. 10.
1117. COPE, Steven R.
"The Birds in My Window." [PoetryNW] (28:3) Aut 87, p. 39.
"A Burial." [CumbPR] (6:2) Spr 87, p. 4.
"Death of W." (on the tenth anniversary). [Confr] (35/36) Spr-Fall 87, p. 221.
"The Meaning of the Moon." [HolCrit] (24:4) O 87, p. 12-13.
"What We Have Heard on High." [PoetryNW] (28:3) Aut 87, p. 40-41.
1118. COPE, Wendy
"The New Regime." [LightY] '87, c86, p. 226.
"Strugnell's Bargain." [PikeF] (8) Fall 87, p. 35.
1119. COPELAND, Helen
"Healing." [Pembroke] (19) 87, p. 131.
1120. COPELAND, Robert F.
"Muscle Tension." [JamesWR] (4:3) Spr 87, p. 4.
1121. COPITHORNE, Judith
"Bookcases." [CapilR] (45) 87 [Ap 88], p. 83.
"Interface." [CapilR] (45) 87 [Ap 88], p. 78.
"Moving." [CapilR] (45) 87 [Ap 88], p. 82.
"Settle Down." [CapilR] (45) 87 [Ap 88], p. 84.
"Signature Ligature Significate." [CrossC] (9:3/4) 87, p. 11.
"Untitled: August 4, 1987, Yew Street, Vancouver." [CapilR] (45) 87 [Ap 88], p. 81.
"Untitled: I don't have time for language." [CapilR] (45) 87 [Ap 88], p. 80.
"Untitled: To get down." [CapilR] (45) 87 [Ap 88], p. 79.
1122. CORBETT, William
"Before Dinner." [NewAW] (1) 87, p. 39.
"Hot Mittens Biker." [NewAW] (1) 87, p. 40.
"A Palimpsest." [NewAW] (1) 87, p. 41.
1123. CORBIERE, Tristan
"Paria." [AntigR] (71/72) Aut 87-Wint 88, p. 90, 92.
"Pariah" (tr. by Peter Dale). [AntigR] (71/72) Aut 87-Wint 88, p. 91, 93.
1124. CORBUS, Patricia
"Ashes, Jade Mirrors." [AntigR] (71/72) Aut 87-Wint 88, p. 55.
"The Visit." [AntigR] (71/72) Aut 87-Wint 88, p. 54.
1125. CORCOBA, Víctor
"Paz!, excriben los poetas." [Mairena] (9:24) 87, p. 108-109.
1126. CORDING, Robert (Robert K.)
"After Dante." [TarPR] (27:1) Fall 87, p. 17.
"At the Halfway House." [Crazy] (32) Spr 87, p. 33-34.
"On Thinking about Gilbert White in Our Nuclear Age." [KenR] (NS 9:3) Sum 87, p. 54-58.
1127. COREY, R. R.
"From the Continued *Narration of My Life*." [Lips] (13) 87, p. 34.
"In Search of Myself." [Lips] (13) 87, p. 36.
"July 4, 5, and Other Days." [Lips] (13) 87, p. 35.
1128. COREY, Stephen
"Ars Poetica." [Poetry] (151:1/2) O-N 87, p. 35.
1129. CORMAN, Cid
"God has no authority." [Notus] (2:1) Spr 87, p. 21.
"I may not say." [Notus] (2:1) Spr 87, p. 23.
"My friend Bill Burnett." [Notus] (2:1) Spr 87, p. 20.

"Oppening." [Notus] (2:1) Spr 87, p. 22.
"So then there was you." [Notus] (2:1) Spr 87, p. 19.
CORMIER-SHEKERJIAN, Regina de
   See DeCORMIER-SHEKERJIAN, Regina
1130. CORN, Alfred
   "Archaic Torso of Apollo" (tr. of Rainer Maria Rilke). [Colum] (12) 87, p. 50.
   "The Chi-Rho Page from the Book of Kells." [Poetry] (151:1/2) O-N 87, p. 35-36.
   "Dublin, the Liberties." [Thrpny] (30) Sum 87, p. 9.
   "Letter to Teresa Guiccioli" (Missolonghi, March 3, 1824). [PartR] (54:2) Spr 87, p.
      274-275.
   "New Year." [PartR] (54:4) Fall 87, p. 582-583.
   "'Nina' at the Phoenix Park Zoo." [FourQ] (1:1) Wint 87, p. 8.
   "Paranoiad." [SouthwR] (72:4) Aut 87, p. 512-514.
   "The Poet's Task" (tr. of Pablo Neruda). [Colum] (12) 87, p. 51.
   "Stephen Dedalus: Self-Portrait as a Young Man." [FourQ] (1:1) Wint 87, p. 8.
   "Toward Skellig Michael." [GrandS] (7:1) Aut 87, p. 46.
   "Welcome to Farewell" (Alaska). [Margin] (4) Aut 87, p. 18.
   "An Xmas Murder." [Poetry] (151:3) D 87, p. 276-284.
1131. CORNIS-POP, Marcel
   "A Burning" (for Ion Caraion, tr. of Dorin Tudoran). [PartR] (54:3) Sum 87, p.
      434.
   "A Cross" (tr. of Dorin Tudoran). [PartR] (54:3) Sum 87, p. 433.
   "The Fountains of Serbia" (tr. of Anghel Dumbraveanu, w. Robert J. Ward).
      [MidAR] (7:2) 87, p. 65-83.
   "The Master to His Apprentice" (tr. of Dorin Tudoran). [PartR] (54:3) Sum 87, p.
      434.
   "Of Unforgettable Caligula" (tr. of Dorin Tudoran). [Vis] (25) 87, p. 34.
1132. CORPI, Lucha
   "Canción de Invierno" (A Magdalena Mora, 1952-1981). [Americas] (15:3/4)
      Fall-Wint 87, p. 51.
   "Fuga." [Americas] (15:3/4) Fall-Wint 87, p. 49-50.
   "Indocumentada Angustia." [Americas] (15:3/4) Fall-Wint 87, p. 52.
   "Invernario." [Americas] (15:3/4) Fall-Wint 87, p. 47.
   "Llueve." [Americas] (15:3/4) Fall-Wint 87, p. 55.
   "Recuerdo Intimo" (para Arturo y Finnigan). [Americas] (15:3/4) Fall-Wint 87, p.
      48.
   "Romance Negro." [Americas] (15:3/4) Fall-Wint 87, p. 45-46.
   "Sonata a Dos Voces" (A Mark Greenside). [Americas] (15:3/4) Fall-Wint 87, p.
      53-54.
1133. CORR, Michael
   "Snyder's Mountains & Rivers" (Selection). [RiverS] (24) 87, p. 39.
   "Venus and the Vikings." [RiverS] (24) 87, p. 66.
1134. CORRENTI, Frank
   "Off Broadway." [PennR] (3:1) Spr-Sum 87, p. 67.
1135. CORRIE, Daniel
   "The Fortunate Summer." [CapeR] (22:1) Spr 87, p. 18-19.
1136. CORRY, Charles
   "The Fragile World." [PoeticJ] (17) 87, p. 27.
   "Nomination." [PoeticJ] (17) 87, p. 26.
   "Reminders." [PoeticJ] (17) 87, p. 26.
1137. CORSE, Elizabeth
   "And the Band Plays On." [Amelia] (4:3, issue 10) 87, p. 45-46.
   "Lotusland." [Amelia] (4:3, issue 10) 87, p. 44-45.
   "Pleasures of My Flesh." [Amelia] (4:3, issue 10) 87, p. 43.
   "Wage of Love." [Amelia] (4:3, issue 10) 87, p. 45.
1138. CORTS, Elaine
   "An Excerpt from H" (tr. of Philippe Sollers). [Rampike] (5:3) 87, p. 35-36.
1139. CORY, Jim
   "Bare." [JamesWR] (4:2) Wint 87, p. 12.
   "Clip Elegy." [JamesWR] (4:2) Wint 87, p. 12.
   "Poem for Your Shorts." [JamesWR] (4:4) Sum 87, p. 9.
1140. COSENS, Susan M.
   "Grandmother's Dream, Picking Waterlilies" (Little Gunflint Lake, Minnesota,
      1905). [YellowS] (22) Spr 87, p. 9.
   "Kiwi Fruit Fantasy." [YellowS] (22) Spr 87, p. 8.

99

1141. COSIER, Tony
"Driving Fallowfield." [Germ] (10:2) Spr 87, p. 21.
"Lodgepole." [Germ] (10:2) Spr 87, p. 20.
"Méditation du Nouvel An" (pour George Johnston, tr. by John Palander). [AntigR]
        (68) Wint 87, p. 35.
"New Year Meditation" (for George Johnston). [AntigR] (68) Wint 87, p. 34.
"Timberline." [Blueline] (7:2/3 [i.e. 8:2/3?]) 87, p. 96.
1142. COSSEBOOM, Ray
"The Archer." [Grain] (15:1) Spr 87, p. 45.
"Back There." [Grain] (15:1) Spr 87, p. 45.
"Beyond Hollyhock Hill." [Grain] (15:1) Spr 87, p. 48.
"The Cosmic Woman." [Grain] (15:1) Spr 87, p. 48.
"Hieroglyphics." [Grain] (15:1) Spr 87, p. 46.
"Laurie." [Grain] (15:1) Spr 87, p. 49.
"Quickly Sketched." [Grain] (15:1) Spr 87, p. 47.
"The Subway." [Grain] (15:1) Spr 87, p. 47.
"Waiting." [Grain] (15:1) Spr 87, p. 46.
1143. COSTANZO, Gerald
"For a Stroke Opera Queen." [ColR] (NS 14:1) Spr-Sum 87, p. 62-63.
"Landscape with Unemployed Jockeys" (for Allyson Hunter). [NoDaQ] (55:1) Wint
        87, p. 42-43.
"The Majestic." [Raccoon] (24/25) My 87, p. 171.
"Manhattan as a Latin-American Capital." [NoDaQ] (55:1) Wint 87, p. 42.
"Seeing My Name in *TV Guide*." [NoDaQ] (55:1) Wint 87, p. 43.
1144. COTO, Patricia
"Todo es nada más que un sorbo." [Mairena] (9:24) 87, p. 122.
1145. COUCH, Larry
"Don't Eat" (tr. of Joyce Mansour). [Vis] (25) 87, p. 27.
"Invite Me" (tr. of Joyce Mansour). [Vis] (23) 87, p. 15.
"Night I Am Vagabond" (tr. of Joyce Mansour). [Vis] (24) 87, p. 25.
"The Telephone Rings" (tr. of Joyce Mansour). [Vis] (23) 87, p. 15.
1146. COUGHLIN, Anthony
"Silence." [Footwork] 87, p. 60.
"The Times." [Footwork] 87, p. 60.
1147. COULEHAN, Jack
"The Dust of the West." [GreenfR] (14:3/4) Sum-Fall 87, p. 129.
"The Empress of Ireland." [BellR] (10:2) Fall 87, p. 43.
"Jerusalem." [GreenfR] (14:3/4) Sum-Fall 87, p. 130.
"Mother and Child." [GreenfR] (14:3/4) Sum-Fall 87, p. 131-132.
"Sometimes the Bodies of Women." [BellR] (10:1) Spr 87, p. 26.
1148. COULETTE, Henri
"At the Writers Conference." [Sequoia] (31:1) Centennial [Sequoia] (31:1)
        Centennial issue 87, p. 27.
1149. COULTHARD, Leslie Jean
"Growth." [Comm] (114:19) 6 N 87, p. 618.
"Star to Salt Star." [ManhatPR] (9) Sum 87, p. 48.
1150. COUNTS, Jill Caroline
"Shopping List." [BallSUF] (28:4) Aut 87, p. 69.
COURCY, Lynne H. de
        See DeCOURCY, Lynne H.
1151. COURSEN, Herb
"Revision of the Book: Early 50's." [SmPd] (24:3) Fall 87, p. 17.
1152. COURT, Wesli
"Lamps" (On lines from Emily Dickinson's letters). [TexasR] (7:3/4) 87, p. 26.
"Rondine of the Rare Device." [LightY] '87, c86, p. 151.
"Small Victory" (On lines from Emily Dickinson's letters). [TexasR] (7:3/4) 87, p.
        27.
1153. COURTEAU, Joanna
"Among Those Who Have Gone Away" ("Entre Los Que Se Fueron," tr. of María
        Victoria Atencia). [PoetC] (18:2) Wint 87, p. 33.
"The Day" ("O Dia," tr. of Carlos Felipe Moisés). [PoetC] (18:2) Wint 87, p. 35.
"The Day of Anger" ("Dia de la Ira," tr. of María Victoria Atencia). [PoetC] (18:2)
        Wint 87, p. 32.
"The Hard Bread" ("El Duro Pan," tr. of María Victoria Atencia). [PoetC] (18:2)
        Wint 87, p. 31.
"Journey" (tr. of Arnaldo Saraiva). [PoetC] (18:2) Wint 87, p. 29.

"Knowledge" ("Conhecimento," tr. of Arnaldo Saraiva). [PoetC] (18:2) Wint 87, p. 42.
"Leave Me Alone" ("Dejame," tr. of María Victoria Atencia). [PoetC] (18:2) Wint 87, p. 30.
"An Ox Striped in Shadow" ("Boi Raiado em Penumbra," tr. of Carlos Felipe Moisés). [PoetC] (18:2) Wint 87, p. 39.
"The Sound of the Sea" ("O Rumor do Mar," tr. of Carlos Felipe Moisés). [PoetC] (18:2) Wint 87, p. 36.
"Tense & Mood" ("O Tempo e o Modo," tr. of Arnaldo Saraiva). [PoetC] (18:2) Wint 87, p. 41.
"This Morning" ("Esta Manhã," tr. of Carlos Felipe Moisés). [PoetC] (18:2) Wint 87, p. 34.
"University" ("Universidade," tr. of Arnaldo Saraiva). [PoetC] (18:2) Wint 87, p. 40.
"Your Smile" ("Teu Sorriso," tr. of Carlos Felipe Moisés). [PoetC] (18:2) Wint 87, p. 37-38.

1154. COWEE, William E.
"Meeting Gandhi on the Markleeville Road." [Interim] (6:2) Fall 87, p. 17.

1155. COWING, Sue
"Gagaku, in Kyoto and After." [BambooR] (36) Fall 87, p. 37.

1156. COWSER, Robert
"Bitter Milk." [EngJ] (76:4) Ap 87, p. 42.

1157. COX, Andrew
"A Damn Good Excuse." [Ascent] (12:3) 87, p. 48.
"The Missouri Lottery." [HighP] (2:1) Spr 87, p. 33-34.

1158. COX, Carol
"A City." [HangL] (50/51) 87, p. 57.
"Made by Hand" (6 Poems). [HangL] (50/51) 87, p. 58-61.

1159. COX, Daniel J.
"Portrait of the Artist as Teacher (or the Teacher as Artist)." [EngJ] (76:4) Ap 87, p. 87.

1160. COX, Mark
"Crossings." [IndR] (10:1/2) 87, p. 50-51.
"Horizontals." [IndR] (10:1/2) 87, p. 52-53.
"I Want to Know What Love It." [Poetry] (149:4) Ja 87, p. 210-211.
"Lemon Icing" (After W. H. Auden). [Poetry] (149:4) Ja 87, p. 211.
"Linda's House of Beauty." [AmerPoR] (16:1) Ja-F 87, p. 36.
"The Old Sanctuary Road" (for Nano Chatfield). [IndR] (10:1/2) 87, p. 56-58.
"Poem for the Name Mary." [AmerPoR] (16:1) Ja-F 87, p. 36.
"Prospect, Ohio." [IndR] (10:1/2) 87, p. 49.
"Running My Fingers through My Beard on Bolton Road." [IndR] (10:1/2) 87, p. 54-55.
"Things My Grandfather Must Have Said." [Poetry] (149:4) Ja 87, p. 209-210.
"Why Is That Pencil Always Behind Your Ear." [IndR] (10:1/2) 87, p. 47-48.

1161. COX, Rosemary D.
"Youth and Age." [DekalbLAJ] (20:1/4) 87, p. 63.

1162. COX, Sarah Christensen
"Savoring Paradise." [CrescentR] (5:1) 87, p. 116.

1163. COX, Tom
"Interlude in a Garage." [Shen] (37:4) 87, p. 80-81.

1164. COXE, Louis
"Moving." [TexasR] (7:3/4) 87, p. 28.
"Trial." [TexasR] (7:3/4) 87, p. 29.

CRABBE, Chris Wallace
See WALLACE-CRABBE, Chris

1165. CRAGO, William
"Inquisition." [EngJ] (76:2) F 87, p. 57.

1166. CRAIG, Christine
"December Evening." [Chelsea] (46) 87, p. 305.

1167. CRAIG, David
"Presbyopia" (1986 Finalist, Eve of Saint Agnes Poetry Competition). [NegC] (7:1/2) 87, p. 201.

1168. CRAIG, Eugene A.
"I Hypnotize Bugs." [LightY] '87, c86, p. 247.

1169. CRAIG, Hugh
"Mandala." [Nimrod] (31:1) Fall-Wint 87, p. 83.

1170. CRAIGHEAD, Philip
"Hina Matsuri." [Amelia] (4:1/2, issue 9) 87, p. 14.
1171. CRAIN, W. Caleb
"Sea, Nothing" (tr. of Juan Ramón Jimenez). [HarvardA] (122:1) N 87, p. 37.
1172. CRAM, David
"After Dinner." [LightY] '87, c86, p. 46.
"Alphabet Soup." [LightY] '87, c86, p. 102.
"The Editor Regrets." [LightY] '87, c86, p. 200.
"Limericks" (2 poems). [LightY] '87, c86, p. 173.
"Tunnel Vision." [LightY] '87, c86, p. 166.
1173. CRAM, Roger
"Babies." [HiramPoR] (43) Fall-Wint 87-88, p. 40-41.
"Observation." [HiramPoR] (43) Fall-Wint 87-88, p. 4.
1174. CRAMER, Steven
"For Now." [PartR] (54:1) Wint 87, p. 129-130.
"Head of a Young Girl" (Vermeer). [Agni] (24/25) 87, p. 101-102.
"Mercy." [Pequod] (23/24) 87, p. 267-268.
"The Present Tense." [Pequod] (23/24) 87, p. 266.
1175. CRASE, Douglas
"Dog Star Sale." [ParisR] (29:102) Spr 87, p. 92.
"Refuge." [WilliamMR] (25) Spr 87, p. 7.
"True Solar Holiday." [YaleR] (77:1) Aut 87, p. 25.
1176. CRATER, Theresa L.
"Downpour." [SinW] (31) 87, p. 46.
1177. CRAVEN, Bruce
"On Broadway." [RiverS] (22) 87, p. 70.
1178. CRAWFORD, Robert
"La Bibliotheque de Nora Barnacle." [Verse] (4:2) Je 87, p. 23.
"The Clerk Maxwell Country." [Verse] (4:2) Je 87, p. 22.
"Experiments." [Verse] (4:2) Je 87, p. 23.
"The Grate Tradition." [Verse] (4:2) Je 87, p. 24.
"Text." [Verse] (4:2) Je 87, p. 24.
CREDICO, Jessan Dunn de
See DeCREDICO, Jessan Dunn
1179. CREEDON, Michael
"Blood of the Boboso: Last Tale of Power" (Selections, w. Henry Pelkingford).
[Caliban] (3) 87, p. 69-70.
"Getting Myself Ready for Frances." [ColEng] (49:2) F 87, p. 175-177.
1180. CREELEY, Robert
"Broad Bay." [WestHR] (41:1) Spr 87, p. 19.
"Epic." [WestHR] (41:1) Spr 87, p. 20.
"Le Fou" (for Charles). [TriQ] (68) Wint 87, p. 133.
"I Would Have Known You Anywhere." [Caliban] (2) 87, p. 86.
"Nationalgalerie Berlin." [Conjunc] (11) 87?, p. 213-215.
"The Seasons." [Conjunc] (11) 87?, p. 211-213.
"This World." [NoDaQ] (55:4) Fall 87, p. 95-96.
"World." [WestHR] (41:1) Spr 87, p. 19.
1181. CRENNER, James
"Museums." [Poetry] (150:3) Je 87, p. 161.
1182. CREWE, Jennifer
"A Change of Season." [Pequod] (23/24) 87, p. 99.
"Great-Grandmother." [Pequod] (23/24) 87, p. 100-101.
1183. CREWS, Judson
"A Collage You Tossed Together Like." [WritersF] (13) Fall 87, p. 181.
"God Made Chickens and Children." [Wind] (17:61) 87, p. 23.
"The Good." [WormR] (27:4, issue 108) 87, p. 93.
"The Hidden Dream Masqueraded by the Most." [Interim] (6:2) Fall 87, p. 24.
"I Always Liked Tall Girls — Even in Africa." [WormR] (27:4, issue 108) 87, p.
92.
"I Am Eternally Fallen Between Two Stools, Time." [Pembroke] (19) 87, p. 118.
"I Denied th Destiny of Gender — Denied It." [WormR] (27:4, issue 108) 87, p. 92.
"I Have Cut Myself Apart in Several." [WormR] (27:4, issue 108) 87, p. 93.
"I Lied." [WormR] (27:4, issue 108) 87, p. 93.
"I Sat Down in That Great Blonde Chair." [Amelia] (4:1/2, issue 9) 87, p. 49.
"If Bulltoven Liked Those Girlie-Butt Pictures." [SlipS] (7) 87, p. 102.

"In a 350-Thousand-Word Memoir of Henry." [WormR] (27:4, issue 108) 87, p. 92.

"It Is the Children Who Are Condemned." [Pembroke] (19) 87, p. 118.

"Not That I Had Ever Needed a Horse's Skull." [WormR] (27:4, issue 108) 87, p. 91.

"A Parade of One Person, and no Spec-." [CrescentR] (5:1) 87, p. 63.

"Recently, I Decided to Go on the Wagon." [SlipS] (7) 87, p. 103.

"Some Quay Beside Some Torrential." [WormR] (27:4, issue 108) 87, p. 93.

"There Were Ides of Change, So to Speak." [WritersF] (13) Fall 87, p. 180-181.

"Writing, writing — Henry Miller." [Wind] (17:61) 87, p. 6.

1184. CRIST, Robert (Robert L.)

"The Book" (tr. of Aris Alexandrou). [Raccoon] (24/25) My 87, p. 169.

"From 'I Converse, Therefore I Exist'" (tr. of Aris Alexandrou). [GreenfR] (14:1/2) Wint-Spr, p. 187.

"In Full Knowledge" (tr. of Aris Alexandrou). [GreenfR] (14:1/2) Wint-Spr, p. 188-189.

"In the Rocks" (tr. of Aris Alexandrou). [GreenfR] (14:1/2) Wint-Spr, p. 187.

"No Man's Land" (tr. of Aris Alexandrou). [GreenfR] (14:1/2) Wint-Spr, p. 188.

"Unsent Letters" (tr. of Aris Alexandrou). [Raccoon] (24/25) My 87, p. 162-168.

1185. CROFT, Sally

"The Woman Made from Flowers" (from "The Mabinogion"). [SenR] (17:1) 87, p. 16-18.

1186. CROGHAN, Melissa

"Hothouse in the Snow." [NegC] (7:1/2) 87, p. 80.

"Petrarch, Writing to the Ancients." [NegC] (7:1/2) 87, p. 78-79.

1187. CROKER, Gaylene

"Picking Kiwis." [KanQ] (19:1/2) Wint-Spr 87, p. 152.

1188. CRONIN, Jeremy

"Group Photo from Pretoria Local on the Occasion of a Fourth Anniverary (Never Taken)." [TriQ] (69) Spr-Sum 87, p. 74-75.

"Labyrinth II." [TriQ] (69) Spr-Sum 87, p. 76-77.

"Lullaby." [TriQ] (69) Spr-Sum 87, p. 80.

"Motho Ke Motho Ka Batho Babang (A Person Is a Person Because of Other People)." [TriQ] (69) Spr-Sum 87, p. 73.

"The Naval Base (Part III)." [TriQ] (69) Spr-Sum 87, p. 71-72.

"To Learn How to Speak." [TriQ] (69) Spr-Sum 87, p. 81-82.

"White Face, Black Mask." [TriQ] (69) Spr-Sum 87, p. 79.

"Your Deep Hair." [TriQ] (69) Spr-Sum 87, p. 78.

1189. CRONYN, Hume

"Bushes Could Be Trees." [Waves] (15:4) Spr 87, p. 64-65.

1190. CROOKER, Barbara

"Field Guide to North American Birds." [LightY] '87, c86, p. 35.

"Florida." [Footwork] 87, p. 33.

"Recipe for Grief." [BlueBldgs] (10) 87?, p. 19.

"Summer Women." [GreenfR] (14:3/4) Sum-Fall 87, p. 115.

"Toward the End of the Century." [GreenfR] (14:3/4) Sum-Fall 87, p. 114.

"Turning Forty." [Footwork] 87, p. 33.

1191. CROSS, Elsa

"Bacantes" (Selection: V). [BlackWR] (13:2) Spr 87, p. 162.

"Bacantes" (Selection: V, tr. by Forrest Gander). [BlackWR] (13:2) Spr 87, p. 162.

1192. CROSS, Mary

"Bodies Subject to Its Action." [AmerPoR] (16:1) Ja-F 87, p. 16.

"I Am Told." [Ploughs] (13:4) 87, p. 32-33.

"Nothing Passes Away." [Ascent] (13:1) 87, p. 15.

"Reckoning with the Sheep." [AmerPoR] (16:1) Ja-F 87, p. 16.

"Whisper." [Ascent] (13:1) 87, p. 14.

1193. CROSTON, Julie

"Fork for Knife." [Poem] (58) N 87, p. 26.

"Laughing Mother Laughing Dog, Two Photographs." [Poem] (58) N 87, p. 27.

1194. CROUCH, Jeff

"The Angel at Delphi." [StoneC] (15:1/2) Fall-Wint 87-88, p. 29.

1195. CROW, Mary

"Absence." [HampSPR] Wint 86, p. 24.

"Hard Things." [HampSPR] Wint 86, p. 25.

"Image for a Pool" (tr. of Jorge Teillier). [SouthernHR] (21:4) Fall 87, p. 339.

"In Memory of a Closed House" (tr. of Jorge Teillier). [AmerV] (7) Sum 87, p. 27.

"Letter of Rain" (tr. of Jorge Teillier). [Nimrod] (31:1) Fall-Wint 87, p. 128-129.
"Nahuala." [Abraxas] (35/36) 87, p. 11.
"Not a Sign of Life" (tr. of Jorge Teillier). [AmerPoR] (16:4) Jl-Ag 87, p. 48.
"Story About a Branch of Myrtle" (tr. of Jorge Teillier). [Nimrod] (31:1) Fall-Wint 87, p. 127.
"Story of the Afternoon" (tr. of Jorge Teillier). [WillowS] (19) Wint 87, p. 14.
"To Talk With the Dead" (tr. of Jorge Teillier). [WillowS] (19) Wint 87, p. 14.
"The White Lily." [HampSPR] Wint 86, p. 24-25.
1196. CROZIER, Lorna
"Cat, French Class, Grocery List, etc." [MalR] (80) S 87, p. 87.
"Cat Named Desire." [Dandel] (14:1) Spr-Sum 87, p. 27.
"Cat Named Solitaire." [Dandel] (14:1) Spr-Sum 87, p. 26.
"The Goldberg Variations." [CanLit] (112) Spr 87, p. 59.
"Hands." [Verse] (4:1) Mr 87, p. 20-22.
"The Pacific." [MalR] (80) S 87, p. 88.
1197. CRUM, Robert
"The Miscarriage: Her Dream." [NowestR] (25:1) 87, p. 37.
"The Miscarriage: Her Dream." [NowestR] (25:3) 87, p. 448.
"Taming the Land." [NowestR] (25:1) 87, p. 35-36.
1198. CRUMP, Charles
"Old Roots." [Interim] (6:2) Fall 87, p. 15-16.
1199. CRUNK, T. L.
"Post-Metaphysical Man at Home." [HampSPR] Wint 87, p. 15.
"Winter." [HampSPR] Wint 87, p. 15.
1200. CRUZ, Pete
"Burnt Tongue Ballade." [SnapD] (10:1/2) Wint 87, p. 27.
"Mermaid Love." [SnapD] (10:1/2) Wint 87, p. 26.
1201. CRUZ, Victor Hernandez
"Hot Thought." [RiverS] (22) 87, p. 63.
"Loisaida" (To the memory of the original Nuyurican Poets Cafe on Sixth Street . . .). [RiverS] (22) 87, p. 59-62.
1202. CSAMER, M. E.
"The Hay Bay Calm." [Event] (16:3) Fall 87, p. 59.
1203. CSOORI, Sandor
"All Time" (tr. by Christine Molinari). [Field] (36) Spr 87, p. 46.
"Last Will and Testament — May" (tr. by Christine Molinari). [Field] (36) Spr 87, p. 47.
"Summer and Halo" (tr. by Christine Molinari). [Field] (36) Spr 87, p. 44.
"To Remember Myself" (tr. by Christine Molinari). [Field] (36) Spr 87, p. 45.
1204. CUADRA, Pablo Antonio
"The Black Ship" (tr. by K. H. Anton). [CutB] (27/28) 87, p. 103.
"Lamento de la Doncella en la Muerte del Guerrero." [Abraxas] (35/36) 87, p. 49.
"A Maiden's Lament on the Death of a Soldier" (tr. by Joel Zeltzer). [Abraxas] (35/36) 87, p. 49.
"The Pyramid of Quetzacoat" (tr. by K. H. Anton). [CutB] (27/28) 87, p. 100-102.
CUADRO, Pablo Antonio
See CUADRA, Pablo Antoni
1205. CUDDIHY, Michael
"Addio." [PraS] (61:1) Spr 87, p. 92.
"Artist's Proofs" (For Andrew Rush, printmaker). [PraS] (61:1) Spr 87, p. 91-92.
"Bread." [Ploughs] (13:4) 87, p. 35.
"First Name." [PraS] (61:1) Spr 87, p. 90.
"In Ignorance." [Ploughs] (13:4) 87, p. 34.
"A Question." [Pequod] (23/24) 87, p. 243.
"Some Questions." [Pequod] (23/24) 87, p. 246.
"Steps" (for Andy Meyer). [Pequod] (23/24) 87, p. 245.
"This Body." [Pequod] (23/24) 87, p. 244.
1206. CUDDY, Dan
"Unemployed." [Vis] (25) 87, p. 30.
1207. CULHANE, Charles
"After Almost Twenty Years." [Bomb] (21) Fall 87, p. 74.
"The Ancient One." [Bomb] (21) Fall 87, p. 74.
"Autumn Yard." [Witness] (1:3) Fall 87, p. 133.
"Death Row." [Bomb] (21) Fall 87, p. 74.
"Green Haven Halls." [Bomb] (21) Fall 87, p. 74.
"Paranoia." [Bomb] (21) Fall 87, p. 74.

CULLINAN

1208. CULLINAN, Patrick
"A Dream of Guests." [TriQ] (69) Spr-Sum 87, p. 340-341.
"Easter Transit" (tr. of Phil du Plessis). [TriQ] (69) Spr-Sum 87, p. 345-346.
"Homage to David Livingstone Phakamile Yali-Manisi." [TriQ] (69) Spr-Sum 87, p. 338-339.
"To Have Love." [TriQ] (69) Spr-Sum 87, p. 342.
1209. CULLY, Barbara
"As One Goes, Rain Falls." [AmerPoR] (16:1) Ja-F 87, p. 48.
"By Devotion to the Divine Spirit." [SouthernPR] (27:1) Spr 87, p. 65.
"The Death the Heart Dies." [Sonora] (12) Spr 87, p. 16.
"Heaven: As Near to You As Your Hands and Your Feet." [AntR] (45:1) Wint 87, p. 39.
"A Straw Coat Will Do for the Mist and Rain of a Lifetime." [AnotherCM] (17) 87, p. 17-18.
"Under Your Feet the Moon." [WestHR] (41:2) Sum 87, p. 150-151.
"Up All Night Near the City Without You." [AntR] (45:1) Wint 87, p. 38.
"Wings in Silence." [NoAmR] (272:3) D 87, p. 66.
1210. CUMALI, Necati
"The Hour of the Sun" (tr. by Murat Nemet-Nejat). [Trans] (19) Fall 87, p. 31.
"The Ipek Hotel" (tr. by Murat Nemet-Nejat). [Trans] (19) Fall 87, p. 30.
1211. CUMMING, Peter
"After the Bomb, Madison Avenue." [Waves] (14:4) Spr 86, p. 24.
1212. CUMMINGS, Darcy
"Conversion." [NegC] (7:1/2) 87, p. 64-65.
"The Night of the Weddings." [NegC] (7:1/2) 87, p. 66-67.
1213. CUMMINS, James
"The Grad Student." [Raccoon] (24/25) My 87, p. 114.
"The Little Professor." [NewRep] (196:12) 23 Mr 87, p. 36.
1214. CUNLIFFE, Dave
"Yankees All." [Bogg] (58) 87, p. 13-14.
1215. CUNNINGHAM, J. V.
"Coffee." [SouthernR] (23:1) Ja 87, p. 82-83.
"The Phoenix." [SouthernR] (23:1) Ja 87, p. 69.
"To a Friend." [SouthernR] (23:1) Ja 87, p. 76.
1216. CURBELO, Silvia
"Lilibeth." [Caliban] (3) 87, p. 24.
"Spontaneous Human Combustion." [Caliban] (3) 87, p. 24.
1217. CURRY, Duncan C.
"Diaries." [Bogg] (57) 87, p. 27.
1218. CURRY, Steven
"Why We Need Kites." [HawaiiR] (19) Spr 86, c87, p. 20.
1219. CURTAIN, Edward J., Jr.
"Family Matters." [ManhatPR] (9) Sum 87, p. 38-39.
1220. CURTIS, Jack
"E. E. Cummings, in Memoriam." [StoneC] (15:1/2) Fall-Wint 87-88, p. 69.
1221. CURTIS, Natalie
"Hunting-Song" (tr. of Navaho poem). [CharR] (13:1) Spr 87, p. 97-98.
1222. CURTIS, Tony
"The Last Candles." [KenR] (NS 9:2) Spr 87, p. 69-71.
"Lines at Barry." [KenR] (NS 9:2) Spr 87, p. 71-72.
1223. CUTLER, Bruce
"Doing Justice." [Spirit] (8:2) 87, p. 191-196.
"Eating an Eel." [BelPoJ] (38:2) Wint 87-88, p. 20-21.
"A War Pastoral, 1943." [NewL] (53:3) Spr 87, p. 16.
1224. CUZA MALE, Belkis
"En los Versos de Marina Svetaeva." [Lyra] (1:2) 87, p. 12.
"Miami Beach: 12 AM." [Lyra] (1:2) 87, p. 11.
1225. CZAPLA, Cathy Young
"Emma Lazarus at Concord, 1876" (1985 Alice Jackson Poetry Prize: Second Prize). [Electrum] (39) Fall-Wint 87, p. 8.
"Reborn in Waco, Texas." [Phoenix] (7:1) 87, p. 11.
1226. CZURY, Craig
"Cherry Hill Alien Malled." [PaintedB] (31) 87, p. 68-70.
1227. DACEY, Florence
"After the Attack" (For Rufina Amaya of Mozote, El Salvador). [Nimrod] (30:2) Spr-Sum 87, p. 47.

"Conception." [Nimrod] (30:2) Spr-Sum 87, p. 48.
"My Mother and I Dance, New Year's Eve." [Nimrod] (30:2) Spr-Sum 87, p. 46-47.
"Winter Storm." [Nimrod] (30:2) Spr-Sum 87, p. 49.
1228. DACEY, Philip
"The Blessing" (for Bob Dunn). [LaurelR] (21:1/2) Wint-Sum 87, p. 25.
"Condom's Wife." [LaurelR] (21:1/2) Wint-Sum 87, p. 26.
"The Confession." [BelPoJ] (38:1) Fall 87, p. 15.
"Divorce Court." [PraS] (61:2) Sum 87, p. 65.
"Double Play." [CreamCR] (11:2/3) 87?, p. 96-97.
"Hopkins to Bridges" (From the Lost Correspondence). [NowestR] (25:3) 87, p. 223-224.
"How They Do Things in Wichita." [LaurelR] (21:1/2) Wint-Sum 87, p. 27-28.
"I'd Like to Fuck Your Brains Out." [AnotherCM] (17) 87, p. 19.
"The Movie: A Book of Poems" (2 selections). [CharR] (13:2) Fall 87, p. 87.
"My Father's First Time." [TarRP] (26:2) Spr 87, p. 17.
"Shacking Up." [BelPoJ] (38:1) Fall 87, p. 16.
"Taking My Children to the Movies." [TarRP] (26:2) Spr 87, p. 15-16.
"Training the Puppy." [CreamCR] (11:2/3) 87?, p. 98.
"You Can't Live in a Museum" (for David Pichaske). [TarRP] (26:2) Spr 87, p. 16-17.
1229. DaGAMA, Steven
"By Sunlight Through Clouds." [YellowS] (24) Aut 87, p. 19.
"Proposal." [YellowS] (24) Aut 87, p. 18.
"Winter Riddle." [YellowS] (24) Aut 87, p. 19.
"Your Face." [YellowS] (23) Sum 87, p. 16.
1230. DAGLARCA, Fazil Hüsnü
"Abstract" (tr. by Ahmet Ö. Evin). [Trans] (19) Fall 87, p. 57.
"Cats" (tr. by Murat Nemet-Nejat). [Trans] (19) Fall 87, p. 56.
"Endless Silence" (tr. by Talat Sait Halman). [Trans] (19) Fall 87, p. 58.
"The Heartless" (tr. by Murat Nemet-Nejat). [Trans] (19) Fall 87, p. 56.
"The Lighthouse" (tr. by Murat Nemet-Nejat). [Trans] (19) Fall 87, p. 54-55.
"The Sultan of the Animals Is the Night" (tr. by Ahmet Ö. Evin). [Trans] (19) Fall 87, p. 57.
1231. DAHI, Soheyl
"My Song." [Bogg] (57) 87, p. 30.
1232. DAHL, David
"The Blessed Sacraments." [BellArk] (3:2) Mr-Ap 87, p. 4-5.
1233. DAHLBERG, Nancy
"Hands On." [Shen] (37:3) 87, p. 16.
1234. DAHLEN, Beverly
"A Reading" (Excerpts). [Conjunc] (10) 87, p. 65-71.
"A-reading Spicer." [Act] (7) 87, p. 1.
1235. DAIGON, Ruth
"Back." [KanQ] (19:3) Sum 87, p. 294-295.
"For This." [KanQ] (19:3) Sum 87, p. 294.
1236. DAKESSIAN, Sylvia
"For Elizabeth." [Jacaranda] (2:2) Spr 87, p. 90.
1237. DALACHINSKY, Steve
"The Joy That Music Brings" (Bobby Hutcherson at the Village Vanguard). [AlphaBS] (1) Je 87, p. 41.
"Saxophone Factory" (for Ben Webster). [AlphaBS] (1) Je 87, p. 42.
"Spring St." (for John Giorno). [AlphaBS] (1) Je 87, p. 40.
1238. DALDORPH, Brian'
"Wrong Doing." [Bogg] (58) 87, p. 12.
1239. DALE, Peter
"Pariah" (tr. of Tristan Corbière). [AntigR] (71/72) Aut 87-Wint 88, p. 91, 93.
1240. DALES, Brenda
"Growing." [EngJ] (76:2) F 87, p. 112.
1241. DALEY, Michael
"At Isidoro & Aurora's, an Excerpt." [Electrum] (39) Fall-Wint 87, p. 21-22.
"The Survivalist Looks at Extinction." [CrabCR] (4:2) Spr 87, p. 12.
1242. DALIBARD, Jill
"Fairy Tale." [Waves] (14:4) Spr 86, p. 50.
1243. DALTON, Dorothy
"Statistics." [Amelia] (4:1/2, issue 9) 87, p. 94.

1244. DALTON, Roque
"Alta Hora de la Noche." [InterPR] (13:1) Spr 87, p. 58.
"Jealousy" (tr. by Sylvia Bernstein and Harold Black). [Vis] (23) 87, p. 13.
"Small Hours of the Night" (tr. by Susan Schreibman). [InterPR] (13:1) Spr 87, p. 59.
1245. DALVEN, Rae (Rachel)
"The Down of My First Youth" (tr. of Victoria Theodorou). [ColR] (NS 14:1) Spr-Sum 87, p. 42-43.
"Jealousy" (tr. of Katerina Anghelake Rooke). [LitR] (31:1) Fall 87, p. 47.
"Ode to a Table Lamp" (tr. of Kiki Dhimoula). [LitR] (31:1) Fall 87, p. 48-49.
"The Oleanders" (tr. of Kiki Dhymoula). [ColR] (NS 14:1) Spr-Sum 87, p. 38-39.
"Penelope Says" (tr. of Katerina Anghelake Rooke). [PartR] (54:2) Spr 87, p. 267-269.
"Seashells" (tr. of Zoe Karelli). [LitR] (31:1) Fall 87, p. 50-51.
"The Ship" (tr. of Zoe Karelli). [ColR] (NS 14:1) Spr-Sum 87, p. 40-41.
1246. DALY, Daniel
"Ascension." [SpiritSH] (53:1) 87, p. 17-18.
"Barefoot Boy with Box." [SpiritSH] (53:1) 87, p. 19.
"A Kind of Anniversary." [SpiritSH] (53:1) 87, p. 20.
"The Runner, On." [SpiritSH] (53:1) 87, p. 18-19.
1247. DAMACION, Kenneth Zamora
"The Burn Ward." [NewL] (53:3) Spr 87, p. 17.
1248. DAMALI, Nia
"Hello Mister." [BlackALF] (21:3) Fall 87, p. 246.
"Spirit Songs." [MinnR] (NS 28) Spr 87, p. 26-27.
"Your Song." [BlackALF] (21:3) Fall 87, p. 245-246.
1249. DANGEL, Leo
"Old Man Brunner Country" (special issue). [SpoonRQ] (12:1) Wint 87, 72 p.
1250. DANIEL, Hal J., III
"1951 Mercury." [Lactuca] (8) N 87, p. 15.
"Baby to Bird." [HolCrit] (24:5) D 87, p. 10.
"Mother's Boyfriend." [HolCrit] (24:4) O 87, p. 13.
"Tomatoes and Mayonnaise." [JamesWR] (4:4) Sum 87, p. 8.
"When I Think of Bucknell." [Bogg] (57) 87, p. 51.
1251. DANIEL, John
"Dedication for a New Mirror." [WritersF] (13) Fall 87, p. 96.
"The Gray Whales Passing Point Reyes." [Sequoia] (31:1) Centennial issue 87, p. 110-111.
"Joshua Tree." [WritersF] (13) Fall 87, p. 98.
"Reading." [WritersF] (13) Fall 87, p. 97-98.
"The Tidepool." [SouthernR] (23:2) Ap 87, p. 378-379.
1252. DANIELL, Rosemary
"Valentine's Day, 1982" (for Darcy, and for Zane, Finalist, Eve of St. Agnes Poetry Competition). [NegC] (7:1/2) 87, p. 188-191.
1253. DANIELS, Jim
"5000 Apply for 100 Jobs." [Contact] (9:44/45/46) Fall-Wint 87, p. 64.
"At the Poetry Reading: 'This Is a Poem About That'." [LightY] '87, c86, p. 200-201.
"Below Zero." [RiverS] (23) 87, p. 24.
"Big O." [RiverS] (23) 87, p. 23.
"Eddie's Story, Detroit, 1982." [PoetryE] (23/24) Fall 87, p. 138-139.
"Elegy for Mr. Ed, the Talking Horse." [LightY] '87, c86, p. 74.
"Exile." [KanQ] (19:1/2) Wint-Spr 87, p. 88.
"Fishing Story." [RiverS] (23) 87, p. 25.
"Foreman Fired Joe." [WormR] (27:1, issue 105) 87, p. 35.
"The Help." [PaintedB] (31) 87, p. 7.
"How Much Light Is Enough." [PoetryE] (23/24) Fall 87, p. 136-137.
"Plant Nurse's Story." [WormR] (27:1, issue 105) 87, p. 36.
"Return to My Grandfather's Cabin, Lake Huron" (for my brother Tim, in California). [ColR] (NS 14:1) Spr-Sum 87, p. 13.
"Something." [PoetryE] (23/24) Fall 87, p. 140-141.
"Still Lives in Detroit, #11." [ColR] (NS 14:1) Spr-Sum 87, p. 14.
"Trouble at the Drive-In." [Witness] (1:4) Wint 87, p. 120-121.
"Until Suddenly." [HawaiiR] (21) Spr 87, p. 18.
"Wrapping Bread." [PaintedB] (31) 87, p. 6.

1254. DANK, Bette
"Black Woman Poet." [Footwork] 87, p. 56.
"Mirror Image." [Footwork] 87, p. 55.
"Sisters." [Footwork] 87, p. 55-56.
1255. DANNER, Betsie M.
"Adoption." [ChatR] (8:1) Fall 87, p. 20.
DAO, Bei
See BEI, Dao
DARBY, Candice Cook
See COOK-DARBY, Candice
1256. DARGAN, Joan
"Pause" (tr. of Noemí Escandell). [StoneC] (14:3/4) Spr-Sum 87, p. 67.
1257. DARLING, Charles
"Granville, New York: the Museum of Natural History." [Blueline] (7:2/3 [i.e.
8:2/3?]) 87, p. 15.
1258. DARLING, Michael
"Whose Woods These Are." [CanLit] (115) Wint 87, p. 104-105.
1259. DARLING, Robert
"My Father, in His Sudden Sleep." [NegC] (7:3/4) 87, p. 132-133.
1260. D'ARPINO, Tony
"At Frost's Grave." [Bogg] (57) 87, p. 49.
"Song." [Bogg] (57) 87, p. 18.
1261. DARRAGH, Tine
"Error Bursts." [Bound] (14:1/2) Fall 85-Wint 86 [c87], p. 42.
1262. DARWISH, Mahmud
"Psalms for Palestine" (tr. by Ben Bennani). [Paint] (14:27) Spr 87, p. 42-44.
1263. DASGUPTA, Pranabendu
"You, I and Subinoy." [Vis] (23) 87, p. 25.
1264. DASSANOWSKY-HARRIS, Robert
"Chiaroscuro." [Os] (24) 87, p. 21.
1265. DAUENHAUER, William
"Penny Arcade." [Writer] (99:3) Mr 86, p. 21.
1266. DAVENPORT, Doris
"I useta Say I Was a Writer." [SinW] (31) 87, p. 38.
1267. DAVID, Almitra
"You Want Me White" (tr. of Alfonsina Storni). [Calyx] (10:2/3) Spr 87, p.
170-171.
1268. DAVIDKOV, Ivan
"Spring" (tr. by Ewald Osers). [CrossCur] (7:3) 87, p. 117.
1269. DAVIDSON, Ian
"Christmas." [NegC] (7:1/2) 87, p. 77.
"Point of Departure." [NegC] (7:1/2) 87, p. 76.
1270. DAVIDSON, Michael
"Framing." [Bound] (14:1/2) Fall 85-Wint 86 [c87], p. 33-34.
1271. DAVIDSON, Phebe E.
"Dry Spring Road." [Nimrod] (30:2) Spr-Sum 87, p. 49.
"Pater Noster." [Nimrod] (30:2) Spr-Sum 87, p. 50.
DAVIDSON, Terri Lynette Brown
See BROWN-DAVIDSON, Terri Lynette
1272. DAVIE, Donald
"North & South" (For Emily Grosholz, who asked about meter). [AmerS] (56:4) Aut
87, p. 574-575.
"Romanesque: Bevagna" (Chiesa Di San Silvestro, 1195, Photographs by Dorren
Davie). [TriQ] (68) Wint 87, p. 63-75.
"Two Intercepted Letters" (in memoriam Philip Larkin, ob. December 2nd, 1985).
[Sequoia] (31:1) Centennial issue 87, p. 26.
1273. DAVIE, Sharon
"Harmony." [VirQR] (63:2) Spr 87, p. 272-273.
1274. DAVIES, Alan
"If Words Had Meaning." [Bound] (14:1/2) Fall 85-Wint 86 [c87], p. 79-86.
"It must have been you." [Act] (7) 87, p. 102.
"Modes." [Temblor] (5) 87, p. 114.
"Setset." [Temblor] (5) 87, p. 111-113.
"Sit down. We said sit down." [Act] (7) 87, p. 102.
1275. DAVIGNON, Richard
"Hector Cantando." [MidAR] (7:2) 87, p. 49.

1276. DAVIS, Alan R.
"Not a Lullaby." [SouthernPR] (27:2) Fall 87, p. 33.
1277. DAVIS, Albert
"Cajun Taffeta." [SewanR] (95:2) Spr 87, p. 246.
"Culs-de-Sac." [SewanR] (95:2) Spr 87, p. 244-245.
1278. DAVIS, Archie
"Education." [Witness] (1:3) Fall 87, p. 17.
1279. DAVIS, Christopher
"Clarence White Escapes His Demon Lover." [AmerPoR] (16:2) Mr-Ap 87, p. 4.
"Clarence White's Angel Is a Witch." [DenQ] (22:1) Sum 87, p. 39-40.
"In This Blackout." [AmerPoR] (16:2) Mr-Ap 87, p. 4.
"Jack Frost's Question" (for R.S.). [AmerPoR] (16:2) Mr-Ap 87, p. 4.
"Jojo's." [AmerPoR] (16:2) Mr-Ap 87, p. 3.
"My Grandmother's Manifest Destiny." [AmerPoR] (16:2) Mr-Ap 87, p. 3.
"The Sacrifices." [AmerPoR] (16:2) Mr-Ap 87, p. 4-5.
1280. DAVIS, Ed
"Drink These Memories Down." [Wind] (17:60) 87, p. 5.
"Hawk Thoughts." [Wind] (17:60) 87, p. 5-6.
1281. DAVIS, Frances
"To My Father." [Waves] (15:3) Wint 87, p. 71.
1282. DAVIS, H.
"Chemo-Poet." [PraS] (61:1) Spr 87, p. 68.
"The Generic Oncologist." [PraS] (61:1) Spr 87, p. 69.
"Healing by Computer." [PraS] (61:1) Spr 87, p. 71-72.
"I Dream." [PraS] (61:1) Spr 87, p. 71.
"I Visit the Prosthesis Lady." [PraS] (61:1) Spr 87, p. 73-74.
"My World." [PraS] (61:1) Spr 87, p. 70.
"The Prince." [PraS] (61:1) Spr 87, p. 72.
1283. DAVIS, Jo Culbertson
"Music." [MemphisSR] (8:1) Fall 87, p. 63.
1284. DAVIS, John
"Checklist." [KanQ] (19:1/2) Wint-Spr 87, p. 111.
"In La Paz." [Wind] (17:60) 87, p. 7-6.
"In the Next Apartment." [SnapD] (10:1/2) Wint 87, p. 60.
"Island Mother." [Wind] (17:60) 87, p. 7.
1285. DAVIS, Jon
"Dangerous Amusements." [OntR] (26) Spr-Sum 87, p. 66-76.
"Landscape Assembled from Dreams." [HighP] (2:3) Wint 87, p. 238.
"Note to the Residents of 412 Beechwood Heights." [PikeF] (8) Fall 87, p. 3.
"The Sacred." [HighP] (2:3) Wint 87, p. 237.
1286. DAVIS, Lloyd
"Bob Hosey Is Dead." [Spirit] (8:2) 87, p. 248.
"The Drunk." [LaurelR] (20:1/2) Sum 87, p. 120.
"Going to Bed." [LaurelR] (20:1/2) Sum 87, p. 121.
1287. DAVIS, Lydia
"Clouds in the Sky." [Notus] (2:1) Spr 87, p. 57.
"The Dog Man." [Bound] (14:1/2) Fall 85-Wint 86 [c87], p. 7.
"The Fish." [Bound] (14:1/2) Fall 85-Wint 86 [c87], p. 8.
"The Great-Grandmothers." [Bound] (14:1/2) Fall 85-Wint 86 [c87], p. 7.
"In the Garment District." [Bound] (14:1/2) Fall 85-Wint 86 [c87], p. 8.
"What She Knew." [Bound] (14:1/2) Fall 85-Wint 86 [c87], p. 8.
1288. DAVIS, Raina
"No Tread Left." [Phoenix] (7:1) 87, p. 44.
1289. DAVIS, Robin
"Eating from the Near of My Almost Bones." [Interim] (6:1) Spr 87, p. 8.
"To See the Apple Seller." [Interim] (6:1) Spr 87, p. 7.
1290. DAVIS, William Virgil
"Confession." [Confr] (35/36) Spr-Fall 87, p. 186.
"Days." [SouthwR] (72:1) Wint 87, p. 119.
"Decision." [PoetL] (81:3) Fall 86, p. 190.
"The Frog Pond." [SouthernPR] (27:2) Fall 87, p. 11.
"I-35, South of Waco." [LightY] '87, c86, p. 108.
"Pilgrimage." [WritersF] (13) Fall 87, p. 133.
"Plum." [PaintedB] (31) 87, p. 5.
"Standing Lookout Above Graves End." [SouthwR] (72:1) Wint 87, p. 119.
"The Swifts at Tintern Abbey." [ArizQ] (43:2) Sum 87, p. 140.

"Three Pages from an Impressionist Calendar." [PoetL] (82:3) Fall 87, p. 160.
"A Visit to the Sea." [KanQ] (19:1/2) Wint-Spr 87, p. 65.
"Walk." [LitR] (31:1) Fall 87, p. 52.
1291. DAVISON, Neil
"The Dogwood." [WestB] (20) 87, p. 42.
"Two Moments of Balance." [WestB] (20) 87, p. 43.
1292. DAVISON, Peter
"Equinox 1980." [Poetry] (151:1/2) O-N 87, p. 37-38.
"The Face in the Field." [TexasR] (7:3/4) 87, p. 30-31.
"The Farm Animals' Desertion." [TexasR] (7:3/4) 87, p. 32.
1293. DAWBER, Diane
"Break." [Quarry] (36:1) Wint 87, p. 16.
"Pull Cord." [Quarry] (36:1) Wint 87, p. 15.
1294. DAWE, Gerald
"Elocution Lesson." [Verse] (4:3) N 87, p. 7.
"Speedboats, 1972." [Verse] (4:3) N 87, p. 7.
1295. DAWIDOFF, Sarah
"The Grobot Odes." [HarvardA] (120:2) Mr 87, p. 16.
1296. DAY, Jean
"The Crowd" (from "A Bronzino"). [Bound] (14:1/2) Fall 85-Wint 86 [c87], p. 49-50.
"Dim Sparse" (for BF & PR). [Bound] (14:1/2) Fall 85-Wint 86 [c87], p. 50.
"Never Prose." [Bound] (14:1/2) Fall 85-Wint 86 [c87], p. 49.
1297. DAY, Sandra
"Instructions." [Waves] (15:1/2) Fall 86, p. 75.
De . . .
    See also names beginning with "De" without the following space, filed below in their
        alphabetic positions, e.g., DeFOE.
De ANDRADE, Eugenio
    See ANDRADE, Eugenio de
De ANGELI, Milo
    See De ANGELIS, Milo
1298. De ANGELIS, Milo
"A.S." (tr. by Lawrence Venuti). [ParisR] (29:105) Wint 87, p. 116-117.
"Born on th Earth" (tr. by Lawrence Venuti). [Sulfur] (18) Wint 87, p. 153-154.
"Conversation with Father" (tr. by Lawrence Venuti). [SenR] (17:2) 87, p. 37.
"In the Lungs" (tr. by Lawrence Venuti). [ParisR] (29:105) Wint 87, p. 120.
"The Killing" (tr. by Lawrence Venuti). [Sulfur] (18) Wint 87, p. 154-155.
"Letter from Vignole" (tr. by Lawrence Venuti). [ParisR] (29:105) Wint 87, p. 119.
"No One, Yet They Return" (tr. by Lawrence Venuti). [SenR] (17:2) 87, p. 36.
"Now She Is Unadorned" (tr. by Lawrence Venuti). [ParisR] (29:105) Wint 87, p. 118.
"Stones in the Warm Mud" (tr. by Lawrence Venuti). [Sulfur] (18) Wint 87, p. 152-153.
"Telegram" (tr. by Lawrence Venuti). [Sulfur] (18) Wint 87, p. 153.
"Via Prospero Finzi" (tr. by Lawrence Venuti). [SenR] (17:2) 87, p. 38.
"With Broken Oars They Embark" (tr. by Lawrence Venuti). [Sulfur] (18) Wint 87, p. 152.
De BELLAGENTE LaPALMA, Marina
    See LaPALMA, Marina de Bellagente
De BURGOS, Julia
    See BURGOS, Julia de
De CABESTANH, Guilhem
    See CABESTANH, Guilhem de
De CAMPOS, Alvaro
    See PESSOA, Fernando
1299. De GRAZIA, Emilio
"Fifth Grade Band Concert" (Mayday, 1986). [LakeSR] (21) 87, p. 3.
De JESUS, Teresa
    See JESUS, Teresa de
1300. De JOUX, Alicia
"Cubist Morning." [Vis] (23) 87, p. 18.
"Letter For." [Vis] (24) 87, p. 33.
De la TORRE, Josefina
    See TORRE, Josefina de la

De las CASAS, Walter
    See CASAS, Walter de las
De LEON, Ulalume González
    See GONZALEZ DE LEON, Ulalume
1301. De LISSOVOY, Noah
    "First Thoughts on Hearing the Etude." [HarvardA] (120:2) Mr 87, p. 34.
    "Turnaround" (for Django Reinhardt). [HarvardA] (121:3) My 87, p. 36-37.
1302. De MARIS, Ron
    "Grill and Counter Man." [KanQ] (19:1/2) Wint-Spr 87, p. 332.
De MELO NETO, João Cabral
    See NETO, João Cabral de Melo
De OCA, Marco Antonio Montes
    See MONTES DE OCA, Marco Antonio
De OLIVEIRA, Celso
    See OLIVEIRA, Celso de
De OYENARD, Sylvia Puentes
    See PUENTES DE OYENARD, Sylvia
De PAUT, Elisa
    See PAUT, Elisa de
De PIORNO, Ñusta
    See PIORNO, Ñusta de
De RONSARD, Pierre
    See RONSARD, Pierre de
1303. De ROUS, Peter
    "The New American Poetry Revised." [Bogg] (58) 87, p. 51.
    "Not For." [Bogg] (57) 87, p. 14.
De SENA, Jorge
    See SENA, Jorge de
1304. De SOUZA, Eunice
    "Advice to Women." [Chelsea] (46) 87, p. 224.
    "Searching for Roots." [Chelsea] (46) 87, p. 225.
    "Women in Dutch Paintings." [Chelsea] (46) 87, p. 224.
1305. De VITO, E. B.
    "Double Bind." [AmerS] (56:1) Wint 87, p. 18.
    "Page from a Diary" (Queen Elizabeth I). [SewanR] (95:4) Fall 87, p. 559.
1306. De VRIES, Carrow
    "Nietzsche, Schopenhauer, Kierkegaard, Existentialists." [WindO] (48) Spr 87, p. 7.
1307. De VRIES, Peter
    "To His Importunate Mistress" (Andrew Marvell Updated). [LightY] '87, c86, p. 127-128.
1308. DEAGON, Ann
    "E = MC round." [LightY] '87, c86, p. 107.
    "Pièce de Résistance." [LightY] '87, c86, p. 218.
1309. DEAHL, James
    "Hiorra." [LaurelR] (20:1/2) Sum 87, p. 43-46.
    "Island Trilogy" (for Ros Goss). [Waves] (15:3) Wint 87, p. 72.
1310. DEAN, Debi Kang
    "New Year's Eve." [GreenfR] (14:3/4) Sum-Fall 87, p. 163.
    "Obake." [GreenfR] (14:3/4) Sum-Fall 87, p. 162.
    "Remembering Your Father." [TarPR] (27:1) Fall 87, p. 39-40.
1311. DEANOVICH, Connie
    "80 Degrees Out." [NewAW] (2) Fall 87, p. 104.
    "Ballerina Criminology." [NewAW] (1) 87, p. 106.
    "Fuck 'em County." [NewAW] (2) Fall 87, p. 105.
    "Pure Valentine." [NewAW] (1) 87, p. 107-108.
    "Silver Nakedness in Calumet City." [NewAW] (2) Fall 87, p. 103.
    "Xylophone Luncheonette." [NewAW] (2) Fall 87, p. 102.
1312. DeCASTRO, Victoria Scharf
    "Daytona Beach in Winter." [DekalbLAJ] (20:1/4) 87, p. 63.
1313. DeCLUE, Charlotte
    "Ijajee's Story." [Spirit] (8:2) 87, p. 26.
    "She says." [Contact] (9:44/45/46) Fall-Wint 87, p. 58-59.
1314. DeCORMIER-SHEKERJIAN, Regina
    "Flutes of Bone, Bones of Clay" (3 selections). [Nimrod] (30:2) Spr-Sum 87, p. 56-59.

"Tear Pot." [HighP] (2:1) Spr 87, p. 8-9.
1315. DeCOURCY, Lynne H.
"August Birthing." [Calyx] (11:1) Wint 87-88, p. 30.
1316. DeCREDICO, Jessan Dunn
"Helen" (4 selections). [Nimrod] (30:2) Spr-Sum 87, p. 60-61.
1317. DEDORA, B.
"Fantasy No. 1." [CrossC] (9:3/4) 87, p. 10.
1318. DeFOE, Mark
"The Assassin's Dream." [PoetL] (82:1) Spr 87, p. 27.
"Distance." [NoDaQ] (55:1) Wint 87, p. 44.
"Dream Lover." [Poetry] (150:6) S 87, p. 323-324.
"Driving the 4-Lane: Epiphany Near Ellenboro, W. Va." [PoetL] (82:1) Spr 87, p. 26.
"Heat." [Poetry] (150:6) S 87, p. 324-325.
"Precaution." [NegC] (7:3/4) 87, p. 159-160.
"Precaution" (1986 Finalist, Eve of Saint Agnes Poetry Competition). [NegC] (7:1/2) 87, p. 209-210.
"Spring: The Ethiopian in My Shower." [WestB] (20) 87, p. 63.
1319. DeFREES, Madeline
"Imaginary Ancestors: The Giraffe Women of Burma." [NowestR] (25:3) 87, p. 433-434.
"In the Middle of Priest Lake." [SouthernPR] (27:2) Fall 87, p. 68.
"Spiritual Exercises." [CrabCR] (4:3) Sum 87, p. 21.
"The Ventriloquist's Dummy." [SouthernPR] (27:2) Fall 87, p. 67.
1320. DEGO, Giuliano
"Here and Elsewhere" (tr. by Jack Bevan). [BlueBldgs] (10) 87?, p. 38.
1321. DeGROOTE, Judith
"Plaka." [Phoenix] (7:1) 87, p. 37.
1322. DEGUY, Michel
"At Rush Hour" (tr. by Pierre Joris). [LitR] (30:3) Spr 87, p. 326-332.
"Rims" (tr. by David Kinloch). [Verse] (4:2) Je 87, p. 59.
1323. DEKIN, Timothy
"White Christmas." [Sequoia] (31:1) Centennial issue 87, p. 66-67.
1324. DELAHAYE, Alain
"The Immensity of the Firmament" (tr. by Anthony Barnett). [Temblor] (5) 87, p. 57-59.
1325. DELANO, Page Dougherty
"Ashby Leach Defense Committee." [MinnR] (NS 29) Fall 87, p. 39-41.
"Dora at the Cannery, c. 1936." [MinnR] (NS 29) Fall 87, p. 37-38.
"Two Chairs." [PraS] (61:3) Fall 87, p. 104-105.
"Winter's End." [Raccoon] (24/25) My 87, p. 183.
1326. DELEHANT, Jean E.
"Keeping Vigil." [KanQ] (19:1/2) Wint-Spr 87, p. 300.
1327. DELFINER, Ellen
"The Diary." [Wind] (17:61) 87, p. 9.
1328. DELP, Michael
"Cruising the A & W." [MemphisSR] (8:1) Fall 87, p. 22.
"Fishing for the Dead." [PassN] (8:1) Wint 87, p. 16.
"Gunning." [NoDaQ] (55:2) Spr 87, p. 153.
"Nightfishing at the Homestead Dam." [NoDaQ] (55:2) Spr 87, p. 152.
"Oba Lake, Ontario." [PennR] (3:1) Spr-Sum 87, p. 21.
1329. DELPHIN, Jacques
"Emelda" (tr. by Alice Otis). [Paint] (14:27) Spr 87, p. 15-17.
1330. DEMETRE, Sheila
"Demeter's Autumn." [Calyx] (11:1) Wint 87-88, p. 26.
"When Persephone Leaves." [Calyx] (11:1) Wint 87-88, p. 25.
"When Persephone Leaves." [PoetryNW] (28:1) Spr 87, p. 40.
"Women of Salt." [Calyx] (10:2/3) Spr 87, p. 76.
1331. DEMPSEY, Sandy
"Immigrant." [Raccoon] (24/25) My 87, p. 201-202.
"Virgin." [Raccoon] (24/25) My 87, p. 191.
1332. DENNIS, Carl
"The Booster." [VirQR] (63:1) Wint 87, p. 86-87.
"The Deacon's Complaint." [Poetry] (150:5) Ag 87, p. 268-269.
"Governors and Priests." [VirQR] (63:1) Wint 87, p. 85-86.
"Henry James and Hester Street." [Salm] (73) Wint 87, p. 151-152.

"Horace and I." [Poetry] (151:1/2) O-N 87, p. 38-39.
"Last Words." [Poetry] (150:5) Ag 87, p. 267-268.
"The Pledge." [Sonora] (13) Fall 87, p. 110.
"The Promised Land." [Salm] (73) Wint 87, p. 150-151.
1333. DENNIS, Michael
"Mayakovsky." [Rampike] (5:3) 87, p. 37.
1334. DENNY, Alma
"I Love Every Hair Off Your Head." [LightY] '87, c86, p. 134.
"Oh, Dem Olden Slippers!" [LightY] '87, c86, p. 237.
"School Cheer (Progressive Style)." [LightY] '87, c86, p. 97.
"Tuesday." [LightY] '87, c86, p. 31.
"We and the Weekend." [LightY] '87, c86, p. 227.
1335. DENT, Tory
"Ocean Park." [ParisR] (29:103) Sum 87, p. 181.
"Vissi D'Arte." [ParisR] (29:103) Sum 87, p. 180.
1336. DENTON, Diana
"Your Birthday." [Waves] (15:1/2) Fall 86, p. 82.
1337. DePALMA, Ray
"Whistle Stop." [SpoonRQ] (12:2) Spr 87, p. 33.
1338. DEPPE, Theodore
"The Crucifixion of the Apostle Peter" (anonymous French painting, 15th century).
[KanQ] (19:4) Fall 87, p. 76.
"Game Near Ocotal" (for Paul Graseck). [GreenfR] (14:1/2) Wint-Spr, p. 68.
1339. DEPTA, Victor
"Entering the Priesthood." [CalQ] (30) Wint 87, p. 30.
1340. Der HOVANESSIAN, Diana
"Armenian Gifts for My Daughters." [GrahamHR] (10) Wint-Spr 87, p. 12-13.
"Beyond Desire." [Amelia] (4:1/2, issue 9) 87, p. 105.
"Climb" (tr. of Gevorg Emin). [CrossCur] (7:3) 87, p. 153.
"Diaspora." [Agni] (24/25) 87, p. 222-223.
"Drowning." [TexasR] (7:3/4) 87, p. 34-35.
"Fisherman's Mother." [TexasR] (7:3/4) 87, p. 33.
"In Orange Light." [Amelia] (4:1/2, issue 9) 87, p. 105.
"Not by Design" (tr. of Maria Banus, w. the author). [CrossCur] (7:3) 87, p. 97.
"On Commonwealth Avenue and Brattle Street" (For William Saroyan). [TexasR]
(7:3/4) 87, p. 36.
"Since the Years of Our Love" (tr. of Hamo Sahian). [InterPR] (13:1) Spr 87, p. 75.
"Villanelle to Change the Past." [InterPR] (13:1) Spr 87, p. 110.
"The Yellow Dream." [StoneC] (14:3/4) Spr-Sum 87, p. 70-71.
DERICOTTE, Toi
    See DERRICOTTE, Toi
1341. DeROLLER, Joseph
"Poem Found While I Looked for Something Else." [LightY] '87, c86, p. 178.
DeROUS, Peter
    See De ROUS, Peter
1342. DERRICOTTE, Toi
"Before Making Love." [PoetryE] (23/24) Fall 87, p. 215.
"Heat." [Caliban] (2) 87, p. 57.
"My Father Still Sleeping After Surgery." [PoetryE] (23/24) Fall 87, p. 214.
"The Polishers of Brass." [PoetryE] (23/24) Fall 87, p. 213.
"The Roomer." [Caliban] (2) 87, p. 58.
"The Stupid Girl." [Caliban] (2) 87, p. 56.
1343. DeRUGERIS, C. K.
"High Drama in the Afternoon." [Bogg] (57) 87, p. 60.
1344. DESKINS, David
"Elvis Roger." [Wind] (17:61) 87, p. 10.
DESLEAL, Alvaro Menen
    See MENEN DESLEAL, Alvaro
1345. DESMOND, Walter
"Fox." [Writer] (99:11) N 86, p. 17.
"Indian Summer." [Vis] (24) 87, p. 20.
1346. DESNOS, Robert
"Comme" (tr. by William Kulik). [AmerPoR] (16:3) My-Je 87, p. 33.
1347. DESSI, Gigi
"Ai Lati." [InterPR] (13:2) Fall 87, p. 36.
"Destroyed" (tr. by Dominick Lepore). [InterPR] (13:2) Fall 87, p. 37.

113

Di PIERO

"Distrutte." [InterPR] (13:2) Fall 87, p. 36.
"Forse." [InterPR] (13:2) Fall 87, p. 34.
"Laterally" (tr. by Dominick Lepore). [InterPR] (13:2) Fall 87, p. 37.
"Perhaps" (tr. by Dominick Lepore). [InterPR] (13:2) Fall 87, p. 35.
1348. DESY, Peter
"Anaphylactic Shock." [LitR] (31:1) Fall 87, p. 100-101.
"At Sea." [Pembroke] (19) 87, p. 144.
"Birthday Celebration, Carl's Chop House, Detroit." [RiverS] (22) 87, p. 81.
"Birthday Celebration, Carl's Chop House, Detroit" (for Marcella Desy). [VirQR]
   (63:3) Sum 87, p. 446.
"Body and Soul." [CentR] (31:2) Spr 87, p. 181.
"The Cough." [WritersF] (13) Fall 87, p. 173-174.
"Departmental Party." [Puerto] (22:2) Spr 87, p. 65.
"Going Bald." [Amelia] (4:3, issue 10) 87, p. 85.
"Her Shoes." [FloridaR] (15:1) Spr-Sum 87, p. 24.
"Loren Eiseley's Poems, *Another Kind of Autumn*." [KanQ] (19:1/2) Wint-Spr 87,
   p. 66.
"Mailman." [KanQ] (19:1/2) Wint-Spr 87, p. 65.
"Mother, Moving." [HawaiiR] (20) Fall 86, c87, p. 84.
"Seeing in the Dark." [CentR] (31:2) Spr 87, p. 184.
1349. DEVENISH, Alan
"After the Beep:" [ColEng] (49:7) N 87, p. 773-774.
1350. DEVET, Rebecca McClanahan
"Behold, All Things Are Become New." [Pembroke] (19) 87, p. 190.
"Leah." [Nimrod] (31:1) Fall-Wint 87, p. 36-38.
"Something Calling My Name." [Nimrod] (31:1) Fall-Wint 87, p. 34-35.
1351. DeVRIES, Rachel Guido
"Scavenging Apples." [CrabCR] (4:3) Sum 87, p. 19.
1352. DEWDNEY, Christopher
"Depth Sounding, Lake Windermere." [Verse] (4:1) Mr 87, p. 23.
"Permugenesis" (from "A Natural History of Southwestern Ontario, Book III").
   [Notus] (2:2) Fall 87, p. 16-17.
DEWITT, Susan Kelly
   See KELLY-DEWITT, Susan
1353. DEY, Richard Morris
"Approaching Bequia" (for James F. Mitchell). [HawaiiR] (20) Fall 86, c87, p.
   70-71.
"A Ship Like a Woman." [HawaiiR] (21) Spr 87, p. 4-5.
1354. DeYOUNG, Robert
"Chameleon." [KanQ] (19:1/2) Wint-Spr 87, p. 292.
"Marco." [CrossCur] (6:4) 87, p. 39.
"A Play Illegal Now." [KanQ] (19:1/2) Wint-Spr 87, p. 292.
1355. DeZURKO, Edward
"Jet Contrails over Amber Waves." [KanQ] (19:3) Sum 87, p. 236.
1356. DHARWADKER, Vinay
"Sunday at the Lodi Gardens" (New Delhi, 1978). [Hudson] (40:3) Aut 87, p.
   445-446.
1357. DHIMOULA, Kiki
"Ode to a Table Lamp" (tr. by Rae Dalven). [LitR] (31:1) Fall 87, p. 48-49.
1358. DHOMHNAILL, Nuala Ní
"Amhrán An Fhir Oig." [YellowS] (25) Wint 87, p. 24.
"Song of the Young Man" (tr. by Joe Malone). [YellowS] (25) Wint 87, p. 24.
1359. DHYMOULA, Kiki
"The Oleanders" (tr. by Rachel Dalven). [ColR] (NS 14:1) Spr-Sum 87, p. 38-39.
Di . . .
   See also names beginning with "Di" without the following space, filed below in their
      alphabetic positions, e.g., DiPALMA
1360. Di GIOVANNI, Norman Thomas
"The Aging" (tr. of Horacio Salas). [Trans] (18) Spr 87, p. 47.
"The Children" (tr. of Horacio Salas). [Trans] (18) Spr 87, p. 46.
"The Sick" (tr. of Horacio Salas). [Trans] (18) Spr 87, p. 45.
1361. Di PIERO, W. S.
"Chinese Apples." [Sequoia] (31:1) Centennial issue 87, p. 107.
"Easy February." [Sequoia] (30:3) Wint 87, p. 42.
"The Faery Child." [Thrpny] (29) Spr 87, p. 4.
"To My Old City." [Sequoia] (31:1) Centennial issue 87, p. 106.

1362. DiAMICO, Maureen
"Admiring Maria." [Footwork] 87, p. 80.
1363. DIAMOND, Olivia
"Majorette Stops Accident with Flaming Baton" (news item). [Raccoon] (24/25) My
87, p. 190.
"Walking West." [Amelia] (4:1/2, issue 9) 87, p. 127-128.
DIAS, Robert Vas
See VAS DIAS, Robert
1364. DIAZ, Rosemary
"Black Boots." [GreenfR] (14:1/2) Wint-Spr, p. 26.
1365. DIB, Mohammed
"Shadow of Lightning" (tr. by Eric Sellin). [LitR] (30:3) Spr 87, p. 395.
"Stele" (tr. by Eric Sellin). [LitR] (30:3) Spr 87, p. 395.
1366. DICKEY, James
"Eagles." [AmerPoR] (16:2) Mr-Ap 87, p. 56.
"Gila Bend." [Poetry] (151:1/2) O-N 87, p. 40.
"The Little More." [Poetry] (150:4) Jl 87, p. 208-210.
"The Six." [Poetry] (151:1/2) O-N 87, p. 41-42.
1367. DICKEY, Pat
"Par Nobile Fratrum." [Amelia] (4:3, issue 10) 87, p. 15.
1368. DICKEY, R. P.
"At a Concert." [LightY] '87, c86, p. 32.
"Materialism." [LightY] '87, c86, p. 21.
"On a Compliment." [LightY] '87, c86, p. 232.
"Walking Naked Around the House." [LightY] '87, c86, p. 154.
1369. DICKEY, William
"Doubles." [HiramPoR] (42) Spr-Sum 87, p. 15-17.
"Elpenor." [NewEngR] (9:4) Sum 87, p. 401-405.
"Hesiod at Evening." [NewEngR] (10:1) Aut 87, p. 85-89.
"Hiroshige: Stations of the Tokkaido Road." [NewEngR] (9:4) Sum 87, p. 397-400.
"Ice." [HiramPoR] (42) Spr-Sum 87, p. 18-23.
"January White Sale." [Spirit] (8:2) 87, p. 226-227.
"Like the Beat Beat Beat of a Tom-Tom." [NewEngR] (10:1) Aut 87, p. 89-94.
"Sending the Clock-Radio to Mars." [HiramPoR] (42) Spr-Sum 87, p. 13-14.
"She Rescued Him from Danger as the Bell." [NewEngR] (10:1) Aut 87, p. 94-96.
"Woke." [FiveFR] (5) 87, p. 3-6.
1370. DICKINSON, Laura
"Learning to Dance." [PoetL] (81:3) Fall 86, p. 157-158.
"To a Model." [PoetL] (81:3) Fall 86, p. 159.
1371. DICKSON, Charles B.
"The Question." [PoeticJ] (17) 87, p. 7.
1372. DICKSON, John
"Bathsheba." [SpoonRQ] (12:2) Spr 87, p. 25.
"Delayed Decision." [Poetry] (149:5) F 87, p. 268-269.
"Escape." [SpoonRQ] (12:2) Spr 87, p. 26-27.
"Little Brother." [Poetry] (149:5) F 87, p. 267-268.
"The Maid." [KanQ] (19:3) Sum 87, p. 172.
"The Mouse Funeral." [PikeF] (8) Fall 87, p. 12.
"The Steeple." [AmerS] (56:3) Sum 87, p. 391-392.
"Suicide Pact." [Poetry] (149:5) F 87, p. 266-267.
1373. DICKSON, Nick
"The Alley." [Amelia] (4:1/2, issue 9) 87, p. 87.
1374. DICKSON, Ray Clark
"The Decoys." [BelPoJ] (37:4) Sum 87, p. 17.
"Harry's Somewhere in the Lost Coast Mizzle." [BelPoJ] (37:4) Sum 87, p. 18-19.
"It Takes an Old Woman Screaming *Vietato Fumare!*" [BelPoJ] (37:4) Sum 87, p.
16.
"Kids Calling His Name." [BelPoJ] (38:2) Wint 87-88, p. 7.
"The Political Sawyers." [BelPoJ] (37:4) Sum 87, p. 1.
"Two Love Poems" ("A Taste of Cider," "The Great Blue Heron of the Salt Pond").
[BelPoJ] (37:4) Sum 87, p. 29.
"Where Are the Birds?" (for Rebecca). [BelPoJ] (38:2) Wint 87-88, p. 6.
1375. DIEMER, Gretchen
"The Eggless Woman" (for Barbara). [CutB] (27/28) 87, p. 70-71.
1376. DIETMEIER, Richard
"War Souvenir." [Abraxas] (35/36) 87, p. 67.

1377. DIGGES, Deborah
    "Circadian Rhythms." [NewYorker] (63:5) 23 Mr 87, p. 36.
    "Painting by Number." [Field] (36) Spr 87, p. 111.
    "Sycamores." [NewYorker] (63:39) 16 N 87, p. 44.
1378. DIGMAN, Steven M.
    "A Man Should Be Masculine." [Bogg] (58) 87, p. 64.
    "The Therapist." [Amelia] (4:3, issue 10) 87, p. 60.
1379. DILLARD, Gavin
    "Untitled: Almost a week without his smell on my fingers." [JamesWR] (4:3) Spr
        87, p. 12.
1380. DILLON, Andrew
    "After Teaching *Paradise Lost*." [InterPR] (13:2) Fall 87, p. 46.
    "College Mail Room." [InterPR] (13:2) Fall 87, p. 46.
    "The Dark of a Small Town." [InterPR] (13:2) Fall 87, p. 47.
    "Denying God." [ArizQ] (43:2) Sum 87, p. 100.
    "The Girl in the Bark-Green Shirt." [InterPR] (13:2) Fall 87, p. 49.
    "In My Daughter's Room." [InterPR] (13:2) Fall 87, p. 49.
    "Later, Alone" (1986 Finalist, Eve of Saint Agnes Poetry Competition). [NegC]
        (7:1/2) 87, p. 152.
    "North of Madison, South of Versailles." [WindO] (49) Fall 87, p. 12.
    "Small Town." [InterPR] (13:2) Fall 87, p. 48.
    "St. Augustine." [WindO] (49) Fall 87, p. 13.
    "Stafford's Internal Reaction to the News That He Had Been Elected Poet No. 1 by a
        National Magazine." [PoetL] (82:3) Fall 87, p. 171.
    "Sunday Night" (1986 Honorable Mention, Eve of Saint Agnes Poetry Competition).
        [NegC] (7:1/2) 87, p. 130.
    "While I Was Enacting Damnations." [PoetL] (82:4) Wint 87-88, p. 222.
    "While Marking the Milton Exams." [InterPR] (13:2) Fall 87, p. 50.
1381. DILLON, Enoch
    "Perspective." [PoetL] (82:3) Fall 87, p. 165.
1382. DILSAVER, Paul
    "Divorce." [WritersF] (13) Fall 87, p. 179-180.
    "Fortuna's Wheel." [WritersF] (13) Fall 87, p. 178.
    "Man Alone." [PaintedB] (31) 87, p. 73.
    "Swine Song." [WritersF] (13) Fall 87, p. 176-177.
    "Time As Terrorist." [WritersF] (13) Fall 87, p. 177.
1383. DiMAGGIO, Jill
    "In the Pizzaria." [Lactuca] (7) Ag 87, p. 21.
    "Upper West Side of Manhattan, Sounds in the Night." [Lactuca] (7) Ag 87, p. 22.
1384. DIMITROVA, Blaga
    "Deserts" (tr. by Heather McHugh and Nikolai Popov). [Trans] (18) Spr 87, p. 277.
    "Forbidden Sea" (Excerpt, tr. by Heather McHugh and Nikolai Popov). [Trans] (18)
        Spr 87, p. 280.
    "I Doze off in the Tired Shade of an Afternoon" (tr. by Elizabeth A. Socolow &
        Ludmilla P. Wightman). [NewEngR] (9:4) Sum 87, p. 384.
    "Multidimensional" (tr. by Heather McHugh and Nikolai Popov). [Trans] (18) Spr
        87, p. 276.
    "Nightlight: Eye of the Owl" (tr. by Heather McHugh and Nikolai Popov). [Trans]
        (18) Spr 87, p. 278.
    "Old Song in a New Voice" (tr. by Heather McHugh and Nikolai Popov). [Trans]
        (18) Spr 87, p. 279.
1385. DING, Dennis
    "At Parting" (tr. of Gu Cheng, w. Edward Morin). [Paint] (14:27) Spr 87, p. 45.
    "Early Spring" (tr. of Gu Cheng, w. Edward Morin). [CrossCur] (7:3) 87, p. 135.
    "Ice Carvings" (tr. of Li Qi, w. Edward Morin). [CrossCur] (7:3) 87, p. 155-156.
    "Iron Meteorite" (Beijing Planetarium, tr. of Gao Fa-lin, w. Edward Morin).
        [Ploughs] (13:4) 87, p. 43-44.
1386. DINGS, Fred
    "Crabbing." [Shen] (37:4) 87, p. 42-43.
    "Late Marsh." [NewYorker] (62:51) 9 F 87, p. 38.
1387. DiPALMA, Ray
    "Chan" (5 poems). [Bound] (14:1/2) Fall 85-Wint 86 [c87], p. 57-59.
1388. DiPIETRO, Marylou
    "Sheila Shea" (1986 Finalist, Eve of Saint Agnes Poetry Competition). [NegC]
        (7:1/2) 87, p. 197-198.

1389. DiSANTO, Grace
"Psychic Bridge." [Pembroke] (19) 87, p. 168.
1390. DISCH, Tom
"Advice to Young Cooks." [Salm] (74/75) Spr-Sum 87, p. 53-54.
"Death Wish IV." [Witness] (1:2) Sum 87, p. 124-125.
"Dreams: A Darwinian View." [NewRep] (196:22) 1 Je 87, p. 36.
"In Memoriam." [Boulevard] (2:3) Fall 87, p. 176-177.
"Medusa at Her Vanity." [Poetry] (151:1/2) O-N 87, p. 42.
"Nightmare on Elm Street." [NewRep] (196:19) 11 My 87, p. 36.
"Riddle with Guesses." [LightY] '87, c86, p. 99-100.
"Short-Term Memory Loss." [LightY] '87, c86, p. 190.
"Sweet Clover" (for Jerry Mundis). [Boulevard] (2:3) Fall 87, p. 175-176.
"A Tree in the Dark." [Witness] (1:2) Sum 87, p. 126.
"Waking Early New Year's Day, Without a Hangover." [Boulevard] (2:3) Fall 87, p.
173-175.
1391. DISCHELL, Stuart
"Fool's Gold." [Agni] (24/25) 87, p. 92-93.
"Macbeth." [Ploughs] (13:1) 87, p. 43-44.
"Sleep Neighbors." [Agni] (24/25) 87, p. 91.
"Souvenir." [BostonR] (12:5) O 87, p. 21.
1392. DISERENS, Deborah
"Heart of Stone." [NegC] (7:1/2) 87, p. 68-69.
"Water Lines." [NegC] (7:1/2) 87, p. 70.
1393. DISLER, Jacqui (Jacqueline)
"Epilogue." [NewAW] (1) 87, p. 115.
"Grate of an Opening Jar." [NewAW] (2) Fall 87, p. 97.
"Rhythm Track." [NewAW] (2) Fall 87, p. 98.
1394. DISTELHEIM, Rochelle
"No Muse Is Good Muse." [LightY] '87, c86, p. 134-135.
1395. DITCHOFF, Pamela
"Summer Custody" (1986 Finalist, Eve of Saint Agnes Poetry Competition). [NegC]
(7:1/2) 87, p. 153.
1396. DITSKY, John
"Badlands." [Amelia] (4:3, issue 10) 87, p. 51.
"A Blues." [AntigR] (69/70) 87, p. 125.
"Fruits & Vegetables." [AntigR] (69/70) 87, p. 125.
"Holding Pattern." [Interim] (6:1) Spr 87, p. 39.
"Losses." [NoDaQ] (55:2) Spr 87, p. 113.
"Love in the Last Decade." [Amelia] (4:3, issue 10) 87, p. 51-52.
"Monkey Mountain, Beppu (2)." [MemphisSR] (8:1) Fall 87, p. 58.
"The Naked Man Picks Berries." [YellowS] (22) Spr 87, p. 7.
"Nickel and Dime." [OntR] (26) Spr-Sum 87, p. 89.
"Pas." [MemphisSR] (8:1) Fall 87, p. 57.
"Paul's Case." [Interim] (6:1) Spr 87, p. 39.
"Petoskey Stone." [OntR] (26) Spr-Sum 87, p. 88.
"Sense." [Poem] (58) N 87, p. 1.
"Two Weeks Now, & Blades." [WindO] (49) Fall 87, p. 51.
1397. DITTRICH, Lisa
"Instructions to a Student Trying to Write about Death" (for Joani). [CimR] (78) Ja
87, p. 61-62.
1398. DIXON, Andrea
"The Over-Face." [Interim] (6:2) Fall 87, p. 37.
1399. DJANIKIAN, Gregory
"Alexandria, 1953." [Poetry] (151:1/2) O-N 87, p. 43.
"The Fight." [CimR] (80) Jl 87, p. 46-47.
"For My Daughter." [CimR] (80) Jl 87, p. 48.
"How I Learned English." [Poetry] (149:4) Ja 87, p. 223-224.
"In the Elementary School Choir." [Poetry] (149:4) Ja 87, p. 221-222.
"When I First Saw Snow" (Tarrytown, N.Y.). [Poetry] (149:4) Ja 87, p. 225.
"Where He Is, I Am" (for my son, 10 months). [NewEngR] (10:2) Wint 87, p.
208-209.
1400. DJERASSI, Carl
"Godfather I." [NewL] (54:1) Fall 87, p. 113.
"My Island." [MidwQ] (28:2) Wint 87, p. 214.
"Three Variations on a Theme by Callosobruchus." [NewL] (54:1) Fall 87, p. 112.

1401. DLUGOS, Tim
"Dear heart, wish you or I were here or there." [ParisR] (29:102) Spr 87, p. 211-212.
"July" (for Darragh Park). [ParisR] (29:102) Spr 87, p. 213-215.
1402. DOBYNS, Stephen
"Cecil." [Pequod] (23/24) 87, p. 201.
"Confession." [Ploughs] (13:4) 87, p. 37.
"Delicious Monstrosity." [Ploughs] (13:4) 87, p. 36.
"Ebb Tide." [Pequod] (23/24) 87, p. 206.
"Faces." [Poetry] (150:4) Jl 87, p. 238-239.
"The Gardener." [VirQR] (63:1) Wint 87, p. 72-73.
"The General and the Tango Singer." [VirQR] (63:1) Wint 87, p. 75-77.
"Learning to Think." [Pequod] (23/24) 87, p. 204.
"Long Story." [Poetry] (151:1/2) O-N 87, p. 44-45.
"Loud Music." [Pequod] (23/24) 87, p. 203.
"Missed Chances." [Antaeus] (58) Spr 87, p. 240-241.
"Odysseus's Homecoming." [Crazy] (32) Spr 87, p. 20-21.
"Orpheus." [Crazy] (32) Spr 87, p. 22-23.
"Short Rides." [VirQR] (63:1) Wint 87, p. 73-75.
"Streetlight." [Pequod] (23/24) 87, p. 200.
"Sun Gazers." [Pequod] (23/24) 87, p. 202.
"Waking." [Pequod] (23/24) 87, p. 205.
"What You Should Have Thought About Earlier." [Ploughs] (13:4) 87, p. 38.
1403. DODD, Elizabeth
"To Name It That Way." [Witness] (1:4) Wint 87, p. 166-167.
1404. DODD, Wayne
"Like Deer Our Bodies." [ThRiPo] (29/30) 87, p. 10.
"Love Ranch." [ThRiPo] (29/30) 87, p. 8-9.
"Naming the Winter." [ThRiPo] (29/30) 87, p. 12-13.
"Nothing That Is Not There." [CharR] (13:1) Spr 87, p. 76.
"Of Desire." [ThRiPo] (29/30) 87, p. 11-12.
"The Only Future Any of Us Has." [ThRiPo] (29/30) 87, p. 14.
"Outside My Cabin." [ThRiPo] (29/30) 87, p. 7.
"The Present." [Crazy] (32) Spr 87, p. 39-41.
"There." [Raccoon] (24/25) My 87, p. 228-229.
1405. DOEBLER, Bettie Anne
"The Old Woman" (On the time before ending). [PassN] (8:2) Sum 87, p. 26.
1406. DOERING, Steven
"Flying to David." [Bogg] (58) 87, p. 18.
1407. DOGEN, Zengi
"Snow" (tr. by W. S. Merwin). [RiverS] (23) 87, p. 45-46.
1408. DOHERTY, Tom
"R&R, Manila, May, 1967." [Abraxas] (35/36) 87, p. 31.
1409. DOLSON, Charles
"River Point Nine" (1987 Ratner-Ferber-Poet Lore Honorable Mention). [PoetL] (82:2) Sum 87, p. 77-78.
1410. DÖLZ-BLACKBURN, Inés
"Tres Poemas de Otoño en 1985." [LetFem] (13:1/2) Primavera-Otoño 87, p. 129-130.
1411. DOMINA, Lynn
"Apples." [PassN] (8:2) Sum 87, p. 23.
"Black Cherries." [PennR] (3:2) Fall-Wint 87, p. 28-29.
"Habits of Grief." [Ascent] (12:2) 87, p. 23.
"The Olde World Cafe." [IndR] (10:3) Spr 87, p. 85.
DONAGH, Bernard Mac
See Mac DONAGH, Bernard
1412. DONAHUE, Joseph
"Open All Night." [Act] (7) 87, p. 76-80.
1413. DONALDSON, Jeffery
"At Sea." [Shen] (37:4) 87, p. 22-26.
"Mandelstam." [NewRep] (196:11) 16 Mr 87, p. 30.
DONNA, Bella
See BELLA DONNA
1414. DONNELL, David
"Chocolate." [MalR] (80) S 87, p. 63-65.
"Potato Head." [MalR] (80) S 87, p. 57-59.

"Rowing." [MalR] (80) S 87, p. 60-62.
1415. DONNELLY, Susan
"Thoreau's *Cape Cod*." [BelPoJ] (38:2) Wint 87-88, p. 32-33.
1416. DONOHUE, Sheila P.
"To Dublin." [CarolQ] (40:1) Fall 87, p. 71-72.
1417. DONOVAN, Laurence
"Perhaps." [Boulevard] (2:3) Fall 87, p. 147.
"The Pine." [SpiritSH] (53:1) 87, p. 2-3.
"The Solar Heater Plant" (Miami, 1939). [SpiritSH] (53:1) 87, p. 4-11.
1418. DONOVAN, Stewart
"Cape Breton Christmas" (after Marianne Moore). [AntigR] (71/72) Aut 87-Wint 88,
    p. 185-186.
"Halifax Report on Sydney Cancer Rates." [AntigR] (71/72) Aut 87-Wint 88, p.
    187-188.
1419. DOOLE, John
"Clarse Distinction." [Margin] (4) Aut 87, p. 17.
"Momentarily" (being a rare example of the correct use of this word). [Margin] (4)
    Aut 87, p. 109.
1420. DOOLEY, David
"O'Keefe and Stieglitz" (3 Selections: "Flowers," "Stieglitz: A Conversation,"
    "Judith"). [BelPoJ] (38:1) Fall 87, p. 8-11.
1421. DORAN, Heather
"To William." [CrabCR] (4:3) Sum 87, p. 14.
1422. DORESKI, William
"Allegro." [BelPoJ] (37:4) Sum 87, p. 12.-13.
"Boxcars at the Bellows Falls Crossing." [Salm] (74/75) Spr-Sum 87, p. 57-58.
"Chesquessett Beach." [Footwork] 87, p. 46.
"French Poem." [Footwork] 87, p. 46.
"Greenville." [Wind] (17:60) 87, p. 9-10.
"Harlow Farm." [BelPoJ] (37:4) Sum 87, p. 13-15.
"Hawthorne and Melville." [Salm] (74/75) Spr-Sum 87, p. 59.
"Minerals in the Harvard Museum." [TexasR] (7:3/4) 87, p. 37.
"New England Gothic." [Wind] (17:60) 87, p. 10-11.
"South Ferry." [Salm] (74/75) Spr-Sum 87, p. 60.
"Spring Break." [Footwork] 87, p. 45.
1423. DORF, Carol
"After the Funeral." [FiveFR] (5) 87, p. 39.
"Yellowjackets." [FiveFR] (5) 87, p. 38.
DORMAN, Sonya
    See HESS, Sonya
1424. DORN, Edward
"The Independent Boulder Woman." [WillowS] (20) Spr 87, p. 95-97.
1425. DORNIN, Christopher L.
"The Jefferson State School Personnel Manuel." [Amelia] (4:1/2, issue 9) 87, p.
    33-39.
"Knife." [Amelia] (4:1/2, issue 9) 87, p. 32-33.
1426. DORO, Sue
"Bacon Lettuce Bankruptcy." [LakeSR] (21) 87, p. 6.
1427. DORSETT, Robert
"Another Portrait." [SmPd] (24:3) Fall 87, p. 27.
"Cruelty" (tr. of I-to Wen). [NewOR] (14:1) Spr 87, p. 98.
"Found Poem: Explanation for the Present" (Adapted from "The Concept of Irony"
    by Kierkegaard). [WindO] (48) Spr 87, p. 13.
1428. DOTSON, Raymond
"I come Graymalkin." [InterPR] (13:1) Spr 87, p. 108.
1429. DOTY, Mark
"Harbor Lights." [YaleR] (77:1) Aut 87, p. 26-28.
1430. DOTY, Ruth
"St. Petersburg, a Great Jeweled Wolf Rolls into the Black Sea . . ." (Excerpts).
    [Nimrod] (30:2) Spr-Sum 87, p. 62-66.
1431. DOUBIAGO, Sharon
"The Bridge of San Luis Rey" (from the epic poem, "South America Mi Hija).
    [MidAR] (7:2) 87, p. 130-136.
"Oedipus Drowned" (Selection: 7. "How Do I Love Thee? Let Me Count the
    Ways"). [Calyx] (10:2/3) Spr 87, p. 25-29.
"South America, Mi Hija" (Excerpts). [Calyx] (11:1) Wint 87-88, p. 20-24.

"South America, Mi Hija" (Selection: 1. Pluto and Demeter). [AnotherCM] (17) 87,
    p. 20-24.
1432. DOUGHERTY, Jay
    "Conversation From Another Planet." [SmPd] (24:1) Wint 87, p. 11.
    "Help Wanted — Literary." [Bogg] (58) 87, p. 52.
    "Old Women Are Taking Over the World." [LightY] '87, c86, p. 235.
    "On Poetry Writing and Love Affairs." [Amelia] (4:3, issue 10) 87, p. 88.
    "Physical." [Lactuca] (7) Ag 87, p. 26.
    "A Reply." [LightY] '87, c86, p. 47.
    "There Are Mornings When." [Bogg] (57) 87, p. 46.
    "Unpleasant Surprise." [LightY] '87, c86, p. 194.
1433. DOUGLAS, Ann
    "Dunthorpe." [IndR] (10:3) Spr 87, p. 29-30.
1434. DOUGLAS, David Paul
    "Rubà i I" (tr. of Shamsur Rahman Faruqi, w. Gopi Chand Narang). [Bomb] (18)
        Wint 87, p. 68.
    "Rubà i IV" (tr. of Shamsur Rahman Faruqi, w. Gopi Chand Narang). [Bomb] (18)
        Wint 87, p. 68.
    "Underdone" (tr. of Shamsur Rahman Faruqi, w. Gopi Chand Narang). [Bomb]
        (18) Wint 87, p. 68.
1435. DOUGLASS, Karen
    "Anthem for Cat Lovers." [Confr] (35/36) Spr-Fall 87, p. 140.
1436. DOVE, Rita
    "Adolescence — II." [BostonR] (12:1) F 87, p. 13.
    "Arrow." [MichQR] (26:3) Sum 87, p. 477-478.
    "Ars Poetica." [Poetry] (151:1/2) O-N 87, p. 45.
    "Compendium." [BostonR] (12:1) F 87, p. 13.
    "Crab-Boil" (Ft. Myers, 1962). [PartR] (54:2) Spr 87, p. 263-264.
    "Fantasy and Science Fiction." [Ploughs] (13:1) 87, p. 46-47.
    "Flash Cards." [BostonR] (12:1) F 87, p. 13.
    "Hully Gully." [Ploughs] (13:1) 87, p. 48.
    "Obbligato." [Ploughs] (13:1) 87, p. 45.
    "Parsley." [BostonR] (12:1) F 87, p. 13.
    "Saints." [BostonR] (12:1) F 87, p. 13.
    "Stargazing." [ParisR] (29:103) Sum 87, p. 184-185.
1437. DOWNES, G. V.
    "Pool" (Variations on a Navajo healing ceremony, chants 104-108 of the
        Coyoteway). [Event] (16:3) Fall 87, p. 24.
    "Slippage." [Event] (16:3) Fall 87, p. 23.
1438. DOWNIE, Glen
    "Diagnosis: Heart Failure." [Waves] (15:3) Wint 87, p. 46.
    "Living in Sin: 1." [Waves] (15:3) Wint 87, p. 48.
    "The Marias, Mexico City." [Waves] (15:3) Wint 87, p. 47.
1439. DOXEY, W. S. (William)
    "Hounds." [SouthernHR] (21:3) Sum 87, p. 254.
    "Melody." [Confr] (35/36) Spr-Fall 87, p. 201.
1440. DOYLE, James
    "The Age of Reptiles Arrives, Shooting Sparks" (for Allen Wargo). [PoetL] (81:4)
        Wint 86-87, p. 232.
    "The Cave Artist." [BallSUF] (28:4) Aut 87, p. 34.
    "Coastline." [Interim] (6:1) Spr 87, p. 34.
    "Convert." [HampSPR] Wint 87, p. 50.
    "Dali." [WillowS] (19) Wint 87, p. 9.
    "Europa and the Bull." [Interim] (6:1) Spr 87, p. 33.
    "Evangelist." [InterPR] (13:2) Fall 87, p. 90.
    "The Governor's Office" (Selections: "Meeting Needs," "The Press Secretary").
        [WindO] (49) Fall 87, p. 61.
    "How the Nation Began." [HampSPR] Wint 87, p. 50-51.
    "Icarus." [WillowS] (19) Wint 87, p. 10.
    "The Inexorable." [Raccoon] (24/25) My 87, p. 242.
    "The Moon." [Footwork] 87, p. 52.
    "The Saviour." [WillowS] (19) Wint 87, p. 11.
    "Solitude." [HampSPR] Wint 87, p. 51.
    "The Tribe." [Jacaranda] (2:2) Spr 87, p. 63.
    "Why They Discovered America." [Interim] (6:1) Spr 87, p. 33.

1441. DOYLE, Suzanne J.
    "Season Tickets." [Sequoia] (31:1) Centennial issue 87, p. 32.
1442. DOZIER, Brent
    "A Memory of an Apple Tree in April, in Alabama." [Amelia] (4:3, issue 10) 87, p. 96.
    "Sere, Golden Willows." [SouthernHR] (21:1) Wint 87, p. 35.
    "Write! my little mestizo." [Abraxas] (35/36) 87, p. 26.
1443. DRAGOMOSHCHENKO, Arkadii
    "Nasturium as Reality" (tr. by Lyn Hejinian and Elena Balashova). [Sulfur] (19) Spr 87, p. 94-107.
1444. DRAKE, Jeannette
    "Missing Children" (for Aunt Mattie." [Callaloo] (10:3) Sum 87, p. 480.
1445. DRAKE, Robert
    "Sonnet: You are fire you are burning." [Bogg] (57) 87, p. 16.
1446. DRESMAN, Paul
    "The Lost Woman." [SoDakR] (25:3) Aut 87, p. 76-83.
1447. DREW, Bettina
    "Music." [PennR] (3:1) Spr-Sum 87, p. 22.
1448. DREW, George
    "Burning Candles with Scudder Bates." [Blueline] (7:2/3 [i.e. 8:2/3?]) 87, p. 4-5.
    "The Physics of This Earthly Life." [CumbPR] (7:1) Fall 87, p. 50-53.
    "Running with a Biologist" (for Dick Dinn). [Blueline] (7:2/3 [i.e. 8:2/3?]) 87, p. 101.
1449. DREYER, Lynne
    "The White Museum" (Excerpt). [Bound] (14:1/2) Fall 85-Wint 86 [c87], p. 67-68.
1450. DRISCOLL, Jack
    "Elegy: Charles Atlas (1893-1972)." [Poetry] (149:6) Mr 87, p. 327.
    "Goodwill." [NoDaQ] (55:3) Sum 87, p. 77.
    "Houdini." [Poetry] (149:6) Mr 87, p. 326.
    "Nest Robbers, St. James Cemetery, 1959." [NoDaQ] (55:3) Sum 87, p. 76.
    "Sister's Lecture on the Weakness of the Flesh." [TexasR] (8:3/4) Fall-Wint 87, p. 17.
    "Spying." [Poetry] (149:6) Mr 87, p. 325.
1451. DRISKELL, Leon
    "Going Away Present" (1986 Finalist, Eve of Saint Agnes Poetry Competition). [NegC] (7:1/2) 87, p. 194.
    "Toward the Ancient Walnut" (1986 Finalist, Eve of Saint Agnes Poetry Competition). [NegC] (7:1/2) 87, p. 192-193.
1452. DRIZHAL, Peter M.
    "Mr. Bird Plays Jazz." [HampSPR] Wint 87, p. 14.
1453. DROGE, Gerald
    "Three North." [CapeR] (22:2) Fall 87, p. 23.
1454. DRUCKER, Johanna
    "Against Fiction" (Excerpt). [Bound] (14:1/2) Fall 85-Wint 86 [c87], p. 2-4.
1455. DRURY, John
    "Descant." [Shen] (37:2) 87, p. 24.
    "How It Matters" (For Eric Pankey). [BelPoJ] (38:1) Fall 87, p. 24-25.
    "In Memoriam: Tom Hird." [CimR] (81) O 87, p. 44.
    "Sonnet to Orpheus." [NewRep] (197:21) 23 N 87, p. 30.
    "Sudy." [CimR] (81) O 87, p. 32.
1456. DRUSKA, John
    "Lament of the Impotent Trashman." [Pig] (14) 87, p. 77.
    "Toward a Woodchuck Poetics." [Pig] (14) 87, p. 77.
1457. DU, Fu
    "After the Harvest." [PoetryE] (23/24) Fall 87, p. 82.
    "The Journey North" (tr. by David Hinton). [NewEngR] (10:1) Aut 87, p. 33-35.
1458. Du HAIME, Kathleen
    "Breakdown à la Mode." [Writer] (99:5) My 86, p. 17.
1459. Du PLESSIS, Phil
    "Easter Transit" (tr. by Patrick Cullinan). [TriQ] (69) Spr-Sum 87, p. 345-346.
1460. DUBIE, Norman
    "Accident." [AmerPoR] (16:5) S-O 87, p. 26.
    "The Apocrypha of Jacques Derrida." [Field] (37) Fall 87, p. 76-77.
    "Ars Poetica." [AmerPoR] (16:5) S-O 87, p. 23.
    "Baptismal." [AmerPoR] (16:5) S-O 87, p. 24.

"Buffalo Clouds Over the Maestro Hoon" (for our godson). [Field] (37) Fall 87, p. 78-79.
"Chagall." [AmerPoR] (16:5) S-O 87, p. 24.
"Coyote Creek." [AmerPoR] (16:5) S-O 87, p. 26.
"The Death of the Race Car Driver." [AmerPoR] (16:5) S-O 87, p. 25.
"Jeremiad." [AmerPoR] (16:5) S-O 87, p. 24.
"The Peace of Lodi." [AmerPoR] (16:5) S-O 87, p. 26.
"Poem: A mule kicked out in the trees." [AmerPoR] (16:5) S-O 87, p. 24.
"Trakl" (for Paul). [AmerPoR] (16:5) S-O 87, p. 25.
"Victory" (for my wife). [AmerPoR] (16:5) S-O 87, p. 25.
"The Wine Bowl." [AmerPoR] (16:5) S-O 87, p. 26.
"Women with Children." [AmerPoR] (16:5) S-O 87, p. 25.
1461. DUBNOV, Eugene
"And let me tell you more" (tr. by Anne Stevenson and the Author). [SenR] (17:1) 87, p. 20.
"I Hide My Face Against the Tramcar Window" (tr. by Chris Arkell and John Heath-Stubbs). [SenR] (17:1) 87, p. 19.
"I've Read How" (tr. by John Heath-Stubbs and the author). [SouthernHR] (21:2) Spr 87, p. 167.
"The Legatee" (tr. of Anna Akhmatova, w. John Heath-Stubbs). [ChiR] (35:4) 87, p. 103.
"Marina Tsvetayeva (1892-1941)" (tr. of Anna Akhmatova, w. John Heath-Stubbs). [ChiR] (35:4) 87, p. 104.
"Not the Snow" (tr. by C. Newman and the author). [SouthernHR] (21:2) Spr 87, p. 155.
"On This Warm Midsummer Day" (For Eddie Linden and Nina Alferova, tr. by the author and C. Newman). [Waves] (15:1/2) Fall 86, p. 90.
"Poem of the Hall" (tr. by the author and C. Newman). [WebR] (12:1) Spr 87, p. 81-86.
"Sergei Esenin" (tr. of Anna Akhmatova, w. John Heath-Stubbs). [ChiR] (35:4) 87, p. 106.
"Sergei Esenin (1895-1925)" (tr. of Anna Akhmatova, w. John Heath-Stubbs). [ChiR] (35:4) 87, p. 105.
"To a Future Reader" (tr. of Anna Akhmatova, w. John Heath-Stubbs). [ChiR] (35:4) 87, p. 107.
1462. DUBOVSKY, A.
"Miropol." [NowestR] (25:2) 87, p. 83.
1463. DUCORNET, Rikki
"Desire." [Margin] (1) Wint 86, p. 93.
"Viperweed." [Margin] (3) Sum 87, p. 51-56.
1464. DUDDY, Patrick
"Caribbean Idyll." [Thrpny] (31) Fall 87, p. 20.
1465. DUDLEY, Michael
"Last of the wine." [Bogg] (58) 87, p. 33.
1466. DUEMER, Joseph
"Burn Victim." [MSS] (5:3) 87, p. 128.
"The Loveliness of Two Retarded Girls Eating Lunch." [MSS] (5:3) 87, p. 130.
"Recidivist's Song." [MSS] (5:3) 87, p. 127.
"That's What Friends Are For." [MSS] (5:3) 87, p. 131.
1467. DUER, David
"Starting to Portray the Heart." [Contact] (9:44/45/46) Fall-Wint 87, p. 51.
1468. DUFER, Dennis
"Crowd Scene." [ThRiPo] (29/30) 87, p. 25.
1469. DUFFY, Carol Ann
"Politico." [Stand] (28:3) Sum 87, p. 57.
1470. DUFFY, Patty
"Bald omphalloskeptic sunning." [Amelia] (4:1/2, issue 9) 87, p. 53.
"T'was once a gay whale we dubbed Cisco." [Amelia] (4:1/2, issue 9) 87, p. 16.
1471. DUGAN, Alan
"Pro-Nuke Blues." [NowestR] (25:3) 87, p. 365.
1472. DUGAN, Lawrence
"Stone Harbor." [Jacaranda] (2:2) Spr 87, p. 16-17.
1473. DUHAIME, A.
"In the rain" (tr. by Dorothy Howard). [CrossC] (9:3/4) 87, p. 9.
"Sous la pluie." [CrossC] (9:3/4) 87, p. 9.

1474. DUHAMEL, Denise
"On Being Born the Same Exact Day of the Same Exact Year as Boy George."
[Ploughs] (13:4) 87, p. 39-40.
1475. DUKES, Norman
"Two Pictures of a Rose in the Dark." [Agni] (24/25) 87, p. 116-117.
1476. DUMARAN, Adele
"The World Is a Wedding" (for my father, 1987 Ratner-Ferber-Poet Lore Honorable
Mention). [PoetL] (82:2) Sum 87, p. 89-90.
1477. DUMBRAVEANU, Anghel
"The Fountains of Serbia" (in Romanian and English, tr. by Robert J. Ward and
Marcel Cornis-Pop). [MidAR] (7:2) 87, p. 65-83.
1478. DUNCAN, Graham
"Blue Spruce." [Blueline] (7:2/3 [i.e. 8:2/3?]) 87, p. 54.
"Floater." [PoeticJ] (17) 87, p. 36.
"Spring Disorder." [Blueline] (7:2/3 [i.e. 8:2/3?]) 87, p. 53.
1479. DUNCAN, Julia Nunnally
"Breakdown." [Vis] (24) 87, p. 34-36.
1480. DUNGEY, Christopher
"Fort Michilimacinac from a Modern Promontory." [Jacaranda] (2:2) Spr 87, p.
84-85.
1481. DUNHAM, Vera
"The More You Tear Off, the More You Keep" (tr. of Andrei Voznesensky, w.
William Jay Smith). [Trans] (18) Spr 87, p. 314-315.
1482. DUNN, Ann
"Candle." [HampSPR] Wint 86, p. 50.
"The Formal Pond." [MidAR] (7:2) 87, p. 23.
"Tea Pot." [HampSPR] Wint 86, p. 51.
1483. DUNN, Douglas
"The Dark Crossroads." [Verse] (4:2) Je 87, p. 8-9.
"Daylight." [Verse] (4:2) Je 87, p. 7.
"Jig of the Week No. 21." [KenR] (NS 9:2) Spr 87, p. 73-74.
"Supreme Death." [BostonR] (12:1) F 87, p. 27.
1484. DUNN, Millard
"Skylight." [OhioR] (38) 87, p. 114.
"Sleeping with Bees." [OhioR] (38) 87, p. 115.
1485. DUNN, R. S.
"Cartography's Harsh Realities, or, My Heart Faces Where the Wild Goose
Chases." [Paint] (14:28) Aut 87, p. 16.
1486. DUNN, Stephen
"After Listening in the Car to Those Who Call the Radio Psychologist." [Antaeus]
(58) Spr 87, p. 244-245.
"Among Men." [ParisR] (29:105) Wint 87, p. 97.
"Beginnings" (for Larry Raab). [QW] (24) Wint 87, p. 44-45.
"Cleanliness." [Poetry] (150:3) Je 87, p. 152.
"Collecting Future Lives." [Nat] (245:3) 1-8 Ag 87, p. 102.
"Companionship." [Nat] (244:4) 31 Ja 87, p. 122.
"Corners." [LitR] (30:4) Sum 87, p. 562.
"Desire." [LitR] (30:4) Sum 87, p. 568-569.
"Disquisition in an Empty House." [LaurelR] (21:1/2) Wint-Sum 87, p. 7-8.
"Emptiness." [Poetry] (150:3) Je 87, p. 155.
"Essay on the Personal." [LitR] (30:4) Sum 87, p. 559-560.
"Flaws." [QW] (24) Wint 87, p. 42-43.
"From the Manifesto of the Selfish." [LaurelR] (21:1/2) Wint-Sum 87, p. 5.
"Hawk." [Poetry] (149:5) F 87, p. 291.
"Improvisation on Lines Overheard on a Train." [PoetryNW] (28:1) Spr 87, p.
46-47.
"The Kisser and Teller." [GeoR] (41:2) Sum 87, p. 384.
"The Listener." [Ploughs] (13:1) 87, p. 49-50.
"Loveliness." [Poetry] (150:3) Je 87, p. 153-154.
"On the Way to Work." [Poetry] (149:5) F 87, p. 292-293.
"Poetry" (To a Young Poet Who Asked." [Poetry] (149:5) F 87, p. 293.
"The Sixties." [LaurelR] (21:1/2) Wint-Sum 87, p. 6.
"The Soul Boat." [PoetryNW] (28:1) Spr 87, p. 45-46.
"Stories." [KenR] (NS 9:2) Spr 87, p. 110-111.
"The Substitute." [LitR] (30:4) Sum 87, p. 565-566.
"Sweetness." [Poetry] (150:3) Je 87, p. 149-150.

"Tenderness." [Poetry] (150:3) Je 87, p. 150-151.
"Why I Think I'm a Writer." [Poetry] (151:1/2) O-N 87, p. 46-47.
1487. DUNNE, Carol
"The Jilt." [SmPd] (24:1) Wint 87, p. 26.
"Lunch Date: Two/Twenty-two/Eighty-three." [NewRena] (7:1, #21) Fall 87, p. 30.
"Woman of Caramel, Bitten Too Easily Down." [StoneC] (14:3/4) Spr-Sum 87, p. 68.
1488. DUNSMORE, Roger
"Jack's Poem." [GreenfR] (14:1/2) Wint-Spr, p. 57-58.
"The Junk Store, Lines from a Paragraph by Sauer" (for Siguenza). [GreenfR] (14:1/2) Wint-Spr, p. 59.
"News from the Park" (for Rick). [GreenfR] (14:1/2) Wint-Spr, p. 54-56.
1489. DUNWOODY, Michael
"Eyeless in Babylon." [Event] (16:1) Mr 87, p. 8-11.
"Litany." [Waves] (15:4) Spr 87, p. 40-43.
1490. DuPLESSIS, Rachel Blau
"Draft #1: It." [Temblor] (5) 87, p. 22-28.
"Draft #2: She." [Temblor] (5) 87, p. 29-33.
"Draft #3: Of." [Sulfur] (20) Fall 87, p. 23-27.
1491. DuPREE, Don Keck
"Spring." [SouthernR] (23:2) Ap 87, p. 382.
"That Quickening" (a gardener's garland). [SouthernR] (23:2) Ap 87, p. 383.
"Winter." [SouthernR] (23:2) Ap 87, p. 381.
1492. DURCAN, Paul
"Before the Celtic Yoke." [Pembroke] (19) 87, p. 84.
"Doris Fashions." [AntigR] (69/70) 87, p. 205.
"EI Flight 106: New York - Dublin." [Stand] (28:4) Aut 87, p. 10-11.
"EI Flight 106: New York - Dublin" (after J.M.W. Turner). [AntigR] (71/72) Aut 87-Wint 88, p. 67-68.
"Nora Dreaming of Kilcash." [AntigR] (69/70) 87, p. 204.
1493. DUTTON, Paul
"Else." [CrossC] (9:3/4) 87, p. 13.
1494. DUVAL, Quinton
"Crows at Evening." [Raccoon] (24/25) My 87, p. 235.
DUYN, Mona van
See Van DUYN, Mona
1495. DWELLER, Cliff
"The Eternal Grief." [SlipS] (7) 87, p. 115-116.
"The Ferryboat." [SlipS] (7) 87, p. 113-114.
"The Gray Horse." [SlipS] (7) 87, p. 111-112.
1496. DWYER, David
"The Railroad Station at Sabattis, NY" (21 June 86). [SoDakR] (25:2) Sum 87, p. 54-55.
1497. DWYER, Deirdre
"Questions for My Father." [Event] (16:1) Mr 87, p. 61-63.
"Summer's Gone South." [Germ] (10:2) Spr 87, p. 22-23.
1498. DWYER, Frank
"The Mystery." [Salm] (72) Fall 86, p. 203.
1499. DWYER, William
"The Chosen Simple Things." [Wind] (17:59) 87, p. 11.
"Dove Season." [Wind] (17:59) 87, p. 12.
1500. DYBEK, Stuart
"Childhood Scenes." [Caliban] (2) 87, p. 107.
"Island." [Poetry] (151:1/2) O-N 87, p. 48.
"The Playground." [Caliban] (2) 87, p. 107.
"Shaving." [Caliban] (2) 87, p. 107.
1501. DYC, Gloria
"Dreams in a Season of Drought." [PraS] (61:4) Wint 87, p. 20-21.
"On the Fourth Day." [PraS] (61:4) Wint 87, p. 18-19.
"Thinning the Herd" (for Beth Windsor). [PraS] (61:4) Wint 87, p. 16-18.
1502. DYCK, E. F.
"Fall Days." [PraF] (8:1) Spr 87, p. 75.
1503. DYE, Bru
"10 Hearts." [JamesWR] (4:2) Wint 87, p. 8.
"Black Rock Androgyny." [CentralP] (12) Fall 87, p. 51.
"No Nocturnes." [YellowS] (25) Wint 87, p. 18.

1504. DYER, Linda
    "God and New Clothes." [BellR] (10:1) Spr 87, p. 49.
    "Technology Speaking." [BellR] (10:1) Spr 87, p. 50.
1505. DYKEWOMON, Elana
    "Carnal Knowledge." [SinW] (31) 87, p. 43-44.
    "Knowledge in the Biblical Sense." [SinW] (31) 87, p. 42.
1506. EADY, Cornelius
    "Fun" (for Michael Collier). [WilliamMR] (25) Spr 87, p. 25.
    "Grace." [WilliamMR] (25) Spr 87, p. 81.
    "Nothing." [WilliamMR] (25) Spr 87, p. 24.
    "The Sweet Smell" (for the victims of Howard Beach). [WilliamMR] (25) Spr 87, p. 82.
1507. EARLY, Gerald
    "The Dreadful Bop of Flyers." [NowestR] (25:3) 87, p. 394-398.
    "Flamingo or the Making of Salad" (a poem for parents who have lost young children). [SenR] (17:2) 87, p. 39-42.
    "How Being a Prizefighter Is Like Painting Signs . . ." [Raccoon] (24/25) My 87, p. 265-267.
    "How the War in the Streets Is Won." [LitR] (30:4) Sum 87, p. 605.
    "Something for the Union Dead." [SenR] (17:2) 87, p. 43.
    "Specific Jazz, or, How Birdland Got Its Name." [Raccoon] (24/25) My 87, p. 271-272.
    "The Staff Writer's Quest for an Historical Yardbird." [Wind] (17:59) 87, p. 13.
1508. EASON, Wayne
    "Wake Forest Nursing Home: Interview, Albert, Bron 1888." [Pembroke] (19) 87, p. 134.
    "Wake Forest Nursing Home: Interview, Ramsey, Born 1910." [Pembroke] (19) 87, p. 133.
1509. EATON, Charles Edward
    "The Ablution." [Pembroke] (19) 87, p. 124.
    "The Amazon." [ConcPo] (20) 87, p. 18.
    "The Bit." [AnotherCM] (17) 87, p. 33-34.
    "The Brain Trust." [CrossCur] (6:4) 87, p. 57-58.
    "The Clutch." [SouthernPR] (27:1) Spr 87, p. 29.
    "The Crane." [CrossCur] (7:3) 87, p. 29-30.
    "The Crop Duster." [ChatR] (8:1) Fall 87, p. 21.
    "Flaws." [Confr] (35/36) Spr-Fall 87, p. 87.
    "The Grommet." [AnotherCM] (17) 87, p. 35.
    "Hair of the Dog." [Salm] (73) Wint 87, p. 146-147.
    "The Hand Grenade." [CharR] (13:1) Spr 87, p. 81.
    "The Leash." [HolCrit] (24:1) F 87, p. 18.
    "The Love Boat." [HawaiiR] (19) Spr 86, c87, p. 30.
    "The Probe." [Pembroke] (19) 87, p. 125.
    "Quicksand." [CharR] (13:1) Spr 87, p. 80-81.
    "The Turn-On." [Paint] (14:28) Aut 87, p. 5.
1510. EATON, Elizabeth A.
    "I Feel Like a Kid Again." [HiramPoR] (43) Fall-Wint 87-88, p. 30.
    "Looking for the Way." [HiramPoR] (43) Fall-Wint 87-88, p. 6.
1511. EBALO, Dan
    "The Star Story." [NewYorker] (63:22) 20 Jl 87, p. 34.
1512. EBERHART, Richard
    "All of Us." [SewanR] (95:1) Wint 87, p. 1.
    "At Archie Peisch's Funeral." [TexasR] (7:3/4) 87, p. 39.
    "Brief Candle." [TexasR] (7:3/4) 87, p. 38.
    "Millennia." [TexasR] (7:3/4) 87, p. 40.
    "Singular, Desolate, Out of It." [Poetry] (151:1/2) O-N 87, p. 49.
    "Speech of Acceptance." [Poetry] (151:1/2) O-N 87, p. 49.
    "Stone Fence." [PartR] (54:3) Sum 87, p. 423.
    "Sun-Make." [NewEngR] (9:3) Spr 87, p. 265.
    "Wind Blowing Around." [NegC] (7:3/4) 87, p. 68.
1513. ECEVIT, Bülent
    "Tomorrow" (tr. by Talat Sait Halman). [Trans] (19) Fall 87, p. 104.
1514. ECHAVARREN, Roberto
    "Loves." [Rampike] (5:3) 87, p. 39.
1515. ECONOMOU, George
    "An Evening in Kingfisher." [GrandS] (6:2) Wint 87, p. 194-196.

EDDY, Darlene Mathis
See MATHIS-EDDY, Darlene
1516. EDDY, Elizabeth
"Near-Miss Eddy." [LightY] '87, c86, p. 72-73.
1517. EDDY, Gary
"Relentless." [ColR] (NS 14:2) Fall-Wint 87, p. 49.
1518. EDDY, Lynn
"Mechanical Blue." [DekalbLAJ] (20:1/4) 87, p. 36.
1519. EDELSTEIN, Carol
"Plants and Animals." [ColR] (NS 14:2) Fall-Wint 87, p. 84.
"Rice." [ColR] (NS 14:2) Fall-Wint 87, p. 81-82.
"A Seamstress Remembers the Louisiana State Fair." [ColR] (NS 14:2) Fall-Wint
87, p. 83.
1520. EDKINS, Anthony
"Conveying Regrets." [SpiritSH] (53:1) 87, p. 31.
"A Little Conversation." [SpiritSH] (53:1) 87, p. 31.
"Travel Book" (3 poems, tr. of Santiago Sylvester). [Trans] (18) Spr 87, p.
183-184.
1521. EDMOND, Lauris
"Directions." [Verse] (4:3) N 87, p. 8.
1522. EDMUNDS, Sandra
"Everyone But Me." [Writ] (19) 87, p. 9.
"Nocturne 1-3." [Writ] (19) 87, p. 5-7.
"Opium" (after Jean Cocteau). [Writ] (19) 87, p. 8.
1523. EDSON, Russell
"Angels." [Field] (37) Fall 87, p. 81.
"The Captain's Bath." [Epoch] (36:1) 87-88, p. 48.
"A Childhood." [Witness] (1:2) Sum 87, p. 63.
"Cursing the Dark." [Caliban] (2) 87, p. 88.
"The Family Trust." [Witness] (1:2) Sum 87, p. 64.
"Hammered Chick Pie." [Caliban] (2) 87, p. 88.
"Happiness." [Caliban] (2) 87, p. 87.
"The Method." [Caliban] (2) 87, p. 89.
"The Mistakes of an Old Woman." [Epoch] (36:1) 87-88, p. 46.
"The Old Woman Pot." [Caliban] (2) 87, p. 89.
"The Pilot." [TexasR] (7:3/4) 87, p. 41.
"The Secret Graveyard of Elephants." [Epoch] (36:1) 87-88, p. 45.
"The Twilight of the Gods." [Field] (37) Fall 87, p. 80.
"The Twisted Dog." [Caliban] (2) 87, p. 87.
"Under Things." [Witness] (1:2) Sum 87, p. 63.
"Whiskers." [Epoch] (36:1) 87-88, p. 47.
1524. EDWARDS, R. Geren
"Nascence." [Witness] (1:3) Fall 87, p. 94.
1525. EDWARDS, Susan
"Marsh Walk." [Blueline] (7:2/3 [i.e. 8:2/3?]) 87, p. 24.
1526. EEDS, Maryann
"The Better to Eat You." [EngJ] (76:4) Ap 87, p. 78.
1527. EGERMEIER, Virginia
"The Old Songwriter." [Vis] (24) 87, p. 7.
"Rain in the Dust Bowl." [CrossCur] (7:1) 87, p. 57.
"Raison d'Etre." [CrossCur] (7:1) 87, p. 58.
"Today." [CrossCur] (7:1) 87, p. 55-56.
1528. EHRHART, W. D.
"The Ducks on Wissahickon Creek." [StoneC] (14:3/4) Spr-Sum 87, p. 33.
"For Mrs. Na" (Cu Chi District, 28 December 1985). [VirQR] (63:2) Spr 87, p.
266-267.
"Last Flight Out from the War Zone" (for Bruce Weigl). [VirQR] (63:2) Spr 87, p.
267.
"Meltdown at Chernobyl." [StoneC] (14:3/4) Spr-Sum 87, p. 32.
"Twice Betrayed" (for Nguyen Thi My Huong, Ho Chi Minh City, December 1985).
[ConnPR] (6:1) 87, p. 33-34.
"Water." [VirQR] (63:2) Spr 87, p. 268.
1529. EHRLICH, Shelley
"The Allure of Birdwatching." [Northeast] (Ser. 4:6) Wint 87-88, p. 11.
"The Big Snow." [Northeast] (Ser. 4:6) Wint 87-88, p. 12.
"Constancy." [Northeast] (Ser. 4:6) Wint 87-88, p. 13.

1530. EICHWALD, Richard
"Daguerreotypes." [SewanR] (95:2) Spr 87, p. 247-248.
1531. EIDE, Steve
"I Find Two, Many-Petaled Flowers." [LakeSR] (21) 87, p. 29.
1532. EIMERS, Nancy
"Aslant." [QW] (24) Wint 87, p. 99.
"Magnolia Season." [Nat] (244:16) 25 Ap 87, p. 544.
1533. EINBOND, Bernard Lionel
"A Bit of an Englishman." [Bogg] (58) 87, p. 32.
1534. EINHORN, Sharone
"Black Wind." [AmerPoR] (16:4) Jl-Ag 87, p. 42.
"Love Ends." [AmerPoR] (16:4) Jl-Ag 87, p. 42.
"Mexico." [AmerPoR] (16:4) Jl-Ag 87, p. 42.
1535. EINZIG, Barbara
"Clearing." [Bound] (14:1/2) Fall 85-Wint 86 [c87], p. 41.
1536. EISELE, Midge
"Everything We Learn to Live Without" (4 selections). [Nimrod] (31:1) Fall-Wint
87, p. 66-69.
1537. EISELEY, Loren
"For Alice." [PraS] (61:3) Fall 87, p. 19.
"Lizard's Eye." [PraS] (61:3) Fall 87, p. 26.
1538. EISENBERG, Barry S.
"On Any Given Day." [WoosterR] (7) Spr 87, p. 68.
1539. EISENBERG, Ruth F.
"The Clearing." [PoeticJ] (17) 87, p. 43.
1540. EISIMINGER, Skip
"Among the Widow's Weeds." [SoCaR] (19:2) Spr 87, p. 58.
"Child of Violence." [SoCaR] (19:2) Spr 87, p. 58.
1541. EKHOLM, John
"The Rage of the Wounded Bear." [LakeSR] (21) 87, p. 5.
1542. EKLUND, Jane
"New Brunswick." [PoetryNW] (28:2) Sum 87, p. 41-42.
"While Reading Robinson Crusoe." [PoetryNW] (28:2) Sum 87, p. 42-43.
1543. EKSTROM, Margareta
"Loving Couples" (tr. by Daniel Ogden). [Vis] (23) 87, p. 16.
1544. ELENBOGEN, Dina
"Say a Prayer, But the Sea Wind Blows Them Out" (1987 Ratner-Ferber-Poet Lore
Honorable Mention). [PoetL] (82:2) Sum 87, p. 91-92.
1545. ELIOT, Kt
"The Homefire." [BellArk] (3:5) S-O 87, p. 10.
1546. ELIZABETH, Martha
"Aubade: In Progress." [BellArk] (3:1) Ja-F 87, p. 10.
"Nanci: Two Dances" (Solo & Ensemble). [BellArk] (3:3) My-Je 87, p. 10.
"Secular Harassment." [PoetL] (81:3) Fall 86, p. 172.
1547. ELIZONDO, Salvador
"An Incomprehensible Occurence" (tr. by Bruce Holling Roberts). [CreamCR]
(11:2/3) 87?, p. 1.
1548. ELKIN, Roger
"Omaha Beach." [CrossCur] (7:3) 87, p. 73.
1549. ELKIND, Sue Saniel
"The Artist." [CentR] (31:3) Sum 87, p. 279.
"Hidden Memories." [Wind] (17:60) 87, p. 12.
"My Rage." [CrossCur] (6:4) 87, p. 103.
"No Save Place." [Wind] (17:60) 87, p. 12-13.
"Silence." [CrossCur] (7:2) 87, p. 79.
1550. ELLEDGE, Jim
"Bath Spa: *Aquae Sulis:* Whitsun 1984" (1986 Finalist, Eve of Saint Agnes Poetry
Competition). [NegC] (7:1/2) 87, p. 178-179.
"For Frank O'Hara's Ghost." [NoAmR] (272:1) Mr 87, p. 18.
"On Earth as It Is" (For the Rev. James Sherman Elledge, 1 Sept. 1900 - 29 Jan.
1986). [TexasR] (8:3/4) Fall-Wint 87, p. 20-21.
ELLEN, Patricia Ver
See VerELLEN, Patricia
1551. ELLENBOGEN, George
"The End of the Affair." [PartR] (54:3) Sum 87, p. 432-433.

1552. ELLIOT, Alistair
"Reasons for Happiness in San Francisco." [Margin] (2) Spr 87, p. 5-7.
1553. ELLIOTT, Andrew
"The Fairy Tale." [BostonR] (12:1) F 87, p. 23.
1554. ELLIOTT, David
"The Time Is Right." [PassN] (8:2) Sum 87, p. 23.
1555. ELLIOTT, Harley
"For Farmers." [Spirit] (8:2) 87, p. 335.
"Guitar." [HangL] (50/51) 87, p. 62.
"Hot Pig in Clover." [HangL] (50/51) 87, p. 65.
"The Mourning Cloak Academy." [HangL] (50/51) 87, p. 64.
"Priorities." [HangL] (50/51) 87, p. 63.
1556. ELLIOTT, William I.
"Ball of Yarn" (tr. of Shuntaro Tanikawa, w. Kazuo Kawamura). [Amelia] (4:3,
issue 10) 87, p. 102.
"A Friend Who Leapt to His Death" (tr. of Shuntaro Tanikawa, w. Kazuo
Kawamura). [Amelia] (4:3, issue 10) 87, p. 102.
"Pictures at an Exhibition." [Amelia] (4:3, issue 10) 87, p. 109.
1557. ELLIS, Carol
"Yankaway." [NoDaQ] (55:1) Wint 87, p. 65.
1558. ELLIS, Mayne
"Ice is uncertain" (Award Poem — 1st Place). [Phoenix] (7:1) 87, p. 1.
1559. ELLIS, Melanie
"Returning." [GreenfR] (14:1/2) Wint-Spr, p. 25.
1560. ELLSWORTH, Priscilla
"Reading the Signs." [ManhatPR] (9) Sum 87, p. 6.
1561. ELMAN, Richard
"Cool Lighting over Tucson." [NewYorker] (63:14) 25 My 87, p. 87.
"The Old Poet" (a map poem of Nicaragua, tr. of Mario Cajina-Vega). [Witness]
(1:4) Wint 87, p. 76-77.
1562. ELMENDORF, Robert
"Change of Diet." [Bogg] (57) 87, p. 10.
1563. ELMER, E. F.
"Antoinette." [ChatR] (8:1) Fall 87, p. 22.
1564. ELMUSA, Sharif S.
"Bookishness." [Vis] (23) 87, p. 32.
"Come with Me." [Vis] (23) 87, p. 32.
"In the Refugee Camp." [PoetryE] (23/24) Fall 87, p. 153.
1565. ELON, Florence
"A Familiar Ghost Story." [CarolQ] (39:2) Wint 87, p. 18.
"Odd Birds." [CarolQ] (39:2) Wint 87, p. 19-20.
1566. ELOVIC, Barbara
"At Parties." [GreenfR] (14:3/4) Sum-Fall 87, p. 96.
"Getting Off the Track." [GreenfR] (14:3/4) Sum-Fall 87, p. 95.
1567. ELROD, John
"This Is the Way." [BellArk] (3:5) S-O 87, p. 19.
1568. ELSBERG, John
"After Attending a Bly Workshop." [Bogg] (58) 87, p. 18.
"Her Knowledge of the Future." [Wind] (17:61) 87, p. 11.
"Quiet." [Wind] (17:61) 87, p. 11.
1569. ELSON, Virginia
"Heron at Islamorada." [PraS] (61:1) Spr 87, p. 86.
"Shadows for Traction." [PraS] (61:1) Spr 87, p. 87.
1570. ELSTED, Crispin
"Crystallography." [Margin] (1) Wint 86, p. 22-34.
1571. ELVIR SANDOVAL, Jorge
"Pequeñeces." [Mairena] (9:24) 87, p. 119.
1572. ELYTIS, Odysseus
"Diary of an Invisible April" (Selections, tr. by Jeffrey Carson). [AmerPoR] (16:2)
Mr-Ap 87, p. 34.
"The Gloria" (Excerpt, tr. by Edward Morin and Lefteris Pavlides). [CrossCur] (7:3)
87, p. 152.
"With Both Light and Death" (Selections, tr. by Jeffrey Carson). [AmerPoR] (16:2)
Mr-Ap 87, p. 35.
1573. EMANS, Elaine V.
"The Cats of Dame Edith." [BallSUF] (28:4) Aut 87, p. 42.

"Coleridge, Praise." [CentR] (31:4) Fall 87, p. 384.
"Honeybee." [TexasR] (8:1/2) Spr-Sum 87, p. 62.
"Interview with *Rover's* Ghost." [LitR] (30:4) Sum 87, p. 608.
"Letter to an Environmentalist." [KanQ] (19:1/2) Wint-Spr 87, p. 101.
"Night Heron." [Wind] (17:59) 87, p. 15.
"People Are Getting Into Plants These Days." [Wind] (17:59) 87, p. 14.
"Puffins." [Wind] (17:59) 87, p. 14-15.
"What Bird?" [TexasR] (8:1/2) Spr-Sum 87, p. 63.
1574. EMANUEL, Lynn
"A Blond Bombshell." [OhioR] (38) 87, p. 61.
"Drawing Rosie's Train Trip." [OhioR] (38) 87, p. 66.
"For Me at Sunday Sermons, the Serpent." [OhioR] (38) 87, p. 62.
"The Night Man at the Blue Lite." [OhioR] (38) 87, p. 63.
"One Summer Hurricane Lynn Spawns Tornados As Far West As Ely." [OhioR]
(38) 87, p. 67.
"A Riddle." [OhioR] (38) 87, p. 68.
"Rita and the Fires of Love." [OhioR] (38) 87, p. 64.
"Seizure." [OhioR] (38) 87, p. 65.
1575. EMBLEN, D. L.
"The Child Asks About the Sun" (tr. of Werner Aspenström). [CrossCur] (7:3) 87,
p. 133.
"The Lakes in Scandinavia" (tr. of Werner Aspenström). [PoetL] (81:3) Fall 86, p.
180.
1576. EMERY, Michael J.
"19th Century Blues." [WindO] (48) Spr 87, p. 26.
"Another Burning." [WindO] (49) Fall 87, p. 39.
"Jigsaw Puzzles." [KanQ] (19:1/2) Wint-Spr 87, p. 204.
"Lacunae." [WindO] (49) Fall 87, p. 39.
1577. EMIN, Gevorg
"At the Ashtarak Cemetery" (in Armenian & English, tr. by Martin Robbins).
[StoneC] (14:3/4) Spr-Sum 87, p. 46-47.
"Climb" (tr. by Diana Der Hovanessian). [CrossCur] (7:3) 87, p. 153.
"Often I Cringe from a Shooting Pain" (tr. by Martin Robbins). [InterPR] (13:1) Spr
87, p. 74.
"Smart Lamb" (tr. by Martin Robbins). [InterPR] (13:1) Spr 87, p. 74.
1578. EMMONDS, David
"Alisons Laugh." [AntigR] (69/70) 87, p. 130.
1579. EMMOTT, Kirsten
"Deep Underground." [Waves] (15:4) Spr 87, p. 62-63.
1580. ENDO, Russell (Russell Susumu)
"At the Cemetery." [PaintedB] (30) 87, p. 39.
"I Remember Having Dinner with You." [AmerPoR] (16:4) Jl-Ag 87, p. 14.
"Poem: Be still humpback whale, and other beasts of the sea, while I name you."
[AmerPoR] (16:4) Jl-Ag 87, p. 14.
1581. ENDREZZE-DANIELSON, Anita
"I Give You." [YellowS] (24) Aut 87, p. 24.
"The Jester's Daughter." [YellowS] (24) Aut 87, p. 24.
"Sunflower Woman" (A poem to be read in vertical columns or horizontally).
[YellowS] (25) Wint 87, p. 26-27.
"These Are Roses You've Never Given Me." [YellowS] (24) Aut 87, p. 25.
1582. ENGDAHL, Lee
"Hammers." [CrossCur] (7:1) 87, p. 44-45.
1583. ENGEBRETSEN, Alan C.
"Pacific Harbor." [Wind] (17:59) 87, p. 18.
1584. ENGELBERT, Jo Anne
"Guatemala, Your Name" (to Luis Alfredo Arango, tr. of Carmen Matute). [AmerV]
(8) Fall 87, p. 52-53.
1585. ENGELS, Billie R.
"The Hausfrau" (tr. of Angela Sommer). [NewOR] (14:2) Sum 87, p. 64.
1586. ENGELS, John
"In Cedar Grove Cemetery." [TexasR] (7:3/4) 87, p. 42-43.
"Night Cry in Ljubljana." [NewEngR] (9:3) Spr 87, p. 289-290.
1587. ENGLE, John D., Jr.
"Financial Note." [LightY] '87, c86, p. 22.
"Horrorscope." [LightY] '87, c86, p. 131.
"Mower and Mower." [LightY] '87, c86, p. 243.

"Smoker's Epitaph." [LightY] '87, c86, p. 241.
1588. ENGLE, Paul
"Drop of Water." [Poetry] (151:1/2) O-N 87, p. 50.
1589. ENGLEBERT, Michel
"Jack Ruby Believed." [MissouriR] (10:1) 87, p. 70-72.
"The Story That Haldemann Julius Told." [MissouriR] (10:1) 87, p. 68-69.
1590. ENGMAN, John
"Sway." [NewEngR] (10:2) Wint 87, p. 156.
1591. ENOS, Anya Dozier
"Incapacity." [GreenfR] (14:1/2) Wint-Spr, p. 24.
"Slipping Cynicism." [GreenfR] (14:1/2) Wint-Spr, p. 23.
1592. ENRIQUEZ, R.
"V. I stop dying" (tr. of Socorro Leon Femat, w. Thomas Hoeksema). [InterPR]
(13:1) Spr 87, p. 21.
"Cactus" (tr. of Blanca Luz Pulido, w. Thomas Hoeksema). [InterPR] (13:1) Spr
87, p. 15.
"Mauve and amber" (tr. of Adriana Yañez, w. Thomas Hoeksema). [InterPR] (13:1)
Spr 87, p. 19.
1593. ENSLER, Eve
"Images / Messages." [CentralP] (12) Fall 87, p. 101-104.
1594. ENSLIN, Theodore
"Abuse of what I know to use." [Notus] (2:2) Fall 87, p. 39.
"After a blur of snow." [Notus] (2:2) Fall 87, p. 38.
"Antiphony" (Selections: 1-12). [Conjunc] (11) 87?, p. 169-174.
"I go away to find my girl again." [Notus] (2:2) Fall 87, p. 40.
"A paean unafraid." [Notus] (2:2) Fall 87, p. 41.
1595. EORSI, Istvan
"The Applause" (tr. of Tillye Boesche-Zacharow, w. Laszlo Baransky, Anna Saghy
and Bob Rosenthal). [Rampike] (5:3) 87, p. 70.
"Beer: For Leising" (tr. of Karl Mickel, w. Laszlo Baransky, Anna Saghy and Bob
Rosenthal). [Rampike] (5:3) 87, p. 66.
"A Career" (tr. by Laszlo Baransky, Anna Saghy and Bob Rosenthal). [Rampike]
(5:3) 87, p. 69.
"Change of Location" (tr. of Uwe Kolbe, w. Laszlo Baransky, Anna Saghy and Bob
Rosenthal). [Rampike] (5:3) 87, p. 66.
"German Woman '46" (tr. of Karl Mickel, w. Laszlo Baransky, Anna Saghy and
Bob Rosenthal). [Rampike] (5:3) 87, p. 66.
"Metamorphosis" (tr. of Uwe Kolbe, w. Laszlo Baransky, Anna Saghy and Bob
Rosenthal). [Rampike] (5:3) 87, p. 67.
"The Modern Quarter" (tr. of Karl Mickel, w. Laszlo Baransky, Anna Saghy and
Bob Rosenthal). [Rampike] (5:3) 87, p. 67.
"The Myth of the Cave" (tr. of Volker Braun, w. Laszlo Baransky, Anna Saghy and
Bob Rosenthal). [Rampike] (5:3) 87, p. 69.
"Orderly Hair" (tr. of Karl Mickel, w. Laszlo Baransky, Anna Saghy and Bob
Rosenthal). [Rampike] (5:3) 87, p. 67.
"The Question" (tr. by Allen Ginsberg). [Rampike] (5:3) 87, p. 68.
"Zeno Black" (tr. of Noah Zacharin, w. Laszlo Baransky, Anna Saghy and Bob
Rosenthal). [Rampike] (5:3) 87, p. 70.
1596. EPLING, Kathy
"Ordinary Sunlight." [MSS] (5:3) 87, p. 186-187.
1597. EPSTEIN, Daniel Mark
"Raphael." [KenR] (NS 9:2) Spr 87, p. 92-95.
1598. EPSTEIN, Elaine
"Biography." [Pequod] (23/24) 87, p. 320-321.
1599. EQUI, Elaine
"Another Form of Suicidal Behavior." [Gargoyle] (32/33) 87, p. 83.
"Aperture." [Ploughs] (13:4) 87, p. 42.
"Approaching Orgasm." [Gargoyle] (32/33) 87, p. 81-82.
"Cages Sway." [AnotherCM] (17) 87, p. 36.
"Cannibals in Space." [Ploughs] (13:4) 87, p. 41.
"In a Monotonous Dream." [NewAW] (1) 87, p. 104.
"The Myth of Self." [NewAW] (1) 87, p. 103.
"Voodoo Doll." [NewAW] (1) 87, p. 105.
1600. ERB, Elke
"The Squabbles of Children" (tr. by Rosmarie Waldrop). [ColR] (NS 14:2)
Fall-Wint 87, p. 56.

1601. ERDRICH, Louise
"Captivity." [CutB] (27/28) 87, p. 38-39.
"Night Sky." [CutB] (27/28) 87, p. 36-37.
"The Woods." [CutB] (27/28) 87, p. 40.
1602. ERICH, Roman Olaf
"Pleading Your Song." [Bogg] (57) 87, p. 29.
1603. ERICKSON, Lorene
"Mother Speaks the Back-Home Blues." [PassN] (8:1) Wint 87, p. 20.
1604. ERIN, Jacob
"For Ruth." [Wind] (17:59) 87, p. 22.
1605. ERMINI, Flavio
"Aestas" (Selections: III-IV). [Os] (24) 87, p. 28.
1606. ERNST, Kathy
"Fools" (visual poem). [WindO] (49) Fall 87, p. 31.
1607. ERNST, Myron
"Last Conversations with Dad." [WebR] (12:1) Spr 87, p. 12.
"One More Winter Night." [LaurelR] (21:1/2) Wint-Sum 87, p. 54.
"Remain in the K-Mart." [LaurelR] (21:1/2) Wint-Sum 87, p. 53.
"Skaneateles Lake." [HampSPR] Wint 87, p. 39.
"Vermeer." [WebR] (12:1) Spr 87, p. 13.
"The White Life Has Happened to Doris." [HampSPR] Wint 87, p. 39-40.
1608. ESCANDELL, Noemí
"Pausa." [StoneC] (14:3/4) Spr-Sum 87, p. 66.
"Pause" (tr. by Joan Dargan). [StoneC] (14:3/4) Spr-Sum 87, p. 67.
1609. ESCOBAR GALINDO, David
"Yo Sigo Hablando de la Rosa." [Mairena] (9:24) 87, p. 73-74.
1610. ESHE, Aisha
"A Day in the Life of a Child." [Footwork] 87, p. 49.
"Hersey Park 30 Years Later." [Footwork] 87, p. 49.
"Michael, IX." [Footwork] 87, p. 49.
1611. ESHLEMAN, Clayton
"Brown Thrasher." [Sulfur] (19) Spr 87, p. 1098-109.
"Children of the Monosyllable." [Sulfur] (19) Spr 87, p. 109-112.
"During Bacon." [Margin] (5) Wint 87-88, p. 3-4.
"Gisants" (Cathédrale St-Pierre et St-Paul). [MichQR] (26:2) Spr 87, p. 355.
"Impotence Still-Life." [Temblor] (5) 87, p. 36-38.
"Indiana in the Night Sky." [Notus] (2:1) Spr 87, p. 46-48.
"Not one of Rilke's 'early departed'" (testimonial for Porfirio DiDonna, 1942-1986).
[Sulfur] (19) Spr 87, p. 52.
"Outtakes." [Notus] (2:1) Spr 87, p. 43-45.
"The Sprouting Skull." [Temblor] (5) 87, p. 34-35.
"Toledan Self-Portrait" (tr. of Julio Ortega). [Sulfur] (19) Spr 87, p. 46-49.
1612. ESKESEN, Hal
"Fable." [ManhatPR] (9) Sum 87, p. 13.
1613. ESPADA, Martin
"Toque de Queda: Curfew in Lawrence" (Lawrence, Massachusetts, August 1984).
[RiverS] (22) 87, p. 66.
"Waiting for the Cops." [Spirit] (8:2) 87, p. 141-143.
"Where the Disappeared Would Dance" (Ponce, Puerto Rico, 1985). [RiverS] (22)
87, p. 64-65.
1614. ESPAILLAT, Rhina P.
"Presence." [ManhatPR] (9) Sum 87, p. 62.
"Theme and Variations." [Amelia] (4:3, issue 10) 87, p. 53-54.
"A Winter Walk." [ManhatPR] (9) Sum 87, p. 62.
1615. ESSARY, Loris
"Wired" (Excerpts, w. Karl Kempton). [CentralP] (12) Fall 87, p. 4, 15, 85.
1616. ESSEX, David
"Surveillance, 1966." [Jacaranda] (2:2) Spr 87, p. 86.
1617. ESTAVER, Paul
"Assassin." [StoneC] (15:1/2) Fall-Wint 87-88, p. 40-44.
"Bestler Follows Allison to Darkness." [CarolQ] (40:1) Fall 87, p. 82-83.
1618. ESTELLÉS, Vicent Andrés
"LXXIII. Molt discret jove impertinent." [InterPR] (13:2) Fall 87, p. 12.
"Here I Was Born" (tr. by Nathaniel B. Smith). [WebR] (12:2) Fall 87, p. 20.
"Horatians, LXXIII" (tr. by Nathaniel Smith). [InterPR] (13:2) Fall 87, p. 13.

131

"Notebook for No One" (to Francesc Vallverdú, 6 selections tr. by Nathaniel B.
    Smith). [WebR] (12:2) Fall 87, p. 18-19.
"Seràs un Mort." [InterPR] (13:2) Fall 87, p. 14.
"When You're Dead" (tr. by Nathaniel Smith). [InterPR] (13:2) Fall 87, p. 15.
1619. ESTES, Angie
"The Dance of the Sheets" (for my mother). [NegC] (7:3/4) 87, p. 161.
"The Dance of the Sheets" (for my mother, 1986 Finalist, Eve of Saint Agnes Poetry
    Competition). [NegC] (7:1/2) 87, p. 174.
"You Stand There Fishing" (1986 Finalist, Eve of Saint Agnes Poetry Competition).
    [NegC] (7:1/2) 87, p. 175.
1620. ESTES, Carolyn
"An Open Poem for the Guidance Director." [EngJ] (76:3) Mr 87, p. 112.
1621. ESTESS, Sybil P.
"Massage on Christmas Eve." [Shen] (37:4) 87, p. 11-13.
1622. ESTEVES, Sandra María
"A Julia y a Mí" (For Julia De Burgos). [Cond] (14) 87, p. 118-119.
"A la Mujer Borrinqueña." [Cond] (14) 87, p. 117.
1623. ETTER, Dave
"A Bag of Seeds." [Pig] (14) 87, p. 8.
"Cob Shed." [SpoonRQ] (12:2) Spr 87, p. 2-3.
"Crossing Gates." [Raccoon] (24/25) My 87, p. 232.
"Czechoslovakia." [SpoonRQ] (12:2) Spr 87, p. 4-5.
"Fender Sitting." [SpoonRQ] (12:2) Spr 87, p. 1.
"Kirby Quackenbush: September Moon." [MidwQ] (28:3) Spr 87, p. 321-322.
"The Sweetest Little Woman in New Orleans." [SpoonRQ] (12:2) Spr 87, p. 6.
"Thief." [Pig] (14) 87, p. 8.
1624. ETTY, Robert
"Going to America." [Bogg] (58) 87, p. 11.
1625. EVANS, A. C.
"Dawn Chorus." [Gargoyle] (32/33) 87, p. 395.
1626. EVANS, Bradford
"In Town Until Dawn." [Wind] (17:59) 87, p. 16.
"Not Seen in the Picture" (after the painting: "Portrait of Kathy," by Robin
    Freedenfeld). [MidAR] (7:2) 87, p. 88-89.
1627. EVANS, David Allan
"Billy Pablic." [Amelia] (4:1/2, issue 9) 87, p. 129.
1628. EVANS, George
"The Dowser." [Poetry] (150:3) Je 87, p. 132.
"Isaac." [Poetry] (149:6) Mr 87, p. 336.
"Northern Island." [Poetry] (150:3) Je 87, p. 131.
"Study of My Father." [Poetry] (149:6) Mr 87, p. 337.
1629. EVANS, Lynne McIlvride
"In the Morning That Is Still." [Waves] (15:3) Wint 87, p. 49.
"Wormpickers" (illegal immigrants work the night shift). [Waves] (15:3) Wint 87, p.
    49.
1630. EVARTS, Prescott, Jr.
"Grandmother's Watch." [TexasR] (8:1/2) Spr-Sum 87, p. 80.
1631. EVASON, Greg
"A nest for business." [CrossC] (9:3/4) 87, p. 13.
"Symptoms of Collage" (Selection: 319). [CrossC] (9:3/4) 87, p. 13.
1632. EVATT, Julia
"Rosanna." [Confr] (35/36) Spr-Fall 87, p. 106.
1633. EVE, Barbara
"A Letter of Introduction." [Agni] (24/25) 87, p. 89.
1634. EVEREST, Beth
"Hakone." [Quarry] (36:3) Sum 87, p. 28.
"Thru an Open Window." [Quarry] (36:3) Sum 87, p. 29.
1635. EVETTS, Josephine
"Cycle." [Dandel] (14:2) Fall-Wint 87, p. 5-14.
"Jacob Wrestling." [Dandel] (14:1) Spr-Sum 87, p. 22.
1636. EVIN, Ahmet Ö.
"Abstract" (tr. of Fazil Hüsnü Daglarca). [Trans] (19) Fall 87, p. 57.
"The Sultan of the Animals Is the Night" (tr. of Fazil Hüsnü Daglarca). [Trans] (19)
    Fall 87, p. 57.
1637. EWART, Gavin
"The Achievements of Herrings." [LightY] '87, c86, p. 117.

"Cocks and Crows." [LightY] '87, c86, p. 48.
"Home, Sweet Home!" [LightY] '87, c86, p. 172.
"Knopf and Dutton." [LightY] '87, c86, p. 218.
"The Living Masters" (George Barker, David Gascoyne, Gavin Ewart, billed as such at a poetry festival). [LightY] '87, c86, p. 126.
"The Madness of a Headmistress." [LightY] '87, c86, p. 96.
"Mrs. Whitehouse's View of Sexual Intercourse." [LightY] '87, c86, p. 257.
"Scott Joplin" (Clerihew). [LightY] '87, c86, p. 67.
"Shakespeare Sonnets Converted into Couplets." [LightY] '87, c86, p. 204-205.
1638. EWING, Jim
"Birdnesting." [TexasR] (8:1/2) Spr-Sum 87, p. 76.
1639. EXNER, Richard
"The Sharing" (tr. by Jascha Kessler). [CrossCur] (7:1) 87, p. 119.
"Untereinander." [CrossCur] (7:1) 87, p. 118.
1640. FAAS, David
"Captain Neptune." [JamesWR] (4:3) Spr 87, p. 4.
1641. FABRIS, Dino
"Ex Vita" (tr. of Pier Paolo Pasolini). [ParisR] (29:103) Sum 87, p. 129-131.
"Italy" (tr. of Pier Paolo Pasolini). [ParisR] (29:103) Sum 87, p. 122-128.
1642. FABRIZI, Nicolo
"Dogs of Hell." [Caliban] (3) 87, p. 133-134.
"The House" (tr. of Massimo Mori). [Caliban] (3) 87, p. 102-104.
"Mrs. Richmond Gets Sick of Dogs and Leaves for Greenland" (tr. of Nani Balestrini). [Caliban] (3) 87, p. 96-98.
"Mrs. Richmond's Film: The Last Beach" (tr. of Nani Balestrini). [Caliban] (3) 87, p. 99-101.
1643. FAGAN, Cary
"Joanne on Poros." [AntigR] (69/70) 87, p. 88.
"Magog." [AntigR] (69/70) 87, p. 88.
1644. FAGAN, Robert
"Keys." [BellArk] (3:2) Mr-Ap 87, p. 18.
1645. FAIERS, Chris
"Chalk Players." [CrossC] (9:2) 87, p. 3.
1646. FAINLIGHT, Ruth
"The Planetarium." [Thrpny] (30) Sum 87, p. 10.
1647. FAIRBANKS, Lauren
"Screw the Lids." [LitR] (30:4) Sum 87, p. 576.
1648. FAIRCHILD, B. H.
"The Bluebird Cafe." [TexasR] (8:1/2) Spr-Sum 87, p. 73.
"The City of God." [BlackWR] (14:1) Fall 87, p. 45-46.
"The Houses." [KanQ] (19:1/2) Wint-Spr 87, p. 87.
"In Another Life I Encounter My Father." [ColR] (NS 14:1) Spr-Sum 87, p. 17-18.
"My Mother's Dreams." [SouthernR] (23:3) Jl 87, p. 623-624.
"Shorty's Pool Hall." [TexasR] (8:1/2) Spr-Sum 87, p. 72.
"Speaking the Names." [SouthernR] (23:3) Jl 87, p. 622-623.
"The Structures of Everyday Life." [Hudson] (40:2) Sum 87, p. 295.
"West Texas" (1985 Alice Jackson Poetry Prize: Honorable Mention). [Electrum] (39) Fall-Wint 87, p. 13.
1649. FALCO, Edward
"Delivery." [Confr] (35/36) Spr-Fall 87, p. 200.
"Picture from a War Zone." [Confr] (35/36) Spr-Fall 87, p. 200.
1650. FALKOFF, Fontaine
"To Laura" (Christmas, 1985). [PoeticJ] (17) 87, p. 16.
1651. FALLON, Peter
"Caesarean." [MassR] (28:3) Aut 87, p. 416-417.
"Carnaross 2." [MassR] (28:3) Aut 87, p. 413.
"Dipping Day." [MassR] (28:3) Aut 87, p. 415.
"Madelaine." [MassR] (28:3) Aut 87, p. 417-419.
"The Mass-hour." [Pembroke] (19) 87, p. 82-83.
"The Meadow." [MassR] (28:3) Aut 87, p. 414-415.
"My Care." [MassR] (28:3) Aut 87, p. 419-420.
"Neighbours." [MassR] (28:3) Aut 87, p. 416.
"An Open Fire" (For Robert McGlynn). [MassR] (28:3) Aut 87, p. 416.
"The Rag-Tree, Boherard." [MassR] (28:3) Aut 87, p. 412.
1652. FALLON, Teresa
"Routine." [BlueBldgs] (10) 87?, p. 20.

1653. FALQUEZ-CERTAIN, Miguel
"Hermes." [LindLM] (6:4) O-D 87, p. 5.
"Janis" (Para Margarita Abello Villalba). [LindLM] (6:2/3) Ap-S 87, p. 12.
1654. FALSBERG, Elizabeth
"The Turtle's Voice." [BellArk] (3:3) My-Je 87, p. 8.
1655. FANDEL, John
"Memorial Days." [Comm] (114:10) 22 My 87, p. 321.
1656. FANTHORPE, U. A.
"Carthage: An Historical Guide." [CumbPR] (7:1) Fall 87, p. 46-47.
"Washing-up" (for Hilda Cotterill). [CumbPR] (7:1) Fall 87, p. 48-49.
1657. FARALLO, Livio
"9:00 A.M. Bullshit." [SlipS] (7) 87, p. 34-35.
"Presidency." [SlipS] (7) 87, p. 35.
1658. FARGAS, Laura
"Hyperbolae." [Gargoyle] (32/33) 87, p. 91-92.
1659. FARKAS, Endre
"Mumbling" (tr. of Karoly Bari). [Rampike] (5:3) 87, p. 68.
1660. FARLEY, Blanche (Blanche F.)
"A Bride of the 80's, Down the Aisle." [LightY] '87, c86, p. 129.
"In the Artist's House." [Confr] (35/36) Spr-Fall 87, p. 207.
1661. FARLEY, Joseph
"Birds." [PaintedB] (30) 87, p. 66.
"Flag Day." [PaintedB] (30) 87, p. 67.
1662. FARMER, Harold
"For a Dead Cobra." [MalR] (80) S 87, p. 82.
1663. FARNSWORTH, Robert
"At a Sunday Concert." [NewEngR] (9:4) Sum 87, p. 385-386.
"History" (for Arden). [CarolQ] (40:1) Fall 87, p. 7-9.
"Landscape for an Antique Clock." [MissouriR] (10:2) 87, p. 142-143.
"On Leaving a Demonstration to Have My Hair Cut" (after Thoreau). [NewEngR]
    (9:4) Sum 87, p. 386-387.
"Waterworks." [CarolQ] (40:1) Fall 87, p. 10-11.
"Your Left Hand" (for Rory). [CarolQ] (40:1) Fall 87, p. 12-13.
1664. FARRELL, M. A. (Mary Ann)
"Children of the Trail." [Wind] (17:61) 87, p. 12.
"Notre Dame de Lourdes Restaurant Haitien." [Vis] (24) 87, p. 8.
"Sisters Share." [Wind] (17:61) 87, p. 13.
1665. FARUQI, Shamsur Rahman
"Night Falls with a Broken Wing" (tr. by Frances W. Pritchett). [Bomb] (18) Wint
    87, p. 68.
"Rubà i I" (tr. by Gopi Chand Narang and David Paul Douglas). [Bomb] (18) Wint
    87, p. 68.
"Rubà i IV" (tr. by Gopi Chand Narang and David Paul Douglas). [Bomb] (18) Wint
    87, p. 68.
"Underdone" (tr. by Gopi Chand Narang and David Paul Douglas). [Bomb] (18)
    Wint 87, p. 68.
"Untitled: Into the shy, scented ear of the night" (tr. by the author). [Bomb] (18)
    Wint 87, p. 68.
1666. FASCE, Maria de los Angeles
"El Beso." [Mairena] (9:24) 87, p. 67.
1667. FASEL, Ida
"Chapel." [ChrC] (104:21) 15-22 Jl 87, p. 623.
"Cologne." [ChrC] (104:13) 22 Ap 87, p. 379.
"Journeys." [PoeticJ] (17) 87, p. 15.
1668. FAUCHER, Réal
"All-Night Music." [Bogg] (58) 87, p. 38-39.
"Incident at 4 A.M." [WormR] (27:4, issue 108) 87, p. 83.
"The Man Who Jumped Beyond His Time." [WormR] (27:4, issue 108) 87, p. 83.
"The Old Man." [SlipS] (7) 87, p. 87.
"Poetic Touch." [SlipS] (7) 87, p. 88.
"She Wants You Ready." [WormR] (27:4, issue 108) 87, p. 83.
"Survival of One of Us." [Footwork] 87, p. 54.
"Uneasy Divorce." [WormR] (27:4, issue 108) 87, p. 84.
"Why Did You Take So Much." [WormR] (27:4, issue 108) 87, p. 84.
1669. FAY, Julie
"How to Cook Mussels on the Beach." [HighP] (2:2) Fall 87, p. 131-132.

1670. FEDERMAN, Raymond
"Reflections on Ways to Improve Death." [Caliban] (2) 87, p. 103-106.
1671. FEDO, David
"Dreaming of Trotsky." [WritersF] (13) Fall 87, p. 172.
1672. FEELA, David J.
"Growing Pains." [PassN] (8:2) Sum 87, p. 22.
1673. FEENY, Thomas
"Family Reunion." [Puerto] (22:2) Spr 87, p. 70-71.
"February 2." [CapeR] (22:1) Spr 87, p. 9.
"It's Not the Movies." [Event] (16:3) Fall 87, p. 66-67.
"New Moon in Your Waterglass." [Wind] (17:61) 87, p. 14-15.
"When You Grow Up." [Wind] (17:61) 87, p. 14.
1674. FEHLER, Gene
"Eating Out." [LightY] '87, c86, p. 36.
"If E. E. Cummings Followed Baseball, 'Nobody Loses All the Time' Might Have
Been Not About Uncle Sol But . . ." [Pig] (14) 87, p. 43.
"If Edgar Allan Poe Were a Chicago Cubs Fan, 'The Raven' Might Be 'The Cub
Star'." [Pig] (14) 87, p. 40.
"If Hamlet Had Been Watching His Third Base Coach, Shakespeare Might Have
Had Him Wondering . . ." [Pig] (14) 87, p. 41.
"If Oliver Wendell Holmes Had Been a Brooklyn Dodger Fan in the 1950's, 'Old
Ironsides' Might Be 'Ebbets Field'." [Pig] (14) 87, p. 41.
"If Richard Lovelace Knew Baseball, 'To Lucasta, Going to the Wars' Might Be 'To
My Fans . . .'." [Pig] (14) 87, p. 43.
"I'm a Texan Now." [LightY] '87, c86, p. 182.
1675. FEHRMAN, Jan Day
"Songs from the Ancient and Modern." The Best of [BambooR] [(31-32)] 86, p.
27-28.
1676. FEIGERT, Don
"Man Dies in Bizarre Accident." [Vis] (24) 87, p. 31-32.
"Visiting the Pig Farm, I Learned." [Pig] (14) 87, p. 51.
1677. FEIN, Cheri
"Blacklash." [Bomb] (19) Spr 87, p. 75.
"Blue Moon." [Bomb] (19) Spr 87, p. 74.
"For George on My Birthday." [Bomb] (19) Spr 87, p. 75.
"Lucretia." [Bomb] (19) Spr 87, p. 74.
1678. FEIN, Richard J.
"The Old Jewish Cemetery in Warsaw." [LitR] (30:4) Sum 87, p. 574-575.
1679. FEINSTEIN, Robert N.
"The Beer and the Bear." [LightY] '87, c86, p. 117.
"The Court Rests" (News item: Mistrial declared in German court when a magistrate
is found asleep). [LightY] '87, c86, p. 230-231.
"The Fair Fowl" (News item: Mayo Clinic endorses chicken soup as treatment for the
common cold). [LightY] '87, c86, p. 229.
"The First Backache." [Amelia] (4:1/2, issue 9) 87, p. 93.
"Grow! Grow! Grow!" [HolCrit] (24:2) Ap 87, p. 20.
"Older Is Safer." [LightY] '87, c86, p. 237.
"On Pain of Freedom." [Amelia] (4:1/2, issue 9) 87, p. 93-94.
"A Ramble Through the Dictionary." [Bogg] (57) 87, p. 15.
"Scallops and Trollops and Such." [Bogg] (58) 87, p. 10.
"The TV Chef." [LightY] '87, c86, p. 39.
1680. FEIRING, Alice S.
"Now on Stage." [AnotherCM] (17) 87, p. 37-38.
1681. FELDMAN, Irving
"Good Morning America." [GrandS] (6:3) Spr 87, p. 28-30.
"[Sic] Transcript Gloria, or The Body Politician." [LightY] '87, c86, p. 258.
1682. FELDMAN, Ruth
"The Elephant" (tr. of Primo Levi). [InterPR] (13:2) Fall 87, p. 33.
"Equality, Father" (tr. of Edith Bruck). [Spirit] (8:2) 87, p. 164-165.
"Liber Fulguralis" (To the Mav Luceziniai. Selections: 9 poems, tr. of Margherita
Guidacci). [Stand] (28:1) Wint 86-87, p. 4-8.
"To Doctor Z" (tr. of Margherita Guidacci). [CrossCur] (7:3) 87, p. 136.
1683. FELICIANO MENDOZA, Ester
"Poemas de la Vispera" (10 poems). [Mairena] (9:24) 87, p. 92-96.

1684. FELLMAN, Stanley A.
"Christmas: We Started with Reason, Ended in Hate." [Nimrod] (30:2) Spr-Sum 87,
p. 77.
"From the Song Book of the Russian Army, 1937 edition." [InterPR] (13:1) Spr 87,
p. 109.
"How the Gardener Sees It." [Nimrod] (30:2) Spr-Sum 87, p. 77.
"My Best Guess." [Nimrod] (30:2) Spr-Sum 87, p. 78.
1685. FEMAT, Socorro Leon
"V. Dejo de morir." [InterPR] (13:1) Spr 87, p. 20.
"V. I stop dying" (tr. by Thomas Hoeksema and R. Enriquez). [InterPR] (13:1) Spr
87, p. 21.
1686. FEOLE, Glenn
"Poem for My Daughter." [Footwork] 87, p. 62.
1687. FERBER, Al
"Flip Top Desks." [PaintedB] (30) 87, p. 16.
"Giving Up the Ghost." [Gambit] (20) 86, p. 76.
"Partners in Crime." [PaintedB] (30) 87, p. 17.
"Strike: June 1984." [Gambit] (20) 86, p. 75.
1688. FERGUSON, John B.
"Dragon Breath." [EngJ] (76:5) S 87, p. 111.
1689. FERGUSON, Penny L.
"Suffering." [AntigR] (71/72) Aut 87-Wint 88, p. 194.
1690. FERICANO, Paul
"Poem for William Rummel Serving a Life Sentence in a Texas Prison for Not
Fixing an Air Conditioner." [Spirit] (8:2) 87, p. 190.
1691. FERKIN, Lenore J.
"Found." [HolCrit] (24:1) F 87, p. 11.
"Gloopy and Blit." [HolCrit] (24:3) Je 87, p. 20.
1692. FERNANDEZ, Amando J.
"El Amigo." [LindLM] (6:4) O-D 87, p. 5.
"Ya el Otro." [LindLM] (6:4) O-D 87, p. 5.
1693. FERNANDEZ, Raymond Ringo
"Cell-Rapping" (Selections: 10 poems). [Witness] (1:3) Fall 87, p. 80-93.
"Plastic and Steel." [Witness] (1:3) Fall 87, p. 146-147.
1694. FERNANDEZ GILL, Alicia
"Los Heraldos Blancos." [Mairena] (9:24) 87, p. 50.
1695. FERRA, Lorraine
"Desire." [FloridaR] (15:2) Fall-Wint 87, p. 56.
1696. FERRARELLI, Rina
"Deeds" (tr. of Bartolo Cattafi). [Trans] (18) Spr 87, p. 323.
"The Flood" (tr. of Bartolo Cattafi). [Trans] (18) Spr 87, p. 321.
"A Gathering Quietness." [TarRP] (26:2) Spr 87, p. 41-42.
"In There" (tr. of Bartolo Cattafi). [Trans] (18) Spr 87, p. 322.
"The Line the Thread" (tr. of Bartolo Cattafi). [Trans] (18) Spr 87, p. 321.
"The Sand Dunes." [KanQ] (19:3) Sum 87, p. 290-291.
"The Shortcut." [KanQ] (19:3) Sum 87, p. 289.
"Stepfather." [Wind] (17:59) 87, p. 34.
"Thickets of Shade" (tr. of Bartolo Cattafi). [Trans] (18) Spr 87, p. 320.
"The Tin Box" (tr. of Bartolo Cattafi). [Trans] (18) Spr 87, p. 322.
"To My Shadow" (tr. of Bartolo Cattafi). [Trans] (18) Spr 87, p. 321.
"To Repeat the Image" (tr. of Bartolo Cattafi). [Trans] (18) Spr 87, p. 323.
"Venus" (tr. of Bartolo Cattafi). [Trans] (18) Spr 87, p. 322.
1697. FERRARI, Americo
"El Lugar Común (1)." [Inti] (24/25) Otoño 86-Primavera 87, p. 255.
"El Lugar Común (2)." [Inti] (24/25) Otoño 86-Primavera 87, p. 256.
"El Lugar Común (3)." [Inti] (24/25) Otoño 86-Primavera 87, p. 256.
1698. FERREE, Joel
"Business Luncheon." [LightY] '87, c86, p. 228-229.
FERRER, Juan José Prat
See PRAT FERRER, Juan José
1699. FERRY, David
"Abyss" (tr. of Charles Baudelaire). [Raritan] (7:1) Sum 87, p. 31.
"After Spotsylvania Court House." [TexasR] (7:3/4) 87, p. 46.
"Autumn Day" (tr. of Rainer Maria Rilke). [Raritan] (7:1) Sum 87, p. 33.
"The Guest Ellen at the Supper for Street People." [Raritan] (7:1) Sum 87, p. 28-29.

"Out at Lanesville" (In memoriam Mary Ann, 1932-1980). [TexasR] (7:3/4) 87, p. 44-45.

1700. FETHERLING, Doug
"Cool Embraces Warm, the Outcome Is a Fog That Disappears to Reveal Perspective." [AlphaBS] (2) D 87, p. 13.
"Starting with North." [AlphaBS] (2) D 87, p. 12.

1701. FEYERABEND, Barbara
"Hellbrunn Sonnets." [SenR] (17:1) 87, p. 72-78.
"Stradivarius Reclining." [SenR] (17:1) 87, p. 71.

1702. FIBIGER, Walt
"Sanded Roads." [EngJ] (76:5) S 87, p. 111.

1703. FICKERT, Kurt
"Crossing the Equator." [Wind] (17:60) 87, p. 14.
"Saint Helens." [Farm] (4:2) Spr-Sum 87, p. 57.

1704. FIEBER, Glenn
"A Private Enterprise." [Event] (16:2) Sum 87, p. 100-101.

1705. FIELD, Crystal (Crystal MacLean)
"The Dilettante" (After reading *Buried Alive*, Janis Joplin's biography). [NewL] (54:1) Fall 87, p. 90-91.
"Duchamp's Nude." [NewL] (54:1) Fall 87, p. 93.
"Eleanor of the Irises in My Yard." [NewL] (54:1) Fall 87, p. 89.
"I Will Not Look Away." [NewL] (54:1) Fall 87, p. 91.
"Moving First." [HeliconN] (17/18) Spr 87, p. 164.
"Moving First." [NewL] (54:1) Fall 87, p. 94.
"Pose for a Surreal Painter." [NewL] (54:1) Fall 87, p. 92.
"Prufrock Was Wrong." [NewL] (54:1) Fall 87, p. 93.
"Sleeping Dogs." [HeliconN] (17/18) Spr 87, p. 165.
"Sleeping Dogs." [NewL] (54:1) Fall 87, p. 95.

1706. FIELDER, William A.
"Istanbul" (tr. of Cahit Külebi, w. Dionis Coffin Riggs and Özcan Yalim). [StoneC] (15:1/2) Fall-Wint 87-88, p. 36-37.

1707. FIELDS, Kenneth
"And Company Kept." [Sequoia] (31:1) Centennial issue 87, p. 60.
"The Company." [Sequoia] (31:1) Centennial issue 87, p. 60.
"No Moon At All." [Sequoia] (31:1) Centennial issue 87, p. 61.
"Powerhouse." [Sequoia] (31:1) Centennial issue 87, p. 61.

1708. FIELDS, Leslie Leyland
"A Profitable Fishing Season." [PassN] (8:2) Sum 87, p. 20.
"The Whale." [PassN] (8:2) Sum 87, p. 20.

1709. FIFER, Elizabeth
"Dadadd." [Footwork] 87, p. 57.
"Dad's Poverty." [Footwork] 87, p. 56.

1710. FIGMAN, Elliot
"Station Music." [Poetry] (150:1) Ap 87, p. 11.

1711. FILES, Meg
"Fuji-san becomes Mount Sopris." [Amelia] (4:3, issue 10) 87, p. 74.
"Separation." [Amelia] (4:1/2, issue 9) 87, p. 111.

1712. FILIPOWSKA, Patricia
"The Day Lilies of Golf Club Lane." [Farm] (4:2) Spr-Sum 87, p. 68.

1713. FILKINS, Peter
"Rome at Night" (tr. of Ingeborg Bachmann). [Trans] (18) Spr 87, p. 281.
"A Type of Loss" (tr. of Ingeborg Bachmann). [PartR] (54:3) Sum 87, p. 425-426.
"Wood and Shavings" (tr. of Ingeborg Bachmann). [Trans] (18) Spr 87, p. 282.

1714. FINALE, Frank
"To My Mother." [NegC] (7:3/4) 87, p. 76.

1715. FINCH, Roger
"At Gawdawpalin Temple." [CimR] (78) Ja 87, p. 36.
"Bird Vendors at Wat Phra Si Maha That." [WebR] (12:1) Spr 87, p. 25.
"Calle Santa Ursula." [Poem] (58) N 87, p. 62.
"Close Encounters of a Secret Kind." [PoetL] (81:4) Wint 86-87, p. 214.
"Couple with a Wine Glass." [Poem] (58) N 87, p. 63.
"Essentials of Set Design." [Waves] (15:4) Spr 87, p. 56.
"The Fight Between the Jaguar and the Anteater." [WebR] (12:1) Spr 87, p. 26.
"From Gaya to Bodhgaya by Autorickshaw." [WindO] (49) Fall 87, p. 35.
"A Gift of Eloquence." [LitR] (30:4) Sum 87, p. 616-617.
"Hildegard of Bingen and Her man." [PoetL] (81:4) Wint 86-87, p. 213.

"I Never Saw a Saw Like This Saw Saws." [PoetL] (81:4) Wint 86-87, p. 215.
"Papermaking." [AntigR] (69/70) 87, p. 68.
"Pavarotti Recalls Caruso, But Who Will Recall Pavarotti?" [WebR] (12:1) Spr 87,
    p. 24.
"Studies on Arden's *Tamil Grammar*" (Chapter VI: The Order of Words and
    Clauses). [ClockR] (4:1) 87, p. 35.
"Sunset at the Temple of Dawn." [KanQ] (19:3) Sum 87, p. 41.
1716. FINCKE, Gary (*See also* FINKE, Gary)
"The Agnes Child." [PoetL] (82:1) Spr 87, p. 29-30.
"Ants." [PraS] (61:3) Fall 87, p. 92.
"The Appalachian Trail." [MemphisSR] (7:2) Spr 87, p. 23.
"The Asthma Revenge." [CapeR] (22:1) Spr 87, p. 40.
"Beans Are." [WestB] (20) 87, p. 26.
"The Blue People." [WebR] (12:1) Spr 87, p. 46.
"Bourbon, Red Meat, Salt, Grease." [Poetry] (149:4) Ja 87, p. 219.
"Calculus" (1986 Honorable Mention, Eve of Saint Agnes Poetry Competition).
    [NegC] (7:1/2) 87, p. 139-140.
"Coal." [PaintedB] (30) 87, p. 70.
"Enlisting." [Poetry] (149:4) Ja 87, p. 220.
"The Fly." [PennR] (3:1) Spr-Sum 87, p. 25.
"Groaning Boards." [GeoR] (41:2) Sum 87, p. 346-347.
"Levitation." [MemphisSR] (7:2) Spr 87, p. 22-23.
"Listening." [WebR] (12:1) Spr 87, p. 45.
"The Man Who Shot Kennedy Is Aging in Our Town." [CharR] (13:2) Fall 87, p.
    22.
"The Nazi on the Phone." [WestB] (20) 87, p. 26-27.
"Poor Farm." [PoetL] (82:4) Wint 87-88, p. 197.
"Pornography." [PoetL] (82:1) Spr 87, p. 28.
"Skid Marks." [MidAR] (7:2) 87, p. 90-91.
"That's What I Was Thinking." [PraS] (61:3) Fall 87, p. 91.
"Three Hours in the Two-Block Town." [WebR] (12:1) Spr 87, p. 44.
"Where the Bakery Was." [PaintedB] (30) 87, p. 71-72.
1717. FINEBERG, Michael
"Posture" (tr. of Henri Michaux). [LitR] (30:3) Spr 87, p. 421-424.
1718. FINK, Eloise Bradley
"Signature." [WindO] (49) Fall 87, p. 16.
1719. FINK, Robert A.
"Foot Reflexologist, Farmers and Christmas." [TriQ] (68) Wint 87, p. 86-87.
"Mesquite." [Poetry] (150:1) Ap 87, p. 33-34.
"The Meteorologist Explains Tornadoes." [WritersF] (13) Fall 87, p. 149-150.
"Ripley's Wouldn't Touch This." [PoetryNW] (28:1) Spr 87, p. 25.
"They Say the Good Die Young." [PoetryNW] (28:1) Spr 87, p. 24.
"Turning Thirty-Five, I Begin to Look Behind Me." [TexasR] (8:1/2) Spr-Sum 87,
    p. 60-61.
"West Texas Interlude." [TriQ] (68) Wint 87, p. 88-89.
1720. FINKE, Gary (*See also* FINCKE, Gary)
"The Blue People." [BlueBldgs] (10) 87?, p. 50.
1721. FINKEL, Donald
"Addressee Deceased — Return to Sender" (for F.). [CreamCR] (11:2/3) 87?, p. 77.
"Affinities." [SenR] (17:1) 87, p. 14.
"Answer" (tr. of Bei Dao, w. Xueliang Chen). [SenR] (17:2) 87, p. 25.
"Beyond Despair" (Selections: 6 poems). [MissouriR] (10:3) 87, p. 45-50.
"Border" (tr. of Bei Dao, w. Xueliang Chen). [SenR] (17:2) 87, p. 26.
"The Burning of Rome." [GrandS] (6:4) Sum 87, p. 259.
"Country Night" (tr. of Bei Dao, w. Xueliang Chen). [SenR] (17:2) 87, p. 27.
"Departures." [GrandS] (6:4) Sum 87, p. 258.
"Let's Go" (tr. of Bei Dao, w. Xueliang Chen). [Antaeus] (58) Spr 87, p. 160.
"The Oranges Are Ripe" (tr. of Bei Dao, w. Xueliang Chen). [Antaeus] (58) Spr 87,
    p. 158.
"The Phrygian Version." [Poetry] (151:1/2) O-N 87, p. 51-52.
"The Rebuilding of Rome." [GrandS] (6:4) Sum 87, p. 257.
"Separation." [YaleR] (77:1) Aut 87, p. 150.
"Snow Line" (tr. of Bei Dao, w. Xueliang Chen). [SenR] (17:2) 87, p. 24.
"Sufficient Unto the Day." [SenR] (17:1) 87, p. 13.
"Testament" (tr. of Bei Dao, w. Xueliang Chen). [Antaeus] (58) Spr 87, p. 157.
"This Is Where I Draw the Line." [NewRep] (196:15) 13 Ap 87, p. 40.

"A Ticket" (tr. of Bei Dao, w. Xueliang Chen). [Antaeus] (58) Spr 87, p. 159-160.
1722. FINKELSTEIN, Caroline
"The Brave Little Tailleurs of 1935." [AmerPoR] (16:4) Jl-Ag 87, p. 16.
"The Gods." [MassR] (28:4) Wint 87, p. 654.
"The Modes of Our Most Perfect Lady." [AmerPoR] (16:4) Jl-Ag 87, p. 16.
"You Must Not Mix Milk with Meat." [Poetry] (150:2) My 87, p. 103.
1723. FINKELSTEIN, Norman
"Braids." [Salm] (72) Fall 86, p. 176-177.
"A Poem for the Great Heresy." [Salm] (74/75) Spr-Sum 87, p. 51-52.
"A Poem for the Little Shoemakers." [Salm] (72) Fall 86, p. 175-176.
1724. FINLEY, Betty
"My Lover the Plumber." [TexasR] (8:1/2) Spr-Sum 87, p. 96-97.
"What's the Winter For?" [TexasR] (8:1/2) Spr-Sum 87, p. 95.
1725. FINLEY, Jeanne
"The Dam Tender, 1854." [Blueline] (7:2/3 [i.e. 8:2/3?]) 87, p. 39.
"The Dream of Horses." [Blueline] (7:2/3 [i.e. 8:2/3?]) 87, p. 40.
"Nanda Devi." [Blueline] (7:2/3 [i.e. 8:2/3?]) 87, p. 37.
"The Passenger." [Blueline] (7:2/3 [i.e. 8:2/3?]) 87, p. 38.
1726. FINLEY, Michael
"Biker Bob Maniskalko's Living Room Decor." [LakeSR] (21) 87, p. 28.
1727. FINNELL, Dennis
"Bear Skull in the Attic." [NewL] (54:1) Fall 87, p. 18.
"Everybody's Business." [Agni] (24/25) 87, p. 146-147.
"One Hundred and Fifty Springs in Hannibal." [CharR] (13:1) Spr 87, p. 77-78.
"The Peaceable Kingdom." [NewL] (54:1) Fall 87, p. 19.
"The Sentence of Memory." [CharR] (13:1) Spr 87, p. 77.
1728. FINNIGAN, Joan
"Songs from Both Sides of the River" (Selections). [Quarry] (36:3) Sum 87, p.
59-61.
1729. FIRER, Susan
"Midnight Purple Cabbages." [CreamCR] (11:2/3) 87?, p. 66.
1730. FISCHER, Allen C.
"Audience." [PraS] (61:2) Sum 87, p. 98.
"Butterfly Man." [PraS] (61:2) Sum 87, p. 96.
"Hunting Season." [PraS] (61:2) Sum 87, p. 97.
"The Joke." [PraS] (61:2) Sum 87, p. 100-101.
"Metal Fatigue." [PraS] (61:2) Sum 87, p. 99.
"One Night Stanzas." [NegC] (7:3/4) 87, p. 168.
"One Night Stanzas" (1986 Finalist, Eve of Saint Agnes Poetry Competition).
[NegC] (7:1/2) 87, p. 216.
"Opening the City." [PraS] (61:2) Sum 87, p. 99.
1731. FISET, Joan
"What If the River Contained the Sea?" [CrabCR] (4:2) Spr 87, p. 21.
1732. FISH, Karen
"Daylight in the Distance." [AmerPoR] (16:1) Ja-F 87, p. 41.
"Dusk" (in memory of my father, Charlie). [MichQR] (26:1) Wint 87, p. 175-176.
"Irony." [AmerPoR] (16:1) Ja-F 87, p. 41.
"The Middle Ages." [NoAmR] (272:3) S 87, p. 108.
"Orbiting the Sun." [DenQ] (22:1) Sum 87, p. 6.
"Safe House: Brandon, Vermont (Thinking of the Underground Railroad)." [DenQ]
(22:1) Sum 87, p. 7-8.
"The Tub." [PartR] (54:1) Wint 87, p. 132-133.
"The Viaduct." [DenQ] (22:1) Sum 87, p. 9.
1733. FISHER, Sally
"Art History: The Halo." [Field] (37) Fall 87, p. 82-83.
"Courtly Love." [TarPR] (27:1) Fall 87, p. 35.
1734. FISHMAN, Charles
"Again Horizon." [BlueBldgs] (10) 87?, p. 52.
"The Beast." [HighP] (2:2) Fall 87, p. 191-192.
"Eagle Feathers." [Vis] (24) 87, p. 19.
"Hoping for a Boy" (Award Poem). [Phoenix] (7:1) 87, p. 4.
"The Race." [ConnPR] (6:1) 87, p. 36.
1735. FISKE, Ingrid
"Al Wat Kind Is" (All That Is 'Child'"). [TriQ] (69) Spr-Sum 87, p. 92-93.
"Dolphin Eater." [TriQ] (69) Spr-Sum 87, p. 88-89.
"Our Sharpeville." [TriQ] (69) Spr-Sum 87, p. 94-95.

"Small Passing." [TriQ] (69) Spr-Sum 87, p. 90-91.
1736. FISTER, Mary P.
    "Sparrow Hawk over the Phone" (for Mimi White). [CrabCR] (4:3) Sum 87, p. 17.
1737. FITCH, Brian
    "Dancing in the Dark." [SewanR] (95:1) Wint 87, p. 3.
    "Paris Postcard." [SewanR] (95:1) Wint 87, p. 2-3.
1738. FITZGERALD, F. Scott
    "The Boy Who Killed His Mother." [LightY] '87, c86, p. 254-256.
1739. FITZGERALD, Jim
    "L'Obscurite des Eaux" (tr. of Alejandra Pizarnik, w. Frank Graziano). [NewOR]
        (14:3) Fall 87, p. 44.
    "Names and Figures" (tr. of Alejandra Pizarnik, w. Frank Graziano). [NewOR]
        (14:3) Fall 87, p. 17.
1740. FITZGERALD, Judith
    "A Body of Love" (For Daniel Jalowica). [CrossC] (9:1) 87, p. 27.
1741. FITZHUGH, Gwen
    "Poem for My Father." [EngJ] (76:8) D 87, p. 78.
1742. FITZPATRICK, Peter
    "Commission on Pornography." [JamesWR] (4:3) Spr 87, p. 12.
1743. FITZSIMMONS, Thomas
    "Dream." [CrossCur] (7:2) 87, p. 125.
    "Neko-chan, the Cat." [Poem] (57) Mr 87, p. 47.
1744. FIXEL, Lawrence
    "Framis: More or Less Himself." [NewAW] (1) 87, p. 66-67.
    "Life & Death of a Guide." [Caliban] (2) 87, p. 163.
1745. FLAMM, Matthew
    "Midtown." [PoetryE] (23/24) Fall 87, p. 179-180.
    "Super on the West Side." [PoetryE] (23/24) Fall 87, p. 178.
1746. FLANAGAN, Bob
    "Sonnet." [NewAW] (1) 87, p. 116.
1747. FLANAGAN-SIMPSON, Katherine
    "The Burning Woman." [CentR] (31:4) Fall 87, p. 378-379.
1748. FLANDERS, Jane
    "Homage to Leonardo." [Poetry] (150:3) Je 87, p. 158-159.
    "Queen Anne's Legs." [LightY] '87, c86, p. 60.
    "You, Flying." [LitR] (31:1) Fall 87, p. 60.
1749. FLECK, Polly
    "Coyote's Last Trick." [Dandel] (14:1) Spr-Sum 87, p. 28.
1750. FLEISCHMAN, W. C.
    "Invisible." [CutB] (27/28) 87, p. 106-107.
1751. FLEMING, Jack
    "Among Old Dancers." [WebR] (12:1) Spr 87, p. 43.
    "Elementals." [WebR] (12:1) Spr 87, p. 42.
1752. FLESHOOD, Suzy
    "An Antiphon." [HiramPoR] (43) Fall-Wint 87-88, p. 7.
    "The Death of Silence." [HiramPoR] (43) Fall-Wint 87-88, p. 8.
    "Gets." [HiramPoR] (43) Fall-Wint 87-88, p. 21.
    "The Gift." [HiramPoR] (43) Fall-Wint 87-88, p. 45.
1753. FLETCHER, Lynne Yamaguchi
    "Larches" (tr. of Kitahara Hakushu). [ColR] (NS 14:1) Spr-Sum 87, p. 34.
1754. FLEU, Richard
    "Foreplay." [StoneC] (15:1/2) Fall-Wint 87-88, p. 55.
1755. FLINT, Carol
    "A Trois." [Spirit] (8:2) 87, p. 82.
1756. FLIPIKOWSKI, Zoe
    "Looking into a Glass Case at the Museum of Native American Cultures, Spokane,
        Washington." [CentR] (31:1) Wint 87, p. 58.
1757. FLOCK, Miriam
    "Lily in the House." [Shen] (37:4) 87, p. 37.
1758. FLOOK, Maria
    "Household." [Agni] (24/25) 87, p. 105-106.
    "Woodpecker." [MissouriR] (10:3) 87, p. 73.
FLORE, Shirley Le
    See LeFLORE, Shirley
1759. FLORES, Toni
    "Glyph." [SenR] (17:1) 87, p. 38.

"In the Oaxacan Sierra." [SenR] (17:1) 87, p. 37.
"Temple of the Foliated Cross." [SenR] (17:1) 87, p. 36.
1760. FLYNN, Andrew
"Tonight the River." [BlueBldgs] (10) 87?, p. 54.
1761. FLYNN, David
"The Burning House." [KanQ] (19:1/2) Wint-Spr 87, p. 203.
1762. FLYTHE, Starkey (Starkey S.), Jr.
"Paul's Wholesale Florist." [GeoR] (41:1) Spr 87, p. 140-143.
"Pavane pour une Infante défunte." [GreensboroR] (42) Sum 87, p. 66.
"The Plot of *Twelfth Night*, or, What You Will." [GreensboroR] (42) Sum 87, p. 65.
FOE, Mark de
    See DeFOE, Mark
1763. FOERSTER, Richard
"Ghosts." [SouthwR] (72:3) Sum 87, p. 382.
"Halley's Comet." [Nat] (244:18) 9 My 87, p. 620.
"King René's Book of Love, Folio 47v" (for Sophie Wilkins). [Shen] (37:2) 87, p. 23.
"Mozart's Death" (For Robert Phillips). [Poetry] (151:3) D 87, p. 295.
1764. FOGEL, Alice B.
"Back Home." [MinnR] (NS 28) Spr 87, p. 34-35.
"Elemental." [Phoenix] (7:1) 87, p. 42.
"Ice Island." [SouthernPR] (27:1) Spr 87, p. 18-19.
"The Sleepwalker." [SenR] (17:1) 87, p. 60-61.
"Stone Walls." [PoetryNW] (28:1) Spr 87, p. 13.
1765. FOGLE, Richard Harter
"Good Old Southern Boy." [NegC] (7:3/4) 87, p. 171.
1766. FOIX, J. V.
"Four Sonnets" (tr. by M. L. Rosenthal). [AmerPoR] (16:1) Ja-F 87, p. 42.
1767. FOLEY, Louis
"American Dream." [Bogg] (58) 87, p. 28.
1768. FOLEY, Michael
"My Muse." [Pembroke] (19) 87, p. 83.
1769. FOLKESTAD, Marilyn
"Speaking in Tongues." [Calyx] (10:2/3) Spr 87, p. 120-121.
1770. FOLSOM, Eric
"The Old Road to Sydenham." [Quarry] (36:1) Wint 87, p. 112.
1771. FOLSOM, Jack
"The Rune of the Lapwing." [MidwQ] (28:3) Spr 87, p. 357.
1772. FONDANE, Benjamin
"Horizontal Bar — Do Not Enter (a Cine-Poem)" (tr. by Leonard Schwartz). [LitR] (30:3) Spr 87, p. 468-471.
1773. FONTAINE, Arturo
"The Denial" (tr. by the author and James Brasfield). [CutB] (27/28) 87, p. 104.
"Lagoons" (tr. by the author and James Brasfield). [CutB] (27/28) 87, p. 105.
"Your Dresses" (tr. by the author and James Brasfield). [CutB] (27/28) 87, p. 105.
1774. FONTANA, Giovanni
"Poema Pretestvale." [Rampike] (5:3) 87, p. 7.
1775. FONTANAROSA, Paula
"And Fly Little Bird." [HiramPoR] (43) Fall-Wint 87-88, p. 5.
"Colors." [HiramPoR] (43) Fall-Wint 87-88, p. 22.
"The store windows are like a row of mirrors." [HiramPoR] (43) Fall-Wint 87-88, p. 26.
1776. FORBES, Greg
"By Lago Atitlan." [Quarry] (36:1) Wint 87, p. 98-101.
"An Unmarked Car." [Quarry] (36:1) Wint 87, p. 97-98.
1777. FORBES, John
"Europe: A Guide for Ken Searle." [Verse] (4:2) Je 87, p. 57-58.
1778. FORCE, Kathy
"A Man Full of Beer Gets on the Bus, Sits with His Leg Against Mine." [LakeSR] (21) 87, p. 15.
1779. FORD, Denise
"Nietzsche." [Bogg] (57) 87, p. 50.
1780. FORD, Michael C.
"Conversations & the New Poetics." [WormR] (27:1, issue 105) 87, p. 33.

"Happy Anniversary" (after/ Gerald Locklin). [WormR] (27:1, issue 105) 87, p. 32-33.
1781. FORD, Victoria
"Canada Geese" (Horicon Marsh National Wildlife Refuge — For V.J.B.). [Abraxas] (35/36) 87, p. 75.
1782. FORD, William
"Backslider." [Phoenix] (7:1) 87, p. 33.
1783. FOREMAN, Robert
"Competitors." [CrabCR] (4:2) Spr 87, p. 5.
"The Last Gift." [Lactuca] (6) Ap-My 87, p. 12.
"The Traditional Jazz Band." [Lactuca] (6) Ap-My 87, p. 12.
1784. FORER, Bernard
"The Turncoat." [PoeticJ] (17) 87, p. 2.
1785. FORESTIER, Lisa
"The Leaves Are Falling." [PoetL] (82:3) Fall 87, p. 151.
1786. FORSTHOFFER, J. P.
"It's 3 A.M. and All Is Not Well." [Confr] (35/36) Spr-Fall 87, p. 175.
1787. FORT, Charles
"The Poet's Daughter." [CarolQ] (39:3) Spr 87, p. 40.
1788. FORT, Maria Rosa
"In This Night, in this World" (tr. of Alejandra Pizarnik, w. Frank Graziano). [ColR] (NS 14:2) Fall-Wint 87, p. 57-59.
1789. FORTUNATO, Peter
"Caliban, Recalling the Staff." [Nimrod] (30:2) Spr-Sum 87, p. 59.
1790. FOSS, Phillip
"Because Giving Him Away His Eyes." [Notus] (2:2) Fall 87, p. 63-65.
"The Chinese Poems." [Notus] (2:2) Fall 87, p. 66-67.
"Confusing Green with the Color Red: Allegories." [Conjunc] (10) 87, p. 251-252.
1791. FOSSO, D. R.
"Bouquet." [Pembroke] (19) 87, p. 144.
"Hunger." [Pembroke] (19) 87, p. 144.
1792. FOSTER, Barbara (See also BELLA DONNA)
"London." [Bogg] (58) 87, p. 36.
1793. FOSTER, Edward
"Marianne Moore in Egypt." [Lips] (13) 87, p. 37.
1794. FOSTER, Linda Nemec
"Staring at the Brick Wall." [PennR] (3:1) Spr-Sum 87, p. 64-65.
"The Third Secret of Fatima" (1986 Finalist, Eve of Saint Agnes Poetry Competition). [NegC] (7:1/2) 87, p. 183.
1795. FOSTER, Michael
"General Store." [YellowS] (22) Spr 87, p. 23.
1796. FOSTER, Sesshu
"July." [Contact] (9:44/45/46) Fall-Wint 87, p. 45.
1797. FOWLER, Anne Carroll
"First Rites." [KanQ] (19:3) Sum 87, p. 173.
1798. FOWLER, Gene
"Fitting In." [AlphaBS] (1) Je 87, p. 8.
"In Transit." [AlphaBS] (1) Je 87, p. 7.
"Truck Stop Dance: Nov. 73-Feb 74." [AlphaBS] (1) Je 87, p. 6.
1799. FOWLER, Karen Joy
"Glass Houses" (For My Father, Redwood City, Kaiser Hospital, February). [CalQ] (30) Wint 87, p. 53-54.
"The Schwarzschild Radius" (For the Anorectic Karen). [CalQ] (30) Wint 87, p. 52-53.
1800. FOWLER, Russell
"Old Mortality." [SoCaR] (19:2) Spr 87, p. 28.
1801. FOX, Hugh
"Two Sisters." [Bogg] (57) 87, p. 52.
1802. FOX, Susan
"Penelope Gardening." [Poetry] (150:1) Ap 87, p. 35.
1803. FOX, Suzanne
"Luxuries." [Interim] (6:1) Spr 87, p. 36.
1804. FRAIND, Lori
"Paint Me Beautiful" (The Greensboro Review Literary Award, Honorable Mention). [GreensboroR] (41) Wint 86-87, p. 45-46.

FRALEY

1805. FRALEY, Michael
"A Delicate Balance." [PoeticJ] (17) 87, p. 20.
1806. FRAME, Cynthia Solt
"Sundays." [Bogg] (58) 87, p. 64.
"The Tucson Radio DJ." [Bogg] (58) 87, p. 36.
1807. FRANCIS, H. E.
"Chronicles" (for Luis Bassani, tr. of Ofelia Castillo). [BlackWR] (13:2) Spr 87, p. 167.
1808. FRANCIS, Jim
"The Man on the Humber River Bridge." [Rampike] (5:3) 87, p. 75.
1809. FRANCIS, Lee
"Monuments." [Bogg] (57) 87, p. 59.
1810. FRANCIS, Pat Therese
"Primavera." [Spirit] (8:2) 87, p. 58.
1811. FRANCIS, Robert
"Alma Natura." [TexasR] (7:3/4) 87, p. 49.
"Gray Squirrel." [TexasR] (7:3/4) 87, p. 48.
"The Gypsy Moth Man." [TexasR] (7:3/4) 87, p. 47.
"Light and Shadow." [LightY] '87, c86, p. 98.
"The Pumpkin Man." [LightY] '87, c86, p. 33-34.
"Where to Spend the Winter." [LightY] '87, c86, p. 160.
1812. FRANCO OPPENHEIMER, Felix
"Del Tiempo y Su Figura." [Mairena] (9:23) 87, p. 116-117.
"Desde Mi Mismo." [Mairena] (9:23) 87, p. 115.
"Identidad." [Mairena] (9:23) 87, p. 114.
"La Luz, Mi Luz" (II). [Mairena] (9:23) 87, p. 117.
"Nada." [Mairena] (9:23) 87, p. 118.
"Pesadumbre." [Mairena] (9:23) 87, p. 117.
1813. FRANK, Bernhard
"Chess Game" (tr. of Shmu'el Shatal). [WebR] (12:2) Fall 87, p. 43.
"David and Jonathan" (tr. of Else Lasker-Schüler). [WebR] (12:2) Fall 87, p. 42.
"Snow White" (tr. of Guillaume Apollinaire). [WebR] (12:2) Fall 87, p. 42.
"This Is Where She Lived" (tr. of Shmu'el Shatal). [WebR] (12:2) Fall 87, p. 44.
"Venice" (tr. of Shmu'el Shatal). [ColR] (NS 14:2) Fall-Wint 87, p. 67.
1814. FRANKLIN, Walt
"The Hummingbird" (for my son's first birthday). [Blueline] (7:2/3 [i.e. 8:2/3?]) 87, p. 14.
"Three Days in the Bar." [Wind] (17:60) 87, p. 15.
1815. FRANTOM, Marcy
"Robeline Road." [CarolQ] (40:1) Fall 87, p. 18-19.
1816. FRANZEN, Cola
"Bettor" (tr. of Saúl Yurkievich). [NewAW] (1) 87, p. 97-100.
"Crossing" (tr. of Saúl Yurkievich). [NewOR] (14:1) Spr 87, p. 44.
"Donde" (from "Rimbomba," tr. of Saul Yurkievich). [Rampike] (5:3) 87, p. 40.
"En un Bar" (from "Mujeres Timidas," tr. of Alicia Borinsky). [Rampike] (5:3) 87, p. 40.
"I Miss Her Already" (tr. of Alicia Borinsky). [StoneC] (15:1/2) Fall-Wint 87-88, p. 67.
"Immortalities of the Marionette" (tr. of Alicia Borinsky). [StoneC] (15:1/2) Fall-Wint 87-88, p. 65.
"In Buenos Aires" (tr. of Alicia Borinsky). [NewAW] (2) Fall 87, p. 48.
"Mi Estomago (My Belly)" (tr. of Marjorie Agosin). [Calyx] (10:2/3) Spr 87, p. 115-116.
"O" (from "Apuntes," tr. of Juan Cameron). [Rampike] (5:3) 87, p. 41.
"Proverbio" (from "Mujeres Timidas," tr. of Alicia Borinsky). [Rampike] (5:3) 87, p. 41.
"Strip-Tease" (tr. of Alicia Borinsky). [NewAW] (2) Fall 87, p. 47.
1817. FRASER, Sanford
"Fishes." [PoeticJ] (17) 87, p. 32.
FRATRIK, Julie Cooper
See COOPER-FRATRIK, Julie
1818. FRAZE, Candida
"Love in the Dark." [CentR] (31:2) Spr 87, p. 190.
1819. FRAZEE, James
"Blue Elegy." [MSS] (5:3) 87, p. 185.

1820. FRAZIER, Hood
"Benediction." [HampSPR] Wint 87, p. 52-53.
"How We Come to It." [HampSPR] Wint 87, p. 52.
1821. FREDERICK, Lorca Lowe
"Variation" (tr. of Federico Garcia). [YellowS] (23) Sum 87, p. 29.
1822. FREDERICKSON, Kathy
"Boot This in Disk Drive #1." [ColEng] (49:2) F 87, p. 179.
"The Litter." [ColEng] (49:2) F 87, p. 178.
1823. FREDERICKSON, Todd
"Lake Spirit." [GreenfR] (14:3/4) Sum-Fall 87, p. 173.
1824. FREEDMAN, William
"Kidnapped." [WebR] (12:1) Spr 87, p. 40-41.
1825. FREEMAN, Marion
"And the Head Began to Burn" (tr. of Alfonsina Storni). [MinnR] (NS 29) Fall 87,
p. 17-18.
"It Could Well Be" (tr. of Alfonsina Storni). [MinnR] (NS 29) Fall 87, p. 16.
1826. FREERICKS, Charles Avakian
"Rooted In." [ColR] (NS 14:2) Fall-Wint 87, p. 92-93.
FREES, Madeline de
See DeFREES, Madeline
1827. FREIDINGER, Paul
"The Drifts of Winter's Mind." [NoDaQ] (55:2) Spr 87, p. 26.
"Modern Man and the Children of the Sun." [Lactuca] (7) Ag 87, p. 39.
1828. FREISINGER, Randall R.
"The Kirby Man" (for Toby and Laura). [LaurelR] (21:1/2) Wint-Sum 87, p. 88-90.
"Meeting at the Bloody Brook Bar." [LaurelR] (21:1/2) Wint-Sum 87, p. 91.
"On Rereading *The Sun Also Rises*." [NewL] (54:1) Fall 87, p. 65-66.
"Slow-Pitch Tournament, Alston, Michigan" (June 15, 1986). [LaurelR] (21:1/2)
Wint-Sum 87, p. 92-93.
"Spring Burial" (for Bruce Petersen). [NewL] (54:1) Fall 87, p. 66-67.
FRENCH, Dayv James
See JAMES-FRENCH, Dayv
1829. FRENEAU, Philip
"The Indian Burying Ground." [Shen] (37:1) 87, p. 7-8.
1830. FRETWELL, Kathy
"Summer Hiatus." [Quarry] (36:4) Fall 87, p. 34.
1831. FREUDINGER, Paul
"Chiaroscuro." [CrossCur] (6:4) 87, p. 119.
1832. FREY, Cecelia
"The Black Cook." [Event] (16:3) Fall 87, p. 62.
"Darkness Gathers." [Event] (16:3) Fall 87, p. 61.
"The Flip Game." [Event] (16:3) Fall 87, p. 60.
1833. FREY, Gina Bergamino
"October Chill." [Vis] (23) 87, p. 27.
1834. FRIAR, Kimon
"Old Stories" (tr. of Yannis Kondos). [Poetry] (151:1/2) O-N 87, p. 52.
1835. FRIEBERT, Stuart
"Artist" (tr. of Karl Krolow). [Iowa] (17:3) Fall 87, p. 105.
"The Bear He Sees." [PoetL] (82:3) Fall 87, p. 169.
"Beyond" (tr. of Karl Krolow). [Field] (36) Spr 87, p. 36.
"Come & Get It." [PraS] (61:1) Spr 87, p. 17-18.
"The Darmstadt Orchids." [QW] (25) Spr 87, p. 132.
"Don't Think" (tr. of Karl Krolow). [QW] (25) Spr 87, p. 131.
"Endangered Landscape" (tr. of Rainer Brambach). [Iowa] (17:3) Fall 87, p. 106.
"From the Program" (tr. of Bettina Behn). [ConnPR] (6:1) 87, p. 32.
"The House That Holds Everything" (tr. of Karl Krolow). [QW] (25) Spr 87, p.
130.
"The Hungarian Telephonograph." [Iowa] (17:3) Fall 87, p. 110.
"I Don't Quite Understand You." [HawaiiR] (22) Fall 87, p. 33.
"On Biographies" (tr. of Karl Krolow). [HawaiiR] (19) Spr 86, c87, p. 25.
"On Biographies" (tr. of Karl Krolow). [Iowa] (17:3) Fall 87, p. 104.
"On Getting More Than You Give or the Opposite." [FloridaR] (15:1) Spr-Sum 87,
p. 73.
"On Hunting and Other Things" (tr. of Karl Krolow). [Field] (36) Spr 87, p. 35.
"Seasons" (tr. of Karl Krolow). [NoDaQ] (55:2) Spr 87, p. 58.
"Uncle Ross." [PoetL] (82:3) Fall 87, p. 168.

"What to Do with Love" (for Karl Krolow). [FloridaR] (15:1) Spr-Sum 87, p. 72.
"When There's Too Much Love." [Iowa] (17:3) Fall 87, p. 109-110.
1836. FRIED, Philip
"Heretical Testaments" (2 selections: "Old Man among Old Men," "Fragment of a
Heretical Testament"). [BelPoJ] (38:1) Fall 87, p. 38-39.
"The Messiah Cycle" (Selection: "Nathan's Quarrel with the Angels"). [BelPoJ]
(38:1) Fall 87, p. 40.
"My Father Winks." [CapeR] (22:1) Spr 87, p. 28.
1837. FRIEDMAN, Daisy
"Anniversary Poem." [Bomb] (20) Sum 87, p. 80.
"L'Espirit d'Escalier." [Bomb] (20) Sum 87, p. 80.
"Private Routines." [Bomb] (20) Sum 87, p. 80.
"A Sunny Day Response." [Bomb] (20) Sum 87, p. 80.
1838. FRIEDMAN, Dorothy
"The Cold Bare Facts." [Writer] (100:5) My 87, p. 21.
"Last Night in Florida." [Writer] (99:11) N 86, p. 18.
"The Old Oak." [CrossCur] (7:1) 87, p. 60-61.
1839. FRIEDMAN, Jeff
"Bird." [Ascent] (12:3) 87, p. 49.
1840. FRIEDSON, Tony
"Jumping Galley." [HawaiiR] (19) Spr 86, c87, p. 53.
1841. FRIES, Kenny
"In Jerusalem." [JamesWR] (4:2) Wint 87, p. 6.
1842. FRIGGIERI, Oliver
"April Song" (tr. of Mario Azzopardi). [Vis] (25) 87, p. 17.
1843. FRIIS-BAASTAD, Erling
"The Ash Lad." [AlphaBS] (2) D 87, p. 10-11.
"Better Than Nothing." [AlphaBS] (1) Je 87, p. 2.
"Dawson City, Autumn." [AlphaBS] (1) Je 87, p. 4.
"Instructions to a Sleuth." [AlphaBS] (1) Je 87, p. 3.
"The Poet Divides His Time." [AlphaBS] (1) Je 87, p. 5.
1844. FRIMAN, Alice
"Anger, Etc." [CapeR] (22:1) Spr 87, p. 24.
"The Flail." [BelPoJ] (37:4) Sum 87, p. 26.
"Her Son." [BlueBldgs] (10) 87?, p. 28.
"In a Minor Key." [BelPoJ] (37:4) Sum 87, p. 27.
"Looking for the Parts." [CapeR] (22:1) Spr 87, p. 23.
"Nature Walk." [Puerto] (22:2) Spr 87, p. 86.
"The Outcome." [Puerto] (22:2) Spr 87, p. 83.
"Prophecy." [BelPoJ] (37:4) Sum 87, p. 28.
"Street Signs." [Puerto] (22:2) Spr 87, p. 87.
"Subject Matter." [BelPoJ] (37:4) Sum 87, p. 26-27.
"The Surgeon's Wife." [Puerto] (22:2) Spr 87, p. 84-85.
"Turning Fifty." [BlueBldgs] (10) 87?, p. 27.
"Unposted Letter." [SoCaR] (20:1) Fall 87, p. 50.
1845. FRITSCH, Jancie
"Night and I'm the Vagrant" (tr. of Joyce Mansour, w. Elton Glaser). [ColR] (NS
14:1) Spr-Sum 87, p. 32.
1846. FROST, Carol
"Acorns." [Ploughs] (13:1) 87, p. 51-52.
"After Byzantium." [PoetryNW] (28:3) Aut 87, p. 42.
"All I Cannot." [MissouriR] (10:1) 87, p. 193.
"All Summer Long." [MissouriR] (10:1) 87, p. 192.
"A Butterfly and a Day." [PoetryNW] (28:3) Aut 87, p. 41-42.
"The Gardener Eats a Rose." [Raccoon] (24/25) My 87, p. 99.
"In Scarecrow's Garden." [Ploughs] (13:1) 87, p. 53.
"Late Sigh" (for A G). [AmerPoR] (16:3) My-Je 87, p. 6.
"Pot-au-Feu." [Raccoon] (24/25) My 87, p. 95.
"The Procession." [Raccoon] (24/25) My 87, p. 96-97.
"The Twins." [Raccoon] (24/25) My 87, p. 98.
1847. FROST, Kenneth
"Castaway." [Salm] (72) Fall 86, p. 180-181.
"Cezanne." [ManhatPR] (9) Sum 87, p. 45.
"Night Patrol." [SouthwR] (72:3) Sum 87, p. 388.
"Possum on the Highway." [Salm] (72) Fall 86, p. 180.
"Roulette." [Phoenix] (7:1) 87, p. 13.

"Zookeepers know." [Phoenix] (7:1) 87, p. 12.
1848. FROST, Robert
"Birches." [Nimrod] (30:2) Spr-Sum 87, p. 23-24.
"Pertinax." [Iowa] (17:3) Fall 87, p. 87.
"Range-Finding." [Iowa] (17:3) Fall 87, p. 88-89.
1849. FRUMKIN, Gene
"The Brown Dog." [Sulfur] (20) Fall 87, p. 110.
"Love that Careless Word!" [HighP] (2:2) Fall 87, p. 171-172.
1850. FRY, Nan
"An Anglo-Saxon Riddle: 66" (from "The Exeter Book," tr. of anonymous
Anglo-Saxon poem). [StoneC] (14:3/4) Spr-Sum 87, p. 74.
1851. FRYM, Gloria
"The Opening." [Notus] (2:2) Fall 87, p. 43.
"Sleep." [Notus] (2:2) Fall 87, p. 42.
"Who They Were." [Notus] (2:2) Fall 87, p. 44.
FU, Du
    See DU ,Fu
FU, Tu
    See DU ,Fu
1852. FUJIMOTO, Wanda
"Interitance." The Best of [BambooR] [(31-32)] 86, p. 29.
1853. FUKUYAMA, Betty
"November Day." [BellArk] (3:3) My-Je 87, p. 7.
1854. FULKER, Tina
"Snow Storm." [Vis] (24) 87, p. 27.
1855. FULLEN, George
"Escaping Fate." [InterPR] (13:2) Fall 87, p. 78.
"Steinbeck's Lesson." [InterPR] (13:2) Fall 87, p. 78.
1856. FULLER, Roy
"Early and Late Works." [SouthernR] (23:3) Jl 87, p. 740.
1857. FULLER, William
"Otherwise These Days." [NewAW] (1) 87, p. 95-96.
1858. FULLER, Winston
"Two Weeks After My Forty-Third Birthday." [LaurelR] (20:1/2) Sum 87, p. 70.
1859. FULTON, Alice
"Trouble in Mind." [Poetry] (151:1/2) O-N 87, p. 53.
1860. FUNGE, Robert
"Four for Mr. Meyerson." [CharR] (13:2) Fall 87, p. 78-80.
"On the Writing of Small Poems." [SpoonRQ] (12:2) Spr 87, p. 31.
"Runes." [HawaiiR] (22) Fall 87, p. 34.
"A Sense of Lived Time." [CentR] (31:1) Wint 87, p. 58-59.
"Testimony." [HawaiiR] (22) Fall 87, p. 35.
1861. FUNICELLO, Linda
"Center" (after Sylvia Plath). [ManhatPR] (9) Sum 87, p. 53.
1862. FUNKHOUSER, Erika
"The Blue in Beets." [TexasR] (7:3/4) 87, p. 51.
"The Women Who Clean Fish." [TexasR] (7:3/4) 87, p. 50.
1863. FUNSTEN, Kenneth
"Gets Honked At." [SlipS] (7) 87, p. 108.
"The Slender Girl in the Red Leather Jumpsuit." [SlipS] (7) 87, p. 108-109.
"Someone Sd." [SlipS] (7) 87, p. 107.
1864. FURLONG, Waltrina
"Marcus Aurelius." [Interim] (6:1) Spr 87, p. 38.
1865. FUSEK, Serena
"An American Portrait" (cribbed from an interview with Jerry Hall, in *Vanity Fair*,
March, 1985). [PoetL] (81:3) Fall 86, p. 173-174.
"Source" (To Hank Williams and Tony Moffeit). [PoeticJ] (17) 87, p. 24.
"This One's For You." [Bogg] (57) 87, p. 13.
"Touring the Marine Resources Center." [PoeticJ] (17) 87, p. 13.
1866. FUSSELMAN, Amy
"First Dinner with His Mother." [GreenfR] (14:1/2) Wint-Spr, p. 107.
1867. FUTORANSKY, Luisa
"Probable Forgetting of Ithaca" (tr. by Jason Weiss). [ColR] (NS 14:2) Fall-Wint
87, p. 53.
1868. GABBARD, G. N.
"Discount Store." [LightY] '87, c86, p. 232.

"'Fool!' Said My Muse to Me." [LightY] '87, c86, p. 191.
"King Alfred Explains It" (A Poem for Students of Intellectual History). [LightY]
    '87, c86, p. 58-60.
"To a Fringed Genital." [LightY] '87, c86, p. 207.
"Witches' Sabbatical." [LightY] '87, c86, p. 211.
1869. GABIS, Rita
"Deerfield River in Summer." [BlackWR] (14:1) Fall 87, p. 16.
"Missouri." [BelPoJ] (38:1) Fall 87, p. 37.
1870. GABLE, Cate
"Kilauea." [BambooR] (36) Fall 87, p. 45-46.
"Small." [BambooR] (36) Fall 87, p. 47.
1871. GADD, Maxine
"Movement." [Rampike] (5:3) 87, p. 76.
"Riff What Ought?" [WestCR] (22:2) Fall 87, p. 15-16.
1872. GAERTNER, Ken
"Herod." [Poem] (57) Mr 87, p. 62-63.
1873. GALASSI, Jonathan
"Beautiful Loser" (Nineteenth-century family picture). [Nat] (244:5) 7 F 87, p. 158.
"I know the time when the most impassive face" (tr. of Eugenio Montale). [GrandS]
    (6:3) Spr 87, p. 117.
"My life, I ask of you no stable" (tr. of Eugenio Montale). [GrandS] (6:3) Spr 87, p.
    117.
"Wind and Flags" (tr. of Eugenio Montale). [NewYRB] (34:12) 16 Jl 87, p. 4.
GALINDO, David Escobar
    See ESCOBAR GALINDO, David
1874. GALL, Sally M.
"Marking Time." [SouthernR] (23:1) Ja 87, p. 137-139.
1875. GALLAGHER, Diane M.
"Earthworks" (Bill Bruford at the Bottom Line 7-18-87). [SpiritSH] (53:1) 87, p.
    25.
"Redskirt." [SpiritSH] (53:1) 87, p. 24.
1876. GALLAGHER, Tess
"All Day the Light Is Clear." [ParisR] (29:103) Sum 87, p. 186.
"Cougar Meat." [Zyzzyva] (3:3) Fall 87, p. 46-48.
"Dim House, Bright Face." [Poetry] (150:6) S 87, p. 344.
"The Hands of the Blindman." [Caliban] (3) 87, p. 25.
"If Poetry Were Not a Morality." [Poetry] (151:1/2) O-N 87, p. 54-56.
"Message for the Sinecurist." [AmerPoR] (16:4) Jl-Ag 87, p. 13.
"Monologue at the Chinook Bar and Grill." [AmerPoR] (16:4) Jl-Ag 87, p. 12.
"Redwing." [Poetry] (151:1/2) O-N 87, p. 56.
"Rijl." [Poetry] (150:6) S 87, p. 343-344.
"Small Garden Near a Field." [Poetry] (150:6) S 87, p. 345-346.
"The Story of a Citizen." [AmerPoR] (16:4) Jl-Ag 87, p. 13.
"Their Heads Bent Toward Each Other Like Flowers." [AmerPoR] (16:4) Jl-Ag 87,
    p. 14.
1877. GALLAHER, Cynthia
"Bulletin: UFOs Realign Missile Targets." [PikeF] (8) Fall 87, p. 18.
"The Invisible." [PikeF] (8) Fall 87, p. 18.
1878. GALLER, David
"Meyer Levine." [TriQ] (68) Wint 87, p. 116-117.
"The Pickup, 1951." [TriQ] (68) Wint 87, p. 113-115.
"Small Figure at the Foot of a Large Building." [Margin] (4) Aut 87, p. 112.
1879. GALVIN, Brendan
"An American Naturalist Writes to a Londoner, 1758." [NewYorker] (63:14) 25 My
    87, p. 38.
"The Apple Trees." [TexasR] (7:3/4) 87, p. 54.
"Fall Squashes." [StoneC] (14:3/4) Spr-Sum 87, p. 11.
"Great Blue." [TexasR] (7:3/4) 87, p. 52-53.
"Letter Accompanying a Cask of Seeds from America (1723)" (from
    "Sengekontacket Traveler"). [TexasR] (8:3/4) Fall-Wint 87, p. 33-37.
"March 11, 50 Degrees." [KenR] (NS 9:2) Spr 87, p. 108.
"The Patience of White Birches." [NewYorker] (63:4) 16 Mr 87, p. 36.
"Poem of the Towhee." [StoneC] (14:3/4) Spr-Sum 87, p. 7-8.
"Raising Walls in Ireland." [SewanR] (95:3) Sum 87, p. 448-449.
"Rural Mailboxes." [TexasR] (7:3/4) 87, p. 55.
"September Dory Race." [KenR] (NS 9:2) Spr 87, p. 108-109.

"Snakebit (1767)." [Ascent] (12:3) 87, p. 39-41.
"Why There Is Spring Lightning: Letter to B. Franklin" (from "Sengekontacket
    Traveler"). [TexasR] (8:3/4) Fall-Wint 87, p. 30-32.
"Workout." [StoneC] (14:3/4) Spr-Sum 87, p. 9.
1880. GALVIN, James
"At the Sand Creek Bridge." [AmerPoR] (16:3) My-Je 87, p. 4.
"Black Star." [AmerPoR] (16:3) My-Je 87, p. 5.
"Botany" (for Ray Worster, 1918-1984, who died of freezing on Boulder Ridge,
    where he was born). [AmerPoR] (16:3) My-Je 87, p. 5.
"Cartography." [AmerPoR] (16:3) My-Je 87, p. 3.
"Combat Zone." [AmerPoR] (16:3) My-Je 87, p. 4.
"Driving into Laramie." [AmerPoR] (16:3) My-Je 87, p. 5.
"Holy Saturday, an Exercise in Personification." [AmerPoR] (16:3) My-Je 87, p. 4.
"Left Handed Poem." [AmerPoR] (16:3) My-Je 87, p. 3.
"Life Throes." [AmerPoR] (16:3) My-Je 87, p. 3.
"Matins." [AmerPoR] (16:3) My-Je 87, p. 5.
"My Death As a Girl I Knew." [AmerPoR] (16:3) My-Je 87, p. 4.
"No." [AmerPoR] (16:3) My-Je 87, p. 4.
"Original." [AmerPoR] (16:3) My-Je 87, p. 3.
"Regard." [AmerPoR] (16:3) My-Je 87, p. 5.
"A Safe Place." [AmerPoR] (16:3) My-Je 87, p. 5.
"Spring Blizzard." [AmerPoR] (16:3) My-Je 87, p. 4.
1881. GALVIN, Martin
"Jogging by the C&O Canal." [PoetL] (81:4) Wint 86-87, p. 231.
"Learning the Trade." [PoetL] (81:4) Wint 86-87, p. 230.
GAMA, Steven da
    See DaGAMA, Steven
GAMBOA, Manuel Manazar
    See MANAZAR BAMBOA, Manuel
1882. GANASSI, Ian
"Partial Explanation." [ParisR] (29:102) Spr 87, p. 95-96.
"Totem and Taboo." [DenQ] (22:1) Sum 87, p. 24-25.
1883. GANDER, Forrest
"Bacantes" (Selection: V, tr. of Elsa Cross). [BlackWR] (13:2) Spr 87, p. 162.
"The Cases of Forrest Gander." [FiveFR] (5) 87, p. 93.
"The Drowning of Yuko." [Raccoon] (24/25) My 87, p. 282-283.
"Evening Calm." [FiveFR] (5) 87, p. 94.
"Imagining You" (after Jean Follain). [Gargoyle] (32/33) 87, p. 278-279.
"Last Garden" (tr. of Myriam Moscona). [BlackWR] (13:2) Spr 87, p. 161.
"Loiter." [FiveFR] (5) 87, p. 95-96.
"Memory" (tr. of Veronica Volkow). [BlackWR] (13:2) Spr 87, p. 165.
"Parable of the Tinderbox." [Caliban] (3) 87, p. 13-14.
"Rush to the Lake." [Raccoon] (24/25) My 87, p. 243.
1884. GANGEMI, Kenneth
"A Streetcar Named St. Charles." [Confr] (35/36) Spr-Fall 87, p. 148.
1885. GANGOPADHYAY, Sunil
"By Writing a Poem." [Bomb] (18) Wint 87, p. 64.
"Calcutta and I." [Bomb] (18) Wint 87, p. 64.
"Two Curses." [Bomb] (18) Wint 87, p. 64.
1886. GANICK, Peter
"Senescence" (Selection: IX). [Os] (24) 87, p. 20.
1887. GANSZ, David C. D.
"Animadversions" (Selections: III-IV). [Notus] (2:1) Spr 87, p. 38-42.
"Animadversions" (Selections: V-IV). [Notus] (2:2) Fall 87, p. 24-27.
"Sin Tactics" (Part II of Millennial Scriptions). [Temblor] (6) 87, p. 22-32.
1888. GANZEL, Barbara L.
"Angus, the One-Legged Duckling." [GeoR] (41:4) Wint 87, p. 798-799.
1889. GAO, Fa-lin
"Iron Meteorite" (Beijing Planetarium, tr. by Edward Morin and Dennis Ding).
    [Ploughs] (13:4) 87, p. 43-44.
1890. GARCIA, Albert
"Visitor." [TarRP] (26:2) Spr 87, p. 20.
1891. GARCIA, Alberto
"It Doesn't Matter / No Importa." [Contact] (9:44/45/46) Fall-Wint 87, p. 20.
1892. GARCIA, Carlos Ernesto
"A la Perplejidad de un Difunto." [InterPR] (13:1) Spr 87, p. 48.

"Postcard" (in Spanish). [InterPR] (13:1) Spr 87, p. 48.
"Postcard" (tr. by Susan Schreibman). [InterPR] (13:1) Spr 87, p. 49.
"To the Perplexity of One Deceased" (tr. by Susan Schreibman). [InterPR] (13:1)
Spr 87, p. 49.
1893. GARCIA, Douglas
"Arte Mágico" (Homenaje a Borges antes de su Muerte). [Inti] (24/25) Otoño
86-Primavera 87, p. 257.
"Muerte de Shigechiyo Izumi a los 120 Años." [Inti] (24/25) Otoño 86-Primavera
87, p. 258.
1894. GARCIA LORCA, Federico
"Blind Panorama of New York" (tr. by Greg Simon and Steven L. White). [ParisR]
(29:104) Fall 87, p. 89-90.
"Dawn" (tr. by Greg Simon and Steven L. White). [ParisR] (29:104) Fall 87, p. 93.
"Death" (To Luis de la Serna, tr. by Greg Simon and Steven L. White). [ParisR]
(29:104) Fall 87, p. 94.
"Earth and Moon" (tr. by Greg Simon). [NowestR] (25:3) 87, p. 324-325.
"Lament for Ignacio Sanchez Mejias" (tr. by Robin Skelton). [MalR] (79) Je 87, p.
61-69.
"Living Sky" (tr. by Greg Simon and Steven L. White). [ParisR] (29:104) Fall 87,
p. 91-92.
"Ode to Walt Whitman" (tr. by Greg Simon and Steven L. White). [ParisR] (29:104)
Fall 87, p. 95-99.
"Variación." [YellowS] (23) Sum 87, p. 29.
"Variation" (tr. by Frederick Lowe). [YellowS] (23) Sum 87, p. 29.
1895. GARCIA PEREZ, Agustín
"Entre Sombras de Plata." [Mairena] (9:24) 87, p. 114.
1896. GARDINIER, Suzanne
"Fishing Trip." [Agni] (24/25) 87, p. 159.
"Isaac." [MassR] (28:4) Wint 87, p. 738.
"To Mary, Who Is Married Now." [Agni] (24/25) 87, p. 158.
"Tonight" (Soweto, June 1986). [YaleR] (76:3) Spr 87, p. 414.
"Two Traveling Women and the Houdini Man." [Agni] (24/25) 87, p. 156-157.
1897. GARDNER, Dick
"Gears." [Pig] (14) 87, p. 88.
1898. GARDNER, Geoffrey
"Annual." [Hudson] (40:3) Aut 87, p. 450.
1899. GARDNER, Stephen
"Not about Trees." [IndR] (10:3) Spr 87, p. 23.
1900. GARFINKEL, Patricia
"Fat Kenneth." [Vis] (24) 87, p. 38.
1901. GARGANO, Elizabeth
"A Girl's Home Journal." [PraS] (61:3) Fall 87, p. 114-117.
"In Those Days." [Poem] (58) N 87, p. 6.
1902. GARLAND, Max
"Outline for a Baptist History of Highway 305." [SouthernPR] (27:2) Fall 87, p. 10.
1903. GARMON, John
"Aunt Wayne." [PassN] (8:2) Sum 87, p. 21.
"Creekbeds Are Dry Near Mobeetie" (for my Grandmother Burgdorf). [PassN] (8:1)
Wint 87, p. 18.
"Ebb, Ocean of Life, (The Flow Will Return)" (— Walt Whitman). [Interim] (6:2)
Fall 87, p. 19.
"Lake Champlain Confessional." [Interim] (6:2) Fall 87, p. 20.
"A Quality of Loss." [Interim] (6:2) Fall 87, p. 18.
1904. GARRETT, Caroline
"Some years ago." The Best of [BambooR] [(31-32)] 86, p. 30.
1905. GARRETT, Edward Cortez
"The Story." [GreensboroR] (42) Sum 87, p. 54.
1906. GARRETT, George
"York Harbor Morning." [TexasR] (7:3/4) 87, p. xiii-xiv.
1907. GARRISON, David
"My Father, Alone, Driving Home, Thinks of His Two Lost Children" (for Donald
and Carol Anne). [CumbPR] (7:1) Fall 87, p. 82-83.
"The Old Man Is Like Moses" (tr. of Vicente Aleixandre). [CrossCur] (6:4) 87, p.
25.
"We Must Keep Up Courage in These Brief Days." [CumbPR] (7:1) Fall 87, p. 84.

1908. GARRISON, Deborah Gottlieb
"What We Hear toward Morning." [NewYorker] (62:52) 16 F 87, p. 38.
1909. GARSON, Karl
"Choice as a Matter of Dream." [KanQ] (19:3) Sum 87, p. 3-6.
"October Reflection." [KanQ] (19:3) Sum 87, p. 311.
1910. GARTEN, Bill
"Claws." [LaurelR] (20:1/2) Sum 87, p. 51.
1911. GARTON, Victoria
"Wake for Our Dead Love." [Bogg] (58) 87, p. 39.
1912. GARVER, Dan
"An Evening Pastoral." [DenQ] (22:1) Sum 87, p. 18.
1913. GARZA, San Juanita
"After George Herbert." [NewAW] (2) Fall 87, p. 96.
"French Garden." [NewAW] (2) Fall 87, p. 95.
1914. GASH, Sondra
"Daughter in London." [US1] (20/21) Wint 86-87, p. 21.
1915. GASPAR, Nagy
"Old Wave" (tr. by Zsuzsanna Ozsvath and Martha Satz). [Os] (24) 87, p. 4.
"Rég' Hullám." [Os] (24) 87, p. 5.
1916. GASPARINI, Len
"Poem: Although it is cruel, you cannot but marvel." [Waves] (15:4) Spr 87, p. 57.
1917. GASTIGER, Joseph
"For Kimiko." [TriQ] (68) Wint 87, p. 97.
"For Whoever Drops By at The Mai Kai, The Derby or Pete's." [TriQ] (68) Wint 87,
    p. 94-96.
1918. GATES, Beatrix
"Family Tree." [Nimrod] (31:1) Fall-Wint 87, p. 80.
"Wild Blue." [Nimrod] (31:1) Fall-Wint 87, p. 79.
1919. GATES, Edward
"Five Ghazals." [Germ] (10:2) Spr 87, p. 29-33.
GATTUTA, Margo la
    See LaGATTUTA, Margo
1920. GAUTREAUX, Tim
"Of Signs and Signals." [GreensboroR] (39) Wint 85-86, p. 84-87.
"Reminder." [Poem] (58) N 87, p. 60-61.
1921. GAVER, Chasen
"The Beholder." [JamesWR] (4:3) Spr 87, p. 13.
1922. GAYLE, Elizabeth
"The Bog Poem." [GreensboroR] (42) Sum 87, p. 16-17.
"One Friday Afternoon in the Fall." [GreensboroR] (42) Sum 87, p. 19.
"That Spark of Life." [GreensboroR] (42) Sum 87, p. 18.
1923. GEADA, Rita
"Fluir de la Armonía." [Inti] (24/25) Otoño 86-Primavera 87, p. 260.
"Recreamos con los Rostros del Languaje." [Inti] (24/25) Otoño 86-Primavera 87, p.
    259.
"Vivir en los Asombros." [Inti] (24/25) Otoño 86-Primavera 87, p. 259-260.
1924. GEAREN, Barbara
"Buying Lady Lobsters." [BambooR] (33) Spr 87, p. 4-5.
"Collected Letters" (for NH). [HawaiiR] (21) Spr 87, p. 68-70.
1925. GEDDES, Gary
"The Dream Bed." [CapilR] (44) 87, p. 4-10.
"The Last Canto." [Verse] (4:1) Mr 87, p. 25-27.
1926. GEIGER, Nicole Alexandra
"Slowly." [YellowS] (24) Aut 87, p. 9.
1927. GELETA, Greg
"Advance to Go." [PaintedB] (31) 87, p. 50.
"Advice to a Lonely Heart on New Year's Eve." [PaintedB] (31) 87, p. 58.
"The Art of Hailing a Cab." [PaintedB] (31) 87, p. 47-48.
"The Death of Mussolini." [PaintedB] (31) 87, p. 55.
"Donna Lee." [PaintedB] (31) 87, p. 53-54.
"First Kiss." [PaintedB] (31) 87, p. 51.
"Four A.M. at the Mt. Joy Rest Stop." [PaintedB] (31) 87, p. 57.
"Geleta Gets a Second Chance at Adolescence" (for Paul Zimmer). [PaintedB] (31)
    87, p. 59.
"Introducing Mr. Homonym." [PaintedB] (31) 87, p. 49.
"Jamaica Farewell." [PaintedB] (31) 87, p. 52.

"The Man Who Lives Alone." [PaintedB] (31) 87, p. 61.
"Shooting from Half Court." [PaintedB] (31) 87, p. 56.
"Train Set." [PaintedB] (31) 87, p. 60.
1928. GELLAND, Carolyn
"The Sandals of My Ancestors." [CapeR] (22:2) Fall 87, p. 18.
"Smell." [DekalbLAJ] (20:1/4) 87, p. 37.
1929. GENEGA, Paul
"The Problem of Feet in Our Times." [Vis] (25) 87, p. 38.
"Professions." [Outbr] (18/19) Fall 86-Spr 88, p. 32.
1930. GENSLER, Kinereth
"The Last Parent." [FloridaR] (15:2) Fall-Wint 87, p. 91.
1931. GENT, Andrew
"After Visiting the Home of a Famous Poet." [PaintedB] (31) 87, p. 20.
"Poem: It's stupid to be happy in August." [PaintedB] (31) 87, p. 19.
1932. GENTLEMAN, Dorothy Corbett
"My Wedding Ring." [Waves] (14:4) Spr 86, p. 71.
1933. GEORGE, Alice Rose
"Cross Country." [Bomb] (18) Wint 87, p. 76.
"My Man." [Bomb] (18) Wint 87, p. 76.
"Observing Billy." [Bomb] (18) Wint 87, p. 76.
"On the Road." [Bomb] (18) Wint 87, p. 76.
1934. GEORGE, Anne
"The Grist Mill" (1986 Finalist, Eve of Saint Agnes Poetry Competition). [NegC]
(7:1/2) 87, p. 164.
1935. GEORGE, Beth
"Night Lights." [Waves] (15:1/2) Fall 86, p. 81.
1936. GERARDI, Mary-Ellen
"Deaf Mute at the Art Gallery." [Writer] (99:5) My 86, p. 17.
1937. GERBER, Dan
"The Last Bridge Home." [Caliban] (2) 87, p. 120.
"The Rain Beats Down." [Caliban] (2) 87, p. 120.
1938. GERGELY, Agnes
"Prayer Before Turning Off the Light" (tr. by Jascha Kessler, w. Maria Körösy).
[Nimrod] (31:1) Fall-Wint 87, p. 131.
"Shipwreck, from Outside" (tr. by Jascha Kessler, w. Maria Körösy). [Nimrod]
(31:1) Fall-Wint 87, p. 131.
1939. GERMAN, Greg
"House in the Middle of a Field." [KanQ] (19:1/2) Wint-Spr 87, p. 209.
"Seasoning." [NegC] (7:3/4) 87, p. 138.
"Sow 32 in Stall #9." [PoetL] (81:3) Fall 86, p. 181.
"Traveling With the River." [Wind] (17:61) 87, p. 16.
1940. GERNES, Sonia
"Beneath Annie's Gown" (Anna Storcy, Hartford, Michigan, 1823-1904). [NewL]
(54:1) Fall 87, p. 42-43.
"Little Sisters." [SouthernR] (23:4) O 87, p. 802-803.
"The Many Kinds of Doubt." [NewL] (54:1) Fall 87, p. 40-41.
"Possum." [HiramPoR] (42) Spr-Sum 87, p. 24-25.
"Waitomo: The River Under the Earth." [NewL] (54:1) Fall 87, p. 39-40.
"What If a Woman." [SouthernR] (23:4) O 87, p. 801.
1941. GERSHENSON, Bernard
"Inventions in the Public Domain." [FiveFR] (5) 87, p. 22-24.
1942. GERSTLER, Amy
"BZZZZZZZ." [NewAW] (2) Fall 87, p. 101.
"Marriage." [NewAW] (2) Fall 87, p. 99-100.
1943. GERTLER, Pesha
"The Right Thing." [Calyx] (11:1) Wint 87-88, p. 34-35.
"The Season of Bitter Root and Snake Venom." [Calyx] (10:2/3) Spr 87, p. 178.
1944. GERY, John
"For No Music." [Outbr] (18/19) Fall 86-Spr 88, p. 177.
"On the Tip of the Tongue." [Outbr] (18/19) Fall 86-Spr [Outbr] (18/19) Fall 86-Spr
88, p. 176.
"Oral Phenomenology." [Outbr] (18/19) Fall 86-Spr 88, p. 178.
"The Shape of Sadness." [CumbPR] (6:2) Spr 87, p. 10.
"Tears, Idle Tears." [Wind] (17:60) 87, p. 8.

1945. GETSI, Lucia Cordell
"Intensive Care" (Pablo Neruda Prize for Poetry, Second Prize). [Nimrod] (31:1)
Fall-Wint 87, p. 8-17.
"Swimming the Body's Water." [BelPoJ] (38:2) Wint 87-88, p. 1.
1946. GETTY, Sarah
"After a Quarrel: The Julliard String Quartet." [Shen] (37:1) 87, p. 58-59.
"The Oseberg Ship." [Shen] (37:1) 87, p. 59-61.
"Thanksgiving." [Shen] (37:4) 87, p. 63.
1947. GEWANTER, David
"Rock, Paper, Scissors." [NewEngR] (10:1) Aut 87, p. 28-32.
1948. GHIGNA, Charles
"Aries Sideshow." [LightY] '87, c86, p. 123.
"Poetry Pâté." [EngJ] (76:2) F 87, p. 81.
"Seven Little Existential Poems." [Pig] (14) 87, p. 31.
"Who Is this Poet." [Pig] (14) 87, p. 31.
1949. GHIMOSOULIS, Kostís
"Shadow Is the Absence of Light — The Moon Yes and Nothing Is Mutual" (tr. by
Yannis Goumas). [Verse] (4:2) Je 87, p. 60.
1950. GHOSE, Zulfikar
"Bells in Goliad." [Chelsea] (46) 87, p. 216.
"The Last Watermelon in Texas." [Chelsea] (46) 87, p. 214.
"Surprising Flowers." [Chelsea] (46) 87, p. 215.
1951. GIAMMARINO, Jaye
"A Time of Loneliness" (Japanese Sedoka). [Amelia] (4:1/2, issue 9) 87, p. 126.
1952. GIBB, Robert
"Anacreontic." [StoneC] (14:3/4) Spr-Sum 87, p. 44-45.
"Buying Raw Milk." [KanQ] (19:3) Sum 87, p. 195.
"Camp Calvary." [PaintedB] (30) 87, p. 33.
"The Dance." [PaintedB] (30) 87, p. 30.
"The Ecstasy of Maria Rubio." [Raccoon] (24/25) My 87, p. 17.
"Franklin Engine House No. 10." [WestB] (20) 87, p. 61-62.
"Journal of the First Birth" (for Matthew). [PraS] (61:4) Wint 87, p. 24-27.
"Letter to Russell Barron." [PaintedB] (30) 87, p. 31-32.
"Lock Haven: July 3, 1986." [WestB] (20) 87, p. 60-61.
"Newswanger's Roadside Stand and Greenhouses, Kutztown, PA." [KanQ] (19:3)
Sum 87, p. 194.
"Pan de Pueblo." [Raccoon] (24/25) My 87, p. 147-148.
"The Seed-Pod." [KanQ] (19:1/2) Wint-Spr 87, p. 98.
"Stacking Wood." [KanQ] (19:3) Sum 87, p. 193.
"To the First Bees of Spring." [StoneC] (14:3/4) Spr-Sum 87, p. 43.
"Watching for the Next Poem." [HampSPR] Wint 87, p. 12.
1953. GIBBON, Phil
"Highway Survivors." [MoodySI] (18/19) Fall 87, p. 45.
1954. GIBBS, Kathryn
"Walking" (For Sam Ragan). [Pembroke] (19) 87, p. 142.
1955. GIBBS, Robert
"Flyovers / Stopovers." [CanLit] (115) Wint 87, p. 102-104.
"Hearing Again from the Earth Earthy." [Germ] (11:1) Fall 87, p. 38.
"I see." [Germ] (11:1) Fall 87, p. 39.
"My Turn at the Ballet." [Germ] (11:1) Fall 87, p. 37.
"Watching the Watchers in the Reptile House." [CanLit] (115) Wint 87, p. 65.
1956. GIBSON, Becky Gould
"This Child." [CumbPR] (6:2) Spr 87, p. 15.
GIBSON, Elisabeth Grant
See GRANT-GIBSON, Elisabeth
1957. GIBSON, Grace
"At a London Museum" (to a Japanese friend, tr. of Hwang Tong-Gyu, w. John
Chay). [Pembroke] (19) 87, p. 21.
"The Exit" (tr. of Hwang Tong-Gyu, w. John Chay). [InterPR] (13:1) Spr 87, p.
60.
"For Two to Fly Together in the Sky" (tr. of Hwang Tong-Gyu, w. John Chay).
[Pembroke] (19) 87, p. 24.
"From an Alien Land 4" (tr. of Hwang Tong-Gyu, w. John Chay). [Pembroke] (19)
87, p. 22.
"Iowa Diary 1" (to Ma Chinggi, tr. of Hwang Tong-Gyu, w. John Chay).
[Pembroke] (19) 87, p. 22-23.

"A Joyful Letter" (tr. of Hwang Tong-Gyu, w. John Chay). [Pembroke] (19) 87, p. 25.
"The Last Solgo" (tr. of Hwang Tong-Gyu, w. John Chay). [Pembroke] (19) 87, p. 23-24.
"A Little Autumn Day" (tr. of Hwang Tong-Gyu, w. John Chay). [Pembroke] (19) 87, p. 24.
"Separate, But Standing Around Together" (tr. of Hwang Tong-Gyu, w. John Chay). [Pembroke] (19) 87, p. 22.
"Short Poem" (poems 4 & 5, tr. of Hwang Tong-Gyu, w. John Chay). [Pembroke] (19) 87, p. 25.
"A Small Poem #5" (tr. of Hwang Tong-Gyu, w. John Chay). [InterPR] (13:1) Spr 87, p. 60.
"Snowfall on the Harbor" (tr. of Hwang Tong-Gyu, w. John Chay). [Pembroke] (19) 87, p. 26.
"A Snowy Night" (tr. of Kim Do Sung, w. John Chay). [InterPR] (13:1) Spr 87, p. 62.
"Song" (tr. of Hwang Tong-Gyu, w. John Chay). [Pembroke] (19) 87, p. 26.
"Walking the Tightrope" (tr. of Hwang Tong-Gyu, w. John Chay). [Pembroke] (19) 87, p. 21.
"The Wind" (tr. of Pak Yul A, w. John Chay). [InterPR] (13:1) Spr 87, p. 63.
"Wind Burial" (poems 1-11, tr. of Hwang Tong-Gyu, w. John Chay). [Pembroke] (19) 87, p. 26-31.
"Winter Morning" (tr. of Lee Sung Hyung, w. John Chay). [InterPR] (13:1) Spr 87, p. 64.
"The Year Is Getting Late" (tr. of Kim Do Sung, w. John Chay). [InterPR] (13:1) Spr 87, p. 61.
1958. GIBSON, Margaret
"Doing Nothing." [PoetryNW] (28:2) Sum 87, p. 6-7.
"Long Walks in the Afternoon." [TexasR] (7:3/4) 87, p. 56.
"Out in the Open." [TexasR] (7:3/4) 87, p. 57-59.
"A Ripple of Deer, a Metamorphosis of Bear, a Metaphor of Mountains." [GeoR] (41:2) Sum 87, p. 380-381.
"Sensing the Enemy" (Bavaria, 1972). [MichQR] (26:1) Wint 87, p. 32-33.
1959. GIBSON, Stephen
"Andy Warhol: *Suicide*, 1963." [CharR] (13:1) Spr 87, p. 93.
"Indians." [Colum] (12) 87, p. 124.
"Nature." [Colum] (12) 87, p. 123.
1960. GIL, Lourdes
"A las Memorias del Marques de Bradomin." [LindLM] (6:1) Ja-Mr 87, p. 13.
"Los Palisades." [LindLM] (6:1) Ja-Mr 87, p. 13.
"El Sucesor de Drake." [LindLM] (6:1) Ja-Mr 87, p. 13.
1961. GILBERT, Celia
"The Gardener." [TexasR] (7:3/4) 87, p. 61.
"Narcissi in Winter." [TexasR] (7:3/4) 87, p. 62.
"Presbyopia." [MichQR] (26:1) Wint 87, p. 242-243.
"She's Painted a Blue Fish, a Red Apple." [Poetry] (151:1/2) O-N 87, p. 57-58.
"The Silence." [TexasR] (7:3/4) 87, p. 60.
"Wild Asters" (In memory of Beatrice Hawley). [BostonR] (12:2) Ap 87, p. 20.
1962. GILBERT, Sandra M.
"2085." [MissouriR] (10:2) 87, p. 170-171.
"After Thanksgiving." [Poetry] (149:4) Ja 87, p. 204.
"Against Poetry." [Poetry] (151:1/2) O-N 87, p. 59.
"Gold Tooth." [Poetry] (149:4) Ja 87, p. 205.
"Grandpa." [MissouriR] (10:2) 87, p. 172-173.
"The Outsider and Other Poems" (6 poems). [OntR] (26) Spr-Sum 87, p. 15-26.
1963. GILBERT-LECOMTE, Roger
"Crowned Head" (tr. by David Rattray). [LitR] (30:3) Spr 87, p. 472.
"High" (tr. by David Rattray). [LitR] (30:3) Spr 87, p. 472.
"Holy Childhood or Concealment of Birth" (tr. by David Rattray). [LitR] (30:3) Spr 87, p. 473.
"Rebirth Prebirth" (tr. by David Rattray). [LitR] (30:3) Spr 87, p. 474.
1964. GILCHRIST, Ellen
"November." [HeliconN] (17/18) Spr 87, p. 98.
"Running." [HeliconN] (17/18) Spr 87, p. 99.
1965. GILDNER, Gary
"Cleaning the Oven." [Field] (37) Fall 87, p. 92-93.

GILL, Alicia Fernández
    See FERNANDEZ GILL, Alicia
1966. GILL, John
    "Atlantic City, N.J." [HangL] (50/51) 87, p. 73.
    "Encounter with Mayakovsky." [HangL] (50/51) 87, p. 70.
    "Haibun 2/23/85." [HangL] (50/51) 87, p. 72.
    "Nostalgia." [HangL] (50/51) 87, p. 71.
1967. GILLAN, Maria
    "August Serenade." [CrossCur] (7:2) 87, p. 128-129.
    "Dark on Dark." [NegC] (7:3/4) 87, p. 133.
    "Even Then." [CrossCur] (7:2) 87, p. 127.
    "The Faces of Love." [CrossCur] (7:2) 87, p. 130.
    "Foreboding" (To Jennifer, Freshman Year, Georgetown). [Lips] (13) 87, p. 20-21.
    "Poem to My Daughter at 18." [Lips] (13) 87, p. 22-23.
    "The Young Men in Black Leather Jackets." [Lips] (13) 87, p. 19.
1968. GILLESPIE, Amber Coss
    "And I'm here going crazy." [Footwork] 87, p. 36.
    "Eating Cheese." [Footwork] 87, p. 36.
    "Good Poems." [Footwork] 87, p. 36.
    "Stink." [Footwork] 87, p. 36.
1969. GILLESPIE, John
    "The Dangers of Bowling." [Pig] (14) 87, p. 88.
1970. GILLESPIE, Mary
    "Two Poems" (1. "April," 2. "Summer"). [CrossCur] (6:5) 87, p. 54-55.
1971. GILLETT, Michelle
    "Balance." [PassN] (8:1) Wint 87, p. 8.
    "Inside the Cloud" (On the anniversary of the bombing of Hiroshima). [PassN] (8:1)
        Wint 87, p. 8.
1972. GILLIAMS, Maurice
    "Elegy" (tr. by André Lefevere). [Paint] (14:28) Aut 87, p. 36.
    "Spring Poem" (tr. by André Lefevere). [Paint] (14:28) Aut 87, p. 38.
    "Tristitia Ante" (tr. by André Lefevere). [Paint] (14:28) Aut 87, p. 37.
1973. GILLIES, John
    "The Illusion Principle." [AntigR] (69/70) 87, p. 128-129.
1974. GILLILAND, Mary
    "The Bargain." [GreenfR] (14:3/4) Sum-Fall 87, p. 151.
    "Nice Girl." [GreenfR] (14:3/4) Sum-Fall 87, p. 152.
1975. GILMORE, Patricia
    "For My GrandFather: A Hunter Killed by Lightning." [SouthernPR] (27:2) Fall 87,
        p. 18.
    "Grass Snake's Serenade." [Wind] (17:59) 87, p. 17-18.
GINEBRA, Arminda Valdés
    See VALDÉS GINEBRA, Arminda
1977. GINGRICH-PHILBROOK, Craig
    "The Tulip-tree" (For Michael Odom). [CutB] (27/28) 87, p. 54-56.
1978. GINS, Madeline
    "Essay on Multi-Dimensional Architecture" (Excerpt). [Bound] (14:1/2) Fall 85-Wint
        86 [c87], p. 95-98.
1979. GINSBERG, Allen
    "Ayers Rock Uluru Song." [RiverS] (24) 87, p. 27.
    "The Question" (tr. of Istvan Eorsi). [Rampike] (5:3) 87, p. 68.
    "Velocity of Money." [Harp] (274:1640) Ja 87, p. 38.
1980. GIOIA, Dana
    "The Gods of Winter." [Poetry] (151:3) D 87, p. 285.
    "Horoscopes: A Pantoum." [Sequoia] (31:1) Centennial issue 87, p. 77.
    "The Motets" (Selections: II-IV, IX, XI, XIV, XX, tr. of Eugenio Montale).
        [Boulevard] (2:1/2) Spr 87, p. 17-20.
    "Night Watch" (For my uncle, Theodore Ortiz, November, 1955). [Poetry] (151:1/2)
        O-N 87, p. 60-61.
    "Speaking of Love." [Poetry] (151:3) D 87, p. 286.
    "Two Small Songs." [Verse] (4:1) Mr 87, p. 55.
GIOVANNI, Norman Thomas di
    See Di GIOVANNI, Norman Thomas
1981. GIROUX, Joye S.
    "Cosmic Fantasy." [KanQ] (19:3) Sum 87, p. 223.
    "Death Is a White Horse." [KanQ] (19:3) Sum 87, p. 222.

1982. GITZEN, Julian
    "The Eye of the Beholder." [NegC] (7:3/4) 87, p. 108.
1983. GIZZI, Michael
    "Continental Harmony" (Selections: 1, 3, 5, 7). [Temblor] (5) 87, p. 52-56.
1984. GLADDING, Jody
    "Down Pour." [Pembroke] (19) 87, p. 153.
    "Mud Song." [Pembroke] (19) 87, p. 153.
1985. GLADING, Jan
    "Banties." [Kaleid] (15) Sum-Fall 87, p. 62.
    "New Lumbar Spine X-Ray." [Kaleid] (14) Wint-Spr 87, p. 68.
    "Three Bales of Hay." [Kaleid] (14) Wint-Spr 87, p. 68.
1986. GLANCY, Diane
    "After the Loss." [PassN] (8:2) Sum 87, p. 9.
    "Dance Hall Indian." [Farm] (4:2) Spr-Sum 87, p. 56.
    "Demosthenes." [Farm] (4:2) Spr-Sum 87, p. 55.
    "Great Indian Father in the Subway." [Calyx] (10:2/3) Spr 87, p. 68.
    "July 14." [Sulfur] (18) Wint 87, p. 72.
    "Mother GOodbye." [Sulfur] (18) Wint 87, p. 72-73.
    "Not Knowing How." [Farm] (4:2) Spr-Sum 87, p. 54.
    "The Old Trip." [PoetC] (19:1) Fall 87, p. 7.
    "Palace of the Plains." [ColR] (NS 14:2) Fall-Wint 87, p. 13.
    "Peru, Kansas." [Sulfur] (18) Wint 87, p. 70-71.
    "Scarecrow." [PikeF] (8) Fall 87, p. 31.
    "A Walk." [KanQ] (19:1/2) Wint-Spr 87, p. 76-77.
    "You Remember." [ColR] (NS 14:2) Fall-Wint 87, p. 14.
1987. GLANG, Gabrielle
    "Wanderlust." [Vis] (24) 87, p. 28.
1988. GLASER, Elton
    "Chromatic Maladies." [NoDaQ] (55:3) Sum 87, p. 79-81.
    "Clearing the Ground." [SouthernPR] (27:1) Spr 87, p. 17.
    "Dancing Lessons." [Poetry] (149:5) F 87, p. 259.
    "Ditch Lilies." [NoDaQ] (55:1) Wint 87, p. 72-73.
    "Divorce." [Lips] (13) 87, p. 4.
    "Insomniacs at the Feet of Science." [PoetryNW] (28:3) Aut 87, p. 20.
    "The Lesson." [Lips] (13) 87, p. 6-7.
    "Night and I'm the Vagrant" (tr. of Joyce Mansour, w. Jancie Fritsch). [ColR] (NS
        14:1) Spr-Sum 87, p. 32.
    "Prologue to Insomnia." [Gambit] (20) 86, p. 109-110.
    "Report from Downriver." [Lips] (13) 87, p. 5.
    "A Riff for Isadora." [PoetryNW] (28:1) Spr 87, p. 26-27.
    "Underfoot." [NoDaQ] (55:3) Sum 87, p. 78.
    "Winter Inset." [Poetry] (149:5) F 87, p. 260-261.
1989. GLASS, Malcolm
    "Lifting the Veil." [Poem] (58) N 87, p. 53.
    "Little Sonnet for Farewell." [ManhatPR] (9) Sum 87, p. 21.
    "The Lost and Found Department." [ManhatPR] (9) Sum 87, p. 20.
    "Superstitions." [Poetry] (150:2) My 87, p. 90.
    "Winter Park Drive-In Theater." [HighP] (2:1) Spr 87, p. 48-49.
1990. GLASS, William
    "The Comedian As the Letters 'B' and 'G'." [Boulevard] (2:3) Fall 87, p. 126-127.
    "Frailty." [Boulevard] (2:3) Fall 87, p. 127.
1991. GLASSER, Carole
    "All That's Left." [Footwork] 87, p. 24.
    "Eddie." [Footwork] 87, p. 24.
    "Some Days We Are Held." [Footwork] 87, p. 24.
    "Zelda" (for Zelda Fitzgerald). [Footwork] 87, p. 24.
1992. GLATSHTEYN, Yankev (*See also* GLATSTEIN, Jacob)
    "Moyshe-Leyb's Voice" (tr. by Kathryn Hellerstein). [PartR] (54:1) Wint 87, p.
        126-128.
1993. GLATSTEIN, Jacob (*See also* GLATSHTEYN, Yankev)
    "At the Forest Entrance" (tr. by Doris Vidaver). [AnotherCM] (17) 87, p. 39.
    "Morning Subway" (from "Holocaust Poems," tr. by Doris Vidaver). [PraS] (61:3)
        Fall 87, p. 81.
    "Profanation" (tr. by Doris Vidaver). [AnotherCM] (17) 87, p. 40.
    "Twilight of the World" (from "Holocaust Poems," tr. by Doris Vidaver). [PraS]
        (61:3) Fall 87, p. 80.

"The Unsteady House Swims Like an Ark" (from "Holocaust Poems," tr. by Doris
Vidaver). [PraS] (61:3) Fall 87, p. 82-83.
1994. GLAZE, Andrew
"Cat's Cradle." [TriQ] (68) Wint 87, p. 98.
1995. GLAZER, Jane
"All Wool But Rarely a Yard Wide." [BellArk] (3:5) S-O 87, p. 19.
"Magnetic Field." [BellArk] (3:6) N-D 87, p. 6.
"Out of the Same Pajamas" (for my brother, Jess). [BellArk] (3:3) My-Je 87, p. 7.
"Taking Red Emperors to Bed." [BellArk] (3:2) Mr-Ap 87, p. 1.
"To Other Worlds" (For Sören Matsen 1888-1983). [BellArk] (3:3) My-Je 87, p. 6.
1996. GLAZER, Michele
"Blue Paint Causes Stains in Laboratory Rats." [ColEng] (49:3) Mr 87, p. 289.
"Jungle." [DenQ] (22:2) Fall 87, p. 72-73.
"Pueblo." [ColEng] (49:3) Mr 87, p. 288.
1997. GLAZIER, Loss
"Tuesday Mornings in San Leandro." [SlipS] (7) 87, p. 89.
1998. GLAZNER, Greg
"Red Tide, a Beach of Salvage." [Poetry] (150:3) Je 87, p. 143.
1999. GLEASON, James
"Charlie Susel." [Wind] (17:61) 87, p. 15.
"The Iris Bed." [CrossCur] (6:4) 87, p. 121.
2000. GLEASON, Marian
"Better Refrain." [LightY] '87, c86, p. 133.
2001. GLEASON, Paul
"A Song for Jack." [MoodySI] (18/19) Fall 87, p. 37.
2002. GLEN, Emilie
"City Green." [Wind] (17:61) 87, p. 55.
"Once." [Wind] (17:61) 87, p. 55.
"Ping Ping Ping." [Pembroke] (19) 87, p. 185.
2003. GLENN, Helen Trubek
"Moonflowers / Evening Glory" (for Helene Swarts). [PoetL] (82:3) Fall 87, p. 137.
"Rites." [PoetL] (82:3) Fall 87, p. 136.
2004. GLICKFELD, Carole L.
"Interjection" (for G. Erratum: "succession" in line 2 should read "succussion").
[Phoenix] (7:1) 87, p. 31.
2005. GLICKMAN, Susan
"Country Music." [MalR] (81) D 87, p. 16-17.
"Families." [MalR] (81) D 87, p. 18-19.
"Heavy Weather." [MalR] (81) D 87, p. 20-21.
"Metafiction I: Bon Voyage." [Event] (16:1) Mr 87, p. 34.
"Metafiction II: A Familiar Story." [Event] (16:1) Mr 87, p. 35.
"Poem About Your Laugh." [MalR] (81) D 87, p. 22.
"Stone Poem." [CanLit] (113/114) Sum-Fall 87, p. 107-108.
"Who's There?" [MalR] (81) D 87, p. 15.
2006. GLICKSTEIN, Gloria
"A Small Literary Fame." [Boulevard] (2:3) Fall 87, p. 122-123.
2007. GLOEGGLER, Tony
"When Phil Rizzuto." [Bogg] (58) 87, p. 41.
2008. GLOSSER, John L.
"To S. K." [ChrC] (104:3) 28 Ja 87, p. 84.
2009. GLUCK, Louise
"Marathon" (Section 8. "Song of Invisible Boundaries). [AmerPoR] (16:5) S-O 87,
p. 33.
"Portrait." [KenR] (NS 9:3) Sum 87, p. 135.
2010. GOCKER, Paula
"Hiroshima." [FiveFR] (5) 87, p. 7-8.
"Semantics." [PennR] (3:2) Fall-Wint 87, p. 54.
2011. GOEDICKE, Patricia
"After Lovemaking." [MassR] (28:4) Wint 87, p. 701-703.
"Along the Blackfoot." [MemphisSR] (7:2) Spr 87, p. 8-9.
"Biting the Apple." [PoetL] (82:4) Wint 87-88, p. 204.
"The Black Train." [MemphisSR] (7:2) Spr 87, p. 7.
"Black Walnut" (For Sylvanus Daniel Cook). [HampSPR] Wint 87, p. 42-44.
"Cathay" (for Margaret Fox Schmidt). [PraS] (61:4) Wint 87, p. 76-77.
"Charmian & Co." [PraS] (61:4) Wint 87, p. 75-76.
"December of the Gurburs." [Caliban] (3) 87, p. 57-58.

"The Discomfort." [CharR] (13:2) Fall 87, p. 60.
"The Door." [MemphisSR] (7:2) Spr 87, p. 10.
"Left Out." [CharR] (13:2) Fall 87, p. 61-62.
"Now, This Morning, Beaming." [PraS] (61:4) Wint 87, p. 73-74.
"So with Death." [StoneC] (15:1/2) Fall-Wint 87-88, p. 14-15.
"Some Nights of the Mind." [BlackWR] (13:2) Spr 87, p. 93-94.
"Tell Me Another." [PraS] (61:4) Wint 87, p. 71-72.
"Two Winds." [HampSPR] Wint 87, p. 41-42.
"What Was That." [PraS] (61:4) Wint 87, p. 68-70.
"Without Looking." [PoetL] (82:4) Wint 87-88, p. 205-206.
2012. GOINGS, Margaret
      "Here and There." [Bogg] (58) 87, p. 30.
2013. GOLD, Lloyd
      "Rainwalk." [Wind] (17:61) 87, p. 17.
2014. GOLDBARTH, Albert
      "Amaze." [PoetL] (81:3) Fall 86, p. 187-188.
      "April 15." [OhioR] (38) 87, p. 101-102.
      "Assembly." [Poetry] (149:5) F 87, p. 258.
      "At the Heart." [Poetry] (149:5) F 87, p. 257.
      "Donald Duck in Danish." [NewEngR] (9:4) Sum 87, p. 360-366.
      "Dying Away from You." [IndR] (11:1) Wint 87, p. 74-78.
      "A Hum." [Poetry] (149:5) F 87, p. 258.
      "Old Photo." [PoetL] (82:4) Wint 87-88, p. 214.
      "Parnassus." [Poetry] (149:5) F 87, p. 257.
      "Singsong, Whatever It Means." [NowestR] (25:3) 87, p. 316-317.
      "The Snow Owl." [PennR] (3:1) Spr-Sum 87, p. 42.
      "A Toast." [PoetL] (82:4) Wint 87-88, p. 214.
      "The Way the Novel Functions." [Poetry] (151:1/2) O-N 87, p. 62.
      "Why Saints Have to Be Dead." [PraS] (61:1) Spr 87, p. 60-64.
      "The World Trade Center." [OntR] (26) Spr-Sum 87, p. 35-37.
      "Zoran Perisic's." [Crazy] (33) Wint 87, p. 54-56.
2015. GOLDBECK, Janne
      "Cinderella." [WeberS] (4:2) Fall 87, p. 15-16.
      "The Frontier Languages." [CentR] (31:3) Sum 87, p. 289-290.
      "Notes of a Woman, Crossing to Oregon." [WeberS] (4:2) Fall 87, p. 17-19.
2016. GOLDBERG, Barbara
      "Night at the Opera." [PassN] (8:2) Sum 87, p. 13.
      "Two Women." [LightY] '87, c86, p. 148-149.
2017. GOLDBERG, Beckian Fritz
      "L'Age Mûr" (Camille Claudel, 1864-1942). [AmerPoR] (16:4) Jl-Ag 87, p. 5.
      "Fable: The Woman and the Iris." [PoetryNW] (28:2) Sum 87, p. 35-36.
      "Geraniums." [PoetryNW] (28:2) Sum 87, p. 38.
      "Slow Dancing." [PoetryNW] (28:2) Sum 87, p. 37.
      "Walking in the Solstice." [QW] (25) Spr 87, p. 127.
2018. GOLDBERG, Bonni
      "Limited Vision." [PoetryNW] (28:1) Spr 87, p. 33-34.
2019. GOLDBERG, Natalie
      "Coming Together." [Calyx] (10:2/3) Spr 87, p. 154-155.
      "Two Iowa Farmers." [Calyx] (10:2/3) Spr 87, p. 152-153.
2020. GOLDEN, Renny
      "Guatemalan Exodus: Los Naturales." [Calyx] (10:2/3) Spr 87, p. 41-43.
2021. GOLDENHAR, Edith
      "Haibun." [YellowS] (23) Sum 87, p. 40.
2022. GOLDENSOHN, Barry
      "Great Horned Owl." [Ploughs] (13:1) 87, p. 54.
      "Her Husband Speaks After Her Death." [Poetry] (150:4) Jl 87, p. 199.
      "In Flight." [Salm] (72) Fall 86, p. 179.
      "Last Act: Don Giovanni." [Salm] (74/75) Spr-Sum 87, p. 44-45.
      "Margaret Roper" (after Holbein's drawing). [Salm] (72) Fall 86, p. 178-179.
      "The Miracle, with Tour-Guide and Tourists." [Salm] (74/75) Spr-Sum 87, p. 45.
      "The Mirror Stage." [Salm] (74/75) Spr-Sum 87, p. 46.
      "Tarzan & Co." [Salm] (74/75) Spr-Sum 87, p. 47-48.
      "Witness." [Poetry] (150:4) Jl 87, p. 198.
      "You Are Not Yet Asleep." [Ploughs] (13:1) 87, p. 55.
2023. GOLDENSOHN, Lorrie
      "Bald Eagle with a Six Foot Wingspan." [Raccoon] (24/25) My 87, p. 308.

2024. GOLDMAN, Judy
"At a Table across from a Child." [CumbPR] (7:1) Fall 87, p. 8.
"Bite-Size Pieces." [CarolQ] (39:3) Spr 87, p. 80-81.
"Handling the Serpents." [Pembroke] (19) 87, p. 188.
"Laying on of Hands." [TexasR] (8:1/2) Spr-Sum 87, p. 90-91.
"Medicine Women Doing What We Have to Do." [GreensboroR] (40) Sum 86, p. 40.
"Suicide." [SouthernPR] (27:1) Spr 87, p. 53.
"This Year Is a Test and I Am Making a 'C'." [CumbPR] (7:1) Fall 87, p. 9.
2025. GOLDSBY, Marcie
"Precisely." [AmerPoR] (16:5) S-O 87, p. 8.
"Reading an Analysis of Georg Trakl." [AmerPoR] (16:5) S-O 87, p. 8.
2026. GOLDSTEIN, Laurence
"Death Charm, Found in a River." [Boulevard] (2:3) Fall 87, p. 171.
2027. GOLDSTEIN, Marion
"Adoption." [WindO] (49) Fall 87, p. 17-18.
2028. GÖNENÇ, Turgay
"Unexpected Sights" (tr. by Talat Sait Halman). [Trans] (19) Fall 87, p. 105.
2029. GONET, Jill
"Dream of My Birth." [Calyx] (11:1) Wint 87-88, p. 31.
"Screen Memory." [PoetryNW] (28:4) Wint 87-88, p. 15-16.
"Sealing." [Calyx] (11:1) Wint 87-88, p. 32.
2030. GONZALEZ, Angel
"The Conformist" (tr. by Steven Ford Brown and Pedro Gutierrez Revuelta). [CrossCur] (7:3) 87, p. 33.
"Do You Know That Paper Can?" (tr. by Steven Ford Brown and Pedro Gutierrez Revuelta). [CrossCur] (7:3) 87, p. 32.
GONZALEZ, David Lago
See LAGO GONZALEZ, David
2031. GONZALEZ, Otto-Raúl
"Ten New Colors" (tr. by John Oliver Simon). [AmerPoR] (16:1) Ja-F 87, p. 3-6.
2032. GONZALEZ, Ray
"After Reading the Death Poems." [Americas] (15:1) Spr 87, p. 44.
"Letter to Thomas McGrath." [Americas] (15:1) Spr 87, p. 47.
"One Day." [Americas] (15:1) Spr 87, p. 43.
"Saving the Candles." [HighP] (2:1) Spr 87, p. 6-7.
"A Simple Summer Rain." [Americas] (15:1) Spr 87, p. 42.
"Two Wolf Poems." [Americas] (15:1) Spr 87, p. 45-46.
"Walk" (for John Brandi). [Americas] (15:1) Spr 87, p. 41.
GONZALEZ, Salvador Lopez
See LOPEZ GONZALEZ, Salvador
2033. GONZALEZ DE LEON, Ulalume
"The Dancing Key" (tr. by Sara Nelson). [AmerPoR] (16:2) Mr-Ap 87, p. 18.
"Forgotten Shared Jar" (tr. by Sara Nelson). [AmerPoR] (16:2) Mr-Ap 87, p. 18.
"Imaginary Finale 1" (tr. by Sara Nelson). [AmerPoR] (16:2) Mr-Ap 87, p. 18.
"Sign" (tr. by Sara Nelson). [AmerPoR] (16:2) Mr-Ap 87, p. 19.
"Where the Jar, Remembered Only in Dreams, Peers for an Instant . . ." (tr. by Sara Nelson). [AmerPoR] (16:2) Mr-Ap 87, p. 19.
2034. GONZALEZ GUERRERO, Antonio
"Bajo la Agria Luz de los Cerezos" (III, V, VIII). [Mairena] (9:24) 87, p. 75-76.
2035. GOODENOUGH, J. B.
"Adage." [Blueline] (7:2/3 [i.e. 8:2/3?]) 87, p. 66.
"Bone and Beetle." [SpoonRQ] (12:2) Spr 87, p. 29.
"Come Thaw." [SpoonRQ] (12:2) Spr 87, p. 28.
"Drought." [Wind] (17:60) 87, p. 16.
"Dwarf." [PassN] (8:1) Wint 87, p. 14.
"Fear for the Children." [Wind] (17:60) 87, p. 16.
"Fields in Winter." [TexasR] (7:3/4) 87, p. 63.
"Fisherman." [SouthernPR] (27:2) Fall 87, p. 17.
"Gourds." [Northeast] (Ser. 4:5) Sum 87, p. 45.
"Into Winter." [Pembroke] (19) 87, p. 154.
"The Last One." [CentR] (31:3) Sum 87, p. 282.
"Living on Old Land." [TexasR] (7:3/4) 87, p. 65.
"Missing." [Pembroke] (19) 87, p. 153.
"Proximities." [ThRiPo] (29/30) 87, p. 26.
"The Road to the Shore." [CrabCR] (4:2) Spr 87, p. 18.

"She Whom He Took to Wife." [StoneC] (15:1/2) Fall-Wint 87-88, p. 46.
"Sheep on the Town Road." [TexasR] (7:3/4) 87, p. 64.
"Trumpet Vine" (Newburyport). [SouthernPR] (27:2) Fall 87, p. 16.
"Under Water." [NewRena] (7:1, #21) Fall 87, p. 135.
"Visitation." [Blueline] (7:2/3 [i.e. 8:2/3?]) 87, p. 67.
2036. GOODING, C.
"Memory's Trace." [US1] (20/21) Wint 86-87, p. 29.
2037. GOODMAN, Lizbeth L.
"Root-Bound." [CrossCur] (7:2) 87, p. 74.
2038. GOODMAN, Melinda
"The Line." [SinW] (31) 87, p. 87-89.
2039. GOODMAN, Miriam
"Climbing Mt. Israel." [TexasR] (7:3/4) 87, p. 66.
2040. GOODMAN, Ryah Tumarkin
"Ancestors." [InterPR] (13:1) Spr 87, p. 103.
"Choice." [CrossCur] (6:4) 87, p. 12.
"Performance." [Vis] (23) 87, p. 24.
"Portrait." [InterPR] (13:1) Spr 87, p. 102.
"Reply to a Poet." [LitR] (31:1) Fall 87, p. 88.
"Reply to a Poet." [NegC] (7:3/4) 87, p. 87.
"Sound." [InterPR] (13:1) Spr 87, p. 103.
"Today." [CrossCur] (6:4) 87, p. 13.
"Trees." [Amelia] (4:3, issue 10) 87, p. 14.
2041. GOODWIN, Douglas
"Breath." [Bogg] (57) 87, p. 53.
2042. GOODWIN, June
"Marriage and Other Sidereal Relations." [PoetL] (82:4) Wint 87-88, p. 210-212.
"Woman of South Africa." [MinnR] (NS 29) Fall 87, p. 21-22.
2043. GOODWIN, Leslie
"Buzz Words." [Writer] (99:5) My 86, p. 16.
2044. GOON, Nirmalendoo
"The Cuckoo of the Concrete" (tr. by Rabiul Hasan). [InterPR] (13:2) Fall 87, p. 44.
"The Recapture" (tr. by Rabiul Hasan). [InterPR] (13:2) Fall 87, p. 44.
2045. GORCZYNSKI, Renata
"The Blackened River" (tr. of Adam Zagajewski, w. C. K. Williams). [ParisR] (29:105) Wint 87, p. 46.
"Codeword" (tr. of Adam Zagajewski, w. C. K. Williams). [ParisR] (29:105) Wint 87, p. 50.
"The Creation" (tr. of Adam Zagajewski, w. Robert Hass). [Antaeus] (58) Spr 87, p. 91-92.
"Cruel" (for Joseph Czapski, tr. of Adam Zagajewski, w. C. K. Williams). [ParisR] (29:105) Wint 87, p. 47-48.
"A Fence. Chestnut Trees" (tr. of Adam Zagajewski, w. C. K. Williams). [ParisR] (29:105) Wint 87, p. 49.
"The Lullaby" (tr. of Adam Zagajewski, w. Robert Hass). [Antaeus] (58) Spr 87, p. 93-94.
"Russia Comes Into Poland" (for Joseph Brodsky, tr. of Adam Zagajewski, w. C. K. Williams). [ParisR] (29:105) Wint 87, p. 52-53.
"A Warm, Small Rain" (tr. of Adam Zagajewski, w. C. K. Williams). [ParisR] (29:105) Wint 87, p. 51.
"Wind at Night" (tr. of Adam Zagajewski, w. Robert Hass). [Antaeus] (58) Spr 87, p. 92.
2046. GORDETT, Marea
"The Clean White Sleep of Animals." [ColEng] (49:5) S 87, p. 534.
"First Love." [ColEng] (49:5) S 87, p. 533.
"Self Portrait with Imaginary Child." [ColEng] (49:5) S 87, p. 535.
"To My Old Lover, After Many Years." [ColEng] (49:5) S 87, p. 536.
2047. GORDON, Don
"80." [NoDaQ] (55:1) Wint 87, p. 75.
"Childhood." [NoDaQ] (55:1) Wint 87, p. 74.
2048. GORDON, Kirpal
"Flooding Shadows." [Raccoon] (24/25) My 87, p. 44-45.
"Letter in Lady Day Spring Tones to Those Who Can't Make Bail Awaiting Trail in the Brooklyn House of Detention." [CentralP] (11) Spr 87, p. 45-48.
"Under the Gun Tower." [Witness] (1:3) Fall 87, p. 123.

2049. GORDON, Rebecca
"La Revolución Es un Chavala de Cino Años." [Calyx] (10:2/3) Spr 87, p. 181-182.
"Sonnet on a New Bed." [Calyx] (10:2/3) Spr 87, p. 151.
2050. GORDON, Sarah
"Spirituality Today" (for Chris). [Confr] (35/36) Spr-Fall 87, p. 131-132.
2051. GORHAM, Peter
"Desert Rain" (Mt. Hopkins, Arizona, 1984). [HawaiiR] (19) Spr 86, c87, p. 37.
2052. GORMAN, Damian
"The Somme." [Pembroke] (19) 87, p. 95.
2053. GORMAN, LeRoy
"Cr fl ash." [CrossC] (9:3/4) 87, p. 2.
"Haiku: Grey sky nearing." [CrossC] (9:2) 87, p. 23.
2054. GORST, Norma
"Turning Point: Ki'i Pond." [HawaiiR] (22) Fall 87, p. 51.
"'Ulili" (for Bruce). [HawaiiR] (22) Fall 87, p. 50.
2055. GOSSETT, Hattie
"On the Question of Fans / The Slave Quarters Are Never Air Conditioned." [Spirit]
(8:2) 87, p. 52-54.
2056. GOTO, T. M.
"Affinity with Season" (for Dean). [HawaiiR] (22) Fall 87, p. 70.
"Five Billion Animals Capable of Morality." [BambooR] (36) Fall 87, p. 42.
"Incision." [HawaiiR] (19) Spr 86, c87, p. 68-69.
2057. GOTT, George
"Dubedat." [WindO] (49) Fall 87, p. 50.
"Hotel Fabian." [WindO] (49) Fall 87, p. 50.
"Snake Island." [MidwQ] (28:2) Wint 87, p. 215.
2058. GOTTLIEB, Michael
"Wake Up and Smell the Coffee" (Selections: 1-12). [Bound] (14:1/2) Fall 85-Wint
86 [c87], p. 99-101.
2059. GOTTSCHALK, Keith
"Emergency Poems" (Two Excerpts: "First Night," "War Memorial"). [TriQ] (69)
Spr-Sum 87, p. 179.
2060. GOUMAS, Yannis
"Principles." [Waves] (14:4) Spr 86, p. 77.
"Recognition" (tr. of Erríkos Beliés). [Verse] (4:2) Je 87, p. 61.
"Shadow Is the Absence of Light — The Moon Yes and Nothing Is Mutual" (tr. of
Kostís Ghimosoúlis). [Verse] (4:2) Je 87, p. 60.
2061. GOURLAY, Elizabeth
"The Discipline." [Event] (16:2) Sum 87, p. 106.
2062. GRABILL, James
"4 A.M." [GreenfR] (14:3/4) Sum-Fall 87, p. 141.
"Ars Poetica." [Spirit] (8:2) 87, p. 107-108.
"Forest." [Germ] (10:2) Spr 87, p. 47.
"Fuel." [GreenfR] (14:3/4) Sum-Fall 87, p. 137-138.
"In November." [Germ] (10:2) Spr 87, p. 44.
"January 15th." [HighP] (2:3) Wint 87, p. 250-252.
"Late in the Afternoon These Questions Appear." [Germ] (10:2) Spr 87, p. 45.
"Lens." [GreenfR] (14:3/4) Sum-Fall 87, p. 142.
"The Next Light." [HighP] (2:3) Wint 87, p. 249.
"Or." [Germ] (10:2) Spr 87, p. 46.
"Through the Door." [GreenfR] (14:3/4) Sum-Fall 87, p. 140.
"Under Construction." [GreenfR] (14:3/4) Sum-Fall 87, p. 139.
2063. GRACE, George
"Mississippi Overflow." [MoodySI] (18/19) Fall 87, p. 19.
2064. GRADY, Paul
"(Trashin)the Place w/Thoz Eyes." [JamesWR] (4:4) Sum 87, p. 4.
2065. GRAFF, Herman
"The Bloom We Can Not See." [Lactuca] (8) N 87, p. 2-3.
"The Clock." [Lactuca] (8) N 87, p. 1.
"The Stranger." [Lactuca] (8) N 87, p. 4.
2066. GRAFTON, Grace
"To My Love." [BellArk] (3:6) N-D 87, p. 5.
2067. GRAHAM, David (David M.)
"An Arsenal of Deer" (1986 Honorable Mention, Eve of Saint Agnes Poetry
Competition). [NegC] (7:1/2) 87, p. 143-145.

"Aunt Dwindle and Uncle Nothing" (after James Tate's "The Malingerer").
[NewEngR] (9:3) Spr 87, p. 343-344.
"Boys and Fireworks." [HawaiiR] (20) Fall 86, c87, p. 56-57.
"Comfortable Smoke." [Poetry] (150:6) S 87, p. 318-320.
"Instructions for Insomnia." [Caliban] (2) 87, p. 97.
"Kinds of Jazz." [Poetry] (150:6) S 87, p. 322.
"The Mind's Eye." [Poetry] (150:6) S 87, p. 321.
"Mnemosyne." [SouthernPR] (27:1) Spr 87, p. 47.
"Self-Portrait as Author and Citizen." [Caliban] (2) 87, p. 96.
"Self-Portrait with Preferences." [Caliban] (2) 87, p. 95.
2068. GRAHAM, John J.
"To Dorothy, Absent." [Vis] (23) 87, p. 36.
2069. GRAHAM, Jorie
"Act IV, Sc. 1." [Ploughs] (13:1) 87, p. 58.
"The Birth of Beauty." [Ploughs] (13:1) 87, p. 59.
"Untitled: In the city that apparently never was." [Ploughs] (13:1) 87, p. 56-67.
"What the End Is For" (Grand Forks, North Dakota). [NewYorker] (62:51) 9 F 87,
p. 35.
2070. GRAHAM, K. Michael
"Where the Two Converge." [Writer] (99:1) Ja 86, p. 19.
2071. GRAHAM, Loren
"Waking Late at Night to Sirens." [Amelia] (4:3, issue 10) 87, p. 84.
2072. GRAHAM, Neile
"The Prophet as Traveller." [CanLit] (112) Spr 87, p. 84.
"Salamander Pendant." [CanLit] (112) Spr 87, p. 60.
"Settled in Montana for Winter." [Descant] (59) Wint 87, p. 18.
"Sleeping with Lambs." [Descant] (59) Wint 87, p. 19.
2073. GRAHN, Judy
"Spider Webster's Declaration: He Is Singing the End of the World Again." [Spirit]
(8:2) 87, p. 147-149.
2074. GRANATO, Carol
"April in Absentia." [Gambit] (21) 87, p. 55.
2075. GRANET, Roger
"Adverse." [NegC] (7:3/4) 87, p. 81.
2076. GRANT, J. B.
"In Reference to a Young 0300." [Event] (16:1) Mr 87, p. 76-85.
2077. GRANT, Paul
"Dixie." [CarolQ] (40:1) Fall 87, p. 36-38.
"Gloryland" (Swan's Penny Arcade). [PoetryNW] (28:3) Aut 87, p. 15-17.
"Isinglass." [PoetL] (82:3) Fall 87, p. 154.
2078. GRANT-GIBSON, Elisabeth
"The Farmer Teaches His Daughter to Fish." [CimR] (80) Jl 87, p. 4.
2079. GRANTHAM, R. F.
"Headline: Kansas Youth Dies in Undertow." [Writer] (100:1) Ja 87, p. 23.
2080. GRASSI, Carolyn
"The Renoir Retrospective" (Grand Palais, Paris). [PassN] (8:1) Wint 87, p. 19.
2081. GRAVES, Michael
"For Fame." [Wind] (17:59) 87, p. 19-20.
"Meditation, 9." [Wind] (17:59) 87, p. 19.
2082. GRAVLEY, Ernestine
"Refuge." [Phoenix] (7:1) 87, p. 8.
2083. GRAY, Beth
"Bread in the Desert." [BellArk] (3:2) Mr-Ap 87, p. 17.
"Riding Westward." [BellArk] (3:2) Mr-Ap 87, p. 17.
2084. GRAY, Dorothy Randall
"25,000 Women Pyramid." [Cond] (14) 87, p. 169-171.
2085. GRAY, James
"From Index of Facadomy." [Rampike] (5:3) 87, p. 77.
2086. GRAY, Janet
"Murder & Young Girls." [SlipS] (7) 87, p. 27-29.
"Words for the Unborn." [Amelia] (4:1/2, issue 9) 87, p. 60.
2087. GRAY, Jeffrey
"Escuintla." [Atlantic] (260:1) Jl 87, p. 79.
2088. GRAY, Pat
"Diversion." [MinnR] (NS 28) Spr 87, p. 10.

2089. GRAY, Patrick Worth
"Blossoms." [Poem] (58) N 87, p. 30.
"Driving." [CapeR] (22:1) Spr 87, p. 5.
"Four Photographs." [BelPoJ] (38:1) Fall 87, p. 13-14.
"Gunsmoke in Old Tay Ninh." [BelPoJ] (38:1) Fall 87, p. 12.
"How They Left Grant, Oklahoma." [Poem] (58) N 87, p. 31.
"January in Nebraska" (for Theodore Roethke, reprinted from Bogg 28-29). [Bogg]
        (58) 87, p. 42.
"Once There Was a Man." [BelPoJ] (38:1) Fall 87, p. 12-13.
"Potatoes." [WindO] (49) Fall 87, p. 38.
"Snapshot." [Poem] (58) N 87, p. 29.
"Spring in Arnett." [Footwork] 87, p. 49-50.
"Training Accident." [Nimrod] (30:2) Spr-Sum 87, p. 78.
"W.C.W. in the South." [MalR] (80) S 87, p. 112.
"W.C.W. in the South." [Nimrod] (30:2) Spr-Sum 87, p. 79.
2090. GRAZIANO, Frank
"Imaginary Biography of Seymour" (tr. of Darío Jaramillo). [NewOR] (14:3) Fall
        87, p. 76-77.
"In This Night, in this World" (tr. of Alejandra Pizarnik, w. Maria Rosa Fort).
        [ColR] (NS 14:2) Fall-Wint 87, p. 57-59.
"Names and Figures" (tr. of Alejandra Pizarnik, w. Jim Fitzgerald). [NewOR] (14:3)
        Fall 87, p. 17.
"L'Obscurite des Eaux" (tr. of Alejandra Pizarnik, w. Jim Fitzgerald). [NewOR]
        (14:3) Fall 87, p. 44.
2091. GREATHOUSE, Florence
"Camping Trip." [SnapD] (10:1/2) Wint 87, p. 15.
"Small Town Lady." [SnapD] (10:1/2) Wint 87, p. 14.
2092. GREEN, Connie J.
"The Father Dream." [Poem] (58) N 87, p. 54.
"The Goldfish." [Poem] (58) N 87, p. 56.
"Pruning Trees." [Poem] (58) N 87, p. 55.
2093. GREEN, Coppie
"I Dream I Am Molly Bloom." [GreensboroR] (43) Wint 87-88, p. 106.
2094. GREEN, David H.
"Geek." [LightY] '87, c86, p. 80.
2095. GREEN, Kate
"Living Memory." [KanQ] (19:3) Sum 87, p. 143.
"Question for the Newborn." [AmerPoR] (16:2) Mr-Ap 87, p. 36.
2096. GREEN, Melissa
"The Housewright's Mercy" (for Rick and Joyce). [Agni] (24/25) 87, p. 108-114.
2097. GREEN, Peter
"Good Luck with the Syrtes: A Tunisian Propemptikon." [SouthernHR] (21:4) Fall
        87, p. 327-328.
"Persephone" (tr. of Yannis Ritsos, w. Beverly Bardsley). [GrandS] (6:4) Sum 87,
        p. 143-156.
2098. GREEN, William H.
"Apartment Complex Under Construction." [HampSPR] Wint 86, p. 41.
"River Runner: Middle Age." [CrossCur] (6:5) 87, p. 67-68.
"Secret Rooms." [LaurelR] (21:1/2) Wint-Sum 87, p. 87.
"Stepping on a Rusty Nail." [CapeR] (22:1) Spr 87, p. 12.
"The Suicide: A Widow's Question." [HampSPR] Wint 86, p. 41.
"Under a Yardtree on Papermill Land." [CrossCur] (6:5) 87, p. 81.
2099. GREENBAUM, Jessica
"Inventing Difficulty." [PartR] (54:1) Wint 87, p. 122-123.
"The Scimitar-Horned Oryx." [SouthwR] (72:2) Spr 87, p. 270-271.
2100. GREENBERG, Alvin
"Departure." [GeoR] (41:4) Wint 87, p. 720.
"In the Examining Room." [ManhatPR] (9) Sum 87, p. 42.
2101. GREENBERG, Barbara L.
"Judge Kroll." [NowestR] (25:3) 87, p. 277.
2102. GREENBERG, Howard
"Duel." [Shen] (37:1) 87, p. 52.
2103. GREENBERGER, Ann
"Sisyphus Inverted." [Agni] (24/25) 87, p. 134-135.
2104. GREENBLATT, Ray
"Retirement." [InterPR] (13:2) Fall 87, p. 64.

2105. GREENE, Angela
"A Backwards Look." [Verse] (4:3) N 87, p. 15.
2106. GREENE, Ben
"Some Closing Remarks (The Retiring Biologist, to His Colleagues)." [DenQ] (21:3)
Wint 87, p. 52.
2107. GREENE, James
"Impressionism" (tr. of Osip Mandelstam). [NewYorker] (63:13) 18 My 87, p. 40.
"Life-painting." [CumbPR] (6:2) Spr 87, p. 6-7.
"Self-Portrait" (tr. of Osip Mandelstam). [NewYorker] (63:13) 18 My 87, p. 40.
"The Triumph of Middle-Age" (to Abraham Cowley). [CumbPR] (7:1) Fall 87, p.
11-12.
"The Wave Advances" (tr. of Osip Mandelstam). [NewYorker] (63:13) 18 My 87, p.
40.
2108. GREENE, Jeffrey
"The Anatomy of Night." [SewanR] (95:1) Wint 87, p. 5.
"Sail Loft." [SewanR] (95:1) Wint 87, p. 4-5.
"A Self-Portrait for Mary" (Denver Quarterly Poetry Competition Winner, Second
Prize). [DenQ] (22:2) Fall 87, p. 8-17.
2109. GREENE, Ruth
"Swans in Love." [PoetryE] (23/24) Fall 87, p. 164.
"Wildflowers of the Northeast, #49." [PoetryE] (23/24) Fall 87, p. 163.
2110. GREENFIELD, Robert L.
"Concerning the Assassination of John F. Kennedy." [MinnR] (NS 28) Spr 87, p.
7-8.
"The Darling of the Sororities." [WormR] (27:4, issue 108) 87, p. 85.
"Literary Quarrel." [WormR] (27:4, issue 108) 87, p. 84.
"The Red Bear Runneth" (1985 Alice Jackson Poetry Prize: 2nd Honorable
Mention). [Electrum] (39) Fall-Wint 87, p. 12.
2111. GREENLEY, Emily
"Albert & Miranda." [HarvardA] (120:2) Mr 87, p. 39.
"In My Favorite Dream." [HarvardA] (120:2) Mr 87, p. 32.
"My Place." [HarvardA] (122:1) N 87, p. 12.
"Outside in Wichita." [HarvardA] (122:2) D 87, p. 24.
"Two-Step." [HarvardA] (122:1) N 87, p. 9.
"Valentines." [HarvardA] (121:3) My 87, p. 40.
2112. GREENWALD, Robert
"The Silent Ringmaster" (Kaleidoscope International Poetry Awards 1986-87, First
Prize). [Kaleid] (14) Wint-Spr 87, p. 66.
2113. GREENWALD, Roger
"Any day now Willow Lake will be freezing over" (tr. of Jacques Werup). [Pequod]
(23/24) 87, p. 248-249.
"The Four Cradles" (tr. of Pia Tafdrup, w. Poul Borum). [Writ] (19) 87, p. 28-30.
"In Spite of Everything" (tr. of Pia Tafdrup, w. Poul Borum). [Writ] (19) 87, p. 31.
"The Inmost Membrane of My Brain" (tr. of Pia Tafdrup, w. Poul Borum). [Writ]
(19) 87, p. 24.
"Just My Blood" (tr. of Pia Tafdrup, w. Poul Borum). [Writ] (19) 87, p. 26-27.
"No Longer Afraid" (tr. of Pia Tafdrup, w. Poul Borum). [Writ] (19) 87, p. 32.
"Of course Malmö United can win the all-Sweden finals" (tr. of Jacques Werup).
[Pequod] (23/24) 87, p. 247.
"Sharp Tugs" (tr. of Pia Tafdrup, w. Poul Borum). [Writ] (19) 87, p. 33.
"Skin" (tr. of Pia Tafdrup, w. Poul Borum). [Writ] (19) 87, p. 35.
"So As Not to Stand in Our Own Way" (tr. of Pia Tafdrup, w. Poul Borum). [Writ]
(19) 87, p. 25.
"Spring Tide" (tr. of Pia Tafdrup, w. Poul Borum). [Writ] (19) 87, p. 34.
"What Comes" (tr. of Pia Tafdrup, w. Poul Borum). [Writ] (19) 87, p. 23.
2114. GREENWAY, William
"The District of Looking Back." [CarolQ] (39:2) Wint 87, p. 64.
"Dream Life." [CapeR] (22:2) Fall 87, p. 43.
"Five Clichés." [Pig] (14) 87, p. 66.
"Rat." [CapeR] (22:2) Fall 87, p. 42.
"A Woman Brought to Child." [SnapD] (10:1/2) Wint 87, p. 61.
2115. GREER, Jane
"Better Advice to Colonel Valentine" (After Robert Graves). [BellArk] (3:4) Jl-Ag
87, p. 10.
"Full Circle." [BellArk] (3:4) Jl-Ag 87, p. 4.

2116. GREGER, Debora
  "The 1,002nd Night." [Poetry] (150:3) Je 87, p. 140-141.
  "Bees, Los Conquistadores." [Agni] (24/25) 87, p. 48-49.
  "Narcissus." [Poetry] (150:3) Je 87, p. 142.
  "The Opera Companion." [DenQ] (21:3) Wint 87, p. 81-84.
  "Recent Events: The Fossil Record." [Agni] (24/25) 87, p. 50.
2117. GREGERMAN, Debra
  "Tiepolo's St. Mary of Egypt Taken to Heaven." [Colum] (12) 87, p. 122.
2118. GREGERSON, Linda
  "The Bad Physician." [Atlantic] (259:1) Ja 87, p. 67.
2119. GREGG, Linda
  "Both of Us So Poor." [Sonora] (12) Spr 87, p. 10.
  "The Fine Pale Wild Cloth of Love" (7 poems). [IndR] (10:1/2) 87, p. 99-107.
  "Gnostics on Trial." [Spirit] (8:2) 87, p. 110.
  "If It's Not One Thing It's Another." [Sonora] (12) Spr 87, p. 11.
  "Kept Burning and Distant." [Antaeus] (58) Spr 87, p. 151.
  "Night Music." [Ploughs] (13:4) 87, p. 45.
  "On Lesbos Remembering Her Mountain on Paros." [Sonora] (12) Spr 87, p. 12.
  "Persephone to the Other Husband." [Antaeus] (58) Spr 87, p. 151.
  "Surrounded by Sheep and Low Land." [PartR] (54:3) Sum 87, p. 431.
2120. GREGOR, Arthur
  "Mozartian." [Nat] (244:25) 27 Je 87, p. 896.
  "The Threshold, or, My Home in Winter." [SouthernR] (23:1) Ja 87, p. 130-136.
2121. GREGOR, Debora
  "Snow White and Rose Red." [NewYorker] (63:44) 21 D 87, p. 42.
2122. GREGORY, Gina
  "Silence for the Expedition" (Reprinted from Bogg 28-29). [Bogg] (58) 87, p. 42.
2123. GREGORY, Michael
  "The Border of Visible Light" (after Elihu Vedder's painting, "The Cup of Death").
    [WestHR] (41:2) Sum 87, p. 143-144.
  "Gun." [AnotherCM] (17) 87, p. 41-42.
  "Lottery" (for Naomi Shihab Nye). [PassN] (8:1) Wint 87, p. 15.
  "Lottery" (for Naomi Shihab Nye). [PassN] (8:2) Sum 87, p. 30.
  "Lunch in the Islands." [Amelia] (4:1/2, issue 9) 87, p. 128.
2124. GREGORY, Robert
  "Variation on a Line from ZONE." [ManhatPR] (9) Sum 87, p. 50.
2125. GREINER, Betsy
  "President and Mrs. Reagan Visit Ford's Theater, April 8, 1984" (for Byron
    Ringland). [Pig] (14) 87, p. 65.
  "Turn Me On." [Pig] (14) 87, p. 64.
2126. GRENNAN, Eamon
  "Conjunctions." [MissouriR] (10:3) 87, p. 23-25.
  "The Cycle of Their Lives." [MissouriR] (10:3) 87, p. 18-19.
  "A Lack of Epitaphs." [MissouriR] (10:3) 87, p. 26.
  "The Nature of America." [KenR] (NS 9:4) Fall 87, p. 9-10.
  "Traveller." [MissouriR] (10:3) 87, p. 22.
  "Walking Fall." [KenR] (NS 9:4) Fall 87, p. 10-11.
  "Walking to Work." [MissouriR] (10:3) 87, p. 20-21.
  "Winter Morning, Twelve Noon." [Verse] (4:1) Mr 87, p. 7.
  "Woodchuck." [KenR] (NS 9:4) Fall 87, p. 8-9.
GRESTY, David Price
  See PRICE-GRESTY, David
2127. GREY, John
  "Blind Jazz." [Wind] (17:61) 87, p. 18.
  "Cutting Out the Cities." [Farm] (4:2) Spr-Sum 87, p. 69.
  "Harbor One." [SmPd] (24:2) Spr 87, p. 28.
  "Presidents." [Bogg] (58) 87, p. 41.
  "Remembered by Houses." [Outbr] (18/19) Fall 86-Spr 88, p. 67-68.
  "She's the Flower." [BellArk] (3:3) My-Je 87, p. 20.
  "Small Beats in Large Acreage." [Farm] (4:2) Spr-Sum 87, p. 10.
  "Tall Tales Untrue." [Blueline] (7:2/3 [i.e. 8:2/3?]) 87, p. 79.
  "Years of Buzzards." [HawaiiR] (21) Spr 87, p. 33.
2128. GREY, Lucinda
  "Letter to No Address" (1986 Finalist, Eve of Saint Agnes Poetry Competition).
    [NegC] (7:1/2) 87, p. 182.

2129. GREY, Robert
"Salt" (1987 Ratner-Ferber-Poet Lore Honorable Mention). [PoetL] (82:2) Sum 87,
p. 99-101.
2130. GRIFFIN, Gail
"In the Office in the Afternoon following a Class in Women's Literature." [Calyx]
(11:1) Wint 87-88, p. 27.
2131. GRIFFIN, Larry D.
"Grandpa's Attempt to Compliment Mrs. Nugent on Building the Finest House in
Town." [WormR] (27:4, issue 108) 87, p. 113.
"Porch Sitting." [CimR] (81) O 87, p. 23-24.
"What Old Man Johnson Said to Grandpa After Returning Thanks." [WormR] (27:4,
issue 108) 87, p. 112.
2132. GRIFFIN, Sheila
"Man." [Sonora] (13) Fall 87, p. 88.
2133. GRIFFIN, Walter
"Clinic." [Vis] (25) 87, p. 25.
"Day of the Soft Mouth." [MemphisSR] (8:1) Fall 87, p. 32-33.
"Dirt." [PassN] (8:2) Sum 87, p. 27.
"Dirt." [Poem] (58) N 87, p. 58.
"Fish Leaves." [BlueBldgs] (10) 87?, p. 22.
"Fish Leaves." [SewanR] (95:1) Wint 87, p. 7-8.
"Fish Leaves." [Waves] (14:4) Spr 86, p. 48.
"Harmless Blood." [MemphisSR] (8:1) Fall 87, p. 34.
"Harmless Blood." [PraS] (61:4) Wint 87, p. 32.
"Homesick." [KanQ] (19:3) Sum 87, p. 60.
"Homesick." [SewanR] (95:1) Wint 87, p. 6-7.
"Hulls." [KanQ] (19:3) Sum 87, p. 59.
"Moraff, Barbara "Lines." [Abraxas] (35/36) 87, p. 63.
"Speed." [Vis] (24) 87, p. 30.
"The Submariner." [SewanR] (95:1) Wint 87, p. 8.
"The Swimmer." [Poem] (58) N 87, p. 59.
"The Trees Are Falling." [ConnPR] (6:1) 87, p. 24.
"Vogelsang 5." [Poem] (58) N 87, p. 57.
"Wet Pavement." [Abraxas] (35/36) 87, p. 62.
"Wet Pavement." [HighP] (2:1) Spr 87, p. 10.
"Wet Pavement." [MemphisSR] (8:1) Fall 87, p. 33.
"Wet Pavement." [PraS] (61:4) Wint 87, p. 31.
2134. GRIGGS, Jeanne
"That Lack of Indifference." [CapeR] (22:1) Spr 87, p. 44.
2135. GRIGSBY, Gordon
"Work, Love, Salt." [HiramPoR] (42) Spr-Sum 87, p. 40-41.
2136. GRILL, Neil
"February Man." [CrossCur] (6:4) 87, p. 44-45.
2137. GRIMALDI, A. J.
"George Murphy." [SlipS] (7) 87, p. 83.
"Hey James, Let's Play Army." [SlipS] (7) 87, p. 84.
2138. GRIMES, Larry
"A Visitation." [LaurelR] (20:1/2) Sum 87, p. 90.
2139. GRINDE, Olav
"The Church on Wall Street" (tr. of Rolf Jacobsen). [CrossCur] (7:3) 87, p. 121.
"Guardian Angel" (tr. of Rolf Jacobsen). [StoneC] (14:3/4) Spr-Sum 87, p. 31.
2140. GRISWOLD, Jay
"The Duende." [NoDaQ] (55:3) Sum 87, p. 82.
"Fatherhood." [CumbPR] (6:2) Spr 87, p. 5.
"Hills." [PikeF] (8) Fall 87, p. 24.
"How He Remembers." [Poem] (58) N 87, p. 3.
"Lost." [NoDaQ] (55:3) Sum 87, p. 83.
"Requiem for Jonah." [PoetL] (82:2) Sum 87, p. 107.
"Sanctuary." [HawaiiR] (22) Fall 87, p. 52.
"The Skater." [NegC] (7:3/4) 87, p. 82.
"Solitude." [PikeF] (8) Fall 87, p. 24.
2141. GROFF, David
"The Watchdyke." [PoetryNW] (28:1) Spr 87, p. 27.
2142. GROL-PROKOPCZYK, Regina
"In an Empty Parking Lot, Setting the Hand Brake" (tr. of Stanislaw Baranczak).
[Paint] (14:27) Spr 87, p. 35.

2143. GROLLMES, Eugene E.
"At the Vietnam Veterans Memorial, Washington, D.C." [ManhatPR] (9) Sum 87, p. 23.
2144. GRONSETH, Charlotte M.
"Christmas." [ChrC] (104:39) 23-30 D 87, front cover.
2145. GROOMS, Anthony
"Helena." [ChatR] (8:1) Fall 87, p. 23.
2146. GROSHOLZ, Emily
"The Warning." [YaleR] (76:4) Sum 87, p. 554.
2147. GROSJEAN, Jean
"Elegies" (Selections: VII-IX, tr. by Keith Waldrop). [LitR] (30:3) Spr 87, p. 353-355.
"Elegies" (Selections: X-XI, tr. by Keith Waldrop). [Notus] (2:1) Spr 87, p. 31-32.
2148. GROSS, Pamela
"In Pitch Dark." [StoneC] (14:3/4) Spr-Sum 87, p. 55.
"Splitting Wood." [Raccoon] (24/25) My 87, p. 70.
2149. GROSSMAN, Allen
"The Piano Player Explains Himself." [GrandS] (7:1) Aut 87, p. 30.
2150. GROSSMAN, Andrew J.
"Diddle." [CrabCR] (4:2) Spr 87, p. 5.
"The Efficient Nurses of Florida." [CrabCR] (4:2) Spr 87, p. 26-27.
"The Hired Man." [PikeF] (8) Fall 87, p. 7.
"Now Beauty." [PikeF] (8) Fall 87, p. 3.
"Now Beauty." [Vis] (23) 87, p. 10.
"Reconciled." [BallSUF] (28:4) Aut 87, p. 67.
"Reconciled." [Vis] (23) 87, p. 11.
2151. GROSSMAN, Florence
"Spring Sewing." [Nat] (245:13) 24 O 87, p. 464.
"Still Life." [Nat] (244:16) 25 Ap 87, p. 545.
"Weather Radio." [Nat] (245:12) 17 O 87, p. 427.
2152. GROTH, Patricia Celley
"Would You Pee in a Bucket on Mop Day, or, What Constitutes a Lady?" [US1] (20/21) Wint 86-87, p. 19-21.
2153. GROTH, Susan Charles
"Discovering Castle Conway." [Bogg] (58) 87, p. 40.
2154. GROVE, Charles L.
"Beware the Tides of March." [LightY] '87, c86, p. 123.
2155. GROVE, Rex
"November 23, 1984." [EngJ] (76:8) D 87, p. 78.
2156. GROW, Eric
"The Great Writers." [WormR] (27:4, issue 108) 87, p. 112.
"Mucous Membrane." [WormR] (27:4, issue 108) 87, p. 111.
"Regular Guy." [WormR] (27:4, issue 108) 87, p. 112.
2157. GRUBER, Martin
"Mediterranean" (tr. of Eugenio Montale). [ParisR] (29:105) Wint 87, p. 188-194.
2158. GRUENDING, Dennis
"Chucker Chatter." [PraF] (8:1) Spr 87, p. 62-63.
2159. GRUMMAN, Bob
"Creativity" (visual poem). [WindO] (49) Fall 87, p. 33-34.
2160. GRUMMER, Greg
"Perhaps I Should Have Been More Aggressive." [KanQ] (19:1/2) Wint-Spr 87, p. 312.
"What You Must Do." [KanQ] (19:1/2) Wint-Spr 87, p. 311.
2161. GU, Cheng
"At Parting" (tr. by Edward Morin and Dennis Ding). [Paint] (14:27) Spr 87, p. 45.
"Early Spring" (tr. by Edward Morin and Dennis Ding). [CrossCur] (7:3) 87, p. 135.
2162. GUBMAN, G. D.
"Practicing S's in Speech and Hearing." [US1] (20/21) Wint 86-87, p. 10.
2163. GUEREÑA, Jacinto-Luis
"IV. Desde los recuerdos se inventa." [Mester] (16:1) Spr 87, p. 62.
2164. GUERNSEY, Bruce
"The Creek." [Farm] (4:1) Wint 87, p. 28-29.
"Disconnected." [PennR] (3:1) Spr-Sum 87, p. 47.
"Igloo." [MidwQ] (29:1) Aut 87, p. 74.
"Phone Call, 3:00 AM." [Farm] (4:1) Wint 87, p. 30.

"Time and Temperature." [Farm] (4:1) Wint 87, p. 31.
"Tracing the Call." [PennR] (3:1) Spr-Sum 87, p. 46.
GUERRERO, Antonio Gonzalez
  See GONZALEZ GUERRERO, Antonio
2165. GUEST, Barbara
  "Country Cousins." [Temblor] (6) 87, p. 40.
  "Heavy Violets." [NewAW] (1) 87, p. 28.
  "In Medieval Hollow." [Temblor] (6) 87, p. 33-34.
  "Ropes Sway." [Temblor] (6) 87, p. 39.
  "The Screen of Distance." [Temblor] (6) 87, p. 34-38.
  "This Innocent Song." [NewAW] (1) 87, p. 29.
2166. GUGLIELMI, Joseph
  "After Spicer." [Acts] (6) 87, p. 78.
2167. GUIDACCI, Margherita
  "Liber Fulguralis" (To the Mav Luceziniai. Selections: 9 poems, tr. by Ruth
      Feldman). [Stand] (28:1) Wint 86-87, p. 4-8.
  "To Doctor Z" (tr. by Ruth Feldman). [CrossCur] (7:3) 87, p. 136.
2168. GUILFORD, Charles (Chuck)
  "How It Could Happen." [KanQ] (19:3) Sum 87, p. 110.
  "In Memory." [ConcPo] (20) 87, p. 40.
  "Making Time." [ConcPo] (20) 87, p. 10.
2169. GUILLEMIN, Margaret
  "Discus" (tr. of Paul Celan, w. Katherine Washburn). [AntR] (45:1) Wint 87, p. 96.
  "Grown Weary" (tr. of Paul Celan, w. Katherine Washburn). [AntR] (45:1) Wint
      87, p. 97.
2170. GUILLÉN, Jorge
  "Despertar Español" (Spanish Awaking, tr. by Julian Palley). [Salm] (76-77) Fall
      87-Wint 88, p. 79-80.
2171. GUILLÉN, Nicolás
  "El Abuelo." [Callaloo] (10:2) Spr 87, p. 190.
  "Adivinanzas." [Callaloo] (10:2) Spr 87, p. 188.
  "Angustia Segunda." [Callaloo] (10:2) Spr 87, p. 192.
  "Avisos, Mensajes, Pregones." [Callaloo] (10:2) Spr 87, p. 202.
  "Balada de los Dos Abuelos." [Callaloo] (10:2) Spr 87, p. 184, 186.
  "Ballad of the Two Grandfathers" (tr. by Jill Netchinsky). [Callaloo] (10:2) Spr 87,
      p. 185, 187.
  "Búcata Plata." [Callaloo] (10:2) Spr 87, p. 180.
  "Don't Know No English" (tr. by Langston Hughes and Ben Frederic Carruthers).
      [Callaloo] (10:2) Spr 87, p. 171.
  "Epistle" (for the poet Eliseo Diego, tr. by Vera M. Kutzinski). [Callaloo] (10:2) Spr
      87, p. 205, 207.
  "Epistola." [Callaloo] (10:2) Spr 87, p. 204, 206.
  "Esclavos Europeos." [Callaloo] (10:2) Spr 87, p. 208, 210.
  "European Slaves" (tr. by Vera M. Kutzinski). [Callaloo] (10:2) Spr 87, p. 209,
      211.
  "Go Get Some Bread" (tr. by Jill Netchinsky). [Callaloo] (10:2) Spr 87, p. 181.
  "The Grandfather" (tr. by Vera M. Kutzinski). [Callaloo] (10:2) Spr 87, p. 191.
  "High Brown" (tr. by Langston Hughes and Ben Frederic Carruthers). [Callaloo]
      (10:2) Spr 87, p. 175.
  "The Hopeful Voice" (tr. by Kathleen Ross). [Callaloo] (10:2) Spr 87, p. 195-201.
  "Mi Chiquita." [Callaloo] (10:2) Spr 87, p. 178.
  "Mulata." [Callaloo] (10:2) Spr 87, p. 174.
  "My Gal" (tr. by Langston Hughes and Ben Frederic Carruthers). [Callaloo] (10:2)
      Spr 87, p. 179.
  "Negro Bembón." [Callaloo] (10:2) Spr 87, p. 172.
  "Pass On By" (tr. by Langston Hughes and Ben Frederic Carruthers). [Callaloo]
      (10:2) Spr 87, p. 177.
  "Riddles" (tr. by Jill Netchinsky). [Callaloo] (10:2) Spr 87, p. 189.
  "Second Agony" (tr. by Kathleen Ross). [Callaloo] (10:2) Spr 87, p. 193.
  "Sigue." [Callaloo] (10:2) Spr 87, p. 176.
  "Thick-Lipped Cullud Boy" (tr. by Langston Hughes and Ben Frederic Carruthers).
      [Callaloo] (10:2) Spr 87, p. 173.
  "Tú No Sabe Inglé." [Callaloo] (10:2) Spr 87, p. 170.
  "La Voz Esperanzada." [Callaloo] (10:2) Spr 87, p. 194-200.
  "Warnings, Messages, Announcements" (tr. by Vera M. Kutzinski). [Callaloo]
      (10:2) Spr 87, p. 203.

GUIN, Ursula K. le
    See Le GUIN, Ursula K.
2172. GULLAR, Ferreira
    "My Measure" (tr. by Richard Zenith). [AmerPoR] (16:5) S-O 87, p. 30.
    "No Openings" (tr. by Richard Zenith). [CrossCur] (7:3) 87, p. 74-75.
    "The Wind" (tr. by Richard Zenith). [AmerV] (8) Fall 87, p. 43-45.
2173. GULLEDGE, Jo
    "Pontchartrain Window" (for WP). [MemphisSR] (7:2) Spr 87, p. 32.
    "Sebastian's Market." [MemphisSR] (7:2) Spr 87, p. 33.
2174. GUNDY, Jeff
    "The Dream of Home." [PikeF] (8) Fall 87, p. 13.
    "North from Detroit." [Wind] (17:61) 87, p. 19.
    "On the Morning of the Contra Aid Vote I Dream of Invasion." [LaurelR] (21:1/2)
        Wint-Sum 87, p. 67-68.
    "Traveling Through the States." [HiramPoR] (42) Spr-Sum 87, p. 26.
2175. GUNN, Genni
    "The Bankteller." [GreensboroR] (41) Wint 86-87, p. 99.
2176. GUNN, Thom
    "1975." [Zyzzyva] (3:3) Fall 87, p. 37.
    "The Man with Night Sweats." [Sequoia] (31:1) Centennial issue 87, p. 65.
    "Old Meg." [Thrpny] (31) Fall 87, p. 31.
    "Patch Work." [Poetry] (151:1/2) O-N 87, p. 63.
2177. GUNNARS, Kristjana
    "Casualty." [Verse] (4:1) Mr 87, p. 13.
2178. GURAN, Holly
    "Break-In." [Phoenix] (7:1) 87, p. 9.
2179. GURLEY, George H., Jr.
    "Reliquae: Crossing the Nile." [NewL] (54:1) Fall 87, p. 68-69.
2180. GURLEY, James
    "Dance at the Senior Citizen Center." [CrabCR] (4:2) Spr 87, p. 18.
    "The Fisherman's Daughter." [PoetL] (82:4) Wint 87-88, p. 199-200.
    "Isabella Dances and Fills the Universe." [PoetL] (82:4) Wint 87-88, p. 201-202.
    "October." [Pembroke] (19) 87, p. 191-192.
    "Sunrise." [HawaiiR] (22) Fall 87, p. 73.
2181. GUSTAFSON, Jim
    "The Enormous Still-Life." [NewAW] (1) 87, p. 62-63.
    "The Hurt" (Selection: 10). [HangL] (50/51) 87, p. 74.
2182. GUSTAFSON, Joseph
    "A Shooting Star in Summer." [CrossCur] (6:4) 87, p. 77.
2183. GUSTAFSON, Ralph
    "Beethoven as an Example of the Unconditional." [CanLit] (113/114) Sum-Fall 87,
        p. 178.
    "A Dozen More Profound Stanzas." [CanLit] (115) Wint 87, p. 45-47.
    "Exhibition." [CanLit] (113/114) Sum-Fall 87, p. 90-91.
    "Final Disquisition on the Giant Tube-Worm." [Dandel] (14:1) Spr-Sum 87, p. 24.
    "Lest Violence Be Misunderstood." [Dandel] (14:1) Spr-Sum 87, p. 23.
    "The Question of Priority for the Moment." [Dandel] (14:1) Spr-Sum 87, p. 25.
2184. GUSTAFSSON, Lars
    "Ballad of the Trails in Västmanland" (tr. by Robert Hedin). [StoneC] (15:1/2)
        Fall-Wint 87-88, p. 20-21.
    "Ballad om Stigarna in Västmanland." [StoneC] (15:1/2) Fall-Wint 87-88, p. 18-19.
    "Balladen om Giftet." [StoneC] (15:1/2) Fall-Wint 87-88, p. 17-18.
    "Birdsong, Echo of the Original Paradise" (tr. by Christopher Middleton and the
        author). [SouthernHR] (21:4) Fall 87, p. 363.
    "Discussions" (tr. by Christopher Middleton and the author). [SouthernHR] (21:1)
        Wint 87, p. 36-37.
    "Looking at a Portrait of Lou Andreas-Salomé" (tr. by Christopher Middleton and the
        author). [SouthernHR] (21:1) Wint 87, p. 18.
    "On the Deepest Sounds" (tr. by Christopher Middleton and the author).
        [SouthernHR] (21:1) Wint 87, p. 38.
    "The Poison Ballad" (tr. by Robert Hedin). [StoneC] (15:1/2) Fall-Wint 87-88, p.
        16.
    "Turin, January 3, 1889, the Corner of Via Carlo Alberto" (tr. by Robert Hedin).
        [Paint] (14:28) Aut 87, p. 31.
2185. GUTIERREZ, Ernesto
    "Lagoon" (tr. by Erland Anderson). [NewRena] (7:1, #21) Fall 87, p. 53.

"Laguna." [NewRena] (7:1, #21) Fall 87, p. 52.
2186. GUTIERREZ MORALES, Guillermo
"Ausente." [Mairena] (9:24) 87, p. 62.
"Contra el Tiempo." [Mairena] (9:24) 87, p. 61.
"Sin Allende." [Mairena] (9:24) 87, p. 62.
2187. GUTIERREZ REVUELTA, Pedro
"The Conformist" (tr. of Angel González, w. Steven Ford Brown). [CrossCur] (7:3) 87, p. 33.
"Do You Know That Paper Can?" (tr. of Angel González, w. Steven Ford Brown). [CrossCur] (7:3) 87, p. 32.
2188. GWYNN, R. S.
"Randolph Field, 1938." [TarRP] (26:2) Spr 87, p. 18-19.
"Snow White and the Seven Deadly Sins." [NewEngR] (9:4) Sum 87, p. 389-390.
2189. HABOVA, Dana
"Mothers After the War" (for Jaroslav Seifert, tr. of Vladimír Holan, w. C. G. Hanzlicek). [AntR] (45:1) Wint 87, p. 93.
"Snow" (tr. of Vladimír Holan, w. C. G. Hanzlicek). [AntR] (45:1) Wint 87, p. 93.
2190. HABRA, Hedy
"Dive." [LindLM] (6:2/3) Ap-S 87, p. 5.
"Immured." [LindLM] (6:2/3) Ap-S 87, p. 5.
2191. HACKER, Marilyn
"Aubade II." [Calyx] (10:2/3) Spr 87, p. 150.
"La Bougeotte." [RiverS] (22) 87, p. 33.
"Groves of Academe." [OP] (final issue) Sum 87, p. 26.
"Languedocienne." [RiverS] (22) 87, p. 31.
"Les Serpillières." [RiverS] (22) 87, p. 32.
2192. HADAS, Pamela White
"Show and Tell." [PoetL] (82:4) Wint 87-88, p. 220-221.
2193. HADAS, Rachel
"The Brunch, the Broken Heel, the Matinee." [DenQ] (21:3) Wint 87, p. 88-89.
"DeChirico." [Boulevard] (2:3) Fall 87, p. 105-106.
"Desire." [BostonR] (12:5) O 87, p. 4.
"Four Angers." [YaleR] (76:4) Sum 87, p. 552-553.
"Generations" (Selections: 1-6). [Margin] (3) Sum 87, p. 58-60.
"Mortalities." [LitR] (30:4) Sum 87, p. 537-539.
"Nourishment." [Boulevard] (2:3) Fall 87, p. 106-107.
"The Sleeper." [DenQ] (21:3) Wint 87, p. 86-87.
"Summer in White, Green, and Black." [PartR] (54:1) Wint 87, p. 125-126.
"Teaching V." [DenQ] (21:3) Wint 87, p. 90.
"Three Silences." [Shen] (37:3) 87, p. 32-33.
"Visiting the Gypsy" (For Pamela White Hadas). [Thrpny] (29) Spr 87, p. 13.
2194. HADSALL, Pamela
"Dry Spell." [MidwQ] (29:1) Aut 87, p. 76.
"Prairie Winds." [MidwQ] (29:1) Aut 87, p. 75.
2195. HAEBIG, Patricia
"Elegy for Steven Who Has Quietly Entered Adolescence." [Waves] (15:3) Wint 87, p. 64.
2196. HAGEN, Cecelia
"At the Outer Banks, North Carolina." [PoetC] (18:2) Wint 87, p. 49-50.
"Firefighter." [PoetC] (18:2) Wint 87, p. 51-53.
2197. HAHN, Kimiko
"Celluloid." [AnotherCM] (17) 87, p. 43.
"Cruise Missiles." [AnotherCM] (17) 87, p. 44.
"Infra-Red." [Bomb] (19) Spr 87, p. 70.
2198. HAHN, Oscar
"Adolf Hitler Meditates on the Jewish Problem" (tr. by Naomi Lindstrom). [ColR] (NS 14:1) Spr-Sum 87, p. 31.
"Barbara Azul." [InterPR] (13:1) Spr 87, p. 26.
"The Center of the Bedroom" (tr. by James Hoggard). [InterPR] (13:1) Spr 87, p. 29.
"El Centro del Dormitorio." [InterPR] (13:1) Spr 87, p. 28.
"Consumer Society" (tr. by James Hoggard). [InterPR] (13:1) Spr 87, p. 31.
"Dream of Hiroshima" (tr. by Edward Haworth Hoeppner). [BlackWR] (13:2) Spr 87, p. 131, 133.
"Flat Blue" (tr. by James Hoggard). [InterPR] (13:1) Spr 87, p. 27.
"El Reposo del Guerrero." [InterPR] (13:1) Spr 87, p. 30.

"Sociedad de Consumo." [InterPR] (13:1) Spr 87, p. 30.
"Visión de Hiroshima." [BlackWR] (13:2) Spr 87, p. 130, 132.
"The Warrior's Rest" (tr. by James Hoggard). [InterPR] (13:1) Spr 87, p. 31.
2199. HAHN, Robert
"April in L.A." [CarolQ] (40:1) Fall 87, p. 40-41.
"One More Time" (Chicago, 1954). [CarolQ] (40:1) Fall 87, p. 39.
2200. HAHN, Susan
"After Chemotherapy." [RiverS] (23) 87, p. 56.
"Dybbuk." [RiverS] (23) 87, p. 57-58.
"Oral Interpretation." [Poetry] (150:2) My 87, p. 77.
"Small Green." [Poetry] (150:2) My 87, p. 76.
2201. HAI-JEW, Shalin
"About Non-feeling." [Colum] (12) 87, p. 2.
"Comfort for a Muse." [Colum] (12) 87, p. 1.
"How to Read the Poem She Wrote for You" (for Roy Tong). [WebR] (12:1) Spr
87, p. 38-39.
"Kinged." [Footwork] 87, p. 12.
"Three Disasters." [Footwork] 87, p. 13.
"Three Gypsies" (for my mother). [Footwork] 87, p. 13.
"Welcome Spring" (for Hor Chun). [Footwork] 87, p. 13.
HAIME, Kathleen du
See Du HAIME, Kathleen
2202. HAINES, John
"Death and the Miser" (after the painting by Hieronymus Bosch: Excerpts).
[Hudson] (40:3) Aut 87, p. 436-440.
"Head of Sorrow, Head of Thought." [Hudson] (40:3) Aut 87, p. 441-442.
"Meditation on a Skull Carved in Crystal." [Zyzzyva] (3:3) Fall 87, p. 64-70.
"The Sleepwalkers." [Hudson] (40:3) Aut 87, p. 440-441.
2203. HAISLIP, John
"A Dream of the Metro-Goldwyn Years." [NowestR] (25:3) 87, p. 136-137.
"Hunting for 'Blues' in the Rain." [NowestR] (25:2) 87, p. 159.
"Kelp." [NowestR] (25:2) 87, p. 160.
"Late Afternoon, Seal Rock, 1/25/84." [NowestR] (25:3) 87, p. 422.
HAKUSHU, Kitahara
See KITAHARA, Hakushu
2204. HALEY, Vanessa
"For a Former Student Found at Flemings Landing After Two Years at the Bottom of
the Smyrna River." [SouthernPR] (27:2) Fall 87, p. 44.
"Ice" (for the memory of Theresa Gallo). [GreensboroR] (39) Wint 85-86, p. 18-19.
2205. HALL, Dana Naone
"T'ang Fishermen." The Best of [BambooR] [(31-32)] 86, p. 31.
2206. HALL, Donald
"Christmas Eve in Whitneyville" (to my father). [TexasR] (7:3/4) 87, p. 68-69.
"Her Walk in the West Country." [Sequoia] (31:1) Centennial issue 87, p. 73.
"Moishe's Horse." [SewanR] (95:2) Spr 87, p. 249.
"Names of Horses." [TexasR] (7:3/4) 87, p. 70-71.
"Ox Cart Man." [TexasR] (7:3/4) 87, p. 67.
"Prophecy." [Harp] (274:1650) N 87, p. 38-40.
"Prophecy." [ParisR] (29:103) Sum 87, p. 46-49.
2207. HALL, Irving C.
"Pursuit." [NewL] (54:1) Fall 87, p. 111.
2208. HALL, James Baker (See also HALL, Jim)
"Cape Light" (for Patricia Meyer Spacks). [AmerV] (8) Fall 87, p. 10.
"The Dogs." [Hudson] (40:1) Spr 87, p. 89.
"Kneeling at Easter to the Season's First Bloodroot" (For Cia). [KenR] (NS 9:2) Spr
87, p. 105.
"Modigliani's Last Portrait of Jeanne Hébuterne." [OntR] (26) Spr-Sum 87, p. 87.
"The Relinquishments." [KenR] (NS 9:2) Spr 87, p. 107.
"Winter Trees in the Middle Distance." [KenR] (NS 9:2) Spr 87, p. 106.
2209. HALL, Jim (See also HALL, James Baker)
"Maybe Dats Youwr Pwoblem Too." [LightY] '87, c86, p. 23-24.
"Preposterous." [LightY] '87, c86, p. 140.
2210. HALL, John Lee
"Only 36" (1986 Finalist, Eve of Saint Agnes Poetry Competition). [NegC] (7:1/2)
87, p. 150-151.

2211. HALL, John Michael
"Late Afternoon." [NewL] (53:3) Spr 87, p. 31.
2212. HALL, Phil
"Five Minutes." [Germ] (10:2) Spr 87, p. 25.
2213. HALLAMAN, E. G.
"Adult Abduction Can Be Stopped." [Pig] (14) 87, p. 10.
"Bacon Bits." [Pig] (14) 87, p. 11.
"Come Out, Come Out." [Pig] (14) 87, p. 11.
"The Exploding Poem." [Pig] (14) 87, p. 32.
"Steroids." [Pig] (14) 87, p. 32.
"The Weatherman." [Pig] (14) 87, p. 11.
2214. HALLERMAN, Victoria
"A Last Cloud." [SouthernPR] (27:1) Spr 87, p. 58-59.
"Picture Album Circa 1910." [NoDaQ] (55:2) Spr 87, p. 13.
"Talking to God." [NoDaQ] (55:2) Spr 87, p. 12.
2215. HALLEY, Anne
"The Street of Small Porches." [TexasR] (7:3/4) 87, p. 72.
2216. HALLGREN, Stephanie
"For the Russian Astronaut, Valentina Tereshkova." [NoDaQ] (55:1) Wint 87, p. 76-77.
2217. HALLIDAY, David
"I Am a Landscape Painter." [CrossC] (9:3/4) 87, p. 9.
2218. HALLIDAY, Mark
"Being Physical." [Boulevard] (2:3) Fall 87, p. 168-169.
"Winchendon." [NewEngR] (10:2) Wint 87, p. 200-201.
2219. HALMAN, Talat Sait
"Blood Lurks Under All Words" (tr. of Cemal Süreya). [Trans] (19) Fall 87, p. 136-137.
"The Child and the Kid" (tr. of Özdemir Ince). [Trans] (19) Fall 87, p. 17.
"Conflict" (tr. of Oktay Rifat). [Trans] (19) Fall 87, p. 134.
"Crows" (tr. of Sabahattin Kudret Aksal). [Trans] (19) Fall 87, p. 151-153.
"A Diffuse Winter Symphony" (tr. of Fethi Savasçi). [Trans] (19) Fall 87, p. 110.
"Empty Streets" (tr. of Özdemir Ince). [Trans] (19) Fall 87, p. 18.
"Endless Silence" (tr. of Fazil Hüsnü Daglarca). [Trans] (19) Fall 87, p. 58.
"First" (tr. of Sezai Karakoç). [Trans] (19) Fall 87, p. 106.
"The Flute" (tr. of Oktay Rifat). [Trans] (19) Fall 87, p. 133.
"The Heart Inscribed" (tr. of Ismail Uyaroglu). [Trans] (19) Fall 87, p. 110.
"Just Like That" (tr. of Can Yücel). [Trans] (19) Fall 87, p. 114.
"Letters to My Daughter" (Selection: "In Exile" 12-19, tr. of Ataol Behramoglu). [Trans] (19) Fall 87, p. 83-85.
"Like a Flame" (tr. of Kemal Özer). [Trans] (19) Fall 87, p. 29.
"Our Sons" (tr. of Özdemir Ince). [Trans] (19) Fall 87, p. 19.
"Paean to Flowers" (tr. of Ali Yüce). [Trans] (19) Fall 87, p. 112-113.
"Poem: Yellow, Loveliest, enters my city" (tr. of Ilhan Berk). [Trans] (19) Fall 87, p. 126.
"Postcard" (tr. of Aras Ören). [Trans] (19) Fall 87, p. 108.
"Postcard" (tr. of Ömer Nida). [Trans] (19) Fall 87, p. 108.
"Rain" (tr. of Gülten Akin). [Trans] (19) Fall 87, p. 102.
"Responses for Poetry" (tr. of Ülkü Tamer). [Trans] (19) Fall 87, p. 158-161.
"Sisyphus" (tr. of Cengiz Bektas). [Trans] (19) Fall 87, p. 103.
"Startling Encounter" (tr. of Melih Cevdet Anday). [Trans] (19) Fall 87, p. 128.
"A Story of the Sea" (tr. of Cahit Külebi). [Trans] (19) Fall 87, p. 132.
"Those Women" (tr. of Özcan Yalim). [Trans] (19) Fall 87, p. 111.
"Tomorrow" (tr. of Bülent Ecevit). [Trans] (19) Fall 87, p. 104.
"Unexpected Sights" (tr. of Turgay Gönenç). [Trans] (19) Fall 87, p. 105.
"Unknown Love" (tr. of Adnan Özer). [Trans] (19) Fall 87, p. 109-110.
"Vertigo" (tr. of Melih Cevdet Anday). [Trans] (19) Fall 87, p. 129.
"War and Peace" (tr. of Onat Kutlar). [Trans] (19) Fall 87, p. 107.
"Wind, Ant, History" (tr. of Özdemir Ince). [Trans] (19) Fall 87, p. 18.
"Women" (tr. of Ilhan Berk). [Trans] (19) Fall 87, p. 127.
2220. HALME, Kathleen
"English to English." [NoAmR] (272:3) D 87, p. 55.
2221. HALPEARN, M.
"A Name for My Little Daughter" (tr. of Kedarnath Singh). [Bomb] (18) Wint 87, p. 62.

2222. HALSALL, Jalaine
"Chickens." [KanQ] (19:3) Sum 87, p. 314.
"Surgery 101." [KanQ] (19:3) Sum 87, p. 314-315.
2223. HAMASAKI, Richard
"I Don't Write No Haiku." [HawaiiR] (20) Fall 86, c87, p. 36-37.
2224. HAMBURGER, Michael
"Atemwende" (Selections: 3 poems, tr. of Paul Celan). [SouthernHR] (21:3) Sum
87, p. 224-229.
"Treblinka." [NowestR] (25:3) 87, p. 139.
2225. HAMBY, Barbara
"After Kew Gardens" (1986 Finalist, Eve of Saint Agnes Poetry Competition).
[NegC] (7:1/2) 87, p. 205-206.
2226. HAMILL, Janet
"Red Hills and Sky." [KanQ] (19:4) Fall 87, p. 9-10.
2227. HAMILL, Paul
"The Bitch That Killed the Boy." [NegC] (7:3/4) 87, p. 78.
"The Frozen Quarries." [NegC] (7:3/4) 87, p. 77.
2228. HAMILL, Sam
"And when the sea retreats from here . . ." (tr. of Jaan Kaplinski, w. Riina Tamm).
[AmerPoR] (16:6) N-D 87, p. 8.
"Classical Tragedy." [Dandel] (14:2) Fall-Wint 87, p. 15.
"Dialectics is a dialogue, a play of shadows" (tr. of Jaan Kaplinski, w. Riina Tamm).
[AmerPoR] (16:6) N-D 87, p. 8.
"The early autumn, a faded aquarelle" (tr. of Jaan Kaplinski, w. Riina Tamm).
[AmerPoR] (16:6) N-D 87, p. 8.
"From Childhood On" (tr. of Jaan Kaplinski, w. the author). [Zyzzyva] (3:4) Wint
87-88, p. 129.
"No one can put me back together again" (tr. of Jaan Kaplinski, w. Riina Tamm).
[AmerPoR] (16:6) N-D 87, p. 8.
"No one can put me back together again" (tr. of Jaan Kaplinski, w. the author and
Riina Tamm). [Dandel] (14:2) Fall-Wint 87, p. 29.
"Poems" (Selections: II, III, LXXV, LXX, LII, XCVIII, XI, tr. of Gaius Valerius
Catullus). [CrabCR] (4:2) Spr 87, p. 3-4.
"Sometimes I see so clearly the openness of things" (tr. of Jaan Kaplinski, w. Riina
Tamm). [AmerPoR] (16:6) N-D 87, p. 7.
"The sun shines on the red wall and the wall is warm" (tr. of Jaan Kaplinski, w.
Riina Tamm). [AmerPoR] (16:6) N-D 87, p. 8.
"There is no Good, no Evil, no Sin, no Virtue" (tr. of Jaan Kaplinski, w. Riina
Tamm). [AmerPoR] (16:6) N-D 87, p. 8.
"The washing never gets done" (tr. of Jaan Kaplinski, w. Riina Tamm). [AmerPoR]
(16:6) N-D 87, p. 7.
"The wind sways the lilac branches and shadows" (tr. of Jaan Kaplinski, w. Riina
Tamm). [AmerPoR] (16:6) N-D 87, p. 8.
2229. HAMILTON, Alfred Starr
"An Army Wedding Cake." [Lips] (13) 87, p. 9.
"The Cardinal in the Bush." [WormR] (27:1, issue 105) 87, p. 3-4.
"Chinaware." [PoetL] (82:4) Wint 87-88, p. 247.
"Jail Antics." [WormR] (27:1, issue 105) 87, p. 3.
"June Silver." [PoetL] (82:4) Wint 87-88, p. 247.
"The Prickly Shirt." [Lips] (13) 87, p. 10.
"Sheets." [PoetL] (82:4) Wint 87-88, p. 246.
"That Has Been to the City." [PoetL] (82:4) Wint 87-88, p. 246.
"Walden House." [PoetL] (82:4) Wint 87-88, p. 248.
2230. HAMILTON, Carol (See also HAMILTON, Carol S.)
"The Birds Are Not Sure It Is Time to Go." [WebR] (12:1) Spr 87, p. 32.
"Cleansing." [Bogg] (58) 87, p. 46.
"Esau's Birthright." [ChrC] (104:22) 29 Jl-5 Ag 87, p. 661.
"Isaac." [ChrC] (104:14) 29 Ap 87, p. 396.
"Love Letter." [Vis] (24) 87, p. 32.
"Pueblo Site." [Poem] (58) N 87, p. 46.
"Renewal." [ArizQ] (43:2) Sum 87, p. 118.
"Return Visit." [Poem] (58) N 87, p. 47.
"Salt Bread." [ChrC] (104:11) 8 Ap 87, p. 325.
"Viewing Arcturus in Daylight." [SmPd] (24:3) Fall 87, p. 35.
"Window." [ChrC] (104:10) 1 Ap 87, p. 308.

2231. HAMILTON, Carol S. (*See also* HAMILTON, Carol)
"The Dream Mechanic's Wife." [CumbPR] (7:1) Fall 87, p. 65-66.
"Heat Lightning." [CumbPR] (7:1) Fall 87, p. 63-64.
"Neige à Louveciennes" (after Sisley). [CumbPR] (7:1) Fall 87, p. 67.
"The Omega Declination." [CumbPR] (7:1) Fall 87, p. 61-62.
2232. HAMILTON, Fritz
"Airports" (for Kathy). [DekalbLAJ] (20:1/4) 87, p. 38-39.
"Bad Bread." [KanQ] (19:1/2) Wint-Spr 87, p. 27-28.
"Blunderbuss!" (Kansas Quarterly / Kansas Arts Commission Awards Honorable
Mention Poem, 1986/1987). [KanQ] (19:1/2) Wint-Spr 87, p. 26-27.
"Financial Differences." [PikeF] (8) Fall 87, p. 31.
"He Understands." [SmPd] (24:2) Spr 87, p. 33.
"How Wanda Copes!" [AntigR] (69/70) 87, p. 178-179.
"More Research." [WindO] (48) Spr 87, p. 19.
"New York Loving!" [CapeR] (22:1) Spr 87, p. 45.
"On Phoebe's 31st Birthday" (for Phoebe). [Kaleid] (14) Wint-Spr 87, p. 72.
"Phoebe's Meditation!" (for Phoebe). [Kaleid] (15) Sum-Fall 87, p. 21.
"The Suicide!" (for Bill). [SmPd] (24:3) Fall 87, p. 16.
"To Be Merry." [Kaleid] (14) Wint-Spr 87, p. 72.
"Utopia USA." [WindO] (49) Fall 87, p. 23.
"Violinist I" (for Charlie). [HiramPoR] (42) Spr-Sum 87, p. 27-28.
"Violinist II" (for Charlie). [HiramPoR] (42) Spr-Sum 87, p. 29-30.
"What Happens When Anthony Holdsworth Exhibits at Edible Complex." [SmPd]
(24:2) Spr 87, p. 34.
2233. HAMILTON, Jeff
"The Other End." [DenQ] (22:2) Fall 87, p. 40.
2234. HAMILTON, Karen Ann
"Ascension." [Writer] (99:11) N 86, p. 19.
2235. HAMILTON, Suzan G.
"Lessons." [PoetryNW] (28:4) Wint 87-88, p. 19-20.
"Night Fishing." [PoetryNW] (28:4) Wint 87-88, p. 21-22.
"Turning Around Just So." [PoetryNW] (28:4) Wint 87-88, p. 20-21.
2236. HAMMOND, Karla M.
"Exit Piazza" (in rely to J. Tate's "The Plaza"). [Footwork] 87, p. 51-52.
"Meleager." [Footwork] 87, p. 52.
"Onions for Love." [Footwork] 87, p. 52.
2237. HAMMOND, M. V.
"Carry Over / Would I Carry You." [DekalbLAJ] (20:1/4) 87, p. 39.
2238. HAMMOND, Mary Stewart
"Cosmetics." [NewYorker] (63:32) 28 S 87, p. 38.
"Grandmother's Rug." [NewYorker] (63:11) 4 My 87, p. 40-41.
2239. HAMMOND, Ralph
"A Brutalizing Thing." [Amelia] (4:3, issue 10) 87, p. 116.
2240. HANDLIN, Jim
"Dinner at Montoya's." [Footwork] 87, p. 29.
"Irish Landscape." [Footwork] 87, p. 29.
"Velazquez's Boy Clown." [Footwork] 87, p. 29.
2241. HANDY, Nixeon Civille
"Old Paddington Hall" (University of Washington 1963). [Wind] (17:59) 87, p. 21.
"Saul Lambert Enters" (City Center Gallery, N.Y.). [StoneC] (15:1/2) Fall-Wint
87-88, p. 15.
"Still Warm Hands Disconnected." [Wind] (17:59) 87, p. 21-22.
2242. HANFORD, Mary
"Biopsy." [Vis] (25) 87, p. 24.
"Reverie: Wing J." [Farm] (4:2) Spr-Sum 87, p. 15.
2243. HANKINS, Leslie
"Bull." [CarolQ] (40:1) Fall 87, p. 68.
2244. HANLEY, Patricia
"After all." [Dandel] (14:2) Fall-Wint 87, p. 17.
"Somewhere South of Here." [Dandel] (14:2) Fall-Wint 87, p. 16.
2245. HANNERS, LaVerne
"The Section Line." [BallSUF] (28:4) Aut 87, p. 49.
2246. HANNIGAN, Paul
"Acts of Faith." [BostonR] (12:4) Ag 87, p. 24.
"April Fools." [BostonR] (12:4) Ag 87, p. 24.
"Epithalamion." [BostonR] (12:4) Ag 87, p. 24.

"Helen Keller." [BostonR] (12:4) Ag 87, p. 24.
"Political Poem." [BostonR] (12:4) Ag 87, p. 24.
"Scuola Media." [BostonR] (12:4) Ag 87, p. 24.
"The Smartest Guy in the World." [BostonR] (12:4) Ag 87, p. 24.
"State Religion." [BostonR] (12:4) Ag 87, p. 24.

2247. HANSEN, Tom
"All Things at Once." [DekalbLAJ] (20:1/4) 87, p. 40.
"Knowing It." [KanQ] (19:1/2) Wint-Spr 87, p. 48-49.
"My Lawn Is Brown and All My Neighbors Are Painting Their Houses Again."
    [LightY] '87, c86, p. 244.
"October of Green-Falling Leaves." [KanQ] (19:1/2) Wint-Spr 87, p. 47.
"Parable of the Sun and the Moon." [MemphisSR] (7:2) Spr 87, p. 14.
"Thirteen Ways of Looking at a Red Wheelbarrow." [CapeR] (22:2) Fall 87, p.
    48-49.
"Tomorrow Today." [KanQ] (19:3) Sum 87, p. 42.
"What Has Become of Me." [CharR] (13:1) Spr 87, p. 72-73.

2248. HANSEN, Twyla
"Eyewash." [SmPd] (24:2) Spr 87, p. 10.
"Navigating the North Platte from Lingle to Torrington." [SmPd] (24:2) Spr 87, p.
    8.
"Night Shift at the Old Hospital, 1986." [SmPd] (24:2) Spr 87, p. 9.
"The Separator." [SnapD] (10:1/2) Wint 87, p. 28-29.

2249. HANSON, Charles
"Coffee." [Salm] (72) Fall 86, p. 198-199.

2250. HANSON, H. P.
"Dying Gladiator" (tr. of Erik Lindegren). [Vis] (25) 87, p. 33.

2251. HANSON, Julie Jordan
"Small Come-Callings" (for Deb Allbery). [AmerV] (7) Sum 87, p. 45-46.

2252. HANSON, Kenneth O.
"Lighting the Night Sky." [NowestR] (25:3) 87, p. 280-282.

2253. HANZLICEK, C. G.
"The Call." [PoetryNW] (28:4) Wint 87-88, p. 9-10.
"Heron." [PennR] (3:1) Spr-Sum 87, p. 59.
"It Was for This." [PoetryNW] (28:4) Wint 87-88, p. 9.
"Mothers After the War" (for Jaroslav Seifert, tr. of Vladimír Holan, w. Dana
    Hábová). [AntR] (45:1) Wint 87, p. 93.
"Snow" (tr. of Vladimír Holan, w. Dana Hábová). [AntR] (45:1) Wint 87, p. 93.

2254. HARA, Mavis
"Grandfather." [BambooR] (33) Spr 87, p. 36-37.
"Grandma and the Little Fish." [BambooR] (36) Fall 87, p. 25.
"Grandpa." [BambooR] (33) Spr 87, p. 39.
"The Silence." [BambooR] (33) Spr 87, p. 38.
"Taiko Drums." [BambooR] (33) Spr 87, p. 40.

2255. HARADA, Gail
"Letter to Paris." The Best of [BambooR] [(31-32)] 86, p. 32.

2256. HARDER, Naomi
"Confession to a Friend." [Quarry] (36:4) Fall 87, p. 29-31.

2257. HARDING, Deborah
"Cocoons." [Phoenix] (7:2) 87, p. 2.

2258. HARDING-RUSSELL, Gillian
"Amnesia: For Claude Jutra." [CapilR] (43) 87, p. 17.
"Archibald." [Dandel] (14:2) Fall-Wint 87, p. 38-40.
"At the End of the Garden" (Selections: III, IV, V). [Waves] (15:1/2) Fall 86, p. 80.
"Claude Jutra's Note." [CapilR] (43) 87, p. 18-19.
"The Jogger." [CapilR] (43) 87, p. 22-23.
"The Living House." [CapilR] (43) 87, p. 24-25.
"The Old Man in the Vacant Lot." [Event] (16:2) Sum 87, p. 60-61.
"You Have a Wart." [CapilR] (43) 87, p. 20-21.

2259. HARGITAI, Peter
"With All My Heart" (tr. of Attila Jozsef). [SpiritSH] (53:1) 87, p. 34-35.

2260. HARGRAVES, Joseph
"A Beauty." [JamesWR] (5:1) Fall 87, p. 6.
"Hair." [JamesWR] (4:2) Wint 87, p. 6.
"Home." [JamesWR] (5:1) Fall 87, p. 7.

2261. HARJO, Joy
"Crystal Lake." [RiverS] (22) 87, p. 29.

"Fury of Rain" (for Jo). [RiverS] (22) 87, p. 28.
"Hieroglyphic." [Ploughs] (13:4) 87, p. 46-47.
"The Real Revolution Is Love." [Contact] (9:44/45/46) Fall-Wint 87, p. 16-17.
"Strange Fruit" (For Jacqueline Peters). [RiverS] (22) 87, p. 30.
2262. HARLEMAN, Ann
"Aestivating." [KanQ] (19:3) Sum 87, p. 158.
"Deciding to Fall." [SouthernR] (23:4) O 87, p. 817.
"Deciding to Fall." [Writer] (99:7) Jl 86, p. 18.
"Interval." [GreensboroR] (40) Sum 86, p. 49.
"Leaving El Paso." [SouthernR] (23:4) O 87, p. 815-816.
"Letter to My Cousin." [Ascent] (13:1) 87, p. 23.
"Pacific Dream Algorithm." [BellR] (10:2) Fall 87, p. 58.
"Parts of Speech." [Ascent] (13:1) 87, p. 22.
"Prognosis." [HighP] (2:2) Fall 87, p. 133.
"Review" (for Ilona Karmel). [SouthernR] (23:4) O 87, p. 816.
2263. HARLOW, Robert
"Doors." [PoetryNW] (28:4) Wint 87-88, p. 14-15.
"Mr. Moto Takes a Vacation." [PoetryNW] (28:4) Wint 87-88, p. 12-13.
2264. HARMLESS, William
"Footpath over Perdido Bay." [CumbPR] (6:2) Spr 87, p. 39-41.
"Oniondome Nights." [TarRP] (26:2) Spr 87, p. 36.
2265. HARMON, William
"The Laxness Monster, or, I Be Singer, or, Saul Bellow, Well Met, or, Inexplicable
Spending . . ." [LightY] '87, c86, p. 217.
"Libero Pallante." [SewanR] (95:1) Wint 87, p. 9.
"Winter Hills." [CarolQ] (39:3) Spr 87, p. 9.
2266. HARMS, James
"Gravity Hill." [MSS] (5:3) 87, p. 192-193.
"Homecoming." [PoetryE] (23/24) Fall 87, p. 123-124.
"Stories." [PoetryE] (23/24) Fall 87, p. 125-126.
2267. HARN, John
"Beyond Doubt." [KanQ] (19:3) Sum 87, p. 251.
"Map-Conscious." [KanQ] (19:3) Sum 87, p. 252.
"Sprout in This." [CarolQ] (39:2) Wint 87, p. 51.
2268. HARNEY, John
"The Music of Lost Hourse." [NewYorker] (63:4) 16 Mr 87, p. 40.
2269. HARPER, Michael S.
"The Borning Room." [TexasR] (7:3/4) 87, p. 73.
"Certainties." [Ploughs] (13:1) 87, p. 62-63.
"The Fiddle." [Ploughs] (13:1) 87, p. 60.
"Hinton's Silkscreens" (on defense he was a hurricane out of bounds). [GrahamHR]
(10) Wint-Spr 87, p. 46-47.
"History as Apple Tree." [TexasR] (7:3/4) 87, p. 76-77.
"Jest, a Collection of Records" (for Bob Blackmore). [GrahamHR] (10) Wint-Spr
87, p. 48-49.
"Late September Refrain" (a love supreme, for John S. Wright). [GrahamHR] (10)
Wint-Spr 87, p. 44-45.
"Photographic Conversations" (for Roy De Carava). [Ploughs] (13:1) 87, p. 61.
"A Po' Man's Heart Disease" (Poetry Chapbook). [BlackWR] (14:1) Fall 87, p.
49-64.
"Trays: A Portfolio." [TexasR] (7:3/4) 87, p. 74-75.
2270. HARRELL, Ray
"The Bleeding Heart." [EngJ] (76:6) O 87, p. 99.
2271. HARRINGTON, Dorothy
"Grounded." [ArizQ] (43:1) Spr 87, p. 18.
2272. HARRIS, Gail
"But My Sister, My Sister." [CapilR] (45) 87 [Ap 88], p. 76.
"She Rode the Riverboat, I rang the Bell." [CapilR] (45) 87 [Ap 88], p. 77.
2273. HARRIS, Jana
"Sending the Mare to Auction." [Calyx] (11:1) Wint 87-88, p. 15.
"When He Calls, Asking How You Are." [CrabCR] (4:3) Sum 87, p. 24-25.
2274. HARRIS, Ken
"Cleaning Fish Beneath the Pear Tree" (for Tonja, for we fish similar waters).
[GreensboroR] (42) Sum 87, p. 104-105.
"Climbing the Falls" (for Marcia). [GreensboroR] (39) Wint 85-86, p. 52-54.

175

HARTNETT

2275. HARRIS, Leonard Paul
"This Side / That Side." [Bogg] (58) 87, p. 31.
2276. HARRIS, Malanie Gause
"Losing the City." [SouthernPR] (27:2) Fall 87, p. 31-32.
2277. HARRIS, Marie
"Valentine." [PoetL] (82:4) Wint 87-88, p. 219.
2278. HARRIS, Martin
"Glass Fruit." [CarolQ] (39:2) Wint 87, p. 21-22.
"Michael Joseph David's Head." [CarolQ] (39:2) Wint 87, p. 23-24.
"Spanish Olives." [CarolQ] (40:1) Fall 87, p. 69.
2279. HARRIS, Merry
"Pregnant Thought." [LightY] '87, c86, p. 131.
2280. HARRIS, Robert
"A Graustarkian Audit." [Rampike] (5:3) 87, p. 50.
2281. HARRISON, Jeanne
"Blue Irises." [Quarry] (36:1) Wint 87, p. 30.
"Bouquet." [Quarry] (36:1) Wint 87, p. 31.
"The Sacrifice of Actaeon." [Quarry] (36:1) Wint 87, p. 29.
2282. HARRISON, Jeffrey
"Elegy for the Clotheslines." [Boulevard] (2:3) Fall 87, p. 125.
"In Saint John the Divine." [Boulevard] (2:3) Fall 87, p. 124.
"In the Attic." [Hudson] (40:1) Spr 87, p. 86-87.
"Inside the Fish." [WillowS] (20) Spr 87, p. 32-33.
"The Mute Swan" (Cygnus olor). [WillowS] (20) Spr 87, p. 31.
"Reflection on the Vietnam War Memorial." [YaleR] (77:1) Aut 87, p. 148.
"Scallop" (for Charlie Worthen). [Margin] (5) Wint 87-88, p. 71.
"The Singing Underneath." [Margin] (5) Wint 87-88, p. 71.
"Skating in Late Afternoon." [Crazy] (33) Wint 87, p. 62.
"Trading the Alps for the Andes." [SouthwR] (72:4) Aut 87, p. 491.
2283. HARRISON, Pamela
"Evensong at Carriacou Island." [PassN] (8:2) Sum 87, p. 22.
2284. HARRISON, Richard
"Pinocchio As a Man." [Quarry] (36:4) Fall 87, p. 55-56.
2285. HARROD, Lois Marie
"Blood Wolf." [StoneC] (15:1/2) Fall-Wint 87-88, p. 23.
2286. HARROLD, William
"Jukebox Roulette." [NewL] (53:3) Spr 87, p. 98.
"Trails." [CreamCR] (11:2/3) 87?, p. 16.
2287. HARRYMAN, Carla
"The Male." [Bound] (14:1/2) Fall 85-Wint 86 [c87], p. 17-19.
2288. HARSHMAN, Marc
"Almost." [LaurelR] (20:1/2) Sum 87, p. 114-115.
"Climbing." [MidAR] (7:2) 87, p. 128-129.
"Your Words and Mine." [PassN] (8:2) Sum 87, p. 4.
2289. HART, Henry
"The Frog King." [GrahamHR] (10) Wint-Spr 87, p. 39-40.
"Mystery Play" (November 22, 1963). [Poetry] (151:3) D 87, p. 292.
"Notes from Mount Vernon." [SouthernHR] (21:4) Fall 87, p. 360-361.
"Snapper." [GrahamHR] (10) Wint-Spr 87, p. 37-38.
2290. HART, Jonathan
"Dream Songs." [Grain] (15:4) Wint 87, p. 30.
"Letter to India" (From: Breath and Dust). [Grain] (15:4) Wint 87, p. 31.
"Lost in the Telling." [Grain] (15:4) Wint 87, p. 30.
2291. HARTEIS, Richard
"Genetics" (for Audrey Garbisch). [ThRiPo] (29/30) 87, p. 27.
"Mirage" (In Memoriam, Katharine Meredith Goldenberg). [SmPd] (24:3) Fall 87, p. 6.
"Pedagogy." [SmPd] (24:3) Fall 87, p. 7.
2292. HARTER, Penny
"A Man Beside the New Jersey Turnpike, Easter Eve." [Footwork] 87, p. 61.
"Watching My Parents' House." [Lips] (13) 87, p. 24-25.
2293. HARTMAN, Charles O.
"After Kuo Hsi." [YaleR] (76:3) Spr 87, p. 356-357.
2294. HARTNETT, Michael
"A Farewell to English" (for Brendan Kennelly). [Pembroke] (19) 87, p. 91-94.

2295. HARTOG, Diana
"Basho Sets Forth on His Autumn Journey." [MalR] (79) Je 87, p. 45.
"The Family Eyes." [MalR] (79) Je 87, p. 43-44.
"The Mother Inside." [Event] (16:2) Sum 87, p. 97.
"Tender Buttons." [MalR] (79) Je 87, p. 46.
"Two Poems About Rain, One Written After Chernobyl, One Before." [MalR] (79)
Je 87, p. 47.
2296. HARTSFIELD, Carla
"Applause." [Waves] (15:3) Wint 87, p. 63.
"Pearl and Jack." [AntigR] (69/70) 87, p. 157-158.
"To Mozart: A Birthday." [MalR] (81) D 87, p. 84-85.
2297. HARVEY, Andrew
"At Sabre's Point" (tr. of Victor Segalen, w. Iain Watson). [SenR] (17:2) 87, p. 28.
"Command to the Sun" (tr. of Victor Segalen, w. Iain Watson). [SenR] (17:2) 87, p.
31.
"Farewells" (tr. of Luis Cernuda). [SenR] (17:2) 87, p. 35.
"Hymn to the Resting Dragon" (tr. of Victor Segalen, w. Iain Watson). [SenR]
(17:2) 87, p. 32.
"The Lover Babbles" (tr. of Luis Cernuda). [SenR] (17:2) 87, p. 33-34.
"Mongol Libation" (tr. of Victor Segalen, w. Iain Watson). [SenR] (17:2) 87, p. 29.
"Written with Blood" (tr. of Victor Segalen, w. Iain Watson). [SenR] (17:2) 87, p.
30.
2298. HARVEY, Gayle Elen
"After a Coastal Winter Storm." [CapeR] (22:2) Fall 87, p. 14.
"Beaten." [Bogg] (58) 87, p. 32.
"Mantis." [StoneC] (15:1/2) Fall-Wint 87-88, p. 25.
"That Cold." [CapeR] (22:2) Fall 87, p. 15.
"This Landscape, Somber" (after Munch's "Starry Night"). [Phoenix] (7:2) 87, p.
24.
"The Wish" (for Ben). [PikeF] (8) Fall 87, p. 27.
2299. HARVEY, Kay
"Top Secret." [PoeticJ] (17) 87, p. 29.
2300. HARVEY, Ken J.
"Bullet Through the Moon." [Bogg] (57) 87, p. 47.
"Carnival Monster." [AntigR] (69/70) 87, p. 180.
2301. HARVEY, Roger
"Brother Hawk." [Bogg] (58) 87, p. 29.
"President Reagan." [Bogg] (58) 87, p. 28.
2302. HARVEY, Suzanne R.
"Octopus" (Award Poem). [Phoenix] (7:1) 87, p. 21.
2303. HARWAY, Judith
"Principles of Composition." [CapeR] (22:1) Spr 87, p. 3.
"The Silk-Bound Notebook." [CapeR] (22:1) Spr 87, p. 2.
2304. HASAN, Rabiul
"The Cuckoo of the Concrete" (tr. of Nirmalendoo Goon). [InterPR] (13:2) Fall 87,
p. 44.
"The Recapture" (tr. of Nirmalendoo Goon). [InterPR] (13:2) Fall 87, p. 44.
2305. HASEGAWA, Ryusei
"Clock Exercises" (tr. by James Morita). [LitR] (30:2) Wint 87, p. 194-195.
2306. HASHIMOTO, Sharon
"Spruce Street" (for A.C. Arai). [ColR] (NS 14:1) Spr-Sum 87, p. 64-65.
2307. HASHMI, Alamgir
"Fruit." [Chelsea] (46) 87, p. 220-221.
"Inland." [Chelsea] (46) 87, p. 218-220.
"Jahangir." [CapilR] (44) 87, p. 73.
"January Eggnog." [CapilR] (44) 87, p. 74.
"Refugee Girl Makes Good." [Chelsea] (46) 87, p. 217-218.
2308. HASKELL, Dale
"At St. Jude's." [EngJ] (76:4) Ap 87, p. 93.
2309. HASKINS, Lola
"The Dresser." [GeoR] (41:4) Wint 87, p. 692.
"Kate." [BelPoJ] (38:2) Wint 87-88, p. 16-19.
"Myself As Nude." [BelPoJ] (37:3) Spr 87, p. 1.
"Period Piece 2: August 25, 1954." [SouthernPR] (27:1) Spr 87, p. 46.
"Rebecca's Life" (Warren County, Pennsylvania 1854-1880). [BelPoJ] (37:3) Spr
87, p. 25-29.

2310. HASLAM, Thomas
"For Nora Fitzgerald." [Vis] (23) 87, p. 21.
2311. HASLEY, Louis
"Tallyho the Fox." [LightY] '87, c86, p. 171.
2312. HASS, Robert
"The Creation" (tr. of Adam Zagajewski, w. Renata Gorczynski). [Antaeus] (58) Spr
87, p. 91-92.
"In the Bahamas." [Antaeus] (58) Spr 87, p. 150.
"The Lullaby" (tr. of Adam Zagajewski, w. Renata Gorczynski). [Antaeus] (58) Spr
87, p. 93-94.
"On Squaw Peak." [Antaeus] (58) Spr 87, p. 145-147.
"Thin Air." [Antaeus] (58) Spr 87, p. 148-149.
"Wind at Night" (tr. of Adam Zagajewski, w. Renata Gorczynski). [Antaeus] (58)
Spr 87, p. 92.
2313. HASSALL, Dick
"Ordinary Music." [AntR] (45:3) Sum 87, p. 338-339.
2314. HASSELSTROM, Linda (Linda M.)
"Clara: In the Post Office." [Lactuca] (7) Ag 87, p. 20.
"Drying Onions." [PassN] (8:2) Sum 87, p. 4.
"First Poem for George." [PassN] (8:1) Wint 87, p. 18.
"For Pat, Who Wasn't Home." [PaintedB] (30) 87, p. 74.
"How to Find Me." [CharR] (13:2) Fall 87, p. 68-69.
"Late March Blizzard." [Lactuca] (7) Ag 87, p. 20.
"Roadkill" (special issue). [SpoonRQ] (12:3) Sum 87, 74 p.
2315. HASTY, Palmer
"Inside the Seasons." [Confr] (35/36) Spr-Fall 87, p. 291.
2316. HATHAWAY, Dev
"Back to Normal." [WebR] (12:2) Fall 87, p. 48.
2317. HATHAWAY, Jeanine
"Misperceptions." [GreensboroR] (40) Sum 86, p. 39.
"An Urban Cosmology." [GreensboroR] (40) Sum 86, p. 38.
"When the Bough Breaks." [RiverS] (22) 87, p. 84.
2318. HATHAWAY, William
"Consideration." [PoetC] (18:2) Wint 87, p. 58-59.
"Deer Season Again" (for Rob Patton). [NewEngR] (9:3) Spr 87, p. 311-313.
"Idle Tears." [PoetC] (18:2) Wint 87, p. 56-57.
"Jesting Pilate" (for Ruth). [MemphisSR] (8:1) Fall 87, p. 23.
"The Jungle Gym." [PoetC] (18:2) Wint 87, p. 54-55.
"Kipling at Southsea." [MemphisSR] (8:1) Fall 87, p. 24-25.
2319. HAUG, James
"Grounds." [TarRP] (26:2) Spr 87, p. 45.
"Pool Is a Godless Sport" (For Ed). [SouthernPR] (27:1) Spr 87, p. 8.
2320. HAUSER, Gwen
"La Vie Quotidienne." [Waves] (15:4) Spr 87, p. 73.
2321. HAVEN, Stephen
"Silhouette." [MissouriR] (10:1) 87, p. 164-165.
"Zoo" (for Joanie Lippolis, 1958-1985). [WestHR] (41:4) Wint 87, p. 356-357.
2322. HAWKINS, Hunt
"Mourning the Dying American Female Names." [SouthernR] (23:1) Ja 87, p.
155-156.
"My Neighbor's Pants." [SouthernR] (23:1) Ja 87, p. 156-157.
"My Vacuum Cleaner Suffers Remorse." [SouthernR] (23:1) Ja 87, p. 157-158.
"Penguins." [SouthernPR] (27:1) Spr 87, p. 20.
"Water Fear." [SouthernPR] (27:1) Spr 87, p. 21.
2323. HAWKINS, Tom
"Follow Your Heart to the Land of Enchantment" (The Small Print on the Back of the
Tour Brochure). [LightY] '87, c86, p. 161.
"Four Suburban Tribal Folk Stories." [ChatR] (8:1) Fall 87, p. 32-35.
"Grateful." [Outbr] (18/19) Fall 86-Spr 88, p. 16-17.
"Teachers." [Outbr] (18/19) Fall 86-Spr 88, p. 12-15.
"With My Wife at the Vietnam Memorial 1985." [Pembroke] (19) 87, p. 159-161.
2324. HAWKSWORTH, Marjorie
"In Response." [CentR] (31:1) Wint 87, p. 64.
2325. HAXTON, Brooks
"Auspice." [ThRiPo] (29/30) 87, p. 28-29.
"The Blackout." [LitR] (30:4) Sum 87, p. 637.

"My Friends." [Poetry] (150:1) Ap 87, p. 16.
"Northbound." [Poetry] (150:1) Ap 87, p. 16.
"On the Discontinuation of SALT Talks and the Relaxation of Standards . . ."
    [PoetryE] (23/24) Fall 87, p. 211.
"Pang." [ThRiPo] (29/30) 87, p. 32-33.
"Traveling Company." [ThRiPo] (29/30) 87, p. 30-31.
"Under the Purpling Storm." [PoetryE] (23/24) Fall 87, p. 212.
"Virgin." [Descant] (59) Wint 87, p. 22-26.
2326. HAYASHI, R. T.
"Tennis on the Roof." [KanQ] (19:1/2) Wint-Spr 87, p. 175.
"Water." [KanQ] (19:1/2) Wint-Spr 87, p. 174-175.
2327. HAYDEN, Dolores
"Revenge with Ice Palace" (1985 Alice Jackson Poetry Prize: Honorable Mention).
    [Electrum] (39) Fall-Wint 87, p. 14.
2328. HAYDON, Rich (Richard)
"House Burning." [Poem] (58) N 87, p. 14.
"The Land of Fields." [PoeticJ] (17) 87, p. 4-5.
"Medicine for Fossils." [Poem] (58) N 87, p. 13.
2329. HAYES, Jack
"Silent Commuters, 1970." [ManhatPR] (9) Sum 87, p. 35.
"The Winter I Was Ten." [ManhatPR] (9) Sum 87, p. 34.
2330. HAYES, Noreen
"March 24." [SpiritSH] (53:1) 87, p. 14.
"Photograph / Cape May / October, 1941." [SpiritSH] (53:1) 87, p. 15.
2331. HAYFORD, James
"The Light on the Mountain." [TexasR] (7:3/4) 87, p. 78.
"Something Said." [TexasR] (7:3/4) 87, p. 79.
2332. HAYMAN, Dick
"Portrait." [LightY] '87, c86, p. 139.
2333. HAYMON, Ava Leavell
"Bone Fires." [CalQ] (30) Wint 87, p. 56.
"Cottonwood Fluff." [CalQ] (30) Wint 87, p. 57.
"First Grandchild Remembers a Christmas Story" (1987 Ratner-Ferber-Poet Lore
    Honorable Mention). [PoetL] (82:2) Sum 87, p. 75-76.
"A Minke Whale Rolls Three Times Before Sounding" (Peter Beamish, Trinity Bay,
    Newfoundland). [CalQ] (30) Wint 87, p. 55.
"Sighting." [NowestR] (25:2) 87, p. 8.
2334. HAYNA, Lois Beebe
"Weather Forecast." [CrossCur] (7:2) 87, p. 41.
2335. HAYNES, Robert (Robert E.)
"At the Garden of Gethsemane." [Farm] (4:2) Spr-Sum 87, p. 62-63.
"The Man You Are Looking At." [NewL] (53:3) Spr 87, p. 18.
2336. HAYS, Robert
"Mirror, Mirror, on My Motel Wall." [StoneC] (14:3/4) Spr-Sum 87, p. 64.
2337. HAYWARD, Camille
"Air." [BellArk] (3:2) Mr-Ap 87, p. 8.
"Earth." [BellArk] (3:2) Mr-Ap 87, p. 8.
"Earth" (Corrected reprint). [BellArk] (3:3) My-Je 87, p. 2.
"Fire." [BellArk] (3:2) Mr-Ap 87, p. 8.
"Water." [BellArk] (3:2) Mr-Ap 87, p. 9.
2338. HAZARD, James
"Whiskey in Whiting, Indiana." [Spirit] (8:2) 87, p. 27.
2339. HAZELL, Tim
"Unit 410." [WestCR] (21:3) Wint 87, p. 38-39.
2340. HAZO, Samuel
"Anne's." [GreenfR] (14:1/2) Wint-Spr, p. 148-149.
"On the Stroke of Now." [GreenfR] (14:1/2) Wint-Spr, p. 146-147.
"The Quiet Proofs of Love." [AmerS] (56:1) Wint 87, p. 101-102.
"Throes." [GreenfR] (14:1/2) Wint-Spr, p. 140-143.
"Unto the Islands." [GreenfR] (14:1/2) Wint-Spr, p. 144-145.
HE, Li
    See LI, He
2341. HEAD, Robert
"Modern smooth lines it says." [Bogg] (58) 87, p. 44.
2342. HEALY, Eloise Klein
"Public Water." [HighP] (2:1) Spr 87, p. 26.

2343. HEANEY, Seamus
  "Casualty." [Pembroke] (19) 87, p. 78-80.
  "The Cool That Came Off Sheets." [Salm] (74/75) Spr-Sum 87, p. 42.
  "The Disappearing Island." [AmerPoR] (16:4) Jl-Ag 87, p. 6.
  "During Holy Week." [Salm] (74/75) Spr-Sum 87, p. 43.
  "From the Republic of Conscience." [AmerPoR] (16:4) Jl-Ag 87, p. 6.
  "In Memoriam: Robert Fitzgerald." [NewYRB] (34:20) 17 D 87, p. 9.
  "Inferno III." [Ploughs] (13:1) 87, p. 64-69.
  "An Open Letter." [Harp] (274:1642) Mr 87, p. 39.
  "The Peninsula." [Margin] (4) Aut 87, p. 59-60.
  "A Shooting Script." [AmerPoR] (16:4) Jl-Ag 87, p. 6.
  "The Singer's House." [Shen] (37:3) 87, p. 14-15.
2344. HEATH, Terrence
  "Once Upon a Time in Atlantis." [Verse] (4:1) Mr 87, p. 28.
  "Sonnet 1: The window now is a vase of night." [Grain] (15:2) Sum 87, p. 13.
2345. HEATH-STUBBS, John
  "I Hide My Face Against the Tramcar Window" (tr. of Eugene Dubnov, w. Chris
    Arkell). [SenR] (17:1) 87, p. 19.
  "I've Read How" (tr. of Eugene Dubnov, w. the author). [SouthernHR] (21:2) Spr
    87, p. 167.
  "The Legatee" (tr. of Anna Akhmatova, w. Eugene Dubnov). [ChiR] (35:4) 87, p.
    103.
  "Marina Tsvetayeva (1892-1941)" (tr. of Anna Akhmatova, w. Eugene Dubnov).
    [ChiR] (35:4) 87, p. 104.
  "Memories" (Excerpt, tr. of Giacomo Leopardi). [NewYRB] (34:1) 29 Ja 87, p. 43.
  "Pompey and Caesar." [Margin] (1) Wint 86, p. 51.
  "Sergei Esenin" (tr. of Anna Akhmatova, w. Eugene Dubnov). [ChiR] (35:4) 87, p.
    106.
  "Sergei Esenin (1895-1925)" (tr. of Anna Akhmatova, w. Eugene Dubnov). [ChiR]
    (35:4) 87, p. 105.
  "To a Future Reader" (tr. of Anna Akhmatova, w. Eugene Dubnov). [ChiR] (35:4)
    87, p. 107.
  "The Wicked Fairy's Version." [Margin] (1) Wint 86, p. 51.
2346. HÉBERT, Anne
  "The Cicada" (tr. by A. Poulin, Jr.). [TarPR] (27:1) Fall 87, p. 19.
  "If You're Unhappy" (tr. by A. Poulin, Jr.). [TarPR] (27:1) Fall 87, p. 20.
  "Lightning" (tr. by A. Poulin, Jr.). [TarPR] (27:1) Fall 87, p. 19.
2347. HECHT, Harvey
  "Doll House." [CapeR] (22:1) Spr 87, p. 46.
2348. HEDGES, David
  "Dinner Party." [BellArk] (3:6) N-D 87, p. 10.
2349. HEDIN, Mary
  "Star Gazing." [SoDakR] (25:3) Aut 87, p. 75.
2350. HEDIN, Robert
  "Abandoned Mountain Farm" (tr. of Stein Mehren). [Germ] (10:2) Spr 87, p. 40.
  "Along the Shore" (tr. of Stein Mehren). [Paint] (14:28) Aut 87, p. 30.
  "Ballad of the Trails in Västmanland" (tr. of Lars Gustafsson). [StoneC] (15:1/2)
    Fall-Wint 87-88, p. 20-21.
  "Drop" (tr. of Stein Mehren). [Germ] (10:2) Spr 87, p. 41.
  "Image of a Back Pasture" (tr. of Stein Mehren). [Germ] (10:2) Spr 87, p. 38.
  "The Kilesund Woods" (Excerpt, tr. of Stein Mehren). [Germ] (10:2) Spr 87, p. 37.
  "The Poison Ballad" (tr. of Lars Gustafsson). [StoneC] (15:1/2) Fall-Wint 87-88, p.
    16.
  "Tornado." [Raccoon] (24/25) My 87, p. 173.
  "Turin, January 3, 1889, the Corner of Via Carlo Alberto" (tr. of Lars Gustafsson).
    [Paint] (14:28) Aut 87, p. 31.
  "Winter" (tr. of Stein Mehren). [Germ] (10:2) Spr 87, p. 39.
2351. HEDLIN, Robert
  "Autumnal" (tr. of Stein Mehren). [WebR] (12:2) Fall 87, p. 24.
  "From the Depths of This Night" (tr. of Stein Mehren). [WebR] (12:2) Fall 87, p.
    24.
  "Glow of Sunrise" (tr. of Stein Mehren). [WebR] (12:2) Fall 87, p. 24.
2352. HEFFERNAN, Michael
  "The Ad Hoc Committee." [ColR] (NS 14:1) Spr-Sum 87, p. 66.
  "All That You Can Be." [CharR] (13:1) Spr 87, p. 83-84.
  "Answer the Phone." [MemphisSR] (8:1) Fall 87, p. 37.

"Blackbirds." [Iowa] (17:3) Fall 87, p. 71-72.
"Here Lies the Heart." [PoetryNW] (28:2) Sum 87, p. 33-34.
"The House of God." [Iowa] (17:3) Fall 87, p. 70.
"In Prospect of Eden." [CharR] (13:1) Spr 87, p. 82-83.
"Lacrimae Rerum." [PoetryNW] (28:2) Sum 87, p. 32-33.
"Litany Against the Bellyache, Upon St. Brigid's Day." [Iowa] (17:3) Fall 87, p. 75-76.
"The Manhood of Ireland." [Iowa] (17:3) Fall 87, p. 74-75.
"The Neighborhood Crazyman Talks to the President on the Eve of the Libyan Raids." [AmerPoR] (16:2) Mr-Ap 87, p. 14.
"The Postcard." [ColR] (NS 14:1) Spr-Sum 87, p. 67.
"Reading Aquinas." [Iowa] (17:3) Fall 87, p. 72.
"Willow." [Iowa] (17:3) Fall 87, p. 73-74.
2353. HEIGHTON, Steven
"High Jump." [Waves] (15:1/2) Fall 86, p. 79.
"Josef Stalin: Later Works." [Quarry] (36:1) Wint 87, p. 102.
"Rowers." [Waves] (15:1/2) Fall 86, p. 78.
"Sky Burial." [Grain] (15:3) Fall 87, p. 62.
2354. HEINE-KOEHN, Lala
"May I Ask for the Hand of Your Sister" (for my brother). [PraF] (8:2) Sum 87, p. 46.
"Sela, The Bearing Stool." [Dandel] (14:2) Fall-Wint 87, p. 22-23.
"Whoever He Is." [PraF] (8:2) Sum 87, p. 47.
2355. HEINEMAN, W. F.
"The Beach." [BallSUF] (28:4) Aut 87, p. 13.
"The Migration." [BallSUF] (28:4) Aut 87, p. 14.
"Water Beneath Them." [BallSUF] (28:4) Aut 87, p. 12.
2356. HEINLEIN, David A.
"Expostulation on Non-Negativity." [US1] (20/21) Wint 86-87, p. 24.
"Tea in Princeton." [US1] (20/21) Wint 86-87, p. 22-23.
2357. HEISLER, Eva
"In the Aviary" (Edith Sitwell, 1887-1964). [QW] (24) Wint 87, p. 108-113.
2358. HEJINIAN, Lyn
"The Cell." [Caliban] (2) 87, p. 154-156.
"Nasturium as Reality" (tr. of Arkadii Dragomoshchenko, w. Elena Balashova). [Sulfur] (19) Spr 87, p. 94-107.
"The Person." [Bound] (14:1/2) Fall 85-Wint 86 [c87], p. 75-79.
2359. HELLER, Michael
"Constellations of Waking" (on the suicide of Walter Benjamin at the Franco-Spanish border, 1940). [Pequod] (23/24) 87, p. 301-304.
"Strophes from the Writings of Walter Benjamin." [Conjunc] (10) 87, p. 234.
"This Many Colored Brush Which Once Forced the Elements" (to J.A.). [Conjunc] (10) 87, p. 230-233.
2360. HELLERSTEIN, Kathryn
"Moyshe-Leyb's Voice" (tr. of Yankev Glatshteyn). [PartR] (54:1) Wint 87, p. 126-128.
2361. HELLMAN, Sheila
"Attachment." [KanQ] (19:3) Sum 87, p. 139.
"Old Photo." [GreenfR] (14:1/2) Wint-Spr, p. 113.
2362. HEMMINGSON, Michael
"A Poem: At the beach with her." [PoeticJ] (17) 87, p. 3.
2363. HEMPHILL, Essex
"American Hero." [Callaloo] (10:3) Sum 87, p. 365.
"Family Jewels" (for Washington, D.C.). [JamesWR] (5:1) Fall 87, p. 10.
2364. HEMSCHEMEYER, Judith
"I have a certain smile" (No. 70, in Russian and English, tr. of Anna Akhmatova). [Gargoyle] (32/33) 87, p. 54-55.
"It is simple, it is clear" (No. 218, in Russian and English, tr. of Anna Akhmatova). [Gargoyle] (32/33) 87, p. 56-57.
"Parting (2)" (Zh. 328, tr. of Anna Akhmatova). [NowestR] (25:3) 87, p. 423.
"Turning the Earth, the Earth Turning." [NowestR] (25:3) 87, p. 222.
2365. HENDERSON, Brian
"The Screen." [Event] (16:3) Fall 87, p. 32.
2366. HENDERSON, Cindy S.
"Improper Punctuation." [EngJ] (76:1) Ja 87, p. 86.

181

2367. HENDERSON, Mark
"A Sixpack of Beer." [AntigR] (71/72) Aut 87-Wint 88, p. 22.
"Three Lives." [AntigR] (71/72) Aut 87-Wint 88, p. 23.
2368. HENDRICKS, Ron
"Upon G.C. Murphy's Closing, 1986" (Parkersburg, W. Va., c. 1950). [ChatR]
(8:1) Fall 87, p. 36.
2369. HENDRYSON, Barbara
"Mercy Road." [Sequoia] (30:3) Wint 87, p. 58.
2370. HENIGAN, Julie
"After the Fall." [ManhatPR] (9) Sum 87, p. 49.
"Untitled: I cannot be Eurydice." [ManhatPR] (9) Sum 87, p. 49.
2371. HENKE, Doris Kerr
"Polly Swenson" (after Edgar Lee Masters). [Writer] (100:1) Ja 87, p. 23.
2372. HENKE, Mark
"Reunion." [Writer] (99:11) N 86, p. 19.
"Wells." [CapeR] (22:1) Spr 87, p. 41.
"Yearbook." [Writer] (99:7) Jl 86, p. 20.
2373. HENN, Mary Ann
"Feathers." [Writer] (99:9) S 86, p. 26.
"Incompatible, They'd Say Today." [BallSUF] (28:4) Aut 87, p. 71.
"Just So No One Sees." [Bogg] (58) 87, p. 54.
"Little Birds Swooping." [LightY] '87, c86, p. 113.
"My Second Night in a Bar." [Bogg] (58) 87, p. 38.
2374. HENNING, Dianna
"The Painting Above Ella's Treadle Sewing Machine." [CapeR] (22:2) Fall 87, p. 6.
"Sufficiency." [YellowS] (25) Wint 87, p. 16.
"Turning on the Faucet." [CapeR] (22:2) Fall 87, p. 7.
2375. HENRIE, Carol
"The Luck of Black Cats." [PraS] (61:2) Sum 87, p. 78-80.
"The Mountains of China." [PraS] (61:2) Sum 87, p. 80-81.
2376. HENRY, Daniel
"March 1, 1981" (for Cheri Thickstun). [EngJ] (76:6) O 87, p. 99.
2377. HENRY, Eileen Cameron
"Puppet." [AntigR] (68) Wint 87, p. 37.
2378. HENSHAW, Tyler
"Butcher Shop." [LakeSR] (21) 87, p. 30.
"Portrait of a Purchase." [LakeSR] (21) 87, p. 30.
2379. HENSON, David
"The Last Atlantean." [Spirit] (8:2) 87, p. 177-178.
2380. HENSON, Lance
"Near the wichita mountains." [NoDaQ] (55:4) Fall 87, p. 242.
2381. HEPWORTH, James R.
"Editor to Contributor." [GreenfR] (14:1/2) Wint-Spr, p. 208.
"On Being Asked for a Contributor's Note." [GreenfR] (14:1/2) Wint-Spr, p. 210.
"Sonogram: Pediatrics Clinic, Tucson, Arizona 1982." [GreenfR] (14:1/2) Wint-Spr,
p. 109.
2382. HERBERT, W. N.
"Cormundum." [Verse] (4:2) Je 87, p. 26-27.
"A Dream of Buster Keaton" (5 poems). [PoetC] (19:1) Fall 87, p. 19-27.
"Mariposa Pibroch." [Verse] (4:2) Je 87, p. 27.
"Tiger Balm." [Verse] (4:2) Je 87, p. 25.
2383. HERBERT, Zbigniew
"A Knocker." [Shen] (37:3) 87, p. 11-12.
"Mass for the Imprisoned" (tr. by Michael March and Jaroslaw Anders). [NewYRB]
(33:21-22) 15 Ja 87, p. 15.
2384. HERMAN, Peter
"For Elizabeth, in California." [Waves] (15:1/2) Fall 86, p. 87.
"Tonight." [Waves] (15:1/2) Fall 86, p. 87.
2385. HERMSEN, Terry
"Shirts." [Gambit] (21) 87, p. 56.
2386. HERNANDEZ
"Mar de Fondo" (Selection: 17). [Footwork] 87, p. 21-22.
"Sea Bed" (Selections: 17, 8, 11, tr. by Brian Swann). [Footwork] 87, p. 21-22.
2387. HERNANDEZ, Francisco
"Mexico City Diptych" (tr. by Linda Scheer). [Caliban] (2) 87, p. 142-143.
"Two" (tr. by Linda Scheer). [Caliban] (2) 87, p. 141.

2388. HERNANDEZ, Inées
"1st Tuesday of November, Poetry Evening, Election Night." [Americas] (14:3/4)
Fall-Wint 86, p. 94-96.
"Against the Wind." [Americas] (14:3/4) Fall-Wint 86, p. 97-98.
HERNANDEZ CRUZ, Victor
See CRUZ, Victor Hernandez
2389. HEROY, Susan
"The Family, Descending." [ThRiPo] (29/30) 87, p. 34-36.
2390. HERRERA, Juan Felipe
"Story & King Blvd. / Tenn-age Totems." [FiveFR] (5) 87, p. 37.
2391. HERRINGER, Barbara
"The Novice: a Chant for Women's Voices." [SinW] (31) 87, p. 22.
2392. HERSHON, Robert
"9-5-85, 6:00, 81 [degrees]" (for N.E.S. Jarrett). [HangL] (50/51) 87, p. 78.
"Acqua Arzente" (for Ted Kaufman). [HangL] (50/51) 87, p. 77.
"Coats." [Notus] (2:2) Fall 87, p. 75.
"The Crumble-Brain Cafe." [Notus] (2:2) Fall 87, p. 77.
"The Editors Editing" (for Dick, Mark and Ron). [HangL] (50/51) 87, p. 75.
"Except Thou Bless Me." [HangL] (50/51) 87, p. 79.
"The Festive Head." [PoetryNW] (28:2) Sum 87, p. 47.
"Harold in Midtown." [HangL] (50/51) 87, p. 76.
"Harvey Calls." [PoetryE] (23/24) Fall 87, p. 218.
"Minnesota Farmers Blame Bad Crop on Jews." [PoetryNW] (28:2) Sum 87, p.
46-47.
"NYC Country Music." [Notus] (2:2) Fall 87, p. 78.
"The Yellow Door." [Notus] (2:2) Fall 87, p. 76.
2393. HESS, Alice Shoup
"Transformed." [Writer] (99:5) My 86, p. 16.
2394. HESS, Mary
"Edwina." [ManhatPR] (9) Sum 87, p. 41.
2395. HESS, Sonya
"The Ambassador's Daughter." [Caliban] (2) 87, p. 113.
"Carrying What You Love." [Caliban] (2) 87, p. 115.
"Geography." [LitR] (30:4) Sum 87, p. 620.
"Meditation on a Piñon Wood Fire." [KanQ] (19:3) Sum 87, p. 312.
"Siesta" (Tahiti, 1893). [KanQ] (19:3) Sum 87, p. 312-313.
"Think How Long." [Caliban] (2) 87, p. 114.
2396. HESSELMAN, Marcia
"Ona Baker." [Farm] (4:1) Wint 87, p. 16-17.
2397. HESTER, Beth
"Death by Chance." [HolCrit] (24:5) D 87, p. 11.
2398. HESTER, M. L.
"Florida Exterminator." [PikeF] (8) Fall 87, p. 12.
"Jennifer Is an Island." [ManhatPR] (9) Sum 87, p. 40.
"Lardbelly at the Emergency Room." [Pembroke] (19) 87, p. 194.
"What Of It?" [Confr] (35/36) Spr-Fall 87, p. 176.
2399. HESTER, William
"Shark." [Wind] (17:59) 87, p. 20.
2400. HETTICH, Michael
"Project." [Outbr] (18/19) Fall 86-Spr 88, p. 136-137.
"While My Companion Sleeps in Our Path." [Phoenix] (7:2) 87, p. 27.
2401. HEUSINKVELD, Paula
"Let Me Be Your Forest" (tr. of Ramiro Lagos). [InterPR] (13:2) Fall 87, p. 31.
"Poem for Being in the Clouds" (tr. of Ramiro Lagos). [InterPR] (13:2) Fall 87, p.
29.
2402. HEUVING, Jeanne
"On an Ice Blue Field." [SouthernPR] (27:1) Spr 87, p. 19.
2403. HEWITT, Bernard R.
"Silences." [DekalbLAJ] (20:1/4) 87, p. 41.
2404. HEWITT, Christopher
"August." [JamesWR] (4:4) Sum 87, p. 5.
"The Empty House." [Kaleid] (15) Sum-Fall 87, p. 21.
"Ghost" (tr. of Nina Cassian). [NewYorker] (63:7) 6 Ap 87, p. 42.
"The Green Elephant" (tr. of Nina Cassian). [NewYorker] (63:7) 6 Ap 87, p. 42.
"That Animal" (tr. of Nina Cassian). [NewYorker] (63:7) 6 Ap 87, p. 42.
"The Young Bat" (tr. of Nina Cassian). [NewYorker] (63:7) 6 Ap 87, p. 42.

2405. HEWITT, John
"O Country People." [Pembroke] (19) 87, p. 76-777.
2406. HEYD, Michael
"Word Processor." [Outbr] (18/19) Fall 86-Spr 88, p. 10.
2407. HEYEN, William
"Furrows." [ColR] (NS 14:2) Fall-Wint 87, p. 89.
2408. HEYER, Paul
"Rebecca" (Georgia Street Bazaar). [Waves] (14:4) Spr 86, p. 72.
"Rowena" (Georgia Street Bazaar). [Waves] (14:4) Spr 86, p. 73.
2409. HICKMAN, David
"The Girl." [Gargoyle] (32/33) 87, p. 258.
"Significa." [Gargoyle] (32/33) 87, p. 259.
"Variation # 34." [Gargoyle] (32/33) 87, p. 257.
2410. HICKOK, Betsy Snow
"I've Let the Brakes Go." [PoetryE] (23/24) Fall 87, p. 160.
2411. HICKS, John V.
"The Alder Tree." [CrossCur] (7:3) 87, p. 96.
"Beast Without." [AntigR] (69/70) 87, p. 208.
"Cling." [CanLit] (112) Spr 87, p. 31.
"Descant." [Waves] (14:4) Spr 86, p. 35.
"On Having to Thumb Through Pages to Find Ciardi." [Grain] (15:2) Sum 87, p.
10.
"Out of This Dream." [AntigR] (69/70) 87, p. 207.
"Sonnet for a Small Girl." [Grain] (15:2) Sum 87, p. 8.
"Telltale." [Grain] (15:2) Sum 87, p. 6.
2412. HIEBERT, Jennifer
"And, Aside." [AnotherCM] (17) 87, p. 45.
2413. HIEBERT, Paul
"Sarah Binks" (Selection: "Hi, Sooky, Ho, Sooky." [Grain] (15:3) Fall 87, p.
10-11.
2414. HIESTAND, Emily
"Checking Out the Block." [PraS] (61:4) Wint 87, p. 83-84.
"The Fence." [PraS] (61:4) Wint 87, p. 81.
"Likewise." [Atlantic] (259:2) F 87, p. 78.
"Route One." [PraS] (61:4) Wint 87, p. 82.
"These Are for Your Consideration." [Atlantic] (259:6) Je 87, p. 51.
2415. HIGGINS, Mary Rising
"Ullage 1." [CalQ] (30) Wint 87, p. 29.
2416. HIGGINSON, William J.
"In Front of the Veil" (for the poets of "The Dream Book"). [Footwork] 87, p. 42.
"Washing the Snake by the Light of the Full Moon." [Footwork] 87, p. 41-42.
2417. HIGH, John
"I've forgotten nothing" (tr. of Bella Akhmadulina, w. Katya Olmsted). [FiveFR] (5)
87, p. 102.
"Night Fantasies" (tr. of Bella Akhmadulina, w. Katya Olmsted). [FiveFR] (5) 87,
p. 103.
"Such a night isn't chosen" (tr. of Ivan Zhdanov, w. Katya Olmsted). [FiveFR] (5)
87, p. 68.
"The Walker" (tr. of Ivan Zhdanov). [FiveFR] (5) 87, p. 69.
"When My Wife Dances" (tr. of Peter Veghin, w. Katya Olmsted). [FiveFR] (5) 87,
p. 1-2.
2418. HILBERRY, Conrad
"Aubade." [PassN] (8:2) Sum 87, p. 18.
"Fisherman." [PassN] (8:2) Sum 87, p. 17.
"The God in Winter: A Lecture." [PassN] (8:2) Sum 87, p. 18.
"The Monkey." [PassN] (8:2) Sum 87, p. 16.
2419. HILBERT, Donna
"Movie Candy." [Electrum] (39) Fall-Wint 87, p. 47.
2420. HILDEBIDLE, John
"Back Cove." [TexasR] (7:3/4) 87, p. 80-81.
"Descent of Winter." [PraS] (61:1) Spr 87, p. 82-83.
2421. HILL, Gerald
"A Book of Events" (after Jerome Rothenberg's *Technicians of the Sacred*: 5
selections). [MalR] (80) S 87, p. 85-86.
2422. HILL, Jane
"As Daughters Grow" (for Bill and Barbara Koon). [HighP] (2:1) Spr 87, p. 50-52.

2423. HILL, John Meredith
"Aerogramme." [MissouriR] (10:3) 87, p. 72.
2424. HILL, Lindsay
"Minoa." [Raccoon] (24/25) My 87, p. 138-140.
"The Words." [Raccoon] (24/25) My 87, p. 115-116.
2425. HILL, Nellie
"The Artists' Colony." [ManhatPR] (9) Sum 87, p. 43.
2426. HILL, Pamela Steed
"Slow Dancing." [MidAR] (7:2) 87, p. 86.
2427. HILL, Richard
"Apotheosis." [Zyzzyva] (3:1) Spr 87, p. 59-60.
2428. HILL, Sara
"The Harvest." [Puerto] (22:2) Spr 87, p. 72.
2429. HILLARD, Jeffrey
"Talking to Myself." [KanQ] (19:3) Sum 87, p. 212.
2430. HILLES, Robert
"Hell and Some Notes on a Piano." [Quarry] (36:3) Sum 87, p. 18.
"Outlasting the Landscape." [MalR] (80) S 87, p. 37-38.
"A Poem Is a Machine for Making Choices." [PraF] (8:2) Sum 87, p. 32.
"Something Dangerous." [Quarry] (36:3) Sum 87, p. 19.
"A Tender Man." [MalR] (80) S 87, p. 39.
"Walking Across a Graveyard to Mail a Postcard." [Quarry] (36:3) Sum 87, p. 17.
"When Transforms Flesh" (Bow River, Calgary). [Quarry] (36:3) Sum 87, p. 18.
"Words Contain Sleep." [PraF] (8:2) Sum 87, p. 31.
2431. HILLILA, Bernhard
"Ahead of Me I See" (tr. of Rakel Liehu). [ColR] (NS 14:1) Spr-Sum 87, p. 37.
2432. HILLIS, R.
"Hunted Citizens." [CanLit] (115) Wint 87, p. 125.
2433. HILLMAN, Brenda
"The Calf." [Zyzzyva] (3:2) Sum 87, p. 62-63.
"Festival of the Weaving Maiden." [MissouriR] (10:2) 87, p. 64.
"Magnolia." [Field] (36) Spr 87, p. 11.
"Vespers." [Field] (36) Spr 87, p. 9-10.
2434. HILLRINGHOUSE, Mark
"Pantoum" (for a after Michael Palmer [sic]). [Footwork] 87, p. 54.
"Schrecklichkeit." [Footwork] 87, p. 54.
2435. HILTON, David
"The Melmac Year." [PoetL] (82:4) Wint 87-88, p. 215-218.
2436. HINDLEY, Norman
"Arrhythmia." [HawaiiR] (19) Spr 86, c87, p. 1.
"Good Night, October" (for Shawhan). [HawaiiR] (19) Spr 86, c87, p. 2.
"Holding the New Moon for One Hour Near Christmas, She Lighting the Tree" (for K. B. away). [HawaiiR] (20) Fall 86, c87, p. 14-15.
"Monastery." [HawaiiR] (21) Spr 87, p. 74-76.
"That's All for Picasso" (for Barbara). [HawaiiR] (20) Fall 86, c87, p. 16-17.
"Water Born." The Best of [BambooR] [(31-32)] 86, p. 33-34.
"Winter Eel" (for Douglas Hindley). [HawaiiR] (21) Spr 87, p. 77-79.
"Wood Butcher" (for my father). [HawaiiR] (21) Spr 87, p. 72-73.
2437. HINES, Debra
"Audience." [MemphisSR] (7:2) Spr 87, p. 24.
"Codpiece." [NoAmR] (272:2) Je 87, p. 26.
"The Creature Who Will Eat and Eat and Keep Eating Unitl His Life Ends." [PoetL] (82:1) Spr 87, p. 20.
"Gravid with Goodwill." [PoetL] (82:1) Spr 87, p. 19.
"Guest." [Agni] (24/25) 87, p. 71.
"The Heart." [PoetL] (82:1) Spr 87, p. 21.
"Memento Mori." [CarolQ] (39:2) Wint 87, p. 35-36.
"One My Show Without Embarrassment One's Moral Commitment in Strong, Lucid Verse . . ." [CarolQ] (39:2) Wint 87, p. 37.
"The Tailor of Coventry." [CarolQ] (39:2) Wint 87, p. 38-39.
"Yves Saint Laurent and the Black Pullover." [CarolQ] (39:2) Wint 87, p. 40.
2438. HINKAMP, Shirley
"The Super." [Cond] (14) 87, p. 192.
2439. HINTON, David
"The Journey North" (tr. of Tu Fu). [NewEngR] (10:1) Aut 87, p. 33-35.

2440. HIOTT, Judith
"Family Practice" (For my Father). [Wind] (17:61) 87, p. 20.
2441. HIRSCH, Edward
"Cemetery by the Sea" (Ha'iku, Hawaii). [GrandS] (6:4) Sum 87, p. 123-124.
"Evening Star" (Georgia O'Keeffe in Canyon, Texas, 1917). [Nat] (244:12) 28 Mr
87, p. 408.
"For the New World" (Auditorium Building, Chicago, Adler and Sullivan,
1887-1889). [Shen] (37:4) 87, p. 61-62.
"Homage to O'Keeffe." [NewRep] (196:1/2) 5-12 Ja 87, p. 36.
"Infertility." [NewRep] (197:19) 9 N 87, p. 32.
"Proustian." [SouthwR] (72:2) Spr 87, p. 198.
"Rapture." [Agni] (24/25) 87, p. 96-97.
2442. HIRSCH, Thomas L.
"A History of Golf — sort of." [LightY] '87, c86, p. 29.
HIRSCHFIELD, Jane
    See HIRSHFIELD, Jane
2443. HIRSCHFIELD, Ted
"In Memoriam: Jim Hamby." [CapeR] (22:1) Spr 87, p. 1.
2444. HIRSHFIELD, Jane
"1973." [YellowS] (22) Spr 87, p. 37.
"Heat." [AmerPoR] (16:4) Jl-Ag 87, p. 39.
"The Hungry Ghosts." [CalQ] (30) Wint 87, p. 61.
"Justice Without Passion." [Zyzzyva] (3:4) Wint 87-88, p. 131.
"Lullabye." [GeoR] (41:3) Fall 87, p. 553-555.
"The Stream of It." [Calyx] (10:2/3) Spr 87, p. 13.
2445. HIRZEL, David
"At Black Canyon." [CapeR] (22:2) Fall 87, p. 16.
"The Bells." [HampSPR] Wint 86, p. 55.
"Building, Naming, Flying." [HampSPR] Wint 87, p. 17-18.
"Changing Seasons." [HampSPR] Wint 86, p. 55.
"Fireflies." [Wind] (17:59) 87, p. 33.
"Junkyard." [KanQ] (19:1/2) Wint-Spr 87, p. 220.
"Looking for Land." [HampSPR] Wint 87, p. 16-17.
"Smoke, Fire." [KanQ] (19:3) Sum 87, p. 144.
"Venn Diagram." [KanQ] (19:1/2) Wint-Spr 87, p. 219.
2446. HISSOM, James
"Early Dreams." [LaurelR] (20:1/2) Sum 87, p. 26.
2447. HITCHCOCK, George
"Monday After the Last Sunday." [Caliban] (3) 87, p. 49.
"That Which on Opening Your Brain I Least Expected to Discover." [Caliban] (3)
87, p. 50.
"Vexatious Aphorisms." [Caliban] (3) 87, p. 50-51.
"War." [Caliban] (3) 87, p. 49.
2448. HITTLE, Gervase
"Sioux" (tr. of Peter Pabisch). [SoDakR] (25:3) Aut 87, p. 84-85.
2449. HIX, H. L.
"Echoes: A Sonnet Sequence" (to P.R.). [Amelia] (4:1/2, issue 9) 87, p. 106.
"For Cindy, Art, and Warren, Coming Home Through a Snowstorm, Two Hours
Overdue." [Amelia] (4:1/2, issue 9) 87, p. 107.
"The Hill Across the River." [ColR] (NS 14:2) Fall-Wint 87, p. 88.
"A Man Finds Me Dead." [Amelia] (4:1/2, issue 9) 87, p. 107.
2450. HIX, Hubert E.
"Blue Poem." [LightY] '87, c86, p. 200.
"Pastoral." [Vis] (23) 87, p. 27.
2451. HLATSHWAYO, Mi S'dumo
"The Black Mamba Rises." [TriQ] (69) Spr-Sum 87, p. 296-300.
"The Tears of a Creator" (w. Alfred Temba Qabula). [TriQ] (69) Spr-Sum 87, p.
286-293.
2452. HLONGWANE, David
"Mummy Let Me Go." [TriQ] (69) Spr-Sum 87, p. 60.
2453. HOAD, Patricia J.
"Only Lovers." [US1] (20/21) Wint 86-87, p. 7.
2454. HOAG, Barbara
"Germany's Daughter." [NegC] (7:3/4) 87, p. 165-167.
"Germany's Daughter" (1986 Finalist, Eve of Saint Agnes Poetry Competition).
[NegC] (7:1/2) 87, p. 227-229.

2455. HOAGLAND, Bill
"Ascension." [DenQ] (21:3) Wint 87, p. 58-59.
"Hart Crane." [DenQ] (21:3) Wint 87, p. 60.
"Joan Miro's *Person Throwing a Stone at a Bird*." [DenQ] (21:3) Wint 87, p. 57.
"Pastoral." [SoDakR] (25:2) Sum 87, p. 32.
"Voyeur and Exhibitionist." [BellR] (10:1) Spr 87, p. 27.
2456. HOAGLAND, Tony
"Astrology." [Sonora] (12) Spr 87, p. 19-20.
"Doing This." [AmerPoR] (16:5) S-O 87, p. 38.
"Geography." [Sonora] (12) Spr 87, p. 17-18.
"A Love of Learning." [Crazy] (33) Wint 87, p. 35-36.
"Men and Women." [AmerPoR] (16:5) S-O 87, p. 38.
"On Standing Alone." [Crazy] (33) Wint 87, p. 33-34.
"One Season." [Crazy] (33) Wint 87, p. 31-32.
"The Question." [Spirit] (8:2) 87, p. 334.
2457. HOAGWOOD, Terence
"Night Walk." [TexasR] (8:1/2) Spr-Sum 87, p. 83.
2458. HOBBS, Blair
"Dirt Garden." [InterPR] (13:2) Fall 87, p. 106.
"From Parlor to Porch." [InterPR] (13:2) Fall 87, p. 105.
"Wind-Borne." [InterPR] (13:2) Fall 87, p. 104-105.
2459. HOBEN, Sandra
"The Permanent Collection." [YellowS] (24) Aut 87, p. 33.
2460. HOCHMAN, Benjamin
"Sons of the Right Hand." [LightY] '87, c86, p. 70.
2461. HODGE, Margaret
"Saying Goodbye in a Book Store" (to Doug Nordfors). [BellArk] (3:2) Mr-Ap 87, p. 6.
"Waking Up in a Chair in the Home of Friends" (for Frances and Gunnar Fagerlund). [BellArk] (3:3) My-Je 87, p. 20.
2462. HODGEN, John
"Boy Struck by Lightning Survives." [StoneC] (15:1/2) Fall-Wint 87-88, p. 28-29.
2463. HODGES, Gregg
"Outside You." [KanQ] (19:4) Fall 87, p. 75.
2464. HODGSON, Hallie
"Who, Me?" [LightY] '87, c86, p. 133.
2465. HOEFLER, Walter
"I Wouldn't Be Able to Tell the Story" (No Podria Contar la Historia, tr. by Steven White). [Contact] (9:44/45/46) Fall-Wint 87, p. 28.
2466. HOEFT, Robert D.
"An Open Letter to Mother Nature." [CrossCur] (6:4) 87, p. 148-149.
2467. HOEKSEMA, Thomas
"V. I stop dying" (tr. of Socorro Leon Femat, w. R. Enriquez). [InterPR] (13:1) Spr 87, p. 21.
"Cactus" (tr. of Blanca Luz Pulido, w. R. Enriquez). [InterPR] (13:1) Spr 87, p. 15.
"From the fire" (tr. of José Emilio Pacheco). [InterPR] (13:1) Spr 87, p. 17.
"Haikus" (4 poems, tr. of Gabriela Rábago Palafox). [InterPR] (13:1) Spr 87, p. 23.
"Mauve and amber" (tr. of Adriana Yañez, w. R. Enriquez). [InterPR] (13:1) Spr 87, p. 19.
"Poem: The city encloses us, moist" (tr. of Adriana Monroy). [InterPR] (13:1) Spr 87, p. 13.
"Shipwreck" (tr. of Perla Schwartz). [InterPR] (13:1) Spr 87, p. 25.
2468. HOEPPNER, Edward Haworth
"An Audience for the Minotaur." [NoAmR] (272:3) D 87, p. 22.
"Dream of Hiroshima" (tr. of Oscar Hahn). [BlackWR] (13:2) Spr 87, p. 131, 133.
2469. HOEY, Allen
"Alone." [PaintedB] (30) 87, p. 73.
"Dimies." [BelPoJ] (38:1) Fall 87, p. 33-34.
"The Fire." [Phoenix] (7:1) 87, p. 23.
"First Snow." [KanQ] (19:3) Sum 87, p. 262-263.
"For My Son." [NoDaQ] (55:2) Spr 87, p. 151.
"Lone Duck Inlet." [Poem] (58) N 87, p. 40-41.
"Moving Again." [HighP] (2:2) Fall 87, p. 129-130.
"The Original Chaos of Love." [KanQ] (19:3) Sum 87, p. 263.
"A Painter Speaks to Possibilities." [BelPoJ] (38:1) Fall 87, p. 30-32.

187

2470. HOFER, Mariann
"Barns." [KanQ] (19:1/2) Wint-Spr 87, p. 291.
"Living by the Grain Elevator." [Gambit] (20) 86, p. 25.
2471. HOFFER, Mariann
"Camping on the Site of the Victory Hotel" (Put-in-Bay, Ohio). [Farm] (4:1) Wint
87, p. 35.
"Summer Night." [Farm] (4:1) Wint 87, p. 36.
2472. HOFFMAN, Barbara
"Apology." [BelPoJ] (38:2) Wint 87-88, p. 31.
2473. HOFFMAN, Daniel
"Addendum to *Daniel Hoffman: A Comprehensive Bibliography*." [NegC] (7:1/2)
87, p. 13.
"An Apothegm." [LightY] '87, c86, p. 221.
"Fables." [Poetry] (151:1/2) O-N 87, p. 64.
"Her Obedient Servant" (Robert Graves, 1895-1985). [NegC] (7:1/2) 87, p. 12.
"His Steps." [Boulevard] (2:1/2) Spr 87, p. 205.
"Night Fishing." [NegC] (7:1/2) 87, p. 11.
"Reasons." [NegC] (7:1/2) 87, p. 9.
"The Sacred Fount." [NegC] (7:1/2) 87, p. 10.
"A Stone." [Boulevard] (2:1/2) Spr 87, p. 206.
2474. HOFFMAN, H. A.
"March Planting" (For C.T. Lilly, Spanishburg, W. Va.). [LaurelR] (20:1/2) Sum
87, p. 27.
2475. HOFFMANN, Roald
"Carcinoma." [LaurelR] (21:1/2) Wint-Sum 87, p. 60-61.
"June 1944." [PraS] (61:1) Spr 87, p. 81.
"New Traffic Patterns Ahead" (1986 Winner, Eve of Saint Agnes Poetry
Competition). [NegC] (7:1/2) 87, p. 123.
"Of Scatological Interest." [HampSPR] Wint 87, p. 59.
"Touching the Surface." [NewL] (53:2) Wint 86-87, p. 84-85.
2476. HOGAN, Judy
"Welsh Poems - 1985" ("Light-Food," Book XV, August 2, 1985, Pentre-ty-gwyn).
[Pembroke] (19) 87, p. 143-144.
2477. HOGAN, Michael
"Springtime in the Rockies." [HayF] (2) Spr 87, p. 15.
2478. HOGAN, Wayne
"In the Shadows with Trees." [MSS] (5:3) 87, p. 34.
"Max Beckmann's Worker." [CrabCR] (4:2) Spr 87, p. 14.
2479. HOGGARD, James
"The Center of the Bedroom" (tr. of Oscar Hahn). [InterPR] (13:1) Spr 87, p. 29.
"Consumer Society" (tr. of Oscar Hahn). [InterPR] (13:1) Spr 87, p. 31.
"The Dying Gaul" (Museo di Capitolo, Rome). [InterPR] (13:1) Spr 87, p. 111.
"Flat Blue" (tr. of Oscar Hahn). [InterPR] (13:1) Spr 87, p. 27.
"Naiad." [InterPR] (13:1) Spr 87, p. 112.
"Past Me Now the Breezes Ride." [HampSPR] Wint 86, p. 26.
"Stormwatch" (Serriana de Ronda, Spain). [InterPR] (13:1) Spr 87, p. 112.
"The Warrior's Rest" (tr. of Oscar Hahn). [InterPR] (13:1) Spr 87, p. 31.
"White World" (for Ken & Marie-Claude). [HampSPR] Wint 86, p. 27.
2480. HOGUE, Cynthia
"A Romance." [Raccoon] (24/25) My 87, p. 233.
2481. HOLAN, Vladimír
"Mothers After the War" (for Jaroslav Seifert, tr. by C. G. Hanzlicek and Dana
Hábová). [AntR] (45:1) Wint 87, p. 93.
"Snow" (tr. by C. G. Hanzlicek and Dana Hábová). [AntR] (45:1) Wint 87, p. 93.
2482. HOLDEN, Jonathan
"Against Paradise." [Poetry] (149:6) Mr 87, p. 321-323.
"Full Circle" (for Alan Nordby Holden, 1904-1985). [WestHR] (41:1) Spr 87, p.
15-16.
"Goodness." [AmerPoR] (16:2) Mr-Ap 87, p. 11-12.
"Goodness." [MichQR] (26:3) Sum 87, p. 508-509.
"Home." [Poetry] (149:6) Mr 87, p. 324.
"On an Early Evening in Late June, Almost Anywhere" (for Al). [NewEngR] (9:4)
Sum 87, p. 419.
"A Personal History of the Curveball." [Antaeus] (59) Aut 87, p. 120-122.
"Some Basic Aesthetics." [Poetry] (151:1/2) O-N 87, p. 65.
"Unstopping the Pipes." [NewEngR] (9:4) Sum 87, p. 420.

188

HOLDER

2483. HOLDER, Barbara
"Child Out." [Footwork] 87, p. 35.
2484. HOLINGER, Richard
"Counting Grapes." [ManhatPR] (9) Sum 87, p. 44.
"Full Worm Moon." [ManhatPR] (9) Sum 87, p. 44.
"Imagining What's Left." [BallSUF] (28:4) Aut 87, p. 10.
"In a Tiered Garden Over Basel" (In Memory of Otto Finckh). [Outbr] (18/19) Fall
86-Spr 88, p. 40-41.
"Practical Shooting." [Outbr] (18/19) Fall 86-Spr 88, p. 42.
"Tired of Traveling." [OhioR] (39) 87, p. 108-109.
2485. HOLLADAY, Hilary
"Going to the Ocean." [Verse] (4:1) Mr 87, p. 56.
2486. HOLLAND, Chaney
"Bad Trouble." [Electrum] (39) Fall-Wint 87, p. 19.
"Vagabond" (for Eloise Klein Healy). [Jacaranda] (2:2) Spr 87, p. 88-89.
2487. HOLLAND, Larry
"West of Omaha, by Way of New Caldonia." [Wind] (17:61) 87, p. 21-22.
2488. HOLLAND, Michelle
"Memorial Service." [Footwork] 87, p. 34.
"Under the Torch Bearers at Steven's College." [Footwork] 87, p. 55.
2489. HOLLAND-WHEATON, Heather
"Still Life w/ Paper Clip." [SlipS] (7) 87, p. 11-12.
2490. HOLLANDER, Benjamin
"After . Word . Thing . Language." [Acts] (6) 87, p. 76-77.
2491. HOLLANDER, Gadi
"Sleep, Memory / TheXXCenturyBookoftheDead" (Selections). [Act] (7) 87, p.
45-52.
2492. HOLLANDER, Jean
"Correct Blinking." [AmerS] (56:3) Sum 87, p. 367-368.
"A Mistake Once Made." [Footwork] 87, p. 32.
2493. HOLLANDER, John
"By the Sound." [NewYRB] (34:6) 9 Ap 87, p. 30.
"Coordinating Conjunction." [Poetry] (151:1/2) O-N 87, p. 66-67.
"Departure: A View Out the Window." [PartR] (54:2) Spr 87, p. 262.
"Elemental Colloquy." [NewRep] (196:13) 30 Mr 87, p. 34.
"For a Tall Headstone." [Shen] (37:4) 87, p. 18.
"Inviting a Friend to Lunch." [FourQ] (1:1) Wint 87, p. 22.
"Lines for a Simple Computer to Sort Out." [NewRep] (196:13) 30 Mr 87, p. 34.
"The Noisy Neighbor." [FourQ] (1:1) Wint 87, p. 21.
"An Old Story Is Retold." [PartR] (54:2) Spr 87, p. 262-263.
"Quatrains from Harp Lake." [Raritan] (7:4) Spr 87, p. 39-40.
"A Thing So Small." [Raritan] (7:4) Spr 87, p. 41-42.
"To a Forest Pool." [Shen] (37:4) 87, p. 19.
2494. HOLLANDER, Martha
"Agalma." [Shen] (37:1) 87, p. 30-32.
"The Candid Shot." [Shen] (37:3) 87, p. 33-34.
2495. HOLLO, Anselm
"Outlying Districts" (5 selections). [Notus] (2:2) Fall 87, p. 33-38.
"Revolution" (tr. of Pentti Saarikoski). [Spirit] (8:2) 87, p. 28-29.
2496. HOLLOWAY, Geoffrey
"By Way of a Toast." [Bogg] (57) 87, p. 15.
2497. HOLLOWAY, Glenna
"A Hex for My Neighbor's Green Thumb." [LightY] '87, c86, p. 244-245.
2498. HOLLYWOOD, Alexa
"Poet" (for Nancy, who ceased to write when her professor told her she had the
words of a housewife). [Calyx] (10:2/3) Spr 87, p. 12.
2499. HOLM, Bill
"Ernest Oberholzer and Billy McGee Go Canoeing on Rainy Lake" (For Gene
Monahan). [PaintedB] (30) 87, p. 27-28.
"Scott Joplin." [PaintedB] (30) 87, p. 28-29.
2500. HOLMAN, Bob
"Recipe." [NewAW] (1) 87, p. 114.
2501. HOLMES, Elizabeth
"Leaning to Permanence." [Wind] (17:60) 87, p. 17.
2502. HOLMES, Janet
"Pieces for Non-cooperative Ensemble." [NewL] (53:3) Spr 87, p. 100-101.

2503. HOLMES, John Clellon
"Astapovo Railway Station, 1910." [AlphaBS] (1) Je 87, p. 11.
"Dire Coasts." [PoetryNW] (28:2) Sum 87, p. 43-44.
"Lawrence in Taos." [AlphaBS] (1) Je 87, p. 11.
"Northfork October Return." [PoetryNW] (28:2) Sum 87, p. 44-46.
2504. HOLMES, Nancy
"Riding Lesson." [AntigR] (68) Wint 87, p. 39.
"Yseult at 100 KPH." [WestCR] (21:4) Spr 87, p. 51.
2505. HOLST-WARHAFT, Gail
"Gabrielle Didot" (tr. of Nikos Kavadias). [Paint] (14:27) Spr 87, p. 28-29.
2506. HOLSTEIN, Michael
"Copper Bracelet." [KanQ] (19:1/2) Wint-Spr 87, p. 236.
"The Man Who Feeds Ducks" (after a painting by Li Chi-mao). [Vis] (25) 87, p. 4.
"Silk Pyjamas." [LightY] '87, c86, p. 143.
"Tower of the 10,000 Buddhas." [WebR] (12:2) Fall 87, p. 49-50.
2507. HOLTZMAN, Clark
"Toad Stools." [AntigR] (69/70) 87, p. 138.
2508. HOLUB, Miroslav
"Hominization." [Field] (36) Spr 87, p. 70-71.
2509. HOMER, Art
"Anniversaries." [LaurelR] (21:1/2) Wint-Sum 87, p. 50-51.
"Commuter's Log." [Poetry] (150:1) Ap 87, p. 10.
"Conoeing the Jacks Fork." [CharR] (13:1) Spr 87, p. 85-86.
"Summer Solstice." [LaurelR] (21:1/2) Wint-Sum 87, p. 51-52.
2510. HONEA, Jacqueline Bailey
"Computer Evolution." [Outbr] (18/19) Fall 86-Spr 88, p. 7.
"Frijoles Canyon." [ArizQ] (43:4) Wint 87, p. 292.
2511. HONECKER, George
"By the Influence and Risk of Knowing Only Ghosts." [Rampike] (5:3) 87, p.
      58-59.
2512. HONG, Kyongjoo
"Autumnal End, 1985." [Gambit] (20) 86, p. 72.
"Hollow Autumn." [Gambit] (20) 86, p. 73.
"Reflection." [Gambit] (20) 86, p. 71.
"Sea Dream: The Beginning." [Gambit] (20) 86, p. 74.
2513. HONG, Sara
"Childhood." [HampSPR] Wint 86, p. 43.
"Gaps." [HampSPR] Wint 86, p. 43.
2514. HONGO, Garrett Kaoru
"Ass Why Hard." The Best of [BambooR] [(31-32)] 86, p. 35-36.
"C & H Sugar Strike, Kahuku, 1923." The Best of [BambooR] [(31-32)] 86, p.
      37-38.
"Cloud-Catch." [Crazy] (33) Wint 87, p. 9-10.
"Crossing Ka'u Desert." [OhioR] (39) 87, p. 112.
"Eruption: Pu'u O'o." [SouthwR] (72:4) Aut 87, p. 490.
"Fresno Akatsuki." [Caliban] (2) 87, p. 121.
"Mendocino Rose." [Crazy] (33) Wint 87, p. 7-8.
"*Pinoy* at the Coming World" (Waialua Plantation, 1919). [Ploughs] (13:1) 87, p.
      70-73.
"Previous Offender Blues." [Caliban] (2) 87, p. 122.
"The Underworld" (for Robert Mezey). [WestHR] (41:4) Wint 87, p. 368-370.
"Village: Kahuku-Mura." [NewEngR] (9:3) Spr 87, p. 314-315.
"Volcano House." [Antaeus] (58) Spr 87, p. 187-188.
2515. HONIG, Edwin
"Mao's 'Snow'." [GrahamHR] (10) Wint-Spr 87, p. 58.
"Rimbaud's 'Vowels'." [GrahamHR] (10) Wint-Spr 87, p. 57.
2516. HONIGFELD, Gilbert
"22. I grope along the attic rafters" (1986 Honorable Mention, Eve of Saint Agnes
      Poetry Competition). [NegC] (7:1/2) 87, p. 131.
"Crown." [Footwork] 87, p. 36.
"Geo." [SlipS] (7) 87, p. 37.
"An Old, Old Woman in the First Class Cabin." [Outbr] (18/19) Fall 86-Spr 88, p.
      55.
"Room 15." [Vis] (23) 87, p. 22.
2517. HONMA, Dean (Dean H.)
"Arrival" (for CKT). [HawaiiR] (21) Spr 87, p. 67.

"Fish Story." The Best of [BambooR] [(31-32)] 86, p. 41-42.
"To Buddy, on the Edge." The Best of [BambooR] [(31-32)] 86, p. 39-40.
"Waterdancing." [HawaiiR] (21) Spr 87, p. 66.
2518. HOOD, Charles
"Declination." [Jacaranda] (2:2) Spr 87, p. 66-67.
2519. HOOD, Jacoba
"Come Back Here." [Nimrod] (31:1) Fall-Wint 87, p. 77.
"The Sharper." [Nimrod] (31:1) Fall-Wint 87, p. 77.
"A Stepdaughter Once." [Nimrod] (31:1) Fall-Wint 87, p. 78.
2520. HOOD, Wharton
"The highway is a way." [CrossC] (9:3/4) 87, p. 12.
2521. HOOGESTRAAT, Jane
"Croquet." [Poem] (58) N 87, p. 22.
"Morning Fields." [NoDaQ] (55:2) Spr 87, p. 34.
"Recanting." [Poem] (57) Mr 87, p. 23.
"River Roads." [Poem] (57) Mr 87, p. 24.
"Summer Darkness." [SouthernPR] (27:1) Spr 87, p. 14.
"The Vase Painter Called a Truce." [Poem] (58) N 87, p. 23.
"Words Near Morning." [Poem] (58) N 87, p. 21.
2522. HOOPER, Edward L.
"The Visit" (for Ivan Anderson, Kaleidoscope International Poetry Awards 1986-87, Second Prize). [Kaleid] (14) Wint-Spr 87, p. 67.
2523. HOOVER, Paul
"After Cotton Mather." [Notus] (2:2) Fall 87, p. 22-23.
"Compared to What." [Notus] (2:2) Fall 87, p. 21.
"Idea." [Epoch] (36:3) 87-88, p. 193-194.
"The Movie." [Colum] (12) 87, p. 101.
"Others As Ourselves." [Epoch] (36:3) 87-88, p. 194.
"The Story." [Notus] (2:2) Fall 87, p. 20.
2524. HOPE, Warren
"A Private Anniversary" (In memory of the man who wrote under the name Max Nomad). [CumbPR] (7:1) Fall 87, p. 2-3.
2525. HOPES, David
"Elegaic Fragments." [CarolQ] (39:3) Spr 87, p. 67-70.
"Fragments Wound in a Beach Sparrow's Nest." [StoneC] (14:3/4) Spr-Sum 87, p. 60-61.
"In the End I Weary of the Fire in the Rose." [SouthernHR] (21:4) Fall 87, p. 340-342.
"The Saint Francis Poems." [LitR] (30:4) Sum 87, p. 553-558.
"Storm at York Beach." [Pembroke] (19) 87, p. 186.
2526. HOPKINS, Jennifer
"Fall Camping Near Mt. Rainier." [BellArk] (3:1) Ja-F 87, p. 6.
"Poem for Two Sons." [BellArk] (3:1) Ja-F 87, p. 1.
2527. HOPWOOD, Alison
"Love Probably." [AntigR] (71/72) Aut 87-Wint 88, p. 24.
2528. HORACE
"I.5, I.16, III.20" (in Latin and English, tr. by Joseph Salemi). [CumbPR] (7:1) Fall 87, p. 30-35.
2529. HORIGAN, Ethel
"The Thrashing." [CumbPR] (6:2) Spr 87, p. 32-33.
2530. HORNE, Lewis
"Family Reunion." [CumbPR] (6:2) Spr 87, p. 45.
"Speaking in Tongues." [CumbPR] (6:2) Spr 87, p. 48-49.
"Trails." [CumbPR] (6:2) Spr 87, p. 46-47.
2531. HORNIG, Doug
"High School Reunion." [SlipS] (7) 87, p. 77-82.
2532. HORNOSTY, Cornelia
"Discovery." [Waves] (15:3) Wint 87, p. 61.
2533. HOROWITZ, Mikhail
"Unloseable Blues" (for Ray Bremser). [AlphaBS] (2) D 87, p. 2-3.
2534. HORRIGAN, Timothy
"Menu-Tonique d'un sportif Dynamique." [Contact] (9:44/45/46) Fall-Wint 87, p. 52-53.
"Romancero Gitano." [Contact] (9:44/45/46) Fall-Wint 87, p. 53.
2535. HORSTING, Eric
"Swim." [BelPoJ] (38:1) Fall 87, p. 7.

2536. HORTON, Barbara
"From a Window." [WebR] (12:1) Spr 87, p. 31.
2537. HOSAFLOOK, Carrie
"Friendship." [Gambit] (20) 86, p. 40.
2538. HOSKIN, William D.
"Morning in Troy, N.Y." [HiramPoR] (42) Spr-Sum 87, p. 31.
2539. HOUGEN, Judith
"'Muscles' Hougen Comes Out of Softball Retirement." [TarPR] (27:1) Fall 87, p. 42.
"Tomato Growing." [CutB] (27/28) 87, p. 49.
2540. HOUGHTON, Timothy
"Winter Room" (after Beckman's "Family Picture"). [StoneC] (15:1/2) Fall-Wint 87-88, p. 58-59.
2541. HOUSE, Tom
"The Aging Folksinger Takes a Lounge Gig." [Lactuca] (6) Ap-My 87, p. 15.
"The Bust." [Lactuca] (6) Ap-My 87, p. 13.
"A Contradiction in Terms." [Amelia] (4:1/2, issue 9) 87, p. 130.
"Hardcase from Texas." [Lactuca] (6) Ap-My 87, p. 14.
"Nickle Man in the Projects." [Lactuca] (6) Ap-My 87, p. 14.
2542. HOUSTON, Beth
"Fourth of July." [MinnR] (NS 28) Spr 87, p. 11.
2543. HOUSTON, Peyton
"The Becomings" (Selection: IV). [OP] (final issue) Sum 87, p. 76-79.
"Monhegan Space" (For George and Phoebe Palmer). [OP] (final issue) Sum 87, p. 75.
"Ode." [ParisR] (29:102) Spr 87, p. 216-219.
HOUTEN, Lois van
    See Van HOUTEN, Lois
HOVANESSIAN, Diana Der
    See Der HOVANESSIAN, Diana
2544. HOWARD, Ben
"Clearing Out." [SewanR] (95:1) Wint 87, p. 10.
"Fiat Lux" (For Ben and Rose Howard, Ankeny, Iowa, c. 1933). [NewEngR] (10:1) Aut 87, p. 26.
"Signals." [SewanR] (95:1) Wint 87, p. 11.
2545. HOWARD, David
"The Refractory Lazarus." [Chelsea] (46) 87, p. 44.
2546. HOWARD, Dorothy
"In the rain" (tr. of A. Duhaime). [CrossC] (9:3/4) 87, p. 9.
2547. HOWARD, Richard
"Even in Paris" (to the memory of L. Donald Maher, 1921-1966). [Salm] (76-77) Fall 87-Wint 88, p. 134-158.
"Famed Dancer Dies of Phosphorus Poisoning." [Poetry] (151:1/2) O-N 87, p. 68-70.
"Love Which Alters" (For James Merrill). [GrandS] (6:2) Wint 87, p. 142-144.
2548. HOWE, Fanny
"Torn Parts: A Novel." [Temblor] (6) 87, p. 72-75.
2549. HOWE, Marie
"Gretel, from a Sudden Clearing." [Agni] (24/25) 87, p. 8-9.
"How Many Times." [Ploughs] (13:1) 87, p. 74.
"Menses." [Agni] (24/25) 87, p. 13.
"Song of the Spinster." [Agni] (24/25) 87, p. 14.
"The Split." [Agni] (24/25) 87, p. 10-12.
2550. HOWE, Susan
"Body perception thought of perceiving (half-thought." [Bound] (14:1/2) Fall 85-Wint 86 [c87], p. 102.
"I write at night." [Conjunc] (11) 87?, p. 180.
"Nesmejána reflects the wonder of laughter." [Conjunc] (11) 87?, p. 178.
"Ourself answer ourself." [Conjunc] (11) 87?, p. 179.
"Summer Days, a Painting by Georgia O'Keeffe." [KanQ] (19:4) Fall 87, p. 24.
"Thorow." [Temblor] (6) 87, p. 3-21.
2551. HOWELL, Christopher
"Close to the Vein" (for Bill Hunt). [MassR] (28:2) Sum 87, p. 331.
"Elizabeth's Story." [NowestR] (25:3) 87, p. 358.
"For the Fishermen." [NowestR] (25:3) 87, p. 435.
"The Gallery of Plato Hall." [MidwQ] (29:1) Aut 87, p. 77-83.

"I'm Telling You" (For Bob). [BlackWR] (13:2) Spr 87, p. 29-31.
"Night Flight Letter to Weldon Kees." [NowestR] (25:2) 87, p. 36-37.
"Plato Hall." [ColR] (NS 14:2) Fall-Wint 87, p. 30-31.
"Prayer of the Preblind." [BlackWR] (13:2) Spr 87, p. 28.
"Something to Love." [MassR] (28:2) Sum 87, p. 332.
"We Who Have Found Wisdom." [MassR] (28:2) Sum 87, p. 333.
"Why the River Is Always Laughing." [ColR] (NS 14:2) Fall-Wint 87, p. 29.
"Winter Trees: An Interview." [ColR] (NS 14:2) Fall-Wint 87, p. 26-28.
2552. HOWELL, Travis
"Buenos Aires." [Margin] (4) Aut 87, p. 8.
2553. HOWLEY, Michael
"Embers." [MinnR] (NS 28) Spr 87, p. 15.
2554. HRYCIUK, Marshall
"Strand 44." [CrossC] (9:3/4) 87, p. 15.
HUA, Li Min
See LI, Min Hua
2555. HUACO, Enrique
"Celebracion." [InterPR] (13:2) Fall 87, p. 16.
"Celebration" (tr. by Joe Bolton). [InterPR] (13:2) Fall 87, p. 17.
"Historically This Man" (tr. by Joseph Edward Bolton). [WillowS] (20) Spr 87, p. 34-35.
"Little Testament I-III" (tr. by Joe Bolton). [InterPR] (13:2) Fall 87, p. 19-25.
"Pequeño Testamento I-III." [InterPR] (13:2) Fall 87, p. 18-24.
2556. HUDDLE, David
"The Nature of Yearning" (for Lindsey and Elizabeth). [TexasR] (7:3/4) 87, p. 82-84.
"Tour of Duty" (Selections: "Entry," "Work," "R & R," "Vets"). [HampSPR] Wint 87, p. 54-55.
2557. HUDGINS, Andrew
"After the Last War: A Narrative" (Selections). [NewEngR] (10:2) Wint 87, p. 177-182.
"Bloom." [Sequoia] (30:3) Wint 87, p. 11.
"Cargo." [KenR] (NS 9:1) Wint 87, p. 87-88.
"Child on the Marsh." [Nat] (245:15) 7 N 87, p. 532.
"A Christian on the Marsh." [Ploughs] (13:1) 87, p. 75-77.
"Elegy for My Father, Who Is Not Dead." [KenR] (NS 9:1) Wint 87, p. 88-89.
"Grandmother's Spit." [Atlantic] (260:2) Ag 87, p. 40.
"The House on Denmead Street: Sidney Lanier." [Sequoia] (31:1) Centennial issue 87, p. 127-128.
"Psalm Against Psalms." [MissouriR] (10:2) 87, p. 65-67.
2558. HUECKSTEDT, R. A.
"God" (tr. of Sri Sarvesvar Dayal Saxena). [Paint] (14:27) Spr 87, p. 34.
2559. HUFFSTICKLER, Albert
"Blue Heron Lake, New Mexico." [PaintedB] (31) 87, p. 45.
"Closures." [PaintedB] (30) 87, p. 60.
"Dunaya and the Unicorn." [Lactuca] (7) Ag 87, p. 6.
"How You Bury You Dead." [Lactuca] (7) Ag 87, p. 5.
"Vision." [PoetryE] (23/24) Fall 87, p. 129-130.
"A Wake for Nora Belle Ordez." [PaintedB] (30) 87, p. 59-60.
"The Wine of Morning." [Abraxas] (35/36) 87, p. 69.
2560. HUGGINS, Peter
"Eating Angels." [Wind] (17:59) 87, p. 23.
"Eating Mortality." [ChatR] (8:1) Fall 87, p. 43.
"Fear." [LaurelR] (21:1/2) Wint-Sum 87, p. 10.
"Hunting Angels." [LaurelR] (21:1/2) Wint-Sum 87, p. 11.
"The Man Who Thought He Was Dead." [PoetL] (82:1) Spr 87, p. 31-32.
"Monster Story." [ColR] (NS 14:2) Fall-Wint 87, p. 50.
"Riding Mortality." [Wind] (17:59) 87, p. 23-24.
"The Sound of the Trumpet at Loachapoka." [SouthernHR] (21:1) Wint 87, p. 47.
"Standing Mortality." [PassN] (8:1) Wint 87, p. 7.
"Vertigo in Baton Rouge." [NegC] (7:3/4) 87, p. 111.
2561. HUGHES, John Silver
"Sequence." [CarolQ] (39:3) Spr 87, p. 29-30.
2562. HUGHES, Langston
"Don't Know No English" (tr. of Nicolás Guillén, w. Ben Frederic Carruthers). [Callaloo] (10:2) Spr 87, p. 171.

"High Brown" (tr. of Nicolás Guillén, w. Ben Frederic Carruthers). [Callaloo] (10:2) Spr 87, p. 175.
"My Gal" (tr. of Nicolás Guillén, w. Ben Frederic Carruthers). [Callaloo] (10:2) Spr 87, p. 179.
"Pass On By" (tr. of Nicolás Guillén, w. Ben Frederic Carruthers). [Callaloo] (10:2) Spr 87, p. 177.
"Thick-Lipped Cullud Boy" (tr. of Nicolás Guillén, w. Ben Frederic Carruthers). [Callaloo] (10:2) Spr 87, p. 173.
2563. HUGHES, M. R.
"Po." [CrossCur] (6:4) 87, p. 88.
2564. HUGHES, Mary Gray
"Hatching." [StoneC] (15:1/2) Fall-Wint 87-88, p. 35.
"Heart." [SouthernR] (23:4) O 87, p. 828-829.
"Perception." [StoneC] (15:1/2) Fall-Wint 87-88, p. 34.
"Sweater." [SouthernR] (23:4) O 87, p. 827-828.
2565. HUGHES, Ted
"Lovesong." [NowestR] (25:3) 87, p. 130-131.
2566. HUGO, Richard
"Assumptions." [NowestR] (25:3) 87, p. 184-189.
"Crinan Canal" (For Arnie & Adele). [NowestR] (25:3) 87, p. 175.
"Farmer Dying" (for Hank & Nancy). [NowestR] (25:3) 87, p. 183.
2567. HUH, Se-Wook
"Mailman" (tr. by Esther Lee). [Caliban] (2) 87, p. 50.
"The Man with Guts" (tr. by Esther Lee). [Caliban] (2) 87, p. 52.
"On the Terrace" (tr. by Esther Lee). [Caliban] (2) 87, p. 51.
2568. HUIDOBRO, Vicente
"Hours" (tr. by Robert Lima). [Vis] (25) 87, p. 12.
2569. HULBERT, Kate
"Audience." [Vis] (25) 87, p. 23.
2570. HULL, Bob
"Flood." [CumbPR] (6:2) Spr 87, p. 24-25.
2571. HULL, Lynda
"Aubade." [NewEngR] (9:4) Sum 87, p. 444-445.
"Counting in Chinese." [MissouriR] (10:3) 87, p. 112-113.
"One Note Tolling." [AmerV] (6) Spr 87, p. 20-21.
2572. HULME, Edward Maslin
"A Twilight Song." [Sequoia] (31:1) Centennial issue 87, p. 72.
2573. HULSE, Michael
"Abel." [AntigR] (68) Wint 87, p. 52-53.
"Con's Catfish." [AntigR] (68) Wint 87, p. 54.
2574. HUMES, Harry
"Gathering." [PaintedB] (30) 87, p. 13-14.
"My Mother at Evening." [Raccoon] (24/25) My 87, p. 226-227.
"When the Beetle Colony Is Moody." [PoetryNW] (28:2) Sum 87, p. 28-29.
2575. HUMMER, T. R.
"Bluegrass Wasteland" (With Apologies to Bob Cantwell and to Johnny, the mandolin player . . .). [GeoR] (41:1) Spr 87, p. 81-120.
"In Far Light, the Kinship of Sisters." [MissouriR] (10:2) 87, p. 59-61.
2576. HUMPHREY, Paul
"Boobiat." [LightY] '87, c86, p. 206.
"Hat Trick." [LightY] '87, c86, p. 142.
2577. HUMPHRIES, Jefferson
"Love and Death, or Consolation." [NegC] (7:3/4) 87, p. 118.
"Wooster Square, Spring." [SouthernPR] (27:1) Spr 87, p. 48.
2578. HUNT, Clifford
"Blue Smoke." [FiveFR] (5) 87, p. 63.
"The Seconds." [FiveFR] (5) 87, p. 64.
"Sunken Image.." [FiveFR] (5) 87, p. 67.
"This Thing." [FiveFR] (5) 87, p. 65-66.
2579. HUNT, Erica
"Three Fates." [Bound] (14:1/2) Fall 85-Wint 86 [c87], p. 111.
2580. HUNT, Leigh
"The Blinking Obelisk Picture Palace." [GreensboroR] (42) Sum 87, p. 97.
"Cosmic Disneyland." [GreensboroR] (42) Sum 87, p. 96-97.
2581. HUNT, Nan
"December." [CrossCur] (7:1) 87, p. 169.

2582. HUNT, Tim
"Morning Call Cafe, New Orleans." [HighP] (2:1) Spr 87, p. 11.
2583. HUNTER, Bruce
"Light Against Light." [Dandel] (14:2) Fall-Wint 87, p. 34-35.
"Lilacs." [Dandel] (14:2) Fall-Wint 87, p. 36-37.
2584. HUNTER, Donnell
"Leaving Montana." [KanQ] (19:3) Sum 87, p. 155.
"Old Boards." [Vis] (24) 87, p. 7.
"Scherzo." [CumbPR] (7:1) Fall 87, p. 13.
"Songs of the North." [KanQ] (19:3) Sum 87, p. 156.
"The Year of the Brothers." [HawaiiR] (22) Fall 87, p. 14-16.
2585. HUNTER, Nancy
"The Lady in the Moon" (tr. of Li Shang-yin). [CutB] (27/28) 87, p. 94.
"Silk of Scented Phoenix Tail Lies in Thin Folds" (tr. of Li Shang-yin). [CutB]
(27/28) 87, p. 94.
"Things That Ride on Wind." [Wind] (17:60) 87, p. 18.
"Under the Silver River" (tr. of Li Shang-yin). [CutB] (27/28) 87, p. 93.
"Wind" (tr. of Li Shang-yin). [CutB] (27/28) 87, p. 93.
2586. HUNTSBERRY, Randy
"Mylai Village." [SmPd] (24:2) Spr 87, p. 25.
"Tripwire." [Ascent] (13:1) 87, p. 21.
2587. HURLEY, Maureen
"Merwin's Inlet." [Electrum] (39) Fall-Wint 87, p. 44.
2588. HURLOW, Marcia L.
"Carl's Exhibition." [MalR] (80) S 87, p. 83.
"The Dani of Irian Jaya" (for D. Sunda, missionary to the Dani). [InterPR] (13:1)
Spr 87, p. 101.
"Invading Morlaix." [InterPR] (13:1) Spr 87, p. 101.
"Measures." [Abraxas] (35/36) 87, p. 66.
"Stretching the Pension." [Interim] (6:1) Spr 87, p. 30.
"Stretching the Pension." [Lips] (13) 87, p. 8.
2589. HUSS, Sandra
"Of Human Kindness." [RiverS] (22) 87, p. 82-83.
HUTAY'A, al-
See Al-HUTAY'A
2590. HUTCHINGS, Pat
"Bedtime Stories." [Pembroke] (19) 87, p. 162.
"Night Tennis." [Northeast] (Ser. 4:6) Wint 87-88, p. 3.
"October, Route 21." [Wind] (17:59) 87, p. 25.
2591. HUTCHINSON, Joseph
"My Three-Year-Old with His First Conch Shell." [ConcPo] (20) 87, p. 86.
2592. HUTCHISON, Alexander
"'Chacun Me Dit, Ronsard, Ta Maitress N'Est Telle' from the French of Pierre de
Ronsard: 1524-85." [Verse] (4:2) Je 87, p. 17.
2593. HUTCHMAN, Laurence
"Ultrasound." [CanLit] (113/114) Sum-Fall 87, p. 75.
2594. HUTH, Geof A.
"Collection at St. John St." [PoetryNW] (28:2) Sum 87, p. 17-18.
"Fog in Brazil." [MidAR] (7:2) 87, p. 52-55.
"The Lombardy Poplars." [PoetryNW] (28:2) Sum 87, p. 16-17.
"Mauve." [HiramPoR] (42) Spr-Sum 87, p. 32.
"The Metaphoric Turn of Mind." [CapeR] (22:2) Fall 87, p. 50.
2595. HUTSELL, Barbara
"Amy at Nineteen." [ChatR] (8:1) Fall 87, p. 44.
2596. HUTTEL, Richard
"Seeing to It." [AnotherCM] (17) 87, p. 46-47.
"Sonnet" (for Art Lange). [NewAW] (1) 87, p. 117.
2597. HUYETT, Pat
"Infinity." [NewL] (53:3) Spr 87, p. 33.
2598. HWANG, Tong-Gyu
"At a London Museum" (to a Japanese friend, tr. by Grace Gibson and John Chay).
[Pembroke] (19) 87, p. 21.
"The Exit" (tr. by John Chay and Grace Gibson). [InterPR] (13:1) Spr 87, p. 60.
"For Two to Fly Together in the Sky" (tr. by Grace Gibson and John Chay).
[Pembroke] (19) 87, p. 24.

"From an Alien Land 4" (tr. by Grace Gibson and John Chay). [Pembroke] (19) 87, p. 22.
"Iowa Diary 1" (to Ma Chinggi, tr. by Grace Gibson and John Chay). [Pembroke] (19) 87, p. 22-23.
"A Joyful Letter" (tr. by Grace Gibson and John Chay). [Pembroke] (19) 87, p. 25.
"The Last Solgo" (tr. by Grace Gibson and John Chay). [Pembroke] (19) 87, p. 23-24.
"A Little Autumn Day" (tr. by Grace Gibson and John Chay). [Pembroke] (19) 87, p. 24.
"Port of Call" (tr. by Peter Lee). [Pembroke] (19) 87, p. 17.
"Separate, But Standing Around Together" (tr. by Grace Gibson and John Chay). [Pembroke] (19) 87, p. 22.
"A Short Love Story" (tr. by Edward W. Poitras). [Pembroke] (19) 87, p. 14.
"Short Poem" (poems 4 & 5, tr. by Grace Gibson and John Chay). [Pembroke] (19) 87, p. 25.
"A Small Poem #5" (tr. by John Chay and Grace Gibson). [InterPR] (13:1) Spr 87, p. 60.
"Snowfall on the Harbor" (tr. by Grace Gibson and John Chay). [Pembroke] (19) 87, p. 26.
"Song" (tr. by Grace Gibson and John Chay). [Pembroke] (19) 87, p. 26.
"Song of Peace" (tr. by Peter Lee). [Pembroke] (19) 87, p. 17-18.
"Walking the Tightrope" (tr. by Grace Gibson and John Chay). [Pembroke] (19) 87, p. 21.
"Wild Geese" (tr. by Peter Lee). [Pembroke] (19) 87, p. 20.
"Wind Burial" (poems 1-11, tr. by Grace Gibson and John Chay). [Pembroke] (19) 87, p. 26-31.
"Wind Burial 4" (tr. by Kim Myong-yol). [Pembroke] (19) 87, p. 19.
2599. HYKIN, Susan
"Co-operation." [Event] (16:2) Sum 87, p. 58.
"Convergence." [Event] (16:2) Sum 87, p. 59.
2600. HYLAND, Gary
"South America." [Grain] (15:2) Sum 87, p. 21.
HYON-JONG, Chong
See CHONG, Hyon-Jong
HYUNG, Lee Sung
See LEE, Sung Hyung
I-TO, Wen
See WEN, I-to
2601. IBAÑEZ IGLESIAS, Solveig
"Nacimiento." [LetFem] (13:1/2) Primavera-Ontoño 87, p. 133.
"Nunca." [LetFem] (13:1/2) Primavera-Otoño 87, p. 132-133.
IBN AL-RUMI
See Al-RUMI, Ibn
2602. IBN-I-YAMIN
"Eat your fill, dress well, play dice" (tr. by Omar S. Pound). [AntigR] (69/70) 87, p. 75.
2603. IBN ZUHAIR, Ka'b
"Love Prelude from a Quasida" (tr. by Lenore Mayhew). [NewOR] (14:1) Spr 87, p. 68.
2604. IDDINGS, Kathleen
"Another Maria" (In Baja California). [CrossCur] (7:1) 87, p. 69.
2605. IGLEHART, Tara
"Nantucket." [Phoenix] (7:1) 87, p. 28.
IGLESIAS, Solveig Ibáñez
See IBAÑEZ IGLESIAS, Solveig
2606. IGNATOW, David
"An Aesthetic." [CreamCR] (11:2/3) 87?, p. 76.
"Aesthetics." [FourQ] (1:2) Fall 87, p. 52-53.
"Between." [GreenfR] (14:1/2) Wint-Spr, p. 91.
"Dark." [GreenfR] (14:1/2) Wint-Spr, p. 91.
"The Dog." [GreenfR] (14:1/2) Wint-Spr, p. 89.
"For Stanley Kunitz." [Pequod] (23/24) 87, p. 13.
"He has spent the morning studying the leaves." [HampSPR] Wint 86, p. 6.
"In Dream." [Raccoon] (24/25) My 87, p. 225.
"In the Graveyard." [GreenfR] (14:1/2) Wint-Spr, p. 89.

"It is wonderful to die amidst the pleasures I have known." [HampSPR] Wint 86, p. 6.
"Its Name." [Witness] (1:1) Spr 87, p. 76.
"Listening." [Poetry] (149:5) F 87, p. 255.
"Little Friend." [GreenfR] (14:1/2) Wint-Spr, p. 90.
"None." [GreenfR] (14:1/2) Wint-Spr, p. 89.
"The Self." [Poetry] (149:5) F 87, p. 256.
"Suburbia I." [OhioR] (38) 87, p. 105.
"Suburbia II." [GreenfR] (14:1/2) Wint-Spr, p. 90.
"Summer." [OhioR] (38) 87, p. 106.
"To the Poets." [FourQ] (1:2) Fall 87, p. 53.
"A Tuft of Daisies." [OhioR] (38) 87, p. 107.
"The Value of a Song or a Cry." [HampSPR] Wint 86, p. 5.
"The Wedding." [HampSPR] Wint 86, p. 5.
"Witness." [Poetry] (151:1/2) O-N 87, p. 70.
2607. IKAN, Ron
"Darlene Friendship's Boyfriend." [LightY] '87, c86, p. 153.
2608. ILHAN, Attilâ
"The Hour of Murder" (tr. by Murat Nemet-Nejat). [Trans] (19) Fall 87, p. 155.
"Love Is Forbidden" (tr. by Murat Nemet-Nejat). [Trans] (19) Fall 87, p. 154.
"The Poem of the Third Person" (tr. by Murat Nemet-Nejat). [Trans] (19) Fall 87, p. 156.
2609. INCE, Özdemir
"The Child and the Kid" (tr. by Talat Sait Halman). [Trans] (19) Fall 87, p. 17.
"Empty Streets" (tr. by Talat Sait Halman). [Trans] (19) Fall 87, p. 18.
"Our Sons" (tr. by Talat Sait Halman). [Trans] (19) Fall 87, p. 19.
"Wind, Ant, History" (tr. by Talat Sait Halman). [Trans] (19) Fall 87, p. 18.
INDIANA BOB
   See BOB, Indiana
2610. INDREEIDE, Erling
"Freedom, Abstractions, and Poems" (from Vegar, Vatn og Fjell, tr. by the author, w. Deborah Tannen). [PoetL] (81:3) Fall 86, p. 149-153.
2611. INEZ, Colette
"Daughter's Photo in an Old Folks' Home." [Ploughs] (13:1) 87, p. 79.
"Max Is Asked to Reach into the Past for Memories." [Amelia] (4:3, issue 10) 87, p. 56-57.
"Naming the Moons" (The Ngas of Nigeria." [Ploughs] (13:1) 87, p. 78.
"Riverhouse Inventions." [MichQR] (26:1) Wint 87, p. 113-114.
"Seaweed Dream." [SouthwR] (72:1) Wint 87, p. 120.
"When Newts Mate." [Amelia] (4:3, issue 10) 87, p. 56.
"Windpipe and Life Go On Song." [ThRiPo] (29/30) 87, p. 37-38.
2612. ING, Mahealani
"For Kalei, Inmate in Halawa Maximum Security Facility." [BambooR] (36) Fall 87, p. 93-96.
"What My Mother Said to Me." [BambooR] (36) Fall 87, p. 91-92.
2613. INGERSON, Martin I.
"The Feather G-Suit" (a play with four dances for a play cycle, Noh Plays, Just Dramas). [BellArk] (3:5) S-O 87, p. 3-9.
"A Pride of Lions." [BellArk] (3:4) Jl-Ag 87, p. 7.
"Three Trees Bowing in Season." [BellArk] (3:6) N-D 87, p. 1.
2614. INMAN, Will
"Fish Market." [Pembroke] (19) 87, p. 125-128.
2615. IOANNOU, Susan
"Dawn Snow." [Dandel] (14:2) Fall-Wint 87, p. 33.
"Sea Deep" (At St. Kitts). [Dandel] (14:2) Fall-Wint 87, p. 32.
2616. IRBY, Kenneth
"Still Call Steps" (three short odes). [Conjunc] (11) 87?, p. 100-103.
2617. IRIE, Kevin
"Chronology, the Pond." [CrossC] (9:1) 87, p. 10.
"An Immigrant's Son Visits the Homeland." [WindO] (49) Fall 87, p. 44-45.
"Immigrants: The Second Generation." [WindO] (49) Fall 87, p. 43.
"In Hiding." [CrossC] (9:1) 87, p. 10.
"Regeneration." [Waves] (15:1/2) Fall 86, p. 85.
"The Swan's Nest, Winter." [Germ] (11:1) Fall 87, p. 22.
2618. IRION, Mary Jean
"At the Briefing for Creation Day." [LightY] '87, c86, p. 79.

"At the Briefing for the Creation Day." [StoneC] (14:3/4) Spr-Sum 87, p. 75-76.
"In Extremadura." [ChrC] (104:25) 9-16 S 87, p. 748.
"O Boy." [ChrC] (104:28) 7 O 87, p. 846.
2619. IRWIN, Judith
"Czestochowa." [BellR] (10:2) Fall 87, p. 36.
"The Power of Tabwa." [BellR] (10:2) Fall 87, p. 35.
"Stories of Two Women." [BellR] (10:2) Fall 87, p. 37.
2620. IRWIN, Mark
"America." [Nat] (244:10) 14 Mr 87, p. 332.
"Besides." [LightY] '87, c86, p. 250.
"Church." [Pequod] (23/24) 87, p. 160.
"The Fray." [Pequod] (23/24) 87, p. 161.
2621. ISERMAN, Bruce
"Anxiety Above." [CrossC] (9:2) 87, p. 15.
"Father Broke It Up." [AntigR] (71/72) Aut 87-Wint 88, p. 201.
2622. ISLAS, Arturo
"Videosongs." [Sequoia] (31:1) Centennial issue 87, p. 90-92.
2623. ISRAEL, Inge
"The Caretaker." [Quarry] (36:3) Sum 87, p. 32.
"Cosine." [Quarry] (36:3) Sum 87, p. 31.
"Legato." [Quarry] (36:3) Sum 87, p. 30.
"Sanri Matsubara." [Quarry] (36:3) Sum 87, p. 31.
2624. ISRAEL, Jack (Jack K.)
"California by Edward Hopper." [BelPoJ] (37:4) Sum 87, p. 21.
"The Flower." [BelPoJ] (37:4) Sum 87, p. 21.
"Squirrels." [SmPd] (24:1) Wint 87, p. 8.
"Stoning of a Ton-Ton Macoute." [BelPoJ] (37:4) Sum 87, p. 20.
"The Whore's Dream." [BelPoJ] (37:4) Sum 87, p. 20.
2625. ISSA
"Haiku" (41 poems, tr. by Lucien Stryk). [AmerPoR] (16:3) My-Je 87, p. 28.
2626. ISSENHUTH, Jean-Pierre
"A la Clairière et au Café." [Os] (25) 87, p. 8.
"A Mon Frère." [Os] (25) 87, p. 9.
2627. ISTARU, Ana
"Death Is a Retreat" (tr. by Zoë Anglesey). [Cond] (14) 87, p. 205, 207.
"La Muerte Es un Repliegue." [Cond] (14) 87, p. 204, 206.
2628. ISTVAN, Agh
"Blind-Street" (tr. by Zsuzsanna Ozsvath and Martha Satz). [Os] (24) 87, p. 2.
"Vak-utca." [Os] (24) 87, p. 3.
2629. ITO, Sally
"Jews in Old China." [CapilR] (43) 87, p. 4.
"Kyoto." [CapilR] (43) 87, p. 6-8.
"On Meeting the Prophet: Five Stages." [CapilR] (43) 87, p. 9.
"Sansei." [Dandel] (14:1) Spr-Sum 87, p. 17.
"Upon Seeing a Sculpture of Maitreya, the Future Buddha." [CapilR] (43) 87, p. 5.
2630. ITURRALDE, Iraida
"Desde la Frente Noble de Norberto." [LindLM] (6:4) O-D 87, p. 19.
"Disonancia en Pos de Faulkner." [LindLM] (6:4) O-D 87, p. 19.
"Santiago" (Para Antonio Guernica). [LindLM] (6:4) O-D 87, p. 19.
2631. ITZIN, Charles (Charles F.)
"Forget Him" (For Cheryl). [GreenfR] (14:3/4) Sum-Fall 87, p. 177.
"Lies." [Phoenix] (7:1) 87, p. 27.
"Lists." [Vis] (25) 87, p. 28.
2632. IUPPA, M. J.
"Shadows of the Lost Boy" (for George). [Amelia] (4:3, issue 10) 87, p. 54.
2633. IVASK, Ivar
"Finnish Variations." [Nimrod] (30:2) Spr-Sum 87, p. 80.
2634. IVES, Rich
"Horses" (tr. of Joannes Bobrowski). [ColR] (NS 14:2) Fall-Wint 87, p. 6.
2635. IVO, Lêdo
"The Bats" (tr. by Giovanni Pontiero). [Dandel] (14:2) Fall-Wint 87, p. 20.
"Poor Folk at the Bus Station" (tr. by Giovanni Pontiero). [Dandel] (14:2) Fall-Wint 87, p. 18-19.
"The Poor in the Bus Depot" (tr. by Amy Antin). [NewYorker] (63:43) 14 D 87, p. 44.

"Santa Leopoldina Asylum" (tr. by Giovanni Pontiero). [Dandel] (14:2) Fall-Wint 87, p. 21.
2636. IVRY, Benjamin
"What Time Does a Chinaman Go to the Dentist?" [NewRep] (196:25) 22 Je 87, p. 38.
2637. JABES, Edmond
"The Book of Dialogue" (Selections: "Pre-Dialogue, II," "The Dream," tr. by Rosmarie Waldrop). [LitR] (30:3) Spr 87, p. 367-370.
2638. JACKAMAN, Rob
"Shield." [Quarry] (36:3) Sum 87, p. 13-15.
2639. JACKSON, Fleda Brown
"Arch." [BelPoJ] (37:3) Spr 87, p. 3.
"Bed-Buffaloes, Nose-Fairies, Car-Key Gnomes." [CrescentR] (5:1) 87, p. 42.
"Celebrating Your Fortieth Birthday with Conway Twitty." [IndR] (10:3) Spr 87, p. 77.
"Frieda Lawrence Answers the Doubters." [MidwQ] (28:2) Wint 87, p. 216-217.
2640. JACKSON, Gale
"At the Crossroads." [MinnR] (NS 29) Fall 87, p. 25-27.
"Deepwater" (for Sara). [MinnR] (NS 29) Fall 87, p. 28-30.
"So There Is No Poetry in These Nites" (for the children of Soweto). [MinnR] (NS 29) Fall 87, p. 23-24.
JACKSON, Haywood
See JACKSON, William (Haywood)
2641. JACKSON, Jeffrey A.
"Best Seller." [CapeR] (22:1) Spr 87, p. 35.
"The Yearbook." [CapeR] (22:1) Spr 87, p. 34.
2642. JACKSON, Murray
"Tampa Gull." [PassN] (8:1) Wint 87, p. 18.
"Three Tone Poems for Unc Art Stelle." [Callaloo] (10:3) Sum 87, p. 479.
2643. JACKSON, Reuben M.
"Edward." [BlackALF] (21:3) Fall 87, p. 249-250.
"Haiku." [BlackALF] (21:3) Fall 87, p. 250.
2644. JACKSON, Richard
"How We Make Sense of Things" (for Chuck). [ConcPo] (20) 87, p. 74.
"The Message." [Pembroke] (19) 87, p. 162.
"Unable to Refuse." [KenR] (NS 9:3) Sum 87, p. 81-82.
"What to Listen For." [KenR] (NS 9:3) Sum 87, p. 82-83.
"Who We Are, and Where." [MissouriR] (10:3) 87, p. 156-162.
"Wishbone." [NewEngR] (9:3) Spr 87, p. 295-299.
2645. JACKSON, William (Haywood)
"Eve of the Ark." [Wind] (17:60) 87, p. 19.
"Having Given Myself." [Wind] (17:60) 87, p. 19-20.
2646. JACOBIK, Gray
"Florence." [MinnR] (NS 29) Fall 87, p. 45.
"Gardening Questions." [PoetryE] (23/24) Fall 87, p. 161-162.
"Ice Over Snow." [CreamCR] (11:2/3) 87?, p. 99-100.
2647. JACOBOWITZ, Judah
"Born Again." [LakeSR] (21) 87, p. 18.
"A New Top." [Pig] (14) 87, p. 76.
2648. JACOBS, David
"E. C. Bentley" (Clerihew). [LightY] '87, c86, p. 68.
2649. JACOBS, Dennis
"Leda's Revenge." [SpiritSH] (53:1) 87, p. 28-29.
"The Rain Falls Justly." [SpiritSH] (53:1) 87, p. 26-27.
"She Couldn't Believe." [SpiritSH] (53:1) 87, p. 27-28.
2650. JACOBSEN, Josephine
"Poets Dead and Gone." [CrossCur] (7:2) 87, p. 11.
2651. JACOBSEN, Rolf
"The Church on Wall Street" (tr. by Olav Grinde). [CrossCur] (7:3) 87, p. 121.
"Guardian Angel" (tr. by Olav Grinde). [StoneC] (14:3/4) Spr-Sum 87, p. 31.
"Skytsengelen." [StoneC] (14:3/4) Spr-Sum 87, p. 30.
2652. JACOBSON, Bonnie
"My Luck." [LightY] '87, c86, p. 191.
"Things As They Are." [LightY] '87, c86, p. 146.
"Upwardly Mobile Bean Curd." [LightY] '87, c86, p. 41.
"What Did the Midge Say to the Mildew?" [LightY] '87, c86, p. 242.

"When Wyndham Lewis" (Clerihew). [LightY] '87, c86, p. 67.
2653. JACOBSON, Dale
"Hearing the World." [LakeSR] (21) 87, p. 20.
"Three Quizzes for Scholars." [LakeSR] (21) 87, p. 20.
2654. JACOBY, Jay
"Poem as Found" (Thanks to *The Norton Introduction to Literature*, Third Edition).
[EngJ] (76:8) D 87, p. 79.
2655. JACQUES, Ben
"Company." [KanQ] (19:1/2) Wint-Spr 87, p. 259.
"One Day's Job." [KanQ] (19:1/2) Wint-Spr 87, p. 259.
"The Painter." [KanQ] (19:1/2) Wint-Spr 87, p. 258.
2656. JACQUES, Geoffrey
"Detached Retina." [Notus] (2:1) Spr 87, p. 84.
"Distances." [Notus] (2:1) Spr 87, p. 83.
"A Handshake of Dry Ice." [Notus] (2:1) Spr 87, p. 85.
"No Easy Walk." [Notus] (2:1) Spr 87, p. 82.
2657. JAEGER, Lowell
"Distance." [HighP] (2:2) Fall 87, p. 135-136.
"Medicine Tree." [HighP] (2:2) Fall 87, p. 137-138.
"November '69 War Moratorium: Enroute." [Abraxas] (35/36) 87, p. 70-71.
"Where We Went Wrong." [CharR] (13:2) Fall 87, p. 76.
2658. JAEKEL, Linda K.
"Quartz." [Footwork] 87, p. 25.
2659. JAFFE, Harold
"Man Ray." [Bound] (15:1/2) Fall 86-Wint 87, p. 343-349.
2660. JAFFEE, Leonard R.
"Summer's Coming." [NegC] (7:3/4) 87, p. 110.
2661. JAGASICH, Paul
"At the Table" (tr. of Ivan Wernisch). [HampSPR] Wint 87, p. 32.
"Dream About Death" (tr. of Ivan Wernisch). [HampSPR] Wint 87, p. 32.
"It Was Afternoon or Later" (tr. of Jaroslav Seifert, w. Tom O'Grady). [Spirit] (8:2)
87, p. 317.
"The Other Shore" (tr. of Ivan Wernisch). [HampSPR] Wint 87, p. 31-32.
"Walk Around the Brewery" (tr. of Ivan Wernisch). [HampSPR] Wint 87, p. 31.
2662. JALBERT, Marthe
"Something Is Circulating" (tr. by Carrol Coates). [Paint] (14:27) Spr 87, p. 13-14.
2663. JAMES, Colin
"Values." [Amelia] (4:3, issue 10) 87, p. 78.
2664. JAMES, David
"After Years of Giving In" (for Debra Marie). [CimR] (78) Ja 87, p. 55.
"The Air You Left Behind" (for Gaynell James). [HawaiiR] (22) Fall 87, p. 18-19.
"A Father's Song." [PassN] (8:2) Sum 87, p. 21.
"For All the Liars." [PennR] (3:2) Fall-Wint 87, p. 52.
"For This World and Dreams." [PennR] (3:2) Fall-Wint 87, p. 53.
"The Moo Game." [Iowa] (17:2) Spr-Sum 87, p. 92.
"The Politics of an Idiot." [Caliban] (3) 87, p. 44.
"The Revelation of an Idiot." [Caliban] (3) 87, p. 44.
"September Again." [HawaiiR] (19) Spr 86, c87, p. 8-9.
"The Tired of Your Present Life Tree Game." [Iowa] (17:2) Spr-Sum 87, p. 92.
"The Unhooked Star" (for Lindon Davenport James). [InterPR] (13:2) Fall 87, p.
100-101.
2665. JAMES, Elizabeth Ann
"First Poem for the Arabian Gulf at Abu Dhabi." [Gambit] (20) 86, p. 21.
"Fog Poem." [Gambit] (20) 86, p. 18.
"My Father-in-Law Recalls His First Days in the Gulf." [Gambit] (20) 86, p. 19-20.
"Poem for Abla Akhal Dying in Beirut." [Gambit] (20) 86, p. 16-17.
2666. JAMES, Joyce
"Mrs. Stewart's Concentrated Liquid Bluing" (For our Mother, 1913-1987).
[SouthernPR] (27:2) Fall 87, p. 58.
"Playing Pizzicato." [Comm] (114:8) 24 Ap 87, p. 246-247.
"Raising Animals: Esther and Eve." [Comm] (114:8) 24 Ap 87, p. 246-247.
"There Are the Lilacs." [OhioR] (38) 87, p. 116-117.
"What the Bell Told." [Shen] (37:4) 87, p. 45.
2667. JAMES, Kathi
"Susan's Night Song to Her Children." [Bogg] (58) 87, p. 45.

2668. JAMES, Nancy Esther
"The Husband of the Health Nut." [Wind] (17:60) 87, p. 21-22.
"Moon Rabbit." [Wind] (17:60) 87, p. 21.
2669. JAMES, Pat
"McChestney's." [FloridaR] (15:1) Spr-Sum 87, p. 78.
2670. JAMES, Sibyl
"Autumn Chinese Parasol" (tr. of Li Quing Zhao, w. Kang Xue Pei). [TexasR]
(8:3/4) Fall-Wint 87, p. 7.
"Not Trying the Lamps" (tr. of Li Quing Zhao, w. Kang Xue Pei). [TexasR] (8:3/4)
Fall-Wint 87, p. 6.
"The Peace Hotel, Shanghai" (for Suzanne). [Vis] (25) 87, p. 5-6.
"Real Vanilla." [Calyx] (10:2/3) Spr 87, p. 172-173.
"Red Lotus" (tr. of Li Quing Zhao, w. Kang Xue Pei). [TexasR] (8:3/4) Fall-Wint
87, p. 9.
"Song of the Look-Out on the Great Wall." [Vis] (25) 87, p. 6-8.
"Spring's News" (tr. of Li Quing Zhao, w. Kang Xue Pei). [TexasR] (8:3/4)
Fall-Wint 87, p. 8.
2671. JAMES-FRENCH, Dayv
"After the Blade." [Grain] (15:3) Fall 87, p. 29.
"Making Believe." [Quarry] (36:3) Sum 87, p. 54.
"Night Vision." [Quarry] (36:3) Sum 87, p. 53.
"Pro / Choice / Life." [Quarry] (36:3) Sum 87, p. 55.
"Spoons" (Anne Sexton). [Grain] (15:3) Fall 87, p. 28.
2672. JAMIESON, Leland
"Two Blades." [KanQ] (19:1/2) Wint-Spr 87, p. 150.
2673. JAMIS, Fayad
"It Is Better to Get Up" (tr. by Kathleen Weaver). [Zyzzyva] (3:4) Wint 87-88, p.
41.
2674. JANES, Lola Strong
"Well Bed." [LightY] '87, c86, p. 175.
2675. JANOWITZ, Katherine
"The Lost Tribe, XV." [PartR] (54:1) Wint 87, p. 130.
2676. JANOWITZ, Phyllis
"Little Elegy." [Epoch] (36:2) 87-88, p. 140-141.
"Of Course." [BostonR] (12:2) Ap 87, p. 13.
"Orpheus and La Dolce Vita." [Epoch] (36:2) 87-88, p. 137-138.
"Preference." [SouthwR] (72:1) Wint 87, p. 109.
"Temporary Dwellings." [MichQR] (26:3) Sum 87, p. 473-474.
"Tics." [NewYorker] (62:50) 2 F 87, p. 40.
"Voices." [Epoch] (36:2) 87-88, p. 142.
"What to Do While You're Waiting." [MichQR] (26:3) Sum 87, p. 475-476.
"What We Know about Right-Angled Triangles." [Epoch] (36:2) 87-88, p. 139.
2677. JANZEN, Harold R.
"Spirits Fishing in the Night." [PraF] (8:3) Aut 87, p. 51.
2678. JANZEN, Jean
"To My Aunt Dying in Autumn." [PoetL] (81:3) Fall 86, p. 165.
2679. JAQUISH, Karen I.
"Act of Contrition." [CapeR] (22:2) Fall 87, p. 27.
"L'Occupation" (spring, 1944). [PoetL] (82:4) Wint 87-88, p. 224-225.
2680. JARAMILLO, Darío
"Imaginary Biography of Seymour" (tr. by Frank Graziano). [NewOR] (14:3) Fall
87, p. 76-77.
2681. JARAMILLO LEVI, Enrique
"Barco a la Deriva." [Mairena] (9:24) 87, p. 109.
2682. JARMAN, Mark
"Awakened by Sea Lions." [OhioR] (39) 87, p. 88-89.
"Between Flights." [PoetryNW] (28:2) Sum 87, p. 4-6.
"The Children." [PoetryNW] (28:2) Sum 87, p. 3.
"The Home." [Hudson] (40:1) Spr 87, p. 79-84.
"The Next War." [PraS] (61:1) Spr 87, p. 48-49.
"Resurrection." [PoetryNW] (28:2) Sum 87, p. 4.
"Testimony and Postscript." [Pequod] (23/24) 87, p. 14-15.
"Uncle Tenor." [PraS] (61:1) Spr 87, p. 47-48.
2683. JARNOT, Lisa
"Poem for Smart People." [AlphaBS] (2) D 87, p. 19.

2684. JARRARD, Kyle
"San Francisco." [Wind] (17:59) 87, p. 26.
2685. JARRETT, Emmett
"The 25th of August." [HangL] (50/51) 87, p. 81.
"Sunday Morning." [HangL] (50/51) 87, p. 80.
2686. JARVIS, David
"Clouds." [LaurelR] (20:1/2) Sum 87, p. 17.
"Lies." [LaurelR] (20:1/2) Sum 87, p. 16.
2687. JASPER, Pat
"Black Tie Dinner." [Waves] (15:3) Wint 87, p. 69.
"First Spring Away from Home." [Event] (16:1) Mr 87, p. 64-65.
"March: Vernal Equinox" (for Maria). [CanLit] (115) Wint 87, p. 43-44.
"Missing Snapshot." [Quarry] (36:4) Fall 87, p. 32-33.
"The Morning After." [Waves] (15:3) Wint 87, p. 68.
2688. JASTRUN, Tomasz
"Board" (tr. by Daniel Bourne). [NowestR] (25:2) 87, p. 109.
"Elevator" (tr. by Daniel Bourne). [PraS] (61:1) Spr 87, p. 49-50.
"Feathers" (tr. by Daniel Bourne). [PraS] (61:1) Spr 87, p. 50.
"The First Night" (tr. by Daniel Bourne). [NowestR] (25:2) 87, p. 102.
"Five Year Plan" (tr. by Daniel Bourne). [QW] (25) Spr 87, p. 133.
"Forty-Eight Hours" (tr. by Daniel Bourne). [NowestR] (25:2) 87, p. 110-111.
"Interrogation with Map" (tr. by Daniel Bourne). [NowestR] (25:2) 87, p. 106.
"The Journey Forever" (tr. by Daniel Bourne). [QW] (25) Spr 87, p. 133.
"Leaving Prison" (tr. by Daniel Bourne). [NowestR] (25:2) 87, p. 112.
"Light" (tr. by Daniel Bourne). [NowestR] (25:2) 87, p. 107.
"Milk" (tr. by Daniel Bourne). [Salm] (72) Fall 86, p. 196.
"On the Crossroads" (tr. by Daniel Bourne). [NowestR] (25:2) 87, p. 103.
"Our Grammar" (tr. by Daniel Bourne). [NowestR] (25:2) 87, p. 114.
"Scrap" (tr. by Daniel Bourne). [NowestR] (25:2) 87, p. 113.
"A Secret Meeting" (tr. by Daniel Bourne). [Salm] (72) Fall 86, p. 196-197.
"Small Fires" (tr. by Daniel Bourne). [NowestR] (25:2) 87, p. 108.
"Snow" (tr. by Daniel Bourne). [PartR] (54:2) Spr 87, p. 271-272.
"To My Son" (tr. by Daniel Bourne). [NowestR] (25:2) 87, p. 105.
"Trial" (tr. by Daniel Bourne). [PartR] (54:2) Spr 87, p. 272-273.
"Visitation" (tr. by Daniel Bourne). [PartR] (54:2) Spr 87, p. 273.
"Windows" (tr. by Daniel Bourne). [NowestR] (25:2) 87, p. 104.
2689. JAUSS, David
"My Grandfather's Sayings." [SouthernPR] (27:1) Spr 87, p. 43.
"Seeds." [LaurelR] (21:1/2) Wint-Sum 87, p. 62.
"Setting the Traps." [FloridaR] (15:2) Fall-Wint 87, p. 52-53.
2690. JAY, Suzanne
"Losings." [EngJ] (76:6) O 87, p. 99.
2691. JEANNE, Ave
"Large Mural / Philadelphia Art Museum, Miss Emily Among Many." [WindO] (48)
Spr 87, p. 18.
"Mascara & Creme / The Face I Drew This Morning." [Lactuca] (5) Ja 87, p. 17.
"Portrait / the Absurdity of Miss Emily." [WindO] (48) Spr 87, p. 17.
"The Portrait in Oil / the Insanity of Miss Emily." [WindO] (48) Spr 87, p. 17-18.
"Portrait in Pastels & a Few Stars / The American President" (Finalist, Eve of St.
Agnes Poetry Competition). [NegC] (7:1/2) 87, p. 162.
"Tommy's Portrait / Man Unsure How to Pose." [Lactuca] (5) Ja 87, p. 17-18.
2692. JECH, Jon
"Reunion Near Hartz Island." [BellArk] (3:1) Ja-F 87, p. 7.
2693. JEFFERS, Robinson
"Cassandra." [Raccoon] (24/25) My 87, p. 23.
"Home." [AmerPoR] (16:6) N-D 87, p. 25-31.
2694. JEFFERSON, Jennifer
"Inheriting Grandmother's Music Box." [GreenfR] (14:3/4) Sum-Fall 87, p. 90.
"Port Deposit, 1968" (for Yvonne). [GreenfR] (14:3/4) Sum-Fall 87, p. 89.
2695. JEFFIRE, John
"Lea Nicole." [NegC] (7:3/4) 87, p. 112.
JELLOUN, Tahar Ben
See Ben JELLOUN, Tahar
2696. JENKINS, Lewis
"Late October." [Footwork] 87, p. 83.

2697. JENKINS, Paul
"The Birds of Brazil." [PoetryNW] (28:2) Sum 87, p. 19-20.
"The Definition of Joy." [PoetryNW] (28:2) Sum 87, p. 20-21.
"Following the Blind River." [PraS] (61:4) Wint 87, p. 40-41.
"My Father's Signature." [PraS] (61:4) Wint 87, p. 38-39.
"That Jon Boat." [PraS] (61:4) Wint 87, p. 41.
"Underneath Town Hall." [PoetryNW] (28:2) Sum 87, p. 21-23.
"Urban Rhyme." [PraS] (61:4) Wint 87, p. 39-40.
2698. JENKINS, Robin David
"Salt of the Earth." [SouthernPR] (27:1) Spr 87, p. 11.
2699. JENNINGS, Elizabeth
"Clarify." [Poetry] (150:2) My 87, p. 108.
"Saint Augustine." [Stand] (28:1) Wint 86-87, p. 50.
2700. JENNINGS, Kate
"Faithless Moon." [Hudson] (40:3) Aut 87, p. 394.
"Mail Delivery by Moonlight." [Hudson] (40:3) Aut 87, p. 393.
"The Night Wind: Charles Burchfield." [Hudson] (40:3) Aut 87, p. 391-392.
"Pumpkin." [Hudson] (40:3) Aut 87, p. 392.
"Roadside Stand." [SouthernPR] (27:2) Fall 87, p. 65.
"Scan" (for Michael). [PraS] (61:4) Wint 87, p. 21-22.
"Seven." [PraS] (61:4) Wint 87, p. 22-23.
"Vine Wreath." [PraS] (61:4) Wint 87, p. 23.
"Wrist" (for Anne). [Hudson] (40:3) Aut 87, p. 390.
2701. JENSEN, Laura
"1970 — Summer School." [Iowa] (17:3) Fall 87, p. 59-60.
"Absence." [Field] (37) Fall 87, p. 85-86.
"Amazing." [Iowa] (17:3) Fall 87, p. 56-57.
"The Animal Kingdom." [Iowa] (17:3) Fall 87, p. 57-58.
"Anonymity." [Field] (37) Fall 87, p. 88-89.
"Chimes." [NewYorker] (63:45) 28 D 87, p. 46.
"The Crow Flies." [Field] (37) Fall 87, p. 84.
"Notes Toward an Epic Poem." [Raccoon] (24/25) My 87, p. 300-303.
"Pastoral." [Field] (37) Fall 87, p. 87.
"Report on the Panel of Exiles." [PoetryNW] (28:1) Spr 87, p. 6-7.
"Seaport." [Iowa] (17:3) Fall 87, p. 60.
"Summer." [PoetryNW] (28:2) Sum 87, p. 24-25.
2702. JENSEN, Lynne
"Some People Have Dream Mamas." [NewL] (53:2) Wint 86-87, p. 67-68.
2703. JEROME, Judson
"Abhorrent Acts." [NegC] (7:3/4) 87, p. 44-45.
"Birds and Bees." [Bogg] (57) 87, p. 8-9.
"Darkling Plain Revisited: a Carpe Diem" (for my 60th birthday, February 8, 1987).
    [NegC] (7:3/4) 87, p. 9-11.
"Greed on Wall Street" (*Newsweek* headline). [NegC] (7:3/4) 87, p. 43.
"A Handful of Grit." [NegC] (7:3/4) 87, p. 39-42.
"Helium: An Inert Gas." [LightY] '87, c86, p. 32-33.
"Licensed for Love" (for our 38th anniversary). [NegC] (7:3/4) 87, p. 46-48.
"The Tipping." [Bogg] (57) 87, p. 8.
"When You Said 'Enough'." [Bogg] (57) 87, p. 7-8.
2704. JESUS, Teresa de
"Cook Book" (7 poems, tr. by John Carey). [MinnR] (NS 29) Fall 87, p. 7-15.
JEW, Shalin Hai
    See HAI-JEW, Shalin
2705. JEWELL, Terri L.
"Sistah Flo." [Calyx] (10:2/3) Spr 87, p. 117.
2706. JIMÉNEZ, Juan Ramón
"Nocturne" (tr. by Clark Zlotchew and Dennis Maloney). [AmerPoR] (16:6) N-D
    87, p. 47.
"Sea, Nothing" (tr. by W. Caleb Crain). [HarvardA] (122:1) N 87, p. 37.
"Smoke and Gold" (to Enrique and Amparo Granados, tr. by Clark Zlotchew and
    Dennis Maloney). [AmerPoR] (16:6) N-D 87, p. 47.
JIRO, Nakano
    See NAKANO, Jiro
2707. JOANS, Ted
"Full Mooning." [Caliban] (2) 87, p. 85.
"The Glass Wishes" (in memory of Benjamin Perét). [Caliban] (2) 87, p. 83-84.

"What Ever Happened." [MoodySI] (18/19) Fall 87, p. 44.
2708. JOEL, Miriam
"Machu Picchu." [ManhatPR] (9) Sum 87, p. 55.
2709. JOENS, Harley
"What's Left of the Farm." [Northeast] (Ser. 4:5) Sum 87, p. 8.
2710. JOHANNES, Joan
"Phy Ed 1968." [EngJ] (76:8) D 87, p. 80.
2711. JOHANSSEN, Kerry
"Bodies of Water." [MissouriR] (10:3) 87, p. 74-75.
"Mineral Rights." [SouthernPR] (27:2) Fall 87, p. 21-22.
2712. JOHLER, Walt
"Silent Sounds." [Wind] (17:60) 87, p. 13.
2713. JOHNSON, David
"Crossing the Border" (Winner, 1986 Puerto Del Sol Poetry Contest). [Puerto]
(22:2) Spr 87, p. 144-146.
"Small Elegy." [Pembroke] (19) 87, p. 130.
"To the Smokey Pig, a Bar-B-Que Outside Fort Benning..." (for the soldiers who
don't know it exists). [Pembroke] (19) 87, p. 128-129.
2714. JOHNSON, Denis
"Killed in the War I Didn't Go To." [Raccoon] (24/25) My 87, p. 278-279.
"Willits, California." [Raccoon] (24/25) My 87, p. 284.
2715. JOHNSON, Don
"And the River Gathered Around Us." [GeoR] (41:2) Sum 87, p. 332-333.
"Home Game." [Spirit] (8:2) 87, p. 161-162.
"Protection." [LaurelR] (20:1/2) Sum 87, p. 97-98.
2716. JOHNSON, Frank
"Sweetheart I Want You to Know." [BelPoJ] (37:3) Spr 87, p. 14.
2717. JOHNSON, Greg
"Sorrow." [KanQ] (19:3) Sum 87, p. 123.
2718. JOHNSON, Henry
"On Leaving Prison." [GreenfR] (14:3/4) Sum-Fall 87, p. 97.
"Wild Flowers." [GreenfR] (14:3/4) Sum-Fall 87, p. 98.
2719. JOHNSON, Honor
"A Cadence." [NewEngR] (10:1) Aut 87, p. 116-118.
"Feather Duster." [NewAW] (1) 87, p. 55.
"My Literary Life." [NewAW] (1) 87, p. 54.
"Pleasures." [NewEngR] (10:1) Aut 87, p. 114-115.
2720. JOHNSON, Jean Youell
"Angered, you walked slowly." [Bogg] (57) 87, p. 28.
"Loving alone except in fantasies." [Bogg] (57) 87, p. 55.
"Yes, Sir." [Bogg] (58) 87, p. 64.
2721. JOHNSON, Kent
"Doubt of Love" (tr. of Isidoro Tercero). [Contact] (9:44/45/46) Fall-Wint 87, p. 18.
"I Wonder" (tr. of Carlos Pacheco). [Contact] (9:44/45/46) Fall-Wint 87, p. 19.
2722. JOHNSON, Linda Monacelli
"Some Italian!" (to be read with a thick accent). [LightY] '87, c86, p. 135-136.
2723. JOHNSON, Louis
"Lunch-Party." [Chelsea] (46) 87, p. 46.
"Traveller." [Chelsea] (46) 87, p. 47.
"The View from the Front Window." [Chelsea] (46) 87, p. 45.
2724. JOHNSON, Mark (*See also* JOHNSON, Mark Allan)
"A Passion Walk." [Writer] (99:1) Ja 86, p. 19.
2725. JOHNSON, Mark Allan (*See also* JOHNSON, Mark)
"Burlap and Silk." [BellArk] (3:5) S-O 87, p. 19.
"Love Story" (for Jann). [BellArk] (3:2) Mr-Ap 87, p. 18.
2726. JOHNSON, Markham
"Butchers." [PassN] (8:2) Sum 87, p. 19.
"Starlings, Grackles, Redwings." [PennR] (3:2) Fall-Wint 87, p. 55.
2727. JOHNSON, Michael L.
"Cinders" (tr. of Umberto Saba). [HayF] (2) Spr 87, p. 35.
"Piero della Francesca's *Madonna del Parto*." [KanQ] (19:4) Fall 87, p. 49.
"Sun in the Plaza" (tr. of Carlos Sahagún). [WebR] (12:1) Spr 87, p. 79-80.
"Vision in Almería" (tr. of Carlos Sahagún). [WebR] (12:1) Spr 87, p. 78-79.
2728. JOHNSON, Penny K.
"A Beer in the Comet." [BellArk] (3:3) My-Je 87, p. 5.
"Still Life in the Boom Boom Room." [BellArk] (3:3) My-Je 87, p. 10.

2729. JOHNSON, Pyke, Jr.
"Gas Man." [LightY] '87, c86, p. 34.
"The Man Who Loved a Giraffe" (For P. B.). [LightY] '87, c86, p. 114-115.
2730. JOHNSON, Regis
"A Man a Poem, a Beautiful Woman, and a Pitcher of Beer." [SlipS] (7) 87, p. 19.
2731. JOHNSON, Robert G.
"Startime." [PoeticJ] (17) 87, p. 42.
2732. JOHNSON, Robert K.
"The Baseball Player." [WebR] (12:1) Spr 87, p. 29.
2733. JOHNSON, Robin
"New Satellites." [CrossCur] (7:1) 87, p. 67.
2734. JOHNSON, Ronald
"Ark 57, The Gaia Spire." [Conjunc] (10) 87, p. 165-167.
"The Fireworks Spires." [Temblor] (6) 87, p. 60-68.
2735. JOHNSON, Sharon
"In Canning Season, Schoharie County." [GreenfR] (14:3/4) Sum-Fall 87, p. 127-128.
2736. JOHNSON, Sheila Golburgh
"Extend Hands, Not Arms." [PoeticJ] (17) 87, p. 8.
"For Ruby, In Memoriam." [PoeticJ] (17) 87, p. 37.
"Nature Notes." [CapeR] (22:1) Spr 87, p. 48.
2737. JOHNSON, Sören
"Choices in Spain." [NegC] (7:3/4) 87, p. 88.
2738. JOHNSON, Susan Matthis
"At a Cremation." [HampSPR] Wint 87, p. 47.
2739. JOHNSON, Tom
"After the Ice Storm." [SouthernR] (23:1) Ja 87, p. 150-151.
"Fear of Cancer." [SouthernR] (23:1) Ja 87, p. 151-152.
"Wind River Range." [SouthernR] (23:1) Ja 87, p. 152-154.
2740. JOHNSON, W. R.
"Octavian in Alexandria." [AmerS] (56:2) Spr 87, p. 247.
2741. JOHNSTON, Arnold
"What the Earth Taught Us." [TarRP] (26:2) Spr 87, p. 34-35.
2742. JOHNSTON, Bob
"Clear Title." [KanQ] (19:1/2) Wint-Spr 87, p. 202.
"Dialogue." [KanQ] (19:1/2) Wint-Spr 87, p. 203.
2743. JOHNSTON, George
"Artist Drawing" (tr. of Peter Sandelin). [MalR] (78) Mr 87, p. 105.
"Bar Guest" (tr. of Knut Ødegård). [MalR] (78) Mr 87, p. 9.
"Bed-Time." [MalR] (78) Mr 87, p. 25.
"Bee-Buzz, Salmon-Leap" (tr. of Knut Ødegård). [MalR] (78) Mr 87, p. 7.
"Bee Seasons." [MalR] (78) Mr 87, p. 57-66.
"Cathleen Sweeping." [MalR] (78) Mr 87, p. 69.
"Clocks" (tr. of Knut Ødegård). [MalR] (78) Mr 87, p. 11.
"Clouds come up" (tr. of Sigmund Mjelve). [MalR] (78) Mr 87, p. 99.
"Cows and Turtles" (tr. of Knut Ødegård). [MalR] (78) Mr 87, p. 10.
"Crow's Nests in Court Metres" (for P.K.). [MalR] (78) Mr 87, p. 76.
"Do you think I repeat myself?" (tr. of Peter Sandelin). [MalR] (78) Mr 87, p. 104.
"Domestic." [MalR] (78) Mr 87, p. 22.
"The heavens too" (tr. of Sigmund Mjelve). [MalR] (78) Mr 87, p. 98.
"Home Again." [MalR] (78) Mr 87, p. 26.
"Home Free." [MalR] (78) Mr 87, p. 24.
"I am a dead whale" (tr. of Sigmund Mjelve). [MalR] (78) Mr 87, p. 101.
"In It." [MalR] (78) Mr 87, p. 23.
"It is as though the dark has suddenly grown wings" (tr. of Marianne Larsen). [MalR] (78) Mr 87, p. 102.
"It was just such a day" (tr. of Peter Sandelin). [MalR] (78) Mr 87, p. 104.
"January Evening, Frost-Clear" (Molde 1955, tr. of Knut Ødegård). [MalR] (78) Mr 87, p. 8.
"John Olaf." [MalR] (78) Mr 87, p. 133.
"Jonathan." [MalR] (78) Mr 87, p. 132-133.
"Life." [MalR] (78) Mr 87, p. 134.
"November, Storm" (tr. of Knut Ødegård). [MalR] (78) Mr 87, p. 16.
"O Moonlight." [MalR] (78) Mr 87, p. 33.
"October, Orkney" (tr. of Knut Ødegård). [MalR] (78) Mr 87, p. 12-14.
"Often was summer" (tr. of Sigmund Mjelve). [MalR] (78) Mr 87, p. 100.

"Once it was December" (tr. of Sigmund Mjelve). [MalR] (78) Mr 87, p. 99.
"Poems about the Wind." [MalR] (78) Mr 87, p. 135.
"Restored." [MalR] (78) Mr 87, p. 132.
"Snowfall in Still Weather." [MalR] (78) Mr 87, p. 134.
"There." [MalR] (78) Mr 87, p. 68.
"Thora and Ragnar" (tr. of Knut Ødegård). [MalR] (78) Mr 87, p. 17-21.
"Time becomes, always, always" (tr. of Sigmund Mjelve). [MalR] (78) Mr 87, p. 100.
"To bring a glass of wine" (tr. of Marianne Larsen). [MalR] (78) Mr 87, p. 103.
"War, Death" (tr. of Knut Ødegård). [MalR] (78) Mr 87, p. 15.
"We Trundle the Child By" (tr. of Knut Ødegård). [MalR] (78) Mr 87, p. 6.
"When we say nothing" (tr. of Marianne Larsen). [MalR] (78) Mr 87, p. 102.
"You do not see them" (tr. of Peter Sandelin). [MalR] (78) Mr 87, p. 104.
"You sit in a waiting room" (tr. of Marianne Larsen). [MalR] (78) Mr 87, p. 103.
2744. JOHNSTON, Janet
"Lesson Plan." [EngJ] (76:1) Ja 87, p. 89.
2745. JOHNSTON, Mark
"Old Man Losing His Memory." [CentR] (31:2) Spr 87, p. 187-188.
2746. JOHNSTON, Stella
"Andromeda." [Shen] (37:4) 87, p. 20-21.
"Nuclear Medicine." [NewRep] (196:21) 25 My 87, p. 32.
2747. JOHNSTON, Susan
"From Somewhere to the Left of You" (for Jeff, who believes me weak). [CapilR] (44) 87, p. 61.
"The Rain Goddess." [CapilR] (44) 87, p. 62.
"Unable to Make a Poem I Defy Language." [CapilR] (44) 87, p. 60.
2748. JONAS, Gerald
"Electronically Yours." [Atlantic] (260:4) O 87, p. 88.
2749. JONES
"Withdrawing." [Rampike] (5:3) 87, p. 73.
2750. JONES, Andrew McCord
"Freight Master." [Wind] (17:60) 87, p. 23.
"Harlequinade." [Wind] (17:60) 87, p. 23.
2751. JONES, Arlene
"April Sunday, 1986." [CimR] (81) O 87, p. 61-62.
2752. JONES, Daryl (Daryl E.)
"Absolute." [WritersF] (13) Fall 87, p. 79.
"Dolls" (for A.). [WritersF] (13) Fall 87, p. 80.
"The Hotstrip." [TriQ] (68) Wint 87, p. 101-102.
2753. JONES, Douglas
"I Write Dedications." [EngJ] (76:4) Ap 87, p. 28.
2754. JONES, Francis
"Creativity" (tr. of Vyacheslav Kuprianov). [Margin] (1) Wint 86, p. 95.
"Human Injustice" (tr. of Vyacheslav Kuprianov). [Margin] (1) Wint 86, p. 94.
"Last Quarter" (tr. of Ivan V. Lalic). [Margin] (2) Spr 87, p. 61.
"The Legend of the Ocean" (tr. of Vyacheslav Kuprianov). [Margin] (1) Wint 86, p. 96.
"Terrace 2" (tr. of Ivan V. Lalic). [Margin] (2) Spr 87, p. 60.
2755. JONES, Ina
"Cedar Waxwing." [CapeR] (22:1) Spr 87, p. 20.
"Zinnias." [Blueline] (7:2/3 [i.e. 8:2/3?]) 87, p. 25.
2756. JONES, Janis
"19th Century Fiction." [NegC] (7:3/4) 87, p. 170.
2757. JONES, John
"For Kaya." [HangL] (50/51) 87, p. 82.
"Poem for a Stranger." [HangL] (50/51) 87, p. 84.
"Poem, Gaziantep, Turkey." [HangL] (50/51) 87, p. 83.
2758. JONES, Michael
"What They Do." [PassN] (8:1) Wint 87, p. 5.
2759. JONES, Paula
"Cedrelatoona." [Margin] (3) Sum 87, p. 121.
2760. JONES, Richard
"Cloudburst." [NowestR] (25:2) 87, p. 146.
"Cloudburst." [Pembroke] (19) 87, p. 192.
"The Horses." [Field] (36) Spr 87, p. 65-66.
"The Imperfectionist" (Reprinted from Bogg 28-29). [Bogg] (58) 87, p. 42.

"Passion." [Pembroke] (19) 87, p. 193.
"Waiting." [Pembroke] (19) 87, p. 193.
2761. JONES, Robert (*See also* JONES, Robert L.)
"Saying a World." [PoetryNW] (28:2) Sum 87, p. 15.
"Separation." [PoetryNW] (28:2) Sum 87, p. 14-15.
2762. JONES, Robert L. (*See also* JONES, Robert)
"Affairs in Order" (tr. of José Carlos Becerra). [WestHR] (41:3) Aut 87, p. 258.
"Autumn Traverses the Islands" (tr. of José Carlos Becerra). [WestHR] (41:3) Aut 87, p. 260.
"The Drowned Man" (tr. of José Carlos Becerra). [WestHR] (41:3) Aut 87, p. 262.
"Outskirts of the World" (tr. of José Carlos Becerra). [WestHR] (41:3) Aut 87, p. 261.
"Your Face Disappearing" (tr. of José Carlos Becerra). [WestHR] (41:3) Aut 87, p. 259.
2763. JONES, Rodney
"Life of Sundays." [Poetry] (151:1/2) O-N 87, p. 71-72.
"One of the Citizens." [Atlantic] (260:2) Ag 87, p. 44.
2764. JONES, Roger
"The Cellar." [TexasR] (8:1/2) Spr-Sum 87, p. 78-79.
"Elegy: Climbing the Fire Tower" (for J.L.). [TexasR] (8:1/2) Spr-Sum 87, p. 77.
"Infestation." [Wind] (17:61) 87, p. 23.
"Pea Picking." [SmPd] (24:1) Wint 87, p. 27.
"Wasps in the Schoolhouse Eaves." [GreensboroR] (39) Wint 85-86, p. 60.
2765. JONES, Seaborn
"Ceremonies for the Muse." [Amelia] (4:3, issue 10) 87, p. 90.
2766. JONES, Thomas B.
"Return Home." [Footwork] 87, p. 58-59.
2767. JONG, Erica
"The Land of Fuck." [Ploughs] (13:4) 87, p. 48-50.
"Middle Aged Lovers I." [Poetry] (151:1/2) O-N 87, p. 72-73.
JONG-GIL, Kim
See KIM, Jong-gil
2768. JORDAN, Barbara
"An Act of Faith." [Wind] (17:61) 87, p. 24.
2769. JORDAN, Johanna
"Onion Story." [FloridaR] (15:1) Spr-Sum 87, p. 107.
2770. JORDAN, Marean L.
"Tamsen Donner at Alder Creek." [Calyx] (10:2/3) Spr 87, p. 70-71.
2771. JORIS, Pierre
"At Rush Hour" (tr. of Michel Deguy). [LitR] (30:3) Spr 87, p. 326-332.
"Winnetou Old" (Excerpt). [Sulfur] (19) Spr 87, p. 35-39.
2772. JORITZ, Jane
"Among Reasons to Read at Night." [NewAW] (2) Fall 87, p. 110.
"Compliments to the Chef." [NewAW] (2) Fall 87, p. 111.
"Fast Approaching." [NewAW] (2) Fall 87, p. 109.
2773. JORON, Andrew
"Nightdawn." [Caliban] (2) 87, p. 152-153.
2774. JOSEPH, Allison E.
"Calling the Midwives In" (England, 1961). [KenR] (NS 9:1) Wint 87, p. 112-113.
"Dialogue of the Tenement Widow." [KenR] (NS 9:1) Wint 87, p. 110-111.
"Spare Change." [KenR] (NS 9:1) Wint 87, p. 111.
2775. JOSEPH, Lawrence (*See also* JOSEPHS, Laurence)
"Factory Rat." [OntR] (26) Spr-Sum 87, p. 92.
"In the Age of Postcapitalism." [Witness] (1:4) Wint 87, p. 118-119.
"In This Time." [Pequod] (23/24) 87, p. 270-271.
"Let Us Pray." [Pequod] (23/24) 87, p. 269.
"My Eyes Are Black as Hers." [PoetryE] (23/24) Fall 87, p. 183-184.
"My Grandma Weighed Almost Nothing." [OntR] (26) Spr-Sum 87, p. 93.
"On Nature." [Poetry] (151:1/2) O-N 87, p. 74-75.
"Rubaiyat." [OntR] (26) Spr-Sum 87, p. 94-95.
"Stop Me If I've Told You." [Pequod] (23/24) 87, p. 272-274.
"This Is How It Happens." [PoetryE] (23/24) Fall 87, p. 185-188.
"Who to Deny." [PoetryE] (23/24) Fall 87, p. 181-182.
2776. JOSEPHS, Laurence (*See also* JOSEPH, Lawrence)
"In the Ad." [Salm] (72) Fall 86, p. 186-187.
"Lake George" (for Marion Miller). [Salm] (72) Fall 86, p. 187-189.

"Lorca's Grave." [Salm] (72) Fall 86, p. 185.
"Something to Drink From, Made in the Desert." [Salm] (72) Fall 86, p. 185-186.
2777. JOSHI, Prakash
"Acting." [DekalbLAJ] (20:1/4) 87, p. 41.
JOURNOUD, Claude Royet
See ROYET-JOURNOUD, Claude
JOUX, Alicia de
See De JOUX, Alicia
2778. JOVINE, Guiseppe
"Every Night" (tr. by Luigi Bonaffini). [PoetL] (82:3) Fall 87, p. 174.
"The Peacock" (To Miserere, tr. by Luigi Bonaffini). [PoetL] (82:3) Fall 87, p. 173.
2779. JOYCE, Dianne
"Anastasia on the Mountain." [Event] (16:3) Fall 87, p. 88-90.
2780. JOYNER, Hannah
"Windchime." [HarvardA] (122:2) D 87, p. 6.
2781. JOZSEF, Attila
"With a Pure Heart" (tr. by John Bakti). [SpiritSH] (53:1) 87, p. 35.
"With All My Heart" (tr. by Peter Hargitai). [SpiritSH] (53:1) 87, p. 34-35.
2782. JUARROZ, Roberto
"The center isn't a point" (tr. by W. S. Merwin). [OhioR] (38) 87, p. 94.
"The emptiness of the day" (tr. by W. S. Merwin). [Antaeus] (58) Spr 87, p. 99.
"Every silence is a magic space" (tr. by W. S. Merwin). [TriQ] (68) Wint 87, p. 112.
"The glance is a lovely pretext of the eye's" (tr. by W. S. Merwin). [Antaeus] (58) Spr 87, p. 97.
"I found a man writing on his bones" (tr. by W. S. Merwin). [Antaeus] (58) Spr 87, p. 98.
"Its own thirst sustains it" (tr. by W. S. Merwin). [Antaeus] (58) Spr 87, p. 99.
"The prompting of my shadow" (tr. by W. S. Merwin). [Antaeus] (58) Spr 87, p. 98.
"Sixth Vertical Poetry" (In Spanish & English, tr. by W. S. Merwin). [HawaiiR] (20) Fall 86, c87, p. 46-53.
"Things imitate us" (tr. by W. S. Merwin). [TriQ] (68) Wint 87, p. 111.
"Vertical Poetry" (6 selections, tr. by W. S. Merwin). [Trans] (18) Spr 87, p. 203-207.
"Vertical Poetry" (Excerpts, tr. by W. S. Merwin). [Iowa] (17:2) Spr-Sum 87, p. 91.
"Vertical Poetry" (Excerpts, tr. by W. S. Merwin). [MissouriR] (10:2) 87, p. 32-33.
"Vertical Poetry" (Five poems, tr. by W. S. Merwin). [WillowS] (19) Wint 87, p. 55-60.
"Yes, there is a back of things" (tr. by W. S. Merwin). [TriQ] (68) Wint 87, p. 110.
2783. JUDSON, John
"Dawn at Drury Pond." [TexasR] (8:1/2) Spr-Sum 87, p. 81.
2784. JULLICH, Jeffrey
"Fame." [ColEng] (49:4) Ap 87, p. 425.
"Faster Than Vista." [Caliban] (2) 87, p. 148-149.
"Highrise." [ColEng] (49:4) Ap 87, p. 426.
2785. JUNKINS, Donald
"I Am the Reverend Joseph Moody, Removed from My Pulpit in York, Maine for Being 'Incapable.' . . ." [TexasR] (7:3/4) 87, p. 86.
"Joseph Moody, Schoolmaster in York, Maine in My 21st Year, Associate Pastor to My Father Samuel. . ." [TexasR] (7:3/4) 87, p. 85.
2786. JURSZA, Suzana
"Just an Ordinary Monday." [Waves] (15:1/2) Fall 86, p. 72.
2787. JUSTICE, Donald
"Cinema and Ballad of the Great Depression." [Antaeus] (58) Spr 87, p. 84-85.
"Nostalgia of the Lakefronts." [Antaeus] (58) Spr 87, p. 82-83.
"Seawind: A Song" (after Rilke). [AntR] (45:1) Wint 87, p. 40.
"Young Girls Growing Up (1911)" (after Kafka). [Sequoia] (31:1) Centennial issue 87, p. 14.
2788. JUSTICE, Jack
"Country Birthing." [HampSPR] Wint 86, p. 17.
"Dancing." [Wind] (17:60) 87, p. 22.
"Whatever Bloomed in Her Ears." [HampSPR] Wint 86, p. 17.
2789. JUSTIS, Patricia
"Daughter of a Son of a Farmer." [PoeticJ] (17) 87, p. 19.

2790. KABBERT, Jean
"Whatever Happened to Those Orange Crates?" [EngJ] (76:8) D 87, p. 80.
2791. KACHUR, Stephen Patrick
"Awkward Feeling of Self." [HiramPoR] (43) Fall-Wint 87-88, p. 27.
"What I Do with Funny-Looking People." [HiramPoR] (43) Fall-Wint 87-88, p. 34.
2792. KAHANU, Diane
"Ho. Just Cause I Speak Pidgin No Mean I Dumb." The Best of [BambooR] [(31-32)] 86, p. 43.
"Honomalino." [BambooR] (36) Fall 87, p. 83.
"Single Parent Plates." [BambooR] (33) Spr 87, p. 32-33.
"Sometimes He Held My Mom's Hand and Sang Love Songs, Just a Little Flat . . ." [BambooR] (33) Spr 87, p. 34-35.
"Thinking About Peace and About Thinking Globally and Acting Locally." [BambooR] (36) Fall 87, p. 84-85.
2793. KAIKOWSKA, Catherine
"The Metamorphosis." [BelPoJ] (37:4) Sum 87, p. 24-25.
2794. KAIPO, Royal Elementary School
"I am the eyeball looking at you." The Best of [BambooR] [(31-32)] 86, p. 16.
2795. KALAMARAS, George
"An Infinite Place Inside Us Fills the Wide Fields of Space." [HighP] (2:3) Wint 87, p. 232-233.
2796. KALINA, Gail
"Prime: First Hour 6 AM" (from "Canonical Hours"). [Vis] (23) 87, p. 11.
"Sixt: Sixth Hour Noon." [Vis] (24) 87, p. 21.
2797. KALLET, Marilyn
"The White Zombie." [Confr] (35/36) Spr-Fall 87, p. 147.
2798. KALLSEN, T. J.
"The Poem at Destin." [KanQ] (19:1/2) Wint-Spr 87, p. 269.
"Wooing My Muse." [Bogg] (57) 87, p. 54.
2799. KALOGERIS, George
"Following the Village Voices." [Ploughs] (13:1) 87, p. 81.
"The Glass Flowers of the Blashkas" (Harvard Botanical Museum). [Ploughs] (13:1) 87, p. 82-84.
"Winthrop." [Ploughs] (13:1) 87, p. 80.
2800. KAMAL, Daud
"Queen of Ebony" (tr. of Ahmad Nadeem Qasimi). [Vis] (25) 87, p. 12.
2801. KAMENETZ, Rodger
"Daniel da Volterra, 'The Breeches-Maker,' on Michelangelo's Last Judgment." [NewRep] (197:1) 6 Jl 87, p. 40.
"Josie and Joshua: Three Poems." [NewEngR] (10:2) Wint 87, p. 202-203.
"Southern Gothic." [LightY] '87, c86, p. 156.
2802. KAMINSKY, Marc
"American Men." [DevQ] (21:2) Fall 86, p. 78-79.
"Anyone." [CentralP] (12) Fall 87, p. 49.
"Hungry Ghost." [DevQ] (21:2) Fall 86, p. 73-77.
2803. KAMPLEY, Linda
"Fairy Tale." [PoetC] (19:1) Fall 87, p. 10-12.
2804. KANCEWICK, Mary
"The Lynx." [Waves] (15:3) Wint 87, p. 75.
2805. KANE, Paul
"By the Ruins of Carthage at Sunset." [SewanR] (95:3) Sum 87, p. 437-348.
"The Garden Wall" (Assolas House, County Cork). [SewanR] (95:3) Sum 87, p. 450.
"A Letter from Erasmus" (Paris, 1521). [SewanR] (95:4) Fall 87, p. 586-590.
"Rock Creek Cemetery: Washington, D.C." [NewRep] (197:8) 24 Ag 87, p. 32.
"Sequins." [GrandS] (6:3) Spr 87, p. 68.
2806. KANFER, Allen
"The World's Greatest Comedian." [DenQ] (21:3) Wint 87, p. 33-37.
2807. KANG, Xue Pei
"Autumn Chinese Parasol" (tr. of Li Quing Zhao, w. Sibyl James). [TexasR] (8:3/4) Fall-Wint 87, p. 7.
"Not Trying the Lamps" (tr. of Li Quing Zhao, w. Sibyl James). [TexasR] (8:3/4) Fall-Wint 87, p. 6.
"Red Lotus" (tr. of Li Quing Zhao, w. Sibyl James). [TexasR] (8:3/4) Fall-Wint 87, p. 9.

"Spring's News" (tr. of Li Quing Zhao, w. Sibyl James). [TexasR] (8:3/4) Fall-Wint 87, p. 8.
2808. KANTARIS, Sylvia
"The Murmurings." [Stand] (28:1) Wint 86-87, p. 41.
2809. KAPIKIAN, Albert
"Lamentations from the Armenian." [GrahamHR] (10) Wint-Spr 87, p. 7-9.
2810. KAPLAN, Edward
"Whatever Word That Could Mean Whatever Keeps It Together in the First Place." [YellowS] (22) Spr 87, p. 32.
2811. KAPLAN, Howard
"Down." [MSS] (5:3) 87, p. 76.
"In the Middle of Summer Suddenly the Smell of Rain." [MSS] (5:3) 87, p. 77.
2812. KAPLINSKI, Jaan
"And when the sea retreats from here . . ." (tr. by Riina Tamm and Sam Hamill). [AmerPoR] (16:6) N-D 87, p. 8.
"Dialectics is a dialogue, a play of shadows" (tr. by Riina Tamm and Sam Hamill). [AmerPoR] (16:6) N-D 87, p. 8.
"The early autumn, a faded aquarelle" (tr. by Riina Tamm and Sam Hamill). [AmerPoR] (16:6) N-D 87, p. 8.
"From Childhood On" (tr. by the author and Sam Hamill). [Zyzzyva] (3:4) Wint 87-88, p. 129.
"No one can put me back together again" (tr. by Riina Tamm and Sam Hamill). [AmerPoR] (16:6) N-D 87, p. 8.
"No one can put me back together again" (tr. by the author, w. Riina Tamm and Sam Hamill). [Dandel] (14:2) Fall-Wint 87, p. 29.
"Sometimes I see so clearly the openness of things" (tr. by Riina Tamm and Sam Hamill). [AmerPoR] (16:6) N-D 87, p. 7.
"The sun shines on the red wall and the wall is warm" (tr. by Riina Tamm and Sam Hamill). [AmerPoR] (16:6) N-D 87, p. 8.
"There is no Good, no Evil, no Sin, no Virtue" (tr. by Riina Tamm and Sam Hamill). [AmerPoR] (16:6) N-D 87, p. 8.
"The washing never gets done" (tr. by Riina Tamm and Sam Hamill). [AmerPoR] (16:6) N-D 87, p. 7.
"The wind sways the lilac branches and shadows" (tr. by Riina Tamm and Sam Hamill). [AmerPoR] (16:6) N-D 87, p. 8.
2813. KAPPATOS, Rigas
"La Enfermedad y la Merte." [LindLM] (6:1) Ja-Mr 87, p. 7.
"Los Juegos." [LindLM] (6:1) Ja-Mr 87, p. 7.
"Los Sueños de los Gatos." [LindLM] (6:1) Ja-Mr 87, p. 7.
2814. KARAKOÇ, Sezai
"First" (tr. by Talat Sait Halman). [Trans] (19) Fall 87, p. 106.
2815. KARELLI, Zoe
"Seashells" (tr. by Rae Dalven). [LitR] (31:1) Fall 87, p. 50-51.
"The Ship" (tr. by Rachel Dalven). [ColR] (NS 14:1) Spr-Sum 87, p. 40-41.
2816. KARNER, River
"The Lies." [SinW] (31) 87, p. 77.
2817. KARP, Vickie
"Glass." [NewYorker] (63:2) 2 Mr 87, p. 36.
2818. KARR, Mary
"Sad Rite." [Ploughs] (13:4) 87, p. 51.
2819. KASHNER, Sam
"Letter Poem to John Ashbery." [HangL] (50/51) 87, p. 85-86.
"Romantic Notion." [HangL] (50/51) 87, p. 89.
"Special Forces." [HangL] (50/51) 87, p. 87-88.
2820. KASISCHKE, Laura
"The Bride Between Them." [GreensboroR] (42) Sum 87, p. 32-33.
"Give Me a Sign God." [GreensboroR] (42) Sum 87, p. 36.
"St. Peter Blesses the Bastard." [GreensboroR] (42) Sum 87, p. 34-36.
2821. KATCHER, A. (*See also* KATCHER, Antje M.)
"Gathering Butterflies." [PikeF] (8) Fall 87, p. 3.
2822. KATCHER, Antje M. (*See also* KATCHER, A.)
"To My Mother on Her Dying." [ManhatPR] (9) Sum 87, p. 12.
2823. KATES, J.
"Domestic Archaeology." [HawaiiR] (22) Fall 87, p. 26.
"The Horse in the Sea" (tr. of Jean-Pierre Rosnay). [StoneC] (15:1/2) Fall-Wint 87-88, p. 57.

2824. KATROVAS, Richard
    "Elegy for John Van Vleck." [Crazy] (32) Spr 87, p. 7.
2825. KATZ, Susan Bullington
    "Potomac River, 1982." [KanQ] (19:1/2) Wint-Spr 87, p. 268-269.
2826. KAUFFMAN, Jane
    "What Turns Up." [Notus] (2:2) Fall 87, p. 28.
2827. KAUFFMAN, Janet
    "Animal Instruction of the Orphans, or, The Problem of Authority." [Caliban] (3)
        87, p. 11.
    "Loosestrife." [Caliban] (3) 87, p. 10.
    "Where Definition Begins." [Caliban] (3) 87, p. 12.
    "Where the World Is." [Caliban] (3) 87, p. 9.
2828. KAUFMAN, Andrew
    "Etude in Black." [BlackWR] (13:2) Spr 87, p. 67.
    "How to Turn Invisible." [SouthernPR] (27:1) Spr 87, p. 36.
2829. KAUFMAN, Shirley
    "Ganges." [Field] (37) Fall 87, p. 69-71.
2830. KAUFMAN, Stuart
    "The Puncher." [DevQ] (21:2) Fall 86, p. 43.
2831. KAUNE, Gayle Rogers
    "Amnesia." [WindO] (49) Fall 87, p. 24-25.
    "As When a Fly Lands on Your Page and You Can Read the Words It Is Through the
        Wings." [BellArk] (3:4) Jl-Ag 87, p. 3.
    "For Bill." [BellArk] (3:4) Jl-Ag 87, p. 7.
    "Michigan Cemetery." [Raccoon] (24/25) My 87, p. 189.
    "Michigan Childhood." [CentR] (31:4) Fall 87, p. 379-380.
    "Writer's Club." [GreenfR] (14:3/4) Sum-Fall 87, p. 92.
2832. KAURAKA, Kauraka
    "Flying Fish." [HawaiiR] (20) Fall 86, c87, p. 92.
2833. KAVADIAS, Nikos
    "Gabrielle Didot" (tr. by Gail Holst-Warhaft). [Paint] (14:27) Spr 87, p. 28-29.
2834. KAVANAGH, P. J.
    "This Sojourn." [GrandS] (7:1) Aut 87, p. 94.
2835. KAVANAGH, Patrick
    "Epic." [Pembroke] (19) 87, p. 74.
    "Kerr's Ass." [Pembroke] (19) 87, p. 74-75.
    "Prelude." [Pembroke] (19) 87, p. 75-76.
2836. KAVEN, Bob
    "The Struggle." [AmerPoR] (16:4) Jl-Ag 87, p. 34.
2837. KAWAHARADA, Dennis
    "Easy Game." [BambooR] (33) Spr 87, p. 50.
    "Order." The Best of [BambooR] [(31-32)] 86, p. 44.
2838. KAWAMURA, Kazuo
    "Ball of Yarn" (tr. of Shuntaro Tanikawa, w. William I. Elliott). [Amelia] (4:3, issue
        10) 87, p. 102.
    "A Friend Who Leapt to His Death" (tr. of Shuntaro Tanikawa, w. William I.
        Elliott). [Amelia] (4:3, issue 10) 87, p. 102.
2839. KAYE/KANTROWITZ, Melanie
    "Mathematical Model" (for Linda). [SinW] (31) 87, p. 47.
2840. KAZANTZIS, Judith
    "For Example Owen." [Stand] (28:2) Spr 87, p. 4-6.
2841. KAZANTZIS, Judtih
    "Eva." [Verse] (4:1) Mr 87, p. 54.
2842. KEARNS, Josie
    "Father Ghost." [CrossCur] (7:2) 87, p. 107.
2843. KEEFER, Janice Kulyk
    "Cirrus." [Quarry] (36:4) Fall 87, p. 63.
    "Col Tempo." [Quarry] (36:4) Fall 87, p. 64.
    "For Michael, 37." [Descant] (59) Wint 87, p. 20-21.
2844. KEELAN, Claudia
    "Towards." [Ploughs] (13:4) 87, p. 52.
2845. KEELER, Greg
    "Bird Book Blues." [PraS] (61:4) Wint 87, p. 28-29.
    "Easter with Tom: Trabzon, Turkey." [RiverS] (22) 87, p. 79.
    "On Vacation: Orlando, Florida." [RiverS] (22) 87, p. 80.
    "Panfish." [PraS] (61:4) Wint 87, p. 29-30.

2846. KEELER, Julia
"Chores." [Waves] (15:4) Spr 87, p. 48-49.
2847. KEEN, Paul
"Scenes from a Dirty Window." [Event] (16:3) Fall 87, p. 26-27.
2848. KEEN, Suzanne
"December Elegy: Why We Will Go Far." [OhioR] (39) 87, p. 32-33.
"Four Elegies." [OhioR] (39) 87, p. 32-36.
"January Elegy: The Stone Circle." [OhioR] (39) 87, p. 34.
"March Elegy: In Training." [OhioR] (39) 87, p. 35.
"October Elegy: Here Is the Sub-Basement." [OhioR] (39) 87, p. 36.
2849. KEENAN, Deborah
"Open Hands." [Caliban] (3) 87, p. 137.
2850. KEENAN, Gary
"July 4, 1984." [Ploughs] (13:1) 87, p. 85.
2851. KEENER, Earl R.
"Right Field Lines." [WestB] (20) 87, p. 67.
"Wallflower." [WestB] (20) 87, p. 66.
2852. KEENER, LuAnn
"The Bright Arcs." [PoetryNW] (28:1) Spr 87, p. 9.
"Sabra Shatila, Beirut, Summer 1982." [NowestR] (25:1) 87, p. 41.
"Your Name Means Bitter Light" (for my mother). [NowestR] (25:1) 87, p. 39-40.
2853. KEENEY, Bill
"Duello." [SouthernPR] (27:2) Fall 87, p. 28.
2854. KEES, Weldon
"A French Writer Named Sartre." [LightY] '87, c86, p. 56.
"Mitzi." [LightY] '87, c86, p. 178.
2855. KEET, Rose
"Those Jolly Little Beetles" (tr. of Wilma Stockenström). [TriQ] (69) Spr-Sum 87,
            p. 343-344.
KEIHO, Soga
    See SOGA, Keiho
2856. KEITA, Nzadi Zimele
"Poem for Maurice Bishop." [RiverS] (22) 87, p. 58.
2857. KEITH, W. J.
"A. J. M. Smith." [CanLit] (113/114) Sum-Fall 87, p. 92.
"For My Parents." [AntigR] (68) Wint 87, p. 114.
"On Death and Shelter." [AntigR] (68) Wint 87, p. 114-115.
"Penelope." [AntigR] (68) Wint 87, p. 116.
"Small Things" (after seeing an exhibition of engravings by Gerard Brender à
            Brandis). [AntigR] (71/72) Aut 87-Wint 88, p. 7.
"Spirit of Cézanne." [AntigR] (71/72) Aut 87-Wint 88, p. 7.
"Tom Thomson." [CanLit] (113/114) Sum-Fall 87, p. 144.
2858. KEITHLEY, George
"The River's Sister." [WritersF] (13) Fall 87, p. 134.
2859. KEIZER, Arlene R.
"Anna Akhmatova, to Her Second Husband." [Sequoia] (30:3) Wint 87, p. 14.
"Coyoacan" (For Leon Trotsky). [Sequoia] (30:3) Wint 87, p. 12-13.
2860. KELLER, David
"After Supper." [PraS] (61:2) Sum 87, p. 34.
"And We Came to Believe." [Colum] (12) 87, p. 20.
"And We Came to Believe." [US1] (20/21) Wint 86-87, p. 31.
"Argument." [PoetryE] (23/24) Fall 87, p. 174.
"The Bar in the B Movie." [US1] (20/21) Wint 86-87, p. 30.
"Harry Houdini, Condoms, Silence." [SouthernPR] (27:1) Spr 87, p. 67-68.
"Journal." [Footwork] 87, p. 16.
"New Room." [PraS] (61:2) Sum 87, p. 35-36.
"A New Room." [QRL] (Series 8, vol. 27) 87, 69 p.
"Porgy & Bess" (for a friend, uncertain of his work). [Footwork] 87, p. 16.
"Three Pieces for Voice." [PraS] (61:2) Sum 87, p. 36-42.
"Timpani." [Footwork] 87, p. 16.
"To a Young Woman Asking Certainty." [PoetryE] (23/24) Fall 87, p. 172.
2861. KELLER, Tsipi Edith
"The Japanese Man." [SmPd] (24:2) Spr 87, p. 24.
2862. KELLEY, Janine S.
"The Fishermen." [MinnR] (NS 29) Fall 87, p. 19-20.

2863. KELLEY, Tina
"Nourish." [StoneC] (14:3/4) Spr-Sum 87, p. 62.
"Tess Asleep." [StoneC] (15:1/2) Fall-Wint 87-88, p. 32.
2864. KELLMAN, Tony
"After the Rain." [GreenfR] (14:1/2) Wint-Spr, p. 178-179.
"Alpha, Omega." [Chelsea] (46) 87, p. 304.
"Blazing Embers." [GreenfR] (14:1/2) Wint-Spr, p. 182-183.
"Flight." [Chelsea] (46) 87, p. 300-301.
"Nowhere Is Safe." [GreenfR] (14:1/2) Wint-Spr, p. 180-181.
"Sea-Island." [Chelsea] (46) 87, p. 302-303.
2865. KELLY, Brigit Pegeen
"Lost in the Peaceable Kingdom." [PoetryNW] (28:1) Spr 87, p. 10-11.
"Sundays." [NowestR] (25:3) 87, p. 418-421.
"The Thief's Wife." [PoetryNW] (28:1) Spr 87, p. 11-13.
"To the Lost Child" (for Anna). [NowestR] (25:2) 87, p. 6-7.
2866. KELLY, Dave (*See also* KELLY, David M.)
"Mother Teresa." [Raccoon] (24/25) My 87, p. 14.
2867. KELLY, David J.
"The Fugitive." [Pembroke] (19) 87, p. 185.
"Midmorning Groundfog Disappearing." [Pembroke] (19) 87, p. 184-185.
2868. KELLY, David M. (*See also* KELLY, Dave)
"Margarine." [IndR] (11:1) Wint 87, p. 89-90.
2869. KELLY, Mary Lee
"The Egg Trick." [NegC] (7:3/4) 87, p. 137.
"The Oxford Dream Machine." [Bogg] (58) 87, p. 50.
2870. KELLY, Robert
"At the End of the Hudson River." [Notus] (2:1) Spr 87, p. 60.
"The clue to unbounded transmissions from the architects of space." [Notus] (2:2)
    Fall 87, p. 32.
"Hypnogeography." [Notus] (2:1) Spr 87, p. 58-59.
"Not listening." [Notus] (2:1) Spr 87, p. 61.
"The Rube Goldberg Suite." [Conjunc] (11) 87?, p. 20-35.
"Ténèbres" (To the memory of Morton Feldman). [Caliban] (3) 87, p. 59-62.
2871. KELLY-DEWITT, Susan
"Migration." [HawaiiR] (22) Fall 87, p. 56.
"Shadow Woman." [HawaiiR] (22) Fall 87, p. 57-58.
2872. KEMP, Penny
"The Red Convertible" (Excerpts). [CrossC] (9:2) 87, p. 9.
2873. KEMPA, Rick
"Kicking Cairns." [HighP] (2:3) Wint 87, p. 279.
"Pariah." [PoetL] (82:3) Fall 87, p. 158.
2874. KEMPHER, Ruth Moon
"Get-away." [FloridaR] (15:1) Spr-Sum 87, p. 118.
"Looking for Kierkegaard in a Strange Novel." [WindO] (48) Spr 87, p. 12.
"Picking Up Things." [Outbr] (18/19) Fall 86-Spr 88, p. 110.
2875. KEMPTON, Karl
"Wired" (Excerpts, w. Loris Essary). [CentralP] (12) Fall 87, p. 4, 15, 85.
2876. KENAR, Derek
"Tragedy" (Age 11). [PikeF] (8) Fall 87, p. 22.
2877. KENDALL, Robert
"Abstract Expressionism." [Footwork] 87, p. 60-61.
"Certainties." [Raccoon] (24/25) My 87, p. 248.
"From the Bank." [CanLit] (115) Wint 87, p. 63.
"Letter from the End of the World." [CentralP] (11) Spr 87, p. 76.
"A Visit." [KanQ] (19:1/2) Wint-Spr 87, p. 171.
2878. KENDIG, Diane
"Peninsula, Ohio." [Footwork] 87, p. 43.
"Reciting the Old Lord's Prayer." [TarPR] (27:1) Fall 87, p. 32.
2879. KENNEDY, D. G.
"Turn Over Baby." [Bogg] (57) 87, p. 54.
2880. KENNEDY, Maggie
"The Trapeze Artist." [PikeF] (8) Fall 87, p. 6.
2881. KENNEDY, Monique M.
"Between Always and Never" (tr. of Pia Tafdrup, w. Thomas E. Kennedy). [Paint]
    (14:28) Aut 87, p. 32.

"Shadows in the Blood" (tr. of Pia Tafdrup, w. Thomas E. Kennedy). [Paint]
(14:28) Aut 87, p. 33.
2882. KENNEDY, Rebecca
"Tree." [MassR] (28:4) Wint 87, p. 704.
2883. KENNEDY, Stephen
"John's Metamorphoses." [NowestR] (25:3) 87, p. 192-193.
2884. KENNEDY, Thomas E.
"Between Always and Never" (tr. of Pia Tafdrup, w. Monique M. Kennedy). [Paint]
(14:28) Aut 87, p. 32.
"Shadows in the Blood" (tr. of Pia Tafdrup, w. Monique M. Kennedy). [Paint]
(14:28) Aut 87, p. 33.
2885. KENNEDY, X. J.
"A 4th Stanza for Dr. Johnson, Donald Hall, & Louis Phillips." [LightY] '87, c86,
p. 210.
"The Cost of a Sting." [LightY] '87, c86, p. 245.
"Domestic Crisis." [LightY] '87, c86, p. 88.
"English Eats." [LightY] '87, c86, p. 38.
"Finis." [OP] (final issue) Sum 87, p. 7.
"On Being Accused of Wit." [Poetry] (151:1/2) O-N 87, p. 75.
"A Penitent Giuseppe Belli Enters Heaven" (for Miller Williams). [OP] (final issue)
Sum 87, p. 8.
"Pileup." [FourQ] (1:2) Fall 87, p. 26-27.
"A Switched Career." [LightY] '87, c86, p. 216.
"Tending a Cookout in Pouring Rain While Pope John Paul II Arrives in Boston."
[LightY] '87, c86, p. 84-85.
2886. KENNELLY, Brendan
"Straying." [MassR] (28:3) Aut 87, p. 410-411.
2887. KENNEY, Richard
"Ocelots, Etc." [Poetry] (151:1/2) O-N 87, p. 76-77.
2888. KENNY, Maurice
"E. Pauline Johnson (1861-1913): Generations." [GreenfR] (14:1/2) Wint-Spr, p.
49-50.
"From Tekonwatonti / Molly Brant (1735-1795): Poems of War." [GreenfR]
(14:1/2) Wint-Spr, p. 42-50.
"Last Night." [PaintedB] (30) 87, p. 15.
"Marriage Vow." [GreenfR] (14:1/2) Wint-Spr, p. 44.
"Molly." [GreenfR] (14:1/2) Wint-Spr, p. 45-46.
"Moving the Village." [GreenfR] (14:1/2) Wint-Spr, p. 43.
"Sir William Johnson: His Daily Journal." [GreenfR] (14:1/2) Wint-Spr, p. 47-48.
2889. KENT, David W.
"Fallow" (1986 Honorable Mention, Eve of Saint Agnes Poetry Competition).
[NegC] (7:1/2) 87, p. 132.
2890. KENT, Rolly
"The Bluebird." [HayF] (2) Spr 87, p. 36-37.
2891. KENT-STOLL, Marianne
"The Physical Therapist." [GreenfR] (14:3/4) Sum-Fall 87, p. 78.
2892. KENTER, Robert
"Benefaction." [Writ] (19) 87, p. 10.
"Child in the Hourglass." [Writ] (19) 87, p. 11.
"Come Down to the Talking World." [Writ] (19) 87, p. 20.
"Domestic Violence." [Writ] (19) 87, p. 17.
"Father." [AntigR] (69/70) 87, p. 87.
"In First Light." [Writ] (19) 87, p. 13.
"Main Street." [Writ] (19) 87, p. 18.
"Men out of Snow." [Writ] (19) 87, p. 16.
"One Night in Brooklyn I Heard a Voice Calling Out My Name." [Writ] (19) 87, p.
19.
"Planetarium." [Writ] (19) 87, p. 12.
"Wage." [Writ] (19) 87, p. 14-15.
"When Susan Got Out." [Writ] (19) 87, p. 21.
2893. KENYON, Jane
"After an Illness, Walking the Dog." [Poetry] (151:1/2) O-N 87, p. 78.
"The Blue Bowl." [Poetry] (150:3) Je 87, p. 148.
"Homesick." [SenR] (17:1) 87, p. 15.
"On the Aisle." [Poetry] (150:3) Je 87, p. 147.

2894. KEPPLER, Joseph
"Love Swamp." [Bogg] (57) 87, p. 17.
2895. KEROUAC, Jack
"Mexico City Blues" (Selection: "17th Chorus"). [Margin] (2) Spr 87, p. 20.
2896. KERR, Don
"European Ice Berg, Ontario Art Gallery." [Quarry] (36:4) Fall 87, p. 61-62.
"VAG rant." [Quarry] (36:4) Fall 87, p. 59-60.
2897. KERRIGAN, T. S.
"Danae." [Poem] (57) Mr 87, p. 27.
"Dublin Revisited." [CumbPR] (6:2) Spr 87, p. 87.
"Dublin Revisited" (Dublin 1966, 1986). [HawaiiR] (22) Fall 87, p. 63.
"Evening Statuary." [Poem] (57) Mr 87, p. 28.
2898. KERSHNER, Brandon
"3 Dialogues." [Spirit] (8:2) 87, p. 282-284.
2899. KESEY, Ken
"Dark Side." [Sequoia] (31:1) Centennial issue 87, p. 93-94.
2900. KESSLER, Jascha
"Arctic Journey" (tr. of Kirsti Simonsuuri, w. the author). [CrossCur] (7:3) 87, p. 157.
"At First Hand" (tr. of Ottó Orbán, w. Maria Körösy). [VirQR] (63:1) Wint 87, p. 77-78.
"An Awning, the Senses" (tr. of Kirsti Simonsuuri). [Caliban] (2) 87, p. 91.
"Chile" (tr. of Ottó Orbán, w. Maria Körösy). [NewL] (53:3) Spr 87, p. 17.
"The Gate of Teeth" (tr. of Sandor Weöres, w. Mária Körösy). [GrahamHR] (10) Wint-Spr 87, p. 62-63.
"The Golden Fleece" (tr. of Ottó Orbán, w. Maria Körösy). [VirQR] (63:1) Wint 87, p. 78-79.
"The Greeks Are Blinding Polyphemus" (tr. of György Rába, w. Maria Körösy). [HayF] (2) Spr 87, p. 101.
"History of Lit: A Communication" (tr. of István Vas, w. Maria Körösy). [Nimrod] (31:1) Fall-Wint 87, p. 132.
"Idling" (tr. of István Vas, w. Mária Körösy). [GrahamHR] (10) Wint-Spr 87, p. 60-61.
"Intellectuals" (tr. of Ottó Orbán, w. Maria Körösy). [VirQR] (63:1) Wint 87, p. 80.
"Opus" (tr. of Kirsti Simonsuuri). [Caliban] (2) 87, p. 90.
"Poetry" (tr. of Ottó Orbán, w. Maria Körösy). [Nimrod] (31:1) Fall-Wint 87, p. 123.
"Poverty" (tr. of Ottó Orbán, w. Maria Körösy). [PoetryE] (23/24) Fall 87, p. 117.
"Prayer Before Turning Off the Light" (tr. of Agnes Gergely, w. Maria Körösy). [Nimrod] (31:1) Fall-Wint 87, p. 131.
"A Preface to Dying" (tr. of Gyorgy Raba, w. Maria Korosy). [BlueBldgs] (10) 87?, p. 33.
"A Preface to Dying" (tr. of György Rába, w. Maria Körösy). [HayF] (2) Spr 87, p. 102.
"Ruined House" (tr. of Kirsti Simonsuuri). [Caliban] (2) 87, p. 90.
"The Sharing" (tr. of Richard Exner). [CrossCur] (7:1) 87, p. 119.
"Shipwreck, from Outside" (tr. of Agnes Gergely, w. Maria Körösy). [Nimrod] (31:1) Fall-Wint 87, p. 131.
"Song from Kanteletar" (tr. of anonymous Finnish song, collected by Lonrot in the 19th century, w. Kirsti Simonsuuri). [Nimrod] (31:1) Fall-Wint 87, p. 130.
"A Supper" (tr. of Kirsti Simonsuuri). [Caliban] (2) 87, p. 91.
"Turn-of-the-Century Budapest" (tr. of Ottó Orbán, w. Mária Körösy). [GrahamHR] (10) Wint-Spr 87, p. 59.
"The Young Muse." [CrossCur] (7:1) 87, p. 100-101.
2901. KESTENBAUM, Stuart
"Pilgrimage." [TexasR] (7:3/4) 87, p. 87-88.
2902. KESTER, Marcia Gale
"Wagner in Seattle." [BlueBldgs] (10) 87?, p. 51.
2903. KETTNER, M.
"Diet." [WindO] (49) Fall 87, p. 7.
"Nickels." [WindO] (49) Fall 87, p. 7.
2904. KEY, Bruce
"First Mem'ry: A Resurrection" (A Summer Day in 1950). [PoeticJ] (17) 87, p. 33.
2905. KEYES, Robert Lord
"Finding That the Past Is Like a Historical Character." [Wind] (17:59) 87, p. 28-29.
"The Origin of Agriculture." [Wind] (17:59) 87, p. 27-28.

215

KING

2906. KGOSITSILE, Keorapetse
"For Billie Holiday." [TriQ] (69) Spr-Sum 87, p. 349-350.
"Song for Ilva Mackay and Mongane." [TriQ] (69) Spr-Sum 87, p. 351.
2907. KHOMIN, Igor
"Idyll" (tr. by Joseph Langland, w. Tamas Aczel and Laszlo Tikos). [NowestR]
(25:3) 87, p. 132-133.
2908. KIDD, Gordon
"There once was a legal named Blaising." [Amelia] (4:1/2, issue 9) 87, p. 26.
2909. KIERNAN, Rebecca Kelly
"April One." [Amelia] (4:1/2, issue 9) 87, p. 122-123.
"Brighton, Epilogue." [Amelia] (4:1/2, issue 9) 87, p. 123.
"Secrets from Marcus." [Amelia] (4:1/2, issue 9) 87, p. 122.
2910. KIJEWSKI, Bruce
"Bubblegum." [Jacaranda] (2:2) Spr 87, p. 64-65.
2911. KIJNER, Janine
"The Startle of a Deer." [Vis] (25) 87, p. 9.
2912. KIKOT, Mark E.
"Two Thieves." [Waves] (14:4) Spr 86, p. 60.
2913. KIKUCHI, Carl
"Eagle Harbor." [WestB] (20) 87, p. 47.
"My House." [WindO] (49) Fall 87, p. 22.
"Telepathy." [WindO] (49) Fall 87, p. 22.
2914. KILKELLY, Ann Gavere
"Getting Tough with the Muse." [HeliconN] (17/18) Spr 87, p. 96-97.
2915. KILLIAN, Sean
"As Signatures Sag" (Invocation to Kali). [Sulfur] (18) Wint 87, p. 158-160.
"Missive." [Sulfur] (18) Wint 87, p. 161-162.
"Nexus." [Sulfur] (18) Wint 87, p. 158.
"Trigger Finger" (On Translation). [Sulfur] (18) Wint 87, p. 160-161.
2916. KIM, Chiha
"No One" (tr. by David R. McCann). [Pembroke] (19) 87, p. 16-17.
2917. KIM, Do Sung
"A Snowy Night" (tr. by John Chay and Grace Gibson). [InterPR] (13:1) Spr 87, p.
62.
"The Year Is Getting Late" (tr. by John Chay and Grace Gibson). [InterPR] (13:1)
Spr 87, p. 61.
2918. KIM, Jong-gil
"At the Execution Ground" (tr. of Song Sam-mun). [Pembroke] (19) 87, p. 12.
2919. KIM, Jong-sahm
"My Home" (tr. by Hyn-jae Yee Sallee). [HampSPR] Wint 86, p. 30.
2920. KIM, Myong-yol
"Wind Burial 4" (tr. of Hwang Tong-Gyu). [Pembroke] (19) 87, p. 19.
2921. KIM, Sabina
"The House of Babi Yaga." [Grain] (15:4) Wint 87, p. 72-73.
2922. KIM, Sowol
"Azaleas" (tr. by David R. McCann). [Pembroke] (19) 87, p. 13-14.
2923. KIM, Su-yong
"Blue Sky" (tr. by Peter Lee). [Pembroke] (19) 87, p. 15.
"Grass" (tr. by Peter Lee). [Pembroke] (19) 87, p. 16.
"Love" (tr. by Peter Lee). [Pembroke] (19) 87, p. 19.
2924. KIMBALL, Arthur
"Condor." [Waves] (14:4) Spr 86, p. 76.
"Correspondence." [ManhatPR] (9) Sum 87, p. 36.
"Late in the Season." [HawaiiR] (20) Fall 86, c87, p. 85.
"OHM." [Pig] (14) 87, p. 33.
2925. KIMBALL, Chris
"Tropical Island." [Gambit] (20) 86, p. 48.
2926. KIMBLE, James
"The Light the World Appears In" (Selections: 5 poems). [Bound] (15:1/2) Fall
86-Wint 87, p. 255-262.
2927. KIME, Peter
"Louie." [HighP] (2:3) Wint 87, p. 329-330.
2928. KINCAID, Joan Payne
"Miscalculation." [PoeticJ] (17) 87, p. 30.
2929. KING, Kenneth
"The Margins." [PoetryNW] (28:3) Aut 87, p. 47.

"Questions After the Freedom Assignment." [PoetryNW] (28:3) Aut 87, p. 46.
"What to Do About a Dead Grandmother." [PoetryNW] (28:3) Aut 87, p. 45-46.
2930. KING, Lyn
"The Heart Buoyed Up." [Event] (16:3) Fall 87, p. 68-69.
2931. KING, R. D.
"Beating Heart" (1987 Ratner-Ferber-Poet Lore Honorable Mention). [PoetL] (82:2)
      Sum 87, p. 93-94.
"The Big Picture." [LitR] (30:4) Sum 87, p. 608.
"Blue Shoes Downtown." [NowestR] (25:3) 87, p. 431.
"In November." [MissouriR] (10:1) 87, p. 140.
"Jazz Nebraska." [NowestR] (25:3) 87, p. 431.
"The Morning Poems." [MissouriR] (10:1) 87, p. 136.
"On the Plain of Smokes." [MissouriR] (10:1) 87, p. 133.
"Ornamental Horses." [MissouriR] (10:1) 87, p. 134.
"Outside Modesto." [MissouriR] (10:1) 87, p. 137.
"Rivers, Boats, and Cities." [MissouriR] (10:1) 87, p. 138-139.
"Still Life with Jogger." [MissouriR] (10:1) 87, p. 135.
2932. KING, Robert
"Closet Full." [BellArk] (3:6) N-D 87, p. 4.
"Dust in Both Eyes." [BellArk] (3:5) S-O 87, p. 20.
"God Most High." [BellArk] (3:3) My-Je 87, p. 8.
"Letting the Strangers In." [PaintedB] (30) 87, p. 61.
"Logos." [BellArk] (3:6) N-D 87, p. 18.
"Nude Swimming." [PaintedB] (30) 87, p. 61.
"On the Sidewalk." [BellArk] (3:4) Jl-Ag 87, p. 5.
"Once Form Becomes Unshakable." [BellArk] (3:1) Ja-F 87, p. 20.
"The Palouse Underneath." [BellArk] (3:6) N-D 87, p. 3.
"Saying It Happens." [Ascent] (13:1) 87, p. 51.
"Telling Childhood." [PaintedB] (30) 87, p. 62.
2933. KINGSOLVER, Barbara
"Remember the Moon Survives" (for Pamela). [Calyx] (10:2/3) Spr 87, p. 36-38.
"Your Mother's Eyes" (for Maura and Lesbia Lopez). [Calyx] (10:2/3) Spr 87, p.
      39-40.
2934. KINLOCH, David
"The Date-Line." [Verse] (4:2) Je 87, p. 19.
"Epithalamium" (for Nick and Cynthia). [Verse] (4:2) Je 87, p. 20.
"Revolution." [Verse] (4:2) Je 87, p. 21.
"Rims" (tr. of Michel Deguy). [Verse] (4:2) Je 87, p. 59.
2935. KINSELLA, Thomas
"At the Ocean's Edge." [Poetry] (151:1/2) O-N 87, p. 79.
"Magnanimity" (for Austin Clarke's seventieth birthday). [KenR] (NS 9:1) Wint 87,
      p. 45-46.
2936. KINSOLVING, Susan
"The Jellyfish." [Nat] (245:4) 15-22 Ag 87, p. 138.
"Wellers Bridge Road." [Shen] (37:1) 87, p. 43.
2937. KINZIE, Mary
"Dreamchildren." [Salm] (72) Fall 86, p. 172-173.
"Have You Seen Me?" [ThRiPo] (29/30) 87, p. 39-40.
"Intellectual Temptations." [Salm] (72) Fall 86, p. 174.
"Song for a Wedding." [Salm] (72) Fall 86, p. 173.
"Xenophilia." [ThRiPo] (29/30) 87, p. 41-42.
2938. KIRBY, David
"Le Big One de John Dillinger." [SouthernPR] (27:1) Spr 87, p. 69.
"The Breasts of Women." [LightY] '87, c86, p. 153.
"The Death of the Reference Librarian." [LightY] '87, c86, p. 218.
"Fear of Reading." [KanQ] (19:3) Sum 87, p. 77.
"Matthew Arnold on Mars." [HawaiiR] (19) Spr 86, c87, p. 46.
"Pascal's Carriage." [KanQ] (19:3) Sum 87, p. 78.
"White." [SouthernPR] (27:1) Spr 87, p. 70.
2939. KIRBY, Jeff
"Untitled: I'm responsible for AIDS." [JamesWR] (4:4) Sum 87, p. 9.
2940. KIRCHER, Pamela
"The Abandoned World." [TarPR] (27:1) Fall 87, p. 22.
"The Butterfly Caught." [Thrpny] (28) Wint 87, p. 8.
"By the Lilies." [AmerPoR] (16:5) S-O 87, p. 15.
"Desperate Angel." [AmerPoR] (16:5) S-O 87, p. 16.

"Dream of the Rest of My LIfe." [AmerPoR] (16:5) S-O 87, p. 15.
"Every Night." [AmerPoR] (16:5) S-O 87, p. 16.
"If She Spoke." [AmerPoR] (16:5) S-O 87, p. 15.
"No Telling." [TarPR] (27:1) Fall 87, p. 23.
"One Thousand, Ten Thousand Times." [AmerPoR] (16:5) S-O 87, p. 16.
"What Happens." [AmerPoR] (16:5) S-O 87, p. 16.
"Without End." [AmerPoR] (16:5) S-O 87, p. 17.
2941. KIRCHWEY, Karl
    "Bells Above Bretaye." [NewYorker] (63:18) 22 Je 87, p. 32.
    "The Color Known As Provincetown." [Boulevard] (2:3) Fall 87, p. 98-102.
    "For Aëllo" (sculpture from the Harpy Tomb at Xanthos, now in the British
        Museum). [Boulevard] (2:3) Fall 87, p. 102.
    "Museum of Holography." [NewRep] (197:25) 21 D 87, p. 32.
2942. KIRKPATRICK, Robert
    "Double Staves." [CarolQ] (39:3) Spr 87, p. 24-28.
2943. KIRN, Walter
    "The Detective Agency." [Poetry] (150:5) Ag 87, p. 274.
    "No Surmise." [Poetry] (150:5) Ag 87, p. 273.
    "Small Farmer." [Poetry] (150:5) Ag 87, p. 272.
2944. KIRSCH, Sarah
    "In Summer" (tr. by Jean Pearson). [CrossCur] (7:3) 87, p. 37.
2945. KIRSCHENBAUM, Blossom S.
    "Apathy." [LightY] '87, c86, p. 184-185.
    "Imitation Is th Sincerest Flattery, But." [LightY] '87, c86, p. 185.
2946. KIRSCHNER, Phil
    "Perspective." [BellArk] (3:4) Jl-Ag 87, p. 5.
    "To Jonathan." [BellArk] (3:3) My-Je 87, p. 6.
2947. KIRSTEIN, Lincoln
    "Don" (for Paul Taylor). [Raritan] (7:2) Fall 87, p. 21-26.
2948. KISHKAN, Theresa
    "Fields." [WestCR] (22:2) Fall 87, p. 18.
    "In the Event." [WestCR] (22:2) Fall 87, p. 21.
    "Old Scores." [WestCR] (22:2) Fall 87, p. 19-20.
    "A Prayer for Brendan." [WestCR] (22:2) Fall 87, p. 17.
2949. KISS, Anna
    "Emperor Butterfly" (tr. by Nicholas Kolumban). [Spirit] (8:2) 87, p. 50.
2950. KISSICK, Gary
    "Rain Quietude." The Best of [BambooR] [(31-32)] 86, p. 45.
2951. KISTLER, William
    "Mountain Speech Sung As Indian." [Antaeus] (58) Spr 87, p. 192-195.
2952. KITAHARA, Hakushu
    "Larches" (tr. by Lynne Yamaguchi Fletcher). [ColR] (NS 14:1) Spr-Sum 87, p. 34.
2953. KITCHEN, Judith
    "January Thaw." [SenR] (17:1) 87, p. 24.
    "Maps." [SenR] (17:1) 87, p. 21-23.
2954. KITTELL, Linda
    "The Hotel." [SnapD] (10:1/2) Wint 87, p. 25.
    "Long Distances." [KanQ] (19:1/2) Wint-Spr 87, p. 192-193.
    "Madonna Waters." [CentR] (31:3) Sum 87, p. 272.
    "Mercurial." [CentR] (31:3) Sum 87, p. 271-272.
    "My Father, Splitting Wood." [KanQ] (19:1/2) Wint-Spr 87, p. 192.
    "Ransom Holcomb." [SoCaR] (20:1) Fall 87, p. 63-64.
2955. KITTELL, Ronald Edward
    "The Bomb." [SlipS] (7) 87, p. 40.
    "Incumbents." [SlipS] (7) 87, p. 40.
    "Papa." [MidwQ] (29:1) Aut 87, p. 84.
KIVI, Tamara Shulz
    See SHULZ-KIVI, Tamara
2956. KIZER, Carolyn
    "Brother, I Am Here" (tr. of Shu Ting, w. Y. H. Zhao). [MichQR] (26:2) Spr 87, p.
        402-403.
    "Gerda." [ParisR] (29:102) Spr 87, p. 87-91.
    "Missing" (tr. of Shu Ting, w. Y. H. Zhao). [Poetry] (149:5) F 87, p. 253.
    "To the Oak" (tr. of Shu Ting, w. Y. H. Zhao). [Poetry] (149:5) F 87, p. 254.
KLAHR, Frida Lara
    See LARA KLAHR, Frida

2957. KLANDER, Sharon
  "Telling Mother." [NewRep] (197:16) 19 O 87, p. 32.
2958. KLAPPERT, Peter
  "Scattering Carl" (Selection: "Pigface! Pigface! Pigface!). [GreenfR] (14:3/4)
    Sum-Fall 87, p. 29-30.
2959. KLAVAN, Andrew
  "The Night Light." [CrossCur] (7:2) 87, p. 115.
  "On East 35th Street." [SouthernPR] (27:2) Fall 87, p. 30.
2960. KLEIN, Michael
  "Alaska." [JamesWR] (4:3) Spr 87, p. 11.
  "Montana." [JamesWR] (4:3) Spr 87, p. 11.
  "Shaking Places." [JamesWR] (4:3) Spr 87, p. 11.
2961. KLEINSCHMIDT, Edward
  "The Absence of Day." [BlackWR] (13:2) Spr 87, p. 69.
  "Addendum (At the Time of His Death)." [PennR] (3:1) Spr-Sum 87, p. 23.
  "Bad Dreams." [PennR] (3:1) Spr-Sum 87, p. 24.
  "Breakage and Damage." [PoetryNW] (28:1) Spr 87, p. 32-33.
  "Cogito, Cogito, Cogito." [Iowa] (17:1) Wint 87, p. 38.
  "Concordance." [Iowa] (17:1) Wint 87, p. 39-40.
  "Consider / Desire." [Poetry] (149:4) Ja 87, p. 207-208.
  "Departure Tax." [Poetry] (149:4) Ja 87, p. 206-207.
  "Dismissed." [Pequod] (23/24) 87, p. 122.
  "Epidemic (Among People)." [ColEng] (49:8) D 87, p. 889.
  "Ex Post Facto." [Iowa] (17:1) Wint 87, p. 39.
  "Going." [MissR] (15:3, issue 45) Spr-Sum 87, p. 86.
  "Hablar, Apprender, Vivir." [Iowa] (17:1) Wint 87, p. 40-41.
  "Katzenjammer." [NoAmR] (272:2) Je 87, p. 38.
  "Paragrams." [Iowa] (17:1) Wint 87, p. 42-43.
  "The Prime Mover." [Poetry] (150:3) Je 87, p. 133-134.
  "Schubert's Guitar." [Sequoia] (30:3) Wint 87, p. 64.
2962. KLEINZAHLER, August
  "His Neighbor, Her Music." [NewAW] (1) 87, p. 53.
  "Love Poem." [Sulfur] (20) Fall 87, p. 28.
  "Pinned." [Harp] (274:1641) F 87, p. 30.
  "Soda Water with a Boyhood Friend." [NewAW] (1) 87, p. 52.
  "The Tree." [Sulfur] (20) Fall 87, p. 29.
  "Tuesday Morning." [Thrpny] (29) Spr 87, p. 25.
  "Work." [Zyzzyva] (3:3) Fall 87, p. 83.
2963. KLEPETAR, Steve
  "Angel." [Wind] (17:59) 87, p. 30.
2964. KLINE, George L.
  "Eclogue V: Summer" (tr. of Joseph Brodsky, w. the author). [NewYorker] (63:24)
    3 Ag 87, p. 22-24.
2965. KLINE, S. T.
  "Morning at Kyoto's Heian Shrine." [KanQ] (19:1/2) Wint-Spr 87, p. 282.
  "The Year the Winter Broke Willows." [KanQ] (19:1/2) Wint-Spr 87, p. 281.
2966. KLINE, Valerie
  "China Beach in Winter." [AntigR] (69/70) 87, p. 9.
  "Old Woman Who Paints." [AntigR] (69/70) 87, p. 8.
2967. KLOEFKORN, William
  "At Shannon's Creek, Early August." [GeoR] (41:2) Sum 87, p. 382-383.
  "Betting the Dogs." [PennR] (3:2) Fall-Wint 87, p. 8.
  "Do Not Believe All." [LaurelR] (21:1/2) Wint-Sum 87, p. 64-65.
  "Doing It Again." [LaurelR] (21:1/2) Wint-Sum 87, p. 63.
  "On the Road." [Spirit] (8:2) 87, p. 103-104.
  "Plowing." [IndR] (10:3) Spr 87, p. 31-32.
  "Testament." [PennR] (3:2) Fall-Wint 87, p. 9.
2968. KNAPP, Trevor West
  "As Spring Approaches, I Think about Poetry." [KenR] (NS 9:4) Fall 87, p. 92-93.
  "Reporting Back to J.B. on His Handiwork." [KenR] (NS 9:4) Fall 87, p. 91-92.
2969. KNAUTH, Stephen
  "Gathering Christmas Boughs, Guilford Courthouse Battlefield." [Pembroke] (19)
    87, p. 183.
  "Prelude." [Vis] (24) 87, p. 4.
2970. KNIGHT, Arthur Winfield
  "Down to Business." [Interim] (6:2) Fall 87, p. 38-39.

"Ginsberg's Cookies." [AlphaBS] (1) Je 87, p. 33.
"Ginsberg's Cookies." [Interim] (6:2) Fall 87, p. 39.
"Going the Distance." [WindO] (49) Fall 87, p. 62.
"Laughter." [PaintedB] (30) 87, p. 12.
"Morbid Things." [PaintedB] (30) 87, p. 11-12.
"The Outlaw." [AlphaBS] (1) Je 87, p. 35.
"The Outlaw." [Gambit] (21) 87, p. 53-54.
"The Pissing Contest." [SlipS] (7) 87, p. 90.
"The Secret." [PoeticJ] (17) 87, p. 21.
"Tenth Grade English." [AlphaBS] (1) Je 87, p. 34.
"Winter in the Haight." [AlphaBS] (1) Je 87, p. 32.
2971. KNIGHT, Denis
"Odysseus, Lout." [Stand] (28:3) Sum 87, p. 35.
2972. KNIGHT, Etheridge
"The Idea of Ancestry." [Field] (36) Spr 87, p. 76-77.
"On the Birth of a Black / Baby / Boy" (for Isaac BuShie Blackburn-Knight). [Field]
(36) Spr 87, p. 78-79.
"A Poem to Galway Kinnell." [Field] (36) Spr 87, p. 80.
2973. KNIGHT, Tracy G.
"Abandoned Housewife." [Pembroke] (19) 87, p. 182.
"Mister." [Pembroke] (19) 87, p. 182.
2974. KNOEPFLE, John
"World Before Daylight." [ThRiPo] (29/30) 87, p. 43-44.
2975. KNOTT, Kip
"Foreclosure." [Farm] (4:1) Wint 87, p. 14.
"From a Shawnee Burial." [HiramPoR] (42) Spr-Sum 87, p. 34-35.
"Lying in a Field on the Eve of My Wedding." [HiramPoR] (42) Spr-Sum 87, p. 33.
"Mine Shaft." [Gambit] (20) 86, p. 95.
"Potatoes." [Gambit] (20) 86, p. 94.
2976. KNOX, Ann B.
"After a Friend's Wedding." [Blueline] (7:2/3 [i.e. 8:2/3?]) 87, p. 68.
"Map." [Blueline] (7:2/3 [i.e. 8:2/3?]) 87, p. 69.
"On Not Going to China." [PoetL] (82:4) Wint 87-88, p. 213.
"Son's Visit." [Blueline] (7:2/3 [i.e. 8:2/3?]) 87, p. 70.
2977. KNOX, Caroline
"An Acre for Education." [CreamCR] (11:2/3) 87?, p. 25-27.
"Background" (A Poem in Envy of Baudelaire). [Shen] (37:1) 87, p. 76.
"The Deer." [CreamCR] (11:2/3) 87?, p. 29.
"En Passant par la Lorraine." [CreamCR] (11:2/3) 87?, p. 30.
"The Friends of the Friends." [LightY] '87, c86, p. 251.
"The Graph of a Thing." [NewAW] (1) 87, p. 58.
"The Heart." [Shen] (37:1) 87, p. 75.
"Movement Along the Frieze." [NewAW] (2) Fall 87, p. 66.
"Off Gems Bund." [Shen] (37:1) 87, p. 77.
"Religion Poem." [LightY] '87, c86, p. 83.
"To Celeriack Skinner." [CreamCR] (11:2/3) 87?, p. 28.
"The True Meaning." [NewAW] (1) 87, p. 56-57.
"Xerxes and Xanthippe." [LightY] '87, c86, p. 48.
KO, Chang Soo
See CHANG, Soo Ko
2978. KOCH, James S.
"A Short Epic Poem in the English Language Summarizing the Iliad, the Odyssey,
and the Aeneid." [LightY] '87, c86, p. 55.
"A Short Poem." [LightY] '87, c86, p. 192.
2979. KOCH, Kenneth
"The Mediterranean World" (To Fernand Braudel). [GrandS] (6:4) Sum 87, p. 7-17.
"Seasons on Earth." [Raritan] (7:3) Wint 87, p. 42-54.
"What People Say about Paris." [Poetry] (151:1/2) O-N 87, p. 80-82.
2980. KOEHLER, Constance
"Cut Flower in a Beer Bottle Vase." [BellArk] (3:3) My-Je 87, p. 7.
KOEHN, Lala Heine
See HEINE-KOEHN, Lala
2981. KOEPPEL, Fredric
"The Blow Given to Branwen" (from "The Mabinogion"). [Raccoon] (24/25) My
87, p. 264.

2982. KOERTGE, Ronald
   "Diary Cows." [LightY] '87, c86, p. 111.
   "The Sign Said." [Abraxas] (35/36) 87, p. 87.
   "These Students Couldn't Write Their Way Out of a Paper Bag" (— Anonymous).
      [LightY] '87, c86, p. 222-223.
   "The Thing Is to Not Let Go of the Vine" (— Johnny Weissmuller). [Spirit] (8:2)
      87, p. 111.
2983. KOESTENBAUM, Wayne
   "The Answer Is in the Garden." [Agni] (24/25) 87, p. 252-256.
   "Dog Bite." [OntR] (27) Fall-Wint 87, p. 83-88.
   "Fugitive Blue." [Shen] (37:3) 87, p. 47-49.
   "Shéhérazade." [YaleR] (77:1) Aut 87, p. 80-85.
2984. KOETHE, John
   "Mistral." [ParisR] (29:102) Spr 87, p. 46-55.
   "Pining Away." [YaleR] (76:3) Spr 87, p. 417.
2985. KOGAWA, Joy
   "April Christmas Tree." [CrossC] (9:2) 87, p. 7.
   "The Campaign." [CrossC] (9:2) 87, p. 7.
2986. KOLATKAR, Arum
   "Malkhamb." [Bomb] (18) Wint 87, p. 70.
   "Old Newspapers." [Bomb] (18) Wint 87, p. 71.
   "Temperature Normal, Pulse, Respiration Satisfactory." [Bomb] (18) Wint 87, p.
      70.
   "The Turnaround." [Bomb] (18) Wint 87, p. 70-71.
2987. KOLBE, Uwe
   "Change of Location" (tr. by Laszlo Baransky, Istvan Eorsi, Anna Saghy and Bob
      Rosenthal). [Rampike] (5:3) 87, p. 66.
   "Metamorphosis" (tr. by Laszlo Baransky, Istvan Eorsi, Anna Saghy and Bob
      Rosenthal). [Rampike] (5:3) 87, p. 67.
2988. KOLIAS, Helen
   "Penelope Says" (tr. of Katerina Angelaki-Rooke). [Paint] (14:27) Spr 87, p. 30-31.
2989. KOLODNY, Susan
   "Lagoon." [Thrpny] (28) Wint 87, p. 6.
2990. KOLOKITHAS, Dawn
   "Missing You." [Notus] (2:2) Fall 87, p. 71.
   "Relation." [Notus] (2:2) Fall 87, p. 74.
   "There." [Notus] (2:2) Fall 87, p. 72.
   "Words." [Notus] (2:2) Fall 87, p. 73.
2991. KOLUMBAN, Nicholas
   "At a Party." [HawaiiR] (19) Spr 86, c87, p. 28-29.
   "Emperor Butterfly" (tr. of Anna Kiss). [Spirit] (8:2) 87, p. 50.
2992. KOLYBABA, Kathie
   "Red Shoes / A City I've Never Lived In" (Letter Series). [PraF] (8:3) Aut 87, p. 22.
2993. KOMO, Susan
   "Moon." [HawaiiR] (19) Spr 86, c87, p. 44.
2994. KOMUNYAKAA, Yusef
   "Between Days." [Callaloo] (10:3) Sum 87, p. 386.
   "Donut Dollies." [Caliban] (3) 87, p. 148-149.
   "Fragging" (11 poems). [IndR] (10:1/2) 87, p. 137-156.
   "The One-Legged Stool" (prose poem / performance piece). [Callaloo] (10:3) Sum
      87, p. 387-389.
   "Red Pagoda." [Callaloo] (10:3) Sum 87, p. 385.
   "Sunday Morning Over U Minh Forest." [Caliban] (2) 87, p. 47.
   "Thanks." [Caliban] (3) 87, p. 147-148.
   "To Have Danced with Death." [Caliban] (2) 87, p. 48.
   "Until." [Caliban] (2) 87, p. 49.
2995. KONDOS, Yannis
   "Old Stories" (tr. by Kimon Friar). [Poetry] (151:1/2) O-N 87, p. 52.
2996. KONO, Juliet S.
   "The Cane Cutters." The Best of [BambooR] [(31-32)] 86, p. 50.
   "Eggs." [BambooR] (36) Fall 87, p. 23-24.
   "Grandmother and the War." The Best of [BambooR] [(31-32)] 86, p. 49.
   "Tsunami" (April Fool's Day, 1946). [BambooR] (36) Fall 87, p. 20-22.
   "Yonsei." The Best of [BambooR] [(31-32)] 86, p. 51-52.
KOON, Woon
   See WOON, Koon

221

KOWIT

2997. KOONTZ, Tom
    "April 1." [SpoonRQ] (12:2) Spr 87, p. 35.
    "To Will One Thing." [WindO] (48) Spr 87, p. 15.
    "Two Hounds in Fresh Snow." [SpoonRQ] (12:2) Spr 87, p. 34.
2998. KOPEC, Carol
    "Blessing." [Poem] (58) N 87, p. 35.
    "Coming Home from Sieben." [Poem] (58) N 87, p. 36-37.
2999. KÖRÖSY, Mária
    "At First Hand" (tr. of Ottó Orbán, w. Jascha Kessler). [VirQR] (63:1) Wint 87, p.
      77-78.
    "Chile" (tr. of Ottó Orbán, w. Jascha Kessler). [NewL] (53:3) Spr 87, p. 17.
    "The Gate of Teeth" (tr. of Sandor Weöres, w. Jascha Kessler). [GrahamHR] (10)
      Wint-Spr 87, p. 62-63.
    "The Golden Fleece" (tr. of Ottó Orbán, w. Jascha Kessler). [VirQR] (63:1) Wint
      87, p. 78-79.
    "The Greeks Are Blinding Polyphemus" (tr. of György Rába, w. Jascha Kessler).
      [HayF] (2) Spr 87, p. 101.
    "History of Lit: A Communication" (tr. of István Vas, w. Jascha Kessler). [Nimrod]
      (31:1) Fall-Wint 87, p. 132.
    "I Didn't Tell You Then" (tr. of Imre Orvecz, w. Bruce Berlind). [Rampike] (5:3)
      87, p. 70.
    "Idling" (tr. of István Vas, w. Jascha Kessler). [GrahamHR] (10) Wint-Spr 87, p.
      60-61.
    "Intellectuals" (tr. of Ottó Orbán, w. Jascha Kessler). [VirQR] (63:1) Wint 87, p.
      80.
    "Poetry" (tr. of Ottó Orbán, w. Jascha Kessler). [Nimrod] (31:1) Fall-Wint 87, p.
      123.
    "Poverty" (tr. of Ottó Orbán, w. Jascha Kessler). [PoetryE] (23/24) Fall 87, p. 117.
    "Prayer Before Turning Off the Light" (tr. of Agnes Gergely, w. Jascha Kessler).
      [Nimrod] (31:1) Fall-Wint 87, p. 131.
    "A Preface to Dying" (tr. of Gyorgy Raba, w. Jascha Kessler). [BlueBldgs] (10)
      87?, p. 33.
    "A Preface to Dying" (tr. of György Rába, w. Jascha Kessler). [HayF] (2) Spr 87,
      p. 102.
    "Seventh Symphony: The Assumption of Mary" (To my mother's memory, tr. of
      Sandor Weöres, w. Bruce Berlind). [GrahamHR] (10) Wint-Spr 87, p. 64-72.
    "Shipwreck, from Outside" (tr. of Agnes Gergely, w. Jascha Kessler). [Nimrod]
      (31:1) Fall-Wint 87, p. 131.
    "Turn-of-the-Century Budapest" (tr. of Ottó Orbán, w. Jascha Kessler).
      [GrahamHR] (10) Wint-Spr 87, p. 59.
3000. KORP, Maureen
    "The Business Lunch." [AntigR] (69/70) 87, p. 209.
3001. KORSON, Michael
    "This Morning Something Wants to Return." [CalQ] (30) Wint 87, p. 32-33.
3002. KORZUN, L. June
    "Denizen." [SoDakR] (25:3) Aut 87, p. 74.
    "Ten years since the earth took you." [Footwork] 87, p. 57.
    "Working the Fields." [SoDakR] (25:3) Aut 87, p. 46.
3003. KOSHAREK, Pat
    "At the Rim." [SmPd] (24:3) Fall 87, p. 28.
3004. KOSTELANETZ, Richard
    "More Portraits from Memory." [Lips] (13) 87, p. 45.
    "Pitches" (5 rectangular poems, dedicated to Anton Webern). [PikeF] (8) Fall 87, p.
      14-16.
    "Selections from a Cycle of Fictions in Progress." [Caliban] (2) 87, p. 98-102.
3005. KOVACEVICH, Carrie M.
    "Winged Celestial Beings at Seattle Art Museum." [BellArk] (3:1) Ja-F 87, p. 9.
3006. KOVACIK, Karen
    "Abergavenny." [TarRP] (26:2) Spr 87, p. 39.
    "The Poet's Wife" (for Ewa). [TarRP] (26:2) Spr 87, p. 38.
    "Prairie Schooner." [PassN] (8:2) Sum 87, p. 23.
3007. KOVANDA, William James
    "The Drowning." [Wind] (17:61) 87, p. 25-26.
    "Last Rites." [Wind] (17:61) 87, p. 25.
3008. KOWIT, Steve
    "Lurid Confessions." [Spirit] (8:2) 87, p. 60.

3009. KOZER, José
    "La Espera." [Lyra] (1:2) 87, p. 8.
    "Siega." [Lyra] (1:2) 87, p. 9.
3010. KRAINE, Sarah E.
    "Those Still Lions Bleed Green" (in memory of Ernest L. Adams, 1949-1984).
        [ColR] (NS 14:2) Fall-Wint 87, p. 48.
3011. KRAMER, Aaron
    "1928" (tr. of Moishe Nadir). [Vis] (23) 87, p. 36.
    "The Murder of My Mother" (Vilna Ghetto, Oct. 1942, tr. of Avrom Sutzkever).
        [Vis] (25) 87, p. 27.
    "On the Highway." [Vis] (24) 87, p. 30.
    "Someone Has Covered Up" (tr. of Rajzel Zychlinska). [Vis] (25) 87, p. 24.
    "What Comes Home." [CumbPR] (6:2) Spr 87, p. 27.
3012. KRAMER, Joan
    "The Entertainer." [Vis] (24) 87, p. 6.
3013. KRAMER, Larry
    "Big Madge." [MissouriR] (10:1) 87, p. 196-197.
    "Of a Sudden." [MissouriR] (10:1) 87, p. 194-195.
    "Of Our Age." [MissouriR] (10:1) 87, p. 198.
3014. KRAPF, Norbert
    "Narrative on a Four-Poster Bed from Louisiana." [Confr] (35/36) Spr-Fall 87, p.
        166-167.
    "Uncle." [Blueline] (7:2/3 [i.e. 8:2/3?]) 87, p. 11-12.
3015. KRATT, Mary
    "At the British Museum." [Poem] (58) N 87, p. 34.
    "The Beast" (The Greensboro Review Literary Award, Honorable Mention).
        [GreensboroR] (43) Wint 87-88, p. 39-40.
    "Guarding the House." [Raccoon] (24/25) My 87, p. 199.
    "Moon." [Raccoon] (24/25) My 87, p. 193.
    "Real Estate, West Virginia." [Poem] (58) N 87, p. 33.
    "The Simple Life." [LaurelR] (20:1/2) Sum 87, p. 40.
    "Sunday." [ChrC] (104:4) 4-11 F 87, p. 102.
3016. KRAUSE, Judith
    "Berrypicking with the Milkman." [PraF] (8:2) Sum 87, p. 60-61.
3017. KRAUSE, Richard
    "He steps over her almost to position himself on the curb side of the street."
        [AmerPoR] (16:4) Jl-Ag 87, p. 39.
    "Like those stories you hear from time to time of those lovers . . ." [AmerPoR]
        (16:4) Jl-Ag 87, p. 39.
    "The man is writing on the street with a pen." [AmerPoR] (16:4) Jl-Ag 87, p. 39.
    "When you are irritated by something or someone you are never alone." [AmerPoR]
        (16:4) Jl-Ag 87, p. 39.
3018. KRAUSS, Janet
    "The Roofer." [Jacaranda] (2:2) Spr 87, p. 1.
3019. KREBS, Jeffrey
    "Driving the Field." [PassN] (8:1) Wint 87, p. 17.
3020. KREITER-KURYLO, Carolyn
    "Forgive Me, But This Is Just a Smear of Purple." [PoetL] (82:3) Fall 87, p. 153.
    "In the Hills of Les Baux." [Vis] (24) 87, p. 15.
3021. KREMEN, Barbara
    "Pod." [Pembroke] (19) 87, p. 117.
3022. KRETZ, Thomas
    "Margarite Moon of Venus." [KanQ] (19:1/2) Wint-Spr 87, p. 186-187.
    "Stopover." [KanQ] (19:1/2) Wint-Spr 87, p. 187.
3023. KRICH, A. M.
    "Genesis: A Remake." [YellowS] (22) Spr 87, p. 10.
3024. KRICORIAN, Nancy
    "The Angel." [Caliban] (2) 87, p. 140.
3025. KRIESEL, Michael Allen
    "Cancerdance." [PikeF] (8) Fall 87, p. 12.
3026. KRIKAU, Kathy
    "Dignity Gone" (Age 10). [PikeF] (8) Fall 87, p. 22.
3027. KRIM, N. C.
    "Birthing" (Kansas Quarterly / Kansas Arts Commission Awards Honorable Mention
        Poem, 1986/1987). [KanQ] (19:1/2) Wint-Spr 87, p. 35-36.

3028. KROETSCH, Robert
"After Paradise." [PraF] (8:4) Wint 87-88, p. 68-77.
3029. KROG, Antjie
"Lovesong After the Music of K. E. Ntsane" (tr. by David Bunn, Jane Taylor and
the author). [TriQ] (69) Spr-Sum 87, p. 334-335.
3030. KROK, Peter
"Lost." [NegC] (7:3/4) 87, p. 114.
3031. KROLL, Ernest
"Continental Divide." [MidwQ] (28:2) Wint 87, p. 220.
"Ego at the Wheel." [LightY] '87, c86, p. 254.
"The First Cruise." [TexasR] (8:3/4) Fall-Wint 87, p. 19.
"For Regina, Put Off." [WindO] (48) Spr 87, p. 10.
"From the 'Capitol Limited'." [GreensboroR] (40) Sum 86, p. 94.
"Growing Wild in the Capital." [MidwQ] (28:2) Wint 87, p. 218-219.
"Las Vegas." [LightY] '87, c86, p. 178.
"The Melville Scholars." [WindO] (49) Fall 87, p. 30.
"The Nest." [TexasR] (8:1/2) Spr-Sum 87, p. 57.
"Pejorative." [LightY] '87, c86, p. 230.
"Staten Island Ferry." [GreensboroR] (40) Sum 86, p. 94.
"The Vaunting Song of Louis L'Amour." [LightY] '87, c86, p. 56.
3032. KROLL, Judith
"Another Ending." [SouthernR] (23:4) O 87, p. 794-795.
"Betrayals." [SouthernR] (23:4) O 87, p. 795-797.
"On the Train." [Paint] (14:28) Aut 87, p. 24.
"Our Elephant." [SouthernR] (23:4) O 87, p. 797-800.
3033. KROLOW, Karl
"Artist" (tr. by Stuart Friebert). [Iowa] (17:3) Fall 87, p. 105.
"Beyond" (tr. by Stuart Friebert). [Field] (36) Spr 87, p. 36.
"Don't Think" (tr. by Stuart Friebert). [QW] (25) Spr 87, p. 131.
"The House That Holds Everything" (tr. by Stuart Friebert). [QW] (25) Spr 87, p.
130.
"On Biographies" (tr. by Stuart Friebert). [HawaiiR] (19) Spr 86, c87, p. 25.
"On Biographies" (tr. by Stuart Friebert). [Iowa] (17:3) Fall 87, p. 104.
"On Hunting and Other Things" (tr. by Stuart Friebert). [Field] (36) Spr 87, p. 35.
"Seasons" (tr. by Stuart Friebert). [NoDaQ] (55:2) Spr 87, p. 58.
"Über Biographien." [HawaiiR] (19) Spr 86, c87, p. 24.
3034. KRONENBERG, Mindy (Mindy H.)
"C*NC*R." [CrossCur] (7:2) 87, p. 161-162.
"My Mother's Fruitbowl." [CentR] (31:3) Sum 87, p. 276-277.
"Neglect." [Footwork] 87, p. 36-37.
"Winter Thaw." [WebR] (12:2) Fall 87, p. 76.
3035. KRONENFELD, Judy
"2 A.M. and All's Well." [CrescentR] (5:1) 87, p. 118.
"After Touring Many Churches." [MSS] (5:3) 87, p. 190.
"Lente, Lente." [MSS] (5:3) 87, p. 191.
"Poem: A baby thrown from a flaming window." [Electrum] (39) Fall-Wint 87, p.
44.
3036. KRUMBERGER, John
"Lake Pepin." [Germ] (11:1) Fall 87, p. 50.
"The Submission to Silence" (In Memory of James L. White." [Germ] (11:1) Fall
87, p. 51.
3037. KRUSOE, James
"American Popular Song." [Gargoyle] (32/33) 87, p. 80.
"Bow Ties." [US1] (20/21) Wint 86-87, p. 34.
"Poem: Tender is the night my friend" (for Barry Brennan). [Gargoyle] (32/33) 87,
p. 79.
3038. KRYSL, Marilyn
"Grandmother." [PraS] (61:2) Sum 87, p. 56-57.
"Talking All Night." [PraS] (61:2) Sum 87, p. 58.
3039. KUBACK, David
"Rocky Island." [Phoenix] (7:1) 87, p. 32.
3040. KUBY, Lolette
"Early Snow." [Vis] (25) 87, p. 11.
3041. KUHN, Lesley
"A Different Ghost Comes to Tea." [Footwork] 87, p. 43.

3042. KÜLEBI, Cahit
"Istanbul" (in Turkish). [StoneC] (15:1/2) Fall-Wint 87-88, p. 36.
"Istanbul" (tr. by Dionis Coffin Riggs, William A. Fielder and Özcan Yalim).
[StoneC] (15:1/2) Fall-Wint 87-88, p. 37.
"A Story of the Sea" (tr. by Talat Sait Halman). [Trans] (19) Fall 87, p. 132.
3043. KULIK, William
"Comme" (tr. of Robert Desnos). [AmerPoR] (16:3) My-Je 87, p. 33.
"Derniers Vers (Last Poems)" (Excerpts, tr. of Jules Laforgue). [AmerPoR] (16:3)
My-Je 87, p. 33-35.
3044. KULYCKY, Michael
"Untitled: That time in me you can behold." [KanQ] (19:1/2) Wint-Spr 87, p. 330.
3045. KUMIN, Maxine
"A Calling." [TexasR] (7:3/4) 87, p. 89.
"Grappling in the Central Blue." [Nat] (244:21) 30 My 87, p. 718.
"Magellan Street, 1974." [CrossCur] (7:3) 87, p. 38-39.
"Marianne, My Mother, and Me." [Poetry] (150:2) My 87, p. 63-67.
"Night Launch" (Canaveral Seashore National Park). [TexasR] (7:3/4) 87, p. 90-91.
"Nurture." [Poetry] (151:1/2) O-N 87, p. 83.
"Surprises." [MichQR] (26:1) Wint 87, p. 111-112.
"With the Caribou." [Poetry] (151:1/2) O-N 87, p. 84.
3046. KUMMER, John
"Archaeology at 'The Grill'." [BellArk] (3:3) My-Je 87, p. 4-5.
"Le Cinema." [BellArk] (3:2) Mr-Ap 87, p. 3.
3047. KUNENE, Daniel P.
"Kodwa Nkosana (And Yet, Master)" (tr. of M. T. Mazibuko). [TriQ] (69) Spr-Sum
87, p. 208-209.
"Senkatana" (Selection: Act I, Scene 1 (partial), tr. of S. M. Mofokeng). [TriQ] (69)
Spr-Sum 87, p. 336-337.
3048. KUNENE, Mazisi
"Ancient Bonds." [TriQ] (69) Spr-Sum 87, p. 325.
"Cowardice." [TriQ] (69) Spr-Sum 87, p. 327.
"Final Supplication." [TriQ] (69) Spr-Sum 87, p. 330-331.
"The Humanity of All Things." [TriQ] (69) Spr-Sum 87, p. 332.
"A Note to All Surviving Africans." [TriQ] (69) Spr-Sum 87, p. 323-324.
"The Prayer of Ramses II." [TriQ] (69) Spr-Sum 87, p. 328.
"Steve Biko's Anthem." [TriQ] (69) Spr-Sum 87, p. 329.
"The Tyrant." [TriQ] (69) Spr-Sum 87, p. 326.
"The Vision of Life." [TriQ] (69) Spr-Sum 87, p. 333.
3049. KUNTZ, Laurie
"Survival." [Amelia] (4:3, issue 10) 87, p. 71.
3050. KUO, Alex
"The Missing Person." [LitR] (30:4) Sum 87, p. 492.
3051. KUPFERBERG, Tuli
"How Is the Empire?" [AlphaBS] (1) Je 87, p. 43.
3052. KUPRIANOV, Vyacheslav
"Creativity" (tr. by Francis Jones). [Margin] (1) Wint 86, p. 95.
"Human Injustice" (tr. by Francis Jones). [Margin] (1) Wint 86, p. 94.
"The Legend of the Ocean" (tr. by Francis Jones). [Margin] (1) Wint 86, p. 96.
3053. KURIBAYASHI, Laurie
"Freeway Poem." The Best of [BambooR] [(31-32)] 86, p. 54-55.
"Like Love." The Best of [BambooR] [(31-32)] 86, p. 53.
KURYLO, Carolyn Kreiter
See KREITER-KURYLO, Carolyn
3054. KUTLAR, Onat
"War and Peace" (tr. by Talat Sait Halman). [Trans] (19) Fall 87, p. 107.
3055. KUTZINSKI, Vera M.
"Epistle" (for the poet Eliseo Diego, tr. of Nicolás Guillén). [Callaloo] (10:2) Spr 87,
p. 205, 207.
"European Slaves" (tr. of Nicolás Guillén). [Callaloo] (10:2) Spr 87, p. 209, 211.
"The Grandfather" (tr. of Nicolás Guillén). [Callaloo] (10:2) Spr 87, p. 191.
"Warnings, Messages, Announcements" (tr. of Nicolás Guillén). [Callaloo] (10:2)
Spr 87, p. 203.
3056. KUUSISTO, Stephen
"Gogol: Five Portraits." [SenR] (17:1) 87, p. 30-35.
3057. KUZMA, Greg
"Aside from a D." [Epoch] (36:3) 87-88, p. 198.

"Bunny." [VirQR] (63:3) Sum 87, p. 439-441.
"Childhood." [VirQR] (63:3) Sum 87, p. 437-439.
"Childhood Memory." [PoetryNW] (28:3) Aut 87, p. 24.
"A Day in Late November." [Poetry] (151:1/2) O-N 87, p. 85-86.
"Geese Over the Gas Station." [ColR] (NS 14:2) Fall-Wint 87, p. 94-95.
"The last Time I Saw My Brother." [GrahamHR] (10) Wint-Spr 87, p. 41.
"Mike and Sue." [ColR] (NS 14:2) Fall-Wint 87, p. 96-97.
"My Latest Poem." [MSS] (5:3) 87, p. 114.
"Poem: We will make a distinction." [MSS] (5:3) 87, p. 114-116.
"Wildflowers" (for my mother). [BlueBldgs] (10) 87?, p. 46-47.
3058. KYGER, Joanne
       "Ode" (w. Ted Berrigan). [NewAW] (2) Fall 87, p. 34.
LA . . .
       See also names beginning with "La" without the following space, filed below in their
           alphabetic positions, e.g., LaSALLE.
3059. La FONTAINE, Jean de
       "The Man and the Flea" (tr. by Norman R. Shapiro). [LitR] (30:4) Sum 87, p. 591.
       "The Two Bulls and a Frog" (tr. by Norman R. Shapiro). [LitR] (30:4) Sum 87, p.
           590.
La TORRE, Josefina de
       See TORRE, Josefina de la
3060. LABÉ, Louise
       "As Soon As I Have Gone to Take My Rest" (Sonnet, tr. by Marion Shore). [Trans]
           (18) Spr 87, p. 330.
       "If Upon That Fair Breast I Might Lie" (Sonnet, tr. by Marion Shore). [Trans] (18)
           Spr 87, p. 328.
       "While My Eyes Can Shed Another Tear" (Sonnet, tr. by Marion Shore). [Trans]
           (18) Spr 87, p. 329.
3061. LABISI, Dana Hahn
       "I looked at your note." [Footwork] 87, p. 37-38.
3062. LaBOMBARD, Joan
       "The Last Romantic." [PoetryNW] (28:1) Spr 87, p. 41.
3063. LaBONTE, Karen
       "Prayer Into Stone." [MemphisSR] (7:2) Spr 87, p. 43.
3064. LABRADA, Emilio
       "Dalliances #4" (tr. of Odon Betanzos Palacios). [Vis] (25) 87, p. 17.
3065. LACY, Steve
       "Agenda" (Jack Spicer's poem "For Hal" set to music). [Acts] (6) 87, p. 46-48.
3066. LACZI, D. E.
       "Canning." [WindO] (49) Fall 87, p. 14.
3067. LADIN, J.
       "The Akedah." [CalQ] (30) Wint 87, p. 26-27.
3068. LAFORGUE, Jules
       "Derniers Vers (Last Poems)" (Excerpts, tr. by William Kulik). [AmerPoR] (16:3)
           My-Je 87, p. 33-35.
3069. LaGATTUTA, Margo
       "Deaf Kitten." [PassN] (8:1) Wint 87, p. 8.
3070. LAGO, David
       "Surcus." [LindLM] (6:1) Ja-Mr 87, p. 8.
3071. LAGO GONZALEZ, David
       "Las Barcas Bochornosas." [LindLM] (6:4) O-D 87, p. 4.
       "El Hilo Mas Grueso." [LindLM] (6:4) O-D 87, p. 4.
3072. LAGOMARSINO, Nancy
       "400-Yard Girls' Relay." [Ploughs] (13:4) 87, p. 54.
       "On Skimming an Anthology of Contemporary American Poetry." [Ploughs] (13:4)
           87, p. 53.
3073. LAGOS, Ramiro
       "Déjame Ser Tu Selva." [InterPR] (13:2) Fall 87, p. 30.
       "Let Me Be Your Forest" (tr. by Paula Heusinkveld). [InterPR] (13:2) Fall 87, p.
           31.
       "Poem for Being in the Clouds" (tr. by Paula Heusinkveld). [InterPR] (13:2) Fall
           87, p. 29.
       "Poema para Estar en las Nubes." [InterPR] (13:2) Fall 87, p. 28.
LAJOIE, Rhea Mouledoux
       See MOULEDOUX-LAJOIE, Rhea

LAKE

3074. LAKE, Paul
    "The Boat." [Thrpny] (29) Spr 87, p. 11.
    "The Rooster." [SouthwR] (72:2) Spr 87, p. 199-201.
3075. LALIC, Ivan V.
    "Last Quarter" (tr. by Francis Jones). [Margin] (2) Spr 87, p. 61.
    "Terrace 2" (tr. by Francis Jones). [Margin] (2) Spr 87, p. 60.
3076. LALLY, Margaret
    "Tom's Hand." [Kaleid] (14) Wint-Spr 87, p. 69.
3077. LALLY, Michael
    "4.24.86." [HangL] (50/51) 87, p. 90-92.
3078. LaMANNA, Richard
    "Recovery." [FloridaR] (15:1) Spr-Sum 87, p. 30.
    "A Sober Moment." [FloridaR] (15:1) Spr-Sum 87, p. 31-32.
3079. LAMANTIA, Philip
    "Unachieved." [Sulfur] (20) Fall 87, p. 30-33.
3080. LAMPE, Sandra
    "Early Afternoon: Still Life with a Yellow Bucket" (1986 Finalist, Eve of Saint
        Agnes Poetry Competition). [NegC] (7:1/2) 87, p. 226.
3081. LAMPORT, Felicia
    "Pisa Visa." [LightY] '87, c86, p. 61.
    "P$$$$$T." [LightY] '87, c86, p. 213.
3082. LANDAU, Julie
    "Returning to the Farm to Live, #3" (tr. of T'ao Ch'ien). [MSS] (5:3) 87, p. 31.
3083. LANE, Alycee J.
    "The Bottom of Capitol Hill." [Footwork] 87, p. 15.
    "Dreadful." [PaintedB] (31) 87, p. 18.
    "I will cry one thousand tears." [Footwork] 87, p. 14.
    "It Came to Her Children." [Footwork] 87, p. 14.
    "Night bleeds all over day." [Footwork] 87, p. 14.
3084. LANE, John
    "Blue Blossoms" (for SV). [Nimrod] (30:2) Spr-Sum 87, p. 87-88.
3085. LANE, Leonora Azouz
    "Traveling Abroad." [KanQ] (19:3) Sum 87, p. 186.
3086. LANE, M. Travis
    "Field." [CanLit] (112) Spr 87, p. 29.
3087. LANE, Patrick
    "Brothers" (for John and Dick). [MalR] (80) S 87, p. 30-31.
    "Dominion Day Dance." [MalR] (80) S 87, p. 32.
    "Emblems." [Verse] (4:1) Mr 87, p. 11.
    "The Meadow." [Verse] (4:1) Mr 87, p. 10.
    "Night." [MalR] (80) S 87, p. 33.
    "Nunc Dimittis" (for Mary Drover). [MalR] (80) S 87, p. 34.
    "Nunc Dimittis" (for Mary Drover). [Verse] (4:1) Mr 87, p. 10.
3088. LANE, William
    "Salamander." [HangL] (50/51) 87, p. 93.
3089. LANG, Leonard
    "The Drought." [Farm] (4:2) Spr-Sum 87, p. 12.
    "In the House Below Zero." [Farm] (4:2) Spr-Sum 87, p. 13-14.
    "The Way of Water." [CimR] (81) O 87, p. 54.
3090. LANGE, Art
    "Blue Studio." [NewAW] (2) Fall 87, p. 59-60.
    "A Fine Line." [NewAW] (2) Fall 87, p. 61-64.
    "Mbizo" (Johnny Mbizo Dyani, 1946-1986, expatriate South African musician).
        [NewAW] (2) Fall 87, p. 58.
3091. LANGLAND, Joseph
    "Idyll" (tr. of Igor Khomin, w. Tamas Aczel and Laszlo Tikos). [NowestR] (25:3)
        87, p. 132-133.
3092. LANGLEY, Michael McCaffrey
    "Rem Trip." [Vis] (25) 87, p. 39.
3093. LANGTHORNE, Michael
    "Voice 21." [CarolQ] (39:2) Wint 87, p. 99.
3094. LANGTON, Daniel J.
    "December." [NoDaQ] (55:2) Spr 87, p. 50.
    "Near the Water." [StoneC] (15:1/2) Fall-Wint 87-88, p. 55.
    "Rainy Day." [Zyzzyva] (3:4) Wint 87-88, p. 55.

3095. LANIER, Parks, Jr.
"Proverbs for a Child." [Wind] (17:59) 87, p. 29.
3096. LANSING, Gerrit
"Reading *My Life* on a Greyhound Bus from Boston to New York." [Notus] (2:1)
Spr 87, p. 24-25.
"Three Anecdotes of the Uncanny." [Conjunc] (11) 87?, p. 121-122.
3097. LaPALMA, Marina de Bellagente
"Abode." [Rampike] (5:3) 87, p. 36.
3098. LAPE, Sue
"Feeding from the Earth." [Gambit] (20) 86, p. 114.
"Georgia O'Keefe: Tao." [Gambit] (20) 86, p. 116.
"Venus' Basket" (two tiny crustaceans . . . given as a symbol of happy marriage in
Japan). [Gambit] (20) 86, p. 115.
"Watersleep." [Gambit] (20) 86, p. 117.
3099. LAPIDUS, Jacqueline
"Mithymna/Molyvos." [HangL] (50/51) 87, p. 94.
3100. LAPOINT, John
"Copper Gunpowder." [Gambit] (20) 86, p. 50.
3101. LARA KLAHR, Frida
"Día II." [Mester] (16:1) Spr 87, p. 63.
3102. LARDAS, Konstantinos
"The Mourning Songs of Greece" (tr. of anonymous selections). [AmerPoR] (16:5)
S-O 87, p. 28-29.
"The Mourning Songs of Greek Women" (tr. of anonymous poems). [ColEng]
(49:1) Ja 87, p. 37-41.
3103. LARDNER, Ted
"Legends." [HawaiiR] (20) Fall 86, c87, p. 69.
3104. LARKIN, Joan
"Risks." [Calyx] (10:2/3) Spr 87, p. 158.
3105. LARKIN, Philip
"High Windows." [HawaiiR] (21) Spr 87, p. 101.
3106. LARSEN, Jeanne
"After the Slide." [PraS] (61:3) Fall 87, p. 86.
"Burning a Portrait of the Ex-Dictator's Wife." [PraS] (61:3) Fall 87, p. 85-86.
3107. LARSEN, Marianne
"It is as though the dark has suddenly grown wings" (tr. by George Johnston).
[MalR] (78) Mr 87, p. 102.
"To bring a glass of wine" (tr. by George Johnston). [MalR] (78) Mr 87, p. 103.
"When we say nothing" (tr. by George Johnston). [MalR] (78) Mr 87, p. 102.
"You sit in a waiting room" (tr. by George Johnston). [MalR] (78) Mr 87, p. 103.
3108. LARSEN, Wendy (Wendy Wilder)
"Blueberry Point." [Nimrod] (30:2) Spr-Sum 87, p. 92-93.
"Coming Home." [HawaiiR] (19) Spr 86, c87, p. 6-7.
"Mealtimes in Virginia." [Nimrod] (30:2) Spr-Sum 87, p. 89.
"Now We Are Shrunk." [Nimrod] (30:2) Spr-Sum 87, p. 90-91.
"The Stove." [ParisR] (29:105) Wint 87, p. 98.
3109. LARSON, Rustin
"The Calling." [LitR] (31:1) Fall 87, p. 72.
3110. LaRUE, Dorie
"Leda." [MassR] (28:2) Sum 87, p. 350.
Las CASAS, Walter de
See CASAS, Walter de las
3111. LASDUN, James
"A Dinosaur in Rome." [ParisR] (29:103) Sum 87, p. 38-39.
"Jumping." [ParisR] (29:103) Sum 87, p. 36-37.
"Picture of a Girl." [ParisR] (29:103) Sum 87, p. 41.
"Tea with a Politician." [ParisR] (29:103) Sum 87, p. 40.
"The Two of Them." [ParisR] (29:103) Sum 87, p. 34-35.
3112. LASHER, Susan
"The Dig." [Shen] (37:2) 87, p. 40-41.
"In the Teater." [WilliamMR] (25) Spr 87, p. 92-93.
"The Martyr." [WilliamMR] (25) Spr 87, p. 90-91.
3113. LASKA, P. J.
"The Oldest Widow on Coal Run." [LaurelR] (20:1/2) Sum 87, p. 72.
"The Wino Lounge." [LaurelR] (20:1/2) Sum 87, p. 71.

3114. LASKER-SCHÜLER, Else
"David and Jonathan" (tr. by Bernhard Frank). [WebR] (12:2) Fall 87, p. 42.
3115. LASKIN, Pamela L.
"At the Park." [BallSUF] (28:4) Aut 87, p. 51.
"First Sorrow." [Writer] (99:11) N 86, p. 19.
3116. LASSELL, Michael
"How to Visit the Grave of a Friend" (for Kenneth Fermoyle). [KanQ] (19:3) Sum 87, p. 122-123.
"Times Square Poems." [HangL] (50/51) 87, p. 98-102.
3117. LAU, Evelyn
"Bobby-Pin Scratches." [Waves] (14:4) Spr 86, p. 59.
3118. LAUDUN, John
"Xeroxis" (for Julia Rae Nilsen, 21 October, 1986). [SmPd] (24:3) Fall 87, p. 28.
3119. LAUGHLIN, James
"Absolute Love." [Poetry] (149:5) F 87, p. 251.
"The Bible Lady." [AntigR] (69/70) 87, p. 136-137.
"The Blue Footprints." [WestCR] (21:4) Spr 87, p. 50.
"The Care and Feeding of a Poet." [LightY] '87, c86, p. 196.
"Herodotus Reports." [Antaeus] (59) Aut 87, p. 162-163.
"Holes." [Conjunc] (10) 87, p. 185.
"The Importance of Silence." [WestCR] (21:4) Spr 87, p. 48.
"La Langue Enfantine." [AntigR] (69/70) 87, p. 132-133.
"My Ambition" (For Wade Hall). [Poetry] (151:1/2) O-N 87, p. 87.
"Oh Yes." [WestCR] (21:4) Spr 87, p. 49.
"Poets." [AmerV] (9) Wint 87, p. 18.
"Request for Confirmation." [Poetry] (149:5) F 87, p. 252.
"Saxo Cere." [Antaeus] (59) Aut 87, p. 164.
"A Suggestion." [AntigR] (69/70) 87, p. 132.
3120. LAUNIUS, Carl Judson
"The Barflies at Roger's Pool Hall Supplicate for an Anorexic Girl." [TexasR] (8:3/4) Fall-Wint 87, p. 75.
"Job's Turkey: a Commentary." [LightY] '87, c86, p. 106-107.
"Paolo's Version." [LightY] '87, c86, p. 206.
3121. LAUREL, Hya
"Instead Of." [DekalbLAJ] (20:1/4) 87, p. 42.
"The Post Office." [DekalbLAJ] (20:1/4) 87, p. 43-44.
3122. LAUTERBACH, Ann
"Dream Stencils." [NewAW] (1) 87, p. 30-31.
"Forgetting the Lake." [Boulevard] (2:1/2) Spr 87, p. 149-150.
"The French Girl." [Conjunc] (11) 87?, p. 218-219.
"Of the Meadow." [Conjunc] (11) 87?, p. 216-218.
"Revenant" (for Jennifer). [Conjunc] (10) 87, p. 241.
"Tock." [Conjunc] (10) 87, p. 242.
3123. LAUTERMILCH, Steven
"I Have Been Watching" (for David Kostenko, 1954-1986). [CarolQ] (39:3) Spr 87, p. 39.
"The Ninth Elegy" (tr. of Rainer Maria Rilke). [ColR] (NS 14:1) Spr-Sum 87, p. 50-56.
3124. LAUX, Dorianne
"The Laundromat." [Electrum] (39) Fall-Wint 87, p. 40.
"Return." [FiveFR] (5) 87, p. 106.
3125. LAVIERA, Tato
"Bochinche Bilingüe." [Americas] (15:1) Spr 87, p. 67.
"Latero Story." [Americas] (15:1) Spr 87, p. 62-63.
"Melao." [Americas] (15:1) Spr 87, p. 66.
"Viejo." [Americas] (15:1) Spr 87, p. 64-65.
3126. LAVIN, S. R.
"Perdido" (for Piero Heliczer). [Stand] (28:4) Aut 87, p. 51.
3127. LAVIS, E. D.
"I Should Always Wear This Color." [AmerPoR] (16:4) Jl-Ag 87, p. 29.
"Letters" (for Dean). [AmerPoR] (16:4) Jl-Ag 87, p. 28.
"Resolution." [AmerPoR] (16:4) Jl-Ag 87, p. 28.
"What Is Revealed Is Enough." [AmerPoR] (16:4) Jl-Ag 87, p. 29.
3128. LAW, L. Bradley
"Sausalito Winds." [WoosterR] (7) Spr 87, p. 61.

3129. LAWRENCE, Aline
"Pilgrimage." [MoodySI] (18/19) Fall 87, p. 40.
3131. LAWRENCE, Joe B.
"Graduation Gift (I'd Like to Give to You)." [EngJ] (76:2) F 87, p. 96.
"Spring Stream." [EngJ] (76:7) N 87, p. 99.
3132. LAWRENCE, Sean A.
"Cats." [DekalbLAJ] (20:1/4) 87, p. 45.
3133. LAWRY, Mercedes
"Aspirations to Beauty." [BellArk] (3:2) Mr-Ap 87, p. 3.
"An Evening Out." [CrabCR] (4:2) Spr 87, p. 19.
"To Find You." [BellArk] (3:3) My-Je 87, p. 20.
3134. LAWSON, D. S.
"Kenneth." [JamesWR] (4:3) Spr 87, p. 13.
3135. LAWSON, David
"Uncle Buzzie." [BallSUF] (28:4) Aut 87, p. 62-63.
3136. LAWTHER, Marcia
"Here You Find It." [Margin] (5) Wint 87-88, p. 69.
"Say It." [Margin] (5) Wint 87-88, p. 70.
3137. LAX, Robert
"Ar Gu Men Ta Tion." [HangL] (50/51) 87, p. 103-106.
3138. LAYTON, Irving
"Fellini." [Verse] (4:1) Mr 87, p. 25.
"Inter-View." [CrossC] (9:2) 87, p. 13.
"The Paddler." [Verse] (4:1) Mr 87, p. 24.
"Socrates at the Centaur." [CanLit] (112) Spr 87, p. 16-17.
3139. LAZARD, Naomi
"What Is Keeping the Clouds?" (tr. of Nina Cassian). [CrossCur] (7:3) 87, p. 120.
3140. LAZARO, Felipe
"Una Noche de Verano en una Casita de Adorno Navideño." [LindLM] (6:1) Ja-Mr 87, p. 8.
3141. LAZARUS, A. L.
"I Wish I Were Living in Your Century." [LightY] '87, c86, p. 62.
"Memo to My Music Dealer." [LightY] '87, c86, p. 185.
3142. Le GUIN, Ursula K.
"In That Ohio." [KenR] (NS 9:2) Spr 87, p. 99-100.
"The Menstrual Lodge." [Calyx] (10:2/3) Spr 87, p. 34-35.
"Pane." [KenR] (NS 9:2) Spr 87, p. 100-101.
"Spring, Robinsons' Farm." [KenR] (NS 9:2) Spr 87, p. 99.
3143. LEA, Sydney
"After George's Axe Was Stolen." [LaurelR] (21:1/2) Wint-Sum 87, p. 73-74.
"Annual Report" (For my wife). [KenR] (NS 9:2) Spr 87, p. 87-91.
"Arrangement." [Crazy] (32) Spr 87, p. 31-32.
"At the Edge" (Monte Tremezzo). [SewanR] (95:1) Wint 87, p. 12.
"Envoi: To the Dead Poet Whose Poems My Children Wanted Me to Include in This Volume." [Crazy] (32) Spr 87, p. 28-30.
"Five Chapters in Historical Present." [LaurelR] (21:1/2) Wint-Sum 87, p. 69-71.
"Leonora's Kitchen." [TexasR] (7:3/4) 87, p. 92-93.
"Oosh." [MissouriR] (10:3) 87, p. 108-109.
"Over Brogno." [Poetry] (150:2) My 87, p. 93-96.
"Riverfront." [LaurelR] (21:1/2) Wint-Sum 87, p. 71-72.
3144. LEASE, Joseph
"Down River." [Paint] (14:28) Aut 87, p. 18.
"A Few Days in March." [Notus] (2:2) Fall 87, p. 62.
"The Rival." [Paint] (14:28) Aut 87, p. 19.
"Sorcerer-Hedin." [Notus] (2:2) Fall 87, p. 61.
"Sound Shot Through the Heart." [Notus] (2:2) Fall 87, p. 60.
"Whether or Not I Follow You." [NewAW] (2) Fall 87, p. 106.
3145. LEAX, John
"Clearing Trail." [Nimrod] (30:2) Spr-Sum 87, p. 94.
"Planting Beets." [Nimrod] (30:2) Spr-Sum 87, p. 94.
3146. LEDBETTER, J. T.
"I Know a Lady." [KanQ] (19:3) Sum 87, p. 91-92.
"A Lady in Winter." [KanQ] (19:3) Sum 87, p. 92.
3147. LEE, David
"Bargains." [WillowS] (20) Spr 87, p. 85-89.
"Faith Tittle" (Hebrews 11:1-3). [WillowS] (20) Spr 87, p. 90-94.

"September 1st." [SpoonRQ] (12:2) Spr 87, p. 38-41.
3148. LEE, Esther
    "Mailman" (tr. of Huh Se-Wook). [Caliban] (2) 87, p. 50.
    "The Man with Guts" (tr. of Huh Se-Wook). [Caliban] (2) 87, p. 52.
    "On the Terrace" (tr. of Huh Se-Wook). [Caliban] (2) 87, p. 51.
3149. LEE, John B.
    "Looking at the In-Memoriam Issue of Writers' Quarterly" (for Milton Acorn).
        [CrossC] (9:2) 87, p. 3.
3150. LEE, Lance
    "Glimpsed Through the Window of the Paris Express" (author corrected in 7:2, p.
        175). [CrossCur] (7:1) 87, p. 31.
3151. LEE, Li-Young
    "Eating Alone." [MemphisSR] (7:2) Spr 87, p. 49.
    "Rain Diary." [MemphisSR] (7:2) Spr 87, p. 50-52.
LEE, Louis
    See LEE, Lance
3152. LEE, Peter
    "Blue Sky" (tr. of Kim Su-yong). [Pembroke] (19) 87, p. 15.
    "Grass" (tr. of Kim Su-yong). [Pembroke] (19) 87, p. 16.
    "Love" (tr. of Kim Su-yong). [Pembroke] (19) 87, p. 19.
    "Port of Call" (tr. of Hwang Tong-Gyu). [Pembroke] (19) 87, p. 17.
    "Song of Peace" (tr. of Hwang Tong-Gyu). [Pembroke] (19) 87, p. 17-18.
    "Wild Geese" (tr. of Hwang Tong-Gyu). [Pembroke] (19) 87, p. 20.
3153. LEE, Sung Hyung
    "Winter Morning" (tr. by John Chay and Grace Gibson). [InterPR] (13:1) Spr 87, p.
        64.
3154. LEE, Won-sup
    "Pearl" (tr. by Hyn-jae Yee Sallee). [HampSPR] Wint 86, p. 31.
3155. LEE, Yay Seok
    "Moving in water." [Amelia] (4:1/2, issue 9) 87, p. 62.
3156. LEEPER, Kurt
    "Storms." [Gambit] (20) 86, p. 47.
3157. LEFCOWITZ, Barbara F.
    "Villages: for Erling Indreeide, Who Can Still Return." [LitR] (31:1) Fall 87, p. 22.
    "Xerox." [Outbr] (18/19) Fall 86-Spr 88, p. 11.
3158. LEFEVERE, André
    "All's Well That Ends Well" (tr. of Richard Minne). [Paint] (14:28) Aut 87, p. 26.
    "Elegy" (tr. of Maurice Gilliams). [Paint] (14:28) Aut 87, p. 36.
    "Portrait" (tr. of Richard Minne). [Paint] (14:28) Aut 87, p. 27.
    "Spring Poem" (tr. of Maurice Gilliams). [Paint] (14:28) Aut 87, p. 38.
    "Tristitia Ante" (tr. of Maurice Gilliams). [Paint] (14:28) Aut 87, p. 37.
    "We Stood in a Circle" (tr. of Richard Minne). [Paint] (14:28) Aut 87, p. 28.
    "Writing Poetry" (tr. of Richard Minne). [Paint] (14:28) Aut 87, p. 29.
3159. LEFLER, Peggy
    "Minds aged to survive a crime of you." [CrossC] (9:3/4) 87, p. 14.
3160. LeFLORE, Shirley
    "Drum." [RiverS] (24) 87, p. 81.
3161. LEFTWICH, Jim
    "Here We Are." [FiveFR] (5) 87, p. 70-73.
3162. LEGENDRE, Janis
    "Intensive Care." [BallSUF] (28:4) Aut 87, p. 52.
3163. LEGGETT, Stephen
    "The Ribbon." [PassN] (8:1) Wint 87, p. 20.
3164. LEHBERT, Margitt
    "Mayakowski's Vacation with Lilya and Ossip Brik, Summer of 1929" (tr. of
        Steffen Mensching). [Ploughs] (13:4) 87, p. 71-72.
    "Siqueiros: Our Countenance" (tr. of Steffen Mensching). [Ploughs] (13:4) 87, p.
        73-74.
3165. LEHMAN, David
    "Cambridge, 1972." [YaleR] (76:2) Wint 87, p. 234-237.
    "Four Versions of the End." [ParisR] (29:105) Wint 87, p. 102-103.
    "Gallery Notes." [PartR] (54:3) Sum 87, p. 423-425.
    "New York City, 1974." [Boulevard] (2:1/2) Spr 87, p. 124-128.
    "Operation Memory." [Shen] (37:2) 87, p. 41-42.
    "Plato's Retreat." [Shen] (37:2) 87, p. 43-44.
    "Wystan Hugh Auden: A Villanelle." [LightY] '87, c86, p. 214.

3166. LEINART, Virginia
"Leavetaking." [KanQ] (19:1/2) Wint-Spr 87, p. 318.
3167. LEIPER, Esther M.
"Approach to the Second Coming." [Amelia] (4:3, issue 10) 87, p. 86-88.
"The Music Was Always There." [Vis] (23) 87, p. 35.
"Superskin." [Amelia] (4:1/2, issue 9) 87, p. 97.
"The Wars of Faery" (Book 1, Cantos III-IV, for C.S. Lewis). [Amelia] (4:3, issue 10) 87, p. 17-26.
"The Wars of Faery: An Epic Romance in Rhyme Royal" (Book 1, Cantos I-II). [Amelia] (4:1/2, issue 9) 87, p. 5-14.
3168. LEITHAUSER, Brad
"Two Four-Liners" ("Anonymous' Lament," "Parallel Lifelines"). [Poetry] (151:1/2) O-N 87, p. 88.
3169. LELAND, Blake
"Breath." [Epoch] (36:2) 87-88, p. 156-165.
3170. LEMAIRE, Jean-Pierre
"The Violinist" (tr. by Dorothy Aspinwall). [CumbPR] (6:2) Spr 87, p. 9.
"Le Violoniste." [CumbPR] (6:2) Spr 87, p. 8.
3171. LeMON, Richard
"Tea Store." [SoCaR] (20:1) Fall 87, p. 57.
3172. LENFESTEY, James P.
"Dreams of Property Tax Relief." [LakeSR] (21) 87, p. 17.
3173. LENHART, Gary
"Change of Wife." [NewAW] (2) Fall 87, p. 65.
3174. LENHART, Michael
"Age of Miracles." [PoeticJ] (17) 87, p. 44.
3175. LENIHAN, Dan
"Burgers: Ruth and Ellis." [Bogg] (58) 87, p. 43-44.
3176. LENIHAN, Jean
"I Sweep Around the Bed." [StoneC] (14:3/4) Spr-Sum 87, p. 42.
3177. LENSE, Edward
"f/0.95." [GreenfR] (14:3/4) Sum-Fall 87, p. 86.
"Halley's Comet." [GreenfR] (14:3/4) Sum-Fall 87, p. 87.
"Steel Clock." [AntR] (45:1) Wint 87, p. 41.
3178. LENT, John
"Artifice of Eternity." [PraF] (8:2) Sum 87, p. 54-55.
"Ghost in the Vortex." [Event] (16:2) Sum 87, p. 103-105.
"Lament." [Waves] (14:4) Spr 86, p. 46-47.
"Original Sins." [Waves] (14:4) Spr 86, p. 4546.
LEON, Ulalume González de
See GONZALEZ DE LEON, Ulalume
3179. LEONE, Dan
"Ed's Idea." [WormR] (27:1, issue 105) 87, p. 28.
"Ed's Redeeming Qualities." [WormR] (27:1, issue 105) 87, p. 27.
"Life." [WormR] (27:1, issue 105) 87, p. 27.
"Poem: 1. I never write poems." [WormR] (27:1, issue 105) 87, p. 27.
3180. LEOPARDI, Giacomo
"Memories" (Excerpt, tr. by John Heath-Stubbs). [NewYRB] (34:1) 29 Ja 87, p. 43.
"Le Ricordanze" (Excerpt). [NewYRB] (34:1) 29 Ja 87, p. 43.
3181. LEPORE, Dominick (Dominick J.)
"Destroyed" (tr. of Gigi Dessi). [InterPR] (13:2) Fall 87, p. 37.
"Laterally" (tr. of Gigi Dessi). [InterPR] (13:2) Fall 87, p. 37.
"Mourning." [Wind] (17:59) 87, p. 31.
"Perhaps" (tr. of Gigi Dessi). [InterPR] (13:2) Fall 87, p. 35.
3182. LEPOVETSKY, Lisa
"Dear Mother." [Interim] (6:1) Spr 87, p. 35.
"Egg-Plant." [Interim] (6:2) Fall 87, p. 35.
"Emily in Glass." [Interim] (6:2) Fall 87, p. 36.
3183. LERNER, Laurence
"Vacant Possession." [SewanR] (95:1) Wint 87, p. 14.
"Writing the Date." [SewanR] (95:1) Wint 87, p. 13-14.
3184. LERNER, Linda
"The Body Talks." [Writer] (99:3) Mr 86, p. 22.
"A Friend's Possible Illness" (Again, for Jean). [CentR] (31:2) Spr 87, p. 190-191.

3185. LesCARBEAU, Mitchell
"Bodysurfer." [HawaiiR] (19) Spr 86, c87, p. 4-5.
3186. LESLIE, Naton
"In Brush and Throttle of Briar" (At the Hanging Tree on Peach Ridge, Athens,
Ohio." [StoneC] (15:1/2) Fall-Wint 87-88, p. 70.
3187. LESSING, Karin
"Li Santo." [Conjunc] (10) 87, p. 72-77.
3188. LESTER-MASSMAN, Gordon
"I Want." [KanQ] (19:3) Sum 87, p. 232-233.
"Mistakes in Paradise." [Abraxas] (35/36) 87, p. 58-62.
"Praying for Resolution." [HampSPR] Wint 87, p. 13.
"Returning." [KanQ] (19:3) Sum 87, p. 233-234.
3189. LEURGANS, Lois
"Epitaph." [LightY] '87, c86, p. 242.
LEV, Dina Ben
    See BEN-LEV, Dina
3190. LEVENSON, Christopher
"Colonist." [AntigR] (69/70) 87, p. 46.
3191. LEVENTHAL, Ann Z.
"Mending Time" (Corrected reprint of poem appearing in 7:2). [PassN] (8:1) Wint
87, p. 23.
3192. LEVER, Bernice
"Sometimes the Distance." [Waves] (15:1/2) Fall 86, p. 115.
3193. LEVERING, Donald
"As the Dream-Time Bees Looked On." [BlueBldgs] (10) 87?, p. 55-56.
"Bones." [CapeR] (22:1) Spr 87, p. 37.
"Mother Works in the Dark." [PoetL] (81:4) Wint 86-87, p. 218-219.
"My Father Has Left a Pair of His Walking Shoes in the Homes of His Five Sons."
[PoetL] (81:4) Wint 86-87, p. 220-221.
"On Her First Tooth" (for Camas). [PoetL] (81:4) Wint 86-87, p. 216.
"Summer Birthday." [PoetL] (81:4) Wint 86-87, p. 217.
3194. LEVERONI, Rosa
"Absence, VII" (tr. by Lynette McGrath and Nathaniel B. Smith). [WebR] (12:2)
Fall 87, p. 22.
3195. LEVERTOV, Denise
"Athanor." [OP] (final issue) Sum 87, p. 22.
"Ceremonies." [HangL] (50/51) 87, p. 108.
"An Estrangement." [HangL] (50/51) 87, p. 107.
"From the Image-Flow — Death of Chausson, 1899." [OP] (final issue) Sum 87, p.
21.
"Girls." [Sequoia] (31:1) Centennial issue 87, p. 105.
"A Lost Poem." [CreamCR] (11:2/3) 87?, p. 63-64.
"A Stone from Iona." [Shen] (37:4) 87, p. 41.
"The Stricken Children." [Sequoia] (31:1) Centennial issue 87, p. 104.
"Variation on a Theme by Rilke (The Book of Hours, Bk I, 1)." [HangL] (50/51)
87, p. 109.
LEVI, Enrique Jaramillo
    See JARAMILLO LEVI, Enrique
3196. LEVI, Jan Heller
"A Day." [RiverS] (22) 87, p. 72-73.
"What It Is." [RiverS] (22) 87, p. 74.
3197. LEVI, Primo
"Craft" (tr. by Gaia Servadio and A. Alvarez). [NewYorker] (63:34) 12 O 87, p. 46.
"The Elephant" (tr. by Ruth Feldman). [InterPR] (13:2) Fall 87, p. 33.
"L'Elefante" (from "Ad Ora Incerta"). [InterPR] (13:2) Fall 87, p. 32.
3198. LEVI, Toni Mergentime
"Two Bees." [SmPd] (24:2) Spr 87, p. 29.
3199. LEVIN, David
"An Apology for First Children." [CarolQ] (39:3) Spr 87, p. 84.
3200. LEVIN, Harriet
"The Christmas Show." [PartR] (54:3) Sum 87, p. 435-436.
3201. LEVIN, John
"Not Unlike the Honeymooners." [WormR] (27:4, issue 108) 87, p. 94.
"Right Up There with Herzog's Dwarfs." [WormR] (27:4, issue 108) 87, p. 94.
3202. LEVIN, Phillis
"Autumn Book." [SouthwR] (72:3) Sum 87, p. 388.

"The Border Guard." [SouthwR] (72:3) Sum 87, p. 387.
"The Brooklyn Botanic Garden." [NewEngR] (9:4) Sum 87, p. 423-424.
"Dark Horse." [Boulevard] (2:1/2) Spr 87, p. 202.
"Grace." [Poetry] (150:1) Ap 87, p. 5.
"Indian Restaurant." [Boulevard] (2:1/2) Spr 87, p. 203.
"The Little Boy Who Fell." [PartR] (54:2) Spr 87, p. 270-271.
"Machines." [Poetry] (150:1) Ap 87, p. 4.
"A Meeting of Friends." [Boulevard] (2:1/2) Spr 87, p. 199-201.
"On Marble." [Poetry] (150:1) Ap 87, p. 3.
"Out of Chaos." [PartR] (54:2) Spr 87, p. 269-270.
"A Song." [Boulevard] (2:1/2) Spr 87, p. 201.
"What the Intern Saw." [NewEngR] (9:4) Sum 87, p. 424-2425.
3203. LEVINE, Miriam
"Getting Ready for Winter." [TexasR] (7:3/4) 87, p. 94-95.
"Goodnight." [MSS] (5:3) 87, p. 136.
"Shampoo After Surgery." [MSS] (5:3) 87, p. 135.
"The Tuber-Cutter." [TexasR] (7:3/4) 87, p. 96.
"Winter Days." [KenR] (NS 9:1) Wint 87, p. 28-32.
3204. LEVINE, Norm
"The Pharmacist." [CrossCur] (7:1) 87, p. 147.
3205. LEVINE, Philip
"Above the World." [NewYorker] (63:40) 23 N 87, p. 39.
"Animals Are Passing From Our Lives." [NowestR] (25:3) 87, p. 140.
"Bitterness." [MissouriR] (10:2) 87, p. 58.
"Buying and Selling." [NewYorker] (63:29) 7 S 87, p. 32.
"Don't Ask." [Caliban] (2) 87, p. 160-162.
"The Fourth Star." [WestHR] (41:2) Sum 87, p. 138.
"Growth." [WestHR] (41:2) Sum 87, p. 139-140.
"In Saxony." [NowestR] (25:3) 87, p. 138.
"Keats in California." [Poetry] (151:1/2) O-N 87, p. 88-89.
"The Kingdom." [WestHR] (41:1) Spr 87, p. 17-18.
"Long Gone March." [Poetry] (149:6) Mr 87, p. 313-314.
"Lost." [Field] (37) Fall 87, p. 65.
"Lost." [MemphisSR] (7:2) Spr 87, p. 4-5.
"On the River." [NewYorker] (63:36) 26 O 87, p. 36.
"The Rat of Faith." [MissouriR] (10:2) 87, p. 56-57.
"Searching for Us." [MemphisSR] (7:2) Spr 87, p. 6.
"A Theory of Prosody." [OhioR] (38) 87, p. 81.
"This Day." [Field] (37) Fall 87, p. 66-68.
"A Walk with Tom Jefferson." [ParisR] (29:104) Fall 87, p. 28-43.
3206. LEVINE, Toni L.
"Room 25." [EngJ] (76:1) Ja 87, p. 94.
3207. LEVITIN, Alexis
"IV. You lean your face on sorrow, don't even" (tr. of Eugenio de Andrade).
[StoneC] (14:3/4) Spr-Sum 87, p. 23.
"XLVI. It is winter, hands can hardly hold" (tr. of Eugenio de Andrade). [StoneC]
(14:3/4) Spr-Sum 87, p. 22.
"Against the Shadow" (tr. of Eugenio de Andrade). [BostonR] (12:3) Je 87, p. 4.
"The Color of Those Days" (tr. of Eugenio de Andrade). [GrahamHR] (10)
Wint-Spr 87, p. 55.
"The Desired Tomb" (tr. of Jorge de Sena). [GrahamHR] (10) Wint-Spr 87, p. 56.
"For Jonathan Griffin" (In English & Spanish, tr. of Jorge de Sena). [HawaiiR] (19)
Spr 86, c87, p. 38-41.
"Just a Glance" (tr. of Eugenio de Andrade). [SenR] (17:1) 87, p. 45.
"March Has Returned" (tr. of Eugenio de Andrade). [GrahamHR] (10) Wint-Spr 87,
p. 54.
"No, I Cannot Find the Photograph" (tr. of Eugenio de Andrade). [GrahamHR] (10)
Wint-Spr 87, p. 53.
"September Sea" (tr. of Eugenio de Andrade). [CrossCur] (7:3) 87, p. 95.
"The Smooth Beach with Eurydice Dead" (tr. of Sophia de Mello Breyner
Andresen). [Vis] (24) 87, p. 4.
"They Touched the Earth" (tr. of Eugenio de Andrade). [SenR] (17:1) 87, p. 44.
"White on White" (tr. of Eugenio de Andrade). [QRL] (Series 8, vol. 27) 87, 60 p.
"With the Birds" (tr. of Eugenio de Andrade). [SenR] (17:1) 87, p. 46.
3208. LEVY, Andrew
"Earnest Because There Are Alibi." [CentralP] (12) Fall 87, p. 99.

"Some Order of Ash." [CentralP] (12) Fall 87, p. 98.
3209. LEVY, Emily
"One Hundred and Fifty-Seven Ways to Tell My Incest Story." [SinW] (31) 87, p. 6-9.
3210. LEVY, Robert J.
"The Actress." [Boulevard] (2:1/2) Spr 87, p. 151-152.
"Praying Hands" (after Durer). [CrossCur] (7:2) 87, p. 59.
"The Voice." [Boulevard] (2:1/2) Spr 87, p. 152-153.
3211. LEWANDOWSKI, Stephen
"Drenched." [Vis] (23) 87, p. 34.
3212. LEWIS, J. Patrick
"Edward Lear Finds Paradise (And Loses It)." [LightY] '87, c86, p. 64.
"The Elephant." [Event] (16:3) Fall 87, p. 28.
"A Night at the Garden." [NewL] (53:3) Spr 87, p. 91.
"Old Foss (the Cat) Recalls His Life with Mr. Lear." [LightY] '87, c86, p. 65.
"A Poem Beginning with a Line by Zorba." [Event] (16:3) Fall 87, p. 29.
"The Queen Takes Drawing Lessons from Edward Lear." [LightY] '87, c86, p. 62-63.
"The Reddleman" (After reading Hardy's *The Return of the Native*). [Amelia] (4:1/2, issue 9) 87, p. 117.
"The Woman Sleeping Across the Hall." [MSS] (5:3) 87, p. 113.
3213. LEWIS, Janet
"For Emily." [Sequoia] (31:1) Centennial Issue 87, p. 13.
"For Nancy Bray and Gladys Mears, Elegy." [Thrpny] (30) Sum 87, p. 10.
"Sunday Morning at the Artists' House." [Poetry] (151:1/2) O-N 87, p. 90-91.
3214. LEWIS, Jeffery
"Quahog Creation Ballet." [YellowS] (25) Wint 87, p. 19.
3215. LEWIS, Joel
"Minus Water." [Caliban] (2) 87, p. 59.
"Ringer." [Caliban] (2) 87, p. 59.
"White Summer." [Caliban] (2) 87, p. 60-62.
3216. LEWIS, Justin
"Car to California." [MalR] (79) Je 87, p. 104-110.
3217. LEWIS, Katherine (*See also* LEWIS, Kathy)
"I Write on the Sky. I Write on the Sea." [BellArk] (3:6) N-D 87, p. 4.
"On Courting." [BellArk] (3:1) Ja-F 87, p. 6.
"Quirk of the Splendor." [BellArk] (3:1) Ja-F 87, p. 1.
3218. LEWIS, Kathy (*See also* LEWIS, Katherine)
"How to Believe Is to Move." [MSS] (5:3) 87, p. 30.
3219. LEWIS, Lisa
"The Poet, La Bourgeoisie." [MissouriR] (10:1) 87, p. 160-161.
"Revisions." [MissouriR] (10:1) 87, p. 162-163.
3220. LEZAMA LIMA, José
"And My Body?" (tr. by Joseph Chadwick). [HawaiiR] (20) Fall 86, c87, p. 13.
"Las Barbas de un Rey." [HawaiiR] (20) Fall 86, c87, p. 10.
"A King's Whiskers" (tr. by Joseph Chadwick). [HawaiiR] (20) Fall 86, c87, p. 11.
"Y Mi Cuerpo?" [HawaiiR] (20) Fall 86, c87, p. 12.
3221. LI, Chi
"On Arriving at Ling-Nan, January, 1949" (Two tz'u, tr. by Li Chi and Michael O'Connor). [Calyx] (10:2/3) Spr 87, p. 78-79.
3222. LI, He
"Autumn Cold, a Poem to My Cousin" (tr. by Jodi Varon). [Trans] (19) Fall 87, p. 235-236.
"Ballad of an Aching Heart" (tr. by Jodi Varon). [Trans] (19) Fall 87, p. 236.
"Cry of a Heng T'ang Woman" (tr. by Jodi Varon). [Trans] (19) Fall 87, p. 237.
"A Poem I Showed to My Pa Servant" (tr. by Jodi Varon). [ColR] (NS 14:2) Fall-Wint 87, p. 65.
3223. LI, Min Hua
"In Old Milwaukee." [Contact] (9:44/45/46) Fall-Wint 87, p. 50.
"Queer Power." [Contact] (9:44/45/46) Fall-Wint 87, p. 50.
"Sound Effect." [NewL] (54:1) Fall 87, p. 103.
"A Wet, Salty Chinese Secret Impossible to Write in Chinese." [JamesWR] (4:2) Wint 87, p. 6.
3224. LI, Qi
"Ice Carvings" (tr. by Edward Morin and Dennis Ding). [CrossCur] (7:3) 87, p. 155-156.

3225. LI, Quing Zhao
"Autumn Chinese Parasol" (tr. by Kang Xue Pei and Sibyl James). [TexasR] (8:3/4)
Fall-Wint 87, p. 7.
"Not Trying the Lamps" (tr. by Kang Xue Pei and Sibyl James). [TexasR] (8:3/4)
Fall-Wint 87, p. 6.
"Red Lotus" (tr. by Kang Xue Pei and Sibyl James). [TexasR] (8:3/4) Fall-Wint 87,
p. 9.
"Spring's News" (tr. by Kang Xue Pei and Sibyl James). [TexasR] (8:3/4) Fall-Wint
87, p. 8.
3226. LI, Shang-yin
"The Lady in the Moon" (tr. by Nancy Hunter). [CutB] (27/28) 87, p. 94.
"Silk of Scented Phoenix Tail Lies in Thin Folds" (tr. by Nancy Hunter). [CutB]
(27/28) 87, p. 94.
"Under the Silver River" (tr. by Nancy Hunter). [CutB] (27/28) 87, p. 93.
"Wind" (tr. by Nancy Hunter). [CutB] (27/28) 87, p. 93.
LI-YOUNG, Lee
See LEE, Li-Young
3227. LIANNE, Lenny
"When Tomatoes Are Illegal." [SouthernPR] (27:2) Fall 87, p. 64.
3228. LIATSOS, Sandra
"In My Childhood Yard." [DekalbLAJ] (20:1/4) 87, p. 46.
3229. LIBBEY, Elizabeth
"After the Fact" (for Richard Hugo). [AmerS] (56:3) Sum 87, p. 369-370.
"Bringing Home the Groceries." [Crazy] (33) Wint 87, p. 57-58.
"Depression Windfall." [NoAmR] (272:3) S 87, p. 24.
"Spring And." [Atlantic] (260:3) S 87, p. 69.
3230. LIDDELL, Eleanor P.
"Twilight and Dawn." [PoeticJ] (17) 87, p. 11.
3231. LIDDY, James
"The Enchanter of Yellow Gold to the Old Friend." [CreamCR] (11:2/3) 87?, p.
23-24.
"Love Is a Good Read in Bed." [Gargoyle] (32/33) 87, p. 67-68.
3232. LIDDY, John
"Scarecrow." [Margin] (2) Spr 87, p. 77.
3233. LIEBERMAN, David
"Men's Bodies." [JamesWR] (5:1) Fall 87, p. 14.
"Parable of the Goddess: Her Dues." [HolCrit] (24:1) F 87, p. 19.
3234. LIEBERMAN, Laurence
"Twin Pitons: The Conic Isles" (St. Lucia, West Indies). [Boulevard] (2:1/2) Spr 87,
p. 73-103.
3235. LIEBERT, Dan
"Mayan Woman Grinding Corn." [GreensboroR] (40) Sum 86, p. 63.
3236. LIEHU, Rakel
"Ahead of Me I See" (tr. by Bernhard Hillila). [ColR] (NS 14:1) Spr-Sum 87, p. 37.
3237. LIETZ, Robert
"Fire." [Pequod] (23/24) 87, p. 95-96.
"House." [CharR] (13:1) Spr 87, p. 73-75.
"Suburban Man Tracing His Steps Back." [Pequod] (23/24) 87, p. 97-98.
3238. LIFSHIN, Lyn
"47th Year Anniversary." [Boulevard] (2:1/2) Spr 87, p. 209-210.
"After the President Visits Bitberg and ETV Shows the Liberation of the Camps."
[WormR] (27:4, issue 108) 87, p. 87.
"Afterward." [BellR] (10:1) Spr 87, p. 48.
"Afterward." [Grain] (15:1) Spr 87, p. 71.
"Annie Drowning in Tubes like Seaweed." [Event] (16:1) Mr 87, p. 69.
"Annie in Her Last Morphine Daze in the White Room Even Blood Dissolves from."
[Event] (16:1) Mr 87, p. 68.
"Annie in the Spring." [Grain] (15:1) Spr 87, p. 65.
"Annie, Those Last Days in the Hospital in a Snow of Morphine." [AntigR] (69/70)
87, p. 155.
"Artist Colony Applications." [Ploughs] (13:4) 87, p. 56-57.
"Basil." [Grain] (15:1) Spr 87, p. 72.
"Beale Street, Memphis." [Grain] (15:1) Spr 87, p. 66.
"Bible Thumpers Madonna." [WormR] (27:4, issue 108) 87, p. 87.
"Chain Letter Madonna: 1-2." [WormR] (27:4, issue 108) 87, p. 86.
"Christmas 1980." [AntigR] (69/70) 87, p. 156.

"Coffee Madonna." [WormR] (27:4, issue 108) 87, p. 86.
"Cotton Candy Madonna." [WormR] (27:4, issue 108) 87, p. 86.
"Cynical Madonna." [WormR] (27:4, issue 108) 87, p. 86.
"Cynical Madonna." [WormR] (27:4, issue 108) 87, p. 87.
"The Day After Bitburg." [PaintedB] (30) 87, p. 37.
"Dear Janice." [Ploughs] (13:4) 87, p. 58-59.
"Deep Purple." [Lips] (13) 87, p. 38-39.
"Dream of Ivy." [Ploughs] (13:4) 87, p. 55.
"Dream of Shoplifting a Cherry Cloisonne Bottle." [Puerto] (22:2) Spr 87, p. 25-26.
"During the Cold Spell: frost turns light." [Grain] (15:1) Spr 87, p. 67.
"During the Cold Spell: her blond hair." [Grain] (15:1) Spr 87, p. 64.
"During the Cold Spell: she wonders what." [Grain] (15:1) Spr 87, p. 63.
"The Elderberry All Glass Beads Dripping." [Vis] (23) 87, p. 8.
"Facing Away from Where You're Going." [Blueline] (7:2/3 [i.e. 8:2/3?]) 87, p. 58.
"February 22 Light." [DekalbLAJ] (20:1/4) 87, p. 27.
"The Flame Swallower's Woman." [HawaiiR] (20) Fall 86, c87, p. 93.
"Going Past Rapple." [Grain] (15:1) Spr 87, p. 68.
"He Said in the Hospital It." [HawaiiR] (21) Spr 87, p. 52-53.
"Hiroshima." [CentR] (31:2) Spr 87, p. 184-185.
"I Didn't Get Your Violin Back to You I've." [HawaiiR] (19) Spr 86, c87, p. 74-75.
"I Remember Haifa Being Lovely But." [Calyx] (10:2/3) Spr 87, p. 69.
"If You Read the Poem of This Marriage Backward." [Electrum] (39) Fall-Wint 87, p. 41.
"In 1923." [Grain] (15:1) Spr 87, p. 62.
"In the VA Hospital." [HawaiiR] (21) Spr 87, p. 51.
"The Jesuit's Letters Moulder in a Bag Near the Soot." [Bogg] (57) 87, p. 24.
"Joanie, 17." [Grain] (15:1) Spr 87, p. 69.
"Linden Flowers." [Pembroke] (19) 87, p. 172.
"Louise James Africa, Move Survivor." [Contact] (9:44/45/46) Fall-Wint 87, p. 56.
"The Mad Girl Hears the President Say He'd Pardon Those Who Bombed the Abortion Clinic." [BellR] (10:1) Spr 87, p. 46.
"The Mad Girl Remembers How the Record Stuck on 'Juarez'." [Grain] (15:1) Spr 87, p. 70.
"Madonna Introduces the Stamp Poem, Dedicates It to Writers." [WormR] (27:4, issue 108) 87, p. 86.
"Madonna of the Edges." [WormR] (27:4, issue 108) 87, p. 87.
"Madonna Who Is Tired of Trying to Get Thru." [WormR] (27:4, issue 108) 87, p. 85.
"Madonna Who Promised Something She Shouldn't Have." [BellR] (10:1) Spr 87, p. 47.
"Madonna Who Sands Things Away." [WindO] (49) Fall 87, p. 37.
"Madonna Who'd Choose Her House Over a Lover." [WindO] (49) Fall 87, p. 38.
"Margaret Mary." [Grain] (15:1) Spr 87, p. 73.
"May, 1970." [SlipS] (7) 87, p. 88.
"Men and Cars: 1-2." [WormR] (27:4, issue 108) 87, p. 86.
"My Mother and the Down Quilt." [Lips] (13) 87, p. 40-42.
"My Mother and the Heat." [Grain] (15:1) Spr 87, p. 61.
"My Mother and the Pots." [Waves] (15:1/2) Fall 86, p. 70.
"My Mother Who Was Never Lonely or Bored." [CentR] (31:3) Sum 87, p. 274-275.
"On His Last Night in Town." [Puerto] (22:2) Spr 87, p. 27.
"Onion Ring Madonna: 1-5." [WormR] (27:4, issue 108) 87, p. 87.
"Passover Madonna." [Bogg] (58) 87, p. 7.
"The Photographs in a Strip." [Footwork] 87, p. 41.
"Poetry in the Schools." [CentR] (31:3) Sum 87, p. 275-276.
"Pregnant Madonna." [WormR] (27:4, issue 108) 87, p. 86.
"Saturday Night Grand Union Parking Lot." [Waves] (15:1/2) Fall 86, p. 70.
"The Smallest Orange." [Lips] (13) 87, p. 43-44.
"South End." [Abraxas] (35/36) 87, p. 64-65.
"Spoon Night, Crystal Night." [Farm] (4:1) Wint 87, p. 37.
"Stamp Madonna." [WormR] (27:4, issue 108) 87, p. 86.
"Texas Ranch." [Caliban] (2) 87, p. 78-79.
"That Summer Before My Wedding." [HampSPR] Wint 86, p. 32.
"Those Phone Calls." [Abraxas] (35/36) 87, p. 65.
"To Stop Poems About You from Spilling Dropping All Over the Bed Blue Hail." [CrabCR] (4:2) Spr 87, p. 17.

"To the Daughter I Don't Have." [CrossCur] (7:2) 87, p. 148.
"Tomato Sandwiches." [PaintedB] (30) 87, p. 36.
"Unease." [WindO] (49) Fall 87, p. 37.
"Vietnam." [Lactuca] (7) Ag 87, p. 6.
"Wolf Moon, Icicles." [CrossCur] (7:2) 87, p. 149.
3239. LIFSON, Martha (Martha Ronk)
"It's a Desert Still." [AntR] (45:4) Fall 87, p. 436.
"Rhetoric" (10 poems). [Temblor] (5) 87, p. 97-100.
"The Seitz Theater." [Hudson] (40:1) Spr 87, p. 88.
3240. LIGI
"5 Lines." [SlipS] (7) 87, p. 10.
"Going Through Reams." [SlipS] (7) 87, p. 10.
"Reading a Headline" (for Jean). [SlipS] (7) 87, p. 9.
3241. LIGNELL, Kathleen
"Alejandra Among the Lilacs" (tr. of Cristina Peri Rossi). [Nimrod] (30:2) Spr-Sum
87, p. 128-132.
"From the Summer" (tr. of Cristina Peri Rossi). [AnotherCM] (17) 87, p. 105.
"Iconoclastic Landscape" (tr. of Cristina Peri Rossi). [AnotherCM] (17) 87, p. 104.
3242. LILLARD, Charles
"100 Mile House." [AntigR] (68) Wint 87, p. 25.
"Jones Creek." [AntigR] (68) Wint 87, p. 24.
"Kitsumkalum." [Waves] (15:4) Spr 87, p. 67.
"Meziadin." [Event] (16:2) Sum 87, p. 11.
"St. Anne's Crossing." [CanLit] (112) Spr 87, p. 47.
"Williams Lake." [AntigR] (68) Wint 87, p. 26.
3243. LILLEY, Kate
"Song After *Five Easy Pieces*." [Verse] (4:1) Mr 87, p. 5.
LILLYWHITE, Eileen Silver
See SILVER-LILLYWHITE, Eileen
3244. LILLYWHITE, Harvey
"Turning to Darkness." [PoetryNW] (28:1) Spr 87, p. 22-23.
3245. LIM, Shirley Geok-Lin
"Arak." [Chelsea] (46) 87, p. 246.
"Cross-Cultural Exchange" (Singapore 1986). [Chelsea] (46) 87, p. 247.
LIMA, José Lezama
See LEZAMA LIMA, José
3246. LIMA, Robert
"Angel." [CrossCur] (7:2) 87, p. 45.
"Helix." [CrossCur] (7:2) 87, p. 43-44.
"Hours" (tr. of Vicente Huidobro). [Vis] (25) 87, p. 12.
"Island." [CrossCur] (7:2) 87, p. 46.
3247. LIMAN, Claude G.
"Three Pictures from a Family Album." [NowestR] (25:3) 87, p. 180-181.
3248. LIMEHOUSE, Ezekiel
"Pas de Dieu: An Eclogue." [LakeSR] (21) 87, p. 14.
3249. LINDAHL, David
"Cigarettes." [JamesWR] (5:1) Fall 87, p. 5.
"Scream." [JamesWR] (5:1) Fall 87, p. 5.
3250. LINDEGREN, Erik
"Dying Gladiator" (tr. by H. P. Hanson). [Vis] (25) 87, p. 33.
3251. LINDHOLDT, Paul (*See also* LINDHOLDT, Paul J.)
"Brood Slave." [BelPoJ] (37:3) Spr 87, p. 5-6.
3252. LINDHOLDT, Paul J. (*See also* LINDHOLDT, Paul)
"Bounty" (for Darryl). [Interim] (6:1) Spr 87, p. 32.
"Forest Service." [Interim] (6:1) Spr 87, p. 31.
3253. LINDNER, Carl
"The Redtwig Dogwood in Winter." [KanQ] (19:3) Sum 87, p. 313.
"Teaching Checkers to My Son." [SoCaR] (20:1) Fall 87, p. 31.
3254. LINDOW, Sandra J.
"Life Bearing." [MidwQ] (29:1) Aut 87, p. 85-87.
"On Leaving." [MidwQ] (29:1) Aut 87, p. 88-89.
3255. LINDSAY, Frannie
"Wanting You To." [Agni] (24/25) 87, p. 104.
3256. LINDSTROM, Naomi
"Adolf Hitler Meditates on the Jewish Problem" (tr. of Oscar Hahn). [ColR] (NS
14:1) Spr-Sum 87, p. 31.

238

LINEHAN

3257. LINEHAN, Don
"Allspice." [Waves] (15:4) Spr 87, p. 68.
"And the Students Asked, 'What Does the Poem Mean?'." [Germ] (10:2) Spr 87, p. 19.
"Poem in the Old Gaelic Style." [Waves] (15:4) Spr 87, p. 68.
3258. LINEHAN, Moira
"Blessed Is the Fruit." [Writer] (99:7) Jl 86, p. 19.
3259. LINTHICUM, John
"The Dancing God." [LitR] (31:1) Fall 87, p. 17-19.
3260. LINZMEIER, Joe
"Your Hair Cascades." [JamesWR] (4:2) Wint 87, p. 8.
LIONY E BATISTA
See BATISTA, Liony e
3261. LIPMAN, Joel
"In the Opening Between." [YellowS] (22) Spr 87, p. 19.
"My Love's Inventions." [YellowS] (22) Spr 87, p. 18.
3262. LIPSCHUTZ, Kurt
"The Errand Boy's Day Off." [LightY] '87, c86, p. 108.
3263. LIPSITZ, Lou (Louis)
"Autobiographika Politika." [Caliban] (2) 87, p. 13-14.
"Hungarian Aunts" (for Dennis Szakacs). [KanQ] (19:3) Sum 87, p. 278.
"King Kong." [Witness] (1:4) Wint 87, p. 176-177.
"Watching the TV Version of the Holocaust, Interrupted by Commercials." [KanQ] (19:3) Sum 87, p. 277.
"Why the Poet Always Reads First and the Fiction-Writer Second . . ." (for Paul Jones). [Caliban] (2) 87, p. 8-10.
"You Want to Do Something Great." [Caliban] (2) 87, p. 11-12.
3264. LISHAN, Stuart
"Deli." [QW] (25) Spr 87, p. 128-129.
3265. LISITZA, Lorinda
"Tough Dancing." [Grain] (15:4) Wint 87, p. 65.
3266. LISK, Thomas
"Madame Bovary on a Curve." [ChatR] (8:1) Fall 87, p. 62-64.
3267. LISOWSKI, Joseph
"Hua-Tzu Hill" (tr. of P'ei Ti). [NegC] (7:1/2) 87, p. 247.
"Hua-Tzu Hill" (tr. of Wang Wei). [NegC] (7:1/2) 87, p. 248-249.
"Hyacinths." [WindO] (49) Fall 87, p. 57.
"Night Fishing on the James." [Amelia] (4:3, issue 10) 87, p. 65.
"Self Portrait." [Amelia] (4:1/2, issue 9) 87, p. 60.
LISSOVOY, Noah de
See De LISSOVOY, Noah
3268. LITTLE, Geraldine C.
"Madrigal for Margaret Retrieving the Head of Sir Thomas More." [Colum] (12) 87, p. 65.
"Manse." [Nimrod] (30:2) Spr-Sum 87, p. 107.
"Meditation and Celebration for Rainer Maria Rilke: Canzone." [Nimrod] (30:2) Spr-Sum 87, p. 108-109.
"Mette-Sophie Gad (Mrs. Gauguin)." [Raccoon] (24/25) My 87, p. 197.
"Phillis Wheatley: Soliloquy." [LitR] (30:4) Sum 87, p. 572-573.
"Poem for Annette Vallon, French Mistress of Wordsworth . . ." [Nimrod] (30:2) Spr-Sum 87, p. 110-111.
"Quiz." [CrossCur] (7:2) 87, p. 25.
"Scullery." [GreenfR] (14:3/4) Sum-Fall 87, p. 154.
"Triptych: Essex, England." [Shen] (37:4) 87, p. 5-8.
"Watching Sailboats" (for my brother, who was a minister). [Nimrod] (30:2) Spr-Sum 87, p. 106.
3269. LIVINGSTONE, Douglas
"Coronach at Cave-Rock." [TriQ] (69) Spr-Sum 87, p. 347-348.
LLOSA, Ricardo Pau
See PAU-LLOSA, Ricardo
3270. LLUCH MORA, Francisco
"A la ceniza vengo, dolorido." [Mairena] (9:23) 87, p. 121-122.
"A Ti Señor de Cielo y Tierra." [Mairena] (9:23) 87, p. 120-121.
"Del Barro a Dios." [Mairena] (9:23) 87, p. 119.
"Poema del Tiempo." [Mairena] (9:23) 87, p. 122.

"Polvo." [Mairena] (9:23) 87, p. 119-120.
"Saludo a Cesar Vallejo." [Mairena] (9:24) 87, p. 45.
"Sin Quererlo Lo He Ido Comprendiendo." [Mairena] (9:23) 87, p. 120.
3271. LOBANOV-ROSTOVSKY, Sergei
    "Cabaret Voltaire." [AmerPoR] (16:4) Jl-Ag 87, p. 43.
3272. LOCHHEAD, Douglas
    "Vigils & Mercies" (Selections: 11-20). [AntigR] (68) Wint 87, p. 61-76.
    "Vigils & Mercies" (Selections: 21-30). [AntigR] (71/72) Aut 87-Wint 88, p. 33-46.
3273. LOCKE, Duane
    "The Dwarf." [CapeR] (22:2) Fall 87, p. 2.
    "With Byron at Diodati." [Bogg] (58) 87, p. 21.
3274. LOCKE, Edward
    "Diavolezza." [WebR] (12:1) Spr 87, p. 14-15.
    "Midwest." [MidwQ] (28:3) Spr 87, p. 358-359.
    "On the Road." [Poem] (57) Mr 87, p. 19.
3275. LOCKETT, Reginald
    "405 Scott Street." [YellowS] (22) Spr 87, p. 40.
3276. LOCKLIN, Gerald
    "Children of a Lesser Demagogue" (A Wormwood Chapbook). [WormR] (27:2/3,
        issues 106-107) 87, p. 41-80.
    "Eddie Murphy." [BellR] (10:2) Fall 87, p. 25.
    "Enough Already." [BellR] (10:2) Fall 87, p. 26.
    "Equality, 1981." [SlipS] (7) 87, p. 86.
    "For Eleanor Roosevelt." [SlipS] (7) 87, p. 85.
    "For the Christening of Aaron Sjørn Ziolkowksi, June 20, 1986" (son of Rod and
        Heidi Ziolkowski). [Abraxas] (35/36) 87, p. 18.
    "From the Mouths of Boobs." [SlipS] (7) 87, p. 86.
    "How Our Pets Choose Us." [BellR] (10:2) Fall 87, p. 24.
    "I Only Write for Myself." [BellR] (10:2) Fall 87, p. 23.
    "Pardom Me a Little Parental Pride." [Electrum] (39) Fall-Wint 87, p. 48-49.
    "Questionnaire." [BellR] (10:2) Fall 87, p. 22.
    "Yes, But Don't Change the 'Big' to 'Little'." [BellR] (10:2) Fall 87, p. 21.
3277. LOCKWOOD, Virginia
    "Aquarium / Honolulu." [US1] (20/21) Wint 86-87, p. 34.
3278. LOEB, Ellen
    "Winter." [PoetL] (82:2) Sum 87, p. 108.
3279. LOESCH, Cheryl
    "New York." [CrossCur] (6:5) 87, p. 41.
3280. LOFTIS, Norman
    "Self-Portrait at Forty-Two." [AmerPoR] (16:4) Jl-Ag 87, p. 27.
3281. LOGAN, John
    "Three Poems on Morris Grave's Paintings." [NowestR] (25:3) 87, p. 107-108.
3282. LOGAN, William
    "The Advent of Common Law in Littoral Disputes." [Agni] (24/25) 87, p. 32-33.
    "Ambassador of Imperfect Mood." [Agni] (24/25) 87, p. 31.
    "The Ancient Economy." [SouthwR] (72:3) Sum 87, p. 355-356.
    "Animal Actors on the English Stage After 1642." [Poetry] (151:1/2) O-N 87, p. 91.
    "Coleridge in the Hurricane." [GrandS] (6:2) Wint 87, p. 38.
    "On the Late Murders." [GrandS] (6:2) Wint 87, p. 35-36.
    "Pears in Solitude." [SouthwR] (72:3) Sum 87, p. 354-355.
    "Political Song." [GrandS] (6:2) Wint 87, p. 37.
    "Political Song." [Harp] (274:1643) Ap 87, p. 34.
3283. LOGGHE, Joan
    "Sophia's Breasts." [Vis] (23) 87, p. 38-39.
3284. LOGUE, Christopher
    "Homer's 'Iliad,' updated." [Harp] (274:1644) My 87, p. 25-26.
3285. LOGUE, Mary
    "Small Wish" (for James L. White, 1936-1981). [JamesWR] (4:2) Wint 87, p. 3.
3286. LOHMANN, Jeanne
    "Poetry Reading." [CrossCur] (7:1) 87, p. 59.
3287. LOKENSGARD, Ole
    "Porgy and Bass." [PoetryE] (23/24) Fall 87, p. 217.
3288. LOM, Iain
    "The Battle of Inverlochy." [Margin] (3) Sum 87, p. 43-46.
3289. LOMAX, Dave
    "Isn't It Nice to Think So." [Waves] (15:4) Spr 87, p. 55.

3290. LONDON, Jonathan
"Approaching Infinity" (for Maureen). [HawaiiR] (22) Fall 87, p. 12-13.
"Semana Santa in Antingua Guatemala." [HawaiiR] (22) Fall 87, p. 8-9.
"Standing on the Edge of Ritual." [CrossCur] (7:1) 87, p. 11.
"There's a Season." [CrossCur] (7:1) 87, p. 12.
"Two Widows and a Widower." [HawaiiR] (22) Fall 87, p. 10-11.
"When the Dark Comes On" (for Gene Berson). [CrossCur] (7:1) 87, p. 13.
3291. LONDON, Rick
"Abjections: A Suite" (11 selections). [Act] (7) 87, p. 62-66.
"Mudrā." [FiveFR] (5) 87, p. 133.
3292. LONG, Brenda (Brenda Canipe)
"After the Flood." [CarolQ] (39:3) Spr 87, p. 98.
"Betrayal" (for John Paul). [ChatR] (8:1) Fall 87, p. 65.
3293. LONG, John Wingo
"Comeuppance." [HampSPR] Wint 87, p. 24.
"Exorcism." [HampSPR] Wint 87, p. 25.
3294. LONG, Keith
"A Ketchum Morning." [WeberS] (4:2) Fall 87, p. 56-57.
"Killing Puppies." [WeberS] (4:2) Fall 87, p. 54-55.
"Mount Scott Sestina." [WeberS] (4:2) Fall 87, p. 57-58.
3295. LONG, Richard
"Arm's Length" (1986 Finalist, Eve of Saint Agnes Poetry Competition). [NegC]
    (7:1/2) 87, p. 208.
"In the Bath Mirror, Naked." [GreensboroR] (43) Wint 87-88, p. 114.
3296. LONG, Robert Hill
"30 Looks at 20." [BlueBldgs] (10) 87?, p. 31-32.
"Approaching Independence Pass." [NewL] (53:3) Spr 87, p. 73.
"Beverly Carneiro" (Towns in Kansas, on I-70). [LightY] '87, c86, p. 156-158.
"Black Oak" (For Ki Davis, d. 1983). [KenR] (NS 9:3) Sum 87, p. 116-117.
"The Effigies" (Selections). [NewEngR] (10:2) Wint 87, p. 229-232.
"Fin de Siècle." [Poetry] (150:1) Ap 87, p. 20-21.
"Hatteras." [Poetry] (150:1) Ap 87, p. 17-19.
"Miracle Play." [NewEngR] (9:4) Sum 87, p. 421-422.
"The Official Frisbee-Chasing Champion of Colorado." [LightY] '87, c86, p.
    179-181.
"The Power to Die." [KenR] (NS 9:3) Sum 87, p. 117-118.
"Rilke and the Stout Angel." [BlueBldgs] (10) 87?, p. 29-30.
"Two Travelers, Maroon Lake, Colorado." [KenR] (NS 9:3) Sum 87, p. 119.
3297. LONG, Virginia
"Mrs. Wilson, Who Never Loved." [LightY] '87, c86, p. 243.
"Poverty's Pall." [Amelia] (4:1/2, issue 9) 87, p. 55.
3298. LONGLEY, Judy
"My Journey Toward You" (1986 Honorable Mention, Eve of Saint Agnes Poetry
    Competition). [NegC] (7:1/2) 87, p. 126-127.
"Polio Season" (For Teddy). [SouthernPR] (27:1) Spr 87, p. 35-36.
"That Summer She Thought of Dying" (1987 Ratner-Ferber-Poet Lore Honorable
    Mention). [PoetL] (82:2) Sum 87, p. 74.
3299. LONGLEY, Michael
"Conversations." [MassR] (28:3) Aut 87, p. 381-382.
"The King of the Island." [MassR] (28:3) Aut 87, p. 381.
"Wounds." [Pembroke] (19) 87, p. 80-81.
3300. LOOMIS, Sabra
"For Ishi." [AmerV] (6) Spr 87, p. 77.
3301. LOONEY, George
"Acts of Erasure, Acts of Acceptance" (for Anita Zombec). [PraS] (61:4) Wint 87, p.
    77-80.
"Conversation at a Late Hour." [CimR] (79) Ap 87, p. 54.
"Dark Water Rising." [BlackWR] (14:1) Fall 87, p. 11.
"White Explosions." [TarPR] (27:1) Fall 87, p. 28.
3302. LOPES, Michael
"In the Blue Dolphin." [HangL] (50/51) 87, p. 110.
3303. LOPEZ, Adelaida
"Bunraku." [LindLM] (6:4) O-D 87, p. 3.
"Piedras." [LindLM] (6:4) O-D 87, p. 3.
"Los Pinos." [LindLM] (6:4) O-D 87, p. 3.

3304. LOPEZ-ADORNO, Pedro
"Donde Cesar Vallejo Habla entre Sueños al Que Escribe." [Mairena] (9:24) 87, p. 53.
3305. LOPEZ ANGLADA, Luis
"El Caminante Llega a la Rabida" (Antes de entrar en el Monasterio, C. Colón habla a su hijo). [Mairena] (9:24) 87, p. 57-58.
"Tripulantes de las Carabelas" (3 de agosto de 1492, Frescos de Vásques Días en La Rábida . . .). [Mairena] (9:24) 87, p. 58-60.
3306. LOPEZ GONZALEZ, Salvador
"Elegia por una Niña." [Mairena] (9:24) 87, p. 80-81.
3307. LOPEZ SURIA, Violeta
"Isabel Allende." [Mairena] (9:24) 87, p. 110.
LORCA, Federico García
See GARCIA LORCA, Federico
3308. LORDE, Audre
"From the Cave." [Field] (36) Spr 87, p. 89.
"Outlines." [Field] (36) Spr 87, p. 82-87.
3309. LOTT, Rick
"The Engineer." [KanQ] (19:3) Sum 87, p. 210.
"The Gardener." [KanQ] (19:3) Sum 87, p. 210-211.
"Lucy Audubon Speaks to the Night." [SouthernPR] (27:1) Spr 87, p. 15.
3310. LOURIE, Dick
"Friends in Dreams." [HangL] (50/51) 87, p. 111-112.
"Rock and Roll Rhythm and Blues." [HangL] (50/51) 87, p. 113.
3311. LOUTER, David
"The Movements of Horses." [MalR] (79) Je 87, p. 116-117.
3312. LOVE, B. D.
"Dialogue." [Poem] (58) N 87, p. 5.
"His Girl." [HighP] (2:1) Spr 87, p. 12-13.
"His Mirror." [KanQ] (19:3) Sum 87, p. 124-125.
"Lust." [HighP] (2:1) Spr 87, p. 14.
"Seurat: La Cirque." [StoneC] (14:3/4) Spr-Sum 87, p. 48-49.
"Sweethearts Vanish in Tunnel of Love." [LitR] (31:1) Fall 87, p. 32-33.
3313. LOVELOCK, Yann
"The Meon Hill Picket." [Stand] (28:1) Wint 86-87, p. 40.
3314. LOVITT, Robert
"Downtown." [Phoenix] (7:2) 87, p. 38.
"Mr. Doppler and the Speeding Hearts." [Phoenix] (7:2) 87, p. 39.
3315. LOW, Denise
"How to Read Petroglyphs." [Phoenix] (7:1) 87, p. 34.
"Inside the River." [KanQ] (19:1/2) Wint-Spr 87, p. 137.
"Learning the Language of Rivers" (26 Poems). [MidwQ] (28:4) Sum 87, p. 473-510.
"Mastodon Treasure." [KanQ] (19:1/2) Wint-Spr 87, p. 138.
3316. LOW, Jackson Mac
"Pieces o' Six" (VIII, XIII, XIV, XXVII). [Temblor] (5) 87, p. 5-6, 39-40, 92-93, 132-133.
"Pieces o' Six — XXV." [Act] (7) 87, p. 82-84.
"Pieces o' Six — XXVIII." [Conjunc] (11) 87?, p. 145-148.
"Pieces o' Six — XXXII" (Merzgedicht in Memoriam Kurt Schwitters). [Sulfur] (20) Fall 87, p. 123-128.
"Words nd Ends from Ez" (VI. From the Pisan Cantos: LXXIV-LXXXIV, 8/1/81, Ezra Pound). [Temblor] (5) 87, p. 152-156.
3317. LOWE, Frederick
"The Grand Hotel 'Magie de la Lune'." [BelPoJ] (37:3) Spr 87, p. 30.
3318. LOWELL, Douglas
"Desire." [Sulfur] (19) Spr 87, p. 41-42.
"For Max." [Sulfur] (19) Spr 87, p. 42-45.
3319. LOWERY, Joanne
"How Long Is a Long Time." [ManhatPR] (9) Sum 87, p. 14.
"Lady Crane." [ManhatPR] (9) Sum 87, p. 15.
"May 30." [WoosterR] (7) Spr 87, p. 81.
3320. LOWREY, Malcolm
"The Wounded Bat." [NowestR] (25:3) 87, p. 38.
3321. LOY, S. (See also LOY, Sandra)
"The Bottom of the Mountain" (to you, Jack). [MoodySI] (18/19) Fall 87, p. 41.

3322. LOY, Sandra (*See also* LOY, S.)
"Walk step walk step mom in the snow." [PraS] (61:2) Sum 87, p. 86.
3323. LUCAS, Barbara
"First Love." [Outbr] (18/19) Fall 86-Spr 88, p. 96.
"Long Island." [KanQ] (19:3) Sum 87, p. 182-183.
"The Mapmaker's Daughter." [KanQ] (19:3) Sum 87, p. 183.
"Pilgrim State Hospital." [Outbr] (18/19) Fall 86-Spr 88, p. 95.
"Split Custody." [Outbr] (18/19) Fall 86-Spr 88, p. 94.
LUCAS, Eugenio Rentas
See RENTAS LUCAS, Eugenio
3324. LUCIA, Joseph
"Circuit." [PaintedB] (30) 87, p. 63.
"Praising the Geese." [PaintedB] (30) 87, p. 64.
3325. LUCINA, Mary
"Flowers." [AntigR] (68) Wint 87, p. 22.
"Out of the West." [Amelia] (4:3, issue 10) 87, p. 111.
"To Eat #2." [AntigR] (68) Wint 87, p. 21.
3326. LUDVIGSON, Susan
"The Dream of Birds." [Nat] (244:8) 28 F 87, p. 268.
"Dreaming the Latest Version." [MemphisSR] (8:1) Fall 87, p. 30-31.
"The Man Who Loves Coal." [QW] (25) Spr 87, p. 135-136.
"Portrait." [QW] (25) Spr 87, p. 134.
"This Beginning." [SouthernPR] (27:2) Fall 87, p. 70-73.
3327. LUGN, Kristina
"Nobody's Kids" (tr. by Daniel Ogden). [Vis] (25) 87, p. 36.
"SSN" (tr. by Daniel Ogden). [Vis] (23) 87, p. 14.
3328. LUGONES, Leopoldo
"El Pañuelo." [Mairena] (9:24) 87, p. 121.
3329. LUM, Anna
"To an Octogenerian Doing Tai Chi." [RiverS] (24) 87, p. 44.
3330. LUM, Wing Tek
"But My Smile." [BambooR] (33) Spr 87, p. 18-19.
"The Car." [HawaiiR] (20) Fall 86, c87, p. 38.
"Chinese Hot Pot." The Best of [BambooR] [(31-32)] 86, p. 63.
"Expounding the Doubtful Points" (57 poems, for T'ao Ch'ien, for Frank Chin,
    special issue). [BambooR] (34/35) Sum-Fall 87, 107 p.
"I Caught Him Once." The Best of [BambooR] [(31-32)] 86, p. 58.
"Kindergarten." [BambooR] (36) Fall 87, p. 18-19.
"Poet." [BambooR] (36) Fall 87, p. 16-17.
"The Poet Imagines His Grandfather's Thoughts on the Day He Died." The Best of
    [BambooR] [(31-32)] 86, p. 59.
"Resemblances." [HawaiiR] (20) Fall 86, c87, p. 39.
"Riding the North Point Ferry." The Best of [BambooR] [(31-32)] 86, p. 60-62.
"Taking Her to the Open Market." The Best of [BambooR] [(31-32)] 86, p. 56-57.
3331. LUNDAY, Robert
"Cape Fear." [NewEngR] (9:4) Sum 87, p. 388.
"In Mainz, on the Rhine." [CutB] (27/28) 87, p. 74-75.
3332. LUNDE, David
"Beach Blanket Morgan." [BallSUF] (28:4) Aut 87, p. 28.
"Instead." [LightY] '87, c86, p. 194.
"It's Not Easy." [KanQ] (19:1/2) Wint-Spr 87, p. 210.
"Morgan Andretti." [BallSUF] (28:4) Aut 87, p. 28.
"Morgan in the Dark." [BallSUF] (28:4) Aut 87, p. 29.
3333. LUNDY, Tamara
"Group of Shirts Sunning." [Writer] (100:5) My 87, p. 20.
3334. LUNN, Jean
"Rat." [StoneC] (14:3/4) Spr-Sum 87, p. 54.
3335. LUSCHEI, Glenna
"How Will I Care for This Baby?" [GreenfR] (14:1/2) Wint-Spr, p. 213-214.
3336. LUSH, Laura
"The Diver." [Event] (16:1) Mr 87, p. 36-37.
3337. LUSK, Daniel
"Bread and Water." [NoAmR] (272:1) Mr 87, p. 53.
"The Cow Wars: A Homage." [NewL] (53:3) Spr 87, p. 74-77.
"Grieving." [PaintedB] (30) 87, p. 5.
"Northern Lights." [PassN] (8:1) Wint 87, p. 4.

"Reason." [PassN] (8:1) Wint 87, p. 17.
"Work" (for Phil & Cecily). [PaintedB] (30) 87, p. 6.
3338. LUTHER, Susan
"Eclipse." [WindO] (49) Fall 87, p. 53-54.
"To Save the Countryside." [WindO] (49) Fall 87, p. 52-53.
3339. LUTON, Mildred
"Bovine Town." [LightY] '87, c86, p. 179.
"Coup de Grace." [LightY] '87, c86, p. 60.
"Jennifer Blass." [LightY] '87, c86, p. 139.
3340. LUX, Thomas
"Black Road Over Which Green Trees Grow." [VirQR] (63:4) Aut 87, p. 635-636.
"The Perfect God." [AnotherCM] (17) 87, p. 60.
"Still." [Antaeus] (58) Spr 87, p. 243.
"Tarantulas on the Lifebuoy." [Field] (36) Spr 87, p. 104-105.
"Up Late Reading Re WW I." [Antaeus] (58) Spr 87, p. 242.
"Upon Seeing an Ultrasound Photo of an Unborn Child." [VirQR] (63:4) Aut 87, p.
    637-638.
"Voyeur Every Sense." [VirQR] (63:4) Aut 87, p. 636-637.
"Winter River." [BostonR] (12:1) F 87, p. 4.
3341. LUZI, Mario
"And the Wolf" (tr. by Ned Condini). [PartR] (54:3) Sum 87, p. 427-428.
3342. LUZZARO, Susan
"El Otro Lado." [AmerPoR] (16:5) S-O 87, p. 14.
3343. LYLES, Peggy Willis
"All the Way to Heaven: A Revision." [WindO] (48) Spr 87, p. 28.
"And Also Whales." [CapeR] (22:2) Fall 87, p. 37.
3344. LYNCH, Annette
"Lessons." [Poem] (57) Mr 87, p. 39.
"Song of a 118-Year-Old Man." [Poem] (57) Mr 87, p. 40-41.
"Terrain for Guaylin, China" (aboard the launch sailing the Li River). [Poem] (57)
    Mr 87, p. 42.
3345. LYNCH, Charles
"Cables for Your Babel Tour." [BlackALF] (21:3) Fall 87, p. 248.
"Magic Marker Mystifies Manhattan." [BlackALF] (21:3) Fall 87, p. 247-248.
3346. LYNCH, Lawrence W.
"Punctuations" (tr. of Claude Aveline). [AntR] (45:3) Sum 87, p. 297.
3347. LYNCH, Mary Ann
"Something That Stays." [Blueline] (7:2/3 [i.e. 8:2/3?]) 87, p. 56.
3348. LYNCH, Thomas
"Noon on Saturday." [MSS] (5:3) 87, p. 188-189.
3349. LYNSKEY, Edward C.
"Bad Apples." [SnapD] (10:1/2) Wint 87, p. 13.
"Bartholomew's Cobbler." [PoetL] (82:3) Fall 87, p. 161.
"The Diving Bell." [PoetL] (82:1) Spr 87, p. 39.
"Getting Mad and Even." [SouthernPR] (27:1) Spr 87, p. 54.
"Hanging Laundry." [WindO] (49) Fall 87, p. 47.
"Hôpital Albert Schweitzer." [HayF] (2) Spr 87, p. 30.
"If He Hollers, Let Him Go." [WindO] (49) Fall 87, p. 45.
"Kiss of Kin." [CapeR] (22:2) Fall 87, p. 10.
"Kiss of Kin." [MidAR] (7:2) 87, p. 56.
"Kiss of Kin." [Poem] (58) N 87, p. 32.
"The Lame Shall Enter First." [PikeF] (8) Fall 87, p. 12.
"Lillian's Chair." [Blueline] (7:2/3 [i.e. 8:2/3?]) 87, p. 83.
"Little Haiti." [Amelia] (4:3, issue 10) 87, p. 114.
"Little Haiti." [PoetL] (82:1) Spr 87, p. 38.
"Mrs. Lincoln Enters Bellevue Place." [CarolQ] (40:1) Fall 87, p. 53.
"Mrs. Lincoln Enters Bellevue Place." [ColEng] (49:8) D 87, p. 891.
"The Night Light." [HayF] (2) Spr 87, p. 31.
"The Night Light." [SmPd] (24:2) Spr 87, p. 23.
"Polio Summers." [CapeR] (22:2) Fall 87, p. 11.
"Seasons of the Hunter." [Outbr] (18/19) Fall 86-Spr 88, p. 139.
"Shade Tree Mechanics." [AntigR] (71/72) Aut 87-Wint 88, p. 52.
"Shade Tree Mechanics." [Outbr] (18/19) Fall 86-Spr 88, p. 138.
"Storm Windows." [WindO] (49) Fall 87, p. 46.
"The Strange Case of Doctor Mudd." [SouthernHR] (21:2) Spr 87, p. 116.
"Summons to Enigma." [AntigR] (71/72) Aut 87-Wint 88, p. 53.

"The Whore's Coo." [HolCrit] (24:2) Ap 87, p. 19.
"Winter Fields: Getting Through." [HawaiiR] (21) Spr 87, p. 32.
3350. LYON, George Ella
"Choice." [SinW] (31) 87, p. 102.
3351. LYON, Hilary (Hillary)
"The Secret Field." [MidwQ] (29:1) Aut 87, p. 90.
"The Flowers of Spring." [Poem] (58) N 87, p. 18-19.
3352. LYON, Wendy
"A Fable." [LitR] (30:4) Sum 87, p. 618.
"Yet Another Fable." [LitR] (30:4) Sum 87, p. 619.
3353. LYONS, Richard
"About Face." [SoDakR] (25:3) Aut 87, p. 17.
"Appetite" (2 versions). [SoDakR] (25:3) Aut 87, p. 10-11.
"Bus." [SoDakR] (25:3) Aut 87, p. 18.
"Chichikov's Driver." [NewRep] (196:24) 15 Je 87, p. 36.
"Communication." [SoDakR] (25:3) Aut 87, p. 16.
"Dinner Party." [SoDakR] (25:3) Aut 87, p. 14.
"The Doctor & the Young Groom." [Shen] (37:3) 87, p. 59-63.
"Drug Store." [SoDakR] (25:3) Aut 87, p. 19.
"Heritage." [SoDakR] (25:3) Aut 87, p. 20.
"Home." [AntR] (45:3) Sum 87, p. 332-333.
"Inside." [SoDakR] (25:3) Aut 87, p. 9.
"Landscape." [SoDakR] (25:3) Aut 87, p. 12.
"Perspective." [SoDakR] (25:3) Aut 87, p. 15.
"Reality." [SoDakR] (25:3) Aut 87, p. 13-14.
"The Sounds of Music." [SoDakR] (25:3) Aut 87, p. 17.
"These Modern Nights" (to Paul). [IndR] (10:1/2) 87, p. 33-43.
"Windless." [SoDakR] (25:3) Aut 87, p. 19.
"Working." [SoDakR] (25:3) Aut 87, p. 10.
3354. LYONS, Robert
"The Visitors." [BellArk] (3:2) Mr-Ap 87, p. 6.
"The War Years." [BellArk] (3:1) Ja-F 87, p. 10.
3355. MAC, Kathy
"What Is This Thing Called, Love?" [AntigR] (68) Wint 87, p. 132.
Mac . . .
    See also names beginning with Mc . . .
3356. Mac DONAGH, Bernard
"Amber." [Stand] (28:3) Sum 87, p. 58.
Mac LOW, Jackson
    See LOW, Jackson Mac
3357. MacCORNACK, Jonathan
"Tennessee (2)." [AmerPoR] (16:4) Jl-Ag 87, p. 15.
"Toulouse Lautrec." [AmerPoR] (16:4) Jl-Ag 87, p. 15.
3358. MacDONALD, Cynthia
"A Past-Due Notice." [NewRep] (197:20) 16 N 87, p. 38.
3359. MacDONALD, Kathryn
"Emmeline Encounters the Angel of Death and Is Shown the Seven Deadly Sins."
    [BellArk] (3:3) My-Je 87, p. 3.
"Muse." [BellArk] (3:4) Jl-Ag 87, p. 3.
3360. MACHADO, Antonio
"Death of a Wounded Child" (tr. by Joel Zeltzer). [Abraxas] (35/36) 87, p. 48.
"La Muerte del Niño Herido." [Abraxas] (35/36) 87, p. 48.
3361. MACIOCI, R. Nikolas
"Port Clinton Portrait." [WindO] (49) Fall 87, p. 19.
"Rabbit Hunter." [WindO] (49) Fall 87, p. 19.
"Sea Gull Survival." [WindO] (49) Fall 87, p. 18.
3362. MacISAAC, Dan
"Foundations of Cages." [AntigR] (69/70) 87, p. 28.
3363. MACK, Robin
"Love Is a Lot Like Quicksand." [Calyx] (11:1) Wint 87-88, p. 38-39.
"North of Birmingham." [MichQR] (26:1) Wint 87, p. 86.
3364. MACKENZIE, Gareth Morgan
"Mexico City — 1986" (Selection: I). [JamesWR] (4:3) Spr 87, p. 13.
3365. MacKENZIE, Ginny
"Aunt Lena Is Committed to Bellefonte State Hospital." [Ploughs] (13:4) 87, p.
    60-61.

3366. MACKENZIE, Nancy
"At Strome Glen Farm." [CapilR] (43) 87, p. 86.
"Psalmistry." [CapilR] (43) 87, p. 84-85.
"The Yarn." [CapilR] (43) 87, p. 82-83.
3367. MacKENZIE, Robert
"Tearfilm: Lewis 1987." [Verse] (4:2) Je 87, p. 28.
3368. MACKEY, Nathaniel
"Degree Four." [Conjunc] (10) 87, p. 243-245.
"Melin." [Conjunc] (10) 87, p. 245-247.
"Out Island." [Conjunc] (10) 87, p. 247-250.
3369. MacLEOD, Scott
"Twilight." [FiveFR] (5) 87, p. 125-127.
MacLOW, Jackson
    See LOW, Jackson Mac
3370. MacQUEEN, Don
"Good Love Poetry." [Bogg] (58) 87, p. 13.
3371. MacSWEEN, R. J.
"Adam." [AntigR] (71/72) Aut 87-Wint 88, p. 155.
"Crime." [AntigR] (68) Wint 87, p. 51.
"The Fault." [AntigR] (68) Wint 87, p. 49.
"Flying." [AntigR] (69/70) 87, p. 139.
"That Country." [AntigR] (68) Wint 87, p. 50.
"When Time Ceases." [AntigR] (71/72) Aut 87-Wint 88, p. 156.
3372. MADDEN, David
"The Day's Images." [NowestR] (25:3) 87, p. 134-135.
3373. MADDOX, Marjorie
"Threading the Needle." [KanQ] (19:3) Sum 87, p. 252-253.
3374. MADIGAN, Mark
"Letter to Monet." [Poetry] (150:3) Je 87, p. 160.
3375. MADRAZO, Jorge Ariel
"Escribe la Azalea." [Inti] (24/25) Otoño 86-Primavera 87, p. 262.
"Gertrude Stein Dixit." [Inti] (24/25) Otoño 86-Primavera 87, p. 263.
"Jauría." [Inti] (24/25) Otoño 86-Primavera 87, p. 261.
3376. MADSON, Arthur
"Antepenultimate." [CapeR] (22:2) Fall 87, p. 15.
"How to Make a Bear-Claw Necklace." [CapeR] (22:2) Fall 87, p. 20-21.
"Priapus Impotens." [KanQ] (19:3) Sum 87, p. 196-199.
"Saguaro." [KanQ] (19:3) Sum 87, p. 200.
"Still Life." [PoetL] (82:1) Spr 87, p. 13.
3377. MADZELAN, Pete
"Seasons: Let Me Give You" (for Laurie). [Wind] (17:61) 87, p. 28.
3378. MAGARRELL, Elaine
"Loosestrife." [LightY] '87, c86, p. 85-86.
"Reunion." [NewEngR] (10:2) Wint 87, p. 233.
"Wise." [Bogg] (58) 87, p. 48.
3379. MAGDER, Steven
"Sonnet #3 to Baudelaire." [CapeR] (22:1) Spr 87, p. 14.
3380. MAGEE, Kevin
"After Whitman (Gramsci's Whitman)." [Ploughs] (13:4) 87, p. 63.
"The Boss & His Beauty." [Ploughs] (13:4) 87, p. 62.
3381. MAGER, Don
"The Bowl of Roses" (tr. of Rainer Maria Rilke). [BlackWR] (13:2) Spr 87, p. 70-72.
MAGGIO, Jill di
    See DiMAGGIO, Jill
3382. MAGINNES, Al
"Bull Town." [TarPR] (27:1) Fall 87, p. 21.
"Sleepwalking Boy." [GreensboroR] (43) Wint 87-88, p. 126.
3383. MAGOWAN, Robin
"A Hundred Sentences Written on Fans" (Excerpts, tr. of Paul Claudel). [Margin] (1) Wint 86, p. 14-21.
3384. MAGWOOD, Chris
"With a Lake for a Hat." [Rampike] (5:3) 87, p. 74.
3385. MAHAFFEY, Phillip
"Dodson" (the Dodson Ranch, Big Bend). [WritersF] (13) Fall 87, p. 150-151.

3386. MAHAPATRA, Jayanta
"All the Poetry There Is." [WestHR] (41:2) Sum 87, p. 141-142.
"Another Autumn." [Hudson] (40:3) Aut 87, p. 443-444.
"Behind." [Chelsea] (46) 87, p. 210.
"December." [Chelsea] (46) 87, p. 208.
"Doors." [Poetry] (151:1/2) O-N 87, p. 96.
"The Hill." [CrossCur] (7:3) 87, p. 27.
"House." [Chelsea] (46) 87, p. 209.
"A Morning Walk in Bhopal." [SewanR] (95:1) Wint 87, p. 16.
"An October Morning." [Chelsea] (46) 87, p. 213.
"Of Independence Day." [Poetry] (150:4) Jl 87, p. 203-204.
"A Time." [Chelsea] (46) 87, p. 211.
"Twilight." [Chelsea] (46) 87, p. 212.
"Unreal Country." [SewanR] (95:1) Wint 87, p. 15.
3387. MAHON, Derek
"A Garage in Co. Cork." [Pembroke] (19) 87, p. 85-86.
"Night Drive" (after Rilke — St. Peterburg, 1900). [Hudson] (39:4) Wint 87, p. 614.
"October." [Hudson] (39:4) Wint 87, p. 615.
3388. MAHON, Robert L.
"A Gloss Upon King Lear." [CapeR] (22:1) Spr 87, p. 39.
"Telemachus." [CapeR] (22:1) Spr 87, p. 38.
3389. MAHONEY, Denis
"Black Pig" (Selections: 3 sections). [Temblor] (6) 87, p. 51-59.
3390. MAIER, Carol
"Doorknob" (tr. of Octavio Armand). [NewOR] (14:1) Spr 87, p. 55.
3391. MAILMAN, Leo
"The All-Purpose Stomach." [WormR] (27:4, issue 108) 87, p. 108-109.
"Victorian Times." [WormR] (27:4, issue 108) 87, p. 107-108.
3392. MAIN, Pamela
"Self-Portrait of a Dyslexic Child" (for Kristen at twenty). [Outbr] (18/19) Fall 86-Spr 88, p. 18.
3393. MAIO, Samuel
"Glass House." [CharR] (13:2) Fall 87, p. 92.
3394. MAITA, Carlos Jesus
"Caballo Confuso II." [Mairena] (9:24) 87, p. 65.
"Caballo Confuso VI." [Mairena] (9:24) 87, p. 66.
"Pared Informe III." [Mairena] (9:24) 87, p. 65-66.
3395. MAIZELL, Sylvia
"Song About a Dog" (tr. of Sergey Esenin, w. Robert L. Smith). [BlueBldgs] (9) 85?, p. 24. Erratum in [BlueBldgs] (10) 87?, p. 2.
3396. MAJ, Bronislaw
"The Air Between Us" (tr. by Daniel Bourne). [StoneC] (14:3/4) Spr-Sum 87, p. 59.
"Is It Right" (tr. by Daniel Bourne). [CrossCur] (7:3) 87, p. 58.
"Wspólne Powietrze" (Excerpts). [StoneC] (14:3/4) Spr-Sum 87, p. 58.
3397. MAJER, Gerald
"After Dark." [PennR] (3:2) Fall-Wint 87, p. 27.
3398. MAJOR, Alice
"Boxes." [Waves] (14:4) Spr 86, p. 70.
"Palliative Care." [Event] (16:1) Mr 87, p. 75.
3399. MAKI, Wendy
"Learning to Live on the Edge of a Precipice." [Waves] (15:1/2) Fall 86, p. 74.
3400. MAKOFSKE, Mary
"A House Is Only a Possession." [Lactuca] (5) Ja 87, p. 18-19.
"Storm on Good Friday." [CumbPR] (6:2) Spr 87, p. 26.
"An Unbeliever Who Watched from Her Garden the Pentecostals Waiting for the Lord's Last Judgment." [Raccoon] (24/25) My 87, p. 46.
3401. MAKUCK, Peter
"Ceremony." [LaurelR] (21:1/2) Wint-Sum 87, p. 55-56.
"Equations." [GeoR] (41:4) Wint 87, p. 691.
"Heaven." [LaurelR] (21:1/2) Wint-Sum 87, p. 58.
"Phantoms at Swan Quarter." [PoetL] (82:1) Spr 87, p. 14-15.
"Picnic at St. Remy." [StoneC] (14:3/4) Spr-Sum 87, p. 57.
"Valluris: Cafe des Voyageurs." [StoneC] (14:3/4) Spr-Sum 87, p. 56-57.
"With My Father at Emerald Island." [LaurelR] (21:1/2) Wint-Sum 87, p. 57-58.

3402. MALANGA, Gerard
"Forty-One Line Poem" (for Sarah Greenleaf Whittier). [Raccoon] (24/25) My 87, p. 172-173.
"Two Variations and 3 Additional Parts" (for Lindsay). [Caliban] (3) 87, p. 71-74.
3403. MALANGE, Nise
"I, the Unemployed." [TriQ] (69) Spr-Sum 87, p. 294-295.
3404. MALDONADO, Rosa Elena
"Coronary" (In Memoriam, tr. by Claudette Columbus and David Weiss). [SenR] (17:1) 87, p. 40.
"Desire" (tr. by Claudette Columbus and David Weiss). [SenR] (17:1) 87, p. 42.
"Dreams on a Nonexistent Shore" (tr. by Claudette Columbus and David Weiss). [SenR] (17:1) 87, p. 43.
"Inheritance" (tr. by Claudette Columbus and David Weiss). [SenR] (17:1) 87, p. 39.
"Not the City" (tr. by Claudette Columbus and David Weiss). [SenR] (17:1) 87, p. 41.
MALE, Belkis Cuza
   See CUZA MALE, Belkis
3405. MALKUS, Steven (See also MALKUS, Steven W.)
"Stones in Domino." [HarvardA] (120:2) Mr 87, p. 11.
3406. MALKUS, Steven W. (See also MALKUS, Steven)
"Fog on Vineyard Sound." [Outbr] (18/19) Fall 86-Spr 88, p. 81.
"My Eagle." [Outbr] (18/19) Fall 86-Spr 88, p. 79-80.
"Strings of a Blue Guitar." [Outbr] (18/19) Fall 86-Spr 88, p. 82.
3407. MALLORY, Norman
"Fiddler in the Surgery (Enloe Hospital, 1966)." [AntigR] (68) Wint 87, p. 93.
"The Idiot (Enloe Hospital, 1966)." [AntigR] (68) Wint 87, p. 92-93.
3408. MALONE, E. T., Jr.
"Stuck in the Middle of the Comfort Zone." [Pembroke] (19) 87, p. 171-172.
3409. MALONE, Eileen
"Our Coyote." [GreenfR] (14:1/2) Wint-Spr, p. 41.
3410. MALONE, Jacquelyn
"A Quantum Elegy" (for E.K.M., 1940-1986). [PoetryNW] (28:1) Spr 87, p. 7.
3411. MALONE, Joe
"Song of the Young Man" (tr. of Nuala Ní Dhomhnaill). [YellowS] (25) Wint 87, p. 24.
"YaΔe." [Lips] (13) 87, p. 28.
3412. MALONE, Pamela Altfeld
"I Went in Search." [BellArk] (3:3) My-Je 87, p. 10.
"Summer." [BellArk] (3:2) Mr-Ap 87, p. 1.
3413. MALONEY, Dennis
"Nocturne" (tr. of Juan Ramón Jiménez, w. Clark Zlotchew). [AmerPoR] (16:6) N-D 87, p. 47.
"Smoke and Gold" (to Enrique and Amparo Granados, tr. of Juan Ramón Jiménez, w. Clark Zlotchew). [AmerPoR] (16:6) N-D 87, p. 47.
3414. MALYON, Carol
"In Retrospect." [Event] (16:3) Fall 87, p. 82-84.
3415. MAMO, Catherine
"Argument." [Waves] (14:4) Spr 86, p. 61-62.
"Resurrection." [Waves] (14:4) Spr 86, p. 63.
3416. MANABE, Jody
"Dear Reiko, 1968/1978." The Best of [BambooR] [(31-32)] 86, p. 46-48.
3417. MANAZAR GAMBOA, Manuel
"Buttonwillow." [Electrum] (39) Fall-Wint 87, p. 33.
"Till the Bumpers Fall Off" (for Kathy). [Electrum] (39) Fall-Wint 87, p. 35.
3418. MANCILLA, Yolanda
"Niña." [Calyx] (10:2/3) Spr 87, p. 65-66.
3419. MANDEL, Charlotte
"My Mother Giving Orders on the Day Before She Died." [Lips] (13) 87, p. 29.
"Pietà." [Raccoon] (24/25) My 87, p. 200.
3420. MANDEL, Tom
"Hungry and Waiting." [Sulfur] (20) Fall 87, p. 79-81.
"In Empire Camp" (from "Realism"). [Bound] (14:1/2) Fall 85-Wint 86 [c87], p. 5-6.
"These stars, they lock together." [Sulfur] (20) Fall 87, p. 82.

3421. MANDELSTAM, Osip
"Below Thunderclouds There Floats" (in Russian and English, tr. by R. H. Morrison). [AntigR] (71/72) Aut 87-Wint 88, p. 124-125.
"Impressionism" (tr. by James Greene). [NewYorker] (63:13) 18 My 87, p. 40.
"Like a Serpent, I Am Hidden" (in Russian and English, tr. by R. H. Morrison). [AntigR] (71/72) Aut 87-Wint 88, p. 124-125.
"Self-Portrait" (tr. by James Greene). [NewYorker] (63:13) 18 My 87, p. 40.
"The Wave Advances" (tr. by James Greene). [NewYorker] (63:13) 18 My 87, p. 40.
"What Steepness There Is in the Crystal Pool" (in Russian and English, tr. by R. H. Morrison). [AntigR] (71/72) Aut 87-Wint 88, p. 122-123.
3422. MANFRED, Freya
"May in Minnesota." [Farm] (4:1) Wint 87, p. 41.
3423. MANG, Ke
"Darling" (tr. by Willis and Tony Barnstone). [AmerPoR] (16:4) Jl-Ag 87, p. 40.
"Return" (tr. by Willis and Tony Barnstone). [AmerPoR] (16:4) Jl-Ag 87, p. 40.
"To Children" (tr. by Willis and Tony Barnstone). [AmerPoR] (16:4) Jl-Ag 87, p. 40.
"Yesterday and Today" (tr. by Willis and Tony Barnstone). [AmerPoR] (16:4) Jl-Ag 87, p. 41.
3424. MANGAN, Kathy
"A Perfect Day." [SenR] (17:2) 87, p. 60.
"Winter Solstice, Without You." [Raccoon] (24/25) My 87, p. 159.
3425. MANGANELLI, Giorgio
"The Architect, the Commander and the Lily Creature" (tr. by John Satriano). [Rampike] (5:3) 87, p. 38-39.
3426. MANGER, Itzik
"Execution" (tr. by Murray Wolfe). [WebR] (12:2) Fall 87, p. 9.
3427. MANICOM, David
"In a Station of the Montréal Metro." [Event] (16:1) Mr 87, p. 66-67.
"Love Alight." [Grain] (15:4) Wint 87, p. 33.
"Lunacy" (Li Po, 701-62). [Grain] (15:4) Wint 87, p. 32.
"Salisbury Plain." [Shen] (37:4) 87, p. 79-80.
3428. MANIS, William Michael
"Sad Bear" (for Richard Hugo). [PoetL] (81:3) Fall 86, p. 182.
3429. MANLEY, Frank
"Noah's Birds." [CanLit] (112) Spr 87, p. 59.
3430. MANN, Jeff
"Late December Sunset." [LaurelR] (20:1/2) Sum 87, p. 118.
"The Margarita Party." [JamesWR] (4:4) Sum 87, p. 15.
"Summer Ghazal #5." [JamesWR] (4:4) Sum 87, p. 15.
"Yams." [LaurelR] (20:1/2) Sum 87, p. 119.
MANNA, Richard la
See LaMANNA, Richard
3431. MANOUSOS, Anthony
"The Correct Way" (for Richard Shrobe). [AntigR] (68) Wint 87, p. 10.
"First Noble Truth." [AntigR] (68) Wint 87, p. 11.
3432. MANRIQUE, Jaime
"El Cielo Encima de la Casa de Mi Madre." [LindLM] (6:4) O-D 87, p. 13.
"Dias de Barcelona" (Para Miguel Falquez). [LindLM] (6:4) O-D 87, p. 13.
"Tu Arte Inmaculado, Billie Holiday." [LindLM] (6:4) O-D 87, p. 13.
3433. MANROE, Candace Ord
"Elusive." [TexasR] (8:3/4) Fall-Wint 87, p. 88-89.
3434. MANSELL, Chris
"Dialogue." [Waves] (15:1/2) Fall 86, p. 73.
3435. MANSOUR, Joyce
"Don't Eat" (tr. by Larry Couch). [Vis] (25) 87, p. 27.
"Invite Me" (tr. by Larry Couch). [Vis] (23) 87, p. 15.
"Night and I'm the Vagrant" (tr. by Elton Glaser and Jancie Fritsch). [ColR] (NS 14:1) Spr-Sum 87, p. 32.
"Night I Am Vagabond" (tr. by Larry Couch). [Vis] (24) 87, p. 25.
"The Telephone Rings" (tr. by Larry Couch). [Vis] (23) 87, p. 15.
3436. MANSOUR, Mónica
"La Disco del Pueblo" (tr. of John Oliver Simon). [Electrum] (39) Fall-Wint 87, p. 29, 31.

3437. MAO, Douglas
"Two Autumns." [HarvardA] (121:3) My 87, p. 16.
"The Uncarved Block as Fallacy." [HarvardA] (120:2) Mr 87, p. 29.
3438. MARCANO MONTAÑEZ, Jaime
"Amor del Siglo XX." [Mairena] (9:24) 87, p. 79-80.
"En la Noche de los Siglos." [Mairena] (9:24) 87, p. 78.
3439. MARCH, Michael
"Mass for the Imprisoned" (tr. of Zbigniew Herbert, w. Jaroslaw Anders).
[NewYRB] (33:21-22) 15 Ja 87, p. 15.
3440. MARCHAMPS, Guy
"Sédiments de l'Amnésie" (extrait). [Os] (25) 87, p. 23.
3441. MARCUS, Mordecai
"A Careful Celebration." [TarPR] (27:1) Fall 87, p. 37.
"A Debate Between Yvor Winters and Charles Bukowski." [PoetL] (81:4) Wint
86-87, p. 237-238.
"Full-Bodied." [Poem] (57) Mr 87, p. 14.
"Indelicacy Exposed." [TarPR] (27:1) Fall 87, p. 36.
"Lech Walesa." [PoetL] (81:4) Wint 86-87, p. 235-236.
3442. MARCUS, Stanley
"Airraid Drill." [ColEng] (49:5) S 87, p. 538.
"At the Office." [NoDaQ] (55:3) Sum 87, p. 84-85.
"Bad News." [ColEng] (49:5) S 87, p. 537-538.
"Recovery Room." [ColEng] (49:5) S 87, p. 539.
"Summer Journal." [ColEng] (49:5) S 87, p. 540-541.
"War Babies." [MinnR] (NS 28) Spr 87, p. 14.
3443. MARGOLIS, Gary
"Did You Bring Me Anything?" [Poetry] (151:1/2) O-N 87, p. 97.
3444. MARGOSHES, Dave
"Arguing with Science." [CanLit] (113/114) Sum-Fall 87, p. 91-92.
"On Being 40." [Waves] (15:1/2) Fall 86, p. 84.
3445. MARIA, Barbara
"Second Generation." [SinW] (31) 87, p. 23.
3446. MARIANI, Paul
"Catalpa." [Agni] (24/25) 87, p. 58-59.
"The Gospel According to Walter." [Ploughs] (13:4) 87, p. 64-65.
"Landscape with Visionary Blue." [Ploughs] (13:4) 87, p. 66-67.
"The Note." [Raccoon] (24/25) My 87, p. 68-69.
3447. MARIE, Tydal
"A Smile for Mrs. McWethy" (1986 Finalist, Eve of Saint Agnes Poetry
Competition). [NegC] (7:1/2) 87, p. 219.
3448. MARINDAHL, Michael
"How Can Anyone." [Pig] (14) 87, p. 66.
3449. MARINO, Olivia
"Interpretation" (for Bryan, and his class, at Cascia). [Nimrod] (31:1) Fall-Wint 87,
p. 113-114.
3450. MARION, Jeff Daniel
"Stroke by Stroke." [SouthernPR] (27:1) Spr 87, p. 16.
3451. MARION, Paul
"Merrimack Street." [MoodySI] (18/19) Fall 87, p. 41.
MARIS, Ron de
See De MARIS, Ron
3452. MARKERT, Lawrence
"Bringing Back the Dead." [BlackWR] (13:2) Spr 87, p. 68.
"Standing Mute." [Wind] (17:59) 87, p. 32-33.
3453. MARKHAM, Jacquelyn
"Peeling Apples" (for Mother). [Poem] (57) Mr 87, p. 38.
3454. MARKS, Gigi
"Approach." [CarolQ] (40:1) Fall 87, p. 56.
"Surface Water." [SouthernPR] (27:2) Fall 87, p. 49.
3455. MARKS, S. J.
"Clouded Sky" (tr. of Miklós Radnóti, w. Steven Polgar and Stephen Berg. Entire
issue). [PoetryE] (22) Spr 87, 113 p.
"Losing Myself." [AmerPoR] (16:6) N-D 87, p. 45.
"November Woods" (for Masao Abe). [AmerPoR] (16:6) N-D 87, p. 45.
"The Poem." [AntR] (45:4) Fall 87, p. 441.
"Poem in Three Parts." [AmerPoR] (16:6) N-D 87, p. 44.

"Poem with Two Seasons Right Now." [AmerPoR] (16:6) N-D 87, p. 45.
"Returning in Wind and Drizzle to My Home." [AmerPoR] (16:6) N-D 87, p. 45.
"To Go Through Life Is to Walk Across a Field." [AmerPoR] (16:6) N-D 87, p. 44.
"To the Ocean." [AmerPoR] (16:6) N-D 87, p. 46-47.
3456. MARKS, Sharon
"A Little Death." [Vis] (23) 87, p. 29.
3457. MARLATT, Daphne
"Channel time." [CrossC] (9:3/4) 87, p. 14.
"River run." [CrossC] (9:3/4) 87, p. 15.
3458. MARLIS, Stefanie
"The Force of His Sadness." [BlackWR] (14:1) Fall 87, p. 40.
"Masseuse." [Zyzzyva] (3:2) Sum 87, p. 130.
"Remembering About Love." [BlackWR] (14:1) Fall 87, p. 90.
"Turning from the News." [MinnR] (NS 28) Spr 87, p. 16.
"Weight Lifter." [Thrpny] (31) Fall 87, p. 8.
3459. MARMON, Sharon
"At the Park." [PoetL] (81:3) Fall 86, p. 164.
"Only the Rich Give Birth to Angels." [PoetL] (81:4) Wint 86-87, p. 225.
"Sally's First Train Ride — 1910." [PoetL] (81:3) Fall 86, p. 163.
3460. MARSDEN, Carolyn
"On Hubbel's Constant." [Sonora] (12) Spr 87, p. 31.
3461. MARSH, Tony
"On Reading a Recent Biography." [KanQ] (19:1/2) Wint-Spr 87, p. 114.
3462. MARSH, William
"Still Born." [PoetL] (81:3) Fall 86, p. 179.
3463. MARSHALL, Ernest
"How to Bake Bread." [GreensboroR] (43) Wint 87-88, p. 116.
3464. MARSHALL, Gregory
"The Left Atrium." [PraS] (61:1) Spr 87, p. 18-21.
3465. MARSHALL, J. M.
"Oncoming Season." [KanQ] (19:3) Sum 87, p. 174.
3466. MARSHALL, Jack
"Deal." [FiveFR] (5) 87, p. 107-109.
"The Rest of It." [Zyzzyva] (3:3) Fall 87, p. 116-117.
3467. MARSHBURN, Sandra
"Here in This Room." [Wind] (17:60) 87, p. 24.
"River Rat." [LaurelR] (20:1/2) Sum 87, p. 94.
"South Shore Bus Driver." [LaurelR] (20:1/2) Sum 87, p. 96.
"While You Were Asleep." [LaurelR] (20:1/2) Sum 87, p. 95.
3468. MARTEAU, Robert
"Août sur les chaumes abandonnés, aux antennes." [Os] (25) 87, p. 29.
"Au bord de l'étang les peupliers soufflent." [Os] (25) 87, p. 15.
"Corot s'éclaire du premier rayon de jour." [Os] (25) 87, p. 27.
"Le lavis mouvant dont les nuages s'imprègnent." [Os] (25) 87, p. 28.
"Le mond fut fabuleux, l'univers unique." [Os] (25) 87, p. 14.
"Paris scintille: c'est le matin sur la Seine." [Os] (25) 87, p. 16.
3469. MARTEL, Richard
"Performance Danois" (text from a perfomance piece executed while on tour in
    Denmark). [Rampike] (5:3) 87, p. 45.
"Performance Italien" (text from a perfomance piece presented while on tour in Italy).
    [Rampike] (5:3) 87, p. 44.
MARTHA CHRISTINA
    See CHRISTINA, Martha
MARTHA ELIZABETH
    See ELIZABETH, Martha
3470. MARTIAL
"Epigrams" (8 poems, tr. by Joseph S. Salemi). [Trans] (18) Spr 87, p. 300-303.
3471. MARTIN, Charles
"Design." [Boulevard] (2:1/2) Spr 87, p. 161.
"Easter Sunday, 1985." [Boulevard] (2:1/2) Spr 87, p. 159.
"Metaphor of Grass in California." [Boulevard] (2:1/2) Spr 87, p. 160.
3472. MARTIN, J.
"The Hurt." [MassR] (28:2) Sum 87, p. 293-297.
"My Friend, Ludwig Wittgenstein, and the Force of My Friendship with
    Wittgentstein . . ." [ParisR] (29:102) Spr 87, p. 149-153.

3473. MARTIN, Jeffrey
"And There Are Sundays." [Footwork] 87, p. 57.
3474. MARTIN, Jennifer
"Sunday Painting." [ParisR] (29:105) Wint 87, p. 101.
3475. MARTIN, Kathi
"Homebodies / Statement of Intent / Introduction." [BlueBldgs] (10) 87?, p. 34.
3476. MARTIN, Lindsey
"Truckdriver's Wife." [NewL] (53:3) Spr 87, p. 99.
3477. MARTIN, Lynn
"Lenten Sequence" (for Abby Niebauer 1937-1985). [IndR] (11:1) Wint 87, p. 85-88.
"The Woman Who Married Forever." [CentR] (31:3) Sum 87, p. 273-274.
3478. MARTIN, Mary E.
"I Could Waltz Across Texas with You" (for T. R.). [SouthernPR] (27:1) Spr 87, p. 9.
3479. MARTIN, Reginald
"In September." [BallSUF] (28:4) Aut 87, p. 57.
3480. MARTIN, Richard
"They." [AnotherCM] (17) 87, p. 61.
3481. MARTIN, Sharon (See also MARTIN, Sharon E.)
"Brandywine." [LaurelR] (20:1/2) Sum 87, p. 87.
"Coming by Train, Through Orchards." [LaurelR] (20:1/2) Sum 87, p. 86.
3482. MARTIN, Sharon E. (See also MARTIN, Sharon)
"Untitled: The cold's here, settling in." [Amelia] (4:1/2, issue 9) 87, p. 29.
3483. MARTIN, Stephen-Paul
"Cellular Mythologies" (for Beth). [CentralP] (11) Spr 87, p. 90-102.
"Condo Buena Vista." [Act] (7) 87, p. 81.
3484. MARTINEZ, Dionisio D.
"By Closing Time Even the Angels Are Out of Luck." [Sonora] (13) Fall 87, p. 89.
"Desire on a Street Called Texas." [Sonora] (13) Fall 87, p. 90-91.
"Imaginary Cargo: El Mariel, 1980." [Caliban] (3) 87, p. 127.
"Real Life." [Caliban] (3) 87, p. 128.
3485. MARTINEZ, Jan
"Canción del Diverso Tiempo." [Inti] (24/25) Otoño 86-Primavera 87, p. 251-253.
3486. MARTINEZ, Mirna
"Ars Poetica" (tr. by Zoe Anglesey). [StoneC] (15:1/2) Fall-Wint 87-88, p. 51.
"Arte Poetica." [StoneC] (15:1/2) Fall-Wint 87-88, p. 50.
"Palabra Amor Mío." [Cond] (14) 87, p. 196.
"Word" (tr. by Zoë Anglesey). [Cond] (14) 87, p. 197.
3487. MARTINEZ, Ramón E.
"After Lorca." [BlackWR] (13:2) Spr 87, p. 65.
"Compass at True North." [GreenfR] (14:3/4) Sum-Fall 87, p. 39.
"Dandelion Fireworks" (for Norman Dubie). [VirQR] (63:4) Aut 87, p. 640-641.
"Drowning Poem." [GrahamHR] (10) Wint-Spr 87, p. 27.
"Mexican Gold Poppies at Picacho Peak." [GrahamHR] (10) Wint-Spr 87, p. 26.
"Rorschach Poem Number One." [MidwQ] (28:3) Spr 87, p. 360.
"Seeing in the True Light." [GreenfR] (14:3/4) Sum-Fall 87, p. 40.
"Zipper." [Electrum] (39) Fall-Wint 87, p. 40.
3488. MARTINI, Stelio Maria
"E/Mana/Azione N.5" (E/Mana/Ation No.5). [Caliban] (2) 87, p. 67.
3489. MARTINO, Mauro
"Tonight It's My Grandfather." [CrossC] (9:2) 87, p. 15.
3490. MARTINS, Max
"Black and Black" (tr. by James Bogan). [NewL] (53:3) Spr 87, p. 115.
"Musicstone" (tr. by James Bogan). [NewL] (53:3) Spr 87, p. 113.
"This for That" (tr. by James Bogan). [NewL] (53:3) Spr 87, p. 113.
"To Shan-Hui" (tr. by James Bogan). [NewL] (53:3) Spr 87, p. 115.
3491. MARTINSON, Harry
"Tussock" (tr. by William Jay Smith and Leif Sjöberg). [GreenfR] (14:1/2) Wint-Spr, p. 92.
3492. MARTINUIK, Lorraine
"Far Enough Down Any Road." [Dandel] (14:1) Spr-Sum 87, p. 18.
3493. MARTY, Sid
"At the Breaking of Drought." [MalR] (80) S 87, p. 110.
"Funny How Things Go On." [PraF] (8:2) Sum 87, p. 21.
"Medicine." [Grain] (15:4) Wint 87, p. 74-75.

"Sky Humour." [MalR] (80) S 87, p. 111.
"You Had to Be There." [PraF] (8:2) Sum 87, p. 20.
3494. MARX, Anne
"Girl Aloft with Longing." [NegC] (7:3/4) 87, p. 154.
3495. MARZANO, Nick
"Rx." [JamesWR] (4:2) Wint 87, p. 3.
3496. MASARIK, Al
"Blue Claw." [PaintedB] (30) 87, p. 57-58.
"The First Line of a Poem." [Raccoon] (24/25) My 87, p. 60.
"Reading You My New Poems." [Raccoon] (24/25) My 87, p. 61.
"Red-Winged Blackbird." [Raccoon] (24/25) My 87, p. 108.
"Truck Farmer." [Raccoon] (24/25) My 87, p. 59.
3497. MASIZA, Zolisa
"The Pain." [AmerPoR] (16:5) S-O 87, p. 21.
3498. MASON, David
"The Old Brit." [CumbPR] (6:2) Spr 87, p. 16-17.
"A Textbook of Navigation and Nautical Astronomy." [Boulevard] (2:1/2) Spr 87, p.
207-208.
3499. MASON, Kenneth C.
"Carnivore." [KanQ] (19:3) Sum 87, p. 185.
3500. MASSARO, Sheryl
"Awaiting Crickets" (1987 Ratner-Ferber-Poet Lore Honorable Mention). [PoetL]
(82:2) Sum 87, p. 83-84.
MASSMAN, Gordon Lester
See LESTER-MASSMAN, Gordon
3501. MASTERSON, Dan
"Bygones." [MemphisSR] (8:1) Fall 87, p. 61-62.
"Heron." [Ploughs] (13:1) 87, p. 86-88.
"White-Tail." [NoDaQ] (55:2) Spr 87, p. 127-128.
3502. MASUNAGA, Lynn
"At Jefferson Park" (for Jeff). [BellArk] (3:6) N-D 87, p. 5.
3503. MATAS, Julio
"Paseo del Oscuro." [LindLM] (6:2/3) Ap-S 87, p. 8.
3504. MATÉ, Sarah
"Advice to a Poet" (for L.P.). [PoetL] (81:4) Wint 86-87, p. 224.
"Junkyard Man." [PoetL] (81:4) Wint 86-87, p. 222.
"Secrets." [PoetL] (81:4) Wint 86-87, p. 223.
3505. MATHAI, Anna Sujatha
"Families." [Chelsea] (46) 87, p. 240.
"Ishvari's Voice." [Chelsea] (46) 87, p. 241.
3506. MATHIS, Cleopatra
"Eve: Twelve Lessons in Clarity and Grace." [GreenfR] (14:1/2) Wint-Spr, p.
97-102.
"In a White Absence: Fog and Earthlight." [DenQ] (22:1) Sum 87, p. 43-44.
"In a White Absence: Fog and Earthlight." [SenR] (17:1) 87, p. 7-8.
"July Run." [SenR] (17:1) 87, p. 9.
"Living Next Door to the Center for Cold Weather." [MichQR] (26:1) Wint 87, p.
89-91.
"A Summer Anatomy." [TexasR] (7:3/4) 87, p. 97-98.
3507. MATHIS-EDDY, Darlene
"Widow's Walk." [Calyx] (10:2/3) Spr 87, p. 118-119.
3508. MATOS PAOLI, Francisco
"A Ramon Zapata Acosta." [Mairena] (9:23) 87, p. 104.
"Cesar Vallejo." [Mairena] (9:24) 87, p. 44-45.
3509. MATSON, Clive
"Amazing." [YellowS] (24) Aut 87, p. 16.
"Bedside." [YellowS] (24) Aut 87, p. 5.
"Dream of Rebirth." [HangL] (50/51) 87, p. 115-117.
"Early Love." [HangL] (50/51) 87, p. 114.
3510. MATSUEDA, Pat
"Donnie's Poem" (d, 1954). [BambooR] (33) Spr 87, p. 60.
"Wave of Cereus." [BambooR] (33) Spr 87, p. 61.
3511. MATTHEWS, William
"April in the Berkshires." [ParisR] (29:102) Spr 87, p. 191.
"Herd of Buffalo Crossing the Missouri River on Ice." [Atlantic] (259:4) Ap 87, p.
66.

"School Days." [Poetry] (151:1/2) O-N 87, p. 98.
3512. MATTHIAS, John
"Ballad" (tr. of Branko Miljkovic, w. Vladeta Vukovic). [Margin] (2) Spr 87, p. 59.
"Earth and Fire" (tr. of Branko Miljkovic, w. Vladeta Vukovic). [Margin] (2) Spr 87, p. 58.
"Facts from an Apocryphal Midwest" (For Ken Smith and Michael Anania). [AnotherCM] (17) 87, p. 62-80.
"In Praise of Fire" (tr. of Branko Miljkovic, w. Vladeta Vukovic). [Margin] (2) Spr 87, p. 57.
"An Orphic Legacy" (tr. of Branko Miljkovic, w. Vladeta Vukovic). [Margin] (2) Spr 87, p. 58.
3513. MATTSON, Nancy
"Maps." [CapilR] (45) 87 [Ap 88], p. 16-17.
"Snapshot." [CapilR] (45) 87 [Ap 88], p. 15.
3514. MATUTE, Carmen
"Guatemala, Your Name" (to Luis Alfredo Arango, tr. by Jo Anne Engelbert). [AmerV] (8) Fall 87, p. 52-53.
3515. MAVIGLIA, Joe
"Navigation." [Event] (16:1) Mr 87, p. 40.
3516. MAXMIN, Jody
"Ancient Manners, Ancient Folds." [PraS] (61:2) Sum 87, p. 104.
"Illuminated Manuscript" (for Lorenz Eitner). [PraS] (61:2) Sum 87, p. 105-106.
3517. MAXSON, Gloria A.
"Elegies in a City Churchyard." [LightY] '87, c86, p. 239-240.
"Worshiper." [LightY] '87, c86, p. 84.
3518. MAXWELL, Glyn
"Second Son in Exile." [Verse] (4:2) Je 87, p. 51.
3519. MAY, Kathy
"My Grandmother's Hands." [ChatR] (8:1) Fall 87, p. 69.
3520. MAY, Kerry Paul
"A Portrait of My Father." [NowestR] (25:1) 87, p. 38.
3521. MAY, Wong
"The Difficulty of Moonlight in the 6th Arrondissement." [NewYorker] (63:20) 6 Jl 87, p. 36.
3522. MAYHALL, Jane
"Asparagus Nuns." [Interim] (6:2) Fall 87, p. 31.
"Daisies." [Interim] (6:2) Fall 87, p. 32.
"Oslo." [Interim] (6:2) Fall 87, p. 33.
3523. MAYHEW, Lenore
"Love Prelude from a Quasida" (tr. of Ka'b ibn Zuhair). [NewOR] (14:1) Spr 87, p. 68.
3524. MAYNE, Robert L.
"Van Gogh's Last." [Writer] (100:5) My 87, p. 19.
3525. MAYRÖCKER, Friederike
"Franz Schubert, Or: Notes on the Weather, Vienna" (tr. by Rosmarie Waldrop). [Sulfur] (20) Fall 87, p. 116-122.
3526. MAZANDERANI, Nosratollah Kazemi
"Said Wasp to Bee" (tr. by Omar S. Pound). [AntigR] (69/70) 87, p. 75.
3527. MAZIBUKO, M. T.
"Kodwa Nkosana (And Yet, Master)" (tr. by Daniel P. Kunene). [TriQ] (69) Spr-Sum 87, p. 208-209.
3528. MAZUR, Gail
"Ice." [Poetry] (151:3) D 87, p. 270.
"A Small Plane from Boston to Montpelier." [Poetry] (150:4) Jl 87, p. 216-217.
"Ware's Cove." [Poetry] (150:4) Jl 87, p. 215-216.
3529. MAZZARO, Jerome
"Near Sisyphus." [YaleR] (76:3) Spr 87, p. 357-358.
"Now, Though, the Dreams." [SouthwR] (72:3) Sum 87, p. 376.
"Off Naxos." [Hudson] (40:3) Aut 87, p. 448.
"Our Time Among the Figured Vases." [Salm] (72) Fall 86, p. 190.
Mc . . .
    See also names beginning with Mac . . .
3530. McADAM, Rhona
"Viewing the New World." [AntigR] (68) Wint 87, p. 111.
3531. McARTHUR, Cathy
"How to Have a Miscarriage." [MemphisSR] (7:2) Spr 87, p. 36.

"Love." [BellArk] (3:2) Mr-Ap 87, p. 18.
3532. McARTHUR, Mary J.
"Mssrs. Mice and Co." [LightY] '87, c86, p. 118-119.
3533. McAULEY, James J.
"Coming and Going." [WillowS] (19) Wint 87, p. 13.
"The Explorer." [WillowS] (19) Wint 87, p. 12.
3534. McBRIDE, Elizabeth
"Linguistics." [OhioR] (38) 87, p. 95.
3535. McBRIDE, Mark
"Finally It Is Morning." [Poem] (58) N 87, p. 43-45.
3536. McBRIDE, Mekeel
"The Earliest Maps." [Poetry] (150:2) My 87, p. 74.
"The Influence." [ThRiPo] (29/30) 87, p. 45-46.
"My Story as Told by Someone Else." [Poetry] (150:2) My 87, p. 72-73.
"Onion." [ThRiPo] (29/30) 87, p. 47.
"The Relative Distance of the Stars." [SenR] (17:1) 87, p. 12.
"Strauss and the Cows of Ireland." [Agni] (24/25) 87, p. 90.
3537. McCABE, Michael
"A Night Moon Knows." [GreenfR] (14:1/2) Wint-Spr, p. 21.
3538. McCABE, Victoria
"Bedtime." [WeberS] (4:1) Spr 87, p. 30.
"The Belly Thinks of Itself as *Guts*." [WeberS] (4:1) Spr 87, p. 28.
"Grief: The Arm's Song." [WeberS] (4:1) Spr 87, p. 29.
"Landor." [Shen] (37:4) 87, p. 67.
"Rat Terrier in Old Age." [WeberS] (4:1) Spr 87, p. 31.
"Targets Seeking Out the Projectiles." [WeberS] (4:1) Spr 87, p. 30.
"Teeth." [ColEng] (49:7) N 87, p. 770-771.
"The Tongue's Complaint." [ColEng] (49:7) N 87, p. 772.
3539. McCAFFERY, Steve
"An Effect of Cellophane" (Excerpt). [Bound] (14:1/2) Fall 85-Wint 86 [c87], p.
60-61.
3540. McCAFFREY, Phillip
"Apprehension." [Spirit] (8:2) 87, p. 93.
3541. McCALLUM, Paddy
"Close-Up Magic." [CanLit] (115) Wint 87, p. 24-25.
"Gifts." [CanLit] (115) Wint 87, p. 24.
"The Lost Son." [CanLit] (115) Wint 87, p. 25-26.
"The Poetry of George Jehoshaphat Mountain (1789-1863)." [CanLit] (115) Wint
87, p. 26-27.
3542. McCANN, David R.
"Azaleas" (tr. of Kim Sowol). [Pembroke] (19) 87, p. 13-14.
"No One" (tr. of Kim Chiha). [Pembroke] (19) 87, p. 16-17.
"Winter Sky" (tr. of So Chong-ju). [Pembroke] (19) 87, p. 15.
3543. McCANN, Janet
"For Elizabeth." [BellArk] (3:4) Jl-Ag 87, p. 7.
"Frontier Dream" (Award Poem). [Phoenix] (7:1) 87, p. 26.
"In Our Parents' House." [MidwQ] (28:3) Spr 87, p. 361.
"Tolstoy." [PoetC] (18:3) Spr 87, p. 21.
3544. McCAREY, Peter
"Rehabs and Reconstructions" (w. Edwin Morgan). [Verse] (4:2) Je 87, p. 10-16.
3545. McCARRISTON, Linda
"Aubade: November." [BostonR] (12:3) Je 87, p. 15.
"Bucked." [BostonR] (12:3) Je 87, p. 15.
"Hotel Nights with My Mother." [BostonR] (12:3) Je 87, p. 15.
"The Stardust." [BostonR] (12:3) Je 87, p. 15.
"To Judge Faolain, Dead Long Enough: A Summons." [BostonR] (12:3) Je 87, p.
15.
3546. McCARTHY, Eugene J.
"Fawn Hall Among the Antinomians." [NewRep] (197:11/12) 14-21 S 87, p. 14.
3547. McCARTHY, Julia
"How I Spent My Christmas Holidays." [Waves] (15:1/2) Fall 86, p. 71.
"My Father-in-Law." [Waves] (15:1/2) Fall 86, p. 71.
3548. McCARTHY, Penny
"Unraveller." [Stand] (28:3) Sum 87, p. 34.
3549. McCARTHY, Thomas
"State Funeral." [Pembroke] (19) 87, p. 95.

255

3550. McCARTIN, Jim
"Explorations." [Footwork] 87, p. 23.
"Sometimes I Wonder What I'm Talking About." [Footwork] 87, p. 22.
"To a Poet Fretting About Fame." [Footwork] 87, p. 23.
3551. McCARTNEY, Sharon
"Alaska." [Event] (16:3) Fall 87, p. 30.
"Ilsebill." [Event] (16:3) Fall 87, p. 31.
3552. McCASLIN, Susan
"Dream Child" (18 poems). [BellArk] (3:4) Jl-Ag 87, p. 8-9.
"Hymn to the Father." [BellArk] (3:5) S-O 87, p. 10.
"Muse's Coda." [BellArk] (3:2) Mr-Ap 87, p. 20.
"Paradox." [BellArk] (3:3) My-Je 87, p. 10.
"A Place of Permanence." [BellArk] (3:6) N-D 87, p. 5.
"A Sharing of Space." [BellArk] (3:2) Mr-Ap 87, p. 18.
3553. McCLATCHY, J. D.
"Achill Island." [Poetry] (151:1/2) O-N 87, p. 92-93.
"Kilim." [GrandS] (6:4) Sum 87, p. 75-82.
3554. McCLAURIN, Irma
"Old Age Sequence" (for Gwendolyn Brooks). [BlackALF] (21:3) Fall 87, p. 252.
3555. McCLELLAN, Jane
"Henry Becker, D. O. A." [BallSUF] (28:4) Aut 87, p. 64-66.
3556. McCLELLAND, Bruce
"Corn Ouija." [Notus] (2:1) Spr 87, p. 50-52.
"Lines." [Notus] (2:1) Spr 87, p. 49.
"Second Corn Ouija." [Notus] (2:1) Spr 87, p. 53-56.
3557. McCLOSKEY, Mark
"Hand." [LightY] '87, c86, p. 254.
3558. McCLUNG, Kathleen
"Hospice" (for Robin). [PoetryNW] (28:4) Wint 87-88, p. 10.
3559. McCLURE, Michael
"For Jack Spicer." [Acts] (6) 87, p. 49.
"Fortunate Fault." [Caliban] (3) 87, p. 21.
"Looking at the Sheep's Brain." [Caliban] (3) 87, p. 22.
"Miracle or Crime." [Caliban] (3) 87, p. 23.
"Newspaper Death Photo of Marilyn Monroe: The Calgary Sun." [Caliban] (3) 87, p. 20-21.
3560. McCLURG, Kayla L.
"Assignment: Poetry." [EngJ] (76:8) D 87, p. 79.
3561. McCOLLEY, Beverly A.
"Word War." [EngJ] (76:6) O 87, p. 98.
3562. McCOMBS, Judith
"Inside the Color Print." [RiverS] (23) 87, p. 60.
"Perception." [RiverS] (23) 87, p. 62.
"Territory." [RiverS] (23) 87, p. 63.
"Things Happen." [RiverS] (23) 87, p. 59.
"The Traveller." [RiverS] (23) 87, p. 61.
3563. McCORD, Howard
"Folk-Tales from the Face of Mount Asgaard, Baffin Island." [Gambit] (20) 86, p. 120.
3564. McCORD, Teresa
"The Shape of Getting Along." [Wind] (17:60) 87, p. 20.
3565. McCORKLE, James
"Fishing on the River at Evening" (for Jane Staw). [PoetC] (19:1) Fall 87, p. 15-16.
"Oya." [AnotherCM] (17) 87, p. 81-92.
"Some Details of Autumn." [Boulevard] (2:1/2) Spr 87, p. 157-158.
3566. McCORKLE, Jennifer Jones
"The Green Volkswagen Dream." [Northeast] (Ser. 4:6) Wint 87-88, p. 8.
"Resurrection I." [Northeast] (Ser. 4:6) Wint 87-88, p. 6.
"Resurrection II." [Northeast] (Ser. 4:6) Wint 87-88, p. 7.
3567. McCORMACK, Catherine Savoy
"Excuses." [Amelia] (4:1/2, issue 9) 87, p. 121.
3568. McCORMACK, James E.
"Leaving Belfast Lough, 1930." [AntigR] (68) Wint 87, p. 7.
"New Life, 1930." [AntigR] (68) Wint 87, p. 8.
"Ulster From Here." [AntigR] (68) Wint 87, p. 9.

3569. McCRAE, John
"The Anxious Dead." [Waves] (15:1/2) Fall 86, p. 98.
"In Flanders Fields." [Waves] (15:1/2) Fall 86, p. 96.
"Isandhlwawa." [Waves] (15:1/2) Fall 86, p. 97.
"The Night Cometh." [Waves] (15:1/2) Fall 86, p. 98.
3570. McCREDIE, Marcie
"Grocery Shopping." [Wind] (17:60) 87, p. 25.
3571. McCROSSIN, Dana L.
"And You Have Come to Know Love" (for my brother). [StoneC] (14:3/4) Spr-Sum
87, p. 63.
3572. McCUE, Frances
"In Single Moments." [PoetryNW] (28:3) Aut 87, p. 11-12.
3573. McCUE, Frances A.
"Travelling North by Car Past the Spoon Factory." [PoetC] (19:1) Fall 87, p. 5-6.
3574. McCULLOUGH, Ken
"My Foot Finds." [Abraxas] (35/36) 87, p. 8.
"Respite." [Abraxas] (35/36) 87, p. 9.
"Richard." [Abraxas] (35/36) 87, p. 10.
"Vietnam Veterans Memorial, Washington, D.C." (for Jim McGreevey). [Abraxas]
(35/36) 87, p. 7-8.
3575. McCURDY, Harold
"Notes for an Approaching Quadricentennial." [Pembroke] (19) 87, p. 113-114.
3576. McDADE, Thomas Michael
"Systems." [MoodySI] (18/19) Fall 87, p. 11.
3577. McDANIEL, Tom
"Continuance." [KanQ] (19:1/2) Wint-Spr 87, p. 102.
"How to Help Each Other Up." [KanQ] (19:1/2) Wint-Spr 87, p. 102.
3578. McDANIEL, Wilma Elizabeth
"Farm Children in the Grip of 1933." [HangL] (50/51) 87, p. 118.
"Hired Girl's Pet." [HangL] (50/51) 87, p. 120.
"The Long Wait." [HangL] (50/51) 87, p. 121.
"Lumbago." [PoetL] (82:4) Wint 87-88, p. 251.
"Scouting with Playmates, 1932." [HangL] (50/51) 87, p. 119.
"Theatrical Names." [HangL] (50/51) 87, p. 122.
"Wings." [HangL] (50/51) 87, p. 123.
3579. McDERMOTT, Maura
"Physics." [Phoenix] (7:1) 87, p. 46.
3580. McDONALD, Agnes
"Waiting Out the Storm." [GreensboroR] (43) Wint 87-88, p. 71-72.
3581. McDONALD, Daniel
"Going Home for the High School Reunion: The Class of '45" (Finalist, Eve of St.
Agnes Competition). [NegC] (7:1/2) 87, p. 163.
3582. McDONALD, Walter
"Across the Fence." [Phoenix] (7:2) 87, p. 53.
"After the Noise of Saigon." [CutB] (27/28) 87, p. 69.
"After the Noise of Saigon." [PoetL] (81:3) Fall 86, p. 191.
"After Watching the Space Shuttle Explode." [Raccoon] (24/25) My 87, p. 304.
"Bait." [HayF] (2) Spr 87, p. 104.
"Balance." [SouthernPR] (27:1) Spr 87, p. 10.
"Behind the Boathouse." [CimR] (80) Jl 87, p. 32.
"Between Barns." [RiverS] (23) 87, p. 48.
"Bluejays in Summer." [LitR] (31:1) Fall 87, p. 63.
"A Brief Familiar Story of Webs." [Pembroke] (19) 87, p. 99.
"Bulls at Sundown." [WestB] (20) 87, p. 40.
"Crawling through Caverns." [PraS] (61:1) Spr 87, p. 25-26.
"Doves at Dawn." [Puerto] (22:2) Spr 87, p. 140-141.
"Driving at Night Through Hardscrabble." [TexasR] (8:1/2) Spr-Sum 87, p. 34.
"Faces We Never Forget." [HampSPR] Wint 86, p. 13.
"The Farm at Auction." [ColR] (NS 14:1) Spr-Sum 87, p. 60-61.
"Finding My Father's Hands in Mid-life." [ColEng] (49:7) N 87, p. 774.
"First View of the Enemy." [AntigR] (71/72) Aut 87-Wint 88, p. 94.
"The Flying Dutchman." [CentR] (31:2) Spr 87, p. 185-187.
"Games." [Raccoon] (24/25) My 87, p. 244.
"Grandmother's Last Years." [Waves] (14:4) Spr 86, p. 49.
"The Groves, the High Places." [PassN] (8:1) Wint 87, p. 15.
"Hardscrabble." [RiverS] (23) 87, p. 49.

"Having a Mind of Winter." [CapeR] (22:1) Spr 87, p. 30.
"Learning to Aim Well." [NewL] (54:1) Fall 87, p. 71.
"Living Near Oak Creek Dam." [WeberS] (4:2) Fall 87, p. 34.
"Living on Buried Water." [SouthwR] (72:2) Spr 87, p. 237.
"Living on Open Plains." [KanQ] (19:3) Sum 87, p. 154-155.
"Loading a Shotgun, at Twelve." [KanQ] (19:3) Sum 87, p. 154.
"Lord Hawk." [WritersF] (13) Fall 87, p. 121.
"Losing a Boat on the Brazos." [Poetry] (149:5) F 87, p. 281.
"The Middle Years." [CimR] (78) Ja 87, p. 30.
"Midnight at Dillon." [FloridaR] (15:2) Fall-Wint 87, p. 34.
"The Mind Is a Hawk." [FloridaR] (15:2) Fall-Wint 87, p. 33.
"Morning Coffee." [Pembroke] (19) 87, p. 100.
"Nearing the End of a Century." [AntR] (45:4) Fall 87, p. 437.
"An Old Familiar Story of Summer." [CimR] (80) Jl 87, p. 62.
"On a Screened Porch in the Country." [WeberS] (4:2) Fall 87, p. 34.
"The One That Got Away." [Stand] (28:4) Aut 87, p. 50.
"Ranching in the San Juan." [WeberS] (4:2) Fall 87, p. 33.
"Reasons for Desiring Drought." [WoosterR] (7) Spr 87, p. 41.
"Riding on Hardscrabble." [WritersF] (13) Fall 87, p. 122.
"Splitting Wood for Winter." [PraS] (61:1) Spr 87, p. 24-25.
"The Sting of the Visible." [WritersF] (13) Fall 87, p. 123.
"Stories We Seem to Remember." [HampSPR] Wint 86, p. 12.
"Tracking on Hardscrabble." [MidAR] (7:2) 87, p. 22.
"Trophies." [WebR] (12:1) Spr 87, p. 47.
"Trying to Understand the Weather." [MidwQ] (28:2) Wint 87, p. 221.
"The Way a Dog Leaves Home." [WeberS] (4:2) Fall 87, p. 35.
"When Children Think You Can Do Anything." [Poetry] (149:5) F 87, p. 280.
"The Wild Swans of Da Lat." [WestB] (20) 87, p. 41.
"Witching on Canvas." [CrossCur] (7:2) 87, p. 93.

3583. McDOUGALL, Jo
"Reporting Back." [Spirit] (8:2) 87, p. 179.

3584. McELROY, Colleen J.
"Confessions of a Woman Who Sucks Baby Toes." [Nimrod] (30:2) Spr-Sum 87,
p. 119-120.
"For Want of a Male the Shoe Was Lost." [Nimrod] (30:2) Spr-Sum 87, p. 116.
"Learning to Swim at Forty-Five." [Calyx] (10:2/3) Spr 87, p. 176-177.
"Memoirs of American Speech" (Excerpt). [Spirit] (8:2) 87, p. 145-146.
"Sweet with Wonder, My Feet Upon Air." [Nimrod] (30:2) Spr-Sum 87, p.
117-118.

3585. McEUEN, James
"Incarnatus Est." [Vis] (25) 87, p. 21.

3586. McEWEN, R. F.
"Night Watch — Day Break." [KanQ] (19:4) Fall 87, p. 58-59.

3587. McFADDEN, David
"Blue Irises." [MalR] (80) S 87, p. 29.
"Consciousness." [WestCR] (22:1) Sum 87, p. 33.
"Crime Prevention Measures." [WestCR] (22:1) Sum 87, p. 34.
"Elephants." [MalR] (80) S 87, p. 25.
"The Inchworm." [MalR] (80) S 87, p. 27.
"Love's Like Milk." [MalR] (80) S 87, p. 23.
"The Piano Player." [WestCR] (22:1) Sum 87, p. 36.
"The Poetry of Our Age." [WestCR] (22:1) Sum 87, p. 31-32.
"Sailing in Perfect Space." [WestCR] (22:1) Sum 87, p. 35-36.
"Shantideva." [MalR] (80) S 87, p. 26.
"Terrible Storm on Lake Erie." [MalR] (80) S 87, p. 28.
"A Visit to the Zoo." [MalR] (80) S 87, p. 24.

3588. McFALL, Gardner
"Blue Raft." [MissouriR] (10:2) 87, p. 119-120.
"Field Trip to Fort Story." [MissouriR] (10:2) 87, p. 115-116.
"Four Corners." [MissouriR] (10:2) 87, p. 117.
"Identity." [MissouriR] (10:2) 87, p. 121-122.
"Missing." [MissouriR] (10:2) 87, p. 118.

3589. McFARLAND, Ron
"The Beautiful Waitress." [BellR] (10:2) Fall 87, p. 56.
"Ceteris Paribus" (other things being equal). [Ascent] (12:2) 87, p. 40.
"Early Morning Episode." [HampSPR] Wint 87, p. 10-11.

"The Family Farm." [HighP] (2:2) Fall 87, p. 194-195.
"Flood in Oklahoma." [CimR] (81) O 87, p. 10.
"Just Someone I Met at a Party." [HampSPR] Wint 87, p. 10.
"A Perfect Day." [Ascent] (12:2) 87, p. 39.
"Waitress from Burley." [BellR] (10:2) Fall 87, p. 57.
3590. McFEE, Michael
"1926." [SouthernPR] (27:1) Spr 87, p. 44-45.
"Family Reunion Near Grape Creek Church, Four Miles West of Murphy, N.C.,
1880." [VirQR] (63:3) Sum 87, p. 443-444.
"First Radio." [Poetry] (149:6) Mr 87, p. 329.
"Little Elegy" (for Johnny Olson, d. October 1985). [LightY] '87, c86, p. 73.
"Sliding Rock." [VirQR] (63:3) Sum 87, p. 444-446.
"Snow Goat." [NewYorker] (62:48) 19 Ja 87, p. 69.
"Uncle Homer Mets Carl Sandburg." [CarolQ] (39:3) Spr 87, p. 95-96.
3591. McFERREN, Martha
"The Best Advice I Received as an Adolescent." [HeliconN] (17/18) Spr 87, p. 95.
"Clouds / Fire / Clouds." [HeliconN] (17/18) Spr 87, p. 93.
"Tripartite." [HeliconN] (17/18) Spr 87, p. 94.
3592. McGARA, Bonnie
"Montauk." [BallSUF] (28:4) Aut 87, p. 7-8.
3593. McGARTLAND, Nancy
"Seven Years After the War." [CapeR] (22:2) Fall 87, p. 26.
3594. McGEHEE, J. Pittman
"Traveling Man." [CimR] (78) Ja 87, p. 56.
3595. McGOVERN, Martin
"For Delia" (Denver Quarterly Poetry Competition Winner, Third Prize). [DenQ]
(22:2) Fall 87, p. 18-19.
3596. McGOWAN, James D.
"The Sasha Sequence" (in collaboration with the Apple II program *The Catalyst Kid*
by Hale Chatfield). [HiramPoR] (42) Spr-Sum 87, p. 50-51.
3597. McGRATH, Campbell
"Dust" (Chapbook of Poems). [OhioR] (39) 87, p. 65-80.
3598. McGRATH, Carmelita
"Avondale." [Waves] (15:4) Spr 87, p. 69.
"Spring?" [Waves] (15:4) Spr 87, p. 70.
"Western Cove Revisited." [Waves] (15:4) Spr 87, p. 70-71.
3599. McGRATH, Kristina
"Last House on January Road, Off Route 8" (for Fredda). [Epoch] (36:2) 87-88, p.
112-125.
"The Removal: From Magopa to Bethanie." [PennR] (3:2) Fall-Wint 87, p. 30-32.
3600. McGRATH, Lynette
"Absence, VII" (tr. of Rosa Leveroni, w. Nathaniel B. Smith). [WebR] (12:2) Fall
87, p. 22.
"A Day Like This" (tr. of Francesc Parcerisas, w. Nathaniel Smith). [InterPR] (13:2)
Fall 87, p. 11.
"Distant Deaths" (tr. of Clementina Arderiu, w. Nathaniel B. Smith). [WebR] (12:2)
Fall 87, p. 22.
"Parting" (tr. of Francesc Parcerisas, w. Nathaniel Smith). [InterPR] (13:2) Fall 87,
p. 7.
"Roman Heads" (tr. of Francesc Parcerisas, w. Nathaniel Smith). [InterPR] (13:2)
Fall 87, p. 7.
"Song of Perfect Trust" (tr. of Clementina Arderiu, w. Nathaniel B. Smith). [WebR]
(12:2) Fall 87, p. 21.
"Summer Vacation" (tr. of Francesc Parcerisas, w. Nathaniel Smith). [InterPR]
(13:2) Fall 87, p. 9.
"Virgil's Hand" (tr. of Francesc Parcerisas, w. Nathaniel Smith). [InterPR] (13:2)
Fall 87, p. 9.
3601. McGRATH, Thomas
"Ah, to the Villages!" [PoetryE] (23/24) Fall 87, p. 23.
"Ambitions." [TriQ] (70) Fall 87, p. 218.
"Another Christmas Carol." [PoetryE] (23/24) Fall 87, p. 37.
"Ars Poetica: Or: Who Lives in the Ivory Tower?" [PoetryE] (23/24) Fall 87, p.
9-10.
"At Port Townsend" (for Sam and Tree). [NoDaQ] (55:1) Wint 87, p. 27.
"The Black Train." [TriQ] (70) Fall 87, p. 212-213.
"The Bravest Boat." [NoDaQ] (55:1) Wint 87, p. 28.

"The Bread of This World, Praises III." [PoetryE] (23/24) Fall 87, p. 31.
"Celebration." [PoetryE] (23/24) Fall 87, p. 113.
"The Citizen Dreaming." [TriQ] (68) Wint 87, p. 76-77.
"A Coal Fire in Winter." [PoetryE] (23/24) Fall 87, p. 24.
"Deprivation." [Caliban] (3) 87, p. 17.
"Driving Toward Boston I Run Across One of Robert Bly's Old Poems." [PoetryE] (23/24) Fall 87, p. 27-28.
"The End of the World." [PoetryE] (23/24) Fall 87, p. 30.
"Even Song." [TriQ] (68) Wint 87, p. 80.
"The Excursion: or, O Columbus!" [NoDaQ] (55:1) Wint 87, p. 23-24.
"Faithfully Yours." [PoetryE] (23/24) Fall 87, p. 38.
"The Fatigue of Objects." [Caliban] (3) 87, p. 17.
"Get Out of Town." [PoetryE] (23/24) Fall 87, p. 7.
"Guerrillas" (for Don Gordon). [PoetryE] (23/24) Fall 87, p. 36.
"In Dream Time." [TriQ] (70) Fall 87, p. 219.
"In Praise of Necessity." [PoetryE] (23/24) Fall 87, p. 17-18.
"In the Confusion of Empires." [TriQ] (70) Fall 87, p. 214.
"The Inheritance." [PoetryE] (23/24) Fall 87, p. 35.
"The Landscape Inside Me." [PoetryE] (23/24) Fall 87, p. 21.
"Last Will and Testament" (for Tomasito). [NoDaQ] (55:1) Wint 87, p. 30.
"Letter to an Imaginary Friend" (Selections). [TriQ] (70) Fall 87, p. 16-37.
"The Little Odyssey of Jason Quint, of Science, Doctor." [PoetryE] (23/24) Fall 87, p. 13-15.
"A Little Song About Charity" (Tune of Matty Grove). [PoetryE] (23/24) Fall 87, p. 11-12.
"A Long Way Outside Yellowstone" (Cheyenne, Wyoming, 1940). [PoetryE] (23/24) Fall 87, p. 8.
"Look on My Works!" [TriQ] (70) Fall 87, p. 211.
"Mediterranean." [TriQ] (68) Wint 87, p. 78-79.
"Ordonnance." [PoetryE] (23/24) Fall 87, p. 33.
"Poem: How could I have come so far?" [PoetryE] (23/24) Fall 87, p. 113.
"Praises." [PoetryE] (23/24) Fall 87, p. 25-26.
"Praises IV. On the Beauty and the Wonders of Women and Some of the Problems Attendant Thereunto." [TriQ] (70) Fall 87, p. 215-217.
"Proletarian in Abstract Light." [PoetryE] (23/24) Fall 87, p. 29.
"Rediscovery." [Caliban] (3) 87, p. 15-16.
"Remembering the Children of Auschwitz." [Spirit] (8:2) 87, p. 91-92.
"The Return." [PoetryE] (23/24) Fall 87, p. 34.
"That's the Way It Goes." [PoetryE] (23/24) Fall 87, p. 22.
"Think of This Hour." [PoetryE] (23/24) Fall 87, p. 16.
"Trail Blazers" (remembering Stephen Vincent Benét). [NoDaQ] (55:1) Wint 87, p. 29-30.
"Transformations of Old Silver Crossing the Continent." [NoDaQ] (55:1) Wint 87, p. 25-26.
"When We Say Goodbye." [PoetryE] (23/24) Fall 87, p. 32.
"You Can Start the Poetry Now, Or: News from Crazy Horse." [PoetryE] (23/24) Fall 87, p. 19-20.
"You Taught Me." [PoetryE] (23/24) Fall 87, p. 112.
3602. McGUCKIAN, Medbh
"Amelia." [FourQ] (1:2) Fall 87, p. 58.
3603. McGUFFIN, Aaron
"The Desert Travelers." [LaurelR] (20:1/2) Sum 87, p. 88.
3604. McGUINN, Rex
"Artist Brooding on the Porch of the National Theatre." [KanQ] (19:4) Fall 87, p. 49.
3605. McGUIRK, Kevin
"Snowy Night." [AntigR] (69/70) 87, p. 10.
3606. McGURL, Mark
"Yellow Hesitations." [HarvardA] (122:2) D 87, p. 9.
3607. McHUGH, Heather
"20-200 on 737." [Thrpny] (30) Sum 87, p. 5.
"Deserts" (tr. of Blaga Dimitrova, w. Nikolai Popov). [Trans] (18) Spr 87, p. 277.
"Forbidden Sea" (Excerpt, tr. of Blaga Dimitrova, w. Nikolai Popov). [Trans] (18) Spr 87, p. 280.
"From 20,000 Feet." [MichQR] (26:2) Spr 87, p. 314.

"Multidimensional" (tr. of Blaga Dimitrova, w. Nikolai Popov). [Trans] (18) Spr 87,
    p. 276.
"Nightlight: Eye of the Owl" (tr. of Blaga Dimitrova, w. Nikolai Popov). [Trans]
    (18) Spr 87, p. 278.
"Old Song in a New Voice" (tr. of Blaga Dimitrova, w. Nikolai Popov). [Trans] (18)
    Spr 87, p. 279.
"Unfamiliar." [Thrpny] (28) Wint 87, p. 10.
3608. McINNIS, Michael
"Downtown Kerouac Lowell." [MoodySI] (18/19) Fall 87, p. 40.
3609. McINTOSH, James
"Chair Music." [LaurelR] (20:1/2) Sum 87, p. 116.
"My Father's Garage, in the Rain." [LaurelR] (20:1/2) Sum 87, p. 117.
3610. McKAIN, David
"Elk Lick Bible Camp." [GreenfR] (14:3/4) Sum-Fall 87, p. 135.
"Harm's Way." [TarRP] (26:2) Spr 87, p. 37.
"Sundials." [TexasR] (7:3/4) 87, p. 100-101.
"Witching." [TexasR] (7:3/4) 87, p. 99.
3611. McKAY, Don
"Domestic Animals." [MalR] (81) D 87, p. 28-29.
"Ink Lake." [Dandel] (14:1) Spr-Sum 87, p. 29-35.
"Luke & Co." [MalR] (81) D 87, p. 23-25.
"Plantation." [MalR] (81) D 87, p. 26-27.
3612. McKAY, Linda Back
"Bill of Goods." [Farm] (4:1) Wint 87, p. 32.
"Social Blunder." [Vis] (23) 87, p. 20.
3613. McKEAN, James
"Solstice." [CalQ] (30) Wint 87, p. 58-59.
3614. McKEE, Louis
"Redemption." [PikeF] (8) Fall 87, p. 3.
"Scarecrow." [CapeR] (22:2) Fall 87, p. 13.
"Song and Dance" (for Etheridge Knight). [StoneC] (14:3/4) Spr-Sum 87, p. 69.
"A Twenty Dollar Story." [Raccoon] (24/25) My 87, p. 246.
"What Comes of Dance." [StoneC] (14:3/4) Spr-Sum 87, p. 69.
3615. McKENNA, J. J.
"Celebration." [HawaiiR] (22) Fall 87, p. 72.
3616. McKENTY, Bob
"E Pluribus Ovum." [LightY] '87, c86, p. 230.
"The Lamb." [LightY] '87, c86, p. 113.
"The Zebra." [LightY] '87, c86, p. 114.
3617. McKERNAN, John
"Cézanne Was Not Very Good at Inter-." [Agni] (24/25) 87, p. 88.
3618. McKERNAN, Llewellyn
"The Dreamer." [LaurelR] (20:1/2) Sum 87, p. 29.
"The Hunter." [LaurelR] (20:1/2) Sum 87, p. 28.
"The Killer." [LaurelR] (20:1/2) Sum 87, p. 28.
"The Maker." [LaurelR] (20:1/2) Sum 87, p. 29.
3619. McKIM, Elizabeth
"Sense of Place." [Phoenix] (7:2) 87, p. 56.
3620. McKINNEY, Irene
"Solitude in the Oneida Community: Victor Cragin Noyes, 1866." [Salm] (73) Wint
    87, p. 153-154.
3621. McKINNON, Patrick
"All the Young Guys." [SlipS] (7) 87, p. 29.
"Connie Larson." [WormR] (27:1, issue 105) 87, p. 7-8.
"Duckstrut Willie." [Lactuca] (5) Ja 87, p. 27.
"Every Sunday." [WormR] (27:1, issue 105) 87, p. 7.
"The Fingerprint Story." [Bogg] (57) 87, p. 10.
"Little Known Fact." [WormR] (27:1, issue 105) 87, p. 7.
"The Michaletti Poem." [Lactuca] (5) Ja 87, p. 28.
"Poem for Mother." [Lactuca] (7) Ag 87, p. 1-2.
"Rose." [SlipS] (7) 87, p. 30.
"The Shaving Poem." [Lactuca] (7) Ag 87, p. 2-3.
"Terrible Tom." [Abraxas] (35/36) 87, p. 72-73.
3622. McKINSEY, Martin
"Strange Days" (tr. of Yannis Ritsos). [Verse] (4:3) N 87, p. 16.
"Sunday" (tr. of Yannis Ritsos). [Verse] (4:3) N 87, p. 16.

3623. McLAUGHLIN, John
"The Baby." [Footwork] 87, p. 38.
"Fallen Fruit." [Footwork] 87, p. 38.
3624. McLAUGHLIN, William
"Chinese Bridges." [HampSPR] Wint 86, p. 14-15.
"Emil Is Puzzled by His Movie-Going." [HolCrit] (24:3) Je 87, p. 19.
"Heavy Tea." [HampSPR] Wint 86, p. 15-16.
"Views on Aerial Irrigation." [CapeR] (22:1) Spr 87, p. 16.
3625. McLAURIN, Ken
"Before Swimming." [SouthernPR] (27:2) Fall 87, p. 9.
"More Autobiography." [SouthernPR] (27:1) Spr 87, p. 30.
3626. McLEOD, Don (Donald)
"Fisherman's lined face." [Amelia] (4:3, issue 10) 87, p. 37.
"Winter night sky." [MoodySI] (18/19) Fall 87, p. 19.
3627. McLEOD, Milt
"Lines." [ManhatPR] (9) Sum 87, p. 37.
"Man and Dolphin" (Ancient Corinth, 1980). [WebR] (12:2) Fall 87, p. 84.
3628. McMAHAN, Brendan
"Golan" (reprinted from Bogg 28-29). [Bogg] (58) 87, p. 42.
3629. McMAHON, Lynne
"Autumnal." [NewEngR] (10:2) Wint 87, p. 199.
"Futureworld." [QW] (24) Wint 87, p. 91.
"Going Back." [Nat] (244:20) 23 My 87, p. 695.
"The Hotel de Dream (Myself at Twenty)." [DenQ] (21:3) Wint 87, p. 85.
"Missouri Box-Step." [PraS] (61:1) Spr 87, p. 95-96.
"Notre Dame." [AntR] (45:1) Wint 87, p. 42-44.
"Our First Porno Movie." [PraS] (61:1) Spr 87, p. 93-94.
"The Paris Women's Peace March." [AmerPoR] (16:6) N-D 87, p. 43.
"Poems at Christmastime." [Field] (36) Spr 87, p. 48-53.
"Rippled Window." [PraS] (61:1) Spr 87, p. 94-95.
"Unbuilding." [Atlantic] (260:2) Ag 87, p. 43.
3630. McMANIS, Ed
"Fire for Fire." [Writer] (99:1) Ja 86, p. 20.
3631. McMASTER, Susan
"Nucleic acid." [CrossC] (9:3/4) 87, p. 18.
3632. McMILLAN, Ian
"Tall in the Saddle." [Harp] (274:1648) S 87, p. 27.
3633. McMULLEN, Richard E.
"Hitler Is Dead in This." [CrossCur] (6:5) 87, p. 12-13.
3634. McNAIR, Joseph
"The Moon." [FloridaR] (15:1) Spr-Sum 87, p. 123.
3635. McNAIR, Wesley
"The Man with the Radios." [Poetry] (151:1/2) O-N 87, p. 93-94.
"The Name." [KenR] (NS 9:3) Sum 87, p. 80.
"Seeing Cooch." [KenR] (NS 9:3) Sum 87, p. 78.
"What It Is." [KenR] (NS 9:3) Sum 87, p. 79.
3636. McNALLY, Stephen
"Our Story." [PoetryNW] (28:4) Wint 87-88, p. 28-29.
"We Were Beyond Help." [PoetryNW] (28:4) Wint 87-88, p. 27-28.
3637. McNAMARA, Devon
"Opening Day." [LaurelR] (20:1/2) Sum 87, p. 109-110.
"Sacred Heart" (letter to my father while teaching in a Catholic school). [LaurelR]
(20:1/2) Sum 87, p. 111-113.
3638. McNAMARA, Robert
"The White Breast of the Dim Sea." [PoetryNW] (28:4) Wint 87-88, p. 41.
3639. McNARIE, Alan Decker
"Raising the Dead." [CapeR] (22:1) Spr 87, p. 13.
3640. McNAUGHTON, Elnora
"Los Angeles Visit." [Wind] (17:59) 87, p. 34.
3641. McPETERS, Annette
"Migration." [PoetL] (81:3) Fall 86, p. 166.
3642. McPHERSON, Michael
"Inspector." [HawaiiR] (21) Spr 87, p. 57.
"Junior Got the Snakes." The Best of [BambooR] [(31-32)] 86, p. 64-65.
"Traveller." [HawaiiR] (19) Spr 86, c87, p. 3.
"Visit." [HawaiiR] (20) Fall 86, c87, p. 54.

"White Horse in the Far Pasture." [HawaiiR] (21) Spr 87, p. 56.
"The White Volvo" (for Paul). [HawaiiR] (20) Fall 86, c87, p. 55.
3643. McPHERSON, Sandra
"Alder, 1982." [Zyzzyva] (3:2) Sum 87, p. 104-105.
"Alpine Two-step." [Antaeus] (58) Spr 87, p. 87-88.
"Keeping House." [NowestR] (25:3) 87, p. 173.
"Of Birds and Their Metaphors." [Thrpny] (28) Wint 87, p. 22.
"The Pantheist to His Child." [Field] (37) Fall 87, p. 63-64.
"Presbyterian, 1983." [Poetry] (151:1/2) O-N 87, p. 93-94.
"Ridge Road." [Ploughs] (13:4) 87, p. 68-69.
"Sonnet for a Singer." [Ploughs] (13:4) 87, p. 70.
3644. McPHILEMY, Kathleen
"Fat Dad." [Pembroke] (19) 87, p. 86-91.
3645. McQUEEN, David
"I Touch." [Interim] (6:1) Spr 87, p. 22.
"A Sister's Elegy." [Interim] (6:1) Spr 87, p. 21.
3646. McQUILKIN, Rennie
"Balancing" (for Hugh). [BelPoJ] (37:3) Spr 87, p. 22-23.
"In Wyeth." [TexasR] (7:3/4) 87, p. 106.
"The Rev. Robert Walker Skates." [Atlantic] (259:2) F 87, p. 60-61.
"The Rev. Robert Walker Skates." [TexasR] (7:3/4) 87, p. 102-103.
"A Rouse for the Widow Corrigan." [HampSPR] Wint 86, p. 36.
"Sister Marie Angelica Plays Badminton." [TexasR] (7:3/4) 87, p. 104-105.
3647. McQUILLAN, Kathleen
"To the Woman Who Danced." [YellowS] (24) Aut 87, p. 22.
3648. McRAY, Paul
"Landscape, 1986." [PassN] (8:1) Wint 87, p. 5.
"Remembering My Father's Tattoos." [PassN] (8:1) Wint 87, p. 5.
3649. McREYNOLDS, Douglas J.
"Incident in Kansas, 1871" (Seaton Honorable Mention Poem 1987). [KanQ] (19:3) Sum 87, p. 184-185.
3650. McROBERTS, Robert
"Michael, Ten Months." [TarPR] (27:1) Fall 87, p. 38.
3651. McSEVENY, Angela
"Colin." [Verse] (4:2) Je 87, p. 6.
3652. McWHIRTER, George
"Blasphemy of Don Juan in the Flames of Hell" (tr. of José Emilio Pacheco). [Margin] (2) Spr 87, p. 103.
"Cocteau Through the Looking Glass" (tr. of José Emilio Pacheco). [Margin] (2) Spr 87, p. 101.
"Contra Kodak" (tr. of José Emilio Pacheco). [Margin] (2) Spr 87, p. 103.
"New Sisyphus" (tr. of José Emilio Pacheco). [Margin] (2) Spr 87, p. 99.
"Transfigurations" (tr. of José Emilio Pacheco). [Margin] (2) Spr 87, p. 99.
"Written in Red Ink" (tr. of José Emilio Pacheco). [Margin] (2) Spr 87, p. 101.
3653. MEAD, Stephen X.
"Minutes of the Compass." [Wind] (17:61) 87, p. 29.
"This Winter." [Paint] (14:28) Aut 87, p. 17.
3654. MEADE, Mary Ann
"The Feather-Duster Salesman." [BallSUF] (28:4) Aut 87, p. 41.
"Snow Angel." [FloridaR] (15:1) Spr-Sum 87, p. 122.
3655. MEADOR, Roger
"The Walk." [SmPd] (24:2) Spr 87, p. 16.
3656. MEANS-YBARRA, Ricardo
"A Framing Job" (1985 Alice Jackson Poetry Prize: Honorable Mention). [Electrum] (39) Fall-Wint 87, p. 15.
3657. MEATS, Stephen
"The Pipe" (tr. of Charles Baudelaire). [PoetryE] (23/24) Fall 87, p. 219.
3658. MECKEL, Christoph
"Saüre" (Selections: 10, 36, 57, tr. by Carol Bedwell). [PoetL] (81:3) Fall 86, p. 175-177.
3659. MEDINA, Pablo
"The Arrival." [KanQ] (19:3) Sum 87, p. 172.
"March 9th." [KanQ] (19:3) Sum 87, p. 173.
3660. MEDINA, Ramón Felipe
"Breve Elegia para Cesar Vallejo." [Mairena] (9:24) 87, p. 47.

3661. MEEHAN, Maude
"El Barracuda, Santa Rita Jail, June 1983." [SinW] (31) 87, p. 95.
"Maria Sez." [SinW] (31) 87, p. 94.
3662. MEEK, Jay
"Big Bang." [LightY] '87, c86, p. 79.
"The Dalton Gang." [MemphisSR] (7:2) Spr 87, p. 12-13.
"Heroics." [KanQ] (19:3) Sum 87, p. 91.
"Mirrors." [KanQ] (19:3) Sum 87, p. 90.
"Various the Works That Rise Among Us." [MemphisSR] (7:2) Spr 87, p. 11.
"Words." [Raccoon] (24/25) My 87, p. 57-58.
3663. MEHREN, Stein
"Abandoned Mountain Farm" (tr. by Robert Hedin). [Germ] (10:2) Spr 87, p. 40.
"Along the Shore" (tr. by Robert Hedin). [Paint] (14:28) Aut 87, p. 30.
"Autumnal" (tr. by Robert Hedlin). [WebR] (12:2) Fall 87, p. 24.
"Drop" (tr. by Robert Hedin). [Germ] (10:2) Spr 87, p. 41.
"From the Depths of This Night" (tr. by Robert Hedlin). [WebR] (12:2) Fall 87, p.
    24.
"Glow of Sunrise" (tr. by Robert Hedlin). [WebR] (12:2) Fall 87, p. 24.
"Image of a Back Pasture" (tr. by Robert Hedin). [Germ] (10:2) Spr 87, p. 38.
"The Kilesund Woods" (Excerpt, tr. by Robert Hedin). [Germ] (10:2) Spr 87, p. 37.
"Winter" (tr. by Robert Hedin). [Germ] (10:2) Spr 87, p. 39.
3664. MEHROTRA, Arvind Krishna
"Don't Ask Me Why." [Chelsea] (46) 87, p. 223.
"Fragment." [Chelsea] (46) 87, p. 223.
"So Where Does One Go." [Chelsea] (46) 87, p. 222.
MEI, Yuan
    See YUAN, Mei
3665. MEIER, Kay
"Ruins" (to Ellie). [PassN] (8:2) Sum 87, p. 19.
"Song for My Father." [EngJ] (76:8) D 87, p. 78.
3666. MEINKE, Peter
"The Chipmunk Center." [LightY] '87, c86, p. 112.
"The Examiner's Death." [LightY] '87, c86, p. 258-259.
"Old Backboards." [CrossCur] (7:2) 87, p. 108-109.
"Twenty Years Later." [CrossCur] (6:4) 87, p. 27-28.
3667. MEIRELES, Cecilia
"Ancient Music" (tr. by Cecelia Burokas). [ColR] (NS 14:1) Spr-Sum 87, p. 36.
3668. MEISTER, Peter
"18th Century London Rain." [HampSPR] Wint 87, p. 26.
3669. MEISTER, Shirley Vogler
"Bingoholic." [LightY] '87, c86, p. 232.
3670. MELARTIN, Riika
"Being Followed." [SouthernPR] (27:2) Fall 87, p. 12.
3671. MELCHER, Nannette Swift
"First Born." [PoeticJ] (17) 87, p. 31.
"Moving Would Be Easier If I Were a Turtle." [PoeticJ] (17) 87, p. 10.
"Senior Citizen." [PoeticJ] (17) 87, p. 31.
3672. MELFI, Mary
"Life Sentence." [AntigR] (68) Wint 87, p. 94.
3673. MELIS, Amelia
"Still." [PoetC] (18:3) Spr 87, p. 19.
3674. MELNICK, David
"Men in Aida" (Excerpt, Book II, "Iliad," Book II: 1-30). [Bound] (14:1/2) Fall
    85-Wint 86 [c87], p. 43-46.
3675. MELNYCZUK, Askold
"And So." [Ploughs] (13:1) 87, p. 89.
"Forsythia." [Ploughs] (13:1) 87, p. 90.
MELO NETO, João Cabral de
    See NETO, João Cabral de Melo
MENA, Carlos E. Quirós
    See QUIROS MENA, Carlos E.
3676. MENDELL, Olga
"Departure." [Americas] (14:3/4) Fall-Wint 86, p. 99-100.
"Listening to Mongo Santamaría Calling the Spirits from Buffalo." [Americas]
    (14:3/4) Fall-Wint 86, p. 102.
"Veinte Años Después." [Americas] (14:3/4) Fall-Wint 86, p. 101.

MENDOZA, Ester Feliciano
   See FELICIANO MENDOZA, Ester
3677. MENEBROKER, Ann
   "Homeowner with Backyard." [Bogg] (58) 87, p. 27.
3678. MENEMENCIOGLU, Nermin
   "Avalanche" (tr. of Metin Altiok). [Trans] (19) Fall 87, p. 127.
3679. MENEN DESLEAL, Alvaro
   "Las Manos." [NewRena] (7:1, #21) Fall 87, p. 58.
   "My Two Hands" (tr. by Erland Anderson). [NewRena] (7:1, #21) Fall 87, p. 59.
3680. MENES, Orlando
   "Cat's Cradle without a String." [FloridaR] (15:1) Spr-Sum 87, p. 33-34.
3681. MENFI, John
   "Two Antiques" (1986 Finalist, Eve of Saint Agnes Poetry Competition). [NegC]
      (7:1/2) 87, p. 148-149.
3682. MENSCHING, Steffen
   "Mayakowski's Vacation with Lilya and Ossip Brik, Summer of 1929" (tr. by
      Margitt Lehbert). [Ploughs] (13:4) 87, p. 71-72.
   "Siqueiros: Our Countenance" (tr. by Margitt Lehbert). [Ploughs] (13:4) 87, p.
      73-74.
3683. MERASTY, Billy
   "Beaded, Flower-Designed Wrist-Band." [PraF] (8:3) Aut 87, p. 86.
   "Reindeer Lake." [PraF] (8:3) Aut 87, p. 87.
   "Worry." [PraF] (8:3) Aut 87, p. 87.
3684. MEREDITH, Joseph
   "Belfield, October, Early Morning." [FourQ] (1:2) Fall 87, p. 46.
   "The Glass Cutter." [FourQ] (1:1) Wint 87, p. 28-29.
   "Making Ends Meet." [FourQ] (1:2) Fall 87, p. 45-46.
3685. MEREDITH, William
   "A Couple of Trees." [PartR] (54:2) Spr 87, p. 264-265.
   "Grace." [Poetry] (151:1/2) O-N 87, p. 99-100.
   "In the Rif Mountains" (Northern Morocco). [PartR] (54:2) Spr 87, p. 265-266.
   "The Jain Bird Hospital in Delhi." [PartR] (54:2) Spr 87, p. 266-267.
   "A Mild-Spoken Citizen Finally Writes to the White House." [SenR] (17:2) 87, p.
      63-65.
   "Partial Accounts." [NewYorker] (62:52) 16 F 87, p. 34.
   "What I Remember the Writers Telling Me When I Was Young." [Atlantic] (259:5)
      My 87, p. 67.
3686. MERRIAM, Eve
   "Subway Seasoning." [LightY] '87, c86, p. 183.
3687. MERRILL, Christopher
   "Concert." [DenQ] (22:1) Sum 87, p. 45.
   "Scotch Broom: An Inventory." [SenR] (17:2) 87, p. 59.
3688. MERRILL, James
   "The Afternoon Sun." [GrandS] (6:2) Wint 87, p. 124.
   "Alessio and the Zinnias." [Poetry] (151:1/2) O-N 87, p. 101.
   "Days of 1908." [GrandS] (6:2) Wint 87, p. 126.
   "Farewell Performance" (For David Kalstone, 1932-1986). [GrandS] (6:3) Spr 87,
      p. 12-13.
   "Grace." [AntR] (45:1) Wint 87, p. 45.
   "Here Today." [Margin] (1) Wint 86, p. 1-2.
   "Investiture at Cecconi's" (for David Kalstone, 1932-1986). [Raritan] (7:3) Wint 87,
      p. 23.
   "Menu." [FourQ] (1:1) Wint 87, p. 19.
   "On an Italian Shore." [GrandS] (6:2) Wint 87, p. 125.
   "A Preface to the Memoirs." [NowestR] (25:3) 87, p. 111.
   "Three Cavafy Poems." [GrandS] (6:2) Wint 87, p. 124-126.
3689. MERRILL, Thomas
   "Prelude" (1986 Honorable Mention, Eve of Saint Agnes Poetry Competition).
      [NegC] (7:1/2) 87, p. 128-129.
3690. MERWIN, W. S.
   "After the Alphabets." [Poetry] (151:1/2) O-N 87, p. 102.
   "Airport." [NewYorker] (63:35) 19 O 87, p. 46.
   "Ashikaga Tadayoshi's Palace" (tr. of Muso Soseki, w. Soiku Shigematsu).
      [AmerPoR] (16:2) Mr-Ap 87, p. 30.
   "At Ei's Departure for Choho-ji" (tr. of Muso Soseki, w. Soiku Shigematsu).
      [AmerPoR] (16:2) Mr-Ap 87, p. 32.

265

MERWIN

"At the Nachi Kannon Hall" (tr. of Muso Soseki, w. Soiku Shigematsu).
    [AmerPoR] (16:2) Mr-Ap 87, p. 27.
"At the Same Time." [Iowa] (17:1) Wint 87, p. 36-37.
"At Whole-World-In-View Hut" (tr. of Muso Soseki, w. Soiku Shigematsu).
    [AmerPoR] (16:2) Mr-Ap 87, p. 30.
"Being Early." [ParisR] (29:105) Wint 87, p. 153.
"Berryman." [RiverS] (23) 87, p. 46-47.
"Beyond Light (Zessho Chiko)" (tr. of Muso Soseki, w. Soiku Shigematsu).
    [AmerPoR] (16:2) Mr-Ap 87, p. 32.
"Beyond the World" (tr. of Muso Soseki, w. Soiku Shigematsu). [AmerPoR] (16:2)
    Mr-Ap 87, p. 32.
"A Biding Mountain" (tr. of Muso Soseki, w. Soiku Shigematsu). [AmerPoR]
    (16:2) Mr-Ap 87, p. 29.
"The Bridge Where the Moon Crosses" (tr. of Muso Soseki, w. Soiku Shigematsu).
    [AmerPoR] (16:2) Mr-Ap 87, p. 31.
"Buddha's Satori" (tr. of Muso Soseki, w. Soiku Shigematsu). [AmerPoR] (16:2)
    Mr-Ap 87, p. 25.
"The center isn't a point" (tr. of Roberto Juarroz). [OhioR] (38) 87, p. 94.
"Chord." [Atlantic] (260:1) Jl 87, p. 41.
"Clear Valley (Seikei Tsutetsu)" (tr. of Muso Soseki, w. Soiku Shigematsu).
    [AmerPoR] (16:2) Mr-Ap 87, p. 32.
"Climbing Down the Snowy Montain" (tr. of Muso Soseki, w. Soiku Shigematsu).
    [AmerPoR] (16:2) Mr-Ap 87, p. 30.
"Conquerer." [ParisR] (29:105) Wint 87, p. 155.
"Digging Out the Buddha Relic" (tr. of Muso Soseki, w. Soiku Shigematsu).
    [AmerPoR] (16:2) Mr-Ap 87, p. 31.
"Dry Tree (Koboku Joei)" (tr. of Muso Soseki, w. Soiku Shigematsu). [AmerPoR]
    (16:2) Mr-Ap 87, p. 26.
"The Duck." [Field] (37) Fall 87, p. 74.
"East Peak" (tr. of Muso Soseki, w. Soiku Shigematsu). [AmerPoR] (16:2) Mr-Ap
    87, p. 27.
"Elegy." [RiverS] (23) 87, p. 39.
"Emigre." [RiverS] (23) 87, p. 31-32.
"The emptiness of the day" (tr. of Roberto Juarroz). [Antaeus] (58) Spr 87, p. 99.
"Empty Water." [PartR] (54:1) Wint 87, p. 121.
"Every silence is a magic space" (tr. of Robert Juarroz). [TriQ] (68) Wint 87, p. 112.
"Exercise." [RiverS] (23) 87, p. 38-39.
"Finally." [RiverS] (23) 87, p. 42-43.
"The Finding of Reasons." [RiverS] (23) 87, p. 41-42.
"Flat Mountain (Heizan Zenkin)" (tr. of Muso Soseki, w. Soiku Shigematsu).
    [AmerPoR] (16:2) Mr-Ap 87, p. 32.
"For Gen the New Head Priest of Erin-ji" (tr. of Muso Soseki, w. Soiku
    Shigematsu). [AmerPoR] (16:2) Mr-Ap 87, p. 29.
"For Myo's Departure for Shofuku-ji" (tr. of Muso Soseki, w. Soiku Shigematsu).
    [AmerPoR] (16:2) Mr-Ap 87, p. 29.
"For Sho the New Head Priest of Erin-ji" (tr. of Muso Soseki, w. Soiku
    Shigematsu). [AmerPoR] (16:2) Mr-Ap 87, p. 30.
"The Fragrance of the Udumbara (Dompo Shuo)" (tr. of Muso Soseki, w. Soiku
    Shigematsu). [AmerPoR] (16:2) Mr-Ap 87, p. 30.
"The glance is a lovely pretext of the eye's" (tr. of Roberto Juarroz). [Antaeus] (58)
    Spr 87, p. 97.
"Great Verse Valley" (tr. of Muso Soseki, w. Soiku Shigematsu). [AmerPoR] (16:2)
    Mr-Ap 87, p. 31.
"Hall of the Guardian God" (tr. of Muso Soseki, w. Soiku Shigematsu). [AmerPoR]
    (16:2) Mr-Ap 87, p. 31.
"Hearing the Names of the Valleys." [Field] (37) Fall 87, p. 72.
"The Horizons of Rooms." [GrandS] (7:1) Aut 87, p. 65-66.
"House of Spring (Shun-oku Myoha)" (tr. of Muso Soseki, w. Soiku Shigematsu).
    [AmerPoR] (16:2) Mr-Ap 87, p. 30.
"Hut in Harmony (Tekian Hojun)" (tr. of Muso Soseki, w. Soiku Shigematsu).
    [AmerPoR] (16:2) Mr-Ap 87, p. 32.
"I found a man writing on his bones" (tr. of Roberto Juarroz). [Antaeus] (58) Spr
    87, p. 98.
"Inauguration of Fukusan Dormitory" (tr. of Muso Soseki, w. Soiku Shigematsu).
    [AmerPoR] (16:2) Mr-Ap 87, p. 27.
"The Inevitable Lightness." [PartR] (54:1) Wint 87, p. 122.

"It" (tr. of Muso Soseki, w. Soiku Shigematsu). [AmerPoR] (16:2) Mr-Ap 87, p. 30.
"Its own thirst sustains it" (tr. of Roberto Juarroz). [Antaeus] (58) Spr 87, p. 99.
"Journey." [NewYorker] (63:38) 9 N 87, p. 132.
"Kanaloa." [NewYorker] (63:8) 13 Ap 87, p. 32.
"A Last Look." [Poetry] (151:1/2) O-N 87, p. 102-103.
"Laughing Mountain (Shozan Shunen)" (tr. of Muso Soseki, w. Soiku Shigematsu). [AmerPoR] (16:2) Mr-Ap 87, p. 27.
"Learning." [Caliban] (2) 87, p. 46.
"Living in the Mountains: Ten Poems" (tr. of Muso Soseki, w. Soiku Shigematsu). [AmerPoR] (16:2) Mr-Ap 87, p. 28.
"Losing a Language." [YaleR] (76:3) Spr 87, p. 358-359.
"The Lost Originals." [Caliban] (2) 87, p. 46.
"Lover of Mountains (Ninzan)" (tr. of Muso Soseki, w. Soiku Shigematsu). [AmerPoR] (16:2) Mr-Ap 87, p. 29.
"Magnificent Peak" (tr. of Muso Soseki, w. Soiku Shigematsu). [AmerPoR] (16:2) Mr-Ap 87, p. 30.
"Memory." [Field] (37) Fall 87, p. 73.
"Moon Mountain" (tr. of Muso Soseki, w. Soiku Shigematsu). [AmerPoR] (16:2) Mr-Ap 87, p. 27.
"Moon Tree Cliff (Keigan)" (tr. of Muso Soseki, w. Soiku Shigematsu). [AmerPoR] (16:2) Mr-Ap 87, p. 29.
"Mourning for the Layman Named Cloud Peak" (tr. of Muso Soseki, w. Soiku Shigematsu). [AmerPoR] (16:2) Mr-Ap 87, p. 27.
"Native." [YaleR] (76:3) Spr 87, p. 359-360.
"No Gain" (tr. of Muso Soseki, w. Soiku Shigematsu). [AmerPoR] (16:2) Mr-Ap 87, p. 31.
"No Word Hut (Mokuan Shuyu)" (tr. of Muso Soseki, w. Soiku Shigematsu). [AmerPoR] (16:2) Mr-Ap 87, p. 29.
"Note in a Guide Book." [Iowa] (17:1) Wint 87, p. 37.
"Old Creek" (tr. of Muso Soseki, w. Soiku Shigematsu). [AmerPoR] (16:2) Mr-Ap 87, p. 26.
"Old Hut (Koan Fusho)" (tr. of Muso Soseki, w. Soiku Shigematsu). [AmerPoR] (16:2) Mr-Ap 87, p. 27.
"Old Man Advancing" (tr. of Muso Soseki, w. Soiku Shigematsu). [AmerPoR] (16:2) Mr-Ap 87, p. 29.
"Old Man at Leisure (Kanso Ankan)" (tr. of Muso Soseki, w. Soiku Shigematsu). [AmerPoR] (16:2) Mr-Ap 87, p. 32.
"Old Man in Retirement" (tr. of Muso Soseki, w. Soiku Shigematsu). [AmerPoR] (16:2) Mr-Ap 87, p. 26.
"Old Man of Few Words (Mohuo Myokai)" (tr. of Muso Soseki, w. Soiku Shigematsu). [AmerPoR] (16:2) Mr-Ap 87, p. 32.
"Old Man To-The-Point" (tr. of Muso Soseki, w. Soiku Shigematsu). [AmerPoR] (16:2) Mr-Ap 87, p. 29.
"Ox Turned Loose (Hogo Korin)" (tr. of Muso Soseki, w. Soiku Shigematsu). [AmerPoR] (16:2) Mr-Ap 87, p. 32.
"Paper." [Nat] (244:5) 7 F 87, p. 152.
"The Peak of the Help Up Flower" (tr. of Muso Soseki, w. Soiku Shigematsu). [AmerPoR] (16:2) Mr-Ap 87, p. 31.
"Pine Shade" (tr. of Muso Soseki, w. Soiku Shigematsu). [AmerPoR] (16:2) Mr-Ap 87, p. 28.
"Place." [Nat] (244:7) 21 F 87, p. 230.
"The Pond at Hui-Neng's Spring" (tr. of Muso Soseki, w. Soiku Shigematsu). [AmerPoR] (16:2) Mr-Ap 87, p. 31.
"Print Fallen out of Somewhere." [Antaeus] (58) Spr 87, p. 246.
"The prompting of my shadow" (tr. of Roberto Juarroz). [Antaeus] (58) Spr 87, p. 98.
"Rain at Night." [Antaeus] (58) Spr 87, p. 247.
"Refugee" (From the Arabic of Salem Tubram, a version by Nasser Aruri and Edmund Ghareeb). [Nat] (244:5) 7 F 87, p. 152.
"Reizan Osho Visits Me" (tr. of Muso Soseki, w. Soiku Shigematsu). [AmerPoR] (16:2) Mr-Ap 87, p. 25.
"Reply to Bukko Zenji's Poem at Seiken-ji" (tr. of Muso Soseki, w. Soiku Shigematsu). [AmerPoR] (16:2) Mr-Ap 87, p. 30.
"Reply to Genno Osho's Poem" (Excerpts, tr. of Muso Soseki, w. Soiku Shigematsu). [AmerPoR] (16:2) Mr-Ap 87, p. 27.

"Reply to Suzan Osho's Snow Poem" (tr. of Muso Soseki, w. Soiku Shigematsu).
    [AmerPoR] (16:2) Mr-Ap 87, p. 29.
"The Rose Beetle." [NewYorker] (63:15) 1 Je 87, p. 32.
"Sibyl." [RiverS] (23) 87, p. 35-36.
"Sixth Vertical Poetry" (tr. of Robert Juarroz). [HawaiiR] (20) Fall 86, c87, p.
    47-53.
"Snow" (tr. of Muso Soseki, w. Soiku Shigematsu). [AmerPoR] (16:2) Mr-Ap 87,
    p. 30.
"Snow" (tr. of Zengi Dogen). [RiverS] (23) 87, p. 45-46.
"Snow at Rohatsu Sesshin" (tr. of Muso Soseki, w. Soiku Shigematsu). [AmerPoR]
    (16:2) Mr-Ap 87, p. 30.
"Snow Garden" (tr. of Muso Soseki, w. Soiku Shigematsu). [AmerPoR] (16:2)
    Mr-Ap 87, p. 29.
"Snow Valley" (tr. of Muso Soseki, w. Soiku Shigematsu). [AmerPoR] (16:2)
    Mr-Ap 87, p. 26.
"The Solstice." [ParisR] (29:105) Wint 87, p. 154.
"Spring Cliff" (tr. of Muso Soseki, w. Soiku Shigematsu). [AmerPoR] (16:2)
    Mr-Ap 87, p. 27.
"The Strangers from the Horizon." [Caliban] (2) 87, p. 45.
"Suspicor Speculum" (To Sysiphus). [RiverS] (23) 87, p. 43-44.
"Suzan Osho's Visit" (tr. of Muso Soseki, w. Soiku Shigematsu). [AmerPoR]
    (16:2) Mr-Ap 87, p. 29.
"Suzan Osho's Visit to My West Mountain Hut" (tr. of Muso Soseki, w. Soiku
    Shigematsu). [AmerPoR] (16:2) Mr-Ap 87, p. 31.
"Temple of Serene Light" (tr. of Muso Soseki, w. Soiku Shigematsu). [AmerPoR]
    (16:2) Mr-Ap 87, p. 31.
"Tengan Osho's Visit to Erin-ji" (tr. of Muso Soseki, w. Soiku Shigematsu).
    [AmerPoR] (16:2) Mr-Ap 87, p. 28.
"Thanks." [Nat] (244:10) 14 Mr 87, p. 336.
"Thanks for Daisen Osho's Visit" (Excerpts, tr. of Muso Soseki, w. Soiku
    Shigematsu). [AmerPoR] (16:2) Mr-Ap 87, p. 26.
"Thanks Sent to Taihei Osho" (Excerpts, tr. of Muso Soseki, w. Soiku Shigematsu).
    [AmerPoR] (16:2) Mr-Ap 87, p. 26.
"Things imitate us" (tr. of Robert Juarroz). [TriQ] (68) Wint 87, p. 111.
"Three Step Waterfall" (tr. of Muso Soseki, w. Soiku Shigematsu). [AmerPoR]
    (16:2) Mr-Ap 87, p. 31.
"Tiger Valley" (tr. of Muso Soseki, w. Soiku Shigematsu). [AmerPoR] (16:2)
    Mr-Ap 87, p. 31.
"To Kengai Osho of Engaku-ji" (tr. of Muso Soseki, w. Soiku Shigematsu).
    [AmerPoR] (16:2) Mr-Ap 87, p. 27.
"To the Emperor's Messenger" (tr. of Muso Soseki, w. Soiku Shigematsu).
    [AmerPoR] (16:2) Mr-Ap 87, p. 26.
"To the Riverside Temple (Rinsen-ji)" (tr. of Muso Soseki, w. Soiku Shigematsu).
    [AmerPoR] (16:2) Mr-Ap 87, p. 29.
"Toki-No-Ge (Satori Poem)" (tr. of Muso Soseki, w. Soiku Shigematsu).
    [AmerPoR] (16:2) Mr-Ap 87, p. 31.
"Truth Hall (Gido Shushin)" (tr. of Muso Soseki, w. Soiku Shigematsu).
    [AmerPoR] (16:2) Mr-Ap 87, p. 28.
"Utterance." [Nat] (244:5) 7 F 87, p. 152.
"Vertical Poetry" (6 selections, tr. of Roberto Juarroz). [Trans] (18) Spr 87, p.
    203-207.
"Vertical Poetry" (Excerpts, tr. of Roberto Juarroz). [Iowa] (17:2) Spr-Sum 87, p.
    91.
"Vertical Poetry" (Excerpts, tr. of Roberto Juarroz). [MissouriR] (10:2) 87, p.
    32-33.
"Vertical Poetry" (Five poems, tr. of Roberto Juarroz). [WillowS] (19) Wint 87, p.
    55-60.
"Visiting My Old Hut in Late Spring" (tr. of Muso Soseki, w. Soiku Shigematsu).
    [AmerPoR] (16:2) Mr-Ap 87, p. 27.
"Wandering" (tr. of Muso Soseki, w. Soiku Shigematsu). [AmerPoR] (16:2) Mr-Ap
    87, p. 25.
"Ways." [Iowa] (17:1) Wint 87, p. 36.
"Withered Zen" (tr. of Muso Soseki, w. Soiku Shigematsu). [AmerPoR] (16:2)
    Mr-Ap 87, p. 30.
"Yes, there is a back of things" (tr. of Robert Juarroz). [TriQ] (68) Wint 87, p. 110.

3691. MESA, Lauren
"The Flower Vendor" (after Diego Rivera). [CumbPR] (7:1) Fall 87, p. 68.
"Shelter." [LaurelR] (21:1/2) Wint-Sum 87, p. 66.
"Woman Weighing Gold." [CutB] (27/28) 87, p. 78.
3692. MESLER, Corey
"Dominoes" (for Allison). [Wind] (17:59) 87, p. 41.
"Savages." [Wind] (17:59) 87, p. 26.
3693. MESSER, Virginia
"The Sow's Ear." [Writer] (100:5) My 87, p. 20.
3694. MESSERLI, Douglas
"Hymns to Him" (3 selections). [Notus] (2:1) Spr 87, p. 26-28.
"Maxims from My Mother's Milk" (2 selections). [Notus] (2:1) Spr 87, p. 29-30.
"Scared Cows." [Bound] (14:1/2) Fall 85-Wint 86 [c87], p. 94.
3695. METZGER, Deena
"Heat." [YellowS] (24) Aut 87, p. 20.
"Lilith." [Electrum] (39) Fall-Wint 87, p. 23-24.
"Raspberries." [YellowS] (24) Aut 87, p. 21.
"What Feeds Us." [YellowS] (24) Aut 87, p. 21.
MEULEN, Jim Vander
See Vander MEULEN, Jim
3696. MEYER, Bruce
"Somewhere Short of Home." [Waves] (14:4) Spr 86, p. 68-69.
3697. MEYER, Thomas
"The Nichol Suite." [Conjunc] (10) 87, p. 168-172.
3698. MEYER, William (William E., Jr.)
"How Much Should You Write, S. K." [WindO] (48) Spr 87, p. 22, 25.
"If = Repetition, Søren." [WindO] (48) Spr 87, p. 21.
"The Kierkegaardian Drewn Poem." [WindO] (48) Spr 87, p. 21.
"Kierkegaardian/Texas Haiku." [WindO] (48) Spr 87, p. 20.
"Red Dastardly Night and Concrete Girl on Indian Fence." [WindO] (48) Spr 87, p. 20.
"Soren Kirkegaard Hitchhiking." [WindO] (48) Spr 87, p. 25.
"A Talk with My Mother." [WindO] (49) Fall 87, p. 49.
"Two Ducks." [BallSUF] (28:4) Aut 87, p. 18.
"Two Ducks." [SmPd] (24:1) Wint 87, p. 9.
"Two Gulls: Bill and Mary Anne." [SmPd] (24:1) Wint 87, p. 9.
3699. MEYERS, Joan Rohr
"Apples." [Comm] (114:3) 13 F 87, p. 87.
"At Dawn." [Comm] (114:3) 13 F 87, p. 87.
"Finish Line." [Comm] (114:3) 13 F 87, p. 87.
"Summer's Majesty." [Comm] (114:3) 13 F 87, p. 87.
"Windows." [Comm] (114:3) 13 F 87, p. 87.
3700. MEYERS, Kent
"Straw" (For My Father). [PoetL] (82:3) Fall 87, p. 163-164.
3701. MICHAEL, Ann E.
"Reason." [Poem] (58) N 87, p. 2.
3702. MICHAEL KARL (RITCHIE)
"May Day in China, Xi'An." [Gambit] (20) 86, p. 113.
3703. MICHAELSON, Caren Lee
"T - Stop." [AlphaBS] (2) D 87, p. 5.
3704. MICHALSKA, BethMarie
"Peaches and War." [Quarry] (36:1) Wint 87, p. 26.
3705. MICHAUX, Henri
"Posture" (tr. by Michael Fineberg). [LitR] (30:3) Spr 87, p. 421-424.
3706. MICHELINE, Jack
"Poems for the Ringing of the Bells." [AlphaBS] (1) Je 87, p. 12.
MICHIKO, Saeki
See SAEKI, Michiko
3707. MICKEL, Karl
"Beer: For Leising" (tr. by Laszlo Baransky, Istvan Eorsi, Anna Saghy and Bob Rosenthal). [Rampike] (5:3) 87, p. 66.
"German Woman '46" (tr. by Laszlo Baransky, Istvan Eorsi, Anna Saghy and Bob Rosenthal). [Rampike] (5:3) 87, p. 66.
"The Modern Quarter" (tr. by Laszlo Baransky, Istvan Eorsi, Anna Saghy and Bob Rosenthal). [Rampike] (5:3) 87, p. 67.

"Orderly Hair" (tr. by Laszlo Baransky, Istvan Eorsi, Anna Saghy and Bob
Rosenthal). [Rampike] (5:3) 87, p. 67.
3708. MIDDLEBROOK, Diane
"After Klee's *Geschwister*." [Sequoia] (31:1) Centennial issue 87, p. 108.
"Buddhist Prayer Flags from Bhutan." [Sequoia] (31:1) Centennial issue 87, p. 108.
3709. MIDDLETON, Christopher
"Birdsong, Echo of the Original Paradise" (tr. of Lars Gustafsson, w. the author).
[SouthernHR] (21:4) Fall 87, p. 363.
"Discussions" (tr. of Lars Gustafsson, w. the author). [SouthernHR] (21:1) Wint
87, p. 36-37.
"Looking at a Portrait of Lou Andreas-Salomé" (tr. of Lars Gustafsson, w. the
author). [SouthernHR] (21:1) Wint 87, p. 18.
"On the Deepest Sounds" (tr. of Lars Gustafsson, w. the author). [SouthernHR]
(21:1) Wint 87, p. 38.
"A Revenant." [HangL] (50/51) 87, p. 124.
3710. MIDDLETON, David
"Thomas Tallis to William Byrd" (on the dissolution of the English abbeys).
[SewanR] (95:4) Fall 87, p. 525-527.
3711. MIECZKOWSKI, Rondo
"That Crazy Woman Who Lived Next Door." [DekalbLAJ] (20:1/4) 87, p. 48.
MIELES, Edgardo Nieves
See NIEVES MIELES, Edgardo
MIHARU NO ARISUKE
See ARISUKE, Miharu No
3712. MIKOLOWSKI, Ken
"Big Enigmas" (Excerpt). [Notus] (2:1) Spr 87, p. 81.
"Chaos" (for Bob Sestok). [Notus] (2:1) Spr 87, p. 79.
"Ecology." [Notus] (2:1) Spr 87, p. 80.
3713. MIKULEC, Patrick B.
"At the Firing Range." [Phoenix] (7:1) 87, p. 14.
"Origins (At Buck Hollow Graveyard)." [Outbr] (18/19) Fall 86-Spr 88, p. 140.
"Recapitulating Stars." [GreensboroR] (43) Wint 87-88, p. 92.
"When the Mountain Blew." [EngJ] (76:3) Mr 87, p. 59.
3714. MILBERG, Jennie
"Homeless." [Wind] (17:60) 87, p. 26.
"What Can I Give Now." [Wind] (17:60) 87, p. 26-27.
3715. MILBURN, Michael
"The Funeral." [Ploughs] (13:4) 87, p. 75-76.
"Last Letter." [Agni] (24/25) 87, p. 107.
3716. MILES, Jeffrey
"Zen Slug." [CarolQ] (39:3) Spr 87, p. 82.
3717. MILES, S. P.
"Beside and With You." [Pembroke] (19) 87, p. 154-155.
"Recognition." [Pembroke] (19) 87, p. 155-156.
3718. MILJKOVIC, Branko
"Ballad" (tr. by John Matthias and Vladeta Vukovic). [Margin] (2) Spr 87, p. 59.
"Earth and Fire" (tr. by John Matthias and Vladeta Vukovic). [Margin] (2) Spr 87, p.
58.
"In Praise of Fire" (tr. by John Matthias and Vladeta Vukovic). [Margin] (2) Spr 87,
p. 57.
"An Orphic Legacy" (tr. by John Matthias and Vladeta Vukovic). [Margin] (2) Spr
87, p. 58.
3719. MILLER, Bill
"Being Alone." [Contact] (9:44/45/46) Fall-Wint 87, p. 60.
"A New Con." [Contact] (9:44/45/46) Fall-Wint 87, p. 60.
"The Yard Shimmers." [Contact] (9:44/45/46) Fall-Wint 87, p. 60.
3720. MILLER, Carl
"Snail-Watching." [KanQ] (19:1/2) Wint-Spr 87, p. 210.
3721. MILLER, Carolyn
"At the End of Summer." [YellowS] (22) Spr 87, p. 29.
3722. MILLER, Carolyn Reynolds
"Chagall's Three Angels: Three Repaintings." [MalR] (81) D 87, p. 74-76.
"Coming and Going." [MalR] (81) D 87, p. 77-80.
"Forced Marches." [CutB] (27/28) 87, p. 76-77.
"Rising and Falling." [ColR] (NS 14:1) Spr-Sum 87, p. 58-59.

3723. MILLER, Chuck
"Harvesters." [GreenfR] (14:3/4) Sum-Fall 87, p. 56-60.
3724. MILLER, D. Patrick
"Dream of the Shebear." [YellowS] (24) Aut 87, p. 23.
3725. MILLER, David
"Door of Paradise." [Act] (7) 87, p. 60-61.
3726. MILLER, Derek
"Not a Tornado Warning." [HangL] (50/51) 87, p. 213.
3727. MILLER, E. Ethelbert
"New York (for Egberto)." [BlackALF] (21:3) Fall 87, p. 235.
"New York (for Enid)." [BlackALF] (21:3) Fall 87, p. 235-236.
"New York (for Marie)." [BlackALF] (21:3) Fall 87, p. 236.
"New York (for Richard)." [BlackALF] (21:3) Fall 87, p. 236.
3728. MILLER, E. S.
"The Costume." [OP] (final issue) Sum 87, p. 73.
"Egghead." [OP] (final issue) Sum 87, p. 74.
3729. MILLER, Errol
"Druid City." [Lactuca] (7) Ag 87, p. 12.
"Far Far Away" (For Sylvia Plath). [Interim] (6:1) Spr 87, p. 11.
"He Can't Pull Free Beyond the Circle." [Interim] (6:1) Spr 87, p. 12.
"The Interior Designer." [SmPd] (24:3) Fall 87, p. 25.
"She Lies Down in Tall Grasses." [InterPR] (13:2) Fall 87, p. 79.
3730. MILLER, Frances
"Pray, You, Love, Remember" (Honorary Mention 1987 John Williams Andrews
Narrative Poetry Prize). [PoetL] (82:4) Wint 87-88, p. 230-233.
3731. MILLER, Hugh
"Camping Out." [AntigR] (69/70) 87, p. 140-141.
"A Froward Broadside" (matinee for Kathleen, Corky, & Nadine). [AntigR] (69/70)
87, p. 140.
"The Nature of Things." [AntigR] (71/72) Aut 87-Wint 88, p. 138.
3732. MILLER, James A.
"Beauty." [BellArk] (3:6) N-D 87, p. 5.
"Before the Rain" (for Elie Wiesel). [ManhatPR] (9) Sum 87, p. 60.
"Coda on an Amish Teleology." [Poem] (57) Mr 87, p. 57.
"In the Land of Meade and Lee." [BellArk] (3:1) Ja-F 87, p. 10.
"Injunction on the Thought of Woman Even After Having Been Up for One and One
Half Day." [HawaiiR] (21) Spr 87, p. 47.
"Mystic Journey of the Unknown Magus." [Poem] (57) Mr 87, p. 56.
"Negative Capability." [BellArk] (3:1) Ja-F 87, p. 2.
"On the Salutary Effect of Coffee (Good Such) and Other Certain Cultural
Digressions." [BellArk] (3:4) Jl-Ag 87, p. 6.
"Saturday Evening, the Idea of Order on Canal St." [Poem] (57) Mr 87, p. 58.
"Substantive Mirage, Candent Aphrodite." [Poem] (57) Mr 87, p. 55.
"Two Avenues to the Past" (On Looking at the Only Extant Photograph). [BellArk]
(3:1) Ja-F 87, p. 4.
"Two Avenues to the Past" (On Looking at the Only Extant Photograph). [Poem]
(57) Mr 87, p. 51-54.
3733. MILLER, Jane
"Any Two Wheels." [AmerPoR] (16:6) N-D 87, p. 5.
"Approaching Forty Devils." [Agni] (24/25) 87, p. 94-95.
"August Zero." [AmerPoR] (16:6) N-D 87, p. 6.
"Betrayal." [AmerPoR] (16:6) N-D 87, p. 4.
"Broken Garland of Months" (after Folgore da San Gemignano). [AmerPoR] (16:6)
N-D 87, p. 4.
"Intestine of Taos." [AntR] (45:1) Wint 87, p. 48-49.
"Lengthening Day." [AmerPoR] (16:6) N-D 87, p. 3.
"Let Three Days Pass." [AmerPoR] (16:6) N-D 87, p. 5.
"Lost White Brother." [HighP] (2:2) Fall 87, p. 169-170.
"Mona Lisa." [AmerPoR] (16:6) N-D 87, p. 7.
"Outer Space." [AmerPoR] (16:6) N-D 87, p. 3.
"Picnic." [AmerPoR] (16:6) N-D 87, p. 5.
"The Purple Robe." [AmerPoR] (16:6) N-D 87, p. 4.
"Scattered Alphabet." [Sonora] (13) Fall 87, p. 92-93.
"Semantic Field." [AmerPoR] (16:6) N-D 87, p. 6.
"Sonnet Against Nuclear Weapons." [Sonora] (13) Fall 87, p. 94-95.
"Stravinsky." [AntR] (45:1) Wint 87, p. 47.

"Topos." [AntR] (45:1) Wint 87, p. 46.
3734. MILLER, Jauren
"Late December, San Joaquin." [Zyzzyva] (3:4) Wint 87-88, p. 108.
3735. MILLER, Jeanette
"Magritte's Red Curtain: A Villanelle on Decalcomania." [Shen] (37:3) 87, p. 64.
3736. MILLER, John N.
"Between Home and Abroad." [Outbr] (18/19) Fall 86-Spr 88, p. 74.
"Three-Pony Opera" (Fall, 1982). [SmPd] (24:1) Wint 87, p. 12-14.
3737. MILLER, Leslie Adrienne
"Epithalamium." [OP] (final issue) Sum 87, p. 58-59.
"Primary Colors." [OP] (final issue) Sum 87, p. 56-57.
"Tracks Were on the Frosty Lawn." [OP] (final issue) Sum 87, p. 60-61.
3738. MILLER, Michael
"Buckets." [HawaiiR] (19) Spr 86, c87, p. 10.
"Changing Light." [SouthernR] (23:3) Jl 87, p. 610.
3739. MILLER, Pat
"Maybe the Trees." [Gambit] (21) 87, p. 20.
3740. MILLER, Philip
"Bitter." [Poem] (57) Mr 87, p. 6.
"Father's Day." [NegC] (7:3/4) 87, p. 89-90.
"Four Leaf Clovers." [Raccoon] (24/25) My 87, p. 295.
"Grandma Rose." [Poem] (57) Mr 87, p. 8.
"Houses." [Raccoon] (24/25) My 87, p. 296.
"Pain." [Poem] (57) Mr 87, p. 7.
"Shadow Show." [NegC] (7:3/4) 87, p. 91.
"This Evening" (The Greensboro Review Literary Award, Honorable Mention).
[GreensboroR] (41) Wint 86-87, p. 51.
3741. MILLER, Theresa W.
"Running with Helena." [GreensboroR] (43) Wint 87-88, p. 115.
3742. MILLER, Walter James
"A Sequence of Sequins." [HampSPR] Wint 87, p. 23.
3743. MILLER, Warren C.
"Knowledge." [Outbr] (18/19) Fall 86-Spr 88, p. 31.
"Sixty-Seventh Street Scheherazade." [PaintedB] (30) 87, p. 38.
3744. MILLER, William
"Old Faith." [SouthernHR] (21:4) Fall 87, p. 356-357.
3745. MILLETT, John
"Aran — Recalled from Hackle Back Mount Seaview." [Vis] (24) 87, p. 12.
"Fox in the Pie." [Vis] (23) 87, p. 37.
"Kilronan Stud." [Vis] (25) 87, p. 4.
"Man into Clothesline." [Chelsea] (46) 87, p. 34-35.
3746. MILLIS, Christopher
"After a Walk" (tr. of Umberto Saba). [SenR] (17:2) 87, p. 7.
"Invitation." [Pig] (14) 87, p. 21.
"Letter to a Friend Studying Piano at the Conservatory of" (tr. of Umberto Saba).
[SenR] (17:2) 87, p. 11-13.
"Messages." [Pig] (14) 87, p. 20.
"To My Wife" (tr. of Umberto Saba). [SenR] (17:2) 87, p. 8-10.
3747. MILLS, Christopher
"Happiness" (tr. of Umberto Saba). [Paint] (14:28) Aut 87, p. 34.
"In the Courtyard" (tr. of Umberto Saba). [Paint] (14:28) Aut 87, p. 35.
3748. MILLS, George
"Empery." [Ascent] (13:1) 87, p. 41-42.
"Hearsay." [PoetL] (82:1) Spr 87, p. 18.
"Quite a Guy." [Ascent] (13:1) 87, p. 42.
3749. MILLS, Paul
"Adoration of the Shepherds." [Stand] (28:2) Spr 87, p. 66-67.
3750. MILLS, Ralph J., Jr.
"9/2" (for Diane Wakoski). [AnotherCM] (17) 87, p. 93.
"10/27." [Northeast] (Ser. 4:6) Wint 87-88, p. 5.
"11/9." [SpoonRQ] (12:2) Spr 87, p. 16.
"By the / Road" (for Martin Wine). [SpoonRQ] (12:2) Spr 87, p. 15.
"Even If." [SpoonRQ] (12:2) Spr 87, p. 14.
"A Morning For." [Northeast] (Ser. 4:6) Wint 87-88, p. 4.
3751. MILLS, Sparling
"Old Bruce." [AntigR] (71/72) Aut 87-Wint 88, p. 204.

3752. MILOSZ, Czeslaw
"All Hallows' Eve" (tr. by the author and Leonard Nathan). [NewYorker] (63:37) 2
N 87, p. 42.
"And Yet the Books." [CrossCur] (7:3) 87, p. 57.
"La Belle Époque" (tr. by the author). [Antaeus] (58) Spr 87, p. 231-239.
"Incantation." [KenR] (NS 9:4) Fall 87, p. 21.
"Mary Magdalene and I." [NewYorker] (63:1) 23 F 87, p. 40.
3753. MILTNER, Robert
"Class Notes." [EngJ] (76:4) Ap 87, p. 49.
3754. MIMS, Spencer
"Sphere." [MoodySI] (18/19) Fall 87, p. 7.
3755. MINET, Lawrence
"Daphne Beating Apollo to the Laurel Tree." [Poem] (57) Mr 87, p. 26.
"A Part of the Forest." [Wind] (17:61) 87, p. 30.
"Portrait of the Artist as an Old Man." [Wind] (17:61) 87, p. 30.
3756. MINNE, Richard
"All's Well That Ends Well" (tr. by André Lefevere). [Paint] (14:28) Aut 87, p. 26.
"Portrait" (tr. by André Lefevere). [Paint] (14:28) Aut 87, p. 27.
"We Stood in a Circle" (tr. by André Lefevere). [Paint] (14:28) Aut 87, p. 28.
"Writing Poetry" (tr. by André Lefevere). [Paint] (14:28) Aut 87, p. 29.
3757. MINOR, James
"Haiku" (4 poems). [Northeast] (Ser. 4:6) Wint 87-88, p. 14.
3758. MINTON, Helena
"At the Construction Site of the Hydro-Electric Plant" (Lowell, Massachuetts, 1984).
[HampSPR] Wint 86, p. 38.
"From the Same Cloth" (form the mill girls, Lowell, Massachusetts, circa 1840).
[TexasR] (7:3/4) 87, p. 108-109.
"Lent." [HampSPR] Wint 86, p. 39.
"Linen." [HampSPR] Wint 86, p. 39.
"Negroe Cloth" (Lowell, Massachusetts circa 1940). [HampSPR] Wint 86, p. 40.
"Wife of Millhand" (Lowell, Massachusetts, circa 1875). [TexasR] (7:3/4) 87, p.
107.
3759. MINUS, Ed
"The Bees." [ChatR] (8:1) Fall 87, p. 75.
3760. MIRIKITANI, Janice
"Love Canal." [Contact] (9:44/45/46) Fall-Wint 87, p. 46-47.
"Soul Food." [Zyzzyva] (3:2) Sum 87, p. 93-94.
3761. MIRSKIN, Jerry
"Blue Mornings." [MSS] (5:3) 87, p. 63-64.
"Cyclops." [SenR] (17:2) 87, p. 58.
"Digging." [MSS] (5:3) 87, p. 62.
"Diner." [MSS] (5:3) 87, p. 59-60.
"Dream After Rain." [MSS] (5:3) 87, p. 64-65.
"In Its Mercy." [GreenfR] (14:3/4) Sum-Fall 87, p. 43.
"In November." [MSS] (5:3) 87, p. 60-61.
"Outside Fargo, North Dakota." [GreenfR] (14:3/4) Sum-Fall 87, p. 44.
3762. MITCHAM, Judson
"How the Story Goes On." [PraS] (61:4) Wint 87, p. 95.
"In the Kingdom of the Air." [GeoR] (41:3) Fall 87, p. 529.
"Laments." [GeoR] (41:1) Spr 87, p. 173-175.
"Late in October." [PraS] (61:4) Wint 87, p. 94-95.
"Refusing to Cry." [PraS] (61:4) Wint 87, p. 92-93.
3763. MITCHELL, Ben
"Migration of the Hare Across Eurasia" (In memoriam, Joseph Beuys, 1921-1986).
[PassN] (8:1) Wint 87, p. 22.
3764. MITCHELL, Hugh P.
"Decline to Sleep." [StoneC] (14:3/4) Spr-Sum 87, p. 63.
3765. MITCHELL, Roger
"Afternoon at the Guide Museum." [Abraxas] (35/36) 87, p. 5-6.
"Fantasia, with John Locke." [PoetryNW] (28:3) Aut 87, p. 10.
"Motels." [NoAmR] (272:1) Mr 87, p. 72-73.
"Rain." [PoetryNW] (28:3) Aut 87, p. 9.
"Spring Wind." [PoetryNW] (28:3) Aut 87, p. 10-11.
"Things." [PoetryE] (23/24) Fall 87, p. 119.

3766. MITCHELL, Stephen
"Last Poems" (Selections: 5 poems, tr. of Rainer Maria Rilke). [Thrpny] (30) Sum 87, p. 20.
3767. MITCHELL, Susan
"Women in Profile: Bas-Relief, Left Section Missing." [NewYorker] (63:9) 20 Ap 87, p. 38.
3768. MITCHELL, Wendy
"Fever." [NegC] (7:3/4) 87, p. 156-157.
3769. MIZE, R. W.
"Man Farming." [Pembroke] (19) 87, p. 118-120.
3770. MIZEJEWSKI, Linda
"At Thirty, Learning To Garden" (Academy of American Poets Prize, 1986). [PennR] (3:1) Spr-Sum 87, p. 1-2.
3771. MJELVE, Sigmund
"Clouds come up" (tr. by George Johnston). [MalR] (78) Mr 87, p. 99.
"The heavens too" (tr. by George Johnston). [MalR] (78) Mr 87, p. 98.
"I am a dead whale" (tr. by George Johnston). [MalR] (78) Mr 87, p. 101.
"Often was summer" (tr. by George Johnston). [MalR] (78) Mr 87, p. 100.
"Once it was December" (tr. by George Johnston). [MalR] (78) Mr 87, p. 99.
"Time becomes, always, always" (tr. by George Johnston). [MalR] (78) Mr 87, p. 100.
3772. MLADINIC, Peter
"The Fugitive." [Wind] (17:61) 87, p. 31.
3773. MNOTOZA, Zim
"Evicted by the Farmer." [AmerPoR] (16:5) S-O 87, p. 20-21.
3774. MOE, H. D.
"Into the Deep Past Toward Now." [FiveFR] (5) 87, p. 134-136.
3775. MOELLER, Eileen
"Barn Fire." [Footwork] 87, p. 27-28.
"Confessions." [Footwork] 87, p. 28.
"Linda." [Calyx] (11:1) Wint 87-88, p. 33.
"My Mother Always Seemed Bigger Than Me." [Footwork] 87, p. 28.
"Tree of Heaven (Ailanthus)." [Outbr] (18/19) Fall 86-Spr 88, p. 26-27.
"When the Junk Man Came Down Summer Street." [Outbr] (18/19) Fall 86-Spr 88, p. 28-30.
3776. MOFFEIT, Tony
"Drifter in a Dark Wind." [PoeticJ] (17) 87, p. 22.
"Hank." [Gargoyle] (32/33) 87, p. 356.
"Hank Williams." [Vis] (24) 87, p. 5.
"Nothing to Say." [PoeticJ] (17) 87, p. 22.
"Walking on Space." [PoeticJ] (17) 87, p. 23.
3777. MOFFETT, Judith
"Choosing Tarzan." [MichQR] (26:3) Sum 87, p. 479-482.
3778. MOFFITT, John
"Mating Flight." [KanQ] (19:1/2) Wint-Spr 87, p. 112.
"Rites of Change." [KanQ] (19:1/2) Wint-Spr 87, p. 112-113.
3779. MOFOKENG, S. M.
"Senkatana" (Selection: Act I, Scene 1 (partial), tr. by Daniel P. Kunene). [TriQ] (69) Spr-Sum 87, p. 336-337.
3780. MOHR, Bill
"The Will to Live" (1985 Alice Jackson Poetry Prize: Honorable Mention). [Electrum] (39) Fall-Wint 87, p. 16-18.
3781. MOHRBACHER, Bob
"Contract." [BellArk] (3:6) N-D 87, p. 3.
"The Silk Trees." [BellArk] (3:6) N-D 87, p. 4.
3782. MOISÉS, Carlos Felipe
"The Day," ("O Dia," tr. by Joanna Courteau). [PoetC] (18:2) Wint 87, p. 35.
"An Ox Striped in Shadow" ("Boi Raiado em Penumbra," tr. by Joanna Courteau). [PoetC] (18:2) Wint 87, p. 39.
"The Sound of the Sea" ("O Rumor do Mar," tr. by Joanna Courteau). [PoetC] (18:2) Wint 87, p. 36.
"This Morning" ("Esta Manhã," tr. by Joanna Courteau). [PoetC] (18:2) Wint 87, p. 34.
"Your Smile" ("Teu Sorriso," tr. by Joanna Courteau). [PoetC] (18:2) Wint 87, p. 37-38.

3783. MOK, Maurits
    "Return Trip" (tr. by Constance Studer). [Vis] (24) 87, p. 20.
3784. MOLARSKY, Margaret G.
    "Fog, you have stolen the hill." [Kaleid] (14) Wint-Spr 87, p. 69.
    "Little sleeping slug." [Kaleid] (14) Wint-Spr 87, p. 69.
    "Precious gravity." [Kaleid] (14) Wint-Spr 87, p. 69.
MOLEN, Robert Vander
    See VanderMOLEN, Robert
3785. MOLINARI, Christine
    "All Time" (tr. of Sandor Csoóri). [Field] (36) Spr 87, p. 46.
    "Last Will and Testament — May" (tr. of Sandor Csoóri). [Field] (36) Spr 87, p. 47.
    "Summer and Halo" (tr. of Sandor Csoóri). [Field] (36) Spr 87, p. 44.
    "To Remember Myself" (tr. of Sandor Csoóri). [Field] (36) Spr 87, p. 45.
3786. MOLLOY-OLUND, Barbara
    "Night and Effort." [Ploughs] (13:4) 87, p. 77-78.
3787. MOLTON, Warren Lane
    "He Descended into Hell." [ChrC] (104:12) 15 Ap 87, p. 351.
    "Maundy Thursday." [ChrC] (104:9) 18-25 Mr 87, p. 264.
    "Waking in Winter." [ChrC] (104:8) 11 Mr 87, p. 236.
3788. MOMADAY, N. Scott
    "Mogollon Morning." [Sequoia] (31:1) Centennial issue 87, p. 46.
MON, Richard le
    See LeMON, Richard
3789. MONACO, Cory
    "The Animal Test." [WormR] (27:4, issue 108) 87, p. 107.
    "Dennis the Menace the Marine." [WormR] (27:4, issue 108) 87, p. 106.
    "Dropped." [WormR] (27:1, issue 105) 87, p. 10.
    "Had." [WormR] (27:1, issue 105) 87, p. 9.
    "His (1974)." [WormR] (27:1, issue 105) 87, p. 9.
    "It Is Interesting." [WormR] (27:4, issue 108) 87, p. 105.
    "John Wayne." [StoneC] (14:3/4) Spr-Sum 87, p. 49.
    "Last Night." [WormR] (27:4, issue 108) 87, p. 106.
    "Nervous Kid's." [WormR] (27:1, issue 105) 87, p. 8.
    "Saw." [WormR] (27:1, issue 105) 87, p. 8.
    "Stay Up Through the Night Then." [WormR] (27:1, issue 105) 87, p. 8-9.
    "Warning." [WormR] (27:1, issue 105) 87, p. 9.
    "Yeah, Right." [WormR] (27:1, issue 105) 87, p. 10.
3790. MONARDO, Anna F.
    "Some Moments Are a Long Time Coming." [Outbr] (18/19) Fall 86-Spr 88, p. 127.
3791. MONETTE, Paul
    "The Very Same." [AmerPoR] (16:6) N-D 87, p. 55.
3792. MONROE, Kent, Jr.
    "Armageddon." [StoneC] (15:1/2) Fall-Wint 87-88, p. 62-63.
3793. MONROY, Adriana
    "Poem: The city encloses us, moist" (tr. by Thomas Hoeksema). [InterPR] (13:1) Spr 87, p. 13.
    "Poema: La ciudad nos enclava, húmeda." [InterPR] (13:1) Spr 87, p. 12.
3794. MONSEN, Jocelyn G.
    "Beach Walk." [PraF] (8:3) Aut 87, p. 71.
    "Bush Pilot." [PraF] (8:3) Aut 87, p. 71.
    "Spring of the High Water." [PraF] (8:3) Aut 87, p. 70.
3795. MONTAGUE, John
    "The Siege of Mullingar." [Pembroke] (19) 87, p. 78.
3796. MONTALE, Eugenio
    "Above the Scribbled Writing" (tr. by Antony Oldknow). [SoDakR] (25:2) Sum 87, p. 16.
    "Arsenio" (tr. by William Arrowsmith). [Pequod] (23/24) 87, p. 295-296.
    "Don't ask us the word that will give shape" (tr. by Ned Condini). [PraS] (61:3) Fall 87, p. 70-71.
    "Eclogue" (tr. by William Arrowsmith). [SouthernHR] (21:2) Spr 87, p. 156-157.
    "End of Childhood" (tr. by William Arrowsmith). [Pequod] (23/24) 87, p. 292-294.
    "Falsetto" (tr. by William Arrowsmith). [SouthernHR] (21:2) Spr 87, p. 132-133.
    "I know the time when the most impassive face" (tr. by Jonathan Galassi). [GrandS] (6:3) Spr 87, p. 117.
    "I often met evil in life" (tr. by Ned Condini). [PraS] (61:3) Fall 87, p. 72.

"I would have liked to feel scoured, bared" (tr. by Ned Condini). [PraS] (61:3) Fall
    87, p. 72.
"A Kind of Fantasy" (tr. by Antony Oldknow). [SoDakR] (25:2) Sum 87, p. 17.
"Mediterranean" (tr. by Martin Gruber). [ParisR] (29:105) Wint 87, p. 188-194.
"The Motets" (Selections: II-IV, IX, XI, XIV, XX, tr. by Dana Gioia). [Boulevard]
    (2:1/2) Spr 87, p. 17-20.
"My life, I ask of you no stable" (tr. by Jonathan Galassi). [GrandS] (6:3) Spr 87, p.
    117.
"North Wind" (tr. by Ned Condini). [PraS] (61:3) Fall 87, p. 71.
"Now and Then" (tr. by William Arrowsmith). [SouthernHR] (21:2) Spr 87, p. 134.
"Ossi di Seppia" (Selections: 4 poems in Italian and English, tr. by William
    Arrowsmith). [CrossCur] (7:2) 87, p. 26-33.
"Satura" (Selections: 4 poems, tr. by William Arrowsmith). [Interim] (6:2) Fall 87,
    p. 3-6.
"Seacoasts" (tr. by William Arrowsmith). [Pequod] (23/24) 87, p. 290-291.
"A Wild Squall" (tr. by William Arrowsmith). [SouthernHR] (21:3) Sum 87, p. 230.
"Wind and Flags" (tr. by Jonathan Galassi). [NewYRB] (34:12) 16 Jl 87, p. 4.
MONTAÑEZ, Jaime Marcano
    See MARCANO MONTAÑEZ, Jaime
3797. MONTE, Bryan
    "Paragraphs." [JamesWR] (5:1) Fall 87, p. 7.
3798. MONTEIRO, George
    "Pity the Flowers" (tr. of Fernando Pessoa). [Nimrod] (31:1) Fall-Wint 87, p. 135.
    "Poem — Straight to the Point" (tr. of Fernando Pessoa). [Nimrod] (31:1) Fall-Wint
        87, p. 134-135.
    "Transactions." [DevQ] (21:2) Fall 86, p. 41-42.
3799. MONTES DE OCA, Marco Antonio
    "Bells" (To Pablo Antonio Cuadra, tr. by Brian Swann). [Footwork] 87, p. 21.
3800. MONTGOMERY, Carol
    "Haiku" (3 poems). [Amelia] (4:1/2, issue 9) 87, p. 100.
3801. MONTGOMERY, George
    "Billboards Could Even Be Vacant" (A love poem for James Dean). [AlphaBS] (2) D
        87, p. 7.
    "Buddha's Junkyard Along the Highway Near the Railroad Yards" (for Neal
        Cassady). [MoodySI] (18/19) Fall 87, p. 27.
    "In and Out Windows." [AlphaBS] (1) Je 87, p. 26.
    "The Perfect Fool." [AlphaBS] (1) Je 87, p. 25.
    "Somehow Paradise" (a poem for Ray Bremser). [Footwork] 87, p. 44.
    "Two Gathered Angels." [MoodySI] (18/19) Fall 87, p. 27.
3802. MONTGOMERY, John
    "The Cairn of Presidents" (for Gary Snyder). [AlphaBS] (1) Je 87, p. 16.
    "How It Was at the Conference." [AlphaBS] (2) D 87, p. 23.
    "Lullaby Before 1988." [AlphaBS] (2) D 87, p. 22.
    "Untitled: This is the story of the country that could." [AlphaBS] (1) Je 87, p. 14-15.
3803. MOODY, Rodger
    "I Want, I Want" (For Denise Wallace). [SnapD] (10:1/2) Wint 87, p. 70-71.
    "Searching Out the Past." [Wind] (17:61) 87, p. 32.
3804. MOODY, Shirley
    "We Are All Heart" (for Ron Bayes). [Pembroke] (19) 87, p. 224.
3805. MOOLTEN, David
    "Trajectories." [NegC] (7:1/2) 87, p. 88-89.
    "Vietnamization." [NegC] (7:1/2) 87, p. 87.
3806. MOON, Jay
    "Her." [Amelia] (4:1/2, issue 9) 87, p. 23.
3807. MOORE, Alison
    "Distractions." [PoetryNW] (28:3) Aut 87, p. 18-19.
3808. MOORE, Barbara
    "Crowed Up." [Salm] (72) Fall 86, p. 204-205.
    "River." [MidwQ] (28:2) Wint 87, p. 222.
    "Suburbs." [MidwQ] (28:2) Wint 87, p. 223.
3809. MOORE, Edward
    "Landscape." [NewAW] (2) Fall 87, p. 108.
    "Untitled Novel." [NewAW] (2) Fall 87, p. 107.
3810. MOORE, Gene M.
    "Autumnal." [ArizQ] (43:4) Wint 87, p. 378.

3811. MOORE, George B.
"The New Decade." [SouthwR] (72:1) Wint 87, p. 134.
MOORE, Jackie Warren
See WARREN-MOORE, Jackie
3812. MOORE, Janice Townley
"Fidelity." [Confr] (35/36) Spr-Fall 87, p. 209.
"West of Tuscaloosa." [SouthernPR] (27:1) Spr 87, p. 28.
3813. MOORE, Lenard D.
"Breaking Ground: Jacksonville, North Carolina." [GreenfR] (14:3/4) Sum-Fall 87,
     p. 172.
"For Dudley Randall." [BlackALF] (21:3) Fall 87, p. 242.
"On Hearing Gerald W. Barrax." [BlackALF] (21:3) Fall 87, p. 241-242.
"On Hearing Gerald W. Barrax" (Erratum notice). [BlackALF] (21:4) Wint 87, p.
     449.
"Poor Old Mr. Toothpick." [BlackALF] (21:3) Fall 87, p. 243.
"Power lines all down." [Pembroke] (19) 87, p. 100.
"Raleigh Jazz Festival, 1986." [BlackALF] (21:3) Fall 87, p. 243-244.
"A Summer Stroll." [BlackALF] (21:3) Fall 87, p. 242-243.
3814. MOORE, Marianne
"By Disposition of Angels." [Field] (37) Fall 87, p. 35.
"The Fish" (Excerpts). [AmerPoR] (16:2) Mr-Ap 87, p. 46-47.
"The Frigate Pelican." [Field] (37) Fall 87, p. 39-42.
"A Grave." [Field] (37) Fall 87, p. 24.
"New York." [AmerPoR] (16:2) Mr-Ap 87, p. 43.
"Nine Nectarines and Other Porcelain." [Field] (37) Fall 87, p. 15-17.
"Poetry." [Iowa] (17:3) Fall 87, p. 159-160.
"Poetry" (revised). [Iowa] (17:3) Fall 87, p. 160.
"Silence." [Field] (37) Fall 87, p. 30.
"The Steeple-Jack." [Field] (37) Fall 87, p. 9-11.
"To a Snail." [AmerPoR] (16:2) Mr-Ap 87, p. 47.
3815. MOORE, Miles David
"Watching Charlie's Angels." [Bogg] (57) 87, p. 55.
3816. MOORE, Nicholas
"Coffee-Coloured Horses of the Moon." [Poetry] (151:1/2) O-N 87, p. 103.
3817. MOORE, Richard
"Affluence." [LightY] '87, c86, p. 138.
"The New Courtship." [LightY] '87, c86, p. 138-139.
"TV." [TexasR] (7:3/4) 87, p. 111.
"The Visitors." [TexasR] (7:3/4) 87, p. 110.
"What Comes Naturally." [Salm] (74/75) Spr-Sum 87, p. 49-50.
3818. MOORE, Roger
"Death and the Maiden." [AntigR] (69/70) 87, p. 154.
"Family Portrait." [Waves] (15:4) Spr 87, p. 72.
3819. MOORE, Todd
"Baxter Was." [SlipS] (7) 87, p. 103.
"The Game Was." [Bogg] (58) 87, p. 44.
"I Was Never." [Bogg] (57) 87, p. 22.
3820. MOORHEAD, Andrea
"And It Was at Aachen." [Os] (24) 87, p. 23.
"Earth Song." [Os] (25) 87, p. 26.
"Harmony." [Os] (24) 87, p. 15.
"The Journal of Nights" (tr. of Claude Beausoleil). [Os] (24) 87, p. 7-9.
"Passage to the Sea." [Os] (25) 87, p. 19.
"The Road to Sinsheim." [Os] (25) 87, p. 18.
"Shadow of Snow." [Os] (24) 87, p. 14.
"Somewhere in Magog." [Os] (25) 87, p. 25.
"Split Light." [Os] (25) 87, p. 10.
3821. MOORMAN, Charles
"Four Christmas Love Songs." [TexasR] (8:1/2) Spr-Sum 87, p. 18-21.
3822. MOOSE, Ruth
"Eleven." [ColR] (NS 14:1) Spr-Sum 87, p. 11.
"Guy in Paris." [Pembroke] (19) 87, p. 131-132.
"Mill on the Pond." [ColR] (NS 14:1) Spr-Sum 87, p. 10.
MORA, Francisco Lluch
See LLUCH MORA, Francisco

3823. MORA, Pat
"Bruja: Witch." [Calyx] (10:2/3) Spr 87, p. 179-180.
3824. MORAES, Dom
"Absences." [Chelsea] (46) 87, p. 205.
"Babur." [Chelsea] (46) 87, p. 202-203.
"Casualties." [Chelsea] (46) 87, p. 204.
"Monsters" (Selections: "Dracula," "Naiad"). [Chelsea] (46) 87, p. 206-207.
3825. MORAFF, Barbara
"The cats are falling off." [WormR] (27:4, issue 108) 87, p. 96.
"She Rambled All Around" (for "Monty"). [AlphaBS] (1) Je 87, p. 9.
"To the Lady #1." [AlphaBS] (1) Je 87, p. 10.
"To the Lady #2, Moon." [AlphaBS] (1) Je 87, p. 10.
MORALES, Guillermo Gutierrez
See GUTIERREZ MORALES, Guillermo
3826. MORAN, Angelin
"The Tryst." [Waves] (15:4) Spr 87, p. 61.
"Upon Learning of a High Suicide Rate Among Dentists." [Waves] (15:4) Spr 87, p. 60.
3827. MORAN, Duncan
"Rocks." [CumbPR] (7:1) Fall 87, p. 69.
"What's Done." [PassN] (8:1) Wint 87, p. 19.
3828. MORAN, Ronald
"Double Passage in Mid Life." [Wind] (17:60) 87, p. 28-29.
"Nathan's Fortune." [Wind] (17:60) 87, p. 28.
3829. MORAND, Paul
"El Paso (Texas)" (tr. by Ron Padgett and Bill Zavarsky). [NewAW] (1) 87, p. 36-37.
"Southern Pacific" (tr. by Ron Padgett and Bill Zavarsky). [NewAW] (1) 87, p. 37-38.
3830. MORCATE, Daniel
"Al Surcar el Primer Trazo" (Para Arturo). [LindLM] (6:2/3) Ap-S 87, p. 17.
3831. MORDENSKI, Jan
"At Point Pelee." [Waves] (15:1/2) Fall 86, p. 83.
3832. MOREHEAD, Maureen
"On a Sculpture by Henry Moore: Wondering Why the Head Is So Small." [AmerPoR] (16:5) S-O 87, p. 42.
"Shining the Eyes" (for Rebecca Bryant Boone). [AmerPoR] (16:5) S-O 87, p. 42.
"This Is Not How Leaving the World Is Supposed to Be." [KanQ] (19:4) Fall 87, p. 26.
3833. MORGAN, David R.
"Faust." [Bogg] (58) 87, p. 55.
3834. MORGAN, Edwin
"Rehabs and Reconstructions" (w. Peter McCAREY). [Verse] (4:2) Je 87, p. 10-16.
3835. MORGAN, Elizabeth (*See also* MORGAN, Elizabeth Seydel)
"Macho/Psyche" (The Greensboro Review Literary Award, Honorable Mention). [GreensboroR] (41) Wint 86-87, p. 48-49.
3836. MORGAN, Elizabeth Seydel (*See also* MORGAN, Elizabeth)
"The Adamsons' Peacocks." [GeoR] (41:4) Wint 87, p. 751.
3837. MORGAN, Frederick
"The Loss." [Boulevard] (2:1/2) Spr 87, p. 190-194.
3838. MORGAN, John
"The Siege of Leningrad, 1941-42." [DevQ] (21:2) Fall 86, p. 8-10.
3839. MORGAN, Robert
"Firecrackers at Christmas." [AmerS] (56:1) Wint 87, p. 68-69.
"Hayfield." [Poetry] (150:1) Ap 87, p. 12.
"Moving the Bees." [Poetry] (150:1) Ap 87, p. 13.
"Overalls." [Confr] (35/36) Spr-Fall 87, p. 104.
"Prehistoric Lamp." [Confr] (35/36) Spr-Fall 87, p. 103.
"The Road from Elmira." [TriQ] (68) Wint 87, p. 90-92.
"Soul Sleep." [Confr] (35/36) Spr-Fall 87, p. 105.
"When He Spoke Out of the Dark." [TriQ] (68) Wint 87, p. 93.
3840. MORGAN, Robert C.
"Emptiness." [MoodySI] (18/19) Fall 87, p. 9.
3841. MORGAN, Robin
"Phobiphilia." [Spirit] (8:2) 87, p. 71-74.

3842. MORGAN, S. K.
"Sucker Punch." [SlipS] (7) 87, p. 82.
3843. MORI, Kyoko
"Toward Harvest." [Farm] (4:2) Spr-Sum 87, p. 50-53.
3844. MORI, Massimo
"The House" (tr. by Nicolo Fabrizi). [Caliban] (3) 87, p. 102-104.
3845. MORIARTY, Laura
"And to brave clearness I'd have given." [Bound] (14:1/2) Fall 85-Wint 86 [c87], p. 15.
"La Quinta del Sordo" (After Goya). [Bound] (14:1/2) Fall 85-Wint 86 [c87], p. 16.
"Though you complain about your bruises." [Bound] (14:1/2) Fall 85-Wint 86 [c87], p. 15.
3846. MORIN, Edward
"At Parting" (tr. of Gu Cheng, w. Dennis Ding). [Paint] (14:27) Spr 87, p. 45.
"Early Spring" (tr. of Gu Cheng, w. Dennis Ding). [CrossCur] (7:3) 87, p. 135.
"The Gloria" (Excerpt, tr. of Odysseus Elytis, w. Lefteris Pavlides). [CrossCur] (7:3) 87, p. 152.
"Ice Carvings" (tr. of Li Qi, w. Dennis Ding). [CrossCur] (7:3) 87, p. 155-156.
"Iron Meteorite" (Beijing Planetarium, tr. of Gao Fa-lin, w. Dennis Ding). [Ploughs] (13:4) 87, p. 43-44.
3847. MORISAKI, Tracy
"A Cat on the Wall." [HawaiiR] (21) Spr 87, p. 59.
3848. MORISON, Ted
"Proust Wrote the *Only*." [Wind] (17:61) 87, p. 33-34.
"Small Mercies." [Wind] (17:61) 87, p. 33.
3849. MORITA, James
"Clock Exercises" (tr. of Hasegawa Ryusei). [LitR] (30:2) Wint 87, p. 194-195.
"Ode to Soil" (tr. of Shinkawa Kazue). [LitR] (30:2) Wint 87, p. 257-258.
3850. MORITZ, A. F.
"An Afternoon in Illinois." [Shen] (37:4) 87, p. 71.
3851. MORLEY, Hilda
"Epidaurus." [Spirit] (8:2) 87, p. 316.
"Song of the Terrible." [Poetry] (151:1/2) O-N 87, p. 104.
3852. MORRILL, Donald
"Back to Normal." [FloridaR] (15:1) Spr-Sum 87, p. 106.
"Sentient Being" (Tibet, 1986). [CutB] (27/28) 87, p. 72-73.
3853. MORRIS, Carol
"Pastoral." [ManhatPR] (9) Sum 87, p. 22.
3854. MORRIS, Elizabeth
"Running in Place." [Bogg] (57) 87, p. 28.
3855. MORRIS, Herbert
"629 West 173rd Street" (for Nancy Wilner). [IndR] (10:1/2) 87, p. 125-136.
"Cold." [Agni] (24/25) 87, p. 85-87.
"The Day the Poet Came to Read." [Shen] (37:4) 87, p. 48-61.
"French" (For Joseph Gabriel). [Poetry] (149:6) Mr 87, p. 315-320.
"Lincoln's Hat." [Hudson] (39:4) Wint 87, p. 607-610.
"The Wait" (Russell Lee: "Saturday afternoon street scene," Welch, McDowell Co., WV, Aug. 24, 1946). [Pequod] (23/24) 87, p. 34-42.
3856. MORRIS, John N.
"The Alterations." [SewanR] (95:2) Spr 87, p. 250-251.
"The Disappearance of Sideshows." [SewanR] (95:2) Spr 87, p. 251-252.
"On the List." [NewYorker] (63:42) 7 D 87, p. 49.
"The Turing Game." [GrandS] (6:4) Sum 87, p. 217-218.
"Untrimming the Tree." [GrandS] (6:2) Wint 87, p. 220-221.
3857. MORRIS, Peter
"Apprentice." [Writer] (100:1) Ja 87, p. 23-24.
"The Bookmark." [Writer] (100:5) My 87, p. 19-20.
"The Poet Laureate of the South Pole." [Writer] (99:7) Jl 86, p. 21.
3858. MORRISON, Boby
"Tu beso hizo alvidarme de la agonía de los pájaros." [Mairena] (9:24) 87, p. 119.
3859. MORRISON, Lillian
"Sailing, Sailing" (Lines written to keep the mind off incipient seasickness). [LightY] '87, c86, p. 164.
3860. MORRISON, R. H.
"Below Thunderclouds There Floats" (tr. of Osip Mandelstam). [AntigR] (71/72) Aut 87-Wint 88, p. 125.

"Like a Serpent, I Am Hidden" (tr. of Osip Mandelstam). [AntigR] (71/72) Aut
87-Wint 88, p. 125.
"What Steepness There Is in the Crystal Pool" (tr. of Osip Mandelstam). [AntigR]
(71/72) Aut 87-Wint 88, p. 123.
MORRISON, Tamara Wong
See WONG-MORRISON, Tamara
3861. MORRISSEY, Stephen
"Feel Nothing." [AntigR] (69/70) 87, p. 39-40.
3862. MORROW, M. E.
"Obit for Sally E." [AmerS] (56:1) Wint 87, p. 86.
3863. MORSE, Beatrice
"On River." [SmPd] (24:2) Spr 87, p. 28.
3864. MORSE, Carl
"Contra Naturam." [JamesWR] (4:3) Spr 87, p. 1.
3865. MORSE, Ruth
"The Avenue of Limes, St. John's." [Verse] (4:2) Je 87, p. 18.
"A Birthday Greeting." [SouthernR] (23:4) O 87, p. 811-812.
"From the Poet, Making Time." [SouthernR] (23:4) O 87, p. 813-814.
"The Selfish Gene." [SouthernR] (23:4) O 87, p. 812-813.
3866. MORTON, Colin
"Auditory Camouflage." [CanLit] (112) Spr 87, p. 31.
"London, Certainly." [CanLit] (112) Spr 87, p. 30.
"That's True." [CrossC] (9:3/4) 87, p. 17.
3867. MORTON, Grace
"Winter Evening." [YellowS] (25) Wint 87, p. 9.
3868. MORTON, W. C.
"Dafney's Lamentation." [Spirit] (8:2) 87, p. 315.
3869. MOSBY, George, Jr.
"As Oceans Tear Apart" (for demos antos). [HangL] (50/51) 87, p. 130.
"A Cold Day: A Last Song." [HangL] (50/51) 87, p. 129.
3870. MOSCONA, Myriam
"Last Garden" (tr. by Forrest Gander). [BlackWR] (13:2) Spr 87, p. 161.
"Ultimo Jardin." [BlackWR] (13:2) Spr 87, p. 160.
3871. MOSER, Kathleen
"Axiomatic." [PaintedB] (30) 87, p. 49-50.
"Beside the Wide River." [PaintedB] (30) 87, p. 52-53.
"Holding Suns." [PaintedB] (30) 87, p. 51.
"Morning Whistle." [PaintedB] (30) 87, p. 55.
"Not Even." [PaintedB] (30) 87, p. 47.
"Pearl Makers." [PaintedB] (30) 87, p. 48.
"Sand." [PaintedB] (30) 87, p. 56.
"Snow on the Boulevard." [PaintedB] (30) 87, p. 53-54.
3872. MOSER, Sandy
"They Call Me Lucy." [Wind] (17:59) 87, p. 35.
3873. MOSES, Daniel David
"Our Lady of the Glacier." [AntigR] (69/70) 87, p. 11-12.
"An Oval Moon." [Waves] (15:4) Spr 87, p. 66.
3874. MOSLER, Charlie
"Silent Comedy." [Footwork] 87, p. 40.
3875. MOSS, Howard
"At One." [Boulevard] (2:1/2) Spr 87, p. 218.
"The Cardinal." [Poetry] (151:1/2) O-N 87, p. 105.
"Naming a Painting." [NewRep] (196:18) 4 My 87, p. 32.
3876. MOSS, Stanley
"The Bathers." [NewYorker] (63:15) 1 Je 87, p. 38.
"Elegy for Myself." [Poetry] (151:1/2) O-N 87, p. 105.
"Exchange of Gifts." [Poetry] (149:4) Ja 87, p. 227.
"Following the Saints." [Poetry] (149:4) Ja 87, p. 229.
"Hannibal Crossing the Alps." [NewRep] (197:22) 30 N 87, p. 38.
"Lullaby." [Poetry] (149:4) Ja 87, p. 230.
"New York Song." [Nat] (245:1) 18-25 Jl 87, p. 60.
"Songs of Imaginary Arabs." [Poetry] (149:4) Ja 87, p. 229.
"To Ariel Bloch, My Arabist Friend." [Poetry] (149:4) Ja 87, p. 228.
"Work Song." [Poetry] (149:4) Ja 87, p. 226.
3877. MOSS, Stella
"Four Letter Words." [LightY] '87, c86, p. 135.

3878. MOSSIN, Andrew
   "Love Poem" (for Elizabeth). [Confr] (35/36) Spr-Fall 87, p. 187.
3879. MOTIER, Donald
   "On the Hound" (for M.S. & in memory of Jack Kerouac and Neal Cassady).
      [MoodySI] (18/19) Fall 87, p. 42.
3880. MOTT, Elaine
   "Along the Hudson." [PoetL] (82:3) Fall 87, p. 135.
   "Anna's Tree." [Raccoon] (24/25) My 87, p. 195.
   "A Casualty of the Atomic Age, January 3, 1961." [PennR] (3:2) Fall-Wint 87, p.
      76-77.
   "First Love." [CrossCur] (6:4) 87, p. 75.
   "The Food of Hiroshima." [LaurelR] (21:1/2) Wint-Sum 87, p. 13.
   "Graduation Picture." [Wind] (17:59) 87, p. 24.
   "Passages." [Raccoon] (24/25) My 87, p. 198.
   "Second Twin." [HighP] (2:1) Spr 87, p. 15-16.
   "Ten Treatments." [PoetL] (82:3) Fall 87, p. 133-134.
   "The Way Home." [CrossCur] (6:4) 87, p. 101.
3881. MOTT, Michael
   "Mirrors of Shakespeare." [SewanR] (95:4) Fall 87, p. 557-558.
3882. MOULEDOUX-LAJOIE, Rhea
   "On My Body." [AntigR] (68) Wint 87, p. 36.
3883. MOYE, Tom
   "The Seashell Scarcely Knows." [NegC] (7:3/4) 87, p. 162.
3884. MUELLER, Ilze
   "Afro-German" (tr. of May Opitz). [Cond] (14) 87, p. 5.
3885. MUELLER, Lisel
   "When I Am Asked." [Poetry] (151:1/2) O-N 87, p. 106.
3886. MUELLER, Marnie
   "Issei Women at Tule Lake." [Footwork] 87, p. 57.
MUIN, Ozaki
   See OZAKI, Muin
3887. MULDOON, Paul
   "Anseo." [Pembroke] (19) 87, p. 84-85.
   "The Coney." [Antaeus] (58) Spr 87, p. 80-81.
   "My Grandfather's Wake." [Antaeus] (58) Spr 87, p. 78.
   "Ontario." [Antaeus] (58) Spr 87, p. 79.
   "The Soap-Pig." [MassR] (28:3) Aut 87, p. 383-386.
3888. MULHOLLAND, Mary Jane
   "Khmer Children in School." [EngJ] (76:5) S 87, p. 110.
3889. MULLEN, Laura
   "The Holmes Poems." [Thrpny] (31) Fall 87, p. 23.
   "The Motions." [DevQ] (21:2) Fall 86, p. 13-15.
   "Passport." [DenQ] (22:1) Sum 87, p. 48-50.
   "The Poet Explains to Her Favorite Literary Critic the Theft of the Hat." [DenQ]
      (22:1) Sum 87, p. 46-47.
   "The Surface." [ParisR] (29:102) Spr 87, p. 93-94.
   "Three Way Mirror." [Boulevard] (2:1/2) Spr 87, p. 148.
   "Toy." [Boulevard] (2:1/2) Spr 87, p. 147.
3890. MULLEN, Michael
   "The Scientist's Escape: Version 1." [ThRiPo] (29/30) 87, p. 48.
3891. MULLER, Marlene
   "Couple on the Pier." [BellArk] (3:4) Jl-Ag 87, p. 7.
   "First Elegy" (R.J.M 1925-1986). [BellArk] (3:3) My-Je 87, p. 6.
   "Untying Knots." [BellArk] (3:4) Jl-Ag 87, p. 3.
3892. MULLIN, Anne
   "Old Light." [ColEng] (49:8) D 87, p. 890.
3893. MULLINS, Cecil J.
   "In Europe." [CapeR] (22:2) Fall 87, p. 8.
3894. MULLOY, Marcia
   "Barely, a Man Lives." [ManhatPR] (9) Sum 87, p. 58.
3895. MULRANE, Scott H.
   "Cutting Oil Tanks" (For Charles Courtney). [Wind] (17:60) 87, p. 32.
   "Epilogue." [FloridaR] (15:1) Spr-Sum 87, p. 79.
3896. MUNCIE, Mary K.
   "I Thought" (Reprinted from Bogg 28-29). [Bogg] (58) 87, p. 42.

3897. MUNFORD, Christopher
"The Harvest (Driving Through Oklahoma)." [Outbr] (18/19) Fall 86-Spr 88, p. 22-23.
"I Am Here to Feed the Cat." [Outbr] (18/19) Fall 86-Spr 88, p. 20-21.
"Taxco." [Outbr] (18/19) Fall 86-Spr 88, p. 19.
3898. MUNN, Pier
"Armed Conflict." [LightY] '87, c86, p. 74.
"Home Owner's Lament." [LightY] '87, c86, p. 243.
3899. MUÑOZ QUIROS, Jose Maria
"El Naufrago (1) y (2)." [Mairena] (9:24) 87, p. 71.
3900. MURA, David
"Grandfather and Grandmother in Love." [Nat] (244:16) 25 Ap 87, p. 545.
3901. MURABITO, Stephen
"Alone with the Artichokes." [TarPR] (27:1) Fall 87, p. 33.
"Bless You for Yesterday's Rolls." [MissR] (15:3, issue 45) Spr-Sum 87, p. 53-54.
"The Bright Young Poets of America Twirl Spaghetti and Beat It for the County Line." [Phoenix] (7:2) 87, p. 12-14.
"In the Store" (for Sebastian Murabito). [GreenfR] (14:3/4) Sum-Fall 87, p. 133-134.
"Little Louisiana Tabasco Hot Pepper" (for Schwartz, the Hot Pepper Man). [Pig] (14) 87, p. 15.
"The Lost Digits of My Ancestors" (For Ed Ochester). [BelPoJ] (37:3) Spr 87, p. 7-13.
"To Come Close" (for Gerald Stern). [Phoenix] (7:2) 87, p. 10-11.
"Traditions" (for John O'Brien). [MinnR] (NS 28) Spr 87, p. 24.
3902. MURAI, Karen
"Little Known About These Parts." [NewAW] (2) Fall 87, p. 88.
"A Middle Class Monologue." [NewAW] (1) 87, p. 109.
"Ode to the Survival Knife." [NewAW] (2) Fall 87, p. 89.
"Sitting on Zero." [NewAW] (1) 87, p. 110.
3903. MURAT, Fernando
"La distancia anulada por la distancia" (de Las Veces de Isla). [Os] (25) 87, p. 2.
"La progresión del viento arroja sus muñecos" (de Las Veces de Isla). [Os] (25) 87, p. 2.
3904. MURATORI, Fred
"After Meredith." [Outbr] (18/19) Fall 86-Spr 88, p. 166.
"On Ruining Beethoven's Fifth Piano Concerto." [Outbr] (18/19) Fall 86-Spr 88, p. 165.
"The Two Poetries." [PoetryNW] (28:2) Sum 87, p. 28.
3905. MURAWSKI, Elisabeth
"The Bath." [MSS] (5:3) 87, p. 182-183.
"Connections." [OhioR] (38) 87, p. 93.
"Hopi Wedding." [CrabCR] (4:3) Sum 87, p. 6.
"The Road to Christ in the Desert." [GrandS] (6:4) Sum 87, p. 115-116.
"Solution." [CrabCR] (4:3) Sum 87, p. 6.
"To Be Continued." [CumbPR] (6:2) Spr 87, p. 36.
"Tut Exhibit — Washington, D. C." [CumbPR] (6:2) Spr 87, p. 37-38.
"Two Poets: A Sequel." [TarPR] (27:1) Fall 87, p. 34.
"Waxing, As the Moon." [AmerV] (7) Sum 87, p. 82.
"White." [LitR] (30:4) Sum 87, p. 594.
3906. MURCKO, Terry
"Flies." [Pig] (14) 87, p. 26.
"Hair." [Pig] (14) 87, p. 26.
3907. MURPHY, Daryl
"The Wife's Lament." [PassN] (8:2) Sum 87, p. 25.
3908. MURPHY, Frank
"And All the Ships at Sea." [HangL] (50/51) 87, p. 131.
"Fire Island." [HangL] (50/51) 87, p. 132.
3909. MURPHY, Gordon
"Independence." [Footwork] 87, p. 30.
3910. MURPHY, James
"Before Dawn." [KanQ] (19:3) Sum 87, p. 224.
"The Math Teacher's Love Poem." [KanQ] (19:3) Sum 87, p. 225.
3911. MURPHY, Julie
"Wendy." [Cond] (14) 87, p. 193.

3912. MURPHY, Kay
"Early Forties Song." [ColEng] (49:4) Ap 87, p. 424.
"Serial Murders." [Outbr] (18/19) Fall 86-Spr 88, p. 172.
3913. MURPHY, Maureen
"Deluxe Diner." [Wind] (17:59) 87, p. 5.
3914. MURPHY, Peter E.
"The Bridge." [YellowS] (24) Aut 87, p. 16.
"Murphy Confronts Himself." [PaintedB] (31) 87, p. 43.
"Murphy, Furiously content." [PaintedB] (31) 87, p. 42.
"Murphy's Porch." [PaintedB] (31) 87, p. 41.
"The Painters" (for Sonya). [PassN] (8:2) Sum 87, p. 13.
3915. MURPHY, Ray
"Animal Magnetism." [PoetL] (82:2) Sum 87, p. 113.
"Theft." [PoetL] (82:2) Sum 87, p. 111-112.
3916. MURPHY, Remington
"Courting the Black Widow." [TexasR] (8:1/2) Spr-Sum 87, p. 89.
"Petition." [TexasR] (8:1/2) Spr-Sum 87, p. 88.
3917. MURPHY, Rich
"Standard Royal Flush." [GreenfR] (14:3/4) Sum-Fall 87, p. 174.
3918. MURPHY, Sheila E.
"Another Life." [PassN] (8:1) Wint 87, p. 8.
"Tone Prayer." [DekalbLAJ] (20:1/4) 87, p. 49.
3919. MURRAY, G. E.
"Haunts." [NowestR] (25:2) 87, p. 58.
"Mid-Winter Love Lyric." [Hudson] (39:4) Wint 87, p. 618.
"Persuasions" (after Django Reinhardt). [NowestR] (25:2) 87, p. 59.
"The Rounds" (for my father, 1917-1981). [Jacaranda] (2:2) Spr 87, p. 24-27.
"The Rounds" (for my father, 1917-81). [PraS] (61:4) Wint 87, p. 65-68.
"A Year's Time, Its Music Baroque As Cancer." [SouthernHR] (21:4) Fall 87, p. 361.
3920. MURRAY, Joan
"My Father's Last Words During the Breeders' Cup" (November 1985). [OntR] (27) Fall-Wint 87, p. 29-30.
"The Precarious Nest." [PraS] (61:2) Sum 87, p. 19-22.
"The Same Water." [OntR] (27) Fall-Wint 87, p. 31-33.
"The Unmolested Child." [ParisR] (29:103) Sum 87, p. 194-204.
3921. MURRAY, Lachlan
"Antigonish Summer." [CanLit] (115) Wint 87, p. 61-62.
"For Miss Cooke." [CanLit] (115) Wint 87, p. 123.
3922. MURRAY, Les A.
"Freshwater and Salt." [Verse] (4:1) Mr 87, p. 4.
"The Kitchens." [Verse] (4:3) N 87, p. 3-5.
"Low Down Sandcastle Blues." [Verse] (4:3) N 87, p. 5.
"Max Fabre's Yachts." [NewYRB] (34:19) 3 D 87, p. 25.
"Max Fabre's Yachts." [Verse] (4:1) Mr 87, p. 5.
"The Megaethon: 1850, 1906-1929." [Atlantic] (260:3) S 87, p. 74-75.
"Mercurial September." [NewYRB] (34:19) 3 D 87, p. 25.
"To the Soviet Americans." [Verse] (4:3) N 87, p. 6.
3923. MUSGRAVE, Susan
"Rolling Boil." [Event] (16:2) Sum 87, p. 51-55.
3924. MUSGRAVES, Leroy
"I Was Looking." [BlackWR] (14:1) Fall 87, p. 102.
"What Is Left." [BlackWR] (14:1) Fall 87, p. 41.
3925. MUSKAT, Timothy
"Deuteronomy." [AntigR] (68) Wint 87, p. 112.
3926. MUSKE, Carol
"Pediatrics." [Thrpny] (28) Wint 87, p. 4.
"Vermont Farmhouse, 3 A.M." [Field] (37) Fall 87, p. 90-91.
"The Wish Foundation." [WestHR] (41:4) Wint 87, p. 358-360.
3927. MUSO, Soseki
"Ashikaga Tadayoshi's Palace" (tr. by W. S. Merwin and Soiku Shigematsu). [AmerPoR] (16:2) Mr-Ap 87, p. 30.
"At Ei's Departure for Choho-ji" (tr. by W. S. Merwin and Soiku Shigematsu). [AmerPoR] (16:2) Mr-Ap 87, p. 32.
"At the Nachi Kannon Hall" (tr. by W. S. Merwin and Soiku Shigematsu). [AmerPoR] (16:2) Mr-Ap 87, p. 27.

"At Whole-World-In-View Hut" (tr. by W. S. Merwin and Soiku Shigematsu).
[AmerPoR] (16:2) Mr-Ap 87, p. 30.
"Beyond Light (Zessho Chiko)" (tr. by W. S. Merwin and Soiku Shigematsu).
[AmerPoR] (16:2) Mr-Ap 87, p. 32.
"Beyond the World" (tr. by W. S. Merwin and Soiku Shigematsu). [AmerPoR]
(16:2) Mr-Ap 87, p. 32.
"A Biding Mountain" (tr. by W. S. Merwin and Soiku Shigematsu). [AmerPoR]
(16:2) Mr-Ap 87, p. 29.
"The Bridge Where the Moon Crosses" (tr. by W. S. Merwin and Soiku
Shigematsu). [AmerPoR] (16:2) Mr-Ap 87, p. 31.
"Buddha's Satori" (tr. by W. S. Merwin and Soiku Shigematsu). [AmerPoR] (16:2)
Mr-Ap 87, p. 25.
"Clear Valley (Seikei Tsutetsu)" (tr. by W. S. Merwin and Soiku Shigematsu).
[AmerPoR] (16:2) Mr-Ap 87, p. 32.
"Climbing Down the Snowy Montain" (tr. by W. S. Merwin and Soiku
Shigematsu). [AmerPoR] (16:2) Mr-Ap 87, p. 30.
"Digging Out the Buddha Relic" (tr. by W. S. Merwin and Soiku Shigematsu).
[AmerPoR] (16:2) Mr-Ap 87, p. 31.
"Dry Tree (Koboku Joei)" (tr. by W. S. Merwin and Soiku Shigematsu).
[AmerPoR] (16:2) Mr-Ap 87, p. 26.
"East Peak" (tr. by W. S. Merwin and Soiku Shigematsu). [AmerPoR] (16:2) Mr-Ap
87, p. 27.
"Flat Mountain (Heizan Zenkin)" (tr. by W. S. Merwin and Soiku Shigematsu).
[AmerPoR] (16:2) Mr-Ap 87, p. 32.
"For Gen the New Head Priest of Erin-ji" (tr. by W. S. Merwin and Soiku
Shigematsu). [AmerPoR] (16:2) Mr-Ap 87, p. 29.
"For Myo's Departure for Shofuku-ji" (tr. by W. S. Merwin and Soiku Shigematsu).
[AmerPoR] (16:2) Mr-Ap 87, p. 29.
"For Sho the New Head Priest of Erin-ji" (tr. by W. S. Merwin and Soiku
Shigematsu). [AmerPoR] (16:2) Mr-Ap 87, p. 30.
"The Fragrance of the Udumbara (Dompo Shuo)" (tr. by W. S. Merwin and Soiku
Shigematsu). [AmerPoR] (16:2) Mr-Ap 87, p. 30.
"Great Verse Valley" (tr. by W. S. Merwin and Soiku Shigematsu). [AmerPoR]
(16:2) Mr-Ap 87, p. 31.
"Hall of the Guardian God" (tr. by W. S. Merwin and Soiku Shigematsu).
[AmerPoR] (16:2) Mr-Ap 87, p. 31.
"House of Spring (Shun-oku Myoha)" (tr. by W. S. Merwin and Soiku
Shigematsu). [AmerPoR] (16:2) Mr-Ap 87, p. 30.
"Hut in Harmony (Tekian Hojun)" (tr. by W. S. Merwin and Soiku Shigematsu).
[AmerPoR] (16:2) Mr-Ap 87, p. 32.
"Inauguration of Fukusan Dormitory" (tr. by W. S. Merwin and Soiku Shigematsu).
[AmerPoR] (16:2) Mr-Ap 87, p. 27.
"It" (tr. by W. S. Merwin and Soiku Shigematsu). [AmerPoR] (16:2) Mr-Ap 87, p.
30.
"Laughing Mountain (Shozan Shunen)" (tr. by W. S. Merwin and Soiku
Shigematsu). [AmerPoR] (16:2) Mr-Ap 87, p. 27.
"Living in the Mountains: Ten Poems" (tr. by W. S. Merwin and Soiku
Shigematsu). [AmerPoR] (16:2) Mr-Ap 87, p. 28.
"Lover of Mountains (Ninzan)" (tr. by W. S. Merwin and Soiku Shigematsu).
[AmerPoR] (16:2) Mr-Ap 87, p. 29.
"Magnificent Peak" (tr. by W. S. Merwin and Soiku Shigematsu). [AmerPoR]
(16:2) Mr-Ap 87, p. 30.
"Moon Mountain" (tr. by W. S. Merwin and Soiku Shigematsu). [AmerPoR] (16:2)
Mr-Ap 87, p. 27.
"Moon Tree Cliff (Keigan)" (tr. by W. S. Merwin and Soiku Shigematsu).
[AmerPoR] (16:2) Mr-Ap 87, p. 29.
"Mourning for the Layman Named Cloud Peak" (tr. by W. S. Merwin and Soiku
Shigematsu). [AmerPoR] (16:2) Mr-Ap 87, p. 27.
"No Gain" (tr. by W. S. Merwin and Soiku Shigematsu). [AmerPoR] (16:2) Mr-Ap
87, p. 31.
"No Word Hut (Mokuan Shuyu)" (tr. by W. S. Merwin and Soiku Shigematsu).
[AmerPoR] (16:2) Mr-Ap 87, p. 29.
"Old Creek" (tr. by W. S. Merwin and Soiku Shigematsu). [AmerPoR] (16:2)
Mr-Ap 87, p. 26.
"Old Hut (Koan Fusho)" (tr. by W. S. Merwin and Soiku Shigematsu). [AmerPoR]
(16:2) Mr-Ap 87, p. 27.

"Old Man Advancing" (tr. by W. S. Merwin and Soiku Shigematsu). [AmerPoR]
    (16:2) Mr-Ap 87, p. 29.
"Old Man at Leisure (Kanso Ankan)" (tr. by W. S. Merwin and Soiku Shigematsu).
    [AmerPoR] (16:2) Mr-Ap 87, p. 32.
"Old Man in Retirement" (tr. by W. S. Merwin and Soiku Shigematsu). [AmerPoR]
    (16:2) Mr-Ap 87, p. 26.
"Old Man of Few Words (Mohuo Myokai)" (tr. by W. S. Merwin and Soiku
    Shigematsu). [AmerPoR] (16:2) Mr-Ap 87, p. 32.
"Old Man To-The-Point" (tr. by W. S. Merwin and Soiku Shigematsu). [AmerPoR]
    (16:2) Mr-Ap 87, p. 29.
"Ox Turned Loose (Hogo Korin)" (tr. by W. S. Merwin and Soiku Shigematsu).
    [AmerPoR] (16:2) Mr-Ap 87, p. 32.
"The Peak of the Help Up Flower" (tr. by W. S. Merwin and Soiku Shigematsu).
    [AmerPoR] (16:2) Mr-Ap 87, p. 31.
"Pine Shade" (tr. by W. S. Merwin and Soiku Shigematsu). [AmerPoR] (16:2)
    Mr-Ap 87, p. 28.
"The Pond at Hui-Neng's Spring" (tr. by W. S. Merwin and Soiku Shigematsu).
    [AmerPoR] (16:2) Mr-Ap 87, p. 31.
"Reizan Osho Visits Me" (tr. by W. S. Merwin and Soiku Shigematsu). [AmerPoR]
    (16:2) Mr-Ap 87, p. 25.
"Reply to Bukko Zenji's Poem at Seiken-ji" (tr. by W. S. Merwin and Soiku
    Shigematsu). [AmerPoR] (16:2) Mr-Ap 87, p. 30.
"Reply to Genno Osho's Poem" (Excerpts, tr. by W. S. Merwin and Soiku
    Shigematsu). [AmerPoR] (16:2) Mr-Ap 87, p. 27.
"Reply to Suzan Osho's Snow Poem" (tr. by W. S. Merwin and Soiku Shigematsu).
    [AmerPoR] (16:2) Mr-Ap 87, p. 29.
"Snow" (tr. by W. S. Merwin and Soiku Shigematsu). [AmerPoR] (16:2) Mr-Ap
    87, p. 30.
"Snow at Rohatsu Sesshin" (tr. by W. S. Merwin and Soiku Shigematsu).
    [AmerPoR] (16:2) Mr-Ap 87, p. 30.
"Snow Garden" (tr. by W. S. Merwin and Soiku Shigematsu). [AmerPoR] (16:2)
    Mr-Ap 87, p. 29.
"Snow Valley" (tr. by W. S. Merwin and Soiku Shigematsu). [AmerPoR] (16:2)
    Mr-Ap 87, p. 26.
"Spring Cliff" (tr. by W. S. Merwin and Soiku Shigematsu). [AmerPoR] (16:2)
    Mr-Ap 87, p. 27.
"Suzan Osho's Visit" (tr. by W. S. Merwin and Soiku Shigematsu). [AmerPoR]
    (16:2) Mr-Ap 87, p. 29.
"Suzan Osho's Visit to My West Mountain Hut" (tr. by W. S. Merwin and Soiku
    Shigematsu). [AmerPoR] (16:2) Mr-Ap 87, p. 31.
"Temple of Serene Light" (tr. by W. S. Merwin and Soiku Shigematsu). [AmerPoR]
    (16:2) Mr-Ap 87, p. 31.
"Tengan Osho's Visit to Erin-ji" (tr. by W. S. Merwin and Soiku Shigematsu).
    [AmerPoR] (16:2) Mr-Ap 87, p. 28.
"Thanks for Daisen Osho's Visit" (Excerpts, tr. by W. S. Merwin and Soiku
    Shigematsu). [AmerPoR] (16:2) Mr-Ap 87, p. 26.
"Thanks Sent to Taihei Osho" (Excerpts, tr. by W. S. Merwin and Soiku
    Shigematsu). [AmerPoR] (16:2) Mr-Ap 87, p. 26.
"Three Step Waterfall" (tr. by W. S. Merwin and Soiku Shigematsu). [AmerPoR]
    (16:2) Mr-Ap 87, p. 31.
"Tiger Valley" (tr. by W. S. Merwin and Soiku Shigematsu). [AmerPoR] (16:2)
    Mr-Ap 87, p. 31.
"To Kengai Osho of Engaku-ji" (tr. by W. S. Merwin and Soiku Shigematsu).
    [AmerPoR] (16:2) Mr-Ap 87, p. 27.
"To the Emperor's Messenger" (tr. by W. S. Merwin and Soiku Shigematsu).
    [AmerPoR] (16:2) Mr-Ap 87, p. 26.
"To the Riverside Temple (Rinsen-ji)" (tr. by W. S. Merwin and Soiku Shigematsu).
    [AmerPoR] (16:2) Mr-Ap 87, p. 29.
"Toki-No-Ge (Satori Poem)" (tr. by W. S. Merwin and Soiku Shigematsu).
    [AmerPoR] (16:2) Mr-Ap 87, p. 31.
"Truth Hall (Gido Shushin)" (tr. by W. S. Merwin and Soiku Shigematsu).
    [AmerPoR] (16:2) Mr-Ap 87, p. 28.
"Visiting My Old Hut in Late Spring" (tr. by W. S. Merwin and Soiku Shigematsu).
    [AmerPoR] (16:2) Mr-Ap 87, p. 27.
"Wandering" (tr. by W. S. Merwin and Soiku Shigematsu). [AmerPoR] (16:2)
    Mr-Ap 87, p. 25.

"Withered Zen" (tr. by W. S. Merwin and Soiku Shigematsu). [AmerPoR] (16:2)
Mr-Ap 87, p. 30.
3928. MUTH, Carol Sue
"Unmentionable." [Amelia] (4:1/2, issue 9) 87, p. 74.
3929. MYCUE, Edward
"Falklands." [Bogg] (58) 87, p. 20.
"Little More Than Sex on a Raft." [YellowS] (22) Spr 87, p. 13.
"Omit Hell, Add Heaven." [Caliban] (2) 87, p. 139.
"The President." [Caliban] (2) 87, p. 138.
"Street Steeple." [Caliban] (2) 87, p. 138.
"The Vapour Zone, Good Morning." [CapilR] (42) 87, p. 64.
"Venus Has an Ulcer." [Margin] (3) Sum 87, p. 20.
"The Voices and Mary Louise." [CapilR] (42) 87, p. 63.
3930. MYERS, Alan
"The Bust of Tiberius" (tr. of Joseph Brodsky, w. the author). [NewYRB] (34:11)
25 Je 87, p. 18.
3931. MYERS, Gary
"Weeping Angel" (for Susan Prospere). [KanQ] (19:3) Sum 87, p. 331.
3932. MYERS, Jack
"The Aesthetes." [PoetryE] (23/24) Fall 87, p. 118.
"The Energy It Takes to Pass Through Solid Objects" (for my son, Jacob). [Crazy]
(33) Wint 87, p. 44-45.
3933. MYERS, Joan Rohr
"Beyond Reach." [Farm] (4:1) Wint 87, p. 15.
"Preliminaries." [ChrC] (104:10) 1 Ap 87, p. 303.
"Towards Morning." [Comm] (114:19) 6 N 87, p. 618.
3934. MYERS, Neil
"In the Bright Day." [CarolQ] (39:2) Wint 87, p. 59-63.
3935. MYLES, Eileen
"Mad Pepper." [ParisR] (29:102) Spr 87, p. 97-100.
"A Poem in Two Homes." [Bomb] (21) Fall 87, p. 76-77.
MYONG-YOL, Kim
See KIM, Myong-yol
3936. NADIR, Moishe
"1928" (tr. by Aaron Kramer). [Vis] (23) 87, p. 36.
3937. NAFFZIGER, Audrey
"Reflections on a Piltdown Man." [Gambit] (21) 87, p. 21.
3938. NAGLE, Alice
"Rebirth." [SouthernPR] (27:1) Spr 87, p. 37-38.
3939. NAGYS, Henrikas
"Terra Incognita" (in Lithuanian & English, tr. by Jonas Zdanys). [StoneC] (14:3/4)
Spr-Sum 87, p. 52-53.
3940. NAKANO, Jiro
"Arrest" (tr. of Sojin Takei, w. Kay Nakano). The Best of [BambooR] [(31-32)] 86,
p. 67.
"At the Volcano Internment Camp" (tr. of Muin Ozaki, w. Kay Nakano). The Best of
[BambooR] [(31-32)] 86, p. 68.
"Death at the Camp" (tr. of Keiho Soga, w. Kay Nakano). The Best of [BambooR]
[(31-32)] 86, p. 72.
"A flock of black birds" (tr. of Sojin Takei, w. Kay Nakano). The Best of
[BambooR] [(31-32)] 86, p. 73.
"Fort Sill Internment Camp" (tr. of Muin Ozaki, w. Kay Nakano). The Best of
[BambooR] [(31-32)] 86, p. 70.
"Homecoming" (tr. of Sojin Takei, w. Kay Nakano). The Best of [BambooR]
[(31-32)] 86, p. 73.
"My hands lightly touch" (tr. of Sojin Takei, w. Kay Nakano). The Best of
[BambooR] [(31-32)] 86, p. 70.
"On the Ship to the Mainland" (tr. of Muin Ozaki, w. Kay Nakano). The Best of
[BambooR] [(31-32)] 86, p. 69.
"Santa Fe Internment Camp" (tr. of Sojin Takei, w. Kay Nakano). The Best of
[BambooR] [(31-32)] 86, p. 71.
3941. NAKANO, Kay
"Arrest" (tr. of Sojin Takei, w. Jiro Nakano). The Best of [BambooR] [(31-32)] 86,
p. 67.
"At the Volcano Internment Camp" (tr. of Muin Ozaki, w. Jiro Nakano). The Best of
[BambooR] [(31-32)] 86, p. 68.

"Death at the Camp" (tr. of Keiho Soga, w. Jiro Nakano). The Best of [BambooR]
    [(31-32)] 86, p. 72.
"A flock of black birds" (tr. of Sojin Takei, w. Jiro Nakano). The Best of
    [BambooR] [(31-32)] 86, p. 73.
"Fort Sill Internment Camp" (tr. of Muin Ozaki, w. Jiro Nakano). The Best of
    [BambooR] [(31-32)] 86, p. 70.
"Homecoming" (tr. of Sojin Takei, w. Jiro Nakano). The Best of [BambooR]
    [(31-32)] 86, p. 73.
"My hands lightly touch" (tr. of Sojin Takei, w. Jiro Nakano). The Best of
    [BambooR] [(31-32)] 86, p. 70.
"On the Ship to the Mainland" (tr. of Muin Ozaki, w. Jiro Nakano). The Best of
    [BambooR] [(31-32)] 86, p. 69.
"Santa Fe Internment Camp" (tr. of Sojin Takei, w. Jiro Nakano). The Best of
    [BambooR] [(31-32)] 86, p. 71.
3942. NAPORA, Joe
"A Broken Limb Upheld by the Light." [GreenfR] (14:1/2) Wint-Spr, p. 64-65.
"Rescue." [GreenfR] (14:1/2) Wint-Spr, p. 66-67.
3943. NARANG, Gopi Chand
"Rubà i I" (tr. of Shamsur Rahman Faruqi, w. David Paul Douglas). [Bomb] (18)
    Wint 87, p. 68.
"Rubà i IV" (tr. of Shamsur Rahman Faruqi, w. David Paul Douglas). [Bomb] (18)
    Wint 87, p. 68.
"Underdone" (tr. of Shamsur Rahman Faruqi, w. David Paul Douglas). [Bomb] (18)
    Wint 87, p. 68.
3944. NARANJO, Carmen
"Cancion de Cuna Para un Niño Salvadoreño." [Cond] (14) 87, p. 178, 180.
"The Cat" (tr. by Zoë Anglesey). [Cond] (14) 87, p. 173, 175.
"La Flor, la Abeja." [Cond] (14) 87, p. 176.
"El Gato." [Cond] (14) 87, p. 172, 174.
"Lullaby for a Salvadoran Child" (tr. by Zoë Anglesey). [Cond] (14) 87, p. 179,
    181.
"Perhaps the Flower, the Bee" (tr. by Zoë Anglesey). [Cond] (14) 87, p. 177.
3945. NARANJO, Teresa Mae
"Standing Rain." [GreenfR] (14:1/2) Wint-Spr, p. 19-20.
3946. NASH, Roger
"The Coppery Weathercock." [AntigR] (69/70) 87, p. 200.
"A Dream." [WestCR] (21:3) Wint 87, p. 36.
"The Dream of the Rood" (tr. by Roger Nash). [AntigR] (69/70) 87, p. 201.
"Family Discussion." [CapilR] (45) 87 [Ap 88], p. 18.
"Maxims." [WestCR] (21:3) Wint 87, p. 37.
"Photo of an Angry Man." [WestCR] (21:3) Wint 87, p. 35.
"This Is My Mother's Camera." [CanLit] (113/114) Sum-Fall 87, p. 167.
"Voyages of a Garden Shed." [Quarry] (36:4) Fall 87, p. 57-58.
3947. NASH, Thomas
"A Little Night Music." [CarolQ] (40:1) Fall 87, p. 87.
3948. NASH, Valery
"Neighbors." [PoetryNW] (28:1) Spr 87, p. 29-30.
"On the Way to School." [SouthernPR] (27:2) Fall 87, p. 34.
"Your Kindness." [StoneC] (15:1/2) Fall-Wint 87-88, p. 45-46.
3949. NASIO, Brenda
"The Andrea Poems." [Amelia] (4:3, issue 10) 87, p. 106-107.
"At the Jersey Shore / Notes from the Front Porch." [Amelia] (4:3, issue 10) 87, p.
    108.
3950. NASLUND, Alan
"Conjectured West." [Amelia] (4:3, issue 10) 87, p. 89-90.
3951. NATHAN, Leonard
"All Hallows' Eve" (tr. of Czeslaw Milosz, w. the author). [NewYorker] (63:37) 2
    N 87, p. 42.
"Chorale." [CrossCur] (7:1) 87, p. 103.
"Climbing Mount Fuji." [NewEngR] (9:3) Spr 87, p. 329-331.
"Cold Ovens." [PoetL] (81:4) Wint 86-87, p. 227-228.
"A Farewell to Good Reasons." [CrossCur] (7:1) 87, p. 104.
"If I Say 'You'." [PoetL] (81:4) Wint 86-87, p. 226.
"In Case You Think I've Forgotten." [CrossCur] (7:2) 87, p. 77.
"Just Looking, Thank You." [Spirit] (8:2) 87, p. 105-106.
"Letter from Pliny." [CrossCur] (7:2) 87, p. 78.

"My Older Brother." [PoetL] (81:4) Wint 86-87, p. 229.
"Second Home." [CrossCur] (6:4) 87, p. 60-61.
"The Tigers of Wrath Are Wiser Than the Horses of Instruction" (— Blake).
    [Zyzzyva] (3:2) Sum 87, p. 85.
3952. NATHAN, Norman
"An Aged Man." [Poem] (57) Mr 87, p. 43.
"Blanketing Nature." [SoCaR] (19:2) Spr 87, p. 50.
"Chinese Screen." [KanQ] (19:1/2) Wint-Spr 87, p. 121.
"Conflict." [Poem] (57) Mr 87, p. 44.
"Dried Leaves Drift." [Poem] (57) Mr 87, p. 45.
"Fading." [Poem] (57) Mr 87, p. 46.
"Fiction." [PoetL] (81:3) Fall 86, p. 189.
"Like a Sea of Grass." [NewRena] (7:1, #21) Fall 87, p. 102.
"Oriental Screen 16." [KanQ] (19:1/2) Wint-Spr 87, p. 121.
"Sheep Nip the Tender." [SoCaR] (19:2) Spr 87, p. 50-51.
"Sometimes the Hill Ends." [SpiritSH] (53:1) 87, p. 22.
"Under Foreign Rule." [KanQ] (19:1/2) Wint-Spr 87, p. 120.
"Where." [SpiritSH] (53:1) 87, p. 23.
"Will's Will." [PoetL] (82:3) Fall 87, p. 159.
3953. NATHANSON, Tenney
"Old-Fashioned Romance on CBS" (Selection: 1). [Sonora] (13) Fall 87, p.
    120-125.
"The Wish to Steal a Baby in a Fifteen Year Old Girl" (Selections: 1-2). [Sonora]
    (13) Fall 87, p. 86-87.
3954. NATIONS, Opal Louis
"The Whiskerbit." [Rampike] (5:3) 87, p. 80.
3955. NAULT, Marianne
"Sisters in Sorrow" (On a line from Marina Tsvetayeva). [Stand] (28:4) Aut 87, p.
    24.
3956. NAVARRE, Martinez Porras
"The Desolated World." [NegC] (7:3/4) 87, p. 75.
3957. NAWAZ, Shuja
"The Buddhist Priest on His Death." [Vis] (25) 87, p. 16.
3958. NAWROCKI, James
"Inland." [Gambit] (21) 87, p. 52.
3959. NAZARETH, Ralph
"Quartet." [Wind] (17:60) 87, p. 30.
3960. NEBT'KATA, Ismima
"Directions." [RiverS] (24) 87, p. 53.
3961. NECAKOV, Lillian
"Remember in the spine milk sours." [CrossC] (9:3/4) 87, p. 2.
3962. NEDEL, Victoria
"Seasonal." [CutB] (27/28) 87, p. 48.
3963. NEELD, Judith
"First Son." [TexasR] (7:3/4) 87, p. 113.
"Homecoming of the North Coast Wife." [TexasR] (7:3/4) 87, p. 112.
"The Last Summer in Llanberis." [ColR] (NS 14:2) Fall-Wint 87, p. 34-35.
"To a Friend in the Hebrides." [CrossCur] (6:4) 87, p. 64.
"To Fit the Heart into the Body." [TarRP] (26:2) Spr 87, p. 31.
"When the Sea Bird Has Gone: Concert." [CrossCur] (6:4) 87, p. 63.
3964. NEELEY, Rebecca
"Anger to Use: The Waitress Poem." [SinW] (31) 87, p. 82-83.
3965. NEELIN, David
"Delivery." [Shen] (37:2) 87, p. 68.
"Greek." [Shen] (37:2) 87, p. 68.
"Groceries." [Shen] (37:2) 87, p. 65-66.
"Science, 227, 375-381." [NewEngR] (10:1) Aut 87, p. 27.
"Short One." [Shen] (37:2) 87, p. 67.
"Talking with the Other Lover." [Shen] (37:2) 87, p. 67.
NEJAT, Murat Nemet
    See NEMET-NEJAT, Murat
3966. NELMS, Sheryl L.
"Air Tight." [Kaleid] (15) Sum-Fall 87, p. 15.
"Deer Jumping." [Kaleid] (15) Sum-Fall 87, p. 44.
"Hunting Pheasants." [Phoenix] (7:2) 87, p. 28.
"In the Sharpening." [Kaleid] (15) Sum-Fall 87, p. 44.

"The Kiamichi Spring." [Abraxas] (35/36) 87, p. 71.
"Meditation." [Kaleid] (15) Sum-Fall 87, p. 15.
"Pickin Strawberries." [Confr] (35/36) Spr-Fall 87, p. 218.
"The Rub." [Confr] (35/36) Spr-Fall 87, p. 219.
"Summer Was." [BallSUF] (28:4) Aut 87, p. 33.
3967. NELSON, Eric
    "Because the Air." [CalQ] (30) Wint 87, p. 60.
    "Natural Selection." [ThRiPo] (29/30) 87, p. 49.
    "Three Die in Seconds." [WestHR] (41:4) Wint 87, p. 366-367.
3968. NELSON, Howard
    "Ancient Dance." [PoetryE] (23/24) Fall 87, p. 216.
3969. NELSON, Leslie
    "Imagining My Parents Spending a Weekend at the Beach." [BlackWR] (14:1) Fall
        87, p. 9-10.
    "My Brothers Telling the Story of Our Father." [TarRP] (26:2) Spr 87, p. 21.
3970. NELSON, Linda
    "Homecoming." [EngJ] (76:7) N 87, p. 93.
3971. NELSON, Liza
    "By the Roots." [HeliconN] (17/18) Spr 87, p. 167.
    "One Kind of Woman Whispers to Another." [HeliconN] (17/18) Spr 87, p. 166.
3972. NELSON, Sandra
    "The Ground Rules." [PassN] (8:2) Sum 87, p. 21.
3973. NELSON, Sara
    "The Dancing Key" (tr. of Ulalume González de León). [AmerPoR] (16:2) Mr-Ap
        87, p. 18.
    "Forgotten Shared Jar" (tr. of Ulalume González de León). [AmerPoR] (16:2)
        Mr-Ap 87, p. 18.
    "Imaginary Finale 1" (tr. of Ulalume González de León). [AmerPoR] (16:2) Mr-Ap
        87, p. 18.
    "Sign" (tr. of Ulalume González de León). [AmerPoR] (16:2) Mr-Ap 87, p. 19.
    "Where the Jar, Remembered Only in Dreams, Peers for an Instant . . ." (tr. of
        Ulalume González de León). [AmerPoR] (16:2) Mr-Ap 87, p. 19.
3974. NELSON, Shannon
    "Self." [DevQ] (21:2) Fall 86, p. 11-12.
3975. NELSON, W. Dale
    "The Lookouts." [Confr] (35/36) Spr-Fall 87, p. 273.
3976. NEMEROV, Howard
    "Authorities." [AmerPoR] (16:4) Jl-Ag 87, p. 4.
    "The Big Bang." [LightY] '87, c86, p. 147.
    "The Bluejay and the Mockingbird." [AmerPoR] (16:4) Jl-Ag 87, p. 3.
    "The Celestial Emperor." [AmerPoR] (16:4) Jl-Ag 87, p. 4.
    "A Christmas Card of Halley's Comet." [YaleR] (76:2) Wint 87, p. 256.
    "Commencement." [SewanR] (95:2) Spr 87, p. 184.
    "Crotchets." [BlackWR] (14:1) Fall 87, p. 47.
    "Deconstructing the Text of Texts." [SewanR] (95:2) Spr 87, p. 184.
    "Economic Man" (for Naomi Lebowitz). [SouthernR] (23:1) Ja 87, p. 3-4.
    "The Faith." [AmerPoR] (16:4) Jl-Ag 87, p. 4.
    "Found Poem" (after information received in The St. Louis Post-Dispatch, 4 v 86).
        [MissouriR] (10:3) 87, p. 71.
    "From the Poetry Exchange, Two Conversations." [LightY] '87, c86, p. 215.
    "IFF." [AmerPoR] (16:4) Jl-Ag 87, p. 3.
    "In the Beginning." [AmerPoR] (16:4) Jl-Ag 87, p. 4.
    "In Transit." [SewanR] (95:2) Spr 87, p. 183.
    "Intimations." [AmerPoR] (16:4) Jl-Ag 87, p. 3.
    "Landscape with Self-Portrait." [RiverS] (23) 87, p. 18.
    "Low-level Cross-country" (for Brooks Baekeland). [SouthernR] (23:1) Ja 87, p. 4.
    "Night Operations, Coastal Command RAF." [LightY] '87, c86, p. 26-27.
    "Night Piece." [SewanR] (95:2) Spr 87, p. 182-183.
    "Parabola." [SouthernR] (23:1) Ja 87, p. 2-3.
    "Philology." [SewanR] (95:2) Spr 87, p. 184.
    "Playing the Machine." [AmerPoR] (16:4) Jl-Ag 87, p. 3.
    "Po Biz." [LightY] '87, c86, p. 192.
    "Remembering the Way." [SouthernR] (23:1) Ja 87, p. 2.
    "The Rent in the Screen." [PraS] (61:3) Fall 87, p. 8.
    "The Revised Version." [PraS] (61:3) Fall 87, p. 70.
    "The Royal Visit." [SewanR] (95:2) Spr 87, p. 182.

"This Present Past." [SouthernR] (23:1) Ja 87, p. 31.
"To Joy Our Student, Bidding Adieu." [SouthernR] (23:1) Ja 87, p. 1.
3977. NEMET-NEJAT, Murat
"All Red" (tr. of Sabahattin Kudret Aksal). [Trans] (19) Fall 87, p. 150.
"A Blind Cat Black" (tr. of Ece Ayhan). [Trans] (19) Fall 87, p. 130.
"Blond" (tr. of Sabahattin Kudret Aksal). [Trans] (19) Fall 87, p. 150.
"Cats" (tr. of Fazil Hüsnü Daglarca). [Trans] (19) Fall 87, p. 56.
"Epitafio" (tr. of Ece Ayhan). [Trans] (19) Fall 87, p. 131.
"The Heartless" (tr. of Fazil Hüsnü Daglarca). [Trans] (19) Fall 87, p. 56.
"The Hour of Murder" (tr. of Attilâ Ilhan). [Trans] (19) Fall 87, p. 155.
"The Hour of the Sun" (tr. of Necati Cumali). [Trans] (19) Fall 87, p. 31.
"The Ipek Hotel" (tr. of Necati Cumali). [Trans] (19) Fall 87, p. 30.
"The Lighthouse" (tr. of Fazil Hüsnü Daglarca). [Trans] (19) Fall 87, p. 54-55.
"Love Is Forbidden" (tr. of Attilâ Ilhan). [Trans] (19) Fall 87, p. 154.
"Masts" (tr. of Sabahattin Kudret Aksal). [Trans] (19) Fall 87, p. 150.
"An Old Pirate in These Waters" (tr. of Ali Püsküllüoglu). [Trans] (19) Fall 87, p. 148.
"The Poem of the Third Person" (tr. of Attilâ Ilhan). [Trans] (19) Fall 87, p. 156.
"Rifle" (tr. of Sabahattin Kudret Aksal). [Trans] (19) Fall 87, p. 149.
"Sleep" (tr. of Ülkü Tamer). [Trans] (19) Fall 87, p. 157.
"Statue of Lions" (tr. of Cemal Süreya). [Trans] (19) Fall 87, p. 135.
"Table" (tr. of Sabahattin Kudret Aksal). [Trans] (19) Fall 87, p. 149.
3978. NEPO, Mark
"Autumn." [IndR] (10:3) Spr 87, p. 24-25.
"Esther Cannot Control Haman and Ahasuerus." [KenR] (NS 9:4) Fall 87, p. 68-73.
"Esther Describes How She Was Chosen Queen." [KenR] (NS 9:4) Fall 87, p. 65-68.
"The Garden" (from "Fire without Witness"). [KanQ] (19:4) Fall 87, p. 89-96.
"Lorenzo and the Pazzi Conspiracy." [MassR] (28:1) Spr 87, p. 7-10.
"Moses Has Trouble with God's Instructions." [MassR] (28:1) Spr 87, p. 10-12.
"A Statue Violent in Its Sadness." [SouthernPR] (27:1) Spr 87, p. 51-52.
3979. NERUDA, Pablo
"Ode to a Village Movie Theater" (tr. by Margaret Peden). [Antaeus] (58) Spr 87, p. 105-106.
"Ode to the Lizard" (tr. by Margaret Sayers Peden). [ParisR] (29:103) Sum 87, p. 173-174.
"Ode to the Voyager Albatross" (tr. by Margaret Peden). [Antaeus] (58) Spr 87, p. 100-104.
"The Poet's Task" (tr. by Alfred Corn). [Colum] (12) 87, p. 51.
"Seaweed (Algas del Oceano)" (tr. by Margaret Sayers Peden). [MissouriR] (10:2) 87, p. 28-31.
3980. NESHEIM, Steven
"The Crow." [PoetL] (82:1) Spr 87, p. 40.
"Marble." [PoetL] (82:2) Sum 87, p. 109.
3981. NESTOR, Jack
"Siberia." [LaurelR] (21:1/2) Wint-Sum 87, p. 77-79.
3982. NETCHINSKY, Jill
"Ballad of the Two Grandfathers" (tr. of Nicolás Guillén). [Callaloo] (10:2) Spr 87, p. 185, 187.
"Go Get Some Bread" (tr. of Nicolás Guillén). [Callaloo] (10:2) Spr 87, p. 181.
"Riddles" (tr. of Nicolás Guillén). [Callaloo] (10:2) Spr 87, p. 189.
3983. NETO, Agostinho
"Western Civilization." [TriQ] (69) Spr-Sum 87, p. 225.
3984. NETO, João Cabral de Melo
"Antiode" (against so-called profound poetry, tr. by Richard Zenith). [PoetL] (81:4) Wint 86-87, p. 253-258.
"Banks & Cathedrals" (tr. by Richard Zenith). [SenR] (17:2) 87, p. 18.
"Cemetery in Pernambuco (Nossa Senhora da Luz)" (tr. by Richard Zenith). [SenR] (17:2) 87, p. 14.
"Cemetery in Pernambuco (São Lourenço de Mata)" (tr. by Richard Zenith). [SenR] (17:2) 87, p. 15.
"Encounter with a Poet" (tr. by Richard Zenith). [PartR] (54:3) Sum 87, p. 429-431.
"For the Book Fair" (tr. by Richard Zenith). [SenR] (17:2) 87, p. 17.
"Horacio" (tr. by Richard Zenith). [Trans] (19) Fall 87, p. 252.
"The Nothing That Is" (tr. by Richard Zenith). [Trans] (19) Fall 87, p. 251.
"On Elizabeth Bishop" (tr. by Celso de Oliveira). [Verse] (4:3) N 87, p. 58.

"The Poet Thomas Hardy Speaks" (tr. by Ashley Brown). [Verse] (4:3) N 87, p. 57.
"Renewed Homage to Marianne Moore" (tr. by Celso de Oliveira). [Verse] (4:3) N
87, p. 57.
"Renewed Homage to Marianne Moore" (tr. by Richard Zenith). [Trans] (19) Fall
87, p. 253.
"Sugar Cane Girl" (tr. by Richard Zenith). [SenR] (17:2) 87, p. 16.
"The Voice of the Canefield" (tr. by Richard Zenith). [Atlantic] (259:2) F 87, p. 52.
3985. NEUER, Kathleen
"Buffalo Grass." [TexasR] (8:3/4) Fall-Wint 87, p. 98.
"Centering." [HawaiiR] (20) Fall 86, c87, p. 68.
"Lost Arts." [PennR] (3:2) Fall-Wint 87, p. 75.
"On the Irresistiblex Allure of Adobe." [TexasR] (8:3/4) Fall-Wint 87, p. 99.
3986. NEUMAN, Scott L.
"All Right, Dear. Goodbye" (on the death of Hart Crane). [WindO] (49) Fall 87, p.
8.
"Valediction for Brendan." [WindO] (49) Fall 87, p. 8.
3987. NEW, Joan
"To a Cousin from Jane Carlyle" (1986 Finalist, Eve of Saint Agnes Poetry
Competition). [NegC] (7:1/2) 87, p. 176-177.
3988. NEWELL, Ann
"Ring of sweat." [Amelia] (4:3, issue 10) 87, p. 32.
3989. NEWLOVE, John
"Don't Give Me Any." [Quarry] (36:3) Sum 87, p. 57.
"Pages of Illustrations." [Quarry] (36:3) Sum 87, p. 56.
"River." [Quarry] (36:3) Sum 87, p. 58.
"The Weather." [Verse] (4:1) Mr 87, p. 12.
3990. NEWMAN, C.
"Not the Snow" (tr. of Eugene Dubnov, w. the author). [SouthernHR] (21:2) Spr
87, p. 155.
"On This Warm Midsummer Day" (For Eddie Linden and Nina Alferova, tr. of
Eugene Dubnov, w. the author). [Waves] (15:1/2) Fall 86, p. 90.
"Poem of the Hall" (tr. of Eugene Dubnov, w. the author). [WebR] (12:1) Spr 87, p.
81-86.
3991. NEWMAN, Gail
"House Near the Sea." [YellowS] (23) Sum 87, p. 49.
3992. NEWMAN, Michael
"Tower Blocks." [Bogg] (57) 87, p. 53.
3993. NEWMAN, P. B.
"Captian Harry Makes a Living." [SouthernPR] (27:1) Spr 87, p. 56.
"Concord." [KanQ] (19:1/2) Wint-Spr 87, p. 151.
"Dogs and Birds." [Pembroke] (19) 87, p. 142.
"Hunters." [TarRP] (26:2) Spr 87, p. 23.
3994. NEWMAN, Wade
"True Love." [LightY] '87, c86, p. 130.
3995. NEWMARK, Brittany
"Snow in April." [QW] (24) Wint 87, p. 98.
3996. NIATUM, Duane
"The Hollows." [Phoenix] (7:1) 87, p. 38.
3997. NICEWONGER, Kirk
"The Army of Emperor Qin." [ChiR] (35:4) 87, p. 119-121.
"One a Signboard in Front of Greenwood Baptist Church, Brooklyn." [LitR] (31:1)
Fall 87, p. 71.
"Twilight Property" (After the Guitar Piece by Leo Kottke). [KanQ] (19:3) Sum 87,
p. 193.
3998. NICHOL, B. P.
"Horizon #11." [CanLit] (113/114) Sum-Fall 87, p. 61.
"The Lungs: A Draft" (for Robert Kroetsch, from "Organ Music"). [PraF] (8:4) Wint
87-88, p. 47-49.
"Martyrology" (Selections: Three poems from Bo(o)ks 7(VII) & (10)8). [CapilR]
(45) 87 [Ap 88], p. 49-55.
"Sine" (Horizon No. 17). [CrossC] (9:3/4) 87, p. 2.
"Single Letter Translation of Basho's 'Frog / Pond / Plop'." [CrossC] (9:3/4) 87, p.
2.
"Water Poem #5." [CanLit] (113/114) Sum-Fall 87, p. 61.
3999. NICHOLS, Cindy
"Garden Story." [KenR] (NS 9:1) Wint 87, p. 63.

"Owl." [KenR] (NS 9:1) Wint 87, p. 64.
4000. NICHOLS, Grace
"In My Name." [Chelsea] (46) 87, p. 295.
"Night Is Her Robe." [Chelsea] (46) 87, p. 294.
"Waterpot." [Chelsea] (46) 87, p. 293.
4001. NICHOLS, Jeff
"Fine Lines." [LaurelR] (20:1/2) Sum 87, p. 41.
4002. NICHOLS, Martha
"Embracing All That Moves." [YellowS] (23) Sum 87, p. 4.
"Shut Your Eyes." [FiveFR] (5) 87, p. 128-132.
4003. NICHOLS, Weeden R.
"Frontenac." [KanQ] (19:3) Sum 87, p. 58-59.
"Musings at the Stock Tank." [MidwQ] (29:1) Aut 87, p. 92.
"Recurrent Nightmare #3." [MidwQ] (29:1) Aut 87, p. 91.
4004. NICKERSON, Sheila
"On Birds, Letters, Distance." [GreenfR] (14:3/4) Sum-Fall 87, p. 179.
"Pelican of the Wilderness." [GreenfR] (14:3/4) Sum-Fall 87, p. 178.
4005. NICKLAS, Deborah Pierce
"Snow and the Streetlight." [PoetL] (82:3) Fall 87, p. 152.
"Walking to School After Snowstorms." [PoetL] (81:3) Fall 86, p. 197.
4006. NICOSIA, Gerald
"Don't Try to Explain Your Past" (to Bob Kaufman). [AlphaBS] (2) D 87, p. 21.
"The Ghost of Swade Bonnet." [AlphaBS] (2) D 87, p. 20.
"The Siren Song of the Red Taillights" (a poem inspired by a line of Kerouac's).
[AlphaBS] (1) Je 87, p. 13.
4007. NIDA, Ömer
"Postcard" (tr. by Talat Sait Halman). [Trans] (19) Fall 87, p. 108.
4008. NIDITCH, B. Z.
"198-." [FiveFR] (5) 87, p. 92.
"The Acts of a Poet." [WindO] (48) Spr 87, p. 9.
"Budapest, 1986." [WritersF] (13) Fall 87, p. 195-196.
"Crisis Center." [Interim] (6:2) Fall 87, p. 42.
"Grandfather." [Footwork] 87, p. 57.
"Grandfather Mendes." [BallSUF] (28:4) Aut 87, p. 36.
"Harbor Town." [AntigR] (69/70) 87, p. 144.
"Maytime" (for Josef Brodsky). [SpiritSH] (53:1) 87, p. 12.
"Nominal Poem." [SpiritSH] (53:1) 87, p. 13.
"Paul Celan." [WritersF] (13) Fall 87, p. 195.
"Phillip Larkin's Evening Gone" (In Memoriam). [Interim] (6:2) Fall 87, p. 43.
"A Poet Requests to See Me Before His Death." [AntigR] (69/70) 87, p. 144.
"Pre-War Cellar Discovery, Budapest." [GreensboroR] (40) Sum 86, p. 62.
"The Wagon Bed." [BallSUF] (28:4) Aut 87, p. 59.
"You Took Me In." [Interim] (6:2) Fall 87, p. 44.
4009. NIEBAUER, Abby
"Say Anything You Want" (On the Ferry Kitsap). [CrossCur] (7:1) 87, p. 73.
"That Which Is Bright Rises Twice." [CrossCur] (7:1) 87, p. 74.
4010. NIEDELMAN, Hilda L.
"Tapestry." [ManhatPR] (9) Sum 87, p. 18-19.
NIELSEN, Kurt Skov
See SKOV-NIELSEN, Kurt
4011. NIELSEN, Nancy L.
"The Sadness of Cicadas." [PoetL] (81:3) Fall 86, p. 178.
4012. NIEVES MIELES, Edgardo
"Todos Estamos a la Espera, Cesar Vallejo" (2). [Mairena] (9:24) 87, p. 54.
4013. NIGHTINGALE, Barbara
"Resemblances Are Things That Can Be Seen." [KanQ] (19:1/2) Wint-Spr 87, p. 348.
4014. NIJMEIJER, Peter
"After Years" (tr. of Eddy van Vliet). [Vis] (25) 87, p. 38.
4015. NILSSEN, Fjaere C.
"Cotton Poison." [BelPoJ] (37:4) Sum 87, p. 32-33.
4016. NIMMO, Kurt
"Dancer." [SlipS] (7) 87, p. 12.
"Miss America." [SlipS] (7) 87, p. 13.
"Sexual Harassment." [SlipS] (7) 87, p. 14.

4017. NIMNICHT, Nona
   "Centaur." [PraS] (61:2) Sum 87, p. 32.
   "The Dwarfs of Velázquez." [PraS] (61:2) Sum 87, p. 32-33.
   "The Red Bison of Altamira." [PraS] (61:2) Sum 87, p. 30-31.
   "To the Paperhanger." [CrossCur] (7:1) 87, p. 98-99.
   "Waking." [CrossCur] (7:1) 87, p. 97.
4018. NIMS, John Frederick
   "The Consolations of Etymology, with Fanfare." [LightY] '87, c86, p. 70.
   "Dropping the Names." [Poetry] (151:1/2) O-N 87, p. 107-108.
   "In Praise of Sobriety." [LightY] '87, c86, p. 145.
   "The Shape of Leaves." [GrandS] (7:1) Aut 87, p. 222.
4019. NIMTZ, Steven
   "A Dangerous Aesthetic." [BambooR] (36) Fall 87, p. 10-13.
   "A Part." [BambooR] (36) Fall 87, p. 9.
   "There Is a Road That." [BambooR] (36) Fall 87, p. 14-15.
4020. NISETICH, Frank J.
   "Chanticleer" (1986 Honorable Mention, Eve of Saint Agnes Poetry Competition).
      [NegC] (7:1/2) 87, p. 137.
4021. NISHIDA, Merle M.
   "Rose." [BambooR] (36) Fall 87, p. 39-41.
4022. NITTIS, Dion
   "Heart and Mind." [AmerPoR] (16:5) S-O 87, p. 39.
   "I Knew a Girl." [AmerPoR] (16:5) S-O 87, p. 39.
4023. NIXON, John, Jr.
   "Honorable Mention." [ArizQ] (43:3) Aut 87, p. 196.
4024. NIXON-JOHN, Gloria D.
   "Bon Voilier." [EngJ] (76:3) Mr 87, p. 85.
4025. NOBLE, Claude Mary
   "Sacred Heart." [Phoenix] (7:1) 87, p. 39.
4026. NOLAN, Husam
   "Everglades Night Crossing." [FloridaR] (15:1) Spr-Sum 87, p. 23.
4027. NOLAN, James
   "End of the Party" (after Neruda). [NewOR] (14:3) Fall 87, p. 84-89.
4028. NOLD, John
   "Crows on the Cornfield" (This poem's title is taken from Van Gogh's last picture).
      [Quarry] (36:3) Sum 87, p. 5-12.
4029. NOLL, Bink
   "The Nap." [CreamCR] (11:2/3) 87?, p. 59.
   "The Ten Best Things About the House." [GreensboroR] (39) Wint 85-86, p. 96-97.
4030. NORD, Gennie
   "White Willow." [CutB] (27/28) 87, p. 57.
4031. NORDBRANDT, Henrik
   "When a Person Dies" (tr. by the author and Alexander Taylor). [NoDaQ] (55:3)
      Sum 87, p. 226-227.
4032. NORDHAUS, Jean
   "The Black Scarf." [ManhatPR] (9) Sum 87, p. 5.
   "Carpenter." [CumbPR] (6:2) Spr 87, p. 28.
   "Eating Crow." [WestB] (20) 87, p. 28.
   "Eskimo with Fish: A Meditation in Jade." [ManhatPR] (9) Sum 87, p. 4.
   "Kindertotenlieder." [KanQ] (19:3) Sum 87, p. 266-267.
   "The Shirts" (for my brothers). [KanQ] (19:3) Sum 87, p. 267-268.
   "Tile Setter." [CumbPR] (6:2) Spr 87, p. 29.
4033. NORDSTROM, Lars
   "Towards the Pole" (tr. of Rolf Aggestam, w. Erland Anderson). [GreenfR] (14:1/2)
      Wint-Spr, p. 103.
4034. NORGREN, Constance
   "Learning." [MinnR] (NS 28) Spr 87, p. 9.
4035. NORMAN, Chad
   "Movement Within the Mustard Seed." [Waves] (15:3) Wint 87, p. 58-59.
4036. NORMOLLE, Sue
   "The Drowning." [Ascent] (12:3) 87, p. 30.
4037. NORRIS, Jeanne
   "Old Faithful." [KanQ] (19:1/2) Wint-Spr 87, p. 236.
4038. NORRIS, Kathleen
   "Burying the Past." [SoDakR] (25:3) Aut 87, p. 52-54.
   "Cement." [SoDakR] (25:3) Aut 87, p. 49-51.

"Getting Lucky." [SoDakR] (25:2) Sum 87, p. 56-57.
"Mrs. Schneider Walks Home on a Night in June." [SoDakR] (25:3) Aut 87, p. 47-48.
"A Poem for My Mother." [SoDakR] (25:2) Sum 87, p. 58.
4039. NORRIS, Ken
"The Agony of Being an Expos Fan." [Descant] (56/57) Spr-Sum 87, p. 140.
"Andre Dawson, at the Height of His Career." [Descant] (56/57) Spr-Sum 87, p. 141.
"The hours go by." [Descant] (56/57) Spr-Sum 87, p. 142.
"You never lose the ability to say your name using the thirteen colours of language." [Descant] (56/57) Spr-Sum 87, p. 143.
4040. NORRIS, Leslie
"A Dying Hawk." [NewYorker] (63:23) 27 Jl 87, p. 34.
"The Summer Hawk." [NewYorker] (63:23) 27 Jl 87, p. 34.
4041. NORTH, Charles
"Fourteen Poems" (2-line poems). [NewAW] (2) Fall 87, p. 41-42.
"Nocturnes." [Colum] (12) 87, p. 3-5.
4042. NORTH, Mary
"To a Lost Child." [Confr] (35/36) Spr-Fall 87, p. 108-109.
"To My Mother As I Feel the First Snow." [Confr] (35/36) Spr-Fall 87, p. 107.
4043. NORTHERN, Michael
"Scream." [Writer] (99:1) Ja 86, p. 18.
4044. NORTHSUN, Nila
"The 1st One I Ever Saw Dead." [Abraxas] (35/36) 87, p. 88.
4045. NORTJE, Arthur
"Exit Visa." [TriQ] (69) Spr-Sum 87, p. 384.
"From the Way I Live Now." [TriQ] (69) Spr-Sum 87, p. 385.
"Horses: Athlone." [TriQ] (69) Spr-Sum 87, p. 382-383.
"The spacious days pass into the neutrality." [TriQ] (69) Spr-Sum 87, p. 386.
4046. NORTON, Scott
"Rain in Monodendri." [US1] (20/21) Wint 86-87, p. 35.
"We Used to Leave the Lights On." [US1] (20/21) Wint 86-87, p. 35.
NOSRATOLLAH KAZEMI MAZANDERANI
See MAZANDERANI, Nosratollah Kazemi
4047. NOSTRAND, Jennifer
"The back gardens of Versailles." [Amelia] (4:3, issue 10) 87, p. 113.
"In the twilight." [Amelia] (4:3, issue 10) 87, p. 112.
"You pick me up in a cab." [Amelia] (4:3, issue 10) 87, p. 112.
"Your hair is lightened." [Phoenix] (7:1) 87, p. 19.
4048. NOVAK, R.
"Terry Fox." [WindO] (48) Spr 87, p. 27.
4049. NOWAK, Darren
"At x27." [WoosterR] (7) Spr 87, p. 73-74.
4050. NOWAK, Nancy
"Sanctuary." [IndR] (10:3) Spr 87, p. 86.
4051. NOYES, H. F.
"Arguing a point." [Amelia] (4:1/2, issue 9) 87, p. 18.
"Ex-boxer." [Amelia] (4:3, issue 10) 87, p. 114.
"Halfway home." [Amelia] (4:3, issue 10) 87, p. 9.
4052. NOYES, Steve
"Herb Schellenberg." [MalR] (79) Je 87, p. 81-82.
4053. NURKSE, D.
"Air Well." [HayF] (2) Spr 87, p. 81.
"Faded Green Card." [HayF] (2) Spr 87, p. 79.
"The Hush." [Footwork] 87, p. 38.
"Interior Wind." [CrossCur] (6:4) 87, p. 22.
"Melody Next Door." [Vis] (24) 87, p. 26.
"Ovid in Exile." [PoetL] (81:3) Fall 86, p. 185-186.
"A Southern Capital." [HayF] (2) Spr 87, p. 80.
"Without Rain." [CrossCur] (6:4) 87, p. 21.
4054. NUTTING, Leslie
"The Kingdom of Trees." [Waves] (15:1/2) Fall 86, p. 76-77.
4055. NYE, Naomi Shihab
"A Definite Shore." [GreenfR] (14:1/2) Wint-Spr, p. 167-168.
"No Wonder." [GreenfR] (14:1/2) Wint-Spr, p. 171.
"Nobody's Newspaper." [Spirit] (8:2) 87, p. 49.

"Soap Does Not Have Supernatural Powers" (Mexican soap label. For Adlai). [GreenfR] (14:1/2) Wint-Spr, p. 169-170.
4056. NYSTROM, Debra
"The Dream of Burning" (Villa of the Mysteries, Pompeii). [Thrpny] (31) Fall 87, p. 18.
"Emily's Ghost." [BostonR] (12:2) Ap 87, p. 8.
4057. OAKES, Randy W.
"My German Shepherd Is Dating." [NoDaQ] (55:3) Sum 87, p. 86.
4058. OAKS, Jeff
"Flesh." [MSS] (5:3) 87, p. 152.
"The Last." [MSS] (5:3) 87, p. 154.
"The Starfish." [Sequoia] (30:3) Wint 87, p. 26.
"White Songs." [MSS] (5:3) 87, p. 152-153.
4059. OATES, Joyce Carol
"Compost." [Antaeus] (58) Spr 87, p. 191.
"The Convalescent." [FourQ] (1:2) Fall 87, p. 14.
"Here, Nights Are Distinct from Days." [SouthwR] (72:3) Sum 87, p. 414.
"How Delicately." [NewEngR] (9:3) Spr 87, p. 288.
"The Insomniac." [Salm] (72) Fall 86, p. 183-184.
"Island, 1949." [VirQR] (63:2) Spr 87, p. 270-271.
"Last Exit Before Bridge." [OhioR] (38) 87, p. 103-104.
"Lines in Substitution for a Eulogy for a Dead Elder." [Iowa] (17:1) Wint 87, p. 106.
"Lost Creek." [VirQR] (63:2) Spr 87, p. 268-270.
"Mania: Early Phase." [Shen] (37:4) 87, p. 35.
"Motive, Metaphor." [Poetry] (151:1/2) O-N 87, p. 109.
"Mutability." [Iowa] (17:1) Wint 87, p. 105.
"Once Upon a Time." [PraS] (61:3) Fall 87, p. 113.
"Playground." [Hudson] (40:1) Spr 87, p. 90.
"Recurring Dream of Childhood." [FourQ] (1:1) Wint 87, p. 9-10.
"Shriven." [Iowa] (17:1) Wint 87, p. 105.
"Silence." [Iowa] (17:1) Wint 87, p. 105.
"Snapshot Album." [Nat] (244:7) 21 F 87, p. 231.
"Terror of Flying." [FourQ] (1:1) Wint 87, p. 10.
"This Morning." [PraS] (61:3) Fall 87, p. 114.
"Undefeated Heavyweight, 20 Years Old (I)." [PraS] (61:3) Fall 87, p. 112.
"Undefeated Heavyweight, 20 Years Old (II)." [PraS] (61:3) Fall 87, p. 112.
"Undertow, Wolf's Head Lake." [Salm] (72) Fall 86, p. 182-183.
"Waiting on Elvis, 1956." [Poetry] (151:1/2) O-N 87, p. 109.
"White Piano" (For Elliot Gilbert). [CalQ] (30) Wint 87, p. 24-25.
"Winslow Homer's 'The Gulf Stream,' 1902." [Iowa] (17:1) Wint 87, p. 104-105.
4060. OBADIAH, Silas
"My Tale." [GreenfR] (14:3/4) Sum-Fall 87, p. 169.
"The Silent Call." [Chelsea] (46) 87, p. 118.
"The Things They Said." [GreenfR] (14:3/4) Sum-Fall 87, p. 170.
4061. OBERC, Lawrence
"Steps." [Bogg] (58) 87, p. 37.
4062. OBERG, Arthur
"Lust." [NowestR] (25:1) 87, p. 105.
"Walking." [NowestR] (25:1) 87, p. 102.
4063. OBERTO, Anna
"Nuova Scrittura" (New Writing). [Caliban] (2) 87, p. 65.
4064. O'BRIEN, Geoffrey
"Off/Center" (Selections: 3 sections). [NewAW] (1) 87, p. 59-61.
4065. O'BRIEN, John
"An Abandoned Cemetery in Pocahontas County, West Virginia" (for Beck). [SouthwR] (72:1) Wint 87, p. 133-134.
"Chimneys." [Wind] (17:61) 87, p. 46.
"The Generic Poem." [Pig] (14) 87, p. 33.
"Saxophones." [Wind] (17:61) 87, p. 22.
4066. O'BRIEN, Mark
"For Clifford Bernel." [Margin] (2) Spr 87, p. 78-80.
"A Poem for Debby." [Margin] (2) Spr 87, p. 80-83.
O'BRIEN, Susan Roney
See RONEY-O'BRIEN, Susan

4067. O'BRIEN, Sylvia
     "Convalescence." [Amelia] (4:3, issue 10) 87, p. 79.
     "Senescence." [Amelia] (4:3, issue 10) 87, p. 79-80.
OCA, Marco Antonio Montes de
     See MONTES DE OCA, Marco Antonio
4068. OCHESTER, Ed
     "Changing the Name to Ochester." [AntR] (45:1) Wint 87, p. 52-54.
     "Duke." [LightY] '87, c86, p. 77.
     "The Heart of Owl Country." [AntR] (45:1) Wint 87, p. 50-51.
     "The Latin American Solidarity Committee Fundraising Picnic." [LightY] '87, c86,
          p. 202.
     "Mary Mihalik." [SouthernPR] (27:2) Fall 87, p. 40-41.
     "New Day." [Poetry] (150:4) Jl 87, p. 224-225.
4069. O'CONNELL, Bill
     "Last Night Out." [KanQ] (19:1/2) Wint-Spr 87, p. 204.
     "Late One Night." [Jacaranda] (2:2) Spr 87, p. 9.
4070. O'CONNOR, Deirdre
     "Skellig." [GrahamHR] (10) Wint-Spr 87, p. 36.
4071. O'CONNOR, J. F.
     "On the Rhyming of Four-Line Verses." [LightY] '87, c86, p. 193.
4072. O'CONNOR, Mark
     "Frigate-Birds." [Chelsea] (46) 87, p. 33.
     "North Head Quarantine Station (Sydney)." [Chelsea] (46) 87, p. 25-32.
4073. O'CONNOR, Michael
     "On Arriving at Ling-Nan, January, 1949" (Two tz'u, tr. of Chi Li, w. Li Chi).
          [Calyx] (10:2/3) Spr 87, p. 78-79.
4074. O'CONNOR, Sheila M.
     "Tangled Bedsheets." [ThRiPo] (29/30) 87, p. 50.
4075. ODAM, Joyce
     "Solitaires." [Bogg] (58) 87, p. 25.
4076. ØDEGÅRD, Knut
     "Bar Guest" (tr. by George Johnston). [MalR] (78) Mr 87, p. 9.
     "Bee-Buzz, Salmon-Leap" (tr. by George Johnston). [MalR] (78) Mr 87, p. 7.
     "Clocks" (tr. by George Johnston). [MalR] (78) Mr 87, p. 11.
     "Cows and Turtles" (tr. by George Johnston). [MalR] (78) Mr 87, p. 10.
     "January Evening, Frost-Clear" (Molde 1955, tr. by George Johnston). [MalR] (78)
          Mr 87, p. 8.
     "November, Storm" (tr. by George Johnston). [MalR] (78) Mr 87, p. 16.
     "October, Orkney" (tr. by George Johnston). [MalR] (78) Mr 87, p. 12-14.
     "Thora and Ragnar" (tr. by George Johnston). [MalR] (78) Mr 87, p. 17-21.
     "War, Death" (tr. by George Johnston). [MalR] (78) Mr 87, p. 15.
     "We Trundle the Child By" (tr. by George Johnston). [MalR] (78) Mr 87, p. 6.
4077. O'DELL, John
     "Tall Grass." [Writer] (99:3) Mr 86, p. 21-22.
4078. O'DELL, Mary Ernestine
     "The Truth in February." [PassN] (8:1) Wint 87, p. 19.
4079. O'DONNELL, Mary
     "Catching Up" (for Ann). [GreensboroR] (39) Wint 85-86, p. 70.
     "Cutting Loose." [GreensboroR] (39) Wint 85-86, p. 71.
4080. OGDEN, Daniel
     "Game of Chance" (tr. of Petter Bergman). [Vis] (23) 87, p. 14.
     "Loving Couples" (tr. of Margareta Ekstrom). [Vis] (23) 87, p. 16.
     "Nobody's Kids" (tr. of Kristina Lugn). [Vis] (25) 87, p. 36.
     "SSN" (tr. of Kristina Lugn). [Vis] (23) 87, p. 14.
OGDEN, David
     See OGDEN, Daniel
4081. OGDEN, Hugh
     "In the Woods Near Most Any City" (for D. B., 1986 Finalist, Eve of Saint Agnes
          Poetry Competition). [NegC] (7:1/2) 87, p. 212-214.
     "Martha" (for Olive on her 94th birthday). [StoneC] (14:3/4) Spr-Sum 87, p. 20-21.
4082. OGLOZA, Darius
     "So Goes the Conversation." [Bogg] (57) 87, p. 56.
4083. O'GRADY, James J.
     "Doris-Billy-Richard." [Zyzzyva] (3:3) Fall 87, p. 51-53.
4084. O'GRADY, Tom
     "Deep Mud" (tr. of Pavel Srut, w. the author). [HampSPR] Wint 87, p. 33.

"It Was Afternoon or Later" (tr. of Jaroslav Seifert, w. Paul Jagasich). [Spirit] (8:2) 87, p. 317.
"My Love" (tr. of Pavel Srut, w. the author). [HampSPR] Wint 87, p. 34-37.
"Not Long Before April" (tr. of Pavel Srut, w. the author). [HampSPR] Wint 87, p. 33-34.
4085. O'HARA, Edgar
"Cometa Malherido." [Inti] (24/25) Otoño 86-Primavera 87, p. 266-267.
"The Lighthouse Invites the Storm." [Inti] (24/25) Otoño 86-Primavera 87, p. 265-266.
4086. O'HARA, Mark
"Beethoven and the Alder." [CumbPR] (6:2) Spr 87, p. 3.
"Eleventh Graders on Saint-Saens' 'Rondo and Capricioso'." [CumbPR] (6:2) Spr 87, p. 1-2.
4087. O'HARA, Pat
"Where Rain-Crows Call" (1986 Finalist, Eve of Saint Agnes Poetry Competition). [NegC] (7:1/2) 87, p. 165-166.
4088. O'HARA, Scott
"Broken Circle." [JamesWR] (4:2) Wint 87, p. 7.
4089. O'HARRA, Deborah
"Stalking the Invisible Man." [CutB] (27/28) 87, p. 66-68.
4090. OHMANN-KRAUSE, Joseph
"I. Siracusa." [WebR] (12:2) Fall 87, p. 46.
"II. Messina." [WebR] (12:2) Fall 87, p. 47.
"III. Venice." [WebR] (12:2) Fall 87, p. 47.
"The Gleaning." [WebR] (12:2) Fall 87, p. 48.
4091. OHNESORGE-FICK, Karen
"Ma's Ghost." [Ploughs] (13:4) 87, p. 79.
4092. OIJER, Bruno K.
"Deceived" (tr. by the author). [Vis] (23) 87, p. 19.
"He Wanted You" (tr. by the author). [Vis] (23) 87, p. 19.
4093. OJAIDE, Tanure
"I Am a Bird." [Chelsea] (46) 87, p. 123.
"In the Sahel." [Chelsea] (46) 87, p. 120.
"Memories of Famine." [Chelsea] (46) 87, p. 121.
"Supplies." [Chelsea] (46) 87, p. 122.
4094. O'KEEFE, Richard R.
"My Dog, My Death." [ThRiPo] (29/30) 87, p. 51.
4095. OLASON, Sara
"Death by Disorder." [BelPoJ] (37:3) Spr 87, p. 4-5.
"Helping My Sister with a Research Project About Coots on the Cedar River." [BellArk] (3:3) My-Je 87, p. 9.
"My Usual Place at the Table" (to Mr. Little). [BellArk] (3:3) My-Je 87, p. 1.
"Song of the Disappearing Woman" (for Liz). [BellArk] (3:4) Jl-Ag 87, p. 10.
"A Walk on Queen Anne Hill." [BellArk] (3:4) Jl-Ag 87, p. 4.
4096. OLDER, Julia
"My Rumi-nation" (Sufi poet Jalal al-Din Rumi, 1207-73, expressed mystical thought through symbols). [LightY] '87, c86, p. 55.
4097. OLDKNOW, Antony
"Above the Scribbled Writing" (tr. of Eugenio Montale). [SoDakR] (25:2) Sum 87, p. 16.
"Horse Race." [MinnR] (NS 28) Spr 87, p. 36-37.
"Interlude." [CreamCR] (11:2/3) 87?, p. 109-110.
"A Kind of Fantasy" (tr. of Eugenio Montale). [SoDakR] (25:2) Sum 87, p. 17.
4098. OLDS, Jennifer
"Counting to Nine (Not Getting There)" (1985 Alice Jackson Poetry Prize: First Prize). [Electrum] (39) Fall-Wint 87, p. 6.
"Smallest Town." [NewL] (53:2) Wint 86-87, p. 68-69.
4099. OLDS, Sharon
"After Making Love in Winter." [Poetry] (150:2) My 87, p. 82.
"The Animals." [RiverS] (22) 87, p. 48.
"The Camp Bus, with My Son on It, Pulls Away from the Curb." [RiverS] (22) 87, p. 47.
"The Ceremony" (Partisan woods near Smolensk, 1941). [OP] (final issue) Sum 87, p. 65.
"Crab." [Ploughs] (13:4) 87, p. 82-83.
"The Daughter Goes to Camp." [Ploughs] (13:4) 87, p. 84.

"The Day They Tied Me Up." [Poetry] (151:1/2) O-N 87, p. 110-111.
"Death and Murder." [RiverS] (22) 87, p. 44.
"The Empire State Building as the Moon." [NewYorker] (62:52) 16 F 87, p. 91.
"The Ferryer." [ParisR] (29:105) Wint 87, p. 95-96.
"For My Mother." [OP] (final issue) Sum 87, p. 62-63.
"History of Medicine." [Field] (37) Fall 87, p. 59.
"The Language of the Brag." [Calyx] (10:2/3) Spr 87, p. 8-9.
"May 1968." [Poetry] (150:2) My 87, p. 80-81.
"The Mortal One." [Ploughs] (13:4) 87, p. 85-86.
"Mrs. Krikorian." [Nat] (245:20) 12 D 87, p. 727.
"Natural History." [Field] (37) Fall 87, p. 62.
"Necking." [Field] (37) Fall 87, p. 60-61.
"R. I. P." [OP] (final issue) Sum 87, p. 64.
"The Return." [OP] (final issue) Sum 87, p. 63.
"The Sash." [Ploughs] (13:4) 87, p. 80-81.
"Six Weeks after My Father's Death." [RiverS] (22) 87, p. 45-46.
"The Things of This World" (6 poems). [IndR] (10:1/2) 87, p. 21-32.
4100. O'LEARY, Dawn
"Winter, Black and White." [PoetryNW] (28:3) Aut 87, p. 25.
4101. O'LEARY, Thomas
"Soliloquy for Rough Beast." [ColR] (NS 14:1) Spr-Sum 87, p. 72-73.
4102. OLES, Carole
"Early." [GeoR] (41:2) Sum 87, p. 334-335.
"On Greyhound, Boston to New York." [Poetry] (151:1/2) O-N 87, p. 111-112.
"Preparing for Weather." [TexasR] (7:3/4) 87, p. 114.
"The Unteaching." [TexasR] (7:3/4) 87, p. 115.
4103. OLINKA, Sharon
"South Was the Promise We Were Born With." [Confr] (35/36) Spr-Fall 87, p. 164-165.
4104. OLIPHANT, Dave
"Maria's Bath." [CreamCR] (11:2/3) 87?, p. 8.
4105. OLIVE, Harry
"The Day His Father Died." [CrossCur] (6:4) 87, p. 9.
"Listening to the Man with the Lee-Enfield Rifle." [Puerto] (22:2) Spr 87, p. 109.
"Rock Men." [WebR] (12:1) Spr 87, p. 50.
4106. OLIVEIRA, Celso de
"On Elizabeth Bishop" (tr. of João Cabral de Melo Neto). [Verse] (4:3) N 87, p. 58.
"Renewed Homage to Marianne Moore" (tr. of João Cabral de Melo Neto). [Verse] (4:3) N 87, p. 57.
4107. OLIVER, Mary
"The Buddha's Last Instruction." [VirQR] (63:4) Aut 87, p. 632-633.
"Fish Bones." [KenR] (NS 9:4) Fall 87, p. 23-24.
"The Hermit Crab." [Poetry] (151:1/2) O-N 87, p. 112-113.
"Indonesia." [KenR] (NS 9:4) Fall 87, p. 24.
"The Lilies Break Open Over the Dark Water." [VirQR] (63:4) Aut 87, p. 631-632.
"Maybe." [Ploughs] (13:4) 87, p. 87-88.
"Moccasin Flowers." [Atlantic] (259:6) Je 87, p. 64.
"Nature." [Antaeus] (58) Spr 87, p. 89-90.
"Orion." [Poetry] (150:2) My 87, p. 114.
"The Other." [MemphisSR] (8:1) Fall 87, p. 7.
"The Terns." [KenR] (NS 9:4) Fall 87, p. 25.
4108. OLIVER, Merrill
"The Way Things Click." [WestB] (20) 87, p. 103.
4109. OLIVER, Michael Brian
"Poor Bastard" (Remembering Alden). [CanLit] (112) Spr 87, p. 71.
4110. OLIVER, Raymond
"Epitaph." [Sequoia] (31:1) Centennial issue 87, p. 28.
"Journey into Spring" (for Mary Anne, in spite of her preference for short poems). [NegC] (7:3/4) 87, p. 70-75.
"Some Immortality." [Sequoia] (31:1) Centennial issue 87, p. 29.
"The World Theatre." [Sequoia] (31:1) Centennial issue 87, p. 28.
4111. OLIVEROS, Chuck
"The Fall of Adam and Eve." [Wind] (17:60) 87, p. 31-32.
"Invoking Amnesia." [Caliban] (2) 87, p. 134-135.
"Poison Water." [Wind] (17:60) 87, p. 31.

4112. OLLIVIER, Larry
"The Iron Cross at Christ Church." [BellArk] (3:2) Mr-Ap 87, p. 9.
4113. OLMSTED, Katya
"I've forgotten nothing" (tr. of Bella Akhmadulina, w. John High). [FiveFR] (5) 87,
p. 102.
"Night Fantasies" (tr. of Bella Akhmadulina, w. John High). [FiveFR] (5) 87, p.
103.
"Such a night isn't chosen" (tr. of Ivan Zhdanov, w. John High). [FiveFR] (5) 87,
p. 68.
"When My Wife Dances" (tr. of Peter Veghin, w. John High). [FiveFR] (5) 87, p.
1-2.
4114. OLOFSSON, Tommy
"Dream Seeds" (tr. by Jean Pearson). [PaintedB] (30) 87, p. 18.
"Freeing the Shadow" (tr. by Jean Pearson). [PaintedB] (30) 87, p. 19.
"On Leash" (tr. by Jean Pearson). [CrossCur] (7:3) 87, p. 61.
"The Shadow Inside Me" (tr. by Jean Pearson). [PaintedB] (30) 87, p. 18.
"The Waves with You" (tr. by Jean Pearson). [PaintedB] (30) 87, p. 19.
4115. OLSEN, William
"The Dead Monkey." [PoetryNW] (28:3) Aut 87, p. 7-8.
"Tomorrow." [Shen] (37:4) 87, p. 15-17.
"Water." [PoetryNW] (28:3) Aut 87, p. 6-7.
4116. OLSON, Elder
"Shark and Cockroach." [Poetry] (151:1/2) O-N 87, p. 114.
4117. OLSON, Kirby
"The Encyclopedist's Conundrum." [LightY] '87, c86, p. 184.
"Insects Blind to History." [LightY] '87, c86, p. 246.
4118. OLSON, Matt
"The Desert Retreat." [CentR] (31:1) Wint 87, p. 65.
4119. OLSON, Nancy A.
"Vermont Schoolyard." [EngJ] (76:7) N 87, p. 99.
4120. OLSON, Toby
"Unfinished Building." [Temblor] (5) 87, p. 158-163.
4121. O'MELVENY, Regina
"The Butterfly Collector" (1985 Alice Jackson Poetry Prize: 1st Honorable Mention).
[Electrum] (39) Fall-Wint 87, p. 11.
4122. O'NEILL, Alexandre
"Legacy" (tr. by Richard Zenith). [MassR] (28:4) Wint 87, p. 651.
"An Unoriginal Poem About Fear" (tr. by Richard Zenith). [MassR] (28:4) Wint 87,
p. 652-653.
4123. O'NEILL, Brian
"Phenomenology." [OhioR] (38) 87, p. 98-100.
"The Stock Girl." [Crazy] (32) Spr 87, p. 35-36.
4124. O'NEILL, John
"Beluga Whale Birth." [MalR] (79) Je 87, p. 128.
"Her Fear Is Whale." [MalR] (79) Je 87, p. 127.
"Inuit Hunters." [AntigR] (68) Wint 87, p. 40.
"The Moose." [MalR] (79) Je 87, p. 125.
"Moose II." [MalR] (79) Je 87, p. 126.
4125. O'NEILL, Patrick
"Two Different Deer Camps." [Paint] (14:28) Aut 87, p. 22-23.
ONO, Tosaburo
See TOSABURO, Ono
4126. OOSAHWE, Linda Relacion
"Rain-in-the-Face Nainoa Goingsnake." [HawaiiR] (21) Spr 87, p. 42.
4127. OPENGART, Bea
"Forgive, Forgive." [GreensboroR] (42) Sum 87, p. 83.
4128. OPITZ, May
"Afro-German" (tr. by Ilze Mueller). [Cond] (14) 87, p. 5.
OPPENHEIMER, Felix Franco
See FRANCO OPPENHEIMER, Felix
4129. ORBAN, Ottó
"At First Hand" (tr. by Jascha Kessler, w. Maria Körösy). [VirQR] (63:1) Wint 87,
p. 77-78.
"Chile" (tr. by Jascha Kessler, w. Maria Körösy). [NewL] (53:3) Spr 87, p. 17.
"The Golden Fleece" (tr. by Jascha Kessler, w. Maria Körösy). [VirQR] (63:1) Wint
87, p. 78-79.

299

"Intellectuals" (tr. by Jascha Kessler, w. Maria Körösy). [VirQR] (63:1) Wint 87, p. 80.
"Poetry" (tr. by Jascha Kessler, w. Maria Körösy). [Nimrod] (31:1) Fall-Wint 87, p. 123.
"Poverty" (tr. by Jascha Kessler, w. Maria Körösy). [PoetryE] (23/24) Fall 87, p. 117.
"Turn-of-the-Century Budapest" (tr. by Jascha Kessler, w. Mária Körösy). [GrahamHR] (10) Wint-Spr 87, p. 59.
4130. ORBELL, Margaret
"A Man Dreams of His Dead Wife" (tr. of Moa Tetua). [Trans] (19) Fall 87, p. 173.
"Marquesas Islands Songs" (tr. of Anonymous poems). [Trans] (19) Fall 87, p. 174-176.
4131. ORELLANA, Carlos
"The City Is Going to Explode, Flora" (tr. by John Oliver Simon). [Vis] (23) 87, p. 8.
4132. ÖREN, Aras
"Postcard" (tr. by Talat Sait Halman). [Trans] (19) Fall 87, p. 108.
4133. ORFALEA, Gregory
"The Capital of Solitude" (for E. Ethelbert Miller). [GreenfR] (14:1/2) Wint-Spr, p. 152-153.
"Sparrows in the Snow." [GreenfR] (14:1/2) Wint-Spr, p. 150-151.
4134. ORLOWSKY, Dzvinia
"Growing Up Ukrainian." [Agni] (24/25) 87, p. 220-221.
4135. ORMSBY, Eric
"Forgetful Lazarus." [Shen] (37:4) 87, p. 77.
"Lazarus and Basements." [Shen] (37:4) 87, p. 76.
"Lazarus in Sumatra." [Shen] (37:4) 87, p. 78.
"Lazarus Listens." [Shen] (37:4) 87, p. 77.
"The Pine at Auger Falls." [Blueline] (7:2/3 [i.e. 8:2/3?]) 87, p. 55.
"Railyard in Winter." [Blueline] (7:2/3 [i.e. 8:2/3?]) 87, p. 93.
"Starfish." [AntigR] (69/70) 87, p. 7.
4136. OROZCO, Olga
"Brillos, Soplos, Rumores." [LetFem] (13:1/2) Primavera-Otoño 87, p. 15.
"Esbozos Frente a un Modelo." [LetFem] (13:1/2) Primavera-Otoño 87, p. 16-17.
"Jonah's Lament" (tr. by Eliot Weinberger). [AmerPoR] (16:2) Mr-Ap 87, p. 20.
"Personal Stamp" (tr. by Eliot Weinberger). [AmerPoR] (16:2) Mr-Ap 87, p. 20.
"Sphinxes Accustomed to Being" (tr. by Eliot Weinberger). [AmerPoR] (16:2) Mr-Ap 87, p. 19-20.
"The Sunken Continent" (tr. by Eliot Weinberger). [ColR] (NS 14:2) Fall-Wint 87, p. 54-55.
4137. ORR, Ed
"Appearances." [YellowS] (22) Spr 87, p. 34.
"Hot Humid Night." [YellowS] (22) Spr 87, p. 35.
"Strawberry Patch" (after Anna Akhmatova). [WritersF] (13) Fall 87, p. 189.
"What's in a Name." [LightY] '87, c86, p. 28.
4138. ORR, Gregory
"After Botticelli's 'Birth of Venus'." [IndR] (10:3) Spr 87, p. 18.
"Available Now: Archaic Torsos of Both Sexes." [Poetry] (150:5) Ag 87, p. 285.
"The City and the Barbarians." [Ploughs] (13:4) 87, p. 89-92.
"The Lost Children." [IndR] (10:3) Spr 87, p. 12.
"On a Highway East of Selma, Alabama, July, 1965." [SenR] (17:1) 87, p. 57-59.
"The Teachers." [OhioR] (39) 87, p. 90.
4139. ORR, Pam
"Joan of Arc." [SouthernPR] (27:1) Spr 87, p. 52.
4140. ORR, Priscilla
"Cafe Tres Bien" (for Carley). [Footwork] 87, p. 18.
"Legacy" (for Mother). [Footwork] 87, p. 18.
4141. ORR, Verlena
"Blackbirds at Mt. Zion." [ColR] (NS 14:2) Fall-Wint 87, p. 25.
"Stars." [ColR] (NS 14:1) Spr-Sum 87, p. 19.
4142. ORTEGA, Julio
"Toledan Self-Portrait" (tr. by Clayton Eshleman). [Sulfur] (19) Spr 87, p. 46-49.
4143. ORTH, Kevin
"Amazing Grace." [Gambit] (21) 87, p. 65.
"Association." [Gambit] (20) 86, p. 123.
"A Blues." [WestB] (20) 87, p. 85.

"The Dream in the Stone." [Gambit] (20) 86, p. 121-122.
"The Hour Has Come." [Gambit] (21) 87, p. 66-67.
"In Memory of Dmitri Shostakovich." [WestB] (20) 87, p. 84.
"One Night." [Gambit] (20) 86, p. 124.
"The Other Life." [Bogg] (58) 87, p. 20.
"The Other Life." [Gambit] (20) 86, p. 125.
"A Report from the Air." [Gambit] (20) 86, p. 126.
4144. ORTIZ, Simon J.
"Mid-America Prayer." [RiverS] (24) 87, p. 84.
4145. ORTOLANI, Al
"Grace." [LightY] '87, c86, p. 83.
"Jessa's Late Assignment." [LightY] '87, c86, p. 223.
"The Price of Change." [EngJ] (76:4) Ap 87, p. 44.
"Taco Vendor's Advice." [Wind] (17:60) 87, p. 50.
4146. ORVECZ, Imre
"I Didn't Tell You Then" (tr. by Bruce Berlind, w. Maria Körösy). [Rampike] (5:3) 87, p. 70.
4147. OSAKI, Mark
"Tradecraft." [CrossCur] (7:1) 87, p. 146.
4148. OSBEY, Brenda Marie
"Anoher Time and Farther South" (for Clyde R. Taylor, a Mourning Poem). [SouthernR] (23:4) O 87, p. 804-805.
"Elvena." [AmerPoR] (16:6) N-D 87, p. 23-24.
"The Godchild." [SouthernR] (23:4) O 87, p. 805-807.
"The House." [GreenfR] (14:1/2) Wint-Spr, p. 172-175.
"Speaking of Trains" (for Moses Nkondo). [AmerPoR] (16:6) N-D 87, p. 21-22.
"Writing Home." [GreenfR] (14:1/2) Wint-Spr, p. 176-177.
4149. OSBORN, Andrew
"Ashes, Ashes." [HarvardA] (120:2) Mr 87, p. 6.
4150. OSBORN, Karen
"Blood and Light." [PoetL] (82:3) Fall 87, p. 149.
"The Language of Fields." [PoetL] (82:3) Fall 87, p. 150.
"Lost in the Spindle." [CentR] (31:4) Fall 87, p. 378.
"When a Woman Dreams of Mountains." [SoCaR] (19:2) Spr 87, p. 23.
"The Witching." [CentR] (31:4) Fall 87, p. 377.
4151. OSBORNE, Bud
"For the Kids Who Kill Themselves Because of Braces." [MinnR] (NS 28) Spr 87, p. 31-32.
4152. OSERS, Ewald
"Spring" (tr. of Ivan Davidkov). [CrossCur] (7:3) 87, p. 117.
4153. O'SHAUGHNESSY, Kathleen
"Picture-Taking at Cow Creek." [GreensboroR] (39) Wint 85-86, p. 51.
4154. OSING, Gordon
"The Water Radical." [SouthernR] (23:3) Jl 87, p. 625-627.
4155. OSLIN, Irv
"A Supermarket in New York City." [Pig] (14) 87, p. 35.
4156. OSTRIKER, Alicia
"Boil." [MissouriR] (10:3) 87, p. 137.
"Boil." [US1] (20/21) Wint 86-87, p. 33.
"Hating the World." [MissouriR] (10:3) 87, p. 136.
"A Meditation in Seven Days." [MichQR] (26:1) Wint 87, p. 188-195.
"Mid-February" (for Maxine Kumin). [OntR] (27) Fall-Wint 87, p. 68.
"Move." [NewYorker] (63:8) 13 Ap 87, p. 38.
"Stream." [Poetry] (151:1/2) O-N 87, p. 115-116.
"Stream." [US1] (20/21) Wint 86-87, p. 32.
"Words for a Wedding." [OntR] (27) Fall-Wint 87, p. 69.
"A Young Woman, a Tree." [Poetry] (150:6) S 87, p. 331-334.
4157. OSTROM, Hans
"From Another Part of the Forest." [PoetryNW] (28:1) Spr 87, p. 37.
"Paid Mourner." [CreamCR] (11:2/3) 87?, p. 115.
"Sierra Nevada in March." [CreamCR] (11:2/3) 87?, p. 116.
4158. OSWALD, Ernest J.
"Melancholy Breakfast" (after Frank O'Hara). [Pig] (14) 87, p. 15.
4159. OTIS, Alice
"Emelda" (tr. of Jacques Delphin). [Paint] (14:27) Spr 87, p. 15-17.

4160. OTIS, Emily
"Drawbacks." [LightY] '87, c86, p. 113.
4161. OTORIÑO, Rafael Felipe
"Night Guest" (tr. by Jason Wilson). [Trans] (18) Spr 87, p. 185.
"Stairs" (tr. by Jason Wilson). [Trans] (18) Spr 87, p. 186.
4162. OTT, Gil
"My hand more than my eye, as it passes over." [CentralP] (12) Fall 87, p. 87.
4163. OTT, Rita
"Berry-Picking." [BellArk] (3:2) Mr-Ap 87, p. 7.
"Journey to Your Family." [BellArk] (3:4) Jl-Ag 87, p. 4.
"The Legacy of Anna's Ugly Quilt." [BellArk] (3:1) Ja-F 87, p. 3.
4164. OUGHTON, John
"Playing Piano After Mother's Funeral" (from the "Mata Hari" series)." [Waves] (15:1/2) Fall 86, p. 66-67.
"Stroke / Oblique" (for my mother). [Waves] (15:1/2) Fall 86, p. 67-68.
4165. OVERTON, Ron
"7-Eleven." [HangL] (50/51) 87, p. 143.
"The Branch Will Not Break, But the Jay Might." [HangL] (50/51) 87, p. 139.
"The Economics of Small Losses." [HangL] (50/51) 87, p. 144.
"Invitation." [HangL] (50/51) 87, p. 145.
"Narrative." [HangL] (50/51) 87, p. 140.
"Quicksand." [HangL] (50/51) 87, p. 141.
"Real Musicians" (for Carla Bley). [HangL] (50/51) 87, p. 142.
4166. OWEN, Maureen
"To Love Even Now the Summer." [FiveFR] (5) 87, p. 52.
4167. OWEN, Sue
"My Name Is Snow." [Ploughs] (13:1) 87, p. 93-94.
"Pain Is Certain." [SouthernR] (23:4) O 87, p. 823.
"The Wolf." [Ploughs] (13:1) 87, p. 91-92.
4168. OWENS, Clarke
"After Washing My Dead Father's Pickup Truck." [CapeR] (22:1) Spr 87, p. 47.
4169. OWENS, Derek
"For Teresa" (after Breton). [YellowS] (25) Wint 87, p. 29.
4170. OWENS, June
"Normandy Revisited" (Award Poem — 2nd Place). [Phoenix] (7:1) 87, p. 2.
4171. OWENS, Rochelle
"Eat Bookstore!" [MoodySI] (18/19) Fall 87, p. 34-36.
4172. OWER, John
"Sonnet 2." [KanQ] (19:3) Sum 87, p. 57.
"Sonnet 5." [KanQ] (19:3) Sum 87, p. 57.
4173. OXENHANDLER, Noelle
"The One Who Listens." [SenR] (17:1) 87, p. 28.
4174. OXLEY, William
"The Sea Wall." [Interim] (6:2) Fall 87, p. 41.
OYENARD, Sylvia Puentes de
See PUENTES DE OYENARD, Sylvia
4175. OZAKI, Muin
"At the Volcano Internment Camp" (in Romanized Japanese and English, tr. by Jiro & Kay Nakano). The Best of [BambooR] [(31-32)] 86, p. 68.
"Fort Sill Internment Camp" (in Romanized Japanese and English, tr. by Jiro & Kay Nakano). The Best of [BambooR] [(31-32)] 86, p. 70.
"On the Ship to the Mainland" (in Romanized Japanese and English, tr. by Jiro & Kay Nakano). The Best of [BambooR] [(31-32)] 86, p. 69.
4176. ÖZER, Adnan
"Unknown Love" (tr. by Talat Sait Halman). [Trans] (19) Fall 87, p. 109-110.
4177. ÖZER, Kemal
"Like a Flame" (tr. by Talat Sait Halman). [Trans] (19) Fall 87, p. 29.
4178. OZSVATH, Zsuzsanna
"Abandonment" (tr. of Weöres Sándor, w. Martha Satz). [Os] (24) 87, p. 12.
"After Creation" (tr. of Weöres Sándor, w. Martha Satz). [Os] (24) 87, p. 10.
"Blind-Street" (tr. of Agh István, w. Martha Satz). [Os] (24) 87, p. 2.
"The Magicians' Parade Under Our Castles" (tr. of Gyula Takats, w. Martha Satz). [WebR] (12:1) Spr 87, p. 87.
"Old Wave" (tr. of Nagy Gáspár, w. Martha Satz). [Os] (24) 87, p. 4.
"Vault" (tr. of Zsuzsa Albert, w. Martha Satz). [WebR] (12:1) Spr 87, p. 87.

4179. OZUG, Charles
    "Breaking Surface" (to Matthew). [StoneC] (15:1/2) Fall-Wint 87-88, p. 52.
4180. PABISCH, Peter
    "Sioux" (tr. by Gervase Hittle). [SoDakR] (25:3) Aut 87, p. 84-85.
4181. PACERNICK, Gary
    "Moose Watching on the Road to Rangeley." [Gambit] (20) 86, p. 32.
    "The Open Door." [CrossCur] (6:4) 87, p. 122.
4182. PACHECO, Carlos
    "I Wonder" (tr. by Kent Johnson). [Contact] (9:44/45/46) Fall-Wint 87, p. 19.
4183. PACHECO, José Emilio
    "Blasfemias de Don Juan en los Infiernos." [Margin] (2) Spr 87, p. 102.
    "Blasphemy of Don Juan in the Flames of Hell" (tr. by George McWhirter).
        [Margin] (2) Spr 87, p. 103.
    "Cocteau Se Mira en el Espejo." [Margin] (2) Spr 87, p. 100.
    "Cocteau Through the Looking Glass" (tr. by George McWhirter). [Margin] (2) Spr
        87, p. 101.
    "Contra Kodak" (tr. by George McWhirter). [Margin] (2) Spr 87, p. 103.
    "Contra la Kodak." [Margin] (2) Spr 87, p. 102.
    "Del Fuego." [InterPR] (13:1) Spr 87, p. 16.
    "Escrito con Tinta Roja." [Margin] (2) Spr 87, p. 100.
    "From the fire" (tr. by Thomas Hoeksema). [InterPR] (13:1) Spr 87, p. 17.
    "New Sisyphus" (tr. by George McWhirter). [Margin] (2) Spr 87, p. 99.
    "Le Nouvel Mythe de Sisyphe." [Margin] (2) Spr 87, p. 98.
    "Preguntas sobre los Cerdos e Imprecaciones de los Mismos." [NewRena] (7:1,
        #21) Fall 87, p. 56.
    "Questions about Hogs and Their Abusive Names" (tr. by Erland Anderson).
        [NewRena] (7:1, #21) Fall 87, p. 56.
    "Ratus Norvegicus" (in Spanish). [Abraxas] (35/36) 87, p. 50.
    "Ratus Norvegicus" (tr. by John Oliver Simon). [Abraxas] (35/36) 87, p. 51.
    "Transfiguraciones." [Margin] (2) Spr 87, p. 98.
    "Transfigurations" (tr. by George McWhirter). [Margin] (2) Spr 87, p. 99.
    "Written in Red Ink" (tr. by George McWhirter). [Margin] (2) Spr 87, p. 101.
PACHECO, Irving Sepúlveda
    See SEPULVEDA PACHECO, Irving
4184. PACK, Robert
    "Autumn Warmth." [TexasR] (7:3/4) 87, p. 116-118.
    "Breaking." [PraS] (61:4) Wint 87, p. 63-64.
    "Intending Words." [HampSPR] Wint 87, p. 5-6.
    "Mozart." [HampSPR] Wint 87, p. 7-8.
4185. PACKARD, William
    "The anachronistic bliss of waking late." [NegC] (7:3/4) 87, p. 66.
    "Chain Poem." [Pig] (14) 87, p. 27.
    "Come break my cups." [NegC] (7:3/4) 87, p. 65.
    "Following Are the Answers to the Word Problems Which Were Assigned Last
        Week." [Pig] (14) 87, p. 95.
    "They are doing it in Africa, black over black." [ConnPR] (6:1) 87, p. 31.
    "Virgil to Dante." [NegC] (7:3/4) 87, p. 67.
4186. PACKIE, Susan
    "Correction." [SlipS] (7) 87, p. 110.
    "Early Maine Snows." [InterPR] (13:2) Fall 87, p. 86.
    "Giraffe." [Lactuca] (8) N 87, p. 28.
    "Labors." [InterPR] (13:2) Fall 87, p. 87-88.
    "Stains / Eighteen and Graduating." [Lactuca] (6) Ap-My 87, p. 24.
    "The Tent Dwellers." [InterPR] (13:2) Fall 87, p. 89.
4187. PADEL, Ruth
    "Deus Absconditus." [KenR] (NS 9:4) Fall 87, p. 99-100.
    "Shards." [KenR] (NS 9:4) Fall 87, p. 100-101.
4188. PADGETT, Ron
    "A Brief Correspondence Course." [ParisR] (29:102) Spr 87, p. 199.
    "El Paso (Texas)" (tr. of Paul Morand, w. Bill Zavarsky). [NewAW] (1) 87, p.
        36-37.
    "Euphues." [ParisR] (29:102) Spr 87, p. 200.
    "Light As Air." [Boulevard] (2:1/2) Spr 87, p. 53-57.
    "Smoke." [ParisR] (29:102) Spr 87, p. 201.
    "Southern Pacific" (tr. of Paul Morand, w. Bill Zavarsky). [NewAW] (1) 87, p.
        37-38.

"Wisconsin." [Sulfur] (20) Fall 87, p. 115.
4189. PADHI, Bibhu
"Explaining to My Son the Nature of Zero." [Chelsea] (46) 87, p. 235.
"Pigeons." [Chelsea] (46) 87, p. 233.
"Places" (for Don Goodyear). [Chelsea] (46) 87, p. 234.
4190. PADUA, Jose
"On the Far Edge of the European Theater." [AnotherCM] (17) 87, p. 101.
4191. PAGANO, Eva
"Portuguese Men-of-War." [PoetL] (82:3) Fall 87, p. 156.
"Vanishing Points." [PoetL] (82:3) Fall 87, p. 157.
4192. PAGE, Deborah Carty
"Quiet Desperation on Leave." [BallSUF] (28:4) Aut 87, p. 56.
4193. PAGE, P. K.
"Crow's Nest." [MalR] (78) Mr 87, p. 73-74.
"Deaf-Mute in the Pear Tree." [Verse] (4:1) Mr 87, p. 17-18.
"Eden." [WestCR] (22:2) Fall 87, p. 39-40.
"Goodbye." [WestCR] (22:2) Fall 87, p. 41.
"The Hidden Components." [WestCR] (22:2) Fall 87, p. 35-36.
"Kaleidoscope." [WestCR] (22:2) Fall 87, p. 27-30.
"Remembering George Johnston Reading." [MalR] (78) Mr 87, p. 75.
"The Tree." [WestCR] (22:2) Fall 87, p. 37-38.
"Two Dreams." [WestCR] (22:2) Fall 87, p. 31-34.
"Winter Morning." [CanLit] (113/114) Sum-Fall 87, p. 45.
4194. PAGE, Tom
"Gove County, Kansas." [MinnR] (NS 28) Spr 87, p. 30.
4195. PAGE, William
"Air." [SouthernR] (23:2) Ap 87, p. 371.
"The Bearing Tree." [Wind] (17:61) 87, p. 35.
"Hamlet's Gertrude." [NoDaQ] (55:2) Spr 87, p. 98.
"Invocation." [KanQ] (19:3) Sum 87, p. 87.
"Smoke." [SouthernR] (23:2) Ap 87, p. 370.
"The Subject." [Wind] (17:61) 87, p. 35-36.
4196. PAHMEIER, Gailmarie
"And I Like the Sucking Sound the Air Brakes Make." [Interim] (6:1) Spr 87, p. 4.
"For My Younger Sister, Brenda: To Be Read While Riding in the Pickup to North
Carolina." [Interim] (6:1) Spr 87, p. 5.
"Miracle of Earth." [Interim] (6:1) Spr 87, p. 3.
"This, the Body." [Interim] (6:1) Spr 87, p. 6.
4197. PAK, Yul A
"The Wind" (tr. by John Chay and Grace Gibson). [InterPR] (13:1) Spr 87, p. 63.
4198. PALACIOS, Odon Betanzos
"Dalliances #4" (tr. by Emilio Labrada). [Vis] (25) 87, p. 17.
PALAFOX, Gabriela Rábago
See RABAGO PALAFOX, Gabriela
4199. PALANDER, John
"Méditation du Nouvel An" (pour George Johnston, tr. of Tony Cosier). [AntigR]
(68) Wint 87, p. 35.
4200. PALEN, John
"It Won't Last Long, We Thought." [PassN] (8:1) Wint 87, p. 7.
4201. PALEY, Grace
"Somewhere." [RiverS] (23) 87, p. 13.
4202. PALLEY, Julian
"Despertar Español" (Spanish Awaking, tr. of Jorge Guillén). [Salm] (76-77) Fall
87-Wint 88, p. 79-80.
PALMA, Marina de Bellagente La
See LaPALMA, Marina de Bellagente
PALMA, Ray di
See DiPALMA, Ray
4203. PALMER, Daryl
"Dry Thaumaturgy." [KanQ] (19:3) Sum 87, p. 39.
4204. PALMER, Leslie
"On Outdueling Byron." [WindO] (49) Fall 87, p. 27.
4205. PALMER, Lisa
"The Poet." [SinW] (31) 87, p. 39.
"What You Can't Feel, I Do." [Electrum] (39) Fall-Wint 87, p. 22.

4206. PALMER, M. D.
   "Nude Beach Picnic." [SpiritSH] (53:1) 87, p. 29-30.
4207. PALMER, Michael
   "Baudelaire Series" (Three Poems). [Bound] (14:1/2) Fall 85-Wint 86 [c87], p.
      10-12.
   "Sun." [Sulfur] (20) Fall 87, p. 4-22.
   "Ten Definitions (for the Spicer Conference)." [Acts] (6) 87, p. 74.
4208. PALMER, William
   "Dear Wife: Just Enough." [WindO] (49) Fall 87, p. 11.
   "The Heart of an Elephant" (at Toronto's Science Center). [PassN] (8:2) Sum 87, p.
      26.
   "The Kaiku Salesman." [WindO] (49) Fall 87, p. 10.
   "Shorts." [WindO] (49) Fall 87, p. 9.
4209. PANDE, Mrinal
   "The Bullock" (tr. of Kedarnath Singh). [Bomb] (18) Wint 87, p. 62.
4210. PANKEY, Eric
   "After It's Spent." [Shen] (37:2) 87, p. 22.
   "Afterward." [Shen] (37:2) 87, p. 22.
   "As We Forgive Those." [Iowa] (17:3) Fall 87, p. 78-79.
   "For the End of the World." [SenR] (17:1) 87, p. 65-66.
   "Metaphor." [WestHR] (41:1) Spr 87, p. 51-54.
   "Natural History" (For David). [KenR] (NS 9:4) Fall 87, p. 42-43.
   "Over His Sleeping and His Waking." [Iowa] (17:3) Fall 87, p. 78.
   "Permanence." [KenR] (NS 9:4) Fall 87, p. 43-47.
   "Redemption Songs." [AmerV] (7) Sum 87, p. 17-18.
   "Within a Circle of Rain, My Father." [Iowa] (17:3) Fall 87, p. 77-78.
4211. PANKOWSKI, Elsie
   "Drilling the Well." [Amelia] (4:3, issue 10) 87, p. 109.
   "Migrations." [WritersF] (13) Fall 87, p. 133-134.
4212. PAOLA, Suzanne
   "Denials." [SenR] (17:1) 87, p. 69-70.
   "The Lost Twin." [QW] (24) Wint 87, p. 88-90.
   "A Suicide in Early Spring." [SouthernPR] (27:2) Fall 87, p. 41.
   "The White." [NewEngR] (10:2) Wint 87, p. 187.
   "Willow." [AmerV] (7) Sum 87, p. 11.
PAOLI, Francisco Matos
   See MATOS PAOLI, Francisco
4213. PAPADIMITRAKOPOULOS, Elias
   "The Dream" (tr. by John Taylor). [WebR] (12:2) Fall 87, p. 45.
4214. PAPE, Greg
   "Flight." [PoetryNW] (28:1) Spr 87, p. 38-39.
4215. PAPELL, Helen
   "My Neighbor's Fig Trees." [Outbr] (18/19) Fall 86-Spr 88, p. 83.
PAPPAS, Rita Signorelli
   See SIGNORELLI-PAPPAS, Rita
4216. PAPPAS, Theresa
   "Black Nets." [IndR] (11:1) Wint 87, p. 79.
   "From the Tower." [WebR] (12:2) Fall 87, p. 67-68.
   "Return to the Island." [WebR] (12:2) Fall 87, p. 68-69.
4217. PARADIS, Philip
   "Comet Watch." [Poetry] (149:6) Mr 87, p. 338-340.
   "Lesson for the Day: Sincerity." [KanQ] (19:1/2) Wint-Spr 87, p. 317.
   "The Man Who Knew Things." [GreenfR] (14:3/4) Sum-Fall 87, p. 50.
   "Pickerel." [Pembroke] (19) 87, p. 154.
   "To Patricia Upon Learning of Her Cancer." [KanQ] (19:3) Sum 87, p. 276.
   "Tremor." [ThRiPo] (29/30) 87, p. 52.
   "What the Citizenry Knows About You." [LaurelR] (21:1/2) Wint-Sum 87, p.
      29-30.
4218. PARCERISAS, Francesc
   "Colonia D'Estiueig." [InterPR] (13:2) Fall 87, p. 8.
   "Comiat." [InterPR] (13:2) Fall 87, p. 6.
   "A Day Like This" (tr. by Nathaniel Smith and Lynette McGrath). [InterPR] (13:2)
      Fall 87, p. 11.
   "Un Dia Com Aquest." [InterPR] (13:2) Fall 87, p. 10.
   "La Mà de Virgili." [InterPR] (13:2) Fall 87, p. 8.

305

"Parting" (tr. by Nathaniel Smith and Lynette McGrath). [InterPR] (13:2) Fall 87, p. 7.
"Roman Heads" (tr. by Nathaniel Smith and Lynette McGrath). [InterPR] (13:2) Fall 87, p. 7.
"Summer Vacation" (tr. by Nathaniel Smith and Lynette McGrath). [InterPR] (13:2) Fall 87, p. 9.
"Testes Romanes." [InterPR] (13:2) Fall 87, p. 6.
"Virgil's Hand" (tr. by Nathaniel Smith and Lynette McGrath). [InterPR] (13:2) Fall 87, p. 9.
4219. PARENZEE, Donald
"An Apparent Loss." [TriQ] (69) Spr-Sum 87, p. 159.
"In the Morgue." [TriQ] (69) Spr-Sum 87, p. 163.
"Interview" (for Megan, at ten years). [TriQ] (69) Spr-Sum 87, p. 160-161.
"Pain Isn't Something." [TriQ] (69) Spr-Sum 87, p. 162.
4220. PARHAM, Robert
"Mr Poole." [Wind] (17:60) 87, p. 33.
"Penis." [KanQ] (19:1/2) Wint-Spr 87, p. 244.
"Sending the Dog for Bones." [SouthernPR] (27:1) Spr 87, p. 32.
"A Sunday School Play, Sorta." [Wind] (17:60) 87, p. 33.
"A Wife and Her Weeds." [KanQ] (19:1/2) Wint-Spr 87, p. 244.
4221. PARINI, Jay
"Another Version of Our Love." [GrahamHR] (10) Wint-Spr 87, p. 23-24.
"At the Ice Cream Parlor." [ChiR] (35:4) 87, p. 112-114.
"At the Ruined Monastery in Amalfi" (for Charles Wright). [SouthernR] (23:3) Jl 87, p. 612-613.
"Boys." [GrahamHR] (10) Wint-Spr 87, p. 25.
"Grandmother in Heaven." [PartR] (54:3) Sum 87, p. 431-432.
"History." [AmerS] (56:3) Sum 87, p. 414.
"Piazza." [GrahamHR] (10) Wint-Spr 87, p. 21-22.
"Portrait of the Artist as a Young Lover" (On Rhodes, 1972). [Poetry] (151:1/2) O-N 87, p. 117-118.
"Portrait of the Artist Underground" (in 2063)." [NewEngR] (10:2) Wint 87, p. 213-214.
"Reading Through the Night." [YaleR] (76:2) Wint 87, p. 259.
"Things of This World." [VirQR] (63:3) Sum 87, p. 447-449.
"The White Town." [SouthernR] (23:3) Jl 87, p. 611-612.
4222. PARISH, Barbara Shirk
"Dark Rain." [SnapD] (10:1/2) Wint 87, p. 58.
"Legacy." [SnapD] (10:1/2) Wint 87, p. 69.
4223. PARKER, Aleksandra
"History" (tr. of Stanislaw Baranczak, w. Michael Parker). [Verse] (4:1) Mr 87, p. 6.
"The Return to Order" (tr. of Stanislaw Baranczak, w. Michael Parker). [Verse] (4:3) N 87, p. 9-14.
4224. PARKER, Christopher
"After the Masters Are Astounded." [Footwork] 87, p. 30.
"Biological Clock." [StoneC] (14:3/4) Spr-Sum 87, p. 65.
"Falling." [Footwork] 87, p. 29-30.
"The Gift." [CrossCur] (6:4) 87, p. 23.
"Gravel." [Phoenix] (7:1) 87, p. 7.
4225. PARKER, Lizbeth
"Person to Person." [KanQ] (19:3) Sum 87, p. 235.
"Race Memory." [KanQ] (19:3) Sum 87, p. 235.
4226. PARKER, Martha
"Going Home." [PoetL] (82:1) Spr 87, p. 16.
4227. PARKER, Melinda
"Mrs. Grunsons." [BellR] (10:1) Spr 87, p. 25.
"The Search for Herman MacGrueder." [BellR] (10:1) Spr 87, p. 24.
4228. PARKER, Michael
"History" (tr. of Stanislaw Baranczak, w. Aleksandra Parker). [Verse] (4:1) Mr 87, p. 6.
"The Return to Order" (tr. of Stanislaw Baranczak, w. Aleksandra Parker). [Verse] (4:3) N 87, p. 9-14.
4229. PARKER, Richard
"On One Digging Ditches for the Laying of Drains." [Poem] (57) Mr 87, p. 17.
"Song of the Blackbird." [Poem] (57) Mr 87, p. 18.

"Sonnet to Girlfriend, Overseas, Who Won't Write." [Poem] (57) Mr 87, p. 16.
4230. PARKER, Susan
"In the Garden." [CrabCR] (4:3) Sum 87, p. 20.
4231. PARKIN, Andrew
"Spitting on the Fire." [AntigR] (69/70) 87, p. 165-166.
"Tadanori." [Margin] (1) Wint 86, p. 3.
4232. PARLATORE, Anselm
"Azimuth at Mecox." [Abraxas] (35/36) 87, p. 24.
"Mecox Dune Heath with Viaduct and Isthmus." [Caliban] (2) 87, p. 118-119.
"Seduction at Mecox." [Caliban] (2) 87, p. 116-117.
4233. PARRIS, Ed
"Tornado." [ColR] (NS 14:2) Fall-Wint 87, p. 47.
"Unterecker's Guavas." [HawaiiR] (20) Fall 86, c87, p. 45.
4234. PARRIS, P. B.
"Letter from Spain." [SouthernR] (23:1) Ja 87, p. 145-146.
4235. PARRY, Marian
"Pasiphaë" (from "The Memoirs of a Diva"). [Shen] (37:2) 87, p. 90-101.
4236. PARSONS, Jeff
"Departure Lane, 27." [WormR] (27:4, issue 108) 87, p. 113-115.
"Strip Show." [WormR] (27:4, issue 108) 87, p. 115-116.
4237. PARTHASARATHY, R.
"Bharati at One Hundred." [Chelsea] (46) 87, p. 232.
"Speaking of Places." [Chelsea] (46) 87, p. 230-231.
4238. PARTRIDGE, Dixie
"After Drought." [CharR] (13:2) Fall 87, p. 89.
"Current: A Wyoming Farm in the Fifties" (for my younger brother). [GreensboroR]
    (40) Sum 86, p. 130.
"Legacy." [CrossCur] (6:4) 87, p. 78-79.
"Lynne Orchard at Equinox." [KanQ] (19:1/2) Wint-Spr 87, p. 230.
"Papering: At Grandmother's." [SouthernHR] (21:3) Sum 87, p. 271.
"Piano Pieces" (for J.). [CentR] (31:3) Sum 87, p. 285.
"Remission, n." [GreensboroR] (40) Sum 86, p. 129.
"Returning Late." [LaurelR] (21:1/2) Wint-Sum 87, p. 31.
"What Changes." [CentR] (31:3) Sum 87, p. 283-284.
4239. PARUN, Vesna
"Gold" (tr. by Ivana Spalatin). [PaintedB] (31) 87, p. 71.
"Sound of Wings, Sound of Water" (Excerpt, tr. by Ivana Spalatin). [PaintedB] (31)
    87, p. 72.
"Sum Krila I Sum Vode" (Excerpt). [PaintedB] (31) 87, p. 72.
"Zlato." [PaintedB] (31) 87, p. 71.
4240. PASOLINI, Pier Paolo
"Ex Vita" (tr. by Dino Fabris). [ParisR] (29:103) Sum 87, p. 129-131.
"Italy" (tr. by Dino Fabris). [ParisR] (29:103) Sum 87, p. 122-128.
4241. PASOS, Joaquin
"Blind Indians" (tr. by Erland Anderson). [NewRena] (7:1, #21) Fall 87, p. 55.
"Los Indios Ciegos." [NewRena] (7:1, #21) Fall 87, p. 54.
4242. PASS, John
"A Clue." [Event] (16:2) Sum 87, p. 99.
"Coil." [PraF] (8:1) Spr 87, p. 86.
"A Drink of Water." [Event] (16:2) Sum 87, p. 98.
"Sagittarius A West." [WestCR] (21:3) Wint 87, p. 12-13.
"Something as Difficult as Someone New." [WestCR] (21:3) Wint 87, p. 11.
4243. PASSANTINO, Patricia
"Good Night, My Love." [BellArk] (3:3) My-Je 87, p. 20.
"Thank God for Randy." [BellArk] (3:4) Jl-Ag 87, p. 7.
4244. PASSARO, Vincent
"Meat." [NewAW] (1) 87, p. 64-65.
4245. PASTAN, Linda
"The Accident." [TriQ] (68) Wint 87, p. 84-85.
"Accidents." [Poetry] (150:1) Ap 87, p. 15.
"The Angel of Death." [VirQR] (63:4) Aut 87, p. 644-645.
"At Great Point." [VirQR] (63:4) Aut 87, p. 644.
"Balancing Act: for N." [CrossCur] (7:3) 87, p. 71-72.
"Ceremony." [Nimrod] (30:2) Spr-Sum 87, p. 121.
"Circe." [GeoR] (41:1) Spr 87, p. 65-66.
"The Descent." [TriQ] (68) Wint 87, p. 83.

"The Dogwoods." [Poetry] (150:1) Ap 87, p. 14.
"Family Tree." [Poetry] (151:1/2) O-N 87, p. 119-120.
"The Floozie Clause." [PaintedB] (31) 87, p. 16.
"Fractured." [CrossCur] (7:2) 87, p. 12-13.
"Fruit of the Tree." [GeoR] (41:3) Fall 87, p. 532.
"Late February." [PaintedB] (31) 87, p. 17.
"Lessons." [Nimrod] (30:2) Spr-Sum 87, p. 122.
"Memorial Gardens, Queens." [DenQ] (22:2) Fall 87, p. 38.
"On the Question of Free Will." [Nimrod] (30:2) Spr-Sum 87, p. 120.
"The Ordinary Weather of Summer." [Agni] (24/25) 87, p. 47.
"Rereading the Odyssey in Middle Age." [PennR] (3:1) Spr-Sum 87, p. 39.
"Root Pruning." [TriQ] (68) Wint 87, p. 81-82.
"The Sirens." [ParisR] (29:103) Sum 87, p. 183.
"Snapshot of My Mother at 15." [DenQ] (22:2) Fall 87, p. 39.
"The Son." [PennR] (3:1) Spr-Sum 87, p. 41.
"The Suitor." [PennR] (3:1) Spr-Sum 87, p. 40.
"Turnabout." [NewRep] (196:23) 8 Je 87, p. 46.
"Vacation." [VirQR] (63:4) Aut 87, p. 643-644.
4246. PASTOR, Ned
"(914) 555-4144." [LightY] '87, c86, p. 150.
"Curriculum Change." [LightY] '87, c86, p. 232.
"Dial-a-Shrink" (News item: Shrink Link, a telephone counseling service for
executives . . .). [LightY] '87, c86, p. 234.
"Have You? I Have Never!" [LightY] '87, c86, p. 71.
"Lucky Dilemma." [LightY] '87, c86, p. 128.
"Two Hoorays for Holidays." [LightY] '87, c86, p. 227.
"What's All This Fuss About Tax Reform?" [LightY] '87, c86, p. 22.
"Yuppies Vs. Nopies." [LightY] '87, c86, p. 130.
4247. PATERSON, Evangeline
"A Letter from Kiev." [Stand] (28:4) Aut 87, p. 31.
4248. PATIL, J. Birje
"The Secunderabad Club." [NoDaQ] (55:3) Sum 87, p. 175.
4249. PATRICK, Kathleen
"Chain Letter." [LakeSR] (21) 87, p. 16.
4250. PATTEN, Brian
"Burning Genius." [NewL] (53:3) Spr 87, p. 94-95.
4251. PATTEN, Karl
"Skinnydipping: Cambridgeshire." [CharR] (13:2) Fall 87, p. 88.
4252. PATTEN, Leslie
"The Story Behind Blackberry Sour Cream Pie." [CrabCR] (4:3) Sum 87, p. 25.
4253. PATTERSON, David
"I Wonder How I Look." [HiramPoR] (43) Fall-Wint 87-88, p. 42.
"Incorrect Grammar." [HiramPoR] (43) Fall-Wint 87-88, p. 43.
"What I Do with Funny Looking People." [HiramPoR] (43) Fall-Wint 87-88, p. 35.
4254. PATTERSON, Veronica
"The Other Side of the Ice." [ColR] (NS 14:1) Spr-Sum 87, p. 69.
4255. PATTON, Patti Ann
"Cookeville." [Jacaranda] (2:2) Spr 87, p. 68.
4256. PAU-LLOSA, Ricardo
"Fog's Edge." [AmerPoR] (16:4) Jl-Ag 87, p. 26.
"The Island of Mirrors." [DenQ] (21:3) Wint 87, p. 31-32.
4257. PAUL, Arthur
"Closure." [HarvardA] (122:2) D 87, p. 28.
"We Will Bury You." [HarvardA] (121:3) My 87, p. 12.
4258. PAUL, Gary
"He Slashed His Wrists Three Times & Said Goodbye Goodbye Goodbye."
[Rampike] (5:3) 87, p. 49.
4259. PAUL, Jay
"Crazy." [StoneC] (15:1/2) Fall-Wint 87-88, p. 39.
4260. PAULENICH, Craig
"The Goat-Man." [SoCaR] (19:2) Spr 87, p. 40-41.
"Waiting." [SoCaR] (19:2) Spr 87, p. 41.
"When the Neighbor Butchers." [SoCaR] (19:2) Spr 87, p. 40.
"Working the Lunar Eclipse." [SoCaR] (19:2) Spr 87, p. 41.
4261. PAULI, Kenneth
"Waiting for Eagles." [Pembroke] (19) 87, p. 132-133.

4262. PAULIN, Tom
"Belling the Cat" (from *Piers Plowman*). [KenR] (NS 9:2) Spr 87, p. 75-76.
"Landsflykt" (August Strindberg: Excerpt). [Verse] (4:1) Mr 87, p. 3.
"Let No Man Write My Epitaph." [KenR] (NS 9:2) Spr 87, p. 77.
4263. PAULSON, Ron
"I look across the table at my grandfather's mouth." [Quarry] (36:1) Wint 87, p. 103.
4264. PAUT, Elisa de
"Sábana." [LetFem] (13:1/2) Primavera-Otoño 87, p. 125.
4265. PAVELIS, Kelly
"After a March Rain." [Wind] (17:60) 87, p. 43.
"A Nocturne." [Wind] (17:60) 87, p. 29.
4266. PAVESE, Cesar
"Creation" (tr. by Daniel Tiffany). [ChiR] (35:4) 87, p. 118.
"The Friend Who Is Asleep" (tr. by Daniel Tiffany). [ChiR] (35:4) 87, p. 117.
"Habits" (tr. by Daniel Tiffany). [ChiR] (35:4) 87, p. 115-116.
4267. PAVLICH, Walter
"Near Winter, St. Regis, Montana" (for Melinda and Bruce). [Interim] (6:1) Spr 87, p. 44-46.
"A Theory of Birds." [HighP] (2:3) Wint 87, p. 280-281.
"Three Hearts of the Octopus." [Raccoon] (24/25) My 87, p. 179-180.
"We toss our offerings." [SmPd] (24:3) Fall 87, p. 23.
4268. PAVLIDES, Lefteris
"The Gloria" (Excerpt, tr. of Odysseus Elytis, w. Edward Morin). [CrossCur] (7:3) 87, p. 152.
4269. PAWLAK, Mark
"Chalatenango 1980." [HangL] (50/51) 87, p. 146-154.
4270. PAWLOWSKI, Robert
"Funerary." [MissR] (15:3, issue 45) Spr-Sum 87, p. 51-52.
"The Homestead Act." [TexasR] (8:1/2) Spr-Sum 87, p. 41.
"Margaret Sleeping." [TexasR] (8:3/4) Fall-Wint 87, p. 18.
"Minnesota Burial." [TexasR] (8:1/2) Spr-Sum 87, p. 40.
"Recovery." [MissR] (15:3, issue 45) Spr-Sum 87, p. 50.
4271. PAYNE, John Burnett
"The Canvas" (For Marsha Gurell). [Wind] (17:59) 87, p. 36.
4272. PAYNE, Michelle
"First Calf." [SpoonRQ] (12:2) Spr 87, p. 22-23.
"Hotspot." [SpoonRQ] (12:2) Spr 87, p. 20-21.
"Poor Boy." [SpoonRQ] (12:2) Spr 87, p. 19.
"To a Ruined Maid Dying Young" (after Hardy and Housman). [SpoonRQ] (12:2) Spr 87, p. 24.
4273. PAZ, Octavio
"1930: Scenic Views" (tr. by Eliot Weinberger). [BostonR] (12:5) O 87, p. 24.
"Axis" (tr. by Eliot Weinberger). [YellowS] (25) Wint 87, p. 5.
"Eje." [YellowS] (25) Wint 87, p. 5.
"Full Wind" (tr. by Sharon Sieber). [NowestR] (25:3) 87, p. 319-323.
"I Speak of the City" (for Eliot Weinberger, tr. by Eliot Weinberger). [Sulfur] (20) Fall 87, p. 75-78.
"Letter of Testimony Cantata" (tr. by Eliot Weinberger). [ParisR] (29:105) Wint 87, p. 133-141.
"Maithuna" (tr. by Eliot Weinberger). [YellowS] (25) Wint 87, p. 6-7.
4274. PEACOCK, Molly
"Art Buzzards" (At the Albright Knox Art Gallery, Buffalo, New York). [Boulevard] (2:3) Fall 87, p. 22-23.
"Better to Be Naked Than a Dutch Painting." [Pequod] (23/24) 87, p. 90-91.
"Blank Paper." [Pequod] (23/24) 87, p. 94.
"Clean It Up Immediately." [Pequod] (23/24) 87, p. 93.
"Feeling Sorry for Yourself." [Pequod] (23/24) 87, p. 89.
"How I Had to Act." [ParisR] (29:102) Spr 87, p. 94-95.
"I Must Have Learned This Somewhere." [Boulevard] (2:3) Fall 87, p. 26.
"Lost with a Map." [SouthwR] (72:4) Aut 87, p. 530.
"My God, Why Are You Crying?" [ParisR] (29:102) Spr 87, p. 93.
"Oh, You Stupid Girl." [Boulevard] (2:3) Fall 87, p. 25.
"The Only Choice." [Pequod] (23/24) 87, p. 88.
"A Product of Us." [Boulevard] (2:3) Fall 87, p. 23-34.
"Reunion." [ParisR] (29:102) Spr 87, p. 192.

"Screaming at My Student." [Pequod] (23/24) 87, p. 87.
"A Simple Purchase." [Poetry] (149:4) Ja 87, p. 190-191.
"The Spell." [Poetry] (149:4) Ja 87, p. 189.
"That Leaf." [MissouriR] (10:3) 87, p. 114.
"Two Peonies / Two Girls." [SouthwR] (72:4) Aut 87, p. 529.
"The Unexpected Freedom." [Pequod] (23/24) 87, p. 92.
"When I Love You" (For Marc). [Poetry] (151:1/2) O-N 87, p. 121.
4275. PEARL, Dan
    "Old Battles." [BellArk] (3:1) Ja-F 87, p. 10.
4276. PEARSON, Jean
    "Dream Seeds" (tr. of Tommy Olofsson). [PaintedB] (30) 87, p. 18.
    "Freeing the Shadow" (tr. of Tommy Olofsson). [PaintedB] (30) 87, p. 19.
    "In Summer" (tr. of Sarah Kirsch). [CrossCur] (7:3) 87, p. 37.
    "On Leash" (tr. of Tommy Olofsson). [CrossCur] (7:3) 87, p. 61.
    "The Shadow Inside Me" (tr. of Tommy Olofsson). [PaintedB] (30) 87, p. 18.
    "The Waves with You" (tr. of Tommy Olofsson). [PaintedB] (30) 87, p. 19.
4277. PEARSON, Marlene
    "Divorce." [Calyx] (11:1) Wint 87-88, p. 36-37.
4278. PECK, David W.
    "Truth Gives Birth." [JamesWR] (5:1) Fall 87, p. 7.
4279. PECK, Gail J.
    "Across the Table." [GreensboroR] (39) Wint 85-86, p. 95.
4280. PECK, John
    "Animula." [Salm] (72) Fall 86, p. 166.
    "Before a Journey." [Salm] (72) Fall 86, p. 168-169.
    "Border." [Salm] (72) Fall 86, p. 169-170.
    "The Capital 1980." [Salm] (72) Fall 86, p. 167-168.
    "Evening Concert." [Salm] (72) Fall 86, p. 170-171.
    "Towards Neuchâtel." [Salm] (72) Fall 86, p. 167.
4281. PECK, Mary
    "What I Wear Hides Me." [ManhatPR] (9) Sum 87, p. 33.
    "Who But You?" [ManhatPR] (9) Sum 87, p. 33.
4282. PECZYNSKI, Joseph
    "Untitled: The best thing about Vietnam was the smoke." [Lactuca] (7) Ag 87, p. 7.
4283. PEDEN, Margaret (Margaret Sayers)
    "Ode to a Village Movie Theater" (tr. of Pablo Neruda). [Antaeus] (58) Spr 87, p.
        105-106.
    "Ode to the Lizard" (tr. of Pablo Neruda). [ParisR] (29:103) Sum 87, p. 173-174.
    "Ode to the Voyager Albatross" (tr. of Pablo Neruda). [Antaeus] (58) Spr 87, p.
        100-104.
    "Seaweed (Algas del Oceano)" (tr. of Pablo Neruda). [MissouriR] (10:2) 87, p.
        28-31.
4284. PEDERSON, Cynthia S.
    "After WaKeeney." [SpoonRQ] (12:2) Spr 87, p. 46.
    "Along Highway 18." [SpoonRQ] (12:2) Spr 87, p. 48-49.
    "Drowning at the Dutch Goose." [Phoenix] (7:2) 87, p. 9.
    "Falling Asleep in Kansas." [SpoonRQ] (12:2) Spr 87, p. 45.
    "Sunflowers." [Farm] (4:2) Spr-Sum 87, p. 74.
    "Tall Tale: A Kansas Legend of Life." [SpoonRQ] (12:2) Spr 87, p. 47.
4285. PEDERSON, Miriam
    "Taking on the Season." [PassN] (8:2) Sum 87, p. 23.
4286. PEDRINAN, Elena Maria
    "Allende" (tr. by Helen Peterson). [InterPR] (13:1) Spr 87, p. 35.
    "Corazon de Aquino." [InterPR] (13:1) Spr 87, p. 32.
    "Heart in My Homeland" (tr. by Helen Peterson). [InterPR] (13:1) Spr 87, p. 33.
    "Santos, Santos, Santos." [InterPR] (13:1) Spr 87, p. 34.
PEENEN, H. J. Van
    See Van PEENEN, H. J.
4287. PEFFER, George
    "Reprise: Insomnia." [Pig] (14) 87, p. 93.
    "Worried." [Pig] (14) 87, p. 93.
PEI, Kang Xue
    See KANG, Xue Pei
4288. P'EI, Ti
    "Hua-Tzu Hill" (in Chinese & English, tr. by Joseph Lisowski). [NegC] (7:1/2) 87,
        p. 247.

PELKINGFORD

4289. PELKINGFORD, Henry
"Blood of the Boboso: Last Tale of Power" (Selections, w. Michael Creedon).
[Caliban] (3) 87, p. 69-70.
4290. PELOSO, Vincent Frank
"Driving in the Summer." [Outbr] (18/19) Fall 86-Spr 88, p. 160-164.
4291. PENGILLY, Gordon
"The Cow Poems" (Selections: 1-6, 8-10, 13, 16). [Dandel] (14:1) Spr-Sum 87, p.
5-16.
4292. PENNANT, Edmund
"The Reprieve" (1986 Finalist, Eve of Saint Agnes Poetry Competition). [NegC]
(7:1/2) 87, p. 181.
4293. PENNEY, Scott
"Last Call." [Shen] (37:3) 87, p. 17.
4294. PENNISI, Eugene
"Rilke Variation." [LitR] (31:1) Fall 87, p. 52.
4295. PENNY, Michael
"Pellagra, Geophysicist." [MalR] (80) S 87, p. 109.
4296. PENSAK, Susan
"Against" (tr. of Alejandra Pizarnik). [SinW] (31) 87, p. 99.
"Poem for Emily Dickinson" (tr. of Alejandra Pizarnik). [SinW] (31) 87, p. 99.
4297. PEOPLES, Peg
"Late Spring." [GrahamHR] (10) Wint-Spr 87, p. 34.
4298. PEPPER, Patric
"The Willow Trees." [Wind] (17:60) 87, p. 48.
4299. PERCHIK, Simon
"8. I teach my thumbs to fill this branch." [AnotherCM] (17) 87, p. 102.
"15. And the tracks as branches each Fall." [AnotherCM] (17) 87, p. 103.
"84. Falling where the sun refills, its light." [PoetL] (81:4) Wint 86-87, p. 240.
"86. The breeze almost extinct." [PoetL] (81:4) Wint 86-87, p. 241.
"87. Each leaf yellow though it's not the sun." [PoetL] (81:4) Wint 86-87, p. 242.
"122. You will fatten your fingers on mud." [PartR] (54:1) Wint 87, p. 133-134.
"125. Bloated with seas it never wanted." [MSS] (5:3) 87, p. 155.
"150. 'The dormitory wall!' carved by commands." [ManhatPR] (9) Sum 87, p. 16.
"156. Jutting from my neck its dorsal fin." [Bogg] (57) 87, p. 12.
"174. And your black eyes again their night." [Pembroke] (19) 87, p. 184.
"180. So rounded a season: the sky." [BallSUF] (28:4) Aut 87, p. 55.
"207. Motionless, covering what's in back." [InterPR] (13:1) Spr 87, p. 78.
"212. Still gathering the moonlight." [InterPR] (13:1) Spr 87, p. 79.
"215. I destroyed the bridge, this fog." [InterPR] (13:1) Spr 87, p. 80.
"216. Trimmed for bank, for lift." [InterPR] (13:1) Spr 87, p. 80.
"As if I too had swallowed a star: a cry." [Os] (25) 87, p. 12.
"As if my lips have learned to weep." [Os] (25) 87, p. 13.
"Death likes to kneel, work." [SmPd] (24:2) Spr 87, p. 17.
"The Embattled Gunpowder." [CharR] (13:1) Spr 87, p. 79.
"Focus the Sun." [SoDakR] (25:3) Aut 87, p. 43.
"Hooves High, Necks Pulled Back." [ColEng] (49:8) D 87, p. 886-887.
"The Lamb's Half-Buried." [ColEng] (49:8) D 87, p. 887.
"Not the Birds." [SoDakR] (25:3) Aut 87, p. 44.
"A stain that never heals — at the wond." [Os] (25) 87, p. 5.
"Still in a trance, this photograph." [Os] (25) 87, p. 4.
"These wings I smooth: a dim light." [Os] (24) 87, p. 26.
"These Wires Want to be Exact, Leave." [ColEng] (49:8) D 87, p. 888.
"This granite has sea in it, each splash." [Os] (24) 87, p. 27.
"This room needs a door, a knob." [WindO] (49) Fall 87, p. 25.
"This watch already gathering." [Os] (25) 87, p. 30.
4300. PEREL, Jane Lunin
"Bolero." [PoetryNW] (28:4) Wint 87-88, p. 35.
"Equinox: October Wasps from a Library Window." [PoetryNW] (28:4) Wint 87-88,
p. 36.
4301. PERELMAN, Bob
"Appetite." [NewAW] (2) Fall 87, p. 78.
"Back to the Present." [Ploughs] (13:4) 87, p. 95-96.
"Either/And." [Ploughs] (13:4) 87, p. 93-94.
"Face Value." [Sulfur] (18) Wint 87, p. 74-80.
"Face Value" (Selections: 5 poems). [Temblor] (6) 87, p. 117-121.
"Motion." [Ploughs] (13:4) 87, p. 97-98.

"Repeat, said no one in particular, repeat after me." [Bound] (14:1/2) Fall 85-Wint 86 [c87], p. 72-74.
"The Story of My Life." [Zyzzyva] (3:2) Sum 87, p. 68-69.
PÉREZ, Agustín García
        See GARCIA PÉREZ, Agustín
PEREZ, Elena Clavijo
        See CLAVIJO PEREZ, Elena
PÉREZ, Rebeca Campo
        See CAMPO PÉREZ, Rebeca
4302. PÉREZ ALMEDA, Antonio
        "Polvo Seran, Mas Polvo Enamorado." [Mairena] (9:24) 87, p. 117.
4303. PERI ROSSI, Cristina
        "Alejandra Among the Lilacs" (tr. by Kathleen Lignell). [Nimrod] (30:2) Spr-Sum 87, p. 128-132.
        "From the Summer" (tr. by Kathleen Lignell). [AnotherCM] (17) 87, p. 105.
        "Iconoclastic Landscape" (tr. by Kathleen Lignell). [AnotherCM] (17) 87, p. 104.
4304. PERKINS, James A. (James Ashbrook)
        "Dalliance." [CapeR] (22:1) Spr 87, p. 7.
        "Fruit Cellar." [PassN] (8:2) Sum 87, p. 24.
        "Odysseus and the Highway Patrol" (For Lynda L. Scott). [US1] (20/21) Wint 86-87, p. 11.
4305. PERLBERG, Mark
        "The Thought Garden." [PraS] (61:1) Spr 87, p. 26.
4306. PERONARD, Kai
        "First Light." [Wind] (17:61) 87, p. 37.
4307. PERREAULT, Dwayne
        "The Forest in Our Minds" (for Patrick Lane). [AntigR] (71/72) Aut 87-Wint 88, p. 118.
        "The Mortician." [AntigR] (71/72) Aut 87-Wint 88, p. 117.
        "On June 24 There Were Church Bells Ringing in Montreal and I Was Watching Television." [AntigR] (71/72) Aut 87-Wint 88, p. 119.
4308. PERREAULT, George
        "Out Here." [HighP] (2:2) Fall 87, p. 134.
4309. PERRIE, Walter
        "City Man" (Selections: 1, 4, 6-7, 11-14). [Margin] (1) Wint 86, p. 78-79.
        "Eight Sonnets and a Finale." [Margin] (1) Wint 86, p. 73-77.
4310. PERRIN, Jane
        "March Fifth" (For Ron Bayes). [Pembroke] (19) 87, p. 224.
4311. PERRINE, Laurence
        "Limericks" (6 poems). [LightY] '87, c86, p. 173-174.
        "On a Deceased Office-Seeker." [LightY] '87, c86, p. 240.
        "On a Late Schoolboy." [LightY] '87, c86, p. 241.
        "On a Reformed Sinner." [LightY] '87, c86, p. 241.
        "Q.E.D." [LightY] '87, c86, p. 138.
4312. PERRON, Lee
        "Red-Necked Lummox." [CharR] (13:1) Spr 87, p. 89.
        "Shatterproof." [CharR] (13:1) Spr 87, p. 88.
        "Wheeper! Wheeper!." [CharR] (13:1) Spr 87, p. 88.
4313. PERRY, Elaine
        "Earth Mama." [WoosterR] (7) Spr 87, p. 27.
        "Goodnight Ladies." [YellowS] (23) Sum 87, p. 24.
        "Women's Work." [YellowS] (24) Aut 87, p. 40.
4314. PERSUN, Terry L.
        "My Wet Spring." [Wind] (17:60) 87, p. 34-35.
        "No One Notices." [KanQ] (19:1/2) Wint-Spr 87, p. 290.
        "Railroad Memories." [Wind] (17:60) 87, p. 34.
        "Self Indulged in Flesh and Darkness." [KanQ] (19:1/2) Wint-Spr 87, p. 290-291.
4315. PERTH, Elizabeth Charlotte
        "Capistrano once had a swallow." [Amelia] (4:1/2, issue 9) 87, p. 64.
4316. PESCE, Tom, Jr.
        "Fresh Air, Give Me Fresh Air." [Pig] (14) 87, p. 91.
4317. PESEROFF, Joyce
        "A Dog in the Lifeboat" (example from Tom Regan's *The Case for Animal Rights*). [MassR] (28:1) Spr 87, p. 30.
4318. PESSOA, Fernando
        "Pity the Flowers" (tr. by George Monteiro). [Nimrod] (31:1) Fall-Wint 87, p. 135.

"Poem — Straight to the Point" (tr. by George Monteiro). [Nimrod] (31:1) Fall-Wint 87, p. 134-135.
4319. PETERFREUND, Stuart
"Below the Ice." [TexasR] (7:3/4) 87, p. 119.
"Monday After Easter." [TexasR] (7:3/4) 87, p. 120-121.
"Waiting for the 7:12." [NewOR] (14:2) Sum 87, p. 38.
4320. PETERS, Patrick
"The History of High School Basketball." [Farm] (4:1) Wint 87, p. 38-39.
4321. PETERS, Robert
"Christmas Snow for Mitchum." [JamesWR] (4:2) Wint 87, p. 9.
"Eskimo Haiku." [LightY] '87, c86, p. 233.
"Existential Rag." [JamesWR] (5:1) Fall 87, p. 10.
"Shaker Light" (Selections: 5 poems). [ConnPR] (6:1) 87, p. 3-10.
"A Singular Man." [PoetL] (82:3) Fall 87, p. 170.
"Testicles." [JamesWR] (4:2) Wint 87, p. 9.
4322. PETERSEN, Paulann Whitman
"Exposure." [Calyx] (11:1) Wint 87-88, p. 18.
"Groom of the Animal-Bride." [Calyx] (11:1) Wint 87-88, p. 16-17.
"I Listen to Alice Walker on a Pocket Radio." [Calyx] (10:2/3) Spr 87, p. 175.
"The Moon Recounts the Birth of the Sun." [Sequoia] (30:3) Wint 87, p. 56-57.
"Pity." [CutB] (27/28) 87, p. 43.
"Root." [Calyx] (11:1) Wint 87-88, p. 19.
"Then I Am the Garden." [CutB] (27/28) 87, p. 42.
4323. PETERSON, Allan
"Preparing for Loons." [HayF] (2) Spr 87, p. 38.
4324. PETERSON, Helen
"Allende" (tr. of Elena Maria Pedrinan). [InterPR] (13:1) Spr 87, p. 35.
"Heart in My Homeland" (tr. of Elena Maria Pedrinan). [InterPR] (13:1) Spr 87, p. 33.
4325. PETERSON, Jim
"The Ax." [AntR] (45:3) Sum 87, p. 329.
"Enough." [GeoR] (41:1) Spr 87, p. 17-18.
4326. PETERSON, Robert
"A Memory of the War." [Caliban] (3) 87, p. 152.
4327. PETERSON, Susan
"Handwritten Envelope." [SpoonRQ] (12:2) Spr 87, p. 17.
"Wisconsin Confessions." [SpoonRQ] (12:2) Spr 87, p. 18.
4328. PETERSON, Walt
"My Son's First Poetry Reading." [NegC] (7:3/4) 87, p. 164.
4329. PETIT, Michael
"Louisiana New Year." [DenQ] (22:1) Sum 87, p. 31-32.
4330. PETREMAN, David A.
"J.W.R. Visits Merida in the Yucatan." [PikeF] (8) Fall 87, p. 34.
"Monologue of Death." [Pembroke] (19) 87, p. 187.
4331. PETRIE, Paul
"The Composition." [ChrC] (104:36) 2 D 87, p. 1076.
"Genealogy." [TexasR] (7:3/4) 87, p. 122-123.
"Mickelsson's Ghosts" (For John Gardner). [MSS] (5:3) 87, p. 134.
"The Skaters." [TexasR] (7:3/4) 87, p. 124.
"The Trip to the Island." [LitR] (30:4) Sum 87, p. 592-593.
4332. PETROSKY, Anthony
"Two Mornings, Shanghai, 5 A.M." (for E. B.). [OhioR] (39) 87, p. 37-39.
4333. PETROUSKE, Rosalie Sanara
"Dolls." [PassN] (8:1) Wint 87, p. 11.
"Footprints." [WindO] (49) Fall 87, p. 49.
"When She Calls." [WindO] (49) Fall 87, p. 48.
4334. PETTEYS, D. F.
"Compensation." [LitR] (31:1) Fall 87, p. 61.
4335. PETTIT, Michael
"The Beyond." [MassR] (28:2) Sum 87, p. 267-268.
"Cardinal Points." [MissouriR] (10:1) 87, p. 34-40.
"Man Walking Downstairs Backwards, Turning, Walking Away . . ." (Plate 16, The Human Figure in Motion). [Agni] (24/25) 87, p. 144.
"Valentine Show at the Lingerie Shop." [OhioR] (38) 87, p. 96.
"Woman Turning and Lifting Train" (Plate 152, The Human Figure in Motion). [Agni] (24/25) 87, p. 143.

"Woman Turning, Throwing Kiss, and Walking Upstairs" (Plate 117, The Human Figure in Motion). [Agni] (24/25) 87, p. 145.
4336. PFAFF, John
"City at 5." [GreensboroR] (39) Wint 85-86, p. 61.
4337. PFEFFERLE, W. T.
"Breakfast." [MissR] (15:3, issue 45) Spr-Sum 87, p. 62.
"Emily at the Playground." [MissR] (15:3, issue 45) Spr-Sum 87, p. 59.
"Hero." [MissR] (15:3, issue 45) Spr-Sum 87, p. 60-61.
"How to Throw a Baby Chicken." [MissR] (15:3, issue 45) Spr-Sum 87, p. 65.
"Reclining." [MissR] (15:3, issue 45) Spr-Sum 87, p. 63-64.
4338. PFEIFER, Michael
"Anyone Could." [MalR] (80) S 87, p. 40.
"The Dead." [CutB] (27/28) 87, p. 79.
"Finality." [CutB] (27/28) 87, p. 79.
"Moths." [BellR] (10:2) Fall 87, p. 14.
"Mourning Doves." [BellR] (10:2) Fall 87, p. 12.
"Red Cadillac" (1987 Ratner-Ferber-Poet Lore Prize Co-Winner). [PoetL] (82:2) Sum 87, p. 71-72.
"The Screen Door." [BellR] (10:2) Fall 87, p. 13.
"Unemployment: An Ode." [NegC] (7:3/4) 87, p. 155.
4339. PHILBRICK, Nathaniel
"Alone Together." [ManhatPR] (9) Sum 87, p. 47.
"Burying Ground in Winter." [ManhatPR] (9) Sum 87, p. 47.
"Funeral." [ManhatPR] (9) Sum 87, p. 46.
PHILBROOK, Craig Gingrich
    See GINGRICH-PHILBROOK, Craig
4340. PHILLIPS, Dennis
"Survey Surveillance." [Act] (7) 87, p. 14-15.
"A World" (Selections: 7 pieces). [Temblor] (6) 87, p. 76-82.
4341. PHILLIPS, Frances
"Before Naming You." [HangL] (50/51) 87, p. 158.
"Gino and Carlo." [HangL] (50/51) 87, p. 157.
"Things Missing Mysterious." [HangL] (50/51) 87, p. 155-156.
4342. PHILLIPS, James
"Fountains Move." [Vis] (23) 87, p. 4.
4343. PHILLIPS, Kathy
"Crack Seed." The Best of [BambooR] [(31-32)] 86, p. 74.
"Kuan Yin Mingles with the Ghosts, Now on Guided Tour, of the Slave Population . . ." The Best of [BambooR] [(31-32)] 86, p. 75.
"Kuan Yin Turns Her Photo Album to a Certain Point." The Best of [BambooR] [(31-32)] 86, p. 76.
4344. PHILLIPS, Kris
"And Now Meet Daddy's Girl." [Gambit] (20) 86, p. 97.
4345. PHILLIPS, Louis
"As If Our Days Would Never End." [NoDaQ] (55:2) Spr 87, p. 59.
"Better Than a Wine Cellar." [NoDaQ] (55:2) Spr 87, p. 60.
"Beyond Postmodernism." [AntigR] (69/70) 87, p. 22.
"Da Locum Melioribus." [HawaiiR] (22) Fall 87, p. 84.
"Everybody in America Is at the Movies." [LightY] '87, c86, p. 76-77.
"Fang Death Solo." [BallSUF] (28:4) Aut 87, p. 68.
"Freud Listens to the Sad Jazz of Job But Offers No Comfort." [Phoenix] (7:2) 87, p. 41.
"Heartbreak in Tuktoyaktuk." [LightY] '87, c86, p. 171.
"The Human Mind." [HawaiiR] (22) Fall 87, p. 85.
"Kilroy in the Twine Factory." [DekalbLAJ] (20:1/4) 87, p. 49.
"Love-Deep in Crossword Puzzles." [LightY] '87, c86, p. 144-145.
"The Middle-aged Poet Suns Himself by a Lake and Idly Peruses Larousse's . . . ." [AntigR] (69/70) 87, p. 23.
"Sigmund Freud Meets Robinson Crusoe." [Phoenix] (7:2) 87, p. 42.
"Study for the Left Hand Alone." [HawaiiR] (21) Spr 87, p. 43.
"To the Director of the Metropolitan Transportation Union." [HawaiiR] (20) Fall 86, c87, p. 82.
"The Trans-World Courier Express Is on the Move." [HawaiiR] (20) Fall 86, c87, p. 83.
"Why Contemporary American Poets Rarely Write Epigrams of the Quality of Ben Jonson's 'On Gut'." [LightY] '87, c86, p. 209.

4346. PHILLIPS, Michael Lee
"The Women on Rhodes." [BelPoJ] (37:4) Sum 87, p. 34-35.
4347. PHILLIPS, Robert
"An Aged Rector Named Fiddle." [LightY] '87, c86, p. 71.
"Letter from the County." [Poetry] (150:5) Ag 87, p. 279.
"Suburban Interior." [Poetry] (151:1/2) O-N 87, p. 122.
"Survivor's Lament." [SouthwR] (72:2) Spr 87, p. 269.
"Wish You Were Here." [Poetry] (150:5) Ag 87, p. 278.
4348. PHILLIPS, Walt
"Awash." [Amelia] (4:1/2, issue 9) 87, p. 119-120.
"Miles." [Amelia] (4:1/2, issue 9) 87, p. 120-121.
"Novelette." [Amelia] (4:1/2, issue 9) 87, p. 120.
"Ukulele." [Footwork] 87, p. 35.
4349. PHILLIS, Randy
"The House." [PassN] (8:2) Sum 87, p. 27.
"Summer in Europe." [Wind] (17:61) 87, p. 38-39.
4350. PICCIONE, Anthony
"After a Day of Patching Little Things." [Raccoon] (24/25) My 87, p. 175.
4351. PICHASKE, D.
"The Cheerleaders." [Northeast] (Ser. 4:5) Sum 87, p. 38-39.
"Exercise Against Retirement #4" (for Rev. Arthur J. Larson, 6/22/80). [Northeast]
(Ser. 4:5) Sum 87, p. 35.
"Fathers and Sons." [Northeast] (Ser. 4:5) Sum 87, p. 37.
"Home Visit." [Northeast] (Ser. 4:5) Sum 87, p. 36.
"Pilgrim at Ten Years' Remove." [Northeast] (Ser. 4:5) Sum 87, p. 41.
"Playing the Strings of Guilt (II)." [Northeast] (Ser. 4:5) Sum 87, p. 40.
"The Raised Fist of the Father." [Northeast] (Ser. 4:5) Sum 87, p. 34.
"Visiting the Father." [Northeast] (Ser. 4:5) Sum 87, p. 42.
4352. PICKARD, Tom
"My Pen." [Margin] (1) Wint 86, p. 97-98.
4353. PIEPHOFF, Bruce
"Don Like No Poultry." [GreensboroR] (40) Sum 86, p. 75.
"Help Wanted." [Pembroke] (19) 87, p. 116-117.
"Hot Bixtit." [GreensboroR] (39) Wint 85-86, p. 88.
"The Miner's Son." [Pembroke] (19) 87, p. 115-116.
4354. PIERCY, Marge
"Absolute Zero in the Brain." [Gargoyle] (32/33) 87, p. 371.
"Arles, 7 P.M." [LightY] '87, c86, p. 162-163.
"The Carrot." [Lips] (13) 87, p. 54.
"Joy Road and Livernois." [OP] (final issue) Sum 87, p. 66-69.
"Morning Love Song." [YellowS] (22) Spr 87, p. 4.
"Raisin Pumpernickel." [Lips] (13) 87, p. 55-56.
"Le Sacre du Printemps." [MassR] (28:2) Sum 87, p. 193-196.
"Six Underrated Pleasures." [Spirit] (8:2) 87, p. 94-99.
"Vegetable Love." [YellowS] (22) Spr 87, p. 5.
4355. PIERMAN, Carol J.
"The Changelings." [CarolQ] (40:1) Fall 87, p. 67.
"How We Learned About Fiction." [ThRiPo] (29/30) 87, p. 53.
"Night Thoughts." [CharR] (13:2) Fall 87, p. 93.
PIERO, W. S. di
See Di PIERO, W. S.
PIETRO, Marylou di
See DiPIETRO, Marylou
4356. PIFER, Don
"Rainbow Land." [Gambit] (20) 86, p. 37.
PIGNO, Antonia Quintana
See QUINTANA PIGNO, Antonia
4357. PIKE, Earl C.
"Dream: we are in a gallery." [Amelia] (4:3, issue 10) 87, p. 55.
"Untitled: i. dream: we are in a gallery." [BlueBldgs] (10) 87?, p. 21.
"What Has Been Taken and Taken Back." [CrossCur] (6:5) 87, p. 42.
4358. PIKE, Lawrence
"Services." [PassN] (8:2) Sum 87, p. 20.
4359. PILCHER, Barry Edgar
"Looking." [Bogg] (57) 87, p. 15.

4360. PILIBOSIAN, Helene
"Made in America." [HighP] (2:3) Wint 87, p. 326-328.
4361. PILKINGTON, Ace G.
"Richard II and Other Emperors." [WeberS] (4:2) Fall 87, p. 69.
"Van Gogh's Long Grass with Butterflies." [WeberS] (4:2) Fall 87, p. 68.
"William Stafford: The Poet's Task in a Power Failure." [WeberS] (4:2) Fall 87, p. 68.
4362. PILKINGTON, Kevin
"In a Bar on 2nd." [MemphisSR] (8:1) Fall 87, p. 28-29.
4363. PINARD, Karel
"Disdainful of the Ideal Theorem" (1986 Poetry Award). [Lyra] (1:1) 87, p. 18.
4364. PINGARRON, Michael
"The Big Zero." [Lactuca] (7) Ag 87, p. 4.
"Fork It Over." [Lactuca] (7) Ag 87, p. 4.
"Of Ruined Cities." [Lactuca] (7) Ag 87, p. 4.
4365. PINI, Robert
"Concerto." [CrabCR] (4:3) Sum 87, p. 14.
4366. PINKERTON, Helen
"On Jan van Huysum's 'Vase of Flowers' (1722) in the J. Paul Getty Museum." [Sequoia] (31:1) Centennial issue 87, p. 47.
"On Rembrandt's Etching of Joseph Telling His Dream (1636)." [Sequoia] (31:1) Centennial issue 87, p. 47.
PIÑON, Evangelina Vigil
See VIGIL-PIÑON, Evangelina
4367. PINSKER, Sanford
"At the Greenwich Village Reunion Concert, I Think of the Strange Word 'Hurt'." [NoDaQ] (55:2) Spr 87, p. 49.
"Sunday Dinner, in Flanders." [KanQ] (19:3) Sum 87, p. 200.
4368. PINSKY, Robert
"The Figured Wheel." [NewEngR] (10:1) Aut 87, p. 68-69.
"The Hearts." [NewRep] (196:4) 26 Ja 87, p. 40.
"Memoir." [AmerPoR] (16:5) S-O 87, p. 7.
"Picture." [ParisR] (29:105) Wint 87, p. 100.
"Voyage to the Moon." [Poetry] (151:1/2) O-N 87, p. 123-126.
"What Why When How Who." [AmerPoR] (16:5) S-O 87, p. 6-7.
4369. PINSON, Ken R.
"Asylum." [Nimrod] (30:2) Spr-Sum 87, p. 124.
"Ice." [Nimrod] (30:2) Spr-Sum 87, p. 123.
4370. PIOMBINO, Nick
"Slowed Reason" (w. Charles Bernstein). [NewAW] (1) 87, p. 82-83.
"Stet." [Bound] (14:1/2) Fall 85-Wint 86 [c87], p. 90-92.
4371. PIORNO, Nusta de
"Aquel de la Larga Fama." [Mairena] (9:24) 87, p. 64.
"En Cada Abril." [Mairena] (9:24) 87, p. 63.
"El Sauce." [Mairena] (9:24) 87, p. 64.
4372. PIORO, Tadeusz
"Dead Poets" (tr. of Tadeusz Borowski). [Trans] (19) Fall 87, p. 224.
"Dear Diary" (tr. of Tadeusz Borowski). [Trans] (19) Fall 87, p. 219.
"Friends" (tr. of Tadeusz Borowski). [Trans] (19) Fall 87, p. 223.
"I Think of You" (tr. of Tadeusz Borowski). [Trans] (19) Fall 87, p. 219.
"It's the Same Each Night" (tr. of Tadeusz Borowski). [Trans] (19) Fall 87, p. 220.
"My Friend, I Think of You at Night" (tr. of Tadeusz Borowski). [Trans] (19) Fall 87, p. 222.
"Night Over Birkenau" (tr. of Tadeusz Borowski). [Trans] (19) Fall 87, p. 221.
"Return to Life" (tr. of Tadeusz Borowski). [Trans] (19) Fall 87, p. 221.
4373. PITCHFORD, Kenneth
"Archaic Torso of Apollo (after Rilke)." [ManhatPR] (9) Sum 87, p. 27.
4374. PITKETHLY, Lawrence
"Return of the Native." [Ploughs] (13:1) 87, p. 95-106.
4375. PITKIN, Anne
"Aeronauts." [PraS] (61:2) Sum 87, p. 26-27.
"Blue Morning Glory." [PraS] (61:2) Sum 87, p. 25.
"Casualties." [Amelia] (4:1/2, issue 9) 87, p. 85-86.
"Paper Boy." [Amelia] (4:1/2, issue 9) 87, p. 84-85.
"The Poet in Adolescence." [Amelia] (4:3, issue 10) 87, p. 132.
"Want." [PraS] (61:2) Sum 87, p. 27-28.

4376. PITT, Jo Jane
"The Girl Next Door." [GreensboroR] (40) Sum 86, p. 99.
"Predawn." [GreensboroR] (40) Sum 86, p. 100.
4377. PITTENGER, Gary
"Social Zoology: Prep for a Field Trip." [LightY] '87, c86, p. 182.
4378. PITTOCK, Murray
"Thoor Ballylee." [CumbPR] (6:2) Spr 87, p. 89.
4379. PITZEN, Jim
"To Liver Not to Live." [Pig] (14) 87, p. 75.
4380. PITZER, Jack
"Redoubt." [BallSUF] (28:4) Aut 87, p. 60-61.
4381. PIZARNIK, Alejandra
"Against" (tr. by Susan Pensak). [SinW] (31) 87, p. 99.
"In This Night, in this World" (tr. by Maria Rosa Fort and Frank Graziano). [ColR]
(NS 14:2) Fall-Wint 87, p. 57-59.
"L'Obscurite des Eaux" (tr. by Jim Fitzgerald and Frank Graziano). [NewOR] (14:3)
Fall 87, p. 44.
"Names and Figures" (tr. by Jim Fitzgerald and Frank Graziano). [NewOR] (14:3)
Fall 87, p. 17.
"Poem for Emily Dickinson" (tr. by Susan Pensak). [SinW] (31) 87, p. 99.
4382. PLAICE, Stephen
"Lines Written at Bunyan's Cottage." [CumbPR] (6:2) Spr 87, p. 31.
4383. PLATH, James
"From This 5th Floor Office Window." [WindO] (49) Fall 87, p. 21.
"Refrain." [WindO] (49) Fall 87, p. 20.
4384. PLAYER, William
"The Hardboiled Detective Watches a Rich Dame." [HiramPoR] (42) Spr-Sum 87, p.
36.
PLESSIS, Phil du
See Du PLESSIS, Phil
PLESSIS, Rachel Blau du
See DuPLESSIS, Rachel Blau
4385. PLINER, Susan
"A Distant Tree." [GreenfR] (14:1/2) Wint-Spr, p. 106.
4386. PLOTZ, John
"On Veteran's Day." [HarvardA] (120:2) Mr 87, p. 30-31.
4387. PLOUNT, Michael
"They stood on the roadside holding buckwheat honey colored babies." [Notus]
(2:1) Spr 87, p. 77-78.
4388. PLUMLY, Stanley
"Hedgerows." [Atlantic] (259:6) Je 87, p. 46-47.
"The Wyoming Poetry Tour." [NewYorker] (63:41) 30 N 87, p. 38.
4389. PLUMMER, Deb (Deborah)
"Amazed." [PassN] (8:1) Wint 87, p. 18.
"Natchez." [CapeR] (22:1) Spr 87, p. 32.
4390. PLYMELL, Charles
"Was Poe Afraid?" [Bogg] (58) 87, p. 27.
4391. POBO, Kenneth
"Comet Hitting the Sun." [Outbr] (18/19) Fall 86-Spr 88, p. 153.
"Directed by the Poet." [BlueBldgs] (10) 87?, p. 23.
"H. D., the Rain, and the Pear Tree." [CumbPR] (6:2) Spr 87, p. 12-13.
"Leaves Burning." [ColR] (NS 14:2) Fall-Wint 87, p. 36.
"Pluto." [CumbPR] (6:2) Spr 87, p. 14.
"What Do You Think Sara Jane's Lighter Was Doing Under Lou Christie's Seat" (Or
a Paean to 60s Pop Music). [JamesWR] (4:4) Sum 87, p. 8.
4392. POENARU, Vasile
"Adolescents on the Sea" (tr. of Nichita Stanescu, w. Tom Carlson). [LitR] (30:4)
Sum 87, p. 589.
"Autumn Twilight" (tr. of Nichita Stanescu, w. Tom Carlson). [LitR] (30:4) Sum
87, p. 588.
"Distance" (tr. of Nichita Stanescu, w. Tom Carlson). [LitR] (30:4) Sum 87, p. 588.
"The Market" (tr. by Thomas C. Carlson). [Raccoon] (24/25) My 87, p. 294.
"Ninth Elegy: Of the Egg" (tr. of Nichita Stanescu, w. Thomas C. Carlson).
[Raccoon] (24/25) My 87, p. 106-107.
"Song" (tr. of Nichita Stanescu, w. Tom Carlson). [LitR] (30:4) Sum 87, p. 589.

"Unwords" (tr. of Nichita Stanescu, w. Thomas C. Carlson). [Raccoon] (24/25) My
      87, p. 105.
4393. POITRAS, Edward W.
      "A Short Love Story" (tr. of Hwang Tong-Gyu). [Pembroke] (19) 87, p. 14.
4394. POKORNOWSKI, Debra
      "The Amnesiac." [Ascent] (12:2) 87, p. 41-42.
      "Eclipse." [Ascent] (12:2) 87, p. 42.
4395. POLGAR, Steven
      "Clouded Sky" (tr. of Miklós Radnóti, w. Stephen Berg and S. J. Marks. Entire
      issue). [PoetryE] (22) Spr 87, 113 p.
4396. POLITE, Frank
      "Mummy with an Erection." [Pig] (14) 87, p. 7.
4397. POLITO, Robert
      "Cathy's Braces." [Ploughs] (13:4) 87, p. 99-101.
4398. POLKINHORN, Harry
      "Public and Private." [Rampike] (5:3) 87, p. 51.
4399. POLLAK, Felix
      "Adam and Eve, Old." [Northeast] (Ser. 4:5) Sum 87, p. 6.
      "The Common cold" (Riding with a friend, age four). [Northeast] (Ser. 4:6) Wint
      87-88, p. 1.
      "Mirror Reflections." [Northeast] (Ser. 4:5) Sum 87, p. 3-5.
4400. POLLET, Sylvester
      "Triolet, After Titian." [LightY] '87, c86, p. 143.
4401. POLLITT, Katha
      "An Anthology of Socialist Verse." [Poetry] (151:1/2) O-N 87, p. 126.
      "Fishbowl." [Poetry] (151:1/2) O-N 87, p. 127.
      "Mandarin Oranges." [NewYorker] (63:1) 23 F 87, p. 36.
4402. POLSON, Don
      "Another Straw." [AntigR] (69/70) 87, p. 47.
4403. POMERANCE, Bernard
      "Custer Dreams the Tongiht Show." [Harp] (274:1643) Ap 87, p. 31-32.
4404. PONSOT, Marie
      "(For William Cook, Drowned in Maine, and for Roy Huss, Lost in Indonesia)."
      [Comm] (114:9) 8 My 87, p. 289.
      "I Ask Myself a Few Real Historical Questions" (On a Library of Congress photo of
      Eunice B. Winkless, 1904). [OP] (final issue) Sum 87, p. 16-17.
      "In Favor of Good Dreams." [OP] (final issue) Sum 87, p. 20.
      "Not This Year." [Comm] (114:13) 17 Jl 87, p. 421.
      "The Problem of Fiction." [OP] (final issue) Sum 87, p. 18-19.
      "Proserpine, Packing." [Comm] (114:1) 16 Ja 87, p. 13.
      "Reminder." [Comm] (114:3) 13 F 87, p. 84.
4405. PONTIERO, Giovanni
      "The Bats" (tr. of Lêdo Ivo). [Dandel] (14:2) Fall-Wint 87, p. 20.
      "Poor Folk at the Bus Station" (tr. of Lêdo Ivo). [Dandel] (14:2) Fall-Wint 87, p.
      18-19.
      "Santa Leopoldina Asylum" (tr. of Lêdo Ivo). [Dandel] (14:2) Fall-Wint 87, p. 21.
POP, Marcel Cornis
      See CORNIS-POP, Marcel
4406. POPA, Vasko
      "Heaven's Ring: A Cycle of Poems" (tr. by Charles Simic). [Field] (36) Spr 87, p.
      37-43.
4407. POPE, Mary McGehee
      "The Drought." [DekalbLAJ] (20:1/4) 87, p. 50.
      "A High Pitched Tone." [DekalbLAJ] (20:1/4) 87, p. 50.
4408. POPOV, Nikolai
      "Deserts" (tr. of Blaga Dimitrova, w. Heather McHugh). [Trans] (18) Spr 87, p.
      277.
      "Forbidden Sea" (Excerpt, tr. of Blaga Dimitrova, w. Heather McHugh). [Trans]
      (18) Spr 87, p. 280.
      "Multidimensional" (tr. of Blaga Dimitrova, w. Heather McHugh). [Trans] (18) Spr
      87, p. 276.
      "Nightlight: Eye of the Owl" (tr. of Blaga Dimitrova, w. Heather McHugh). [Trans]
      (18) Spr 87, p. 278.
      "Old Song in a New Voice" (tr. of Blaga Dimitrova, w. Heather McHugh). [Trans]
      (18) Spr 87, p. 279.

4409. PORAD, Francine
"Spite House." [Amelia] (4:1/2, issue 9) 87, p. 97.
4410. PORRITT, R.
"Read This Poem from the Bottom Up." [LaurelR] (21:1/2) Wint-Sum 87, p. 32.
4411. PORTA, Antonio
"Human Relations" (Selections: XX, XXII). [Caliban] (3) 87, p. 86.
"New Journal" (Excerpts). [Caliban] (3) 87, p. 87.
4412. PORTER, Anne
"La Bella Notizia." [Comm] (114:22) 18 D 87, p. 732.
"Native Americans." [Comm] (114:12) 19 Je 87, p. 386.
4413. PORTER, Caryl
"Philosophy I." [ChrC] (104:22) 29 Jl-5 Ag 87, p. 644.
4414. PORTER, Pamela Rice
"Ruth's Love Letters, 1918-1919." [Comm] (114:16) 25 S 87, p. 529.
4415. PORTER, Peter
"Pontormo's Sister." [Poetry] (151:1/2) O-N 87, p. 127-128.
4416. POTASH, Larry
"Bare Dancing." [LaurelR] (20:1/2) Sum 87, p. 92.
POTTER, Alicia Rivero
See RIVERO-POTTER, Alicia
4417. POULIN, A., Jr.
"The Cicada" (tr. of Anne Hébert). [TarPR] (27:1) Fall 87, p. 19.
"If You're Unhappy" (tr. of Anne Hébert). [TarPR] (27:1) Fall 87, p. 20.
"Lightning" (tr. of Anne Hébert). [TarPR] (27:1) Fall 87, p. 19.
"A Momentary Order." [KenR] (NS 9:3) Sum 87, p. 97-104.
4418. POUND, Ezra
"The Coming of War: Actaeon." [SouthernR] (23:3) Jl 87, p. 546.
4419. POUND, Omar S.
"An Arab Chieftain to His Young Wife" (tr. of Abid Ibn al-Abras). [AntigR] (69/70)
87, p. 72.
"An Arab on Cauteries (ca. 980 A.D.)" (Adapted from a prose treatise on medicine,
tr. of Albucasis). [AntigR] (69/70) 87, p. 74.
"Eat your fill, dress well, play dice" (tr. of Ibn-I-Yamin). [AntigR] (69/70) 87, p.
75.
"It Is New, Therefore a Pleasure" (tr. of Al-Hutay'a). [AntigR] (69/70) 87, p. 73.
"Said Wasp to Bee" (tr. of Nosratollah Kazemi Mazanderani). [AntigR] (69/70) 87,
p. 75.
"Slow Giving" (tr. of Ibn al-Rumi). [AntigR] (69/70) 87, p. 73.
4420. POWELL, Jim
"Circe" (for Olga Rudge). [Thrpny] (30) Sum 87, p. 31.
4421. POWELL, Joseph
"Only at Night." [CrabCR] (4:3) Sum 87, p. 27.
"X-18025." [PassN] (8:2) Sum 87, p. 22.
4422. POWELL, Shawn
"Under the Carpet." [Gambit] (21) 87, p. 43.
4423. POWER, Marjorie
"Crow Lesson." [StoneC] (14:3/4) Spr-Sum 87, p. 14.
"During an Evening Walk." [CrossCur] (6:4) 87, p. 87.
"A History of Dreams." [PoetC] (18:2) Wint 87, p. 12.
"The Mother and the Daughter." [CrabCR] (4:3) Sum 87, p. 20.
"On an Upper Branch." [CapeR] (22:2) Fall 87, p. 3.
"Reading the Class News." [Outbr] (18/19) Fall 86-Spr 88, p. 52.
4424. POWER, Nicholas
"Underneath Jim's truck." [CrossC] (9:3/4) 87, p. 12.
4425. POWERS, Dan
"December." [PikeF] (8) Fall 87, p. 7.
4426. POWERS, William
"To Be on the Ice at First Light." [CentR] (31:4) Fall 87, p. 376.
4427. POYNER, Ken
"This Hope." [Wind] (17:60) 87, p. 37-38.
"War Fever and the First Strike." [Wind] (17:60) 87, p. 36-37.
POZNAK, Joan van
See Van POZNAK, Joan
4428. PRADO, Adélia
"Mobiles" (tr. by Ellen Watson). [Antaeus] (58) Spr 87, p. 199-200.
"Praise for a Color" (tr. by Ellen Watson). [ParisR] (29:103) Sum 87, p. 178.

"Purple" (tr. by Ellen Watson). [ParisR] (29:103) Sum 87, p. 177.
"Two Ways" (tr. by Ellen Watson). [Antaeus] (58) Spr 87, p. 196.
"The Way Things Talk" (tr. by Ellen Watson). [Antaeus] (58) Spr 87, p. 197-198.
4429. PRADO, Holly
   "Ariadne Speaks of Dionysus, of Life Beyond the Old Story." [Temblor] (5) 87, p.
      41-44.
4430. PRAT FERRER, Juan José
   "Sonetos de la Noche" (Selection: IV, VII). [Mester] (16:1) Spr 87, p. 59-60.
4431. PRATT, Brian
   "From the Back of the Bus." [Waves] (15:3) Wint 87, p. 62.
4432. PRATT, Charles W.
   "Another Fable in Two Languages." [LightY] '87, c86, p. 116.
   "Porcupine Sonnet." [LightY] '87, c86, p. 247.
   "Postcard from Civilization." [LightY] '87, c86, p. 21.
4433. PRAY, Toni
   "Imagined in a House at Amherst." [Writer] (99:1) Ja 86, p. 18.
4434. PRAYSON, Michael
   "A Blue Sky." [HiramPoR] (43) Fall-Wint 87-88, p. 25.
4435. PRECIOUS, Joc
   "Snow Poem '84." [Bogg] (58) 87, p. 11.
PREE, Don Keck du
   See DuPREE, Don Keck
4436. PREIL, Gabriel
   "Two Fogels" (in Hebrew & English, tr. by Nikki Stiller). [InterPR] (13:2) Fall 87,
      p. 40-41.
   "Words About Her, 1983" (in Hebrew & English, tr. by Nikki Stiller). [InterPR]
      (13:2) Fall 87, p. 38-39.
4437. PRESTON, Daniel S.
   "Negotiations." [PennR] (3:2) Fall-Wint 87, p. 3.
4438. PRETTI, Emma
   "La notte a volte è arancione e diventa una strana stazione." [Os] (24) 87, p. 30.
4439. PRICE, Barrett R.
   "Avoiding Enlightenment in Gloucester, Mass." [Kaleid] (14) Wint-Spr 87, p. 69.
4440. PRICE, Elizabeth A.
   "At the Sound of the Tone." [DenQ] (22:1) Sum 87, p. 36.
4441. PRICE, Larry
   "Crude Thinking." [Bound] (14:1/2) Fall 85-Wint 86 [c87], p. 20-23.
   "The Fully-Clothed Excess Generator (World Version)." [NewAW] (2) Fall 87, p.
      84-86.
4442. PRICE, Reynolds
   "31 December 1985" (For R.L.C.). [Poetry] (151:3) D 87, p. 293.
   "Ben Long's Drawing of Me." [AmerV] (7) Sum 87, p. 54.
   "The Dream of Salt." [AmerV] (7) Sum 87, p. 53.
   "Near a Milestone" (Fifty-third birthday). [Poetry] (151:3) D 87, p. 294.
   "Paid." [AmerV] (7) Sum 87, p. 55.
   "Sky, Dark." [AmerV] (7) Sum 87, p. 55.
   "Thicket." [AmerV] (7) Sum 87, p. 54.
   "Unbeaten Play" (For Ross Quaintance, 1957-1985). [Poetry] (151:1/2) O-N 87, p.
      129-132.
4443. PRICE, Ron
   "Cobb's Lake." [Raccoon] (24/25) My 87, p. 37-39.
   "Healing the Chosen Betrayal." [Raccoon] (24/25) My 87, p. 280-281.
4444. PRICE-GRESTY, David
   "Sonogram." [Amelia] (4:3, issue 10) 87, p. 64.
4445. PRICHARD, Dael
   "Above a Bright Yellow Table Cloth." [SmPd] (24:1) Wint 87, p. 17-19.
   "By the Pool." [Waves] (15:4) Spr 87, p. 47.
   "Past Young, a Little." [DekalbLAJ] (20:1/4) 87, p. 51.
4446. PRINCE, Diana
   "Parachutist." [ThRiPo] (29/30) 87, p. 54.
4447. PRINZMETAL, Donna
   "Cunt." [YellowS] (23) Sum 87, p. 37.
   "Distances, a Letter." [Electrum] (39) Fall-Wint 87, p. 42.
4448. PRITCHETT, Frances W.
   "Night Falls with a Broken Wing" (tr. of Shamsur Rahman Faruqi). [Bomb] (18)
      Wint 87, p. 68.

4449. PRIVITERA, Rodolfo
"De Tarde." [Inti] (24/25) Otoño 86-Primavera 87, p. 270-271.
"Futura Pleza de Museo." [Inti] (24/25) Otoño 86-Primavera 87, p. 269.
"Vigilia." [Inti] (24/25) Otoño 86-Primavera 87, p. 269-270.
4450. PROCTOR, Clint
"Wind Dreams." [Wind] (17:59) 87, p. 37.
PROKOPCZYK, Regina Grol
    See GROL-PROKOPCZYK, Regina
4451. PROPER, Stan
"Bloody Memories: Kent State 1970" (for Lyn Lifshin). [Lactuca] (7) Ag 87, p. 10.
"In the Belly of the Hill." [Lactuca] (7) Ag 87, p. 9.
"July Roses." [PoeticJ] (17) 87, p. 28.
"Memories are Stored in Tupperware." [Lactuca] (6) Ap-My 87, p. 20.
"The New Vandals." [Lactuca] (6) Ap-My 87, p. 19.
"U. Mass Campus — 1971: Kent State Postlude" (for Lyn Lifshin). [Lactuca] (7) Ag
    87, p. 10.
"The White Heat of Night." [Lactuca] (6) Ap-My 87, p. 19.
"The White heat of Night." [Lactuca] (7) Ag 87, p. 9.
4452. PROPP, Karen
"7-Eleven." [Agni] (24/25) 87, p. 160-161.
4453. PROSPERE, Susan
"The Pool of Tears." [NewYorker] (63:18) 22 Je 87, p. 36.
4454. PROULX, Sylvain
"Waiting." [AntigR] (71/72) Aut 87-Wint 88, p. 51.
4455. PRUITT, Gladys
"Letters to My Mother." [Writer] (99:11) N 86, p. 18.
4456. PRUYNE, Rose
"Bird Stories." [PoetL] (82:1) Spr 87, p. 10.
"Cleaning the Garden in November." [PoetL] (82:1) Spr 87, p. 11-12.
"Trying to Catch the Horse." [PoetL] (82:1) Spr 87, p. 9.
4457. PUENTES DE OYENARD, Sylvia
"Delirio." [LetFem] (13:1/2) Primavera-Otoño 87, p. 127-128.
"Mi Pequeño Pájaro." [LetFem] (13:1/2) Primavera-Otoño 87, p. 126-127.
"Rose Exigida." [LetFem] (13:1/2) Primavera-Otoño 87, p. 127.
4458. PULIDO, Blanca Luz
"Cactus." [InterPR] (13:1) Spr 87, p. 14.
"Cactus" (tr. by Thomas Hoeksema and R. Enriquez). [InterPR] (13:1) Spr 87, p.
    15.
4459. PULLEY, Nancy L.
"Friends Talk About Moving to the East Coast." [PassN] (8:1) Wint 87, p. 16.
4460. PULTZ, Constance
"Love Near City Hall." [Vis] (23) 87, p. 9.
"Making Things Real." [StoneC] (14:3/4) Spr-Sum 87, p. 34.
4461. PURDY, Al
"Flying Over Vancouver Island" (from Port Renfrew to Tofino). [MalR] (79) Je 87,
    p. 113-114.
"The Gossamer Ending." [MalR] (79) Je 87, p. 111-112.
"I Think of John Clare." [Rampike] (5:3) 87, p. 42.
"Yes and No." [Verse] (4:1) Mr 87, p. 16-17.
4462. PURSIFULL, Deborah
"Poking the Dead with a Stick." [OP] (final issue) Sum 87, p. 33-34.
4463. PÜSKÜLLÜOGLU, Ali
"An Old Pirate in These Waters" (tr. by Murat Nemet-Nejat). [Trans] (19) Fall 87, p.
    148.
4464. QABULA, Alfred Temba
"Africa." [TriQ] (69) Spr-Sum 87, p. 284-285.
"Migrants' Lament — A Song." [TriQ] (69) Spr-Sum 87, p. 281-283.
"The Tears of a Creator" (w. Mi S'dumo Hlatshwayo). [TriQ] (69) Spr-Sum 87, p.
    286-293.
4465. QASIMI, Ahmad Nadeem
"Queen of Ebony" (tr. by Daud Kamal). [Vis] (25) 87, p. 12.
4466. QUAGLIANO, Tony
"Recollections of a Coot." [HawaiiR] (22) Fall 87, p. 7.
4467. QUALLS, Suzanne
"Early in a Rotten Summer." [Thrpny] (30) Sum 87, p. 23.

4468. QUERENGESSER, Neil
"Waves." [Dandel] (14:2) Fall-Wint 87, p. 24.
QI, Li
See LI, Qi
4469. QUINN, Bernetta
"Day Goes Shut." [LitR] (30:4) Sum 87, p. 510.
"For Brother Thadee Matura, OFM." [Pembroke] (19) 87, p. 130-131.
4470. QUINN, Harold
"Broken Places." [HolCrit] (24:5) D 87, p. 12.
4471. QUINN, Jeannette
"Optic Nerve." [Bogg] (57) 87, p. 11.
4472. QUINN, John
"Deep Autumn." [ColEng] (49:4) Ap 87, p. 428.
4473. QUINN, John Robert
"Album." [SpiritSH] (53:1) 87, p. 32.
"Mole." [SpiritSH] (53:1) 87, p. 33.
"Mrs. Overholt's Garden." [ChrC] (104:12) 15 Ap 87, p. 356.
"Nightfall." [SpiritSH] (53:1) 87, p. 32.
"Reminiscence." [KanQ] (19:1/2) Wint-Spr 87, p. 135.
"Winter Aconite." [ChrC] (104:8) 11 Mr 87, p. 245.
4474. QUINTANA PIGNO, Antonia
"La Jornada." [WritersF] (13) Fall 87, p. 31-59.
QUIROS, Jose Maria Muñoz
See MUÑOZ QUIROS, Jose Maria
4475. QUIROS MENA, Carlos E.
"Genesis." [Mairena] (9:24) 87, p. 116.
4476. RAAB, Lawrence
"Night Song." [DenQ] (21:3) Wint 87, p. 27-28.
"Revision." [DenQ] (21:3) Wint 87, p. 29-30.
"Revision." [DevQ] (21:2) Fall 86, p. 71-72.
"Stories in Which the Past Is Made" (To my brother). [Poetry] (151:1/2) O-N 87, p. 133.
4477. RABA, György
"The Greeks Are Blinding Polyphemus" (tr. by Jascha Kessler w. Maria Körösy). [HayF] (2) Spr 87, p. 101.
"A Preface to Dying" (tr. by Jascha Kessler, w. Maria Korosy). [BlueBldgs] (10) 87?, p. 33.
"A Preface to Dying" (tr. by Jascha Kessler, w. Maria Körösy). [HayF] (2) Spr 87, p. 102.
4478. RABAGO PALAFOX, Gabriela
"Haikus" (4 poems in Spanish). [InterPR] (13:1) Spr 87, p. 22.
"Haikus" (4 poems, tr. by Thomas Hoeksema). [InterPR] (13:1) Spr 87, p. 23.
4479. RABASSA, Gregory
"Curriculum Vitae" (tr. of Blanca Varela). [AmerPoR] (16:2) Mr-Ap 87, p. 21.
"Everyday Light" (tr. of Blanca Varela). [AmerPoR] (16:2) Mr-Ap 87, p. 21.
"Lady's Journal" (tr. of Blanca Varela). [AmerPoR] (16:2) Mr-Ap 87, p. 21.
"Listening to Billie Holiday" (tr. of Blanca Varela). [AmerPoR] (16:2) Mr-Ap 87, p. 21.
4480. RACEVSKIS, Karlis
"Laundry for Marie-Jo" (tr. of Michel Butor). [AntR] (45:3) Sum 87, p. 286-290.
4481. RACEY, Susan L
"Looking at Love from a Different Angle." [Writer] (99:9) S 86, p. 24.
4482. RACHEL, Naomi
"The Embrace." [HampSPR] Wint 86, p. 44.
"Our Own Seasons." [HampSPR] Wint 86, p. 45.
"The Process of Poetry." [DevQ] (21:2) Fall 86, p. 67-68.
"The Ritual." [DevQ] (21:2) Fall 86, p. 69-70.
4483. RADIN, Doris
"His Kokeshi." [Jacaranda] (2:2) Spr 87, p. 23.
"Poem Written on His Typewriter." [NewL] (54:1) Fall 87, p. 70.
4484. RADISON, Gary
"In My Passing." [WestCR] (21:3) Wint 87, p. 34.
4485. RADNER, Rebecca
"— End —." [NewEngR] (10:1) Aut 87, p. 137-140.
"If It's Allowed to Say." [NewEngR] (10:1) Aut 87, p. 134-136.
"Lighten Up Why." [Caliban] (2) 87, p. 16-17.

"Our Bodies Burning." [Caliban] (2) 87, p. 18-21.
"What We Saw of Each Other." [CentralP] (12) Fall 87, p. 27-29.
4486. RADNOTI, Miklós
"Clouded Sky" (tr. by Steven Polgar, Stephen Berg and S. J. Marks. Entire issue).
[PoetryE] (22) Spr 87, 113 p.
"I Lived in an Age on This Earth" (tr. by Susan Tomory and Reynold Stone).
[AntigR] (71/72) Aut 87-Wint 88, p. 158.
"Seventh Eclogue" (tr. by Susan Tomory and Reynold Stone). [AntigR] (71/72) Aut
87-Wint 88, p. 158.
4487. RADU, Kenneth
"Sleep." [Event] (16:1) Mr 87, p. 92-94.
4488. RAFFA, Joseph
"Death Depends on Our Dark Silence." [CrossCur] (6:5) 87, p. 52-53.
"Final Nightmare of the Future." [MidwQ] (28:2) Wint 87, p. 224.
"The Mulberry Picker." [CrabCR] (4:3) Sum 87, p. 16.
"On Red Hill." [Vis] (25) 87, p. 31-32.
"Public Relations." [Footwork] 87, p. 49.
4489. RAFFELD, David
"Downpour." [PoetryE] (23/24) Fall 87, p. 203.
"A Fable." [PoetryE] (23/24) Fall 87, p. 202.
"Room at Arles." [PoetryE] (23/24) Fall 87, p. 204.
4490. RAFIKA, Merini
"Harrouda" (Excerpt, tr. of Tahar Ben Jelloun). [Paint] (14:27) Spr 87, p. 8-10.
4491. RAGAN, James
"Birthing the Stillborn." [MissouriR] (10:1) 87, p. 159.
"The Falling Accidental." [NoAmR] (272:3) S 87, p. 101.
"Third Grade Sister of Charity" (for H. M.). [CrossCur] (7:1) 87, p. 105.
4492. RAGOSTA, Ray
"The Varieties of Religious Experience" (Selections: 5-9). [Notus] (2:1) Spr 87, p.
33-37.
4493. RAIL, DeWayne
"Okada's Choice." [PoetryNW] (28:3) Aut 87, p. 37-38.
4494. RAINE, Craig
"Baize Doors." [AmerS] (56:4) Aut 87, p. 546-547.
"A Chest of Drawers." [Ploughs] (13:4) 87, p. 167-170.
"In the Kalahari Desert." [Ploughs] (13:4) 87, p. 159-161.
"In the Mortuary." [Ploughs] (13:4) 87, p. 149-150.
"Inca." [Ploughs] (13:4) 87, p. 164-166.
"The Trout Farm." [Ploughs] (13:4) 87, p. 151-152.
4495. RAINE, Kathleen
"I, Who Am You." [Stand] (28:3) Sum 87, p. 40.
4496. RAKOSI, Carl
"The Lobster." [Conjunc] (11) 87?, p. 223-224.
4497. RALEIGH, Richard
"Mounting Suspicion." [HawaiiR] (19) Spr 86, c87, p. 47.
4498. RALSTON, Andrea Beth
"Hidden." [Gambit] (20) 86, p. 36.
4499. RAMANUJAN, A. K.
"Elements of Composition." [Chelsea] (46) 87, p. 190-191.
"Fear." [Chelsea] (46) 87, p. 192-193.
"Highway Stripper." [Chelsea] (46) 87, p. 198-201.
"Looking for the Center." [Chelsea] (46) 87, p. 196-197.
"Zoo Gardens Revisited." [Chelsea] (46) 87, p. 194-195.
4500. RAMKE, Bin
"Better Late Than Never." [Crazy] (33) Wint 87, p. 50-51.
"The Botanical Gardens." [AmerV] (8) Fall 87, p. 23-24.
"Es Könnte Auch Anders Sein." [Shen] (37:4) 87, p. 64-65.
"The Fine Prospect." [Crazy] (33) Wint 87, p. 48-49.
"The Last Refuge of the Shy Man." [Shen] (37:4) 87, p. 66.
"Life Raft." [GeoR] (41:3) Fall 87, p. 473-474.
"One View of the Wide, Wide World." [Poetry] (151:1/2) O-N 87, p. 134-136.
"Sex Object." [OhioR] (39) 87, p. 85.
RAMOS, Jesús Tomé
See TOMÉ RAMOS, Jesús
4501. RAMPP, Charles
"Compass Directions." [Poem] (58) N 87, p. 11.

"No Difference." [Poem] (58) N 87, p. 12.
4502. RAMSEY, Jarold
"Four-Handed: For My Daughters." [SenR] (17:1) 87, p. 27.
"The Man of Grass" (David Douglas 1798-1834). [NowestR] (25:3) 87, p. 190-191.
4503. RAMSEY, Paul
"Elegy." [HawaiiR] (19) Spr 86, c87, p. 27.
"Five O'Clock Song" (A Love Poem). [HawaiiR] (19) Spr 86, c87, p. 26.
"Logistics." [Pembroke] (19) 87, p. 181.
"Pompous." [LightY] '87, c86, p. 240.
"Song of Obedience." [Pembroke] (19) 87, p. 181.
"Trialogue." [Pembroke] (19) 87, p. 181.
4504. RANDALL, Julia
"Gone Missing." [MichQR] (26:1) Wint 87, p. 244-245.
4505. RANDALL, Margaret
"Blood Loosens Its Strangle-Hold." [Cond] (14) 87, p. 203.
"Kaleidoscope." [Cond] (14) 87, p. 202.
"Under the Stairs." [ColR] (NS 14:2) Fall-Wint 87, p. 44-46.
4506. RANDOLPH, Sally
"Tea with Rita." [YellowS] (22) Spr 87, p. 15.
4507. RANKIN, Paula
"Chipping Icicles." [SenR] (17:1) 87, p. 62.
"Luck: West Side Market, Cleveland." [MemphisSR] (8:1) Fall 87, p. 12-13.
"Unemployment." [SenR] (17:1) 87, p. 63-64.
4508. RAPTOSH, Diane
"Casualty." [KanQ] (19:3) Sum 87, p. 231.
"Just West of Now." [MichQR] (26:1) Wint 87, p. 115-116.
"Stuttering." [MalR] (80) S 87, p. 114.
4509. RAS, Barbara
"Letting Go of Land." [MassR] (28:4) Wint 87, p. 684.
"Pregnant Poets Swim Lake Tarleton, New Hampshire" (for Emily Wheeler).
[MassR] (28:4) Wint 87, p. 683.
4510. RASH, Ron
"After." [NegC] (7:3/4) 87, p. 103-104.
"Among the Believers." [SouthernPR] (27:2) Fall 87, p. 11.
4511. RASMUSSEN, Tamara
"Toes." [AntigR] (69/70) 87, p. 206.
4512. RATCLIFFE, Stephen
"1100 People Are Said to Live Below Grand Central Station." [NewAW] (1) 87, p.
111.
"Ode to Joy." [NewAW] (1) 87, p. 112.
"Present Tense" (Selection: Part Six). [NewAW] (2) Fall 87, p. 67-71.
4513. RATHBUN, Victoria
"Uncool." [Spirit] (8:2) 87, p. 260.
4514. RATNER, Rochelle
"Borders." [MinnR] (NS 28) Spr 87, p. 17-19.
"Lilacs, Asparagus, a Broken Pear Tree." [HangL] (50/51) 87, p. 159-160.
"Mr. Rubin." [Bogg] (58) 87, p. 17.
4515. RATON, W. S.
"Raspberries in Chocolate." [CarolQ] (39:2) Wint 87, p. 78.
4516. RATTRAY, David
"Crowned Head" (tr. of Roger Gilbert-Lecomte). [LitR] (30:3) Spr 87, p. 472.
"High" (tr. of Roger Gilbert-Lecomte). [LitR] (30:3) Spr 87, p. 472.
"Holy Childhood or Concealment of Birth" (tr. of Roger Gilbert-Lecomte). [LitR]
(30:3) Spr 87, p. 473.
"Opening the Eyelid." [Conjunc] (10) 87, p. 173-176.
"Rebirth Prebirth" (tr. of Roger Gilbert-Lecomte). [LitR] (30:3) Spr 87, p. 474.
"To the Consciousness of a Shooting Star" (w. Gérard Charrière). [Bomb] (18) Wint
87, p. 44-47.
4517. RATUSHINSKAYA, Irina
"Give Me a Nickname, Prison." [Harp] (274:1644) My 87, p. 28.
"I'll live through this, survive, and they'll ask me" (tr. by Frances Padorr Brent and
Carol Avins). [NewYRB] (34:8) 7 My 87, p. 19.
"Two Poems from Prison" (tr. by Frances Padorr Brent and Carol Avins).
[NewYRB] (34:8) 7 My 87, p. 19.
"Well, we'll live as the soul directs" (tr. by Frances Padorr Brent and Carol Avins).
[NewYRB] (34:8) 7 My 87, p. 19.

4518. RATZLAFF, Keith
"Theme and Variation." [PoetryNW] (28:4) Wint 87-88, p. 46-47.
4519. RAWLES, Richard
"Horses." [YellowS] (23) Sum 87, p. 34.
"Seven Falls." [YellowS] (23) Sum 87, p. 35.
"Sophia." [YellowS] (23) Sum 87, p. 34.
4520. RAWLS, Bonnie
"The Suburban Habit of Going Home." [StoneC] (14:3/4) Spr-Sum 87, p. 25.
4521. RAY, Amitava
"Tristessa." [Chelsea] (46) 87, p. 253.
"Walk Me Out in the Morning Dew, My Honey." [Chelsea] (46) 87, p. 254.
4522. RAY, David
"Ajanta." [Amelia] (4:3, issue 10) 87, p. 28-29.
"A Cigarette Likened to a Soldier in Winter Whites" (In Memoriam, John Kiely,
    1946-1986). [Iowa] (17:3) Fall 87, p. 45-46.
"A Consultation Without Fee." [Pequod] (23/24) 87, p. 318-319.
"The Death of Chekhov." [Ascent] (13:1) 87, p. 50-51.
"Ennui." [LightY] '87, c86, p. 184.
"Firestarter." [HampSPR] Wint 86, p. 18.
"First Ice." [Iowa] (17:3) Fall 87, p. 46-47.
"For Madame Bloch, in Vence." [CreamCR] (11:2/3) 87?, p. 65.
"From Horseheads to Watkins Glen in the Old Days" (For Jim Myers). [WritersF]
    (13) Fall 87, p. 132.
"Gossipy Poem: Honolulu, 1/29/87." [HawaiiR] (22) Fall 87, p. 64.
"The Hammering." [Event] (16:1) Mr 87, p. 33.
"In the Kitchen After the Funeral." [Iowa] (17:3) Fall 87, p. 47.
"Leaving the Bistro." [Iowa] (17:3) Fall 87, p. 48-49.
"The Leper." [GreenfR] (14:3/4) Sum-Fall 87, p. 165.
"The Lesson." [HampSPR] Wint 86, p. 19.
"The Lovers." [Iowa] (17:3) Fall 87, p. 48.
"Memorial Day." [GreenfR] (14:3/4) Sum-Fall 87, p. 164.
"Moment by the Pool." [NewL] (54:1) Fall 87, p. 115.
"Our Wailing Wall." [NewL] (53:3) Spr 87, p. 20-23.
"Passport Photo." [GreenfR] (14:3/4) Sum-Fall 87, p. 166.
"Portrait of Charles 1930." [ColEng] (49:4) Ap 87, p. 422.
"The Prayer." [ColEng] (49:4) Ap 87, p. 423.
"The Red Shoes." [DenQ] (22:1) Sum 87, p. 19-20.
"Sprinkled with Grace." [NewL] (54:1) Fall 87, p. 115.
"Syllabics." [Amelia] (4:3, issue 10) 87, p. 29.
"Waiting in the Mountains." [Pequod] (23/24) 87, p. 317.
4523. RAY, Judy
"Falling Flowers." [WritersF] (13) Fall 87, p. 118.
"Offering." [HampSPR] Wint 86, p. 20.
4524. RAY, Lila
"A Medical Mishap Perhaps." [NewL] (54:1) Fall 87, p. 109.
4525. RAYMOND, Elizabeth
"Things My Mother Loved." [Writer] (99:7) Jl 86, p. 19.
4526. RAYMOND, Kathy
"The Worst That Could Happen on Vacation." [Wind] (17:61) 87, p. 39.
4527. REA, Susan
"Pennsylvania Graveyard." [PassN] (8:2) Sum 87, p. 9.
4528. READER, Willie
"The Last Tango." [NegC] (7:3/4) 87, p. 134.
4529. REAGLER, Robin
"All Life." [Iowa] (17:3) Fall 87, p. 54.
"Big Swim." [Ploughs] (13:4) 87, p. 102-103.
"If I'm Bored Saying If I Tell." [Iowa] (17:3) Fall 87, p. 51-54.
"I'm Talking to You." [Iowa] (17:3) Fall 87, p. 54-55.
"Warning to Bridge Trolls, in at Least Five Voices." [NoAmR] (272:1) Mr 87, p.
    64.
"The Yellow Store." [Iowa] (17:3) Fall 87, p. 50-51.
4530. REARDON, Patrick
"Response." [Wind] (17:60) 87, p. 11.
4531. REARICK, John
"The End of Religion As We Know It." [US1] (20/21) Wint 86-87, p. 39.

4532. RECHNITZ, Emily
    "Steam Engines in Scranton." [PoetL] (82:3) Fall 87, p. 139-140.
4533. RECIPUTI, Natalie
    "Abstract Portrait." [BellArk] (3:6) N-D 87, p. 8.
    "He Says He's in Love." [BellArk] (3:6) N-D 87, p. 4.
    "Song for a Small Boat Leaving Biloxi on a Night in June, 1979." [BellArk] (3:4)
        Jl-Ag 87, p. 2.
4534. RECTOR, K. K.
    "Fanatic." [KanQ] (19:1/2) Wint-Spr 87, p. 301.
    "Running Away." [KanQ] (19:1/2) Wint-Spr 87, p. 302.
4535. RECTOR, Liam
    "Him, His Place" (for Donald Hall). [AmerPoR] (16:4) Jl-Ag 87, p. 22.
4536. REDDY, Kathleen
    "Blue-Eyed Boy." [WebR] (12:1) Spr 87, p. 16.
    "Up There." [WebR] (12:1) Spr 87, p. 17.
4537. REDGROVE, Peter
    "Great Powers." [Stand] (28:1) Wint 86-87, p. 16.
    "The Stained-Glass Students." [Stand] (28:1) Wint 86-87, p. 14-15.
    "The Stranger Miner." [Stand] (28:1) Wint 86-87, p. 16-17.
    "Treehouse Bible." [Stand] (28:1) Wint 86-87, p. 14.
    "The Widow Considers the Correspondence." [Stand] (28:1) Wint 86-87, p. 18.
4538. REDMOND, Eugene B.
    "Double Clutch Lover." [BlackALF] (21:4) Wint 87, p. 447-449.
4539. REDMOND, Mary Anne
    "The Opal." [Abraxas] (35/36) 87, p. 15.
4540. REDWINE, Nancy
    "In the temple of willow bend." [YellowS] (22) Spr 87, p. 31.
4541. REED, Alison T.
    "Eunuch." [MalR] (81) D 87, p. 64.
    "Misunderstanding." [MidwQ] (28:2) Wint 87, p. 225.
    "Point-of-View." [Wind] (17:60) 87, p. 27.
4542. REED, Diana
    "At the Glove Counter." [HampSPR] Wint 86, p. 46-47.
    "The Invisible Children of the Peacock." [NewEngR] (10:2) Wint 87, p. 207.
4543. REED, John R.
    "Sunday Morning, Bari." [SouthwR] (72:3) Sum 87, p. 414-415.
4544. REEVE, F. D.
    "Concrete Music." [AmerPoR] (16:1) Ja-F 87, p. 14-15.
    "Making Do." [SouthwR] (72:4) Aut 87, p. 454.
4545. REEVES, Trish
    "Broken Ground." [PoetC] (18:3) Spr 87, p. 20.
    "Collect Calls." [QW] (24) Wint 87, p. 107.
    "The Elements." [PassN] (8:2) Sum 87, p. 22.
    "Freedom." [NewL] (54:1) Fall 87, p. 21.
    "Infidelity." [QW] (24) Wint 87, p. 106.
    "A Thought Remembered Is a Thought Forgotten." [NewL] (54:1) Fall 87, p. 20.
    "What Do I Have of You." [NewL] (54:1) Fall 87, p. 21.
4546. REGALBUTO, G.
    "Breaking Beans" (for Eoin). [Gambit] (21) 87, p. 39.
4547. REGAN, J. M.
    "The Bone Islands." [JamesWR] (4:2) Wint 87, p. 10.
    "The Good Victim." [JamesWR] (4:4) Sum 87, p. 5.
    "Partial Luetic History of an Individual at Risk." [JamesWR] (4:3) Spr 87, p. 5.
    "Spring 1986" (for Alex, tr. of Gennady Trifonov). [JamesWR] (4:4) Sum 87, p. 5.
4548. REGAN, Jennifer
    "The Brother Poems" (Selections: 7 poems). [PraS] (61:3) Fall 87, p. 105-111.
4549. REGIER, Gail
    "Penelope Speaks" (The Greensboro Review Literary Award, Honorable Mention).
        [GreensboroR] (41) Wint 86-87, p. 16-17.
4550. REHMAN, Salim-ur
    "The Night Gasps for Breath" (tr. of Amjad Islam Amjad). [Vis] (23) 87, p. 12.
4551. REID, Alastair
    "Daedalus." [BostonR] (12:6) D 87, p. 10.
    "The Figures on the Frieze." [BostonR] (12:6) D 87, p. 10.
    "A Lesson in Music." [BostonR] (12:6) D 87, p. 10.
    "Once at Piertarvit." [BostonR] (12:6) D 87, p. 10.

"The Syntax of Seasons." [BostonR] (12:6) D 87, p. 10.
4552. REID, Bethany
"The Hayrake." [BellArk] (3:2) Mr-Ap 87, p. 7.
"Siblings, Strangers." [BellArk] (3:3) My-Je 87, p. 7.
"What the Bees Said." [BellArk] (3:3) My-Je 87, p. 6.
4553. REID, D. C.
"Dear Aldous." [AntigR] (69/70) 87, p. 202.
4554. REID, Kendall
"Balloon Frame." [CrescentR] (5:1) 87, p. 64-65.
4555. REILLY, Kathleen
"Cat's Eyes." [SouthernPR] (27:2) Fall 87, p. 14.
4556. REILLY, Stephen
"Pygmalion's Complaint." [FloridaR] (15:1) Spr-Sum 87, p. 48.
4557. REINFELD, Linda
"Foundations." [Sulfur] (19) Spr 87, p. 40.
4558. REINHARD, John
"When Fathers Speak for Daughters." [PassN] (8:2) Sum 87, p. 5.
4559. REISNER, Barbara
"The Exchange." [GrahamHR] (10) Wint-Spr 87, p. 30-31.
"The Fruit of Goodly Trees." [BlueBldgs] (10) 87?, p. 35-36.
"The Margin the Light Falls on." [GrahamHR] (10) Wint-Spr 87, p. 29.
"A Taste of Honey." [GrahamHR] (10) Wint-Spr 87, p. 28.
"Until the Day Breathe." [LaurelR] (21:1/2) Wint-Sum 87, p. 85-86.
4560. REISS, James
"The Amanuensis." [OntR] (26) Spr-Sum 87, p. 90-91.
"Castrati in Caesar's Court." [NewRep] (197:2/3) 13-20 Jl 87, p. 34.
4561. REITER, David
"Our Bones Get Stiff." [Dandel] (14:2) Fall-Wint 87, p. 31.
"The Snow in Us." [Dandel] (14:2) Fall-Wint 87, p. 30.
4562. REITER, Thomas
"Completing the New Lake." [SouthernHR] (21:4) Fall 87, p. 359.
"The Death Watch Beetle." [PoetC] (19:1) Fall 87, p. 8-9.
"Rainbarrel" (To my grandmother). [ThRiPo] (29/30) 87, p. 55.
4563. RENAUD, Jorge A.
"I Want You." [Americas] (14:3/4) Fall-Wint 86, p. 88.
"Misery Comes Cheap." [Americas] (14:3/4) Fall-Wint 86, p. 89.
"Nothing, Really." [Americas] (14:3/4) Fall-Wint 86, p. 93.
"One for #12." [Americas] (14:3/4) Fall-Wint 86, p. 90-91.
"She Walks in Shadows." [Americas] (14:3/4) Fall-Wint 86, p. 92.
4564. RENDLEMAN, Danny
"Rosalie." [Raccoon] (24/25) My 87, p. 268-270.
4565. RENKL, Margaret
"After Rain." [Shen] (37:4) 87, p. 39.
"Shrew." [SouthernPR] (27:2) Fall 87, p. 13.
"Small Comforts." [SouthernPR] (27:1) Spr 87, p. 60.
4566. RENNER, Bruce
"Body Light." [ClockR] (4:1) 87, p. 13.
4567. RENNING, Charles H.
"Possession." [ArizQ] (43:2) Sum 87, p. 164.
4568. RENSBERGER, David
"A Political Prisoner." [ChatR] (8:1) Fall 87, p. 82.
4569. RENTAS LUCAS, Eugenio
"Desesperacion." [Mairena] (9:23) 87, p. 125-126.
"Hacia Adentro." [Mairena] (9:23) 87, p. 124-125.
"Saldra el Arco Iris." [Mairena] (9:23) 87, p. 123-124.
4570. REVELL, Donald
"The Children's Undercroft." [PoetC] (18:2) Wint 87, p. 45-46.
"From Cuiseaux." [PoetC] (18:2) Wint 87, p. 47-48.
"A Heart's Instruments." [Pequod] (23/24) 87, p. 158.
"A Home Made Saint." [IndR] (10:3) Spr 87, p. 81.
"The Next Marriage." [Pequod] (23/24) 87, p. 157.
"Polygamy." [Ploughs] (13:4) 87, p. 104.
"Prague." [Pequod] (23/24) 87, p. 159.
"St. Lucy's Day." [Poetry] (151:3) D 87, p. 267-269.
REVUELTA, Pedro Gutierrez
See GUTIERREZ REVUELTA, Pedro

4571. REWAK, William J.
"Good Taste." [KanQ] (19:1/2) Wint-Spr 87, p. 149.
"Jersey Cokesbury." [AntigR] (69/70) 87, p. 36.
"A Piece of Rag." [KanQ] (19:1/2) Wint-Spr 87, p. 150.
"The Shape-Shifters." [AntigR] (69/70) 87, p. 37.
"Strategy." [AntigR] (69/70) 87, p. 37.
4572. REYES, Carlos
"The Sky's Green Willow" (Spanish and English, tr. of Josefina de la Torre).
[BlackWR] (13:2) Spr 87, p. 186-209.
4573. REYNOLDS, Craig A.
"Watch What You Make of Me." [BlackALF] (21:3) Fall 87, p. 251.
4574. REYNOLDS, Katherine
"Bromeliads." [PoetryNW] (28:1) Spr 87, p. 44-45.
4575. REYNOLDS, Richard G.
"To the Stream without a Name." [KanQ] (19:3) Sum 87, p. 236.
4576. RHENISCH, Harold
"Brushwork." [Grain] (15:3) Fall 87, p. 52-57.
"The Koan" (Excerpt). [AntigR] (69/70) 87, p. 61-67.
"The Light in the Fingers." [Event] (16:2) Sum 87, p. 14-15.
"The Threshing Floor." [Event] (16:2) Sum 87, p. 12-13.
"We Will Not Be Read." [Grain] (15:3) Fall 87, p. 58-61.
"The Wind and the Moon." [Event] (16:3) Fall 87, p. 33-35.
4577. RHETT, Kathryn
"A Black Beret." [AntR] (45:1) Wint 87, p. 55.
"Two Women." [AntR] (45:1) Wint 87, p. 56.
4578. RHOADES, Lisa
"Eclipses." [SmPd] (24:3) Fall 87, p. 26.
"The evening came magenta." [Abraxas] (35/36) 87, p. 53.
4579. RHODENBAUGH, Suzanne
"The Carbide Lamp." [PennR] (3:1) Spr-Sum 87, p. 43.
4580. RHODES, Dee Schenck
"Three Children: Listening." [NegC] (7:3/4) 87, p. 113.
4581. RIBOVICH, John
"Greed." [Poem] (58) N 87, p. 28.
4582. RICE, Bruce
"Wedding Picture" (Annie Bissell). [Grain] (15:2) Sum 87, p. 19.
4583. RICE, Stan
"Authority." [Zyzzyva] (3:1) Spr 87, p. 141.
"Madness Evicted." [FiveFR] (5) 87, p. 77-78.
"The Rain of Reason." [FiveFR] (5) 87, p. 76.
"We Must Assiduously Remember the Invisible Joys of the Torments of Hell."
[FiveFR] (5) 87, p. 74-75.
4584. RICH, Adrienne
"Children Playing Checkers at the Edge of the Forest." [Field] (37) Fall 87, p. 52.
"Death and Taxes." [Sequoia] (31:1) Centennial issue 87, p. 122.
"Dreamwood." [Poetry] (151:1/2) O-N 87, p. 136.
"English Poetry Remembered." [Sequoia] (31:1) Centennial issue 87, p. 121.
"In Memoriam." [YaleR] (76:3) Spr 87, p. 411.
"The Novel." [Field] (37) Fall 87, p. 51.
"A Story." [Field] (37) Fall 87, p. 50.
4585. RICH, Mark
"Clocks and Locks." [LightY] '87, c86, p. 186-187.
"Even the Mourning Doves." [Poem] (58) N 87, p. 10.
"The Face Is a Face." [Poem] (58) N 87, p. 9.
4586. RICHARDS, Anne
"The Villa Goshen" (for D.L.B.). [Jacaranda] (2:2) Spr 87, p. 58-61.
4587. RICHARDS, Marilee
"The Memory." [MidwQ] (28:3) Spr 87, p. 362.
4588. RICHARDS, Melanie
"The Arrow Suspended in Midair." [Farm] (4:2) Spr-Sum 87, p. 29.
"The Postcard." [Farm] (4:2) Spr-Sum 87, p. 28.
"The Rooms She Will Not Enter." [Farm] (4:2) Spr-Sum 87, p. 30.
4589. RICHARDS, Tad
"He Becomes Reacquainted with Solitude." [BellR] (10:2) Fall 87, p. 8.
"Red River." [BellR] (10:2) Fall 87, p. 7.

"Stagecoach" (for Dr. Manny Rich's Wednesday night group, 1970). [BellR] (10:2) Fall 87, p. 9-11.
4590. RICHARDSON, Emma
"Beginnings." [SouthernHR] (21:2) Spr 87, p. 158.
4591. RICHARDSON, James
"The Mind-Body Problem." [NewRep] (197:18) 2 N 87, p. 34.
"The Mind-Body Problem" (Corrected reprint). [NewRep] (197:23) 7 D 87, p. 36.
4592. RICHMAN, Elliot
"After the Poems of Anonymous Japanese Courtesans" (The Rexroth Translations). [WindO] (49) Fall 87, p. 4.
"Along the Banks Where Alph the Sacred River Runs." [Bogg] (58) 87, p. 17.
"Closing my eyes to inhale." [Bogg] (58) 87, p. 64.
"A Host of Shadows." [WindO] (48) Spr 87, p. 31.
"It Was Such Fun." [Vis] (23) 87, p. 20.
"The Night of Kierkegaard's Burial, November 11, 1855." [WindO] (48) Spr 87, p. 30.
"The Nighthawk." [WindO] (49) Fall 87, p. 5.
"On First Reading Tu Fu." [WindO] (49) Fall 87, p. 5.
"The Sweeper." [Amelia] (4:1/2, issue 9) 87, p. 73.
"There was a young man from Copenhagen." [WindO] (48) Spr 87, p. 30.
4593. RICHMAN, Jan
"Parting the Waters." [FiveFR] (5) 87, p. 104-105.
4594. RICHMOND, Steve
"The." [WormR] (27:4, issue 108) 87, p. 88.
"Ears." [Wind] (17:59) 87, p. 38.
"Gagaku" (6 poems). [WormR] (27:4, issue 108) 87, p. 88-91.
"Gagaku: The correct way for me to create." [Bogg] (57) 87, p. 29.
"Gagaku: Demons behind the wheel." [Lactuca] (8) N 87, p. 39.
"Gagaku: It's woman's dream to be Queen." [Bogg] (58) 87, p. 47.
"Gagaku: Maybe I've exorcised all of 'em." [Lactuca] (8) N 87, p. 38.
"Gagaku: Middle of May 87." [Lactuca] (8) N 87, p. 38.
"Gagaku: Now they walk somewhat strut in a circle." [Lactuca] (6) Ap-My 87, p. 21.
"Gagaku: Schopenhauer." [Lactuca] (8) N 87, p. 37.
"Gagaku: Their eyes enlarge." [Lactuca] (8) N 87, p. 39.
"Gagaku: They come forward." [Lactuca] (8) N 87, p. 36.
"Life." [WormR] (27:4, issue 108) 87, p. 90.
4595. RICHSTONE, May
"Not What We Had in Mind." [LightY] '87, c86, p. 235.
4596. RICHTER, Harvena
"Skins." [SoDakR] (25:2) Sum 87, p. 82-83.
4597. RICKABAUGH, René
"Digging." [NowestR] (25:3) 87, p. 326.
4598. RICKERTSEN, Anne
"Sliding." [SinW] (31) 87, p. 48.
4599. RICKETTS, Marijane G.
"Lilliput Magic." [PoeticJ] (17) 87, p. 35.
4600. RIDDELL, John
"Now Wise Will Expect." [CrossC] (9:3/4) 87, p. 15.
4601. RIDL, Jack
"50s Blues." [Wind] (17:61) 87, p. 40.
"At Home." [Paint] (14:28) Aut 87, p. 13.
"Coach's Kid's Summer." [PennR] (3:1) Spr-Sum 87, p. 45.
"Everything You Do Is a Reflection." [PennR] (3:1) Spr-Sum 87, p. 44.
"Late in His Career." [Wind] (17:61) 87, p. 40.
"The Men in the Family." [SouthernPR] (27:1) Spr 87, p. 42.
"Watching the Virginia Reel: A Fugue." [Paint] (14:28) Aut 87, p. 12.
4602. RIDLAND, John
"Literary Anecdote (Apocryphal)." [Iowa] (17:2) Spr-Sum 87, p. 129-130.
"Mountain Music." [Iowa] (17:2) Spr-Sum 87, p. 127-129.
4603. RIFAT, Oktay
"Conflict" (tr. by Talat Sait Halman). [Trans] (19) Fall 87, p. 134.
"The Flute" (tr. by Talat Sait Halman). [Trans] (19) Fall 87, p. 133.
4604. RIFENBURGH, D. C.
"My Father's Will." [Shen] (37:4) 87, p. 44-45.

4605. RIGGS, Dionis Coffin
"The Cliff Dwellers" (tr. of Gülten Akin). [InterPR] (13:2) Fall 87, p. 42-43.
"Istanbul" (tr. of Cahit Külebi, w. William A. Fielder and Özcan Yalim). [StoneC] (15:1/2) Fall-Wint 87-88, p. 36-37.
4606. RIGSBEE, David
"Fireflies." [Pembroke] (19) 87, p. 156-157.
"God's Tumbler." [SouthernR] (23:1) Ja 87, p. 141-144.
"Half Lives." [SouthernR] (23:1) Ja 87, p. 140-141.
"The Mermaid." [Poetry] (149:5) F 87, p. 271-275.
"Midnight." [Pembroke] (19) 87, p. 157-158.
"Platonic." [Pembroke] (19) 87, p. 158-159.
"To a Mother." [GreensboroR] (43) Wint 87-88, p. 70.
"White." [Poetry] (149:5) F 87, p. 270-271.
4607. RILEY, Joanne M.
"The Builder's Daughter." [Outbr] (18/19) Fall 86-Spr 88, p. 72.
"Colors of Yarrow." [Footwork] 87, p. 16.
"Death of a Sparrow." [Outbr] (18/19) Fall 86-Spr 88, p. 70.
"Dream Thief." [Footwork] 87, p. 17.
"Leaving the Treehouse." [Outbr] (18/19) Fall 86-Spr 88, p. 71.
"Piano Dances for Mother and Daughter." [Footwork] 87, p. 17.
"Summer: Bagpipes and Cicadas." [Phoenix] (7:1) 87, p. 10.
"Turtles and a Ghost Story." [Footwork] 87, p. 17.
4608. RILEY, Michael D.
"W. B. Yeats." [BlueBldgs] (10) 87?, p. 18.
"Words: Update at Eleven." [HighP] (2:3) Wint 87, p. 331-333.
4609. RILEY, Tom
"A Bit of Enlightenment." [LightY] '87, c86, p. 228.
"Clerihews" (2 poems). [LightY] '87, c86, p. 68.
"The Primitive Astronomer." [LightY] '87, c86, p. 78.
4610. RILKE, Rainer Maria
"Archaic Torso of Apollo" (tr. by Alfred Corn). [Colum] (12) 87, p. 50.
"Autumn Day" (tr. by David Ferry). [Raritan] (7:1) Sum 87, p. 33.
"The Bowl of Roses" (tr. by Don Mager). [BlackWR] (13:2) Spr 87, p. 70-72.
"Herbsttag." [Raritan] (7:1) Sum 87, p. 32.
"The Island" (tr. by Walter Arndt). [NewEngR] (10:2) Wint 87, p. 215-216.
"Last Poems" (Selections: 5 poems, tr. by Stephen Mitchell). [Thrpny] (30) Sum 87, p. 20.
"Das Lied des Idioten." [StoneC] (14:3/4) Spr-Sum 87, p. 16.
"The Ninth Elegy" (tr. by Steven Lautermilch). [ColR] (NS 14:1) Spr-Sum 87, p. 50-56.
"The Simpleton's Song" (tr. by Martin Robbins). [StoneC] (14:3/4) Spr-Sum 87, p. 17.
4611. RIND, Sherry
"Another Anniversary Poem for John." [PoetryNW] (28:1) Spr 87, p. 5.
"The Fall Shuffle of the Ruffed Grouse." [PoetryNW] (28:1) Spr 87, p. 4-5.
4612. RINGER, Darby
"NCS." [BellArk] (3:3) My-Je 87, p. 1.
4613. RIOS, Alberto
"The Corner Uncle." [NoAmR] (272:1) Mr 87, p. 71.
"Juan Rulfo Moved Away." [OhioR] (38) 87, p. 92.
"The Man, Fat and Cigar." [Sonora] (13) Fall 87, p. 111-112.
"Secret Prune." [Sonora] (13) Fall 87, p. 113-114.
RIOS, Andrés Castro
        See CASTRO RIOS, Andrés
4614. RIQUELME, María
"Hermana." [Mairena] (9:24) 87, p. 122.
4615. RISDEN, E. L.
"Questions After the Late Show." [NegC] (7:3/4) 87, p. 119.
4616. RISSET, Jacqueline
"Seven Passages from a Woman's Life" (tr. by Rosmarie Waldrop). [LitR] (30:3) Spr 87, p. 356-358.
4617. RISTAU, Harland
"Great Game of Baseball." [Bogg] (58) 87, p. 20.
4618. RITCHEY, Matthew
"Skyscraper at Night." [Gambit] (20) 86, p. 42.

4619. RITCHIE, Elisavietta
"Challenges." [LightY] '87, c86, p. 152.
"Elegy for the Other Woman." [LightY] '87, c86, p. 147.
RITCHIE, Michael Karl
See MICHAEL KARL (RITCHIE)
4620. RITCHINGS, Joan Drew
"Attic Dance." [LightY] '87, c86, p. 176-177.
"Happy Ending." [Writer] (100:5) My 87, p. 21.
"Lament." [Writer] (100:1) Ja 87, p. 24.
"Mantis Gravestone." [Writer] (99:3) Mr 86, p. 20.
"Reading Outdoors." [LightY] '87, c86, p. 245.
4621. RITSOS, Yannis
"Helen" (tr. by Marianthe Colakis). [WebR] (12:1) Spr 87, p. 59-77.
"Persephone" (tr. by Peter Green and Beverly Bardsley). [GrandS] (6:4) Sum 87, p. 143-156.
"Strange Days" (tr. by Martin McKinsey). [Verse] (4:3) N 87, p. 16.
"Sunday" (tr. by Martin McKinsey). [Verse] (4:3) N 87, p. 16.
4622. RITTY, Joan
"At Sea." [InterPR] (13:1) Spr 87, p. 86.
"I Ching, Ha!" [InterPR] (13:1) Spr 87, p. 85.
"Sestina: Carolina Mountains." [InterPR] (13:1) Spr 87, p. 84-85.
"Song from Fortitude." [InterPR] (13:1) Spr 87, p. 87.
4623. RIVARD, David
"How It Will Always Seem" (for David Guennette). [IndR] (10:3) Spr 87, p. 78-79.
"Secured Town." [Sonora] (12) Spr 87, p. 24.
"Soul." [IndR] (10:3) Spr 87, p. 80.
4624. RIVAS, María Emma
"Una Aventura Cosmica." [LetFem] (13:1/2) Primavera-Otoño 87, p. 134-141.
4625. RIVERA, Diana
"The Garden." [MSS] (5:3) 87, p. 4.
"Ice." [MSS] (5:3) 87, p. 1-2.
"Light." [MSS] (5:3) 87, p. 8.
"The Rose." [MSS] (5:3) 87, p. 5-6.
RIVERA, R. Barreto
See BARRETO-RIVERA, R.
4626. RIVERA-RODAS, Oscar
"El Arribo a la Transparencia." [Inti] (24/25) Otoño 86-Primavera 87, p. 275-278.
4627. RIVERO-POTTER, Alicia
"El Angelus de Millet" (A Richard). [Inti] (24/25) Otoño 86-Primavera 87, p. 274.
"Como los paganos." [Inti] (24/25) Otoño 86-Primavera 87, p. 273-274.
4628. RIVERS, J. W.
"April in a Mountain Cabin: Swiss Pine Lake, North Carolina" (For Mercedes, my wife). [Poetry] (151:1/2) O-N 87, p. 137.
"Basil Norris Recounts to Great-Grandson Leslie Incidents of His Travel in Virginia and Carolina." [SoCaR] (19:2) Spr 87, p. 26-28.
"Basil Norris, Squire of Aldingbourne, Recounts to Great-Grandson Leslie Incidents of His Travel . . ." [SoCaR] (19:2) Spr 87, p. 24-26.
"The Gertz Family." [SoCaR] (20:1) Fall 87, p. 18-21.
"The Philadelphia Project." [Pembroke] (19) 87, p. 101-102.
"President Polk Addresses Congress." [Pembroke] (19) 87, p. 110.
"Sleepy Hollow Revisited: The True Ending of Rip van Winkle's Dreams." [Pembroke] (19) 87, p. 100-101.
4629. RIVETTE, Elizabeth
"The Work (Skidding Song)." [Blueline] (7:2/3 [i.e. 8:2/3?]) 87, p. 99.
4630. RIXON, Bob
"The Cloistered Nuns." [Lactuca] (7) Ag 87, p. 27-28.
"To a Friend in Crete." [Lactuca] (7) Ag 87, p. 27.
4631. ROBBINS, Anthony
"February." [SouthernR] (23:2) Ap 87, p. 375-376.
"Marrakesh." [Abraxas] (35/36) 87, p. 53.
4632. ROBBINS, Doren
"Time of the Devils." [Caliban] (3) 87, p. 31-32.
4633. ROBBINS, Martin
"At the Ashtarak Cemetery" (tr. of Gevorg Emin). [StoneC] (14:3/4) Spr-Sum 87, p. 46-47.
"Blue Window." [Os] (24) 87, p. 24.

"Evening Prayers." [InterPR] (13:1) Spr 87, p. 107.
"February Mirror." [WebR] (12:1) Spr 87, p. 34.
"For Abbie Huston Evans, Poet, at 100." [TexasR] (7:3/4) 87, p. 126.
"Kite Flying." [Pembroke] (19) 87, p. 176.
"Often I Cringe from a Shooting Pain" (tr. of Gevorg Emin). [InterPR] (13:1) Spr 87, p. 74.
"On an October Pond." [Os] (25) 87, p. 6.
"On Finding an Eye in Houghton Library, Harvard." [TexasR] (7:3/4) 87, p. 125.
"Portrait." [Pembroke] (19) 87, p. 176.
"Reunion." [InterPR] (13:1) Spr 87, p. 106.
"Seasonal Readings." [Os] (24) 87, p. 25.
"The Simpleton's Song" (tr. of Rainer Maria Rilke). [StoneC] (14:3/4) Spr-Sum 87, p. 17.
"Smart Lamb" (tr. of Gevorg Emin). [InterPR] (13:1) Spr 87, p. 74.
"Sparring Partners." [Pembroke] (19) 87, p. 175.
"Weather Update." [WebR] (12:1) Spr 87, p. 34.
"Winter Inventory." [Os] (25) 87, p. 11.
"With an Outstretched Arm." [WebR] (12:1) Spr 87, p. 33.
4634. ROBBINS, Mary Susannah
"Here." [StoneC] (14:3/4) Spr-Sum 87, p. 73.
4635. ROBBINS, Richard
"Bidding on Fulton Street." [PoetryNW] (28:1) Spr 87, p. 21-22.
"July." [PoetryNW] (28:1) Spr 87, p. 20-21.
"May on the Wintered-Over Ground." [NoAmR] (272:1) Mr 87, p. 10.
"Near Pocatello with My Great-Grandfather, 1918." [Puerto] (22:2) Spr 87, p. 82.
"Opening." [PennR] (3:2) Fall-Wint 87, p. 1.
"Small Song." [PennR] (3:2) Fall-Wint 87, p. 2.
4636. ROBBINS, Tim
"The Comb." [JamesWR] (4:3) Spr 87, p. 13.
"Comet." [HangL] (50/51) 87, p. 161.
"On the Quai." [HangL] (50/51) 87, p. 162.
"Place de la République May 2." [HangL] (50/51) 87, p. 163.
4637. ROBERSON, Ed
"Hotei: The Fullness." [Callaloo] (10:3) Sum 87, p. 366.
"Lucid Interval as Integral Music" (Selections). [Callaloo] (10:3) Sum 87, p. 367-368.
4638. ROBERTS, Betty
"Unwritten." [Bogg] (57) 87, p. 25.
"Walk Away" (In memory of a climber killed in New Zealand). [Bogg] (58) 87, p. 45.
4639. ROBERTS, Bonnie
"Ice Cream." [SmPd] (24:1) Wint 87, p. 15.
"My Lovemaking Is Autobiographical." [YellowS] (24) Aut 87, p. 8.
4640. ROBERTS, Bruce Holling
"An Incomprehensible Occurence" (tr. of Salvador Elizondo). [CreamCR] (11:2/3) 87?, p. 1.
4641. ROBERTS, Charles
"The First Night." [Confr] (35/36) Spr-Fall 87, p. 149.
"Kandinsky's Moscow in the Early Morning." [Confr] (35/36) Spr-Fall 87, p. 149.
"Marbot." [MidAR] (7:2) 87, p. 48.
"Variations on Gauguin." [MidAR] (7:2) 87, p. 46-47.
4642. ROBERTS, Dorothy
"Moving In." [AntigR] (71/72) Aut 87-Wint 88, p. 137.
"The Snowflakes." [AntigR] (69/70) 87, p. 167.
4643. ROBERTS, Janet
"Clear as Glass." [ManhatPR] (9) Sum 87, p. 51.
4644. ROBERTS, Kevin
"101 South S.F." [CanLit] (113/114) Sum-Fall 87, p. 206.
"San Francisco Sonnet." [CanLit] (113/114) Sum-Fall 87, p. 144.
"Where Is Here?" [CanLit] (113/114) Sum-Fall 87, p. 206.
4645. ROBERTS, Kim
"It Was Years." [Bomb] (20) Sum 87, p. 84.
"Minor League." [GreenfR] (14:3/4) Sum-Fall 87, p. 37.
"On This Map." [Bomb] (20) Sum 87, p. 84.
"The Social Games." [GreenfR] (14:3/4) Sum-Fall 87, p. 38.
"Something Autumn." [Bomb] (20) Sum 87, p. 84.

"Timothy Grass." [OhioR] (38) 87, p. 97.
"Under the Night Sky." [Sonora] (13) Fall 87, p. 115.
4646. ROBERTS, Len
"At Lavender Harvest" (For Vido). [Wind] (17:59) 87, p. 39-40.
"Blacktop." [Raccoon] (24/25) My 87, p. 231.
"Hvar, 1943, 1985." [Wind] (17:59) 87, p. 39.
"Lighting Candles in the Lake George Narrows" (for Hayden Carruth). [HolCrit] (24:4) O 87, p. 12.
"The Naming Field." [ColR] (NS 14:1) Spr-Sum 87, p. 12.
"On Edisto Island." [SouthernPR] (27:2) Fall 87, p. 29.
"On the Third Tier." [StoneC] (15:1/2) Fall-Wint 87-88, p. 53.
"Polishing the Work Boots." [PennR] (3:2) Fall-Wint 87, p. 33.
"Shoveling Snow." [PennR] (3:2) Fall-Wint 87, p. 34.
"Shoveling the Sidewalk in Cohoes, New York." [PoetryNW] (28:1) Spr 87, p. 36-37.
"Sunday Morning Sink Bath." [Raccoon] (24/25) My 87, p. 230.
"What the Hell, February, Wassergass." [CarolQ] (40:1) Fall 87, p. 57.
4647. ROBERTS, Steven
"Crane" (from "Aquatics: Bay"). [Bound] (14:1/2) Fall 85-Wint 86 [c87], p. 93.
4648. ROBERTSON, Harry
"To One of Them" (On Seeing a Picture of 3 Dead Soldiers on a Beach at Buna, New Guinea, 1943). [StoneC] (14:3/4) Spr-Sum 87, p. 15.
4649. ROBERTSON, Robin
"Balefire." [GrandS] (6:2) Wint 87, p. 76.
"Brattach." [GrandS] (6:2) Wint 87, p. 75.
"Embankment." [GrandS] (6:2) Wint 87, p. 73-74.
"Hill-Fort." [GrandS] (6:2) Wint 87, p. 74-75.
4650. ROBINS, Tonja
"Old Lady Eve" (The Greensboro Review Literary Award Poem). [GreensboroR] (41) Wint 86-87, p. 3.
"What She Says About Love." [GreensboroR] (39) Wint 85-86, p. 98-99.
4651. ROBINSON, Bruce
"The El." [StoneC] (14:3/4) Spr-Sum 87, p. 27.
4652. ROBINSON, Elizabeth
"Mica." [Epoch] (36:1) 87-88, p. 5-16.
"Socks." [Notus] (2:1) Spr 87, p. 94.
4653. ROBINSON, Ethel Winter
"Divorce Court." [Writer] (99:5) My 86, p. 18.
4654. ROBINSON, James Miller
"Excavating." [PoetryE] (23/24) Fall 87, p. 208.
4655. ROBINSON, Jamey
"Monochrome." [Footwork] 87, p. 80.
4656. ROBINSON, John
"As a Young Bicyclist." [Epoch] (36:3) 87-88, p. 190.
"A Dream Cannot Leave." [Epoch] (36:3) 87-88, p. 191.
"Modern Ghosts." [Epoch] (36:3) 87-88, p. 192.
4657. ROBINSON, Kit
"Autochthonous Redaction" (3 selections). [Bound] (14:1/2) Fall 85-Wint 86 [c87], p. 56.
"Simples" (to Lyn Hejinian). [NewAW] (2) Fall 87, p. 76-77.
4658. ROBISON, Margaret
"Letter Poem." [MinnR] (NS 29) Fall 87, p. 44.
4659. ROBSON, Ruthann
"The Animus of Diane Arbus, the Photographer." [NewL] (53:2) Wint 86-87, p. 15.
"The Aquarium." [Phoenix] (7:2) 87, p. 54.
"Kathe Kollwitz, Graphic Artist, Sketches a German Working-Class Woman." [NewL] (53:2) Wint 86-87, p. 12-13.
"Mary Cassatt, After Destroying the Letters of Edgar Degas." [NewL] (53:2) Wint 86-87, p. 13-14.
"Neolithic Masks." [FloridaR] (15:2) Fall-Wint 87, p. 5-16.
4660. ROBY, Gayle
"Faith Healing." [OhioR] (38) 87, p. 110-111.
"Mispronunciation." [OhioR] (38) 87, p. 112.
4661. ROCKWELL, Jeanne
"Brooklyn Dodger." [Phoenix] (7:1) 87, p. 6.

4662. RODAS, Ana María
"Being Guerrillera" (tr. by Zoë Anglesey). [Cond] (14) 87, p. 191.
"Cualquiera Tiene Derecho." [Cond] (14) 87, p. 184.
"The Days Are the Cities" (tr. by Zoë Anglesey). [Cond] (14) 87, p. 187.
"Los Días Son las Ciudades." [Cond] (14) 87, p. 186.
"Everyone Has the Right" (tr. by Zoë Anglesey). [Cond] (14) 87, p. 185.
"Look at Me" (tr. by Zoë Anglesey). [Cond] (14) 87, p. 189.
"Mirame." [Cond] (14) 87, p. 188.
"Ser Guerrillera." [Cond] (14) 87, p. 190.
4663. RODD, Laurel Rasplica
"Tangled Hair" (Selections: Two Waka, tr. of Yosano Akiko). [Paint] (14:27) Spr
87, p. 41.
4664. RODEFER, Stephen
"In the American Tree and Out the Other." [Zyzzyva] (3:1) Spr 87, p. 107-108.
"Passing Duration" (2 selections: "Enclosure of Elk," "Avery"). [Bound] (14:1/2)
Fall 85-Wint 86 [c87], p. 38-40.
4665. RODITI, Edouard
"Das Ewig Weibliche" (for E.M. Cioran, tr. by David Applefield). [LitR] (30:3) Spr
87, p. 434.
"Fabeltier" (tr. by David Applefield). [LitR] (30:3) Spr 87, p. 434.
"Windesbraut" (for Kenneth Rexroth, tr. by David Applefield). [LitR] (30:3) Spr 87,
p. 435.
4666. RODNING, Charles B.
"A smooth bough." [BallSUF] (28:4) Aut 87, p. 9.
4667. RODRIGUEZ, Blanca
"Nispero." [Os] (25) 87, p. 21.
"Saudade." [Os] (25) 87, p. 22.
"Sonrisas." [Os] (25) 87, p. 20.
4668. RODRIGUEZ, Carlos
"Llama de Amore Vivita: Jarchas" (Selección de poemas de un libro de próxima
aparición). [CuadP] (4:12) Mayo-Agosto 87, p. 57-68.
4669. RODRIGUEZ, Lesbia
"Poem to a Neighborhood Organizer / Poema a un Cedecista." [Contact] (9:44/45/46)
Fall-Wint 87, p. 21.
4670. RODRIGUEZ, Linda
"Reading at Night." [NewL] (54:1) Fall 87, p. 17.
4671. ROE, Margie McCreless
"As if in Prayer." [ChrC] (104:33) 11 N 87, p. 997.
4672. ROE, Michael
"The Critical Eye." [NegC] (7:3/4) 87, p. 135.
4673. ROEMERSDOCHTER, Maria Tesselschade
"Challenge" (tr. by Ria Vanderauwera). [Paint] (14:27) Spr 87, p. 40.
4674. ROESKE, Paulette
"Again." [KanQ] (19:3) Sum 87, p. 329.
"Aquarium." [VirQR] (63:4) Aut 87, p. 634-635.
"Island." [HawaiiR] (21) Spr 87, p. 6.
"Under Glass" (Santa Maria della Vittoria). [VirQR] (63:4) Aut 87, p. 633-634.
4675. ROETHKE, Theodore
"The Dark Angel" (from the Notebooks of Theodore Roethke — 1950-53, arranged
by David Wagoner). [NowestR] (25:3) 87, p. 141-143.
4676. ROFFMAN, Rosaly DeMaios
"A Story of Cups: With Appended Prayer." [CentR] (31:3) Sum 87, p. 270.
"The Way a Ten-Year-Old Prays." [Outbr] (18/19) Fall 86-Spr 88, p. 106-107.
4677. ROGACKI, Joanne M.
"Aunt Jenny's Farm." [EngJ] (76:7) N 87, p. 98.
4678. ROGAL, Stan
"Auntie." [AlphaBS] (2) D 87, p. 26.
4679. ROGERS, Del Marie
"Dry Arrangement in a Domed Jar" (For Ruth, my daughter). [HighP] (2:3) Wint 87,
p. 240.
"Mountain Lion." [HighP] (2:3) Wint 87, p. 239.
4680. ROGERS, Linda
"Setting the Hook." [CanLit] (113/114) Sum-Fall 87, p. 75.
4681. ROGERS, Pattiann
"The Eyes of the Gardener in the Villa of the Blind." [Raccoon] (24/25) My 87, p.
134-135.

"The Grooming." [Shen] (37:4) 87, p. 27-28.
"The Laying-On of Hands." [Poetry] (151:1/2) O-N 87, p. 138-139.
"Lifting the Soles of the Feet to the Sky." [Nimrod] (30:2) Spr-Sum 87, p. 126-127.
"Making Love with the Gods." [ClockR] (4:1) 87, p. 26-27.
"March 20th, 11:59 PM." [ClockR] (4:1) 87, p. 24.
"Old Bard: The Progression of Seasons." [Nimrod] (30:2) Spr-Sum 87, p. 125-126.
"On Being Eaten Alive." [Iowa] (17:2) Spr-Sum 87, p. 20-21.
"The Sense God Gave." [Iowa] (17:2) Spr-Sum 87, p. 19-20.
"There Is a Way to Walk on Water." [MichQR] (26:2) Spr 87, p. 400-401.
"War Horses." [ClockR] (4:1) 87, p. 25.
"What the Sun God Saw One Summer Afternoon." [Iowa] (17:2) Spr-Sum 87, p.
    21-22.
"When You Watch Us Sleeping." [Iowa] (17:2) Spr-Sum 87, p. 23-24.
4682. ROGOFF, Jay
"Ritual." [Salm] (72) Fall 86, p. 200.
"The Rock and Roll Angel" (for Mark Roberts and B. D. Love). [Salm] (74/75)
    Spr-Sum 87, p. 56.
4683. ROHRKEMPER, John
"Two Grammarians Make Love." [CentR] (31:2) Spr 87, p. 191.
4684. ROITMAN, Judith
"The Death of King David." [KanQ] (19:3) Sum 87, p. 141-142.
"Prospectus for a Kansas Wind Festival in the Flint Hills" (for Bill and Laurie).
    [KanQ] (19:3) Sum 87, p. 140-141.
4685. ROLL, Elizabeth J.
"Orange." [Raccoon] (24/25) My 87, p. 192.
ROLLER, Joseph de
    See DeROLLER, Joseph
4686. ROLLER, Tom
"My Case for Going On" (for S.J.R.). [BellArk] (3:4) Jl-Ag 87, p. 7.
4687. ROLLINGS, Alane
"The Age of Great Vocations." [GeoR] (41:2) Sum 87, p. 394-396.
"Ideal Forms." [Raccoon] (24/25) My 87, p. 119-120.
"In Your Own Sweet Time." [AmerPoR] (16:5) S-O 87, p. 36.
"Problems in Astronomy." [Raccoon] (24/25) My 87, p. 123-124.
"Sweet Luck." [Raccoon] (24/25) My 87, p. 121-122.
"Wild for to Hold." [AmerPoR] (16:5) S-O 87, p. 37.
4688. ROMANO, Rose
"Family Reunion." [Footwork] 87, p. 24.
"The First Scent." [SinW] (31) 87, p. 37.
4689. ROMO-CARMONA, Mariana
"Encounter with El Morro of Havana" (tr. of Minerva Salado). [Cond] (14) 87, p.
    213.
"Skirmish" (tr. of Minerva Salado). [Cond] (14) 87, p. 211.
"Word in the Mirror" (tr. of Minerva Salado). [Cond] (14) 87, p. 209.
4690. ROMTVEDT, David
"According to Leek." [Raccoon] (24/25) My 87, p. 10-13.
"Again Yellowstone River, Way Out East" (corrected reprint from 4:1). [CrabCR]
    (4:2) Spr 87, p. 2.
"Bureaucrat." [Raccoon] (24/25) My 87, p. 40-41.
"How Many Horses" (5 selections). [Nimrod] (31:1) Fall-Wint 87, p. 107-111.
"Music Out of a Sigh." [Raccoon] (24/25) My 87, p. 42.
"What I Know." [Raccoon] (24/25) My 87, p. 43.
4691. RONAN, Richard
"After Three Years" (tr. of Paul Verlaine). [AmerPoR] (16:4) Jl-Ag 87, p. 24.
"L'Allée" (tr. of Paul Verlaine). [AmerPoR] (16:4) Jl-Ag 87, p. 25.
"The beautiful falselight gleams all day, my soul" (tr. of Paul Verlaine). [AmerPoR]
    (16:4) Jl-Ag 87, p. 25.
"Faun" (tr. of Paul Verlaine). [AmerPoR] (16:4) Jl-Ag 87, p. 24.
"Hope shines small, a splinter of straw in the stable" (tr. of Paul Verlaine).
    [AmerPoR] (16:4) Jl-Ag 87, p. 25.
"The Hour of the Shepherd" (tr. of Paul Verlaine). [AmerPoR] (16:4) Jl-Ag 87, p.
    25.
"In the interminable ennui of the plains" (tr. of Paul Verlaine). [AmerPoR] (16:4)
    Jl-Ag 87, p. 24.
"Innocent Boys" (tr. of Paul Verlaine). [AmerPoR] (16:4) Jl-Ag 87, p. 25.
"Languor" (tr. of Paul Verlaine). [AmerPoR] (16:4) Jl-Ag 87, p. 25.

"Love Overturned" (tr. of Paul Verlaine). [AmerPoR] (16:4) Jl-Ag 87, p. 26.
"Parisian Sketch" (tr. of Paul Verlaine). [AmerPoR] (16:4) Jl-Ag 87, p. 24.
"Sunset" (tr. of Paul Verlaine). [AmerPoR] (16:4) Jl-Ag 87, p. 24.
"Utterly small, utterly lovely" (tr. of Paul Verlaine). [AmerPoR] (16:4) Jl-Ag 87, p. 26.
4692. RONEY-O'BRIEN, Susan
    "The Light Pilgrim." [BelPoJ] (37:4) Sum 87, p. 2-4.
4693. RONSARD, Pierre de
    "To His Girl Friend" (tr. by Nathaniel B. Smith). [WebR] (12:2) Fall 87, p. 23.
ROOKE, Katerina Angelaki
    See ANGELAKI-ROOKE, Katerina
4694. ROOP, Laura
    "As with Any Death." [HiramPoR] (42) Spr-Sum 87, p. 37-38.
4695. ROOT, William Pitt
    "At Hazard." [Sequoia] (31:1) Centennial issue 87, p. 123-125.
    "Homecoming" (after Albinas Zukauskas). [CutB] (27/28) 87, p. 92.
    "Ordeal by Devotion." [Nat] (244:14) 11 Ap 87, p. 484.
    "Relics of War" (after Vladas Slaitas). [CutB] (27/28) 87, p. 91.
4696. RORIPAUGH, Robert
    "The Lander Hotel and Bar: For Mike Trbovich." [Wind] (17:60) 87, p. 39.
4697. ROSBERG, Rose
    "Double Sight in Bali." [Waves] (14:4) Spr 86, p. 51.
    "Respite on 47th St." [NewRena] (7:1, #21) Fall 87, p. 101.
    "TV Relatives." [Phoenix] (7:2) 87, p. 49.
4698. ROSCOE, Jerry
    "Arnold's." [SoCaR] (19:2) Spr 87, p. 51.
    "Study." [Pig] (14) 87, p. 50.
    "Where There's Smoke." [NewEngR] (10:2) Wint 87, p. 183.
4699. ROSE, Anne Jantzin
    "The Angry Man." [Event] (16:3) Fall 87, p. 63.
4700. ROSE, Jennifer
    "At Dachau with a German Lover." [Ploughs] (13:1) 87, p. 107-108.
    "Cologne's Cathedral" (for Gary Lee and Bob Harris). [Ploughs] (13:1) 87, p. 109-110.
    "Winter, Chicago." [Ploughs] (13:1) 87, p. 111.
4701. ROSE, Wendy
    "Calling Home the Scientists." [RiverS] (24) 87, p. 63.
    "Earth Place" (for Mary Simmons). [Calyx] (10:2/3) Spr 87, p. 75.
4702. ROSE, Wilga
    "At Mackerel Beach." [Bogg] (58) 87, p. 46.
    "Ferry Passing." [Bogg] (57) 87, p. 18.
4703. ROSEN, Kenneth
    "The Hebrew Lion." [DenQ] (22:2) Fall 87, p. 74-77.
    "Whole Horse." [CreamCR] (11:2/3) 87?, p. 56-58.
4704. ROSEN, Michael J.
    "The Burning House." [BostonR] (12:4) Ag 87, p. 4.
    "Catching Himself Aware." [SouthwR] (72:1) Wint 87, p. 73-74.
    "His Acceptance Speech." [GrandS] (6:3) Spr 87, p. 201-202.
    "The Inheritance." [Shen] (37:4) 87, p. 74-75.
4705. ROSENBAUM, Sylvia
    "Miracle." [Wind] (17:61) 87, p. 34.
4706. ROSENBERG, Liz
    "After the Death of a Neighbor's Child." [NewYorker] (62:50) 2 F 87, p. 69.
    "Between Men and Women." [Poetry] (150:2) My 87, p. 100.
    "Fathers and Sons." [Poetry] (150:2) My 87, p. 99.
    "In the Country of Dreamers." [NewYorker] (63:2) 2 Mr 87, p. 32.
    "A Little Poverty." [SouthernPR] (27:1) Spr 87, p. 57.
    "Lovesick." [Nat] (245:9) 26 S 87, p. 318.
    "My Husband Takes Some Photographs of Me." [Poetry] (150:2) My 87, p. 98.
    "The Seed." [TarRP] (26:2) Spr 87, p. 29.
    "Van Gogh's Potato Eaters." [TarRP] (26:2) Spr 87, p. 29.
    "Where Were You?" [Poetry] (150:2) My 87, p. 97.
4707. ROSENBERGER, F. C.
    "At Seventy." [LightY] '87, c86, p. 237.
    "A Slender Book of Verse and Its Purchaser." [LightY] '87, c86, p. 203.

4708. ROSENBLATT, Sarah
"Past Closing Time." [Ploughs] (13:4) 87, p. 106.
"Should I Stay or Should I Go?" [Ploughs] (13:4) 87, p. 105.
4709. ROSENFELD, Natania
"My Father Walking." [GrahamHR] (10) Wint-Spr 87, p. 42.
4710. ROSENQUIST, Karl
"Black and White Dream." [Ploughs] (13:4) 87, p. 107-108.
4711. ROSENTHAL, Bob
"The Applause" (tr. of Tillye Boesche-Zacharow, w. Laszlo Baransky, Istvan Eorsi
and Anna Saghy). [Rampike] (5:3) 87, p. 70.
"Beer: For Leising" (tr. of Karl Mickel, w. Laszlo Baransky, Istvan Eorsi and Anna
Saghy). [Rampike] (5:3) 87, p. 66.
"A Career" (tr. of Istvan Eorsi, w. Laszlo Baransky and Anna Saghy). [Rampike]
(5:3) 87, p. 69.
"Change of Location" (tr. of Uwe Kolbe, w. Laszlo Baransky, Istvan Eorsi and
Anna Saghy). [Rampike] (5:3) 87, p. 66.
"German Woman '46" (tr. of Karl Mickel, w. Laszlo Baransky, Istvan Eorsi and
Anna Saghy). [Rampike] (5:3) 87, p. 66.
"Metamorphosis" (tr. of Uwe Kolbe, w. Laszlo Baransky, Istvan Eorsi and Anna
Saghy). [Rampike] (5:3) 87, p. 67.
"The Modern Quarter" (tr. of Karl Mickel, w. Laszlo Baransky, Istvan Eorsi and
Anna Saghy). [Rampike] (5:3) 87, p. 67.
"The Myth of the Cave" (tr. of Volker Braun, w. Laszlo Baransky, Istvan Eorsi and
Anna Saghy). [Rampike] (5:3) 87, p. 69.
"Orderly Hair" (tr. of Karl Mickel, w. Laszlo Baransky, Istvan Eorsi and Anna
Saghy). [Rampike] (5:3) 87, p. 67.
"Zeno Black" (tr. of Noah Zacharin, w. Laszlo Baransky, Istvan Eorsi and Anna
Saghy). [Rampike] (5:3) 87, p. 70.
4712. ROSENTHAL, M. L.
"At the Last." [Poetry] (151:1/2) O-N 87, p. 140-141.
"Four Sonnets" (tr. of J. V. Foix). [AmerPoR] (16:1) Ja-F 87, p. 42.
"Notes Toward an Unauthorized Autobiography." [Pequod] (23/24) 87, p. 102-104.
4713. ROSENZWEIG, Geri (Gerry)
"Raking a Field" (watercolor by Carl Larsson, 1905). [PoetL] (81:3) Fall 86, p. 160.
"Three Rabbis." [GreensboroR] (43) Wint 87-88, p. 88-89.
4714. ROSIER, R. Peter
"Blindness." [ArizQ] (43:1) Spr 87, p. 78.
4715. ROSNAY, Jean-Pierre
"Le Cheval dans la Mer" (A Michel Monier-Vinard). [StoneC] (15:1/2) Fall-Wint
87-88, p. 56.
"The Horse in the Sea" (tr. by J. Kates). [StoneC] (15:1/2) Fall-Wint 87-88, p. 57.
4716. ROSS, Bob
"The Torpedo Angel." [KanQ] (19:3) Sum 87, p. 249-250.
4717. ROSS, Kathleen
"The Hopeful Voice" (tr. of Nicolás Guillén). [Callaloo] (10:2) Spr 87, p. 195-201.
"Second Agony" (tr. of Nicolás Guillén). [Callaloo] (10:2) Spr 87, p. 193.
4718. ROSSELLI, Amelia
"You would not take responsibility." [Verse] (4:2) Je 87, p. 59.
4719. ROSSER, J. Allyn
"Cold Food." [KanQ] (19:1/2) Wint-Spr 87, p. 254.
"The Dropping of a Name." [Poetry] (150:2) My 87, p. 84-85.
"Equitable Distribution." [NegC] (7:1/2) 87, p. 72.
"How You Know." [KanQ] (19:1/2) Wint-Spr 87, p. 253.
"In the (Subjunctive) Mood." [Poetry] (150:2) My 87, p. 83-84.
"Last Inning." [PraS] (61:2) Sum 87, p. 86-87.
"Letter to the Cracker Company." [GeoR] (41:3) Fall 87, p. 572.
"Premeditation." [NegC] (7:1/2) 87, p. 71.
ROSSI, Cristina Peri
See PERI ROSSI, Cristina
4720. ROSSINI, Clare
"After Your Death." [PoetryNW] (28:4) Wint 87-88, p. 18-19.
"For a Friend Since Youth." [PoetryNW] (28:4) Wint 87-88, p. 17-18.
"'Life Before Birth,' A display" (The Chicago Museum of Science and Industry,
1963). [KenR] (NS 9:2) Spr 87, p. 96.
"A Mourning Dove in New York City." [KenR] (NS 9:2) Spr 87, p. 97.

"Portrait: Woman, Aged Thirty, Posed on Flowered Couch." [KenR] (NS 9:2) Spr 87, p. 98.
"Sleepwalker." [Boulevard] (2:1/2) Spr 87, p. 204.
ROSTOVSKY, Sergei Lobanov
    See LOBANOV-ROSTOVSKY, Sergei
4721. ROSU, Dona
    "1. I lean over the edge of the well" (in Romanian & English, tr. by Ann Woodward). [InterPR] (13:1) Spr 87, p. 66-67.
    "3. My body prepared to endure fire and water" (in Romanian & English, tr. by Ann Woodward). [InterPR] (13:1) Spr 87, p. 68-69.
    "9. I say I want to sleep the night through together" (in Romanian & English, tr. by Ann Woodward). [InterPR] (13:1) Spr 87, p. 68-69.
    "10. My god, I ask you again" (in Romanian & English, tr. by Ann Woodward). [InterPR] (13:1) Spr 87, p. 70-71.
    "17. Stars are too far, one from another" (in Romanian & English, tr. by Ann Woodward). [InterPR] (13:1) Spr 87, p. 70-71.
    "18. Do you remember how, when I was little" (in Romanian & English, tr. by Ann Woodward). [InterPR] (13:1) Spr 87, p. 72-73.
4722. ROTELLA, Alexis
    "Haiku: Flagstone steps." [LightY] '87, c86, p. 123.
4723. ROTELLA, Guy
    "Christmas Eve." [HawaiiR] (21) Spr 87, p. 31.
4724. ROTHENBERG, Jerome
    "First Gematria." [Sulfur] (18) Wint 87, p. 186-188.
    "The Visitation." [RiverS] (24) 87, p. 19.
4725. ROTHMAN, David
    "The Apotheosis of the Saxophonist." [PennR] (3:2) Fall-Wint 87, p. 72.
4726. ROTHMAN, Susan Noe
    "Eddie Clings to the Good Life." [SlipS] (7) 87, p. 36.
ROUS, Peter de
    See De ROUS, Peter
4727. ROWE, Kelly
    "Demon Lover." [PoetryNW] (28:3) Aut 87, p. 32-33.
    "Looking Back." [VirQR] (63:4) Aut 87, p. 638-639.
    "The Shed." [VirQR] (63:4) Aut 87, p. 639-640.
4728. ROY, Lucinda
    "After His Funeral, She Rocks All Afternoon." [GreensboroR] (39) Wint 85-86, p. 68-69.
4729. ROYET-JOURNOUD, Claude
    "I See a Spot Coming Closer and Closer to Where I'm Waiting for It" (tr. by Keith Waldrop). [LitR] (30:3) Spr 87, p. 371-380.
4730. ROZ, Víctor
    "Amor, con Amor Se Paga." [Mairena] (9:24) 87, p. 117.
4731. RUARK, Gibbons
    "North Towards Armagh." [AntR] (45:1) Wint 87, p. 57.
    "Transatlantic Summer Elegy." [AntR] (45:1) Wint 87, p. 58.
    "Wildflower Lullaby." [PoetC] (18:3) Spr 87, p. 22.
    "Words to Accompany a Small Glass Swan." [Salm] (73) Wint 87, p. 144-145.
4732. RUBERG, Merle
    "Supreme Love" (on Danielle Collobert, from *Anawratha*, tr. of Anne-Marie Albiach). [Act] (7) 87, p. 19.
4733. RUBIN, Larry
    "The Bachelor, Giving an Accounting." [ChatR] (8:1) Fall 87, p. 97.
    "An Encounter with the Campus Police." [KanQ] (19:1/2) Wint-Spr 87, p. 84.
    "The Insomniac." [CrossCur] (6:4) 87, p. 102.
    "Lessons of the Sea: Embarkation." [HolCrit] (24:2) Ap 87, p. 19.
    "The Midnight Visitor." [SouthernHR] (21:4) Fall 87, p. 362.
    "On Reaching Fifty." [KanQ] (19:1/2) Wint-Spr 87, p. 84.
4734. RUBIN, Louis D., Jr.
    "Salzburg Variations." [SewanR] (95:2) Spr 87, p. 179-181.
4735. RUBIN, Mark
    "The Arrangement." [Crazy] (33) Wint 87, p. 37-38.
    "Heroes." [Crazy] (33) Wint 87, p. 39-40.
    "Lament of Saint Nicholas." [Crazy] (33) Wint 87, p. 43.
    "On the New York Side of the Hudson." [Crazy] (33) Wint 87, p. 41-42.
    "Sylvia." [KanQ] (19:3) Sum 87, p. 293.

"The Wife." [Boulevard] (2:3) Fall 87, p. 103-104.
4736. RUCKER, Trish
"Movements of the Jupiter Symphony." [HampSPR] Wint 87, p. 48-49.
4737. RUCKS, Carol
"A Change of Address." [Abraxas] (35/36) 87, p. 30.
"East Franklin Avenue." [Abraxas] (35/36) 87, p. 30.
4738. RUDMAN, Mark
"The Bus to the Ruins" (Denver Quarterly Poetry Competition Winner, First Prize).
    [DenQ] (22:2) Fall 87, p. 6-7.
"Casket Closed." [Boulevard] (2:3) Fall 87, p. 128-133.
"Courbet." [DenQ] (21:3) Wint 87, p. 45-51.
"Eventual Claims." [PartR] (54:3) Sum 87, p. 428-429.
"Further Escapes of the Poet at 9." [Pequod] (23/24) 87, p. 207-208.
"My Quarrel with Thoreau." [YaleR] (76:3) Spr 87, p. 354-356.
"The Nowhere Steps: Uxmal, Sayil, Chichen-Itza." [Margin] (4) Aut 87, p. 19-24.
"Winter Solstice." [SouthwR] (72:1) Wint 87, p. 94-95.
4739. RUDOLPH, Lee
"Cockeast Pond: A Change of State." [TexasR] (7:3/4) 87, p. 127-128.
4740. RUDY, D. L.
"Regret." [Wind] (17:61) 87, p. 41.
"Rejection: A Portrait." [Footwork] 87, p. 60.
RUE, Dorie La
    See LaRUE, Dorie
4741. RUEFLE, Mary
"Gulley Farm." [Ploughs] (13:1) 87, p. 116.
"In the Bitter Country." [Ploughs] (13:1) 87, p. 113.
"Lo and Behold." [Ploughs] (13:1) 87, p. 112.
"Love Lies Bleeding." [Ploughs] (13:1) 87, p. 114.
"Success." [Ploughs] (13:1) 87, p. 115.
"Swamp Maples." [ThRiPo] (29/30) 87, p. 57.
"Unaccompanied Brain." [ThRiPo] (29/30) 87, p. 56.
4742. RUESCHER, Scott
"Doug." [Agni] (24/25) 87, p. 56-57.
"Massasoit the Wampanoag." [NewEngR] (10:2) Wint 87, p. 228.
4743. RUFFIN, Paul
"The Ball." [LakeSR] (21) 87, p. 4.
"Circling." [ColR] (NS 14:1) Spr-Sum 87, p. 15-16.
"The Day Hank Williams Died." [StoneC] (14:3/4) Spr-Sum 87, p. 50.
"Dog on a Trotline." [SouthernHR] (21:4) Fall 87, p. 357.
"Pitch-pine." [SouthernR] (23:2) Ap 87, p. 377.
"The Undertaker's Twenty Years." [StoneC] (14:3/4) Spr-Sum 87, p. 51.
4744. RUGAMA, Leonel
"The Earth Is a Satellite of the Moon." [Contact] (9:44/45/46) Fall-Wint 87, p. 21.
RUGERIS, C. K. de
    See DeRUGERIS, C. K.
4745. RUGGIERI, Helen
"Candlemas Dawn Question: Is There Poetry Past Forty?" [Phoenix] (7:1) 87, p. 22.
"Learning to Read." [Outbr] (18/19) Fall 86-Spr 88, p. 8-9.
4746. RUGO, Mariève
"All Over England, Flowers Ignite: 1940-1945." [NoDaQ] (55:1) Wint 87, p.
    151-153.
"Choices." [NoDaQ] (55:1) Wint 87, p. 153.
"The Dog." [Nimrod] (30:2) Spr-Sum 87, p. 134.
"A Geography of My Father." [NoDaQ] (55:1) Wint 87, p. 154.
"Romanian Folk Tale." [Nimrod] (30:2) Spr-Sum 87, p. 133-134.
RUIZ, José O. Colón
    See COLON RUIZ, José O.
RUMI, Ibn al-
    See Al-RUMI, Ibn
4747. RUMMEL, Mary Kay
"Of Clover." [Abraxas] (35/36) 87, p. 29.
"Omen." [Germ] (11:1) Fall 87, p. 23.
4748. RUNGREN, Lawrence
"Committee Meeting." [PoetL] (81:3) Fall 86, p. 156.

4749. RUNOWICZ, Victor T.
  "Abracadabra." [KanQ] (19:3) Sum 87, p. 291.
  "Life, Come Upon Suddenly." [Poem] (58) N 87, p. 8.
  "Love on Public Television." [Poem] (58) N 87, p. 7.
4750. RUSCALLEDA BERCEDONIZ, Jorge María
  "Hablando con Cesar Vallejo." [Mairena] (9:24) 87, p. 52-53.
4751. RUSS, Biff
  "Healing a Dead Grandfather." [PassN] (8:1) Wint 87, p. 11.
4752. RUSS, Lisa
  "The Adulterous Man Runs." [GreenfR] (14:3/4) Sum-Fall 87, p. 116.
  "Blessings, They Find You." [GreenfR] (14:3/4) Sum-Fall 87, p. 117-118.
4753. RUSSELL, CarolAnn
  "New Haven" (for Ken Florey). [HawaiiR] (21) Spr 87, p. 58.
RUSSELL, Gillian Harding
  See HARDING-RUSSELL, Gillian
4754. RUSSELL, Hilary
  "The Day Willis Harder Didn't Kill His Beagle." [LightY] '87, c86, p. 110.
  "Earlene Spratt's Lot." [LightY] '87, c86, p. 259-260.
4755. RUSSELL, Jonathan
  "Tea-Leaves in the Sky." [NegC] (7:3/4) 87, p. 98.
4756. RUSSELL, Norman (Norman H.)
  "The Bobcat Bounced." [GreenfR] (14:1/2) Wint-Spr, p. 40.
  "The Earth Is a Closed Mouth of Sounds." [GreenfR] (14:1/2) Wint-Spr, p. 38.
  "Fir Forest." [PraS] (61:4) Wint 87, p. 109-110.
  "Gaia." [PraS] (61:4) Wint 87, p. 110-111.
  "God's Revenge." [WestCR] (21:3) Wint 87, p. 8.
  "In the Morning." [WestCR] (21:3) Wint 87, p. 7.
  "In This Desert." [PraS] (61:4) Wint 87, p. 111.
  "Man and Woman." [WestCR] (21:3) Wint 87, p. 10.
  "The Mountain." [CharR] (13:1) Spr 87, p. 87.
  "My Names." [PraS] (61:4) Wint 87, p. 109.
  "My Strength." [SmPd] (24:2) Spr 87, p. 19.
  "Oak Limbs Dancing." [SmPd] (24:1) Wint 87, p. 29.
  "The Only Enemy." [PraS] (61:4) Wint 87, p. 112-113.
  "Only One Son or Daughter." [SmPd] (24:2) Spr 87, p. 18.
  "Speaking in the Dust." [WormR] (27:4, issue 108) 87, p. 105.
  "The Speaking of a Snail." [GreenfR] (14:1/2) Wint-Spr, p. 39.
  "Spider." [PraS] (61:4) Wint 87, p. 112.
  "The Squirrel and the Panther." [StoneC] (15:1/2) Fall-Wint 87-88, p. 71.
  "Surveillance." [SmPd] (24:2) Spr 87, p. 20.
  "To Thank the Wolves." [WestCR] (21:3) Wint 87, p. 9.
  "The Tree Is Like a Blanket." [WormR] (27:4, issue 108) 87, p. 105.
4757. RUSSELL, Thomas
  "Lavonder." [NowestR] (25:3) 87, p. 315.
  "A Poem on My Son's Birthday." [PoetryNW] (28:4) Wint 87-88, p. 3-4.
4758. RUSSELL, Timothy
  "In Adversum." [GreenfR] (14:3/4) Sum-Fall 87, p. 53.
  "In Alio Loco." [WestB] (20) 87, p. 6-7.
  "In Consideratione Praemissorum." [LaurelR] (20:1/2) Sum 87, p. 39.
  "In Dubio." [WestB] (20) 87, p. 8.
  "In Duplo." [GreenfR] (14:3/4) Sum-Fall 87, p. 53-54.
  "In Embryo." [WestB] (20) 87, p. 5-6.
  "In Excambio." [GreenfR] (14:3/4) Sum-Fall 87, p. 54.
  "In Exitu." [WestB] (20) 87, p. 10.
  "In Folio" (for S.H.). [LaurelR] (20:1/2) Sum 87, p. 38.
  "In His Verbis." [GreenfR] (14:3/4) Sum-Fall 87, p. 55.
  "In Rem Versum." [WestB] (20) 87, p. 9.
4759. RUSSELL, Tom
  "The Life Before Us." [SouthernPR] (27:1) Spr 87, p. 41-42.
4760. RUSSO, Albert
  "Cormorant of Yangshuo." [Amelia] (4:3, issue 10) 87, p. 27.
  "Emergency Call" (1986 Finalist, Eve of Saint Agnes Poetry Competition). [NegC]
    (7:1/2) 87, p. 171.
4761. RUTHER, Barbara
  "Disloyal Lover." [ArizQ] (43:3) Aut 87, p. 263.

4762. RUTHERFORD, Bonnie
"Ballard 1909." [BellArk] (3:2) Mr-Ap 87, p. 3.
"Henry." [BellArk] (3:6) N-D 87, p. 6.
4763. RUTSALA, Vern
"Father Fear." [KenR] (NS 9:1) Wint 87, p. 61-62.
"Field Burning." [Crazy] (32) Spr 87, p. 11-13.
"Raisins." [KenR] (NS 9:1) Wint 87, p. 60-61.
"Talking to Strangers." [Hudson] (40:1) Spr 87, p. 85-86.
"Traffic Watch." [Atlantic] (259:2) F 87, p. 66.
4764. RUVINSKY, Joan
"Let's get out the gun." [Quarry] (36:3) Sum 87, p. 25.
"The question of simple." [Quarry] (36:3) Sum 87, p. 26-27.
4765. RYAN, Gregory A.
"The Oasis Well." [MidwQ] (28:2) Wint 87, p. 226-227.
4766. RYAN, Kay
"The Absolutes." [NewRena] (7:1, #21) Fall 87, p. 133.
"Caryatid." [Comm] (114:19) 6 N 87, p. 618.
"A Certain Meanness of Culture." [KenR] (NS 9:3) Sum 87, p. 52-53.
"Come Dark Ship." [AmerPoR] (16:5) S-O 87, p. 46.
"Duchamp." [SoCaR] (20:1) Fall 87, p. 35.
"Every Painting by Chagall." [AmerPoR] (16:5) S-O 87, p. 46.
"Les Natures Profundement Bonnes Sont Toujours Indecises." [AmerS] (56:4) Aut
87, p. 548.
"New Instruments." [Thrpny] (31) Fall 87, p. 9.
"Seed." [NewRena] (7:1, #21) Fall 87, p. 134.
"Squirrel." [Pembroke] (19) 87, p. 190.
"The Tables Freed." [KenR] (NS 9:3) Sum 87, p. 53.
"Yellow." [ParisR] (29:103) Sum 87, p. 179.
4767. RYAN, Martin
"Transactions." [AmerS] (56:4) Aut 87, p. 470.
4768. RYAN, Michael
"Crossroads Inn." [Nat] (245:21) 19 D 87, p. 766.
4769. RYDER, Phyllis
"At the Elwell Chapel." [AntR] (45:3) Sum 87, p. 330.
4770. RYDER, Salmon
"Cold August Blues." [US1] (20/21) Wint 86-87, p. 40.
"Safe Sex." [US1] (20/21) Wint 86-87, p. 41.
4771. RYEGATE, Lucy
"Picnic — Acadia." [Poem] (57) Mr 87, p. 21.
"Showers, Torrents, Waterworks." [Poem] (57) Mr 87, p. 20.
"We See Less Distinctly at Night But We See Farther." [Poem] (57) Mr 87, p. 22.
4772. SAARIKOSKI, Pentti
"Revolution" (tr. by Anselm Hollo). [Spirit] (8:2) 87, p. 28-29.
4773. SABA, Umberto
"After a Walk" (tr. by Christopher Millis). [SenR] (17:2) 87, p. 7.
"Cinders" (tr. by Michael L. Johnson). [HayF] (2) Spr 87, p. 35.
"Happiness" (tr. by Christopher Millis). [Paint] (14:28) Aut 87, p. 34.
"In the Courtyard" (tr. by Christopher Millis). [Paint] (14:28) Aut 87, p. 35.
"Letter to a Friend Studying Piano at the Conservatory of" (tr. by Christopher
Millis). [SenR] (17:2) 87, p. 11-13.
"To My Wife" (tr. by Christopher Millis). [SenR] (17:2) 87, p. 8-10.
4774. SABATIER, Robert
"Spectacles" (tr. by Eric Sellin). [CrossCur] (7:3) 87, p. 154.
4775. SACKS, Peter
"Arkansas." [Boulevard] (2:3) Fall 87, p. 161-163.
"Autumn." [YaleR] (76:4) Sum 87, p. 514-518.
"Confederate Graveyard: Franklin, Tennessee." [Boulevard] (2:3) Fall 87, p.
164-165.
"For Tim Sutcliffe (1914-1986), Headmaster, Clifton Preparatory School, Durban."
[TriQ] (69) Spr-Sum 87, p. 442-446.
"Medanales" (for Barbara). [Boulevard] (2:3) Fall 87, p. 166-167.
"Virginia." [Boulevard] (2:3) Fall 87, p. 163-164.
4776. SACUTA, Norm
"Summer Windigo." [AntigR] (71/72) Aut 87-Wint 88, p. 56.
4777. SADOFF, Ira
"In the House of the Child." [TexasR] (7:3/4) 87, p. 129.

"Zinfandel." [TexasR] (7:3/4) 87, p. 130-131.
4778. SAEKI, Michiko
"A Tattoo" (The Greensboro Review Literary Award, Honorable Mention).
[GreensboroR] (41) Wint 86-87, p. 31-32.
"Wind." [GreensboroR] (43) Wint 87-88, p. 90.
4779. SAFFORD, June Billings
"The Accordion Player." [Outbr] (18/19) Fall 86-Spr 88, p. 171.
"The Playground at Lindley Park." [Outbr] (18/19) Fall 86-Spr 88, p. 170.
4780. SAGAN, Miriam
"All Hallows." [Ploughs] (13:1) 87, p. 119-121.
"Day. Book." [PaintedB] (31) 87, p. 14.
"Epithalamion." [Footwork] 87, p. 30.
"Full Moon: Ceremony." [Ploughs] (13:1) 87, p. 117-118.
4781. SAGARIS, Lake
"Wind." [Dandel] (14:2) Fall-Wint 87, p. 25.
4782. SAGHY, Anna
"The Applause" (tr. of Tillye Boesche-Zacharow, w. Laszlo Baransky, Istvan Eorsi
and Bob Rosenthal). [Rampike] (5:3) 87, p. 70.
"Beer: For Leising" (tr. of Karl Mickel, w. Laszlo Baransky, Istvan Eorsi and Bob
Rosenthal). [Rampike] (5:3) 87, p. 66.
"A Career" (tr. of Istvan Eorsi, w. Laszlo Baransky and Bob Rosenthal). [Rampike]
(5:3) 87, p. 69.
"Change of Location" (tr. of Uwe Kolbe, w. Laszlo Baransky, Istvan Eorsi and Bob
Rosenthal). [Rampike] (5:3) 87, p. 66.
"German Woman '46" (tr. of Karl Mickel, w. Laszlo Baransky, Istvan Eorsi and
Bob Rosenthal). [Rampike] (5:3) 87, p. 66.
"Metamorphosis" (tr. of Uwe Kolbe, w. Laszlo Baransky, Istvan Eorsi and Bob
Rosenthal). [Rampike] (5:3) 87, p. 67.
"The Modern Quarter" (tr. of Karl Mickel, w. Laszlo Baransky, Istvan Eorsi and
Bob Rosenthal). [Rampike] (5:3) 87, p. 67.
"The Myth of the Cave" (tr. of Volker Braun, w. Laszlo Baransky, Istvan Eorsi and
Bob Rosenthal). [Rampike] (5:3) 87, p. 69.
"Orderly Hair" (tr. of Karl Mickel, w. Laszlo Baransky, Istvan Eorsi and Bob
Rosenthal). [Rampike] (5:3) 87, p. 67.
"Zeno Black" (tr. of Noah Zacharin, w. Laszlo Baransky, Istvan Eorsi and Bob
Rosenthal). [Rampike] (5:3) 87, p. 70.
4783. SAHAGUN, Carlos
"Sun in the Plaza" (tr. by Michael L. Johnson). [WebR] (12:1) Spr 87, p. 79-80.
"Vision in Almería" (tr. by Michael L. Johnson). [WebR] (12:1) Spr 87, p. 78-79.
4784. SAHIAN, Hamo
"Since the Years of Our Love" (tr. by Diana Der Hovanessian). [InterPR] (13:1) Spr
87, p. 75.
4785. SAID, Amina
"The Earth Beats" (tr. by Eric Sellin). [LitR] (30:3) Spr 87, p. 399.
4786. SAINT, Assotto
"Heaven in Hell" (for Counsel Wright, 1933-1983). [JamesWR] (5:1) Fall 87, p.
10.
4787. SAINT, Bernard
"The Cricket Sings." [Interim] (6:1) Spr 87, p. 15.
"Forge Fields." [Interim] (6:1) Spr 87, p. 16.
"Touch." [Interim] (6:1) Spr 87, p. 17.
4788. SAINT-PIERRE, Yves
"Her death mask makeup." [Waves] (15:1/2) Fall 86, p. 34.
4789. SALA, Jerome
"Abstract Barbie Doll Painting." [Ploughs] (13:4) 87, p. 110.
"At the Slave Camp." [NewAW] (1) 87, p. 102.
"Explorer." [Ploughs] (13:4) 87, p. 111.
"The Great." [NewAW] (1) 87, p. 101.
"He Forgot to Remember to Forget." [Ploughs] (13:4) 87, p. 109.
4790. SALADO, Minerva
"Encounter with El Morro of Havana" (tr. by Mariana Romo-Carmona). [Cond] (14)
87, p. 213.
"Encuentro con el Morro de la Habana." [Cond] (14) 87, p. 212.
"Escaramuza." [Cond] (14) 87, p. 210.
"Palabra en el Espejo." [Cond] (14) 87, p. 208.
"Skirmish" (tr. by Mariana Romo-Carmona). [Cond] (14) 87, p. 211.

"Word in the Mirror" (tr. by Mariana Romo-Carmona). [Cond] (14) 87, p. 209.
4791. SALAMONE, Karen
"Blue Gift in Winter." [BellArk] (3:4) Jl-Ag 87, p. 4.
"Construction." [BellArk] (3:5) S-O 87, p. 19.
"Gossamer Strangers." [BellArk] (3:3) My-Je 87, p. 5.
"Illusion of the Moment." [BellArk] (3:2) Mr-Ap 87, p. 1.
"Melting Gracefully into Grass." [BellArk] (3:3) My-Je 87, p. 5.
"Stories Beginning." [BellArk] (3:5) S-O 87, p. 1.
4792. SALAMUN, Tomaz
"I. Are you asleep, a sunflower, black seed, gold" (tr. by the author and Michael
Waltuch). [WillowS] (20) Spr 87, p. 81.
"II. Shouts are words, silent sleep" (tr. by the author and Michael Waltuch).
[WillowS] (20) Spr 87, p. 82.
"III. Don't be afraid of images of the world" (tr. by the author and Michael Waltuch).
[WillowS] (20) Spr 87, p. 83.
"IV. Reflect, children, slide silently" (tr. by the author and Michael Waltuch).
[WillowS] (20) Spr 87, p. 84.
"The Blue Vault" (tr. by Michael Biggins). [Ploughs] (13:4) 87, p. 112.
"The Boat" (tr. by Michael Biggins). [WillowS] (20) Spr 87, p. 80.
"The Cross" (tr. by Michael Biggins). [WillowS] (20) Spr 87, p. 78-79.
"Dead Men" (tr. by Michael Biggins). [MissR] (15:3, issue 45) Spr-Sum 87, p.
28-30.
"Folk Song" (tr. by Charles Simic). [Antaeus] (58) Spr 87, p. 33.
"Help Me!" (tr. by Michael Biggins). [MissR] (15:3, issue 45) Spr-Sum 87, p. 27.
"Light for Hamdija Demiroviç" (tr. by Charles Simic). [Antaeus] (58) Spr 87, p. 38.
"Lips" (tr. by Michael Biggins). [ParisR] (29:105) Wint 87, p. 149.
"Man with the Golden Eye" (tr. by Charles Simic). [Antaeus] (58) Spr 87, p. 35.
"Maria" (tr. by Charles Simic). [Antaeus] (58) Spr 87, p. 39-43.
"Nikola Tesla" (tr. by Charles Simic). [Antaeus] (58) Spr 87, p. 34.
"Pont-Neuf" (tr. by Michael Biggins). [ParisR] (29:105) Wint 87, p. 148.
"Sonnet About Milk" (tr. by Charles Simic). [Antaeus] (58) Spr 87, p. 37.
"Trout" (tr. by Charles Simic). [Antaeus] (58) Spr 87, p. 36.
4793. SALAS, Horacio
"The Aging" (tr. by Norman Thomas di Giovanni). [Trans] (18) Spr 87, p. 47.
"The Children" (tr. by Norman Thomas di Giovanni). [Trans] (18) Spr 87, p. 46.
"The Sick" (tr. by Norman Thomas di Giovanni). [Trans] (18) Spr 87, p. 45.
4794. SALEMI, Joseph (Joseph S.)
"Epigrams" (8 poems, tr. of Martial). [Trans] (18) Spr 87, p. 300-303.
"Horace I.5, I.16, III.20" (tr. of Horace). [CumbPR] (7:1) Fall 87, p. 30-35.
"Miss Crespo's Halloween." [Poem] (58) N 87, p. 48.
"Tibullus I.2" (Excerpts, tr. of Tibullus). [CumbPR] (7:1) Fall 87, p. 26-29.
4795. SALERNO, Joe
"Dark." [Abraxas] (35/36) 87, p. 55-56.
"Near Midnight." [Abraxas] (35/36) 87, p. 54.
4796. SALES, Miguel
"Carcelero." [LindLM] (6:1) Ja-Mr 87, p. 22.
"Monje." [LindLM] (6:1) Ja-Mr 87, p. 22.
"Pintor." [LindLM] (6:1) Ja-Mr 87, p. 22.
"Preso." [LindLM] (6:1) Ja-Mr 87, p. 22.
"Tejedor." [LindLM] (6:1) Ja-Mr 87, p. 22.
4797. SALINAS, Luis Omar
"Middle Age." [Americas] (14:3/4) Fall-Wint 86, p. 83.
"Nights in Fresno." [Americas] (14:3/4) Fall-Wint 86, p. 80.
"Sea Song." [Americas] (14:3/4) Fall-Wint 86, p. 81.
"What Is My Name?" [Americas] (14:3/4) Fall-Wint 86, p. 79.
"When the Evening Is Quiet." [Americas] (14:3/4) Fall-Wint 86, p. 82.
4798. SALISBURY, Ralph
"As Sure As." [HawaiiR] (22) Fall 87, p. 71.
"For Mary Turner Salisbury." [GreenfR] (14:1/2) Wint-Spr, p. 51.
"Salt Petals." [GreenfR] (14:1/2) Wint-Spr, p. 52-53.
"To Someone in Line." [NowestR] (25:3) 87, p. 194.
4799. SALKEY, Andrew
"An Exemplary Exile." [MassR] (28:4) Wint 87, p. 655.
"A House of Exile." [MassR] (28:4) Wint 87, p. 656.
"My Land of Look Behind" (For Roberta Uno Thelwell and Michael Thelwell).
[Chelsea] (46) 87, p. 306.

"Yesterday and Today." [MassR] (28:4) Wint 87, p. 655-656.
4800. SALLAH, Tijan M.
"An Africa." [Callaloo] (10:3) Sum 87, p. 553.
"The Elders Are Gods." [Callaloo] (10:3) Sum 87, p. 551-552.
"Other-Room People." [Callaloo] (10:3) Sum 87, p. 554-555.
4801. SALLEE, Hyn-jae Yee
"My Home" (tr. of Jong-sahm Kim). [HampSPR] Wint 86, p. 30.
"Pearl" (tr. of Won-sup Lee). [HampSPR] Wint 86, p. 31.
4802. SALLEE, Marjorie L.
"Pterodactyls." [EngJ] (76:5) S 87, p. 110.
4803. SALLIS, James
"Altitude." [CharR] (13:2) Fall 87, p. 73-74.
"What We're Born With." [CharR] (13:2) Fall 87, p. 75.
4804. SALTER, Mary Jo
"Aubade for Brad." [SouthwR] (72:4) Aut 87, p. 476-477.
"Emily Wants to Play." [SouthwR] (72:4) Aut 87, p. 475-476.
"Late Spring" (Li Shih-Cho, ca. 1690-1770). [GrandS] (6:4) Sum 87, p. 53-55.
"The Moon and Big Ben." [YaleR] (77:1) Aut 87, p. 79.
"Puzzle Piece." [GrandS] (7:1) Aut 87, p. 114.
4805. SALTMAN, Benjamin
"At 59." [CrossCur] (7:1) 87, p. 127.
4806. SALZMANO, Eva
"Parallel." [MSS] (5:3) 87, p. 184.
SAM-MUN, Song
   See SONG, Sam-mun
4807. SAMMONS, Toni
"Mirror Lake, Yosemite Valley." [InterPR] (13:1) Spr 87, p. 91.
"Nadja Poem." [InterPR] (13:1) Spr 87, p. 92.
"San Luis Obispo." [InterPR] (13:1) Spr 87, p. 90.
"Spring Visual." [InterPR] (13:1) Spr 87, p. 89.
"Untwisting the Visual Purple." [InterPR] (13:1) Spr 87, p. 88-89.
"Waiting for Seals." [MalR] (81) D 87, p. 47-48.
"Wandering through Houses." [MalR] (81) D 87, p. 49-50.
4808. SAMPSON, Dennis
"The Justification." [Crazy] (33) Wint 87, p. 29-30.
"The Vigil." [Crazy] (33) Wint 87, p. 26-28.
4809. SANCHEZ, Ricardo
"En Lo In." [Americas] (15:2) Sum 87, p. 62-66.
"Sentiments Hacia Belén." [Americas] (15:2) Sum 87, p. 45-61.
4810. SANCHEZ, Sonia
"An Anthem" (for the ANC and the Brandywine Peace Community). [Footwork] 87, p. 9-10.
4811. SANDEEN, Ernest
"A Late Twentieth-Century Prayer." [Poetry] (151:1/2) O-N 87, p. 143.
4812. SANDELIN, Peter
"Artist Drawing" (tr. by George Johnston). [MalR] (78) Mr 87, p. 105.
"Do you think I repeat myself?" (tr. by George Johnston). [MalR] (78) Mr 87, p. 104.
"It was just such a day" (tr. by George Johnston). [MalR] (78) Mr 87, p. 104.
"You do not see them" (tr. by George Johnston). [MalR] (78) Mr 87, p. 104.
4813. SANDERS, Bonnie Barry
"Up from the River" (1986 Finalist, Eve of Saint Agnes Poetry Competition). [NegC] (7:1/2) 87, p. 185-187.
4814. SANDERS, David
"Ice." [KanQ] (19:4) Fall 87, p. 60.
4815. SANDERS, Mark
"Flying at Night." [TarPR] (27:1) Fall 87, p. 29.
"Great Plains Lit." [LightY] '87, c86, p. 224.
"No Accounts, 1948." [CharR] (13:1) Spr 87, p. 86-87.
"The Other Two" (Selection: 2. The Marriage gone wrong). [AntigR] (69/70) 87, p. 86.
"The Red-Handled Hatchet." [LightY] '87, c86, p. 204.
"The Turtle." [LightY] '87, c86, p. 115.
4816. SANDMEIER, Dennis D.
"A Petition to the Timekeeper." [EngJ] (76:8) D 87, p. 79.

SANDOR

4817. SANDOR, Weöres
"Abandonment" (tr. by Zsuzsanna Ozsvath and Martha Satz). [Os] (24) 87, p. 12.
"After Creation" (tr. by Zsuzsanna Ozsvath and Martha Satz). [Os] (24) 87, p. 10.
"Elhagyottság." [Os] (24) 87, p. 13.
"A Teremtés Után." [Os] (24) 87, p. 11.
SANDOVAL, Jorge Elvir
See ELVIR SANDOVAL, Jorge
4818. SANDY, Stephen
"Bingham Hill." [Poetry] (150:6) S 87, p. 326-327.
"Command Performance" (for Robert Lowell). [TexasR] (7:3/4) 87, p. 132-133.
"Letter from Stony Creek." [TexasR] (7:3/4) 87, p. 134.
"Little Auden Ode, 1970." [Salm] (73) Wint 87, p. 141-142.
"The News and the Weather." [TexasR] (7:3/4) 87, p. 135.
"Picnic with Morgan" (M.R. 1941-1980). [Salm] (73) Wint 87, p. 136-141.
"Rural Affairs." [Salm] (73) Wint 87, p. 142-143.
"The Sunday Outboard." [MichQR] (26:2) Spr 87, p. 351-352.
"Thatch." [Boulevard] (2:1/2) Spr 87, p. 105-106.
"Words for Dr. Richards." [Poetry] (151:1/2) O-N 87, p. 144-145.
4819. SANELLI, Mary Lou
"Waterfront Photo (Ketchikan, Alaska)." [CrabCR] (4:2) Spr 87, p. 20.
4820. SANER, Reg
"Desert Space." [US1] (20/21) Wint 86-87, p. 8.
"Elizabeth." [GeoR] (41:2) Sum 87, p. 362-363.
"Headwaters." [Poetry] (149:5) F 87, p. 278.
"Reaching Keet Seel." [Poetry] (149:5) F 87, p. 279.
"These Days." [SouthernPR] (27:2) Fall 87, p. 69.
4821. SANFORD, Christy Sheffield
"Our Lady of the Lavender Mist" (For Woman, Men and Reader). [SlipS] (7) 87, p. 104-105.
4822. SANGER, Peter
"Sea Bones." [AntigR] (71/72) Aut 87-Wint 88, p. 184.
SANTIAGO, José Manuel Torres
See TORRES SANTIAGO, José Manuel
SANTIAGO BACA, Jimmy
See BACA, Jimmy Santiago
SANTO, Grace di
See DiSANTO, Grace
4823. SANTOS, Sherod
"All Souls." [Poetry] (150:6) S 87, p. 341-342.
"Angelus." [QW] (24) Wint 87, p. 48-50.
"The Art of Fiction" (after Hardy). [Nat] (244:6) 14 F 87, p. 194.
"The Children of Paradise." [Nat] (244:2) 17 Ja 87, p. 58.
"The Easter Manifestations." [YaleR] (76:3) Spr 87, p. 415-416.
"Genetics." [NewEngR] (9:4) Sum 87, p. 446-447.
"Inspiration." [Poetry] (151:1/2) O-N 87, p. 146.
"Midsummer." [NewYorker] (63:26) 17 Ag 87, p. 26.
"Le Muséum d'Histoire Naturelle." [MemphisSR] (8:1) Fall 87, p. 8-9.
"Nineteen Fifty-five." [NewEngR] (9:4) Sum 87, p. 448-450.
"The Whelk." [NewYorker] (63:35) 19 O 87, p. 112.
"The Woman at the Hotel de Dream." [QW] (24) Wint 87, p. 51-52.
4824. SANZARO, Leonard
"Sue & Ariel." [Interim] (6:2) Fall 87, p. 34-35.
4825. SAPIA, Yvonne
"Aquí." [Americas] (14:3/4) Fall-Wint 86, p. 86.
"Defining the Grateful Gesture." [Americas] (14:3/4) Fall-Wint 86, p. 84-85.
"Talking to the Mirror." [Americas] (14:3/4) Fall-Wint 86, p. 87.
4826. SAPINKOPF, Lisa
"The Art of Poetry" (tr. of Yves Bonnefoy). [HampSPR] Wint 86, p. 29.
"Women by the Seashore" (tr. of Sophia de Mello Breyner Andresen). [HampSPR] Wint 86, p. 28.
4827. SARAH, Robyn
"Shell." [WestCR] (22:1) Sum 87, p. 42.
4828. SARAIVA, Arnaldo
"Journey" (tr. by Joanna Courteau). [PoetC] (18:2) Wint 87, p. 29.
"Knowledge" ("Conhecimento", tr. by Joanna Courteau). [PoetC] (18:2) Wint 87, p. 42.

"Tense & Mood" ("O Tempo e o Modo," tr. by Joanna Courteau). [PoetC] (18:2)
    Wint 87, p. 41.
"University" ("Universidade," tr. by Joanna Courteau). [PoetC] (18:2) Wint 87, p.
    40.
4829. SARAVIA, Juan Ramón
    "Poema para el Cual Jamas Podre Encontrar un Titulo." [Mairena] (9:24) 87, p. 111.
4830. SARCO, Charmagne
    "Moon." [PoetryNW] (28:4) Wint 87-88, p. 23.
    "Weeds." [PoetryNW] (28:4) Wint 87-88, p. 22-23.
4831. SARENCO
    "Poetical Licence." [Caliban] (2) 87, p. 68.
4832. SARGEANT, Lowell E.
    "Self Employment." [LightY] '87, c86, p. 22-23.
4833. SARGENT, Robert
    "Bones." [HampSPR] Wint 87, p. 20.
    "The Etruscan Sculpture." [HampSPR] Wint 87, p. 20.
    "The Goat." [HolCrit] (24:1) F 87, p. 20.
    "The Historians." [LaurelR] (21:1/2) Wint-Sum 87, p. 30.
    "Hull and the Bard." [BallSUF] (28:4) Aut 87, p. 30.
    "The Humming of Tunes." [NegC] (7:3/4) 87, p. 117.
4834. SARTON, May
    "As Does New Hampshire." [TexasR] (7:3/4) 87, p. 138.
    "August Third." [Poetry] (151:1/2) O-N 87, p. 147.
    "Christmas Light." [Poetry] (151:3) D 87, p. 274.
    "The House in Winter." [TexasR] (7:3/4) 87, p. 137.
    "June Wind." [TexasR] (7:3/4) 87, p. 136.
    "The Phoenix Again." [Poetry] (151:3) D 87, p. 272.
    "Wilderness Lost" (For Bramble my cat). [Poetry] (151:3) D 87, p. 273-274.
4835. SARTORELLO, Lori
    "The Mundane." [AntigR] (68) Wint 87, p. 38.
4836. SASANOV, Catherine
    "Catalyst of Little Evolutions." [BlueBldgs] (10) 87?, p. 48.
    "Considering George Mallory (1886-1924) on Mt. Everest Being Survived By."
        [BlueBldgs] (10) 87?, p. 49.
    "Kitty Oppenheimer Defends Her Husband As Not Being a Communist Conspirator,
        1954." [HayF] (2) Spr 87, p. 55.
    "Oppenheimer Contracts Throat Cancer, 1967." [HayF] (2) Spr 87, p. 56.
    "Oppenheimer Leaves His Family for Work Again, Los Alamos, 1945." [HayF] (2)
        Spr 87, p. 54.
4837. SASSO, Laurence J., Jr.
    "Boy Walking Home at Dusk on the Day of the A-Bomb Drill at School" (1953).
        [GreenfR] (14:3/4) Sum-Fall 87, p. 175-176.
4838. SATER, Steven
    "Getting Up So Late in the Afternoon." [SpiritSH] (53:1) 87, p. 30.
    "What Is to Be Life." [SpiritSH] (53:1) 87, p. 30.
4839. SATO, Hiroaki
    "On the Rock Mountain, A Mountain Goat" (tr. of Kazuko Shiraishi). [Dandel]
        (14:2) Fall-Wint 87, p. 41-49.
    "Osiris, the God of Stone" (tr. of Yoshimasu Gozo). [LitR] (30:2) Wint 87, p.
        297-298.
4840. SATRIANO, John
    "The Architect, the Commander and the Lily Creature" (tr. of Giorgio Manganelli).
        [Rampike] (5:3) 87, p. 38-39.
4841. SATTLER, Joel
    "Arrows." [Gargoyle] (32/33) 87, p. 164.
4842. SATZ, Mario
    "Mothers of the Plaza de Mayo" (tr. by Jason Wilson). [Trans] (18) Spr 87, p. 126.
    "W. H. Hudson (1841-1922)" (tr. by Jason Wilson). [Trans] (18) Spr 87, p. 127.
4843. SATZ, Martha
    "Abandonment" (tr. of Weöres Sándor, w. Zsuzsanna Ozsvath). [Os] (24) 87, p. 12.
    "After Creation" (tr. of Weöres Sándor, w. Zsuzsanna Ozsvath). [Os] (24) 87, p.
        10.
    "Blind-Street" (tr. of Agh István, w. Zsuzsanna Ozsvath). [Os] (24) 87, p. 2.
    "The Magicians' Parade Under Our Castles" (tr. of Gyula Takats, w. Zsuzsanna
        Ozsvath). [WebR] (12:1) Spr 87, p. 87.
    "Old Wave" (tr. of Nagy Gáspár, w. Zsuzsanna Ozsvath). [Os] (24) 87, p. 4.

"Vault" (tr. of Zsuzsa Albert, w. Zsuzsanna Ozsvath). [WebR] (12:1) Spr 87, p. 87.
4844. SAULS, Roger
"Spending a Night in the Shenandoah Valley." [Raccoon] (24/25) My 87, p. 21.
4845. SAUNDERS, Josephine
"With Hands Wide Open." [Poetry] (151:1/2) O-N 87, p. 148.
4846. SAUNDERS, Leslie
"Jazz Dream from a Difficult Labour." [Quarry] (36:1) Wint 87, p. 27-28.
"Second Delivery." [Quarry] (36:1) Wint 87, p. 28.
4847. SAUNDERS, Linda
"August." [GreenfR] (14:1/2) Wint-Spr, p. 95.
"Winter." [GreenfR] (14:1/2) Wint-Spr, p. 96.
4848. SAUTTER, Diane Moon
"Freud." [PassN] (8:2) Sum 87, p. 22.
4849. SAVANI, J.
"Domesticity." [US1] (20/21) Wint 86-87, p. 44.
4850. SAVARD, Jeannine
"Angry at No One." [AmerPoR] (16:6) N-D 87, p. 54.
"The Broken Bench" (After André Kertész). [AmerPoR] (16:6) N-D 87, p. 54.
"The Cleaning Girls." [AmerPoR] (16:6) N-D 87, p. 53.
"House-Sitting in New Hampshire." [QW] (25) Spr 87, p. 137.
"The Maintenance Man and the Model." [AmerPoR] (16:6) N-D 87, p. 53.
"The Roomer." [AmerPoR] (16:6) N-D 87, p. 54.
"Speaking Out of Doors." [AmerPoR] (16:6) N-D 87, p. 53.
"Tintype with White Rosebank." [HayF] (2) Spr 87, p. 105-106.
"The Worrying." [AmerPoR] (16:6) N-D 87, p. 56.
4851. SAVARESE, Ralph
"Loons, Water" (1987 Ratner-Ferber-Poet Lore Honorable Mention). [PoetL] (82:2)
Sum 87, p. 102-105.
4852. SAVASÇI, Fethi
"A Diffuse Winter Symphony" (tr. by Talat Sait Halman). [Trans] (19) Fall 87, p.
110.
4853. SAVITT, Lynne
"9-07-86" (for Michael). [AlphaBS] (1) Je 87, p. 24.
"Deal, She Said." [AlphaBS] (1) Je 87, p. 23.
"I Love You." [Pig] (14) 87, p. 63.
"Response to Van Gogh on His Fantasizing the Erotica of the Continental Shift."
[AlphaBS] (1) Je 87, p. 22.
"Sea of Love." [Pig] (14) 87, p. 62.
"To a Married Lover on the Weather." [Pig] (14) 87, p. 63.
"Vacation." [AlphaBS] (1) Je 87, p. 23.
"Why I Love Kissing You." [Pig] (14) 87, p. 62.
4854. SAVOIE, Terrence
"After Sex." [AmerPoR] (16:5) S-O 87, p. 46.
"Father-Milk" (For Pamela). [Poetry] (149:5) F 87, p. 287.
4855. SAWYER, Paul
"Quidiron Pro Quo." [LightY] '87, c86, p. 31.
"Sharper Than a Serpent's Tooth." [LightY] '87, c86, p. 95.
4856. SAXENA, Sri Sarvesvar Dayal
"God" (tr. by R. A. Hueckstedt). [Paint] (14:27) Spr 87, p. 34.
4857. SAXON, Sonia
"In the Oakland Museum." [MinnR] (NS 28) Spr 87, p. 33.
4858. SAXTON, Roger
"Re-echoing Birdsong." [Puerto] (22:2) Spr 87, p. 143.
"Sleep." [Puerto] (22:2) Spr 87, p. 142.
4859. SAYPER, Jerome
"The Fly and the Emperor." [Amelia] (4:1/2, issue 9) 87, p. 118.
4860. SCALAPINO, Leslie
"Chameleon Series" (Excerpt). [Bound] (14:1/2) Fall 85-Wint 86 [c87], p. 27-29.
"Here a Play Done by Dancers." [Zyzzyva] (3:4) Wint 87-88, p. 45-53.
"Jumping-Jack Flash." [Conjunc] (10) 87, p. 43-47.
"Leg, a Play" (Excerpt). [Notus] (2:2) Fall 87, p. 3-15.
"Roll." [Temblor] (5) 87, p. 7-14.
"The Series — As Fragile — 2." [Act] (7) 87, p. 66-71.
"Way" (Selections: Two Sequences, "Bum Series," "Hoofer"). [AmerPoR] (16:3)
My-Je 87, p. 37-40.

4861. SCANLON, Richard
    "Tooth Fairy." [Poem] (57) Mr 87, p. 33.
    "Wooden Floors." [Poem] (57) Mr 87, p. 32.
4862. SCANNELL, Vernon
    "White Witch." [Stand] (28:3) Sum 87, p. 56.
4863. SCATES, Maxine
    "Birthday." [PoetryE] (23/24) Fall 87, p. 168-169.
    "Desire in America." [MassR] (28:1) Spr 87, p. 147-148.
    "Hospital." [Crazy] (33) Wint 87, p. 46-47.
    "Night Sounds." [PoetryE] (23/24) Fall 87, p. 170-171.
4864. SCHAEFFER, Susan Fromberg
    "Drawing" (for Johnny Deneny). [OP] (final issue) Sum 87, p. 12-13.
    "In Dreams." [LitR] (30:4) Sum 87, p. 532-536.
    "Judgment Day." [GreensboroR] (41) Wint 86-87, p. 78-79.
    "Sherlock Holmes." [OP] (final issue) Sum 87, p. 14-15.
    "Writing." [OP] (final issue) Sum 87, p. 9-11.
4865. SCHAIN, Eliot
    "Berkeley, Without Mantras." [AmerPoR] (16:6) N-D 87, p. 24.
4866. SCHAPIRO, Jane
    "Grandpa's High School Class Photo." [CapeR] (22:1) Spr 87, p. 4.
    "The Hologram." [WebR] (12:1) Spr 87, p. 30-31.
    "Water." [PoetryE] (23/24) Fall 87, p. 154.
4867. SCHECHTER, Ruth Lisa
    "Listen to the Grass Moving Outside." [Footwork] 87, p. 51.
    "Worksheets." [Phoenix] (7:1) 87, p. 18.
4868. SCHEER, Linda
    "Mexico City Diptych" (tr. of Francisco Hernández). [Caliban] (2) 87, p. 142-143.
    "Two" (tr. of Francisco Hernández). [Caliban] (2) 87, p. 141.
4869. SCHEFFLEIN, Susan
    "Alone." [BallSUF] (28:4) Aut 87, p. 23.
4870. SCHENKER, Donald
    "Anatomy." [WormR] (27:1, issue 105) 87, p. 1-2.
    "Clouds in the Kitchen, Fire in the Sea" (for Vertigo Play). [WormR] (27:1, issue
        105) 87, p. 2-3.
    "Sic Semper Tyrannis!" [Abraxas] (35/36) 87, p. 16.
    "Stone Lions." [Abraxas] (35/36) 87, p. 17.
    "Symptons." [Abraxas] (35/36) 87, p. 16-17.
    "Tableau: Death in the Family." [PoetryNW] (28:2) Sum 87, p. 34-35.
4871. SCHEXNAYDER, Kenneth
    "An American Story." [MemphisSR] (7:2) Spr 87, p. 42.
4872. SCHIPPER, Jenny
    "Kaleidoscope of Desire" (w. Alex Smith). [SlipS] (7) 87, p. 45-74.
4873. SCHLOSS, David
    "The Anima." [NoAmR] (272:2) Je 87, p. 18.
4874. SCHMIDT, Paulette
    "Poems from St. Pelagia Prison" (Selection: "Poem II," tr. of Philippe Soupault).
        [Gargoyle] (32/33) 87, p. 370.
4875. SCHMITT, Peter
    "Adolescence." [Boulevard] (2:3) Fall 87, p. 96-97.
    "At the East German Border" (near Duderstadt, east of Göttingen). [SpiritSH] (53:1)
        87, p. 21-22.
    "Fundamentalist Funeral." [Boulevard] (2:3) Fall 87, p. 95-96.
    "Milk." [SpiritSH] (53:1) 87, p. 21.
4876. SCHMITTAUER, Jan (Jan E.)
    "Ramada Inn, Virginia Beach." [HolCrit] (24:1) F 87, p. 17.
    "Thoughts While Looking into My Grandmother's Casket." [Gambit] (20) 86, p. 15.
4877. SCHMITZ, Dennis
    "Bird-Watching." [Field] (36) Spr 87, p. 5-6.
    "Blue." [CalQ] (30) Wint 87, p. 22-23.
    "Brand Loyalty." [NowestR] (25:3) 87, p. 363-364.
    "The Frog." [Raccoon] (24/25) My 87, p. 181-182.
    "Frontier." [HayF] (2) Spr 87, p. 34.
    "Halloween Creature." [Field] (36) Spr 87, p. 7-8.
    "Phone-Calls." [Caliban] (3) 87, p. 113.
    "The Spider." [CalQ] (30) Wint 87, p. 21.

"Temporal Aspects of Dying as a Non-Scheduled Status Passage." [Caliban] (3) 87, p. 112-113.
"The Text." [HayF] (2) Spr 87, p. 33.
4878. SCHNEIDRE, P.
"At Her Party." [Zyzzyva] (3:4) Wint 87-88, p. 70.
4879. SCHNOEKER-SHORB, Yvette A.
"In the Hands of the X-Ray Technician." [Phoenix] (7:2) 87, p. 55.
4880. SCHOEBERLEIN, Marion
"The Kite." [Amelia] (4:3, issue 10) 87, p. 26.
4881. SCHOFIELD, Don
"Sarcophagi with Glyphs" (Turkish National Archaeological Museum, Istanbul).
[SouthernPR] (27:2) Fall 87, p. 61-62.
"Star." [Agni] (24/25) 87, p. 68-69.
4882. SCHOONOVER, Amy Jo
"Hot Days and Strange Restaurants." [LaurelR] (20:1/2) Sum 87, p. 42.
4883. SCHOPPERT, Jim
"The Crying Woman." [GreenfR] (14:1/2) Wint-Spr, p. 36.
"The Effect of Alcohol on Indian People." [GreenfR] (14:1/2) Wint-Spr, p. 35.
"Late Quiet Evening." [GreenfR] (14:1/2) Wint-Spr, p. 37.
"Lay the Dark Hills Dreaming." [GreenfR] (14:1/2) Wint-Spr, p. 33-34.
4884. SCHRAUFNAGEL, Lynda
"Mimicry." [Shen] (37:4) 87, p. 68-69.
"Trappings." [Shen] (37:4) 87, p. 69-70.
4885. SCHREIBER, Jan
"From Mr. Bowles' Diary." [TexasR] (7:3/4) 87, p. 139-140.
4886. SCHREIBER, Ron
"4-10-86." [HangL] (50/51) 87, p. 172.
"4-13-86." [HangL] (50/51) 87, p. 173-174.
"4-25-86." [HangL] (50/51) 87, p. 177.
"Back (4-30-86)." [HangL] (50/51) 87, p. 178.
"'Recovery' (5-18-86)." [HangL] (50/51) 87, p. 179.
"The Valley of Death (4-25-86)." [HangL] (50/51) 87, p. 176.
"Your Life." [HangL] (50/51) 87, p. 175.
4887. SCHREIBMAN, Susan
"Among the Ashes" (tr. of Rebeca Campo Pérez). [InterPR] (13:1) Spr 87, p. 53.
"Between" (tr. of Idea Vilariño). [YellowS] (25) Wint 87, p. 32.
"If There Were a Whiteness" (tr. of Rebeca Campo Pérez). [InterPR] (13:1) Spr 87, p. 51.
"Nightdreams" (tr. of Rebeca Campo Pérez). [InterPR] (13:1) Spr 87, p. 51.
"Postcard" (tr. of Carlos Ernesto Garcia). [InterPR] (13:1) Spr 87, p. 49.
"Small Hours of the Night" (tr. of Roque Dalton). [InterPR] (13:1) Spr 87, p. 59.
"The Starry Night." [Amelia] (4:1/2, issue 9) 87, p. 21.
"The Suicide" (tr. of Jorge Luis Borges). [InterPR] (13:1) Spr 87, p. 57.
"Tankas" (6 poems, tr. of Jorge Luis Borges). [InterPR] (13:1) Spr 87, p. 54, 56.
"That Night" (tr. of Idea Vilariño). [YellowS] (25) Wint 87, p. 32.
"To the Perplexity of One Deceased" (tr. of Carlos Ernesto Garcia). [InterPR] (13:1) Spr 87, p. 49.
4888. SCHREY, E.
"Le-Grau-du-roi." [Quarry] (36:1) Wint 87, p. 95-96.
"Lighthouse of La Gacholle." [Quarry] (36:1) Wint 87, p. 94.
"Mas le Paradis." [Quarry] (36:1) Wint 87, p. 94-95.
4889. SCHULER, Robert
"Fantasia for Rain & Guitar." [LakeSR] (21) 87, p. 13.
4890. SCHULMAN, Grace
"After the Division." [Poetry] (149:5) F 87, p. 276-277.
"Easter in Bellagio." [YaleR] (76:2) Wint 87, p. 260.
"Straight Talk, Straight As the Greek" (Ezra Pound and Hilda Doolittle, 1912).
[Poetry] (151:1/2) O-N 87, p. 149.
4891. SCHULTE, Rainer
"Another Low Pressure System?" (tr. of Wolfgang Bächler). [NewOR] (14:3) Fall 87, p. 32.
"Anticipation" (for Michael Krüger, tr. of Wolfgang Bächler). [NewOR] (14:3) Fall 87, p. 22.
"Branching Out" (tr. of Wolfgang Bächler). [NewOR] (14:3) Fall 87, p. 36.
"The Days Are Growing Shorter" (tr. of Wolfgang Bächler). [NewOR] (14:3) Fall 87, p. 26.

"Fruitless Retreat" (tr. of Wolfgang Bächler). [NewOR] (14:3) Fall 87, p. 34.
"I Carry Earth in Me" (tr. of Wolfgang Bächler). [NewOR] (14:3) Fall 87, p. 30.
"Roads" (tr. of Wolfgang Bächler). [NewOR] (14:3) Fall 87, p. 20.
"A Scream" (tr. of Wolfgang Bächler). [NewOR] (14:3) Fall 87, p. 24.
"To Begin the World Again." [NewOR] (14:1) Spr 87, p. 81.
"Untitled: The eye of memory." [NewOR] (14:1) Spr 87, p. 73.
"Veitshöchheim" (tr. of Wolfgang Bächler). [NewOR] (14:3) Fall 87, p. 28.
4892. SCHULTZ, Lee
"Vacation in the 39th Summer." [Amelia] (4:1/2, issue 9) 87, p. 80-81.
"Veteran Prof Speaks to Affluent Student." [Amelia] (4:1/2, issue 9) 87, p. 79-80.
4893. SCHULTZ, Philip
"The Eight-Mile Bike Ride" (For John Cheever). [Poetry] (151:1/2) O-N 87, p. 150-151.
"It's No Small Wonder" (for Rose Graubart Ignatow). [PaintedB] (31) 87, p. 29.
4894. SCHULTZ, Robert O'neal
"The Snowman's Pilgrimage" (dedicated, with love, to John Lennon). [BallSUF] (28:4) Aut 87, p. 17.
4895. SCHUT, Laurie
"Threads of Fire Beads of Light." [Event] (16:1) Mr 87, p. 38-39.
4896. SCHUYLER, James
"Horse-Chestnut Trees and Roses." [NewYorker] (63:16) 8 Je 87, p. 32.
"Let's All Hear It for Mildred Bailey!" [Poetry] (151:1/2) O-N 87, p. 151-153.
"Rain." [NewYorker] (63:27) 24 Ag 87, p. 32.
4897. SCHWARTZ, Hillel
"All Be Riders." [PraS] (61:3) Fall 87, p. 83-84.
"Concerning Mrs. Joe Person's Remedy, a Sure Cure . . . as Advertised in North Carolina in 1915." [PoetryNW] (28:1) Spr 87, p. 3-4.
"Dressage." [BelPoJ] (37:4) Sum 87, p. 5.
"Fantasiestücke 3. Ann Landers Comes to Me for Advice." [Comm] (114:11) 5 Je 87, p. 357.
"Go Fish." [PoetryNW] (28:4) Wint 87-88, p. 45-46.
"Grand Mogul Bus Tours." [PikeF] (8) Fall 87, p. 31.
"Gravel Pit." [PoetryNW] (28:4) Wint 87-88, p. 43-45.
"History Lesson for the Insignificant Year 1823." [HampSPR] Wint 87, p. 45-46.
"Knights of Columbus." [Farm] (4:2) Spr-Sum 87, p. 31.
"Rounds." [HampSPR] Wint 86, p. 53.
"Scale." [HolCrit] (24:1) F 87, p. 10.
"Tree Falling." [HampSPR] Wint 86, p. 52.
"What Dolphins Do and Do Not Do." [PennR] (3:2) Fall-Wint 87, p. 35-37.
4898. SCHWARTZ, Howard
"The Very Beginning" (a South Pacific myth). [RiverS] (24) 87, p. 36.
4899. SCHWARTZ, Jeffery
"On the Boardwalk in Asbury Park." [PennR] (3:1) Spr-Sum 87, p. 20.
4900. SCHWARTZ, Leonard
"Horizontal Bar — Do Not Enter (a Cine-Poem)" (tr. of Benjamin Fondane). [LitR] (30:3) Spr 87, p. 468-471.
4901. SCHWARTZ, Lloyd
"House Hunting." [GrandS] (6:3) Spr 87, p. 75-82.
"Pseudodoxia Epidemica." [Ploughs] (13:4) 87, p. 113-117.
"Vermeers." [MassR] (28:2) Sum 87, p. 221-228.
4902. SCHWARTZ, Naomi
"The Art in Magic." [Thrpny] (28) Wint 87, p. 21.
"Still Life: Marriage." [FiveFR] (5) 87, p. 53-54.
4903. SCHWARTZ, Perla
"Naufragio." [InterPR] (13:1) Spr 87, p. 24.
"Shipwreck" (tr. by Thomas Hoeksema). [InterPR] (13:1) Spr 87, p. 25.
4904. SCHWARZ, Robin
"An Argument with the Terms." [CumbPR] (6:2) Spr 87, p. 19-23.
4905. SCINTO, Helen C.
"Reversal." [EngJ] (76:6) O 87, p. 98.
4906. SCOBIE, Stephen
"Felix Paul Greve." [PraF] (8:4) Wint 87-88, p. 82.
4907. SCOFIELD, Robin
"The Crossing." [Shen] (37:2) 87, p. 38-39.
4908. SCOTT, Herbert
"Grandmother, Waiting for the Mail." [Nimrod] (31:1) Fall-Wint 87, p. 81.

"Oklahoma Pastoral." [Nimrod] (31:1) Fall-Wint 87, p. 82.
4909. SCOTT, Paul
"Junkyard 8:00 A.M." [Abraxas] (35/36) 87, p. 34.
"Never enough the shot." [Abraxas] (35/36) 87, p. 35.
4910. SCRUTON, Jim
"Penknife." [Farm] (4:2) Spr-Sum 87, p. 72.
"Plowland." [Farm] (4:2) Spr-Sum 87, p. 70.
"The Vise." [Farm] (4:2) Spr-Sum 87, p. 71.
4911. SCUTELLARO, Guy
"Winter's Night." [CrossCur] (6:4) 87, p. 59.
SE-WOOK, Huh
See HUH, Se-Wook
4912. SEABURG, Alan
"Act IV: Jean Plays Solitaire." [CapeR] (22:1) Spr 87, p. 36.
"Alone in Marriage." [HawaiiR] (21) Spr 87, p. 19.
"A Bend in Grief, Near Conway." [BallSUF] (28:4) Aut 87, p. 39.
"The City of Love." [BallSUF] (28:4) Aut 87, p. 38.
"The Gift of 26 March." [BallSUF] (28:4) Aut 87, p. 37.
4913. SEATON, J. P.
"Cold Night, Reading" (tr. of Yuan Mei). [LitR] (31:1) Fall 87, p. 39.
"On a Painting" (tr. of Yuan Mei). [LitR] (31:1) Fall 87, p. 39.
"Waning Years: Random Poems IV" (tr. of Yuan Mei). [NegC] (7:1/2) 87, p. 253.
"Waning Years: Random Poems VI" (tr. of Yuan Mei). [NegC] (7:1/2) 87, p. 251.
4914. SEATON, Maureen
"The Bell Tower" (1987 Ratner-Ferber-Poet Lore Prize Co-Winner). [PoetL] (82:2)
Sum 87, p. 73.
"The First Drink." [Iowa] (17:2) Spr-Sum 87, p. 86-87.
"Hudson Sonnets." [Iowa] (17:2) Spr-Sum 87, p. 88-90.
"Swan Lake." [Iowa] (17:2) Spr-Sum 87, p. 85-86.
"Thanksgiving Poem for James Wright." [NewL] (53:3) Spr 87, p. 78-79.
"Three Views of Death." [PoetryNW] (28:3) Aut 87, p. 21-22.
"Two Rhymed Paintings with Sonnets" (for the artist, Libby Robinson).
[PoetryNW] (28:3) Aut 87, p. 22-23.
4915. SEATON, Peter
"Two Words." [Bound] (14:1/2) Fall 85-Wint 86 [c87], p. 103-105.
4916. SEBTI, Youcef
"Wedding Night" (tr. by Eric Sellin). [LitR] (30:3) Spr 87, p. 397.
4917. SEE, Molly
"On the Beach at Spartini, Watching the Medusas." [BellR] (10:2) Fall 87, p. 6.
4918. SEEMAN, Julianne
"Morning in Half Light." [CapeR] (22:2) Fall 87, p. 34-35.
"Roads." [CapeR] (22:2) Fall 87, p. 33.
"Strip Mining." [CapeR] (22:2) Fall 87, p. 36.
4919. SEETCH, Beth
"Dale Arden, Away Too Long, Speaks to *Parade* Magazine." [RiverS] (22) 87, p.
71.
4920. SEGALEN, Victor
"At Sabre's Point" (tr. by Andrew Harvey and Iain Watson). [SenR] (17:2) 87, p.
28.
"Command to the Sun" (tr. by Andrew Harvey and Iain Watson). [SenR] (17:2) 87,
p. 31.
"Hymn to the Resting Dragon" (tr. by Andrew Harvey and Iain Watson). [SenR]
(17:2) 87, p. 32.
"Mongol Libation" (tr. by Andrew Harvey and Iain Watson). [SenR] (17:2) 87, p.
29.
"Written with Blood" (tr. by Andrew Harvey and Iain Watson). [SenR] (17:2) 87, p.
30.
4921. SEGALL, Pearl Bloch
"Tante." [PoeticJ] (17) 87, p. 25.
4922. SEGALL, Sally Bennett
"Finding the Lion." [Poetry] (150:2) My 87, p. 75.
"Indigo Bunting." [SenR] (17:1) 87, p. 26.
4923. SEIDMAN, Hugh
"American." [Pequod] (23/24) 87, p. 147.
"The Dew." [ParisR] (29:102) Spr 87, p. 204.
"Goddesses." [ParisR] (29:102) Spr 87, p. 203.

"Lake." [ParisR] (29:102) Spr 87, p. 202.
"Max." [Pequod] (23/24) 87, p. 145.
"Muse." [Pequod] (23/24) 87, p. 144.
"Poetics." [ParisR] (29:102) Spr 87, p. 203.
"Those Days." [Pequod] (23/24) 87, p. 146.
4924. SEIFERLE, Rebecca
    "Ancestors." [NegC] (7:3/4) 87, p. 158.
    "The Hammer-Headed Foal." [CarolQ] (39:2) Wint 87, p. 8.
    "Hives" (1986 Finalist, Eve of Saint Agnes Poetry Competition). [NegC] (7:1/2) 87,
        p. 167.
    "Is It OK to Say Heart in a Poem?" [CarolQ] (39:2) Wint 87, p. 7.
4925. SEIFERT, Jaroslav
    "It Was Afternoon or Later" (tr. by Paul Jagasich and Tom O'Grady). [Spirit] (8:2)
        87, p. 317.
4926. SEILER, Barry
    "The Public Sleeper." [Jacaranda] (2:2) Spr 87, p. 18-19.
    "Souls." [Jacaranda] (2:2) Spr 87, p. 20.
4927. SEITZER, Carol
    "Body Parts." [CentR] (31:3) Sum 87, p. 277-278.
    "Hushup." [CentR] (31:3) Sum 87, p. 278.
4928. SELAWSKY, John T.
    "The Blackberries." [SoDakR] (25:2) Sum 87, p. 34.
    "Entering the Forest." [SoDakR] (25:2) Sum 87, p. 33.
    "The Frogs." [Poem] (57) Mr 87, p. 4-5.
    "Harvest." [StoneC] (15:1/2) Fall-Wint 87-88, p. 61.
    "The Moths." [Wind] (17:61) 87, p. 42-43.
    "October." [CapeR] (22:1) Spr 87, p. 49.
    "The Salamander." [Poem] (57) Mr 87, p. 3.
    "Secondary Growth." [Wind] (17:61) 87, p. 42.
    "The Wheel." [SmPd] (24:2) Spr 87, p. 16.
4929. SELDEN, Gary
    "Delight in Order, Too." [LightY] '87, c86, p. 205.
    "Red Raspberries." [LightY] '87, c86, p. 40.
4930. SELDIN, Tony
    "Children Are Dancing on Haight Street." [AlphaBS] (2) D 87, p. 27.
4931. SELENDER, Mike
    "Coring a Bog." [Lactuca] (5) Ja 87, p. 38-39.
    "The Flusher." [Lactuca] (8) N 87, p. 34.
    "Francis Farmer, LA County Jail, 1943." [Lactuca] (6) Ap-My 87, p. 23-24.
    "I Am the Stone." [Lactuca] (5) Ja 87, p. 36-37.
    "If Turkey Creek Were Put Underground." [Lactuca] (5) Ja 87, p. 37.
    "Jeremiah." [Lactuca] (8) N 87, p. 35.
    "Largo — Reflections on the Third Movement of Dmitri Shostakovich's Fifth
        Symphony." [Lactuca] (5) Ja 87, p. 39.
    "Passing Through." [Lactuca] (8) N 87, p. 33.
4932. SELLERS, Bettie
    "Farm for Sale." [ChatR] (8:1) Fall 87, p. 98.
4933. SELLIN, Eric
    "The Café" (tr. of Rachid Boudjedra). [LitR] (30:3) Spr 87, p. 400.
    "Destiny" (tr. of Rachid Bey). [LitR] (30:3) Spr 87, p. 398-399.
    "The Earth Beats" (tr. of Amina Saïd). [LitR] (30:3) Spr 87, p. 399.
    "I Might Perhaps Restate Tonight" (tr. of Malek Alloula). [LitR] (30:3) Spr 87, p.
        396.
    "Imperfect and Present Tense" (tr. of Hocine Bouzaher). [LitR] (30:3) Spr 87, p.
        401.
    "Shadow of Lightning" (tr. of Mohammed Dib). [LitR] (30:3) Spr 87, p. 395.
    "Spectacles" (tr. of Robert Sabatier). [CrossCur] (7:3) 87, p. 154.
    "Stele" (tr. of Mohammed Dib). [LitR] (30:3) Spr 87, p. 395.
    "Wedding Night" (tr. of Youcef Sebti). [LitR] (30:3) Spr 87, p. 397.
    "Words from the Star" (Excerpt, tr. of Jean Amrouche). [LitR] (30:3) Spr 87, p.
        396.
4934. SELTZER, Joanne
    "Bravura." [Bogg] (57) 87, p. 11.
    "Response to Keats' Letter of 22 November 1817." [Bogg] (58) 87, p. 14.
4935. SEMANSKY, Chris
    "Marbles." [Outbr] (18/19) Fall 86-Spr 88, p. 125-126.

4936. SEMENOVICH, Joseph
"It's such an ugly bird, the gull." [WebR] (12:2) Fall 87, p. 80.
"Pet." [Wind] (17:61) 87, p. 36.
4937. SEMONES, Charles
"Lament." [Wind] (17:60) 87, p. 40-41.
"Myself, My Body" (after the manner of Whitman's *Song of Myself*). [JamesWR]
(4:2) Wint 87, p. 7.
"Sabbathsong" (for D.D.). [ChatR] (8:1) Fall 87, p. 99.
4938. SENA, Jorge de
"The Desired Tomb" (tr. by Alexis Levitin). [GrahamHR] (10) Wint-Spr 87, p. 56.
"For Jonathan Griffin" (In English & Spanish, tr. by Alexis Levitin). [HawaiiR] (19)
Spr 86, c87, p. 38-41.
4939. SENECHAL, Diana
"Art Seen from Beneath the Brush." [Writer] (99:7) Jl 86, p. 18.
"From the Amazon." [Writer] (99:1) Ja 86, p. 20.
SEOK, Lee Yay
See LEE, Yay Seok
4940. SEPAMLA, Sipho
"Bearer" (from "Hurry Up to It!"). [TriQ] (69) Spr-Sum 87, p. 66.
"Heroes of the Day." [TriQ] (69) Spr-Sum 87, p. 479-480.
4941. SEPULVEDA PACHECO, Irving
"Cesar Vallejo." [Mairena] (9:24) 87, p. 50-51.
4942. SEQUEIRA, Jose
"Freedom." [Electrum] (39) Fall-Wint 87, p. 25.
4943. SERCHUK, Peter
"The Angel on the Backyard Porch." [PoetC] (19:1) Fall 87, p. 14.
4944. SERENI, Vittorio
"December 3" (tr. by Ann Snodgrass). [Trans] (18) Spr 87, p. 318.
"Niccolò" (tr. by Ann Snodgrass). [Trans] (18) Spr 87, p. 319.
"Poet in Black" (tr. by Ann Snodgrass). [Trans] (18) Spr 87, p. 318.
"Years Later" (tr. by Ann Snodgrass). [Trans] (18) Spr 87, p. 317.
4945. SERVADIO, Gaia
"Craft" (tr. of Primo Levi, w. A. Alvarez). [NewYorker] (63:34) 12 O 87, p. 46.
4946. SESHADRI, Vijay
"Made in the Topics." [Antaeus] (58) Spr 87, p. 189-190.
"A Sketch from the Campaign in the North." [Nat] (245:7) 12 S 87, p. 244.
4947. SETH, Vikram
"On the 50th Anniversary of the Golden Gate Bridge." [Thrpny] (31) Fall 87, p. 5.
4948. SETHI, Robbie Clipper
"Field of Water." [Boulevard] (2:3) Fall 87, p. 170.
4949. SETLAK, LeAnne
"From the Catwalk." [LaurelR] (20:1/2) Sum 87, p. 89.
"Three Notes on Negative Entropy." [TarPR] (27:1) Fall 87, p. 44.
4950. SEVICK, Joan
"Vacationing in Pompeii." [CrossCur] (6:4) 87, p. 43.
4951. SEXTON, Tom
"Cutting the Christmas Tree" (1986 Finalist, Eve of Saint Agnes Poetry
Competition). [NegC] (7:1/2) 87, p. 217-218.
"Dawson City, 1899." [TexasR] (8:1/2) Spr-Sum 87, p. 42-43.
4952. SEYFRIED, Robin
"Revenge." [Sonora] (12) Spr 87, p. 1-2.
4953. SHADBOLT, Jack
"Green Fire." [CanLit] (113/114) Sum-Fall 87, p. 58-59.
"The Way In" (for Max). [CanLit] (113/114) Sum-Fall 87, p. 60.
4954. SHADOIAN, Jack
"Please Be Home." [CrabCR] (4:2) Spr 87, p. 12-13.
4955. SHAFFER, Craig
"Harmony." [GreensboroR] (40) Sum 86, p. 23-24.
"The Pasteurization of Uncle." [GreensboroR] (40) Sum 86, p. 25.
4956. SHAFFER, Frank, Jr.
"Marcus Antonius at the Nile." [LaurelR] (20:1/2) Sum 87, p. 91.
4957. SHALIN, Hai-Jew
"Meditation Over a Blue Baby in a Glass Crib." [Contact] (9:44/45/46) Fall-Wint 87,
p. 54.
SHANG-YIN, Li
See LI, Shang-yin

4958. SHANNON, Jeanne
"The Cardboard Man." [YellowS] (22) Spr 87, p. 39.
4959. SHAPIRO, Alan
"During the Wedding Ceremony." [Thrpny] (30) Sum 87, p. 31.
"Maison des Jeunes." [TriQ] (68) Wint 87, p. 107-109.
"Practical Joke." [Thrpny] (31) Fall 87, p. 8.
"Ready or Not." [Sequoia] (31:1) Centennial issue 87, p. 62.
"Rickshaw." [Sequoia] (31:1) Centennial issue 87, p. 63-64.
4960. SHAPIRO, Daniel E.
"Holland." [BlackWR] (14:1) Fall 87, p. 38-39.
"The Yellow Boat" (after Edvard Munch). [BlackWR] (14:1) Fall 87, p. 18-19.
4961. SHAPIRO, David
"The Erratics." [Boulevard] (2:1/2) Spr 87, p. 156.
"Man on a Stone Slab." [Boulevard] (2:1/2) Spr 87, p. 155-156.
4962. SHAPIRO, Gregg
"True Romance." [Vis] (23) 87, p. 21.
4963. SHAPIRO, Harvey
"Before Sleep." [PoetryE] (23/24) Fall 87, p. 190.
"Combat." [PoetryE] (23/24) Fall 87, p. 189.
"Comment." [PartR] (54:3) Sum 87, p. 435.
"From an Autobiography." [PoetryE] (23/24) Fall 87, p. 193-194.
"New York Note." [PoetryE] (23/24) Fall 87, p. 191.
"Questions." [PoetryE] (23/24) Fall 87, p. 192.
"Two Cornell Deaths." [Pequod] (23/24) 87, p. 241-242.
4964. SHAPIRO, Joan
"Generations." [TexasR] (7:3/4) 87, p. 141.
"Ripeness." [TexasR] (7:3/4) 87, p. 142.
4965. SHAPIRO, Karl
"On Being Yanked from a Favorite Anthology" (To Bob Wiggins). [Poetry]
(151:1/2) O-N 87, p. 154.
"Retirement." [Poetry] (151:1/2) O-N 87, p. 153-154.
"The Scarlet Fever." [Confr] (35/36) Spr-Fall 87, p. 33.
"Tableau." [Confr] (35/36) Spr-Fall 87, p. 32.
"Tourists." [Confr] (35/36) Spr-Fall 87, p. 34.
"Virginia Child." [Confr] (35/36) Spr-Fall 87, p. 31.
4966. SHAPIRO, Michael
"God Is a Dishwater Blonde." [SoDakR] (25:3) Aut 87, p. 86.
4967. SHAPIRO, Nancy Hyatt
"The Kiss of a Married Man." [MemphisSR] (7:2) Spr 87, p. 44.
4968. SHAPIRO, Norman R.
"The Man and the Flea" (tr. of Jean de la Fontaine). [LitR] (30:4) Sum 87, p. 591.
"The Two Bulls and a Frog" (tr. of Jean de la Fontaine). [LitR] (30:4) Sum 87, p.
590.
SHARAT CHANDRA, G. S.
See CHANDRA, G. S. Sharat
4969. SHARFMAN, Bern
"Wine Coolers." [LightY] '87, c86, p. 41.
4970. SHARKEY, Lee
"All My Pretty Ones." [BelPoJ] (38:1) Fall 87, p. 17.
4971. SHARP, Loretta
"Poem for the Visiting Poet." [Contact] (9:44/45/46) Fall-Wint 87, p. 55.
"Poem to Make David Smile." [Contact] (9:44/45/46) Fall-Wint 87, p. 55.
4972. SHARPES, Don
"A Basket of Visions." [WeberS] (4:1) Spr 87, p. 51.
"Father Surrogate." [WeberS] (4:1) Spr 87, p. 48-49.
"Ireland, by God." [WeberS] (4:1) Spr 87, p. 49.
"Late Thoughts on *Late Night Thoughts*." [WeberS] (4:1) Spr 87, p. 50-51.
4973. SHATAL, Shmu'el
"Chess Game" (tr. by Bernhard Frank). [WebR] (12:2) Fall 87, p. 43.
"This Is Where She Lived" (tr. by Bernhard Frank). [WebR] (12:2) Fall 87, p. 44.
"Venice" (tr. by Bernhard Frank). [ColR] (NS 14:2) Fall-Wint 87, p. 67.
4974. SHATRAW, Harriet B.
"Broken Goblets." [Wind] (17:60) 87, p. 6.
"Stones of the Field" (1986 Second Prize in Poetry). [Lyra] (1:2) 87, p. 23.
4975. SHAVE, Kar
"Some Guests." [Quarry] (36:4) Fall 87, p. 71.

"Sunwapta Falls." [Quarry] (36:4) Fall 87, p. 72.
4976. SHAW, Catherine
"The Feast of St. Blaise." [Outbr] (18/19) Fall 86-Spr 88, p. 108-109.
4977. SHAW, Robert B.
"Cloudscape." [PartR] (54:1) Wint 87, p. 134.
"Degrees of Resolution." [Ploughs] (13:1) 87, p. 122-123.
"Extended Run." [KenR] (NS 9:2) Spr 87, p. 104.
"The Floater." [PartR] (54:1) Wint 87, p. 134-135.
"Homework." [KenR] (NS 9:2) Spr 87, p. 102.
"Old Burying Ground." [KenR] (NS 9:2) Spr 87, p. 103-104.
"Spring's Awakening." [Poetry] (150:1) Ap 87, p. 1.
"There and Back Again." [YaleR] (76:3) Spr 87, p. 412-414.
"To His Pulse." [Poetry] (151:1/2) O-N 87, p. 155.
4978. SHAWGO, Lucy
"Chrysalis." [DekalbLAJ] (20:1/4) 87, p. 52.
4979. SHAY, M. E.
"The Relationship Talk." [Puerto] (22:2) Spr 87, p. 20-21.
4980. SHEA, John
"Cyclopean Walls and Sheep." [NegC] (7:1/2) 87, p. 85-86.
"A Touch of Sympathy." [NegC] (7:1/2) 87, p. 83-84.
4981. SHEAFFER, M. P. A.
"Bag Lady." [Phoenix] (7:1) 87, p. 17.
4982. SHEARD, Norma Voorhees
"Chernobyl." [US1] (20/21) Wint 86-87, p. 11.
"Preparing to Spend the Night Alone." [US1] (20/21) Wint 86-87, p. 11.
4983. SHEEHAN, Marc J.
"My First Time Drunk." [ManhatPR] (9) Sum 87, p. 63.
"Pheasant Season." [PennR] (3:1) Spr-Sum 87, p. 60.
4984. SHEEHAN, Tom (Thomas F.)
"The Lilac Run." [SoDakR] (25:2) Sum 87, p. 31.
"A Majority of Sound." [SlipS] (7) 87, p. 5.
"Nobody Will Ever Come Up to Me and Say 'I Remember Jack Winters Just Like
You Do'." [SlipS] (7) 87, p. 6-8.
4985. SHEFFER, Roger
"A Man Who Looked Like Robert Garrow." [Blueline] (7:2/3 [i.e. 8:2/3?]) 87, p.
36.
"Parallel Trail." [Blueline] (7:2/3 [i.e. 8:2/3?]) 87, p. 35.
4986. SHEIKH, Mansoor Y.
"Still Life." [Vis] (25) 87, p. 11.
4987. SHEIRER, John Mark
"Depressed by the *Wall Street Journal*, I Urinate in an Unused Pasture and Watch the
Insects Deal in Commodities." [LaurelR] (20:1/2) Sum 87, p. 53.
"Growing Up in the Country: Two Memories." [LaurelR] (20:1/2) Sum 87, p. 52.
SHEKERJIAN, Regina de Cormier
See DeCORMIER-SHEKERJIAN, Regina
4988. SHELDON, Allan
"Cuisin Art." [EngJ] (76:4) Ap 87, p. 30.
4989. SHELDON, Glenn
"When I Think of Iowa" (for Janet Manning). [SpoonRQ] (12:2) Spr 87, p. 37.
4990. SHELLEY, Pat
"Double Vision." [Bogg] (57) 87, p. 59.
4991. SHELLY, Nadine
"Red Ribbon." [Grain] (15:4) Wint 87, p. 34.
"Velvet." [Grain] (15:4) Wint 87, p. 35.
4992. SHELNUTT, Eve
"Civil Engineer in Spain." [ClockR] (4:1) 87, p. 29.
"Daughters Weighing Their Legacy." [SoDakR] (25:2) Sum 87, p. 75.
"Orchard Winter." [PassN] (8:1) Wint 87, p. 5.
"Sentence." [CapeR] (22:2) Fall 87, p. 17.
4993. SHELTON, Richard
"Dog." [PoetryNW] (28:2) Sum 87, p. 8-9.
"Summer's Children." [Atlantic] (260:6) D 87, p. 74.
4994. SHEPARD, Neil
"Condominiums." [WestB] (20) 87, p. 100-101.
"Mission Reef." [PassN] (8:2) Sum 87, p. 25.
"Obedience." [BlueBldgs] (10) 87?, p. 24.

"Obedience." [WestB] (20) 87, p. 99-100.
4995. SHEPARD, Roy
"The Milkman." [Poem] (58) N 87, p. 52.
"You Would Say." [Footwork] 87, p. 57.
4996. SHEPHERD, Gail
"Sisters." [PraS] (61:2) Sum 87, p. 77-78.
4997. SHEPHERD, J. Barrie
"Advent Awakening." [ChrC] (104:38) 16 D 87, p. 1134.
"March." [ChrC] (104:9) 18-25 Mr 87, p. 261.
"Mary at the Manger." [ChrC] (104:36) 2 D 87, p. 1078-1079.
"Maundy Thursday: Thomas's Testimony." [ChrC] (104:11) 8 Ap 87, p. 327-28.
4998. SHEPHERD, Jamie
"Mirror." [SnapD] (10:1/2) Wint 87, p. 72.
4999. SHEPLER, Michael
"For J." [Colum] (12) 87, p. 102.
"Homecoming." [Colum] (12) 87, p. 103-104.
SHEPPARD, Neil
    See SHEPARD, Neil
5000. SHERMAN, Kenneth
"Adam Names the Beast." [MalR] (81) D 87, p. 65-66.
"After." [MalR] (81) D 87, p. 67.
"Black Adam's Blues." [MalR] (81) D 87, p. 69.
"Mad Eve Sings." [MalR] (81) D 87, p. 68.
5001. SHERRILL, Jan Mitchell
"Citizen of Sodom." [JamesWR] (5:1) Fall 87, p. 12.
"For Ann Tyler, Maine: How Could Anyone Actually Go Travelling in Search of
    Winter?" [CarolQ] (40:1) Fall 87, p. 85.
"Killing Cats." [JamesWR] (5:1) Fall 87, p. 12.
"The Theatre: Uncle Vanya." [CarolQ] (40:1) Fall 87, p. 86.
5002. SHERRY, James
"Our Nuclear Heritage" (2 selections). [Bound] (14:1/2) Fall 85-Wint 86 [c87], p.
    51-53.
5003. SHETTY, Manohar
"Domestic Creatures." [Chelsea] (46) 87, p. 242-243.
"Hoarding." [Chelsea] (46) 87, p. 244-245.
5004. SHEVIN, David
"The Korean Gravestone in Connersville, Indiana." [ColR] (NS 14:2) Fall-Wint 87,
    p. 87.
"Lassie" (by Crow, Sylvia Plath's black labrador). [Pig] (14) 87, p. 36.
"Picture: Ochoapa." [Phoenix] (7:2) 87, p. 37.
"Tweety Among the Nightingales" (by Old Possum, T. S. Eliot's cat). [Pig] (14) 87,
    p. 37.
5005. SHEWAN, Kathy S.
"Emma." [AntigR] (69/70) 87, p. 163.
5006. SHIFFRIN, Nancy
"Scheherezade in the Kitchen." [Amelia] (4:3, issue 10) 87, p. 115.
5007. SHIGEMATSU, Soiku
"Ashikaga Tadayoshi's Palace" (tr. of Muso Soseki, w. W. S. Merwin). [AmerPoR]
    (16:2) Mr-Ap 87, p. 30.
"At Ei's Departure for Choho-ji" (tr. of Muso Soseki, w. W. S. Merwin).
    [AmerPoR] (16:2) Mr-Ap 87, p. 32.
"At the Nachi Kannon Hall" (tr. of Muso Soseki, w. W. S. Merwin). [AmerPoR]
    (16:2) Mr-Ap 87, p. 27.
"At Whole-World-In-View Hut" (tr. of Muso Soseki, w. W. S. Merwin).
    [AmerPoR] (16:2) Mr-Ap 87, p. 30.
"Beyond Light (Zessho Chiko)" (tr. of Muso Soseki, w. W. S. Merwin).
    [AmerPoR] (16:2) Mr-Ap 87, p. 32.
"Beyond the World" (tr. of Muso Soseki, w. W. S. Merwin). [AmerPoR] (16:2)
    Mr-Ap 87, p. 32.
"A Biding Mountain" (tr. of Muso Soseki, w. W. S. Merwin). [AmerPoR] (16:2)
    Mr-Ap 87, p. 29.
"The Bridge Where the Moon Crosses" (tr. of Muso Soseki, w. W. S. Merwin).
    [AmerPoR] (16:2) Mr-Ap 87, p. 31.
"Buddha's Satori" (tr. of Muso Soseki, w. W. S. Merwin). [AmerPoR] (16:2)
    Mr-Ap 87, p. 25.

"Clear Valley (Seikei Tsutetsu)" (tr. of Muso Soseki, w. W. S. Merwin).
[AmerPoR] (16:2) Mr-Ap 87, p. 32.
"Climbing Down the Snowy Montain" (tr. of Muso Soseki, w. W. S. Merwin).
[AmerPoR] (16:2) Mr-Ap 87, p. 30.
"Digging Out the Buddha Relic" (tr. of Muso Soseki, w. W. S. Merwin).
[AmerPoR] (16:2) Mr-Ap 87, p. 31.
"Dry Tree (Koboku Joei)" (tr. of Muso Soseki, w. W. S. Merwin). [AmerPoR]
(16:2) Mr-Ap 87, p. 26.
"East Peak" (tr. of Muso Soseki, w. W. S. Merwin). [AmerPoR] (16:2) Mr-Ap 87,
p. 27.
"Flat Mountain (Heizan Zenkin)" (tr. of Muso Soseki, w. W. S. Merwin).
[AmerPoR] (16:2) Mr-Ap 87, p. 32.
"For Gen the New Head Priest of Erin-ji" (tr. of Muso Soseki, w. W. S. Merwin).
[AmerPoR] (16:2) Mr-Ap 87, p. 29.
"For Myo's Departure for Shofuku-ji" (tr. of Muso Soseki, w. W. S. Merwin).
[AmerPoR] (16:2) Mr-Ap 87, p. 29.
"For Sho the New Head Priest of Erin-ji" (tr. of Muso Soseki, w. W. S. Merwin).
[AmerPoR] (16:2) Mr-Ap 87, p. 30.
"The Fragrance of the Udumbara (Dompo Shuo)" (tr. of Muso Soseki, w. W. S.
Merwin). [AmerPoR] (16:2) Mr-Ap 87, p. 30.
"Great Verse Valley" (tr. of Muso Soseki, w. W. S. Merwin). [AmerPoR] (16:2)
Mr-Ap 87, p. 31.
"Hall of the Guardian God" (tr. of Muso Soseki, w. W. S. Merwin). [AmerPoR]
(16:2) Mr-Ap 87, p. 31.
"House of Spring (Shun-oku Myoha)" (tr. of Muso Soseki, w. W. S. Merwin).
[AmerPoR] (16:2) Mr-Ap 87, p. 30.
"Hut in Harmony (Tekian Hojun)" (tr. of Muso Soseki, w. W. S. Merwin).
[AmerPoR] (16:2) Mr-Ap 87, p. 32.
"Inauguration of Fukusan Dormitory" (tr. of Muso Soseki, w. W. S. Merwin).
[AmerPoR] (16:2) Mr-Ap 87, p. 27.
"It" (tr. of Muso Soseki, w. W. S. Merwin). [AmerPoR] (16:2) Mr-Ap 87, p. 30.
"Laughing Mountain (Shozan Shunen)" (tr. of Muso Soseki, w. W. S. Merwin).
[AmerPoR] (16:2) Mr-Ap 87, p. 27.
"Living in the Mountains: Ten Poems" (tr. of Muso Soseki, w. W. S. Merwin).
[AmerPoR] (16:2) Mr-Ap 87, p. 28.
"Lover of Mountains (Ninzan)" (tr. of Muso Soseki, w. W. S. Merwin). [AmerPoR]
(16:2) Mr-Ap 87, p. 29.
"Magnificent Peak" (tr. of Muso Soseki, w. W. S. Merwin). [AmerPoR] (16:2)
Mr-Ap 87, p. 30.
"Moon Mountain" (tr. of Muso Soseki, w. W. S. Merwin). [AmerPoR] (16:2)
Mr-Ap 87, p. 27.
"Moon Tree Cliff (Keigan)" (tr. of Muso Soseki, w. W. S. Merwin). [AmerPoR]
(16:2) Mr-Ap 87, p. 29.
"Mourning for the Layman Named Cloud Peak" (tr. of Muso Soseki, w. W. S.
Merwin). [AmerPoR] (16:2) Mr-Ap 87, p. 27.
"No Gain" (tr. of Muso Soseki, w. W. S. Merwin). [AmerPoR] (16:2) Mr-Ap 87,
p. 31.
"No Word Hut (Mokuan Shuyu)" (tr. of Muso Soseki, w. W. S. Merwin).
[AmerPoR] (16:2) Mr-Ap 87, p. 29.
"Old Creek" (tr. of Muso Soseki, w. W. S. Merwin). [AmerPoR] (16:2) Mr-Ap 87,
p. 26.
"Old Hut (Koan Fusho)" (tr. of Muso Soseki, w. W. S. Merwin). [AmerPoR]
(16:2) Mr-Ap 87, p. 27.
"Old Man Advancing" (tr. of Muso Soseki, w. W. S. Merwin). [AmerPoR] (16:2)
Mr-Ap 87, p. 29.
"Old Man at Leisure (Kanso Ankan)" (tr. of Muso Soseki, w. W. S. Merwin).
[AmerPoR] (16:2) Mr-Ap 87, p. 32.
"Old Man in Retirement" (tr. of Muso Soseki, w. W. S. Merwin). [AmerPoR] (16:2)
Mr-Ap 87, p. 26.
"Old Man of Few Words (Mohuo Myokai)" (tr. of Muso Soseki, w. W. S. Merwin).
[AmerPoR] (16:2) Mr-Ap 87, p. 32.
"Old Man To-The-Point" (tr. of Muso Soseki, w. W. S. Merwin). [AmerPoR]
(16:2) Mr-Ap 87, p. 29.
"Ox Turned Loose (Hogo Korin)" (tr. of Muso Soseki, w. W. S. Merwin).
[AmerPoR] (16:2) Mr-Ap 87, p. 32.

"The Peak of the Help Up Flower" (tr. of Muso Soseki, w. W. S. Merwin).
    [AmerPoR] (16:2) Mr-Ap 87, p. 31.
"Pine Shade" (tr. of Muso Soseki, w. W. S. Merwin). [AmerPoR] (16:2) Mr-Ap 87,
    p. 28.
"The Pond at Hui-Neng's Spring" (tr. of Muso Soseki, w. W. S. Merwin).
    [AmerPoR] (16:2) Mr-Ap 87, p. 31.
"Reizan Osho Visits Me" (tr. of Muso Soseki, w. W. S. Merwin). [AmerPoR]
    (16:2) Mr-Ap 87, p. 25.
"Reply to Bukko Zenji's Poem at Seiken-ji" (tr. of Muso Soseki, w. W. S. Merwin).
    [AmerPoR] (16:2) Mr-Ap 87, p. 30.
"Reply to Genno Osho's Poem" (Excerpts, tr. of Muso Soseki, w. W. S. Merwin).
    [AmerPoR] (16:2) Mr-Ap 87, p. 27.
"Reply to Suzan Osho's Snow Poem" (tr. of Muso Soseki, w. W. S. Merwin).
    [AmerPoR] (16:2) Mr-Ap 87, p. 29.
"Snow" (tr. of Muso Soseki, w. W. S. Merwin). [AmerPoR] (16:2) Mr-Ap 87, p.
    30.
"Snow at Rohatsu Sesshin" (tr. of Muso Soseki, w. W. S. Merwin). [AmerPoR]
    (16:2) Mr-Ap 87, p. 30.
"Snow Garden" (tr. of Muso Soseki, w. W. S. Merwin). [AmerPoR] (16:2) Mr-Ap
    87, p. 29.
"Snow Valley" (tr. of Muso Soseki, w. W. S. Merwin). [AmerPoR] (16:2) Mr-Ap
    87, p. 26.
"Spring Cliff" (tr. of Muso Soseki, w. W. S. Merwin). [AmerPoR] (16:2) Mr-Ap
    87, p. 27.
"Suzan Osho's Visit" (tr. of Muso Soseki, w. W. S. Merwin). [AmerPoR] (16:2)
    Mr-Ap 87, p. 29.
"Suzan Osho's Visit to My West Mountain Hut" (tr. of Muso Soseki, w. W. S.
    Merwin). [AmerPoR] (16:2) Mr-Ap 87, p. 31.
"Temple of Serene Light" (tr. of Muso Soseki, w. W. S. Merwin). [AmerPoR]
    (16:2) Mr-Ap 87, p. 31.
"Tengan Osho's Visit to Erin-ji" (tr. of Muso Soseki, w. W. S. Merwin).
    [AmerPoR] (16:2) Mr-Ap 87, p. 28.
"Thanks for Daisen Osho's Visit" (Excerpts, tr. of Muso Soseki, w. W. S. Merwin).
    [AmerPoR] (16:2) Mr-Ap 87, p. 26.
"Thanks Sent to Taihei Osho" (Excerpts, tr. of Muso Soseki, w. W. S. Merwin).
    [AmerPoR] (16:2) Mr-Ap 87, p. 26.
"Three Step Waterfall" (tr. of Muso Soseki, w. W. S. Merwin). [AmerPoR] (16:2)
    Mr-Ap 87, p. 31.
"Tiger Valley" (tr. of Muso Soseki, w. W. S. Merwin). [AmerPoR] (16:2) Mr-Ap
    87, p. 31.
"To Kengai Osho of Engaku-ji" (tr. of Muso Soseki, w. W. S. Merwin).
    [AmerPoR] (16:2) Mr-Ap 87, p. 27.
"To the Emperor's Messenger" (tr. of Muso Soseki, w. W. S. Merwin). [AmerPoR]
    (16:2) Mr-Ap 87, p. 26.
"To the Riverside Temple (Rinsen-ji)" (tr. of Muso Soseki, w. W. S. Merwin).
    [AmerPoR] (16:2) Mr-Ap 87, p. 29.
"Toki-No-Ge (Satori Poem)" (tr. of Muso Soseki, w. W. S. Merwin). [AmerPoR]
    (16:2) Mr-Ap 87, p. 31.
"Truth Hall (Gido Shushin)" (tr. of Muso Soseki, w. W. S. Merwin). [AmerPoR]
    (16:2) Mr-Ap 87, p. 28.
"Visiting My Old Hut in Late Spring" (tr. of Muso Soseki, w. W. S. Merwin).
    [AmerPoR] (16:2) Mr-Ap 87, p. 27.
"Wandering" (tr. of Muso Soseki, w. W. S. Merwin). [AmerPoR] (16:2) Mr-Ap 87,
    p. 25.
"Withered Zen" (tr. of Muso Soseki, w. W. S. Merwin). [AmerPoR] (16:2) Mr-Ap
    87, p. 30.
5008. SHIKATANI, Gerry
    "The Bend." [Waves] (15:3) Wint 87, p. 52-53.
    "Contexte." [CapilR] (44) 87, p. 54.
    "Guadaquivir." [Waves] (15:3) Wint 87, p. 54.
    "Matapoeic." [CrossC] (9:3/4) 87, p. 13.
    "The Prado: Signs, Secrets and Sacred Objects." [MalR] (79) Je 87, p. 118-121.
    "Restauration." [CapilR] (44) 87, p. 51-52.
    "Texte." [CapilR] (44) 87, p. 53.
    "This Is About Meditation" (For David McFadden, Cordoba, Spain, 1985). [CapilR]
        (44) 87, p. 49-50.

"Umbrian Spring." [MalR] (79) Je 87, p. 122-124.
5009. SHILLING, Grant
"The Steal." [Grain] (15:3) Fall 87, p. 38.
5010. SHIMER, Michael
"The Kiss." [Poem] (57) Mr 87, p. 9.
"Nutcraker Sweet" (To Violet). [Poem] (57) Mr 87, p. 12.
"When Glory Broke." [Poem] (57) Mr 87, p. 10-11.
5011. SHINKAWA, Kazue
"Ode to Soil" (tr. by James Morita). [LitR] (30:2) Wint 87, p. 257-258.
5012. SHIPP, R. D.
"Suspects." [Ploughs] (13:4) 87, p. 118-119.
5013. SHIRAISHI, Kazuko
"On the Rock Mountain, A Mountain Goat" (tr. by Hiroaki Sato). [Dandel] (14:2)
Fall-Wint 87, p. 41-49.
"Yellow Night" (tr. by John Solt). [LitR] (30:2) Wint 87, p. 259-262.
5014. SHIRLEY, Aleda
"21 August 1984." [GeoR] (41:3) Fall 87, p. 570-571.
"A Basketball Game at Newburg Middle School." [AmerV] (6) Spr 87, p. 38-39.
"Cant." [Poetry] (150:4) Jl 87, p. 191.
"The Garden at Giverny." [Poetry] (150:4) Jl 87, p. 192.
5015. SHOAF, Diann Blakely
"Child" (for Toni Saldivar). [SouthernHR] (21:4) Fall 87, p. 355.
"Moving." [SouthernPR] (27:1) Spr 87, p. 55.
5016. SHOEMAKER, John-Bruce
"Haiku" (2 poems). [Amelia] (4:3, issue 10) 87, p. 112.
5017. SHOMER, Enid
"7 A.M.: Getting Down to Work." [HeliconN] (17/18) Spr 87, p. 28.
"August Night." [HeliconN] (17/18) Spr 87, p. 29.
"Harvest." [PassN] (8:2) Sum 87, p. 19.
"Horses." [WindO] (49) Fall 87, p. 42.
"Luncheonette in Live Oak, Florida." [PoetL] (82:3) Fall 87, p. 182.
"Wild Plum." [Poetry] (150:1) Ap 87, p. 28.
5018. SHORE, Jane
"A Clock." [AntR] (45:1) Wint 87, p. 59-60.
"Eighth Notes" (for George Shore). [AntR] (45:1) Wint 87, p. 61-63.
"A Luna Moth" (for Elizabeth Bishop). [AntR] (45:1) Wint 87, p. 64-65.
"Wood." [AntR] (45:1) Wint 87, p. 66-67.
5019. SHORE, Marion
"As Soon As I Have Gone to Take My Rest" (Sonnet, tr. of Louise Labé). [Trans]
(18) Spr 87, p. 330.
"If Upon That Fair Breast I Might Lie" (Sonnet, tr. of Louise Labé). [Trans] (18)
Spr 87, p. 328.
"While My Eyes Can Shed Another Tear" (Sonnet, tr. of Louise Labé). [Trans] (18)
Spr 87, p. 329.
5020. SHORT, Brent
"The Wire." [SpoonRQ] (12:2) Spr 87, p. 30.
5021. SHORT, Gary
"At American Flat Mill" (for Marty and Cathy). [Abraxas] (35/36) 87, p. 88-89.
"Lines on an Autumn Night." [PassN] (8:1) Wint 87, p. 14.
5022. SHORTSLEEVE, Mary
"Black Bird of Prey: Notes to Myself." [NewRena] (7:1, #21) Fall 87, p. 50.
"For Chase" (Killed in the aftermath of the Blizzard of '78). [NewRena] (7:1, #21)
Fall 87, p. 51.
5023. SHREVE, Sandy
"Canadians Driving the I-5 to Seattle While the U.S. Bombed Libya." [Waves]
(15:3) Wint 87, p. 55.
5024. SHU, Ting
"Brother, I Am Here" (tr. by Carolyn Kizer, w. Y. H. Zhao). [MichQR] (26:2) Spr
87, p. 402-403.
"Missing" (tr. by Carolyn Kizer, w. Y. H. Zhao). [Poetry] (149:5) F 87, p. 253.
"To the Oak" (tr. by Carolyn Kizer, w. Y. H. Zhao). [Poetry] (149:5) F 87, p. 254.
5025. SHULZ-KIVI, Tamara
"Picasso in the Catalogue." [PoetL] (82:4) Wint 87-88, p. 207.
5026. SHUMAKER, Peggy
"The Cousin on Holiday." [HayF] (2) Spr 87, p. 29.
"First Thing in the Morning, Eclairs, Lightning." [PraS] (61:1) Spr 87, p. 64-65.

"Owl / Beating." [ColR] (NS 14:1) Spr-Sum 87, p. 68.
"Pastoral: Squash and Rice." [PraS] (61:1) Spr 87, p. 67-68.
"Vespers." [PraS] (61:1) Spr 87, p. 66.
"The Waitress's Kid." [HayF] (2) Spr 87, p. 27-28.
SHUNTARO, Tanikawa
    See TANIKAWA, Shuntaro
5027. SHURIN, Aaron
    "Agora." [Act] (7) 87, p. 29-33.
    "A's Dream." [Conjunc] (11) 87?, p. 119-120.
    "Codex" (Three sections). [Bound] (14:1/2) Fall 85-Wint 86 [c87], p. 9.
5028. SHUTTLEWORTH, Paul
    "And the Dog Is Called Lefty." [HayF] (2) Spr 87, p. 71.
    "Before a Train Robbery." [PennR] (3:2) Fall-Wint 87, p. 73.
    "Black Napkin on Snow." [Wind] (17:61) 87, p. 44.
    "The Deer." [Wind] (17:61) 87, p. 44.
    "Duet for Lost Highway: Vengeance, Murder, Cars Burning in Motel Parking Lots,
        Honky Tonks, and True Love . . ." [HayF] (2) Spr 87, p. 69-70.
    "In Glenwood Springs for the Dedication of a New Tombstone for Doc Holliday."
        [PennR] (3:2) Fall-Wint 87, p. 74.
    "Just Before the Hot, Steamy Guts of June" (for Paul Zarzyski). [WestB] (20) 87, p.
        19-23.
    "Letting Go." [KanQ] (19:1/2) Wint-Spr 87, p. 39.
    "Spring Training" (Kansas Quarterly / Kansas Arts Commission Awards Honorable
        Mention Poem, 1986/1987). [KanQ] (19:1/2) Wint-Spr 87, p. 37.
    "The Very Last Afternoon of Summer." [KanQ] (19:1/2) Wint-Spr 87, p. 38.
5029. SIBLEY, Mary
    "White." [Amelia] (4:3, issue 10) 87, p. 118.
5030. SIBUM, Norm
    "Bulletholes and Bottles of Badacsonyi" (To James Ellis). [AntigR] (71/72) Aut
        87-Wint 88, p. 65-66.
    "Propertius in May." [AntigR] (68) Wint 87, p. 129-131.
5031. SICOLI, Dan
    "Bill Didn't Care." [PikeF] (8) Fall 87, p. 27.
    "Drum." [SlipS] (7) 87, p. 97.
    "Mind." [Lactuca] (8) N 87, p. 16.
    "Moment." [Lactuca] (8) N 87, p. 17.
    "Randiletti Was a Bit." [Lactuca] (8) N 87, p. 17.
    "Terminal." [Amelia] (4:3, issue 10) 87, p. 103-105.
5032. SIEBER, Sharon
    "Full Wind" (tr. of Octavio Paz). [NowestR] (25:3) 87, p. 319-323.
5033. SIEDLECKI, Peter
    "I Like to Think of Kafka." [StoneC] (15:1/2) Fall-Wint 87-88, p. 13.
5034. SIEGEL, June
    "To the Extent That I Haven't a Cat." [LightY] '87, c86, p. 109.
5035. SIEGEL, Robert
    "Straight at the Blue" (for Father Francis MacNutt). [ChrC] (104:26) 23 S 87, p.
        783.
    "The very first dream of morning." [Atlantic] (259:3) Mr 87, p. 43.
5036. SIEGELMAN, Kenneth
    "Secret on Moon Street." [Wind] (17:61) 87, p. 27.
5037. SIGNORELLI-PAPPAS, Rita
    "Riding with Keats." [ColEng] (49:4) Ap 87, p. 427.
5038. SIGURDSSON, Olafur Johann
    "Delicate Scent" (tr. by Alan Boucher). [Vis] (25) 87, p. 36.
5039. SILESKY, Barry
    "Cafe Memoir." [NewAW] (2) Fall 87, p. 87.
    "Finding the Future." [NewL] (53:3) Spr 87, p. 92-93.
    "The First Imperial Egg." [ManhatPR] (9) Sum 87, p. 10-11.
5040. SILKIN, Jon
    "Gifts." [KenR] (NS 9:2) Spr 87, p. 78-79.
    "Paying for Forgiveness." [Bogg] (58) 87, p. 8-9.
5041. SILLIMAN, Ron
    "Hidden" (Selection: "Lucky"). [CentralP] (11) Spr 87, p. 39-43.
    "Lucky" (from "Hidden"). [WestCR] (22:1) Sum 87, p. 37-41.
    "Oz" (Excerpt). [NewAW] (1) 87, p. 84-90.
    "Paradise" (Excerpt). [Bound] (14:1/2) Fall 85-Wint 86 [c87], p. 13-14.

5042. SILVA, Beverly
"Desire." [Vis] (23) 87, p. 28.
"I Dreamed Last Night of the Freeway That Goes Nowhere." [SlipS] (7) 87, p. 38.
"Little Chola." [SlipS] (7) 87, p. 39.
"A Surfer's Body." [SlipS] (7) 87, p. 37.
5043. SILVER, William
"A New Father Briefly Considers the Loss of Eden." [CalQ] (30) Wint 87, p. 28.
5044. SILVER-LILLYWHITE, Eileen
"Another Life." [OhioR] (38) 87, p. 113.
"Blue Moon." [AntR] (45:1) Wint 87, p. 68.
5045. SIMAS, Joseph
"Distance: 'Analogy'" (tr. of Anne-Marie Albiach). [LitR] (30:3) Spr 87, p. 338-347.
"Entire Days" (Selection: Parts I-IV). [Temblor] (5) 87, p. 78-80.
"'H-II' Linear" (tr. of Anne-Marie Albiach, w. Anthony Barnett). [Temblor] (5) 87, p. 66-77.
"Kinderpart." [Act] (7) 87, p. 16-18.
"The Longer Sentiments of Middle, III." [Temblor] (5) 87, p. 85-88.
5046. SIMIC, Charles
"Ancient Engines and Beasts." [Field] (36) Spr 87, p. 95.
"Are Russian cannibals worse than the English?" [NewAW] (2) Fall 87, p. 21.
"Autobiography." [Pequod] (23/24) 87, p. 16-20.
"Back at the Chicken Shack." [Poetry] (151:1/2) O-N 87, p. 157-158.
"The Big Machine." [Sulfur] (19) Spr 87, p. 10.
"The Big War." [ParisR] (29:102) Spr 87, p. 86.
"Bread." [ParisR] (29:102) Spr 87, p. 85.
"Celestial Overseers." [Witness] (1:4) Wint 87, p. 138.
"Collard Greens and Black-Eye Peas" (for Clark Coolidge). [Sulfur] (19) Spr 87, p. 8-9.
"Dear Helen." [Poetry] (150:4) Jl 87, p. 229.
"The Devils." [Antaeus] (58) Spr 87, p. 154.
"Early Evening Algebra." [Poetry] (150:4) Jl 87, p. 229.
"Everything's foreseeable." [NewAW] (2) Fall 87, p. 21.
"First Frost." [TexasR] (7:3/4) 87, p. 144.
"First Thing in the Morning." [Ploughs] (13:4) 87, p. 120.
"Folk Song" (tr. of Tomaz Salamun). [Antaeus] (58) Spr 87, p. 33.
"The Gods." [Ploughs] (13:4) 87, p. 121.
"Heaven's Ring: A Cycle of Poems" (tr. of Vasko Popa). [Field] (36) Spr 87, p. 37-43.
"The Immortal." [Poetry] (151:1/2) O-N 87, p. 156-157.
"In a forest of question marks you were no bigger than an asterisk." [NewAW] (2) Fall 87, p. 22.
"In the Alley." [TexasR] (7:3/4) 87, p. 145.
"Light for Hamdija Demirovic" (tr. of Tomaz Salamun). [Antaeus] (58) Spr 87, p. 38.
"M." [Caliban] (2) 87, p. 39-43.
"Man with the Golden Eye" (tr. of Tomaz Salamun). [Antaeus] (58) Spr 87, p. 35.
"Maria" (tr. of Tomaz Salamun). [Antaeus] (58) Spr 87, p. 39-43.
"My Father's Dream." [Sulfur] (19) Spr 87, p. 9-10.
"Nikola Tesla" (tr. of Tomaz Salamun). [Antaeus] (58) Spr 87, p. 34.
"The old farmer in overalls hanging from a barn beam." [NewAW] (2) Fall 87, p. 19.
"A Place in the Country." [TexasR] (7:3/4) 87, p. 143.
"A Poem about sitting on a New York rooftop on a chill autumn evening." [NewAW] (2) Fall 87, p. 20.
"Police dogs in a dog-groomer's window dressed as children." [NewAW] (2) Fall 87, p. 20.
"Promises of Leniency and Forgiveness." [Field] (36) Spr 87, p. 97-98.
"Shelley." [GrandS] (7:1) Aut 87, p. 78-79.
"Sonnet About Milk" (tr. of Tomaz Salamun). [Antaeus] (58) Spr 87, p. 37.
"St. Thomas Aquinas." [Antaeus] (58) Spr 87, p. 152-153.
"That Bit of Vaudeville" (for Fanny Howe). [Witness] (1:1) Spr 87, p. 130-131.
"Trout" (tr. of Tomaz Salamun). [Antaeus] (58) Spr 87, p. 36.
"A week-long holiday in a glass paperweight bought at Coney Island." [NewAW] (2) Fall 87, p. 19.

5047. SIMMERMAN, Jim
  "A Bluebird in the Rain." [Sonora] (13) Fall 87, p. 116-117.
  "December." [LaurelR] (21:1/2) Wint-Sum 87, p. 36-38.
  "Once out of Nature." [NewEngR] (9:4) Sum 87, p. 426-427.
  "Philly's Garden." [LaurelR] (21:1/2) Wint-Sum 87, p. 38-40.
  "The Public Job of Blood." [Ploughs] (13:4) 87, p. 122.
  "The Swallows, Their Song." [LaurelR] (21:1/2) Wint-Sum 87, p. 35-36.
  "Take It Back." [Sonora] (13) Fall 87, p. 118-119.
5048. SIMMONS, James
  "From the Irish." [Pembroke] (19) 87, p. 59.
  "Husband to Wife." [Pembroke] (19) 87, p. 82.
  "The Influence of Natural Objects" (for Bill Ireland). [Pembroke] (19) 87, p. 81.
5049. SIMMONS, Mary Crescenzo
  "Lady Las Vegas." [Lactuca] (5) Ja 87, p. 26-27.
5050. SIMON, Greg
  "Blind Panorama of New York" (tr. of Federico García Lorca, w. Steven L. White).
    [ParisR] (29:104) Fall 87, p. 89-90.
  "Dawn" (tr. of Federico García Lorca, w. Steven L. White). [ParisR] (29:104) Fall
    87, p. 93.
  "Death" (To Luis de la Serna, tr. of Federico García Lorca, w. Steven L. White).
    [ParisR] (29:104) Fall 87, p. 94.
  "Earth and Moon" (tr. of Federico García Lorca). [NowestR] (25:3) 87, p. 324-325.
  "Living Sky" (tr. of Federico García Lorca, w. Steven L. White). [ParisR] (29:104)
    Fall 87, p. 91-92.
  "Ode to Walt Whitman" (tr. of Federico García Lorca, w. Steven L. White). [ParisR]
    (29:104) Fall 87, p. 95-99.
5051. SIMON, John Oliver
  "The Brain of Ruben Dario" (tr. of Jorge Eduardo Argüello). [PikeF] (8) Fall 87, p.
    30.
  "The Broken-Down Bus" (tr. of Alberto Blanco). [Puerto] (22:2) Spr 87, p. 49-53.
  "The City Is Going to Explode, Flora" (tr. of Carlos Orellana). [Vis] (23) 87, p. 8.
  "Despertador." [Abraxas] (35/36) 87, p. 73.
  "La Disco del Pueblo" (tr. by Mónica Mansour). [Electrum] (39) Fall-Wint 87, p.
    29, 31.
  "The People's Disco." [Electrum] (39) Fall-Wint 87, p. 28, 30.
  "Ratus Norvegicus" (tr. of José Emilio Pacheco). [Abraxas] (35/36) 87, p. 51.
  "Ten New Colors" (tr. of Otto-Raúl González). [AmerPoR] (16:1) Ja-F 87, p. 3-6.
5052. SIMON, Louise
  "The Dawn Swim." [Quarry] (36:1) Wint 87, p. 18.
  "Probie Days." [Quarry] (36:1) Wint 87, p. 17.
5053. SIMON, Marjorie
  "Connect the Dots." [Nimrod] (31:1) Fall-Wint 87, p. 85.
  "Long Distance Talker." [Nimrod] (31:1) Fall-Wint 87, p. 86.
5054. SIMON, Maurya
  "Alligator Shoes." [Raccoon] (24/25) My 87, p. 194.
  "At Mudumalai." [MichQR] (26:3) Sum 87, p. 506-507.
  "Atomic Psalm." [MSS] (5:3) 87, p. 32.
  "Dream Babies." [PoetryE] (23/24) Fall 87, p. 167.
  "Les Fleurs du Printemps." [TriQ] (68) Wint 87, p. 100.
  "Heat Wave." [Interim] (6:1) Spr 87, p. 23.
  "Madras Lament." [PoetryE] (23/24) Fall 87, p. 165-166.
  "Rothko's Black." [TriQ] (68) Wint 87, p. 99.
  "The Sadness of Rivers." [Poetry] (150:1) Ap 87, p. 2.
  "Star-Gazing in Autumn." [HawaiiR] (22) Fall 87, p. 59-60.
  "Twilight." [HawaiiR] (22) Fall 87, p. 61.
  "The Years." [PassN] (8:2) Sum 87, p. 13.
5055. SIMONE, Roberta
  "Clerihew Couples" (4 poems). [LightY] '87, c86, p. 68-69.
  "A Literary History of Cheese." [LightY] '87, c86, p. 207-209.
5056. SIMONI, Wanda D.
  "The King of Sweden." [Writer] (99:3) Mr 86, p. 21.
5057. SIMONS, Mary Crescenzo
  "Beyond the Great Wall." [Phoenix] (7:1) 87, p. 44.
5058. SIMONS, Michelle Blake
  "Burn Victims." [SouthernR] (23:4) O 87, p. 821-822.
  "The Cheat." [SouthernR] (23:4) O 87, p. 819-820.

"Forms of Grief." [SouthernR] (23:1) Ja 87, p. 125-126.
"The Fourth Wall." [Ploughs] (13:4) 87, p. 123-124.
"Gates of Horn." [SouthernR] (23:4) O 87, p. 820-821.
"January 1, 5 PM." [SouthernR] (23:1) Ja 87, p. 126.

5059. SIMONSUURI, Kirsti
"Arctic Journey" (tr. by Jascha Kessler and the author). [CrossCur] (7:3) 87, p. 157.
"An Awning, the Senses" (tr. by Jascha Kessler). [Caliban] (2) 87, p. 91.
"Opus" (tr. by Jascha Kessler). [Caliban] (2) 87, p. 90.
"Ruined House" (tr. by Jascha Kessler). [Caliban] (2) 87, p. 90.
"Song from Kanteletar" (tr. of Finnish anonymous song, collected by Lonrot in the 19th century, w. Jascha Kessler). [Nimrod] (31:1) Fall-Wint 87, p. 130.
"A Supper" (tr. by Jascha Kessler). [Caliban] (2) 87, p. 91.

5060. SIMPSON, Grace
"Levitation." [SouthernPR] (27:1) Spr 87, p. 66.

SIMPSON, Katherine Flanagan
See FLANAGAN-SIMPSON, Katherine

5061. SIMPSON, Louis
"Friends." [Poetry] (149:6) Mr 87, p. 334-335.
"The Masterpiece." [Colum] (12) 87, p. 22.
"Neighbors." [OhioR] (39) 87, p. 86-87.
"O What Can Ail Thee, Knight at Arms?" [Poetry] (149:6) Mr 87, p. 332-333.
"On a Painting by Jimmy Ernst." [OhioR] (38) 87, p. 8.
"Summer Comes to the Three Villages." [MissouriR] (10:1) 87, p. 190-191.

5062. SIMPSON, Megan
"September 13." [FiveFR] (5) 87, p. 36.

5063. SIMPSON, Nancy
"Food Director's Testimony." [LightY] '87, c86, p. 58.
"I Was Fortunate." [Confr] (35/36) Spr-Fall 87, p. 133.
"In the Southern Mountains" (Exchanging Ideas on the Subject of Art for A.J. Zimmermacher). [Confr] (35/36) Spr-Fall 87, p. 134-135.

5064. SIMS, Peter
"On Looking Up a Word in the Dictionary" (for BethMarie Michalska and Allan Brown). [Quarry] (36:1) Wint 87, p. 116-117.
"Ravishing Is Writing." [Grain] (15:1) Spr 87, p. 43-44.
"A Small Box." [Quarry] (36:1) Wint 87, p. 115.

5065. SINCLAIR, Marjorie
"The Old Woman Meditates." [HawaiiR] (19) Spr 86, c87, p. 58.

5066. SINGH, Kedarnath
"The Bullock" (tr. by Mrinal Pande). [Bomb] (18) Wint 87, p. 62.
"A Name for My Little Daughter" (tr. by M. Halpearn). [Bomb] (18) Wint 87, p. 62.

5067. SIRETT, Neff
"How the Argument Began" (for D & D). [Grain] (15:4) Wint 87, p. 42.
"Letters." [Grain] (15:2) Sum 87, p. 15-16.
"Singing Lesson." [Grain] (15:2) Sum 87, p. 17.
"To a Friend Who Was Till He Entered U of T." [Grain] (15:2) Sum 87, p. 14.

5068. SIROWITZ, Hal
"Gazing Out." [PaintedB] (30) 87, p. 34.

5069. SISSMAN, L. E.
"Dying: An Introduction." [BostonR] (12:2) Ap 87, p. 19.

5070. SJÖBERG, Leif
"Isak Dinesen" (On the centennial of her birth, tr. of Thorkild Bjørnvig, w. William Jay Smith). [GrahamHR] (10) Wint-Spr 87, p. 50-52.
"Tussock" (tr. of Harry Martinson, w. William Jay Smith). [GreenfR] (14:1/2) Wint-Spr, p. 92.

5071. SKEEN, Tim
"The Cabin." [Colum] (12) 87, p. 105.

5072. SKELTON, Robin
"Lament for Ignacio Sanchez Mejias" (tr. of Federico Garcia Lorca). [MalR] (79) Je 87, p. 61-69.

5073. SKILLMAN, Judith
"1986, Legend of the Lamed-Vov." [PraS] (61:2) Sum 87, p. 101-103.
"An Incident in the New World." [NowestR] (25:1) 87, p. 10-11.
"On a Local Lake." [CumbPR] (7:1) Fall 87, p. 7.
"Study in Blue." [PraS] (61:2) Sum 87, p. 103-104.
"The Waiting." [NowestR] (25:1) 87, p. 12.
"Weeping Fig." [HawaiiR] (22) Fall 87, p. 42.

5074. SKINNER, Douglas Reid
"The Body Is a Country of Joy and of Pain." [TriQ] (69) Spr-Sum 87, p. 465-467.
"Law and Order." [TriQ] (69) Spr-Sum 87, p. 41-43.
5075. SKINNER, Jeffrey
"Beauty and the Spider." [Iowa] (17:1) Wint 87, p. 73-74.
"Breaking Down on the New England Thruway." [HampSPR] Wint 86, p. 9.
"For Stuart Porter, Who Asked for a Poem That Would Not Depress Him Further."
    [Atlantic] (260:6) D 87, p. 54.
"A Grace." [Iowa] (17:1) Wint 87, p. 76-77.
"Happy Hour with Grady." [Iowa] (17:1) Wint 87, p. 72-73.
"Leveling Ground for the Backyard Pool." [HampSPR] Wint 86, p. 8-9.
"Looking at a Photograph of My Father at My Age." [Iowa] (17:1) Wint 87, p.
    75-76.
"On a Bad Painting in the Lobby of IBM International." [Iowa] (17:1) Wint 87, p.
    74-75.
"Pastoral." [HampSPR] Wint 86, p. 7-8.
"Prayer to Cottonmouth Blocking the Road to the Pond." [Comm] (114:6) 27 Mr 87,
    p. 176.
"Prayer to Sparrow in Two Seasons." [Atlantic] (259:1) Ja 87, p. 72.
"Prayer to Wasp on the Occasion of Its Execution." [Iowa] (17:1) Wint 87, p. 77-78.
"Self Portrait." [ParisR] (29:105) Wint 87, p. 93.
"Summer Guests." [HampSPR] Wint 86, p. 10.
5076. SKINNER, Knute
"At the Church of St. Mary of the Immaculate Conception, Rome." [FloridaR] (15:2)
    Fall-Wint 87, p. 55.
"Bailey." [LightY] '87, c86, p. 101.
"The Girl Next Door." [LightY] '87, c86, p. 239.
"The Obligation." [LightY] '87, c86, p. 165.
"A Social Engagement." [LightY] '87, c86, p. 45.
5077. SKIPPER, Louie
"1955." [KenR] (NS 9:3) Sum 87, p. 31-32.
"Deaths That Travel with the Weather" (Excerpt). [KenR] (NS 9:3) Sum 87, p.
    32-39.
5078. SKLAREW, Myra
"Dreaming of Rain." [DenQ] (21:3) Wint 87, p. 72-74.
"The Messiah Reconsidered." [Poetry] (151:3) D 87, p. 287-289.
5079. SKLOOT, Floyd
"Caring for the Life." [Raccoon] (24/25) My 87, p. 247.
"In the Phoenix Islands." [NowestR] (25:1) 87, p. 16.
"You Asked for It." [NewEngR] (10:1) Aut 87, p. 25.
5080. SKOV-NIELSEN, Kurt
"Easter Monday." [AntigR] (71/72) Aut 87-Wint 88, p. 157.
5081. SKOYLES, John
"43rd Avenue." [AntR] (45:1) Wint 87, p. 70.
"Good Cheer." [TriQ] (68) Wint 87, p. 103-104.
"Holy Cross Church" (W. 42nd Street). [AntR] (45:1) Wint 87, p. 69.
5082. SKRANDE, Eva
"The Bus Driver." [KanQ] (19:3) Sum 87, p. 330.
"The Holy Tree." [CutB] (27/28) 87, p. 52.
5083. SLACK, Ellen
"The City in August: The Coast at Last." [NegC] (7:1/2) 87, p. 73.
"Pheasants Cry." [NegC] (7:1/2) 87, p. 74-75.
5084. SLAVENS, Kerry
"Natalya Longing." [MalR] (81) D 87, p. 81-82.
"A Perfect Day." [MalR] (81) D 87, p. 83.
5085. SLAVITT, David R.
"Consent." [SouthernPR] (27:2) Fall 87, p. 37.
"Fizz." [NegC] (7:3/4) 87, p. 83-84.
"Letter to a Grandchild." [KanQ] (19:3) Sum 87, p. 88-89.
"Sonnet." [KanQ] (19:3) Sum 87, p. 90.
5086. SLAYMAKER, Bob
"Vegetable Seller in Nairobi." [MinnR] (NS 28) Spr 87, p. 22.
5087. SLEIGH, Tom
"Animus." [Poetry] (150:1) Ap 87, p. 22-23.
"First Love." [Poetry] (150:1) Ap 87, p. 25.
"The Seal." [Poetry] (150:1) Ap 87, p. 23-25.

5088. SLICER, Deborah
"Suburbia" (After de Chirico). [HampSPR] Wint 87, p. 19.
5089. SLING, Naomi
"Fire in bat guano." [Amelia] (4:1/2, issue 9) 87, p. 44.
5090. SLOAN, Gerry
"Small Tubes of Uncertain Affinities" (for David Sanders). [PassN] (8:1) Wint 87, p. 17.
5091. SLOAN, Margy
"Abeyance Series" (Excerpts). [Act] (7) 87, p. 41-44.
5092. SLOMKOWSKA, Lusia
"Remembering an Organ Concert: Sopot, Poland." [NewL] (53:3) Spr 87, p. 19.
"Why Cities Have Farmer's Markets" (for my mother). [Agni] (24/25) 87, p. 224-225.
5093. SLOTA, Richard
"Famous Michael." [Abraxas] (35/36) 87, p. 36-45.
5094. SLYMAN, Ernest
"Olecranon." [LightY] '87, c86, p. 95.
5095. SMART, Carolyn
"Multiplication" (for Elizabeth Legge). [Quarry] (36:1) Wint 87, p. 58-60.
"Winnipeg" (for MaryAnn McCrea). [Quarry] (36:1) Wint 87, p. 61-63.
5096. SMETZER, Michael
"Old Man of the Road." [KanQ] (19:3) Sum 87, p. 109.
"On Hearing You Love a Wife Beater Divorced Three Times." [KanQ] (19:3) Sum 87, p. 107.
"Smetzer Graves near Clinton, Kansas" (Seaton First Award Poem 1987). [KanQ] (19:3) Sum 87, p. 108-109.
5097. SMITH, Alex
"Kaleidoscope of Desire" (w. Jenny Schipper). [SlipS] (7) 87, p. 45-74.
5098. SMITH, Arthur
"The Dull Tugs." [PennR] (3:2) Fall-Wint 87, p. 56.
"The Least of Things." [NewYorker] (63:20) 6 Jl 87, p. 30.
"A Little Death." [Crazy] (33) Wint 87, p. 52-53.
"The Recital" (for my sister). [MissouriR] (10:2) 87, p. 140-141.
5099. SMITH, Barbara (See also SMITH, Barbara E. & SMITH, Barbara Elaine)
"Cross-Country." [LaurelR] (20:1/2) Sum 87, p. 50.
"Genuine (with a Long i) Mountain Crafts." [LaurelR] (20:1/2) Sum 87, p. 48-49.
5100. SMITH, Barbara E. (See also SMITH, Barbara & SMITH, Barbara Elaine)
"Candidates." [Writer] (99:9) S 86, p. 25.
5101. SMITH, Barbara Elaine (See also SMITH, Barbara & SMITH, Barbara E.)
"Waste and Want." [Writer] (99:5) My 86, p. 17.
5102. SMITH, Bruce
"Hart Crane: A Coda." [Crazy] (33) Wint 87, p. 12.
"Hart Crane: A Dream for Two Voices." [Crazy] (33) Wint 87, p. 11.
"In the City of Brotherly Love." [ParisR] (29:105) Wint 87, p. 145-147.
"The Present Tense." [Crazy] (33) Wint 87, p. 20-25.
"Self Portrait after Waking." [Crazy] (33) Wint 87, p. 13-19.
5103. SMITH, Charlie
"American Drift." [BlackWR] (13:2) Spr 87, p. 87-88.
"As Far As Living Things Go." [AmerPoR] (16:3) My-Je 87, p. 19.
"At the Forestry Sub-Station." [AmerPoR] (16:3) My-Je 87, p. 19.
"Confederate States." [Sonora] (12) Spr 87, p. 28.
"The Holly Tree." [Nat] (245:11) 10 O 87, p. 387.
"Indistinguishable from the Darkness." [NewYorker] (63:12) 11 My 87, p. 42.
"Kohaku." [Sonora] (12) Spr 87, p. 29-30.
"Monastic." [TarRP] (26:2) Spr 87, p. 44.
"Neither Ornamental Nor True." [AmerPoR] (16:3) My-Je 87, p. 19.
"Redbird." [Crazy] (32) Spr 87, p. 16-17.
"Walking Home Through the Garden." [TarRP] (26:2) Spr 87, p. 43-44.
5104. SMITH, Dave
"Crab House." [Atlantic] (260:5) N 87, p. 76.
"Lake Drummond Dream." [YaleR] (77:1) Aut 87, p. 151-152.
"Local Color." [MissouriR] (10:2) 87, p. 62.
"New Year's Day." [Nat] (245:18) 28 N 87, p. 659.
"Palmetto Special." [Poetry] (151:1/2) O-N 87, p. 158-159.
"Sexual Odor." [MissouriR] (10:2) 87, p. 63.

5105. SMITH, David-Glen
"A Fist of New Moon." [YellowS] (25) Wint 87, p. 35.
"'In Spirit,' They Said." [YellowS] (25) Wint 87, p. 35.
5106. SMITH, Douglas Burnet
"Caterpillars." [AntigR] (71/72) Aut 87-Wint 88, p. 89.
"Walking Shoe." [AntigR] (71/72) Aut 87-Wint 88, p. 86-87.
"A Woman Named Experience" (Port Lorne Cemetery, Nova Scotia). [AntigR]
(71/72) Aut 87-Wint 88, p. 87-88.
5107. SMITH, Francis J.
"Dartmoor at Dusk." [ManhatPR] (9) Sum 87, p. 7.
"Honeymoon in Nice." [LightY] '87, c86, p. 144.
5108. SMITH, Gary
"Fireflies." [BlackALF] (21:3) Fall 87, p. 240.
5109. SMITH, H. Wendell
"Molly Gaunt." [LightY] '87, c86, p. 151.
5110. SMITH, Hugh T.
"By Rent-A-Truck." [Outbr] (18/19) Fall 86-Spr 88, p. 167.
5111. SMITH, Iain Crichton
"Child." [KenR] (NS 9:2) Spr 87, p. 83.
"Death." [Verse] (4:2) Je 87, p. 4.
"Did You See the Modest Girl?" (tr. of anonymous Gaelic poem). [Stand] (28:2) Spr
87, p. 50.
"A Dying." [KenR] (NS 9:2) Spr 87, p. 79-81.
"Even." [Verse] (4:2) Je 87, p. 3.
"Glance." [Verse] (4:2) Je 87, p. 4.
"Pity That I Was Not Born Blind" (tr. of anonymous Gaelic poem). [Stand] (28:2)
Spr 87, p. 49.
"Poem: The sea and the library in this town." [KenR] (NS 9:2) Spr 87, p. 82.
"The Scholar and the Poet." [Verse] (4:2) Je 87, p. 3.
"Seathan Son of the King of Ireland" (tr. of anonymous Gaelic poem). [Stand]
(28:2) Spr 87, p. 50-53.
"Stubble." [Verse] (4:2) Je 87, p. 3.
5112. SMITH, J. D.
"The Wooly Mammoth." [Wind] (17:60) 87, p. 42-43.
5113. SMITH, James Steel
"Clerihews" (3 poems). [LightY] '87, c86, p. 66-67.
"Invitation." [LightY] '87, c86, p. 142.
"Knitting-Sitting Song." [LightY] '87, c86, p. 47.
SMITH, James Sutherland
See SUTHERLAND-SMITH, James
5114. SMITH, Joan Jobe
"Beef and Barley Soup." [WormR] (27:1, issue 105) 87, p. 13-14.
"Getting Drunk with My Third Mother-in-Law." [WormR] (27:1, issue 105) 87, p.
10-11.
"Go-Go Girl Reunion." [WormR] (27:1, issue 105) 87, p. 11-12.
"How You Taste the Apples." [WormR] (27:1, issue 105) 87, p. 12-13.
"Without Grouchy Old Preminger." [WormR] (27:1, issue 105) 87, p. 14.
5115. SMITH, Jodi
"The King of the Butterflies." [Gambit] (20) 86, p. 41.
5116. SMITH, John
"Junco." [StoneC] (15:1/2) Fall-Wint 87-88, p. 47.
5117. SMITH, John Vincent
"Antofagasta" (tr. of Rene Chapero). [Vis] (24) 87, p. 13.
5118. SMITH, Jordan
"After Rozewicz." [Shen] (37:4) 87, p. 73.
"Alberich." [ParisR] (29:105) Wint 87, p. 142-143.
"A Primer for Those Who Have Dealings with the Gods." [Agni] (24/25) 87, p. 103.
"That Idiot." [Shen] (37:4) 87, p. 72.
5119. SMITH, Judy
"Why He Is Not Happy." [AntigR] (71/72) Aut 87-Wint 88, p. 209.
5120. SMITH, Kay
"Old Women and Love." [CanLit] (112) Spr 87, p. 39.
"Orchard Morning." [CanLit] (112) Spr 87, p. 8.
5121. SMITH, Larry E.
"This Is the Buzzards' Roost." [LakeSR] (21) 87, p. 19.

5122. SMITH, Lee A.
"Night as Seen by an Indian." [LaurelR] (20:1/2) Sum 87, p. 108.
"A Night for Believing." [LaurelR] (20:1/2) Sum 87, p. 69.
5123. SMITH, Leonora
"Some Came Home" (for D., 1949-?). [Nimrod] (31:1) Fall-Wint 87, p. 87-90.
5124. SMITH, Macklin
"Why This Obsession?" [MichQR] (26:2) Spr 87, p. 311-313.
5125. SMITH, Maurine
"Folk Lore." [CharR] (13:2) Fall 87, p. 85.
"Hypnosis." [CharR] (13:2) Fall 87, p. 86.
5126. SMITH, Michael
"Mi C-YaaN beLieVe iT." [GrahamHR] (10) Wint-Spr 87, p. 73-75.
5127. SMITH, Nancy
"Another Night on the Town." [Waves] (15:4) Spr 87, p. 58-59.
"Wives of the House." [Waves] (15:4) Spr 87, p. 59.
5128. SMITH, Nathaniel (Nathaniel B.)
"Absence, VII" (tr. of Rosa Leveroni, w. Lynette McGrath). [WebR] (12:2) Fall 87,
    p. 22.
"Between Two Darknesses, One Lightning Flash" (tr. of Vicente Aleixandre).
    [InterPR] (13:1) Spr 87, p. 7, 9.
"Chess, I-II" (tr. of Jorge Luis Borges). [InterPR] (13:2) Fall 87, p. 27.
"A Day Like This" (tr. of Francesc Parcerisas, w. Lynette McGrath). [InterPR]
    (13:2) Fall 87, p. 11.
"Distant Deaths" (tr. of Clementina Arderiu, w. Lynette McGrath). [WebR] (12:2)
    Fall 87, p. 22.
"Here I Was Born" (tr. of Vicent Andrés Estellés). [WebR] (12:2) Fall 87, p. 20.
"Horatians, LXXIII" (tr. of Vicent Andrés Estellés). [InterPR] (13:2) Fall 87, p. 13.
"Notebook for No One" (to Francesc Vallverdú, 6 selections tr. of Vicent Andrés
    Estellés). [WebR] (12:2) Fall 87, p. 18-19.
"Parting" (tr. of Francesc Parcerisas, w. Lynette McGrath). [InterPR] (13:2) Fall 87,
    p. 7.
"Psalm 5" (tr. of Ernesto Cardenal). [InterPR] (13:1) Spr 87, p. 11.
"Roman Heads" (tr. of Francesc Parcerisas, w. Lynette McGrath). [InterPR] (13:2)
    Fall 87, p. 7.
"Song of Perfect Trust" (tr. of Clementina Arderiu, w. Lynette McGrath). [WebR]
    (12:2) Fall 87, p. 21.
"Summer Vacation" (tr. of Francesc Parcerisas, w. Lynette McGrath). [InterPR]
    (13:2) Fall 87, p. 9.
"To His Girl Friend" (tr. of Pierre de Ronsard). [WebR] (12:2) Fall 87, p. 23.
"Virgil's Hand" (tr. of Francesc Parcerisas, w. Lynette McGrath). [InterPR] (13:2)
    Fall 87, p. 9.
"When You're Dead" (tr. of Vicent Andrés Estellés). [InterPR] (13:2) Fall 87, p. 15.
5129. SMITH, Patricia M.
"Ladle." [CrabCR] (4:2) Spr 87, p. 28.
5130. SMITH, R. T.
"Apollo in Appalachia." [InterPR] (13:2) Fall 87, p. 61.
"Bridle." [PoetL] (81:3) Fall 86, p. 183-184.
"Cancun: Dinner in the Tourist Zone." [SoCaR] (20:1) Fall 87, p. 29.
"Carnival Wheels." [GreensboroR] (43) Wint 87-88, p. 105.
"Congregation." [Pembroke] (19) 87, p. 111.
"The Cyclades." [PoetC] (19:1) Fall 87, p. 13.
"Faun." [SoCaR] (20:1) Fall 87, p. 28.
"Fretful, the Last Apostate Grunt Fondles His M-60 and Meditates on Republicans,
    Drought and National Shame." [CimR] (79) Ap 87, p. 38.
"Gargoyle, Forming." [InterPR] (13:2) Fall 87, p. 63.
"Impact." [Wind] (17:60) 87, p. 44.
"Kudzu: Amnesty." [PoetL] (82:1) Spr 87, p. 35-37.
"Making the Snowshoes." [Spirit] (8:2) 87, p. 221.
"March, and Mae Fields Tells of the Most Recent Miracle She Almost Saw." [QW]
    (24) Wint 87, p. 92-93.
"North of Spruce Pine." [GeoR] (41:4) Wint 87, p. 736.
"Poem on a Phrase from Carruth." [Pembroke] (19) 87, p. 111-112.
"Rhubard." [NoDaQ] (55:1) Wint 87, p. 155-156.
"The Scratch" (Honorary Mention 1987 John Williams Andrews Narrative Poetry
    Prize). [PoetL] (82:4) Wint 87-88, p. 234-237.
"Short Story Lesson." [ConcPo] (20) 87, p. 72-73.

"Similes." [SoCaR] (20:1) Fall 87, p. 30.
"This Invasion." [HawaiiR] (22) Fall 87, p. 43.
"Threshold." [Poem] (57) Mr 87, p. 68-69.
"Thrift." [InterPR] (13:2) Fall 87, p. 62.
"Untangling the Vines." [CimR] (79) Ap 87, p. 62.
"Wild Tom Blows Through the 85 Torch, Which Is." [TexasR] (8:1/2) Spr-Sum 87,
    p. 33.
5131. SMITH, Robert Lavett
"An Encounter with God." [Vis] (25) 87, p. 19.
"The Man Who Built a Castle" (For Dan Regan). [Footwork] 87, p. 60.
"Paestum." [Vis] (24) 87, p. 16.
"Portrait of a Lady." [Footwork] 87, p. 59-60.
"Some Kind of Permanence." [Footwork] 87, p. 59.
"Starvation." [Footwork] 87, p. 34-35.
"The Visitors." [Footwork] 87, p. 59.
"What I Wanted to Tell You" (for Lisa). [Footwork] 87, p. 34.
5132. SMITH, Ron
"For Mother, Who Thought Cremation Evil." [PoetryNW] (28:4) Wint 87-88, p.
    30-32.
"Great Granddaddy." [GreensboroR] (40) Sum 86, p. 117.
"Leaving Forever." [Nat] (244:8) 28 F 87, p. 264.
"Sister." [PoetryNW] (28:4) Wint 87-88, p. 29-30.
"War Stories, 1947." [PoetryE] (23/24) Fall 87, p. 131-133.
5133. SMITH, Stephen E.
"Most of What We Take Is Given." [QW] (24) Wint 87, p. 104-105.
5134. SMITH, Steven
"High Density." [CrossC] (9:3/4) 87, p. 20.
SMITH, Sybil Woods
    See WOODS-SMITH, Sybil
5135. SMITH, Thomas R.
"Firefly in the Pines." [Germ] (10:2) Spr 87, p. 10.
"Gratitude" (For Krista). [Germ] (10:2) Spr 87, p. 15.
"In a Canoe on Clearwater Lake." [Germ] (10:2) Spr 87, p. 16.
"Man in the World." [Germ] (10:2) Spr 87, p. 14.
"The Mary Shrine." [Germ] (10:2) Spr 87, p. 12.
"Northern Lights." [Germ] (10:2) Spr 87, p. 17.
"The Sound of Water." [Germ] (10:2) Spr 87, p. 13.
"Summer Solstice." [Germ] (10:2) Spr 87, p. 11.
"Two Poems on the Fear of Love." [Spirit] (8:2) 87, p. 77.
5136. SMITH, William Alexander
"His Day." [GreensboroR] (42) Sum 87, p. 73.
"Job Hunt." [GreensboroR] (42) Sum 87, p. 72.
"Observing the Pulse in the Hollow of My Wrist." [GreensboroR] (42) Sum 87, p.
    73.
5137. SMITH, William Jay
"Isak Dinesen" (On the centennial of her birth, tr. of Thorkild Bjørnvig, w. Leif
    Sjöberg). [GrahamHR] (10) Wint-Spr 87, p. 50-52.
"Journey to the Interior." [Poetry] (151:1/2) O-N 87, p. 160.
"The More You Tear Off, the More You Keep" (tr. of Andrei Voznesensky, w. Vera
    Dunham). [Trans] (18) Spr 87, p. 314-315.
"Over a dark and quiet empire" (tr. of Andrei Voznesensky, w. Patricia Blake).
    [Trans] (18) Spr 87, p. 316.
"Three Views of a Medusa" (tr. of Jean-Max Tixier). [Trans] (19) Fall 87, p.
    197-198.
"To hang bare light bulbs from a ceiling" (tr. of Andrei Voznesensky, w. Patricia
    Blake). [Trans] (18) Spr 87, p. 316.
"Tussock" (tr. of Harry Martinson, w. Leif Sjöberg). [GreenfR] (14:1/2) Wint-Spr,
    p. 92.
"Variations on a Flame" (tr. of Jean-Max Tixier). [Trans] (19) Fall 87, p. 198.
5138. SMITH-BOWERS, Cathy
"Conversation with My Hyphen After the Divorce." [PoetL] (81:4) Wint 86-87, p.
    233-234.
"Markings." [SoCaR] (20:1) Fall 87, p. 64-65.
"Saviours." [SouthernPR] (27:2) Fall 87, p. 25-26.
"Third Child." [SouthernPR] (27:1) Spr 87, p. 39-40.

"To My Nephew, Age 11-1/2, of His Estranged Father." [Pembroke] (19) 87, p. 164.

5139. SMITH-SOTO, Mark
"Easter Wings." [CarolQ] (39:3) Spr 87, p. 71.

5140. SMITS, Ronald
"Crossing the Bayonne Bridge." [Footwork] 87, p. 57.

5141. SMOCK, Frederick
"Basketball Jones." [GreenfR] (14:3/4) Sum-Fall 87, p. 171.
"Incident from the Life of Mandelstam." [Wind] (17:60) 87, p. 45.
"Nabokov Purchases an Émigré Daily." [Wind] (17:60) 87, p. 46.
"Night" (for Marina Tsveteyeva). [Wind] (17:60) 87, p. 45.
"Stone Women" (after Bohdan Boychuk). [Wind] (17:60) 87, p. 46.
"Tsarskoe Selo" (St. Petersburg, 1758). [Wind] (17:60) 87, p. 46.

5142. SMUKLER, Linda
"Mud Wrestlers." [SinW] (31) 87, p. 17-18.

5143. SMYTH, Laura
"Laurel Lake." [SouthernPR] (27:2) Fall 87, p. 43.

5144. SMYTH, Paul
"Trespass." [TexasR] (7:3/4) 87, p. 146-147.

5145. SNEED, E. W.
"Me Wants a Minks." [LightY] '87, c86, p. 129.

5146. SNEFF, Priscilla
"Poem: Here is my poem." [YaleR] (77:1) Aut 87, p. 26.

5147. SNEYD, Steve
"An Unlikely Couple." [Bogg] (57) 87, p. 56.

5148. SNIDER, Clifton
"Following St. Catherine." [Vis] (24) 87, p. 16.

5149. SNIVELY, Susan
"After Anger." [PoetryE] (23/24) Fall 87, p. 156.
"Forgiveness." [PoetryE] (23/24) Fall 87, p. 157.
"The Law of Gravity." [KenR] (NS 9:4) Fall 87, p. 95-98.
"Music Deepens the Distance." [PoetryE] (23/24) Fall 87, p. 155.
"Sledding on Lunatic Hill." [PoetryE] (23/24) Fall 87, p. 158.
"Soldier and Laughing Girl" (A painting by Vermeer). [KenR] (NS 9:4) Fall 87, p. 94.
"The Wish." [PoetryE] (23/24) Fall 87, p. 159.

5150. SNODGRASS, Ann
"December 3" (tr. of Vittorio Sereni). [Trans] (18) Spr 87, p. 318.
"Niccolò" (tr. of Vittorio Sereni). [Trans] (18) Spr 87, p. 319.
"Poet in Black" (tr. of Vittorio Sereni). [Trans] (18) Spr 87, p. 318.
"Years Later" (tr. of Vittorio Sereni). [Trans] (18) Spr 87, p. 317.

5151. SNODGRASS, W. D.
"April Inventory." [Nimrod] (30:2) Spr-Sum 87, p. 35-36.
"Assuming Fine Feathers, W.D. Takes Flight." [AmerPoR] (16:1) Ja-F 87, p. 35.
"Coroner's Inquest." [LightY] '87, c86, p. 93-94.
"Credo" (for Antonia Quintana Pigno). [LightY] '87, c86, p. 90-92.
"Lullaby: The Comforting of Cock Robin." [AmerPoR] (16:1) Ja-F 87, p. 34.
"The Poet Ridiculed by Hysterical Academics" (after the painting by DeLoss McGraw). [LightY] '87, c86, p. 196-197.
"Through the Nursery Window" (for Dylan Taylor McGraw). [MichQR] (26:2) Spr 87, p. 315-316.
"W. D., Don't Fear That Animal" (after the painting by DeLoss McGraw). [LightY] '87, c86, p. 89-90.
"W. D. Lifts Ten Times the Weight of His Own Body" (after DeLoss McGraw's painting . . .). [GrahamHR] (10) Wint-Spr 87, p. 32-33.
"W.D. and Cock Robin Discuss the Dreaded Interrogation." [AmerPoR] (16:1) Ja-F 87, p. 34-35.
"W.D. Consults with Kafka and Dostoevsky Concerning the Whereabouts of Cock Robin." [AmerPoR] (16:1) Ja-F 87, p. 34.
"W.D. Sits in Kafka's Chair and Is Interrogated Concerning the Assumed Death of Cock Robin." [AmerPoR] (16:1) Ja-F 87, p. 35.
"W.D. Tries to Warn Cock Robin." [AmerPoR] (16:1) Ja-F 87, p. 33.

5152. SNOTHERLY, Mary C.
"Mimosa." [Pembroke] (19) 87, p. 112.
"Traveling Backroads, N.C. Highway 307 East." [Pembroke] (19) 87, p. 112-113.

369

5153. SNOW, Karen
"My Gracious Silence" (Coriolanus to his wife, Virgilia — Shakespeare). [BelPoJ]
(37:4) Sum 87, p. 22-23.
5154. SNYDER, Gary
"Foxtail Pine." [NowestR] (25:3) 87, p. 43-44.
"Walking the New York Bedrock Alive in the Sea of Information" (from "Mountains
of Rivers Without End"). [Sulfur] (20) Fall 87, p. 55-59.
5155. SNYDER, J. K.
"Hangzhou in Snow." [AntigR] (71/72) Aut 87-Wint 88, p. 8.
"Remembering Jinan." [AntigR] (71/72) Aut 87-Wint 88, p. 9.
"Shandong: At the University." [AntigR] (71/72) Aut 87-Wint 88, p. 8.
5156. SO, Chong-ju
"Winter Sky" (tr. by David R. McCann). [Pembroke] (19) 87, p. 15.
5157. SOBIN, Anthony
"Another Birthday: The Poet Takes His Laps." [KanQ] (19:3) Sum 87, p. 16.
"Springtime in Alabama." [KanQ] (19:3) Sum 87, p. 16.
"The Thaw." [KanQ] (19:3) Sum 87, p. 15.
5158. SOBIN, Gustaf
"Ferrara Unleavened" (In Memory of My Parents). [Act] (7) 87, p. 11-13.
5159. SOBSEY, Cynthia
"Cups and Saucers." [PassN] (8:1) Wint 87, p. 7.
"Separations." [Wind] (17:61) 87, p. 50.
5160. SOCOLOW, Elizabeth Anne
"Emilie Du Chatelet, Nine Months Pregnant, Addresses Newton: Notes Found . . ."
[US1] (20/21) Wint 86-87, p. 42-43.
"I Doze off in the Tired Shade of an Afternoon" (tr. of Blaga Dimitrova, w. L. P.
Wightman). [NewEngR] (9:4) Sum 87, p. 384.
"Laughing at Gravity: Conversations wih Isaac Newton" (2 selections). [Nimrod]
(31:1) Fall-Wint 87, p. 39-41.
"To Newton on My Purse and the Dryness of the Heavens." [US1] (20/21) Wint
86-87, p. 43.
5161. SOGA, Keiho
"Death at the Camp" (in Romanized Japanese and English, tr. by Jiro & Kay
Nakano). The Best of [BambooR] [(31-32)] 86, p. 72.
SOIKU, Shigematsu
See SHIGEMATSU, Soiku
SOJIN, Takei
See TAKEI, Sojin
5162. SOLARCZYK, Bart
"Poets." [Bogg] (57) 87, p. 48.
5163. SOLE, Kelwyn
"Appointment." [TriQ] (69) Spr-Sum 87, p. 164-165.
"As We Stop Loving." [TriQ] (69) Spr-Sum 87, p. 167-168.
"The Sunlight Has Moved." [TriQ] (69) Spr-Sum 87, p. 166.
5164. SOLHEIM, James
"Kanna Mackett's Tragedy." [ChiR] (35:4) 87, p. 80-86.
5165. SOLLERS, Philippe
"An Excerpt from H" (tr. by Elaine Corts). [Rampike] (5:3) 87, p. 35-36.
5166. SOLLFREY, Stacey
"Poetry Reading Itself Together." [Bogg] (58) 87, p. 55.
5167. SOLOMON, Carl
"Hobo Joe Didn't Survive and Why." [AlphaBS] (1) Je 87, p. 1.
5168. SOLOMON, Jack
"Auld Lang Syne." [Jacaranda] (2:2) Spr 87, p. 57.
5169. SOLONCHE, J. R.
"Blue Heron." [LitR] (30:4) Sum 87, p. 541-542.
"A Drawing by Rembrandt, 'Mercury and Argus'." [PoetryNW] (28:1) Spr 87, p.
36.
"On a Photograph of Charlie Chaplin and Albert Einstein." [AmerS] (56:1) Wint 87,
p. 70.
"Pompeii." [InterPR] (13:1) Spr 87, p. 81.
"Standing on the Bridge Above the Water." [PoetryNW] (28:1) Spr 87, p. 35.
"Three Hawks." [InterPR] (13:1) Spr 87, p. 82-83.
"Three Hawks." [LitR] (30:4) Sum 87, p. 540-541.
"The Wishes of Human Vanity." [CrabCR] (4:2) Spr 87, p. 16.

5170. SOLT, John
"Yellow Night" (tr. of Shiraishi Kazuko). [LitR] (30:2) Wint 87, p. 259-262.
5171. SOLWAY, David
"Antipaxos." [PartR] (54:1) Wint 87, p. 130-132.
"Night." [MalR] (80) S 87, p. 115.
5172. SOMERVILLE, Jane
"The Dawn of the Day Star." [LaurelR] (20:1/2) Sum 87, p. 107.
"A Downwardness All Around Us." [SoDakR] (25:2) Sum 87, p. 84.
"For Arnold Friend, a Fantasy Man Invented by Joyce Carol Oates." [Pembroke]
(19) 87, p. 163.
"The Whole World." [KanQ] (19:3) Sum 87, p. 253.
"Yes Yes Yes It's All So Interesting." [Pembroke] (19) 87, p. 163.
5173. SOMMER, Angela
"The Hausfrau" (tr. by Billie R. Engels). [NewOR] (14:2) Sum 87, p. 64.
5174. SOMMER, Richard
"The Taste." [MalR] (79) Je 87, p. 77.
"A Temple of Bees." [MalR] (79) Je 87, p. 78.
"Time." [MalR] (79) Je 87, p. 79-80.
5175. SONDE, Susan
"Death As Kinds of Weather." [SouthernHR] (21:1) Wint 87, p. 48.
"Letters from the Baja (Selections)." [BallSUF] (28:4) Aut 87, p. 6.
"Ours Is the Legacy of Privation." [HeliconN] (17/18) Spr 87, p. 161.
"Pavane." [HampSPR] Wint 87, p. 38.
"Those Phrases" (from "View from the Doge's Palace"). [StoneC] (14:3/4) Spr-Sum
87, p. 18.
"View North." [HeliconN] (17/18) Spr 87, p. 160.
"Villa Doloroso." [HolCrit] (24:5) D 87, p. 13.
5176. SONG, Cathy
"A Child's Painting." [AmerPoR] (16:4) Jl-Ag 87, p. 5.
"Easter: Wahiawa, 1959." The Best of [BambooR] [(31-32)] 86, p. 79-81.
"Tribe" (for Andrea). The Best of [BambooR] [(31-32)] 86, p. 82-83.
"The White Porch." The Best of [BambooR] [(31-32)] 86, p. 84-85.
"Youngest Daughter." The Best of [BambooR] [(31-32)] 86, p. 77-78.
5177. SONG, Sam-mun
"At the Execution Ground" (tr. by Kim Jong-gil). [Pembroke] (19) 87, p. 12.
5178. SONG, Terry
"Into the Light." [Puerto] (22:2) Spr 87, p. 22-24.
5179. SONIAT, Katherine
"Bedside Story." [SenR] (17:2) 87, p. 62.
"Desire." [Poetry] (151:1/2) O-N 87, p. 161.
"Evening Coming On." [LaurelR] (21:1/2) Wint-Sum 87, p. 33.
"The Future." [SenR] (17:2) 87, p. 61.
"Late Exchanges." [Northeast] (Ser. 4:5) Sum 87, p. 46.
"Lightning Rods." [LaurelR] (21:1/2) Wint-Sum 87, p. 33.
"Other People's Houses." [Outbr] (18/19) Fall 86-Spr 88, p. 182-183.
"Santa Rosa Island." [SouthernR] (23:4) O 87, p. 818.
"Winter Toys." [NewL] (53:2) Wint 86-87, p. 82-83.
5180. SORBY, Angela
"Le Thérapeute" (after Magritte). [Lactuca] (6) Ap-My 87, p. 22.
5181. SORENSEN, Sally Jo
"Equinox." [WestB] (20) 87, p. 39.
5182. SORESTAD, Glen
"Dry Hills." [Waves] (14:4) Spr 86, p. 64.
"Early Morning Sun — Weyburn." [Puerto] (22:2) Spr 87, p. 66.
"Juxtaposition." [Waves] (14:4) Spr 86, p. 64.
"Small Flowers." [Puerto] (22:2) Spr 87, p. 67.
"Sunday Afternoon at De Keulse Pot, Amsterdam." [Quarry] (36:3) Sum 87, p.
47-48.
"Travelling to Dieppe." [Quarry] (36:3) Sum 87, p. 45-46.
5183. SORNBERGER, Judith
"Baptism by Immersion." [GreenfR] (14:1/2) Wint-Spr, p. 166.
"My Diver" (to Perry from Mother, Italy, June 1945). [Calyx] (11:1) Wint 87-88, p.
28-29.
"Visiting the Nation's Capital." [GreenfR] (14:1/2) Wint-Spr, p. 163-165.
5184. SORRENTINO, Gilbert
"Snapshot from Copenhagen." [Sequoia] (31:1) Centennial issue 87, p. 76.

5185. SOSIS, Phil
"Creation." [US1] (20/21) Wint 86-87, p. 44.
5186. SOTO, Gary
"Another Time." [Crazy] (32) Spr 87, p. 37-38.
"Ars Poetica, or Mazatlan, on a Day When Bodies Wash to the Shore." [Poetry]
    (150:3) Je 87, p. 144-145.
"Eve." [Ploughs] (13:4) 87, p. 126-127.
"Good for Nothing." [Caliban] (2) 87, p. 28-29.
"Happy." [Caliban] (2) 87, p. 26-27.
"House, Street, Old Man." [Ploughs] (13:4) 87, p. 125.
"Literary Criticism." [Caliban] (2) 87, p. 32-34.
"Lunch in the Business Park." [Caliban] (2) 87, p. 30-31.
"Memory." [Thrpny] (29) Spr 87, p. 4.
"Rough Translation of a Sabines Poem." [Poetry] (150:3) Je 87, p. 145-146.
"Taking Things Into Our Hands." [Ploughs] (13:4) 87, p. 128.
"Who Will Know Us?" (For Jaroslav Seifert). [Poetry] (151:1/2) O-N 87, p.
    162-163.
SOTO, Mark Smith
    See SMITH-SOTO, Mark
SOSEKI, Muso
    See MUSO, Soseki
5187. SOUPAULT, Philippe
"Poems from St. Pelagia Prison" (Selection: "Poem II," tr. by Paulette Schmidt).
    [Gargoyle] (32/33) 87, p. 370.
5188. SOUSTER, Raymond
"A Cold Wind's Blowing." [Quarry] (36:3) Sum 87, p. 50.
"Declaration." [CapilR] (42) 87, p. 9.
"Don't Cross Me, Cat." [Quarry] (36:3) Sum 87, p. 52.
"Hanlan's Point Holiday." [CapilR] (42) 87, p. 4-5.
"The House Around the Corner." [CapilR] (42) 87, p. 7.
"The Humberside Special." [Quarry] (36:3) Sum 87, p. 51.
"Pictures from a Long-Lost World: Religious Riots, Calcutta, August 1946."
    [Quarry] (36:3) Sum 87, p. 49.
"Plain Fact." [CapilR] (42) 87, p. 8.
5189. SOUTHWICK, Marcia
"Dolls." [MissR] (15:3, issue 45) Spr-Sum 87, p. 57-58.
"Fear of Trains." [PoetC] (18:3) Spr 87, p. 26-27.
"Widower's Song." [MissR] (15:3, issue 45) Spr-Sum 87, p. 55-56.
SOUZA, Eunice de
    See De SOUZA, Eunice
SOWOL, Kim
    See KIM, Sowol
5190. SOYINKA, Wole
"Muhammad Ali at the Ringside, 1985." [SouthernR] (23:3) Jl 87, p. 507-510.
5191. SPACKS, Barry
"Aunts." [Jacaranda] (2:2) Spr 87, p. 83.
"A Father." [CumbPR] (7:1) Fall 87, p. 70-71.
"Flying Not Falling." [CarolQ] (40:1) Fall 87, p. 70.
"Poem for a Wedding." [CumbPR] (7:1) Fall 87, p. 73.
"Poem for X." [CharR] (13:2) Fall 87, p. 86-87.
"War on the Dandelions." [CumbPR] (7:1) Fall 87, p. 72.
5192. SPAIN, Victoria
"Christina's World." [KanQ] (19:4) Fall 87, p. 41.
"Reflections in the Water" (for Richard Ye). [KanQ] (19:4) Fall 87, p. 41.
5193. SPALATIN, Ivana
"Gold" (tr. of Vesna Parun). [PaintedB] (31) 87, p. 71.
"Sound of Wings, Sound of Water" (Excerpt, tr. of Vesna Parun). [PaintedB] (31)
    87, p. 72.
5194. SPANOS, William
"A Letter to Susan on the Way." [MSS] (5:3) 87, p. 66-73.
5195. SPARKS, Amy Bracken
"Jim's Steak House." [SouthernPR] (27:2) Fall 87, p. 24-25.
5196. SPARSHOTT, Francis
"On Turning Tail." [Grain] (15:1) Spr 87, p. 14.
"A Tale from Valéry: Haute Ecole." [Grain] (15:1) Spr 87, p. 13.

5197. SPEAKES, Richard
   "Code of Ethics — Coin Laundry Association." [Poetry] (150:2) My 87, p. 88-89.
   "Mama Loves Janis Joplin." [Poetry] (150:2) My 87, p. 86-87.
5198. SPEAR, Roberta
   "In Just One Day." [Raccoon] (24/25) My 87, p. 15-16.
   "Painting in Fog." [Raccoon] (24/25) My 87, p. 136-137.
   "The Uncles." [Poetry] (151:1/2) O-N 87, p. 163-164.
5199. SPEARS, Heather
   "At the Art Therapist's." [CanLit] (113/114) Sum-Fall 87, p. 108.
5200. SPEARS, Noa
   "Tuning the Trumpet." [LightY] '87, c86, p. 99.
5201. SPEARS, Woodridge
   "Entry." [AmerV] (9) Wint 87, p. 41.
5202. SPECTOR, Al
   "A Class Act." [Wind] (17:61) 87, p. 45.
   "Gladiator." [Wind] (17:61) 87, p. 45-46.
5203. SPEER, Laurel
   "Barbering the Chinese." [DenQ] (21:3) Wint 87, p. 80.
   "Colored Glass." [NegC] (7:3/4) 87, p. 136.
   "A Copybook Found in Rubble." [WindO] (48) Spr 87, p. 44.
   "The Doctors Have Pronounced Frau Engel Gravely Ill." [WindO] (48) Spr 87, p.
      42-43.
   "An Early Draft of the Heiligenstadt Testament." [WindO] (48) Spr 87, p. 43.
   "We Regret." [LaurelR] (21:1/2) Wint-Sum 87, p. 59.
   "We're Not Vegetarian." [WindO] (48) Spr 87, p. 42.
5204. SPEERS, E.
   "Sonnet 18: Listen, friends, and I'll make love to you." [Bogg] (57) 87, p. 30.
5205. SPENCE, Michael
   "Adam Chooses." [Poetry] (149:4) Ja 87, p. 192-193.
   "Card Game." [Poetry] (149:4) Ja 87, p. 194.
   "The Hollow Bargain." [Poetry] (149:4) Ja 87, p. 193.
   "The Lost People." [Spirit] (8:2) 87, p. 258.
   "My Approach." [Shen] (37:3) 87, p. 31-32.
   "Proofreader's Island." [LightY] '87, c86, p. 219.
   "The Right Way to Escape from a Sinking Ship" (The Mary Elinore Smith Poetry
      Prize). [AmerS] (56:3) Sum 87, p. 328-329.
   "The Snow Returns." [Paint] (14:28) Aut 87, p. 8.
   "Stepson." [CharR] (13:2) Fall 87, p. 59.
   "Voyager" (for Sharon Hashimoto). [CharR] (13:2) Fall 87, p. 58-59.
5206. SPENDER, Stephen
   "The Express." [CharR] (13:1) Spr 87, p. 102-103.
   "Farewell to My Student." [Poetry] (151:1/2) O-N 87, p. 165.
5207. SPICER, Bob
   "Kittens." [Waves] (15:1/2) Fall 86, p. 55.
5208. SPICER, David
   "Twins." [NoDaQ] (55:1) Wint 87, p. 157-158.
5209. SPICER, Jack
   "Agenda" (his poem "For Hal" set to music by Steve Lacy). [Acts] (6) 87, p. 46-48.
   "An Answer to Jaime." [Acts] (6) 87, p. 8.
   "Eucalyptus Leaves." [Acts] (6) 87, p. 7.
   "For Russ." [Act] (6) 87, back cover.
   "Hibernation." [Acts] (6) 87, p. 23.
   "The Inheritance: Palm Sundy." [Acts] (6) 87, p. 12.
   "Minneapolis — October 1950." [Acts] (6) 87, p. 13.
   "On Reading Last Year's Love Poems." [Acts] (6) 87, p. 11.
   "Sonnet I." [Acts] (6) 87, p. 12.
   "We find the body difficult to speak." [Acts] (6) 87, p. 8.
   "With fifteen cents and that I could get a subway ride in New York." [Acts] (6) 87,
      p. 79.
5210. SPICHER, Julia
   "Word to Measure Space." [WestB] (20) 87, p. 25.
5211. SPIES, Lynne Davis
   "Appalachian Canon." [HampSPR] Wint 86, p. 54.
5212. SPINA, Vincent
   "All Night." [ConcPo] (20) 87, p. 98.
   "Bridges." [ConcPo] (20) 87, p. 128.

5213. SPINGARN, Lawrence P.
"Moral Tales: 'The Last Colony'." [Bogg] (58) 87, p. 22.
"Where Is England?" [Bogg] (58) 87, p. 50.
5214. SPINNER, Bettye T.
"Kahlib: On Cats and Consequential Things." [EngJ] (76:8) D 87, p. 81.
"When I Write Poetry." [EngJ] (76:6) O 87, p. 99.
5215. SPIRES, Elizabeth
"On the King's Road." [SenR] (17:2) 87, p. 53.
"Profil Perdu." [Poetry] (150:3) Je 87, p. 156-157.
"Saint Teresa in Ecstasy" (Rome, a sculpture by Bernini). [Raccoon] (24/25) My 87,
p. 177.
"The Woman on the Dump." [GeoR] (41:4) Wint 87, p. 677-678.
5216. SPIVACK, Kathleen
"After He Left." [KanQ] (19:3) Sum 87, p. 106-107.
"The Bird-Catcher." [PraS] (61:1) Spr 87, p. 108-110.
"Faraway Music." [KanQ] (19:1/2) Wint-Spr 87, p. 78.
"Letter from Home." [MemphisSR] (7:2) Spr 87, p. 40-41.
"The Suitability Quiz." [PoetL] (81:3) Fall 86, p. 169.
5217. SPIVACK, Susan Fantl
"Honey in the Wall." [Blueline] (7:2/3 [i.e. 8:2/3?]) 87, p. 22.
"Last Night." [Blueline] (7:2/3 [i.e. 8:2/3?]) 87, p. 23.
"Like Pots Hold Stew." [GreenfR] (14:3/4) Sum-Fall 87, p. 143.
5218. SPLAKE, T. Kilgore
"Attack." [Bogg] (57) 87, p. 49.
5219. SPOONER, David
"Four Idiosyncratics on Revolution." [Margin] (3) Sum 87, p. 1-2.
5220. SPOTORNO, Radomiro
"Austin Mini" (tr. by Richard Burns). [Margin] (1) Wint 86, p. 52-53.
5221. SPOTTSWOOD, H. M.
"Crosscut Sawing." [CapeR] (22:1) Spr 87, p. 26.
5222. SPRINKLE, Annie
"Poems by Body Parts." [YellowS] (23) Sum 87, p. 43.
5223. SQUIRE-BURESH, Anne
"Saints Are Not Born to It." [ChrC] (104:15) 6 My 87, p. 431.
5224. SRUT, Pavel
"Deep Mud" (tr. by the author and Tom O'Grady). [HampSPR] Wint 87, p. 33.
"My Love" (tr. by the author and Tom O'Grady). [HampSPR] Wint 87, p. 34-37.
"Not Long Before April" (tr. by the author and Tom O'Grady). [HampSPR] Wint
87, p. 33-34.
5225. ST. ANDREWS, B. A.
"Coastnotes." [Jacaranda] (2:2) Spr 87, p. 28-29.
"Explaining the Sea." [HighP] (2:1) Spr 87, p. 27-28.
"La Guardia: 4 AM." [CarolQ] (39:2) Wint 87, p. 97-98.
"On Vacation." [TarRP] (26:2) Spr 87, p. 40-41.
5226. ST. CLAIR, Philip
"Buffet." [GreenfR] (14:3/4) Sum-Fall 87, p. 48.
"Ce Billet a Cours Legal." [PoetryNW] (28:1) Spr 87, p. 43.
"Elegy." [MalR] (81) D 87, p. 44-46.
"Ghosts." [GreenfR] (14:3/4) Sum-Fall 87, p. 49.
5227. ST. GERMAIN, Sheryl
"Medusa Falls in Love." [Footwork] 87, p. 26.
"Medusa Visits New York City in Winter." [Footwork] 87, p. 26.
5228. ST. JOHN, David
"Divine." [Raccoon] (24/25) My 87, p. 9.
"The Doors" (The Church of San Zeno, Verona). [Poetry] (151:3) D 87, p. 290-291.
"From a Daybook" (In memory of G.). [Poetry] (151:1/2) O-N 87, p. 142.
"The Kama Sutra According to Fiat." [Harp] (274:1647) Ag 87, p. 27.
"Nights in the Villa." [DenQ] (22:2) Fall 87, p. 36-37.
"Quote Me Wrong Again and I'll Slit the Throat of Your Pet Iguana!" [Boulevard]
(2:3) Fall 87, p. 144-146.
"Terraces of Rain." [Antaeus] (58) Spr 87, p. 155-156.
5229. ST. MARTIN, Hardie
"One of Lee's Soldiers" (tr. of Jorge Luis Borges). [AmerV] (9) Wint 87, p. 63.
5230. ST. MAUR, Erin
"Windfall." [Phoenix] (7:2) 87, p. 22.

5231. STACHLER, Ronald T.
"I'm a Kid Again and I'm Alone to Be Called." [HiramPoR] (43) Fall-Wint 87-88, p. 33.
5232. STAFFORD, Kim R.
"Losing One." [NowestR] (25:3) 87, p. 445.
5233. STAFFORD, William
"All the Time." [CrabCR] (4:3) Sum 87, p. 3.
"At a Small College." [LaurelR] (21:1/2) Wint-Sum 87, p. 94.
"Back Home Under the Wind." [WoosterR] (7) Spr 87, p. 45.
"Being Ready." [WoosterR] (7) Spr 87, p. 47.
"Birthdays." [CrossCur] (7:2) 87, p. 95.
"Cold Month." [WoosterR] (7) Spr 87, p. 46.
"The Day Millicent Found the World." [Poetry] (150:6) S 87, p. 330.
"Different Things." [ClockR] (4:1) 87, p. 11.
"Disposal." [CrossCur] (7:3) 87, p. 137.
"Driving the Valley Road." [ClockR] (4:1) 87, p. 12.
"Faux Pas." [LightY] '87, c86, p. 46.
"For Alexis Christa von Hartmann: Proved Not Guilty." [ThRiPo] (29/30) 87, p. 58.
"Forging a Passport." The Best of [BambooR] [(31-32)] 86, p. 87.
"Hearing the Wind." [CrabCR] (4:3) Sum 87, p. 3.
"Late, Late." [CrossCur] (7:2) 87, p. 94.
"Life Work." [WoosterR] (7) Spr 87, p. 44.
"Living Here." [Field] (36) Spr 87, p. 58.
"Lost in the Centuries." [Spirit] (8:2) 87, p. 189.
"Noticing." [Poetry] (151:1/2) O-N 87, p. 166.
"On Being Local." The Best of [BambooR] [(31-32)] 86, p. 86.
"The Origin of *Country*." [WoosterR] (7) Spr 87, p. 43.
"Presenting These Pieces." [Poetry] (151:1/2) O-N 87, p. 166.
"Preservation." [ThRiPo] (29/30) 87, p. 59.
"The Return of the Animal That Drank Up Sound." [NowestR] (25:3) 87, p. 105.
"Seduction River." [Field] (36) Spr 87, p. 57.
"Three Artists on Location." [LaurelR] (21:1/2) Wint-Sum 87, p. 95.
"Twelfth Birthday." [ThRiPo] (29/30) 87, p. 60.
"Waiting for Poems to Come." [OhioR] (38) 87, p. 10-13.
"Your Life." [Poetry] (151:1/2) O-N 87, p. 167.
5234. STALEY, E. O.
"Duo for Voice & Percussion." [LightY] '87, c86, p. 211.
5235. STALEY, Teresa (Teresa M.)
"Act Four, Scene One." [GreensboroR] (39) Wint 85-86, p. 92.
"Folk Arts: City Stage, 1984." [GreensboroR] (39) Wint 85-86, p. 93-94.
"Variations on a Theme" (The Greensboro Review Literary Award, Honorable Mention). [GreensboroR] (41) Wint 86-87, p. 50.
5236. STALLINGS, Tyler
"Christ." [CentralP] (11) Spr 87, p. 103.
5237. STALLWORTHY, Bob
"At Burley's Store." [Waves] (15:3) Wint 87, p. 73.
5238. STAMBLER, Peter
"Unsettled Accounts." [QRL] (Series 8, vol. 27) 87, 63 p.
5239. STANDEN, Michael
"Smile." [Stand] (28:3) Sum 87, p. 41.
5240. STANDING, Sue
"Cellar Door." [Spirit] (8:2) 87, p. 204-205.
"Electra: The Escape Artist." [SouthwR] (72:3) Sum 87, p. 416.
"The Home Counties Posing as the Universe." [Colum] (12) 87, p. 21.
5241. STANESCU, Nichita
"Adolescents on the Sea" (tr. by Tom Carlson and Vasile Poenaru). [LitR] (30:4) Sum 87, p. 589.
"Autumn Twilight" (tr. by Tom Carlson and Vasile Poenaru). [LitR] (30:4) Sum 87, p. 588.
"Distance" (tr. by Tom Carlson and Vasile Poenaru). [LitR] (30:4) Sum 87, p. 588.
"Ninth Elegy: Of the Egg" (tr. by Thomas C. Carlson and Vasile Poenaru). [Raccoon] (24/25) My 87, p. 106-107.
"Second Elegy: The Ghetica" (for Vasile Parvan, tr. by Thomas C. Carlson). [BlueBldgs] (10) 87?, p. 37.
"Song" (tr. by Tom Carlson and Vasile Poenaru). [LitR] (30:4) Sum 87, p. 589.

"Unwords" (tr. by Thomas C. Carlson and Vasile Poenaru). [Raccoon] (24/25) My 87, p. 105.
5242. STANFORD, Ann
"After Rain." [SouthernR] (23:4) O 87, p. 966.
5243. STANFORD, Frank
"Man is so afraid." [Raccoon] (24/25) My 87, p. 262-263.
"There Is No Where in You a Paradise That Is No Place and There You Do Not Enter
. . ." [Raccoon] (24/25) My 87, p. 276-277.
5244. STANFORD, Janet Holmes
"The Fence." [Puerto] (22:2) Spr 87, p. 106.
5245. STANFORD, Michael
"Tunes from a Cracked Cauldron." [GreensboroR] (40) Sum 86, p. 128.
5246. STANIZZI, John L.
"The Mouth of the River" (Mouth of the Scantic River — East Windsor,
Connecticut). [BlueBldgs] (10) 87?, p. 42-44.
5247. STANLEY, Jean W.
"Apostrophe." [Poem] (57) Mr 87, p. 25.
5248. STANTON, Douglas
"A True Story." [HawaiiR] (22) Fall 87, p. 82-83.
5249. STANTON, Joseph
"The Anchor Takes Command" (for Joseph Feher). [BambooR] (36) Fall 87, p. 49.
"The Kim Chee Test" (for En Suk). The Best of [BambooR] [(31-32)] 86, p. 88-89.
"Parrots in Aiea." [HawaiiR] (21) Spr 87, p. 60-61.
"Tsuchi-Gumo." [BambooR] (36) Fall 87, p. 50.
5250. STANTON, Maura
"At Hemingway's House." [AmerS] (56:4) Aut 87, p. 502.
"The Dance." [MichQR] (26:1) Wint 87, p. 30-31.
"The Grocery Store." [MissouriR] (10:2) 87, p. 138-139.
"The Kingdom of the Weeds." [AmerPoR] (16:4) Jl-Ag 87, p. 38.
"Living Apart." [Poetry] (151:1/2) O-N 87, p. 167.
"Peoria." [MichQR] (26:1) Wint 87, p. 29-30.
"Pole Vaulting." [Poetry] (149:4) Ja 87, p. 214.
"Tales of the Supernatural." [AmerPoR] (16:4) Jl-Ag 87, p. 35-38.
"The Village of the Mermaids" (after Paul Delvaux). [Verse] (4:1) Mr 87, p. 50-51.
"Wander Indiana." [Poetry] (149:4) Ja 87, p. 215-216.
5251. STAP, Don
"Crooked Lake, 1978." [FloridaR] (15:1) Spr-Sum 87, p. 22.
"From a Photograph." [AmerS] (56:3) Sum 87, p. 406.
5252. STAPLE, Will
"No More Hot Coffee When I Die." [BelPoJ] (38:2) Wint 87-88, p. 30.
5253. STARBUCK, George
"Catalogue Raisonné of My Refrigerator Door" (For Joshua Starbuck, master of
montage). [Poetry] (151:1/2) O-N 87, p. 168-169.
"Pretty Conundrums, And They Tempt the Eye" (for Amy Clampitt). [AmerPoR]
(16:2) Mr-Ap 87, p. 33.
5254. STARK, Jonathan
"A Modest Apocalypse." [WebR] (12:2) Fall 87, p. 77.
"Thunder and Snow." [WebR] (12:2) Fall 87, p. 78.
5255. STARK, Max
"A Thousand Names." [Phoenix] (7:2) 87, p. 3.
5256. STARZEC, Larry
"The Executioner." [PikeF] (8) Fall 87, p. 6.
"On a Warm Afternoon in Chicago." [KanQ] (19:3) Sum 87, p. 248.
"Under the Bridge." [KanQ] (19:3) Sum 87, p. 249.
5258. STEARNS, Catherine
"Talking Back." [ColEng] (49:6) O 87, p. 653.
5259. STEELE, Craig W.
"Heavy with mouse." [Amelia] (4:3, issue 10) 87, p. 6.
5260. STEELE, Leighton
"95 Seward." [AntigR] (69/70) 87, p. 142.
"Olive Street, Santa Barbara." [AntigR] (69/70) 87, p. 143.
5261. STEELE, Paul Curry
"Clerihews" (2 poems). [LightY] '87, c86, p. 67-68.
5262. STEELE, Timothy
"Education in Music." [Sequoia] (31:1) Centennial issue 87, p. 30.
"Joseph." [Sequoia] (31:1) Centennial issue 87, p. 31.

"Portrait of a Woman in a Museum." [Zyzzyva] (3:1) Spr 87, p. 129.
"Waiting for the Storm." [Field] (36) Spr 87, p. 67.
5263. STEFENHAGENS, Lyn
"David in Pasture." [KanQ] (19:1/2) Wint-Spr 87, p. 194.
"True Gods." [KanQ] (19:1/2) Wint-Spr 87, p. 193.
5264. STEFFEY, Duane
"Against Entropy" (for R.S.). [PennR] (3:1) Spr-Sum 87, p. 62.
"Animals" (for K. P.). [KanQ] (19:3) Sum 87, p. 315-316.
"The Hedonist Speaks." [LaurelR] (21:1/2) Wint-Sum 87, p. 34.
"Letter to a Distant Lover." [KanQ] (19:3) Sum 87, p. 316.
5265. STEFFLER, John
"For a Photographer." [AntigR] (71/72) Aut 87-Wint 88, p. 11-12.
"Lepidoptera." [AntigR] (71/72) Aut 87-Wint 88, p. 10-11.
"Vacation." [AntigR] (71/72) Aut 87-Wint 88, p. 12.
5266. STEIN, Alice P.
"Grounded." [LightY] '87, c86, p. 161.
5267. STEIN, Charles
"Theforestforthetrees" (Selections: 17 poems). [Conjunc] (11) 87?, p. 149-160.
"The Wind Harbours It in Its Belly" (from "The Emerald Seeds"). [Notus] (2:1) Spr
87, p. 66-72.
5268. STEIN, Dona
"Hike." [StoneC] (14:3/4) Spr-Sum 87, p. 41.
"Old Masters." [Sequoia] (30:3) Wint 87, p. 70.
"The Sawmill Fire." [StoneC] (14:3/4) Spr-Sum 87, p. 40.
"Sweeping." [GreenfR] (14:3/4) Sum-Fall 87, p. 79.
5269. STEIN, Hannah
"Walking Up the Hill." [PassN] (8:2) Sum 87, p. 26.
5270. STEIN, Judith A.
"Lesbian Appetites: a Rhyme for Teaching A-B-C's." [SinW] (31) 87, p. 49.
5271. STEIN, Julia
"A Happy Kid." [MinnR] (NS 29) Fall 87, p. 33-34.
"Let Your Courage." [MinnR] (NS 29) Fall 87, p. 31-32.
"The Triangle Fire." [MinnR] (NS 29) Fall 87, p. 35-36.
5272. STEIN, Kevin
"The Argument." [PoetryNW] (28:1) Spr 87, p. 42.
"Birds in a Circle." [Poetry] (149:5) F 87, p. 290.
"Her Flower Garden." [SouthernPR] (27:2) Fall 87, p. 15.
"Terms." [Poetry] (149:5) F 87, p. 288-289.
5273. STEIN, M. D.
"Ward Duty." [Thrpny] (31) Fall 87, p. 17.
5274. STEINARR, Steinn
"The Sun" (tr. by Alan Boucher). [Vis] (24) 87, p. 21.
"Wood" (tr. by Alan Boucher). [Vis] (23) 87, p. 12.
5275. STEINBERG, David
"Spring, San Francisco, 1987." [JamesWR] (4:4) Sum 87, p. 4.
5276. STEINBERGH, Judith W.
"Arguing with Joyce." [Calyx] (10:2/3) Spr 87, p. 10.
"Gem." [TexasR] (7:3/4) 87, p. 148.
5277. STEINER, Louis, Jr.
"Dioboloi." [Quarry] (36:3) Sum 87, p. 16.
"Outcrop." [Quarry] (36:3) Sum 87, p. 16.
5278. STEINGASS, David
"Calf." [PraS] (61:1) Spr 87, p. 46.
"Midnight Call." [ThRiPo] (29/30) 87, p. 61-62.
"Pig-History." [RiverS] (23) 87, p. 21.
"Ratter." [RiverS] (23) 87, p. 22.
5279. STEINGESSER, Martin
"This Is a Safe House" (for Anna Calero de Lopez, Nicaragua Libre 1987).
[Witness] (1:4) Wint 87, p. 90-91.
5280. STEINKE, Paul David
"Introductions." [Vis] (23) 87, p. 5.
"Love Poem for Anne Frances." [Vis] (23) 87, p. 5.
"Le Verrou." [Vis] (23) 87, p. 5.
5281. STEINMAN, Lisa (Lisa M.)
"A Book of Other Days" (Pablo Neruda Prize for Poetry, First Prize). [Nimrod]
(31:1) Fall-Wint 87, p. 1-7.

"Familiarity." [BellR] (10:2) Fall 87, p. 27.
"Getting Things Straight." [BellR] (10:2) Fall 87, p. 29.
"In the Midst of, and Tallying." [ColR] (NS 14:1) Spr-Sum 87, p. 70-71.
"Notes for Speech." [BellR] (10:2) Fall 87, p. 28.
5282. STELLA, Rachel
"Scientia Liberatrix, or, The Exploding Mother-in-Law" (tr. of Alphonse Allais).
[Notus] (2:2) Fall 87, p. 18-19.
5283. STELMACH, Marjorie
"Almost Every Sunday." [RiverS] (22) 87, p. 22.
"Drought." [Ascent] (12:3) 87, p. 19.
"Fire." [CapeR] (22:2) Fall 87, p. 40.
"Ghost Story." [Ascent] (12:3) 87, p. 18.
"I Miss Old Novels." [CapeR] (22:2) Fall 87, p. 39.
"Life Saving." [RiverS] (22) 87, p. 20-21.
"Listen." [RiverS] (22) 87, p. 23.
"Love in Winter." [CapeR] (22:2) Fall 87, p. 41.
"My Calling." [MalR] (79) Je 87, p. 91.
"This Is a Note." [MalR] (79) Je 87, p. 92-93.
5284. STELMACH, Robert
"Night Interior and a Mural." [Vis] (23) 87, p. 29.
5285. STELZIG, Eugene
"Assorted Selfscriptings." [GreenfR] (14:3/4) Sum-Fall 87, p. 80-81.
5286. STEPANCHEV, Stephen
"A Bottle." [PoetL] (82:2) Sum 87, p. 121.
"The Cemetery in Mokrin." [PoetL] (82:2) Sum 87, p. 120-121.
"Courtly." [PoetL] (82:2) Sum 87, p. 119.
"Her Needle." [PoetL] (82:2) Sum 87, p. 122.
"Undressing." [PoetL] (82:2) Sum 87, p. 122.
5287. STEPHENS, Jack
"Shrimping." [MissouriR] (10:1) 87, p. 60-61.
"St. Francis, Hiding." [MissouriR] (10:1) 87, p. 62-63.
"A Visitation: On Finding a Meteorite in My Yard." [PoetC] (19:1) Fall 87, p. 3-4.
5288. STEPTOE, Lamont
"I Want to Paint Tonight." [PaintedB] (30) 87, p. 9-10.
5289. STERITE, Jennie E.
"The Sears Catalog." [SmPd] (24:3) Fall 87, p. 15.
5290. STERLE, Francine
"Eating a Flower." [NegC] (7:3/4) 87, p. 93.
"Great Blue Heron Country." [Interim] (6:1) Spr 87, p. 43.
"Hummingbird." [Interim] (6:1) Spr 87, p. 42.
"My Father's Clothes." [Interim] (6:1) Spr 87, p. 44.
5291. STERLING, Phillip
"The Resurrection of the Body" (for Gene Stack). [SenR] (17:1) 87, p. 29.
"White Birch" (Sarah's poem). [SmPd] (24:1) Wint 87, p. 14.
5292. STERN, Cathy
"Old Loves." [Shen] (37:4) 87, p. 10.
"Once Removed." [NewRep] (196:16) 20 Ap 87, p. 40.
"Thirty-Ninth Anniversary." [Shen] (37:4) 87, p. 9.
"Those Places." [Shen] (37:4) 87, p. 9-10.
5293. STERN, Gerald
"Another Insane Devotion." [Poetry] (150:6) S 87, p. 349-350.
"Bob Summers' Body." [Ploughs] (13:1) 87, p. 126.
"Brain of My Heart." [Poetry] (151:1/2) O-N 87, p. 169-170.
"Hobbes." [Pequod] (23/24) 87, p. 54-56.
"I Hate My Moaning." [ThRiPo] (29/30) 87, p. 63.
"It Was in Houston." [Poetry] (150:6) S 87, p. 350-351.
"My Favorite Farewell." [Nat] (244:11) 21 Mr 87, p. 372.
"No Wind." [NowestR] (25:3) 87, p. 266.
"Nobody Else Living." [ThRiPo] (29/30) 87, p. 64.
"Stopping Schubert." [Nat] (244:11) 21 Mr 87, p. 372.
"There I Was One Day." [Ploughs] (13:1) 87, p. 124-125.
5294. STERN, Richard
"Common Market" (The four sections stray progressively further from their
originals). [Raccoon] (24/25) My 87, p. 117-118.
5295. STERN, Robert
"And What If." [AntigR] (69/70) 87, p. 76.

"Anne Frank." [AntigR] (71/72) Aut 87-Wint 88, p. 120-121.
"The Snowman." [AntigR] (69/70) 87, p. 76.
5296. STERNLIEB, Barry
   "Bathing the Girls." [PoetryE] (23/24) Fall 87, p. 146.
   "Dennisport." [SouthwR] (72:3) Sum 87, p. 417.
   "Full Circle." [CharR] (13:2) Fall 87, p. 57.
   "Growing Season." [GreenfR] (14:3/4) Sum-Fall 87, p. 167.
   "Hunger." [PoetryE] (23/24) Fall 87, p. 150.
   "In the Name of Water." [PoetryE] (23/24) Fall 87, p. 147-148.
   "Instinct." [GreenfR] (14:3/4) Sum-Fall 87, p. 168.
   "The Light" (July 4, 1978). [PoetryE] (23/24) Fall 87, p. 151-152.
   "Return to the Photograph." [PoetryE] (23/24) Fall 87, p. 149.
   "Riverwife." [YellowS] (25) Wint 87, p. 16.
   "Tea Garden." [Poetry] (150:3) Je 87, p. 130.
5297. STEURY, Tim
   "Seventy-five Miles an Hour Across the Top of the World." [SnapD] (10:1/2) Wint
      87, p. 62-63.
5298. STEVENS, Alex
   "Chin." [Shen] (37:3) 87, p. 76.
   "Eye." [Shen] (37:3) 87, p. 77-78.
   "Hand." [Shen] (37:3) 87, p. 80.
   "Nose." [Shen] (37:3) 87, p. 78-79.
5299. STEVENS, C. J.
   "Fall." [StoneC] (14:3/4) Spr-Sum 87, p. 29.
5300. STEVENS, Patricia
   "Saturday Bull in a Michigan Bar." [KanQ] (19:1/2) Wint-Spr 87, p. 254.
5301. STEVENSON, Anne
   "And let me tell you more" (tr. of Eugene Dubnov, w. the Author). [SenR] (17:1)
      87, p. 20.
   "Icon." [Poetry] (151:1/2) O-N 87, p. 172.
   "Jarrow." [KenR] (NS 9:2) Spr 87, p. 85-86.
   "Naming the Flowers." [KenR] (NS 9:2) Spr 87, p. 84.
   "Nightmares, Daymoths" (After writing on Sylvia Plath). [Poetry] (151:1/2) O-N 87,
      p. 171.
5302. STEVENSON, Diane
   "Family Album." [Poetry] (150:4) Jl 87, p. 187-188.
   "Lullaby." [Poetry] (150:4) Jl 87, p. 188-189.
   "Matins." [Poetry] (150:4) Jl 87, p. 189.
   "Sources of Light." [Poetry] (150:4) Jl 87, p. 190.
5303. STEWARD, D. E.
   "Blackbirds." [HampSPR] Wint 86, p. 21.
   "Drifter." [Bogg] (57) 87, p. 58.
   "November." [Conjunc] (11) 87?, p. 181-191.
   "Speaker." [Abraxas] (35/36) 87, p. 68.
   "Trogir." [Puerto] (22:2) Spr 87, p. 107.
5304. STEWART, Dolores
   "Blueberrying." [BallSUF] (28:4) Aut 87, p. 5.
   "A Dog in the Cemetery." [LitR] (31:1) Fall 87, p. 20.
   "February: the Swans, the Children." [LitR] (31:1) Fall 87, p. 21.
   "Runes" (6 selections). [BelPoJ] (38:1) Fall 87, p. 18-23.
5305. STEWART, Frank
   "The Arrival." [Zyzzyva] (3:4) Wint 87-88, p. 72.
   "A Christmas Toast" (for Dean and Julie, 1986). [BambooR] (33) Spr 87, p. 62.
   "To a Friend" (killed in Dragon Valley, Vietnam). [Spirit] (8:2) 87, p. 249.
5306. STEWART, Jack
   "White Lake" (In memory of my father). [AntR] (45:1) Wint 87, p. 71-72.
5307. STEWART, Pamela
   "Good Friday." [Raccoon] (24/25) My 87, p. 22.
   "Our Solitudes." [Raccoon] (24/25) My 87, p. 306.
   "Something, Which Waits, Is Always Telling Lies." [Colum] (12) 87, p. 49.
5308. STEWART, Pat
   "Of Intrinsic Value." [Raccoon] (24/25) My 87, p. 249.
5309. STEWART, Susan
   "The Summer Before the Moon." [Harp] (274:1646) Jl 87, p. 34.
5310. STEWART, W. Gregory
   "Bozo and the Fun Band." [Amelia] (4:3, issue 10) 87, p. 91.

"In the Park." [Amelia] (4:3, issue 10) 87, p. 91.
"Life As Commodity." [Amelia] (4:3, issue 10) 87, p. 92.
"Scotland for the Pipes." [Amelia] (4:3, issue 10) 87, p. 91-92.
5311. STICKNEY, John
"Dear Weatherman." [CrossCur] (6:4) 87, p. 10-11.
5312. STILES, Deborah
"Old Man." [Wind] (17:60) 87, p. 35.
5313. STILLER, Nikki
"A Mixed Blessing." [InterPR] (13:2) Fall 87, p. 57-60.
"Two Fogels" (tr. of Gabriel Preil). [InterPR] (13:2) Fall 87, p. 40-41.
"Words About Her, 1983" (tr. of Gabriel Preil). [InterPR] (13:2) Fall 87, p. 38-39.
5314. STILLMAN, Michael
"Remembering the Sixties." [Sequoia] (31:1) Centennial issue 87, p. 126.
5315. STINE, Peter
"Meditation." [Witness] (1:2) Sum 87, p. 107.
5316. STINSON, Don
"Nuptials." [Phoenix] (7:1) 87, p. 20-21.
5317. STOCK, Norman
"Homeless" (1987 Ratner-Ferber-Poet Lore Honorable Mention). [PoetL] (82:2) Sum 87, p. 97-98.
5318. STOCKENSTRÖM, Wilma
"Those Jolly Little Beetles" (tr. by Rose Keet). [TriQ] (69) Spr-Sum 87, p. 343-344.
5319. STOCKER, Mark
"Vita Longa, Cars Brevis." [LightY] '87, c86, p. 236.
STOLL, Marianne Kent
See KENT-STOLL, Marianne
5320. STOLOFF, Carolyn
"Going Places." [Contact] (9:44/45/46) Fall-Wint 87, p. 48.
"The Redon Boy." [Contact] (9:44/45/46) Fall-Wint 87, p. 49.
"Short Story." [Caliban] (3) 87, p. 45-46.
"When the Sky Smells of Burning Sapphires." [Caliban] (2) 87, p. 24-25.
5321. STONE, Alison
"Brandeis Senior Year." [Poetry] (150:2) My 87, p. 79.
"Foggy Notion." [Poetry] (149:5) F 87, p. 262.
"Rocket to Russia." [Poetry] (149:5) F 87, p. 263.
"Spofford Hall." [Poetry] (150:2) My 87, p. 78-79.
"Walking Home After the Subhumans." [SlipS] (7) 87, p. 36.
5322. STONE, Arlene
"Svengali's Next to Immortal Tongue." [YellowS] (23) Sum 87, p. 18-19.
5323. STONE, Arthur
"Morning Scales" (for Susan, " (1986 Finalist, Eve of Saint Agnes Poetry Competition). [NegC] (7:1/2) 87, p. 211.
5324. STONE, Ira
"In Florida." [Lactuca] (7) Ag 87, p. 11.
"Seattle Smog." [Lactuca] (7) Ag 87, p. 11.
5325. STONE, Jesse
"Shake, Rattle and Roll." [Caliban] (3) 87, p. 153.
"Smack Dab in the Middle." [Caliban] (3) 87, p. 156.
"W.P.A." [Caliban] (3) 87, p. 155.
"Your Cash Ain't Nothin' But Trash." [Caliban] (3) 87, p. 154-155.
5326. STONE, John
"A Trenta-sei for John Ciardi (1916-1986)." [AmerS] (56:2) Spr 87, p. 203-204.
5327. STONE, Ken
"Deep Vows Made." [PoeticJ] (17) 87, p. 17.
5328. STONE, Reynold
"I Lived in an Age on This Earth" (tr. of Miklòs Radnóti, w. Susan Tomory). [AntigR] (71/72) Aut 87-Wint 88, p. 158.
"The Man Spoke" (tr. of József Attila, w. Susan Tomory). [AntigR] (71/72) Aut 87-Wint 88, p. 158.
"Seventh Eclogue" (tr. of Miklòs Radnóti, w. Susan Tomory). [AntigR] (71/72) Aut 87-Wint 88, p. 158.
"You Should Not Be Sorry" (tr. of József Attila, w. Susan Tomory). [AntigR] (71/72) Aut 87-Wint 88, p. 158.
5329. STONE, Ruth
"The Latest Hotel Guest Walks Over Particles That Revolve in Seven Other Dimensions . . ." [AmerPoR] (16:3) My-Je 87, p. 48.

"Message From Your Toes." [Footwork] 87, p. 8.
"Names." [TexasR] (7:3/4) 87, p. 149.
"Nursery Rhyme." [Footwork] 87, p. 8.
"Snow Trivia." [Footwork] 87, p. 8.
"Surviving in Earlysville with a Broken Window." [Footwork] 87, p. 9.
5330. STONE, Thomas R.
"Bloody Pond, Shiloh." [MemphisSR] (8:1) Fall 87, p. 64.
5331. STORACE, Patricia
"His Statue to Pygmalion." [Agni] (24/25) 87, p. 115.
"Song of Salt and Pepper." [NewYorker] (63:3) 9 Mr 87, p. 34.
"Southern Hospitality." [NewYRB] (34:6) 9 Ap 87, p. 4.
5332. STORNI, Alfonsina
"And the Head Began to Burn" (tr. by Marion Freeman). [MinnR] (NS 29) Fall 87,
    p. 17-18.
"Hombres en la Ciudad." [StoneC] (15:1/2) Fall-Wint 87-88, p. 26.
"It Could Well Be" (tr. by Marion Freeman). [MinnR] (NS 29) Fall 87, p. 16.
"Men in the City" (tr. by Maria Bennett). [StoneC] (15:1/2) Fall-Wint 87-88, p. 27.
"Sierra" (tr. by Joel Zeltzer). [Amelia] (4:3, issue 10) 87, p. 81.
"Voy a Dormir." [Mairena] (9:24) 87, p. 139.
"You Want Me White" (tr. by Almitra David). [Calyx] (10:2/3) Spr 87, p. 170-171.
5333. STOWELL, Phyllis
"Winter Landscape: Jas du Bouffan." [Thrpny] (28) Wint 87, p. 10.
5334. STRAHAN, Brad (Bradley R.)
"Appearance." [CrabCR] (4:3) Sum 87, p. 18.
"March Again." [Lips] (13) 87, p. 30.
"Public Romances " (For J.M.). [CrabCR] (4:3) Sum 87, p. 18.
5335. STRAND, Mark
"The Famous Scene." [NewYorker] (63:6) 30 Mr 87, p. 30.
"The History of Poetry" (for Lee Rust Brown). [Shen] (37:4) 87, p. 13.
"To Himself." [Poetry] (151:1/2) O-N 87, p. 173.
5336. STRICKLAND, Stephanie
"Diringer's *The Alphabet: A Key to the History of Mankind.*" [PraS] (61:4) Wint 87,
    p. 56-57.
"Use of Icons." [PraS] (61:4) Wint 87, p. 55-56.
5337. STROFFOLINO, Chris
"Serenade." [Bogg] (58) 87, p. 22.
5338. STRONG, Eithne
"Dublin Bay." [FourQ] (1:2) Fall 87, p. 59.
5339. STRONGIN, Lynn
"Spent." [AntigR] (68) Wint 87, p. 12.
5340. STRUNK, Orlo, Jr.
"Moose." [InterPR] (13:2) Fall 87, p. 93.
5341. STRUTHERS, Ann
"The Fifth of July at Spirit Lake." [PoetC] (18:3) Spr 87, p. 23.
5342. STRYK, Dan
"The Geranium." [CharR] (13:1) Spr 87, p. 94.
"I Am Sitting in a Small Room Watching Snowfall." [BallSUF] (28:4) Aut 87, p.
    21.
"Swallow Evening." [SouthwR] (72:4) Aut 87, p. 554.
5343. STRYK, Lucien
"Botanist" (Sweden, 1986). [Poetry] (151:1/2) O-N 87, p. 174.
"Haiku" (41 poems, tr. of Issa). [AmerPoR] (16:3) My-Je 87, p. 28.
5344. STUART, Dabney
"Franz Kafka Applies for a Literary Fellowship." [ColEng] (49:6) O 87, p. 655-656.
5345. STUART, Katherine Y.
"For Men Only." [PoetL] (82:3) Fall 87, p. 155.
STUBBS, John Heath
    See HEATH-STUBBS, John
5346. STUCKI, Marcia V.
"Vera." [BlueBldgs] (10) 87?, p. 8-15.
5347. STUDER, Constance
"Prayer to a Purple God." [Kaleid] (14) Wint-Spr 87, p. 70.
"Return Trip" (tr. of Maurits Mok). [Vis] (24) 87, p. 20.
"The Touch of Hands" (Kaleidoscope International Poetry Awards 1986-87, Third
    Prize). [Kaleid] (14) Wint-Spr 87, p. 67.
"The Waiting Room." [Kaleid] (14) Wint-Spr 87, p. 70.

5348. STURGIS, Susanna J.
"The Key Sestina" (for Chris). [Outbr] (18/19) Fall 86-Spr 88, p. 86-87.
5349. SU, Adrienne
"The Collector." [HarvardA] (121:3) My 87, p. 11.
SU-YONG, Kim
See KIM, Su-yong
5350. SUBRAMAN, Belinda
"At the Grocery Store." [SlipS] (7) 87, p. 8.
"An Experiment with Carl Sagan." [Bogg] (57) 87, p. 16.
5351. SUDHALTER, Treva R.
"Cupped in Lily." [Phoenix] (7:2) 87, p. 52.
5352. SUEHLA, John
"Frosty Bees." [DekalbLAJ] (20:1/4) 87, p. 53.
"Pelicans." [DekalbLAJ] (20:1/4) 87, p. 53.
"Planet Years." [DekalbLAJ] (20:1/4) 87, p. 53.
5353. SUK, Julie
"The Woman Who Loved Horses." [Vis] (25) 87, p. 10.
5354. SUKNASKI, Andrew
"Divining West" (part II of "Celestial Mechanics" /life fragment in progress//). [PraF]
(8:4) Wint 87-88, p. 50-53.
"Lawn Outside Norcanair in Buffalo Narrows." [PraF] (8:1) Spr 87, p. 61.
5355. SULLAM, Elizabeth
"Avignon, 1984." [Vis] (23) 87, p. 30.
"Garda See (Lake Garda)." [Vis] (24) 87, p. 11.
"Not Blue Roses." [Gargoyle] (32/33) 87, p. 188-189.
"Ravenna, 1985." [Vis] (24) 87, p. 12.
"Transitions." [Vis] (24) 87, p. 10.
5356. SULLIVAN, Chuck
"The Laying on of Hands." [SouthernPR] (27:1) Spr 87, p. 62-64.
5357. SULLIVAN, Gerald
"For the Luggage Room." [KanQ] (19:1/2) Wint-Spr 87, p. 188.
5358. SULLIVAN, Janet
"Pachydermist" (for Dian Fossey). [MichQR] (26:1) Wint 87, p. 87-88.
5359. SULLIVAN, Maggie
"Untitled: They went up and up he thought." [Jacaranda] (2:2) Spr 87, p. 62.
5360. SULLIVAN, Margaret
"The Crier." [Amelia] (4:1/2, issue 9) 87, p. 70.
5361. SULLIVAN, Rosemary
"A Chilean Sequence" (5 selections). [MalR] (81) D 87, p. 39-43.
5362. SULLIVAN, William P.
"Osprey at Beech Fork Lake." [LaurelR] (20:1/2) Sum 87, p. 30-31.
5363. SUMBERG, Chris
"She Squeaked Therefore She's Not." [Bogg] (57) 87, p. 26.
5364. SUMMERHAYES, Don
"Chrome Chairs Recovered." [MalR] (79) Je 87, p. 95-95.
"I Know I Am Smiling." [MalR] (79) Je 87, p. 94.
5365. SUMNER, Melody
"Mona Lisa (Our History)." [Rampike] (5:3) 87, p. 64-65.
5366. SUMRALL, Amber Coverdale
"Infinity." [PassN] (8:2) Sum 87, p. 25.
"Womantides." [SinW] (31) 87, p. 45.
5367. SUNDAHL, Daniel J.
"Approaching an Accident." [PennR] (3:2) Fall-Wint 87, p. 78.
5368. SUNDVALL, Herbert
"Baby." [BellArk] (3:2) Mr-Ap 87, p. 10.
"Love Story." [BellArk] (3:2) Mr-Ap 87, p. 18.
"Stalled Car." [BellArk] (3:4) Jl-Ag 87, p. 10.
SUNG, Kim Do
See KIM, Do Sung
5369. SUPRANER, Robyn
"Ah Baby, You." [PraS] (61:1) Spr 87, p. 75-76.
"Heartwood." [PraS] (61:1) Spr 87, p. 77-78.
"A Question of Happiness." [PraS] (61:1) Spr 87, p. 74-75.
"The Ragman." [BlueBldgs] (10) 87?, p. 45.

5370. SÜREYA, Cemal
"Blood Lurks Under All Words" (tr. by Talat Sait Halman). [Trans] (19) Fall 87, p. 136-137.
"Statue of Lions" (tr. by Murat Nemet-Nejat). [Trans] (19) Fall 87, p. 135.
SURIA, Violeta López
See LOPEZ SURIA, Violeta
5371. SUSIE
"Afternoon" (reprinted from Bogg 28-29). [Bogg] (58) 87, p. 42.
5372. SUSSKIND, Harriet
"The Common Sun." [PraS] (61:4) Wint 87, p. 59-60.
"Memory: Darker." [PraS] (61:4) Wint 87, p. 60-62.
"A New Roof." [GeoR] (41:4) Wint 87, p. 706.
"Not Leafless." [SenR] (17:1) 87, p. 25.
"Rain After a Death." [Nimrod] (30:2) Spr-Sum 87, p. 135.
"Time for the Hollyhocks." [PraS] (61:4) Wint 87, p. 58-59.
"The White Silo." [Nimrod] (30:2) Spr-Sum 87, p. 136.
5373. SUTHERLAND, Robert D.
"The Wonderful World." [LightY] '87, c86, p. 176.
5374. SUTHERLAND, W. Mark
"A Case History." [Waves] (15:3) Wint 87, p. 56.
"The History of Miracles." [Waves] (15:3) Wint 87, p. 57.
5375. SUTHERLAND-SMITH, James
"A Command." [StoneC] (15:1/2) Fall-Wint 87-88, p. 24.
"You." [CumbPR] (7:1) Fall 87, p. 81.
5376. SUTTER, Barton
"Pine Creek Filling Station." [NoDaQ] (55:2) Spr 87, p. 176.
5377. SUTTON, Catherine
"As a Drawing by My Son." [AmerV] (7) Sum 87, p. 63-64.
5378. SUTTON, Dorothy Moseley
"We Shall Rest, and Faith We Shall Need It." [FloridaR] (15:1) Spr-Sum 87, p. 119.
5379. SUTZKEVER, Abraham (Avrom)
"The Murder of My Mother" (Vilna Ghetto, Oct. 1942, tr. by Aaron Kramer). [Vis] (25) 87, p. 27.
"To My Child" (tr. by Murray Wolfe). [WebR] (12:2) Fall 87, p. 8-9.
5380. SUVIN, Darko R.
"A stag cries." [Amelia] (4:3, issue 10) 87, p. 40.
5381. SVEHLA, John
"The Garden." [Wind] (17:61) 87, p. 47.
"The House." [Wind] (17:61) 87, p. 47.
"Span Worms." [Wind] (17:61) 87, p. 47.
"Spring." [Wind] (17:61) 87, p. 47.
5382. SVOBODA, Terese
"American Gothic" (Selection: III). [PraS] (61:2) Sum 87, p. 82-85.
"Captain Andy." [VirQR] (63:4) Aut 87, p. 642-643.
"Conquistador." [YaleR] (77:1) Aut 87, p. 148-149.
"Laughing Africa." [Ploughs] (13:1) 87, p. 127-131.
"Rite." [TarRP] (26:2) Spr 87, p. 22-23.
5383. SWAIM, Alice MacKenzie
"To the Unknown Artist." [Wind] (17:59) 87, p. 3.
5384. SWANBERG, Ingrid
"August." [Abraxas] (35/36) 87, p. 15.
"Homeopathy." [Abraxas] (35/36) 87, p. 14.
5385. SWANGER, David
"Hero." [PoetryNW] (28:2) Sum 87, p. 27.
"These Hearts We Would Name Our Own" (for Max). [PoetryNW] (28:2) Sum 87, p. 26-27.
"We Have Faced Night and Warmed Each Other." [CharR] (13:2) Fall 87, p. 91.
5386. SWANN, Brian
"Bells" (To Pablo Antonio Cuadra, tr. of Marco Antonio Montes de Oca). [Footwork] 87, p. 21.
"A Childhood." [NewL] (54:1) Fall 87, p. 44-45.
"The Clock That Stopped." [ColEng] (49:6) O 87, p. 657.
"Deer Song" (version of Native American poem). [CharR] (13:1) Spr 87, p. 96-97.
"Faust Among the Stars." [ColEng] (49:6) O 87, p. 658.
"Finding a Career." [ColEng] (49:6) O 87, p. 657.

"Io" (version of Native American poem). [CharR] (13:1) Spr 87, p. 99-100.
"Mediterranean." [AntR] (45:4) Fall 87, p. 438-440.
"Mouse Dance Song" (version of Native American poem). [CharR] (13:1) Spr 87, p. 95-96.
"Prayer." [NewEngR] (9:3) Spr 87, p. 291.
"Ruse to Trick the Spirit of the Snow" (version of Native American poem). [CharR] (13:1) Spr 87, p. 100.
"The Sand." [ColEng] (49:6) O 87, p. 656.
"Sea Bed" (Selections: 17, 8, 11, tr. of Hernandez). [Footwork] 87, p. 21-22.
"She Will Gather Roses" (version of Native American poem). [CharR] (13:1) Spr 87, p. 95.
"Thanatopsis." [SouthwR] (72:4) Aut 87, p. 530.
5387. SWANN, Ely
"Hardboiled Wine." [Wind] (17:60) 87, p. 47-48.
"In Broad Daylight." [Wind] (17:60) 87, p. 47.
5388. SWANN, Gethsemane
"A Cymical Marriage." [HawaiiR] (22) Fall 87, p. 24-25.
"Ghazal for John the Baptist." [Vis] (25) 87, p. 14.
5389. SWANN, Roberta
"Grey Fox." [YellowS] (24) Aut 87, p. 9.
5390. SWEENEY, Matthew
"Dog on a Chain." [Stand] (28:4) Aut 87, p. 25.
5391. SWEENEY, Michael
"Imagining Wyoming." [Phoenix] (7:2) 87, p. 23.
5392. SWEET, Mary Logan
"Critic." [BallSUF] (28:4) Aut 87, p. 22.
5393. SWENSEN, Cole
"Our Town." [FiveFR] (5) 87, p. 21.
5394. SWENSON, Karen
"Apollo at LAX." [Salm] (72) Fall 86, p. 194-195.
"Aunt Liz in the Home." [Salm] (72) Fall 86, p. 194.
"The Floating Mormon." [PraS] (61:1) Spr 87, p. 88.
"The Signature of Love." [Salm] (72) Fall 86, p. 193-194.
"Two Trees in Kathmandu." [PraS] (61:1) Spr 87, p. 89.
5395. SWENSON, May
"In Florida." [YaleR] (76:3) Spr 87, p. 353-354.
"Strawberrying." [Atlantic] (259:3) Mr 87, p. 52.
"Third Floor Walk-Up, 1984." [Poetry] (151:1/2) O-N 87, p. 175-176.
5396. SWIFT, Michael
"Agonies in the Garden of Snakes." [JamesWR] (4:4) Sum 87, p. 8-9.
"Poe Poem." [JamesWR] (4:2) Wint 87, p. 3.
5397. SWILKY, Jody
"Balance." [Raccoon] (24/25) My 87, p. 178.
5398. SWINTON, John
"Donor and Recipient." [BallSUF] (28:4) Aut 87, p. 26-27.
5399. SWIST, Wally
"The old man." [WindO] (49) Fall 87, p. 63.
"Whiskey." [Outbr] (18/19) Fall 86-Spr 88, p. 24-25.
5400. SYLVESTER, Santiago
"Travel Book" (3 poems, tr. by Anthony Edkins). [Trans] (18) Spr 87, p. 183-184.
5401. SZE, Arthur
"The Day Can Become a Zen Garden of Raked Sand." [HighP] (2:3) Wint 87, p. 323.
"Parallax." [HighP] (2:3) Wint 87, p. 324-325.
"Shuttle." [Sonora] (12) Spr 87, p. 15.
5402. SZEMAN, Sherri
"Holiday." [CentR] (31:3) Sum 87, p. 280-281.
"The Kommandant." [MSS] (5:3) 87, p. 159-166.
"Letter to Sylvia." [LitR] (30:4) Sum 87, p. 606-607.
"The Toast" (to god who did not save us, after a poem by Anna Ahmatova). [SoCaR] (19:2) Spr 87, p. 49.
5403. SZIRTES, George
"Metro" (Excerpts). [Margin] (5) Wint 87-88, p. 15-22.
5404. SZUMIGALSKI, Anne
"Silent is the cuckoo." [Grain] (15:4) Wint 87, p. 6.
"There's a farm in god's head." [PraF] (8:4) Wint 87-88, p. 9-11.

"Think of a word." [PraF] (8:4) Wint 87-88, p. 10-11.
5405. TACHIYAMA, Gary
  "How the Island Works." [BambooR] (36) Fall 87, p. 4.
  "Reverse Drive Therapy." [BambooR] (36) Fall 87, p. 8.
  "Reviewing the Scene." The Best of [BambooR] [(31-32)] 86, p. 91-93.
  "Someday, But for Now." The Best of [BambooR] [(31-32)] 86, p. 90.
  "Stars." [BambooR] (36) Fall 87, p. 5-7.
5406. TADA, Chimako
  "Song." [CrossCur] (7:2) 87, p. 62-63.
5407. TAFDRUP, Pia
  "Between Always and Never" (tr. by Thomas E. Kennedy and Monique M.
      Kennedy). [Paint] (14:28) Aut 87, p. 32.
  "The Four Cradles" (tr. by Poul Borum and Roger Greenwald). [Writ] (19) 87, p.
      28-30.
  "In Spite of Everything" (tr. by Poul Borum and Roger Greenwald). [Writ] (19) 87,
      p. 31.
  "The Inmost Membrane of My Brain" (tr. by Poul Borum and Roger Greenwald).
      [Writ] (19) 87, p. 24.
  "Just My Blood" (tr. by Poul Borum and Roger Greenwald). [Writ] (19) 87, p.
      26-27.
  "No Longer Afraid" (tr. by Poul Borum and Roger Greenwald). [Writ] (19) 87, p.
      32.
  "Shadows in the Blood" (tr. by Thomas E. Kennedy and Monique M. Kennedy).
      [Paint] (14:28) Aut 87, p. 33.
  "Sharp Tugs" (tr. by Poul Borum and Roger Greenwald). [Writ] (19) 87, p. 33.
  "Skin" (tr. by Poul Borum and Roger Greenwald). [Writ] (19) 87, p. 35.
  "So As Not to Stand in Our Own Way" (tr. by Poul Borum and Roger Greenwald).
      [Writ] (19) 87, p. 25.
  "Spring Tide" (tr. by Poul Borum and Roger Greenwald). [Writ] (19) 87, p. 34.
  "What Comes" (tr. by Poul Borum and Roger Greenwald). [Writ] (19) 87, p. 23.
5408. TAGAMI, Jeff
  "Now It Is Broccoli." [Spirit] (8:2) 87, p. 100-101.
5409. TAGGART, John
  "In Itself." [Sulfur] (19) Spr 87, p. 24.
  "Marvin Gaye Suite." [Conjunc] (10) 87, p. 34-42.
  "Saul and David." [Notus] (2:2) Fall 87, p. 29-31.
  "See What Love." [NowestR] (25:3) 87, p. 283-287.
  "Speeded Up Played Faster." [Sulfur] (19) Spr 87, p. 25.
5410. TAGLIABUE, John
  "3 Poems in 2 Airports: Portland and Boston." [GreenfR] (14:1/2) Wint-Spr, p.
      211-212.
  "Barns as Temporary Fine Smelling Temples." [Epoch] (36:3) 87-88, p. 188.
  "Condominiums Dissolving." [BallSUF] (28:4) Aut 87, p. 25.
  "Distant Cousin of Odysseus in Revery." [ConnPR] (6:1) 87, p. 37.
  "Extended Quixote." [BallSUF] (28:4) Aut 87, p. 24.
  "Furtively and Subliminally Aware of Each Other." [TexasR] (7:3/4) 87, p. 150.
  "Inscape-and Escape of Song." [Epoch] (36:3) 87-88, p. 189.
  "Insurance." [BallSUF] (28:4) Aut 87, p. 24.
  "Paul Valery: 'A Poem Is a Holiday of Mind'." [ManhatPR] (9) Sum 87, p. 26.
  "Spontaneous Plans Helped Out by the Solar System." [Epoch] (36:3) 87-88, p.
      187.
  "Suggested by an Eik-Ibibio Folktale." [NowestR] (25:3) 87, p. 106.
  "Three Typewriter Poems." [Margin] (2) Spr 87, p. 17-19.
  "Wm. James Said the Millennium Would Not Come As Long As a Single Cockroach
      Suffered . . ." [PraS] (61:2) Sum 87, p. 95.
5411. TAKARA, Kathryn
  "Bird's View." [HawaiiR] (20) Fall 86, c87, p. 30-31.
  "Harvest." [HawaiiR] (19) Spr 86, c87, p. 73.
  "Payment." [HawaiiR] (19) Spr 86, c87, p. 72.
5412. TAKATS, Gyula
  "The Magicians' Parade Under Our Castles" (tr. by Zsuzsanna Ozsvath and Martha
      Satz). [WebR] (12:1) Spr 87, p. 87.
5413. TAKEI, Sojin
  "Arrest" (in Romanized Japanese and English, tr. by Jiro & Kay Nakano). The Best
      of [BambooR] [(31-32)] 86, p. 67.

"A flock of black birds" (in Romanized Japanese and English, tr. by Jiro & Kay Nakano). The Best of [BambooR] [(31-32)] 86, p. 73.
"Homecoming" (in Romanized Japanese and English, tr. by Jiro & Kay Nakano). The Best of [BambooR] [(31-32)] 86, p. 73.
"My hands lightly touch" (in Romanized Japanese and English, tr. by Jiro & Kay Nakano). The Best of [BambooR] [(31-32)] 86, p. 70.
"Santa Fe Internment Camp" (in Romanized Japanese and English, tr. by Jiro & Kay Nakano). The Best of [BambooR] [(31-32)] 86, p. 71.
5414. TAKIZAWA, Raynette
"Tansu I." The Best of [BambooR] [(31-32)] 86, p. 94.
5415. TAKSA, Mark
"Bay in the Palms." [Poem] (57) Mr 87, p. 15.
5416. TALBOT, Peter R.
"Riding the Broadway Limited" (1986 Honorable Mention, Eve of Saint Agnes Poetry Competition). [NegC] (7:1/2) 87, p. 134.
5417. TALBOTT, Strobe
"A Toast for a Composer's Widow in Tashkent." [NewYorker] (62:47) 12 Ja 87, p. 30-31.
5418. TALIAFERRO, Merle
"The Real Moral Dilemma." [Writer] (99:5) My 86, p. 17.
5419. TALL, Deborah
"Birdflight." [PoetC] (18:3) Spr 87, p. 24-25.
"Isolation Unit." [NewL] (53:3) Spr 87, p. 30.
5420. TALLMOUNTAIN, Mary
"Birthing." [Calyx] (10:2/3) Spr 87, p. 111.
5421. TAM, Reuben
"Calling Out." [HawaiiR] (21) Spr 87, p. 2.
"To Anahola Mountain." [HawaiiR] (21) Spr 87, p. 3.
"Waimea Canyon." [BambooR] (33) Spr 87, p. 79.
"Waipouli Reef." [HawaiiR] (21) Spr 87, p. 1.
5422. TAMANTHA F., Solomon Elementary School
"Clear Eyes." The Best of [BambooR] [(31-32)] 86, p. 15.
5423. TAMER, Ülkü
"Responses for Poetry" (tr. by Talat Sait Halman). [Trans] (19) Fall 87, p. 158-161.
"Sleep" (tr. by Murat Nemet-Nejat). [Trans] (19) Fall 87, p. 157.
5424. TAMM, Riina
"And when the sea retreats from here . . ." (tr. of Jaan Kaplinski, w. Sam Hamill). [AmerPoR] (16:6) N-D 87, p. 8.
"Dialectics is a dialogue, a play of shadows" (tr. of Jaan Kaplinski, w. Sam Hamill). [AmerPoR] (16:6) N-D 87, p. 8.
"The early autumn, a faded aquarelle" (tr. of Jaan Kaplinski, w. Sam Hamill). [AmerPoR] (16:6) N-D 87, p. 8.
"No one can put me back together again" (tr. of Jaan Kaplinski, w. Sam Hamill). [AmerPoR] (16:6) N-D 87, p. 8.
"No one can put me back together again" (tr. of Jaan Kaplinski, w. the author and Sam Hamill). [Dandel] (14:2) Fall-Wint 87, p. 29.
"Sometimes I see so clearly the openness of things" (tr. of Jaan Kaplinski, w. Sam Hamill). [AmerPoR] (16:6) N-D 87, p. 7.
"The sun shines on the red wall and the wall is warm" (tr. of Jaan Kaplinski, w. Sam Hamill). [AmerPoR] (16:6) N-D 87, p. 8.
"There is no Good, no Evil, no Sin, no Virtue" (tr. of Jaan Kaplinski, w. Sam Hamill). [AmerPoR] (16:6) N-D 87, p. 8.
"The washing never gets done" (tr. of Jaan Kaplinski, w. Sam Hamill). [AmerPoR] (16:6) N-D 87, p. 7.
"The wind sways the lilac branches and shadows" (tr. of Jaan Kaplinski, w. Sam Hamill). [AmerPoR] (16:6) N-D 87, p. 8.
5425. TAMMARO, Thom
"St. Peter's Tears." [SoDakR] (25:2) Sum 87, p. 18-19.
"Union Meeting, 1959." [NoDaQ] (55:2) Spr 87, p. 137-138.
5426. TANA, Patti
"Sewing the Bullet Holes." [HiramPoR] (42) Spr-Sum 87, p. 44-45.
5427. TANCZYN, Dorothy
"Penelope." [Writer] (100:5) My 87, p. 20.
5428. TANGORRA, Joanne
"In Florence." [AntR] (45:3) Sum 87, p. 346-347.
"My Sister's Hair." [AntR] (45:3) Sum 87, p. 343.

"Rose Window" (for my nephew). [AntR] (45:3) Sum 87, p. 344-345.
5429. TANIKAWA, Shuntaro
"Ball of Yarn" (tr. by William I. Elliott and Kazuo Kawamura). [Amelia] (4:3, issue 10) 87, p. 102.
"The Day Birds Vanished from the Sky" (tr. by Harold Wright). [LitR] (30:2) Wint 87, p. 263.
"A Friend Who Leapt to His Death" (tr. by William I. Elliott and Kazuo Kawamura). [Amelia] (4:3, issue 10) 87, p. 102.
"Seeing Off Kenneth Rexroth: The Tokyo American Center, July 8, 1975" (tr. by Harold Wright). [LitR] (30:2) Wint 87, p. 263.
5430. TANNEN, Deborah
"Freedom, Abstractions, and Poems" (from Vegar, Vatn og Fjell, tr. of Erling Indreeide, w. the author). [PoetL] (81:3) Fall 86, p. 149-153.
5431. TANNY, Marlaina
"Inner Scenes." [NegC] (7:3/4) 87, p. 86.
"Slow and Painless Death." [MinnR] (NS 29) Fall 87, p. 42-43.
"Where the Soul goes." [WorldO] (20:2) Wint 85-86 c88, p. 38.
5432. TANZI, Diane
"Memo to My Sister." [Footwork] 87, p. 45.
5433. T'AO, Ch'ien
"Returning to the Farm to Live, #3" (tr. by Julie Landau). [MSS] (5:3) 87, p. 31.
5434. TARACHOW, Michael
"Walking in the Midst of Others." [Spirit] (8:2) 87, p. 83.
5435. TARN, Nathaniel
"Litany of the Names of Lesbos." [Caliban] (2) 87, p. 144-145.
"Narrative of the Men and Women Who Became Stars." [Conjunc] (11) 87?, p. 253-255.
"Narrative of the Vision of Our Lady of Armeiro." [Conjunc] (11) 87?, p. 250-252.
"Persephone West." [Temblor] (5) 87, p. 45-51.
"Protoavia: Narrative of the Pilots." [Conjunc] (10) 87, p. 277-280.
5436. TARVER, John
"No Time" (for Cas Crumb, January 17, 1987). [Ploughs] (13:4) 87, p. 129.
5437. TARWOOD, J.
"A Parochial Education." [LaurelR] (21:1/2) Wint-Sum 87, p. 12.
TASSEL, Katrina van
    See Van TASSEL, Katrina
5438. TATA, Sam
"12 Poems from an Indian Journey." [Descant] (58) Fall 87, p. 19-30.
"Bombay Bohemia: Party at Alberta's" (For M.T.B.). [Descant] (58) Fall 87, p. 22.
"Canvas by Amrita Sher Gil: Bombay" (For Toni). [Descant] (58) Fall 87, p. 23.
"Colaba: Blind Man in the Rain." [Descant] (58) Fall 87, p. 21.
"Death of a Mahatma" (Mohandas Karamchand Gandhi 1869-1948). [Descant] (58) Fall 87, p. 24.
"Exhibition by Shiavax Chavda." [Descant] (58) Fall 87, p. 30.
"Foggy Morning: Calcutta." [Descant] (58) Fall 87, p. 27.
"Girl Singing" (A painting by George Keyt). [Descant] (58) Fall 87, p. 26.
"Old Ruins: Delhi." [Descant] (58) Fall 87, p. 25.
"Rajabai Tower at Noon: Bombay." [Descant] (58) Fall 87, p. 29.
"Temple at Tanjore." [Descant] (58) Fall 87, p. 19.
"To a Lady in an Urban Landscape" (Recollections of a Kangra painting). [Descant] (58) Fall 87, p. 28.
"Train Journey before the Monsoon." [Descant] (58) Fall 87, p. 20.
5439. TATE, James
"A Beer Ain't Got No Bone." [Field] (36) Spr 87, p. 100-101.
"Foreign Airport." [DenQ] (21:3) Wint 87, p. 6.
"Neighbors." [Field] (36) Spr 87, p. 102.
"Nuisance." [Poetry] (151:1/2) O-N 87, p. 177.
"Las Ramblas." [DenQ] (21:3) Wint 87, p. 8.
"The Sunday Driver in Search of Himself." [NowestR] (25:3) 87, p. 110.
"Under Mounting Pressure." [Ploughs] (13:1) 87, p. 132.
"We Go A-Quilting." [DenQ] (21:3) Wint 87, p. 7.
5440. TAYLOR, Alexander
"When a Person Dies" (tr. of Henrik Nordbrandt, w. the author). [NoDaQ] (55:3) Sum 87, p. 226-227.
5441. TAYLOR, Bruce
"After Rumi" (Jala al-Din Rumi, 1207-1273). [HayF] (2) Spr 87, p. 57-58.

"At Munsan on the Imjin River I Think of the Lower East Bank of the Upper St.
   Croix." [HayF] (2) Spr 87, p. 59-60.
"Father Lewis." [NowestR] (25:3) 87, p. 432.
"Middle-Aged Man, Sitting" (for John Cheever). [PassN] (8:2) Sum 87, p. 5.
5442. TAYLOR, Catherine
"Winterchill." [Writer] (99:9) S 86, p. 25.
5443. TAYLOR, D. Scott
"Living Alone." [LightY] '87, c86, p. 44.
5444. TAYLOR, Dabrina
"Ice" (The Greensboro Review Literary Award, Honorable Mention).
   [GreensboroR] (43) Wint 87-88, p. 51-52.
"Snow." [GreensboroR] (43) Wint 87-88, p. 53-54.
"The Vendor's Mare." [Gargoyle] (32/33) 87, p. 228.
5445. TAYLOR, David C.
"Alaskan Vision." [BellArk] (3:4) Jl-Ag 87, p. 1.
5446. TAYLOR, Eleanor Ross
"No." [ParisR] (29:102) Spr 87, p. 82-84.
5447. TAYLOR, Ellen M.
"In the All-Night Laundromat." [PassN] (8:1) Wint 87, p. 17.
5448. TAYLOR, Henry
"Master of None." [Poetry] (151:1/2) O-N 87, p. 178-179.
5449. TAYLOR, James
"Because I Didn't Take the Picture." [Puerto] (22:2) Spr 87, p. 43.
"Dear Paul" (A letter from his godfather in America). [Gargoyle] (32/33) 87, p. 260.
"Last Words for M.W. Johnson." [Lips] (13) 87, p. 50-51.
5450. TAYLOR, Jane
"Lovesong After the Music of K. E. Ntsane" (tr. of Antjie Krog, w. David Bunn and
   the author). [TriQ] (69) Spr-Sum 87, p. 334-335.
5451. TAYLOR, John
"The Dream" (tr. of Elias Papadimitrakopoulos). [WebR] (12:2) Fall 87, p. 45.
5452. TAYLOR, Jonathan
"A Love Poem: A Nuclear Reactor Considers Its Breakdown." [CumbPR] (7:1) Fall
   87, p. 1.
5453. TAYLOR, Keith
"Detroit Dancing." [Notus] (2:1) Spr 87, p. 64.
"Wind Horses." [Notus] (2:1) Spr 87, p. 65.
5454. TAYLOR, Kent
"Bay Bridge." [Abraxas] (35/36) 87, p. 12-13.
"Buying Groceries." [Abraxas] (35/36) 87, p. 12.
"N-Judah." [Abraxas] (35/36) 87, p. 13.
5455. TAYLOR, Linda
"Quilts in Autumn." [Pembroke] (19) 87, p. 114-115.
5456. TAYLOR, Maggie
"John Bible." [PassN] (8:1) Wint 87, p. 15.
5457. TAYLOR, Marilyn
"For Bluebird Woman." [Northeast] (Ser. 4:5) Sum 87, p. 44.
"Late in the Wet Season." [PoetryNW] (28:4) Wint 87-88, p. 41-42.
"Looking for Wild Orchids" (To My Mother). [Northeast] (Ser. 4:5) Sum 87, p. 43.
"The Tenth Avenue Care Home." [PoetryNW] (28:4) Wint 87-88, p. 42-43.
5458. TAYLOR, Sally
"The End of Summer." [CumbPR] (7:1) Fall 87, p. 75.
5459. TAYLOR, Sandra Kay
"An Urge." [YellowS] (22) Spr 87, p. 24.
5460. TCETERA, André
"Jarry au Restau." [Rampike] (5:3) 87, p. 46.
5461. TEDLOCK, Dennis
"Five Days from a Dream Almanac." [Conjunc] (10) 87, p. 235-240.
5462. TEIGEN, Sue
"My Mother's Clock." [PoetL] (82:4) Wint 87-88, p. 208.
"Nightfall, Hay Lake." [PoetL] (82:4) Wint 87-88, p. 209.
5463. TEILLIER, Jorge
"Afternoon Story" (tr. by Carolyne Wright). [SenR] (17:2) 87, p. 21.
"Alegría." [Iowa] (17:2) Spr-Sum 87, p. 70.
"Another Song" (tr. by Carolyne Wright). [AmerPoR] (16:2) Mr-Ap 87, p. 42.
"Aperitif" (tr. by Carolyne Wright). [Iowa] (17:2) Spr-Sum 87, p. 72.
"Bridge in the South" (tr. by Carolyne Wright). [SenR] (17:2) 87, p. 22.

"Dark Lantern" (tr. by Carolyne Wright). [AmerPoR] (16:2) Mr-Ap 87, p. 42.
"Golden Age" (tr. by Carolyne Wright). [AmerPoR] (16:2) Mr-Ap 87, p. 42.
"Historia de un Hijo Prodigo." [BlackWR] (13:2) Spr 87, p. 134-138.
"Image" (tr. by Carolyne Wright). [SenR] (17:2) 87, p. 23.
"Image for a Pool" (tr. by Mary Crow). [SouthernHR] (21:4) Fall 87, p. 339.
"In Memory of a Closed House" (tr. by Mary Crow). [AmerV] (7) Sum 87, p. 27.
"In Order to Talk to the Dead" (tr. by Carolyne Wright). [AmerPoR] (16:2) Mr-Ap
    87, p. 41.
"Joy" (tr. by Carolyne Wright). [Iowa] (17:2) Spr-Sum 87, p. 71.
"The Key" (tr. by Carolyne Wright). [Iowa] (17:2) Spr-Sum 87, p. 73.
"Letter of Rain" (tr. by Mary Crow). [Nimrod] (31:1) Fall-Wint 87, p. 128-129.
"Night Trains" (tr. by Carolyne Wright). [BlackWR] (13:2) Spr 87, p. 141-155.
"Nobody's Died Yet in This House" (tr. by Carolyne Wright). [Iowa] (17:2)
    Spr-Sum 87, p. 72-73.
"Not a Sign of Life" (tr. by Mary Crow). [AmerPoR] (16:4) Jl-Ag 87, p. 48.
"So Long" (tr. by Carolyne Wright). [AmerPoR] (16:2) Mr-Ap 87, p. 42.
"Story About a Branch of Myrtle" (tr. by Mary Crow). [Nimrod] (31:1) Fall-Wint
    87, p. 127.
"Story of a Prodigal Son" (tr. by Carolyne Wright). [BlackWR] (13:2) Spr 87, p.
    135-139.
"Story of the Afternoon" (tr. by Mary Crow). [WillowS] (19) Wint 87, p. 14.
"To a Child in a Tree" (tr. by Carolyne Wright). [SenR] (17:2) 87, p. 20.
"To Talk With the Dead" (tr. by Mary Crow). [WillowS] (19) Wint 87, p. 14.
"Los Trenes de la Noche." [BlackWR] (13:2) Spr 87, p. 140-154.
"When Everyone Goes Away" (tr. by Carolyne Wright). [Iowa] (17:2) Spr-Sum 87,
    p. 74.
5464. TEJADA, Robert
    "A Delta for D.H.L." [Sulfur] (20) Fall 87, p. 83-84.
5465. TEMPLETON, Fiona
    "Hi Cowboy! Enclosed Why You Are Wrong . . ." (Selections: Parts 15, 18).
        [Bound] (14:1/2) Fall 85-Wint 86 [c87], p. 30-32.
5466. TENENBAUM, Molly
    "Blue Willow and Others." [PoetryNW] (28:4) Wint 87-88, p. 32-33.
    "The Body I Left When I Got Up This Morning." [PoetryNW] (28:4) Wint 87-88, p.
        34.
    "Homelife." [PoetryNW] (28:2) Sum 87, p. 40-41.
    "My Father's Dinner." [PoetryNW] (28:2) Sum 87, p. 39-40.
    "Rosie's Book." [BellArk] (3:2) Mr-Ap 87, p. 10.
    "The Suspense of Being a Child." [PoetryNW] (28:4) Wint 87-88, p. 33-34.
5467. TERADA, Wini
    "Faces on the Unpaved Road Past Mokule'ia." The Best of [BambooR] [(31-32)]
        86, p. 95.
5468. TERASHIMA, Robert
    "The Dancers at Obon." [Abraxas] (35/36) 87, p. 28-29.
5469. TERCERO, Isidoro
    "Doubt of Love" (tr. by Kent Johnson). [Contact] (9:44/45/46) Fall-Wint 87, p. 18.
5470. TERENCE, Susan
    "Night Melody." [SouthernPR] (27:2) Fall 87, p. 54.
5471. TERMAN, Philip
    "Bless the Children Who Pass Away." [Gambit] (20) 86, p. 22.
    "Child of God." [PoetryNW] (28:3) Aut 87, p. 34-35.
    "Secrets." [PoetryNW] (28:3) Aut 87, p. 33-34.
    "Your Father's Garage." [PoetryNW] (28:3) Aut 87, p. 36.
5472. TERRANOVA, Elaine
    "Steven." [Outbr] (18/19) Fall 86-Spr 88, p. 173-174.
5473. TERRILL, Richard
    "Variations on Variations on a Summer Day by Wallace Stevens." [HayF] (2) Spr
        87, p. 16-17.
5474. TERRIN BENAVIDES, Manuel
    "Balada del Muchacho Ahogado." [Mairena] (9:24) 87, p. 72.
5475. TERRIS, Virginia R.
    "Sex." [GreenfR] (14:3/4) Sum-Fall 87, p. 46.
    "A Woman." [GreenfR] (14:3/4) Sum-Fall 87, p. 47.
    "Years Later: The Boy Friend." [GreenfR] (14:3/4) Sum-Fall 87, p. 45.
5476. TERRY, Gilmer
    "Aquaba." [Vis] (23) 87, p. 31.

5477. TETI, Ranieri
"Voltaanima" (Excerpt). [Os] (24) 87, p. 29.
5478. TETI, Zona
"After Homer." [AmerPoR] (16:2) Mr-Ap 87, p. 6.
"Alpha Beta." [AmerPoR] (16:2) Mr-Ap 87, p. 6.
"Elizabeth's Sabbath." [AmerPoR] (16:2) Mr-Ap 87, p. 6.
"Gretel and Hansel." [AmerPoR] (16:2) Mr-Ap 87, p. 6.
"I Speak." [ManhatPR] (9) Sum 87, p. 54.
5479. TETUA, Moa
"A Man Dreams of His Dead Wife" (tr. by Margaret Orbell). [Trans] (19) Fall 87, p.
173.
5480. THALMAN, Mark
"The Ants." [LightY] '87, c86, p. 118.
5481. THATCHER, Philip
"Low Tide at Gabriola." [Event] (16:2) Sum 87, p. 62.
5482. THEODOROU, Victoria
"The Down of My First Youth" (tr. by Rachel Dalven). [ColR] (NS 14:1) Spr-Sum
87, p. 42-43.
5483. THIERS, Naomi
"New England: Strictest Winter." [ColR] (NS 14:2) Fall-Wint 87, p. 86.
5484. THOMAS, Calvin
"Climbing Smith Mountain Tower." [NegC] (7:3/4) 87, p. 95-96.
5485. THOMAS, Debra
"The Last Turnings of the Season's Wheel." The Best of [BambooR] [(31-32)] 86,
p. 96-100.
"That Moment." [HawaiiR] (19) Spr 86, c87, p. 45.
"Where You Sleep." The Best of [BambooR] [(31-32)] 86, p. 101.
5486. THOMAS, Elizabeth
"The World and What We Know." [Outbr] (18/19) Fall 86-Spr 88, p. 84-85.
5487. THOMAS, Jim
"After Sleeping." [BallSUF] (28:4) Aut 87, p. 20.
"Desert, Oasis." [BallSUF] (28:4) Aut 87, p. 58.
"Hard Times: A Rock Poem." [MinnR] (NS 28) Spr 87, p. 38.
"Night Work." [KanQ] (19:1/2) Wint-Spr 87, p. 260.
5488. THOMAS, John
"He Despairs of the Poems He Reads." [Margin] (5) Wint 87-88, p. 73.
"He Reflects on History and the Irrelevance of Absolution." [Margin] (5) Wint
87-88, p. 72.
5489. THOMAS, Joyce
"Two-Panel Painting" (for Ben and the others, 1985 Alice Jackson Poetry Prize:
First Prize). [Electrum] (39) Fall-Wint 87, p. 7.
5490. THOMAS, Julia
"Breakfast." [LaurelR] (20:1/2) Sum 87, p. 66.
"The Naming of Parts." [LaurelR] (20:1/2) Sum 87, p. 65.
5491. THOMAS, Larry D.
"Each a Wingless Black Angel." [WebR] (12:1) Spr 87, p. 18.
"In the Icehouse." [WebR] (12:1) Spr 87, p. 19.
"The Parlor." [CapeR] (22:1) Spr 87, p. 29.
5492. THOMAS, Michael W.
"Sudden Lovecry." [Verse] (4:3) N 87, p. 8.
5493. THOMAS, Nancy C.
"Quiet!" [EngJ] (76:4) Ap 87, p. 28.
5494. THOMAS, P. L.
"Thoughts in Silhouette." [Writer] (100:1) Ja 87, p. 22-23.
5495. THOMAS, Robert
"The Ecology of Light." [AmerPoR] (16:4) Jl-Ag 87, p. 30.
5496. THOMAS, Stanley J.
"Soap." [Bogg] (57) 87, p. 11.
5497. THOMAS, Stanley R.
"Entrapment: A Continuing Saga." [BlackALF] (21:4) Wint 87, p. 451.
5498. THOMPSON, Carol
"Fireflies" (for Jonathan). [PoeticJ] (17) 87, p. 34.
5499. THOMPSON, Catherine
"Cracking the Crab." [KanQ] (19:3) Sum 87, p. 276-277.
5500. THOMPSON, Gary
"Bicycle." [CutB] (27/28) 87, p. 47.

"Fallow" (for Dick, Missoula, 1984). [CutB] (27/28) 87, p. back cover.
"Train." [CutB] (27/28) 87, p. 46.
5501. THOMPSON, Jeanie
"Autumn Journal." [Raccoon] (24/25) My 87, p. 103-104.
"A True Story." [Raccoon] (24/25) My 87, p. 101-102.
5502. THOMPSON, Jeri
"Sergio: our smell." [Electrum] (39) Fall-Wint 87, p. 39.
5503. THOMPSON, Julius E.
"Son to Father." [Callaloo] (10:3) Sum 87, p. 481.
5504. THOMPSON, M. E.
"Rose Petals." [JamesWR] (4:4) Sum 87, p. 14.
5505. THOMPSON, Perry
"Solo Sax." [DekalbLAJ] (20:1/4) 87, p. 67.
"Your Hands (Winter Is Green)." [DekalbLAJ] (20:1/4) 87, p. 68.
5506. THOMPSON, Phyllis Hoge
"The Light on the Door." [Hudson] (40:2) Sum 87, p. 296.
"Voyager." [Raccoon] (24/25) My 87, p. 184.
5507. THOMPSON, Rebecca
"Wild Swans." [MidwQ] (28:2) Wint 87, p. 228.
5508. THOMPSON, Sara
"Winter Afternoon." [Stand] (28:2) Spr 87, p. 33.
5509. THOMPSON, Sue Ellen
"The Compliment." [DenQ] (21:3) Wint 87, p. 79.
5510. THORN, Arline R.
"Ethereal Definitions." [LaurelR] (20:1/2) Sum 87, p. 19.
5511. THORNDIKE, Jon
"Arthiritis of the Brain." [WindO] (49) Fall 87, p. 26.
"The Beginning of Wisdom." [SlipS] (7) 87, p. 107.
5512. THORNDIKE, Nick
"After Reading the Detroit News" ("Geneva Talks Stall"). [ChrC] (104:2) 21 Ja 87, p. 47.
"Tomatoes of the Lord." [ChrC] (104:19) 17-24 Je 87, p. 549.
5513. THORNTON, Bruce
"The Angle of Repose." [Jacaranda] (2:2) Spr 87, p. 87.
"The Bones of Paradise." [CutB] (27/28) 87, p. 53.
5514. THORNTON, Russell
"Double." [Germ] (11:1) Fall 87, p. 46.
"Racoons." [Germ] (11:1) Fall 87, p. 48.
"You Want to Talk to Rain." [Germ] (11:1) Fall 87, p. 47.
5515. THORPE, Allison
"Private Journeys." [Wind] (17:60) 87, p. 38.
5516. THORSTON, Pamela
"Washing the Heirlooms." [WindO] (49) Fall 87, p. 15.
"World of Her Own." [WindO] (49) Fall 87, p. 15.
5517. THUMBOO, Edwin
"NTI" (Nanyang Technological Institute). [Chelsea] (46) 87, p. 248-249.
"The Road." [Chelsea] (46) 87, p. 249-250.
TI, P'ei
   See P'EI, Ti
5518. TIBBETTS, Frederick
"Long Summer Evenings." [Jacaranda] (2:2) Spr 87, p. 2.
5519. TIBULLUS
"I.2" (Excerpts in Latin and English, tr. by Joseph Salemi). [CumbPR] (7:1) Fall 87, p. 26-29.
5520. TICHBORNE, Chidiock
"Elegy, Written with His Own Hand in the Tower Before His Execution." [Paint] (14:28) Aut 87, p. 42.
5521. TICHY, Susan
"Antiquities." [Crazy] (32) Spr 87, p. 14-15.
"The Arrest of Dante: Our Chains." [CalQ] (30) Wint 87, p. 48-51.
"Galang." [BelPoJ] (38:2) Wint 87-88, p. 8-12.
"In Fact" (Zambales Mountains, Philippines). [CalQ] (30) Wint 87, p. 47.
5522. TIDD, Cynthia Ann
"The Black Experience." [ArizQ] (43:4) Wint 87, p. 305.
TIEGEN, Sue
   See TEIGEN, Sue

5523. TIEMAN, John Samuel
"Bitter Song for Her." [Americas] (15:2) Sum 87, p. 70.
"Doña Beatriz, una Canción a Dúo." [Americas] (15:2) Sum 87, p. 69.
5524. TIERNEY, Karl
"Homosexuality." [JamesWR] (4:2) Wint 87, p. 11.
"Letting Air." [JamesWR] (4:4) Sum 87, p. 14.
"The Sailors of Hart Crane." [JamesWR] (4:2) Wint 87, p. 11.
"Whore" (After Catullus). [JamesWR] (4:2) Wint 87, p. 11.
5525. TIERNEY, Sallie
"Still Life in Two or More Colors." [BellArk] (3:5) S-O 87, p. 1.
"What Promises There Were." [BellArk] (3:5) S-O 87, p. 10.
5526. TIFFANY, Daniel
"Creation" (tr. of Cesar Pavese). [ChiR] (35:4) 87, p. 118.
"The Friend Who Is Asleep" (tr. of Cesar Pavese). [ChiR] (35:4) 87, p. 117.
"Habits" (tr. of Cesar Pavese). [ChiR] (35:4) 87, p. 115-116.
5527. TIGER, Madeline
"Autumn Poem." [US1] (20/21) Wint 86-87, p. 45.
"In Your Fifties You Grope Through Significant Changes and You Are Afraid.
Never Mind." [Amelia] (4:3, issue 10) 87, p. 101.
5528. TIKOS, Laszlo
"Idyll" (tr. of Igor Khomin, w. Joseph Langland and Tamas Aczel). [NowestR]
(25:3) 87, p. 132-133.
5529. TILLER, Ruth
"Beware the Night." [DekalbLAJ] (20:1/4) 87, p. 54.
5530. TILLINGHAST, David
"The Albino King Snake." [Confr] (35/36) Spr-Fall 87, p. 220.
"Dreaming of Perhaps." [SoCaR] (20:1) Fall 87, p. 42-43.
"With All Due Respect." [SoCaR] (20:1) Fall 87, p. 43.
5531. TIMMINS, Michael
"Missing Children." [Event] (16:1) Mr 87, p. 60.
TING, Shu
See SHU, Ting
5532. TINKHAM, Charles
"The Cripple and the Secretary of State." [Kaleid] (14) Wint-Spr 87, p. 71.
"The Encounter." [Kaleid] (14) Wint-Spr 87, p. 71.
"A last Corner of Prairie (1985)" (for Irene Herlocker). [Kaleid] (14) Wint-Spr 87,
p. 71.
5533. TIPPING, Richard
"Chalk." [Verse] (4:1) Mr 87, p. 53.
5534. TIPTON, Carolyn
"White" (tr. of Rafael Alberti). [Trans] (18) Spr 87, p. 294-297.
"Zurbarán" (tr. of Rafael Alberti). [Trans] (18) Spr 87, p. 298-299.
5535. TIPTON, James
"I Do Not Know What to Do" (For Mary). [HighP] (2:3) Wint 87, p. 236.
"The Imaginary Love Poem." [HighP] (2:3) Wint 87, p. 234-235.
5536. TIRONE, Gail
"In the Empty Hall the Show's Over." [ColEng] (49:4) Ap 87, p. 420-421.
"Taipei." [ColEng] (49:4) Ap 87, p. 419-420.
5537. TISERA, Mary
"Loving Cup" (for Herman and Wilhelmina Steinbacher). [KanQ] (19:3) Sum 87, p.
86.
"A Useful Life." [LaurelR] (20:1/2) Sum 87, p. 18.
5538. TISHMAN, Art
"Postcard from New Jersey." [Pig] (14) 87, p. 75.
5539. TIXIER, Jean-Max
"Three Views of a Medusa" (tr. by William Jay Smith). [Trans] (19) Fall 87, p.
197-198.
"Variations on a Flame" (tr. by William Jay Smith). [Trans] (19) Fall 87, p. 198.
5540. TOBE, Dorothy
"Veri." [PoetL] (81:3) Fall 86, p. 170.
5541. TOBIN, Daniel
"Legend." [Vis] (24) 87, p. 39.
5542. TOHEE, Mahtoh Ge
"American Guns." [GreenfR] (14:1/2) Wint-Spr, p. 22.
5543. TOKARCZYK, Michelle M.
"After Woyko's Disappearance." [Cond] (14) 87, p. 2-01.

"Granny's Death." [Cond] (14) 87, p. 200.
5544. TOKUNO, Ken
"Elegy for My Mother's Mother." [BellArk] (3:1) Ja-F 87, p. 18.
"Hawaiian Sunset." [BellArk] (3:3) My-Je 87, p. 20.
5545. TOLL, Chris
"The Moral Order." [Bogg] (57) 87, p. 48.
5546. TOLL, Katharine
"A Birthday Poem to G. R. F. F." [Salm] (74/75) Spr-Sum 87, p. 55.
5547. TOLLYFIELD, Christine
"Hourglass." [Stand] (28:3) Sum 87, p. 52.
5548. TOMASCH, Morris
"Slum Scape." [Writer] (99:3) Mr 86, p. 20.
5549. TOMÉ RAMOS, Jesús
"La Hora." [Mairena] (9:24) 87, p. 110.
5550. TOMKINS, Rita
"Rosewood Box." [ManhatPR] (9) Sum 87, p. 17.
5551. TOMKIW, Lydia
"Cerebral Dance." [NewAW] (2) Fall 87, p. 92.
"Settling Into Our Bones." [NewAW] (2) Fall 87, p. 93.
"Six of Ox Is." [NewAW] (2) Fall 87, p. 94.
5552. TOMLINSON, Bernard
"Caper Ceilidh." [Margin] (5) Wint 87-88, p. 63.
5553. TOMLINSON, Charles
"February." [CreamCR] (11:2/3) 87?, p. 13.
"Night Ferry." [Poetry] (151:1/2) O-N 87, p. 181.
"North with Lawren Harris" (Lawren Harris, Canadian painter, 1885-1970).
[Poetry] (151:1/2) O-N 87, p. 180.
"Palermo." [CreamCR] (11:2/3) 87?, p. 14.
"Revolution" (Piazza di Spagna). [CreamCR] (11:2/3) 87?, p. 15.
5554. TOMLINSON, Rawdon
"Easter 1954." [DekalbLAJ] (20:1/4) 87, p. 54.
"Louise." [DekalbLAJ] (20:1/4) 87, p. 55.
5555. TOMORY, Susan
"I Lived in an Age on This Earth" (tr. of Miklòs Radnóti, w. Reynold Stone).
[AntigR] (71/72) Aut 87-Wint 88, p. 158.
"The Man Spoke" (tr. of József Attila, w. Reynold Stone). [AntigR] (71/72) Aut
87-Wint 88, p. 158.
"Seventh Eclogue" (tr. of Miklòs Radnóti, w. Reynold Stone). [AntigR] (71/72) Aut
87-Wint 88, p. 158.
"You Should Not Be Sorry" (tr. of József Attila, w. Reynold Stone). [AntigR]
(71/72) Aut 87-Wint 88, p. 158.
5556. TOMPKINS, Leslie C.
"Thinning into Fall" (for M. L'E. September 1986). [SouthernPR] (27:2) Fall 87, p.
42.
TONG-GYU, Hwang
See HWANG, Tong-Gyu
5557. TORGERSEN, Eric
"And now with a haircut and shoes." [NewL] (54:2) Wint 87-88, p. 79.
"An Apple from Walt Whitman." [CentR] (31:4) Fall 87, p. 384-385.
"Left Eye." [NewL] (54:2) Wint 87-88, p. 82-83.
"My Blindness." [NewL] (54:2) Wint 87-88, p. 85.
"The Throne of the Third Heaven of the Nations Millennium General Assembly."
[Notus] (2:1) Spr 87, p. 90-93.
"What Is Your Earliest Memory? What Does It Mean" (for Barbara Drake)."
[HangL] (50/51) 87, p. 180.
"What the Blind Kid Said." [NewL] (54:2) Wint 87-88, p. 80.
5558. TORRE, Josefina de la
"The Sky's Green Willow" (Spanish and English, tr. by Carlos Reyes). [BlackWR]
(13:2) Spr 87, p. 186-209.
5559. TORREN, Asher
"Babi Yar." [NegC] (7:3/4) 87, p. 85.
"Nelly's Inn, Paracas." [Lactuca] (7) Ag 87, p. 12.
"The Y Chromosome." [SmPd] (24:3) Fall 87, p. 27.
5560. TORRES SANTIAGO, José Manuel
"Mensaje a Cesar Vallejo." [Mairena] (9:24) 87, p. 49.

5561. TORRESON, Rodney
"A Pitcher Is a Beautiful Woman in an Old Movie." [CapeR] (22:1) Spr 87, p. 31.
5562. TOSABURO, Ono
"Hands" (tr. by Graeme Wilson). [LitR] (31:1) Fall 87, p. 86.
5563. TOSTESON, Heather
"Brandywine." [SouthernPR] (27:1) Spr 87, p. 22.
"Heaven." [SouthernPR] (27:2) Fall 87, p. 50-52.
5564. TOURÉ, Askia M.
"The Frontier of Rage." [BlackALF] (21:3) Fall 87, p. 234.
"Nefertari: A Priase Song" (for Vickie). [BlackALF] (21:3) Fall 87, p. 232-234.
"Osirian Rhapsody: A Myth" (for Larry Neal & Bob Marley). [BlackALF] (21:3)
Fall 87, p. 227-230.
"Sun / Prince: A Rite (of Passage)." [BlackALF] (21:3) Fall 87, p. 230-231.
5565. TOWELL, Larry
"Highlands." [Waves] (15:3) Wint 87, p. 50-51.
5566. TOWLE, Parker
"Fear of Love." [Vis] (23) 87, p. 24.
"Winter Overnight on the Mountain." [Blueline] (7:2/3 [i.e. 8:2/3?]) 87, p. 65.
5567. TOWNSEND, Ann
"The Braille Woods." [TexasR] (8:1/2) Spr-Sum 87, p. 94.
"Clearing." [WestHR] (41:4) Wint 87, p. 365.
"Dance Around: A Romance." [CharR] (13:2) Fall 87, p. 62-65.
"On Alum Creek." [PoetryNW] (28:1) Spr 87, p. 28-29.
5568. TOWNSEND, Joanne
"Afternoon Song for Jean." [Interim] (6:1) Spr 87, p. 40.
"Iris: The Goddess, the Rainbow, the Flower" (for Phydella Hogan). [Interim] (6:1)
Spr 87, p. 41.
5569. TOY, Judith Baldwin
"A Proposal." [PoetL] (82:1) Spr 87, p. 17.
5570. TOYAMA, Jean Yamasaki
"Etiquette." The Best of [BambooR] [(31-32)] 86, p. 102.
5571. TRACY, Sandra S.
"Expertise." [EngJ] (76:3) Mr 87, p. 45.
5572. TRAINA, Joe
"Working the Stacker at US Tobacco." [Wind] (17:61) 87, p. 48.
5573. TRAINER, Yvonne
"For the Record." [CanLit] (115) Wint 87, p. 27.
"Letters to Mary." [CanLit] (115) Wint 87, p. 6-8.
"Three Rocks Jutting Up from Snow." [CanLit] (115) Wint 87, p. 64.
5574. TRAMONTE, Barbara Paturick
"Language, the Truest Tongue." [NewL] (54:1) Fall 87, p. 124.
5575. TRANQUILLA, Ronald
"Grandma at the Home." [Gambit] (20) 86, p. 24.
5576. TRANTER, John
"Braille." [Verse] (4:2) Je 87, p. 52.
"Crying in Early Infancy" (Selected sonnets: 19, 22, 26-27, 35-37, 39). [NewAW]
(2) Fall 87, p. 72-75.
"Laminex." [Verse] (4:2) Je 87, p. 52-53.
5577. TRASK, Haunani-Kay
"Colonization." [BambooR] (36) Fall 87, p. 88-89.
"Dawn." [BambooR] (36) Fall 87, p. 90.
"Makua Kane" (Waimanalo, 1986). [HawaiiR] (20) Fall 86, c87, p. 32-35.
"Racist White Woman." [BambooR] (36) Fall 87, p. 86-87.
5578. TRAUNSTEIN, Russ
"Up Fair Kilties!" [LightY] '87, c86, p. 168-169.
5579. TRAWICK, Leonard M.
"At the Flying School." [BelPoJ] (37:4) Sum 87, p. 9.
"A Cold Day." [BelPoJ] (37:4) Sum 87, p. 11.
"Earth." [BelPoJ] (37:4) Sum 87, p. 10.
5580. TRAXLER, Patricia
"At the New World Donut Shop." [HangL] (50/51) 87, p. 181.
"Cicadas in August." [HangL] (50/51) 87, p. 182.
"Heart at the Window." [HangL] (50/51) 87, p. 183.
"How I Got This Way." [HangL] (50/51) 87, p. 184-185.
5581. TREFETHEN, Florence
"Australia: Orion Upside Down." [TexasR] (7:3/4) 87, p. 152.

"Getting into the Picture." [TexasR] (7:3/4) 87, p. 151.
5582. TREGEBOV, Rhea
"National Portrait Gallery, London." [CanLit] (113/114) Sum-Fall 87, p. 10.
5583. TREININ, Avner
"School" (tr. by Rachel Berghash). [ColR] (NS 14:1) Spr-Sum 87, p. 35.
5584. TREITEL, Margot
"Abandoned Vehicles / 2." [Poem] (57) Mr 87, p. 59.
"The Exile's Manifesto." [AnotherCM] (17) 87, p. 111.
"An Hour of Feeling." [Footwork] 87, p. 40.
"The New Realism" (New York, August 1980). [Salm] (72) Fall 86, p. 202.
"Open Boat." [SmPd] (24:1) Wint 87, p. 30.
"A Return to Decency." [Salm] (72) Fall 86, p. 201-202.
"Scenes in Bronze" (Benin Expedition, 1897). [ColEng] (49:6) O 87, p. 650-651.
"The Simple Present." [Poem] (57) Mr 87, p. 60.
"Soap Opera." [LaurelR] (21:1/2) Wint-Sum 87, p. 41.
"Start Here." [Poem] (57) Mr 87, p. 61.
5585. TREITEL, Renata
"A Wife's Dream" (Award Poem). [Phoenix] (7:1) 87, p. 5.
5586. TREMBLAY, Gail
"Urban Indians, Pioneer Square, Seattle." [Calyx] (10:2/3) Spr 87, p. 67.
5587. TREMMEL, Robert
"The Words of Your Life." [NoDaQ] (55:2) Spr 87, p. 106.
5588. TRENA, Laynie
"Plainfield." [Footwork] 87, p. 44-45.
5589. TRETHEWEY, Eric
"Armadillos" (to Randolph Bates). [SouthernR] (23:3) Jl 87, p. 619-621.
"Celka." [PraS] (61:4) Wint 87, p. 96-97.
"Elegy" (for Shannon). [PaintedB] (31) 87, p. 77.
"Hell on Wheels." [AntigR] (71/72) Aut 87-Wint 88, p. 32.
"Life Story." [PraS] (61:4) Wint 87, p. 97-98.
"Old Love, Old Times, Driving Through." [PaintedB] (31) 87, p. 76.
"Reconnaissance." [AntigR] (71/72) Aut 87-Wint 88, p. 32.
"Snowbound." [PaintedB] (31) 87, p. 75.
5590. TRIFONOV, Gennady
"Spring 1986" (for Alex, tr. by J. M. Regan). [JamesWR] (4:4) Sum 87, p. 5.
5591. TRIVELPIECE, Laurel
"Lost in the Shine." [MassR] (28:2) Sum 87, p. 351.
"October." [MassR] (28:2) Sum 87, p. 352.
5592. TROPP, Gloria R.
"Coltrane." [AlphaBS] (1) Je 87, p. 45.
"No One Owns Nefertiti." [AlphaBS] (1) Je 87, p. 44.
5593. TROPP, Stephen
"The McCarthy Years." [AlphaBS] (1) Je 87, p. 46.
"Talking Shoes." [AlphaBS] (1) Je 87, p. 46.
"With George Orwell in Vietnam." [AlphaBS] (1) Je 87, p. 46.
5594. TROTSKY, Dana
"Milk and Honey." [DekalbLAJ] (20:1/4) 87, p. 68.
5595. TROWBRIDGE, William
"100 of the World's Favorite Melodies." [TarPR] (27:1) Fall 87, p. 41-42.
"American Gothic." [NewL] (54:1) Fall 87, p. 106-107.
"Home Front." [NewL] (54:1) Fall 87, p. 108-109.
"Self Help." [LightY] '87, c86, p. 24-26.
"Viet Kong." [LightY] '87, c86, p. 257.
5596. TRUSSELL, Donna
"Cakewalk." [PoetryNW] (28:3) Aut 87, p. 13.
"Snow." [PoetryNW] (28:3) Aut 87, p. 12-13.
5597. TSVETAEVA, Marina
"Mileposts II" (tr. by Mary Jane White). [WillowS] (20) Spr 87, p. 7-30.
"Mileposts, Part 1" (To Anna Akhmatove, tr. by Mary Jane White). [AmerPoR] (16:3) My-Je 87, p. 24-27.
TU, Fu
        See DU, Fu
5598. TUCKER, David
"After Fighting #2." [SouthernPR] (27:2) Fall 87, p. 28.
"Hog Killing." [CumbPR] (7:1) Fall 87, p. 74.

5599. TUCKER, Martin
"Two Poems on St. Simon's Island, Georgia." [Confr] (35/36) Spr-Fall 87, p.
191-192.
5600. TUCKER, Memye Curtis
"Airport Phone Booth." [LightY] '87, c86, p. 146.
"Genesis." [AntigR] (68) Wint 87, p. 23.
"Separation." [Confr] (35/36) Spr-Fall 87, p. 262.
5601. TUDORAN, Dorin
"A Burning" (for Ion Caraion, tr. by Marcel Cornis-Pop). [PartR] (54:3) Sum 87, p.
434.
"A Cross" (tr. by Marcel Cornis-Pop). [PartR] (54:3) Sum 87, p. 433.
"The Master to His Apprentice" (tr. by Marcel Cornis-Pop). [PartR] (54:3) Sum 87,
p. 434.
"Of Unforgettable Caligula" (tr. by Marcel Cornis-Pop). [Vis] (25) 87, p. 34.
5602. TULLOSS, Rod
"Learning." [US1] (20/21) Wint 86-87, p. 46.
"My Father." [US1] (20/21) Wint 86-87, p. 45.
5603. TUMBALÉ, Elkion
"Ch-alice." [Bogg] (58) 87, p. 54.
"Eat This." [Bogg] (57) 87, p. 12.
5604. TUPPER, Jean L.
"Raccoons, the Most Articulate." [SouthernPR] (27:1) Spr 87, p. 12.
5605. TURCO, Lewis
"Amherst Neighbors" (On lines from Emily Dickinson's letters). [LightY] '87, c86,
p. 187-188.
"The Gift" (On lines from Emily Dickinson's letters). [LightY] '87, c86, p. 31.
"Just God" (On lines from Emily Dickinson's letters). [LightY] '87, c86, p. 82.
"The Kite." [Nat] (244:9) 7 Mr 87, p. 300.
"The Naked Eye" (On lines from Emily Dickinson's letters). [LightY] '87, c86, p.
124.
"A Sampler of Hours: Poems on Lines from Emily Dickinson's Letters" (Selections:
3 Pieces). [HampSPR] Wint 86, p. 22-23.
"Werewind." [Raccoon] (24/25) My 87, p. 305.
5606. TURETZKY, Philip
"Daedalethics" (A Manifesto, w. William Bogard). [ColR] (NS 14:2) Fall-Wint 87,
p. 68-80.
5607. TURNBULL, Becky
"Poem: When the bird sings, I am a child" (to Frank O'Hara, 1926-1966, poet &
perfectly nice man). [PaintedB] (30) 87, p. 65.
5608. TURNER, Alberta
"For a Good Man" (Selections: II, IV). [Stand] (28:2) Spr 87, p. 26-27.
"Tell Them." [SouthernPR] (27:1) Spr 87, p. 38.
"Trying to Be Human." [Stand] (28:2) Spr 87, p. 25.
5609. TURNER, Doug
"Gifts." [Waves] (15:1/2) Fall 86, p. 40.
"Hitching." [HawaiiR] (21) Spr 87, p. 34-35.
"The Kid." [AntigR] (68) Wint 87, p. 113.
"This Game." [AntigR] (71/72) Aut 87-Wint 88, p. 162.
5610. TURNER, Laura
"Daedalus." [HiramPoR] (43) Fall-Wint 87-88, p. 9.
"I Dream My Grandmother." [HiramPoR] (43) Fall-Wint 87-88, p. 39.
"Nothing." [HiramPoR] (43) Fall-Wint 87-88, p. 44.
5611. TURNER, Michael B.
"Sure Sign of Fish." [AntigR] (69/70) 87, p. 194.
5612. TURNER, Myron
"Ark: Voyage and Recollection." [Margin] (5) Wint 87-88, p. 14.
"Whorls." [Margin] (5) Wint 87-88, p. 13.
5613. TURPIN, Mark
"The Box." [ParisR] (29:105) Wint 87, p. 92.
"Pickwork." [ParisR] (29:105) Wint 87, p. 90-91.
5614. TUSIANI, Joseph
"Epitaph for a Little Girl." [SpiritSH] (53:1) 87, p. 17.
"In Memoriam W.H. Auden." [SpiritSH] (53:1) 87, p. 16.
5615. TWICHELL, Chase
"The Givens." [SenR] (17:2) 87, p. 47-48.
"Let X." [Field] (36) Spr 87, p. 114.

"The Other Knife." [SenR] (17:2) 87, p. 44.
"Religious Water." [Field] (36) Spr 87, p. 115-116.
"The White Mercedes." [SenR] (17:2) 87, p. 46.
"Window in the Shape of a Diamond." [SenR] (17:2) 87, p. 45.
5616. TYLER, Robert L.
"The Courage of the People." [KanQ] (19:1/2) Wint-Spr 87, p. 122.
5617. TYNDALL, Paul
"The Door." [AntigR] (69/70) 87, p. 168.
"Driving Westward into Val D'Or." [AntigR] (69/70) 87, p. 168.
5618. TYSH, Chris
"Coats of Arms" (Selections: 2 sections). [NewAW] (1) 87, p. 76.
5619. UCEDA, Julia
"The Stranger" (tr. by Noël M. Valis). [NewOR] (14:1) Spr 87, p. 31.
5620. UCHIDA, Jo Ann
"Fever." The Best of [BambooR] [(31-32)] 86, p. 103-105.
5621. UCHMANOWICZ, Pauline
"Flowers, an Empty House and a Breakfast Roll." [NewAW] (1) 87, p. 113.
"The Motion." [GreensboroR] (40) Sum 86, p. 50.
5622. ULLMAN, Leslie
"Dawn Feeding." [Poetry] (150:5) Ag 87, p. 260-261.
"Desire." [DenQ] (22:2) Fall 87, p. 78.
"Election." [DenQ] (22:2) Fall 87, p. 79-80.
"Heat." [NewYorker] (63:22) 20 Jl 87, p. 28.
"Peace." [Poetry] (150:5) Ag 87, p. 261-262.
5623. ULLMAN, Michelle
"Lust." [Electrum] (39) Fall-Wint 87, p. 39.
5624. ULMER, James
"Crabbing for Blue Claws." [NewYorker] (63:37) 2 N 87, p. 48.
"Windfalls." [MissouriR] (10:3) 87, p. 135.
5625. UNDERWOOD, Corinne
"Pulling Bindweed." [NewL] (53:3) Spr 87, p. 32.
5626. UNDERWOOD, Jane
"Speak of It." [YellowS] (23) Sum 87, p. 32.
5627. UNDERWOOD, Robert
"The Chiropractor." [WormR] (27:4, issue 108) 87, p. 82.
"Keepig Up with the Past." [WormR] (27:4, issue 108) 87, p. 82.
"Poets Don't Wear Ties." [WormR] (27:4, issue 108) 87, p. 82-83.
"Tricia's Skillet." [WormR] (27:4, issue 108) 87, p. 81.
5628. UNDERWOOD, Susan O'Dell
"Cats Mating." [GreensboroR] (42) Sum 87, p. 46.
"The Child in Winter." [GreensboroR] (42) Sum 87, p. 45-46.
5629. UNTERECKER, John
"Flight Letter." [HawaiiR] (19) Spr 86, c87, p. 60-61.
"Found." [HawaiiR] (19) Spr 86, c87, p. 59.
"Physical." [Salm] (72) Fall 86, p. 191-192.
"Ruined Bridge Seen from a Plane — Theme and Six Variations." [WillowS] (19) Wint 87, p. 16.
"The Valley." [Blueline] (7:2/3 [i.e. 8:2/3?]) 87, p. 100.
5630. UPDIKE, John
"Goodbye, Göteborg." [NewYorker] (63:36) 26 O 87, p. 42.
"Snowdrops 1987." [OntR] (27) Fall-Wint 87, p. 20.
"The Sometime Sportsman Greets the Spring." [LightY] '87, c86, p. 30.
"Switzerland." [Nat] (244:21) 30 My 87, p. 740.
5631. UPTON, Lee
"Coffee Break." [PennR] (3:1) Spr-Sum 87, p. 5.
"Empathy." [PennR] (3:1) Spr-Sum 87, p. 4.
"A Turban." [PennR] (3:1) Spr-Sum 87, p. 3.
5632. URDANG, Constance
"The Apparition." [RiverS] (22) 87, p. 10.
"A Life You Might Say You Might Live." [RiverS] (22) 87, p. 9.
"My Father's Death." [OntR] (26) Spr-Sum 87, p. 40.
"Sic Transit." [RiverS] (22) 87, p. 11.
"That Life." [RiverS] (22) 87, p. 12.
5633. URTECHO, José Coronel
"Ode to Rubén Dario." [Contact] (9:44/45/46) Fall-Wint 87, p. 11-13.

5634. UTLEY, Constance
"Children's Home, 1955." [Outbr] (18/19) Fall 86-Spr 88, p. 175.
5635. UTLEY, J. L.
"In the Blur of Movement." [Caliban] (3) 87, p. 18-19.
5636. UU, David
"Data supplies." [CrossC] (9:3/4) 87, p. 11.
"The Language Fetishist." [CrossC] (9:3/4) 87, p. 11.
"Report on Spatial Poem No. 4: Shadow Event" (Historical Document #8537).
[Rampike] (5:3) 87, p. 56.
5637. UYAROGLU, Ismail
"The Heart Inscribed" (tr. by Talat Sait Halman). [Trans] (19) Fall 87, p. 110.
5638. UYEMATSU, Amy
"Local Wisdom." [BambooR] (36) Fall 87, p. 66.
"The Old Woman Who Dances with Me." [BambooR] (36) Fall 87, p. 67-69.
"Three Pulls of the Loom." [GreenfR] (14:3/4) Sum-Fall 87, p. 82-85.
5639. VACLAVICEK, Susan
"The Gift." [GreenfR] (14:3/4) Sum-Fall 87, p. 91.
"Liturgy" (for my mother). [Blueline] (7:2/3 [i.e. 8:2/3?]) 87, p. 80-81.
"Sledding." [Blueline] (7:2/3 [i.e. 8:2/3?]) 87, p. 82-83.
5640. VAJPEYI, Ashok
"Apocalypse" (tr. by Krishna Paldeva Wide). [Bomb] (18) Wint 87, p. 67.
"By Words Too" (tr. by Krishna Paldeva Wide). [Bomb] (18) Wint 87, p. 67.
"For Guillevick and Genevieve" (tr. by Krishna Paldeva Wide). [Bomb] (18) Wint
87, p. 66.
"In Bhilai" (tr. by Krishna Paldeva Wide). [Bomb] (18) Wint 87, p. 66.
"A Prayer" (tr. by Krishna Paldeva Wide). [Bomb] (18) Wint 87, p. 67.
5641. VALDÉS GINEBRA, Arminda
"Quisiera que mi casa toda fuera." [Mairena] (9:24) 87, p. 115.
5642. VALIS, Noël M.
"The Stranger" (tr. of Julia Uceda). [NewOR] (14:1) Spr 87, p. 31.
5643. VALLEJO, César
"Los Heraldos Negros." [Mairena] (9:24) 87, p. 4.
5644. VALLONE, Anthony
"Peach Blossom Snow." [MSS] (5:3) 87, p. 26-27.
"Snow Angels." [MSS] (5:3) 87, p. 28-29.
"Stadium Lights" (for Dave Gaskill). [KanQ] (19:1/2) Wint-Spr 87, p. 349.
VALVERDE, Alfonso Barrera
See BARRERA VALVERDE, Alfonso
Van . . .
See also names beginning with "Van" without the following space, filed below in
their alphabetic positions.
Van BRUNT, H. L.
See Van BRUNT, Lloyd
5645. Van BRUNT, Lloyd
"A Bible, A Torah, and a Koran." [SouthernPR] (27:2) Fall 87, p. 48-49.
"First Draft." [PoetL] (82:4) Wint 87-88, p. 227-228.
"Leftovers." [PoetL] (82:4) Wint 87-88, p. 229.
"Notes toward a Poem about the National Zoo." [GreenfR] (14:1/2) Wint-Spr, p.
154-162.
"A Seabird Poem for Children." [PoetL] (82:4) Wint 87-88, p. 226.
"Speech After Long Silence." [Blueline] (7:2/3 [i.e. 8:2/3?]) 87, p. 94-95.
5646. Van DUYN, Mona
"At the New Orleans Zoo" (for Viktor Hamburger). [RiverS] (23) 87, p. 19-20.
"A Bouquet of Zinnias." [Poetry] (151:1/2) O-N 87, p. 182-183.
"The Ferris Wheel." [GrandS] (6:4) Sum 87, p. 35-38.
"Mockingbird Month." [Ploughs] (13:4) 87, p. 130-131.
5647. Van HOUTEN, Lois
"Courtship." [Footwork] 87, p. 31.
"Crows As an Emissary of Fate." [Footwork] 87, p. 32.
"Family Dynamics." [Footwork] 87, p. 32.
"Levels." [StoneC] (14:3/4) Spr-Sum 87, p. 28.
"Something to Fly With." [Footwork] 87, p. 32.
"Speaking to Stars." [Footwork] 87, p. 31.
"Why We Need the Dead." [Lips] (13) 87, p. 27.
5648. Van PEENEN, H. J.
"Existence" (tr. of Alfonso Barrera Valverde). [SenR] (17:1) 87, p. 47.

"A Letter to My Brother from the Old Quarter" (tr. of Alfonso Barrera Valverde). [SenR] (17:1) 87, p. 48-49.
"Penumbra" (tr. of Alfonso Barrera Valverde). [SenR] (17:1) 87, p. 56.
"Regards to a White Mare" (tr. of Alfonso Barrera Valverde). [SenR] (17:1) 87, p. 50-52.
"Sonnet: You have copied water's way of voyaging" (tr. of Alfonso Barrera Valverde). [SenR] (17:1) 87, p. 55.
"The Sparrow's Daily Round" (tr. of Alfonso Barrera Valverde). [SenR] (17:1) 87, p. 53.
"Stone Cross" (For My Brother Wilfrido, tr. of Alfonso Barrera Valverde). [SenR] (17:1) 87, p. 54.
5649. Van POZNAK, Joan
"Gertrude and Alice." [LightY] '87, c86, p. 212.
"Love Portions." [LightY] '87, c86, p. 43.
"On Seeing Gavin Ewart in Sainsbury's." [LightY] '87, c86, p. 212-213.
"Viola D'Amore." [LightY] '87, c86, p. 132.
5650. Van TASSEL, Katrina
"Age of Innocence." [Footwork] 87, p. 47.
"Discovery." [Footwork] 87, p. 48.
Van VLIET, Eddy
See VLIET, Eddy van
5651. Van WALLEGHEN, Michael
"The Afterlife." [Hudson] (39:4) Wint 87, p. 602-603.
"Peach Isle." [Hudson] (39:4) Wint 87, p. 604-605.
"Prayer to a Guardian Angel" (tr. of Dmitri Bobyshev). [Vis] (25) 87, p. 18.
"Starship Lands in Cornfield" (Headline, *Weekly World News*). [Hudson] (39:4) Wint 87, p. 601-602.
"Who's There?" [Hudson] (39:4) Wint 87, p. 605-606.
5652. Van WERT, William F.
"Her Dying Eyes." [HampSPR] Wint 86, p. 33.
"In the Beginning." [KanQ] (19:3) Sum 87, p. 304-305.
"On Reading: *Hop on Pop*." [CentR] (31:4) Fall 87, p. 382-384.
5653. Van WINCKEL, Nance
"All He Asks" (Nome, Alaksa. 1907). [Iowa] (17:1) Wint 87, p. 107-108.
"Apology." [Iowa] (17:1) Wint 87, p. 109.
"Autumn Nostalgia." [PoetryNW] (28:1) Spr 87, p. 14-15.
"Bad Girl, with Hawk." [AmerPoR] (16:5) S-O 87, p. 47.
"Basket with Blue Ox" (for Donna). [Iowa] (17:1) Wint 87, p. 110.
"Boy in Tree in Storm." [Ascent] (12:2) 87, p. 26-27.
"Calendar Girls." [PoetryNW] (28:4) Wint 87-88, p. 16-17.
"Counting Towards Sleep." [Poetry] (149:4) Ja 87, p. 218.
"Fast-Driving Dream." [PoetryNW] (28:1) Spr 87, p. 16-17.
"Goodnight" (For Charles Wright). [Poetry] (149:4) Ja 87, p. 217.
"House of Clues." [Iowa] (17:1) Wint 87, p. 111-112.
"Just Be Home Before Sundown." [Iowa] (17:1) Wint 87, p. 110-111.
"Lake of Resolve." [PoetryNW] (28:1) Spr 87, p. 18-19.
"The Many Beds of Martha Washington." [PoetryNW] (28:1) Spr 87, p. 15-16.
"Talking with Ginger in Studyhall." [SenR] (17:1) 87, p. 68.
5654. Van WYK, Chris
"The Ballot and the Bullet." [TriQ] (69) Spr-Sum 87, p. 65.
"Helping My Father Make a Cupboard." [TriQ] (69) Spr-Sum 87, p. 64.
"The Road." [TriQ] (69) Spr-Sum 87, p. 62-63.
5655. VANCE, Richard
"Shampoo." [AntigR] (71/72) Aut 87-Wint 88, p. 176.
5656. VANDEMARR, Lee
"Edward Thomas" (For Roger Bowen). [CalQ] (30) Wint 87, p. 54.
5657. Vander MEULEN, Jim
"Me an pete sometimes fish." [Grain] (15:3) Fall 87, p. 30.
5658. VANDERAUWERA, Ria
"Challenge" (tr. of Maria Tesselschade Roemersdochter). [Paint] (14:27) Spr 87, p. 40.
5659. VanderMOLEN, Robert
"Farm House." [Sulfur] (20) Fall 87, p. 111-112.
"From Here to There." [Sulfur] (20) Fall 87, p. 113-114.
"Up North." [Sulfur] (20) Fall 87, p. 112-113.

5660. VANEK, M. C.
"The Gentleman Ponders Lady's Concern." [CimR] (79) Ap 87, p. 39.
"The Gentleman Protests." [CimR] (79) Ap 87, p. 41.
"Lady" (to R.S.). [CimR] (78) Ja 87, p. 22.
"Lady Changes Her Strategy." [CimR] (79) Ap 87, p. 42.
"Lady Replies." [CimR] (79) Ap 87, p. 40.
5661. VANGELISTI, Paul
"Los Alephs." [Temblor] (5) 87, p. 101-106.
5662. VANNATTA, Dennis
"Old Ladies, in Their Dying." [Paint] (14:28) Aut 87, p. 20-21.
5663. VARDON, Beth
"To A. E. Housman on My Seventieth Birthday." [EngJ] (76:2) F 87, p. 109.
5664. VARELA, Blanca
"Curriculum Vitae" (tr. by Gregory Rabassa). [AmerPoR] (16:2) Mr-Ap 87, p. 21.
"Everyday Light" (tr. by Gregory Rabassa). [AmerPoR] (16:2) Mr-Ap 87, p. 21.
"Lady's Journal" (tr. by Gregory Rabassa). [AmerPoR] (16:2) Mr-Ap 87, p. 21.
"Listening to Billie Holiday" (tr. by Gregory Rabassa). [AmerPoR] (16:2) Mr-Ap
87, p. 21.
5665. VARON, Jodi
"Autumn Cold, a Poem to My Cousin" (tr. of Li He). [Trans] (19) Fall 87, p.
235-236.
"Ballad of an Aching Heart" (tr. of Li He). [Trans] (19) Fall 87, p. 236.
"Cry of a Heng T'ang Woman" (tr. of Li He). [Trans] (19) Fall 87, p. 237.
"A Poem I Showed to My Pa Servant" (tr. of Li He). [ColR] (NS 14:2) Fall-Wint
87, p. 65.
5666. VAS, István
"History of Lit: A Communication" (tr. by Jascha Kessler, w. Maria Körösy).
[Nimrod] (31:1) Fall-Wint 87, p. 132.
"Idling" (tr. by Jascha Kessler, w. Mária Körösy). [GrahamHR] (10) Wint-Spr 87,
p. 60-61.
5667. VAS DIAS, Robert
"A Maze." [Margin] (1) Wint 86, p. 35.
5668. VASSILAKIS, Nico
"Eavesdropping 4/5's into the century." [Caliban] (3) 87, p. 75-76.
"Father's Dead Sister." [Lactuca] (6) Ap-My 87, p. 20.
VASSILIADIS, Aristotelis
See ALEXANDROU, Aris
5669. VEACH, Cindy
"The Dogfish" (1987 Ratner-Ferber-Poet Lore Honorable Mention). [PoetL] (82:2)
Sum 87, p. 95-96.
5670. VEAZEY, Mary
"For a Good Ole Boy." [LightY] '87, c86, p. 145.
5671. VEENENDAAL, Cornelia
"The Block Print." [HangL] (50/51) 87, p. 186.
"Passing Strange." [HangL] (50/51) 87, p. 187-188.
5672. VEGA, Janine Pommy
"The Ancient Waltz." [AlphaBS] (1) Je 87, p. 39.
"Bread vs. Poem" (for Raymond the Cabdrver). [AlphaBS] (2) D 87, p. 4.
"Human Prayer." [Witness] (1:3) Fall 87, p. 132.
"Little Ghost in the Station" (for Richard Manuel). [AlphaBS] (1) Je 87, p. 38.
"Lurigancho" (a men's prison, Lima Peru, September 1982). [Witness] (1:3) Fall
87, p. 28-29.
"The Walk." [AlphaBS] (1) Je 87, p. 36-37.
VEGA, Mario Cajina
See CAJINA-VEGA, Mario
5673. VEGHIN, Peter
"When My Wife Dances" (tr. by John High and Katya Olmsted). [FiveFR] (5) 87, p.
1-2.
5674. VEINBERG, Jon
"Catacombs of Saint Callistus." [AntR] (45:3) Sum 87, p. 341.
"Refugee." [Poetry] (150:4) Jl 87, p. 221-222.
"Slicing Peaches." [MissouriR] (10:1) 87, p. 200-201.
"Spirits of the Wind." [Poetry] (150:4) Jl 87, p. 218-220.
"Stray Dog in the Rain." [AntR] (45:3) Sum 87, p. 342.
"Winter Eclipse." [MissouriR] (10:1) 87, p. 199.

5675. VEINSTEIN, Alain
"Introducing the Spade" (tr. by Rosmarie Waldrop). [LitR] (30:3) Spr 87, p.
359-366.
5676. VELIE, Edward
"Jack-of-All-Trades." [Writer] (99:9) S 86, p. 25.
5677. VENUTI, Lawrence
"A.S." (tr. of Milo De Angelis). [ParisR] (29:105) Wint 87, p. 116-117.
"Born on th Earth" (tr. of Milo De Angeli). [Sulfur] (18) Wint 87, p. 153-154.
"Conversation with Father" (tr. of Milo De Angelis). [SenR] (17:2) 87, p. 37.
"In the Lungs" (tr. of Milo De Angelis). [ParisR] (29:105) Wint 87, p. 120.
"The Killing" (tr. of Milo De Angeli). [Sulfur] (18) Wint 87, p. 154-155.
"Letter from Vignole" (tr. of Milo De Angelis). [ParisR] (29:105) Wint 87, p. 119.
"No One, Yet They Return" (tr. of Milo De Angelis). [SenR] (17:2) 87, p. 36.
"Now She Is Unadorned" (tr. of Milo De Angelis). [ParisR] (29:105) Wint 87, p.
118.
"Stones in the Warm Mud" (tr. of Milo De Angeli). [Sulfur] (18) Wint 87, p.
152-153.
"Telegram" (tr. of Milo De Angeli). [Sulfur] (18) Wint 87, p. 153.
"Via Prospero Finzi" (tr. of Milo De Angelis). [SenR] (17:2) 87, p. 38.
"With Broken Oars They Embark" (tr. of Milo De Angeli). [Sulfur] (18) Wint 87, p.
152.
Ver ELLEN, Patricia
See VerELLEN, Patricia
5678. VERDICCHIO, Pasquale
"Winter Insect, Summer Grass." [Temblor] (6) 87, p. 148-151.
5679. VerELLEN, Patricia
"Children Learning Their Alphabet." [Outbr] (18/19) Fall 86-Spr 88, p. 6.
"Saul." [Outbr] (18/19) Fall 86-Spr 88, p. 5.
5680. VERLAINE, Paul
"After Three Years" (tr. by Richard Ronan). [AmerPoR] (16:4) Jl-Ag 87, p. 24.
"L'Allée" (tr. by Richard Ronan). [AmerPoR] (16:4) Jl-Ag 87, p. 25.
"The beautiful falselight gleams all day, my soul" (tr. by Richard Ronan).
[AmerPoR] (16:4) Jl-Ag 87, p. 25.
"Faun" (tr. by Richard Ronan). [AmerPoR] (16:4) Jl-Ag 87, p. 24.
"Hope shines small, a splinter of straw in the stable" (tr. by Richard Ronan).
[AmerPoR] (16:4) Jl-Ag 87, p. 25.
"The Hour of the Shepherd" (tr. by Richard Ronan). [AmerPoR] (16:4) Jl-Ag 87, p.
25.
"In the interminable ennui of the plains" (tr. by Richard Ronan). [AmerPoR] (16:4)
Jl-Ag 87, p. 24.
"Innocent Boys" (tr. by Richard Ronan). [AmerPoR] (16:4) Jl-Ag 87, p. 25.
"Languor" (tr. by Richard Ronan). [AmerPoR] (16:4) Jl-Ag 87, p. 25.
"Love Overturned" (tr. by Richard Ronan). [AmerPoR] (16:4) Jl-Ag 87, p. 26.
"Parisian Sketch" (tr. by Richard Ronan). [AmerPoR] (16:4) Jl-Ag 87, p. 24.
"Sunset" (tr. by Richard Ronan). [AmerPoR] (16:4) Jl-Ag 87, p. 24.
"Utterly small, utterly lovely" (tr. by Richard Ronan). [AmerPoR] (16:4) Jl-Ag 87,
p. 26.
5681. VERNON, Lorraine
"Japanese Painting." [Germ] (11:1) Fall 87, p. 44-45.
"The Walking Poem." [Germ] (11:1) Fall 87, p. 42.
"Whistlers." [Germ] (11:1) Fall 87, p. 43.
5682. VERNON, William J.
"The Fallen Brick." [Outbr] (18/19) Fall 86-Spr 88, p. 69.
5683. VERTREACE, Martha M.
"Black Tulips." [HampSPR] Wint 87, p. 9.
"Trade Secrets." [Phoenix] (7:1) 87, p. 45.
5684. VICKERS, Edward Davin
"Too Many Chocolate-Covered Cherries" (1986 Finalist, Eve of Saint Agnes Poetry
Competition). [NegC] (7:1/2) 87, p. 184.
5685. VICUÑA, Cecilia
"And if I devoted my life" ("Untitled," tr. by Eliot Weinberger). [AmerPoR] (16:2)
Mr-Ap 87, p. 16.
"Luxumei" (tr. by Eliot Weinberger). [AmerPoR] (16:2) Mr-Ap 87, p. 15.
"Solitude" (tr. by Eliot Weinberger). [AmerPoR] (16:2) Mr-Ap 87, p. 16.
"Topac Inca Yupanqui" (tr. by Eliot Weinberger). [AmerPoR] (16:2) Mr-Ap 87, p.
16.

"Wikuna" (tr. by Eliot Weinberger). [AmerPoR] (16:2) Mr-Ap 87, p. 15.
5686. VIDAVER, Doris
"At the Forest Entrance" (tr. of Jacob Glatstein). [AnotherCM] (17) 87, p. 39.
"Morning Subway" (from "Holocaust Poems," tr. of Jacob Glatstein). [PraS] (61:3)
Fall 87, p. 81.
"Profanation" (tr. of Jacob Glatstein). [AnotherCM] (17) 87, p. 40.
"Twilight of the World" (from "Holocaust Poems," tr. of Jacob Glatstein). [PraS]
(61:3) Fall 87, p. 80.
"The Unsteady House Swims Like an Ark" (from "Holocaust Poems," tr. of Jacob
Glatstein). [PraS] (61:3) Fall 87, p. 82-83.
5687. VIERECK, Peter
"Autumn Dialogue." [TexasR] (7:3/4) 87, p. 153-154.
"Massachusetts Three-Lines" (In this form, each three-line poem has exactly 17
words). [Ploughs] (13:4) 87, p. 134-136.
"Songs: I" (from the German of Gottfried Benn). [Ploughs] (13:4) 87, p. 133.
"White-Haired in the Abominated Regions." [Ploughs] (13:4) 87, p. 132.
5688. VIGIL-PIÑON, Evangelina
"Equinox." [Americas] (15:3/4) Fall-Wint 87, p. 61.
"The Giving." [Americas] (15:3/4) Fall-Wint 87, p. 59.
"Hacia un Invierno." [Americas] (15:3/4) Fall-Wint 87, p. 62-63.
"In Its Absence." [Americas] (15:3/4) Fall-Wint 87, p. 58.
"The Parting" (to the memory of Chichimeca). [Americas] (15:3/4) Fall-Wint 87, p.
57.
"Spillage." [Americas] (15:3/4) Fall-Wint 87, p. 60.
5689. VILARIÑO, Idea
"Between" (tr. by Susan Schreibman). [YellowS] (25) Wint 87, p. 32.
"Entre." [YellowS] (25) Wint 87, p. 32.
"La Noche." [YellowS] (25) Wint 87, p. 32.
"That Night" (tr. by Susan Schreibman). [YellowS] (25) Wint 87, p. 32.
5690. VILLALOBOS CHINCHILLA, Freddy
"Centro América." [Mairena] (9:24) 87, p. 118.
5691. VILLALONGO, Jose
"How Can I Occupy a Place?" [Footwork] 87, p. 83.
5692. VILLANI, Jim
"Carlo Rossi's Dream." [Pig] (14) 87, p. 81.
"Turtles Do It." [Pig] (14) 87, p. 10.
5693. VILMURE, Kathleen
"Destructible Milieux." [PoetL] (82:3) Fall 87, p. 143-145.
"For My Grandfather." [PoetL] (82:3) Fall 87, p. 141-142.
5694. VINCIGUERRA, Theresa
"Cover Me." [YellowS] (22) Spr 87, p. 16.
5695. VINZ, Mark
"Bedtime Story." [NoDaQ] (55:2) Spr 87, p. 88.
"Clotheslines." [SpoonRQ] (12:2) Spr 87, p. 10.
"Missing You." [SpoonRQ] (12:2) Spr 87, p. 13.
"Night Man." [SpoonRQ] (12:2) Spr 87, p. 8.
"Nightfishing." [NoDaQ] (55:2) Spr 87, p. 87-88.
"One Size Fits All." [SpoonRQ] (12:2) Spr 87, p. 7.
"Sam Hill, Jack Robinson, and Me." [SpoonRQ] (12:2) Spr 87, p. 12.
"Sleeping Till Noon." [SpoonRQ] (12:2) Spr 87, p. 11.
"True Believer." [SpoonRQ] (12:2) Spr 87, p. 9.
"What I Remember About the 6th Grade." [AnotherCM] (17) 87, p. 112.
5696. VISSER, Richard
"I Wondered." [WritersF] (13) Fall 87, p. 176.
VITO, E. B. de
See De VITO, E. B.
5697. VLASOPOLOS, Anca
"After the Summer Solstice." [Interim] (6:1) Spr 87, p. 29-30.
"Dénouement." [SenR] (17:2) 87, p. 49.
"Divestitures." [Interim] (6:1) Spr 87, p. 27-28.
"Lesson." [Interim] (6:1) Spr 87, p. 25.
"No Other Plot." [Interim] (6:1) Spr 87, p. 26.
"Stakes." [Interim] (6:1) Spr 87, p. 28-29.
5698. VLIET, Eddy van
"After Years" (tr. by Peter Nijmeijer). [Vis] (25) 87, p. 38.

5699. VOGELSANG, Arthur
"Lee." [DenQ] (22:1) Sum 87, p. 21-23.
"Never Ask for Advice." [ParisR] (29:105) Wint 87, p. 144.
"Versailles, Two Banks." [DenQ] (21:3) Wint 87, p. 94-95.
5700. VOIGT, Ellen Bryant
"At the Movie: Virginia, 1956." [VirQR] (63:2) Spr 87, p. 277-279.
"The Field Trip." [VirQR] (63:2) Spr 87, p. 274-276.
"For My Father." [TexasR] (7:3/4) 87, p. 155-156.
"Frog." [Atlantic] (259:5) My 87, p. 40.
"Good News." [VirQR] (63:2) Spr 87, p. 279-280.
"The Happiness Poems." [TexasR] (7:3/4) 87, p. 157-158.
"May." [Thrpny] (28) Wint 87, p. 22.
"Nightshade." [PartR] (54:1) Wint 87, p. 128-129.
"The Visitor." [VirQR] (63:2) Spr 87, p. 276-277.
5701. VOLKOW, Veronica
"La Memoria." [BlackWR] (13:2) Spr 87, p. 164.
"Memory" (tr. by Forrest Gander). [BlackWR] (13:2) Spr 87, p. 165.
Von ALBRECHT, Michael
See ALBRECHT, Michael von
5702. VOSS, Fred
"At Goodstone Aircraft Company." [WormR] (27:1, issue 105) 87, p. 29-30.
"Liberation." [WormR] (27:1, issue 105) 87, p. 31.
"The Lifers." [WormR] (27:1, issue 105) 87, p. 30.
"Making America Strong." [WormR] (27:1, issue 105) 87, p. 28-29.
"Revenge." [WormR] (27:1, issue 105) 87, p. 30.
"A Threat." [WormR] (27:1, issue 105) 87, p. 29.
"Three Women." [WormR] (27:1, issue 105) 87, p. 28.
5703. VOZNESENSKY, Andrei
"The More You Tear Off, the More You Keep" (tr. by William Jay Smith and Vera
Dunham). [Trans] (18) Spr 87, p. 314-315.
"Over a dark and quiet empire" (tr. by William Jay Smith and Patricia Blake). [Trans]
(18) Spr 87, p. 316.
"To hang bare light bulbs from a ceiling" (tr. by William Jay Smith and Patricia
Blake). [Trans] (18) Spr 87, p. 316.
VRIES, Carrow de
See De VRIES, Carrow
VRIES, Peter de
See De VRIES, Peter
VRIES, Rachel Guido de
See DeVRIES, Rachel Guido
5704. VUKOVIC, Vladeta
"Ballad" (tr. of Branko Miljkovic, w. John Matthias). [Margin] (2) Spr 87, p. 59.
"Earth and Fire" (tr. of Branko Miljkovic, w. John Matthias). [Margin] (2) Spr 87,
p. 58.
"In Praise of Fire" (tr. of Branko Miljkovic, w. John Matthias). [Margin] (2) Spr 87,
p. 57.
"An Orphic Legacy" (tr. of Branko Miljkovic, w. John Matthias). [Margin] (2) Spr
87, p. 58.
5705. VVEDENSKY, Aleksandr
"How the Hours Talk to Each Other" (from "God May Be Around," tr. by Ivan
Burkin). [FiveFR] (5) 87, p. 25-26.
5706. WADDINGTON, Miriam
"Journey to Winnipeg, 1940." [Grain] (15:3) Fall 87, p. 6-7.
5707. WADE, Seth
"The Patriarch." [SlipS] (7) 87, p. 106.
5708. WADE, Sidney
"Hanging in the Balance." [GrandS] (6:2) Wint 87, p. 185.
"Kansas Weather." [YaleR] (76:2) Wint 87, p. 258.
"Seabirds." [SouthwR] (72:4) Aut 87, p. 528.
"Setting the Angel Free." [VirQR] (63:3) Sum 87, p. 441-442.
5709. WADSWORTH, William
"The Physicist on a Cold Night Explains." [YaleR] (77:1) Aut 87, p. 150-151.
5710. WAGNER, Anneliese
"Irish Summer." [GreenfR] (14:1/2) Wint-Spr, p. 115.
"Table, Co. Monaghan." [GreenfR] (14:1/2) Wint-Spr, p. 116.

5711. WAGNER, Catherine
"I pinch your nostrils shut." [WindO] (49) Fall 87, p. 57.
"Mom Loses Twins in Poker Game!" [WindO] (49) Fall 87, p. 56.
"Sandoway." [WindO] (49) Fall 87, p. 55.
5712. WAGNER, Shari
"The Lighthouse Keeper." [SouthernPR] (27:2) Fall 87, p. 27-28.
5713. WAGONER, David
"Blindman." [NowestR] (25:3) 87, p. 267-268.
"For the Young Vine Maples." [Poetry] (151:1/2) O-N 87, p. 184.
5714. WAH, Fred
"Music at the Heart of Thinking" (Selections: 5 poems, #70-74). [PraF] (8:4) Wint
87-88, p. 43-45.
"Music at the Heart of Thinking No. 19." [CrossC] (9:3/4) 87, p. 11.
5715. WAHLE, F. Keith
"The Job Interview." [WormR] (27:1, issue 105) 87, p. 4-5.
"To a Serious Editor." [WormR] (27:1, issue 105) 87, p. 5-6.
"To Jon Anderson." [WormR] (27:1, issue 105) 87, p. 7.
WAHN, Yoon
See YOON, Wahn
5716. WAKOSKI, Diane
"Emerald Ice." [Sulfur] (19) Spr 87, p. 76-77.
"The Good World." [Raccoon] (24/25) My 87, p. 34-36.
"Listening to Whales." [OhioR] (38) 87, p. 18-19.
"The Marine Story" (for David R. Smith). [Raccoon] (24/25) My 87, p. 298-299.
5717. WALCOTT, Derek
"French Colonial: Vers de Société." [RiverS] (22) 87, p. 13.
"Summer Elegy." [NewRep] (196:3) 19 Ja 87, p. 40.
"Summer Elegy II." [NewRep] (196:3) 19 Ja 87, p. 40.
"Sunday in the Old Republic." [Atlantic] (259:1) Ja 87, p. 43.
"Sundays." [NewYorker] (62:48) 19 Ja 87, p. 37.
5718. WALDEN, Gale Renee
"Each New Moon." [Puerto] (22:2) Spr 87, p. 110-111.
5719. WALDMAN, Anne
"The Problem" (after Laura Riding). [NewAW] (1) 87, p. 75.
"Star Dust" (In memory: Mabel Mercer & Jackie Curtis). [NewAW] (1) 87, p. 74.
5720. WALDNER, Liz
"The Au Pair Girl's Speech." [Shen] (37:1) 87, p. 26.
5721. WALDOR, Peter
"Picking Up Vauxhall Rd. During Rush Hour Just Past the Red Devil Paint
Factory." [Footwork] 87, p. 61.
5722. WALDROP, Keith
"An Apparatus." [Caliban] (2) 87, p. 146-147.
"Elegies" (Selections: VII-IX, tr. of Jean Grosjean). [LitR] (30:3) Spr 87, p.
353-355.
"Elegies" (Selections: X-XI, tr. of Jean Grosjean). [Notus] (2:1) Spr 87, p. 31-32.
"The Growth of Private Worlds from Unattached Feelings." [CentralP] (12) Fall 87,
p. 83-84.
"I See a Spot Coming Closer and Closer to Where I'm Waiting for It" (tr. of Claude
Royet-Journoud). [LitR] (30:3) Spr 87, p. 371-380.
"Plurality of Worlds." [NewAW] (2) Fall 87, p. 49-51.
"The Ring: a Legend of Charlemagne." [OP] (final issue) Sum 87, p. 27-30.
"Transcendental Studies" (Excerpts). [Temblor] (6) 87, p. 69-71.
5723. WALDROP, Rosmarie
"The Book of Dialogue" (Selections: "Pre-Dialogue, II," "The Dream," tr. of
Edmond Jabès). [LitR] (30:3) Spr 87, p. 367-370.
"A Form/ Of Taking/ It All." [Temblor] (6) 87, p. 152-178.
"Franz Schubert, Or: Notes on the Weather, Vienna" (tr. of Friederike Mayröcker).
[Sulfur] (20) Fall 87, p. 116-122.
"Inserting the Mirror" (Excerpts). [Act] (7) 87, p. 9-10.
"Introducing the Spade" (tr. of Alain Veinstein). [LitR] (30:3) Spr 87, p. 359-366.
"The Reproduction of Profiles" (Excerpts). [CentralP] (11) 87, p. 5-6.
"The Reproduction of Profiles" (Selections). [OP] (final issue) Sum 87, p. 31-32.
"The Reproduction of Profiles" (Selections: 4 sections). [NewAW] (1) 87, p. 68-69.
"Seven Passages from a Woman's Life" (tr. of Jacqueline Risset). [LitR] (30:3) Spr
87, p. 356-358.

"The Squabbles of Children" (tr. of Elke Erb). [ColR] (NS 14:2) Fall-Wint 87, p. 56.
"A Visit to Samarkand" (for and from Angela Carter). [Caliban] (2) 87, p. 92-94.
5724. WALISH, Marjorie
"Carpet within the Figure." [Sulfur] (18) Wint 87, p. 43-44.
"The Lute Player." [Sulfur] (18) Wint 87, p. 42-43.
5725. WALKER, Jeanne (Jeanne Murray)
"The Bag of Stones." [PassN] (8:1) Wint 87, p. 10.
"Coming Into History." [Poetry] (150:2) My 87, p. 91.
"Invocation to Convince a Baby Already Twelve Days Overdue to Come Out of the Womb." [Poetry] (150:2) My 87, p. 92.
"Shirt." [PassN] (8:1) Wint 87, p. 10.
"Theater." [Poetry] (151:1/2) O-N 87, p. 185.
"Writing to Get Through the Night While the Baby Cries." [LightY] '87, c86, p. 195.
5726. WALKER, Leon
"Leaving." [PoeticJ] (17) 87, p. 39.
5727. WALKER, Lynne
"Winter Poem." [Pig] (14) 87, p. 82.
5728. WALL, Dorothy
"The Daily Life of Nuns." [PraS] (61:2) Sum 87, p. 76-77.
"The Weight of Women." [PraS] (61:2) Sum 87, p. 75-76.
"What Survives." [PraS] (61:2) Sum 87, p. 74-75.
5729. WALLACE, Bronwen
"Gifts." [Event] (16:1) Mr 87, p. 25-27.
"Houses" (for Jim Rhodes). [Quarry] (36:1) Wint 87, p. 40-41.
"Idyll." [MalR] (79) Je 87, p. 31-34.
"Koko." [MalR] (79) Je 87, p. 28-30.
"Lifelines." [MalR] (79) Je 87, p. 39-42.
"Neighbours" (for Lorna Crozier, who asked). [Quarry] (36:1) Wint 87, p. 8-11.
"Ordinary Moving." [MalR] (79) Je 87, p. 35-38.
"Seeing Is Believing" (for Kathie). [Quarry] (36:1) Wint 87, p. 73-76.
"Stunts" (inspired by *The Guinness Book of World Records* and an interview with Phillippe Petit). [Event] (16:1) Mr 87, p. 28-29.
5730. WALLACE, Bruce
"The Fearful Eye of Little-God" (1986 Finalist, Eve of Saint Agnes Poetry Competition). [NegC] (7:1/2) 87, p. 207.
"Pausing in the Woods at Midnight by a Forgotten Cemetery." [PoetL] (82:2) Sum 87, p. 110.
5731. WALLACE, Chick
"Double Messages." [NegC] (7:3/4) 87, p. 92.
5732. WALLACE, Keith
"Martyrs." [Bogg] (57) 87, p. 43.
5733. WALLACE, Naomi
"Ballad for Gallipoli." [HayF] (2) Spr 87, p. 73.
"The Windsurfers." [MassR] (28:4) Wint 87, p. 739.
5734. WALLACE, Robert
"Cecil." [Pembroke] (19) 87, p. 168-169.
"Ice Cream." [Pembroke] (19) 87, p. 170-171.
"Winter Morning." [Pembroke] (19) 87, p. 169-170.
5735. WALLACE, Ronald
"1001 Nights." [Spirit] (8:2) 87, p. 200.
"Birdsong, Anyway." [SouthernR] (23:1) Ja 87, p. 162-163.
"Breakdown." [Atlantic] (260:2) Ag 87, p. 45.
"Camp Calvary." [PoetryNW] (28:4) Wint 87-88, p. 24.
"Kids." [TarRP] (26:2) Spr 87, p. 24.
"A Murder of Crows." [KanQ] (19:1/2) Wint-Spr 87, p. 86.
"Prayer." [SouthernR] (23:1) Ja 87, p. 162.
"Professor of Plums" (for Ricardo Quintana). [KanQ] (19:1/2) Wint-Spr 87, p. 85.
"Sen-Sen." [TarRP] (26:2) Spr 87, p. 24.
"Smoking." [Poetry] (149:6) Mr 87, p. 328.
"Song" (for my father). [KanQ] (19:1/2) Wint-Spr 87, p. 86-87.
"Turning Forty." [NegC] (7:3/4) 87, p. 69.
5736. WALLACE, T. S.
"Begging Stones." [Footwork] 87, p. 19.
"The Harsh Angel." [Footwork] 87, p. 20.

"Jonah." [Vis] (25) 87, p. 23.

"The Way of Trees." [Footwork] 87, p. 19.

5737. WALLACE-CRABBE, Chris

"City" (for Bella Akhmadulina and Boris Messerer). [Nimrod] (31:1) Fall-Wint 87, p. 126.

"Double Concerto." [Nimrod] (31:1) Fall-Wint 87, p. 125.

"Dry Goods." [Nimrod] (31:1) Fall-Wint 87, p. 124.

5738. WALLACH, Martin

"Impressionism." [SmPd] (24:1) Wint 87, p. 8.

WALLEGHEN, Michael van

See Van WALLEGHEN, Michael

5739. WALLER, Gary

"Artist's Studio." [DenQ] (21:3) Wint 87, p. 38.

5740. WALLS, Doyle Wesley

"The Long Rain." [WoosterR] (7) Spr 87, p. 11.

"On Beauty" (going after Edna St. Vincent Millay). [Pig] (14) 87, p. 34.

"On Our Son's Graduation from the Crib." [AntigR] (71/72) Aut 87-Wint 88, p. 210.

5741. WALSH, Ann L.

"Still Waters." [Quarry] (36:4) Fall 87, p. 65-68.

5742. WALSH, Phyllis

"Difficulties of Cultivating Shooting Stars." [SpoonRQ] (12:2) Spr 87, p. 36.

5743. WALTNER, Thomas R.

"How-To Return to Prison." [GreenfR] (14:3/4) Sum-Fall 87, p. 94.

"Reggie: The Prison Poet." [GreenfR] (14:3/4) Sum-Fall 87, p. 93.

5744. WALTON, Ian A.

"Excerpts from the Broken Biscuit Factory" (#33, #37). [Bogg] (57) 87, p. 55.

5745. WALTUCH, Michael

"I. Are you asleep, a sunflower, black seed, gold" (tr. of Tomaz Salamun, w. the author). [WillowS] (20) Spr 87, p. 81.

"II. Shouts are words, silent sleep" (tr. of Tomaz Salamun, w. the author). [WillowS] (20) Spr 87, p. 82.

"III. Don't be afraid of images of the world" (tr. of Tomaz Salamun, w. the author). [WillowS] (20) Spr 87, p. 83.

"IV. Reflect, children, slide silently" (tr. of Tomaz Salamun, w. the author). [WillowS] (20) Spr 87, p. 84.

5746. WAMSLEY, Ellen

"Each Day." [Gambit] (21) 87, p. 18.

"Pearl." [Gambit] (21) 87, p. 40.

5747. WANG, Wei

"Hua-Tzu Hill" (in Chinese & English, tr. by Joseph Lisowski). [NegC] (7:1/2) 87, p. 248-249.

5748. WANIEK, Marilyn Nelson

"The Grebe" (tr. of Thorkild Bjørnvig). [LitR] (30:4) Sum 87, p. 509-510.

"Morning Darkness" (tr. of Thorkild Bjørnvig). [LitR] (30:4) Sum 87, p. 507-508.

5749. WARD, Diane

"Concept Lyrics" (Selections: 4 poems). [Temblor] (6) 87, p. 128-129.

"Cracks." [Bound] (14:1/2) Fall 85-Wint 86 [c87], p. 106-108.

5750. WARD, Elizabeth

"Van Gelder's Secret." [BellArk] (3:2) Mr-Ap 87, p. 10.

5751. WARD, Robert

"Black Lucy" (Victory Lake Nursing Home, 1974). [WillowS] (19) Wint 87, p. 42-43.

"Camera Obscura" (11 poems, for Philip Booth). [SilverFR] (14) 87, 32 p.

5752. WARD, Robert J.

"The Fountains of Serbia" (tr. of Anghel Dumbraveanu, w. Marcel Cornis-Pop). [MidAR] (7:2) 87, p. 65-83.

5753. WARD, Robert R.

"Dèja Vu." [Amelia] (4:1/2, issue 9) 87, p. 58-59.

"Late Spring." [HawaiiR] (22) Fall 87, p. 54-55.

"Shadows." [HawaiiR] (22) Fall 87, p. 53.

5754. WARDEN, Marine Robert

"Miller Canyon." [Abraxas] (35/36) 87, p. 52.

5755. WARE, Marianne

"Understanding Guyana." [Spirit] (8:2) 87, p. 198-199.

WARHAFT, Gail Holst
  See HOLST-WARHAFT, Gail
5756. WARLAND, Betsy
  "Serpent (W)rite, Turn Seven" (Excerpt). [CrossC] (9:3/4) 87, p. 5.
5757. WARREN, Charlotte Gould
  "Looking Out the Window." [KanQ] (19:3) Sum 87, p. 181.
5758. WARREN, Robert Penn
  "After the Dinner Party." [Salm] (72) Fall 86, p. 254-255.
  "Skiers" (to Baudouin and Annie de Moustier). [NowestR] (25:3) 87, p. 109.
5759. WARREN, Rosanna
  "Daily Mail." [Ploughs] (13:1) 87, p. 134.
  "Girl by Minoan Wall." [YaleR] (76:2) Wint 87, p. 231.
  "Ice." [Ploughs] (13:1) 87, p. 133.
  "Jacob Burckhardt, August 8, 1897." [YaleR] (76:2) Wint 87, p. 232-233.
5760. WARREN-MOORE, Jackie
  "A Death Wish for Uncle Joe." [SenR] (17:2) 87, p. 56.
  "Starlight." [SenR] (17:2) 87, p. 57.
5761. WARSAW, Irene
  "Sheep That Pass in the Night." [LightY] '87, c86, p. 116.
5762. WARSH, Sylvia Maultash
  "Lost in Banff, Alberta." [Waves] (15:3) Wint 87, p. 60.
5763. WARWICK, Joanna
  "An Apple Tree for Osip Mandelstam." [Jacaranda] (2:2) Spr 87, p. 3.
  "Letter from C.G. Jung." [Jacaranda] (2:2) Spr 87, p. 6-8.
  "Lorelei." [Jacaranda] (2:2) Spr 87, p. 4-5.
  "My Mother Shows Me the Human Brain." [TexasR] (8:1/2) Spr-Sum 87, p. 92-93.
  "Picasso: 'The Dwarf Dancer'." [BlueBldgs] (10) 87?, p. 7.
  "Rose, O Pure Contradiction." [Ascent] (13:1) 87, p. 34-37.
5764. WASEM, Connie
  "Shots of Hungry Eyes." [BellR] (10:1) Spr 87, p. 51-52.
5765. WASHBURN, Katherine
  "Discus" (tr. of Paul Celan, w. Margaret Guillemin). [AntR] (45:1) Wint 87, p. 96.
  "Grown Weary" (tr. of Paul Celan, w. Margaret Guillemin). [AntR] (45:1) Wint 87, p. 97.
5766. WASHBURN, Laura
  "If You Go to Bly." [Bogg] (58) 87, p. 19.
5767. WASSERMAN, E. H.
  "Grading the Pale Boy's Paper." [HampSPR] Wint 87, p. 21-22.
5768. WASSERMAN, Rosanne
  "Buskins and Robins." [Sulfur] (20) Fall 87, p. 65-66.
  "Dark Furniture" (for Mimi Bess). [Sulfur] (20) Fall 87, p. 61-62.
  "Interview with Elpenor." [Sulfur] (20) Fall 87, p. 63-64.
  "Inuit and Seal" (for Gaëtan and Jim). [Sulfur] (20) Fall 87, p. 60-61.
  "A Provincial Synagogue" (for Sara Levitch Wasserman). [Gambit] (21) 87, p. 35-38.
5769. WASSON, Kirsten
  "Eavesdropping." [KanQ] (19:1/2) Wint-Spr 87, p. 316.
  "Voyeur." [KanQ] (19:1/2) Wint-Spr 87, p. 316-317.
5770. WATERMAN, Cary
  "The Eve of All Saints' Day." [LakeSR] (21) 87, p. 27.
5771. WATERS, Mary Ann
  "The Night He Died, My Father." [GreenfR] (14:1/2) Wint-Spr, p. 197-198.
  "Travelling Highway 97: Biggs Junction to Weed" (For Richard Hugo). [Poetry] (151:1/2) O-N 87, p. 186-188.
5772. WATERS, Michael
  "Brooklyn Waterfall" (for Stephen Dunn). [MemphisSR] (8:1) Fall 87, p. 14-15.
  "The Burden Lifters." [Crazy] (32) Spr 87, p. 26-27.
  "Certain Signs." [TarRP] (26:2) Spr 87, p. 32-33.
  "On the Eve of the Assumption." [NoDaQ] (55:3) Sum 87, p. 87.
  "One Last spider." [TarRP] (26:2) Spr 87, p. 33-34.
  "The Spirit of Siena." [Raccoon] (24/25) My 87, p. 18-20.
  "Toward a Definition of Desire." [IndR] (10:3) Spr 87, p. 26-27.
  "Umbrellas with Souls." [MemphisSR] (8:1) Fall 87, p. 16.
  "Well Water" (Ios, 1985). [MemphisSR] (8:1) Fall 87, p. 17.
5773. WATKINS, Edward
  "The Daily Planet." [LightY] '87, c86, p. 183.

"Silent Lover." [LightY] '87, c86, p. 75.
5774. WATKINS, William John
"Love Poem for Sandra #10,001." [CumbPR] (7:1) Fall 87, p. 80.
"The Sexual Grammarian." [CumbPR] (7:1) Fall 87, p. 78-79.
"The Well." [BallSUF] (28:4) Aut 87, p. 50.
5775. WATSON, Craig
"Discipline" (for John Taggart). [Bound] (14:1/2) Fall 85-Wint 86 [c87], p. 35-37.
5776. WATSON, Ellen
"Mobiles" (tr. of Adélia Prado). [Antaeus] (58) Spr 87, p. 199-200.
"Praise for a Color" (tr. of Adélia Prado). [ParisR] (29:103) Sum 87, p. 178.
"Purple" (tr. of Adélia Prado). [ParisR] (29:103) Sum 87, p. 177.
"Two Ways" (tr. of Adélia Prado). [Antaeus] (58) Spr 87, p. 196.
"The Way Things Talk" (tr. of Adélia Prado). [Antaeus] (58) Spr 87, p. 197-198.
5777. WATSON, Iain
"At Sabre's Point" (tr. of Victor Segalen, w. Andrew Harvey). [SenR] (17:2) 87, p. 28.
"Command to the Sun" (tr. of Victor Segalen, w. Andrew Harvey). [SenR] (17:2) 87, p. 31.
"Hymn to the Resting Dragon" (tr. of Victor Segalen, w. Andrew Harvey). [SenR] (17:2) 87, p. 32.
"Mongol Libation" (tr. of Victor Segalen, w. Andrew Harvey). [SenR] (17:2) 87, p. 29.
"Written with Blood" (tr. of Victor Segalen, w. Andrew Harvey). [SenR] (17:2) 87, p. 30.
5778. WATSON, Lawrence
"Houses." [StoneC] (15:1/2) Fall-Wint 87-88, p. 71.
5779. WATSON, M. T.
"Then Nothing." [Verse] (4:1) Mr 87, p. 55-56.
5780. WATSON, Roderick
"Holiday Cottage." [Verse] (4:2) Je 87, p. 17-18.
5781. WATSON, W. D.
"Red-Haired Mary" (1986 Finalist, Eve of Saint Agnes Poetry Competition). [NegC] (7:1/2) 87, p. 202-204.
5782. WATTERSON, William Collins
"Nightscape with Doves." [NewYorker] (62:51) 9 F 87, p. 77.
5783. WATTS, Anthony
"Safari Notes." [CrossCur] (7:3) 87, p. 151.
5784. WAUGAMAN, Charles A.
"Seneca Point." [CapeR] (22:1) Spr 87, p. 27.
5785. WAUGH, Robert H.
"The Senate Met at Noon." [InterPR] (13:2) Fall 87, p. 72.
"Snow, Early November." [InterPR] (13:2) Fall 87, p. 73-74.
"Wrestling the Breaker." [InterPR] (13:2) Fall 87, p. 74.
5786. WAYMAN, Tom
"Cost Plus." [MassR] (28:4) Wint 87, p. 685-686.
"Defective Parts of Speech: Have You Really Read All These?" [OntR] (26) Spr-Sum 87, p. 38-39.
"The Poet Milton Acorn Crosses into the Republic of Heaven." [MalR] (80) S 87, p. 125-129.
"Snowing." [Quarry] (36:4) Fall 87, p. 76.
"Unemployed." [Event] (16:2) Sum 87, p. 107-109.
"A Yellow Cottage." [Hudson] (40:2) Sum 87, p. 279-285.
5787. WAYNE, Jane O.
"At the High School's Winter Musical." [WebR] (12:1) Spr 87, p. 5.
"Drinking Tea with the Gypsies." [WebR] (12:1) Spr 87, p. 7.
"Freeze Warning." [MichQR] (26:2) Spr 87, p. 354.
"Going in for Tests." [WebR] (12:1) Spr 87, p. 6.
"In Flood's Cove." [WebR] (12:1) Spr 87, p. 8-9.
"In September." [PoetryNW] (28:2) Sum 87, p. 9-10.
"In the Shower." [WebR] (12:1) Spr 87, p. 11.
"Isoptera." [Poetry] (149:4) Ja 87, p. 199.
"The Last Visit." [Poetry] (149:4) Ja 87, p. 200-201.
"The Regular." [WebR] (12:1) Spr 87, p. 9.
"The Short." [WebR] (12:1) Spr 87, p. 10.
"The Takeover." [MichQR] (26:2) Spr 87, p. 353.
"Waiting." [AmerS] (56:3) Sum 87, p. 342.

"Walking Into the Wind." [Poetry] (149:4) Ja 87, p. 202.
"Watermark." [WebR] (12:1) Spr 87, p. 10.
5788. WEATHERFORD, Carole Boston
"Day's Work." [BlackALF] (21:3) Fall 87, p. 239.
"The Ladies of Dimbaza" (for two voices). [Calyx] (11:1) Wint 87-88, p. 44-45.
"Migrant Man." [BlackALF] (21:3) Fall 87, p. 238-239.
"Shejazz." [BlackALF] (21:3) Fall 87, p. 237-238.
"This Blood." [BlackALF] (21:3) Fall 87, p. 237.
5789. WEATHERS, Winston
"Trinity." [SouthwR] (72:1) Wint 87, p. 95.
5790. WEAVER, Kathleen
"It Is Better to Get Up" (tr. of Fayad Jamis). [Zyzzyva] (3:4) Wint 87-88, p. 41.
5791. WEAVER, Michael S.
"The Dancing Veil" (for Roy DeCarava). [HangL] (50/51) 87, p. 197-199.
"Luxembourg Garden." [HangL] (50/51) 87, p. 200.
5792. WEBB, Bernice Larson
"Paper Dreams." [KanQ] (19:1/2) Wint-Spr 87, p. 176.
5793. WEBB, Charles
"Faces of Age." [KanQ] (19:3) Sum 87, p. 153.
"For All I Know." [Electrum] (39) Fall-Wint 87, p. 45.
"Memento Mori." [KanQ] (19:1/2) Wint-Spr 87, p. 114.
"No." [SlipS] (7) 87, p. 109.
"October 1." [WindO] (49) Fall 87, p. 51.
"Once." [Wind] (17:59) 87, p. 41.
"A Strong Impression." [KanQ] (19:1/2) Wint-Spr 87, p. 113.
5794. WEBB, James F.
"Charge." [Amelia] (4:1/2, issue 9) 87, p. 90.
5795. WEBB, Martha
"The Anatomy of the Infinite." The Best of [BambooR] [(31-32)] 86, p. 107.
"Song at Hanalei" (for Robert Cazimero). The Best of [BambooR] [(31-32)] 86, p. 106.
5796. WEBB, Phyllis
"Attend" (for Sharon Thesen). [Grain] (15:4) Wint 87, p. 12-13.
"Gwendolyn MacEwen 1941-1987." [MalR] (81) D 87, preceding title page.
"Poetics Against the Angel of Death." [CanLit] (115) Wint 87, p. 52-53.
5797. WEBER, Jan
"To a Friend Who Talks of Suicide from Time to Time." [ManhatPR] (9) Sum 87, p. 56-57.
5798. WEBER, Maria
"Descent." [Footwork] 87, p. 26-27.
"Fear." [Footwork] 87, p. 27.
"Strange Bird" (Party at Prattley's). [Footwork] 87, p. 27.
5799. WEBER, Ron
"The Stranger." [GreenfR] (14:1/2) Wint-Spr, p. 108-109.
"The Transfusion" (for Dennis Gaughan). [GreenfR] (14:1/2) Wint-Spr, p. 110.
5800. WEBSTER, Dianne
"Wind Wonders." [Wind] (17:60) 87, p. 4.
5801. WEDGE, George F.
"Second Sight." [StoneC] (14:3/4) Spr-Sum 87, p. 39.
5802. WEDGE, Philip
"Natural" (for Bert). [KanQ] (19:3) Sum 87, p. 40.
"On a February Morning." [KanQ] (19:3) Sum 87, p. 40-41.
5803. WEEKLEY, Richard J.
"11:20 A.M." [BlueBldgs] (10) 87?, p. 39.
"For the first Four Months." [MidwQ] (28:2) Wint 87, p. 229.
"There Is Nothing New." [CrossCur] (7:1) 87, p. 70-71.
"Writing a Poem With One Hand While Driving to San Francisco . . ., or, Truck Stop Pie." [WestCR] (21:3) Wint 87, p. 14-16.
"You Enter the Mirror." [BlueBldgs] (10) 87?, p. 40-41.
"The Young Backpack Women." [KanQ] (19:1/2) Wint-Spr 87, p. 312.
5804. WEEKS, Laurie
"Anamorphosis." [Act] (7) 87, p. 73.
"Vivisections for Piano" (Selections: #1, #2). [Act] (7) 87, p. 72.
5805. WEEKS, Ramona
"Eclipse." [CapilR] (44) 87, p. 64.
"The Future of Potatoes" (A Welsh englyn). [WestB] (20) 87, p. 86.

409

WEISNER

"Nahuatl Poem." [CapilR] (44) 87, p. 65.
"Rebirth and Belonging." [CapilR] (44) 87, p. 66.
"Streets of Laredo Revisited." [CapilR] (44) 87, p. 63.
5806. WEEKS, Robert Lewis
"Gig." [PoetC] (18:2) Wint 87, p. 18.
"Jess Dennison's Garage." [StoneC] (14:3/4) Spr-Sum 87, p. 72-73.
"Odysseus Through Owl Land." [NegC] (7:3/4) 87, p. 99-101.
"Sunday Song." [Northeast] (Ser. 4:5) Sum 87, p. 7.
WEI, Wang
See WANG, Wei
5807. WEIGL, Bruce
"The Black Hose." [MissouriR] (10:3) 87, p. 138-139.
"The Last Lie." [GreenfR] (14:3/4) Sum-Fall 87, p. 185.
"Meditation at Buckroe Beach" (for Dave Smith). [QW] (24) Wint 87, p. 81-82.
"Temptation." [QW] (24) Wint 87, p. 79-80.
5808. WEINBERGER, Eliot
"1930: Scenic Views" (tr. of Octavio Paz). [BostonR] (12:5) O 87, p. 24.
"And if I devoted my life" ("Untitled," tr. of Cecilia Vicuña). [AmerPoR] (16:2)
Mr-Ap 87, p. 16.
"Axis" (tr. of Octavio Paz). [YellowS] (25) Wint 87, p. 5.
"I Speak of the City" (for Eliot Weinberger, tr. of Octavio Paz). [Sulfur] (20) Fall
87, p. 75-78.
"Jonah's Lament" (tr. of Olga Orozco). [AmerPoR] (16:2) Mr-Ap 87, p. 20.
"Letter of Testimony Cantata" (tr. of Octavio Paz). [ParisR] (29:105) Wint 87, p.
133-141.
"Luxumei" (tr. of Cecilia Vicuña). [AmerPoR] (16:2) Mr-Ap 87, p. 15.
"Maithuna" (tr. of Octavio Paz). [YellowS] (25) Wint 87, p. 6-7.
"Personal Stamp" (tr. of Olga Orozco). [AmerPoR] (16:2) Mr-Ap 87, p. 20.
"Solitude" (tr. of Cecilia Vicuña). [AmerPoR] (16:2) Mr-Ap 87, p. 16.
"Sphinxes Accustomed to Being" (tr. of Olga Orozco). [AmerPoR] (16:2) Mr-Ap 87,
p. 19-20.
"The Sunken Continent" (tr. of Olga Orozco). [ColR] (NS 14:2) Fall-Wint 87, p.
54-55.
"Topac Inca Yupanqui" (tr. of Cecilia Vicuña). [AmerPoR] (16:2) Mr-Ap 87, p. 16.
"Wikuna" (tr. of Cecilia Vicuña). [AmerPoR] (16:2) Mr-Ap 87, p. 15.
5809. WEINER, Harte
"The Vodka and the Gin." [ParisR] (29:103) Sum 87, p. 182.
5810. WEINER, Joshua
"Casting Back" (for my father). [AmerS] (56:2) Spr 87, p. 248-249.
5811. WEINER, Rachel
"Landscapes." [CapeR] (22:2) Fall 87, p. 1.
5812. WEINER, Rebecca
"The Payment." [Ploughs] (13:4) 87, p. 137.
5813. WEINGARTEN, Roger
"Florida." [MissouriR] (10:1) 87, p. 64-65.
"Just Another Sunset." [Poetry] (151:1/2) O-N 87, p. 189-190.
"Moment of Vaulted Chambers." [Shen] (37:1) 87, p. 27-29.
"Nightwatch." [Poetry] (150:5) Ag 87, p. 263-264.
"The Noonday Witch." [MissouriR] (10:1) 87, p. 66-67.
"Persona Non Grata." [Poetry] (150:5) Ag 87, p. 265-266.
"Saffron Pig Piñata." [LightY] '87, c86, p. 170.
"Shadow Shadow." [TexasR] (7:3/4) 87, p. 160-161.
"Sometimes, at Thirty-Six." [TexasR] (7:3/4) 87, p. 159.
5814. WEINMAN, Paul
"That Patched-Up Ball." [SlipS] (7) 87, p. 84.
5815. WEIR, Virginia
"Bad Water." [FiveFR] (5) 87, p. 124.
5816. WEIS, R.
"One Moment Rain." [Lyra] (1:2) 87, p. 22.
5817. WEISNER, Ken
"Firefly Sestina." [AntR] (45:3) Sum 87, p. 337.
"The Hats My Father Wore." [AntR] (45:3) Sum 87, p. 336.
"Poem of the Other World." [AntR] (45:3) Sum 87, p. 335.
"Winter in the Old Country." [AntR] (45:3) Sum 87, p. 334.

5818. WEISS, David
"Coronary" (In Memoriam, tr. of Rosa Elena Maldonado, w. Claudette Columbus).
[SenR] (17:1) 87, p. 40.
"Desire" (tr. of Rosa Elena Maldonado, w. Claudette Columbus). [SenR] (17:1) 87,
p. 42.
"Dreams on a Nonexistent Shore" (tr. of Rosa Elena Maldonado, w. Claudette
Columbus). [SenR] (17:1) 87, p. 43.
"Inheritance" (tr. of Rosa Elena Maldonado, w. Claudette Columbus). [SenR] (17:1)
87, p. 39.
"Not the City" (tr. of Rosa Elena Maldonado, w. Claudette Columbus). [SenR]
(17:1) 87, p. 41.
5819. WEISS, Dora
"Macbeth." [Lactuca] (5) Ja 87, p. 23.
5820. WEISS, Jason
"Probable Forgetting of Ithaca" (tr. of Luisa Futoransky). [ColR] (NS 14:2)
Fall-Wint 87, p. 53.
5821. WEISS, Sigmund
"Arriving." [Lactuca] (7) Ag 87, p. 38.
"The Horizon." [Lactuca] (5) Ja 87, p. 24.
"Insight into Silence" (for Dora). [Lactuca] (8) N 87, p. 4.
"Steel for Light in the Night." [Lactuca] (5) Ja 87, p. 24.
"We Could Not Go Far." [Lactuca] (5) Ja 87, p. 25.
5822. WEISS, Theodore
"Eve Before Adam." [CrossCur] (7:2) 87, p. 147.
"An Old Cart" (For an anthology limited to thirteen-line poems). [Poetry] (151:1/2)
O-N 87, p. 190.
5823. WEISSBORT, Daniel
"Finally." [Stand] (28:3) Sum 87, p. 15.
"Sanatorium." [Stand] (28:3) Sum 87, p. 12-14.
5824. WEITZMAN, Sarah Brown
"If I Were There." [YellowS] (22) Spr 87, p. 6.
5825. WELBOURN, Cynthia
"The Boomerang of Geese." [DekalbLAJ] (20:1/4) 87, p. 56.
"High Summer." [CrossCur] (6:5) 87, p. 22.
"The Open Window." [CrossCur] (6:5) 87, p. 24.
"Rich South African Tourists." [Amelia] (4:1/2, issue 9) 87, p. 102.
"Slow Fuse." [CrossCur] (6:5) 87, p. 23.
"Valentine's Day in Key West." [DekalbLAJ] (20:1/4) 87, p. 56.
5826. WELCH, Don
"Buzzard." [Nimrod] (30:2) Spr-Sum 87, p. 140.
"The Marginalist." [Nimrod] (30:2) Spr-Sum 87, p. 141.
"Old German Woman." [Nimrod] (30:2) Spr-Sum 87, p. 139.
5827. WELCH, Jennifer
"When Editors Go Dancing." [Pig] (14) 87, p. 85.
5828. WELISH, Marjorie
"A Full Hand." [Conjunc] (11) 87?, p. 246-249.
"Shown Against Red-Curtained Backgrounds." [NewAW] (1) 87, p. 34-35.
5829. WELLS, Will
"The Ancient." [Gambit] (20) 86, p. 119.
"Hedgeapples." [CharR] (13:2) Fall 87, p. 31.
"Northamptonshire Moss, an Elegy" (for Martyn Smith, 1986 Finalist, Eve of St.
Agnes Poetry Competition). [NegC] (7:1/2) 87, p. 199-200.
5830. WELTNER, Jane Simpson
"No One Sleeps" (1987 Ratner-Ferber-Poet Lore Honorable Mention). [PoetL]
(82:2) Sum 87, p. 79.
5831. WEN, I-to
"Cruelty" (tr. by Robert Dorsett). [NewOR] (14:1) Spr 87, p. 98.
5832. WENDELL, Julia
"Hypersomnia: Exhaustion After a Long Night's Rest." [AmerPoR] (16:1) Ja-F 87,
p. 22.
"Sometimes the Body's Unwilling." [GreenfR] (14:3/4) Sum-Fall 87, p. 183.
"Suburban Voices." [GreenfR] (14:3/4) Sum-Fall 87, p. 180-182.
5833. WENDT, Ingrid
"Having Given Brith." [Calyx] (10:2/3) Spr 87, p. 112.
5834. WENNER, Mary
"Water Music." [BellArk] (3:1) Ja-F 87, p. 5.

5835. WEÖRES, Sandor
"The Gate of Teeth" (tr. by Jascha Kessler, w. Mária Körösy). [GrahamHR] (10)
Wint-Spr 87, p. 62-63.
"Seventh Symphony: The Assumption of Mary" (To my mother's memory, tr. by
Bruce Berlind, w. Mária Körösy). [GrahamHR] (10) Wint-Spr 87, p. 64-72.
5836. WERDINGER, Roberta
"Mechanics." [YellowS] (25) Wint 87, p. 10.
"Poem: Give me your blood your bone." [YellowS] (25) Wint 87, p. 11.
5837. WERNHAM, Guy
"To Have Done with the Judgment of God" (Excerpt, tr. of Antonin Artaud).
[NowestR] (25:3) 87, p. 65-67.
5838. WERNISCH, Ivan
"At the Table" (tr. by Paul Jagasich). [HampSPR] Wint 87, p. 32.
"Dream About Death" (tr. by Paul Jagasich). [HampSPR] Wint 87, p. 32.
"The Other Shore" (tr. by Paul Jagasich). [HampSPR] Wint 87, p. 31-32.
"Walk Around the Brewery" (tr. by Paul Jagasich). [HampSPR] Wint 87, p. 31.
WERT, William F. van
See Van WERT, William F.
5839. WERUP, Jacques
"Any day now Willow Lake will be freezing over" (tr. by Roger Greenwald).
[Pequod] (23/24) 87, p. 248-249.
"Of course Malmö United can win the all-Sweden finals" (tr. by Roger Greenwald).
[Pequod] (23/24) 87, p. 247.
5840. WESCOTT, Mary
"Bear Dance." [ManhatPR] (9) Sum 87, p. 24.
5841. WESLOWSKI, Dieter
"The Bird Who Steals Everything Shining" (41 poems, Winner of the Gardner
Poetry Award). [MSS] (6:1) 87, 50 p.
"Canto Azules" (for B. Jean Hunter). [GreensboroR] (41) Wint 86-87, p. 120.
"Curzio Malaparte Addresses the Constellation of the Dog." [MSS] (5:3) 87, p. 111.
"Diabolique." [Puerto] (22:2) Spr 87, p. 137.
"The Feather of the Crow." [InterPR] (13:1) Spr 87, p. 100.
"General Sherman in Hell." [KenR] (NS 9:4) Fall 87, p. 48.
"Holy Thursday." [Event] (16:3) Fall 87, p. 65.
"If Everytime We Spoke." [Pembroke] (19) 87, p. 194.
"In a Memo, Colette Bids Herself, Adieu." [BostonR] (12:4) Ag 87, p. 12.
"Last Spring, This Spring, Last Spring." [KenR] (NS 9:4) Fall 87, p. 49.
"Leaves." [InterPR] (13:1) Spr 87, p. 100.
"The Map of Spain." [WebR] (12:2) Fall 87, p. 79.
"Maura Paints the Deer Skulls" (for M. Shuttleworth). [KanQ] (19:4) Fall 87, p. 42.
"Night Is the Actuality of Things." [KenR] (NS 9:4) Fall 87, p. 50.
"November Lines for Blaise Pascal." [TexasR] (8:1/2) Spr-Sum 87, p. 74.
"The November Miracle." [CumbPR] (6:2) Spr 87, p. 18.
"Resurrection, with Apology to George Herbert." [KenR] (NS 9:4) Fall 87, p.
48-49.
"Spring, Mrs. Kazmerski Enters the Garden." [MalR] (80) S 87, p. 84.
"This Is the Dream in Which." [Gambit] (20) 86, p. 23.
"What Winter Branches Remember." [KenR] (NS 9:4) Fall 87, p. 49-50.
"While Sitting at the Edge of a Grove." [MSS] (5:3) 87, p. 112.
"Why I Won't Sit in Your Churches." [Puerto] (22:2) Spr 87, p. 136.
"You Know You've Been Living in One Place Too Long." [Gambit] (21) 87, p. 42.
5842. WEST, Charles
"Henny Youngman Haiku" (1 & 2). [Amelia] (4:1/2, issue 9) 87, p. 116.
"Limerick: A man once made a mistake." [Bogg] (57) 87, p. 13.
"Three" (3 Haiku). [LightY] '87, c86, p. 233.
5843. WEST, John Foster
"Rams in Thickets." [ChatR] (8:1) Fall 87, p. 104.
5844. WEST, Richard M.
"The Human Condition." [BellR] (10:2) Fall 87, p. 42.
"The Old Philosopher Plays Some Music." [BellR] (10:2) Fall 87, p. 41.
"A Winter on Bainbridge Island, Washington." [BellR] (10:2) Fall 87, p. 40.
5845. WESTBROOK, Lisa
"Fourth of July." [Gambit] (20) 86, p. 38.
5846. WESTERFIELD, Nancy G.
"Amortization." [Comm] (114:19) 6 N 87, p. 618.
"Bro." [FourQ] (1:1) Wint 87, p. 60.

"The Campers." [Poem] (58) N 87, p. 20.
"Cinna the Poet." [TexasR] (8:1/2) Spr-Sum 87, p. 64.
"Estrangement." [KanQ] (19:1/2) Wint-Spr 87, p. 97.
"The Godmother." [EngJ] (76:8) D 87, p. 81.
"Smoke." [Comm] (114:1) 16 Ja 87, p. 19.
"Spoilage." [NegC] (7:3/4) 87, p. 115.
"Walking the Overpass." [NegC] (7:3/4) 87, p. 116.
5847. WESTFALL, Marilyn
"Room with Parrots." [CrabCR] (4:2) Spr 87, p. 19.
5848. WESTON, Mildred
"Dust Storm." [NowestR] (25:2) 87, p. 133.
"Landscape." [NowestR] (25:2) 87, p. 129.
5849. WESTWOOD, Norma
"Artist's Conception." [Interim] (6:2) Fall 87, p. 14.
"Cedar Waxwings." [ManhatPR] (9) Sum 87, p. 25.
"To Fall." [Interim] (6:2) Fall 87, p. 13.
"Untouchable." [Interim] (6:2) Fall 87, p. 12.
5850. WETTEROTH, Bruce
"Cult of Dirt Roads." [SouthernPR] (27:1) Spr 87, p. 61.
"Out-Takes from South Dakota." [Field] (36) Spr 87, p. 54.
"Petroglyphs." [Field] (36) Spr 87, p. 55-56.
"Waking." [StoneC] (15:1/2) Fall-Wint 87-88, p. 59.
5851. WEXELBLATT, Robert
"Clothespins." [HawaiiR] (22) Fall 87, p. 75.
"In the Days of the Kalda Railroad." [HawaiiR] (22) Fall 87, p. 76-81.
"One Day with Mortality." [PoetryNW] (28:4) Wint 87-88, p. 26-27.
5852. WHALEN, Damian
"Fishing Rock Creek" (For Rod Heckaman). [HighP] (2:2) Fall 87, p. 165-166.
5853. WHALEN, Philip
"One of My Favorite Songs Is 'Stormy Weather'." [NowestR] (25:3) 87, p. 48.
5854. WHALEN, Tom
"Plant Life." [NewOR] (14:3) Fall 87, p. 70-71.
"You Who Let Me." [YellowS] (25) Wint 87, p. 4.
5855. WHATLEY, Wallace
"Eighth and Broad." [LightY] '87, c86, p. 250.
"Highway 80." [MinnR] (NS 28) Spr 87, p. 25.
5856. WHEATCROFT, John
"First Time in the Forest." [GrahamHR] (10) Wint-Spr 87, p. 18-20.
"On the Cornish Coast." [DenQ] (22:2) Fall 87, p. 56-57.
"Retrospective: William De Kooning's Imaginary Brother Speaking." [GrahamHR]
(10) Wint-Spr 87, p. 14-17.
5857. WHEATLEY, Pat (Patience)
"The Conquest of Mexico — Montreal 1980." [Quarry] (36:1) Wint 87, p. 91-92.
"Mica Mine." [Germ] (11:1) Fall 87, p. 52.
"Snaps of the Trip" (Selection: 2. "Makhtar"). [Quarry] (36:1) Wint 87, p. 92-93.
WHEATON, Heather Holland
See HOLLAND-WHEATON, Heather
5858. WHEDON, Tony
"Fling." [IndR] (11:1) Wint 87, p. 84.
"The Guitar Lesson." [IndR] (11:1) Wint 87, p. 80-81.
"Paper Girl." [IndR] (11:1) Wint 87, p. 82-83.
"Poem for the End of November." [StoneC] (15:1/2) Fall-Wint 87-88, p. 33.
5859. WHEELER, Susan
"The Man with the Green Card" (for Marc Giordano). [Sulfur] (19) Spr 87, p.
92-93.
"To Deify." [MassR] (28:2) Sum 87, p. 269-270.
"What Memory Reveals." [Sulfur] (19) Spr 87, p. 91-92.
5860. WHISLER, Robert F.
"Driftwood." [Footwork] 87, p. 37.
"Gathering Bones." [PoeticJ] (17) 87, p. 9.
"Lyke-Wake." [ArizQ] (43:1) Spr 87, p. 28.
"Mercutio by the Garden Wall." [Amelia] (4:3, issue 10) 87, p. 117.
"Moon Talk." [Footwork] 87, p. 37.
"Russell Elias." [Poem] (58) N 87, p. 49-51.
"Soubrette." [CapeR] (22:2) Fall 87, p. 31.
"Turning without a Signal." [HawaiiR] (22) Fall 87, p. 32.

"Two Aspirin Days." [Footwork] 87, p. 37.
5861. WHITE, Boyd
"Fenton River Breakdown." [TarRP] (26:2) Spr 87, p. 25-26.
"For the Bricklayer's Daughter." [TarRP] (26:2) Spr 87, p. 27-28.
5862. WHITE, Calvin
"Ralph." [AntigR] (71/72) Aut 87-Wint 88, p. 126-128.
5863. WHITE, Gail
"Miracles." [WindO] (48) Spr 87, p. 8.
"Miss Dickinson Goes to the Office." [Pig] (14) 87, p. 34.
5864. WHITE, J. P.
"The Black Cat of Hilltop Provence." [NoAmR] (272:1) Mr 87, p. 76.
"In Ecclesiastes I Read." [Poetry] (151:1/2) O-N 87, p. 191.
"On Mallarmé's Plan." [Agni] (24/25) 87, p. 277-278.
"Playing for the Pickerel One August Night." [Poetry] (150:5) Ag 87, p. 259.
"There Is a Prairie River" (for Tom McGrath). [AnotherCM] (17) 87, p. 137.
"To Confucius." [Poetry] (150:5) Ag 87, p. 257-258.
5865. WHITE, James L.
"For Those Who Are Horses Underneath." [JamesWR] (5:1) Fall 87, p. 13.
"An Ordinary Composure." [JamesWR] (5:1) Fall 87, p. 13.
5866. WHITE, Kathy M.
"Haiku" (2 poems). [WindO] (49) Fall 87, p. 63.
5867. WHITE, Mary Jane
"Mileposts II" (tr. of Marina Tsvetaeva). [WillowS] (20) Spr 87, p. 7-30.
"Mileposts, Part 1" (To Anna Akhmatove, tr. of Marina Tsvetaeva). [AmerPoR]
(16:3) My-Je 87, p. 24-27.
5868. WHITE, Mike
"The Island." [NewEngR] (10:1) Aut 87, p. 21-24.
5869. WHITE, Mimi
"Indigo Bunting." [CrabCR] (4:3) Sum 87, p. 16.
5870. WHITE, Nancy
"Tongue." [Ploughs] (13:1) 87, p. 135.
"Walking Down Court Street." [Ploughs] (13:1) 87, p. 136-137.
"Winter." [Ploughs] (13:1) 87, p. 138.
5871. WHITE, Pat
"The Motel in Paxton." [CrescentR] (5:1) 87, p. 83.
5872. WHITE, Shelley
"The Healing." [Spirit] (8:2) 87, p. 163.
5873. WHITE, Steven (See also WHITE, Steven F. & WHITE, Steven L.)
"I Wouldn't Be Able to Tell the Story" (No Podria Contar la Historia, tr. of Walter
Hoefler). [Contact] (9:44/45/46) Fall-Wint 87, p. 28.
5874. WHITE, Steven F. (See also WHITE, Steven & WHITE, Steven L.)
"Tahirassawichi in Washington" (tr. of Ernesto Cardenal). [Spirit] (8:2) 87, p.
244-246.
5875. WHITE, Steven L. (See also WHITE, Steven & WHITE, Steven F.)
"Blind Panorama of New York" (tr. of Federico García Lorca, w. Greg Simon).
[ParisR] (29:104) Fall 87, p. 89-90.
"Dawn" (tr. of Federico García Lorca, w. Greg Simon). [ParisR] (29:104) Fall 87,
p. 93.
"Death" (To Luis de la Serna, tr. of Federico García Lorca, w. Greg Simon).
[ParisR] (29:104) Fall 87, p. 94.
"Living Sky" (tr. of Federico García Lorca, w. Greg Simon). [ParisR] (29:104) Fall
87, p. 91-92.
"Ode to Walt Whitman" (tr. of Federico García Lorca, w. Greg Simon). [ParisR]
(29:104) Fall 87, p. 95-99.
5876. WHITE, Terry
"Standing Dogwatch on the West Fork River, Clarksburg, Halloween." [Wind]
(17:61) 87, p. 49-50.
5877. WHITEBIRD, J.
"The Find." [CrossCur] (7:2) 87, p. 131.
5878. WHITEHEAD, James
"At the Roadhouse He Turns to His Wife with an Observation on Mortality, Then
Asks Her to Dance." [SouthernHR] (21:3) Sum 87, p. 253.
"He's Living Through the Subject of Abortion." [SouthernR] (23:2) Ap 87, p. 372.
"A Report — After They're Dead — By Someone Who Knew Both Bob and Sue . .
." [SouthernR] (23:2) Ap 87, p. 373-374.

5879. WHITEHEAD, Jeffrey
"The Blind." [ColEng] (49:3) Mr 87, p. 285-287.
"Division with Zero." [ColEng] (49:3) Mr 87, p. 281.
"Portrait of the Artist with *Objets Trouvés*." [PoetryNW] (28:4) Wint 87-88, p. 40.
"Stone Work." [Agni] (24/25) 87, p. 242.
"Twisted Child." [ColEng] (49:3) Mr 87, p. 284.
"Velcro Prayer Stone." [ColEng] (49:3) Mr 87, p. 282-284.
5880. WHITEHEAD, Thomas
"A Lunist and His Lunism." [Interim] (6:2) Fall 87, p. 21.
"Sing, Columnar Muse, of Me the Last in This Bin." [BelPoJ] (38:1) Fall 87, p. 5.
5881. WHITEMAN, Bruce
"The Invisible World Is in Decline" (Selection: Book IV, Part 5). [CapilR] (45) 87
[Ap 88], p. 56-65.
5882. WHITEMAN, Roberta Hill
"Storm Warning." [CharR] (13:1) Spr 87, p. 91.
5883. WHITING, Nathan
"Fashion Appreciation Session." [KanQ] (19:1/2) Wint-Spr 87, p. 315.
"Rats, America Is Moderate." [HangL] (50/51) 87, p. 201.
5884. WHITLOW, Carolyn Beard
"Black, I." [Callaloo] (10:3) Sum 87, p. 415.
"On Charlevoix: Detroit, 1961." [Callaloo] (10:3) Sum 87, p. 414.
5885. WHITMAN, Ruth
"Clara Schumann." [PraS] (61:1) Spr 87, p. 23.
"Fool's Thread." [AmerV] (8) Fall 87, p. 29.
"Losing a City." [PraS] (61:1) Spr 87, p. 22.
"Poetry Reading in Nazareth." [PraS] (61:1) Spr 87, p. 21-22.
"A Questionnaire." [TexasR] (7:3/4) 87, p. 162-163.
"The Testing of Hanna Senesh" (Selections). [Witness] (1:1) Spr 87, p. 45-57.
5886. WHITMAN, Walt
"A Clear Midnight." [Antaeus] (59) Aut 87, p. 21-22.
5887. WHITNEY, Jennifer
"The Dead at Timberline." [SpoonRQ] (12:2) Spr 87, p. 42.
5888. WHITTEMORE, Reed
"The Boy and the Wolf." [LightY] '87, c86, p. 54.
"The City Mouse and the Country Mouse." [LightY] '87, c86, p. 251-253.
"In Memory of an English Professor." [LightY] '87, c86, p. 224.
"The Mocking Bird and the Owl." [LightY] '87, c86, p. 102-104.
5889. WHITTINGTON, Janice D.
"Winter in a West Texas Town." [WritersF] (13) Fall 87, p. 148.
5890. WICKERS, Brian
"A Seashell from the Seychelles." [Atlantic] (260:2) Ag 87, p. 66.
5891. WIDE, Krishna Paldeva
"Apocalypse" (tr. of Ashok Vajpeyi). [Bomb] (18) Wint 87, p. 67.
"By Words Too" (tr. of Ashok Vajpeyi). [Bomb] (18) Wint 87, p. 67.
"For Guillevick and Genevieve" (tr. of Ashok Vajpeyi). [Bomb] (18) Wint 87, p.
66.
"In Bhilai" (tr. of Ashok Vajpeyi). [Bomb] (18) Wint 87, p. 66.
"A Prayer" (tr. of Ashok Vajpeyi). [Bomb] (18) Wint 87, p. 67.
5892. WIDEMAN, John
"For James Baldwin: (1924-87)." [MassR] (28:4) Wint 87, p. 560.
5893. WIDNER, Jill (Jill E.)
"Gunman." [HawaiiR] (21) Spr 87, p. 50.
"Las Horas de Verdad (The Hours of Truth)." The Best of [BambooR] [(31-32)] 86,
p. 108-109.
"The Lure." [HawaiiR] (20) Fall 86, c87, p. 86-87.
"Trembling." The Best of [BambooR] [(31-32)] 86, p. 110.
5894. WIEDER, Laurence
"A Song That Lies the Least to the Most." [Boulevard] (2:1/2) Spr 87, p. 195-198.
5895. WIEGNER, Kathleen
"The Bill Collector." [HangL] (50/51) 87, p. 209.
"Childhood's End" (for Christine). [HangL] (50/51) 87, p. 210.
"For Rosella, Who Says She Is Becoming Invisible." [HangL] (50/51) 87, p.
206-207.
"Two People." [HangL] (50/51) 87, p. 208.
5896. WIER, Dara
"Euthanasia." [MassR] (28:4) Wint 87, p. 698-700.

"Past Sorrow." [MassR] (28:4) Wint 87, p. 697-698.
"Rolando's Fissure." [DenQ] (22:1) Sum 87, p. 16-17.
5897. WIESELTIER, Leon
  "Robert Bly Quelling Riots in Miami." [NewRep] (197:9) 31 Ag 87, p. 38.
5898. WIGGINS, Jean
  "Grandma's Fern." [BallSUF] (28:4) Aut 87, p. 47.
5899. WIGHTMAN, Ludmilla Popova
  "I Doze off in the Tired Shade of an Afternoon" (tr. of Blaga Dimitrova, w. E. A.
    Socolow). [NewEngR] (9:4) Sum 87, p. 384.
5900. WIGINGTON, Nan
  "Billie's Roses." [PassN] (8:2) Sum 87, p. 21.
5901. WIGUTOW, Warren
  "An die Musik" (for Gerrit, after hearing the Concord String Quartet perform
    Beethoven's Op. 127). [Notus] (2:2) Fall 87, p. 45.
  "Old Ming Huang, What Fine Horses" (for E.P. at 100). [Notus] (2:2) Fall 87, p.
    46-47.
5902. WILBORN, William
  "On Seeing the 'Human Skeleton, Lateral View, in Crawing Posture' by Mr.
    Stubbs." [Thrpny] (31) Fall 87, p. 22.
5903. WILBUR, Richard
  "The Catch." [TexasR] (7:3/4) 87, p. 164-165.
  "Orchard Trees, January." [TexasR] (7:3/4) 87, p. 169.
  "Shad-Time." [TexasR] (7:3/4) 87, p. 166-167.
  "Trolling for Blues" (For John and Barbara). [Poetry] (151:1/2) O-N 87, p. 192.
  "Wyeth's Milk Cans." [TexasR] (7:3/4) 87, p. 168.
5904. WILD, Peter
  "Arden, Delaware." [MemphisSR] (8:1) Fall 87, p. 35-36.
  "Artichokes." [BellR] (10:1) Spr 87, p. 20.
  "Cauliflower." [BellR] (10:1) Spr 87, p. 22.
  "Celebration." [ColR] (NS 14:2) Fall-Wint 87, p. 51.
  "Circus People." [ColR] (NS 14:2) Fall-Wint 87, p. 52.
  "Duck Girl." [Colum] (12) 87, p. 19.
  "Famous Trumpet Players." [LaurelR] (21:1/2) Wint-Sum 87, p. 83.
  "Farmers." [Raccoon] (24/25) My 87, p. 250.
  "Father Flanagan." [Colum] (12) 87, p. 17-18.
  "Gold." [OhioR] (39) 87, p. 31.
  "Hungarian Folk Dances." [CharR] (13:2) Fall 87, p. 71.
  "Lascaux." [CharR] (13:2) Fall 87, p. 72.
  "Novitiates." [CharR] (13:2) Fall 87, p. 73.
  "Storms." [LaurelR] (21:1/2) Wint-Sum 87, p. 84.
  "Train Wreck" (The Greensboro Review Literary Award, Honorable Mention).
    [GreensboroR] (41) Wint 86-87, p. 47.
  "Trimming Trees." [KanQ] (19:3) Sum 87, p. 124.
  "Turnips." [BellR] (10:1) Spr 87, p. 21.
  "Walnuts." [BellR] (10:1) Spr 87, p. 23.
  "Wives." [CharR] (13:2) Fall 87, p. 71-72.
  "A Woman Offers a Man She Had Considered Brutish a Stick of Gum." [HiramPoR]
    (42) Spr-Sum 87, p. 39.
5905. WILDER, Rex
  "Snails." [BelPoJ] (38:2) Wint 87-88, p. 13.
5906. WILJER, Robert
  "Afterward." [Poetry] (150:1) Ap 87, p. 27.
  "Ice Storm" (for Elizabeth). [AmerS] (56:1) Wint 87, p. 99-100.
  "Quick Dip." [Poetry] (150:1) Ap 87, p. 26.
5907. WILKINSON, Claude
  "Jukehouse." [DekalbLAJ] (20:1/4) 87, p. 57.
5908. WILKINSON, Nicole
  "Free As the Sun Is Free." [LitR] (30:4) Sum 87, p. 571.
  "Some Tailors Seeking Wisdom." [CarolQ] (40:1) Fall 87, p. 54.
5909. WILL, Frederic
  "Blocknotes" (Selections: 2, 11, 10, 6). [PaintedB] (30) 87, p. 7-8.
5910. WILLARD, Nancy
  "Aquarium." [NewYorker] (63:31) 21 S 87, p. 108.
  "Charm of the Gold Road, the Silver Road, and the Hidden Road." [Caliban] (2) 87,
    p. 137.
  "The Feast of St. Tortoise." [Field] (37) Fall 87, p. 75.

"How Biddy Called Back Friday, Her Lost Pig." [Caliban] (2) 87, p. 137.
"How Biddy Put Her Shadow in Its Place." [Caliban] (2) 87, p. 136.
"Little Elegy with Books and Beasts" (In memory of Martin Provensen, 1916-1987).
    [NewYorker] (63:27) 24 Ag 87, p. 28.
"The Potato Picker." [NewYorker] (63:43) 14 D 87, p. 48.
5911. WILLEMS, S. F.
"Hans Is Locked in the House!" [SmPd] (24:3) Fall 87, p. 29.
"Shoes!" [SmPd] (24:3) Fall 87, p. 29.
5912. WILLEMSE, Hein
"Poem: The storm troopers are in the streets" (tr. by David Bunn and the author).
    [TriQ] (69) Spr-Sum 87, p. 180-181.
5913. WILLEY, Edward
"At Home." [LightY] '87, c86, p. 137.
5914. WILLIAMS, C. K.
"Altzheimer's: The Husband" (for Jean Mauger). [AmerPoR] (16:1) Ja-F 87, p. 23.
"Alzheimer's" (For Renée Mauger). [Atlantic] (259:4) Ap 87, p. 55.
"The Blackened River" (tr. of Adam Zagajewski, w. Renata Gorczynski). [ParisR]
    (29:105) Wint 87, p. 46.
"The Body." [Pequod] (23/24) 87, p. 126.
"Codeword" (tr. of Adam Zagajewski, w. Renata Gorczynski). [ParisR] (29:105)
    Wint 87, p. 50.
"The Color of Time." [CrossCur] (6:5) 87, p. 132-134.
"The Critic." [AmerPoR] (16:1) Ja-F 87, p. 23.
"Cruel" (for Joseph Czapski, tr. of Adam Zagajewski, w. Renata Gorczynski).
    [ParisR] (29:105) Wint 87, p. 47-48.
"Experience." [AmerPoR] (16:1) Ja-F 87, p. 23.
"Failure." [CrossCur] (6:5) 87, p. 146.
"Fast Food." [CrossCur] (6:5) 87, p. 153.
"Fat." [AmerPoR] (16:1) Ja-F 87, p. 24.
"A Fence. Chestnut Trees" (tr. of Adam Zagajewski, w. Renata Gorczynski).
    [ParisR] (29:105) Wint 87, p. 49.
"Fifteen" (for Jessie). [CrossCur] (6:5) 87, p. 154.
"Flight." [CrossCur] (6:5) 87, p. 139-141.
"From My Window." [CrossCur] (6:5) 87, p. 129-131.
"Gardens." [AmerPoR] (16:1) Ja-F 87, p. 25.
"Good Mother: Out." [AmerPoR] (16:1) Ja-F 87, p. 25.
"Good Mother: The Bus." [Pequod] (23/24) 87, p. 124.
"Good Mother: The Car." [Pequod] (23/24) 87, p. 124.
"Good Mother: Home." [Pequod] (23/24) 87, p. 123.
"Good Mother: The Metro." [Pequod] (23/24) 87, p. 125.
"Good Mother: The Plane." [Pequod] (23/24) 87, p. 125.
"Good Mother: The Street." [Pequod] (23/24) 87, p. 123.
"Greed." [AmerPoR] (16:1) Ja-F 87, p. 26.
"Halves." [CrossCur] (6:5) 87, p. 119.
"Herakles." [AmerPoR] (16:1) Ja-F 87, p. 26.
"Jews." [Pequod] (23/24) 87, p. 127.
"Keep It." [CrossCur] (6:5) 87, p. 122.
"The Lens." [AmerPoR] (16:1) Ja-F 87, p. 23.
"Like Little Birds." [CrossCur] (6:5) 87, p. 121.
"Love: Sight." [CrossCur] (6:5) 87, p. 151.
"Love: The Dance." [CrossCur] (6:5) 87, p. 152.
"Love: Wrath." [CrossCur] (6:5) 87, p. 149.
"The Lover." [Pequod] (23/24) 87, p. 128.
"Men." [CrossCur] (6:5) 87, p. 142.
"Midas." [CrossCur] (6:5) 87, p. 148.
"The Mistress." [Pequod] (23/24) 87, p. 128.
"Native Americans." [AmerPoR] (16:1) Ja-F 87, p. 25.
"Neglect." [CrossCur] (6:5) 87, p. 135-137.
"One Morning in Brooklyn." [CrossCur] (6:5) 87, p. 145.
"The Orchid." [AmerPoR] (16:1) Ja-F 87, p. 24.
"The Past." [CrossCur] (6:5) 87, p. 143.
"Peace." [AmerPoR] (16:1) Ja-F 87, p. 26.
"Penance." [CrossCur] (6:5) 87, p. 120.
"The Rabbit Fights for His Life, the Leopard Eats Lunch" (For Harvey Finkle).
    [CrossCur] (6:5) 87, p. 124-125.
"Reading: Early Sorrow." [AmerPoR] (16:1) Ja-F 87, p. 25.

"Reading: The Bus." [AmerPoR] (16:1) Ja-F 87, p. 24.
"Reading: The Cop." [AmerPoR] (16:1) Ja-F 87, p. 25.
"Reading: The Gym." [AmerPoR] (16:1) Ja-F 87, p. 24.
"Reading: The Subway." [AmerPoR] (16:1) Ja-F 87, p. 25.
"Resentment." [Pequod] (23/24) 87, p. 127.
"Rush Hour." [AmerPoR] (16:1) Ja-F 87, p. 26.
"Russia Comes Into Poland" (for Joseph Brodsky, tr. of Adam Zagajewski, w.
    Renata Gorczynski). [ParisR] (29:105) Wint 87, p. 52-53.
"Some of Us." [Pequod] (23/24) 87, p. 126.
"The Spirit the Triumph." [CrossCur] (6:5) 87, p. 123.
"Spit." [CrossCur] (6:5) 87, p. 126-128.
"Suicide: Anne" (for Anne Sexton). [Pequod] (23/24) 87, p. 130.
"Suicide: Elena." [Pequod] (23/24) 87, p. 129.
"Suicide: Ludie." [Pequod] (23/24) 87, p. 129.
"The Telephone." [CrossCur] (6:5) 87, p. 147.
"Two: Resurrections." [AmerPoR] (16:1) Ja-F 87, p. 24.
"Vehicle: Absence." [CrossCur] (6:5) 87, p. 155.
"Vehicle: Forgetting." [AmerPoR] (16:1) Ja-F 87, p. 26.
"Vehicle: Indolence." [AmerPoR] (16:1) Ja-F 87, p. 26.
"Vehicle: Insecurity." [CrossCur] (6:5) 87, p. 156.
"A Warm, Small Rain" (tr. of Adam Zagajewski, w. Renata Gorczynski). [ParisR]
    (29:105) Wint 87, p. 51.
"Work." [AmerPoR] (16:1) Ja-F 87, p. 24.
5915. WILLIAMS, Clive
    "Any Girl." [Bogg] (57) 87, p. 58.
5916. WILLIAMS, Daniel
    "Father's Lunch Box." [Outbr] (18/19) Fall 86-Spr 88, p. 53-54.
5917. WILLIAMS, David
    "Bush." [PassN] (8:1) Wint 87, p. 8.
    "In praise of the potato." [Atlantic] (259:3) Mr 87, p. 74.
    "Listening to Guy Dull Knife Sing." [MidwQ] (28:3) Spr 87, p. 363.
5918. WILLIAMS, Dawn
    "Two Opposite But Same Ends." [ChatR] (8:1) Fall 87, p. 105.
5919. WILLIAMS, Dennis
    "If" (for Duncan Robertson). [Spirit] (8:2) 87, p. 16.
5920. WILLIAMS, Diane
    "Conversation." [NewAW] (2) Fall 87, p. 113.
    "Unstuck." [NewAW] (2) Fall 87, p. 112.
5921. WILLIAMS, Jonathan
    "Twits Gits Moles Proles & Odd Sods of Dreary Little Sebber" (8 poems).
        [Conjunc] (10) 87, p. 269-276.
5922. WILLIAMS, Lenny
    "The Ostrich Lectures." [BlackALF] (21:4) Wint 87, p. 452.
5923. WILLIAMS, Mark
    "What the Neighbors Don't See." [Hudson] (39:4) Wint 87, p. 611-612.
5924. WILLIAMS, Merryn
    "Hound of the Baskervilles." [CrossCur] (7:3) 87, p. 119.
5925. WILLIAMS, Miller
    "My Wife Reads the Paper at Breakfast on the Birthday of the Scottish Poet."
        [LightY] '87, c86, p. 203.
    "On a Photograph of My Mother at Seventeen." [Boulevard] (2:1/2) Spr 87, p. 154.
    "When I Am Dead, My Dearest." [ChatR] (8:1) Fall 87, p. 67.
5926. WILLIAMS, Norman
    "The Birth of the Miraculous Child." [BostonR] (12:5) O 87, p. 15.
    "The Genius of Small-town America." [BostonR] (12:5) O 87, p. 15.
    "Giants of the Midwest." [BostonR] (12:5) O 87, p. 15.
    "Mrs. Nietfeldt Alone at Midnight." [BostonR] (12:5) O 87, p. 15.
    "Skonoke's Barber Chair." [BostonR] (12:5) O 87, p. 15.
    "Those Crabapples." [BostonR] (12:5) O 87, p. 15.
5927. WILLIAMS, William
    "A Trip to the Planetarium." [Gambit] (20) 86, p. 44.
5928. WILLIAMS, William Carlos
    "The Girl." [OhioR] (39) 87, p. 17-18.
    "Love Song." [Iowa] (17:3) Fall 87, p. 99.
    "The Red Wheelbarrow." [Iowa] (17:3) Fall 87, p. 93-94.
    "Spring and All" (part XVIII, "To Elsie). [Shen] (37:1) 87, p. 21-24.

"These." [Iowa] (17:3) Fall 87, p. 97-98.
5929. WILLIAMSON, Alan
"From an Airplane." [MissouriR] (10:2) 87, p. 168-169.
"The Muse of Distance." [ParisR] (29:103) Sum 87, p. 82-95.
"Recitation for the Dismantling of a Hydrogen Bomb." [AmerPoR] (16:6) N-D 87,
p. 42.
"Two People in Two Houses on a Hill." [AntR] (45:1) Wint 87, p. 73.
"Wires at Inspiration Point." [AntR] (45:1) Wint 87, p. 74.
5930. WILLIAMSON, Don T.
"Backing Up to Check the Gate." [BelPoJ] (37:3) Spr 87, p. 24.
5931. WILLITTS, Martin, Jr.
"Ma and Pa Kettle Meet Godzilla." [Pig] (14) 87, p. 86.
5932. WILLMOT, Rod
"Haiku" (5 poems). [CanLit] (113/114) Sum-Fall 87, p. 127.
5933. WILLMOTT, Glenn
"Other Echoes Inhabit the Dust." [Waves] (15:1/2) Fall 86, p. 86.
5934. WILLSON, Julie
"Buster Keaton." [Sonora] (12) Spr 87, p. 14.
"The Love-lost World." [Sonora] (12) Spr 87, p. 13.
"Points to Remember." [BlackWR] (13:2) Spr 87, p. 66.
5935. WILMARTH, Richard N.
"Burned." [SlipS] (7) 87, p. 41.
"November Saturday." [SlipS] (7) 87, p. 43.
"Paranoia." [SlipS] (7) 87, p. 43.
"Rene's Little Girl." [SlipS] (7) 87, p. 42.
5936. WILNER, Eleanor
"Bailing Out — A Poem for the 1970s." [Calyx] (10:2/3) Spr 87, p. 57.
"Going the Rounds" (for Dr. Janet Abrams). [Boulevard] (2:3) Fall 87, p. 110-112.
"The Last Man" (for Vivian). [Calyx] (10:2/3) Spr 87, p. 44-45.
5937. WILSON, Alan R.
"Counting to 100" (Selections: 43-46). [AntigR] (69/70) 87, p. 190-193.
"From Counting to 100." [CanLit] (115) Wint 87, p. 78-80.
5938. WILSON, D. H.
"Against Heaven" (tr. of Hans Georg Bulla, w. the author). [PoetL] (81:4) Wint
86-87, p. 250.
"Back in Cellars" (tr. of Hans Georg Bulla, w. the author). [PoetL] (81:4) Wint
86-87, p. 244.
"Back to Happiness" (tr. of Hans Georg Bulla, w. the author). [PoetL] (81:4) Wint
86-87, p. 249.
"Dog-Paddle" (tr. of Hans Georg Bulla, w. the author). [PoetL] (81:4) Wint 86-87,
p. 251.
"Father" (tr. of Hans Georg Bulla, w. the author). [PoetL] (81:4) Wint 86-87, p.
248.
"Father from the Tree" (tr. of Hans Georg Bulla, w. the author). [PoetL] (81:4) Wint
86-87, p. 247.
"Fresh Loam" (tr. of Hans Georg Bulla, w. the author). [PoetL] (81:4) Wint 86-87,
p. 248.
"From Dernekamp" (tr. of Hans Georg Bulla, w. the author). [PoetL] (81:4) Wint
86-87, p. 252.
"From the Shore" (tr. of Hans Georg Bulla, w. the author). [PoetL] (81:4) Wint
86-87, p. 249.
"Greetings to Rafael Alberti" (tr. of Hans Georg Bulla, w. the author). [PoetL]
(81:4) Wint 86-87, p. 246.
"Landscape with Feather" (tr. of Hans Georg Bulla, w. the author). [PoetL] (81:4)
Wint 86-87, p. 243.
"Late Ice" (tr. of Hans Georg Bulla, w. the author). [PoetL] (81:4) Wint 86-87, p.
244.
"Night Return" (tr. of Hans Georg Bulla, w. the author). [PoetL] (81:4) Wint 86-87,
p. 247.
"Night Train" (tr. of Hans Georg Bulla, w. the author). [PoetL] (81:4) Wint 86-87,
p. 245.
"The Old Man" (tr. of Hans Georg Bulla, w. the author). [PoetL] (81:4) Wint 86-87,
p. 246.
"Snowfall" (tr. of Hans Georg Bulla, w. the author). [PoetL] (81:4) Wint 86-87, p.
252.

"Through the Village" (tr. of Hans Georg Bulla, w. the author). [PoetL] (81:4) Wint 86-87, p. 243.
"Toads on the March" (tr. of Hans Georg Bulla, w. the author). [PoetL] (81:4) Wint 86-87, p. 245.
"Village End" (tr. of Hans Georg Bulla, w. the author). [PoetL] (81:4) Wint 86-87, p. 250.
"The Wicked Village" (tr. of Hans Georg Bulla, w. the author). [PoetL] (81:4) Wint 86-87, p. 251.
5939. WILSON, Graeme
"Hands" (tr. of Ono Tosaburo). [LitR] (31:1) Fall 87, p. 86.
"Images" (tr. of anonymous Japanese poem). [LitR] (31:1) Fall 87, p. 87.
"Light" (tr. of Yamamura Bocho). [LitR] (31:1) Fall 87, p. 87.
"The Power of Suggestion" (tr. of Miharu No Arisuke). [LitR] (31:1) Fall 87, p. 86.
5940. WILSON, Jason
"Mothers of the Plaza de Mayo" (tr. of Mario Satz). [Trans] (18) Spr 87, p. 126.
"Night Guest" (tr. of Rafael Felipe Otoriño). [Trans] (18) Spr 87, p. 185.
"Stairs" (tr. of Rafael Felipe Otoriño). [Trans] (18) Spr 87, p. 186.
"This Bitter Matter" (9 poems, tr. of Horacio Castillo). [Trans] (18) Spr 87, p. 90-94.
"W. H. Hudson (1841-1922)" (tr. of Mario Satz). [Trans] (18) Spr 87, p. 127.
5941. WILSON, Jeanne
"Camping Out." [Gambit] (20) 86, p. 91.
"Eleanor Roosevelt." [Gambit] (20) 86, p. 92.
5942. WILSON, Jill
"Allhollows Eve." [CentR] (31:3) Sum 87, p. 282-283.
5943. WILSON, John
"Not Hope But Delight" (1986 Winner, Eve of Saint Agnes Poetry Competition). [NegC] (7:1/2) 87, p. 117.
5944. WILSON, Joseph
"What There Is in Dark." [PaintedB] (30) 87, p. 79.
5945. WILSON, Rob
"Anita Sky." The Best of [BambooR] [(31-32)] 86, p. 111.
"Kogan." [BambooR] (33) Spr 87, p. 15.
"Soliloquy in Waikiki." [HawaiiR] (21) Spr 87, p. 48.
5946. WILSON, Robert
"Cleaning Shoreline." [WindO] (49) Fall 87, p. 40.
"Hunters and Gatherers." [WindO] (49) Fall 87, p. 40.
"Lost Farm in November." [WindO] (49) Fall 87, p. 41.
5947. WILSON, Robley, Jr.
"What You See." [Poetry] (151:1/2) O-N 87, p. 193.
5948. WILSON, Ruth
"Strike." [Waves] (14:4) Spr 86, p. 53.
5949. WILSON, Steve
"Bodhisattva." [LitR] (30:4) Sum 87, p. 615.
"Missive to Wallenberg." [Wind] (17:59) 87, p. 42.
5950. WILSON, William J.
"After a Painting by Renoir." [Writer] (99:3) Mr 86, p. 22.
5951. WINANS, A. D.
"Bar Room Scene, 1987." [Bogg] (58) 87, p. 37.
"Class Reunion" (1986 Honorable Mention, Eve of Saint Agnes Poetry Competition). [NegC] (7:1/2) 87, p. 141-142.
"Family Man." [Outbr] (18/19) Fall 86-Spr 88, p. 105.
"For Jack Micheline." [AlphaBS] (1) Je 87, p. 28.
"For Jackie." [YellowS] (23) Sum 87, p. 43.
"For Joyce." [Vis] (23) 87, p. 26.
"For the Young Turks of North Beach." [AlphaBS] (1) Je 87, p. 29-31.
"The Last Cowboy." [AlphaBS] (1) Je 87, p. 27.
"Politics." [Contact] (9:44/45/46) Fall-Wint 87, p. 63.
5952. WINBURN, Rae
"Mentor." [Bogg] (57) 87, p. 24.
5953. WINCH, Terence
"Betrayal." [HangL] (50/51) 87, p. 212.
"Night Court." [HangL] (50/51) 87, p. 211.
WINCKEL, Nance van
    See Van WINCKEL, Nance

5954. WIND, Chris
"Chryseis and Briseis." [AntigR] (69/70) 87, p. 38.
5955. WINDER, Barbara
"El Campo Santo." [NewL] (54:1) Fall 87, p. 116-117.
5956. WINDERL, Carl
"Refrigerator Parents." [SmPd] (24:2) Spr 87, p. 22.
5957. WINDO, Pam
"Down to the Marrow." [Writer] (99:1) Ja 86, p. 20.
5958. WINFIELD, William
"Murmur of Blue." [Colum] (12) 87, p. 106.
"Nuit Blanche." [Abraxas] (35/36) 87, p. 20.
"Vase." [Abraxas] (35/36) 87, p. 20.
"Voyages." [Colum] (12) 87, p. 107.
WING, Tek Lum
        See LUM, Wing Tek
5959. WINK, Johnny
"Susan Among the Mosquitoes." [Pig] (14) 87, p. 17.
5960. WINN, Howard
"Photograph of My Father Taken During World War I." [BallSUF] (28:4) Aut 87, p.
        43-44.
5961. WINTERS, Anne
"Pearl." [MissouriR] (10:2) 87, p. 174.
5962. WINWOOD, David
"Chickens." [FloridaR] (15:2) Fall-Wint 87, p. 92.
"Cows." [Pig] (14) 87, p. 51.
"Dive for Cover." [CrossCur] (6:4) 87, p. 147.
5963. WIRE, Gale
"Nervous Crickets, Furious Stars." [HiramPoR] (43) Fall-Wint 87-88, p. 16.
"Take Something." [HiramPoR] (43) Fall-Wint 87-88, p. 10.
5964. WIRSIG, Kirk
"I Remember." [AntigR] (69/70) 87, p. 54.
5965. WISEMAN, Christopher
"Beneath the Visiting Moon." [PraF] (8:2) Sum 87, p. 12.
"Still Fighting, Almost Down." [PraF] (8:2) Sum 87, p. 11-12.
5966. WITT, Harold
"American Lit." [Interim] (6:1) Spr 87, p. 9-10.
"The Anglophile." [Bogg] (58) 87, p. 12.
"Briefer Days." [CrossCur] (7:1) 87, p. 10.
"Dorothy Parker." [CharR] (13:2) Fall 87, p. 90.
"Heraclitan." [CrossCur] (7:1) 87, p. 9.
"Rip." [CharR] (13:2) Fall 87, p. 90.
"Sonnets." [WritersF] (13) Fall 87, p. 191.
5967. WITTE, John
"Anna." [OhioR] (39) 87, p. 111.
"Sparrows." [OhioR] (39) 87, p. 110.
"The War Effort." [PoetryNW] (28:3) Aut 87, p. 31-32.
5968. WITZSCHE, Margaret
"Survival Device." [CapilR] (45) 87 [Ap 88], p. 47.
"The white of the river." [CapilR] (45) 87 [Ap 88], p. 38.
5969. WIXON, Vincent A.
"Killing Roosters." [BellR] (10:2) Fall 87, p. 55.
5970. WOESSNER, Warren
"Master Locksmith." [Lips] (13) 87, p. 49.
"Mr. Comet." [Abraxas] (35/36) 87, p. 32-33.
"New York Saturday." [Lips] (13) 87, p. 48.
"The Tree on the Curve." [Raccoon] (24/25) My 87, p. 245.
"Walter Dexter 1868-1948." [Abraxas] (35/36) 87, p. 32.
5971. WOHLFELD, Valerie
"An Echo of Crows" (Selection: II. "The Black Bird's Golden House). [BlackWR]
        (13:2) Spr 87, p. 89-92.
"Songs for the Unborn." [Nimrod] (31:1) Fall-Wint 87, p. 71-76.
5972. WOJAHN, David
"After" (Hurricane Gloria). [PraS] (61:3) Fall 87, p. 73-74.
"Departures" (P.L., 1922-1985). [PoetryE] (23/24) Fall 87, p. 177.
"A Fifteenth Anniversary: John Berryman" (January, 1987). [Poetry] (151:1/2) O-N
        87, p. 194-195.

"Garry Owen" (Port Townsend: The Bluffs). [PraS] (61:3) Fall 87, p. 78-80.
"In Hiding" (After Franco's victory, Manuel Cortes spent 30 years in hiding in the attic of his home). [PraS] (61:3) Fall 87, p. 74-77.
"Riding the Empire Builder, 1948." [Poetry] (150:4) Jl 87, p. 240.
"Shroud." [NewEngR] (9:4) Sum 87, p. 451-452.
"Signs and Wonders." [PoetryE] (23/24) Fall 87, p. 175-176.
5973. WOLD, Norman H.
"Halsfjord" (1987 Ratner-Ferber-Poet Lore Honorable Mention). [PoetL] (82:2) Sum 87, p. 80.
5974. WOLF, Abby
"The History of the World: A Mixtec Version." [QW] (25) Spr 87, p. 140-144.
5975. WOLF, Michele
"The Keeper of Light." [Boulevard] (2:3) Fall 87, p. 80.
"Women at Thirty" (On a theme after Donald Justice). [GreenfR] (14:3/4) Sum-Fall 87, p. 153.
5976. WOLFE, Ellen
"Travelling." [KanQ] (19:1/2) Wint-Spr 87, p. 348-349.
5977. WOLFE, Murray
"Execution" (tr. of Itzik Manger). [WebR] (12:2) Fall 87, p. 9.
"To My Child" (tr. of Abraham Sutzkever). [WebR] (12:2) Fall 87, p. 8-9.
5978. WOLFF, Daniel
"Work Sonnets" (3 selections). [Agni] (24/25) 87, p. 203-205.
5979. WOLFF, Henry
"Words." [Shen] (37:4) 87, p. 14.
5980. WOLFF, Rebecca
"The Rich Own Us." [HangL] (50/51) 87, p. 214.
5981. WOLPER, Page Kerry
"Shining Shoes." [HarvardA] (122:1) N 87, p. 15.
WONG, May
See MAY, Wong
5982. WONG-MORRISON, Tamara
"Honomalino." [BambooR] (36) Fall 87, p. 82.
"Strange Scent" (Written 1978 — Hawaii's Bicentennial). The Best of [BambooR] [(31-32)] 86, p. 112.
"Volcano Morning, Before Breakfast." [BambooR] (36) Fall 87, p. 81.
5983. WONGAR, B.
"The Dry Country." [NewRena] (7:1, #21) Fall 87, p. 71.
"Poor Fellow Dingo." [NewRena] (7:1, #21) Fall 87, p. 70.
"Soul's Return" (to Sandy, the Dingo). [NewRena] (7:1, #21) Fall 87, p. 69.
5984. WOOD, Barbara Parker
"The Spring That I Wanted to Die." [FloridaR] (15:1) Spr-Sum 87, p. 121.
5985. WOOD, Clifford
"Tulip Child." [BelPoJ] (38:2) Wint 87-88, p. 34.
5986. WOOD, Peter
"Canada Gander." [PraS] (61:2) Sum 87, p. 23.
"House Finch." [PraS] (61:2) Sum 87, p. 23.
"Losing Ground." [PraS] (61:2) Sum 87, p. 24.
5987. WOOD, Sandra
"Wild Poppies" (after Claude Monet). [Gambit] (21) 87, p. 41.
5988. WOOD, Susan
"On Fire." [Poetry] (150:4) Jl 87, p. 201-202.
"Sunday Nights." [Poetry] (150:4) Jl 87, p. 200-201.
"Witness." [Spirit] (8:2) 87, p. 202-203.
5989. WOODBURY, Marjorie
"Thin Line." [PoetryE] (23/24) Fall 87, p. 142.
"To Paula Modersohn-Becker." [PoetryE] (23/24) Fall 87, p. 144-145.
"When I'm With You." [PoetryE] (23/24) Fall 87, p. 143.
5990. WOODFORD, Bruce P.
"Smoky Sundays." [Wind] (17:60) 87, p. 49-50.
5991. WOODLEY, Ken
"Broken Mirror." [HampSPR] Wint 86, p. 35.
"Waiting on the Fall-Out." [HampSPR] Wint 86, p. 34.
5992. WOODS, Christopher
"Country House by a River" (After Cezanne). [Puerto] (22:2) Spr 87, p. 28-29.
5993. WOODS, John
"The Hanging Wave." [SouthernPR] (27:1) Spr 87, p. 45.

"The Village Constable." [HawaiiR] (22) Fall 87, p. 62.
5994. WOODS, Phil
"The Sheep and the Pine Cone." [HighP] (2:3) Wint 87, p. 255-256.
5995. WOODS-SMITH, Sybil
"The Bruise." [CumbPR] (7:1) Fall 87, p. 76-77.
5996. WOODWARD, Ann
"1. I lean over the edge of the well" (tr. of Dona Rosu). [InterPR] (13:1) Spr 87, p. 66-67.
"3. My body prepared to endure fire and water" (tr. of Dona Rosu). [InterPR] (13:1) Spr 87, p. 68-69.
"9. I say I want to sleep the night through together" (tr. of Dona Rosu). [InterPR] (13:1) Spr 87, p. 68-69.
"10. My god, I ask you again" (tr. of Dona Rosu). [InterPR] (13:1) Spr 87, p. 70-71.
"17. Stars are too far, one from another" (tr. of Dona Rosu). [InterPR] (13:1) Spr 87, p. 70-71.
"18. Do you remember how, when I was little" (tr. of Dona Rosu). [InterPR] (13:1) Spr 87, p. 72-73.
5997. WOODWARD, Jeffrey
"A Breast in a Wood." [Poem] (58) N 87, p. 16-17.
"Odysseus." [Poem] (58) N 87, p. 15.
5998. WOODY, Elizabeth
"Hand into Stone." [GreenfR] (14:1/2) Wint-Spr, p. 29.
"Our Reverence and Difficult Return." [GreenfR] (14:1/2) Wint-Spr, p. 30-32.
"Speaking Hands." [GreenfR] (14:1/2) Wint-Spr, p. 27-28.
5999. WOON, Koon
"The Question I Want to Ask." [BellArk] (3:4) Jl-Ag 87, p. 3.
"Riddle." [BellArk] (3:4) Jl-Ag 87, p. 5.
6000. WORLEY, Jeff
"Biographical Note." [MidAR] (7:2) 87, p. 28.
"Connecting Flight." [Thrpny] (30) Sum 87, p. 16.
"Early Morning Fare." [MidAR] (7:2) 87, p. 29.
"For Gregory Moore." [BelPoJ] (37:3) Spr 87, p. 15-16.
"Hands." [PassN] (8:2) Sum 87, p. 9.
"Horoscope." [NoDaQ] (55:3) Sum 87, p. 88-89.
"Item Buried in 'Financial Times' Section." [WritersF] (13) Fall 87, p. 190-191.
"Separation." [PoetryNW] (28:3) Aut 87, p. 14-15.
"Spoons." [BelPoJ] (37:3) Spr 87, p. 16-19.
"Surprise Attacks" (for Linda). [WestB] (20) 87, p. 104-105.
"To the Long Distance Caller Who Keeps Hanging Up." [ThRiPo] (29/30) 87, p. 66.
"Winter Refusing to Leave Altoona" (for Kjell Meling). [LitR] (31:1) Fall 87, p. 34.
6001. WORLEY, Stella
"The Drought Is Here." [Bogg] (57) 87, p. 53.
6002. WORMHOUDT, Arthur
"Hair" (tr. of Amir Manjak Ibn Muhammad al-Yusufi). [Paint] (14:27) Spr 87, p. 39.
6003. WORMSER, Baron
"Adultery." [MichQR] (26:2) Spr 87, p. 350.
"American Poem of the Senior Citizenry." [Poetry] (151:1/2) O-N 87, p. 196-198.
"Dropping Acid at Aunt Bea and Uncle Harry's 40th Wedding Anniversary Celebration." [ParisR] (29:102) Spr 87, p. 198.
"Dropping Acid at Aunt Bea's." [Harp] (274:1647) Ag 87, p. 31.
"Embracing a Cloud: Rural Commune, 1971." [ParisR] (29:102) Spr 87, p. 196-197.
"Porno." [MichQR] (26:2) Spr 87, p. 349-350.
6004. WOROZBYT, Theodore, Jr.
"Carving." [QW] (25) Spr 87, p. 138-139.
"The Fifth Force." [SouthernPR] (27:2) Fall 87, p. 46-47.
6005. WORSHAM, Fabian
"Transition." [SouthernHR] (21:4) Fall 87, p. 354.
6006. WORTH, Jan
"Canning Beans." [PassN] (8:1) Wint 87, p. 16.
6007. WOZENCRAFT, Kimberly
"Give & Take." [Witness] (1:3) Fall 87, p. 95.

6008. WREGGITT, Andrew
    "The Lawn Bowlers." [Waves] (15:4) Spr 87, p. 45-46.
    "Twelve of My Own." [Waves] (15:4) Spr 87, p. 44-45.
6009. WRIGHT, A. J.
    "Snake Catcher." [Amelia] (4:3, issue 10) 87, p. 63.
6010. WRIGHT, C. D.
    "The Body's Temperature at Rest." [PennR] (3:2) Fall-Wint 87, p. 4-5.
    "Humidity." [Epoch] (36:3) 87-88, p. 195.
    "Kings' Daughters, Home for Unwed Mothers, 1948." [Raccoon] (24/25) My 87, p.
        273-275.
    "The Legend of Hell" (homage ot Barbara McClintock). [Field] (36) Spr 87, p.
        119-120.
    "Narrativity Scenes." [Epoch] (36:3) 87-88, p. 196-197.
    "One Summer." [ThRiPo] (29/30) 87, p. 65.
    "Personals." [Caliban] (2) 87, p. 75.
    "Remarks on Colour." [PennR] (3:2) Fall-Wint 87, p. 6-7.
6011. WRIGHT, Carolyne
    "After We Received the News of the 100-Mile Wind." [LitR] (31:1) Fall 87, p. 64.
    "Afternoon Story" (tr. of Jorge Teillier). [SenR] (17:2) 87, p. 21.
    "Another Song" (tr. of Jorge Teillier). [AmerPoR] (16:2) Mr-Ap 87, p. 42.
    "Aperitif" (tr. of Jorge Teillier). [Iowa] (17:2) Spr-Sum 87, p. 72.
    "Bridge in the South" (tr. of Jorge Teillier). [SenR] (17:2) 87, p. 22.
    "Commission" (tr. of Rosario Castellanos). [AmerPoR] (16:2) Mr-Ap 87, p. 41.
    "Dark Lantern" (tr. of Jorge Teillier). [AmerPoR] (16:2) Mr-Ap 87, p. 42.
    "Eulene's *Broken Lifeline*." [WillowS] (19) Wint 87, p. 46-48.
    "Eulene's *Noche Oscura*." [WillowS] (19) Wint 87, p. 44-45.
    "Flowers in Winter" (Excerpt). [Nimrod] (31:1) Fall-Wint 87, p. 112.
    "Golden Age" (tr. of Jorge Teillier). [AmerPoR] (16:2) Mr-Ap 87, p. 42.
    "Image" (tr. of Jorge Teillier). [SenR] (17:2) 87, p. 23.
    "In Order to Talk to the Dead" (tr. of Jorge Teillier). [AmerPoR] (16:2) Mr-Ap 87, p.
        41.
    "Joy" (tr. of Jorge Teillier). [Iowa] (17:2) Spr-Sum 87, p. 71.
    "The Key" (tr. of Jorge Teillier). [Iowa] (17:2) Spr-Sum 87, p. 73.
    "Night Trains" (tr. of Jorge Teillier). [BlackWR] (13:2) Spr 87, p. 141-155.
    "Nobody's Died Yet in This House" (tr. of Jorge Teillier). [Iowa] (17:2) Spr-Sum
        87, p. 72-73.
    "An Ordinary Evening in New Orleans — Eulene's Significant Other Speaks."
        [WillowS] (19) Wint 87, p. 51-52.
    "So Long" (tr. of Jorge Teillier). [AmerPoR] (16:2) Mr-Ap 87, p. 42.
    "Spectre and Emanation at JFK." [WillowS] (19) Wint 87, p. 53-54.
    "Story of a Prodigal Son" (tr. of Jorge Tellier). [BlackWR] (13:2) Spr 87, p.
        135-139.
    "To a Child in a Tree" (tr. of Jorge Teillier). [SenR] (17:2) 87, p. 20.
    "When Everyone Goes Away" (tr. of Jorge Teillier). [Iowa] (17:2) Spr-Sum 87, p.
        74.
    "Woman, Money, Watch, Gun" (For Margaret Hasse). [PennR] (3:1) Spr-Sum 87,
        p. 66.
    "Woman, Money, Watch, Gun" (for Margaret Hasse). [WillowS] (19) Wint 87, p.
        49-50.
6012. WRIGHT, Charles
    "Ars Poetica." [TarRP] (26:2) Spr 87, p. 1-2.
    "December Journal." [ParisR] (29:104) Fall 87, p. 201-203.
    "Dog Creek Mainline." [TarRP] (26:2) Spr 87, p. 11-13.
    "From a Journal of the Year of the Ox." [NewYorker] (62:46) 5 Ja 87, p. 26-27.
    "Georg Trakl Journal." [WestHR] (41:4) Wint 87, p. 349-350.
    "Halflife / A commonplace Notebook." [Field] (36) Spr 87, p. 18-34.
    "A Journal of One Significant Landscape." [Field] (36) Spr 87, p. 12-17.
    "Language Journal." [ParisR] (29:104) Fall 87, p. 205-208.
    "Last Journal." [ParisR] (29:104) Fall 87, p. 209.
    "May Journal." [OntR] (27) Fall-Wint 87, p. 37-38.
    "The New Poem." [TarRP] (26:2) Spr 87, p. 1.
    "Primitive Journal." [ParisR] (29:104) Fall 87, p. 204.
    "Silent Journal." [ParisR] (29:104) Fall 87, p. 200.
    "To a Friend Who Wished Always to Be Alone" (William Martin, Dead in Georgia).
        [NowestR] (25:3) 87, p. 68.
    "Visiting Emily Dickinson." [NewYorker] (63:10) 27 Ap 87, p. 36.

6013. WRIGHT, Connie
"Floral Arrangements." [Waves] (15:1/2) Fall 86, p. 69.
6014. WRIGHT, Franz
"Duration." [ParisR] (29:103) Sum 87, p. 42.
"Entry in an Unknown Hand." [ParisR] (29:103) Sum 87, p. 43-44.
"North Country Entries." [ParisR] (29:103) Sum 87, p. 45.
6015. WRIGHT, Harold
"The Day Birds Vanished from the Sky" (tr. of Tanikawa Shuntaro). [LitR] (30:2)
Wint 87, p. 263.
"Seeing Off Kenneth Rexroth: The Tokyo American Center, July 8, 1975" (tr. of
Tanikawa Shuntaro). [LitR] (30:2) Wint 87, p. 263.
6016. WRIGHT, James
"Autumn Begins in Martins Ferry, Ohio." [Shen] (37:3) 87, p. 82-83.
"A Blessing." [Field] (36) Spr 87, p. 66.
6017. WRIGHT, K. Siobhan
"Mending." [CrabCR] (4:2) Spr 87, p. 14.
6018. WRIGHT, Nora D.
"This Photo Is Untouched." [PoetL] (82:1) Spr 87, p. 33-34.
6019. WRIGHT, Suzanne
"Dragonfly in a Jar." [Confr] (35/36) Spr-Fall 87, p. 208.
6020. WRIGLEY, Robert
"Burning the Black Locust." [NowestR] (25:2) 87, p. 9.
"Drills." [PoetryNW] (28:3) Aut 87, p. 44.
"For the Orchardist." [CharR] (13:2) Fall 87, p. 66.
"On the Way to the Dump." [PoetryNW] (28:3) Aut 87, p. 44-45.
"There." [PoetryNW] (28:3) Aut 87, p. 43-44.
"The Walking Man." [CharR] (13:2) Fall 87, p. 68.
"Welcome to Weiser" (after Dick Hugo). [CharR] (13:2) Fall 87, p. 67.
"Winter Love" (from the diary of D.D. Pye, 1871-1900). [CutB] (27/28) 87, p.
80-82.
6021. WURSTER, Michael
"The Documentarist." [Pig] (14) 87, p. 95.
"The O's." [GreenfR] (14:1/2) Wint-Spr, p. 112.
"Two Poems about Stones" ("The Theology of Stones," "Stones at Night"). [Pig]
(14) 87, p. 17.
WYK, Chris van
See Van WYK, Chris
6022. WYNAND, Derk
"Animal Kingdom." [MalR] (79) Je 87, p. 12.
"A Deal We Could Live With." [MalR] (81) D 87, p. 56-57.
"Earthquake." [MalR] (79) Je 87, p. 5-6.
"Engagement." [Dandel] (14:1) Spr-Sum 87, p. 20.
"Failing Words." [MalR] (79) Je 87, p. 8.
"Imprecise Moment." [Dandel] (14:1) Spr-Sum 87, p. 21.
"In December." [CanLit] (115) Wint 87, p. 126.
"In Estoril, and Not Only There." [Dandel] (14:1) Spr-Sum 87, p. 19.
"In the Gardens at Queluz." [MalR] (79) Je 87, p. 7.
"Old Town." [MalR] (79) Je 87, p. 9-10.
"One Arsonist, Two Firemen." [MalR] (79) Je 87, p. 14-15.
"One Version of Love." [MalR] (81) D 87, p. 60-61.
"Seascape with Donkey." [MalR] (81) D 87, p. 62-63.
"Some Lines in the Morning." [MalR] (79) Je 87, p. 13.
"Stormy Night." [MalR] (81) D 87, p. 58-59.
"Vital Distractions." [CanLit] (115) Wint 87, p. 47.
"When I Grew Up." [MalR] (79) Je 87, p. 16.
"Widow." [MalR] (79) Je 87, p. 11.
XUELIANG, Chen
See CHEN, Xueliang
6023. YALIM, Özcan
"Istanbul" (tr. of Cahit Külebi, w. Dionis Coffin Riggs and William A. Fielder).
[StoneC] (15:1/2) Fall-Wint 87-88, p. 36-37.
"Those Women" (tr. by Talat Sait Halman). [Trans] (19) Fall 87, p. 111.
6024. YAMADA, Leona
"Fourth Grade." [HawaiiR] (21) Spr 87, p. 38.
"Grandfather." [BambooR] (33) Spr 87, p. 52.

"Mother and Daughter Summer: Maple Leaves Brought to Hawaii." [HawaiiR] (22) Fall 87, p. 20-21.
"Moving Day." [BambooR] (33) Spr 87, p. 51.
"Sister." [BambooR] (36) Fall 87, p. 35-36.
"Smoke Rings." [HawaiiR] (19) Spr 86, c87, p. 56.
"Stein." [HawaiiR] (21) Spr 87, p. 39.
"Stones in Winds: An Invitation to Dance." [BambooR] (33) Spr 87, p. 53.
6025. YAMAMOTO, Traise
"Clear Gray." [PoetryNW] (28:4) Wint 87-88, p. 5-7.
"The Inland House" (for Nils). [PoetryNW] (28:4) Wint 87-88, p. 8.
"Interval." [PoetryNW] (28:4) Wint 87-88, p. 5.
YAMAMURA, Bocho
    See BOCHO, Yamamura
YAMIN, Ibn-I
    See IBN-I-YAMIN
6026. YAMRUS, John
"I Always Get Defensive." [Bogg] (57) 87, p. 26.
6027. YANDELL, Ben
"At Midnight or Later." [WormR] (27:1, issue 105) 87, p. 32.
"Coupons." [WormR] (27:1, issue 105) 87, p. 31.
6028. YAÑEZ, Adriana
"Malva ay ambar." [InterPR] (13:1) Spr 87, p. 18.
"Mauve and amber" (tr. by Thomas Hoeksema and R. Enriquez). [InterPR] (13:1) Spr 87, p. 19.
6029. YAÑEZ, Mirta
"Contextos de Sor Juana Ines." [Cond] (14) 87, p. 214.
"Contexts of Sor Juana Ines." [Cond] (14) 87, p. 215.
"Generational Task." [Cond] (14) 87, p. 217.
"Quehacer Generacional." [Cond] (14) 87, p. 216.
6030. YARROW, J.
"Fish Story." [BellArk] (3:2) Mr-Ap 87, p. 18.
"Night Sounds." [CrabCR] (4:3) Sum 87, p. 15.
"The River's Lesson." [BellArk] (3:1) Ja-F 87, p. 10.
6031. YATES, Ross
"Spectres." [Writer] (99:9) S 86, p. 24.
6032. YAU, John
"The Case." [Sulfur] (19) Spr 87, p. 5.
"Choral Amphisbaena." [Sulfur] (19) Spr 87, p. 6-7.
"Ghengis Chan, Private Eye." [Sulfur] (19) Spr 87, p. 4.
YBARRA, Ricardo Means
    See MEANS-YBARRA, Ricardo
6033. YEATS, W. B. (William Butler)
"The Circus Animals' Desertion." [AntigR] (71/72) Aut 87-Wint 88, p. 63-64.
"The Lover Tells of the Rose in His Heart." [MassR] (28:3) Aut 87, in unpaged section ff. p. 524.
"Oil and Blood." [KanQ] (19:3) Sum 87, p. 180.
"The Second Coming." [Nimrod] (30:2) Spr-Sum 87, p. 31.
"To a Friend Whose Work Has Come to Nothing." [Antaeus] (59) Aut 87, p. 22.
6034. YENSER, Pamela
"The Art of Love." [Ascent] (12:2) 87, p. 25.
"A Dream of Deputations." [Ascent] (12:2) 87, p. 24-25.
6035. YERPE, Dale G.
"Neighbors." [CrossCur] (6:4) 87, p. 89.
6036. YESELSON, Ruth
"Amaryllis (II)." [FloridaR] (15:1) Spr-Sum 87, p. 50.
"Medea." [FloridaR] (15:1) Spr-Sum 87, p. 49.
6037. YOON, Wahn
"Perversion" (A Studied Misbreeding of Pervert's "La Cène"). [HarvardA] (120:2) Mr 87, p. 35.
6038. YORK, John
"Always in the Middle of Things." [GreensboroR] (39) Wint 85-86, p. 50.
"Johnny's Cosmology." [GreensboroR] (39) Wint 85-86, p. 3-4.
6039. YOSANO, Akiko
"Tangled Hair" (Selections: Two Waka, tr. by Laurel Rasplica Rodd). [Paint] (14:27) Spr 87, p. 41.

6040. YOSHIMASU, Gozo
"Osiris, the God of Stone" (tr. by Hiroaki Sato). [LitR] (30:2) Wint 87, p. 297-298.
6041. YOUNG, Al
"Jazz As Was." [RiverS] (23) 87, p. 72.
"The Moon Up Close in Winter by Telescope." [RiverS] (23) 87, p. 71.
"Moonlessness." [Sequoia] (30:3) Wint 87, p. 69.
"The October Variations." [Sequoia] (31:1) Centennial issue 87, p. 95-97.
6042. YOUNG, Anne
"Drowning." [Calyx] (10:2/3) Spr 87, p. 31.
6043. YOUNG, Carolyn
"The Road." [Footwork] 87, p. 31.
6044. YOUNG, Dean
"Aesthetics Late in the Century." [GeoR] (41:2) Sum 87, p. 360-361.
"Allowance." [PoetryE] (23/24) Fall 87, p. 127-128.
"The Breakers." [IndR] (11:1) Wint 87, p. 91-92.
"Chicken Little." [Iowa] (17:2) Spr-Sum 87, p. 123-124.
"Dissecting the Breast" (after the journal of Andreas Vesalius, Bologna, 1540).
[QW] (24) Wint 87, p. 86-87.
"Failures at 1010 East First" (for Roger Mitchell). [MSS] (5:3) 87, p. 156-157.
"Lace." [OhioR] (38) 87, p. 119.
"Not Now Those Little Goodbye Stories." [Iowa] (17:2) Spr-Sum 87, p. 122-123.
"Presentation to the King." [NoAmR] (272:2) Je 87, p. 5.
"Pulling Through." [OhioR] (38) 87, p. 120-121.
"Revive" (for David Wojahn). [IndR] (11:1) Wint 87, p. 93-94.
"The Save." [Crazy] (32) Spr 87, p. 24-25.
"Second Reception." [MSS] (5:3) 87, p. 157-158.
"Where Do We Come From? What Are We? Where Are We Going?" [Iowa] (17:2)
Spr-Sum 87, p. 124-125.
6045. YOUNG, Ellen Roberts
"Hard-earned Harvest." [Footwork] 87, p. 33.
6046. YOUNG, Gary
"Burning." [MissouriR] (10:1) 87, p. 167.
"Dawn at Las Gaviotas." [MissouriR] (10:1) 87, p. 168.
6047. YOUNG, Geoffrey
"Drive, It Said." [NewAW] (2) Fall 87, p. 79-83.
6048. YOUNG, Patricia
"Bath Water." [Event] (16:2) Sum 87, p. 7.
"Dinner Conversation." [AntigR] (68) Wint 87, p. 90-91.
"Indian Summer." [Event] (16:2) Sum 87, p. 10.
"No Hands." [Event] (16:2) Sum 87, p. 9.
"Sex Is." [Event] (16:2) Sum 87, p. 8-9.
6049. YOUNG, Ree
"Mad Bricey's Widow." [Pembroke] (19) 87, p. 134-135.
"That God Isn't Fair." [Vis] (25) 87, p. 22.
YOUNG, Robert de
See DeYOUNG, Robert
6050. YOUNG, Sandra
"Twelfth Night." [Wind] (17:61) 87, p. 51.
6051. YOUNG BEAR, Ray A.
"The Dream of Purple Birds in Marshall, Washington." [Caliban] (2) 87, p. 55.
"If the Word for Whale Is Right." [CharR] (13:2) Fall 87, p. 80-81.
"Quail and His Role in Agriculture." [WillowS] (20) Spr 87, p. 1-2.
6052. YOURIL, John A.
"Hieroglyph 43." [StoneC] (14:3/4) Spr-Sum 87, p. 19.
"An Inequivalence of the Times." [StoneC] (14:3/4) Spr-Sum 87, p. 19.
"Last Entry." [Wind] (17:61) 87, p. 31.
6053. YRAGUI, Yvonne
"The Clam." [KanQ] (19:1/2) Wint-Spr 87, p. 235.
"Late Night Writing." [InterPR] (13:2) Fall 87, p. 76-77.
"The Oyster." [KanQ] (19:1/2) Wint-Spr 87, p. 234.
"Remembering Nicaragua at a Photography Exhibit." [InterPR] (13:2) Fall 87, p.
75-76.
6054. YUAN, Mei
"Cold Night, Reading" (tr. by J. P. Seaton). [LitR] (31:1) Fall 87, p. 39.
"On a Painting" (tr. by J. P. Seaton). [LitR] (31:1) Fall 87, p. 39.

"Waning Years: Random Poems IV" (tr. by J. P. Seaton). [NegC] (7:1/2) 87, p. 253.
"Waning Years: Random Poems VI" (tr. by J. P. Seaton). [NegC] (7:1/2) 87, p. 251.
6055. YÜCE, Ali
"Paean to Flowers" (tr. by Talat Sait Halman). [Trans] (19) Fall 87, p. 112-113.
6056. YÜCEL, Can
"Just Like That" (tr. by Talat Sait Halman). [Trans] (19) Fall 87, p. 114.
6057. YURKIEVICH, Saúl
"Bettor" (tr. by Cola Franzen). [NewAW] (1) 87, p. 97-100.
"Crossing" (tr. by Cola Franzen). [NewOR] (14:1) Spr 87, p. 44.
"Donde" (from "Rimbomba," tr. by Cola Franzen). [Rampike] (5:3) 87, p. 40.
6058. YURMAN, R. (See also YURMAN, Rich)
"Marriage." [BelPoJ] (38:2) Wint 87-88, p. 2-3.
6059. YURMAN, Rich (See also YURMAN, R.)
"Boarding at 3 A.M." [Wind] (17:61) 87, p. 52.
"Fathering." [Wind] (17:61) 87, p. 52.
6060. ZACHARIN, Noah
"Zeno Black" (tr. by Laszlo Baransky, Istvan Eorsi, Anna Saghy and Bob Rosenthal). [Rampike] (5:3) 87, p. 70.
ZACHAROW, Tillye Boesche
See BOESCHE-ZACHAROW, Tillye
6061. ZAGAJEWSKI, Adam
"The Blackened River" (tr. by C. K. Williams and Renata Gorczynski). [ParisR] (29:105) Wint 87, p. 46.
"Codeword" (tr. by C. K. Williams and Renata Gorczynski). [ParisR] (29:105) Wint 87, p. 50.
"The Creation" (tr. by Robert Hass and Renata Gorczynski). [Antaeus] (58) Spr 87, p. 91-92.
"Cruel" (for Joseph Czapski, tr. by C. K. Williams and Renata Gorczynski). [ParisR] (29:105) Wint 87, p. 47-48.
"A Fence. Chestnut Trees" (tr. by C. K. Williams and Renata Gorczynski). [ParisR] (29:105) Wint 87, p. 49.
"The Lullaby" (tr. by Robert Hass and Renata Gorczynski). [Antaeus] (58) Spr 87, p. 93--94.
"Russia Comes Into Poland" (for Joseph Brodsky, tr. by C. K. Williams and Renata Gorczynski). [ParisR] (29:105) Wint 87, p. 52-53.
"A Warm, Small Rain" (tr. by C. K. Williams and Renata Gorczynski). [ParisR] (29:105) Wint 87, p. 51.
"Wind at Night" (tr. by Robert Hass and Renata Gorczynski). [Antaeus] (58) Spr 87, p. 92.
6062. ZAHNISER, Ed
"The Sacrifice of Memory." [LaurelR] (20:1/2) Sum 87, p. 47.
"Taking Stock of Feelings." [SouthernPR] (27:2) Fall 87, p. 66.
6063. ZANDER, William
"After Goya." [WritersF] (13) Fall 87, p. 194.
"Ancient Rhythms." [Wind] (17:61) 87, p. 54-55.
"Family." [Wind] (17:61) 87, p. 53-54.
6064. ZANES, John P.
"Bhuddist Meditation." [SoCaR] (20:1) Fall 87, p. 44.
6065. ZAPATA ACOSTA, Ramon
"Andanza por lo Bello." [Mairena] (9:23) 87, p. 127.
"Definicion." [Mairena] (9:23) 87, p. 130.
"Definida." [Mairena] (9:23) 87, p. 127.
"Desde Aqui." [Mairena] (9:23) 87, p. 129-130.
"En Poder de la Noche." [Mairena] (9:23) 87, p. 128-129.
6066. ZARENSKY, Hope F. T.
"Wild iris in the rain." [Amelia] (4:3, issue 10) 87, p. 49.
6067. ZARIN, Cynthia
"Saturn." [ParisR] (29:105) Wint 87, p. 104-105.
"Wildlife." [NewYorker] (63:3) 9 Mr 87, p. 74.
6068. ZARZYSKI, Paul
"Champagne on the M" (For Sara). [CutB] (27/28) 87, p. 41.
"Measuring." [Poetry] (149:5) F 87, p. 285-286.

6069. ZAVARSKY, Bill
"El Paso (Texas)" (tr. of Paul Morand, w. Ron Padgett). [NewAW] (1) 87, p. 36-37.
"Southern Pacific" (tr. of Paul Morand, w. Ron Padgett). [NewAW] (1) 87, p. 37-38.
6070. ZAVRIAN, Suzanne Ostro
"Early Memory." [RiverS] (22) 87, p. 86.
"Leaf-Turn." [RiverS] (22) 87, p. 85.
6071. ZAWADIWSKY, Christina
"Colliding Passions." [Abraxas] (35/36) 87, p. 19.
"Cow Poison." [CentralP] (11) Spr 87, p. 57.
"D-E-D Spells Dead." [Raccoon] (24/25) My 87, p. 86-87.
"The Fog Never Parts." [Raccoon] (24/25) My 87, p. 84-85.
"Kissing the Ring." [Raccoon] (24/25) My 87, p. 82-83.
"Knowledge and Misinformation." [Raccoon] (24/25) My 87, p. 79-80.
"Lucky Accidents." [Raccoon] (24/25) My 87, p. 77.
"Truth." [Raccoon] (24/25) My 87, p. 78.
"Words." [Raccoon] (24/25) My 87, p. 81.
6072. ZBOCH, Nancy
"The Figure." [Rampike] (5:3) 87, p. 65.
6073. ZDANYS, Jonas
"Freight Trains" (for my brothers). [StoneC] (14:3/4) Spr-Sum 87, p. 26.
"Freight Trains" (for my brothers. Winner of The Phillips Award, Spring/Summer 1987/88). [StoneC] (15:1/2) Fall-Wint 87-88, p. 2.
"Terra Incognita" (tr. of Henrikas Nagys). [StoneC] (14:3/4) Spr-Sum 87, p. 52-53.
"Touching the Moon." [Poem] (58) N 87, p. 38-39.
6074. ZEGERS, Kip
"A King of Ancient Egypt." [Shen] (37:4) 87, p. 19.
6075. ZEIDENSTEIN, Sondra
"The One Dream." [YellowS] (24) Aut 87, p. 35.
6076. ZEIDNER, Lisa
"Bach's Other Sixteen Children." [WestB] (20) 87, p. 64-65.
"A Bomb." [Poetry] (150:2) My 87, p. 101.
"Child's Moon." [NewRep] (196:14) 6 Ap 87, p. 40.
"The Collector's Fire." [Boulevard] (2:1/2) Spr 87, p. 129-134.
"Decisions, Decisions." [Shen] (37:4) 87, p. 38-39.
"Pothole." [ThRiPo] (29/30) 87, p. 69-70.
"Transvestite." [ThRiPo] (29/30) 87, p. 67-68.
6077. ZEIGER, David
"Homage to Twyla Tharp and Company." [WindO] (49) Fall 87, p. 3.
6078. ZEIGER, Gene
"One Way the Faithful Learn to Dance." [Agni] (24/25) 87, p. 70.
"Still Life" (for Lisa, age 22, who said, "They never told me it would be this way). [BellR] (10:2) Fall 87, p. 34.
"White Hearts." [GeoR] (41:3) Fall 87, p. 508.
6079. ZEIGER, L. L.
"Days Ex Machina: Appliances in a Minor Key." [Pig] (14) 87, p. 6.
"Envoi." [LightY] '87, c86, p. 198-199.
"Food Processor" (after Edna St. Vinent Millay). [LightY] '87, c86, p. 55.
"Misfortune's Darlings." [LightY] '87, c86, p. 167.
6080. ZELTZER, Joel
"The Dead of the Revolution" (tr. of Homero Aridjis). [Abraxas] (35/36) 87, p. 47.
"Death of a Wounded Child" (tr. of Antonio Machado). [Abraxas] (35/36) 87, p. 48.
"A Maiden's Lament on the Death of a Soldier" (tr. of Pablo Antonio Cuadro). [Abraxas] (35/36) 87, p. 49.
"Sierra" (tr. of Alfonsina Storni). [Amelia] (4:3, issue 10) 87, p. 81.
6081. ZEMAIDUK, Nick R.
"All the Peaks and Valleys." [Footwork] 87, p. 39.
"The Freemen." [Footwork] 87, p. 38-39.
"The Lean." [Footwork] 87, p. 39.
"Losing Teeth." [Outbr] (18/19) Fall 86-Spr 88, p. 151.
"On the Preservation of Roses." [Footwork] 87, p. 39-40.
"The Rest of Us" (only the chosen hears the trump — Pottawattomie legend). [InterPR] (13:2) Fall 87, p. 97.
"Roanoke" (c. 1587). [InterPR] (13:2) Fall 87, p. 98-99.
"The Wind Lashed Out." [PoeticJ] (17) 87, p. 6.

6082. ZENITH, Richard
"Another Sky" (tr. of Mario Benedetti). [PoetL] (81:3) Fall 86, p. 155.
"Antiode" (against so-called profound poetry, tr. of João Cabral de Melo Neto).
[PoetL] (81:4) Wint 86-87, p. 253-258.
"Banks & Cathedrals" (tr. of João Cabral de Melo Neto). [SenR] (17:2) 87, p. 18.
"The Bicycle." [NegC] (7:3/4) 87, p. 79.
"Cemetery in Pernambuco (Nossa Senhora da Luz)" (tr. of João Cabral de Melo
Neto). [SenR] (17:2) 87, p. 14.
"Cemetery in Pernambuco (São Lourenço de Mata)" (tr. of João Cabral de Melo
Neto). [SenR] (17:2) 87, p. 15.
"Encounter with a Poet" (tr. of João Cabral de Melo Neto). [PartR] (54:3) Sum 87,
p. 429-431.
"For the Book Fair" (tr. of João Cabral de Melo Neto). [SenR] (17:2) 87, p. 17.
"Horacio" (tr. of João Cabral de Melo Neto). [Trans] (19) Fall 87, p. 252.
"Legacy" (tr. of Alexandre O'Neill). [MassR] (28:4) Wint 87, p. 651.
"Love Is a Center" (tr. of Mario Benedetti). [PoetL] (81:3) Fall 86, p. 154.
"My Measure" (tr. of Ferreira Gullar). [AmerPoR] (16:5) S-O 87, p. 30.
"No Openings" (tr. of Ferreira Gullar). [CrossCur] (7:3) 87, p. 74-75.
"The Nothing That Is" (tr. of João Cabral de Melo Neto). [Trans] (19) Fall 87, p.
251.
"Renewed Homage to Marianne Moore" (tr. of João Cabral de Melo Neto). [Trans]
(19) Fall 87, p. 253.
"Sugar Cane Girl" (tr. of João Cabral de Melo Neto). [SenR] (17:2) 87, p. 16.
"To Maine." [PoetL] (82:4) Wint 87-88, p. 198.
"An Unoriginal Poem About Fear" (tr. of Alexandre O'Neill). [MassR] (28:4) Wint
87, p. 652-653.
"The Voice of the Canefield" (tr. of João Cabral de Melo Neto). [Atlantic] (259:2) F
87, p. 52.
"The Wind" (tr. of Ferreira Gullar). [AmerV] (8) Fall 87, p. 43-45.
6083. ZEPEDA, Rafael
"On Balance in Long Beach" (special section: 11 poems). [WormR] (27:1, issue
105) 87, p. 15-26.
6084. ZETTLEMOYER, Martha
"Chinese Water Torture." [GreensboroR] (43) Wint 87-88, p. 91.
ZHAO, Li Quing
See LI, Quing Zhao
6085. ZHAO, Y. H.
"Brother, I Am Here" (tr. of Shu Ting, w. Carolyn Kizer). [MichQR] (26:2) Spr 87,
p. 402-403.
"Missing" (tr. of Shu Ting, w. Carolyn Kizer). [Poetry] (149:5) F 87, p. 253.
"To the Oak" (tr. of Shu Ting, w. Carolyn Kizer). [Poetry] (149:5) F 87, p. 254.
6086. ZHDANOV, Ivan
"Such a night isn't chosen" (tr. by Katya Olmsted and John High). [FiveFR] (5) 87,
p. 68.
"The Walker" (tr. by John High). [FiveFR] (5) 87, p. 69.
6087. ZIENTEK, James
"John Doe's Father Died This A.M." [Witness] (1:3) Fall 87, p. 145.
6088. ZIEROTH, Dale
"Afternoon and Evening." [CanLit] (115) Wint 87, p. 124.
"All My Friends Have Sex I Know." [WestCR] (21:3) Wint 87, p. 29.
"Aphasia." [CanLit] (115) Wint 87, p. 122.
"Debbie's Piano." [WestCR] (21:3) Wint 87, p. 31.
"The Man with the Lawn Mower." [Margin] (1) Wint 86, p. 89-90.
"The Months of July & August." [WestCR] (21:3) Wint 87, p. 32-33.
"November Sun." [CanLit] (115) Wint 87, p. 105-106.
"On the Morning of My Wife's 39th." [WestCR] (21:3) Wint 87, p. 30.
"We're Sailing into Exception Bay." [Margin] (1) Wint 86, p. 91.
6089. ZILLES, Luke
"Outhouse." [SmPd] (24:1) Wint 87, p. 15.
6090. ZIMMER, Paul
"The Elements of Zimmer." [CharR] (13:1) Spr 87, p. 68-69.
"The Explanation." [ThRiPo] (29/30) 87, p. 72.
"The Flowering." [CharR] (13:1) Spr 87, p. 70.
"For L.C.Z., 1903-1986." [ThRiPo] (29/30) 87, p. 73.
"Winter." [ThRiPo] (29/30) 87, p. 71.
"Zimmer North." [PoetryNW] (28:1) Spr 87, p. 19.

"Zimmer on Zimmer on Zimmer." [CharR] (13:1) Spr 87, p. 71.
"Zimmer's Corner." [CharR] (13:1) Spr 87, p. 70-71.
6091. ZIMMERMAN, Jean
"The History of Sexuality." [Colum] (12) 87, p. 48.
"The Lost Poem." [Paint] (14:28) Aut 87, p. 14-15.
6092. ZIMMERMAN, Ken
"The Stream." [AntR] (45:3) Sum 87, p. 331.
6093. ZIMROTH, Evan
"She Wakes Up." [DenQ] (22:1) Sum 87, p. 51.
6094. ZINSSER, Anne
"Concerns." [Blueline] (7:2/3 [i.e. 8:2/3?]) 87, p. 71.
6095. ZIOLKOWSKI, Heidi
"Somewhere Beyond Good-Bye." [Electrum] (39) Fall-Wint 87, p. 46.
6096. ZIOLKOWSKI, Thad
"Inside the Wind." [Sulfur] (20) Fall 87, p. 85.
"Rules." [Sulfur] (20) Fall 87, p. 85.
6097. ZIPTER, Yvonne
"The Cupola." [Cond] (14) 87, p. 198.
"Structures." [Cond] (14) 87, p. 199.
6098. ZIVKOVIC, Peter D.
"The Ages of Thunder." [Wind] (17:61) 87, p. 56.
6099. ZLOTCHEW, Clark
"Nocturne" (tr. of Juan Ramón Jiménez, w. Dennis Maloney). [AmerPoR] (16:6)
N-D 87, p. 47.
"Smoke and Gold" (to Enrique and Amparo Granados, tr. of Juan Ramón Jiménez,
w. Dennis Maloney). [AmerPoR] (16:6) N-D 87, p. 47.
6100. ZOLLER, Ann L.
"Wings." [Phoenix] (7:1) 87, p. 15.
6101. ZUCKER, David
"Late November." [GreenfR] (14:3/4) Sum-Fall 87, p. 160.
"Ohio Towns." [GreenfR] (14:3/4) Sum-Fall 87, p. 161.
6102. ZUCKERMAN, Anne
"Telephone." [NewL] (53:3) Spr 87, p. 95.
ZUHAIR, Ka'b ibn
See IBN ZUHAIR, Ka'b
6103. ZUKOR-COHEN, Maree
"Letter to Albrigo" (Guatemala, 1980). [Vis] (23) 87, p. 6.
6104. ZULAUF, Sander
"For a Kid Alone in Succasunna." [Footwork] 87, p. 49.
"Separation in Succasunna." [Lips] (13) 87, p. 26.
6105. ZVIBLEMAN, Jana
"When She Is 18, of Whichever Moon." [Calyx] (10:2/3) Spr 87, p. 113.
6106. ZYCHLINSKA, Rajzel
"Someone Has Covered Up" (tr. by Aaron Kramer). [Vis] (25) 87, p. 24.
6107. ZYDEK, Fredrick
"29th Meditation: Things I've Said at My Papa's Grave" (for Bertha). [KanQ]
(19:1/2) Wint-Spr 87, p. 172-173.
"Body Language." [KanQ] (19:1/2) Wint-Spr 87, p. 173.
"Camping near Grove Lake" (for RCTT). [CumbPR] (7:1) Fall 87, p. 6.
"Pulmonary Explosions." [SpoonRQ] (12:2) Spr 87, p. 32.
"Scarecrow." [Amelia] (4:1/2, issue 9) 87, p. 56.
"Storm Warning." [Amelia] (4:1/2, issue 9) 87, p. 57.
"Touring the State Institution." [DekalbLAJ] (20:1/4) 87, p. 58.

Title Index

Titles are arranged alphanumerically, with numerals filed in numerical order before letters. Each title is followed by one or more author entry numbers, which refer to the numbered entries in the first part of the volume. Poems which were untitled are represented by first lines.

mands : 4299.
156. Jutting from my neck its dorsal fin :
4299.
174. And your black eyes again their night :
4299.
180. So rounded a season: the sky : 4299.
198- : 4008.
207. Motionless, covering what's in back :
4299.
212. Still gathering the moonlight : 4299.
215. I destroyed the bridge, this fog : 4299.
216. Trimmed for bank, for lift : 4299.
400-Yard Girls' Relay : 3072.
405 Scott Street : 3275.
629 West 173rd Street : 3855.
(914) 555-4144 : 4246.
1001 Nights : 5735.
The 1,002nd Night : 2116.
1100 People Are Said to Live Below Grand
Central Station : 4512.
1926 : 3590.
1928 : 3011, 3936.
1929: Y You Ask? : 307.
1930-32 : 382.
1930: Scenic Views : 4273, 5808.
1951 Mercury : 1250.
1955 : 5077.
1970 — Summer School : 2701.
1973 : 2444.
1975 : 2176.
1986, Legend of the Lamed-Vov : 5073.
2085 : 1962.
8287 : 434.
5000 Apply for 100 Jobs : 1253.
25,000 Women Pyramid : 2084.
161286 : 434.
A. J. M. Smith : 2857.
A Julia y a Mí : 1622.
A la ceniza vengo, dolorido : 3270.
A la Clairière et au Café : 2626.
A la Mujer Borrinqueña : 1622.
A la Perplejidad de un Difunto : 1892.
A la Primavera : 340.
A las Memorias del Marques de Bradomin :
1960.
A Mon Frère : 2626.
A Ramon Zapata Acosta : 3508.
A-reading Spicer : 1234.
A.S. : 1298, 5677.
A Teremtés Után : 4817.
A Terra e o Mar : 306.
A Ti Señor de Cielo y Tierra : 3270.
A Trois : 1755.
AA : 628.
Abandonada : 960.
An Abandoned Cemetery in Pocahontas
County, West Virginia : 4065.
Abandoned Farm, Hop Bottom, Pa : 552.
Abandoned Housewife : 2973.
Abandoned Mountain Farm : 2350, 3663.
Abandoned Slaughterhouse : 816.
Abandoned Vehicles / 2 : 5584.
The Abandoned World : 2940.

Abandonment : 4178, 4817, 4843.
The Abductors : 871.
Abel : 2573.
Abergavenny : 3006.
Abeyance Series : 5091.
Abhorrent Acts : 2703.
Abjections: A Suite : 3291.
The Ablution : 1509.
Abode : 3097.
Abortion : 31.
About Face : 3353.
About Lazarus : 569.
About Non-feeling : 2201.
Above a Bright Yellow Table Cloth : 4445.
Above the Scribbled Writing : 3796, 4097.
Above the World : 3205.
Abracadabra : 4749.
Abraham's Wife : 459.
Absence : 372, 1195, 2701.
Absence, VII : 3194, 3600, 5128.
The Absence of Day : 2961.
Absences : 3824.
The Absent : 938.
Absolute : 2752.
Absolute Love : 3119.
Absolute Zero in the Brain : 4354.
The Absolutes : 4766.
Abstract : 1080, 1230, 1636.
Abstract Barbie Doll Painting : 4789.
Abstract Expressionism : 2877.
Abstract Portrait : 4533.
El Abuelo : 2171.
Abuse of what I know to use : 1594.
Abyss : 376, 1699.
Accident : 330, 1460.
The Accident : 4245.
Accidents : 4245.
According to Leek : 4690.
The Accordion Player : 4779.
Accusation : 674.
The Achievements of Herrings : 1637.
Achill Island : 3553.
Acorns : 1846.
Acqua Arzente : 2392.
An Acre for Education : 2977.
Acreage and Distance : 167.
Across the Fence : 3582.
Across the Table : 4279.
Acrostic: gentle creatures such as these : 313.
Act IV: Jean Plays Solitaire : 4912.
Act IV, Sc. 1 : 2069.
Act Four, Scene One : 5235.
Act of Contrition : 2679.
An Act of Faith : 2768.
Acting : 2777.
Actors' Night : 63.
The Actress : 3210.
Acts : 821, 1035.
The Acts of a Poet : 4008.
Acts of Erasure, Acts of Acceptance : 3301.
Acts of Faith : 2246.
Acuity : 76.
The Ad Hoc Committee : 2352.

Blacktop : 4646.
Blanche's Dream : 622.
Blank Paper : 4274.
Blanketing Nature : 3952.
Blasfemias de Don Juan en los Infiernos :
    4183.
Blasphemy of Don Juan in the Flames of Hell
    : 3652, 4183.
Blazing Embers : 2864.
The Bleeding Heart : 2270.
Bless the Children Who Pass Away : 5471.
Bless You for Yesterday's Rolls : 3901.
Blessed Is the Fruit : 3258.
The Blessed Sacraments : 1232.
Blessing : 2998.
A Blessing : 6016.
The Blessing : 1228.
Blessings, They Find You : 4752.
The Blind : 5879.
A Blind Cat Black : 254, 3977.
Blind Indians : 135, 4241.
Blind Jazz : 2127.
Blind Panorama of New York : 1894, 5050,
    5875.
Blind Passenger : 558.
Blind-Street : 2628, 4178, 4843.
Blindman : 5713.
Blindness : 4714.
The Blinking Obelisk Picture Palace : 2580.
Bliss : 702.
Blizzard : 981.
Bloated with seas it never wanted : 4299.
The Block Print : 5671.
Blocknotes : 5909.
Blond : 52, 3977.
A Blond Bombshell : 1574.
Blood and Light : 4150.
Blood Loosens Its Strangle-Hold : 4505.
Blood Lurks Under All Words : 2219, 5370.
Blood of the Boboso: Last Tale of Power :
    1179, 4289.
Blood Wolf : 2285.
Bloody Memories: Kent State 1970 : 4451.
Bloody Pond, Shiloh : 5330.
Bloom : 2557.
The Bloom We Can Not See : 2065.
Bloomsday in Provincetown : 462.
Blossoms : 2089.
The Blow : 464, 593.
The Blow Given to Branwen : 2981.
Blow-Me-Down Etude : 483.
Blue : 4877.
Blue Autumn : 743.
Blue Blossoms : 3084.
The Blue Bowl : 2893.
Blue Claw : 3496.
Blue Elegy : 1819.
Blue-Eyed Boy : 4536.
The Blue Footprints : 3119.
Blue Galahad : 486.
Blue Gift in Winter : 4791.
Blue Heron : 5169.
Blue Heron Lake, New Mexico : 2559.

The Blue in Beets : 1862.
Blue Irises : 2281, 3587.
Blue Jay : 495.
Blue Monk : 280.
Blue Moon : 1677, 5044.
Blue Morning Glory : 4375.
Blue Mornings : 3761.
Blue Paint Causes Stains in Laboratory Rats :
    1996.
The Blue People : 1716, 1720.
Blue Poem : 2450.
Blue Raft : 3588.
Blue Shoes Downtown : 2931.
Blue Sky : 2923, 3152.
A Blue Sky : 4434.
Blue Smoke : 2578.
Blue Spruce : 1478.
Blue Studio : 3090.
Blue Table / Stay Cool : 840.
The Blue Vault : 506, 4792.
Blue Willow and Others : 5466.
Blue Window : 4633.
The Blue World : 584.
Blueberry Point : 3108.
Blueberrying : 5304.
The Bluebird : 2890.
The Bluebird Cafe : 1648.
Bluebird for My Garden : 458.
A Bluebird in the Rain : 5047.
Bluegrass Wasteland : 2575.
The Bluejay and the Mockingbird : 3976.
Bluejays in Summer : 3582.
Blueprint for a Scenario (1) : 961.
A Blues : 1396, 4143.
Blunderbuss! : 2232.
Board : 620, 2688.
Boarding at 3 A.M : 6059.
The Boat : 506, 3074, 4792.
Boats Out of Water : 836.
Bob Hosey Is Dead : 1286.
Bob Summers' Body : 5293.
Bobby-Pin Scratches : 3117.
The Bobcat Bounced : 4756.
Bochinche Bilingüe : 3125.
Bodhisattva : 5949.
Bodies of Water : 2711.
Bodies Subject to Its Action : 1192.
The Body : 5914.
Body and Soul : 36, 1348.
Body Craters : 1056.
The Body I Left When I Got Up This Morn-
    ing : 5466.
The Body Is a Country of Joy and of Pain :
    5074.
Body Language : 6107.
Body Light : 4566.
A Body of Love : 1740.
Body Parts : 4927.
Body perception thought of perceiving (half-
    thought : 2550.
The Body Talks : 3184.
The Body's Temperature at Rest : 6010.
Bodysurfer : 3185.

Country Cousins : 2165.
Country House by a River : 5992.
Country Music : 1090, 2005.
Country Night : 424, 953, 1721.
The Country of Here Below : 1114.
The Country Turns Inside Out : 733.
Coup de Grace : 3339.
Coup de Hache : 512.
A Couple of Trees : 3685.
Couple on the Pier : 3891.
Couple with a Wine Glass : 1715.
Coupons : 6027.
The Courage of Children : 1112.
The Courage of the People : 5616.
Courbet : 4738.
The Court Rests : 1679.
Courtesan : 462.
Courting the Black Widow : 3916.
Courting the Chatham Girls : 371.
Courtly : 5286.
Courtly Love : 1733.
Courtship : 5647.
The Cousin on Holiday : 5026.
Cover Me : 5694.
Covey : 488.
The Cow Poems : 4291.
Cow Poison : 6071.
The Cow Wars: A Homage : 3337.
Cowardice : 3048.
Cows : 5962.
Cows and Turtles : 2743, 4076.
A Cow's Life : 449.
Coyoacan : 2859.
Coyote Creek : 1460.
Coyote's Last Trick : 1749.
Cr fl ash : 2053.
Crab : 4099.
Crab-Boil : 1436.
Crab House : 5104.
Crabbing : 1386.
Crabbing for Blue Claws : 5624.
Crack Seed : 4343.
Cracking the Crab : 5499.
Cracks : 5749.
Craft : 109, 3197, 4945.
Crane : 4647.
The Crane : 1509.
Crawling through Caverns : 3582.
Crazy : 4259.
Crazy Horse Names His Daughter : 1024.
Creation : 4266, 5185, 5526.
The Creation : 2045, 2312, 6061.
Creativity : 2159, 2754, 3052.
The Creature Who Will Eat and Eat and Keep
     Eating Unitl His Life Ends : 2437.
Credo : 5151.
The Creek : 2164.
Creekbeds Are Dry Near Mobeetie : 1903.
The Cricket Sings : 4787.
The Crier : 5360.
Crime : 3371.
Crime Prevention Measures : 3587.
Crinan Canal : 2566.

The Cripple and the Secretary of State : 5532.
Crisis Center : 4008.
Criteria for Post-Interrogation Status : 167.
Critic : 5392.
The Critic : 5914.
The Critical Eye : 4672.
Cronicas : 908.
Crooked Lake, 1978 : 5251.
The Crop Duster : 1509.
Cropduster : 507.
Croquet : 2521.
A Cross : 1131, 5601.
The Cross : 506, 4792.
Cross Country : 1933.
Cross-Country : 5099.
Cross-Cultural Exchange : 3245.
Cross Words : 1093.
Crosscut Sawing : 5221.
Crossing : 1816, 6057.
The Crossing : 4907.
Crossing Gates : 1623.
Crossing Ka'u Desert : 2514.
Crossing the Bayonne Bridge : 5140.
Crossing the Border : 2713.
Crossing the Equator : 1703.
Crossings : 1160.
Crossroads Inn : 4768.
Crotchets : 3976.
The Crow : 3980.
The Crow Flies : 2701.
Crow Lesson : 4423.
The Crowd : 1296.
Crowd Scene : 1468.
Crowed Up : 3808.
Crown : 2516.
Crowned Head : 1963, 4516.
Crows : 52, 2219.
Crows As an Emissary of Fate : 5647.
Crows at Evening : 1494.
Crow's Nest : 4193.
Crow's Nests in Court Metres : 2743.
Crows on the Cornfield : 4028.
The Crucifixion of the Apostle Peter : 1338.
Crude Thinking : 4441.
Cruel : 2045, 5914, 6061.
Cruelty : 1427, 5831.
Cruelty. Don't talk to me about cruelty : 1024.
Cruise Missiles : 2197.
Cruising the A & W : 1328.
The Crumble-Brain Cafe : 2392.
Cry of a Heng T'ang Woman : 3222, 5665.
Crying in Early Infancy : 5576.
The Crying Woman : 4883.
A Crystal : 491.
Crystal Lake : 2261.
Crystallography : 1570.
Cualquiera Tiene Derecho : 4662.
Cuánto Te Amara : 795.
Un Cuarto Oscuro Blanco : 57.
Cubist Morning : 1300.
Cuckoo Death Chime : 949.
The Cuckoo of the Concrete : 2044, 2304.
Cuisin Art : 4988.

Families : 2005, 3505.
Family : 969, 970, 1094, 6063.
Family Album : 229, 5302.
The Family, Descending : 2389.
Family Discussion : 3946.
Family Dynamics : 5647.
The Family Eyes : 2295.
The Family Farm : 3589.
Family History : 701.
The Family in the Suburbs: A Situation
    Comedy : 994.
Family Jewels : 2363.
A Family Likeness : 470.
Family Man : 5951.
Family Matters : 1219.
Family Portrait : 39, 3818.
Family Practice : 2440.
The Family Rage : 484.
Family Reading : 467.
Family Reunion : 1673, 2530, 4688.
Family Reunion Near Grape Creek Church,
    Four Miles West of Murphy, N.C., 1880
    : 3590.
Family Tree : 1918, 4245.
The Family Trust : 1523.
Famous Michael : 5093.
The Famous Scene : 5335.
Famous Trumpet Players : 5904.
Fanatic : 4534.
Fang Death Solo : 4345.
Fanta-Scene : 390.
Fantasia : 294.
Fantasia for Rain & Guitar : 4889.
Fantasia, with John Locke : 3765.
Fantasiestücke 3. Ann Landers Comes to Me
    for Advice : 4897.
The Fantasy : 476.
Fantasy and Science Fiction : 1436.
Fantasy No. 1 : 1317.
Far Cry : 280.
Far Enough Down Any Road : 3492.
Far Far Away : 3729.
Faraway Music : 5216.
Farewell Performance : 3688.
A Farewell to English : 2294.
A Farewell to Good Reasons : 3951.
Farewell to My Student : 5206.
Farewells : 928, 2297.
Farm-aid, Champaign-Urbana, September,
    1985 : 1081.
The Farm Animals' Desertion : 1292.
The Farm at Auction : 3582.
Farm Children in the Grip of 1933 : 3578.
Farm for Sale : 4932.
Farm House : 5659.
Farmer Dying : 2566.
The Farmer Teaches His Daughter to Fish :
    2078.
Farmers : 5904.
A Farmstead with a Hayrick and Weirs Beside
    a Stream : 871.
The Farthest House : 868.
Fashion Appreciation Session : 5883.

Fast Approaching : 2772.
Fast-Driving Dream : 5653.
Fast Food : 5914.
Faster Than Vista : 2784.
Fat : 5914.
Fat Dad : 3644.
Fat Kenneth : 1900.
Fate, a Hindi Movie : 938.
Father : 750, 2892, 5938.
A Father : 5191.
Father, 4-F, 1941 : 286.
Father Broke It Up : 2621.
A Father Considers His Infant Son : 738.
Father Demo Square : 1070.
The Father Dream : 2092.
Father Fear : 4763.
Father Flanagan : 5904.
Father from the Tree : 750, 5938.
Father Ghost : 2842.
Father Lewis : 5441.
Father-Milk : 4854.
Father Surrogate : 4972.
Fatherhood : 2140.
Fathering : 6059.
Fathers and Sons : 1104, 4351, 4706.
Father's Day : 317, 3740.
Father's Dead Sister : 5668.
Father's Lunch Box : 5916.
A Father's Song : 2664.
The Fatigue of Objects : 3601.
The Fault : 3371.
Faun : 4691, 5130, 5680.
Faust : 3833.
Faust Among the Stars : 5386.
Faux Pas : 5233.
Fawn Hall Among the Antinomians : 3546.
Fear : 2560, 4499, 5798.
Fear for the Children : 2035.
Fear of Cancer : 2739.
Fear of Love : 5566.
The Fear of Love : 489.
Fear of Reading : 2938.
Fear of Trains : 5189.
The Fearful Eye of Little-God : 5730.
Feast : 943.
The Feast of St. Blaise : 4976.
The Feast of St. Tortoise : 5910.
Feather Duster : 2719.
The Feather-Duster Salesman : 3654.
The Feather G-Suit : 2613.
The Feather of the Crow : 5841.
Feathers : 289, 620, 2373, 2688.
February : 4631, 5553.
February 2 : 1673.
February 22 Light : 3238.
February Fog : 237.
February Man : 2136.
February Mirror : 4633.
February: the Swans, the Children : 5304.
Feedback : 1061.
Feeding Cattle at Night, Jan. 16 : 1050.
Feeding from the Earth : 3098.
Feeding Geese : 816.

Feel Nothing : 3861.
Feeling for Seatbels : 438.
The Feeling of Going On : 949.
Feeling Sorry for Yourself : 4274.
Felix Paul Greve : 4906.
Fellini : 3138.
Female Learning : 542.
The Fence : 2414, 5244.
A Fence. Chestnut Trees : 2045, 5914, 6061.
Fender Sitting : 1623.
Fenton River Breakdown : 5861.
Ferrara Unleavened : 5158.
The Ferris Wheel : 5646.
Ferry : 292.
Ferry Passing : 4702.
The Ferryboat : 1495.
The Ferryer : 4099.
Festival of the Weaving Maiden : 2433.
The Festive Head : 2392.
Fever : 582, 3768, 5620.
A Few Days in March : 3144.
Fiat Lux : 2544.
Fiction : 3952.
Fiction Class: Exercise One (with Credit to
    John Gardner) : 668.
The Fiddle : 2269.
Fiddle Time : 611.
Fiddler in the Surgery (Enloe Hospital, 1966)
    : 3407.
Fidelity : 3812.
Field : 3086.
Field Burning : 4763.
Field Guide to North American Birds : 1190.
Field of Water : 4948.
The Field Pansy : 996.
The Field Trip : 5700.
Field Trip to Fort Story : 3588.
Field Work : 971.
Fields : 688, 2948.
Fields III : 948.
Fields in Winter : 2035.
Fifteen : 5914.
A Fifteenth Anniversary: John Berryman :
    5972.
The Fifth Anniversary : 686.
The Fifth Bullet : 1112.
The Fifth Force : 6004.
Fifth Grade Band Concert : 1299.
The Fifth of July at Spirit Lake : 5341.
The Fight : 1399.
The Fight Between the Jaguar and the
    Anteater : 1715.
The Figure : 6072.
The Figured Wheel : 4368.
The Figures on the Frieze : 4551.
Fin de Siècle : 3296.
A Final Decree : 349.
Final Disquisition on the Giant Tube-Worm :
    2183.
Final Nightmare of the Future : 4488.
Final Supplication : 3048.
Finality : 4338.
Finally : 3690, 5823.

Finally It Is Morning : 3535.
Financial Differences : 2232.
Financial Note : 1587.
The Find : 5877.
Finding a Career : 5386.
Finding My Father's Hands in Mid-life :
    3582.
The Finding of Reasons : 3690.
Finding That the Past Is Like a Historical
    Character : 2905.
Finding the Future : 5039.
Finding the Lion : 4922.
A Fine Line : 3090.
Fine Lines : 4001.
The Fine Pale Wild Cloth of Love : 2119.
The Fine Prospect : 4500.
The Fingerprint Story : 3621.
Finis : 2885.
Finish Line : 3699.
Finnish Rhapsody : 216.
Finnish Variations : 2633.
Fir Forest : 4756.
Fire : 2337, 3237, 5283.
The Fire : 2469.
Fire Color : 542.
Fire for Fire : 3630.
Fire in bat guano : 5089.
The Fire in Our Neighbourhood : 582.
Fire in the Onion field : 773.
Fire Island : 3908.
Firecrackers at Christmas : 3839.
Firefighter : 2196.
Fireflies : 2445, 4606, 5108, 5498.
Firefly in the Pines : 5135.
Firefly Sestina : 5817.
Firemen's Picnic : 38.
Firenze from the 'Dickens View' : 237.
Firestarter : 4522.
Firewood : 1112.
The Fireworks Spires : 2734.
The Firing Squad : 1116.
First : 2219, 2814.
The First Backache : 1679.
First Born : 3671.
First Calf : 4272.
The First Cruise : 3031.
First Day, First Job : 749.
First Days at Bear Creek Ranch : 252.
First Dinner with His Mother : 1866.
First Draft : 5645.
The First Drink : 4914.
First Elegy : 3891.
First Frost : 5046.
First Gematria : 4724.
First Gentleman : 1074.
First Grandchild Remembers a Christmas
    Story : 2333.
First Ice : 4522.
The First Imperial Egg : 5039.
First Kiss : 1927.
First Light : 4306.
The First Line of a Poem : 3496.
First Love : 2046, 3323, 3880, 5087.

3927, 5007.
For Nana : 284.
For Nancy Bray and Gladys Mears, Elegy :
    3213.
For No Music : 1944.
For Nora Fitzgerald : 2310.
For Now : 1174.
For Pat, Who Wasn't Home : 2314.
For Regina, Put Off : 3031.
For Robt. Creeley : 486.
For Rosella, Who Says She Is Becoming
    Invisible : 5895.
For Ruby, In Memoriam : 2736.
For Russ : 5209.
For Ruth : 1604.
For Sho the New Head Priest of Erin-ji :
    3690, 3927, 5007.
For Spicer : 409.
For Stanley Kunitz : 2606.
For Stuart Porter, Who Asked for a Poem
    That Would Not Depress Him Further :
    5075.
For Teresa : 4169.
For the American Dead : 642.
For the Angel of Memory, in Her Sickness
    and in Her Grief : 642.
For the Bayman : 178.
For the Book Fair : 3984, 6082.
For the Bricklayer's Daughter : 5861.
For the Christening of Aaron Sjørn
    Ziolkowksi, June 20, 1986 : 3276.
For the Dreamer Who Makes Nothing of
    Dreams : 229.
For the Duration : 708.
For the End of the World : 4210.
For the first Four Months : 5803.
For the Fishermen : 2551.
For the Kids Who Kill Themselves Because
    of Braces : 4151.
For the Luggage Room : 5357.
For the New World : 2441.
For the Orchardist : 6020.
For the Piano Tuner : 629.
For the Record : 5573.
For the Russian Astronaut, Valentina Ter-
    eshkova : 2216.
For the South : 629.
For the Young Turks of North Beach : 5951.
For the Young Vine Maples : 5713.
For This : 1235.
For This World and Dreams : 2664.
For Those Who Are Horses Underneath :
    5865.
For Tim Sutcliffe (1914-1986), Headmaster,
    Clifton Preparatory School, Durban :
    4775.
For Two to Fly Together in the Sky : 950,
    1957, 2598.
For Want of a Male the Shoe Was Lost :
    3584.
For Whoever Drops By at The Mai Kai, The
    Derby or Pete's : 1917.
(For William Cook, Drowned in Maine, and

for Roy Huss, Lost in Indonesia) : 4404.
For Working Fifty Years on the B&O,
    Grandfather Receives a Watch : 994.
Forbidden Sea : 1384, 3607, 4408.
The Force of His Sadness : 3458.
Forced Marches : 3722.
Foreboding : 1967.
Foreclosure : 2975.
Foreign Airport : 5439.
Foreign Territory : 258.
Foreigner : 592.
Foreman Fired Joe : 1253.
Foreplay : 1754.
Forerunners : 118.
Forest : 2062.
The Forest : 183.
The Forest in Our Minds : 4307.
Forest Service : 3252.
Forge Fields : 4787.
Forget Him : 2631.
Forget Horses : 791.
Forgetful Lazarus : 4135.
Forgetting : 280.
Forgetting the Lake : 3122.
Forging a Passport : 5233.
Forgive, Forgive : 4127.
Forgive Me, But This Is Just a Smear of
    Purple : 3020.
Forgiveness : 897, 5149.
Forgotten Sex : 216.
Forgotten Shared Jar : 2033, 3973.
Fork for Knife : 1193.
Fork It Over : 4364.
A Form/ Of Taking/ It All : 5723.
The Formal Pond : 1482.
Forms of Grief : 5058.
Forse : 1347.
Forsythia : 3675.
Fort Michilimacinac from a Modern Promon-
    tory : 1480.
Fort Sill Internment Camp : 3940, 3941, 4175.
Fortuna's Wheel : 1382.
Fortunate Fault : 3559.
The Fortunate Summer : 1135.
Forty-Eight Hours : 620, 2688.
Forty-One Line Poem : 3402.
Fossils : 392.
Le Fou : 1180.
Found : 1691, 5629.
Found Poem : 3976.
Found Poem: Explanation for the Present :
    1427.
Found Synthetic Adventure Clues : 532.
Foundations : 4557.
Foundations of Cages : 3362.
Fountains Move : 4342.
The Fountains of Serbia : 1131, 1477, 5752.
Four A.M. at the Mt. Joy Rest Stop : 1927.
Four Angers : 2193.
Four Christmas Love Songs : 3821.
Four Corners : 3588.
The Four Cradles : 605, 2113, 5407.
Four Elegies : 2848.

From Mr. Bowles' Diary : 4885.
From My Window : 5914.
From Nicaragua, with Love: Poems 1979-
    1986 : 851, 1045.
From Parlor to Porch : 2458.
From Prague : 367.
From Somewhere to the Left of You : 2747.
From Tekonwatonti / Molly Brant (1735-
    1795): Poems of War : 2888.
From the Amazon : 4939.
From the Back of the Bus : 4431.
From 'The Ballad of Geordie' : 1116.
From the Bank : 2877.
From the 'Capitol Limited' : 3031.
From the Catwalk : 4949.
From the Cave : 3308.
From the Continued *Narration of My Life* :
    1127.
From the Depths of This Night : 2351, 3663.
From the fire : 2467, 4183.
From the Fisherman I Learn : 755.
From the Hymn to Persephone : 192.
From the Image-Flow — Death of Chausson,
    1899 : 3195.
From the Irish : 5048.
From the Manifesto of the Selfish : 1486.
From the Mouths of Boobs : 3276.
From the Poem of Houses : 782.
From the Poet, Making Time : 3865.
From the Poetry Exchange, Two Conversa-
    tions : 3976.
From the Program : 418, 1835.
From the Republic of Conscience : 2343.
From the Same Cloth : 3758.
From the Shore : 750, 5938.
From the Song Book of the Russian Army,
    1937 edition : 1684.
From the Summer : 3241, 4303.
From the Tower : 4216.
From the Way I Live Now : 4045.
From This 5th Floor Office Window : 4383.
Frontenac : 4003.
Frontier : 4877.
Frontier Dream : 3543.
The Frontier Languages : 2015.
The Frontier of Rage : 5564.
Frost : 216.
Frosty Bees : 5352.
A Froward Broadside : 3731.
The Frozen Quarries : 2227.
Fruit : 2307.
Fruit Cellar : 4304.
The Fruit of Goodly Trees : 4559.
Fruit of the Tree : 4245.
The *Fruition* of Berneray, Hebrides : 381.
Fruitless Retreat : 263, 4891.
Fruits & Vegetables : 1396.
Fuck 'em County : 1311.
Fuel : 2062.
Fuga : 1132.
The Fugitive : 2867, 3772.
Fugitive Blue : 2983.
Fuji-san becomes Mount Sopris : 1711.

Full-Bodied : 3441.
Full Circle : 2115, 2482, 5296.
A Full Hand : 5828.
Full Measure : 669.
Full Moon: Ceremony : 4780.
Full Moon Man : 1063.
Full Mooning : 2707.
Full Wind : 4273, 5032.
Full Worm Moon : 2484.
The Fully-Clothed Excess Generator (World
    Version) : 4441.
Fun : 1506.
Fundamentalist Funeral : 4875.
Funeral : 4339.
A Funeral : 181, 607.
The Funeral : 574, 3715.
Funeral Parlor Flowers : 412.
Funerary : 4270.
Funny How Things Go On : 3493.
The Funny Looking Biscuit : 604.
Funny Man : 749.
Furrows : 2407.
Further Escapes of the Poet at 9 : 4738.
Furtively and Subliminally Aware of Each
    Other : 5410.
Fury of Rain : 2261.
Futility Sestina: Getting Housing in Kano,
    Nigeria : 517.
Futura Pleza de Museo : 4449.
The Future : 5179.
The Future of Potatoes : 5805.
Futureworld : 3629.
Futurist Exhibit : 270.
Gabrielle Didot : 2505, 2833.
Gagaku : 4594.
Gagaku: Demons behind the wheel : 4594.
Gagaku, in Kyoto and After : 1155.
Gagaku: It's woman's dream to be Queen :
    4594.
Gagaku: Maybe I've exorcised all of 'em :
    4594.
Gagaku: Middle of May 87 : 4594.
Gagaku: Now they walk somewhat strut in a
    circle : 4594.
Gagaku: Schopenhauer : 4594.
Gagaku: The correct way for me to create :
    4594.
Gagaku: Their eyes enlarge : 4594.
Gagaku: They come forward : 4594.
Gaia : 4756.
Galang : 5521.
Gallery : 630.
The Gallery : 688.
Gallery Notes : 3165.
The Gallery of Plato Hall : 2551.
Galleynipper : 888.
The Game : 304.
Game Near Ocotal : 1338.
Game of Chance : 471, 4080.
The Game Was : 3819.
Games : 3582.
Ganges : 2829.
Gaps : 2513.

The glance is a lovely pretext of the eye's :
    2782, 3690.
Glass : 2817.
The Glass Blower : 380.
The Glass Cutter : 3684.
The Glass Flowers of the Blashkas : 2799.
Glass Fruit : 2278.
Glass House : 3393.
Glass Houses : 1799.
The Glass King : 582.
The Glass Wishes : 2707.
The Gleaning : 4090.
Glimpsed Through the Window of the Paris
    Express : 3150.
Gloopy and Blit : 1691.
The Gloria : 1572, 3846, 4268.
Gloryland : 2077.
A Gloss Upon King Lear : 3388.
Glossolalia : 187.
Glow of Sunrise : 2351, 3663.
Glyph : 1759.
Gnostics on Trial : 2119.
Go Fish : 4897.
Go Get Some Bread : 2171, 3982.
Go-Go Girl Reunion : 5114.
Goal : 682.
The Goat : 4833.
The Goat-Man : 4260.
Goats : 967.
God : 2558, 4856.
God and New Clothes : 1504.
God has no authority : 1129.
The God in Winter: A Lecture : 2418.
God Is a Dishwater Blonde : 4966.
God Made Chickens and Children : 1183.
God Most High : 2932.
The Godchild : 4148.
Goddesses : 4923.
Godfather I : 1400.
The Godmother : 5846.
The Gods : 1722, 5046.
The Gods of Winter : 1980.
God's Revenge : 4756.
God's Tumbler : 4606.
Gogol: Five Portraits : 3056.
Going : 2961.
Going Away Present : 1451.
Going Back : 242, 3629.
Going Bald : 1348.
Going Downtown to Draw Up Our Will : 994.
Going Home : 4226.
Going Home for the High School Reunion:
    The Class of '45 : 3581.
Going in for Tests : 5787.
Going On : 749.
Going Past Rapple : 3238.
Going Places : 5320.
Going the Distance : 2970.
Going the Rounds : 5936.
Going Through Reams : 3240.
Going to America : 1624.
Going to Bed : 1286.
Going to the Ocean : 2485.

Golan : 3628.
Gold : 4239, 5193, 5904.
Gold Tooth : 1962.
The Goldberg Variations : 1196.
Golden Age : 5463, 6011.
The Golden Boys : 1044.
The Golden Fleece : 2900, 2999, 4129.
Golden Valley : 541.
The Goldfish : 2092.
Gone : 977.
Gone Missing : 4504.
Gone to Ground : 161.
The Good : 1183.
Good As Dad : 183.
Good-By and Keep Cold : 1116.
Good Cheer : 5081.
Good for Nothing : 5186.
Good Friday : 239, 5307.
Good Love Poetry : 3370.
Good Luck with the Syrtes: A Tunisian
    Propemptikon : 2097.
Good Morning America : 1681.
Good Mother: Home : 5914.
Good Mother: Out : 5914.
Good Mother: The Bus : 5914.
Good Mother: The Car : 5914.
Good Mother: The Metro : 5914.
Good Mother: The Plane : 5914.
Good Mother: The Street : 5914.
Good News : 5700.
Good Night, My Love : 4243.
Good Night, October : 2436.
Good Old Southern Boy : 1765.
Good Poems : 1968.
Good Taste : 4571.
The Good Time Is Now : 957.
The Good Victim : 4547.
The Good World : 5716.
Goodbye : 4193.
The Goodbye Look : 861.
Goodbye, Göteborg : 5630.
Goodness : 2482.
Goodnight : 3203, 5653.
Goodnight Ladies : 4313.
Goodwill : 1450.
The Gospel According to Walter : 3446.
The Gossamer Ending : 4461.
Gossamer Strangers : 4791.
Gossipy Poem: Honolulu, 1/29/87 : 4522.
The Gothic Cathedral At Bourges : 1116.
Le Gouffre : 376.
Gourds : 2035.
Gove County, Kansas : 4194.
Governors and Priests : 1332.
The Governor's Office : 1440.
Grace : 1016, 1506, 3202, 3685, 3688, 4145.
A Grace : 5075.
The Grad Student : 1213.
Grading the Pale Boy's Paper : 5767.
The Graduate of Harvard University, One-
    onta, N.Y : 918.
Graduation Gift (I'd Like to Give to You) :
    3131.

Graduation Picture : 3880.
Gramercy Park : 13.
The Grand Hotel 'Magie de la Lune' : 3317.
Grand Mogul Bus Tours : 4897.
Grandfather : 2254, 4008, 6024.
The Grandfather : 2171, 3055.
Grandfather and Grandmother in Love : 3900.
Grandfather Mendes : 4008.
Grandma and the Little Fish : 2254.
Grandma at the Home : 5575.
Grandma, On Rose Street : 1053.
Grandma Rose : 3740.
Grandma's Fern : 5898.
Grandmother : 3038.
Grandmother and the War : 2996.
Grandmother in Heaven : 4221.
Grandmother, Waiting for the Mail : 4908.
Grandmother's Dream, Picking Waterlilies :
    1140.
Grandmother's Last Years : 3582.
Grandmother's Rug : 2238.
Grandmother's Spit : 2557.
Grandmother's Watch : 1630.
Grandpa : 1962, 2254.
Grandpa's Attempt to Compliment Mrs.
    Nugent on Building the Finest House in
    Town : 2131.
Grandpa's High School Class Photo : 4866.
Granny's Death : 5543.
Granville, New York: the Museum of Natural
    History : 1257.
The Graph of a Thing : 2977.
Grappling in the Central Blue : 3045.
Grass : 2923, 3152.
Grass Snake's Serenade : 1975.
Grate of an Opening Jar : 1393.
The Grate Tradition : 1178.
Grateful : 2323.
Gratitude : 5135.
Le-Grau-du-roi : 4888.
A Graustarkian Audit : 2280.
A Grave : 3814.
Gravel : 4224.
Gravel Pit : 4897.
Gravid with Goodwill : 2437.
Gravitational Attraction : 1108.
Gravity Hill : 2266.
The Gray Horse : 1495.
Gray Squirrel : 1811.
The Gray Whales Passing Point Reyes : 1251.
The Great : 4789.
Great Blue : 1879.
Great Blue Heron Country : 5290.
Great Game of Baseball : 4617.
Great Granddaddy : 5132.
Great-Grandmother : 1182.
The Great-Grandmothers : 1287.
Great Horned Owl : 2022.
Great Indian Father in the Subway : 1986.
Great Plains Lit : 4815.
Great Powers : 4537.
Great Verse Valley : 3690, 3927, 5007.
The Great Writers : 2156.

The Grebe : 521, 5748.
Greed : 924, 4581, 5914.
Greed on Wall Street : 2703.
Greek : 3965.
The Greeks Are Blinding Polyphemus : 2900,
    2999, 4477.
Green : 698.
Green Chile : 261.
The Green Elephant : 902, 2404.
Green Fire : 4953.
Green Haven Halls : 1207.
Green Sky at Late Night : 293.
The Green Volkswagen Dream : 3566.
Greenville : 1422.
Greetings, Friends! : 164.
Greetings to Rafael Alberti : 750, 5938.
Gregorio Cortez : 261.
Gretel and Hansel : 5478.
Gretel, from a Sudden Clearing : 2549.
The Grey Fleece : 752.
Grey Fox : 5389.
Greyhound Bus Depot : 482.
Grief: The Arm's Song : 3538.
Grieving : 3337.
Grill and Counter Man : 1302.
The Grist Mill : 1934.
Groaning Boards : 1716.
The Grobot Odes : 1295.
Groceries : 3965.
Grocery Shopping : 3570.
The Grocery Store : 5250.
The Grommet : 1509.
Groom of the Animal-Bride : 4322.
The Grooming : 4681.
The Ground Rules : 3972.
Grounded : 2271, 5266.
Grounds : 2319.
Group of Shirts Sunning : 3333.
Group Photo from Pretoria Local on the
    Occasion of a Fourth Anniverary
    (Never Taken) : 1188.
Groves of Academe : 2191.
The Groves, the High Places : 3582.
Grow! Grow! Grow! : 1679.
Growing : 1240.
Growing Pains : 1672.
Growing Season : 5296.
Growing Up in the Country: Two Memories :
    4987.
Growing Up Ukrainian : 4134.
Growing Wild in the Capital : 3031.
Grown Weary : 926, 2169, 5765.
Growth : 1149, 3205.
The Growth of Private Worlds from Unat-
    tached Feelings : 5722.
Guadaquivir : 5008.
La Guardia: 4 AM : 5225.
Guardian Angel : 2139, 2651.
Guardian of the Dump : 701.
Guarding the House : 3015.
Guatemala, Your Name : 1584, 3514.
Guatemalan Exodus: Los Naturales : 2020.
The Guava Garden at Lahainaluna : 816.

Guerrillas : 3601.
Guest : 2437.
The Guest Ellen at the Supper for Street
     People : 1699.
Guests : 269.
Guide to Paris: Eiffel Tower, Versailles : 370.
Guilty as Charged : 144.
Guises: A Chainsong to the Muse : 388.
Guitar : 1555.
The Guitar Lesson : 5858.
Gulley Farm : 4741.
Gun : 2123.
Gunman : 5893.
Gunning : 1328.
Gunsmoke in Old Tay Ninh : 2089.
Gutes and Eulas : 555.
Guy in Paris : 3822.
Gwendolyn MacEwen 1941-1987 : 5796.
The Gypsy Moth Man : 1811.
'H-II' Linear : 61, 333, 5045.
H. D., the Rain, and the Pear Tree : 4391.
Habits : 4266, 5526.
Habits of Grief : 1411.
Hablando con Cesar Vallejo : 4750.
Hablar, Apprender, Vivir : 2961.
Hacia Adentro : 4569.
Hacia un Invierno : 5688.
Had : 3789.
Haibun : 2021.
Haibun 2/23/85 : 1966.
Haiku : 433, 2625, 2643, 3757, 3800, 5016,
     5343, 5866, 5932.
Haiku: Flagstone steps : 4722.
Haiku: Grey sky nearing : 2053.
Haiku: How do I love thee? : 1093.
Haiku: Seventeen sylla- : 1093.
Haikus : 2467, 4478, 4478.
Hair : 56, 2260, 3906, 6002.
Hair of the Dog : 1509.
Hakone : 1634.
Half an Hour : 921.
Half Lives : 4606.
Half-Sized Violin : 115, 548.
Half-Way There : 381.
Halflife / A commonplace Notebook : 6012.
Halfway home : 4051.
Halifax Report on Sydney Cancer Rates :
     1418.
Hall of the Guardian God : 3690, 3927, 5007.
Halley's Comet : 1763, 3177.
Halloween Creature : 4877.
Halsfjord : 5973.
Halves : 5914.
Hamlet's Gertrude : 4195.
The Hammer-Headed Foal : 4924.
Hammered Chick Pie : 1523.
The Hammering : 4522.
Hammers : 1582.
Hand : 3557, 5298.
The Hand Grenade : 1509.
Hand into Stone : 5998.
A Handful of Grit : 2703.
Handling the Serpents : 2024.

Hands : 791, 1196, 5562, 5939, 6000.
The Hands of the Blindman : 1876.
Hands On : 1233.
A Handshake of Dry Ice : 2656.
Handwritten Envelope : 4327.
Hanging in the Balance : 5708.
Hanging Laundry : 3349.
Hanging Up Clothes : 1050.
The Hanging Wave : 5993.
Hangzhou in Snow : 5155.
Hank : 3776.
Hank Williams : 3776.
Hanlan's Point Holiday : 5188.
Hannibal Crossing the Alps : 3876.
Hans Is Locked in the House! : 5911.
Happenstance : 175.
Happiness : 1523, 3747, 4773.
The Happiness Poems : 5700.
Happy : 5186.
Happy Anniversary : 1780.
Happy Ending : 4620.
Happy Hour with Grady : 5075.
A Happy Kid : 5271.
The Happy New Year : 924.
Harbor Lights : 1429.
Harbor One : 2127.
Harbor Town : 4008.
The Hard Bread : 226, 1153.
Hard Dollars : 974.
Hard-earned Harvest : 6045.
Hard Things : 1195.
Hard Times: A Rock Poem : 5487.
The Hardboiled Detective Watches a Rich
     Dame : 4384.
Hardboiled Wine : 5387.
Hardcase from Texas : 2541.
Hardscrabble : 3582.
Harlequinade : 2750.
Harlow Farm : 1422.
Harmless Blood : 2133.
Harmony : 1273, 3820, 4955.
Harm's Way : 3610.
Harold in Midtown : 2392.
Harp Boys : 721.
Harrouda : 437, 4490.
Harry Houdini, Condoms, Silence : 2860.
Harry's Somewhere in the Lost Coast Mizzle :
     1374.
The Harsh Angel : 5736.
Hart Crane : 2455.
Hart Crane: A Coda : 5102.
Hart Crane: A Dream for Two Voices : 5102.
Harvest : 1090, 4928, 5017, 5411.
The Harvest : 2428.
The Harvest (Driving Through Oklahoma) :
     3897.
Harvest Landscape: Blue Cart : 1104.
Harvest Scene : 590.
Harvesters : 3723.
Harvey Calls : 2392.
Hasidic Wedding : 474.
Hat Trick : 2576.
Hatching : 2564.

Hating the World : 4156.
The Hats My Father Wore : 5817.
Hatteras : 3296.
Haunts : 3919.
The Hausfrau : 1585, 5173.
Have You? I Have Never! : 4246.
Have You Seen Me? : 2937.
Haven House, Pasadena : 779.
Having a Mind of Winter : 3582.
Having Given Brith : 5833.
Having Given Myself : 2645.
Hawaiian Sunset : 5544.
Hawk : 1486.
Hawk Thoughts : 1280.
Hawks Are Always from Somewhere Else :
    442.
The Hawk's Cry in Autumn : 686.
Hawthorne and Melville : 1422.
The Hay Bay Calm : 1202.
Hayfield : 3839.
The Hayrake : 4552.
Hazel Tells Laverne : 1.
He Becomes Reacquainted with Solitude :
    4589.
He Can't Pull Free Beyond the Circle : 3729.
He Descended into Hell : 3787.
He Despairs of the Poems He Reads : 5488.
He Forgot to Remember to Forget : 4789.
He has spent the morning studying the leaves
    : 2606.
He Never Wrote : 542.
He Reflects on History and the Irrelevance of
    Absolution : 5488.
He Said : 1014.
He Said in the Hospital It : 3238.
He Says He's in Love : 4533.
He Slashed His Wrists Three Times & Said
    Goodbye Goodbye Goodbye : 4258.
He steps over her almost to position himself
    on the curb side of the street : 3017.
He Understands : 2232.
He Wanted You : 4092.
Head of a Young Girl : 1174.
Head of Sorrow, Head of Thought : 2202.
Headline: Kansas Youth Dies in Undertow :
    2079.
Headwaters : 4820.
Healing : 1119.
The Healing : 5872.
Healing a Dead Grandfather : 4751.
Healing by Computer : 1282.
Healing the Chosen Betrayal : 4443.
Hearing Again from the Earth Earthy : 1955.
Hearing of Nakasone's Apology in the UN for
    Japanese Involvement in World War
    Two : 619.
Hearing That My Piano Teacher Died : 1050.
Hearing the Names of the Valleys : 3690.
Hearing the Wind : 5233.
Hearing the World : 2653.
Hearsay : 3748.
Heart : 2564.
The Heart : 2437, 2977.

Heart and Mind : 4022.
Heart at the Window : 5580.
The Heart Buoyed Up : 2930.
Heart in My Homeland : 4286, 4324.
The Heart Inscribed : 2219, 5637.
The Heart of an Elephant : 4208.
The Heart of Owl Country : 4068.
The Heart of Quang Duc : 560.
Heart of Stone : 1392.
Heartbreak in Tuktoyaktuk : 4345.
The Heartless : 1230, 3977.
The Hearts : 4368.
Hearts and Flowers : 799.
A Heart's Instruments : 4570.
Heartwood : 5369.
Heat : 1318, 1342, 2444, 3695, 5622.
Heat Lightning : 2231.
Heat Wave : 5054.
Heaven : 3401, 5563.
Heaven: As Near to You As Your Hands and
    Your Feet : 1209.
Heaven in Hell : 4786.
The Heavenly Hell of It : 205.
Heaven's Ring: A Cycle of Poems : 4406,
    5046.
The heavens too : 2743, 3771.
Heavy Tea : 3624.
Heavy Violets : 2165.
Heavy Weather : 2005.
Heavy with mouse : 5259.
The Hebrew Lion : 4703.
Hector Cantando : 1275.
Hedgeapples : 5829.
Hedgerows : 4388.
The Hedonist Speaks : 5264.
Helen : 1049, 1316, 4621.
Helen Keller : 2246.
Helena : 2145.
Helendale : 326.
Helium: An Inert Gas : 2703.
Helix : 3246.
Hell and Some Notes on a Piano : 2430.
Hell on Wheels : 5589.
Hellbrunn Sonnets : 1701.
Hello Mister : 1248.
The Help : 1253.
Help Me! : 506, 4792.
Help Wanted : 4353.
Help Wanted — Literary : 1432.
Helping My Father Make a Cupboard : 5654.
Helping My Sister with a Research Project
    About Coots on the Cedar River : 4095.
Henny Youngman Haiku : 5842.
Henry : 4762.
Henry Becker, D. O. A : 3555.
Henry James and Hester Street : 1332.
Her : 3806.
Her Children : 852.
Her death mask makeup : 4788.
Her Dying Eyes : 5652.
Her Fear Is Whale : 4124.
Her Flower Garden : 5272.
Her Garden : 75.

The Jellyfish : 2936.
Jennifer Blass : 3339.
Jennifer Is an Island : 2398.
Jeremiad : 1460.
Jeremiah : 4931.
Jersey Cokesbury : 4571.
Jerusalem : 1147.
Jess Dennison's Garage : 5806.
Jessa's Late Assignment : 4145.
Jesse James in Hell : 629.
Jest, a Collection of Records : 2269.
The Jester's Daughter : 1581.
Jesting Pilate : 2318.
The Jesuit's Letters Moulder in a Bag Near
    the Soot : 3238.
Jet Contrails over Amber Waves : 1355.
Jewel: A Conceit : 289.
Jewish Mother : 589.
Jews : 5914.
Jews in Old China : 2629.
Jig of the Week No. 21 : 1483.
Jigsaw Puzzles : 1576.
The Jilt : 1487.
Jim's Steak House : 5195.
Joan Miro's *Person Throwing a Stone at a*
    Bird : 2455.
Joan of Arc : 4139.
Joanie, 17 : 3238.
Joanne on Poros : 1643.
Job Hunt : 5136.
The Job Interview : 5715.
Job's Turkey: a Commentary : 3120.
The Jogger : 385, 2258.
Jogging by the C&O Canal : 1881.
John Bible : 5456.
John Doe's Father Died This A.M : 6087.
John Muir Remembers Eliza Hendricks : 298.
John Olaf : 2743.
John Wayne : 3789.
Johnny Appleseed Gets a Sign : 224.
Johnny's Cosmology : 6038.
John's Metamorphoses : 2883.
Jojo's : 1279.
The Joke : 1730.
Jonah : 474, 5736.
Jonah's Lament : 4136, 5808.
Jonathan : 2743.
Jones Creek : 3242.
Jonquils : 183.
La Jornada : 4474.
Jose: d. 1985 : 436.
Josef Stalin: Later Works : 2353.
Joseph : 5262.
Joseph Moody, Schoolmaster in York, Maine
    in My 21st Year, Associate Pastor to
    My Father Samuel. . : 2785.
Joshua Tree : 1251.
Josie and Joshua: Three Poems : 2801.
Journal : 2860.
The Journal of Nights : 401, 3820.
A Journal of One Significant Landscape :
    6012.
Journal of the First Birth : 1952.

Journey : 1153, 3690, 4828.
The Journey : 582.
Journey After Passing : 498.
A Journey Back to Where It Started : 1046.
A Journey by Railroad : 136.
The Journey Forever : 620, 2688.
Journey into Spring : 4110.
The Journey North : 1457, 2439.
Journey to the Interior : 5137.
Journey to Winnipeg, 1940 : 5706.
Journey to Your Family : 4163.
Journeys : 1667.
Joy : 5463, 6011.
Joy Road and Livernois : 4354.
The Joy That Music Brings : 1237.
A Joyful Letter : 950, 1957, 2598.
Juan Rulfo Moved Away : 4613.
Judge Kroll : 2101.
Judgment Day : 4864.
Judith : 644.
Los Juegos : 2813.
Jukebox Blues : 317.
Jukebox Roulette : 2286.
Jukehouse : 5907.
Julius Dithers in the Morning : 944.
July : 1401, 1796, 4635.
July 4, 1984 : 2850.
July 4, 5, and Other Days : 1127.
July 5, 1985 : 1090.
July 14 : 1986.
July Roses : 4451.
July Run : 3506.
Jumper Moon : 169.
Jumping : 3111.
Jumping Galley : 1840.
Jumping-Jack Flash : 4860.
Junco : 5116.
June 1944 : 2475.
June Silver : 2229.
June Wind : 4834.
Jungle : 1996.
The Jungle Gym : 2318.
Junior Got the Snakes : 3642.
The Junk Store, Lines from a Paragraph by
    Sauer : 1488.
Junkyard : 2445.
Junkyard 8:00 A.M : 4909.
Junkyard Man : 3504.
Just a Glance : 147, 3207.
Just an Ordinary Monday : 2786.
Just Another Sunset : 5813.
Just Be Home Before Sundown : 5653.
Just Before the Hot, Steamy Guts of June :
    5028.
Just God : 5605.
Just Like That : 2219, 6056.
Just Looking, Thank You : 3951.
Just My Blood : 605, 2113, 5407.
Just Recently in California, Where Else : 881.
Just So No One Sees : 2373.
Just Someone I Met at a Party : 3589.
Just the Right Tree : 445.
Just West of Now : 4508.

The Korean Gravestone in Connersville, Indiana : 5004.
Krazy Kat's Confession : 981.
Kuan Yin Mingles with the Ghosts, Now on Guided Tour, of the Slave Population . . : 4343.
Kuan Yin Turns Her Photo Album to a Certain Point : 4343.
Kudzu: Amnesty : 5130.
Kyoto : 2629.
L. at Gettysburg : 1024.
L. at Jonestown : 1024.
L. at Nagasaki : 1024.
Laborare Est Orare : 660.
Labors : 4186.
Labyrinth II : 1188.
Lace : 582, 6044.
A Lack of Epitaphs : 2126.
Lacrimae Rerum : 2352.
Lacunae : 1576.
Ladders : 73, 320.
The Ladies of Dimbaza : 5788.
Ladle : 5129.
Lady : 1000, 5660.
Lady Canute : 13.
Lady Changes Her Strategy : 5660.
Lady Crane : 3319.
The Lady in the Moon : 2585, 3226.
Lady in White : 638.
A Lady in Winter : 3146.
Lady Las Vegas : 5049.
Lady Leicester Miscarries, 1776 : 1116.
Lady Murasaki : 192.
Lady Replies : 5660.
Lady's Journal : 4479, 5664.
Lagaña of Lace : 949.
Lagoon : 135, 2185, 2989.
Lagoons : 650, 1773.
Laguna : 2185.
Lake : 4923.
The Lake : 527.
Lake Alice : 62.
Lake Champlain Confessional : 1903.
Lake Drummond Dream : 5104.
Lake George : 2776.
Lake of Resolve : 5653.
Lake Pepin : 3036.
Lake Spirit : 1823.
The Lakes in Scandinavia : 221, 1575.
Lakescape: After the Funeral : 1057.
The Lamb : 3616.
The Lamb's Half-Buried : 4299.
Lambs in Spring : 630.
The Lame Shall Enter First : 3349.
Lament : 3178, 4620, 4937.
A Lament : 948.
Lament for Ignacio Sanchez Mejias : 1894, 5072.
Lament for Lorca : 900.
Lament of Saint Nicholas : 4735.
Lament of the Banyan Tree : 13.
Lament of the Impotent Trashman : 1456.
Lament upon Hearing of a Wedding : 762.

Lamentations from the Armenian : 2809.
Lamento de la Doncella en la Muerte del Guerrero : 1204.
Laments : 3762.
Laminex : 5576.
Lamps : 1152.
The Land of Fields : 2328.
The Land of Fuck : 2767.
The Lander Hotel and Bar: For Mike Trbovich : 4696.
Landor : 3538.
Land's End : 419.
Landscape : 3353, 3809, 5848.
Landscape, 1986 : 3648.
Landscape Assembled from Dreams : 1285.
Landscape for an Antique Clock : 1663.
The Landscape Inside Me : 3601.
Landscape with Feather : 750, 5938.
Landscape with Self-Portrait : 3976.
Landscape with Unemployed Jockeys : 1143.
Landscape with Visionary Blue : 3446.
Landscapes : 5811.
Landsflykt : 4262.
The Language Fetishist : 5636.
Language Journal : 6012.
The Language of Fields : 4150.
The Language of the Brag : 4099.
Language, the Truest Tongue : 5574.
La Langue Enfantine : 3119.
Languedocienne : 2191.
Languor : 4691, 5680.
Lapse : 86.
Larches : 1753, 2952.
Lardbelly at the Emergency Room : 2398.
Large Mural / Philadelphia Art Museum, Miss Emily Among Many : 2691.
Largo — Reflections on the Third Movement of Dmitri Shostakovich's Fifth Symphony : 4931.
Las Vegas : 3031.
Lascaux : 5904.
Lassie : 5004.
The Last : 4058.
Last Act: Don Giovanni : 2022.
The Last Atlantean : 2379.
The Last Bridge Home : 1937.
Last Call : 4293.
The Last Candles : 1222.
The Last Canto : 1925.
A Last Cloud : 2214.
Last Conversations with Dad : 1607.
A last Corner of Prairie (1985) : 5532.
The Last Cowboy : 5951.
Last Entry : 6052.
Last Exit Before Bridge : 4059.
Last Flight Out from the War Zone : 1528.
Last Garden : 1883, 3870.
The Last Gift : 194, 1783.
Last House on January Road, Off Route 8 : 3599.
Last Inning : 4719.
Last Journal : 6012.
The Last Kiss : 21.

Mar de Fondo : 2386.
Marathon : 2009.
Marble : 3980.
Marbles : 4935.
Marbot : 4641.
Marcel : 459.
March : 4997.
March 1, 1981 : 2376.
March 9th : 3659.
March 11, 50 Degrees : 1879.
March 20th, 11:59 PM : 4681.
March 24 : 2330.
March, 1724 : 988.
March Again : 5334.
March, and Mae Fields Tells of the Most
     Recent Miracle She Almost Saw : 5130.
The March Buds : 562.
March Elegy: In Training : 2848.
March Fifth : 4310.
March Has Returned : 147, 3207.
March Planting : 2474.
March: Vernal Equinox : 2687.
Marco : 1354.
Marcus Antonius at the Nile : 4956.
Marcus Aurelius : 71, 1864.
Margaret Bope Perkins : 789.
Margaret Mary : 3238.
Margaret Roper : 2022.
Margaret Sleeping : 4270.
Margarine : 2868.
The Margarita Party : 3430.
Margarite Moon of Venus : 3022.
Marge Margerie : 631.
The Margin : 490.
The Margin the Light Falls on : 4559.
The Marginalist : 5826.
The Margins : 2929.
Maria : 4792, 5046.
Maria Sez : 3661.
Marianne Moore in Egypt : 1793.
Marianne, My Mother, and Me : 3045.
Maria's Bath : 4104.
The Marias, Mexico City : 1438.
Marilyn : 482.
Marina Tsvetayeva : 971.
Marina Tsvetayeva (1892-1941) : 50, 1461,
     2345.
The Marine Story : 5716.
Mariposa Pibroch : 2382.
The Market : 865, 4392.
Marking Time : 1874.
Markings : 5138.
Maroon : 491.
Marquesas Islands Songs : 170, 4130.
Marrakesh : 4631.
Marriage : 1942, 6058.
Marriage and Other Sidereal Relations : 2042.
Marriage Couplet : 1055.
Marriage Vow : 2888.
Married : 542.
Marsh Walk : 1525.
Martha : 4081.
The Martyr : 3112.

Martyrdom of the Onions : 967.
Martyrology : 3998.
Martyrs : 5732.
Marvin Gaye Suite : 5409.
Mary at the Manger : 4997.
Mary Cassatt, After Destroying the Letters of
     Edgar Degas : 4659.
Mary Magdalene and I : 3752.
Mary Mihalik : 4068.
Mary of Bethany : 569.
The Mary Shrine : 5135.
Mary's Color : 832.
Ma's Ghost : 4091.
Mas le Paradis : 4888.
Mascara & Creme / The Face I Drew This
     Morning : 2691.
Mass for the Imprisoned : 124, 2383, 3439.
The Mass-hour : 1651.
Massachusetts Three-Lines : 5687.
Massage on Christmas Eve : 1621.
Massasoit the Wampanoag : 4742.
Masseuse : 3458.
Master Locksmith : 5970.
Master of None : 5448.
The Master to His Apprentice : 1131, 5601.
The Masterpiece : 5061.
Mastodon Treasure : 3315.
Masts : 52, 3977.
Matapoeic : 5008.
Materialism : 1368.
The Math Teacher's Love Poem : 3910.
Mathematical Model : 2839.
Mathematics : 974.
Mating Flight : 3778.
Matins : 1880, 5302.
Matisse: The Red Studio : 587.
Matthew Arnold on Mars : 2938.
Maundy Thursday : 3787.
Maundy Thursday: Thomas's Testimony :
     4997.
Maura Paints the Deer Skulls : 5841.
Mauve : 2594.
Mauve and amber : 1592, 2467, 6028.
Max : 4923.
Max Beckmann's Worker : 2478.
Max Fabre's Yachts : 3922.
Max Is Asked to Reach into the Past for
     Memories : 2611.
Maxims : 3946.
Maxims from My Mother's Milk : 3694.
May : 5700.
May 30 : 3319.
May 1968 : 4099.
May, 1970 : 3238.
May Day in China, Xi'An : 3702.
May I Ask for the Hand of Your Sister : 2354.
May in Minnesota : 3422.
May Journal : 6012.
May on the Wintered-Over Ground : 4635.
Mayakovsky : 1333.
Mayakowski's Vacation with Lilya and Ossip
     Brik, Summer of 1929 : 3164, 3682.
Mayan Woman Grinding Corn : 3235.

Montana : 2960.
Montauk : 3592.
Montezuma's Revenge : 486.
The Months of July & August : 6088.
Monuments : 650, 1809.
The Moo Game : 2664.
Mood for Grief: Autumn : 498.
A Mood of Quiet Beauty : 216.
Moon : 604, 2993, 3015, 4830.
The Moon : 1440, 3634.
The Moon and Big Ben : 4804.
The Moon in the Phonebooth : 1099.
The Moon Is Visible Tonight : 434.
Moon, Love: Whereof I Swear Never Again
    to Write : 747.
Moon Mountain : 3690, 3927, 5007.
Moon Rabbit : 2668.
The Moon Recounts the Birth of the Sun :
    4322.
Moon Talk : 5860.
Moon Tree Cliff (Keigan) : 3690, 3927, 5007.
The Moon Up Close in Winter by Telescope :
    6041.
Moonflowers / Evening Glory : 2003.
Moonlessness : 6041.
Moonrise: Hernandez, New Mexico, 1941 :
    642.
Moose : 5340.
The Moose : 4124.
Moose II : 4124.
Moose Watching on the Road to Rangeley :
    4181.
Moraff, Barbara : 2133.
Moral : 747.
The Moral Order : 5545.
Moral Tales: 'The Last Colony' : 5213.
Morbid Things : 2970.
More Autobiography : 3625.
More Portraits from Memory : 3004.
More Repartee with the Mummy : 802.
More Research : 2232.
The More You Tear Off, the More You Keep
    : 1481, 5137, 5703.
Morgan Andretti : 3332.
Morgan in the Dark : 3332.
Morituri : 529.
The Morning After : 2687.
Morning at Kyoto's Heian Shrine : 2965.
Morning Call Cafe, New Orleans : 2582.
Morning Coffee : 3582.
Morning Darkness : 521, 5748.
Morning Fields : 2521.
A Morning For : 3750.
Morning in Half Light : 4918.
Morning in Troy, N.Y : 2538.
Morning Jitters : 216.
Morning Love Song : 4354.
The Morning Poems : 2931.
Morning Scales : 5323.
Morning Subway : 1993, 5686.
Morning Tactics : 368.
A Morning Walk in Bhopal : 3386.
Morning Whistle : 3871.

Morphine : 880.
The Mortal One : 4099.
Mortalities : 2193.
The Mortician : 4307.
Moses Has Trouble with God's Instructions :
    3978.
Most of All : 852.
Most of What We Take Is Given : 5133.
Most People Have Some Brown : 72.
The Motel in Paxton : 5871.
Motels : 3765.
The Motets : 1980, 3796.
Mother and Child : 1147.
Mother and Daughter Summer: Maple Leaves
    Brought to Hawaii : 6024.
The Mother and the Daughter : 4423.
Mother GOodbye : 1986.
The Mother Inside : 2295.
Mother, Moving : 1348.
A Mother Pauses Before a Photograph : 599.
Mother Speaks the Back-Home Blues : 1603.
Mother Teresa : 2866.
Mother Works in the Dark : 3193.
Mothers After the War : 2189, 2253, 2481.
Mother's Boyfriend : 1250.
A Mother's Death : 181, 607.
Mother's Earrings : 1020.
Mothers of the Plaza de Mayo : 4842, 5940.
The Mother's Song : 1067.
Motho Ke Motho Ka Batho Babang (A Person
    Is a Person Because of Other People) :
    1188.
Moths : 4338.
The Moths : 4928.
Motion : 4301.
The Motion : 5621.
Motion Which Disestablishes Organizes
    Everything : 118.
Motionless, covering what's in back : 4299.
The Motions : 3889.
Motive, Metaphor : 4059.
Mound Presence : 764.
Mount Scott Sestina : 3294.
The Mountain : 4756.
Mountain Lion : 4679.
Mountain Music : 4602.
Mountain Speech Sung As Indian : 2951.
Mountain Temple : 690.
Mountain Village : 355.
The Mountains of China : 2375.
Mounting Suspicion : 4497.
Mourning : 3181.
The Mourning Cloak Academy : 1555.
A Mourning Dove in New York City : 4720.
Mourning Doves : 4338.
Mourning for the Layman Named Cloud Peak
    : 3690, 3927, 5007.
The Mourning Songs of Greece : 170, 3102.
The Mourning Songs of Greek Women : 170,
    3102.
Mourning the Dying American Female Names
    : 2322.
Mouse Dance Song : 5386.

My Tale : 4060.
My Three-Year-Old with His First Conch
    Shell : 2591.
My Turn at the Ballet : 1955.
My Two Hands : 135, 3679.
My Underwear : 451.
My Usual Place at the Table : 4095.
My Vacuum Cleaner Suffers Remorse : 2322.
My Wedding Ring : 1932.
My Wet Spring : 4314.
My Wife Reads the Paper at Breakfast on the
    Birthday of the Scottish Poet : 5925.
My World : 1282.
Mylai Village : 2586.
Myself As Nude : 2309.
Myself, My Body : 4937.
The Mystery : 1498.
Mystery Play : 2289.
Mystic Journey of the Unknown Magus :
    3732.
A Myth of Absence : 517.
The Myth of Self : 1599.
The Myth of the Cave : 310, 655, 1595, 4711,
    4782.
N C S : 4612.
N-Judah : 5454.
N T I : 5517.
N Y C Country Music : 2392.
Nabokov Purchases an Émigré Daily : 5141.
Nacimiento : 2601.
Nada : 761, 1812.
Nadja Poem : 4807.
Nahuala : 1195.
Nahuatl Poem : 5805.
Naiad : 2479.
Nairobi : 303.
The Naked Eye : 5605.
The Naked Man Picks Berries : 1396.
The Name : 3635.
A Name, A Shape, A Stasis : 409.
A Name for My Little Daughter : 2221, 5066.
Names : 5329.
Names and Figures : 1739, 2090, 4381.
Names of Horses : 2206.
Naming a Painting : 3875.
The Naming Field : 4646.
The Naming of Parts : 5490.
The Naming of Trees : 857.
Naming the Flowers : 5301.
Naming the Moons : 2611.
Naming the Winter : 1404.
Nanci: Two Dances : 1546.
Nanda Devi : 1725.
Nantucket : 2605.
The Nap : 4029.
Napa: August : 816.
Napping in Trees : 604.
Narcissi in Winter : 1961.
Narcissus : 2116.
Narrative : 4165.
Narrative of the Men and Women Who
    Became Stars : 5435.
Narrative of the Vision of Our Lady of

Armeiro : 5435.
Narrative on a Four-Poster Bed from Louisi-
    ana : 3014.
Narrativity Scenes : 6010.
The Narrow Roads of Oku : 963.
Nascence : 1524.
Nasturium as Reality : 287, 1443, 2358.
Natalya Longing : 5084.
Natchez : 4389.
Nathan's Fortune : 3828.
National Portrait Gallery, London : 5582.
Nationalgalerie Berlin : 1180.
Natirar : 442.
Native : 3690.
The Native : 1090.
Native Americans : 4412, 5914.
Natural : 5802.
Natural History : 4099, 4210.
Natural Selection : 3967.
Nature : 1959, 4107.
Nature Notes : 2736.
The Nature of America : 2126.
The Nature of Things : 3731.
The Nature of Yearning : 2556.
Nature Walk : 1844.
Les Natures Profundement Bonnes Sont
    Toujours Indecises : 4766.
Naufragio : 4903.
El Naufrago (1) y (2) : 3899.
The Naval Base (Part III) : 1188.
Navigating the North Platte from Lingle to
    Torrington : 2248.
Navigation : 3515.
Nazareth : 377, 904, 904.
The Nazi on the Phone : 1716.
The Nazi's Widow : 1111.
NCS : 4612.
Near a Milestone : 4442.
Near Midnight : 4795.
Near-Miss Eddy : 1516.
Near Pocatello with My Great-Grandfather,
    1918 : 4635.
Near Sisyphus : 3529.
Near the Water : 3094.
Near the wichita mountains : 2380.
Near Winter, St. Regis, Montana : 4267.
Nearing Divorce : 1.
Nearing the End of a Century : 3582.
Necessities of Two : 104.
Necking : 4099.
Necktie Moan : 463.
The Necropolis at St. Pierre L'Estrier : 771.
Needles : 665.
Nefertari: A Priase Song : 5564.
Negative Capability : 3732.
Neglect : 3034, 5914.
Negotiations : 4437.
Negro Bembón : 2171.
Negroe Cloth : 3758.
Neige à Louveciennes : 2231.
The Neighborhood Crazyman Talks to the
    President on the Eve of the Libyan
    Raids : 2352.
Neighbors : 3948, 5061, 5439, 6035.

Rubà i I : 1434, 1665, 3943.
Rubà i IV : 1434, 1665, 3943.
Rubaiyat : 2775.
The Rube Goldberg Suite : 2870.
Ruined Bridge Seen from a Plane — Theme
    and Six Variations : 5629.
Ruined House : 2900, 5059.
Ruins : 3665.
Rules : 6096.
Rumours of Moving : 519.
The Rune of the Lapwing : 1771.
Runes : 1860, 5304.
The Runner, On : 1246.
Running : 1964.
Running Away : 4534.
Running in Place : 3854.
Running My Fingers through My Beard on
    Bolton Road : 1160.
Running with a Biologist : 1448.
Running with Helena : 3741.
Rural Affairs : 4818.
Rural Mailboxes : 1879.
Ruse to Trick the Spirit of the Snow : 5386.
Rush Hour : 5914.
Rush to the Lake : 1883.
Russell Elias : 5860.
Russia Comes Into Poland : 2045, 5914, 6061.
Ruth's Love Letters, 1918-1919 : 4414.
Rx : 3495.
S S N : 3327, 4080.
Sábana : 4264.
Sabbathsong : 4937.
Sabra Shatila, Beirut, Summer 1982 : 2852.
Sacramento : 662.
Le Sacre du Printemps : 4354.
The Sacred : 1285.
The Sacred Fount : 2473.
Sacred Heart : 671, 3637, 4025.
The Sacrifice of Actaeon : 2281.
The Sacrifice of Memory : 6062.
The Sacrifices : 1279.
Sad Bear : 3428.
Sad Rite : 2818.
The Sadness of Cicadas : 4011.
The Sadness of Rivers : 5054.
Safari Notes : 5783.
Safe House: Brandon, Vermont (Thinking of
    the Underground Railroad) : 1732.
A Safe Place : 1880.
Safe Sex : 4770.
Saffron Pig Piñata : 5813.
The Sage and the Courtesan : 971.
The Sage, Kien-Wu : 971.
Sagittarius A West : 4242.
Saguaro : 3376.
Said Wasp to Bee : 3526, 4419.
Sail Loft : 2108.
Sailing in Perfect Space : 3587.
Sailing, Sailing : 3859.
The Sailors of Hart Crane : 5524.
Saint . . . : *See also* St. . . . filed below under
    "St."
Saint Augustine : 2699.

The Saint Francis Poems : 2525.
Saint Helens : 1703.
Saint Stephen's Day with the Griffins : 1052.
Saint Teresa in Ecstasy : 5215.
Saints : 1436.
Saints Are Not Born to It : 5223.
Salamander : 37, 3088.
The Salamander : 4928.
Salamander Pendant : 2072.
Saldra el Arco Iris : 4569.
Salisbury Plain : 3427.
Sally's First Train Ride — 1910 : 3459.
Salmo 5 : 851.
Salt : 2129.
Salt Bread : 2230.
Salt of the Earth : 2698.
Salt Petals : 4798.
Saltmines Regained : 483.
Saludo a Cesar Vallejo : 3270.
Salvadore Dali with a Tube Up His Nose :
    100.
Salzburg Variations : 4734.
Sam Hill, Jack Robinson, and Me : 5695.
The Same Wait : 794.
The Same Water : 3920.
A Sampler of Hours: Poems on Lines from
    Emily Dickinson's Letters : 5605.
San Francisco : 2684.
San Francisco Sonnet : 4644.
San Gabriel : 835.
San Luis Obispo : 4807.
Sanatorium : 5823.
Sanctuary : 2140, 4050.
Sand : 3871.
The Sand : 5386.
The Sand Dunes : 1696.
The Sandals of My Ancestors : 1928.
Sanded Roads : 1702.
Sandoway : 5711.
Sandusky River Mornings : 417.
Sanri Matsubara : 2623.
Sansei : 2629.
Santa Fe Internment Camp : 3940, 3941,
    5413.
Santa Leopoldina Asylum : 2635, 4405.
Santa Rosa Island : 5179.
Santiago : 2630.
Santos, Santos, Santos : 4286.
Sapphics (More or Less) : 771.
Sarah Binks : 2413.
Sarcophagi with Glyphs : 4881.
The Sash : 4099.
Sasha : 482.
The Sasha Sequence : 3596.
Sassafras : 208.
Satisfaccion : 909.
Satura : 210, 3796.
Saturday Bull in a Michigan Bar : 5300.
Saturday Evening, the Idea of Order on Canal
    St : 3732.
Saturday Morning : 282.
Saturday Night Grand Union Parking Lot :
    3238.

Socks : 4652.
Socrates at the Centaur : 3138.
Soda Water with a Boyhood Friend : 2962.
Solace : 239.
The Solar Heater Plant : 1417.
Soldier and Laughing Girl : 5149.
Solid : 679.
Soliloquy for Rough Beast : 4101.
Soliloquy in Waikiki : 5945.
Solitaires : 4075.
Solitude : 1440, 2140, 5685, 5808.
Solitude in the Oneida Community: Victor
    Cragin Noyes, 1866 : 3620.
Solo Sax : 5505.
Solstice : 3613.
The Solstice : 3690.
Solstice at the Tidepools : 229.
Solution : 3905.
Some Basic Aesthetics : 2482.
Some Came Home : 5123.
Some Closing Remarks (The Retiring Biolo-
    gist, to His Colleagues) : 2106.
Some Days We Are Held : 1991.
Some Details of Autumn : 3565.
Some Guests : 4975.
Some Immortality : 4110.
Some Italian! : 2722.
Some Kind of Permanence : 5131.
Some Lines in the Morning : 6022.
Some Moments Are a Long Time Coming :
    3790.
Some Nights of the Mind : 2011.
Some of Us : 5914.
Some Order of Ash : 3208.
Some People Have Dream Mamas : 2702.
Some Quay Beside Some Torrential : 1183.
Some Questions : 1205.
Some Tailors Seeking Wisdom : 5908.
Some years ago : 1904.
Someday, But for Now : 5405.
Somehow Paradise : 3801.
Someone Has Covered Up : 3011, 6106.
Someone Sd : 1863.
Someone You Have Seen Before : 216.
Something : 1253.
Something as Difficult as Someone New :
    4242.
Something Autumn : 4645.
Something Calling My Name : 1350.
Something Dangerous : 2430.
Something Else : 702.
Something for the Telling : 733.
Something for the Union Dead : 1507.
Something Inside Us Waits : 852.
Something Is Circulating : 1032, 2662.
Something Said : 2331.
Something That Stays : 3347.
Something to Drink From, Made in the Desert
    : 2776.
Something to Fly With : 5647.
Something to Love : 2551.
Something, Which Waits, Is Always Telling
    Lies : 5307.

Sometime Later : 638.
The Sometime Sportsman Greets the Spring :
    5630.
Sometimes, at Thirty-Six : 5813.
Sometimes He Held My Mom's Hand and
    Sang Love Songs, Just a Little Flat . . :
    2792.
Sometimes I see so clearly the openness of
    things : 2228, 2812, 5424.
Sometimes I Wonder What I'm Talking
    About : 3550.
Sometimes the Bodies of Women : 1147.
Sometimes the Body's Unwilling : 5832.
Sometimes the Distance : 3192.
Sometimes the Hill Ends : 3952.
Somewhat a Visitor : 947.
Somewhere : 4201.
Somewhere Beyond Good-Bye : 6095.
Somewhere in Magog : 3820.
Somewhere Short of Home : 3696.
Somewhere South of Here : 2244.
The Somme : 2052.
The Son : 4245.
Son to Father : 5503.
Sonata a Dos Voces : 1132.
Sonetos de la Noche : 4430.
Song : 865, 950, 1260, 1957, 2598, 4392,
    5241, 5406, 5735.
A Song : 3202.
Song About a Dog : 3395.
Song After *Five Easy Pieces* : 3243.
Song and Dance : 3614.
Song at Hanalei : 5795.
Song for a Small Boat Leaving Biloxi on a
    Night in June, 1979 : 4533.
Song for a Wedding : 2937.
Song for Ilva Mackay and Mongane : 2906.
A Song for Jack : 2001.
Song for My Father : 3665.
Song / For Sanna : 702.
Song from Fortitude : 4622.
Song from Kanteletar : 170, 2900, 5059.
Song of a 118-Year-Old Man : 3344.
Song of a Country Priest : 158.
Song of Obedience : 4503.
Song of Peace : 2598, 3152.
Song of Perfect Trust : 189, 3600, 5128.
Song of Salt and Pepper : 5331.
Song of Silences : 551.
Song of the Blackbird : 4229.
Song of the Disappearing Woman : 4095.
Song of the Earth : 25.
Song of the Last Meeting : 50, 150.
Song of the Look-Out on the Great Wall :
    2670.
Song of the Rails : 561.
Song of the Robin : 630.
Song of the Spinster : 2549.
Song of the Terrible : 3851.
Song of the Young Man : 1358, 3411.
A Song That Lies the Least to the Most :
    5894.
Songs: I : 446, 5687.

Weather : 350.
The Weather : 3989.
Weather Forecast : 2334.
Weather Radio : 2151.
Weather Report : 857.
Weather Update : 4633.
The Weatherman : 2213.
The Wedding : 2606.
The Wedding Gift : 467.
Wedding Night : 4916, 4933.
Wedding Picture : 4582.
Weed : 95.
Weeds : 4830.
A week-long holiday in a glass paperweight
    bought at Coney Island : 5046.
Weeping Angel : 3931.
Weeping Fig : 5073.
Wege : 263.
Weight Lifter : 3458.
The Weight of the Potatoes : 20.
The Weight of Women : 5728.
Welcome Honor to John Coltrane : 280.
Welcome Spring : 2201.
Welcome to Farewell : 1130.
Welcome to Weiser : 6020.
A Welder's Dream : 944.
The Well : 5774.
Well Bed : 2674.
Well Water : 5772.
Well, we'll live as the soul directs : 249, 664,
    4517.
Wellers Bridge Road : 2936.
Wells : 2372.
Welsh Poems - 1985 : 2476.
Wendy : 3911.
We're constantly floating past each other into
    new lights : 457.
We're Not Vegetarian : 5203.
We're Sailing into Exception Bay : 6088.
Werewind : 5605.
Werewolf Movies : 234.
West of Omaha, by Way of New Caldonia :
    2487.
West of Tuscaloosa : 3812.
West Texas : 1648.
West Texas Interlude : 1719.
Western Civilization : 3983.
Western Cove Revisited : 3598.
Westward : 996.
Wet Dream : 898.
Wet Pavement : 2133.
A Wet, Salty Chinese Secret Impossible to
    Write in Chinese : 3223.
We've Been Domesticated, I Tell You : 454.
The Whale : 1708.
What a Friend We Have in Cheeses! or Sing a
    Song of Liederkranz : 1055.
What Being Responsible Means to Me : 691.
What Bird? : 1573.
What Can I Give Now : 3714.
What Changes : 4238.
What Comes : 605, 2113, 5407.
What Comes Home : 3011.

What Comes Naturally : 3817.
What Comes of Dance : 3614.
What Did the Midge Say to the Mildew? :
    2652.
What Do I Have of You : 4545.
What Do You Think Sara Jane's Lighter Was
    Doing Under Lou Christie's Seat :
    4391.
What Dolphins Do and Do Not Do : 4897.
What Ever Happened : 2707.
What Feeds Us : 3695.
What Happens : 2940.
What Happens When Anthony Holdsworth
    Exhibits at Edible Complex : 2232.
What Has Become of Me : 2247.
What Has Been Taken and Taken Back :
    4357.
What He Says : 726.
What I Do with Funny-Looking People :
    2791.
What I Do with Funny Looking People :
    4253.
What I Know : 4690.
What I Remember About the 6th Grade :
    5695.
What I Remember the Writers Telling Me
    When I Was Young : 3685.
What I Wanted to Tell You : 5131.
What I Wear Hides Me : 4281.
What If a Woman : 1940.
What If the River Contained the Sea? : 1731.
What Is Keeping the Clouds? : 902, 3139.
What Is Left : 3924.
What Is My Name? : 4797.
What Is Revealed Is Enough : 3127.
What Is This Thing Called, Love? : 3355.
What Is to Be Life : 4838.
What Is Your Earliest Memory? What Does
    It Mean : 5557.
What It Is : 3196, 3635.
What Memory Reveals : 5859.
What My Mother Said to Me : 2612.
What Of It? : 2398.
What Old Man Johnson Said to Grandpa After
    Returning Thanks : 2131.
What People Say about Paris : 2979.
What Promises There Were : 5525.
What She Knew : 1287.
What She Says About Love : 4650.
What spells raccoon to me : 1024.
What Steepness There Is in the Crystal Pool :
    3421, 3860.
What Survives : 5728.
What the Bees Said : 4552.
What the Bell Told : 2666.
What the Blind Kid Said : 5557.
What the Citizenry Knows About You : 4217.
What the Earth Taught Us : 2741.
What the End Is For : 2069.
What the God Says Through Me : 175.
What the Hell, February, Wassergass : 4646.
What the Intern Saw : 3202.
What the Neighbors Don't See : 5923.

Elvis Makes Love to Me: Now I Carry His Baby : 994.
While Hitchhiking on Monroe Street : 314.
While I Was Enacting Damnations : 1380.
While Marking the Milton Exams : 1380.
While My Companion Sleeps in Our Path : 2400.
While My Eyes Can Shed Another Tear : 3060, 5019.
While Reading Robinson Crusoe : 1542.
While Sitting at the Edge of a Grove : 5841.
While U.S. Helicopters Land as 'Gifts' in Costa Rica : 167.
While You Were Asleep : 3467.
The Whiskerbit : 3954.
Whiskers : 1523.
Whiskey : 5399.
Whiskey in Whiting, Indiana : 2338.
Whisper : 1192.
Whistle Stop : 1337.
Whistlers : 5681.
White : 60, 96, 2938, 3905, 4606, 5029, 5534.
The White : 4212.
White Birch : 5291.
The White Breast of the Dim Sea : 3638.
White Christmas : 1323.
White City Poems : 509.
White Explosions : 3301.
White Face, Black Mask : 1188.
White Geraniums : 36.
White-Haired in the Abominated Regions : 5687.
White Hearts : 6078.
The White Heat of Night : 4451.
The White heat of Night : 4451.
White Horse in the Far Pasture : 3642.
White Lake : 5306.
The White Life Has Happened to Doris : 1607.
The White Lily : 1195.
The White Mercedes : 5615.
The White Museum : 1449.
The white of the river : 5968.
White on White : 147, 3207.
White Piano : 4059.
The White Ponies : 504.
The White Porch : 5176.
White Rose : 604.
White Shadows : 1095.
White Shoulders : 271.
The White Silo : 5372.
White Songs : 4058.
White Summer : 3215.
White-Tail : 3501.
The White Town : 4221.
The White Volvo : 3642.
White Willow : 4030.
White Witch : 4862.
White World : 2479.
The White Zombie : 2797.
Who But You? : 4281.
Who Is This One? : 562.
Who Is this Poet : 1948.

Who, Me? : 2464.
Who They Were : 1851.
Who to Deny : 2775.
Who We Are, and Where : 2644.
Who Will Know Us? : 5186.
Whoever He Is : 2354.
Whole Horse : 4703.
The Whole World : 5172.
Whore : 5524.
The Whore's Coo : 3349.
The Whore's Dream : 2624.
Whorls : 5612.
Who's There? : 2005, 5651.
Whose Language : 483.
Whose Woods These Are : 1258.
Why : 542.
Why All These Answers : 132, 729.
Why Cities Have Farmer's Markets : 5092.
Why Contemporary American Poets Rarely Write Epigrams of the Quality of Ben Jonson's 'On Gut' : 4345.
Why Did You Take So Much : 1668.
Why Gray : 855.
Why He Is Not Happy : 5119.
Why I Don't Speak Italian : 1015.
Why I Love Kissing You : 4853.
Why I Teach Senior English by Ann Hammond : 274.
Why I Think I'm a Writer : 1486.
Why I Wear Two Wedding Rings : 918.
Why I Won't Contribute to the Renovation of the Pike Place Market : 735.
Why I Won't Sit in Your Churches : 5841.
Why Is It Always the Way It Always Is : 118.
Why Is That Pencil Always Behind Your Ear : 1160.
Why Saints Have to Be Dead : 2014.
Why Sing of a Father Unathletic : 517.
Why the Poet Always Reads First and the Fiction-Writer Second . . : 3263.
Why the River Is Always Laughing : 2551.
Why There Is Spring Lightning: Letter to B. Franklin : 1879.
Why They Discovered America : 1440.
Why This Obsession? : 5124.
Why We Need Kites : 1218.
Why We Need the Dead : 5647.
The Wicked Fairy's Version : 2345.
The Wicked Village : 750, 5938.
Widow : 6022.
The Widow Considers the Correspondence : 4537.
Widower's Song : 5189.
Widow's Walk : 3507.
The Wife : 4735.
A Wife and Her Weeds : 4220.
Wife of Millhand : 3758.
A Wife's Dream : 5585.
The Wife's Lament : 3907.
Wikuna : 5685, 5808.
Wild and Free : 24.
Wild Asters : 1961.
Wild Beauty Annie : 876.